Age	Milestone	Age	Milestone
13 months	Pats toy in imitation Vocalizes four different vowel- consonant combinations Stands alone Walks alone	31 months	Builds tower of eight cubes Swings leg to kick ball Jumps distance of 4 inches

16 months	Scribbles spontaneously
	Imitates single words
	Walks alone with good
	  coordination
	Throws ball while standing
		34 months	Imitates vertical and horizontal
			  strokes
			Poses question
			Walks on tiptoe for four steps

19 months	Builds tower of two cubes
	Uses word(s) to make wants
	  known
	Walks up stairs or down stairs with
	  help
		37 months	Understands concept of one
			Understands two prepositions
			Walks up stairs, alternating feet

22 months	Combines word(s) and gesture(s)
	Points to three of doll's body parts
	Stands on right foot or left foot
	  with help
		42 months	Names four colors
			Understands four prepositions
			Copies a circle, a plus sign, or a
			  square

25 months	Uses a two-word utterance Imitates a two-word sentence Runs with coordination	48 months	Goes to toilet alone Hops on one foot Throws ball overhand Climbs well

28 months	Builds tower of six cubes
	Uses a three-word sentence
	Walks up stairs or down stairs
	  alone, placing both feet on each
	  step
		60 months	Skips
			Ties shoes
			Follows three commands
			Dresses and undresses self

Source: Ages 1 month through 42 months adapted from N. Bayley (1993), *Bayley Scales of Infant Development–Second Edition,* Copyright © 1993 by Harcourt Assessment, Inc. Reproduced by permission. All rights reserved. Ages 48 months and 60 months from Lewis (1991), Northern and Downs (1991), and Shapiro (1991).

Assessment of Children
Behavioral, Social, and Clinical Foundations
Fifth Edition

Jerome M. Sattler
San Diego State University

Robert D. Hoge
Carleton University

Jerome M. Sattler, Publisher, Inc.
San Diego

DEDICATED TO

Heidi, David, Deborah, Keith, Walter, Nicole, and Justin

AND TO

Lynda, Andrew, Brenda, Rick, Marta, and Matti

Editorial Services: Sally Lifland and Quica Ostrander, Lifland et al., Bookmakers
Interior Design: Jerome M. Sattler and Sally Lifland
Cover Design: Jerome M. Sattler, Kadir Samuel, and John Rizzo
Proofreaders: Denise Throckmorton and David N. Sattler
Indexers: Madge Schworer and Kadir Samuel
Production Coordinators: Sally Lifland and Jerome M. Sattler
Compositor: Omegatype, Champaign, Illinois
Cover Printer: Phoenix Color
Printer and Binder: Maple-Vail Book Manufacturing Group

This text was set in Times Roman and Helvetica, printed on Restorecote Thin, Smyth sewn, with post embossed Type 2 cover stock. The finish is matte polyester with spot gloss UV.

Cover image: Quilted cloth titled "Shapes and Sizes" by Julie Hirota of Roseville, California © 2003. Finished size 30" x 40". To see more of Julie's contemporary quilted cloths, visit www.jhiro.com.

ISBN: 0-9702671-3-4

16   15   14   13   12   11   10   9   8   7   6   5   4
Printed in the United States of America

CONTENTS

SECTION VI. REPORT WRITING

LIST OF TABLES

LIST OF EXHIBITS

LIST OF FIGURES

PREFACE

A person who is severely impaired never knows his hidden sources of strength until he is treated like a normal human being and encouraged to shape his own life.

—Helen Keller, American author, lecturer,
and blind and deaf activist (1880–1968)

The fifth edition of *Assessment of Children: Behavioral, Social, and Clinical Foundations* is designed to be used as an independent text in such courses as personality assessment, behavioral assessment, and child clinical assessment. It can also be used together with *Assessment of Children: Cognitive Applications, Fourth Edition* and *Assessment of Children: WISC–IV and WPPSI–III Supplement* to provide in-depth coverage of assessment of children.

Like former editions, the fifth edition of *Assessment of Children: Behavioral, Social, and Clinical Foundations* is designed not only as a teaching text but also as a reference book for students and professionals. This is a major revision. Every chapter has been rewritten to make the text more comprehensive, relevant, readable, up to date, and informative. The book contains new chapters on assessment theory, psychometrics, culturally and linguistically diverse children, and report writing. We have given expanded coverage to broad measures of behavioral, social, and emotional functioning and to parenting and family variables. In addition, we have included reviews of specific measures for assessing antisocial behavior disorders, anxiety disorders, depressive disorders, risk of suicide, and substance abuse disorders.

Assessment of Children: Behavioral, Social, and Clinical Foundations, Fifth Edition also contains several useful assessment aids and intervention guidelines:

- Background Questionnaire to obtain information from parents
- Personal Data Questionnaire to obtain information from adolescents
- School Referral Questionnaire to obtain information from teachers
- Semistructured interviews to obtain information from children with special needs, their parents, and their teachers
- Forms for conducting systematic behavioral observations
- Form for conducting self-monitoring assessments
- Forms for recording functional behavioral assessments
- Forms for the assessment of brain injury
- Forms for the assessment of risk factors and protective factors

- Forms for establishing a *DSM-IV–TR* diagnosis of attention-deficit/hyperactivity disorder, autistic disorder, and Asperger's disorder
- Forms for the assessment of giftedness and creativity
- Guidelines for observing children in a classroom
- Guidelines for observing children who may have attention-deficit/hyperactivity disorder or autistic disorder
- Informal measures of phonological ability
- IQ–achievement discrepancy scores necessary to establish a significant difference in cases of learning disability
- Detailed intervention guidelines for helping children with attention-deficit/hyperactivity disorder, learning disabilities, mental retardation, autistic disorder, and brain injury

Assessment of Children: Behavioral, Social, and Clinical Foundations, Fifth Edition contains several useful learning aids:

- At the beginning of each chapter, a list of major headings and goals and objectives
- At the end of each chapter, a Thinking Through the Issues section; a summary of each major topic area; a list of key terms, concepts, and names and the page on which each appears; and a series of study questions
- Exercises in several chapters to help students master the material
- A checklist for evaluating an examiner's interview techniques

The text also includes cartoons touching on assessment, psychology, and education. The cartoons provide comic relief and serve as teaching and learning tools.

This book is based on the philosophy that a psychologist cannot be a competent clinical assessor unless he or she has the relevant information about the child's presenting problem, assets and limitations, family, classroom, and environment, as well as knowledge of the techniques needed to perform the assessments and interventions that might help the child and family. In this text, you will find information to help you become a competent clinical assessor.

Clinical assessors must be mindful of the prominent place that litigation occupies in American society. Those who seek legal recourse to change a diagnosis or recommendation may question assessment results and the decisions reached on the basis of assessment results. Therefore, we strongly urge you to assume that everything you do has potential legal consequences. The best strategy is to be prepared. You can do this by (a) using the most appropriate assessment techniques and instruments, (b) maintaining accurate and complete records, and (c) keeping up with the research and clinical literature in your field.

Underlying any assessment should be respect for children and their families and a desire to help children. A thorough assessment should allow assessors to learn something about the child that they could not learn from simply talking to others about the child, observing the child, or reviewing the child's records. Assessment makes a difference in the lives of children and their families, as well as in the actions of the professionals, including educators, who work with children and their families.

Note to instructors: An *Instructor's Manual* accompanies *Assessment of Children: Behavioral, Social, and Clinical Foundations, Fifth Edition.* The manual contains multiple-choice questions useful for objective examinations.

ACKNOWLEDGMENTS

No Passion on Earth
No Love or Hate
Is Equal to the Passion to Change
Someone Else's Draft.
　　　　　　—H. G. Wells, English author (1866–1946)

We wish to acknowledge the contributions of numerous individuals who have written original material for the book or who have assisted in updating various parts of the book:

Dr. David Breiger, who is co-author of the chapter on the assessment of brain injury

Carol A. Evans, MA, who is co-author of the chapter on visual impairments

Steven Hardy-Braz, Psy.S., who is co-author of the chapter on hearing impairments

Dr. Barbara Lowenthal, who is co-author of the two chapters on learning disability

Dr. Lisa Weyandt, who is co-author of the chapter on attention-deficit/hyperactivity disorder

Dr. John O. Willis, who is co-author of the chapters on attention-deficit/hyperactivity disorder and hearing impairments

We also have been fortunate in receiving the wisdom, guidance, and suggestions of several individuals who willingly gave of their time and energy to read one or more chapters of the book or to assist in other ways. We wish to express our thanks and appreciation to

Dr. Shawn K. Acheson, Western Carolina University
Dr. Mitylene Arnold, Texas A&M University–Kingsville
Dr. Thomas J. Boll, Neuropsychology Institute
Dr. Jeffery P. Braden, North Carolina State University
Dr. Ron Dumont, Fairleigh Dickenson University
Dr. Ruth Ervin, University of British Columbia
Dr. Chris Gruber, Western Psychological Services
Dr. William A. Hillix, San Diego State University
Dr. Dave Madsen, Riverside Publishing Company
Dr. Nancy Mather, Arizona State University
Dr. Thomas Oakland, University of Florida
Dr. Lisa Jane Rapport, Wayne State University
Dr. Christina Rinaldi, University of Alberta
Dr. Mary Ann Roberts, University of Iowa
Dr. David N. Sattler, Western Washington University
Dr. Barry Schneider, University of Ottawa
Dr. Robert J. Volpe, University of Vermont
Dr. John O. Willis, Rivier College

Kadir Samuel, assistant to Jerome M. Sattler at San Diego State University, has helped in numerous ways in getting the book into production. Kadir not only has excellent word processing and graphic skills, but also did the name index. Kadir also is co–office manager at Jerome M. Sattler, Publisher, Inc. Kadir, thanks for all you do. Your dependability and dedication to getting this book published are much appreciated.

Sharon Drum, co–office manager at Jerome M. Sattler, Publisher, Inc., has been an exceptional staff member. Thanks, Sharon, for keeping the company office going and helping with the various details involved in getting this book into production.

We wish to thank the able secretarial staff of the Psychology Department at San Diego State University for their excellent support. Thank you, Darlene Pickrel, Kendrea Hilend, and Maureen Crawford. Jon Rizzo from Instructional Technology Services at San Diego State University has been helpful in assisting us in editing the graphic images. Thank you, Jon. We also want to thank Herman Zielinski for his help in drawing several of the cartoons in the book.

We want to acknowledge Roy A. Wallace, West Coast representative for Maple-Vail Book Manufacturing Group. Roy, thank you for your help in getting this book printed. It has always been a pleasure working with you.

Our families have been supportive throughout this 4-year project. Jerome M. Sattler wishes to thank Heidi, David, Deborah, Keith, and Walter, and Robert D. Hoge wishes to thank Lynda, Andrew, Brenda, Rick, Marta, and Matti for their encouragement and support.

We have been fortunate in having a superb copyediting and production staff help get this book ready for publication. The folks at Lifland et al., Bookmakers are craftspersons and, as the title of their firm indicates, truly "bookmakers." Thank you, Sally Lifland and Quica Ostrander, for your patience and tolerance and for working with us during a 10-month period to make the book clear and readable, grammatically correct, organized, coherent, as free from error as possible, and a work that we can be proud of.

We want to thank Yoram Mizrahi and the staff at Omegatype for putting our galleys into pages with exceptional expertise. Thank you, Yoram, for doing such an excellent job.

Finally, Jerome M. Sattler wishes to acknowledge the role that San Diego State University has played in his life. For 40 years, this great university has given him the support and academic freedom needed to pursue his interests in teaching, research, writing, and consultation. Thank you, San Diego State University, for all that you have given him. He hopes that in his small way he has returned something to his students and to the university community at large. Robert D. Hoge wishes to thank Carleton University in Ottawa for assisting with this book and for allowing him to teach, perform research, and engage in consultation activities throughout the world.

ABOUT THE AUTHORS

Jerome M. Sattler, Ph.D., is a Diplomate in Clinical Psychology and a Fellow of the American Psychological Association. In 1972, he was a Fulbright lecturer. In 1998, he received the Senior Scientist Award from the Division of School Psychology of the APA. In 2003, he received an honorary Doctor of Science degree from Central Missouri State University. In 2005, he received the Gold Medal Award for Life Achievement in the Application of Psychology from the American Psychological Foundation. He is a co-author of the *Stanford-Binet Intelligence Scale–Fourth Edition* and served as an expert witness in the *Larry P. v. Wilson Riles* case involving cultural bias of intelligence tests.

Sattler received his BA degree from the City College of New York and his MA and Ph.D. degrees from the University of Kansas. He has taught at Fort Hays Kansas State College, at the University of North Dakota, and at San Diego State University, where he is professor emeritus and an adjunct professor.

Sattler has written seven textbooks, including *Assessment of Children: Cognitive Applications (Fourth Edition), Clinical and Forensic Interviewing of Children and Families: Guidelines for the Mental Health, Education, Pediatric, and Child Maltreatment Fields,* and *Assessment of Children: WISC–IV and WPPSI–III Supplement* (with Ron Dumont). Five of his textbooks have been translated into Spanish. He also has published over 100 journal articles and has given over 250 speeches and workshops. Since 2000, Sattler has created several endowments to help battered women and children, homeless children, and children in need of special services.

Robert D. Hoge, Ph.D., is Emeritus Professor of Psychology and Distinguished Research Professor at Carleton University in Ottawa, Ontario. He grew up in Bethlehem, a small village near Wheeling, West Virginia, and received his BA from Kenyon College and his MA and Ph.D. degrees in psychology from the University of Delaware. After obtaining his Ph.D., he taught for 2 years at St. Lawrence University in New York. In 1967, he started teaching at Carleton University in Ottawa, Ontario.

Before he switched to child psychology, his early interest was social psychology. His teaching, research, and clinical interests have focused on children and adolescents with special needs, including children who are gifted, have a conduct disorder, or have an emotional disorder. Over the past 15 years, his primary interest has been in the assessment and treatment of juvenile offenders. Hoge provides services to children and adolescents in community-based groups and is involved in an advisory capacity with juvenile justice and child-care organizations in the United States, Canada, and other countries.

Hoge is a Fellow of the Canadian Psychological Association and a registered member of the College of Psychologists of Ontario. He has published three books: *Assessing the Youthful Offender: Issues and Applications* (with D. A. Andrews), *Assessing Adolescents in Educational, Counseling, and Other Settings,* and *The Juvenile Offender: Theory, Research, and Applications.* He is also co-author, with D. A. Andrews, of the *Youth Level of Service/Case Management Inventory,* a widely used instrument for assessing juvenile offenders, and has published widely in international journals.

1

INTRODUCTION

All children need:

To be free from discrimination
To develop physically and mentally in freedom and dignity
To have a name and nationality
To have adequate nutrition, housing, recreation, and medical services
To receive special treatment if handicapped
To receive love, understanding, and material security
To receive an education and develop [their] abilities
To be the first to receive protection in disaster
To be protected from neglect, cruelty, and exploitation
To be brought up in a spirit of friendship among people
—United Nations' Declaration of the Rights of the Child

Terminology

Goals of a Behavioral and Clinical Assessment

Guidelines for Conducting Behavioral and Clinical Assessments

Theoretical Perspectives for Behavioral and Clinical Assessments

Assessment Dimensions and Categories

Children with Special Needs

Role of Parenting in Child Development

How Psychological Problems Develop in Children

Risk and Resiliency

Ethical Considerations

Regulating the Profession

Educational Qualifications of Psychologists

Concluding Comments

Thinking Through the Issues

Summary

Key Terms, Concepts, and Names

Study Questions

Goals and Objectives

This chapter is designed to enable you to do the following:

* Understand the purposes of this book

* Become familiar with assessment terminology

* Understand the basic processes of psychological assessment

* Become familiar with theoretical perspectives underlying assessment

* Understand the way in which diagnostic categories and dimensions are formed

* Become familiar with children with special needs

* Become familiar with how psychological problems develop in children

* Understand the importance of risk and resiliency

* Become familiar with ethical considerations in assessment

1

The goal of this text is to help you make effective decisions about children with special needs. To do this, you will need to learn how to select appropriate assessment measures; administer, score, and interpret the measures; develop good interviewing and observational skills; and develop effective recommendations and interventions. Good assessment practices rest on a foundation of knowledge of measurement theory, statistics, child development, personality theory, child psychopathology, ethical guidelines, and appropriate assessment measures. If you are evaluating children with severe sensory or motor disabilities (e.g., deafness, blindness, or cerebral palsy), you may need to work collaboratively with teachers or other experts knowledgeable about these disabilities. Learning about remedial and educational techniques used to treat and educate children with special abilities will be useful. Note that in this text we use the terms *child, children,* and *youth* to refer to children of all ages, from infancy through adolescence.

The clinical and technical skills needed to be a competent behavioral and clinical assessor include the abilities to do the following:

1. Establish and maintain rapport with children, parents, and teachers
2. Use effective assessment techniques appropriate for evaluating children's behavior
3. Use effective techniques for obtaining accurate and complete information from parents and teachers
4. Evaluate the psychometric properties of tests and other psychological measures
5. Select an appropriate assessment battery
6. Administer and score tests and other assessment tools by following standardized procedures
7. Observe and evaluate behavior objectively
8. Perform informal assessments
9. Interpret assessment results
10. Use assessment findings to develop effective interventions
11. Communicate assessment findings effectively, both orally and in writing
12. Adhere to ethical standards
13. Read and interpret research in behavioral and clinical assessment
14. Keep up with laws and regulations concerning the assessment and placement of children with special needs

In using this text, consider the following cautions. First, it is not a substitute for test manuals or for texts on child development or child psychopathology; it supplements material contained in test manuals and summarizes major findings in the areas of child development and psychopathology. Second, it cannot substitute for clinically supervised experiences. Each student should receive supervision in all phases of assessment, including test selection, administration, scoring, and interpretation; report writing; and communication of results and recommendations. Ideally, every student should examine children who have mental retardation, learning disabilities, and developmental delays, as well as normal and gifted children, in order to develop skills with different populations. Third, although this text covers the major psychological instruments used in behavioral and clinical assessment of children, it does not cover every psychological assessment instrument currently published or even a fraction of the thousands of informal assessment procedures used by clinicians and researchers. However, the principles you will learn in using this text will enable you to select appropriate assessment tools.

In discussing individual measures, we have not attempted a comprehensive review of all psychometric research conducted with each measure. We do, however, summarize the reliability and validity information presented in the test manuals. Table 1-1 lists some of the major sources of information about psychological measures.

It is also important to keep abreast of current research concerning assessment and intervention throughout your training and career. You will want to pay close attention to research on the reliability and validity of tests, behavioral ratings and

---

Table 1-1
Some Sources of Information About Psychological Assessment Instruments

Books

Keyser, D. J., & Sweetland, R. C. (1984–1994). *Test critiques* (Vols. 1–10). Austin, TX: PRO-ED.

Maddox, T. (2003). *Tests: A comprehensive reference for assessments in psychology, education, and business* (5th ed.). Austin, TX: PRO-ED.

Plake, B. S., Impara, J. C., & Spies, R. A. (2003). *The Fifteenth Mental Measurements Yearbook.* Lincoln, NB: University of Nebraska and Buros Institute of Mental Measurement.

Stoloff, M. L., & Couch, J. V. (Eds.). (1992). *Computer use in psychology: A directory of software* (Vol. 3). Washington, DC: American Psychological Association.

Journals

Applied Psychological Measurement (Sage Publications)

Educational and Psychological Measurement (Sage Publications)

Journal of Clinical Psychology (Wiley)

Journal of Educational Measurement (National Council on Measurement in Education)

Journal of Personality Assessment (Society for Personality Assessment)

Journal of Psychoeducational Assessment (The Psychoeducational Corporation)

Journal of School Psychology (Elsevier)

Psychological Assessment (American Psychological Association)

Psychology in the Schools (Wiley)

checklists, interview procedures, observational techniques, and other assessment techniques that you use. Research findings will provide you with a base from which you can evaluate your assessment techniques and recommendations. You also may want to conduct research on personality tests, tests in other relevant areas, behavioral checklists, interviewing, observation, and other assessment procedures. Although much of the material in this text is relevant to this task, you will need to be familiar with the latest research findings before you can perform meaningful research.

In order to work with children with special needs, you will have to become thoroughly knowledgeable about legal and policy regulations concerning assessment procedures, particularly if the assessment is to be the basis for placement in educational programs. Especially important are regulations related to nonbiased assessment, classification of disabling conditions, eligibility criteria for special programs, designing individualized educational programs, rights of parents, confidentiality, and safekeeping of records. Those of you working in school settings will need to follow as precisely as possible the requirements of the Individuals with Disabilities Education Improvement Act of 2004 (Public Law 108-446; referred to as IDEA 2004). Exhibit 1-1 shows the law's requirements for assessment and related activities.

Exhibit 1-1
IDEA 2004 Requirements for Assessment and Related Activities

Sec. 614. EVALUATIONS, ELIGIBILITY DETERMINATIONS, INDIVIDUALIZED EDUCATION PROGRAMS, AND EDUCATIONAL PLACEMENTS.

(b) EVALUATION PROCEDURES—

(1) NOTICE—The local educational agency shall provide notice to the parents of a child with a disability, in accordance with subsections (b)(3), (b)(4), and (c) of section 615, that describes any evaluation procedures such agency proposes to conduct.

(2) CONDUCT OF EVALUATION—In conducting the evaluation, the local educational agency shall—

(A) use a variety of assessment tools and strategies to gather relevant functional, developmental, and academic information, including information provided by the parent, that may assist in determining—

(i) whether the child is a child with a disability; and

(ii) the content of the child's individualized education program, including information related to enabling the child to be involved in and progress in the general education curriculum, or, for preschool children, to participate in appropriate activities;

(B) not use any single measure or assessment as the sole criterion for determining whether a child is a child with a disability or determining an appropriate educational program for the child; and

(C) use technically sound instruments that may assess the relative contribution of cognitive and behavioral factors, in addition to physical or developmental factors.

(3) ADDITIONAL REQUIREMENTS—Each local educational agency shall ensure that—

(A) assessments and other evaluation materials used to assess a child under this section—

(i) are selected and administered so as not to be discriminatory on a racial or cultural basis;

(ii) are provided and administered in the language and form most likely to yield accurate information on what the child knows and can do academically, developmentally, and functionally, unless it is not feasible to so provide or administer;

(iii) are used for purposes for which the assessments or measures are valid and reliable;

(iv) are administered by trained and knowledgeable personnel; and

(v) are administered in accordance with any instructions provided by the producer of such assessments;

(B) the child is assessed in all areas of suspected disability;

(C) assessment tools and strategies that provide relevant information that directly assists persons in determining the educational needs of the child are provided; and

(D) assessments of children with disabilities who transfer from 1 school district to another school district in the same academic year are coordinated with such children's prior and subsequent schools, as necessary and as expeditiously as possible, to ensure prompt completion of full evaluations.

(4) DETERMINATION OF ELIGIBILITY AND EDUCATIONAL NEED—Upon completion of the administration of assessments and other evaluation measures—

(A) the determination of whether the child is a child with a disability as defined in section 602(3) and the educational needs of the child shall be made by a team of qualified professionals and the parent of the child in accordance with paragraph (5); and

(B) a copy of the evaluation report and the documentation of determination of eligibility shall be given to the parent.

(5) SPECIAL RULE FOR ELIGIBILITY DETERMINATION—In making a determination of eligibility under paragraph (4)(A), a child shall not be determined to be a child with a disability if the determinant factor for such determination is—

(A) lack of appropriate instruction in reading, including in the essential components of reading instruction (as defined in section 1208(3) of the Elementary and Secondary Education Act of 1965);

(B) lack of instruction in math; or

(C) limited English proficiency.

(Continued)

Exhibit 1-1 (*Continued*)

(6) SPECIFIC LEARNING DISABILITIES—

   (A) IN GENERAL—Notwithstanding section 607(b), when determining whether a child has a specific learning disability as defined in section 602, a local educational agency shall not be required to take into consideration whether a child has a severe discrepancy between achievement and intellectual ability in oral expression, listening comprehension, written expression, basic reading skill, reading comprehension, mathematical calculation, or mathematical reasoning.

   (B) ADDITIONAL AUTHORITY—In determining whether a child has a specific learning disability, a local educational agency may use a process that determines if the child responds to scientific, research-based intervention as a part of the evaluation procedures described in paragraphs (2) and (3).

(c) ADDITIONAL REQUIREMENTS FOR EVALUATION AND REEVALUATIONS—

   (1) REVIEW OF EXISTING EVALUATION DATA—As part of an initial evaluation (if appropriate) and as part of any reevaluation under this section, the IEP Team and other qualified professionals, as appropriate, shall—

      (A) review existing evaluation data on the child, including—

         (i) evaluations and information provided by the parents of the child;

         (ii) current classroom-based, local, or State assessments, and classroom-based observations; and

         (iii) observations by teachers and related services providers; and

      (B) on the basis of that review, and input from the child's parents, identify what additional data, if any, are needed to determine—

         (i) whether the child is a child with a disability as defined in section 602(3), and the educational needs of the child, or, in case of a reevaluation of a child, whether the child continues to have such a disability and such educational needs;

         (ii) the present levels of academic achievement and related developmental needs of the child;

         (iii) whether the child needs special education and related services, or in the case of a reevaluation of a child, whether the child continues to need special education and related services; and

         (iv) whether any additions or modifications to the special education and related services are needed to enable the child to meet the measurable annual goals set out in the individualized education program of the child and to participate, as appropriate, in the general education curriculum.

   (2) SOURCE OF DATA—The local educational agency shall administer such assessments and other evaluation measures as may be needed to produce the data identified by the IEP Team under paragraph (1)(B).

TERMINOLOGY

There is a certain amount of confusion and inconsistency in the literature regarding assessment terminology. We cannot resolve the confusion and inconsistency, but we will describe the terminology that we will use as consistently as we can throughout the text.

The most general term we employ is *psychological assessment,* and we use it to refer to any activity designed to further the process of accumulating information and forming a judgment about the behavioral, emotional, or social characteristics of an individual. This might involve diagnosing a youth on the basis of an interview, deriving a personality profile on the basis of personality test scores, or forming a judgment of a youth's likelihood of engaging in continued criminal activity on the basis of a social history, interview, and assessment information.

We can distinguish among three types of psychological assessments, although the lines separating these assessments are not always clear.

1. *Cognitive/ability assessments* rely on responses that are classified as correct or incorrect and usually are numerically scored (e.g., 0 or 1; 0, 1, or 2; or 0 or 2). Because the construct measured by the instrument is "tightly bound," each item's relationship to the target construct will be clear; that is, the items will have a high degree of face validity. Generally, standards for internal consistency and reliability are high (perhaps .95 for long tests or .85 to .90+ for shorter tests and subtests). Examples of cognitive/ability assessment instruments are intelligence tests, neuropsychological tests, aptitude tests, and achievement tests.

2. *Objective personality assessments* rely on test items that focus on external behavior or on internal emotional states. Responses are not scored as correct or incorrect; rather, they reflect the presence or absence of positive qualities (e.g., social skills, autonomy, persistence) or negative qualities (e.g., depression, aggression, anxiety). A single scale may have a mix of positive and negative items (the latter usually are reverse scored). In general, standards for internal consistency reliability are moderate (perhaps .85 or higher for long tests of more easily identified characteristics, but often below .80 for shorter tests of constructs that are more difficult to objectify). Examples of such assessment instruments are personality inventories such as the MMPI and the PIC–2, broad

behavioral surveys such as the BASC–2 and the CBCL, and specific behavioral surveys such as the Conners' Rating Scales–Revised and the Reynolds Depression Scales (see Chapters 10 and 14).

3. *Clinical assessments* rely on collecting more open-ended information through, for example, parents' reports of their child's developmental history, interviews, and unstructured observational techniques. Projective measures and apperception tests frequently are used in clinical assessments (see Chapter 10). Usually, the collected information is intended as descriptive evidence to accompany more formal assessment data. In other cases, there may be procedures that allow some degree of classification of responses. Even when responses can be classified, the psychometric properties of the scores cannot be evaluated because the statistical procedures do not yield conventionally scaled scores. However, the accuracy of classification can be evaluated by comparing rates of correct classification with rates of incorrect classification.

Psychological assessments may employ a combination of cognitive, objective personality, and clinical procedures. This is particularly true when the goal is to evaluate a complex phenomenon such as developmental delay, attention-deficit/hyperactivity disorder, or neuropsychological functioning.

GOALS OF A BEHAVIORAL AND CLINICAL ASSESSMENT

A behavioral and clinical assessment is intended to obtain relevant, reliable, and valid information about a child and his or her problems that can be used to assist the child and the people in his or her social world. The information you obtain will depend on the questions asked by the referral source, the ability of the referral source to provide relevant information, the records that are available, the degree of cooperation shown by the child and his or her family, the child's and parents' abilities to communicate, how the child and family perceive you, the type of assessment procedures you use, the atmosphere you establish, and your professional and personal style.

The major goals of a behavioral and clinical assessment are to (a) communicate information about the assessment process and administrative matters, (b) gather relevant background information, (c) conduct a formal evaluation, (d) evaluate the assessment information, and (e) recommend interventions and instructional programs.

COMMUNICATING INFORMATION ABOUT THE ASSESSMENT PROCESS AND ADMINISTRATIVE MATTERS

1. To clear up any misconceptions the child and family may have about the assessment process
2. To convey information to the parents and child (where relevant) about policies related to the assessment or treatment (either your policies or those of the clinic regarding fees, missed appointments, treatment of child and parents, frequency of visits, types of treatment, and related matters)

GATHERING BACKGROUND INFORMATION

1. To establish rapport with the child and parents
2. To identify the child's major problem areas (including a description of the problem, antecedent events and consequences, and factors that may have contributed to the problem)
3. To obtain the child's developmental history (including information about physical, intellectual, emotional, educational, and social development) by interviewing the parents
4. To find out about prior assessments and treatments that the child has had, including dates and treatment outcomes
5. To learn about the child's current family situation (including information about the child's relationship with parents, siblings, and relatives and the relationship between the parents)
6. To obtain information about the child's experiences and behavior at home, at school, and in the community (including information about interests, activities, hobbies, jobs, and relationships with others)
7. To interview the child and observe the child

CONDUCTING A FORMAL EVALUATION

1. To select a battery of psychological measures that will allow you to obtain information about the child's personality, temperament, motor skills, cognitive skills, study habits, work habits, interpersonal behavior, daily living skills, interests, and/or difficulties in living
2. To administer, score, and interpret the assessment battery

EVALUATING THE ASSESSMENT INFORMATION

1. To evaluate the nature, presence, and degree of the child's disabling conditions
2. To evaluate whether the child is at risk for psychopathology or other types of behavioral disturbance
3. To determine the conditions that inhibit and support the acquisition and maintenance of appropriate skills
4. To evaluate the extent to which other problems the child may have make it difficult to assess the child's primary problem. (For example, significant medical problems may make it difficult to evaluate a behavior problem; a parent's own problem, such as alcoholism, may make it difficult for the parent to discuss the child's problem.)
5. To arrive at a tentative formulation of the child's problem
6. To provide baseline information prior to an intervention program
7. To generate hypotheses about the development and maintenance of the child's problem behaviors
8. To evaluate the child's and family's need for and motivation to obtain help

RECOMMENDING INTERVENTIONS AND INSTRUCTIONAL PROGRAMS

1. To answer the referral question
2. To develop useful intervention and instructional programs
3. To guide individuals in selecting appropriate intervention, educational, and vocational programs
4. To monitor changes in the child and parents
5. To measure the impact of the intervention and instructional programs

To meet these goals, we advocate a *multimethod assessment approach* (see Figure 1-1). The approach involves (a) obtaining information from several sources and reviewing the child's records and previous evaluations, (b) using several assessment techniques, including norm-referenced tests, interviews, observations, and informal assessment procedures, and (c) assessing several areas (e.g., adaptive behavior, intelligence, memory, achievement, visual skills, auditory skills, motor skills, oral language, and social-emotional-personality functioning). A thorough assessment will provide information about the child's medical, developmental, academic, familial, and social history, together with information about the child's current behavioral, social, interpersonal, cognitive, and academic functioning.

As a behavioral and clinical examiner, you must appreciate the worth and dignity of each examinee. An assessment represents a mutual engagement between you and the examinee. It should be a collaborative effort and not something done *to* the examinee. It will entail your following ethical guidelines for informed consent and informed refusal. This means that you must fully inform families (and children, where applicable) about the assessment process and what will happen to the information you obtain, and let them decide whether they want to participate. Note, however, that if a court refers a family for assessment, they may have less choice about their participation. If they refuse to participate in such cases, they may face consequences associated with their refusal.

GUIDELINES FOR CONDUCTING BEHAVIORAL AND CLINICAL ASSESSMENTS

When you evaluate a child, never focus exclusively on her or his test scores or numbers; instead, interpret the scores by asking yourself what they suggest about the child's competencies and limitations. Each child has a range of competencies and limitations that you can evaluate by both quantitative and qualitative means. Note that your aim is to assess both limitations *and* competencies; the focus should not be on limitations only.

The following guidelines form an important foundation for the clinical and psychoeducational use of tests and for the assessment process.

BACKGROUND CONSIDERATIONS

1. Assessment techniques should be used for the benefit of the child.

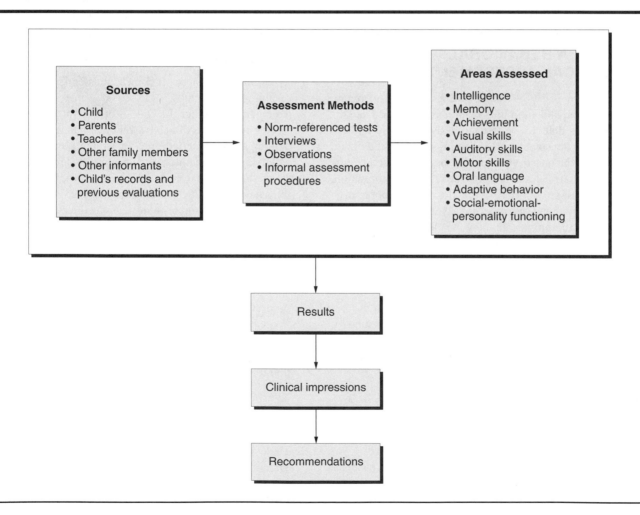

Figure 1-1. Multimethod assessment approach.

2. Assessment should be a systematic process of arriving at an understanding of a child.

TEST ADMINISTRATION CONSIDERATIONS

1. Psychological measures should be administered under standard conditions (e.g., using the exact wording in manuals and following administrative instructions and time limits precisely).
2. Measures should be scored according to well-defined rules.

TEST INTERPRETATION CONSIDERATIONS

1. Scores may be adversely affected by numerous factors in the child, such as poor comprehension of English; temporary states of fatigue, anxiety, or stress; uncooperative behavior and limited motivation; disturbances in temperament or personality; or physical illnesses or disorders.
2. Evidence should indicate that measures have adequate reliability and validity for the situation in which they are being applied.
3. Useful assessment strategies include comparing a youth's performance with that of other children (i.e., normative comparisons) and evaluating the youth's unique profile of scores (i.e., examining individual patterns, which is referred to as the *idiographic approach*).
4. Assessment interpretations are developed by use of *inductive methods* (i.e., gathering information about a child and then drawing conclusions) as well as *deductive methods* (i.e., proposing a hypothesis about the child's behavior and then collecting information that relates to it).
5. Results from psychological measures should be interpreted in relation to other behavioral data and case history information (including a child's cultural background and primary language) and never in isolation. Assessment conclusions and recommendations should be based on all sources of information obtained about a child, not on any single piece of information.
6. Psychological measures represent samples of behavior; they do not directly reveal traits or capacities, but they allow you to make inferences about these characteristics.
7. Tests and other measures assess a child's performance based on her or his answers to a set of items administered at a particular time and place.
8. Reevaluations may be needed after a child has been in a specific program for a period of time (e.g., after 1 year). However, reevaluations should be conducted only when there is a good reason to do so.
9. Measures intended to assess the same area may yield different scores (e.g., two different personality tests purporting to measure similar constructs may give scores that differ).

Tests and other assessment procedures are powerful tools, but their effectiveness will depend on your knowledge and skill. Behavioral and clinical evaluations lead to decisions and actions that affect the lives of children and their families. When used wisely and cautiously, assessment procedures can help you to help children, parents, teachers, and other professionals obtain valuable insights. When used inappropriately, they can mislead those who must make important life decisions, thus causing harm and grief. You must be careful about the words you choose when you write reports and when you communicate with children, their families, and other professionals. Your work represents a major professional contribution to the lives of children and their families, to their schools, and to society.

THEORETICAL PERSPECTIVES FOR BEHAVIORAL AND CLINICAL ASSESSMENTS

Five perspectives are useful in guiding the behavioral and clinical assessment process: the developmental perspective, the normative-developmental perspective, the cognitive-behavioral perspective, the family-systems perspective, and the eclectic perspective. Let us briefly examine each perspective.

Developmental Perspective

A *developmental perspective* proposes that the interplay between genetic disposition and environmental influences follows a definite, nonrandom form and direction. This interplay assures that development proceeds toward specific goals: learning to walk and talk, developing complex coordinated movements, gradually developing more complex thinking skills, applying skills to the understanding of other persons, and reaching sexual maturity. However, there are *intraindividual* (i.e., within the individual) and *interindividual* (i.e., between individuals) differences in the rate and timing of development. Thus, both within individuals and across individuals, different abilities—such as physical, cognitive, and social skills and language and speech—develop at different rates. A developmental perspective focuses both on individual differences in the rate or sequence of development and on general changes common to most individuals at a given age or stage.

The developmental perspective also emphasizes that biological, psychological, and social factors constantly interact to shape and modify children's development. The environments that play a role in children's development—including family, peer, school, and work environments—are interdependent. Children "evoke differential reactions from the environment as a result of their physical and behavioral characteristics, and environments contribute to individual development through the feedback they provide" (Compas, Hinden, & Gerhardt, 1995, p. 270). Maladaptive behaviors may be manifested, at least in part, when there is a mismatch between children's needs and the opportunities afforded them by their environments. This may happen, for example, when the expectations or demands of the environments either exceed or conflict with children's abilities.

Another important principle of the developmental perspective is that growth is both qualitative (involving the appearance of new processes or structures) and quantitative (involving changes in the degree or magnitude of a capacity). At first, children's thoughts are dominated by what they see and touch. By approximately 2 years of age, they begin to develop expressive language recognizable to adults and to recall some prior actions and responses; thinking tends to be egocentric. By about age 7 years, thought processes become more systematic and skills needed to solve concrete problems develop. By age 11 years or so, most children can think abstractly and make logical deductions. Newly developed skills present children with challenges, especially at critical points in development such as puberty.

Normative-Developmental Perspective

A *normative-developmental perspective* evaluates changes in children's cognitions, affect, and behavior in relation to a reference group, usually composed of children of the same age and gender as the referred child (Edelbrock, 1984). *Cognitions* refer to mental processes, including perception, memory, and reasoning, by which children acquire knowledge, make plans, and solve problems. *Affect* refers to the experience of emotion or feeling. The normative-developmental perspective considers demographic variables, such as the child's age, grade, gender, ethnicity, and socioeconomic status (SES); developmental variables, such as language, motor, social, and self-help skills; and the influence of prior development on current and future development.

Normative data are useful in various ways (Edelbrock, 1984). First, normative data provide information about how a particular child's development compares with that of average children. Norms allow you to establish reasonable treatment goals and evaluate the clinical significance of changes resulting from interventions. Second, normative data guide you in selecting appropriate target areas and behaviors that need change—for example, determining that a child is not growing as expected or is not developing age-appropriate skills. Third, normative data allow you to compare information acquired from different sources. Comparing information from parents and teachers, for example, will help you learn about the consistency of children's behavior in different settings. Fourth, normative data may help you to identify behaviors with unusually low or high rates (i.e., behaviors that occur more or less often than expected), transient behaviors (e.g., anxiety associated with enrolling at school), behaviors that are relatively normal for a particular age group (e.g., fear of strangers in very young children), and situational variables that may place the child at risk for developing problem behaviors (e.g., adverse home or classroom environments). Finally, normative data assist in research investigations by allowing investigators to form relatively homogeneous groups and to compare samples across studies.

Cognitive-Behavioral Perspective

A *cognitive-behavioral perspective* focuses on the importance of cognitions as major determinants of emotion and be-

havior; cognitions include both the child's thoughts and his or her ways of processing information. This perspective also looks at the role that cognitions such as values, beliefs, self-statements, perceived self-confidence or self-efficacy based on prior experiences, problem-solving strategies, expectancies, images, and goals play in the development of maladaptive behavior (e.g., withdrawal or task avoidance can result when a child believes that she or he has little self-worth). Finally, this perspective emphasizes the individual and environmental influences that may shape and control the child's thoughts, feelings, and behavior (e.g., auditory stimuli such as sounds from spinning objects may reinforce the child to continue a stereotyped activity, or responses from others, such as verbal comments elicited by a child's aggressive behavior, may increase that behavior).

The cognitive-behavioral perspective emphasizes the importance of empirical validation throughout the assessment and treatment processes. Quantitative measures such as frequency counts, measures of duration, measures of intensity, and records of times of occurrence are used to document the relevant behavior of a child (see Chapters 8 and 9). In addition, self-monitoring assessment can provide data about the child's thoughts, feelings, and behavior (see Chapter 9). Self-monitoring assessment also provides the child with a sense that he or she is an active participant in the assessment and intervention.

The *cognitive aspect* of a cognitive-behavioral perspective acknowledges that cognitions, although private, mediate learning and behavior. Cognitions and behavior also are functionally related: Changes in one can cause changes in the other. The primary concerns are how behavior varies as a function of changes in a child's cognitions and how cognitions and behavior can be modified to produce a desired outcome.

The *behavioral aspect* of a cognitive-behavioral perspective proposes that environmental contingencies, such as setting factors (e.g., temperature, sound level), natural reinforcers (e.g., food, social contact), and distractors (e.g., excessive heat or cold, crowded conditions) also mediate behavior and learning. Thus, for example, acting out can result when environmental stimuli such as teasing from a peer become associated with aversive experiences such as anger. Particular attention is given to the antecedents and consequences of a specific behavior—that is, the events that precede and follow the behavior. The assumption underlying this approach, termed *functional behavioral analysis,* can be represented as follows: antecedents → behavior → consequences. Functional behavioral analysis looks at behavior as it occurs in a given setting; indirect measures are not used (see Chapter 13).

A cognitive-behavioral assessment can assist in interventions. First, asking a child about the factors that exacerbate or reduce a problem behavior implicitly suggests that the problem behavior is subject to various controlling forces. Second, asking a child to monitor his or her thoughts and feelings related to the problem behavior or to describe the circumstances surrounding the problem behavior may help the child identify environmental events that instigate the problem behavior. Third, asking the child to monitor others' responses to the problem behavior highlights the importance of others' roles in relationship to the problem behavior. Thus, by means of the cognitive-behavioral assessment process, a child can come to understand that a problem behavior is explicable and controllable.

Family-Systems Perspective

A *family-systems perspective* focuses on the structure and dynamics of the family. From this perspective, a well-functioning family can be characterized as follows (Turk & Kerns, 1985):

> The members are related to one another in a network of interactions. The four basic characteristics of a family system are (a) it is an open, rather than a closed, system and has a continuous interchange with the external social and physical environment; (b) it is complex, with an intricate organizational structure; (c) it is self-regulating, in the sense of containing homeostatic mechanisms to restore balance; and (d) it is capable of transformation. The family system, confronted with continuous internal and external demand for change, may be able to respond with growth, flexibility, and structural evolution. . . . Consequently, the family is a powerful determinant of behavior and can foster adaptive as well as maladaptive activities. (pp. 6–7)

Characteristics such as the family's structure, functions, resources, history, and life cycle and the individual members' assigned roles, modes of interaction, and unique histories are important elements of a family-systems perspective (Turk & Kerns, 1985, pp. 3–4, with changes in notation):

1. *Structure.* The structure, or configuration, of a family refers to characteristics of the individual members who make up the family unit. It encompasses gender, age distribution, spacing, and size or number of members.
2. *Functions.* Function refers to the tasks the family performs for society and its members (such as educational, economic, and reproductive functions).
3. *Assigned roles.* Assigned roles concern the prescribed responsibilities, expectations, and rights of the individual members. Thus, one family member may be designated the breadwinner, another the overseer of health care, and still another the manager of household operations. Roles do not have to be mutually exclusive, and they seldom are. For example, in many families the mother is the custodian of health as well as the manager of the household.
4. *Modes of interaction.* Mode of interaction relates to the style adopted by the family members to deal with the environment and with one another in both problem solving and decision making.
5. *Resources.* Resources include the general health of family members, social support and skills, personality characteristics, and financial support. These resources will influence the ways the family interprets events.
6. *Family history.* Family history refers to sociocultural factors as well as prior illnesses and modes of coping with stress. The history of the family will affect the ways the family interprets and responds to various events.
7. *Life cycle.* Families also have a life cycle that changes over time. In brief, the family progresses through a reasonably well-defined set of developmental phases, beginning with a courtship phase and ending with the death of parents or parent figures. Each phase is associated with certain developmental tasks, the successful completion of which leads to somewhat different levels of family functioning.
8. *Individual members' unique histories.* Families are composed of individual members who have unique experiences beyond the family. These members each have their own unique conceptions and behavioral repertoires that account for a substantial portion of what is observed within the family contexts. Considerable information is acquired by both children and adults from peers, school, television, books and magazines, radio, the Internet, coworkers, and so forth. Thus, it should *not* be assumed that the family comprises all of the individuals' experiences or is the exclusive shaper of individuals' conceptions of themselves and the world. The unique characteristics of individual family members need to be considered in thinking about families and family functioning.

The key assumptions of a family-systems perspective are that (a) the parts of the family are interrelated, (b) one part of the family cannot be understood in isolation from the rest of the family, (c) family functioning cannot be fully understood simply by understanding each part, (d) changes in one part of the family will affect the other parts, (e) the family is greater than the sum of its parts, (f) the family's structure and organization are important factors determining the behavior of family members, and (g) interactions among family members shape the behavior of the family members (Epstein & Bishop, 1981).

Ideally, during all phases of childhood development, the family provides the food, shelter, and safety a child needs to survive and develop. During infancy, the family helps the child develop a sense of trust and acquire a sense of others as reliable and nurturing. During preschool years, the family encourages the child to explore his or her environment and to develop skills needed for school. During the middle childhood years, the family encourages the child to learn about the wider culture, to distinguish himself or herself from others, and to gain a sense of competence and skill. During adolescence, the family helps the adolescent to establish a positive sense of self-identity and to accept increased responsibility. Although the influence of the family is large, you must recognize that children's behavior is influenced by genetics, culture, school, and peer group experiences as well.

Eclectic Perspective

An *eclectic perspective,* which is based on elements from the four other perspectives, emphasizes that (a) individual, familial, and environmental determinants are critical factors in children's development, (b) children are shaped by their environments and by their genetic constitutions, (c) what can be observed in children may not always reflect their potentials, and (d) children also shape their environments. An eclectic perspective is not a new perspective, nor does it offer an in-depth interpretive system that replaces other systems; it does offer, however, a meaningful perspective for conducting a behavioral and clinical assessment. An eclectic perspective may be especially helpful in interpreting problem behavior.

An eclectic perspective focuses on the following:

1. Taking a medical and social history from the child, parents, teachers, and other relatives
2. Considering genetic factors as they might affect the child's development, recognizing that even if these factors cannot be diagnosed or modified, they can help explain the child's problem to parents and others
3. Looking at the interaction of environmental and biological factors in accounting for the child's development
4. Considering the child's behavior in relation to normative data
5. Evaluating a broad range of behaviors, cognitions, and affects as they relate to the child's development, including the development of personality, temperament, intelligence, language, motor skills, social skills, adaptive behavior, self-help skills, emotions, and interpersonal skills
6. Looking at the frequency, duration, and intensity of the problem behaviors and the situational contexts in which the behaviors occur
7. Noting how the problem behaviors affect the child, the parents, and the family
8. Evaluating the child's and parents' motivation for change and treatment
9. Considering ways to measure the child's problem behaviors, such as by standardized tests, checklists, interviews, systematic observation, and self-monitoring
10. Recording the ways in which the child, parents, and family members see themselves, others, and their environment
11. Noting the family's structure and dynamics, including the family's decision-making style, communication patterns, roles, affective responses and involvement, values and norms, patterns of interaction, means of conflict resolution, and ability to meet the needs of its members

Propositions Based on the Four Perspectives

The propositions that follow—which are based on the developmental, normative-developmental, cognitive-behavioral, and family-systems perspectives—serve as an important foundation for the assessment of children (Bornstein & Lamb, 1999; Bretherton, 1993; Campbell, 1989; Edelbrock, 1984; Luiselli, 1989; Mash & Wolfe, 2002; Masten & Braswell, 1991; Millon, 1987; Turk & Kerns, 1985).

NORMAL FUNCTIONING

1. Children change and evolve rapidly, experiencing changes that are both quantitative and qualitative.
2. Children possess relatively enduring biological dispositions that give a consistent coloration and direction to their experiences.
3. Children's temperaments, early experiences, learning histories, and cultural backgrounds simultaneously interact to affect the development and nature of their emerging psychological structures, abilities, and functions.
4. Children develop relatively stable behaviors, cognitions, and affects that stem partially from generalized learning and partially from similarities among related situations.
5. Children's cognitions can be major determinants of emotion and behavior.
6. Children gradually replace reflexive, sensory-bound, and concrete behavior with more conceptual, symbolic, and cognitively mediated behavior.
7. Children may develop abilities that are not fully expressed in their behavior at a particular stage of development but that may be expressed at a later stage of development.
8. Children's behavior is influenced by their chronological age and their developmental status (including physical maturation).
9. Children's motives and emotions become more refined, advanced, and controlled over the course of their development.
10. Children engage in behaviors and seek situations that are rewarding.
11. Children's behavior that is appropriate at one age may be inappropriate at another age.
12. Children's sense of self and capacity for interpersonal relationships develop, in part, from the parent-child relationship.
13. Children can be stimulated by sensory events, such as pleasant sounds or sights that encourage them to continue a behavior in which they are engaged.
14. Children's development can be better understood by reference to normative data.
15. Children's environments during their formative years are usually highly structured (except possibly in highly dysfunctional families) and closely monitored by parents and other caregivers. Children's interactions with others in their environments contribute to shaping their behavior, and children, in turn, also shape their environments.
16. Children's families function on a continuum from highly functional to highly dysfunctional.
17. Families that function well overall may continue to function adequately during stressful periods. For example, well-functioning families cope with stress successfully, protect their members, adjust to role changes within the family, and continue to carry out their functions. Supportive intervention may nevertheless be beneficial for these families.

DEVIANT FUNCTIONING

1. Children's problems are influenced by complex interactions of biological, psychological, and environmental factors.

2. Children's maladaptive behavior may be related to their cognitions (e.g., emotional problems may be caused by distortions or deficiencies in thinking).

3. The most serious long-term consequences tend to be associated with problems that occur early, express themselves in several forms, are pervasive across settings, and persist throughout the children's development.

4. Children with similar psychological disorders may have different behavioral symptoms, and children with different psychological disorders may have similar behavioral symptoms.

5. Children's referrals for assessment and treatment are influenced by their parents' perceptions and interpretations of behavior and by their parents' psychological and emotional states.

6. Children may have transient problems (such as fears and worries, nightmares, bedwetting, and tantrums) characteristic of a particular developmental period; these problems, if atypical for the child's developmental period, may serve as a warning signal for the development of more serious problems and, therefore, must be handled skillfully. Because some problems disappear or abate with maturity, premature labeling should be avoided.

7. Children may have developmental problems that reflect (a) an exaggeration or distortion of age-appropriate behaviors (e.g., attachment problems in infancy), (b) difficult transitions from one developmental period to the next (e.g., noncompliance in toddlers and preschoolers), or (c) age-related but maladaptive reactions to environmental, particularly familial, stress (e.g., school difficulties among older children associated with moving or with a parent's loss of a job).

8. Families that function poorly may make their members more susceptible to stress. For example, a family may induce in its members maladaptive behavior, illness, or persistent problems that are likely to require treatment; or, a family may be unable to protect its members from maladaptive reactions.

9. Children will likely have difficulty communicating with parents who have distorted thought processes; similarly, parents with distorted thought processes will likely have difficulty communicating with their children. In such situations, children's abilities to adapt flexibly and appropriately to new situations will be restricted.

10. Children must receive interventions appropriate to their developmental level.

Exercise 1-1
Identifying Perspectives

Read each question and identify the theoretical perspective that it most closely reflects: developmental, normative-developmental, cognitive-behavioral, family-systems, or eclectic. Recognize, however, that assigning each question to one perspective is a matter of relative emphasis, because there is considerable overlap among the perspectives. Compare your answers with those following the questions.

1. What role does the child have in the family, and what is the family's structure?
2. What were the child's thoughts and feelings at the time the problem was occurring, and what environmental contingencies are related to the problem behavior?
3. How does the child's self-concept affect the frequency of her acting-out behavior and the roles she assumes in the family?
4. How does the child's behavior compare with that of other children of the same age?
5. Have the child's physical size and level of maturity affected how his peers relate to him?

Suggested Answers

1. Family-systems   2. Cognitive-behavioral   3. Eclectic
4. Normative-developmental   5. Developmental

ASSESSMENT DIMENSIONS AND CATEGORIES

The instruments described in this text measure constructs related to personality, behavior, or social functioning. Some of these constructs are expressed in *dimensional terms*. That is, scores are expressed as the degree to which a youth exhibits a characteristic (e.g., degree of dependence, level of aggressiveness, level of intelligence). Other constructs are expressed in *categorical terms*. In this case, the child is placed in a diagnostic category (e.g., conduct disordered, developmentally delayed, dyslexic, autistic). Both types of constructs are important, because they not only are used to describe the child but also serve as a basis for decision making. For example, a child who is highly aggressive might be placed in a separate class for children with a conduct disorder, or a child with dyslexia might be provided with special education services. In later chapters, we discuss practical issues involved in categorization and labeling and present information related to dimensions and categories for specific measures. Below we present a general introduction to the development of constructs.

Empirical Approach

The *empirical approach* involves the application of factor analytic or multivariate statistical procedures to data and the derivation of constructs through those analyses. This approach has been particularly important in the development of certain cognitive, personality, and behavioral constructs and the measures used to assess them. For example, the personality constructs represented in the Minnesota Multiphasic Personality Inventory (e.g., depression, social introversion) were derived through empirical procedures, and the dimensions of behavioral pathology represented in the Child Behavior Checklist family of instruments were originally derived through factor analytic procedures. Most, although not all, empirically derived personality and behavioral constructs are represented in dimensional terms. The dimensions can reflect relatively specific traits or behaviors (e.g., degree of anger) or higher-order constructs (e.g., degree of pathology).

The *internalizing-externalizing continuum* has proven useful in understanding behavioral, social, and emotional disorders. It is a type of higher-order personality/behavioral construct particularly important in many assessment measures (Achenbach & McConaughy, 1992). The internalizing-externalizing continuum does not relate to the underlying psychological processes or causes of disorders; rather, it is oriented to the expression of symptoms.

Internalizing disorders usually are covert and not easily observable and thus are difficult to evaluate and identify. Although they typically are distressing to the child or adolescent, they are less likely than externalizing disorders to come to the attention of parents and teachers. The severity of internalizing disorders is, in large part, a function of the child's subjective experience. For example, depressive symptoms might include suicidal ideation, fatigue, and feelings of low self-worth. A child may suffer from two or more internalizing disorders simultaneously, such as generalized anxiety disorder and posttraumatic stress disorder (PTSD).

Externalizing disorders of childhood and adolescence are characterized by overt behavioral excesses or disturbances. They are generally distressing to the child's parents, teachers, peers, and others. Represented in conditions involving aggression, anger, defiance, and other antisocial acts, externalizing disorders are likely to cause difficulties in the home, school, and community. A child may suffer from two or more externalizing disorders, such as attention-deficit/hyperactivity disorder and conduct disorder. Some children have both an internalizing and an externalizing disorder, such as major depression and conduct disorder.

Clinical Approach

With the clinical approach to assessment, constructs are based on the experience of clinicians. An important focus of the clinical approach has been efforts to derive diagnostic categories of mental or emotional disorders. The most important source of information about these disorders is the *Diagnostic and Statistical Manual of Mental Disorders* (*DSM-IV–TR;* American Psychiatric Association, 2000), the official diagnostic system of the American Psychiatric Association. Many of the personality tests and rating systems discussed in later chapters of this text reflect *DSM-IV–TR* diagnostic categories. Table 1-2 identifies the major diagnostic categories relevant to infancy, childhood, and adolescence. There are several other disorders whose essential features are considered to be the same in children and adults; therefore, no special categories are provided for children. Examples are depression, gender identity disorder, substance-abuse-related disorders, mood disorders, and schizophrenia.

The Individuals with Disabilities Education Act (IDEA) uses the following 13 categories to classify children who have disabilities: autism, deaf-blindness, developmental delays, emotional disturbance, hearing impairments, mental retardation, multiple disabilities, orthopedic impairments, other health impairments, specific learning disabilities, speech or language impairments, traumatic brain injury, and visual impairments. Table 1-3 describes the 13 categories, which overlap with those of *DSM-IV–TR.*

Table 1-4 shows, by disability, the number and percentage of students ages 6 to 21 years served under IDEA during the 2000–2001 school year. The largest group of students

Calvin and Hobbes   by Bill Watterson

Table 1-2
Major Disorders Usually First Diagnosed in Infancy, Childhood, or Adolescence

Disorder	Description
Mental Retardation	Significantly subaverage intellectual functioning (an IQ of approximately 70 or below) with onset before age 18 years and concurrent deficits or impairments in adaptive functioning
Mild Mental Retardation	IQ level 50–55 to approximately 70
Moderate Mental Retardation	IQ level 35–40 to 50–55
Severe Mental Retardation	IQ level 20–25 to 35–40
Profound Mental Retardation	IQ level below 20 or 25
Learning Disorders	Academic functioning substantially below that expected, given the child's chronological age, measured intelligence, and age-appropriate education
Reading Disorder	Reading achievement substantially below that expected
Mathematics Disorder	Mathematical ability substantially below that expected
Disorder of Written Expression	Writing skills substantially below those expected
Motor Skills Disorder	
Developmental Coordination Disorder	Performance of daily activities that require motor coordination substantially below that expected, given the child's chronological age and measured intelligence
Communication Disorders	Difficulties in speech or language, including expressive language disorder, mixed receptive-expressive language disorder, phonological disorder, and stuttering
Expressive Language Disorder	Impairment in expressive language
Mixed Receptive-Expressive Language Disorder	Impairment in both receptive and expressive language development
Phonological Disorder	Failure to use speech sounds that are developmentally appropriate for the child's age and dialect
Stuttering	Disturbance in normal fluency and time patterning of speech that is inappropriate for the child's age
Pervasive Developmental Disorders	Severe and pervasive impairment in several areas of development: reciprocal social interaction skills, communication skills, or the presence of stereotyped behavior, interests, and activities
Autistic Disorder	Markedly abnormal or impaired development in social interaction and communication and markedly restricted repertoire of activities and interests
Rett's Disorder	Development of multiple specific deficits such as deceleration of head growth, loss of acquired purposeful hand skills, loss of social engagement, poorly coordinated gait or trunk movements, and severely impaired expressive and receptive language development following a period of normal functioning after birth
Childhood Disintegrative Disorder	Marked regression in multiple areas of functioning following a period of at least 2 years of apparently normal development (e.g., significant loss of previously acquired skills in expressive or receptive language, social skills, bowel or bladder control, play, or motor skills)
Asperger's Disorder	Severe and sustained impairment in social interaction (e.g., impaired multiple nonverbal behaviors, poor peer relationships, lack of spontaneous seeking to share interests, or lack of social or emotional reciprocity)
Attention-Deficit and Disruptive Behavior Disorders	
Attention-Deficit/Hyperactivity Disorder	Persistent pattern of inattention and/or hyperactivity-impulsivity that is more frequent and severe than is typically observed in children at a comparable level of development
Conduct Disorder	Repetitive and persistent pattern of behavior in which the basic rights of others or major age-appropriate societal norms or rules are violated
Oppositional Defiant Disorder	Recurrent pattern of negativistic, defiant, disobedient, and hostile behavior toward authority figures that occurs more frequently than is typically observed in children of comparable age and developmental level and that leads to significant impairment in social, academic, or occupational functioning

(*Continued*)

Table 1-2 (*Continued*)

Disorder	Description
Feeding and Eating Disorders of Infancy or Early Childhood	Persistent feeding and eating disturbances
Pica	Persistent eating of nonnutritive substances, including paint, plaster, string, hair, or cloth (younger children) or animal droppings, sand, insects, leaves, and pebbles (older children)
Rumination Disorder	Repeated regurgitation and rechewing of food that develops in an infant or child after a period of normal functioning
Feeding Disorder of Infancy or Early Childhood	Persistent failure to eat adequately, as reflected in significant failure to gain weight or significant weight loss, absent any gastrointestinal or other general medical condition severe enough to account for the feeding disturbance
Tic Disorders	
Tourette's Disorder	Multiple motor or vocal tics (sudden, rapid, recurrent, nonrhythmic, stereotyped motor movements or vocalizations)
Chronic Motor or Vocal Tic Disorder	Either motor tics *or* vocal tics, but *not both*
Transient Tic Disorder	Single or multiple motor tics and/or vocal tics
Elimination Disorders	
Encopresis	Involuntary or intentional expulsion of feces in inappropriate places
Enuresis	Repeated voiding of urine during the day or at night into bed or clothes, which most often is involuntary but occasionally may be intentional
Other Disorders of Infancy, Childhood, or Adolescence	
Separation Anxiety Disorder	Excessive anxiety (beyond that expected for the child's developmental level) concerning separation from the home or from those to whom the child is attached
Selective Mutism	Persistent failure to speak in specific social situations (e.g., at school, with playmates) where speaking is expected, despite speaking in other situations
Reactive Attachment Disorder of Infancy or Early Childhood	Markedly disturbed and developmentally inappropriate social relatedness in most contexts that begins before age 5 years and is associated with grossly pathological care by caregivers
Stereotypic Movement Disorder	Motor behavior that is repetitive, often seemingly driven, and nonfunctional

Source: Adapted from *DSM-IV–TR* (American Psychiatric Association, 2000).

receiving services was those with specific learning disabilities (49.99%), followed by students with speech or language impairments (18.94%), mental retardation (10.61%), and emotional disturbance (8.20%). These four categories represented 87.74% of all students receiving services. The remaining 12.26% had multiple disabilities, hearing impairments, orthopedic impairments, other health impairments, visual impairments, autism, deaf-blindness, traumatic brain injury, or developmental delay. The 5,775,722 students served under IDEA represented about 8.7% of the 66,211,355 children and young adults who were in the U.S. population during 2000–2001, according to the U.S. Census.

We will discuss practical problems in using the diagnostic categories in assessment situations in Chapter 3; here we simply note that there is some controversy regarding the meaning and relevance of these diagnostic systems (Follete & Houts, 1996; Wakefield, 1992). There is a question, for example, about the consistency with which clinical conditions can be diagnosed. Objections have also been raised regarding the possibility that cultural differences have not been sufficiently recognized in defining diagnostic categories. Fortunately, we are seeing increasing efforts to verify and extend the clinically based categorizations through empirical procedures (Scotti, Morris, McNeil, & Hawkins, 1996).

Table 1-3
Thirteen Disability Categories of the Individuals with Disabilities Education Act (IDEA)

1. *Autism.* A developmental disability, generally evident before age 3, that significantly affects verbal and nonverbal communication and social interaction and that adversely affects a child's educational performance. Symptoms may range from mild to severe. Other characteristics often associated with autism are engagement in repetitive activities and stereotyped movements, resistance to environmental change or change in daily routines, and unusual responses to sensory experiences. The term does not apply if a child's educational performance is adversely affected primarily because the child has an emotional disturbance.

2. *Deaf-blindness.* Concomitant hearing and visual impairments, the combination of which causes such severe communication and other developmental and educational needs that a child cannot be accommodated in special education programs solely for children with deafness or children with blindness.

3. *Developmental delays.* Delays in physical development, cognitive development, communication development, social or emotional development, and/or adaptive development experienced by children between 3 and 9 years of age who, by reason thereof, need special education and related services.

4. *Emotional disturbance.* A condition in which one or more of the following characteristics are exhibited over a long period of time and to a marked degree, which adversely affects a child's educational performance: (a) an inability to learn that cannot be explained by intellectual, sensory, or health factors, (b) an inability to build or maintain satisfactory interpersonal relationships with peers and teachers, (c) inappropriate types of behavior or feelings under normal circumstances, (d) a general pervasive mood of unhappiness or depression, and (e) a tendency to develop physical symptoms or fears associated with personal or school problems. The term includes schizophrenia, but does not apply to children who are socially maladjusted unless it is determined that they have an emotional disturbance.

5. *Hearing impairments.* An impairment in hearing, whether permanent or fluctuating, that adversely affects a child's educational performance but does not meet the definition of deafness.

6. *Mental retardation.* Significantly subaverage general intellectual functioning, existing concurrently with deficits in adaptive behavior and manifested during the developmental period, that adversely affects a child's educational performance.

7. *Multiple disabilities.* Concomitant impairments (such as mental retardation and blindness, mental retardation and orthopedic impairment, etc.) that, in combination, cause such severe educational needs that the child cannot be accommodated in special education programs solely for one of the impairments. The term does not include deaf-blindness.

8. *Orthopedic impairments.* A severe orthopedic impairment that adversely affects a child's educational performance. The term includes impairments caused by congenital anomaly (e.g., clubfoot, absence of some limb, etc.), impairments caused by disease (e.g., poliomyelitis, bone tuberculosis, etc.), and impairments from other causes (e.g., cerebral palsy, amputations, and fractures or burns that cause contractures).

9. *Other health impairments.* Limited strength, vitality, or alertness (or heightened alertness to environmental stimuli that results in limited alertness with respect to the educational environment) that adversely affects a child's educational performance. The impairment may be caused by a chronic or acute health problem, such as asthma, attention-deficit disorder or attention-deficit/hyperactivity disorder, diabetes, epilepsy, a heart condition, hemophilia, lead poisoning, leukemia, nephritis, rheumatic fever, or sickle cell anemia.

10. *Specific learning disabilities.* A disorder in one or more of the basic psychological processes involved in understanding or in using language, spoken or written, that may manifest itself in an imperfect ability to listen, think, speak, read, write, spell, or do mathematical calculations. The category includes perceptual disabilities, brain injury, minimal brain dysfunction, dyslexia, and developmental aphasia. It does not include learning problems that are primarily the result of visual, hearing, or motor disabilities; of mental retardation; of emotional disturbance; or of environmental, cultural, or economic disadvantage.

11. *Speech or language impairments.* A communication disorder, such as dysfluency (stuttering), impaired articulation, a language impairment, or a voice impairment, that adversely affects a child's educational performance.

12. *Traumatic brain injury.* An acquired injury to the brain caused by an external physical force, resulting in total or partial functional disability or psychosocial impairment or both, that adversely affects a child's educational performance. The term applies to open- or closed-head injuries resulting in impairments in one or more areas such as cognition; language; memory; attention; reasoning; abstract thinking; judgment; problem solving; sensory, perceptual, and motor abilities; psychosocial behavior; physical functions; information processing; and speech. The term does not apply to brain injuries that are congenital or degenerative or that were induced by birth trauma.

13. *Visual impairments.* An impairment in vision that, even with correction, adversely affects a child's educational performance. The term includes both partial sight and blindness.

Note: These definitions have been adapted from the *Federal Register,* March 12, 1999, pp. 12421–12422.

Table 1-4
Number of Students Ages 6 to 21 Years Served Under the Individuals with Disabilities Education Act (IDEA) in 2000–2001, by Disability

Disability	N	%
Specific learning disabilities	2,887,217	49.99
Speech or language impairments	1,093,808	18.94
Mental retardation	612,978	10.61
Emotional disturbance	473,663	8.20
Multiple disabilities	122,559	2.12
Hearing impairments	70,767	1.23
Orthopedic impairments	73,057	1.26
Other health impairments	291,850	5.05
Visual impairments	25,975	0.45
Autism	78,749	1.36
Deaf-blindness	1,320	0.02
Traumatic brain injury	14,844	0.26
Developmental delay	28,935	0.50
All disabilities	5,775,722	100.00

Source: Adapted from U.S. Department of Education (2003), p. II–20.

CHILDREN WITH SPECIAL NEEDS

Children with special needs are a heterogeneous group. They may have problems involving cognitive functions (such as impaired ability to reason or learn), affect (such as anxiety or depressive reactions), or behavior (such as socially inappropriate behavior, hyperactivity, or violence toward self or others). In addition, they may have physical disabilities, medical problems, or other conditions.

Generalizations about children with special needs must be made with caution, because each child has unique temperament and personality characteristics, cognitive skills, social skills, adaptive-behavior skills, and support systems. *Each child should be viewed as an individual and never only as representing a particular disorder.* If you stereotype the child, your ability to obtain accurate information will be impaired. Your goal is to learn as much about a child's positive coping strategies and accomplishments and the protective factors in her or his life—including those provided by the immediate and extended family—as you do about the symptoms, negative coping strategies, and other factors that may hinder her or his development.

Children who have special needs may have more than one disorder. Children with multiple disorders are said to suffer from *co-morbidity* or to have *co-occurring disorders.* Examples of disorders that commonly occur together are conduct disorder and attention-deficit/hyperactivity disorder, autistic disorder and mental retardation, and childhood depression

and anxiety (Mash & Dozois, 1996). Children with co-occurring disorders are likely to have more complex and longer-lasting psychological problems than children with only a single disorder. Always consider whether children have more than one type of disorder; disorders in childhood may not be "pure."

Children with special needs *usually* go through the same developmental sequences as children without special needs, although sometimes at a different rate. For example, some children may be delayed in reaching developmental milestones (see the table on the inside front cover), and those with severe behavioral or developmental problems, such as autistic disorder or mental retardation, may never reach more mature stages of language development or conceptual thinking.

Children with special needs form their self-concepts in ways similar to those of other children. Parents are the primary source of feedback, followed by siblings and other relatives, friends and neighbors, and teachers and other professionals. You will want to learn about children's self-concepts, how their self-concepts affect their relationships with others, their feelings about having problems, and their aspirations. You also will want to learn how their parents view these same characteristics and the parents' aspirations for their children. Children with special needs are likely to have more negative self-concepts and to experience more frustration, rejection, teasing, prejudice, depression, anxiety, and motivational deficiencies than children without special needs (Cobb, 1989).

Children with special needs who also have physical impairments may be limited in their ability to obtain a full range of sensory information, to socialize, and to engage in sports and other physical activities. These limitations may interfere with the development of cognitive, affective, and interpersonal skills. Physical impairments, in conjunction with behavioral disorders, pose considerable challenges for children's care and development.

The lifetime costs, both direct and indirect, of raising a child with disabilities also must be considered. Direct costs include those for medical expenses (e.g., for doctor fees, travel to medical providers, prescription drugs, inpatient hospital stays, outpatient hospital visits, emergency department visits, and rehabilitation services) and nonmedical expenses (e.g., for home modifications, special education, and residential care). Indirect costs include the value of lost wages when the children become adults and cannot work, are limited in the amount or type of work they can do, or die early, as well as the loss of salary by family members. It has been estimated that "the average lifetime cost for one person with mental retardation is $1,014,000 (in 2003 dollars), and the lifetime costs for all people with mental retardation who were born in 2000 will total $51.2 billion (in 2003 dollars)" (National Center on Birth Defects and Developmental Disabilities, 2005, p. 4, with changes in notation). Later in the chapter, we discuss ways to reduce risk and enhance resiliency, which, if implemented, could reduce the lifetime costs of caring for children with disabilities.

ROLE OF PARENTING IN CHILD DEVELOPMENT

Parenting practices are embedded within a family system, which in turn is embedded within the larger social system. Cultural conflicts, unemployment, economic deprivation, and political events (e.g., the attack on the World Trade Center on September 11, 2001 and its repercussions) are examples of external factors that may affect parenting. Also affecting parenting are structural features of the family, such as whether the family has a mother and a father, a single mother, a single father, same-sex parents, or children from former marriages (i.e., a blended family). Finally, parents influence the child's behavior, and the child in turn influences the parents' behavior. For example, in a coercive family environment a parent's aggressive response to a child's misbehavior will sometimes create a cycle of increasingly aggressive acts on the part of both parent and child.

Let's look at some principal ways parents relate to, control, communicate with, and discipline their children.

1. *Type of relationship.* Parents can have a warm and affectionate relationship with their children and show love and acceptance, or they can have a hostile and rejecting relationship with their children and show anger, be critical, and even possibly be abusive or negligent. Most parents are somewhere in the middle of these extremes. Although an individual parent's behaviors will be variable, they likely will be within a narrow range. For example, affectionate and accepting parents may sometimes be angry and express negative feelings, while hostile parents may sometimes be pleasant and express positive feelings. Finally, the emotional tone underlying parent-child relationships may be expressed overtly or covertly.

2. *Type of child-rearing style.* Parents have different styles of child rearing. Parents with a *permissive style* are inconsistent and overindulgent and exert minimum control over their children's behavior. Parents with an *authoritarian style* are cold and rigid, impose strict rules of behavior, and are physically punitive. Finally, parents with an *authoritative style* are warm and consistent, have clear rules of behavior, and follow appropriate disciplinary practices.

3. *Type of communication.* Parents may be effective in communicating with their children (e.g., clear communication), ineffective (e.g., ambiguous communication), or somewhere in between. In addition, any one communication pattern may have both clear and ambiguous elements.

4. *Type of discipline.* Parents may use positive practices, such as rewards and reasoning, to discipline their child and control the child's behavior. Or, they may use negative practices, such as punishment or threats of punishment. Although no parent is totally consistent in his or her use of disciplinary practices, one form of practice usually predominates (Maccoby, 1980).

Research indicates that authoritative parenting is associated with more positive social and emotional development in children than is either authoritarian or permissive parenting (Baumrind, 1967; 1978). In addition, these findings hold across childhood ages and across cultures (Steinberg, 1999; Steinberg & Morris, 2001).

HOW PSYCHOLOGICAL PROBLEMS DEVELOP IN CHILDREN

Psychological problems in children develop from the interaction among genetic and biological factors, environmental factors (such as inadequate caregiving, parents with psychological problems, stress, and exposure to violence), and individual characteristics (such as personality, emotional reactions, self-concept, coping strategies, motivations, and beliefs). It is the interactive and cumulative effect of several variables, and not the mere presence of one or two variables, that affects children's psychological development. Let's first consider genetic and biological factors and then environmental factors.

Genetic and Biological Factors

Genetic and biological vulnerabilities may limit children's development and may make it more difficult for them to acquire needed competencies and cope with stress. Chapter 18 describes several genetic and biological disorders that affect children's physical and psychological development.

One critical factor affecting children's prenatal development is whether their mothers used or abused drugs or alcohol during pregnancy. Children born to mothers who abuse substances are at risk for birth defects, as well as for motor, cognitive, language, social, and emotional deficits (Cunningham, 1992; Phelps & Cox, 1993). As infants, they may tremble; be agitated, restless, hyperactive, or rigid; have sleep and respiratory difficulties; or be difficult to console. As toddlers and preschoolers, they may have subtle cognitive delays and show deficits in fine-motor control, self-organization and initiation, activity level, attention, speech, and language. As school-age children and adolescents, they may exhibit mild mental retardation, developmental learning disorders, attention difficulties, hyperactivity, and conduct disorders. Heavy alcohol use by a mother during pregnancy is a particularly serious risk factor that may be associated with *fetal alcohol syndrome* or other less severe disabilities (Mattson, Riley, Gramling, Delis, & Jones, 1998). Children born to drug- or alcohol-abusing mothers will need a comprehensive assessment of their physical and psychological functioning.

Environmental Factors

The primary way in which infants and young children learn about themselves and others is through their experiences in the family environment. These experiences may be encoded in memory as a set of beliefs about themselves and others and as expectations about future relationships with others.

Poor parenting behaviors.
Let's look at some parenting behaviors that may adversely affect children's adjustment and the possible reasons for these parenting behaviors.

EXAMPLES

1. *Engaging in child maltreatment.* Parents may engage in child maltreatment. Child maltreatment includes physical abuse, sexual abuse, psychological abuse, or neglect. *Physical abuse* refers to parental behavior that causes physical harm to the child, such as hitting, spanking, burning, or other acts. *Sexual abuse* refers to any type of parental behavior involving sexual activity with the child. *Psychological abuse* refers to parental behavior that causes the child emotional harm, such as overt rejection, ridicule, shaming, and use of threats. *Neglect* refers to parents' failure to meet the child's emotional and physical needs.

Children who have been maltreated are at increased risk for delinquency and for adult criminality (higher arrest rates, higher rates of violent crime), mental health problems (suicide attempts, PTSD), educational problems (low IQ, poor reading ability), occupational difficulties (unemployment, low-level service jobs), and public health and safety issues (prostitution in both males and females, alcohol problems) (English, Widom, & Brandford, 2002; Graham-Bermann, 2001; Widom & Maxfield, 2001). However, the majority of children who have been maltreated do not engage in criminal behavior or have mental health, educational, occupational, or public health and safety problems. The short- and long-term consequences of child maltreatment depend on the personal characteristics and resources of the child, the availability of emotional and social supports for the child, and the availability of therapeutic treatment for the child and parent (Wolfe & McGee, 1991; Zahn-Waxler, Cole, Welsh, & Fox, 1995).

2. *Handling behavioral problems ineffectively.* Parents may inadvertently encourage their children's inappropriate behavior, be unable to establish reasonable limits on their children's behavior, be inconsistent with them and have difficulty handling situations that call for discipline, delay dealing with any misbehavior, or use overly harsh or overly lax disciplinary procedures.

3. *Failing to provide emotional support.* Parents may be cold and insensitive to their children's needs.

4. *Communicating poorly.* Parents may communicate poorly with their children, may not understand the communication of their children, or may give their children mixed messages.

REASONS

1. *History of troubled childhood.* Parents may themselves have been raised in families with much discord (such as domestic violence), had parents who abused substances, or had parents who, as children, were victims of neglect, physical abuse, sexual abuse, or emotional abuse.

2. *Psychological problems.* Parents may have a psychological disorder, a drug or alcohol problem, poor impulse control, sexual identity conflicts, an inability to express emotions appropriately, low tolerance for frustration, excessive dependency needs, arrested development, or a pattern of displacing feelings. Parents with psychological problems may have difficulty helping their children feel emotionally secure, gain an understanding of social causes and effects, develop planning ability, learn the importance of delayed gratification, and learn to take responsibility for their own actions (Clarke & Clarke, 1994). They also may have difficulty coping with developmental changes in their children and are more likely to be thrown into a crisis by stressful events (Frude, 1991).

Although children whose parents become addicted to drugs *after* the children are born are not considered "drug exposed," this kind of exposure to drugs or alcohol nevertheless places them at risk for developing psychological difficulties. Parents who use alcohol or drugs or who have sustained organic deficits as a result of excessive use of substances not only are likely to have poor parenting skills but also may be at risk for neglecting their children or for physically, sexually, or psychologically maltreating them (Cunningham, 1992).

3. *Inadequate affective processes.* Parents may be depressed or have inappropriate or blunted emotions, negative attitudes toward children, fears of mature sexuality, poor relationships with others, or feelings of jealousy when the child associates with other children.

4. *Inadequate cognitive processes.* Parents may rationalize poor parenting practices, have inaccurate beliefs about discipline or unrealistic expectations of the child, show irresponsibility in decision making, minimize the severity of inappropriate behavior, engage in self-deception, have low intelligence, have poor judgment, or be poorly educated.

5. *Inadequate personal resources.* Parents may have low self-esteem, inadequate social skills, inadequate ability to cope with stress, or little emotional support from other adults.

6. *Personal stressors.* Parents may have family conflicts, suffer from personal illnesses, have financial pressures, be involved in domestic violence, have work-related problems, be involved in criminal activity, or have difficulty raising a child who engages in disruptive behavior or who has a physical or intellectual disability. Unemployment, unstable employment, or inadequate income often induces depression and anxiety in parents, which in turn can interfere with their ability to relate to their children and to provide the conditions essential for normal child development (Conger, Conger, Elder, Lorenz, Simons, & Whitbeck, 1993; Magnuson & Duncan, 2002; McLoyd, 1998). Economic stresses can also lead to marital conflict and parental substance abuse, which have a negative impact on parenting and, in extreme cases, may lead to child abuse or neglect.

Children's reactions.
Children reared in adverse family circumstances may come to think of themselves as incompetent or unworthy, to think of others as hostile or unresponsive,

and to think of relationships with others as aversive or unpredictable. These negative thoughts about self and others may interfere with the development of their emotions and behavior-regulation skills. Children may find it particularly difficult to cope with parental rejection, which can arise when a parent is absent physically or emotionally. Children may experience loss of love, care, protection, guidance, and a model to emulate. Under such conditions, children are at risk for depression and other forms of behavior disorders (LaRoche, 1986; Odgers, Vincent, & Corrado, 2002).

Inadequate parenting is always a risk factor, but it does not inevitably cause children to become maladjusted. As noted in the next section of this chapter, children are resilient, and whether inadequate parenting negatively affects their development depends on the presence of protective factors, such as alternative positive role models, and the child's temperament and emotional maturity (Benson, Scales, & Mannes, 2003; Cummings, Davies, & Campbell, 2000; Harris, 2002; Masten, 2001; Masten & Curtis, 2000).

In addition to poor parenting behavior, children may face stresses associated with other environmental events. Such events include the birth of a sibling, moving to a new home or apartment, changing schools, failing classes, being suspended, being exposed to cultural clashes or community violence, being a victim of violence (e.g., being maltreated, mugged, or sexually assaulted), having peers involved with drugs or alcohol, being rejected by peers, confronting racial or religious prejudice, having a friend or relative commit suicide, having a best friend move, losing a job, having a parent lose a job, being homeless, having a relative or close friend die, having parents divorce, experiencing a natural disaster, or becoming pregnant or impregnating someone.

Stress is a key factor in the development of behavior disorders in children. Stress can exacerbate problems that children face and bring about new problems by, for example, leading to acting-out behavior or a breakdown in behavior and producing changes in various neurochemicals in the body.

Direct exposure to violence may affect children's psychological adjustment. In a national survey of a representative sample of 2,000 American children (1,042 boys and 958 girls) ages 10 to 16 years, one-third of the children reported having been the victim of an assault (Boney-McCoy & Finkelhor, 1995). Assaults were characterized as aggravated assault (12.3%), simple assault (11.5%), sexual assault (10.5%), genital violence (7.5%), attempted kidnapping (6.1%), nonparental family assault (5.1%), parental assault (2.2%), and other (44.8%). Extrapolating these results to the entire nation suggests that over 6.1 million youths ages 10 to 16 years have suffered some form of assault. The *victimized children* reported more psychological and behavioral symptoms than did the nonvictimized children, including more symptoms of *posttraumatic stress disorder* during the past week, increased sadness during the past month, and more trouble with teachers during the past year. (Posttraumatic stress disorder, or PTSD, is a psychological reaction to a highly distressing event, such as a natural disaster, an accident, war, or rape; symptoms include frightening thoughts and images, trouble falling asleep, and uncontrollable temper outbursts.)

The survey's authors concluded (Boney-McCoy & Finkelhor, 1995):

> Evidence suggests that violent victimization is a major traumagenic [trauma-causing] influence in child development, and it may account for a substantial portion of mental health morbidity in both childhood and later adult life. These are powerful arguments for the need to quell the tide of violence in society and to protect children from its consequences. (p. 735)

The experience of being victimized and its associated trauma may interfere with or distort several developmental tasks of childhood (Boney-McCoy & Finkelhor, 1995). For example, victimized children may have impaired attachment to a caregiver or impaired self-esteem, may adopt highly sexualized or highly aggressive modes of relating to others, may fail to develop competence in peer relations, or may deal with anxiety in dysfunctional ways, such as by using drugs, dissociating, or engaging in self-injurious behavior. The developmental effects of being victimized are likely to be more severe when the victimization is repetitive and ongoing; when it changes the nature of the child's relationship with her or his caregivers; when it adds to other serious stressors, such as bereavement, parental divorce, or racial discrimination; or when it interferes with a crucial developmental transition (such as when a child is sexually abused during adolescence). Other research has shown that children exposed to community violence may have poor academic performance, depression, or conduct disorders (Schwartz & Gorman, 2003).

Indirect exposure to violence also may affect children's adjustment (U.S. Department of Health & Human Services, 2001). Children who observe violent events in their homes tend to have more behavior problems (such as aggressive and delinquent behavior) and more adjustment problems (such as sleep disturbances, bed-wetting, eating disturbances, fears of abandonment) than children who are not exposed to violent behavior in their homes; they also tend to be more withdrawn and anxious. In addition, children who witness family violence are more likely to be maltreated themselves. Finally, children who both witness family violence and are the victims of maltreatment tend to have more behavior and adjustment problems than children experiencing either event alone.

Comment

Psychological problems may lead children to experience a diminished sense of mastery and control, affecting interpersonal interactions with family and friends, and to suffer impairments in biological functioning. Psychological problems—by inducing stress, disrupting important social bonds, and undermining their existing competencies, self-concept, and view of the world—may compromise children's future development (Hammen & Rudolph, 1996).

Recent research on humans and animals indicates that life experiences can alter some gene-based traits once thought to be innate, a phenomenon referred to as "developmental plasticity" (Begley, 2005). Exercise, diet, and other life style choices, for example, can determine whether the traits associated with some genes will be expressed. For example, (a) the type of environmental risk a person experiences will determine whether the genes hypothesized to be connected with aggression or depression are expressed, (b) the amount of dietary fat a person consumes will determine whether the gene hypothesized to be associated with cholesterol levels is expressed, (c) how much a person smokes will determine whether the gene hypothesized to be connected with gum disease is expressed, and (d) the type of maternal care a child receives will determine whether the gene hypothesized to be associated with neuroticism is expressed. Thus, how genes are expressed can be related to the person's experiences; it is not always a matter of nature versus nurture.

RISK AND RESILIENCY

The concepts of *at-risk children* and *developmental risk* refer to the probability that children with certain characteristics or life experiences may be vulnerable to psychological, physical, or adaptive difficulties during their developmental years and beyond. These difficulties include dropping out of school, drug and alcohol abuse, delinquency, suicide, and psychiatric and behavioral problems (Athey & Ahearn, 1991; Hoge, 2001; Rutter, Giller, & Hagell, 1998). Risk factors are the conditions producing this vulnerability.

Risk factors may be found in the child, in the family, and in the environment (the child's neighborhood, school, peer group, or nation; U.S. Department of Health and Human Services, 2001). Some risk factors come into play during infancy and childhood, whereas others do not appear until adolescence or later years. Some become less important as a child matures, while others persist throughout the life span.

The concept of *resiliency* refers to the ability children have to cope with risk factors or stressors. Some children suffer serious consequences when they are exposed to risk factors such as abuse or poverty, while others, the resilient ones, deal better with risk factors and manifest few emotional or behavioral effects. The factors that moderate the effects of risk or stress are termed *protective factors*.

Risk Factors

Risk factors refer to characteristics of the child or of her or his circumstances that are associated with the development of maladaptive behaviors (see Table 1-5). The same factors that place children "at risk" can also be viewed as "outcome" factors, depending on whether you look at the problem's cause or its outcome—that is, where in the cycle the factors are considered. For example, poor prenatal care (a risk) can lead to low birth weight in an infant (an outcome), low birth weight (a risk) can lead to illness (an outcome), illness (a risk) can lead to problems in school (an outcome), problems in school (a risk) can lead to dropping out of school (an outcome), dropping out of school (a risk) can limit a person to a low-paying job (an outcome), a low-paying job (a risk) can lead to poverty (an outcome), and poverty (a risk) can lead to poor prenatal care (an outcome). The cycle that began with poor prenatal care is now complete (see Figure 1-2).

Major indicators of risk. Let's look at some statistics on 10 major risk factors (see Table 1-6). The statistics were collected by the Annie E. Casey Foundation (2001, 2002, 2003) and the Office of Juvenile Justice and Delinquency Prevention of the U.S. Department of Justice (2004).

1. *Low birth weight.* Babies who weigh less than 5.5 pounds at birth are considered to have low birth weight. Low-birth-weight babies have a greater chance of dying at birth, and those who survive are more likely than normal-birth-weight babies to have medical and school problems. In 2000, 7.6% of all babies had low birth weight.

2. *Infant mortality.* Infant deaths are commonly associated with complications during pregnancy and often occur within 28 days after birth. In 2001, 6.8 infants died per 1,000 live births. The infant mortality rate in the United States in 2000 was higher than that in 20 other developed nations.

3. *Child mortality.* The death rate for children between 1 and 14 years old was 22 per 100,000 in 2000. The highest percentage of child deaths was associated with accidents, most of which involved motor vehicles. Parents who are disadvantaged socially and economically are less likely than their nondisadvantaged counterparts to use infant car seats, follow safety precautions around the home, and engage in other prevention-related activities.

4. *Teenage parenthood.* In 2001, the teen birth rate was 25 births per 100,000 female adolescents 15 to 17 years old. "Children born to teenage mothers are less likely to receive the emotional and financial resources that support their development into independent, productive, and well-adjusted adults" (Annie E. Casey Foundation, 2003, p. 1).

5. *Arrest and incarceration.* Only a minority of youths engage in criminal activity, and an even smaller number commit serious crimes. Nevertheless, FBI statistics indicate that 438,291 youths under the age of 15 were arrested in 2002, while 1,421,948 youths under 18 years of age were arrested in 2002. Only about 4% of those arrests were for violent crimes. The growth in juvenile crime rates that began in the late 1980s peaked in 1994. The youth crime rate has declined significantly in the years since then. For example, juvenile arrests for violent crime declined 44% between 1994 and 2001.

Table 1-5
Risk Factors Checklist

RISK FACTORS CHECKLIST

Child's name: _____   Examiner's name: _____

Age: _____   Grade: _____

School: _____   Date: _____

	Check one				Check one	
I. Individual	Yes	No			Yes	No
1. Genetic vulnerabilities	☐	☐	6. Parents with mental illness		☐	☐
2. Birth deficiencies	☐	☐	7. Parents with physical problems		☐	☐
3. Failure to bond with primary caregiver	☐	☐	8. Parents who are antisocial		☐	☐
4. Exposure to toxins	☐	☐	9. Parents who are poorly educated		☐	☐
5. Medical problems	☐	☐	10. Parents who are substance abusers		☐	☐
6. Chronic underarousal	☐	☐	11. Parents under considerable stress		☐	☐
7. Mental illness	☐	☐	12. Parents who maltreat their children		☐	☐
8. Exposure to violence	☐	☐	13. Parents who reject or neglect their children		☐	☐
9. Aggressive and hostile behavior	☐	☐	14. Parents who are noninvolved with their children		☐	☐
10. Antisocial attitudes or beliefs	☐	☐	15. Lax and ineffective parental discipline		☐	☐
11. Antisocial behavior	☐	☐	16. Parents who use inconsistent, harsh, or permissive methods of parenting		☐	☐
12. Cognitive delays or disorders	☐	☐	17. Parents who provide poor supervision		☐	☐
13. Poor problem-solving skills	☐	☐	18. Parents with inappropriate expectations for their children		☐	☐
14. Anxiety	☐	☐	19. Disruptive family relationships		☐	☐
15. Hyperactivity	☐	☐	20. Delinquent siblings		☐	☐
16. Restlessness	☐	☐	21. Domestic violence		☐	☐
17. Impulsivity	☐	☐	22. Residential mobility		☐	☐
18. Attention difficulties	☐	☐	23. Homelessness		☐	☐
19. Concentration difficulties	☐	☐	24. Large family size		☐	☐
20. Shallow affect	☐	☐	25. Single parent		☐	☐
21. Risk-taking	☐	☐				
22. Victim of violence	☐	☐	**III. School/Community/Environment**			
23. Under considerable stress	☐	☐	1. Inferior schools		☐	☐
24. Depression	☐	☐	2. Inferior teachers		☐	☐
25. Substance abuse	☐	☐	3. Community disorganization and violence		☐	☐
26. Academic failure	☐	☐	4. Access to firearms and drugs in community		☐	☐
27. Learning difficulties	☐	☐	5. No access to health care and social services		☐	☐
28. Language deficits	☐	☐	6. No mentors in community		☐	☐
29. High truancy rates	☐	☐	7. Rejection by peers		☐	☐
30. Failure to understand consequences of actions	☐	☐	8. Antisocial peers		☐	☐
31. Maladaptive methods of handling stress	☐	☐	9. No supportive church community		☐	☐
32. Poor coping ability	☐	☐	10. No leisure or sport facilities in community		☐	☐
II. Family			11. Racism		☐	☐
1. Maternal substance use during pregnancy	☐	☐	12. Residential segregation		☐	☐
2. Obstetrical complications	☐	☐	13. Presence of environmental toxins		☐	☐
3. Low socioeconomic status	☐	☐	14. Recent natural disaster		☐	☐
4. Unemployed parents	☐	☐	15. Economic recession		☐	☐
5. Poverty	☐	☐				

From *Assessment of Children: Behavioral, Social, and Clinical Foundations (Fifth Edition)* by Jerome M. Sattler and Robert D. Hoge. Copyright 2006 by Jerome M. Sattler, Publisher, Inc. Permission to photocopy this table is granted to purchasers of this book for personal use only (see copyright page for details).

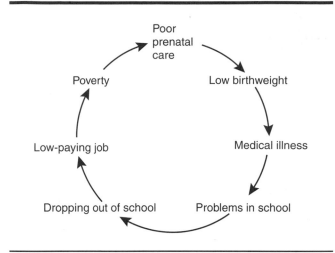

Figure 1-2.   An example of a cycle of risk and outcome factors. The diagram illustrates that factors can be risk factors or outcome factors, depending on where in the cycle the factors are considered.

Table 1-6
Ten Indicators of Child Risk

Indicator	Total U.S. population
1. Percentage of low-birth-weight babies	7.6%
2. Infant mortality rate (number of deaths per 1,000 live births)	6.8
3. Child death rate (number of deaths per 100,000 children ages 1 to 14)	22
4. Teen birth rate (number of births per 100,000 females ages 15 to 17)	25
5. Number of arrests and incarcerations (children under age 15)	0.73% (438,291)
6. Percentage of teens who are high school dropouts (ages 16 to 19)	9%
7. Percentage of teens not attending school and not employed (ages 16 to 19)	8%
8. Teen death rate by accident, homicide, and suicide (number of deaths per 100,000 teens ages 15 to 19)	51
9. Percentage of families with children headed by a single parent	28%
10. Percentage of children in poverty	16.2%

Note. Indicators 1, 3, and 6–10 are based on the year 2000, indicators 2 and 4 are based on the year 2001, and indicator 5 is based on the year 2002.
Source: Indicators 1–4 and 6–10 obtained from Annie E. Casey Foundation (2001, 2002, 2003); indicator 5 obtained from Office of Juvenile Justice and Delinquency Prevention (2004).

6. *Dropping out of school.* In 2000, 9% of youths ages 16 to 19 years dropped out of high school. Because of chronic school failure, adolescents may lose the "hope of attaining a secure and challenging job with economic security and a moderate degree of status" (Kagan, 1991, p. 593).

7. *Teenage unemployment.* In 2000, about 8% of youths between 16 and 19 were neither enrolled in school nor working. The rate for African American and Hispanic American youths was approximately 13%; this rate represented a decline from the 1984 rate of 19%.

8. *Teenage violent death.* The teenage violent death rate in 2000 was 51 per 100,000 youths between 15 and 19 years of age. The leading cause of death for Euro American youths was motor vehicle accidents, whereas the leading cause of death for African American youths was murder. Young people 12 to 17 years of age are more often victims of violent crimes than any other age group. Males are nearly twice as likely as females to be victims of serious violent crimes. Children are at risk for violent death when they live in neighborhoods where violence and other forms of antisocial behavior are common or that provide few, if any, positive support networks.

9. *Single-parent families.* Close to 28% of all children were living with only one parent in 2000. Almost 58% of African American children lived in single-parent families, followed by about 30% of Hispanic American children and 17% of Euro American children. Children living in single-parent households are five times more likely to be poor than children living with both parents.

10. *Low socioeconomic status (SES)/poverty.* Approximately 16% of all children lived below the poverty line in 2000. Almost 33% of African American children lived in poverty, followed by 27.8% of Hispanic American children and 11.2% of Euro American children. Poverty rates are even higher for single-parent families. While 6% of children from intact families were living below the poverty line, 34% of children raised in single-mother families and 17% of children in single-father families were living below the poverty line.

Low SES is probably the single most significant factor placing children at risk for becoming maladjusted. Poverty does not directly cause children to have problems; rather, it exposes children to risk. In comparison to nondisadvantaged children, children from low-SES backgrounds (called "economically disadvantaged children," "disadvantaged children," or "poor children") are more likely to suffer from, for example, growth retardation and anemia, high levels of lead in the blood (because of exposure to lead from old paint and from the air), developmental problems or delays and behavioral problems, learning problems, mild mental retardation, injuries, asthma, dental problems, and childhood diseases (because of lack of vaccinations). Many of these problems may be caused by poor nutrition and poor health care. Homeless children are at even greater risk for many of these problems (Tarnowski & Rohrbeck, 1993).

Research suggests that "low SES status coupled with membership in a minority group is the strongest predictor of school dropout. It is also related to juvenile delinquency and is the strongest predictor of teenage pregnancy" (McWhirter, McWhirter, McWhirter, & McWhirter, 1993, p. 37). Low-SES adolescents may engage in delinquent activities because they see little hope of finding a good job or of being accepted in society. Becoming pregnant may ensure that a female adolescent receives welfare and perhaps gives her a sense of responsibility and belonging.

The sociocultural context of poverty and the life circumstances with which it is typically associated make it difficult for a young child to acquire the skills and values that are prerequisites for success in educational settings. Raising a child in poverty makes it extremely difficult for a parent to provide a background that is conducive to success in school. The stressors encountered as a part of everyday life often force parents to focus their energies on the attainment of short-term outcomes (e.g., providing adequate food and shelter), leaving them little time to concentrate on facilitating the development of skills and attitudes that will allow the child to function well outside the family. And, considering the limited financial resources and limited effectiveness of programs, schools responsible for educating large populations of children in poverty are faced with a nearly impossible task.

The Family Risk Index has four criteria that reflect the overall level of risk confronting children in families (Annie E. Casey Foundation, 2002): living in a family with income below the poverty line, with only one parent, in which no parent has full-time employment, and with a household head who is a high school dropout. Using data from the 2000 U.S. Census, researchers at the Annie E. Casey Foundation (2002) concluded that 12% of American children are living in conditions exhibiting at least three of the four risk factors.

Resilience/Protective Factors

No one knows why children exposed to the same environmental stresses respond differently—some become criminals, for example, and others become productive citizens. However, we do know that how children cope with stressors is influenced by the presence of resilience or protective factors. These factors include psychological resources (e.g., emotional maturity, good problem-solving skills, good interpersonal skills, and high self-esteem) and positive relationships with parents, siblings, peers, and others. Table 1-7 presents a checklist of protective factors.

Children who exhibit some of the protective factors shown in Table 1-7 will cope better with stress and be better able to master and overcome adversity. There are still unanswered questions about the ways in which these factors operate (Rutter, 2000). And even highly resilient children are not invulnerable to risk; they may succumb to the ravages of extreme and persistent stress.

No one risk factor (or even combination of factors) necessarily causes a child to become maladjusted. Similarly, no one protective factor (or even combination of factors) guar-

antees that a child will not become maladjusted. However, protective factors reduce the probability that a child experiencing a risk factor will become maladjusted. In addition, both risk factors and protective factors may interact and exert cumulative effects.

Reducing Risk and Enhancing Resiliency

In order to help children who may be at risk for developing psychological disorders or adjustment problems, society must find ways to reduce risk and enhance protective factors in youths and their families. The following strategies may be useful.

1. *Reduce children's exposure to risk factors.* The aim is to reduce exposure to "malnutrition, toxic substances, illnesses, accidents, and other preventable risk factors" (Masten, 1994, p. 15). This can be done by (a) promoting and establishing "programs to reduce childbirth in early adolescence and to promote healthy pregnancies and child development" (Masten, 1994, p. 15), (b) promoting public health measures designed to reduce children's exposure to lead and mercury and laws requiring the construction of safer automobiles, and (c) reducing poverty and homelessness, which in turn is likely to reduce risks for chronic illnesses, emotional and behavioral problems, and academic delays.

2. *Reduce stressors and the pileup of multiple stressors.* The aim is "to reduce exposure to adversity or the piling up of multiple stressors" (Masten, 1994, p. 16). This can be done by (a) reducing the stress associated with going from elementary school to junior high school by establishing middle schools, (b) stabilizing the school environment for highly mobile families by establishing magnet schools, district-wide school choice, and open enrollment policies, and (c) improving public safety in dangerous urban areas. These changes have important implications for families as well, because even resilient children and families may have times in their lives during which they cannot cope with overwhelming life events.

3. *Increase available resources.* The aim is "to increase the availability of resources to children at risk" (Masten, 1994, p. 17). This can be done by (a) increasing personal resources (e.g., improving children's social and problem-solving skills), (b) increasing material resources (e.g., providing breakfast at school to help children learn better) and community resources (e.g., providing tutors and encouraging teachers to give additional attention to children), and (c) establishing health clinics in schools. In addition, we need to help at-risk children and their families take advantage of available resources. We need to give young people opportunities to succeed in challenging tasks, to teach them positive coping strategies and skills, to expose them to career opportunities, and to provide them with positive peer group experiences. Providing income, food, education, job training, and child management skills to parents also can increase children's resources.

Table 1-7
Protective Factors Checklist

PROTECTIVE FACTORS CHECKLIST

Child's name: _____   Examiner's name: _____

Age: _____   Grade: _____

School: _____   Date: _____

	Check one				Check one	
I. Individual	Yes	No			Yes	No
1. Close bond with primary caregiver	☐	☐	3. Competent parents		☐	☐
2. Physical health	☐	☐	4. Stable, cohesive, and well-adjusted family		☐	☐
3. Emotional maturity	☐	☐	5. Warm, nurturant, or supportive relationship			
4. Mental health	☐	☐	with at least one parent		☐	☐
5. Positive, prosocial attitudes	☐	☐	6. Supportive and caring other family members		☐	☐
6. High self-esteem	☐	☐	7. Parents provide competent supervision and			
7. Good problem-solving skills	☐	☐	direction		☐	☐
8. Good social skills	☐	☐	8. Small family size		☐	☐
9. Good school performance	☐	☐	9. Financially stable family		☐	☐
10. Participates in positive leisure or sport			10. Stable and attractive home environment		☐	☐
activities	☐	☐	11. Assigned chores		☐	☐
11. Highly motivated to address problems	☐	☐				
12. Nonexposure to violence	☐	☐	**III. School/Community/Environment**			
13. Good coping ability	☐	☐	1. Good schools		☐	☐
14. Self-discipline	☐	☐	2. Good teachers		☐	☐
15. Adaptable	☐	☐	3. Good neighborhood		☐	☐
16. Compassionate	☐	☐	4. Limited accessibility to firearms and drugs			
17. "Easy," engaging temperament	☐	☐	in community		☐	☐
18. Special talent	☐	☐	5. Access to health care and social services		☐	☐
19. Impulse control	☐	☐	6. Mentors in community		☐	☐
20. Achievement motivation	☐	☐	7. Peer acceptance		☐	☐
21. Persistence	☐	☐	8. Supportive peers		☐	☐
22. Faith	☐	☐	9. Supportive church community		☐	☐
23. Internal locus of control	☐	☐	10. Leisure or sport facilities in community		☐	☐
24. Intolerant attitude toward deviance	☐	☐	11. Tolerance of ethnic groups		☐	☐
25. Understands consequences of actions	☐	☐	12. Integrated neighborhood		☐	☐
			13. Nonpolluted environment		☐	☐
II. Family			14. No major natural disasters		☐	☐
1. Good prenatal care	☐	☐	15. Economic prosperity		☐	☐
2. Educated parents	☐	☐				

From *Assessment of Children: Behavioral, Social, and Clinical Foundations (Fifth Edition)* by Jerome M. Sattler and Robert D. Hoge. Copyright 2006 by Jerome M. Sattler, Publisher, Inc. Permission to photocopy this table is granted to purchasers of this book for personal use only (see copyright page for details).

Improving the school environment is critical in this respect. Schools should not only provide knowledge and teach problem-solving skills, but also provide a setting where children can become connected with caring, competent adults (Masten, 1994). Adults at effective schools have high expectations combined with high positive regard and support. Effective schools provide children with opportunities to achieve, either academically or in extracurricular activities. This may involve providing services for children with special learning needs and opportunities for all youths to participate in physical activities. A given school's actions will vary according to context, culture, and the needs of its children. Good schools vary, just as good parents do. Effective schools, however, exhibit the strengths discussed above (Reynolds, Creemers, Nesselrod, Schaffer, Stringfield, & Teddlie, 1994; Rutter, 1983).

Services should also be available for youths in trouble with the law or at high risk for antisocial behaviors. There is ample evidence that behaviorally based skill training, focused substance abuse treatments, and multimodal interventions directed toward a range of risk factors are effective in addressing antisocial behaviors (Hoge, 2001; Krisberg & Howell, 1998; Lipsey & Wilson, 1998).

4. *Mobilize protective resources.* The aim is to mobilize protective resources in order to foster resilience. This can be done by (a) establishing programs designed to improve parent-child relationships, (b) offering children relationships with other adults (such as grandparents, older siblings, childcare providers, members of Big Brother/Big Sister organizations) and encouraging children to participate in other mentoring programs, and (c) promoting children's social and intellectual development (such as in the Head Start program).

5. *Create a culture of nonviolence.* The aim is to create "a culture with zero tolerance for violence—one that promotes peaceful conflict resolution; rejects the use of power and control over children, women, and minorities; and respects racial, cultural, and class difference. It is also a culture that values and supports caregiving and parenting and recognizes the importance of relationships between children and their parents and other caregivers, especially in the early years" (U.S. Department of Justice, 2000, p. 46).

Parents and other caregivers can help a child become a more competent individual by doing the following (Masten, 1994, p. 14, with changes in notation; Werner, 2000):

• Make the child feel worthwhile and valued through consistent nurturing behavior and by engendering trust in people.
• Provide "an organized and predictable environment that combines warmth and caring with a clearly defined structure and an established setting of explicit limits that are consistently enforced" (Werner, 2000, p. 129).
• Model competent behavior.
• Provide information and access to knowledge.
• Coach competent behavior, providing guidance and constructive feedback.
• Steer the child away from wasteful or dangerous situations.
• Support the undertaking of new challenges that they believe the child can meet.
• Function as advocates when the child needs community services.
• Provide opportunities for competence- and confidence-building experiences.

ETHICAL CONSIDERATIONS

Whether you are currently in training or are a professional psychologist, you are obligated to follow state and municipal statutes governing the practice of psychology and the ethical guidelines of your professional organization (see Table 1-8). The most important guidelines for psychological assessments are found in two publications: *Standards for Educational and Psychological Testing* (American Educational Research As-

Table 1-8
Examples of Ethical and Professional Guidelines Relevant to Psychological Assessment

Code of Fair Testing Practices in Education (American Psychological Association, 2004)

Ethical Principles of Psychologists and Code of Conduct (American Psychological Association, 2002)

Guidelines for Child Custody Evaluations in Divorce Proceedings (American Psychological Association, 1994a)

Guidelines for Computer-Based Tests and Interpretations (American Psychological Association, 1986)

Guidelines for Providers of Psychological Services to Ethnic, Linguistic, and Culturally Diverse Populations (American Psychological Association, 1990)

Record Keeping Guidelines (American Psychological Association, 1993)

Report of the Task Force on Test User Qualifications (DeMers, Turner, Andberg, Foote, Hough, Ivnik, Meier, Moreland, & Rey-Casserly, 2000)

Responsibilities of Users of Standardized Tests (Association for Assessment in Counseling, 2003)

Standards for Educational and Psychological Testing (American Educational Research Association, American Psychological Association, and National Council on Measurement in Education, 1999)

Standards for Qualifications of Test Users (American Counseling Association, 2003)

sociation, American Psychological Association, & National Council on Measurement in Education, 1999) and *Ethical Principles of Psychologists and Code of Conduct* (American Psychological Association, 2002). The standards include guidelines for the construction, evaluation, and administration of psychological measures. Psychologists who violate state or municipal licensing regulations may lose their licenses, while members of the American Psychological Association (APA) who violate the APA ethical code may face disciplinary actions, including expulsion.

Some key ethical guidelines for conducting assessments of children and their families follow (adapted from the American Psychological Association, 1994a).

1. *Training.* The examiner who conducts a psychological (or psychoeducational) assessment with children and their families has sufficient education, training, and expertise in psychological assessment, child and family development, child psychopathology, and adult psychopathology to conduct assessments. Those working in a specialty area, such as neuropsychology, behavioral medicine, visitation and custody proceedings, or child maltreatment, need additional training in that area. The examiner also keeps abreast of the latest developments in the field.

2. *Consultation.* The examiner who conducts a psychological (or psychoeducational) assessment consults with other professionals when in doubt about assessment findings.

3. *Knowledge of federal and state law.* The examiner who conducts a psychological (or psychoeducational) assessment is knowledgeable about the relevant federal and state laws concerning assessment, such as laws governing children with disabilities, child maltreatment, family violence, and custody evaluations.

4. *Awareness of personal and societal biases and non-discriminatory practice.* The examiner who conducts a psychological (or psychoeducational) assessment is aware of any personal biases regarding age, gender, race, ethnicity, national origin, religion, sexual orientation, disability, language, culture, or socioeconomic status that may interfere with an objective evaluation and recommendations. The examiner recognizes and strives to overcome any such biases or withdraws from the evaluation if the biases cannot be overcome.

5. *Avoidance of multiple relationships.* The examiner who conducts a psychological (or psychoeducational) assessment avoids potential conflicts of interest. For example, the examiner would not take on a new client if doing so would affect the relationship the examiner has with a present client.

6. *Informed consent.* The examiner who conducts a psychological (or psychoeducational) assessment obtains informed consent from parents (or caregivers) to conduct the assessment.

7. *Confidentiality and disclosure of information.* The examiner who conducts a psychological (or psychoeducational) assessment informs the child and his or her parents about the limits of confidentiality and the situations in which information must be revealed (see below).

8. *Multiple methods of data gathering.* The examiner who conducts a psychological (or psychoeducational) assessment uses several sources to gather information about the child, including psychological tests, interviews, observation, psychological and psychiatric reports, and records from schools, hospitals, and other agencies when these are available.

9. *Interpretation of data.* The examiner who conducts a psychological (or psychoeducational) assessment interprets data cautiously and appropriately, considers alternative interpretations, and avoids overinterpreting data.

10. *Explanation of assessment findings.* The examiner who conducts a psychological (or psychoeducational) assessment explains the results of the assessment and the recommendations in a clear and understandable manner to the referral source, to the parents, and to the child, when appropriate.

11. *Records and data.* The examiner who conducts a psychological (or psychoeducational) assessment maintains the raw data, written records, and copies of all recordings, such as audiotapes, videotapes, or CDs.

Confidentiality must be suspended in the following cases (Federal law, 42 C.F.R, Part 2, 1993):

1. *When there is a reasonable suspicion of child maltreatment* (i.e., child abuse or neglect), you are legally obliged to report your suspicion to the authorities.
2. *When the examinee poses a physical threat to another person,* you must warn the prospective victim.
3. *When the examinee is a minor and poses a threat to himself or herself* (e.g., in any situation where the minor is in danger of death, where the delay of medical treatment would pose a health risk to the minor, or where treatment is needed to decrease physical pain), you are required to notify those responsible for the child.

These three exceptions reflect the principle that *when there is a clear and imminent danger to another individual, to society, or to the child directly, confidentiality must be breached.* However, you will need to use considerable judgment in deciding when confidentiality should be breached. First, what behaviors or conditions are grounds for "reasonable suspicion" that the child has been maltreated? Second, what behaviors indicate that the child poses a "physical threat to another person"? And third, what behaviors indicate that the child poses a "threat to himself or herself"?

Strict confidentiality cannot be maintained within schools, clinics, hospitals, prisons, and other agencies because agency personnel involved in the case usually have access to the child's records. You must explain this to the examinee. Review your state law for guidance about confidentiality and privileged communications and the exceptions that may call for breaking confidentiality.

REGULATING THE PROFESSION

Let's now look at how regulatory bodies and professional organizations regulate the profession of psychology.

Regulatory Bodies

Legislatures in each state in the United States and in each province in Canada have established bodies to regulate the activities of psychologists who provide clinical services to the public. Obtaining a license from or registering with a regulatory body allows the recipient to practice as a psychologist.

Regulatory bodies protect the public from unqualified practitioners by screening applicants, by determining the entry requirements for licensure or registration, by investigating complaints from clients, by enforcing ethical and professional conduct standards, by disciplining those who violate the professional code of conduct, by informing the public about the regulation of psychology, and by periodically reviewing and updating the standards and procedures (Edwards, 1994). Discipline procedures range from issuing a cautionary notice to revoking the offender's license or registration.

Licensing or registration is based on the educational qualifications, internship experience, and professional knowledge of the applicant. The education criterion is satisfied through a Ph.D. or Psy.D. degree, although an M.A. degree is sometimes accepted as the minimum educational qualification. Advanced degrees in education or social work and medical programs may also be recognized. The internship requirement is met by supervised experience in a clinical setting (preferably accredited by a professional organization) under the direction of a qualified professional. The professional knowledge requirement is met by successful performance on a standardized examination, such as the Examination for Professional Practice in Psychology, a national test that covers assessment and diagnosis, biological bases of behavior, cognitive-affective bases of behavior, ethical and legal professional issues, research methods, social and multicultural bases of behavior, and treatment and intervention.

States vary in their licensing requirements, and licensing in one jurisdiction does not necessarily mean that one can practice in another jurisdiction. However, efforts are being made by the APA to encourage uniformity in standards across jurisdictions. When standards become more uniform, it will be easier for psychologists to practice in more than one state without having to be relicensed.

National and Regional Professional Organizations

Many nations have national organizations that promote professional and scientific developments in the field of psychology. Among those in the United States, Canada, England, and Australia are the APA, the American Educational Research Association, the Canadian Psychological Association, the British Psychological Society, and the Australian Psychological Society. In addition, specialty organizations such as the National Association of School Psychologists, the Association of Black Psychologists, the Society for Research in Child Development, and the Psychonomic Society promote the field of psychology. States and regions in the United States also usually have organizations devoted to the practice of psychology. Three examples of regional organizations are the Western Psychological Association, the Eastern Psychological Association, and the Midwestern Psychological Association. Provinces in Canada, and other nations as well, have professional organizations that promote the field of psychology.

Professional organizations support scientific and clinical developments, serve as advocates for psychologists with policy makers and the public, develop ethical guidelines for the profession, publish journals and newsletters, organize conferences, and develop accreditation standards for graduate programs in psychology.

The American Psychological Association is organized into divisions, several of which are relevant to the psychological assessment of children. These include Division 5 (Evaluation, Measurement, and Statistics), Division 12 (Society of Clinical Psychology), Division 16 (School Psychology),

Division 17 (Society of Counseling Psychology), Division 33 (Mental Retardation and Developmental Disabilities), Division 37 (Child, Youth, and Family Services), Division 40 (Clinical Neuropsychology), Division 53 (Society of Clinical Child and Adolescent Psychology), and Division 54 (Society of Pediatric Psychology).

EDUCATIONAL QUALIFICATIONS OF PSYCHOLOGISTS

A Ph.D. degree in psychology is based on a research-practitioner program that provides a grounding in psychological research and in one or more clinical specialties. The Psy.D. degree provides training in research methodology but places a greater emphasis on practical training in clinical specialties; a Psy.D. program usually does not require a dissertation. The doctor of education degree (Ed.D.) may qualify as an entry-level degree, particularly for school psychologists. Controversy over the status of individuals with an M.A. degree continues. Some regulatory bodies allow those with the degree to have limited independent practice, while others do not. Regulatory bodies generally require that the entry-level graduate degree be from a recognized psychology graduate program, but there is some ambiguity about this matter, because there are no criteria universally accepted by all state licensing programs (Pryzwansky & Wendt, 1999). The debate over the criteria for evaluating excellence in psychology graduate training programs continues (Altmaier, 2003).

The APA has responded to this problem by developing a set of standards for graduate programs in school, clinical, and counseling psychology (American Psychological Association, 1996). Adhering to these standards is voluntary. Graduate schools may invite the APA to send a team to evaluate their programs. Approval by the APA lends credibility to a program, makes it easier for the university to obtain federal funds, and helps students when they apply for a license. The APA accreditation procedure focuses on seven domains: eligibility; program philosophy, objectives, and curriculum; program resources; student-faculty relations; quality enhancement; public disclosure; and relationship (i.e., a program's commitment to APA's policies and procedures). The APA also accredits doctoral internship programs.

CONCLUDING COMMENTS

This text provides guidelines for promoting the usefulness and fairness of a psychological (or psychoeducational) assessment. We believe that psychological (or psychoeducational) assessments can promote the mental health and help meet the educational needs of children from all ethnic backgrounds. Each youth and her or his parents will represent a new challenge; this text aims to increase your ability to rise effectively to the challenge.

Assessment plays a critical role in all fields that offer services to children with special needs and their families. Assessment is critical, because you cannot even begin an intervention until you know what problems the youth and family are having and what resources are available to them. And once the intervention begins, you can judge its effectiveness only by monitoring and assessing changes in the youth's adjustment. The initial assessment serves as a baseline relative to which you can evaluate changes and plan future interventions.

The assessment results reflect a child's performance at a particular time and place. Learning *why* the child performed as he or she did requires a careful study of the entire clinical history and assessment results. The assessment results usually will not tell you what the child might be able to do under a different set of testing conditions.

Assessments should not end with the report; make every attempt to be available to work with the child, parents, and referral source as needed. You may be in the best position to monitor the recommended interventions and modify them as needed.

All assessment techniques have both strengths and limitations. Although you will obtain valuable information from both formal and informal assessment techniques, neither approach provides perfectly reliable and valid information or completely samples a child's repertoire of behaviors, feelings, and abilities. In addition, assessment techniques vary in their degree of precision. Measurement error, for example, may be associated with the tests you use; the setting in which you conduct the evaluation; the child's motivation, willingness to guess, or level of alertness; and your alertness, biases, or administrative errors. Measurement error may also vary in different parts of the same test and with different age groups. The less objective the assessment technique (e.g., informal checklists, unstructured interviews), the more care you will need to exercise in using it and in interpreting the results. Consequently, it is best to view assessment results as *approximations* of the domains that they pertain to.

In evaluating assessment results and in formulating interventions, you also must consider the context in which the child functions. To be effective, an intervention plan must have *ecological validity*. This means that you must consider how the child's environment—including immediate family, extended family, subculture, neighborhood, school, and even the larger community—affects the child. The environmental contingencies that a child faces play a crucial role in affecting his or her behavior, not only during the testing situation but also outside the testing situation. If you focus exclusively on test results and fail to consider the child's environment, the proposed interventions may fail.

THINKING THROUGH THE ISSUES

1. What are some of the technical and clinical skills needed to become a competent behavioral and clinical assessor?
2. Discuss the differences among clinical, objective personality, and cognitive/ability assessments.
3. Which of the theoretical perspectives do you favor? Why?

4. What can we do as a society to reduce the incidence of mental illness in children?
5. Do you think society should devote more resources to helping at-risk families and children? If so, what resources are most needed?
6. What are some examples of unethical uses of psychological assessments?
7. What qualifies a person to administer psychological tests?

SUMMARY

1. The goal of this text is to help you make effective decisions about children with special needs. To do this, you will need to learn how to select appropriate assessment measures; administer, score, and interpret the measures; develop good interviewing and observational skills; and develop effective recommendations and interventions.
2. Good assessment practices rest on a foundation of knowledge of measurement theory, statistics, child development, personality theory, child psychopathology, ethical guidelines, and appropriate assessment measures.
3. This text is not a substitute for test manuals or for texts on child development or child psychopathology; it supplements material contained in test manuals and summarizes major findings in the areas of child development and psychopathology.
4. Although this text covers the major psychological instruments used in behavioral and clinical assessment of children, it does not cover every psychological assessment instrument currently published or even a fraction of the thousands of informal assessment procedures used by clinicians and researchers.
5. It is important to keep abreast of current research concerning assessment and intervention throughout your training and career.
6. In order to work with children with special needs, you will have to become thoroughly knowledgeable about legal and policy regulations concerning assessment procedures.
7. Those of you working in school settings will need to follow as precisely as possible the requirements of the Individuals with Disabilities Education Improvement Act of 2004 (Public Law 108-446; referred to as IDEA 2004).

Terminology

8. Psychological assessment refers to any activity designed to further the process of accumulating information and forming a judgment about the behavioral, emotional, or social characteristics of an individual.
9. Cognitive/ability assessments rely on responses that are classified as correct or incorrect and usually are numerically scored.
10. Objective personality assessments rely on test items that focus on external behavior or on internal emotional states. Rather than being scored as correct or incorrect, responses reflect the presence or absence of positive qualities (e.g., social skills, autonomy, persistence) or negative qualities (e.g., depression, aggression, anxiety).
11. Clinical assessments rely on collecting more open-ended information through, for example, parents' reports of their child's developmental history, interviews, and unstructured observational techniques. Projective measures and apperception tests frequently are used in clinical assessment.
12. Psychological assessments may employ a combination of cognitive, objective personality, and clinical procedures.

Goals of a Behavioral and Clinical Assessment

13. A behavioral and clinical assessment is intended to obtain relevant, reliable, and valid information about a child and his or her problems that can be used to assist the child and the people in his or her social world.

14. The major goals of a behavioral and clinical assessment are to (a) communicate information about the assessment process and administrative matters, (b) gather relevant background information, (c) conduct a formal evaluation, (d) evaluate the assessment information, and (e) recommend interventions and instructional programs.

15. The multimethod assessment approach involves (a) obtaining information from several sources and reviewing the child's records and previous evaluations, (b) using several assessment techniques, including norm-referenced tests, interviews, observations, and informal assessment procedures, and (c) assessing several areas (e.g., social-emotional-personality functioning, adaptive behavior, intelligence, memory, achievement, visual skills, auditory skills, motor skills, and oral language).

16. As a behavioral and clinical examiner, you must appreciate the worth and dignity of each examinee.

Guidelines for Conducting Behavioral and Clinical Assessments

17. When you evaluate a child, never focus exclusively on his or her test scores or numbers; instead, interpret the scores by asking yourself what they suggest about the child's competencies and limitations.

18. Each child has a range of competencies and limitations that you can evaluate by both quantitative and qualitative means.

19. Note that your aim is to assess both limitations and competencies; the focus should not be on limitations only.

20. Assessment techniques should be used for the benefit of the child.

21. Psychological measures should be administered under standard conditions and scored according to well-defined rules.

22. Scores may be adversely affected by numerous factors in the child (e.g., poor comprehension of English; temporary states of fatigue, anxiety, or stress; physical illnesses or disorders).

23. Evidence should indicate that measures have adequate reliability and validity.

24. Results from psychological measures should be interpreted in relation to other behavioral data and case history information. Assessment conclusions and recommendations should be based on all sources of information obtained about a child, not on any single piece of information.

25. Tests and other assessment procedures are powerful tools, but their effectiveness will depend on your knowledge and skill.

Theoretical Perspectives for Behavioral and Clinical Assessments

26. Five perspectives are useful in guiding the behavioral and clinical assessment process.

27. A developmental perspective proposes that the interplay between genetic disposition and environmental influences follows a definite, nonrandom form and direction.

28. A normative-developmental perspective evaluates changes in children's cognitions, affect, and behavior in relation to a reference group, usually composed of children of the same age and gender as the referred child.

29. A cognitive-behavioral perspective focuses on the importance of cognitions as major determinants of emotions and behavior. This perspective also looks at the role that cognitions such as values, beliefs, self-statements, self-confidence or self-efficacy, problem-solving strategies, expectancies, images, and goals play in the development of maladaptive behavior. Finally, this perspective emphasizes the individual and environmental influences that may shape and control the child's thoughts, feelings, and behavior.

30. A family-systems perspective focuses on the structure and dynamics of the family as determinants of the child's behavior.

31. An eclectic perspective, which is based on elements from the four other perspectives, emphasizes that (a) individual, familial, and environmental determinants are critical factors in children's development, (b) children are shaped by their environments and by their genetic constitutions, (c) what can be observed in children may not always reflect their potentials, and (d) children also shape their environments.

Assessment Dimensions and Categories

32. Assessment constructs may be expressed in dimensional or categorical terms.

33. Assessment constructs expressed in dimensional terms represent the degree to which a youth exhibits a characteristic.

34. Assessment constructs expressed in categorical terms place the child in a diagnostic category.

35. The empirical approach involves the application of factor analytic or multivariate statistical procedures.

36. Many empirically derived constructs reflect either externalizing or internalizing disorders.

37. Internalizing disorders of childhood usually are covert and not easily observable.

38. Externalizing disorders of childhood are characterized by overt behavioral excesses or disturbances.

39. Assessment constructs derived through the clinical approach are based on the experience of clinicians.

40. The *Diagnostic and Statistical Manual of Mental Disorders (DSM-IV-TR)* is the official diagnostic system of the American Psychiatric Association and is widely used in clinical assessments.

41. The Individuals with Disabilities Education Act (IDEA) uses 13 categories to classify children who have disabilities; these categories overlap with those of *DSM-IV-TR.*

42. During the 2000–2001 school year, the largest group of students receiving services was those with specific learning disabilities (49.99%), followed by students with speech or language impairments (18.94%), mental retardation (10.61%), and emotional disturbance (8.20%). These four categories represented 87.74% of all students receiving services.

43. The 5,775,722 students served under IDEA represented about 8.7% of the 66,211,355 children and young adults who were in the U.S. population during 2000–2001, according to the U.S. Census.

Children with Special Needs

44. Children with special needs are a heterogeneous group.

45. Generalizations about children with special needs must be made with caution, because each child has unique temperament and personality characteristics, cognitive skills, social skills, adaptive-behavior skills, and support systems.

46. Each child should be viewed as an individual and never only as representing a particular disorder.

47. Children who have special needs may have more than one disorder. Such children are said to suffer from co-morbidity or to have co-occurring disorders.

48. Children with special needs usually go through the same developmental sequences as children without special needs, although sometimes at a different rate.

49. Children with special needs form their self-concepts in ways similar to those of other children.

50. Children with special needs who also have physical impairments may be limited in their ability to obtain a full range of sensory information, to socialize, and to engage in sports and other physical activities.

51. The lifetime costs, both direct and indirect, of raising a child with disabilities also must be considered.

Role of Parenting in Child Development

52. Parenting practices are embedded within a family system, which in turn is embedded within the larger social system.

53. Cultural conflicts, unemployment, economic deprivation, and political events are examples of external factors that may affect parenting. Also affecting parenting are structural features of the family, such as whether the family has a mother and a father, a single mother, a single father, same-sex parents, or children from former marriages.

54. Parents can have a warm and affectionate relationship with their children and show love and acceptance, or they can have a hostile and rejecting relationship with their children and show anger, be critical, and even possibly be abusive or negligent.

55. Parents have different styles of child rearing. Parents with a permissive style are inconsistent and overindulgent and exert minimum control over their children's behavior. Parents with an authoritarian style are cold and rigid, impose strict rules of behavior, and are physically punitive. Parents with an authoritative style are warm and consistent, have clear rules of behavior, and follow appropriate disciplinary practices.

56. Parents may be effective in communicating with their children, ineffective, or somewhere in between.

57. Parents may use positive practices, such as rewards and reasoning, to discipline their child and control the child's behavior. Or, they may use negative practices, such as punishment or threats of punishment.

58. Research indicates that authoritative parenting is associated with more positive social and emotional development of children than is either authoritarian or permissive parenting.

How Psychological Problems Develop in Children

59. Psychological problems in children develop from the interaction among genetic and biological factors, environmental factors (such as inadequate caregiving, parents with psychological problems, stress, and exposure to violence), and individual characteristics (such as personality, emotional reactions, self-concept, coping strategies, motivations, and beliefs).

60. Genetic and biological vulnerabilities may limit children's development and may make it more difficult for them to acquire needed competencies and cope with stress.

61. A critical factor affecting children's prenatal development is whether their mothers used or abused drugs or alcohol during pregnancy.

62. The primary way in which infants and young children learn about themselves and others is through their experiences in the family environment.

63. Children reared in adverse family circumstances may come to think of themselves as incompetent or unworthy, to think of others as hostile or unresponsive, and to think of relationships with others as aversive or unpredictable.

64. Inadequate parenting is always a risk factor, but it does not inevitably cause children to become maladjusted.

65. Children also may face stresses associated with other environmental events, such as the birth of a sibling, moving, changing schools, or failing classes.

66. Stress is a key factor in the development of behavior disorders in children.

67. Direct exposure to violence may affect children's psychological adjustment.

68. "Evidence suggests that violent victimization is a major traumagenic [trauma-causing] influence in child development, and it may account for a substantial portion of mental health morbidity in both childhood and later adult life. These are powerful arguments for the need to quell the tide of violence in society and to protect children from its consequences" (Boney-McCoy & Finkelher, 1995, p. 735).

69. The experience of being victimized and its associated trauma may interfere with or distort several developmental tasks of childhood.

70. Indirect exposure to violence also may affect children's adjustment.

71. Psychological problems may lead children to experience a diminished sense of mastery and control, affecting interpersonal interactions with family and friends, and to suffer impairments in biological functioning.

72. Psychological problems—by inducing stress, disrupting important social bonds, and undermining their existing competencies, self-concept, and view of the world—may compromise children's future development.

73. How genes are expressed can be related to a person's experiences; it is not always a matter of nature versus nurture.

Risk and Resiliency

74. The concepts of at-risk children and developmental risk refer to the probability that children with certain characteristics or life experiences may be vulnerable to psychological, physical, or adaptive difficulties during their developmental years and beyond.

75. The concept of resiliency refers to the ability children have to cope with risk factors or stressors.

76. Risk factors refer to characteristics of the child or of her or his circumstances that are associated with the development of maladaptive behaviors.

77. Among the major indicators of risk are statistics on low birth weight, infant mortality, child mortality, teenage parenthood, arrest and incarceration, dropping out of school, teenage unemployment, teenage violent death, single-parent families, and low socioeconomic status (SES).

78. Low SES is probably the single most significant factor placing children at risk for becoming maladjusted.

79. Protective factors include psychological resources (e.g., emotional maturity, good problem-solving skills, good interper-

sonal skills, and high self-esteem) and positive relationships with parents or others.

80. We can enhance resiliency by reducing children's exposure to risk factors, reducing stressors and the pileup of multiple stressors, increasing available resources, mobilizing protective resources, and creating a culture of nonviolence.

Ethical Considerations

81. Whether you are in training or are a professional psychologist, you are obligated to follow state and municipal statutes governing the practice of psychology and the ethical guidelines of your professional organization.
82. The most important guidelines for psychological assessments are found in two publications: *Standards for Educational and Psychological Testing* and *Ethical Principles of Psychologists and Code of Conduct.*
83. The standards include guidelines for the construction, evaluation, and administration of psychological measures.
84. Psychologists who violate state or municipal licensing regulations may lose their license, while members of the APA who violate the APA ethical code may face disciplinary actions, including expulsion.
85. Confidentiality must be suspended when there is a reasonable suspicion of child maltreatment, when the examinee poses a physical threat to another person, or when the examinee is a minor and poses a threat to himself or herself.

Regulating the Profession

86. Legislatures in each state in the United States and in each province in Canada have established bodies to regulate the activities of psychologists who provide clinical services to the public.
87. Obtaining a license from or registering with a regulatory body allows the recipient to practice as a psychologist.
88. Regulatory bodies protect the public from unqualified practitioners by screening applicants, by determining the entry requirements for licensure or registration, by investigating complaints from clients, by enforcing ethical and professional conduct standards, by disciplining those who violate the professional code of conduct, by informing the public about the regulation of psychology, and by periodically reviewing and updating the standards and procedures.
89. Licensing or registration is based on the educational qualifications, internship experience, and professional knowledge of the applicant.
90. States vary in their licensing requirements, and licensing in one jurisdiction does not necessarily mean that one can practice in another jurisdiction.
91. Professional organizations support scientific and clinical developments, serve as advocates for psychologists with policy makers and the public, develop ethical guidelines for the profession, publish journals and newsletters, organize conferences, and develop accreditation standards for graduate programs in psychology.

Educational Qualifications of Psychologists

92. A Ph.D. degree in psychology is based on a research-practitioner program that provides a grounding in psychological research and in one or more clinical specialties.
93. The Psy.D. degree provides training in research methodology but places a greater emphasis on practical training in clinical specialties; a Psy.D. program usually does not require a dissertation.
94. The doctor of education degree (Ed.D.) may serve as an entry-level degree, particularly for school psychologists.

Concluding Comments

95. Psychological (or psychoeducational) assessments can promote the mental health and help meet the educational needs of children from all ethnic backgrounds.
96. Assessment is critical, because you cannot even begin an intervention until you know what problems the youth and family are having and what resources are available to them.
97. The assessment results usually will not tell you what the child might be able to do under a different set of testing conditions.
98. Assessments should not end with the report; make every attempt to be available to work with the child, parents, and referral source as needed.
99. All assessment techniques have both strengths and limitations.
100. To be effective, an intervention plan must have ecological validity.

KEY TERMS, CONCEPTS, AND NAMES

Individuals with Disabilities Education Improvement Act of 2004 (IDEA 2004) (p. 3)
Psychological assessment (p. 4)
Cognitive/ability assessment (p. 4)
Objective personality assessment (p. 4)
Clinical assessment (p. 5)
Goals of a behavioral and clinical assessment (p. 5)
Multimethod assessment approach (p. 6)
Assessment guidelines (p. 6)
Idiographic approach (p. 7)
Inductive methods (p. 7)
Deductive methods (p. 7)
Developmental perspective (p. 7)
Intraindividual (p. 7)
Interindividual (p. 7)
Normative-developmental perspective (p. 8)
Cognitions (p. 8)
Affect (p. 8)
Cognitive-behavioral perspective (p. 8)
Cognitive aspect of a cognitive-behavioral perspective (p. 8)
Behavioral aspect of a cognitive-behavioral perspective (p. 8)
Functional behavioral analysis (p. 8)
Family-systems perspective (p. 9)
Structure (p. 9)
Function (p. 9)
Assigned roles (p. 9)
Mode of interaction (p. 9)
Resources (p. 9)
Family history (p. 9)
Life cycle (p. 9)
Individual members' unique histories (p. 9)
Eclectic perspective (p. 9)

STUDY QUESTIONS

1. What do the following terms mean: psychological assessment, cognitive/ability assessment, objective personality assessment, and clinical assessment?
2. Discuss the goals of behavioral and clinical assessments.
3. Discuss the general guidelines for conducting behavioral and clinical assessments.
4. Compare the following theoretical perspectives useful for a behavioral and clinical assessment: (a) developmental, (b) normative-developmental, (c) cognitive-behavioral, (d) family-systems, and (e) eclectic.
5. Distinguish between dimensional and categorical assessment constructs. Include in your discussion the empirical approach and the clinical approach.
6. Discuss children with special needs and why they are a heterogeneous group. Include in your discussion co-occurring disorders, developmental sequences, development of self-concepts, and physical impairments.
7. Discuss how psychological problems develop in children. Include in your discussion genetic and biological factors and environmental factors.
8. Discuss the concept of developmental risk and list some major risk categories.
9. Discuss the concept of resiliency and list some major protective factors.
10. Discuss some key ethical guidelines for conducting assessments. Include in your discussion some sources of legal and ethical guidelines, some professional skills and competencies needed to conduct an ethical assessment, and issues surrounding gathering, interpreting, and reporting data.
11. Discuss the purposes of regulating the profession of psychology and the roles of regulatory bodies and national and regional organizations.
12. Discuss the educational qualifications needed to conduct assessments.

2

BASIC STATISTICAL AND PSYCHOMETRIC CONSTRUCTS

We conquer the facts of nature when we observe and experiment upon them. When we measure them we have made them our servants. A little statistical insight trains them for invaluable work.
—Edward L. Thorndike, American psychologist (1874–1949)

Scales of Measurement

Descriptive Statistics

Correlation and Regression

Statistical Significance

Meta-Analysis

Norm-Referenced Measurement

Derived Scores

Reliability

Validity

Standardization Data

Comment on Useful Statistical and Psychometric Concepts

Thinking Through the Issues

Summary

Key Terms, Concepts, and Names

Study Questions

Goals and Objectives

This chapter is designed to enable you to do the following:

- Become familiar with basic statistical concepts and procedures

- Become familiar with the meaning of reliability and the procedures for evaluating it

- Understand the different forms of validity

In this chapter, we have two goals. First, we will familiarize you with some basic statistical concepts and procedures. Second, we will introduce you to the major psychometric concepts. A knowledge of statistical and psychometric concepts will enhance your understanding of psychological tests and measures, test manuals, and research reports about the tests and measures. The basic concepts reviewed in this chapter will also help you understand the material covered in many other chapters of the text.

Table 2-1
Properties of Scales of Measurement

Scale	Property			
	Classification	Order	Equal units	True zero
Nominal	X	—	—	—
Ordinal	X	X	—	—
Interval	X	X	X	—
Ratio	X	X	X	X

SCALES OF MEASUREMENT

Data can be ordered by various methods. In most cases, we use one of four types of scales: nominal, ordinal, interval, or ratio. A *scale* is a system for assigning values or scores to some measurable trait or characteristic. Once data have been ordered, we can then subject the values to various mathematical procedures to determine relationships between the traits or characteristics of interest and other measured behaviors. Scales range from lower-order ones (nominal, ordinal) to higher-order ones (interval, ratio). The higher-order scales possess all the properties of lower-order ones but have additional properties of their own (see Table 2-1).

Nominal Scale

At the lowest level of measurement is a *nominal measurement scale*. *Nominal* means "name." A nominal scale consists of a set of nonordered categories, with one name, number, or letter given to each item being scaled. The numbers, letters, or names usually represent mutually exclusive categories, cannot be arranged in a meaningful order, and are merely labels or classifications. An example of nominal scaling is the assignment of numbers to baseball players (the numbers do not reflect the players' abilities) or of names to schools. Although nominal scales are of limited usefulness because they allow only for classification, they are still valuable. Some variables, such as sex, ethnicity, and geographic area, can only be described by nominal scales.

Ordinal Scale

At the next level of measurement is an *ordinal measurement scale*. Like a nominal scale, it classifies items, but it has the property of order (or magnitude) as well. The variable being measured is ranked or ordered according to the amount of some characteristic or along some dimension, without regard for differences in the distances between scores. An example of ordinal scaling is the ranking of students from highest to lowest, based on class standing. An ordinal scale tells us who is first, second, and third; it does not tell us, however, whether the distance between the first- and second-ranked scores is the same as the distance between the second- and third-ranked scores. The difference between the first- and second-

ranked grade point averages could be .10 (e.g., 3.30 versus 3.20), and the difference between the second- and third-ranked grade point averages could be .80 (e.g., 3.20 versus 2.40). Another type of ordinal scale is a rating scale, such as

No Anxiety	Mild Anxiety	Moderate Anxiety	Severe Anxiety	Extreme Anxiety
1	2	3	4	5

Interval Scale

At the third level of measurement is an *interval measurement scale*. It classifies, as a nominal scale does, and orders, as an ordinal scale does, but it adds an arbitrary zero point and equal units. Examples of interval scales are the Wechsler Intelligence Scale for Children–IV (WISC–IV), which measures intelligence and provides test scores (or standard scores), and the Fahrenheit scale, which measures temperature. On the WISC–IV, an increase of 10 IQ points from 100 to 110 reflects the same amount of change as an increase from 120 to 130. However, it makes no sense to say that a child with an IQ of 150 is twice as intelligent as a child with an IQ of 75, because interval scales lack a true zero point and because an IQ of zero has no meaning. Similarly, it makes no sense to say that a temperature reading of 0° reflects a complete lack of temperature, although you can say that the difference between 10°F and 20°F is the same as the difference between 60°F and 70°F.

Ratio Scale

At the highest level of measurement is a *ratio measurement scale*. It has a true zero point, equal intervals between adjacent units, and equality of ratios, in addition to allowing ordering and classification. Because there is a meaningful zero point, there is a true ratio between measurements made on a ratio scale. Weight is one example of a characteristic measured on a ratio scale; an individual who weighs 150 pounds is twice as heavy as one who weighs 75 pounds. Like weight, reaction time is measured on a ratio scale with a true zero point and equal ratios: A reaction time of 2,000 milliseconds is exactly twice as long as one of 1,000 milliseconds. Because most psychological characteristics do not permit the determination of an absolute zero point (such as "zero intelligence"), ratio scales are rarely used in psychology. Often we must be content with interval scales or the weaker ordinal and nominal scales.

DESCRIPTIVE STATISTICS

Descriptive statistics summarize data obtained about a sample of individuals. Descriptive statistics include frequency distributions, normal curves, standard scores, and measures of central tendency, dispersion, correlation, and regression. Some descriptive statistics are covered below; others are discussed later in the chapter. Table 2-2 shows symbols and abbreviations commonly used in statistics and

psychometrics. These symbols provide a shorthand method of describing important characteristics of a test formula or norm group. This list is for reference; it is not necessary to memorize the symbols. As you gain more experience in the field, the symbols will become familiar to you.

Measures of Central Tendency

The three most commonly used *measures of central tendency* are the mean, the median, and the mode. These statistics are used to describe the average, center, and most common scores of a set of scores, respectively.

Mean. The *mean* (M or $\overline{X}$) is the arithmetic average of all the scores in a set of scores. To compute the mean, divide the

---

Table 2-2
Common Statistical and Psychometric Symbols and Abbreviations

Symbol	Definition	Symbol	Definition
a	Intercept constant in a regression equation	SE_E or SE_{est}	Standard error of estimate
b	Slope constant in a regression equation		
c	Any unspecified constant	SEM,	Standard error of measurement
CA	Chronological age	SE_m,	
cf	Cumulative frequency	SE_{meas},	
DQ	Developmental quotient	S_m, s_m,	
f	Frequency	s_{meas},	
F	Test statistic in analysis of variance and covariance	or s_{err}	
		t	t test
IQ	Intelligence quotient	T	T score; standard score with a mean of 50 and standard deviation of 10
M	Mean (see also $\overline{X}$)		
MA	Mental age	x	Deviation score $X - \overline{X}$; indicates how far the score falls above or below the mean of the group
Mdn or *Md*	Median		
		X	Raw score
n	Number of cases in a subsample	$\overline{X}$	Mean (see also M)
N	Number of cases in a sample	Y	A second raw score
p	Probability or proportion	z	z score; standard score with a mean of 0 and standard deviation of 1
P	Percentile		
Q	Semi-interquartile range; half the difference between Q_3 and Q_1	σ	Standard deviation of a population
		σ^2	Variance of a population
Q_1	First quartile score (25th percentile score)	Σ	"Sum of"; ΣX means to add up all the Xs (scores)
Q_3	Third quartile score (75th percentile score)	ΣX	Sum of Xs
r	Pearson correlation coefficient	ΣX^2	Sum of squared Xs (square first, then add)
r^2	Coefficient of determination; the proportion of variance in Y attributable to X	$(\Sigma X)^2$	Squared sum of Xs (add first, then square the total)
		ΣXY	Sum of cross products of X and Y (multiply each $X \times Y$, then add)
r_{pb}	Point biserial correlation coefficient		
r_s or ρ	Spearman rank-difference correlation coefficient (also referred to as rho)	ϕ	Phi coefficient; a correlation coefficient for a 2×2 contingency table
r_{xx}	Reliability coefficient	χ^2	Chi square
r_{xy}	Validity coefficient (x represents the test score and y the criterion score)	$<$	Less than
		$>$	Greater than
R	Coefficient of multiple correlation	$\geq$	Greater than or equal to
rel. f	Relative frequency	$\leq$	Less than or equal to
S, s, or SD	Standard deviation of the sample	$\pm$	Plus or minus
		$\sqrt{\ }$	Square root
S^2	Variance of the sample	$\neq$	Not equal to

sum of all the scores by the total number of scores in the set (*N*). The formula is as follows:

$$M = \frac{\Sigma X}{N}$$

where M = mean of the scores
ΣX = sum of the scores
N = number of scores

Example: The mean for the four scores 2, 4, 6, 8 is 5:

$$M = \frac{2 + 4 + 6 + 8}{4} = \frac{20}{4} = 5$$

The mean is responsive to the exact position of each score in a distribution, including extreme scores. However, extreme scores in a data set can affect the mean, so it may not be the best measure of central tendency. For example, three individuals with incomes of $30,000, $40,000, and $2,000,000 have an average income of $900,000. Yet it is unlikely that any of them have anywhere near a $900,000 life style. In this case, the median value (see below) of $40,000 probably reflects a life style more characteristic of this small sample. Still, with this exception, the mean is the preferred measure of central tendency. It is appropriate for both interval and ratio scale data.

Median. The *median* (*Mdn* or *Md*) is the middle point in a set of scores arranged in order of magnitude. Fifty percent of the scores lie at or above the median, and 50% of the scores lie at or below the median. If there is an even number of scores, the median is the number halfway between the two middlemost scores and, therefore, is not any of the actual scores. If there is an odd number of scores, the median is simply the middlemost score.

To compute the median, arrange the scores in order of magnitude from highest to lowest. Then count up (or down) through half the scores. Table 2-3 illustrates the procedure for

calculating the median of an even number and an odd number of scores in a distribution. In the first column, there are eight scores. To obtain the median, count up four scores from the bottom and then determine the number that lies halfway between the fourth and fifth scores (the two middlemost scores). In the second column, there are seven scores. To obtain the median, count up four scores from the bottom; the median is the fourth score. The median divides a distribution into two equal halves; the number of scores above the median is the same as the number below.

When distributions are "skewed" (i.e., the bulk of the scores are at either the high end or the low end of the set), the median is a better measure of central tendency than the mean. The median is not affected disproportionately by outliers—scores that deviate extremely from the other scores in the set. The median is an appropriate measure of central tendency for ordinal, interval, or ratio scale data.

Mode. The *mode* is the score in a set of scores that occurs more frequently than any other. In some sets, two scores occur more often than any other score but with the same frequency as each other; in such cases, we say that the distribution is *bimodal*—there are two modes in the set. When more than two scores occur more frequently than any other score and with the same frequency as each other, the distribution is said to be *multimodal*—there are multiple modes in the set.

The mode is greatly affected by chance and has little or no mathematical usefulness. However, it does tell us what score is most likely to occur and is therefore useful in analyzing data that have been measured on a nominal scale (e.g., "What was the most frequently occurring classification in the group?").

Measures of Dispersion

Dispersion refers to the variability of scores in a set of scores. The range is the simplest measure of the dispersion of a group of scores. More frequently used *measures of dispersion* are the variance and standard deviation.

Range. The *range* is the distance between the highest and lowest scores in a set. We compute the range by subtracting the lowest score in the set from the highest score. The formula is

$$R = H - L$$

where R = range
H = highest score
L = lowest score

Example: The range for the distribution 50, 80, 97, 99 is 49:

$$R = 99 - 50 = 49$$

The range is easily calculated; however, it is not a sensitive measure of dispersion because it is determined by the lo-

Table 2-3
Calculation of the Median

X (even number of scores)	X (odd number of scores)
130	130
128	128
125	125
124	124 ← 124 median
123 ← 123.5 median	123
120	120
110	110
108	

cations of only two scores. The range tells us nothing about the distribution of scores located between the high and low scores, and a single score can grossly change the result. Still, the range provides some information that can be useful in understanding a set of scores.

Variance. *Variance* (S^2) is a statistical measure of the amount of spread in a set of scores—the greater the spread, the greater the variance. Unlike the range, the variance takes into account every score in the group. When two different sets of scores have the same mean but different variances, it means that one set has a larger spread of scores than the other. The variance is obtained by comparing every score in a distribution to the mean of the distribution. The variance is the average squared deviation of scores from the mean. To compute the deviation of an individual score, subtract the mean from that score. Scores that have values greater than the mean will yield positive values, whereas scores that have values less than the mean will yield negative values. The variance is computed in the following way:

$$S^2 = \frac{\Sigma(X - \bar{X})^2}{N}$$

where S^2 = variance of the scores
Σ = sum
X = raw score
$\bar{X}$ = mean
N = number of scores

Example: The variance for the four scores 2, 4, 6, 8 is 5:

$$S^2 = \frac{(2 - 5)^2 + (4 - 5)^2 + (6 - 5)^2 + (8 - 5)^2}{4}$$

$$= \frac{9 + 1 + 1 + 9}{4} = \frac{20}{4} = 5$$

Squaring the distance from the mean has two important benefits. One is that it makes all the variances positive so that they can be summed (rather than canceling each other out). The other is that squaring the distance tends to give greater weight to values farther from the mean and thereby signals how accurate or precise a mean is (i.e., how far scores fall from their central indicator). This is a quality captured by the standard error of measurement, a concept discussed later in the chapter.

Standard deviation. The *standard deviation* (*SD*, *S*, or *s*) is the square root of the variance, representing the average of the squared deviations from the mean. Sometimes symbolized by the Greek letter σ (sigma), it is an important and commonly used measure of the extent to which scores deviate from the mean. The standard deviation is often used in the field of testing and measurement. The formula for calculating the standard deviation of a sample is as follows:

$$SD = \sqrt{\frac{\Sigma(X - \bar{X})^2}{N}}$$

Example: The standard deviation for the four scores 2, 4, 6, 8 is 2.236:

$$S^2 = \sqrt{\frac{(2 - 5)^2 + (4 - 5)^2 + (6 - 5)^2 + (8 - 5)^2}{4}}$$

$$= \sqrt{\frac{9 + 1 + 1 + 9}{4}} = \sqrt{\frac{20}{4}} = \sqrt{5} = 2.236$$

The variance and the standard deviation are both useful as measures of dispersion and in the calculation of *z* scores, which are discussed later in the chapter.

Normal Curve

The *normal* (or bell-shaped) *curve* (see Figure 2-1) is a common type of distribution. Many psychological traits are distributed roughly along a normal curve. An important feature of the normal curve is that it enables us to calculate exactly how many cases fall between any two points under the curve. Small deviations do not appreciably affect the conclusions reached by assuming a perfect normal distribution, which is fortunate, for real data are never perfectly normal.

Figure 2-1 shows the precise relationship between the standard deviation and the proportion of cases under a normal curve. It also shows the percentages of cases that fall within one, two, and three standard deviations above and below the mean. Approximately 68% of the cases fall within +1 *SD* and –1 *SD* of the mean (34% of the cases are between the mean and 1 *SD* above the mean, and 34% of the cases are between the mean and 1 *SD* below the mean). As we move away from the mean, the number of cases diminishes. The areas between +1 *SD* and +2 *SD* and between –1 *SD* and –2 *SD* each represent approximately 14% of the cases. Between +2 *SD* and +3 *SD* and between –2 *SD* and –3 *SD* from the mean, there are even fewer cases—each area represents approximately 2% of the distribution. We will return to the normal curve when we consider standard scores.

CORRELATION AND REGRESSION

Correlation and regression constitute two of the most important statistical procedures used in psychological assessment. Let's look at each of these procedures.

Correlation

Correlations tell us about the degree of association or co-relationship between two variables, including the strength and direction of their relationship. The strength of the relationship is expressed by the absolute magnitude of the *correlation coefficient;* the maximum value is +1.00 or –1.00. The sign of the coefficient reflects the direction of the relationship. A positive correlation (+) indicates that higher scores on one

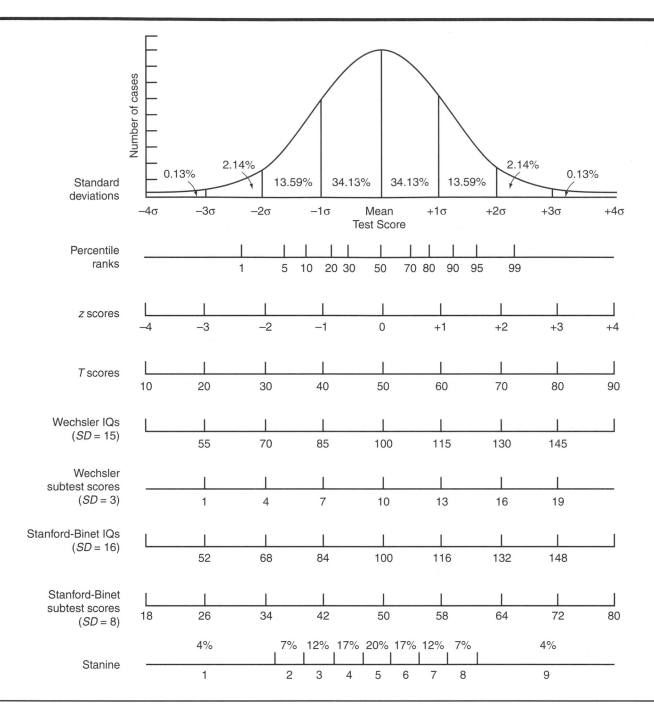

Figure 2-1. Relationship of the normal curve to various types of standard scores.

variable are associated with higher scores on the second variable (e.g., more hours spent studying tend to lead to a higher GPA) and lower scores on one variable are associated with lower scores on the second variable (e.g, fewer hours spent studying tend to lead to a lower GPA). Conversely, a negative correlation (–) signifies an inverse relationship—that is, high scores on one variable are associated with low scores on the other variable (e.g., a large number of days absent tends to be associated with a low GPA). Thus, correlation coefficients range in value from –1.00 to +1.00.

Correlations are used in prediction. The higher the correlation between two variables, the more accurately we can predict the value of one variable when we know the value of the other variable. A correlation of –1.00 or +1.00 means that we can perfectly predict a person's score on one variable if we know the person's score on the other variable (e.g., weight in pounds and weight in kilograms). In contrast, a correlation of .00 indicates that knowing the score on one variable does not help at all in predicting the score on the other variable (e.g., weight and visual acuity).

Variables can be related nonlinearly or curvilinearly. *Curvilinear* means that the relationship between two variables can be portrayed better by a curve than by a straight line. If a curvilinear relationship exists between two variables, the linear correlation coefficient will underestimate the true degree of association. Variables also can be continuous or discrete. A continuous variable is divisible into an infinite number of fractional parts (e.g., temperature, height, age). In contrast, a discrete variable has separate, indivisible categories (e.g., the number of heads in a series of coin tosses). A dichotomous variable is a discrete variable that has two possible values (e.g., head or tail, pass or fail, male or female).

Figure 2-2 shows scatterplots of eight different relationships. A scatterplot presents a visual picture of the relationship between two variables, X and Y. Each point in the scatterplot represents a pair of scores for one examinee—a score on the X variable and a score on the Y variable.

Graph (a) shows a perfect positive linear relationship between X and Y ($r = +1.00$); the dots fall into a straight line from the lower left (low X, low Y) to the upper right (high X, high Y). Graph (b) shows a perfect negative linear relationship ($r = -1.00$); the dots fall into a straight line from the upper left (low X, high Y) to the lower right (high X, low Y). Graphs (c) through (f) show varying degrees of relationship between X and Y. Graph (g) shows no relationship between X and Y ($r = .00$). And Graph (h) shows a curvilinear relationship between X and Y; the dots fall along a curved line. Table 2-4 gives formulas for computing several correlation coefficients.

The most common correlation coefficient is the *Pearson correlation coefficient,* symbolized by r. Pearson's r should be used only when the following conditions are met: (a) the two variables are continuous and normally distributed, (b) there is a linear relationship between the variables, and (c) the predictor variable predicts as well at the high-score ranges as at the low-score ranges. When there is a restriction of range (i.e., the scores are homogeneous), the resulting correlation is lowered. The following are useful terms for describing the strength of a correlation:

- .20 to .29: low
- .30 to .49: moderately low
- .50 to .69: moderate
- .70 to .79: moderately high
- .80 to .99: high

When the conditions for using Pearson's r cannot be met, the Spearman r_s (rank-difference) method can be used (see Table 2-4). This method uses the ranks of the scores instead of the scores themselves. A rank is a number, given to a score, that represents its order in a distribution. For example, in a set of 10 scores, the highest score receives a rank of 1, the fifth score from the top receives a rank of 5, and the lowest score receives a rank of 10.

Correlations should not be used to infer cause and effect. For example, there is an association between hot, wet climates and the incidence of malaria. For a long time, people

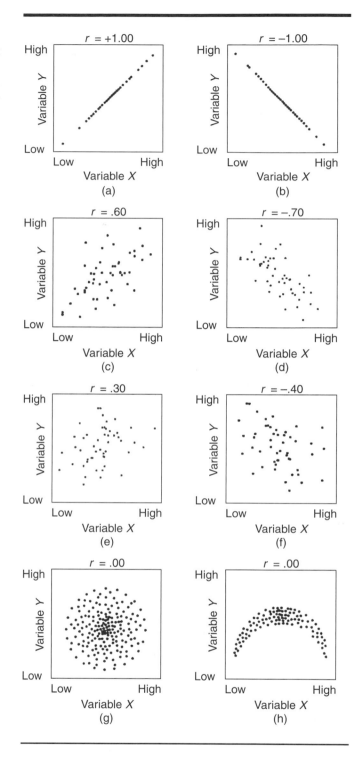

Figure 2-2. Scatter diagrams illustrating various degrees of relationship.

believed that "bad air" caused malaria. (The ancient Romans named the disease for this reason: *Mal aria* means "bad air" in Latin.) We now know that the disease is actually carried by mosquitoes, which flourish in stagnant water in hot climates. Thus, although climate *is* associated with the occurrence of

Table 2-4
Formulas for Computing a Variety of Correlation Coefficients

Name	Description of variables	Formula
Pearson product-moment correlation coefficient (r)	Both variables continuous (on interval or ratio scale)	$$r = \frac{N\,\Sigma XY - (\Sigma X)(\Sigma Y)}{\sqrt{[N\,\Sigma X^2 - (\Sigma X)^2][N\,\Sigma Y^2 - (\Sigma Y)^2]}}$$ where r = correlation coefficient; N = number of paired scores; ΣXY = sum of the products of the paired X and Y scores; ΣX = sum of the X scores; ΣY = sum of the Y scores; ΣX^2 = sum of the squared X scores; $(\Sigma X)^2$ = square of the sum of the X scores; ΣY^2 = sum of the squared Y scores; $(\Sigma Y)^2$ = square of the sum of the Y scores
Spearman rank-difference correlation coefficient (Spearman r, r_s, or ρ)	Both variables on an ordinal scale (rank-ordered)	$$r_s = 1 - \frac{6\,\Sigma D^2}{N(N^2 - 1)}$$ where D = difference between ranks for each person; N = number of paired scores
Point biserial correlation coefficient (r_{pb})	One variable continuous (on interval or ratio scale), the other genuinely dichotomous (usually on nominal scale)	Formula for r can be used (see above). The dichotomous variable can be coded 0 or 1. For example, if sex is the dichotomous variable, 0 can be used for females and 1 for males (0 = females, 1 = males), or vice versa.
Phi (ϕ) coefficient	Both variables dichotomous (on nominal scales)	1. $\phi = \dfrac{BD - AD}{\sqrt{(A+B)(C+D)(A+C)(B+D)}}$ where A, B, C, and D are the four cell frequencies in a contingency table 2. $\phi = \sqrt{\dfrac{\chi^2}{N}}$ where χ^2 = chi square; N = total number of observations

malaria, it is not the *cause* of malaria; the relationship between hot climate and malaria is only an indirect one.

When we want to know how much variance in one variable is explained by its relationship to another variable, we must square the correlation coefficient. For example, if we want to know how much variance in school grades is accounted for by knowing scores on a measure of attentional disorder, we first compute a correlation coefficient. Let's say $r = .40$. Squaring r gives .16, or 16%. Consequently, we can say that knowing the score on the measure of attentional disorder allows us to account for 16% of the variance in school grades. This value may not seem large, but given that other factors—such as the child's intelligence and the number of children in the classroom—account for some of the variance in school grades as well, one's score on a measure of attentional disorder is a significant predictor of academic achievement.

The value r^2 is known as the *coefficient of determination*. Like a correlation coefficient, the coefficient of determination does not establish a cause-and-effect relationship between the two variables.

Regression

You can use the correlation coefficient, together with other information, to construct a linear equation for predicting the score on one variable when you know the score on another variable. (A linear equation is one describing a relationship between the variables that can be represented on a graph by a straight line.) This equation, called the *regression equation*, has the following form:

$$Y_{pred} = bX + a$$

where Y_{pred} = predicted score on Y
b = slope of the regression line
X = known score on X
a = Y intercept of the regression line

The slope of the regression line, b, is defined as

$$b = r\frac{SD_Y}{SD_X}$$

where r = correlation between the X and Y scores
SD_Y = standard deviation of the Y scores
SD_X = standard deviation of the X scores

The formula for calculating b directly from raw data is

$$b = \frac{N\Sigma XY - (\Sigma X)(\Sigma Y)}{N\Sigma X^2 - (\Sigma X)^2}$$

where N = number of paired scores

The intercept a, or regression constant, is determined as follows:

$$a = \bar{Y} - b\bar{X}$$

where $\bar{Y}$ = mean of the Y scores
b = slope of the regression line
$\bar{X}$ = mean of the X scores

Example: To find the regression equation and correlation coefficient for the following pairs of scores (X, Y), we first calculate X^2, Y^2, and XY.

	X	Y	X^2	Y^2	XY
	7	9	49	81	63
	2	3	4	9	6
	6	4	36	16	24
	6	5	36	25	30
	3	1	9	1	3
Σ	24	22	134	132	126

$$\bar{X} = 4.8 \qquad \bar{Y} = 4.4$$

The slope of the regression line is then given by

$$b = \frac{5(126) - 24(22)}{5(134) - (24)^2} = \frac{630 - 528}{670 - 576} = \frac{102}{94} = 1.09$$

and the regression constant is given by

$$a = 4.40 - 1.09(4.80) = 4.40 - 5.23 = -.83$$

These values can now be substituted into the regression equation:

$$Y_{pred} = 1.09X - .83$$

The correlation coefficient for these data is

$$r = \frac{5(126) - 24(22)}{\sqrt{[5(134) - (24)^2][5(132) - (22)^2]}}$$

$$= \frac{102}{\sqrt{94(176)}} = \frac{102}{\sqrt{16,544}} = \frac{102}{128.62} = .79$$

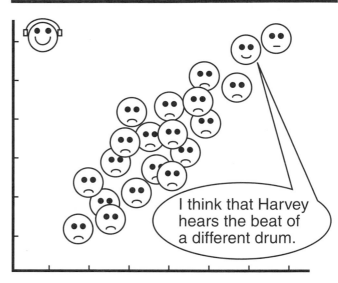

Scatterplot: n = 21; r = +0.63

The Outlier

Courtesy of David Likely.

Standard Error of Estimate

A measure of the accuracy of the predicted Y scores is the standard error of estimate:

$$SE_{est} = SD_Y\sqrt{1 - r_{XY}^2}$$

where SD_Y = standard deviation of the Y scores
r_{XY}^2 = the square of the correlation between the X and Y scores

The *standard error of estimate* is the standard deviation of the error scores, a measure of the amount by which the observed or obtained scores in a sample differ from the predicted scores. The higher the correlation between X and Y, the smaller the standard error of estimate and, hence, the greater the average accuracy of the predictions. You can see from the equation that when $r = +1.00$, the standard error of estimate becomes zero. Thus, a +1.00 correlation coefficient means that you can make perfect predictions of Y if you know X; a .00 correlation means that knowledge of X does not improve your prediction of Y. In the latter case, the standard deviation of the error scores is exactly the same as the standard deviation of the Y scores themselves.

Example: The standard error of estimate for a test with a standard deviation of 15 and a .60 correlation between X and Y is

$$SE_{est} = 15\sqrt{1 - .60^2}$$
$$= 15\sqrt{1 - .36}$$
$$= 15(.80) = 12$$

Multiple Correlation

Multiple correlation is a statistical technique for determining the relationship between one variable and two or more other variables. The coefficient of multiple correlation is represented as *R*. When we use several variables for a prediction, the prediction is likely to be more accurate and powerful than if we based it on a single variable only. A principal drawback to using multiple correlation, however, is that large samples are generally required when several variables are used in the analysis—usually over 100 participants or at least 20 participants per variable. Thus, if 10 variables were being studied, we would need 200 participants to arrive at a stable prediction equation. An example of the use of multiple correlation is in the prediction of success in therapy. Personality test scores, teacher ratings of behavior pathology, and intelligence test scores correlate with a successful outcome. By using these measures in a multiple correlation, we can predict the outcome of therapy with more accuracy than by using any individual measure.

STATISTICAL SIGNIFICANCE

When we want to know whether the difference between two or more scores can be attributed to chance or to some systematic (and perhaps hypothesized) cause, we run a test of *statistical significance*. *Significance* in statistics refers to whether the results differ from what would be expected on the basis of chance alone. Statisticians have agreed that a reasonable criterion for deciding that something is not a chance occurrence is that it would happen by chance 5% of the time or less. Thus, the .05 level (5 times in 100) is the least stringent significance level indicating that observed differences found in a study are real; that is, we would expect the results to occur only 5% of the time by chance. There also are more stringent levels of significance, such as the .01 (1 time in 100) and the .001 (1 time in 1,000) levels. Tests of significance can be used to evaluate differences between two or more means, differences between a score and the mean of the scale, and differences of correlations from zero (or chance). The expression $p < .05$ means that the results have a probability level of less than .05 (or 5 times in 100) of occurring by chance, whereas the expression $p > .05$ means that the results have a probability level of greater than .05 (or more than 5 times in 100) of occurring by chance.

Tests of significance, although highly useful, don't tell the complete story. When we test to see whether two or more means are significantly different, we also need to consider the values of the means, the degree to which they differ, and the direction of the difference. For example, the mean difference between two groups may be statistically significant and yet have no practical significance. If one group has a mean of 100 and the other has a mean of 101, the significance test may yield a p value less than .05, but the difference of only 1 point may have little practical usefulness.

Another way of evaluating the magnitude of difference between two means independent of sample size is by calculating *effect size,* or Cohen's *d* (Cohen, 1988). The formula for computing *d* is as follows:

$$d = \frac{M_1 - M_2}{\sigma_{pooled}}$$

where

M_1 = mean of group 1

M_2 = mean of group 2

σ_{pooled} = square root of the average of the two squared deviations, or $\sigma_{pooled} = \sqrt{\dfrac{SD_1^2 + SD_2^2}{2}}$

Cohen (1988) defined effect size as small if $d = .2$, medium if $d = .5$, and large if $d = .8$.

When we test to see whether a correlation coefficient differs significantly from chance, we also need to know how powerful the coefficient is (or how powerful its strength of association is). When the sample size is large enough, the correlation coefficient may be statistically significant and yet reflect only a weak association between the two variables. Thus, a Pearson correlation coefficient of .20 is significant when the sample size is 100, but the level of variance explained is low ($.20^2 = 4\%$).

META-ANALYSIS

A single study seldom provides definitive answers to research questions. Instead, progress in science is achieved through the accumulation of findings from numerous studies on a particular issue. Traditionally, researchers relied on narrative literature reviews (i.e., on reviewing the research literature by inspecting the findings and arriving at generalizations) to fulfill this function. However, these reviews often suffered from methodological flaws: Narrative reviews of the same body of research sometimes led to different conclusions because of subjective judgments, preferences, and reviewer bias.

Meta-analysis is an alternative to the narrative literature review and avoids many of its flaws. It is used to summarize the results of reliability and validity studies. Meta-analysis makes explicit use of rigorous research techniques (including quantitative methods) to sum up a body of separate but similar studies for the purpose of integrating the findings. Researchers have successfully applied meta-analysis within the social, behavioral, and biomedical sciences.

Meta-analysis is particularly useful in validity generalization studies. Researchers examine, when possible, an entire population of studies that present evidence on the validity of a particular test instrument. The empirical findings from these validity studies (e.g., validity coefficients and scores showing between-group differences) are converted to a common metric (i.e., a standard of measurement) and then evaluated for consistency (i.e., generalizability, or robustness) across different populations, test conditions, criterion measures, and the like. Findings from meta-analyses highlight trends in data and allow researchers and practitioners to obtain valuable information about the validity of the test under study.

Although meta-analysis has many potential benefits and is widely used to synthesize research findings, its conclusions may be compromised by shortcomings in the studies reviewed and in the meta-analytic methods. Matt and Cook (1994) provide a careful examination of factors that may decrease the validity of meta-analysis and offer methods for handling these difficulties. For further information about meta-analysis, see Cooper (1989), Hunter and Schmidt (1990), Light and Pillemer (1984), Rosenthal (1991), and Wolf (1986).

NORM-REFERENCED MEASUREMENT

In *norm-referenced measurement,* an examinee's performance is compared with the performance of a specific group of participants. A norm provides an indication of the average or typical performance of a specified group and the spread of scores above and below the average. Norms are needed because the number of responses in itself is not very meaningful. For example, a teacher's report that a child displayed two incidences of aggressive behavior in a 1-week period is of little value in itself. To interpret that information, we would

"I could have done better, but I didn't want to depart too far from the accepted norm."

Courtesy of Germaine Vanselow; Cartoonist, Bill Vanselow.

want to know the level of aggressive behavior typically displayed by comparable groups of children, and for this we would need a relevant normative population. We could compare the child's score with those of a representative population of children in the United States, those of the children in the child's school, or those of a special population. We can make such a comparison by converting the child's raw score into some relative measure, called a derived score. A *derived score* indicates the child's standing relative to the norm group and allows us to compare the child's performance on one measure with her or his performance on other measures.

DERIVED SCORES

The major types of derived scores used in norm-referenced personality and behavioral measures are standard scores and percentile ranks. Let's look at these two types of derived scores.

Standard Scores

Standard scores are raw scores that have been transformed so that they have a predetermined mean and standard deviation. Once transformed, an examinee's score can be expressed as a value on this standardized scale.

A *z score* is one type of standard score. It has a mean of 0 and a standard deviation of 1. Therefore, almost all z scores lie between −3.0 and +3.0. A z score of −2.5 would indicate that a raw score fell below the mean score of the group by 2½ standard deviations. Frequently, we convert z scores into other standard scores to eliminate the + and − signs. For example, a T score is a standard score based on a distribution with a mean of 50 and a standard deviation of 10. T scores almost always fall between 20 and 80, and a z score of 0 is equivalent to a T score of 50.

Table 2-5 shows formulas for computing various standard scores. A general formula for converting standard scores from one system to another is as follows:

$$\text{New standard score} = \left(\frac{X_{\text{old}} - M_{\text{old}}}{SD_{\text{old}}}\right)SD_{\text{new}} + M_{\text{new}}$$

where
X_{old} = score on old system
M_{old} = mean of old system
SD_{old} = standard deviation of old system
SD_{new} = standard deviation of new system
M_{new} = mean of new system

Example: A standard score of 60 in a T distribution ($M = 50$, $SD = 10$) is converted to a standard score distribution with $M = 100$ and $SD = 15$ as follows:

$$\text{Standard score} = \left(\frac{60 - 50}{10}\right)$$

$$= \left(\frac{10}{10}\right)15 + 100 = (1)15 + 100 = 115$$

Table 2-5
Formulas for Computing Various Standard Scores

Score	Example
z score $$z = \frac{X - \bar{X}}{SD}$$ where z = z score corresponding to the individual raw score X X = individual raw score $\bar{X}$ = mean of sample SD = standard deviation of sample	The z score for an individual with a raw score of 50 in a group having a mean of 30 and standard deviation of 10 is calculated as follows: $$z = \frac{50 - 30}{10} = 2$$ Thus, the z score for this individual is 2.
T score $$T = 10(z) + 50$$ where T = T score corresponding to the individual raw score X 10 = standard deviation of the T distribution z = z score corresponding to the individual raw score X 50 = mean of the T distribution	The T score for an individual with a z score of 2 is calculated as follows: $$T = 10(2) + 50 = 70$$ Thus, the T score for this individual is 70.
Standard score distribution $$SS = 15(z) + 100$$ where SS = standard score corresponding to the individual raw score X 15 = standard deviation of the standard score distribution z = z score corresponding to the individual raw score X 100 = mean of the standard score distribution	The standard score for an individual with a z score of 2 is calculated as follows: $$SS = 15(2) + 100 = 130$$ Thus, the standard score for this individual is 130.

Percentile Ranks

Percentile ranks are derived scores that permit us to determine an individual's position relative to the standardization sample (or any other specified sample). A percentile rank is a point in a distribution at or below which the scores of a given percentage of individuals fall. If 63% of the scores fall at or below a given score, then that score is at the 63rd percentile rank. *Quartiles* are percentile ranks that divide a distribution into four equal parts, with each part containing 25% of the norm group. *Deciles,* a less common percentile rank, contain 10 bands, with each band containing 10% of the norm group. Exhibit 2-1 shows some procedures for calculating percentile ranks.

Interpretation of percentile ranks is simple and straightforward. For example, a child who obtains a percentile rank of 35 on a measure of anxiety has scored higher than 35% of the children in the norm sample. However, the psychometric properties of percentile ranks limit their usefulness in data analysis. Raw score differences between percentile ranks are smaller near the mean than at the extremes of the distribution. *Therefore, percentile ranks cannot be added, subtracted, multiplied, or divided.* In order to use them in statistical tests, we must normalize percentile ranks by converting them to another scale.

A major problem with percentile ranks is that we can't assume that the units along the percentile-rank distribution are equal. Thus, the difference between a person at the 51st percentile rank and one at the 55th percentile rank may be very small. However, there are generally fewer cases at the extremes (people are more spread out), and so here small dif-ferences in percentile ranks (say, between the 95th and 99th percentile ranks) may be meaningful. Percentile ranks are often used in discussing results with parents, but this problem of imprecise units must always be kept in mind.

SCHOOLIES © 1999 by John P. Wood

Sorry—I'm not allowed to talk to anyone outside of my percentile.

Exhibit 2-1
Calculating Percentile Ranks

The following formula is used to determine the percentile rank for a score in a distribution:

$$\text{Percentile rank} = \frac{\left(\dfrac{X - \text{lrl}}{i}\right)\text{fw} + \Sigma\text{fb}}{N} \times 100$$

where
X = raw score
lrl = lower real limit of the target interval or score
i = width of the target interval or score
fw = frequency within the target interval or score
Σfb = sum of frequencies (number of scores occurring) below the target interval or score
N = total number of scores

To compute the lower real limit of a whole number, simply subtract .5 from the number; to get the upper real limit, add .5 to the number. The width of the target interval or score (i) is obtained by subtracting the lower real limit from the upper real limit.

Example 1

Let's compute the percentile rank for a score of 110 in the following distribution:

X	f
120	5
119	10
Target interval for a score of 110 → 110	20
100	40
90	10
80	5
	$N = 90$

where
lrl = 109.5
i = 1
fw = 20
Σfb = 55
N = 90

Substituting these values into the percentile rank formula yields the following:

$$\text{Percentile rank} = \frac{\left(\dfrac{X - \text{lrl}}{i}\right)\text{fw} + \Sigma\text{fb}}{N} \times 100$$

$$= \frac{\left(\dfrac{110 - 109.5}{1}\right)20 + 55}{90} \times 100$$

$$= \frac{\left(\dfrac{.5}{1}\right)20 + 55}{90} \times 100$$

$$= \frac{(.5)20 + 55}{90} \times 100$$

$$= \frac{10 + 55}{90} \times 100$$

$$= \frac{65}{90} \times 100$$

$$= .72 \times 100$$

The percentile rank is the 72nd percentile, or 72. Thus, a score of 110 exceeds 72% of the scores in the distribution.

The formula given here for calculating percentile rank can be used with both grouped (organized into classes of more than one value) and ungrouped (organized into classes of single values) data. When the distribution is ungrouped and all the intervals are 1, a simplified version of the formula can be used:

$$\text{Percentile rank} = \left(\frac{.5\text{fw} + \Sigma\text{fb}}{N}\right) \times 100$$

Example 2

Let us compute the percentile rank for a score of 4 in the following distribution:

X	f
5	3
Target interval for a score of 4 → 4	5
3	4
2	3
1	2
	$N = 17$

where
fw = 5
Σfb = 9
N = 17

Substituting these values into the percentile rank formula for ungrouped data with intervals of 1 yields

$$\text{Percentile rank} = \left(\frac{.5\text{fw} + \Sigma\text{fb}}{N}\right) \times 100$$

$$= \frac{(.5)5 + 9}{17} \times 100$$

$$= \frac{2.5 + 9}{17} \times 100$$

$$= \frac{11.5}{17} \times 100$$

$$= .68 \times 100$$

The percentile rank is the 68th percentile, or 68. Thus, a score of 4 exceeds 68% of the scores in the distribution.

Choice of Derived Scores

We have seen that there are various ways of forming derived scores. Recognize, however, that derived scores are obtained from raw scores and are merely different expressions of a child's performance. Which derived score is used in a given field is more or less an arbitrary historical convention:

- Scores on cognitive measures tend to be expressed as standard scores with $M = 100$ and $SD = 15$.
- Scores on personality and behavioral measures tend to be expressed as T scores with $M = 50$ and $SD = 10$.
- Scores on other assessment measures, such as those used by speech and hearing professionals, tend to be expressed as z scores with $M = 0$ and $SD = 1$.

The mathematical formulas described in this section make it easy to transform one type of derived score into another.

The psychometric model is the one most commonly used in evaluating psychological measures, and it is the one we follow in this text. We now turn to two key constructs of this model: reliability and validity.

RELIABILITY

A psychological measure must be reliable if it is to be useful. *Reliability* refers to the consistency of measurements. A measure may be (a) consistent within itself (thus exhibiting internal reliability), (b) consistent over time (test-retest reliability), (c) consistent with a parallel form of the measure (parallel-forms reliability, sometimes referred to as *alternate-forms reliability*), or (d) consistent when used by another rater or observer (interrater or interobserver reliability). We can quantify the various forms of reliability, as shown below.

Theory of Reliability of Measurement

When we administer the same test to an examinee on several occasions, the examinee will likely earn different scores. Sometimes the score changes in a systematic way (i.e., there is a regular increase or decrease in scores), and sometimes the score changes in a random or unsystematic way. A test is considered unreliable if scores are subject to large random, unsystematic fluctuations; obviously, a test is not dependable if the scores change significantly on readministration. Reliability of measurement refers to the extent to which random or unsystematic variation affects the measurement of a trait, characteristic, or quality.

According to classical psychometric theory, a test score is composed of two components: a *true score* and an *error score*. The concept of a true score refers to the measurement process, not to the underlying content of the test. Thus, the true score represents a combination of all the factors that lead to consistency in measurement of a characteristic. An examinee's true score is a hypothetical construct; we cannot observe it. However, we can hypothesize that if we repeatedly gave the examinee the test, a distribution of scores around the true score would result. The mean of this distribution, which is assumed to be normal, would approximate the true score. The theory assumes that (a) the examinee possesses stable traits, (b) errors are random, and (c) the observed test score results from the addition of the true score and the error score. The reliability coefficient, then, represents a ratio of the true score variance to the observed score variance.

Reliability Coefficients

The *reliability coefficient* expresses the degree of consistency in the measurement of test scores. The reliability coefficient is denoted by the letter r with a subscript consisting of two identical letters (e.g., r_{xx} or r_{tt}). Reliability coefficients range from 1.00 (indicating perfect reliability) to .00 (indicating the absence of reliability). As noted earlier, types of reliability include internal consistency reliability, test-retest reliability, parallel-forms reliability, and interrater reliability. We use the Pearson product-moment correlation formula (see Table 2-4) to compute test-retest and parallel-forms reliability coefficients, specialized formulas to compute internal consistency reliability coefficients, and several different methods to compute interrater reliability coefficients. Table 2-6 shows some procedures for determining reliability.

Reliability is essential in a psychological measure. Low levels of reliability signify that meaningful sources of error are operating in the measure, and the measure cannot be considered stable across time or consistent across situations. Test results need to be reliable—that is, dependable, reproducible, and stable. High reliabilities, usually .80 or higher, are particularly important for tests used in individual assessment.

The following are useful ways to describe reliability coefficients:

- .00 to .59: unreliable
- .60 to .69: marginally reliable
- .70 to .79: relatively reliable
- .80 to .99: reliable

Procedures for Determining Reliability

Different procedures are available for determining three types of reliability.

Internal consistency reliability.   Internal consistency reliability is based on the scores that individuals obtain during a single test administration. One type of internal consistency reliability coefficient uses intercorrelations among comparable parts of the same test. The most general measure of reliability is *Cronbach's coefficient alpha,* which can be used for different scoring systems and is based on the variance of the test scores and the variance of the item scores. Coefficient alpha measures the uniformity or homogeneity of items

Table 2-6
Some Procedures Used to Determine Reliability

Procedure	Description
Cronbach's coefficient alpha (a) formula $$r_{tt} = \left(\frac{n}{n-1}\right)\left(\frac{S_t^2 - \Sigma S_i^2}{S_t^2}\right)$$ where $\quad r_{tt}$ = coefficient alpha reliability estimate $\quad n$ = number of items on the test $\quad S_t^2$ = variance of the total scores on the test $\quad \Sigma S_i^2$ = sum of the variances of individual item scores	An *internal consistency reliability* formula used when a test has no right or wrong answers. This formula provides a general reliability estimate. It is an efficient method of measuring internal consistency. Coefficient alpha essentially indicates the average intercorrelation between test items and any set of items drawn from the same domain.
Kuder-Richardson formula 20 (KR_{20}) $$r_{tt} = \left(\frac{n}{n-1}\right)\left(\frac{S_t^2 - \Sigma pq}{S_t^2}\right)$$ where $\quad r_{tt}$ = reliability estimate $\quad n$ = number of items on the test $\quad S_t^2$ = variance of the total scores on the test $\quad \Sigma pq$ = sum of the product of p and q for each item $\quad p$ = proportion of people getting an item correct $\quad q$ = proportion of people getting an item incorrect	An *internal consistency reliability* formula used for calculating the reliability of a test in which the items are scored 1 or 0 (or right or wrong). It is a special form of the coefficient alpha formula for use with dichotomous items.
Spearman-Brown correction formula $$r_{nn} = \frac{kr_{tt}}{1 + (k-1)r_{tt}}$$ where $\quad r_{nn}$ = estimated reliability coefficient $\quad k$ = number of items on the revised version of the test divided by number of items on the original version of the test $\quad r_{tt}$ = reliability coefficient before correction	An *internal consistency reliability* formula used to evaluate the effect that lengthening or shortening a test will have on the reliability coefficient. The formula increases the reliability estimate when the test is lengthened.
Product-moment correlation coefficient formula See Table 2-4 for the formula.	A formula used to estimate *test-retest reliability* or *parallel-forms reliability*

throughout the test (see Table 2-6). The values obtained by using the *Kuder-Richardson formula 20 coefficient,* a special case of coefficient alpha, are useful for tests scored as pass/fail or right/wrong. The values obtained from the Spearman-Brown correction formula, used to estimate reliability by the split-half method, can be interpreted in the same way as coefficient alpha. The split-half method consists of correlating pairs of scores obtained from equivalent halves of a test administered only once.

Test-retest reliability. The test-retest method involves administering a test, rating scale, observation schedule, or other measure twice to the same group of individuals, with a time interval between the two assessments. The results provide an index of the stability of the measure over time.

The test-retest method is a powerful way of evaluating reliability, but the test-retest reliability coefficient may not be an appropriate measure to use for behavioral checklists and scales, observational procedures, and related forms of measurement. A low test-retest reliability coefficient indicates that the instrument provided different readings each time

measurement was conducted. However, this does not automatically mean that the instrument is faulty—that is, that there is measurement error. It may be that the behaviors being measured have changed. Consequently, you should carefully consider whether low test-retest reliabilities are associated with poorly designed instruments or with actual changes in children's behavior, attitudes, temperament, or other characteristics being measured.

Parallel-forms reliability. One procedure for determining parallel-forms reliability, or alternate-forms reliability, involves creating two different but parallel forms of a measure. The extent of agreement between the forms is used as an index of reliability. For example, two forms of a self-report measure of social competence would be created, with different items in the two forms measuring the same construct. The two forms would be completed by the same respondents and scores from the two measures correlated to establish a reliability coefficient.

Another type of parallel-forms procedure is the *method of interrater agreement.* Interrater reliability refers to the degree to which the ratings are free from error variance associated with either raters or examiners. We assess interrater reliability by having two (or more) raters independently evaluate examinees' behaviors and then comparing the two sets of ratings. A similar procedure used with observational measures is referred to as the *method of interobserver agreement.* We evaluate the extent of agreement between two observers who collect data from the same respondent using the same instrument. Issues associated with the reliability of interview measures and observational measures are discussed in Chapters 7 and 9, respectively.

Standard Error of Measurement

Because some measurement error is usually associated with any test score, there is almost always some uncertainty about an examinee's true score. The *standard error of measurement* (SEM), or standard error of a score, is an estimate of the amount of error associated with an examinee's obtained score. It is directly related to the reliability of a test: the lower the reliability, the higher the standard error of measurement, and conversely, the higher the reliability, the lower the standard error of measurement. Large standard errors of measurement reflect less precise measurements. Of course, the size of the SEM is also related to the standard deviation of the metric—the larger the standard deviation, the larger the SEM. Thus, for example, the SEM will be larger when the total score has a mean of 100 and a standard deviation of 15 than when the total score has a mean of 50 and a standard deviation of 10.

To compute the standard error of measurement, or the standard deviation of the distribution of error scores, from the reliability coefficient of the test, we multiply the standard deviation (SD) of the test by the square root of 1 minus the reliability coefficient (r_{xx}) of the test:

$$\text{SEM} = SD\sqrt{1 - r_{xx}}$$

This equation indicates that as the reliability of a test increases, the standard error of measurement decreases. With a reliability coefficient of 1.00, the standard error of measurement would be zero. With a reliability coefficient of .00, the standard error of measurement would be equal to the standard deviation of the scores in the sample.

VALIDITY

Validity is more difficult to define than reliability (Messick, 1989a, 1989b, 1995). Unlike reliability, validity has no single definition. A related problem is that there is a great deal of inconsistency in the assessment literature regarding validity terminology. We will employ one set of terms in our discussions, but you should understand that these terms and definitions are not universally agreed on (although the definition of construct validity to be given below is widely accepted).

A good way to determine whether a test has validity is to understand what the test measures and then decide the mea-

sures with which it should correlate highly and the measures with which it should correlate poorly. For example, a valid test of anxiety might show a negligible correlation with social intelligence, a moderate correlation with depression (or other internalizing disorder), a negative correlation with aggressiveness (or other externalizing disorder), and perhaps a curvilinear relationship to performance on a test of over-learned motor skills.

Unlike what we observe in the field of ability testing, objective measures of personality may use positive or negative scores, depending on whether we are measuring socially desirable or socially undesirable characteristics. It gets even more confusing when individual items run counter to the direction of the scale as a whole (e.g., "My child laughs and smiles a lot" is negatively coded on a depression scale). If examiners are accustomed to interpreting high test scores as indicating negative attributes, they may make critical mistakes when high test scores indicate positive attributes on a particular instrument (e.g., high scores on a self-esteem test mean positive self-esteem, not negative self-esteem).

Content Validity

Content validity refers to the extent to which the items within a measure represent the domain being assessed. For example, we may ask whether the items from a personality test of bipolar disorder reflect current understanding of that diagnostic category or whether the items from an intelligence test represent a particular definition of the construct of intelligence. The concept of content validity applies as well to rating, checklist, and observational measures. We might ask, for example, whether the content of an observation schedule designed to measure aggressive behavior actually corresponds to our definition of the aggression construct. Content validity is usually evaluated through relatively subjective and unsystematic procedures. That is, we examine the content of a measure and attempt to evaluate the extent to which it corresponds with our understanding of the concept being measured. This represents a good starting point in developing a measure, but more systematic procedures are also required to evaluate a measure's validity.

Face Validity

Face validity refers to whether a test looks valid "on the face of it." In this case, we are asking whether the examinee perceives the instrument as measuring what it claims to measure. This, too, involves judgment, but face validity is important for an individual's motivation to participate in the assessment process. For example, employers sometimes run into resistance in employment screening situations because an examinee believes that the assessment tools have no relevance to the job in question. However, face validity is not considered a true form of validity.

Construct Validity

Construct validity is a key concept within the traditional psychometric model because it gets at the core of the meaning of scores (Messick 1989b, 1995). Construct validity refers to the theoretical meaning of a measure, or the accuracy with which scores from a measure reflect the construct of interest. For example, what does a score within the clinical range on the psychopathic deviate dimension of the MMPI–A personality test tell us about the functioning of the examinee? Similarly, what does it mean to say that a child has a low or high social competence score on a teacher rating measure? What does the score tell us about the child's social functioning? These are the kinds of questions that arise in connection with construct validity.

Psychological assessments help us describe, label, and categorize children and make decisions about them, and construct validity is critical for these functions. If we are going to diagnose a youth as having attention-deficit/hyperactivity disorder and assign her or him to a treatment program for that disorder, then we should be able to defend the basis for our diagnosis.

Although construct validity is important, it is difficult to evaluate. First, and perhaps most important, constructs are difficult to define. There are often controversies over the constructs being assessed by instruments reviewed in this text, such as emotional pathology, attention-deficit/hyperactivity disorder, developmental delay, and antisocial personality traits.

A second problem in evaluating construct validity is that empirical procedures, although useful, are limited. The following are the types of evidence typically used to evaluate construct validity:

- We find a relationship between scores on a particular measure and a theory about how the items were selected. For example, we can say that a measure of adaptive functioning has construct validity if children who obtain high scores on the measure display more success in dealing with daily tasks, schoolwork, and social relationships than those who have low scores on the test.
- We conduct a factor analysis and find that a measure assesses the constructs underlying the measure. For example, you will see in Chapter 10 that analyses of several of the checklist measures of behavioral pathology, including the Child Behavior Checklist and Revised Behavior Problem Checklist, yield factors that correspond to meaningful dimensions of pathology (e.g., social withdrawal, anxiety, aggressiveness).
- We find that the scores from a measure correlate with related measures. For example, suppose we give a test of leadership quality to a sample of high school students, then place them in small groups of six students, and give each group a task to solve. We then have raters who are unfamiliar with the students' test scores rate each student on his or her leadership qualities. A positive correlation between the test scores and the observers' ratings provides evidence that the test has construct validity.

- We find that scores on a measure relate more closely to those on other tests assessing the same construct (referred to as *convergent validation*) than to those on tests that are supposed to measure different constructs (referred to as *discriminant validation*). Thus, when a measure of aggressive tendencies correlates more highly with other measures of aggressive behaviors than with measures of social withdrawal, we can say that the aggression measure has convergent and discriminant validity.
- We design and conduct experimental studies to evaluate the construct underlying the measure and find that the results are consistent with those provided by the measure.
- If the trait being measured is expected to increase in magnitude with age or experience, we show that there are developmental changes in scores from the measure.

Criterion-Related Validity

Criterion-related validity refers to the extent to which scores on a measure relate to some performance criterion. *Concurrent validity* and *predictive validity* constitute the two forms of criterion-related validity. To establish concurrent validity, we collect scores on both a predictor and a criterion at the same time. We might, for example, correlate scores from a measure of learning disability (the predictor) with scores on a measure of school performance (the criterion) collected at about the same time. In the case of predictive validity, the predictor scores are collected at one time and the criterion scores are collected later. For example, we might relate scores from a personality test (the predictor) to measures of criminal activity (the criterion) collected two years after the personality test. In this case, we are evaluating how well the test scores predict later behavior.

Results from criterion-related validity studies are usually expressed as correlation coefficients. For example, a relationship between a teacher rating measure of social maturity and scores on a standardized achievement test might be expressed as $r = .53, p < .01$. The correlation of .53 provides us with information about the degree of association between the predictor and the criterion, and the confidence index (p value) tells us that there is less than 1 chance in 100 of obtaining an association of that magnitude by chance (given a particular number of observations).

STANDARDIZATION DATA

One other basis for evaluating psychological measures relates to the quality of the standardization sample. Most of the instruments considered in this text are norm-referenced measures; that is, an individual's score is compared to the scores earned by a sample of individuals. Factors important in the evaluation of normative groups include the representativeness of the norm group, the size of the norm group, and the relevance of the norm group.

Representativeness

The representativeness of a norm group reflects the extent to which the characteristics of the group match those of the population of interest. With respect to major demographic characteristics, the norm group should match as closely as possible the population as a whole. For psychological and psychoeducational assessment, the most salient of these characteristics are age, grade level, gender, geographic region, ethnicity, and socioeconomic status (SES). SES is usually determined by ascertaining the educational attainment or occupational level of parents (if the tests are for children) or of the examinee (if the tests are for adults). We also need to know when the norms were established to determine whether the norms are current and useful.

Size

The number of participants in the norm group should be large enough to ensure that the test scores are stable and that the subgroups in the population are adequately represented. Usually, the larger the number of participants in the norm group, the more stable the norms. If the test is going to be used for several age groups, then the sample should contain at least 100 participants in each age group.

Relevance

To interpret an examinee's scores properly, the examiner needs a relevant norm group against which to evaluate them. For some purposes, national norms may be most appropriate (e.g., when you want to find out how an examinee ranks within a national population), whereas for other purposes, local norms may be preferred (e.g., when you want to find out how an examinee ranks within a local population). The examiner interpreting the test should have the skill and insight needed to select the proper norm group for each examinee being evaluated. If the norm group is different from the one customarily used, the report should clearly state which norm group was used.

COMMENT ON USEFUL STATISTICAL AND PSYCHOMETRIC CONCEPTS

Despite all the effort devoted to developing reliable and valid assessment instruments, all such instruments have their limitations. Keep in mind the following:

- No instrument is completely reliable (i.e., without error).
- Validity does not exist in the abstract but must be anchored to the specific purposes for which the instrument is used.
- Every examinee's behavior fluctuates from time to time and from situation to situation (e.g., an examinee might perform differently with different examiners).
- Any assessment instrument contains only a sample of all possible questions related to the domain of interest.

- Assessment instruments purporting to measure the same construct may give different results for a particular examinee.
- Instruments measure samples of behavior or constructs at one point in time.
- Assessment scores will likely change to some degree during an examinee's development.

THINKING THROUGH THE ISSUES

1. Even though you will seldom compute standard deviations and carry out significance tests when you administer and score assessment measures, you will often use standard scores and other statistical concepts to interpret results. How will knowledge of statistics and psychometric concepts be useful to you as a clinician?
2. Before you use a measure, how important is it that you become familiar with its reliability, validity, and standardization?
3. Under what circumstances would you use measures that do not have adequate reliability or validity?

SUMMARY

1. A knowledge of statistical and psychometric concepts will enhance your understanding of tests and measures, test manuals, and research reports.

Scales of Measurement

2. Data can be ordered by various methods. In most cases, we use one of four types of scales: nominal, ordinal, interval, or ratio.
3. A nominal measurement scale consists of a set of nonordered categories, with one name, number, or letter given to each item being scaled.
4. Like a nominal scale, an ordinal measurement scale classifies items, but the items are ordered as well. The variable being measured is ranked or ordered according to the amount of some characteristic or along some dimension, without regard for differences in the distances between scores.
5. An interval measurement scale classifies, as a nominal scale does, and orders, as an ordinal scale does, but it adds an arbitrary zero point and equal units.
6. A ratio measurement scale has a true zero point, equal intervals between adjacent units, and equality of ratios, in addition to allowing ordering and classification.

Descriptive Statistics

7. Descriptive statistics summarize data obtained about a sample of individuals.
8. Descriptive statistics include frequency distributions, normal curves, standard scores, and measures of central tendency, dispersion, correlation, and regression.
9. The three most commonly used measures of central tendency are the mean, the median, and the mode.
10. The mean is the arithmetic average of all the scores in a set of scores.
11. The median is the middle point in a set of scores arranged in order of magnitude.
12. The mode is the score in a set of scores that occurs more frequently than any other.
13. Dispersion refers to the variability of scores in a set of scores.

14. The range is the distance between the highest and lowest scores in a set.
15. Variance (S^2) is a statistical measure of the amount of spread in a set of scores—the greater the spread, the greater the variance.
16. The standard deviation (SD) is the square root of the variance, representing the average of the squared deviations from the mean.
17. The normal (or bell-shaped) curve is a common type of distribution. Many psychological traits are distributed roughly along a normal curve.

Correlation and Regression

18. Correlations tell us about the degree of association or co-relationship between two variables, including the strength and direction of their relationship.
19. The strength of the relationship is expressed by the absolute magnitude of the correlation coefficient; the maximum value is +1.00 or −1.00.
20. If a curvilinear relationship exists between two variables, the linear correlation coefficient will underestimate the true degree of association.
21. The most common correlation coefficient is the Pearson correlation coefficient, symbolized by r.
22. Pearson's r should be used only when the following conditions are met: (a) the two variables are continuous and normally distributed, (b) there is a linear relationship between the variables, and (c) the predictor variable predicts as well at the high-score ranges as at the low-score ranges.
23. When the conditions for using Pearson's r cannot be met, the Spearman r_s (rank-difference) method can be used.
24. Correlations should not be used to infer cause and effect.
25. The square of the correlation coefficient represents the proportion of variance in one variable that is accounted for by the other variable.
26. You can use the correlation coefficient, together with other information, to construct a linear equation for predicting the score on one variable when you know the score on another variable. This equation is called the regression equation.
27. A measure of the accuracy of the predicted Y scores in a regression equation is the standard error of estimate.
28. Multiple correlation is a statistical technique for determining the relationship between one variable and two or more other variables.
29. The coefficient of multiple correlation is represented as R.

Statistical Significance

30. When we want to know whether the difference between two or more scores can be attributed to chance or to some systematic (or perhaps hypothesized) cause, we run a test of statistical significance.
31. *Significance* in statistics refers to whether the results differ from what would be expected on the basis of chance alone.
32. Statisticians have agreed that a reasonable criterion for deciding that something is not a chance occurrence is that it would happen by chance 5% of the time or less.
33. When we test to see whether two or more means are significantly different, we also need to consider the values of the means, the degree to which they differ, and the direction of the difference.
34. Another way of evaluating the magnitude of difference between two means independent of sample size is by calculating effect size, or Cohen's d.

Meta-Analysis

35. Meta-analysis is a procedure that makes explicit use of rigorous research techniques (including quantitative methods) to sum up a body of separate but similar studies for the purpose of integrating the findings.
36. Meta-analysis is particularly useful in validity generalization studies.
37. Conclusions from meta-analysis may be compromised by methodological shortcomings in the studies reviewed and in the meta-analytic techniques.

Norm-Referenced Measurement

38. In norm-referenced measurement, an examinee's performance is compared with the performance of a specific group of participants.
39. We make comparisons by converting raw scores on a measure into derived scores based on the norm group.

Derived Scores

40. Standard scores are raw scores that have been transformed so that they have a predetermined mean and standard deviation.
41. A z score is one type of standard score. It has a mean of 0 and a standard deviation of 1.
42. A T score is a standard score based on a distribution with a mean of 50 and a standard deviation of 10.
43. Percentile ranks are derived scores that permit us to determine an individual's position relative to a standardization sample (or any other specified sample).
44. A major problem with percentile ranks is that we can't assume that the units along the percentile-rank distribution are equal.

Reliability

45. Reliability refers to the consistency of measurements.
46. A measure may be (a) consistent within itself (thus exhibiting internal reliability), (b) consistent over time (test-retest reliability), (c) consistent with a parallel form of the measure (parallel-forms reliability, sometimes referred to as alternate-forms reliability), or (d) consistent when used by another rater or observer (inter-rater or interobserver reliability).
47. Reliability of measurement refers to the extent to which random or unsystematic variation affects the measurement of a trait, characteristic, or quality.
48. According to classical psychometric theory, a test score is composed of two components: a true score and an error score. The concept of a true score refers to the measurement process, not to the underlying content of the test.
49. The symbol used to denote a reliability coefficient is the letter r with a subscript consisting of two identical letters.
50. Internal consistency reliability is based on the scores that individuals obtain during a single test administration.
51. The most general measure of reliability is Cronbach's coefficient alpha.
52. Test-retest reliability is an index of stability, a measure of how consistent scores are over time.
53. The test-retest reliability coefficient may not be an appropriate measure to use for behavioral checklists and scales, observational procedures, and related forms of measurement.
54. Parallel-forms reliability, or alternate-forms reliability, can be determined by administering two different but parallel forms of a measure to the same group of examinees.
55. Interrater reliability refers to the degree to which the ratings are free from error variance associated with either raters or examiners.

56. The standard error of measurement (SEM), or standard error of a score, is an estimate of the amount of error associated with an examinee's obtained score. It is directly related to the reliability of a test: the lower the reliability, the higher the standard error of measurement, and conversely, the higher the reliability, the lower the standard error of measurement.

Validity

57. Validity is a difficult concept to define. A related problem is that there is a great deal of inconsistency in the assessment literature regarding validity terminology.
58. Content validity refers to the extent to which the items within a measure represent the domain being assessed.
59. Face validity refers to whether a test looks valid "on the face of it."
60. Construct validity refers to the theoretical meaning of a measure, or the accuracy with which scores from a measure reflect the construct of interest.
61. Criterion-related validity refers to the extent to which scores on a measure relate to some performance criterion.
62. Concurrent validity and predictive validity constitute the two forms of criterion-related validity.
63. Concurrent validity refers to the extent to which assessment scores are related to some currently available criterion measure.
64. Predictive validity refers to the correlation between assessment scores collected at one time and criterion scores collected later.

Standardization Data

65. One other basis for evaluating psychological measures relates to the quality of the standardization sample.
66. Norm-referenced measures are those in which an individual's score is compared to the scores earned by a sample of individuals.
67. Factors important in the evaluation of normative groups include their representativeness, size, and relevance.

KEY TERMS, CONCEPTS, AND NAMES

Scale (p. 34)
Nominal measurement scale (p. 34)
Ordinal measurement scale (p. 34)
Interval measurement scale (p. 34)
Ratio measurement scale (p. 34)
Descriptive statistics (p. 35)
Measures of central tendency (p. 35)
Mean (p. 35)
Median (p. 36)
Mode (p. 36)
Measures of dispersion (p. 36)
Range (p. 36)
Variance (p. 37)
Standard deviation (p. 37)
Normal curve (p. 37)
Correlations (p. 37)
Correlation coefficient (p. 37)
Pearson correlation coefficient (p. 39)
Coefficient of determination (p. 40)
Regression equation (p. 40)
Standard error of estimate (p. 41)
Multiple correlation (p. 42)
Statistical significance (p. 42)

Effect size (p. 42)
Meta-analysis (p. 42)
Norm-referenced measurement (p. 43)
Derived score (p. 43)
Standard scores (p. 43)
z score (p. 43)
T score (p. 43)
Percentile ranks (p. 44)
Quartiles (p. 44)
Deciles (p. 44)
Reliability (p. 46)
True score (p. 46)
Error score (p. 46)
Reliability coefficient (p. 46)
Internal consistency reliability (p. 46)
Cronbach's coefficient alpha (p. 46)
Kuder-Richardson formula 20 coefficient (p. 47)
Test-retest reliability (p. 47)
Parallel-forms reliability (p. 47)
Alternate-forms reliability (p. 47)
Method of interrater agreement (p. 47)
Method of interobserver agreement (p. 48)
Standard error of measurement (p. 48)
Validity (p. 48)
Content validity (p. 48)
Face validity (p. 48)
Construct validity (p. 49)
Convergent validation (p. 49)
Discriminant validation (p. 49)
Criterion-related validity (p. 49)
Concurrent validity (p. 49)
Predictive validity (p. 49)
Standardization data (p. 49)
Representativeness (p. 50)
Size (p. 50)
Relevance (p. 50)

STUDY QUESTIONS

1. Discuss why psychological measurement and statistics are useful.
2. Compare and contrast nominal, ordinal, interval, and ratio scales.
3. Describe the three measures of central tendency.
4. Discuss measures of dispersion.
5. Explain the importance of correlations in psychological assessment.
6. Discuss the regression equation.
7. What is the standard error of estimate?
8. Briefly discuss the concept of statistical significance.
9. Define meta-analysis and describe its usefulness in validity studies.
10. What are some important features of norm-referenced measurement?
11. Describe and evaluate standard scores and percentile ranks.
12. Discuss the concept of reliability, including the theory of reliability and the methods for evaluating reliability.
13. What is the standard error of measurement?
14. Discuss the concept of validity. Include in your discussion the various types of validity.
15. Discuss the factors that should be considered in evaluating standardization data.

3

CONDUCTING THE ASSESSMENT

Children are ever the future of a society. Every child who does not function at a level commensurate with his or her possibilities, every child who is destined to make fewer contributions to society than society needs, and every child who does not take his or her place as a productive adult diminishes the power of that society's future.
—Frances Degen Horowitz, American psychologist (1932–   ),
and Marion O'Brien, American psychologist (1943–   )

Goals and Objectives

This chapter is designed to enable you to do the following:

- Understand the classification and labeling process
- Understand the factors that affect assessment data
- Become familiar with practical issues in conducting assessments
- Learn about the steps in the assessment process
- Understand the role of computers in assessment, scoring, and interpretation
- Become aware of the qualities needed to be an effective examiner
- Understand the challenges of being an expert witness

Our goal in this chapter is to introduce you to some topics associated with a behavioral, social, and clinical assessment. We first discuss issues in classification and labeling. Then we look at factors that may affect the assessment data and the steps in the assessment process. Finally, we discuss effective examiner skills and some of the challenges of being an expert witness.

ISSUES IN CLASSIFICATION AND LABELING

In Chapter 1, you saw that the results of a psychological assessment can be expressed in dimensional terms (e.g., "The youth's score was at the 70th percentile rank on the Externalizing Problem scale from the Child Behavior Checklist") or in categorical terms (e.g., "The youth is diagnosed as having an attention-deficit/hyperactivity disorder"). Descriptions, whether dimensional or categorical, are important, because they are used as a basis for decisions. Categorical descriptions also carry connotations beyond the construct being assessed. For example, children labeled "gifted" may be assumed to have high levels of emotional maturity, academic motivation, and creativity, even though the assessment from which the label was derived was geared to the evaluation of cognitive aptitudes only.

Diagnostic labels have several advantages. For example, they facilitate communication between professionals, parents, and teachers, and in some cases they help point to interventions. Further, a child who learns at a significantly slower rate than his or her classmates may, if his or her teacher is not aware of this, be assigned work that is too difficult; the child may respond to such assignments with maladaptive behaviors (e.g., disrupting the class, noncompliance). Similarly, a child who is depressed may perform below capacity and experience adjustment problems. When a teacher is aware of the diagnosis of developmental delay or depression, she or he can adjust the instructional milieu appropriately.

It has been alleged that placing a label such as "mentally retarded" or "attention-deficit/hyperactivity disordered" on a child initiates a *self-fulfilling prophecy.* In other words, individuals may lower their expectations of children who are so labeled to such an extent that the children are minimally encouraged to achieve. Although negative stereotypes are often associated with labels indicating behavioral deviancy (e.g., conduct disorder) and with labels indicating low levels of intellectual functioning (e.g., mental retardation), research indicates that children's *actual* classroom performance is a more potent force in influencing teachers' expectancies than are labels assigned to the children (Good & Brophy, 1986; Kirsch, 1999). This is so because observation of a child's classroom behavior over weeks and months plays the pivotal role in the formation of the teacher's expectancies. When a teacher learns that a new student in the class has been diagnosed as having a learning disability or a conduct disorder, the teacher is likely to form *provisional* expectations on the

basis of the label. The teacher will modify these expectations, however, if the child performs at grade level and shows satisfactory adjustment. Thus, although labels may initiate expectations, they often hold little power once the observer obtains *direct* information about the child's functioning.

In using a classification system when reporting assessment results, you should adhere to the specific cutoff points and labels in the system, reporting exactly where the child fits with respect to these cutoffs. Similarly, if you are using the *DSM–IV–TR* criteria to make a diagnosis, you must adhere to the specific criteria set forth in its classification system. However, use all assessment findings, not just the child's diagnosis, to develop your recommendations.

The use of labels and classifications should not cloud your ability to recognize and respect children's resiliency. Even when you arrive at an accurate label to characterize a child's problems or disabilities, you still know relatively little about (a) how the child processes, stores, and retrieves information, (b) how differing environments affect the child's personality development, temperament, and learning, and (c) how the child's personality development, temperament, and intellectual growth are best nurtured. You should *not* expect children who receive the same label to perform in exactly the same ways. Children classified as having mental retardation, for example, differ among themselves in their abilities, learning styles, and temperaments. They may surprise you with their intelligence and humanity if you view them without preconceptions. Finally, you must not allow labels to regiment and restrict the ways you observe and work with children. Remember that diagnostic labels do not define the whole person.

VARIABLES THAT AFFECT THE ASSESSMENT

A behavioral and clinical assessment of a child (and his or her family) should consider the following variables (as shown in Figure 3-1):

INPUT

- Innate factors—general inherited ability and specific inherited ability
- Background variables—(a) culture, race, and ethnicity, (b) family background and parental reactions, (c) health history and current health appraisal, (d) educational history and current performance in school, (e) previous assessments and records, and (f) behavioral patterns and mental health

INTERVENING VARIABLES

- Personality and temperament characteristics—interest in the assessment task, anxiety level, degree of impulsiveness, and achievement motivation
- Assessment situation—(a) reason for referral, (b) setting variables, (c) social desirability considerations, (d) reac-

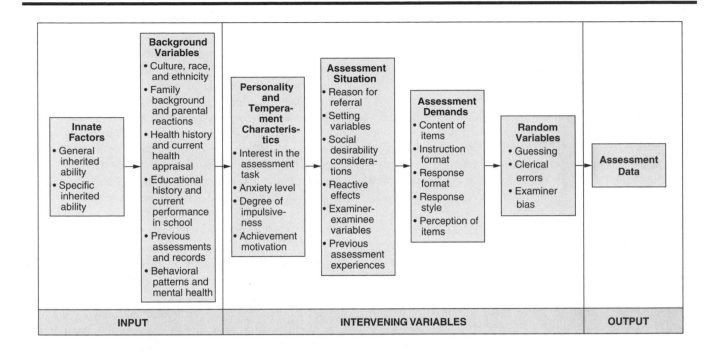

Figure 3-1. Factors influencing assessment data.

tive effects, (e) examiner-examinee variables, and (f) previous assessment experiences
- Assessment demands—content of items, presentation format, response format, response style, and perception of items
- Random variables—guessing, clerical errors, and examiner bias

OUTPUT

- Assessment data

Let's look at these factors in more detail.

Innate Factors

Genetic programming, maturational status, and environmental influences interact to affect the course of development. The genetic influence for many behaviors reflects a high degree of preorganization and priming laid down in brain structures through evolution. Gene actions are associated with the patterns of various human behaviors, with precocity, and with deficits in developmental status. Distinctive cycles of gene action operate at different stages in a child's maturation. The epigenetic process (the process of continuous feedback and modulation that directs development toward specific targets, or end states) is characterized by individual differences in the rate of development and in the timing of particular phases. Thus, personality development, temperament, and intelligence for any given child reflect the interaction of many complex factors.

There is considerable evidence that some personality and temperament characteristics—such as adjustment, extraver-

sion, aggression, inhibition, anger proneness, and emotional regulation—are under genetic influence (Phares, 2003). Genetically related family members show higher correlations on specific characteristics than do genetically unrelated individuals who share the same family environments. In other words, the more similar people are genetically, the more highly related are several personality and temperament characteristics.

Genetic influences also may play a role in the development of psychological disorders such as schizophrenia, bipolar affective disorder, autism, attention-deficit/hyperactivity disorder, conduct disorder, anxiety disorder, fears, stuttering, and specific language disorders (Mash & Wolfe, 2002; Phares, 2003). Current work suggests that psychological disorders arise in part from the interaction of many genes, each of which makes a relatively small contribution to a disorder (Mash & Wolfe, 2002).

Background Variables

Culture, race, and ethnicity. See Chapter 4 for a discussion of culture, race, and ethnicity.

Family background and parental reactions. Forces within the home play an important role in the development of children's personality, temperament, and intelligence. These forces include (a) stimulation in the home (such as encouraging high achievement, intellectual pursuits, and independence), (b) type of punishment regime (e.g., very severe or very mild), (c) the presence of family risk factors (such as parental unemployment, limited parental education, authoritarian parental attitudes, rigid parental behavior, father's absence from the home, and large family size), and (d) the intellectual environment of the home (such as the quality of language models available, opportunities for enlarging vocabulary, feedback about appropriate language usage, and opportunities for language practice).

Although heredity sets the foundation for a child's personality, temperament, and intelligence, it does not set the final limits on these characteristics; it is the environment that either permits these characteristics to be expressed or hinders their expression. Children determine their own experiences by both selecting and eliciting reactions from environmental stimuli, and children "vary in their susceptibility to environmental events and contingencies" (Scarr, 1991, p. 70).

Children's families play a critical role in their development. You will learn much about children by interviewing their parents or caregivers, siblings, and other persons who are close to them. Elicit information that will help you understand how the family members view the child, their concerns about and problems with the child, and what they have done to alleviate their concerns and problems. Ideally, you should visit a child's home to gain additional information about the child and the family.

Within one family, there may be differences between the mother and the father, not only in the way they perceive the child's problem but also in the way they report it. Therefore, you will want to interview both parents to get a thorough picture of how each views the child.

You need to be sensitive to how you communicate assessment results to parents. Some parents may become defensive when they learn about the findings and resent suggestions that they modify their parenting behavior (because, for example, they may fear that their behavior is being criticized). Some parents genuinely want help, whereas others may be uncertain about wanting help, may fear receiving help, or may not want help at all. When parents resist getting help, they may deny that their child has problems, disagree with teachers' reports that their child has problems, feel embarrassed or guilty because they believe that their child's problems reflect poorly on them, become defensive because they believe that a mental health professional will uncover their own problems, or prefer to have problems handled within their immediate and extended families rather than by outsiders.

Some parents, unable to tolerate any undesirable behavior in their child, will immediately seek professional help when any misbehavior occurs. These parents may not have an understanding of normal developmental patterns. Other parents are able to tolerate a wide range of behavior in their child and will not seek professional help until their child's behavior is seriously disturbed.

Overall, your findings and intervention plans must have *ecological validity*. This means that you must consider the child's environment—including his or her immediate family, extended family, peers, culture, home, neighborhood, school,

and larger community—in evaluating assessment findings and in planning interventions.

Health history and current health appraisal.   Parents' genetic backgrounds and mothers' health and health-related behaviors influence the development of fetuses. Several developmental disabilities are directly linked to genetic factors; for example, Down syndrome and Klinefelter's syndrome are forms of mental retardation associated with chromosomal abnormalities. Similarly, a mother's alcohol or drug usage may affect the development of her fetus. You also will need to consider children's health history, including illnesses, accidental injuries, and hospitalizations, and incorporate the medical findings in your evaluation. For example, an examinee with visual defects may have difficulty seeing pictorial items.

Educational history and current performance in school.   A child's performance in school over several years may be a key indicator of his or her adjustment. Fluctuations in grades or test scores, for example, may indicate the presence of stress. And the timing of a severe or sudden drop in school performance may give you clues about when the stress arose. Also, the numbers of absences, instances of tardiness, and relocations noted in the child's school records may give you clues to changes in his or her performance. We recommend that you interview the child's teachers to obtain information about how they view the child and his or her family.

Previous assessments and records.   Review the results of any previous medical, psychological, neuropsychological, psychoeducational, mental health, or psychiatric evaluations of the child before you begin your own assessment. Also examine any other relevant information from the child's records and personal documents. For minor children, you will need the parent's (or guardian's) permission to review or obtain a copy of these records; older children can provide permission for themselves.

Cumulative school records provide a summary of the child's academic performance and school behavior. Study the records, and note the child's academic grades, attendance, work habits, behavior, and degree of cooperativeness. Be sure to note any trends in the records. Be aware that you may need to review several different school records, including a cumulative file, a health file, and a special education file.

Following are some items to consider:

1. Grades obtained by the child in each subject
2. Citizenship ratings
3. Changes in the child's grades and behavior as he or she progressed from grade to grade
4. Relationships between the child's academic grades and his or her behavior
5. Retention in grade
6. Numbers of absences and instances of tardiness and reasons for them, if excessive

7. Disciplinary problems, reasons for the problems, and disciplinary actions taken
8. Results of any psychoeducational or other assessments of the child
9. Any interventions and their results

It may be helpful to make a chart of the child's grades, with rows for subjects and columns for years. Related subjects (e.g., language arts and English) might be placed in adjacent rows. Information from cumulative school records should be compared with other information that you have about the child and his or her family.

Personal documents written by a child—such as an autobiography, a diary, a journal, letters, essays, compositions, or poems—may be useful in evaluating the child's behavioral, social, and emotional competencies. Information obtained from these documents can be explored further during an interview. Before you read any personal document, ask the child and a parent for permission to do so and have the child and parent sign a form granting you permission. Personal documents may give you insight about the child's home, school, friends, activities, attitudes and feelings (including self-concept), and related matters. If possible, evaluate whether the information in the personal document reflects what has happened in the child's life. Personal documents may contain intimate information, and you must establish a trusting relationship with the child if you are to make use of them. Be sure that the child understands your duty to report information about danger to self or others. You should also check with the school administration concerning district policy about examining personal documents.

Behavioral patterns and mental health. Pay close attention to any unusual behavioral patterns, and note any deviations in behavior that are reported. For example, an older child who was confident, outgoing, and sociable but who becomes withdrawn, anxious, and depressed may be at risk for suicide. The examinee's mental health likely plays a role in how she or he responds to assessment items. For example, an examinee who has a pervasive developmental disorder may give unusual responses. Chapters 14 to 24 contain discussions of behavioral and psychological disorders.

Personality and Temperament Characteristics

A child's coping mechanisms, values, interests, interpersonal relationships, problem-solving style, and ability to withstand stress are important areas to evaluate in a behavioral and clinical assessment. For example, a moderately anxious child with limited coping skills may exhibit behavior problems when faced with stress, whereas a highly anxious child with strong coping skills may show no outward behavior problems when faced with the same stress. Personality characteristics that may influence the examinee's performance in the assessment include interest in the assessment tasks, anxiety level, degree of impulsiveness, and achievement motivation.

Assessment Situation

Important aspects of the assessment situation include reason for referral, setting variables, social desirability considerations, reactive effects, examiner-examinee variables, and previous assessment experiences. Let's look at these aspects in more detail.

Reason for referral. Although the reason for referral may be of importance, it may not be the most important issue affecting the child's behavior. A child rarely presents a single problem, and problems may be much more complex than referral sources recognize. You will need to clarify the referral question when it is vague. Referral questions are the "tickets" into a behavioral and clinical assessment, where other important issues may emerge. Identifying the critical issues and arranging them in order of importance become a critical part of a behavioral and clinical assessment.

Setting variables. Setting variables include the level of noise, heat, light, comfort of furniture in the assessment room, the child's degree of hunger or thirst, the location of the assessment (school, home, clinic, jail, hospital), time of day when the assessment takes place, seating arrangements, and related factors; all of these may affect the examinee's responses. For example, an examinee may be more anxious when evaluated in an intimidating environment such as a juvenile detention center than when evaluated in a public school.

Social desirability considerations. Social desirability considerations refer to any possible attempts by the examinee to try to present herself or himself or someone else in a favorable light. For example, in response to an examiner's question, an examinee may say that she has good study habits because she thinks that it is socially desirable to have good study habits.

Reactive effects. Reactive effects are said to occur when an examinee's response pattern is altered by the assessment procedure itself. For example, an examinee may begin to view his or her problems differently by the time the tenth interview question is asked.

Examiner-examinee variables. Characteristics of the examiner-examinee relationship that may affect the examinee's *and* the examiner's performance include age, culture, gender, and appearance. For example, a 16-year-old examinee may view an examiner who is 25 years old as being less competent than a middle-aged examiner. Or a male examiner may interview an attractive female examinee in a different way than he interviews a less attractive female examinee.

Two models can help us better understand the examiner-examinee relationship. One is the *restrictive examiner-examinee model,* which has three subsidiary models. The subsidiary models are (a) an *autocratic model,* in which the examiner believes she or he is responsible for everything that goes on in the assessment and removes all decision-making power from the examinee, (b) a *"pure" scientist model,* in which the examiner is concerned with facts only, and (c) a *collegial model,* in which the examiner tries to become a colleague or buddy of the examinee, despite differences in interests and values. We strongly advise against using any subsidiaries of the restrictive examiner-examinee model. It is important for you to recognize when you are behaving in accordance with one of the restrictive models and to change focus as needed.

Another model, the *collaborative model,* is characterized by an open and responsible collaborative partnership between the examiner and the examinee. The examiner shows respect and concern for the examinee, recognizing that the examinee must maintain freedom and control over his or her life; this holds even with young children. The examinee, in turn, shows respect for the examiner, sharing his or her concerns with the examiner and providing the requested information.

The preferred model may be difficult to establish when examinees fear you, fear the results of the assessment, or fear appearing foolish or ignorant. Even when examinees want to please you, to have successful outcomes, to unburden themselves, to confirm opinions, or to learn better ways of doing things, the assessment may still arouse anxiety. Examinees may be reluctant to talk with you about highly personal matters or answer test questions that reveal negative thoughts or feelings. They may recognize that there is a problem but not be ready to face it. And they may not want you to make judgments about their competency or fitness. Assessing adolescents may present special challenges because they are sometimes working through feelings and attitudes toward adults that interfere with communication. You should be prepared, then, for some awkward moments in the assessment and be ready to reduce any anxiety, fear, or embarrassment that examinees may have. Remember, you are a professional and are expected to behave in a rational and mature manner.

Mutual trust and respect may be more difficult to achieve when the examinee's educational or ethnic background differs from yours. Differences in language and customs may hamper communication. In such situations, you should exercise even more patience and attempt to understand examinees from their perspective (see Chapter 4).

When examinees see you as all-powerful—perhaps thinking that you can provide miracle cures—an ideal relationship will be difficult to establish. Because these beliefs may foster dependency and limit the examinee's involvement, try to mitigate them when they are present. You also don't want to encourage examinees, either overtly or subtly, to be unduly influenced by your ideas and attitudes or to express extreme gratitude to you for your help. *You should want to help examinees, not win their gratitude.*

Previous assessment experiences. Previous experiences with assessment may affect how an examinee responds to the assessment tasks. For example, an examinee who has taken the same personality test in the recent past may remember some of the items and try to answer the same way, even though the answers may not reflect his or her current feelings.

Assessment Demands

Let's look at several assessment variables that may affect the examinee's replies.

Content of items. Responses may be affected by characteristics of the items' content. For example, an examinee may respond differently to items that can be answered with neutral information than to those involving personal details. Or, questions about one parent may elicit qualitatively different responses than those about the other parent.

Presentation format. Responses may be affected by how items are presented, such as orally, in writing, or by computer. For example, an examinee's hearing difficulties may affect her or his ability to answer oral questions, or an examinee's reading difficulties may affect how he or she answers printed questions.

Response format. Responses may be affected by the type of response that is required, such as oral or written one-word answers, essays, true/false answers, or pointing responses. For example, an examinee may be more anxious when an essay response, rather than a one-word response, is required, or an examinee with motor impairment of the upper extremities may not be able to easily write answers that she or he could easily express orally.

Response style. Responses may be affected by the examinee's response style—for example, whether the examinee tends to agree with positively stated questions but disagree with negatively stated questions, to select the last choice in a series, to be open or defensive, to be truthful or lie, to engage in impression formation, or to malinger. Some examinees may show *response bias:* The examinee's response to one item influences his or her response to the next item. For example, after saying "yes" to several items in a row, the examinee says "yes" to the next item when the response otherwise would be "no."

Perception of items. Responses may be affected by how the examinee perceives the items. For example, examinees will likely offer inaccurate responses if they have memory difficulties, misperceive questions, or attend to irrelevant parts of a question. Also, a parent may misinterpret the instructions on a behavior checklist. For example, if the instruction is to check specific behavior problems that occur "frequently," a parent may assume that "frequently" means three or more times a day. In this case, he or she will not report behavior problems that occur only once or twice a day.

Random Variables

Random variables that may affect the assessment data include guessing on the part of the examinee, clerical errors on the part of the examiner, and examiner bias. You have little control over guessing but greater control of the examiner variables.

Assessment Data

The assessment data include all of the information collected in the course of the assessment, including case history data.

STEPS IN A BEHAVIORAL AND CLINICAL ASSESSMENT

You can think of the assessment process as comprising the 11 steps shown in Figure 3-2. These steps represent a multistage assessment process involving planning, collecting data, evaluating results, formulating hypotheses, developing recommendations, communicating results and recommendations, conducting reevaluations, and following up on the child's performance as needed.

Step 1: Review Referral Information

When you receive a referral, read it carefully and, if necessary, consult with the referral source to clarify any ambiguous or vague information. For example, if a teacher asks you to find out why a child is having difficulty in class, you will want to know what kind of difficulty the teacher is referring to in order to keep from going off in the wrong direction. You may find it necessary to reconceptualize or redefine the referral question. You will want to know what the referral source expects you to accomplish and identify the areas that the referral source is most concerned about. If you can't identify these areas, you will have difficulty formulating an appropriate assessment strategy. If you understand the referral question and the referral source's expectations about what you can and cannot accomplish, then you will begin the assessment on a firm footing.

You want to establish a good working relationship with the referral source. Communication and decision making will be easier if you and the referral source share a common vocabulary and agree about the referral question.

Discuss the reasons for individual assessment with the referral source, and spell out any potential benefits and limitations. Some school districts have pre-referral committees, established to work with teachers who have concerns about students' academic performance or behavior. Pre-referral committees may recommend possible interventions. They may also reduce the number of children unnecessarily referred for individual psychoeducational assessment, making it easier to provide prompt and intensive services to those most in need of individual assessment.

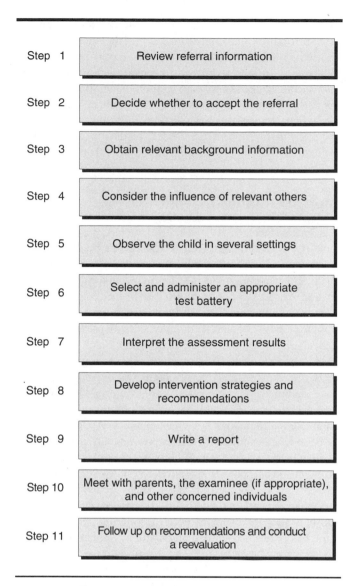

Figure 3-2. Steps in the assessment process.

Step 2: Decide Whether to Accept the Referral

You are not obligated to accept all referrals, nor do you need to give all children who are referred to you a complete assessment battery. Ask yourself questions such as these: Are there other professionals who are more competent to handle the referral because of its highly specialized nature? (For example, a child who has recently sustained a head injury would be best served by a neuropsychological and neurological assessment rather than by a psychoeducational assessment.) Is formal testing needed? Can I answer the concerns of the referral source with assessment procedures other than formal testing? Do I need to refer the child for a medical evaluation because the referral indicates (or you discover in the course of your evaluation) that the child has had a sudden change in personality or cognitive behavior, certain physical complaints (e.g., nausea, dizziness, headache, vomiting, undue sleepless-ness, difficulty in arousal from sleep, listlessness, easy fati-gability, blurred or double vision, motor weakness or clumsiness, loss or reduction in sensory acuities), or alter-ations in sensations (e.g., pain, numbness, tingling, ringing in the ears)? Generally, if you think the examinee's problem is likely neurological or physiological, refer the examinee to a specialist in the appropriate area. If you decide to conduct the evaluation, obtain permission from the parents to do so.

Step 3: Obtain Relevant Background Information

Obtain information relevant to the child's medical, social, psychological, linguistic, educational, and physical develop-ment. You can obtain this information from the child, the par-ents, teachers, and others familiar with the child's problem; from the child's cumulative school records (including records from previous schools); from reports of any previous psycho-logical evaluations; from medical reports; and from reports from other agencies (if applicable). Have the parents com-plete the Background Questionnaire (see Appendix A-1), have the teacher complete the School Referral Questionnaire (see Appendix A-3), and have older children and adolescents complete the Personal Data Questionnaire (Appendix A-2).

   Note whether the child was exposed to any risk factors or predisposing factors for psychological or psychoeducational problems during pregnancy and delivery, early childhood, or later developmental periods and whether the family has a his-tory of any disorders related to the referral question. In school settings, you will want to note information about what the child has or has not learned and about any corrective instruc-tional actions taken by the school staff (such as the remedial approaches used, changes in curricula, and changes in instruc-tional approach). Also obtain samples of the child's classroom work (e.g., essays, writing samples, drawings, constructions). If you plan to contact other sources to obtain information about the child, be sure to have the parents sign a release-of-information consent form. If the child was recently hospital-ized, ask the hospital staff about their opinion of the child's readiness to return to school and about any factors that might interfere with the child's schooling and adjustment.

Step 4: Consider the Influence of Relevant Others

To evaluate a child's problems fully, it is critical that you in-terview the parents, teachers, and other relevant adults and siblings (see Chapters 5, 6, and 7 for information on inter-viewing and Appendix B for suggested semistructured inter-view questions). Determine each parent's preferred language and use an interpreter as needed (see Chapter 4 for informa-tion about using an interpreter). Carefully explain to the par-ents the policies of the clinic, school, or your own practice; limits of confidentiality; fees; time constraints; and what you think you can accomplish. Give them the opportunity to ask questions, and answer their questions as simply, clearly, and directly as possible.

   If you interview the child's parents and teachers, find out about how they view the problem, what they have done to al-leviate the problem, and their role in maintaining the problem. Because different adults see the child in different settings and play different roles with the child, do not be surprised to find that adults' reports about the same child disagree. When the assessment findings do not agree with the parents' or teachers' accounts of what the child can do, investigate the reasons for the disagreement. Do not assume that conflicting reports are wrong; rather, consider them to be based on different samples of behavior. Ideally, you should observe how the behaviors of parents, teachers, and siblings affect the child.

Step 5: Observe the Child in Several Settings

As you administer tests, you also need to observe a child's behavior. Knowing *how* the child performs on a test—infor-mation that supplements the more objective test information—will help you individualize the clinical evaluation. Careful observation also may help you, for example, to develop hy-potheses about the child's coping behaviors and to learn about the child's flexibility and willingness to communicate clearly with others. You will want to observe the child in other set-tings as well.

   Home and classroom visits provide added benefits, in-cluding the opportunity to establish rapport with the child, parents, and teachers and observe the physical characteristics of the child's environments, such as the layout and structure of the home and the classroom (see Chapters 8 and 9 on be-havior observations). Developing a collaborative relationship with the child's parents and teachers will be important both during assessment and during any subsequent interventions. When you conduct an observation, avoid interfering with reg-ular home or classroom routines, and remind the teacher that you don't want the child to know that you are there to observe him or her. Ask teachers or parents to follow their usual rou-tine when you are present. As a result of your visit to the classroom, you should be able to answer questions such as these: How would you describe the classroom environment? Is the curriculum appropriate for the child and is it being im-plemented effectively? What instructional strategies and re-wards are being used? Although you should make every effort to reduce the parents' or teachers' anxiety about your visit, parents and teachers must understand that their behavior may be part of the problem and that changes in their behavior may be part of the solution. The behaviors of the child and parents or the child and teachers are usually so intertwined that it is almost impossible to examine one without the other.

Step 6: Select and Administer an Appropriate Assessment Battery

An effective assessment strategy requires that you develop a plan and choose tests and other assessment procedures to meet your goal. Table 3-1 presents questions to consider in evaluating tests and other assessment procedures. You should also consider the following issues.

1. *How much information should I obtain?* The amount of information needed may be one of your initial concerns; however, there are no simple answers. Your goal is to obtain the information needed to answer the referral question. In some cases, the child's file may contain an extensive case history.

2. *How many tests and procedures are necessary and how long should the assessment be?* The number of tests and procedures and the length of each assessment will be determined by such factors as the seriousness and the nature of the child's problem, the child's age, the amount of time the child can spend without feeling fatigued or stressed, and the time available to you to conduct the assessment. Again, there are no firm or absolute guidelines about these issues. You will need to use clinical judgment in each case.

3. *How broad should the assessment be?* You or other members of the clinical staff will need to decide the type of assessment needed for each case. You will want to consider, for example, which tests and checklists to administer, whether some or all of the family members should be interviewed, whether teachers should be interviewed, whether self-monitoring procedures are necessary, or whether other types of evaluation are needed. Sometimes, you will not make these decisions until you obtain some assessment information.

4. *What procedures are appropriate?* Throughout this text, you will find suggestions for conducting a behavioral and clinical assessment. For example, there are reviews of tests and checklists; semi-structured interview questions; systematic behavior observation forms; functional behavioral assessment forms; forms geared to obtaining a *DSM-IV–TR* diagnosis, such as for attention-deficit/hyperactivity disorder or for autistic disorder; a questionnaire for older children; a questionnaire for parents; a questionnaire for teachers; and descriptions of informal tests. The intent of the text is to serve as a source to which you can turn for ideas to facilitate the assessment. With experience, you will learn to judge when to use specific techniques and which techniques are most useful.

You should carefully study the information contained in the manual for each test you use, including evidence on the reliability and validity of the test and normative data. Handbooks and journals containing information on specific

---

Table 3-1
Questions to Consider When Reviewing an Assessment Instrument

Information about the Assessment Instrument
1. What is the name of the assessment instrument?
2. Who are the authors?
3. Who published it?
4. When was it published?
5. Is an alternative form available?
6. How much does it cost (including the costs of the assessment instrument, answer sheets, scoring services, etc.)?
7. How long does it take to administer?
8. Is there an assessment instrument manual?
9. How recently was the assessment instrument revised?
10. What is the purpose of the assessment instrument?
11. What are the qualifications needed to administer and interpret the assessment instrument?
12. What was the standardization group?
13. How representative was the standardization group?
14. What is the reliability of the assessment instrument?
15. What reliability measures are provided?
16. How valid is the assessment instrument for its stated purposes?
17. What validity measures are provided?
18. If a factor analysis has been performed, what were the results?
19. How clear are the directions for administration and scoring?
20. Are the scoring procedures clear?
21. Are the scales used for reporting scores clearly and carefully described?
22. Are norms reported in an appropriate form (usually as standard scores or percentile ranks)?
23. Are the populations to which the norms refer clearly defined and described?
24. If more than one form is available, are there tables showing equivalent scores on the different forms?
25. Is computer scoring available?

Examinee Considerations
26. What prerequisite skills are needed by the examinee to complete the assessment instrument?
27. In what languages or modes of communication can the assessment instrument be administered?
28. Is the vocabulary level of the assessment instrument's directions appropriate for the examinee?
29. How are the assessment instrument items presented?
30. How does an examinee respond to the assessment items?
31. What stated and unstated adaptations can be made in presentation and response modes?
32. How much is the assessment instrument affected by gender and ethnic bias?
33. Will the assessment instrument materials be interesting to the examinee?
34. Is the assessment instrument suitable for individual or group administration?

measures were identified in Chapter 1; it may be useful to consult some of these. Colleagues working in your school or agency also can be helpful sources of information. Listserv groups on the Internet—such as NASP-Listserv@yahoogroups.com, sponsored by the National Association of School Psychologists (NASP)—are another source of information about tests, other assessment procedures, and public laws governing special education. In the NASP listserv group, individual school psychologists share information and ask questions about issues that arise in their work.

Step 7: Interpret the Assessment Results

After you have administered and scored the tests, gathered the background and observational information, and conducted the interviews, you will need to interpret the findings. Interpretations should never rely solely on scores from formal procedures. Scores are valuable, but so are your judgments of the child's speech, voice quality, language, motor skills, physical appearance, posture, gestures, and affect, as well as interview findings and observational findings. Interpreting the findings is one of the most challenging of all assessment activities, as it will draw on your knowledge of developmental psychology, personality theory, psychopathology, psychometrics, and individual tests. The interpretive process involves integrating the assessment data, making judgments about the meaning of the data, and exploring the implications of the data regarding diagnosis, placement, and intervention.

As you integrate and interpret the assessment data, you will want to consider questions such as the following:

- Are the test scores from similar measures congruent or incongruent? For example, if you administered two different motor tests, are the percentile ranks similar? How might you account for any discrepancies between the two measures? Were there differences in the standardization groups, differences in item types, or differences in the times at which the two tests were administered to the child?
- Are the test results congruent with the other pieces of information about the examinee, such as his or her educational level, academic grades, teacher and parent reports, or occupational level (in the case of adolescents)? What patterns are present in the assessment results?
- Are there any discrepancies in the information you obtained from the child, parents, teachers, and other sources? If so, what might account for the discrepancies? Is it possible that, rather than being discrepancies, the differences simply reflect different behaviors of the child in different settings or contexts? In many cases, self-report data may be the best measure of internal emotional states, while information from teachers and parents may be the best description of externalized behaviors.
- Do the current findings appear to be reliable and valid? For example, did the examinee have motivational difficulties or difficulties understanding the English language? Were there problems administering the tests? Did any other factors affect the reliability and validity of the assessment results?
- Do the assessment results suggest approaches to remediation and intervention?

All of the information you gather should be interpreted in relation to the child as a whole. Because the information will come from many different sources, the information may not be easy to integrate. But integration is essential, particularly in sorting out findings and in establishing trends. The entire text will assist you with interpreting assessment results. As you interpret the findings, consider the extent to which biological and environmental factors may have contributed to the problem and the relative importance of each. Additionally, you want to determine the child's strengths and weaknesses and the adaptive resources available to the child and his or her family to cope with the problem and make changes.

In making interpretations, you will also formulate hypotheses and seek independently verifiable confirming evidence. You should either regard as tentative or drop any hypotheses supported by only one piece of minor evidence. You should retain hypotheses supported by more than one piece of evidence—especially if the supporting data come from more than one source (e.g., test results *and* observations). Also, seek evidence that may disconfirm each hypothesis. At the end of this process, you should have *only* meaningful hypotheses. Keep in mind that these are still hypotheses—that is, tentative and unproven explanations of a complex set of data—but if supported by the data, they are explanations that you can offer with some degree of confidence. Use your judgment in deciding whether a response reflects the examinee's habitual style or is a temporary and transient expression. For example, is the impulsiveness demonstrated by the child related to the test question, to the psychological evaluation, to temporary conditions, or to a habitual style? Although you must be careful not to overinterpret every minuscule aspect of the examinee's performance, there are occasions when hypotheses developed from single responses may prove to be valuable. For example, if, in response to a sentence completion item, a child says that he or she was sexually molested, you will want to follow up this response.

Recognize that test scores do not tell you about the child's home and school environment, the quality of the instruction that the child has received in school, the quality of the child's textbooks, peer pressures, the SES of the family, community mores, and other factors that may influence the child's test performance. You will need to obtain information about these factors from caregivers and teachers and consider their effects on the child's performance.

As a beginning examiner, you are not expected to have the fully developed clinical skills and insights needed to make sophisticated interpretations. Developing these skills takes time. With experience, you will learn how to integrate knowledge obtained from various sources—including class lectures, textbooks, test manuals, practicum, and internship—and will begin to feel more comfortable about making interpretations.

Step 8: Develop Intervention Strategies and Recommendations

In addition to interpreting the assessment findings, you may need to formulate interventions and recommendations; in school settings, you may also need to determine eligibility for a special education program and to work with an educational team to formulate an individualized education program (IEP; see Chapter 3 in *Assessment of Children: Cognitive Applications, Fourth Edition;* Sattler, 2001). To formulate interventions and recommendations, you will need to rely on the same body of information you used to interpret the findings, as well as on information from the fields of school psychology, abnormal psychology, clinical psychology, developmental psychology, educational psychology, and special education. This text provides general information on how to formulate recommendations. However, it is not designed to cover remediation or intervention procedures in depth. You will obtain this knowledge from other texts and sources that cover behavioral interventions, educational interventions, psychotherapy, counseling techniques, and rehabilitation counseling, as well as from supervision and clinical experience.

The assessment report in which you present your recommendations should not merely enumerate the examinee's deficits, or areas of failure, and list behaviors that should be targeted for change; it should also specify abilities that the examinee might be able to use to cope with problems. By identifying compensatory abilities, you establish a basis for developing intervention strategies. Consider, for example, how the examinee's deficits can be circumvented, which sensory processing modalities are most intact, and the examinee's specific needs and capacities. For example, children with severe social skills deficits may benefit from individual treatment programs initially and group treatment programs later. Similarly, with highly distractible children, short intervention sessions conducted in a minimally distracting environment might be appropriate.

You also should consider factors in the school that may interfere with the child's ability to learn and profit from schooling. Consider, for example, whether modifications are needed in the courses the child is taking, the teaching methods used in the classroom, the scheduling of courses, or the physical layout of the building. Also consider whether the child needs any type of assistance, can tolerate a full day or only a half day, needs special equipment to help with communication, or needs to be reassigned to another teacher or to a new school. Evaluate how flexible, accepting, and patient the child's present teacher is, and whether she or he has a positive attitude and is willing to take suggestions and work with other professionals.

Schools may offer speech and language training; remedial classes in basic academic subjects; adaptive physical education; computer-assisted instruction; tutoring for mainstream classes; social skills retraining; mobility and transportation assistance; academic, vocational, and personal counseling; and career development and employment assistance (Sink & Tracy, 1988). You will need to consider which of these or other resources are available in a particular school district. To the extent possible, recommendations should be practical and take into account the realities of classroom and home life. Also consider what resources the family and community have to help the child. In addition, determine the services the parents would like their child to receive and their reactions to the proposed interventions.

Diagnosing behavioral, social, and emotional difficulties is a complex and difficult task. It is often even more difficult to specify with certainty the procedures needed to ameliorate an examinee's problems and to create appropriate conditions to foster behavioral change, learning, social adjustment, and successful participation in the community. Concern with intervention should not tempt us to go beyond the limits of our present knowledge. However, we can suggest treatment interventions, apply these interventions in a careful and thoughtful manner, and then evaluate whether the interventions produce the desired effect.

Step 9: Write a Report

Shortly after you complete the evaluation, you need to write a report that clearly communicates your findings, interpretations, and recommendations. The value of your assessment results and recommendations will depend, in part, on your communicative ability. Your report may be read by a wide range of people—including parents, teachers, counselors, speech and language therapists, psychiatrists, probation officers, pediatricians, neurologists, social workers, attorneys, prosecutors, judges, other professionals, and the examinee (depending on his or her level of development). Therefore, the report should be understandable to any relevant parties. Although your report may be used for purposes other than those originally intended, it is important to specify what the original intent was; this may help prevent misuse.

One of the best ways to learn how to write a report is to study reports written by competent clinicians. Use these reports as general guides; ideally, you should develop your own style and approach to report writing. Because the psychological report or psychoeducational report is a crucial part of the assessment process, it deserves your care and attention (see Chapter 25).

Step 10: Meet with Parents, the Examinee (If Appropriate), and Other Concerned Individuals

After you have written the report, you may want to discuss the results with the child (if appropriate), the child's parents, and the referral source. You may also be called on to present your results at a staff conference, at a due process hearing conducted under IDEA 2004 regulations, or even in court.

All of these face-to-face contacts will require that you be skillful in explaining your findings and recommendations. If children or parents are at the conference, you will need to help them understand the findings, encourage their participation, and reduce any anxiety or defensiveness. By becoming familiar with the content of this text, you will be better able to present and support your findings. Chapter 6 provides guidelines for conferring with parents.

Step 11: Follow Up on Recommendations and Conduct a Reevaluation

Effective delivery of services requires close monitoring of recommendations, interventions, and changes in the child's development. Both short- and long-term follow-ups are important components of the assessment process. Short-term follow-ups (within 2 to 6 weeks) are needed to identify interventions that prove to be ineffective because the situation changed, because they were inadequate from the beginning, or because they were not followed. You also may discover other issues requiring additional assessment after you review the initial response to the intervention.

Long-term follow-ups are important because examinees change as a result of development, life experiences, and treatment; consequently, you should not consider the initial assessment to be an end point. For example, an evaluation conducted when a child is 2 years old may have little meaning a year later, except as a basis for comparison. Reevaluation is an important means of monitoring and documenting a child's response to an intervention, the stability of symptoms, the progression of a disease process, or the course and rate of recovery. Repeated assessment is especially important when a medical intervention procedure (e.g., chemotherapy or brain surgery) or a behavioral intervention procedure (e.g., a cognitive rehabilitation program) is used. Repeated assessment is also required when you place children in special education programs or when preschool children have developmental disabilities. If the child has an IEP, you will want to determine whether the goals and objectives of the plan are being met and how best to change the plan if change is needed.

Assessment recommendations are not the final solution to a child's difficulties. Recommendations are starting points for the clinician and for those responsible for implementing the interventions. Assessment should be an ongoing process, with modifications made to the intervention plans as the child's needs change or when the plans are or become ineffective. Effective consultation requires monitoring the child's progress with both short-term and long-term follow-up contacts as needed.

Comment on Steps in the Assessment Process

Formulating an assessment plan begins with selecting an appropriate battery of tests, deciding on whom to interview, de-

ciding on what types of observations are needed, and modifying the original plan as additional questions develop from the assessment findings. Sometimes you will want to change or add tests or other assessment procedures as a result of the information you obtain early in the assessment process and schedule further assessments in order to gain additional needed information. For example, suppose your original plan does not call for an in-depth developmental history interview with the mother. However, the interview with the child reveals a period of hospitalization last summer. Consequently, you decide that you need to interview the mother to obtain more detailed developmental information. Finally, as you review your findings, you may decide that the child needs a specialized assessment, such as a neuropsychological evaluation or a speech and language evaluation. In this case, you would refer the child to an appropriate specialist.

The steps in the assessment process are not necessarily fixed in the order presented here. For example, sometimes you might formulate hypotheses after you review the referral and background information rather than after you have all of the findings. Your hypotheses will guide you in your selection of assessment tools. As you conduct the examination and review the results, your initial hypotheses may be modified and new ones may emerge.

COMPUTER-BASED ADMINISTRATION, SCORING, AND INTERPRETATION

Computers are having an impact on several phases of the assessment process, including instrument development and test interpretation. Efforts to develop procedures for administering aptitude and achievement tests via computer have been under way for some time (see Sattler, 2001), and similar efforts are being made with interview and observational procedures. Computer-based administration—whereby items are presented on a computer monitor and the examinee responds by using a keyboard, mouse, or touch-screen—is now available for some of the personality tests and rating and behavior checklists described in this text (e.g., the Conners' Rating Scales–Revised). You can expect to see more activity along these lines in the future.

Computer-based scoring of personality tests and rating and checklist measures is widely available. Scoring programs generally provide raw scores and standard scores, and they often produce a graphic presentation of the scores. Figure 3-3 shows a computer-generated plot of subscores on the Child Behavior Checklist/1.5–5, based on normative data from clinical and nonclinical samples of children.

There are several advantages to computer scoring. First, it saves time for the examiner, although this advantage is mitigated if the forms must be sent away for scoring. Second, data can be easily stored and analyzed for research purposes. Third, scores are calculated accurately (assuming there are no computer glitches). This is an important consideration with tests requiring complex scoring procedures. The potential

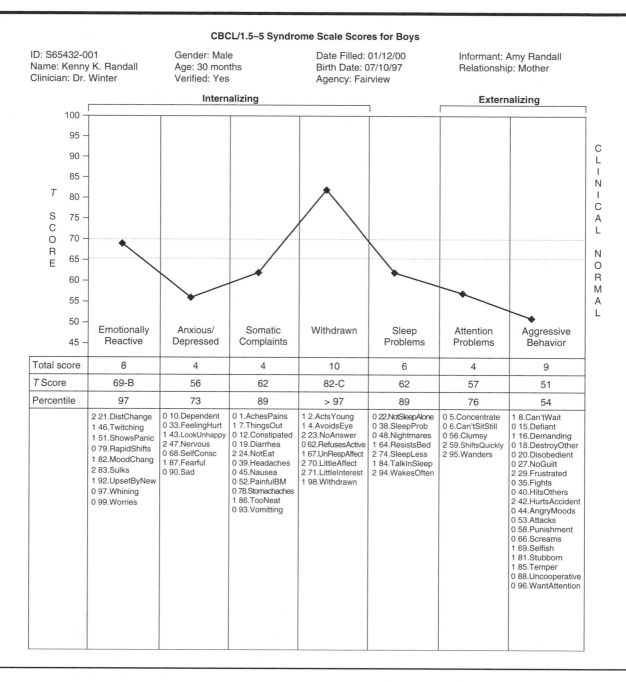

CBCL/1.5–5 Syndrome Scale Scores for Boys

ID: S65432-001
Name: Kenny K. Randall
Clinician: Dr. Winter

Gender: Male
Age: 30 months
Verified: Yes

Date Filled: 01/12/00
Birth Date: 07/10/97
Agency: Fairview

Informant: Amy Randall
Relationship: Mother

	Emotionally Reactive	Anxious/ Depressed	Somatic Complaints	Withdrawn	Sleep Problems	Attention Problems	Aggressive Behavior
Total score	8	4	4	10	6	4	9
T Score	69-B	56	62	82-C	62	57	51
Percentile	97	73	89	> 97	89	76	54
	2 21.DistChange 1 46.Twitching 1 51.ShowsPanic 0 79.RapidShifts 1 82.MoodChang 2 83.Sulks 1 92.UpsetByNew 0 97.Whining 0 99.Worries	0 10.Dependent 0 33.FeelingHurt 1 43.LookUnhappy 2 47.Nervous 0 68.SelfConsc 1 87.Fearful 0 90.Sad	0 1.AchesPains 1 7.ThingsOut 0 12.Constipated 0 19.Diarrhea 2 24.NotEat 0 39.Headaches 0 45.Nausea 0 52.PainfulBM 0 78.Stomachaches 1 86.TooNeat 0 93.Vomitting	1 2.ActsYoung 1 4.AvoidsEye 0 62.RefusesActive 1 67.UnRespAffect 2 70.LittleAffect 2 71.LittleInterest 1 98.Withdrawn	0 22.NotSleepAlone 0 38.SleepProb 0 48.Nightmares 1 64.ResistsBed 2 74.SleepLess 1 84.TalkInSleep 2 94.WakesOften	0 5.Concentrate 0 6.Can'tSitStill 0 56.Clumsy 2 59.ShiftsQuickly 2 95.Wanders	1 8.Can'tWait 0 15.Defiant 1 16.Demanding 0 18.DestroyOther 0 20.Disobedient 0 27.NoGuilt 2 29.Frustrated 0 35.Fights 0 40.HitsOthers 2 42.HurtsAccident 0 44.AngryMoods 0 53.Attacks 0 58.Punishment 0 66.Screams 1 69.Selfish 1 81.Stubborn 1 85.Temper 0 88.Uncooperative 0 96.WantAttention

Figure 3-3. Child Behavior Checklist/1.5–5 computer-scored syndrome profile for Kenny Randall. Note that B = Borderline clinical range, C = Clinical range, and Broken lines = Borderline clinical range. (Reprinted with permission from T. Achenbach & L. Rescorla, 2000.)

downside of computer-based scoring is that the service costs money. You will need to check the costs of obtaining computer-based scoring and interpretive reports with the publisher of each test you use.

Computer-generated reports are increasingly becoming available for personality and behavioral assessment instruments. For example, interpretive reports are available for the Minnesota Multiphasic Personality Inventory–Adolescent. The reports provide summary scores from all of the primary and supplementary scales of the test as well as a narrative summary of conclusions based on the scores. Diagnoses and treatment recommendations relevant to specific contexts (e.g., inpatient mental health, corrections, drug/alcohol treatment) are also available. The computer-generated report is designed to mimic the conclusions and recommendations that would be produced by a clinician interpreting the instrument.

Computer-based interpretive programs are available for most of the behavioral rating and checklist measures described in Chapters 10 and 14. For example, the Youth Self-Report, a self-report checklist designed to assess various problem behaviors, provides a narrative computerized report that explains the examinee's scores on the YSR problem scales and on the *DSM*-oriented scales.

There are, however, potential problems associated with the use of computer-generated reports. First, computer-generated reports are generally based on expert clinical opinion, not on results from quantitative research. In such cases, empirical support for the interpretive statements, diagnoses, and treatment recommendations is lacking (Garb, 2000; Matarazzo, 1992). For example, although validity data may be available to indicate that high scores on an attention problem subscale of a behavioral checklist are significantly associated with poor academic performance, there may be no empirical support for a computer-generated report that translates a particular high score into a diagnosis of attention-deficit/hyperactivity disorder and recommends a specific educational intervention. According to *Standards for Educational and Psychological Testing* (American Educational Research Association et al., 1999), the reliability and validity of computer-generated interpretations must be independently established.

Second, computer-generated reports might be applied in inappropriate and unprofessional ways. This happens when "canned," computer-generated reports are used as is by unqualified practitioners who provide feedback to clients and make therapeutic decisions. It is especially problematic to base recommendations about a child solely on computer-generated test results, without taking into account other characteristics and circumstances of the examinee.

To circumvent these problems, we advise, first, that computer-generated reports be used only by qualified examiners who know the assessment instrument and who have the expertise to interpret the reports. Second, computer programs should be chosen that allow the examiner to insert, omit, and clarify information about the child with ease, using clinical judgments and insights obtained from a study of all of the assessment information obtained about the child.

New challenges await professionals who use computers in their clinical work. Computer-generated reports raise many legal, ethical, clinical, professional, and philosophical issues (American Educational Research Association et al., 1999). Computer records, like all assessment records, must be kept confidential. Clinical professionals need to establish procedures for determining who has access to computer equipment, where and how information is stored, and whether reports will be sent by e-mail to other parties. One unresolved question pertains to who is responsible for a computerized report. For example, if a computerized report is invalid, who is responsible for any harm caused—the clinician, the software manufacturer, or both? Guidelines are still evolving along with computer technology.

EXAMINER QUALIFICATIONS

Examiners who perform clinical and psychoeducational assessments need to meet core and supplemental requirements proposed by a Task Force of the American Psychological Association on test user qualifications (Turner, DeMers, Fox, & Reed, 2001). The core requirements are knowledge of psychometric and measurement issues; familiarity with the effects of ethnic, racial, cultural, gender, age, and linguistic variables on test scores; and understanding of how to assess examinees with disabilities. Supervised experience also is essential. The supplementary requirements are course work in general psychology, child psychology, psychology of learning, physiological psychology, statistics, personality theory, social psychology, abnormal psychology, and counseling and psychotherapy.

Psychometric and Measurement Knowledge

Examiners must be familiar with classical test theory and, where needed, item response theory. They must understand (a) *descriptive statistics* (e.g., properties of the normal curve, measures of central tendency, measures of variation, indices of relationship, scaled scores, and transformations), (b) *theory of reliability and measurement error* (e.g., internal consistency reliability, test-retest reliability, parallel-forms reliability, standard error of measurement, change scores, characteristics of examinees, characteristics of examiners, characteristics of the testing environment, and scoring accuracy), (c) *theory of validity* (e.g., construct validity, criterion-related validity, convergent validity, and discriminant validity), (d) *how to select appropriate tests* (e.g., what tests are designed to meet which purposes, how the tests were constructed, and how they are to be administered, scored, and interpreted), and (e) *how to use assessment procedures* (e.g., norms, administration procedures, confidentiality of results, communication of results, and test security).

Familiarity with Ethnic, Racial, Cultural, Gender, Age, and Linguistic Variables

Examiners should be familiar with how ethnic, racial, cultural, gender, age, and linguistic variables influence the choice of tests; the scoring, interpretation, and analysis of test data; and the use of test data. For example, examiners need to consider how the testing environment affects performance of different groups, how the orientations and values of different groups affect their test performance, how tests may have differential validity for different racial and cultural groups, and how test bias may occur.

Understanding of Assessment of Examinees with Disabilities

Examiners need to be up to date on the legal, technical, and professional issues governing the use of tests with examinees who have disabilities. Examples of such issues are the need for test accommodations, which tests are most appropriate, how the testing environment may affect the examinee's scores, whether inferences based on test scores accurately reflect what the test is measuring for the examinee, and whether specialized norms are appropriate.

Additional Requirements for Examiners

We propose six additional core requirements for examiners (which are not included in the formal recommendation of the

Task Force): rapport-building skills, oral communication skills, listening skills, interviewing skills, history-taking skills, and report-writing skills.

Examiner Competencies in Five Settings

The Task Force also considered examiner competencies in five settings: employment, educational, career and vocational counseling, health care, and forensic settings (Turner et al., 2001). For each setting, Table 3-2 shows examples of specific skills, the purposes of assessment, and the training and supervision

Table 3-2
Examiner Qualifications and Examples of Purposes of Assessment in Five Settings

Specific skills	Examples of purposes of assessment					Training and supervision
	Classification	Description	Prediction	Intervention planning	Tracking	
Employment						
Understand the work setting Understand the work itself Understand the characteristics required of a person in the work situation	Qualify an examinee as being competent for certain jobs or activities	Evaluate examinee's current abilities, skills, interests, personality, knowledge, and other relevant characteristics	Predict examinee's future training and job performance, trustworthiness, ability to stay on the job, and other work-related criteria	Develop plans to improve examinee's skills and ability to handle current and anticipated work responsibilities Decide whether examinee will be retained or fired Decide whether examinee is at risk for performing at an unacceptable level	Evaluate examinee's performance over time	Learn about industrial psychology; psychology of individual differences; job, work, and practice analysis; performance measurement; and employment law relevant to the assessment Obtain supervised experience in an employment setting where tests are used
Educational						
Understand the cognitive and emotional factors that affect examinee's learning Understand the social and political factors that affect schools as learning environments	Determine whether an examinee qualifies for admission to special programs	Evaluate examinee's current cognitive and achievement abilities, emotional maturity, and personality	Predict examinee's future behavior or academic performance	Develop intervention plans to improve examinee's learning or behavioral skills	Evaluate examinee's performance over time Evaluate any interventions, including effects of educational programming Evaluate the social and instructional context variables that may influence examinee's performance	Learn about developmental and social psychology, diagnostic decision making, child psychopathology, and special education Obtain supervised experience in a school setting where tests are used

(Continued)

Table 3-2 (*Continued*)

Specific skills	Examples of purposes of assessment					
	Classification	Description	Prediction	Intervention planning	Tracking	Training and supervision
Career and Vocational Counseling						
Understand how to help examinee make appropriate educational, occupational, retirement, and recreational choices Understand the difficulties that impede examinee's career decision-making process	Identify examinee's career-related skills, abilities, and characteristics Match these with the require-ments of specific jobs or school programs	Obtain a holistic description of examinee, including examinee's career choice and mental health functioning	Predict outcomes by taking into account examinee's developmental level	Base interventions on career development theories and on educational and career information resources	Compare examinee's patterns of growth or deterioration	Learn about career and mental health assessment Obtain supervised experience in a vocational and career setting where tests are used
Health Care						
Understand how to conduct interviews and behavioral observations of examinees and family members, interpret laboratory results, and use other relevant assessment procedures	Arrive at a mental health, medical, or other diagnosis	Provide a comprehensive description of examinee by focusing on his or her person-ality, emotional, cognitive, and other characteristics	Predict outcomes by considering the examinee's personality, strengths, disabilities, and culture; the course of the medical condition; the likely efficacy of the interventions; and other relevant factors	Plan interventions by considering examinee's problems, strengths, and weaknesses and the efficacy of treatment options	Document how examinee's psychological characteristics change over time or as a result of treatment	Learn about psychopathology, health psy-chology, life-span developmental psychology, and biological bases of behavior Obtain supervised experience in a health care setting where tests are used

(Continued)

needed. All settings have the same core requirements, but each setting has additional requirements unique to that setting.

CHALLENGES OF BEING AN EXPERT WITNESS

You may be called on to testify in court or at a special hearing about a psychological or psychoeducational evaluation. For example, you may be asked to give your opinion about a child's need for a special program, mental status, adaptive skills, or general adjustment. Testifying in court or courtlike settings can be a difficult experience. Court procedures are

radically different from those followed in mental health, medical, or school settings. A witness in court often is asked to respond to questions with a simple one-word answer ("Isn't it true that . . . ?"), and little opportunity is afforded to qualify responses. In the courtroom, issues are framed in black-and-white terms; it is not a place where complex philosophical or educational issues are either debated or resolved.

The goal of the mental health system is to promote mental health, while the goal of the legal system is to promote justice. These goals may seem to be in conflict in the courtroom. Yet the two systems are based on similar basic values, which are particularly evident in both systems' rejection of deceit and exploitive use of power. In addition, both emphasize fairness, honesty, and competence in expert testimony; recog-

Table 3-2 (*Continued*)						
	Examples of purposes of assessment					
Specific skills	*Classification*	*Description*	*Prediction*	*Intervention planning*	*Tracking*	*Training and supervision*
Forensic						
Understand the effects of settings on test administration and interpretation Understand the functioning of applicable administrative systems, correctional systems, or court systems Understand the statutory, administrative, or case law of the specific legal context where testing occurs Understand how to communicate with attorneys and judges Understand how to give testimony in a deposition or in court	Arrive at a diagnosis Evaluate legal competency	Evaluate examinee's ability to stand trial or to execute a legal document Evaluate examinee's eligibility for compensation	Predict future behavior of examinee, depending on the context, such as degree of dangerousness to self and others, potential for recidivism on parole, possible changes in emotional reactions, or reactions to custody arrangements	Develop interventions, such as recommendations for treatment or determination of amount of monetary compensation that should be awarded to examinee	Evaluate how test data are affected by the passage of time and by repeated evaluations Rule out alternative causes of conditions	Learn about, violence, criminality, psychopathology, family dynamics, parenting, and/or child custody factors Learn about relevant laws Obtain supervised experience in a forensic setting where tests are used

Note. The specific skills and training noted in the table are in addition to knowledge of the core requirements discussed in the text.
Source: Adapted from Turner, DeMers, Fox, and Reed (2001).

nize limitations in current scientific knowledge; and stress the advancement of human welfare (Melton, 1994).

In some cases, a judge may ask you to provide an objective opinion about a child (or parent) and answer questions like the following: What psychological problems has the child developed as a result of the accident? Should the child be placed in a psychiatric ward of a hospital? Was the child abused sexually? Which parent should be given custody of the child? Was the adolescent competent to waive his or her Miranda rights (the rights of a person accused of a crime to have counsel and not to incriminate himself or herself) when he or she was arrested?

Testifying as an Expert Witness

Time of discovery. During the information-gathering period before trial—a period known as the *time of discovery*—you may be asked to give a deposition. A *deposition* is the tes-

timony of a witness who is placed under oath and then questioned by the opposing counsel. The responses are written down or recorded for use in court at a later date. At the deposition, the opposing counsel will want to learn about your involvement in the case, your findings, how you arrived at your conclusions and recommendations, and related matters. The opposing counsel is likely to refer to your report and other materials. Questions at the deposition tend to be phrased in an open-ended manner, which invites you to expand on your responses, whereas, as noted above, cross-examination questions at trial tend to be closed-ended and require brief, specific answers.

The purpose of a deposition is for the opposing counsel to gather information that will assist his or her client. You need to answer truthfully, but you usually will be advised by your attorney to give minimal answers—that is, to offer no information whatsoever beyond that needed to answer truthfully the questions asked. (Your attorney is usually the one who asked you to perform the evaluation or who is representing the agency for whom you conducted the evaluation.) Depositions, in some sense, are "fishing expeditions," designed to help the opposing counsel gain information that can be used later in the case. You should give equally careful answers during a deposition and in court. Remember that your answers at the deposition are given under oath and can be used later to impugn you if they differ from those you give in testimony at trial.

The direct examination. When you are sworn in as an expert witness in court or at an administrative hearing and answer the questions posed to you by your attorney, you are under *direct examination.* You will be asked to present your findings, recommendations, and opinions. It is your attorney's responsibility to ask the questions skillfully so that you can present your findings in a clear, logical, and understandable manner. To do this, your attorney must know a great deal about the case.

When you testify as an expert witness, expect to answer questions similar to those asked at the deposition, including questions about (a) your professional background and credentials, (b) your publications and professional experience, (c) your experience as an expert witness, (d) your familiarity with the subject matter of the case, (e) the research you conducted on the subject matter of the case (such as a review of literature), (f) whether you fully complied with the subpoena to produce records, and (g) your evaluation of the child, including recommendations (see Table 3-3). You will probably have included in your report the information needed to answer many of the questions about the child. You will want to review your report, recommendations, and deposition transcript carefully prior to testifying.

As an expert witness, you can and should rely on notes or other materials for information that you cannot readily recall. This process, called *refreshing recollection,* is an acceptable and accurate means of providing information to the court. However, you don't want to read from your notes; use them only to verify facts or other information. It is important that you inform your attorney that you plan to bring notes or other materials to court to assist you with your testimony. Discuss with your attorney whether these documents may be detrimental to the case if and when they are inspected by the opposing counsel.

Your role as an expert witness is to provide information to the court so that the court can reach an appropriate decision. In your testimony, present your findings, the implications of the findings, and your conclusions. A logical, carefully reasoned presentation will help the court reach a decision. In some cases, you may be asked to predict whether a defendant will engage in dangerous behavior in the future. This is an area fraught with difficulty. You must be aware of the current research literature before giving an opinion. For example, long-term predictions of violence by expert witnesses have low accuracy (Poythress, 1992). In other cases, you may be asked to explain to the court the impact of a trauma or an illness on the victim and what future treatment the victim may need. Your role as an expert witness may be critical in deciding the outcome of a case, including a determination of the amount of damages awarded a client. The keys to being an expert witness are to adhere closely to your findings, to be familiar with current research findings in your field, and to make interpretations cautiously.

The cross-examination. During the cross-examination, which follows the direct examination, the opposing counsel will question you. Be prepared for the opposing counsel to scrutinize your credentials, your report, and your recommendations, as well as your expertise and credibility. For example, the opposing counsel may ask you about (a) your education (especially if you do not have a doctoral degree: "Isn't it true that a Ph.D. is the accepted degree for the practice of psychology?"), (b) your experience ("You're not a medical doctor, are you? Then how can you tell us about the effects of brain damage?"), (c) the amount of time that you spent with the child ("Do you mean that you spent only two hours testing the child?"), (d) your ability to make recommendations ("Do you think that you know the child well enough based on a three-hour evaluation to make a recommendation?"), (e) the recommendations that you made ("How can you be sure that the child should be placed with her mother [or has been abused or needs a classroom for children with learning disabilities rather than a special tutor]?"), (f) your publications ("Isn't it true that on page 17 you wrote that children are not reliable informants?"), and (g) your assessment techniques ("Isn't it true that intelligence tests are culturally biased?").

The opposing counsel may attempt to discredit you by trying to show that your assessment procedures were faulty, that you are a "hired gun," that you have a questionable character, that your current testimony conflicts with testimony you gave in prior trials, that your publications are inconsistent, or that you lack knowledge about the subject matter (Schultz, 1990). In short, the opposing counsel may do anything within the legal limits of courtroom procedure to impugn your testimony. Because court hearings are based on the adversarial process, there are few absolute truths; the outcome of the case often depends on which party presents a more convincing argument.

Following are some tactics that the opposing counsel might use during cross-examination, along with ways to deal with them (Barsky & Gould, 2002).

1. *Asking leading questions.* To encourage you to agree with his or her propositions, the opposing counsel may use leading questions. Don't allow the opposing counsel to mold your opinion to fit his or her theory. Correct any questions that are based on faulty assumptions.

2. *Feigning ignorance.* To get you to open up, the opposing counsel may feign ignorance. Don't be lulled into thinking that the opposing counsel changed sides or is unfamiliar with the facts. By answering questions concisely and respectfully, you may avoid this trap.

Table 3-3
Examples of Questions That Might Be Asked of an Expert Witness

Background
1. Please state your name.
2. What is your present occupation?
3. For those unfamiliar with the term *psychologist,* please explain to us what a psychologist is.
4. How does a psychologist differ from other professionals, such as psychiatrists or social workers?
5. By whom and where are you employed?
6. How long have you been so employed?
7. Do you have a particular specialty in your work?
8. What services are provided at your organization?
9. What are your specific duties?
10. Describe your prior work history.
11. What education have you had to allow you to do this work? Tell me about your undergraduate degree and institution, graduate degree and institution, and specialized training in the field while you were in school.
12. (If pertinent to testimony) Did you have to write a thesis or research paper to obtain your graduate degree?
13. What is a thesis?
14. What was the topic of your thesis?
15. How many hours of research were involved?
16. Was your thesis published?
17. (If yes) Where was it published?
18. Have you had any other specialized training in your field, such as on-the-job training and seminars and continuing education?
19. (If yes) Tell me about this specialized training.

Publications and Professional Experience
20. In the state where you reside, what are the licensing procedures for psychologists?
21. Are you licensed in your state?
22. (If no) Why are you not licensed?
23. Have you published any books or articles that deal with your work?
24. (If yes) Please describe each publication, including title, topic, publisher, length, and approximate amount of time spent on the publication.
25. Are you presently on the teaching staff of any college or university?
26. (If yes) What classes do you teach? . . . How long have you been teaching? . . . Do you have other teaching experience?
27. Have you presented any papers on the subject of _____ to professional symposiums?
28. (If yes) When? . . . Where? . . . What specific subjects?
29. Are you a member of any professional organizations?
30. (If yes) What organizations? . . . Have you ever served as an officer or in any special capacity for that organization? . . . (If yes) In what capacity did you serve?
31. Have you received any honors or awards for your work in the field of _____?
32. (If yes) Tell me about them.
33. Have you appeared on local or national television concerning your work in this area?
34. (If yes) Tell me about your appearance.
35. Have there been newspaper or magazine articles written concerning your efforts in the field of _____?
36. (If yes) Tell me about these articles.
37. Have you received any national recognition for your work?
38. (If yes) Tell me about that.

Experience as an Expert Witness
39. Have you previously testified as an expert in the courts of this state regarding (reason for lawsuit or prosecution)?
40. (If yes) Tell me about that.
41. Have you testified as an expert in the courts of any other states?
42. (If yes) Which states?
43. How many times have you testified as an expert on the topic of (reason for lawsuit or prosecution)?

Familiarity with Subject Matter
44. Are you familiar with recent literature/articles/research in the area of (reason for lawsuit or prosecution)?
45. Do you subscribe to any professional journals that deal with (reason for lawsuit or prosecution)?
46. (If yes) What journals?
47. Do you routinely keep up with the literature in this field?
48. What is the present state of knowledge in your profession on the characteristics of the (child with attention-deficit/hyperactivity disorder, child with a brain injury, child with a learning disability, etc.)?
49. Can you give any examples? [Produce a comprehensive bibliography that can be used in court.]
50. Do you devote all of your professional time to this field, or do you do work in other areas?
51. (If other areas) Tell me about these other areas.
52. Please explain how you came to be involved in your area of expertise.
53. Can you estimate the number of children you have talked to who have been (type of child cited)?
54. What services do you offer these children?

Research on Subject Matter
55. Have you participated in any research regarding these children?
    (If yes, go to question 56; if no, go to question 76.)
56. In what way did you participate?
57. Was anyone else involved in this research? . . . (If yes) Who?
58. What was the goal of your study?
59. How many children were involved in the study?
60. Did you use accepted scientific methodology in conducting your research?
61. Did you follow approved and established statistical methods in compiling your data?
62. Please explain those methods.
63. What verification procedures were followed to ensure the reliability and validity of your data?
64. Have other similar studies been conducted?
65. Can you give us some examples?
66. Have you compared the information you gathered with information obtained from the work of other experts in your field?
    (If yes, go to question 67; if no, go to question 69.)
67. How do they compare?
68. Is their information consistent with yours?
69. What use is made of this information within your profession?
70. Have the procedures you used gained general acceptance in your profession?
71. How can you know that to be true?

(Continued)

Table 3-3 (*Continued*)

72. Are the data you collected relied on by members of your profession in forming opinions or in making inferences regarding the diagnosis and treatment of these children?
73. Are they helpful to you in other ways?
74. In your experience, is the information revealed by your studies and those of other researchers in your field known to the average person?
75. On what do you base that opinion?

Compliance with Subpoena
76. Have you complied fully with each and every element of the subpoena to produce material?
77. Are there any items that you did not make available to me?
78. Were any of these documents altered in any way?
79. Were any of them recopied, erased, written over, enhanced, edited, or added to in any way since the time each was originally created?
80. Are the photocopies you gave me true and exact replicas of the original documents without any revision?
81. Have any documents falling within the scope of the subpoena or otherwise relevant to the case been lost, stolen, misplaced, destroyed, or thrown away?
82. Are any documents you made, collected, handled, or received that are within the scope of this subpoena or otherwise relevant to the case absent from the documents made available to me?

Evaluation of Child
83. How many times do you normally like to see a child during an evaluation?
84. Did you have an opportunity to interview/evaluate (child's name)?
85. Who contacted you to evaluate (child's name)?
86. Before meeting with (child's name), what did you do to familiarize yourself with the case?
87. Before meeting with (child's name), did you talk with anyone? (If yes, go to question 88; if no, go to question 90.)
88. With whom?
89. What type of information did you hope to obtain from (person met with)?
90. Did you look at any reports in this case before meeting with (child's name)? (If yes, go to question 91; if no, go to question 94.)
91. From whom did you get the reports?
92. How did you use the information that you obtained from (persons or reports)?
93. How much weight did you attribute to information learned from sources other than the child?
94. Is meeting with an adult before talking to the child an accepted practice within your profession?
95. How long were your meetings with (child's name)?
96. Were your interviews of an acceptable length, considering the child's age and level of development?
97. How many times did you meet with (child's name)?
98. How much time would you estimate that you spent with (child's name) in total?

99. How much time would you estimate that you have spent on this case?
100. Where did your meetings with (child's name) take place?
101. When evaluating a child for (reason for referral), what procedures do you typically use for your evaluation?
102. Tell me about the procedures you use, such as their reliability, validity, norm group, and any other relevant information about them.
103. Why do you use these procedures?
104. Do you typically follow the same protocol?
105. Are the procedures you have just described an accepted means of assessment in your profession? (If yes, go to question 106; if no, go to question 108.)
106. Which procedures are not accepted?
107. Why aren't they accepted?
108. How many children have you evaluated using this protocol?
109. Do you regularly keep records of what you find during your evaluation? (If yes, go to question 110; if no, go to question 112.)
110. Please describe what is kept in these records.
111. When are these records completed?
112. Is there anything you can do or attempt to do to ensure that what a child is telling you is not something that was related to the child by a third person?
113. (If yes) Tell me about that.
114. Please describe how (child's name) appeared during your evaluations and how (he, she) acted during the interview.
115. During the course of your evaluation, did (child's name) express any reluctance to talk about anything? (If yes, go to question 116; if no, go to question 118.)
116. What was the child reluctant to talk about?
117. How did you respond to the child's reluctance?
118. Did you arrive at a diagnosis? (Go to either question 119 or question 120.)
119. (If yes) What was it?... How confident are you of your diagnosis?
120. (If no) Why didn't you arrive at a diagnosis?
121. Would other evaluators arrive at the same (diagnosis, conclusions/recommendations)?
122. (If no) Why not?
123. Do you have any doubts about the reliability or validity of the assessment findings?
124. (If yes) Tell me about your doubts.
125. What recommendations did you make?
126. What was the basis for your recommendations?
127. Is there anything else you want to tell us about your findings?
128. (If yes) Go ahead.
129. After meeting with (child's name), did you offer (him, her) any further services?
130. (If yes) What services did you offer the child?
131. Did you offer or suggest any referral services to (child's name)?
132. (If yes) What referral services did you recommend to the child and family?

Source: Questions 1–73 from *Investigation and Prosecution of Child Abuse* (2nd ed., pp. 353–395), by the American Prosecutors Research Institute of the National Center for the Prosecution of Child Abuse. Copyright 1993 by the American Prosecutors Research Institute. Adapted and reprinted with permission. Questions 76–82 adapted from Pope, Butcher, and Seelen (1993, pp. 140–142). Questions 83–117 and 129–132 adapted and reprinted with permission from *Using Expert Witnesses in Child Abuse and Neglect Cases* (pp. 28–29), by M. Zehnder, St. Paul, Minnesota, County Attorneys Association. Copyright 1994 by the Minnesota County Attorneys Association.

3. *Cutting off answers.* To stop you from saying something detrimental to the opposing counsel's case, he or she may cut off your testimony. Remain polite, but, if necessary, ask the judge whether you may finish your answer.

4. *Asking rapid-fire questions.* To prevent you from having time to think about your answers, the opposing counsel may ask questions in rapid succession. Answer questions with due deliberation. You might say, "I need a moment to think about my answer." You can also wait as long as you need to before answering or ask which question you should answer first. If you are not sure that a question is appropriate, wait about 5 seconds before answering to give your attorney time to raise an objection.

5. *Intentionally phrasing questions ambiguously.* To confuse you, the opposing counsel may use language with double meanings or ask complicated or intentionally ambiguous questions. Break questions into their component parts and answer each part in sequence. If the opposing counsel makes a speech but fails to ask a question, you might say, "I do not understand what question you are asking me."

6. *Using slanted rephrasing.* To reduce the impact of your testimony, the opposing counsel might rephrase or slightly alter your testimony so that it is less harmful to his or her client. Listen carefully to any rephrasing of your testimony. If it is slanted, inform the opposing counsel that the rephrased testimony is not correct.

7. *Implying impropriety.* To make you uncomfortable, the opposing counsel might imply that you have done something wrong. For example, the opposing counsel might ask you about whether you have spoken to anyone about your answers. Give the names of the people to whom you have spoken, because it is perfectly permissible to have spoken with your attorney, the client, your supervisor, and others.

Suggestions for Testifying as an Expert Witness

The following suggestions should help you testify as an expert witness (American Prosecutors Research Institute of the National Center for the Prosecution of Child Abuse, *Investigation and Prosecution of Child Abuse,* 2nd ed., pages 387–389, copyright 1993 by the American Prosecutors Research Institute, adapted and reprinted with permission).

PREPARATION

1. Be prepared. Always make sure you are completely familiar with the pertinent facts of the case. Determine the key legal issues. Also be up to date on empirical findings relevant to the case. Don't rely only on in-depth knowledge of a single case.

2. Confer with your attorney before the trial or hearing to learn what information is expected from you and to inform the attorney about the subject matter of your testimony. In addition, review other cases in which you have given similar testimony, and discuss potential cross-examination questions and answers.

3. Avoid using professional jargon. When preparing your testimony, identify any difficult words and use a thesaurus to find simple and clear alternative words that the judge and jury will understand.

4. Provide your attorney with a list of qualification and foundation questions—that is, questions your attorney can ask to establish your credentials—and an up-to-date resume of your professional credentials and educational background.

5. Maintain a file of literature, including monographs, articles, and books, about the specialty area in which you will be offering expert testimony. Make these available to your attorney so that he or she can learn more about your area of expertise. Also, be sure that your attorney is aware of anything you have written about the subject matter under litigation.

6. If you are deposed by the opposing counsel, avoid holding the deposition in your office. Meeting in your office lets the opposing counsel see your books. The opposing counsel could then challenge you in court by referring to one of your own books. A conference room or an attorney's office is a more neutral place for your meeting.

7. When you arrive for a deposition with opposing counsel, make sure you are fully prepared, know the facts of your case, have spoken to your attorney (who will usually be present during the deposition), and have reviewed the relevant references in the professional literature.

8. Segregate your personal notes and work products from the case file. Do not show them to the opposing counsel without either the permission of your attorney or a court order.

9. At a deposition, have a "game plan." For example, you may want to impress the opposing counsel with *all* the facts that support your position in order to encourage settlement of the case. Another plan is to answer the questions honestly but narrowly if you expect the case to go to trial. Always discuss the "game plan" with your attorney.

10. Always tell the truth, and strive to be fair and objective.

11. If you anticipate that the opposing counsel will also be calling an expert witness, offer to help your attorney prepare to deal with the other expert witness. You can even sometimes sit with your attorney in court and suggest areas of cross-examination on the spot.

COURTROOM BEHAVIOR

1. Wear professional and conservative clothing.

2. Remember, when you are approaching the courthouse or are inside it, anyone you pass may be a judge, juror, hostile witness, or opposing counsel. Always conduct yourself accordingly. Do not discuss the case in any public place, including hallways, over lunch at a nearby restaurant, or in the restroom. Do not chat informally with the opposing counsel or any other person on his or her staff.

3. When you enter the courtroom, do not do anything that will draw attention to your behavior.

4. Before sitting down in the witness stand, make brief eye contact with the judge and jury. Adjust the chair and microphone so you don't have to lean forward to answer questions.

5. Before answering each question, control the situation by consciously pausing. This allows the judge and jury to mentally shift from hearing the attorney's question to listening to your answer. For example:

> Q: State your name and occupation.
> [Three-count pause]
> A: My name is _____. I am a psychologist for the _____.
> Q: How long have you been employed?
> [Three-count pause]
> A: I have been working there for _____ years.

6. Answer each question with a complete sentence rather than a word or phrase. The opposing counsel may want the judge and jury to hear only his or her question. By using the three-count pause and complete sentences and looking directly at the jury, you will take psychological control away from the opposing counsel.

7. When answering questions, don't guess. If you don't know the answer to a question, say so—but don't let the opposing counsel trap you into answering question after question with "I don't know." For example, you might say, "The answer to that question is unknown because there is conflicting research [or no research] on that issue." That will keep you from appearing ignorant when opposing counsel is asking you unanswerable questions.

8. Understand the question before you attempt to give an answer. If necessary, ask that it be repeated. You can't possibly give a truthful and accurate answer unless you understand the question.

9. Listen carefully to each question. Be alert for questions with a double meaning and questions that assume you have testified to a fact when you have not done so.

10. Answer the question asked and then stop, especially on cross-examination. Don't volunteer information not called for by the question you are asked.

11. Your choice of words is important. Use words that not only depict what happened but also convey the impression that you intend. Here are some examples of positive, "soft" words, followed by negative, "hard" words in parentheses: *mother* (woman, respondent, abuser), *father* (subject, suspect, defendant), *child* (juvenile, youth), *cut* (laceration, open wound), *molest* (rape, sexually assault), and *bruise* (contusion). Note how the hard and soft words leave different impressions.

12. Give an audible answer that the court reporter can hear. Don't simply nod your head; say yes or no instead. The court reporter is recording everything you say.

13. Speak loudly enough so that everyone can hear you, yet softly enough so that you can raise your voice to emphasize a point. This is especially important if the proceedings are being audiotaped or videotaped.

14. Avoid distracting behaviors such as eating mints, chewing gum, dangling noisy bracelets, or fumbling through a file.

15. Don't look at your attorney or at the judge for help when you are on the witness stand. You are responsible for your testimony.

16. Think clearly about questions involving distances or intervals of time. If you make an estimate, make sure that everyone understands that you are estimating, and be sure your estimates are reasonable.

17. Don't be afraid to look the jurors in the eye. Jurors are naturally sympathetic to witnesses and want to hear what they have to say. Look at them most of the time and speak to them as frankly and openly as you would to a friend or neighbor.

18. Don't argue with the opposing counsel. He or she has every right to question you. Your attorney should object if the opposing counsel asks an inappropriate question. Don't answer a question with a question unless the question you are asked is not clear.

19. Don't lose your temper, no matter how hard you are pressed. If you lose your temper, you have played right into the hands of the opposing counsel.

20. Be courteous. Courtesy is one of the best ways to make a good impression on the judge and jury. Address the judge as "Your Honor."

21. If asked whether you have talked to your attorney or to an investigator, admit it freely. If you are being paid a fee, admit without hesitation that you are receiving compensation.

22. Avoid joking, wisecracks, and condescending comments or inflections. A trial is a serious matter.

23. Allow your attorney to maintain control of the examination process. Don't try to lead the examination in a different direction.

EXPERT TESTIMONY

1. Most people learn visually. Use blackboards, diagrams, and charts when these are appropriate. While standing at the blackboard or easel, turn around and talk to the judge and jury. You want to avoid having an inaudible conversation with the blackboard.

2. If you must make a drawing when testifying, think before drawing anything. Don't start with the cliché "Well, I am not much of an artist." Draw in proportion, and never refer to "here" and "there." If you use vague terms, anyone reviewing a transcript or audiotape of the proceedings (e.g., an appeals court) will not understand what you mean. Describe what you draw verbally, and number each relevant representation.

3. Never read from notes unless absolutely necessary. If you must, announce that you are doing so and state your reason—that is, to refresh your memory, to make sure your statements are specific, or the like. Be aware that the opposing counsel will likely have a right to see the notes and perhaps all of the documents that you take to the stand. That is why it is important that you tell your attorney that you plan to bring these materials to court.

4. An opposing counsel may cross-examine you by referring to articles, books, other people's opinions, or things you have said. The opposing attorney may confront you with something that appears contradictory in an effort to show

that your opinion is inconsistent with these other sources. If this happens, ask to see the book or article to which the opposing counsel refers. Read it, and compare what you read with what the opposing counsel has said. Often, you will find that the opposing counsel has misinterpreted something or taken it out of context. In such cases you should be able to demonstrate not only that you are correct, but also that the article or book agrees with your statement.

CONCLUSION

1. When you finish testifying, nod to the judge and jury and say "Thank you."
2. After each appearance as an expert witness, check with your attorney or others for a critique of your performance. Use the critique to improve the way you testify in the future. If there are transcripts of your testimony, obtain a copy and critique your testimony yourself.

Effectiveness as an Expert Witness

Your effectiveness as an expert witness will be judged on whether you considered all of the relevant facts, whether the judge and jury are confident about the accuracy of the facts underlying your opinion, whether you showed an adequate understanding of the pertinent clinical and scientific principles involved in the case, whether you used methods of assessment and analysis recognized as appropriate by professionals in your field, whether the inferences you drew were logical, whether your assumptions were reasonable, and whether you were reasonably objective. Therefore, you want your testimony to be thorough, clear, logical, consistent, explainable, and objective. See Barsky and Gould (2002) for more information about testifying in court as an expert witness.

We hope our colleagues will step forward as ethical professionals, as thoughtful experts, and as wise advocates in cases in which their knowledge and expertise can legitimately inform decision makers and advance the well being of children.
—Gerald P. Koocher, American psychologist (1947–   ), and Patricia C. Keith Spiegel, American psychologist (1939–   )

EXAMINER STRESS

You may experience stress in your work as an examiner for several reasons (Kash & Holland, 1989; Lederberg, 1989; Tracy, Bean, Gwatkin, & Hill, 1992):

1. You may find it difficult to deal with children or parents who are excessively dependent, angry, or uncooperative. In addition, it can be stressful to have to address such issues as terminal care, suicidal ideations, third-party conflicts, legal issues, debilitation, and disfigurement.
2. When one of your child clients commits suicide, you may experience feelings of astonishment, grief, anger,

incredulity, guilt, and failure (Moritz, Van Nes, & Brouwer, 1989). Your sense of professional competence may be undermined. Your thoughts may be haunted by questions of whether the suicide might have been prevented and whether you bear responsibility for the suicide. Not every clinician experiences these reactions, however. Some, as a way of protecting themselves emotionally, may see the suicide as the responsibility of the interviewee alone or of his or her family.
3. You may experience stress over how children are treated by their parents or others.
4. You may become overinvolved in your cases. This may happen when you identify with the children or parents or when they remind you of an important person in your life.
5. You may disagree with aspects of intervention plans, such as the choice of treatments or placement of children, and feel hampered when your judgments aren't accepted. This problem is exacerbated when legal issues are involved.
6. Problems in your personal life (e.g., conflict with spouse or children, illness, loss of a family member or friend, or financial problems) may affect your professional work.
7. You may experience stress associated with the agency, clinic, or hospital where you work arising from conflicts with the staff, peers, or supervisors; lack of feedback; a sense of low status and limited power; the difficulty of working with families with multiple problems or chronic and complex problems; or professional isolation.
8. You may experience stresses associated with the demands of your job, including answering phone calls at night, handling crisis calls, making visits in rural or isolated areas, visiting homes of children who are violent or suspected of being violent, receiving threats, visiting children during bad weather, recommending removal of children from their homes, appearing in court, recommending termination of parental rights, or seeing children's difficult living conditions.
9. You may experience a sense of helplessness in dealing with severely ill children.
10. You may feel alienated from your job but have to continue to work in the setting because you have limited job mobility.

Your ability to deal with the stress you encounter as an examiner will in part depend on how you have coped with stress in the past. If you were successful in coping in the past, you may be able to conquer your present stress. However, you will have a more difficult time coping with stress if you avoid talking about it; feel shame, guilt, and anger at the thought that you are vulnerable; think that experiencing job stress is incompatible with your professional image; or think that if other professionals learn of your self-doubts and vulnerability, your reputation will be diminished.

The following strategies will help you cope with stress (Corey, Corey, & Callanan, 1993; Holland, 1989; Lederberg, 1989):

- Recognize and monitor any symptoms of stress
- Exercise
- Eat a balanced diet
- Maintain a sense of humor
- Devote time to hobbies
- Change your pace, making a conscious effort to slow down
- Reduce overtime
- Make efforts to create a manageable workload, resisting the temptation to volunteer for additional work or responsibility
- Keep your work goals realistic
- Clarify ambiguous work assignments
- Vary your work activities and the types of children you work with, if possible
- Attend lectures, seminars, or conferences, where you can renew your energy for the job and meet others in your field who confront similar problems
- Keep lines of communication with other staff members open

(The last strategy will be especially helpful in defining problems, working out solutions, ventilating feelings, providing information, clarifying misunderstandings, and negotiating partial solutions.)

Performing psychological or psychoeducational assessments can offer many rewards. Sources of satisfaction include making a difference in children's lives; establishing satisfying relationships with children, working intensively with them, and seeing them progress; earning a good salary and benefits; earning respect from children, their families, other professionals, and supervisors; feeling that you are accomplishing something; increasing your professional knowledge; and having opportunities for personal growth and development. Our society needs competent psychologists to help children and families in need of services. Handling stresses as they arise, finding daily satisfactions in your work, and feeling proud of your contributions will help you in your professional life.

> *The art of caregiving is the art of interdependence. It's a delicate [and] often precarious balance: being involved and keeping perspective; caring and yet being objective; spending time together and taking time to be alone; giving to ourselves and setting limits.*
>
> —Kairos House

GENERAL GUIDELINES FOR BECOMING AN EFFECTIVE EXAMINER

Here are some general guidelines for becoming an effective examiner.

1. *Become an expert in administering tests, conducting interviews, performing observations, and developing interventions.* The more proficient you become in administering, scoring, and interpreting psychological assessment tools (in-

cluding formal and informal tests, interviews, and observations), the more attention you will be able to devote to the examinee. During an assessment, an expert is likely to be more objective and less susceptible to bias than a novice. Plan to maintain your expertise by reviewing your assessment techniques at least once a year. Also keep abreast of professional developments: Learn which interventions are effective and which ones are most appropriate for which types of examinees with special needs.

2. *Develop self-awareness.* Become aware of personal needs that may affect how you conduct assessments, and find ways to control them. You must be realistic about yourself and what you have to offer and be aware of your strengths and weaknesses. Monitor your own behavior during an assessment. Recognize your attitudes, values, and objectives and how they relate to examinees from different ethnic, cultural, and socioeconomic groups. You will also need to acknowledge and accept the differences between yourself and the children, parents, and families you meet, without making value judgments. You want to understand them from their perspectives. You want to see the child's problems clearly and not deny or minimize them, even if they are remote from your experience. When you encounter children and families with whom you find it difficult to work, you will have to either learn to master your reactions—such as anxiety, anger, disgust, fear, intolerance, or revulsion—or forgo working with them and refer them to another source. Self-awareness will help you maintain enthusiasm for your work.

3. *Learn to relate to the examinee.* You must learn to listen carefully to examinees, give them your undivided attention, and show that you accept them. It is important to maintain an attitude of professional interest and concern. When examinees are fearful and anxious, try even harder to establish rapport. For example, make frequent supportive comments, show them that you understand their fears and anxieties and can accept them even if they are fearful, anxious, hostile, or resentful, listen carefully to them, and take the pressure off by interjecting light conversation. When examinees will not cooperate simply because of who you are, you can do nothing to change your status. You can, however, show them that you can be trusted and want to help them.

4. *Remain objective.* Remaining objective means selecting the most effective tests and checklists for the assessment; being open to what you see, hear, and feel; not prejudging a child or his or her family; carefully considering your interpretations and recommendations; and taking into account all relevant factors in interpreting the assessment results. Being objective, however, doesn't mean being aloof or disregarding your feelings.

5. *Monitor your emotions.* You will be exposed to major forms of psychopathology in your work with exceptional children and their families. If you find that this exposure is upsetting, consider talking with someone about your feelings—a counselor or therapist, a professional in the field, your supervisor, or a mentor. Mastering your anxiety and becoming familiar with the serious problems that children and

their families may face will help you be a better behavioral and clinical assessment examiner.

CONCLUDING COMMENTS

Chapters 1, 2, and 3 have discussed the challenges of conducting psychological assessments. The chapters that follow discuss the skills and strategies needed to work with culturally and linguistically diverse children; conduct interviews and observations; use personality tests, adaptive behavior checklists, and visual-motor tests; conduct a functional behavioral assessment; and evaluate children with special needs, including those who display violent behavior, a learning disability, attention-deficit/hyperactivity disorder, mental retardation, giftedness, a visual or hearing impairment, an autistic disorder, or a brain injury.

The assessment guidelines presented in this text are *guidelines,* not fixed and unalterable procedures. *Always be guided by the child's age and abilities, the nature of the referral, background information, and what develops during the assessment. No set of guidelines can prepare you for every situation that you will face.* The beauty of a behavioral and clinical assessment is that it allows you to follow up leads as they develop during the assessment. This means that you can adapt the assessment to the unique needs of the child and to the purpose of the assessment.

You have already acquired a vast amount of knowledge from your interactions with children, parents, family, and others. You can use this knowledge, coupled with the guidelines offered in this text and other relevant books and materials, when you begin to assess children and their parents. The best way to use this book is to become familiar with its contents and then review the sections of the text that relate to a specific referral question. Our intent is not for you to memorize every step of every procedure with every type of child for every purpose. Your common sense and knowledge, coupled with what you learn as a student, will help you whenever unforeseen circumstances arise in an assessment.

After you have studied this text, the major components of a behavioral and clinical assessment should be clear to you. *It will take considerable training and supervised experience, however, to master behavioral and clinical assessment.*

The guidelines in the text are designed to help you conduct useful and fair behavioral and clinical assessments. We believe that behavioral and clinical assessments can promote the mental health and educational needs of children from all ethnic backgrounds. Each child and his or her parents will represent a separate challenge for you; this text aims to increase your ability to rise effectively to the challenge.

Assessment plays a critical role in all fields that offer services to children with special needs and to their families. Assessment is critical, because you cannot even begin an intervention until you know what problems the child and family are having, how they are coping with their problems, and what resources are available to them. And once an intervention begins, you can judge its effectiveness only by monitoring and assessing changes in the child's and family's behavior. The initial assessment serves as a baseline against which you can evaluate future changes and the effectiveness of any interventions.

THINKING THROUGH THE ISSUES

1. Why is each of the three variations of the restrictive examiner-examinee relationship problematic?
2. What information will you need to arrive at a diagnostic impression? What will it take for you to have confidence in your diagnostic impression, once you reach one?
3. What is your opinion of computer-based reports?
4. What do you expect to be your strengths and weaknesses as an examiner?
5. What can you do to emphasize your strengths and minimize your weaknesses, in order to become a more effective examiner?
6. Given your personal history and training, what concerns you the most about your possible performance as an expert witness? In what areas do you think you would do well? How could you prepare yourself for this experience?
7. How do you think you might cope with an unresponsive and bureaucratic work environment? Do you think, for example, that you would work for change in the organization, tolerate the organization and focus on the satisfaction of helping children, or look for another place to work?
8. If the level of stress you faced as an examiner became overwhelming, how would you go about reducing the stress?

SUMMARY

Issues in Classification and Labeling

1. Descriptions, whether dimensional or categorical, are important, because they are used to make decisions. Categorical descriptions also carry connotations beyond the construct being assessed.
2. Diagnostic labels are a means of facilitating communication of important information between professionals, parents, and teachers.
3. Although negative stereotypes are often associated with labels indicating behavioral deviancy and with labels indicating low levels of intellectual functioning, children's actual classroom performance is the major determinant of teachers' expectancies.
4. Children with the same diagnostic label should *not* be expected to perform in exactly the same ways.
5. Although labels are important in the diagnostic process and in communicating with professionals, parents, and teachers, you must not allow labels to regiment and restrict the ways you observe and work with children.

Variables That Affect the Assessment

6. Variables that affect an assessment include innate and background variables, the child's personality and temperament, the assessment situation, assessment demands, random variables, and assessment data.
7. Distinctive cycles of gene action operate at different stages in a child's maturation.

8. Genetic influences may play a role in the development of some personality and temperament characteristics and psychological disorders.

9. Forces within the home play an important role in the development of children's personality, temperament, and intelligence. These forces include stimulation in the home, type of punishment regime, the presence of family risk factors, and the intellectual environment of the home.

10. Although heredity sets the foundation for a child's personality, temperament, and intelligence, it is the environment that either permits these characteristics to be expressed or hinders their expression.

11. Within one family, there may be differences between the mother and the father, not only in the way they perceive the child's problem but also in the way they report it.

12. Overall, your findings and intervention plans must have ecological validity.

13. You need to consider children's health history and incorporate the medical findings in your evaluation.

14. A child's performance in school over several years may be a key indicator of his or her adjustment.

15. Review the results of any previous medical, psychological, neuropsychological, psychoeducational, mental health, or psychiatric evaluations of the child before you begin your own assessment.

16. Examine any other relevant information from the child's records and personal documents.

17. Pay close attention to any unusual behavioral patterns, and note any deviations in behavior that are reported.

18. A child's coping mechanisms, values, interests, interpersonal relationships, problem-solving style, and ability to withstand stress are important areas to evaluate in a behavioral and clinical assessment.

19. Important aspects of the assessment situation include reason for referral, environmental contingencies, social desirability considerations, setting variables, reactive effects, examiner-examinee variables, and previous assessment experiences.

20. The restrictive examiner-examinee model includes three subsidiary models: an autocratic model, a "pure" scientist model, and a collegial model.

21. The collaborative model is characterized by an open and responsible collaborative partnership between the examiner and the examinee.

22. Assessment variables that may affect an examinee's responses include the content of items, presentation format, response format, response style, and perception of items.

23. Random variables that may affect assessment data include guessing on the part of the examinee, clerical errors on the part of the examiner, and examiner bias.

24. The assessment data include all of the information collected in the course of the assessment, including case history data.

Steps in a Behavioral and Clinical Assessment

25. You can think of the assessment process as comprising the following 11 steps: review the referral information; decide whether to accept the referral; obtain relevant background information; consider the influence of relevant others; observe the child in several settings; select and administer an appropriate assessment battery; interpret the assessment results; develop intervention strategies and recommendations; write a report; meet with parents, the examinee (if appropriate), and other con-

cerned individuals; and follow up on recommendations and conduct a reevaluation.

Computer-Based Administration, Scoring, and Interpretation

26. Computers are having an impact on several phases of the assessment process, including instrument development and test interpretation.

27. Computer-based scoring of personality tests and rating and checklist measures is widely available. Scoring programs generally provide raw scores and standard scores, and they often produce a graphic presentation of the scores.

28. Advantages of computer scoring of assessment instruments are that it saves time for the examiner, information can be stored and analyzed easily, and scores are calculated accurately.

29. Computer-generated reports are increasingly becoming available for personality and behavioral assessment instruments.

30. Potential problems associated with the use of computer-generated reports include the fact that they are generally based on expert clinical opinion, not on results from quantitative research, and the possibility that they might be applied in inappropriate and unprofessional ways.

31. Computer-generated reports should be used only by qualified examiners.

Examiner Qualifications

32. Examiners should be thoroughly knowledgeable about psychometric and measurement issues; the effects of ethnic, racial, cultural, gender, age, and linguistic variables on test scores; and how to assess examinees with disabilities.

Challenges of Being an Expert Witness

33. You may be called on to testify in court or at a special hearing about a psychological or psychoeducational evaluation.

34. The goal of the mental health system is to promote mental health, while the goal of the legal system is to promote justice. These goals may seem to be in conflict in the courtroom.

35. During the information-gathering period before trial—a period known as the time of discovery—you may be asked to give a deposition.

36. A deposition is the testimony of a witness who is placed under oath and then questioned by the opposing counsel.

37. The purpose of a deposition is for the opposing counsel to gather information that will assist his or her client.

38. When you are sworn in as an expert witness in court or at an administrative hearing and answer the questions posed to you by your attorney, you are under direct examination.

39. When you testify as an expert witness, expect to answer questions similar to those asked at the deposition, including questions about (a) your professional background and credentials, (b) your publications and professional experience, (c) your experience as an expert witness, (d) your familiarity with the subject matter of the case, (e) the research you conducted on the subject matter of the case (such as a review of literature), (f) whether you fully complied with the subpoena to produce records, and (g) your evaluation of the child, including recommendations.

40. As an expert witness, you can and should rely on notes or other materials for information that you cannot readily recall. This process, called refreshing recollection, is an acceptable and accurate means of providing information to the court.

41. Your role as an expert witness is to provide information to the court so that the court can reach an appropriate decision.

42. During the cross-examination, which follows the direct examination, the opposing counsel will question you.

43. The opposing counsel may attempt to discredit you by trying to show that your assessment procedures were faulty, that you are a "hired gun," that you have a questionable character, that your current testimony conflicts with testimony you gave in prior trials, that your publications are inconsistent, or that you lack knowledge about the subject matter.

44. Tactics that the opposing counsel might use during the cross-examination include asking leading questions, feigning ignorance, cutting off answers, asking rapid-fire questions, intentionally phrasing questions ambiguously, using slanted rephrasing, and implying impropriety.

45. Your effectiveness as an expert witness will be judged on whether you considered all of the relevant facts, whether the judge and jury are confident about the accuracy of the facts underlying your opinion, whether you showed an adequate understanding of the pertinent clinical and scientific principles involved in the case, whether you used methods of assessment and analysis recognized as appropriate by professionals in your field, whether the inferences you drew were logical, whether your assumptions were reasonable, and whether you were reasonably objective.

Examiner Stress

46. You may experience stress in your work as an examiner for the following reasons: having to deal with difficult clients, seeing how children are treated by their parents or others, becoming overinvolved in your cases, disagreeing with intervention plans, experiencing stress in your personal life, experiencing stress in your work environment, being overburdened by work demands, feeling helpless, and feeling alienated if you have limited job mobility.

47. When one of your child clients commits suicide, you may experience feelings of astonishment, grief, anger, incredulity, guilt, and failure.

48. Your ability to deal with the stress you encounter as an examiner will in part depend on how you have coped with stress in the past.

49. The following strategies will help you cope with stress: recognize and monitor any symptoms of stress; exercise; eat a balanced diet; maintain a sense of humor; devote time to hobbies; change your pace; reduce overtime; make efforts to create a manageable workload; keep your work goals realistic; clarify ambiguous work assignments; vary your work activities and the types of children you work with, if possible; attend lectures, seminars, and conferences; and keep lines of communication with other staff members open.

50. Performing psychological or psychoeducational assessments can offer many rewards. Sources of satisfaction include making a difference in children's lives; establishing satisfying relationships with children, working intensively with them, and seeing them progress; earning a good salary and benefits; earning respect from children, their families, other professionals, and supervisors; feeling that you are accomplishing something; increasing your professional knowledge; and having opportunities for personal growth and development.

51. Our society needs competent psychologists to help children and families in need of services.

52. Handling stresses as they arise, finding daily satisfactions in your work, and feeling proud of your contributions will help you in your professional life.

General Guidelines for Becoming an Effective Examiner

53. To become an effective examiner, you should become an expert in administering tests, conducting interviews, performing observations, and developing interventions; develop self-awareness; learn to relate to the examinee; remain objective; and monitor your emotions.

Concluding Comments

54. The assessment guidelines presented in this text are guidelines, not fixed and unalterable procedures.

55. Always be guided by the child's age and abilities, the nature of the referral, background information, and what develops during the assessment.

56. No set of guidelines can prepare you for every situation that you will face.

57. After you have studied this text, the major components of a behavioral and clinical assessment should be clear to you. It will take considerable training and supervised experience, however, to master behavioral and clinical assessment.

58. Assessment plays a critical role in all fields that offer services to children with special needs and to their families.

59. The initial assessment serves as a baseline against which future changes and the effectiveness of any interventions can be evaluated.

KEY TERMS, CONCEPTS, AND NAMES

Issues in classification and labeling (p. 54)
Self-fulfilling prophecy (p. 54)
Innate factors (p. 55)
Background variables (p. 55)
Culture, race, and ethnicity (p. 55)
Family background and parental reactions (p. 55)
Ecological validity (p. 56)
Health history and current health appraisal (p. 56)
Educational history and current performance in school (p. 56)
Previous assessments and records (p. 56)
Behavioral patterns and mental health (p. 57)
Personality and temperament characteristics (p. 57)
Assessment situation (p. 57)
Reason for referral (p. 57)
Setting variables (p. 57)
Social desirability considerations (p. 57)
Reactive effects (p. 57)
Examiner-examinee variables (p. 57)
Restrictive examiner-examinee model (p. 58)
Autocratic model (p. 58)
"Pure" scientist model (p. 58)
Collegial model (p. 58)
Collaborative model (p. 58)
Previous assessment experiences (p. 58)
Assessment demands (p. 58)
Content of items (p. 58)
Presentation format (p. 58)
Response format (p. 58)
Response style (p. 58)

Response bias (p. 58)
Perception of items (p. 58)
Random variables (p. 59)
Assessment data (p. 59)
Step 1: Review referral information (p. 59)
Step 2: Decide whether to accept the referral (p. 59)
Step 3: Obtain relevant background information (p. 60)
Step 4: Consider the influence of relevant others (p. 60)
Step 5: Observe the child in several settings (p. 60)
Step 6: Select and administer an appropriate assessment battery (p. 61)
Step 7: Interpret the assessment results (p. 62)
Step 8: Develop intervention strategies and recommendations (p. 63)
Step 9: Write a report (p. 63)
Step 10: Meet with parents, the examinee (if appropriate), and other concerned individuals (p. 63)
Step 11: Follow up on recommendations and conduct a reevaluation (p. 64)
Computer-based administration, scoring, and interpretation (p. 64)
Computer-generated reports (p. 65)
Examiner qualifications (p. 66)
Psychometric and measurement knowledge (p. 66)
Descriptive statistics (p. 66)
Theory of reliability and measurement error (p. 66)
Theory of validity (p. 66)
How to select appropriate tests (p. 66)
How to use assessment procedures (p. 66)
Ethnic, racial, cultural, gender, age, and linguistic variables (p. 66)
Examinees with disabilities (p. 66)

Examiner competencies in five settings (p. 67)
Challenges of being an expert witness (p. 68)
Testifying as an expert witness (p. 69)
Time of discovery (p. 69)
Deposition (p. 69)
Direct examination (p. 70)
Refreshing recollection (p. 70)
Cross-examination (p. 70)
Suggestions for testifying as an expert witness (p. 73)
Examiner stress (p. 75)

STUDY QUESTIONS

1. Provide examples of the factors that affect assessment scores.
2. Discuss the conditions under which diagnostic labels may have positive and negative influences on a child's treatment.
3. Contrast the restrictive and collaborative models of the examiner-examiner relationship.
4. Discuss the factors to consider in conducting an assessment.
5. Describe the steps in the behavioral and clinical assessment process.
6. Discuss the advantages and disadvantages of computer-based scoring and computer-generated reports.
7. Discuss the qualifications necessary for psychological examiners.
8. Discuss the challenges of being an expert witness.
9. What are some reasons examiners experience stress?
10. Describe some ways in which examiners can deal with stress.
11. List five rewards of being a clinical assessment or forensic examiner.

4

CULTURALLY AND LINGUISTICALLY DIVERSE CHILDREN

"First of all," he said, "if you can learn a simple trick, Scout, you'll get along a lot better with all kinds of folks. You never really understand a person until you consider things from his point of view—"

"Sir?"

"—until you climb into his skin and walk around in it."
—Harper Lee, American novelist (1926–   )

Background Considerations

Evaluating Bias

Ethical and Clinical Guidelines

Practical Considerations in the Conduct of Assessments

Recommendations

Thinking Through the Issues

Summary

Key Terms, Concepts, and Names

Study Questions

Goals and Objectives

This chapter is designed to enable you to do the following:

- Understand problems faced by culturally and linguistically diverse groups

- Evaluate cultural bias in the assessment of culturally and linguistically diverse groups

- Understand ethical and practical issues in conducting assessments with culturally and linguistically diverse groups

This chapter presents information about culturally and linguistically diverse groups, including relevant research on personality and behavioral assessments and recommendations to help you conduct fair and objective assessments. See *Assessment of Children: Cognitive Applications* (Sattler, 2001) for discussions of cultural factors in cognitive assessments.

In this book, we use the terms *Euro American* (to refer to White Americans, Anglo Americans, or Caucasians), *African American* (to refer to Black Americans), *Hispanic American* (to refer to Latinos, Mexican Americans, and other groups from Latin America), *Asian American* (to refer to Chinese, Japanese, South Sea Islanders, Filipinos, and other Asian groups), and *Native American* (to refer to American Indians and Alaskan Native Americans). The use of these terms does away with color designations and emphasizes the national origin of each group. We recognize, however, that these terms may not adequately describe children of multicultural heritage. When asked to choose an ethnicity in order to complete school forms, children of multicultural heritage are faced with the dilemma of having to select one ethnicity from among those in their background. Obviously, school forms, and other forms as well, should have a multiethnic category or even several multiethnic categories if information about ethnicity is required.

It will not always be easy to evaluate the role that cultural variables play in assessment, in part because members of culturally and linguistically diverse groups differ in their adherence to their group's cultural traditions and practices. Great diversity exists within any cultural group, especially between recent immigrants and those who have had more opportunity to become acculturated into their new society. Even among those who are acculturated, differences exist in patterns of acculturation. Members of culturally and linguistically diverse groups do not need to reject their cultural heritage to adapt to a new culture; they can choose to value their old traditions and practices while also valuing those of the new culture. Our society must recognize and preserve cultural diversity and promote culturally sensitive and culturally relevant clinical services.

Within any cultural group, there are differences in values, motivation, social organization, ways of speaking and thinking, and life styles that vary with education, income, class status, geographic origin, assimilation patterns, religious background, and age. Broad generalizations about cultural practices do not do justice to regional, generational, socioeconomic, and idiosyncratic variations. However, knowledge of a child's and family's cultural mores and customs, possible migration experiences, and level of acculturation will help you conduct a more effective assessment. The generalizations in this chapter about culturally and linguistically diverse groups and the majority group must remain generalizations; do not apply them indiscriminately to each child and family. For example, although Euro Americans may be more individualistic than Hispanic Americans, it is difficult to "predict with any certainty the level of individualism of a particular person" (Okazaki & Sue, 1995, p. 368). Broad prescriptions, based on generalizations that do not take into account individual variability, are likely to be not only misleading but also possibly resented by the child and his or her family. *Use what you know about culturally and linguistically diverse groups and the majority group as background for the assessment, but treat each child as an individual and each family as unique.*

The concept of culture is closely intertwined with the concepts of race, ethnicity, and social class. Here are some definitions of these terms (Betancourt & López, 1993):

> *Culture* is the human-made part of the environment, consisting of highly variable systems of meaning that are learned and shared by a people or an identifiable segment of a population. Culture represents designs and ways of life normally transmitted from one generation to another.
> *Race* refers to the genetic makeup common to a population.
> *Ethnicity* refers to a group's common nationality, culture, or language.
> *Social class* refers to group designations within a society, usually based on occupation, education, or both. (pp. 630–632, with changes in notation)

Personality, temperament, and intelligence, as well as psychological disorders, develop within a cultural context. Cultural variables include ethnic background, language spoken inside and outside the home, gender, family interaction patterns, socioeconomic status, neighborhood characteristics, and peer group influences. Cultures differ in how they value and reinforce personality and temperament characteristics and intellectual abilities. For example, the inability to read is a substantial problem for individuals in our culture, but not for those in a nonliterate society. Academic achievement is valued in some cultures but may not be emphasized in other cultures in which manual skills are more important. Some parents may be concerned about a child who is socially withdrawn, while others, because of religious or cultural factors, may not be concerned because they place a higher value on a more solitary life style. It is important for you to be sensitive to these cultural differences. Culture may also determine the threshold at which a behavior is considered problematic or deviant. For example, what might be considered an offensively loud conversational tone in one culture might be considered quite acceptable in another.

However much we subscribe to the philosophy that well-normed standardized assessment tools provide the most reliable and valid means of assessment, we also must recognize the cultural diversity of children. Ethnic groups have unique mores and customs, languages, and social and familial interaction patterns. Differences among African Americans, Euro Americans, Hispanic Americans, Native Americans, and Asian Americans, for example, may be related to the importance placed on certain types of knowledge in their culture and to their temperaments and patterns of social and familial interactions. And within each ethnic group, there are subgroups with different mores and customs, language dialects, and perhaps even family and social interaction patterns. The types of problems individuals have, their perceptions of mental health professionals and other health professionals, and the interventions they will accept may be related to their culture and ethnicity. You must consider factors related to ethnicity in establishing rapport, in conducting assessments, in interpreting the assessment information and results, in applying normative standards, and in formulating treatment and intervention recommendations.

Horowitz and O'Brien (1989) explain the implications of a multicultural society for our work as clinicians:

> We are a nation of diversity. Though the "melting pot" that would diminish diversity was a metaphor applied to the United States for many years, it has become increasingly apparent that this metaphor does not fit reality. The diversity of the United States, deriving from the presence of strong and different cultures—cultures that shape and form the children they nurture—is unlikely to disappear in the next 100 years. Culture should be viewed as the overriding organizer of environmental stimulation for the child. . . . We must strive to understand the strengths of the different cultures that are the source of these pervasive influences or we will not succeed in educating all children to their maximum capabilities. . . . The cultural backgrounds and heritages of all individuals are reflected in values, in patterns of behavior, in the character of emotional responses, in world views, in historical and ahistorical perspectives, and in compatibility with the institutions of the general society. Understanding, respecting, and working in constructive ways with individuals from the diverse cultures that define the United States go beyond the notions of poverty, disadvantage, or even tolerance; a real attempt to understand and appreciate diversity must inform the design of both research and social policy. (p. 445)

Keep in mind that although Horowitz and O'Brien refer specifically to the United States, other countries, including Canada, Australia, and the United Kingdom, also have multicultural societies.

Recognizing cultural diversity does not mean that we set aside our nation's laws and customs. For example, zoning ordinances apply to everyone living in a city, regardless of their cultural membership.

Because assessment results affect children's self-esteem and influence their chances of having a successful life, biased tests may be detrimental to all children. If tests are found to be biased, they must be changed or eliminated. However, if tests are beneficial to culturally and linguistically diverse children, or at least potentially useful, their elimination would be a disservice to these children. In fact, a critical factor in the assessment of culturally and linguistically diverse children is to ensure that test bias does not distort the assessment. In addition, whenever you use assessment tools, you must ensure that the results are employed for the benefit of the child. This chapter demonstrates how you can accomplish this goal.

Both the *Guidelines for Providers of Psychological Services to Ethnic, Linguistic, and Culturally Diverse Populations* (American Psychological Association, 1990) and the *Standards for Educational and Psychological Testing* (American Education Research Association et al., 1999) provide important principles for the conduct of assessments with members of minority groups. You should be familiar with these guidelines as they pertain to your practice.

BACKGROUND CONSIDERATIONS

The U.S. Bureau of the Census estimates that there were 70.4 million children under age 18 living in the United States as of June 1, 2000. The ethnic affiliations of the children were as follows: Euro American, 64%; African American, 15%; Hispanic American, 16%; Asian American, 4%; and Native American, less than 1%. The Hispanic American children traced their origins to Mexico, Puerto Rico, Cuba, El Salvador, Colombia, Guatemala, Nicaragua, Ecuador, Peru, Honduras, and other Central and South American countries. The Asian American groups included Chinese, Filipino, Japanese, Asian Indian, Korean, Vietnamese, Laotian, Cambodian, Thai, Hmong, and others.

The U.S. Bureau of the Census has projected that Hispanic Americans and Asian Americans will account for more than half the growth in the U.S. population every year for the next half-century and beyond. As a result, the ethnic portrait of America will change dramatically: The population of Euro Americans (non-Hispanic), which as of June 1, 2000 was about 71% of all Americans, will shrink to a bare majority (52.8%) by the year 2050. Because the Hispanic American population is young (the mean age is 29 years, the lowest of any ethnic group) and has a high fertility rate, it will likely become the nation's largest minority group by 2005.

It is estimated that by 2050, Hispanic Americans will form 24.3% of the population, up from the current 11.8%, and Asian Americans will make up 9.3%, an increase from the current 3.8%. The African American population will remain relatively constant, rising to about 14.7% from the current 12.2%. The Native American population will stay about the same, showing a small rise from 0.7% to 1.1%. The population as a whole, it is estimated, will rise from 274 million in 2000 to 403 million in 2050.

Problems Faced by Culturally and Linguistically Diverse Groups

In the United States, culturally and linguistically diverse groups may face (a) racism and discrimination, (b) poverty, (c) conflicts associated with acculturation and assimilation, especially when children begin to identify more closely with the majority culture and reject their ethnic culture, (d) problems in dealing with medical, educational, social, and law enforcement organizations, and (e) problems in using standard English. These underlying problems may affect assessment. In addition, children from culturally and linguistically diverse groups who have a disability can be considered to be minorities within minorities.

Prejudice. Confronting prejudice is a common experience of members of culturally and linguistically diverse groups at all socioeconomic levels in our society. Prejudice is an insidious force that can lead to segregation in housing, inequality before the law, discrimination in employment, and other kinds of social and political discrimination. The experience of prejudice may make culturally and linguistically diverse examinees wary of help offered by members of the majority group.

Poverty. When we look at poverty status as determined by 2000 U.S. Census data, we find that Euro American families had the lowest percentage of children living below the poverty line (11.2%), followed by Asian Americans (14.3%), Hispanic Americans (27.9%), Native Americans (31.6%), and African Americans (33.1%). Over 16% of all children in the United States were living in households with incomes below the poverty line in 2000.

Poverty can raise children's and parents' stress levels and place them at increased risk for health problems such as obesity, suicide, and alcoholism. Poverty affects maternal health as well as the child's health and social functioning, both of which may be related to school failure. Poverty also may affect rate of learning, which in turn influences intelligence and academic success. Among the conditions assaulting the central nervous systems of children born into poverty are (a) prenatal problems such as malnutrition, smoking, drug exposure, alcoholism, and infection on the part of the mother, (b) perinatal problems (those connected with or occurring during the birth process) such as breathing problems, abnormal position of the fetus, and problems with the umbilical cord, and (c) postnatal problems such as malnutrition, infection, anemia, and lead poisoning.

Poverty, as such, is neither a necessary nor a sufficient condition to produce intellectual deficits, especially if nutrition and the home environment are adequate. It is only when these and related factors are inadequate that there are likely to be learning deficits. Imagine, for example, how poor nutrition and health care, substandard housing, low family income, family disorganization, anarchic discipline, diminished sense of personal worth, low expectations, frustrated aspirations, exposure to physical violence in the streets, and other environmental pressures might hinder the development of a child's intellectual skills.

Acculturation

Acculturation is the process of cultural change that occurs in individuals when two cultures meet; it leads individuals to adopt elements of another culture, such as values and social behaviors. The process of acculturation may involve all or some of the following phases:

Phase 1: Traditionalism. Individuals maintain and practice mainly the traditions of their culture of origin.

Phase 2: Transitional period. Individuals partake of both the old and the new culture but question not only their own culture's basic traditional values but also those of the new culture.

Phase 3: Marginality. Individuals develop anxiety as they try, unsuccessfully, to meet the demands of both the old and the new culture. In the process, they may become isolated from the culture of origin and from the new culture.

Phase 4: Assimilation. Individuals embrace traditions of the new culture and reject practices and customs of their old culture.

Phase 5: Biculturalism. Individuals integrate practices of both the old and the new culture by selectively adapting new customs and maintaining former ones, without losing a sense of identity.

Factors affecting acculturation. The extent to which individuals maintain or depart from their traditional cultural practices or allow prior cultural practices to coexist with new ones depends on several variables (Fuligni, 1998; Kumabe, Nishida, & Hepworth, 1985).

1. *History of migration experience.* The nature of the migration experience may influence individuals' self-concepts and how they acculturate to the United States. Culturally and linguistically diverse groups may view themselves as forced to come against their will (e.g., African Americans who were forced to come to the United States as slaves); as conquered (e.g., Native Americans or Hispanic Americans), displaced (e.g., Vietnamese), or oppressed (e.g., Cubans who were oppressed in Cuba); or as voluntary immigrants (e.g., individuals who migrated for professional or personal reasons).

2. *Temporal and geographic distance from the country of origin and its indigenous culture.* Individuals' degree of acculturation may be influenced by their length of residence in the United States, the extent to which they maintain ties with the indigenous culture, and how often they return to their native land. Stronger acculturation to the majority culture is more likely if residence has been long, ties with the indigenous culture are minimal, and returns to the native land are limited. Individuals within the same cultural group who immigrated at the same time may differ with regard to how much of the culture of origin they wish to retain and pass on to their children.

3. *Place of residence and socioeconomic status in the homeland.* Individuals' acculturation may be influenced by where they lived in the homeland (e.g., in an urban or a rural area) and their status in the homeland (e.g., their economic, occupational, and educational strata). Individuals with rural backgrounds and low socioeconomic status may have more difficulty adjusting to U.S. culture than those who have urban backgrounds and high socioeconomic status (e.g., rural Cambodians versus urban Vietnamese).

4. *Type of neighborhood in the United States.* Individuals who live in a neighborhood with others of the same ethnicity and who have primary ties with their own group are more likely to keep their indigenous traditions than those who live in an integrated neighborhood and frequently interact with those from other culturally and linguistically diverse groups, as well as the majority group.

5. *Ties with immediate and extended family.* Individuals may have difficulty becoming acculturated when they have close ties to their immediate and extended families.

6. *Role of the family's power and authority.* Individuals will have difficulty deviating from family norms when their

families insist that they maintain indigenous traditions. In many situations, parents may be less acculturated than their children. Furthermore, in many immigrant societies, grandparents play an important role in child rearing, and these grandparents may be less acculturated than their children or grandchildren. Particular care and sensitivity are needed in working with families whose members differ in their degree of acculturation. This may occur, for example, when only one parent is employed in a setting where he or she comes into extended contact with members of the majority culture.

7. *Language and customs.* Individuals may have difficulty acculturating when they primarily speak the language of their homeland, celebrate the holidays of their homeland, and follow the traditions and customs found there. In addition, acculturation may be difficult when individuals have had limited exposure to Western culture in their homeland. Finally, some individuals employ code-switching—using one language in preference to the other in certain settings, while speaking with certain people, or when discussing certain topics.

8. *Individual aspirations.* Individuals may differ with regard to how much of the culture of origin they wish to retain and pass on to their children.

Tables 4-1 and 4-2 list questions that will help you determine children's and parents' degree of acculturation, including language preference.

Stresses associated with acculturation.

For children and families who have immigrated to the United States, there

---

Table 4-1

Interview Questions for Determining an Adolescent's Degree of Acculturation

1. What language do you usually use when you talk with your mother?
2. What language do you usually use when you talk with your father?
3. (If applicable) What language do you usually use when you talk with your sisters and brothers?
4. (If applicable) What language do you usually use when you talk with your grandmother and grandfather?
5. What language do you usually use when you talk with your friends?
6. What language do you usually use when you talk in school?
7. In what language are the television programs you usually watch?
8. In what language are the radio programs you usually listen to?
9. In which language do you usually think?
10. What language do you use for reading?
11. What language do you use for writing?
12. What cultural or ethnic groups live in your neighborhood?
13. What is the cultural or ethnic background of your close friends?
14. What type of foods do you eat at home?
15. What is the ethnic background of your father?
16. What is the ethnic background of your mother?
17. What ethnic or cultural holidays and traditions do you celebrate?
18. What culture do you feel the most proud of?

Table 4-2

Interview Questions for Determining a Parent's Degree of Acculturation

1. What language do you usually use when you talk with your husband (wife)?
2. What language do you usually use when you talk with your child?
3. (If applicable) What language do you usually use when you talk with your brothers and sisters?
4. What language do you usually use when you talk with your friends?
5. What language do you usually use when you shop at the grocery store?
6. In what language are the television programs you usually watch?
7. In what language are the radio programs you usually listen to?
8. In which language do you usually think?
9. What language do you use for reading?
10. What language do you use for writing?
11. What language did you use as a child?
12. What cultural or ethnic groups live in your neighborhood?
13. What is the cultural or ethnic background of your close friends?
14. What type of foods do you eat?
15. What ethnic or cultural holidays and traditions do you celebrate?
16. What culture do you feel the most proud of?

---

are many aspects of the acculturation process that are likely to bring about stress (Zambrana & Silva-Palacios, 1989):

1. Leaving relatives and friends behind when moving from their homeland to the United States
2. Being exposed to customs and mores that differ from those they are accustomed to
3. Having difficulty understanding English
4. Being taunted because of their ethnic origin
5. Being ridiculed because of the way they dress or speak English
6. Feeling lonely because they have few friends from their cultural and linguistic group
7. Speaking in one language and having their friends answer in another
8. Feeling pressured to speak only the native language at home
9. Being teased at home about not knowing how to speak the native language
10. Feeling pressured to speak only English at home
11. Having to act as mediators, negotiators, or translators for members of the family who do not speak English

Acculturation is a process that occurs over time; it is not a single event. Therefore, in working with children who are from minority groups, you need to consider what phase of acculturation they may be in (Fuligni, 1998). After that, you need to evaluate how they are dealing with the separation from their country of origin, their attitudes toward life in the United States, and their hopes and aspirations, conflicts, and adjustment patterns. Acculturation is a complex and dynamic process, and you need to avoid imposing your values on families struggling with acculturation issues.

Ethnic Identity and Identification

Ethnic identity refers to "one's sense of belonging to an ethnic group and the part of one's thinking, perceptions, feelings, and behavior that is due to ethnic group membership" (Rotheram & Phinney, 1986, p. 13). Children from culturally and linguistically diverse groups may have difficulty developing a clear identity if they must choose between the values of the larger society and those of their own group (Spencer & Markstrom-Adams, 1990). For example, do they choose competition or cooperation? Do they value the family over the individual? Do they celebrate the holidays of their group and miss school, or do they attend school and anger their family?

Stereotypes of children's cultural and linguistic group may also impede their identity formation (Spencer & Markstrom-Adams, 1990). If the majority group, for example, views their group negatively (say, as powerless and primitive), how are they to perceive themselves? In addition to hindering identification with the majority group, stereotypes may create anxieties and doubts about their own group. Children may internalize negative portrayals by the majority culture, which, in turn, may lead to low self-esteem and behavioral problems.

Identity formation is impeded when the family fails to discuss ethnic or racial issues with children (Spencer & Markstrom-Adams, 1990). This is likely to happen when the parents are uncomfortable with issues related to race or ethnicity.

Examinees from the same ethnic background may have different degrees of identification with their ethnic group, reflected, in part, by how they wish to be described. For example, some prefer to be identified as African American rather than Black American, others prefer Latino or Chicano over Hispanic, and still others prefer no specific ethnic identification other than American.

Ethnic identification becomes particularly complex when individuals have a biracial or multicultural heritage (Herring, 1992). One issue is the transmission of a cultural heritage and an ethnic identity from the parents to their children. Parents may emphasize their children's membership in one or another group, or they may simply consider them members of the human race and not focus on race or color. A second issue is how the larger community treats biracial or multicultural children and their families—with acceptance or discrimination, for example. A third issue is how biracial or multicultural children integrate their racial or cultural identifications.

EVALUATING BIAS

Although there is considerable research on the effects of culture, ethnicity, and language on assessment of intelligence

and other cognitive aptitudes (see Sattler, 2001), less research is available on the effect of these variables in personality and clinical assessments. Let's examine the limited research that is available.

Bias in Diagnostic Criteria

Diagnostic criteria may be susceptible to bias because the criteria may reflect middle-class Euro American values and standards of conduct that are not relevant to other cultural groups. For example, the criteria defining attention-deficit/hyperactivity disorder may reflect a bias toward achieving excellence in academic pursuits that may not be shared by all groups. Similarly, in some groups, the criteria defining conduct disorder may represent behaviors valued for their survival purposes.

A related source of potential bias is thresholds for identifying deviance or pathology (Bird, Yager, Staghezza, Gould, Canino, & Rubio-Stipec, 1990). Cut-off scores established for one cultural group may not apply to other cultural groups. There is some evidence, for example, that hyperactivity assessed through behavioral checklists may be overdiagnosed in Chinese youths because some Chinese parents are especially intolerant of elevated activity levels.

A useful way to examine the fairness of diagnostic criteria and clinical cut-off scores is to study differences among cultural and ethnic groups in the incidence of disorders. The presence of differences does not necessarily indicate the presence of bias, but it can alert us to that possibility (Drasgow, 1987; Knight & Hill, 1998).

Some differences in the incidence of certain diagnoses have been reported among cultural and ethnic groups. For example, children who are from minority groups have higher rates of some psychological disorders—such as substance abuse, delinquency, and teenage suicide—than do nonminority children (McLoyd, 1998). African American youths are more likely to be diagnosed with externalizing problems and psychotic disorders than Euro American youths but less likely to receive diagnoses of affective disorders (Canino & Spurlock, 2000; Epstein, March, Conners, & Jackson, 1998; Gibbs, 1988; Reynolds, Plake, & Harding, 1983). In comparison with Euro American youths, Hispanic American youths tend to exhibit higher levels of affective disorders, Native American youths have higher levels of substance abuse disorders, and Asian American youths have higher incidences of affective disorders (Cohen & Kassen, 1999; Jones, Kephart, Langley, Parker, Shenoy, & Weeks, 2001). On the other hand, Achenbach and Edelbrock (1983) reported small and nonsignificant differences between Euro American and African American children in pathological behaviors measured by the Child Behavior Checklist when socioeconomic status was controlled. Nonsignificant differences also were reported between Euro American and African American children in behavior problems evaluated with the School Social Behavior Scales (Merrell, 1993) and in diagnoses of autism and attention-deficit/hyperactivity disorders (Cuccaro, Wright, Rownd, Abramson, Waller, & Fender, 1996).

Because of the small number of research studies, methodological problems in some of the research, and inconsistent results, we cannot draw firm conclusions about differences among ethnic and cultural groups in the incidence of personality and behavioral disorders (Cohen & Kassen, 1999; Dana, 1993; Jones et al., 2001; Reynolds, Lowe, & Saenz, 1999). At present, it appears that few differences emerge in relationship to race or ethnicity once the effects of socioeconomic status, sex, and age are controlled (Mash & Wolfe, 2002). We need additional research on whether ethnic or cultural biases exist in the diagnostic criteria for childhood disorders or in the criteria for establishing thresholds of deviance.

Bias in Normative Data

Standardization samples ideally should represent the population. This means that the proportions of people of different races, ethnicities, genders, and socioeconomic groups in the standardization sample should reflect the proportions in the U.S. Census data at the time of standardization. However, efforts to ensure that all groups for whom a measure is intended are fairly represented in the standardization sample do not necessarily ensure that a measure is free of bias, nor does the absence of the relevant groups in a standardization sample necessarily indicate that the measure is invalid. According to Knight and Hill (1998),

> The standardization fallacy occurs when one takes the fact that a measure was standardized (or developed) in a given population as prima facie evidence that the measure is culturally biased when used in another population. . . . Furthermore, the renorming or rescaling of a measure is trivial and accomplishes nothing of fundamental significance if the selection of items is indeed biased. (p. 186, with changes in notation)

A related problem is that, even where ethnic minorities are proportionally represented in the sample, the absolute numbers may be too low to be meaningful. For example, the MMPI–A normative sample contains 7.4% Asian American youths, a somewhat higher percentage than their proportion in the population. However, that is a sample of only 46 youths to represent a large and diverse population of individuals.

Arguments have also been advanced for creating separate norms for ethnic, cultural, and linguistic minorities. *Pluralistic norms* are norms derived for individual groups, such as Euro Americans, African Americans, Hispanic Americans, Asian Americans, and Native Americans. Those who favor pluralistic norms believe that it is fairer to evaluate a child relative to his or her own ethnic group than relative to the majority group. Those who do not favor pluralistic norms believe that as long as children must function in the culture at large, the norms should represent the culture at large. Perhaps pluralistic norms

may serve a limited purpose in some settings, but the reliability and validity of these norms must be established.

Evaluating Bias Through Validity Procedures

Several procedures are available for evaluating the presence of cultural bias in psychological measures (Knight & Hill, 1998; Sattler, 2001). One procedure involves examining item content for evidence of cultural bias. For example, items on a behavioral checklist referring to "frequent crying" or "overt displays of emotion" may mean something different in a culture that discourages public displays of emotion than in a culture that tolerates or encourages emotional displays. The considerable research conducted on intelligence tests has produced little evidence of the presence of content bias (Sattler, 2001). Although there is some evidence that youths from different ethnic groups respond differently to some items of the Revised Children's Manifest Anxiety Scale, the differences were minor and appeared to have no significant effect on the total scores from the measure (Reynolds et al., 1983). There appear to have been few efforts to systematically explore content bias in behavioral rating scales; it is nevertheless important to be sensitive to the possibility that items in a measure may have a different meaning for a young person from a minority cultural or language community.

A second procedure involves examining construct validity. A test would be considered biased if it could be shown to measure different constructs for different ethnic groups. Unfortunately, few studies have examined the construct validity of personality tests and of behavioral rating scales and checklists, and those available have yielded mixed results. Different factor structures for African American and Euro American children have been reported for the Children's Depression Inventory (Politano, Nelson, Evans, Sorenson, & Zeman, 1986). However, similar factor structures have been found for (a) African American and Euro American youths on the Revised Children's Manifest Anxiety Scale (Reynolds & Paget, 1981) and the Conners' Teacher Rating Scale (Epstein et al., 1998) and (b) Native American and Euro American children on measures of hyperactivity (Beiser, Dion, & Gotowiec, 2000). Evidence has also been presented supporting the use of the Comprehensive System of the Rorschach with Euro American, African American, and Hispanic American children (Ritzler, 2001). This body of research again is too sparse to allow us to reach definitive conclusions about the impact of cultural and linguistic variables on construct validity.

Establishing differences in the criterion-related validity of a measure for cultural or linguistic groups is another means of determining the presence of bias. For example, if it could be shown that a measure of pathology significantly predicted success in treatment for one group but not for another, then it could be asserted that a bias existed in the measure. There are two ways of assessing whether this form of bias is present.

One is the single-group approach: A measure is said to be biased when a validity coefficient is significantly different from zero for one ethnic group but not for another. The other is the differential validity approach: A measure is considered to be biased if there is a significant difference between two validity coefficients. Unfortunately, this issue has been virtually unexplored in connection with personality tests, behavioral rating scales, or checklists.

Translations

Translating a psychological measure from one language to another is difficult because the two languages may not have equivalent concepts, dialectical or regional variations may be difficult to accommodate, and the meanings of words may change in translation (Canino & Bravo, 1999). Nevertheless, several personality and behavior measures have been translated from English into Spanish for use with Hispanic American children, including the ADHD Symptoms Rating Scale, Child Behavior Checklist, Youth Self-Report, Conners' Rating Scales, Millon Adolescent Personality Inventory, and Millon Adolescent Clinical Inventory. However, the manuals for these measures do not include normative or psychometric information for the translated versions; therefore, the translations should be used with caution.

ETHICAL AND CLINICAL GUIDELINES

Guidelines regarding the conduct of assessments with culturally and linguistically diverse children are available from the following sources:

- *Ethical Principles of Psychologists and Code of Conduct* (American Psychological Association, 2002)
- *Report of the Task Force on Test User Qualifications* (DeMers et al., 2000)
- *Guidelines for Providers of Psychological Services to Ethnic, Linguistic, and Culturally Diverse Populations* (American Psychological Association, 1990)
- *Standards for Educational and Psychological Testing* (American Educational Research Association et al., 1999)

The *Ethical Principles of Psychologists and Code of Conduct* (American Psychological Association, 2002) provides general principles to guide the activities of psychologists and includes the following statement regarding services to members of culturally diverse groups:

> Psychologists are aware of and respect cultural, individual, and role differences, including those based on age, gender, gender identity, race, ethnicity, culture, national origin, religion, sexual orientation, disability, language, and socioeconomic status, and consider these factors when working with members of such groups. Psychologists try to eliminate the effect on their work of biases based on those factors, and they do not knowingly participate in or condone activities of others based on such prejudices. (p. 1063)

The *Standards for Educational and Psychological Testing* (American Educational Research Association et al., 1999) provides guidelines for the assessment of culturally and linguistically diverse groups. The guidelines cover the construction, evaluation, administration, and interpretation of psychological measures.

Guidelines regarding culturally sensitive clinical assessments are also provided in *DSM-IV–TR* (American Psychiatric Association, 2000):

> Clinicians are called on to evaluate individuals from numerous different ethnic groups and cultural backgrounds (including many who are recent immigrants). Diagnostic assessment can be especially challenging when a clinician from one ethnic or cultural group uses the *DSM-IV* Classification to evaluate an individual from a different ethnic or cultural group.... *DSM-IV* includes three types of information specifically related to cultural considerations: 1) a discussion in the text of cultural variations in the clinical presentations of those disorders that have been included in the *DSM-IV* Classification; 2) a description of culture-bound syndromes that have not been included in the classification; and 3) an outline for cultural formulation designed to assist the clinician in systematically evaluating and reporting the impact of the individual's cultural context. (p. xxxiv)

As an examiner, you are responsible for reporting your degree of confidence in the findings. This means that you may say that the findings are probably reliable and valid or that they may be of limited value because the child has not been evaluated fairly either in English or in his or her native language.

PRACTICAL CONSIDERATIONS IN THE CONDUCT OF ASSESSMENTS

When you evaluate children and parents who are members of minority groups, be prepared to consider issues related to ethnic and racial identity, acculturation, language, changing family patterns, sex roles, religious and traditional beliefs, customs for dealing with crisis and change, racism, poverty, social class, health care practices, and the interactions among these factors. Children and parents who maintain strong ties to their culture, particularly recent refugees or immigrants, may be influenced by indigenous cultural beliefs and practices that affect the symptoms they develop, how they understand the symptoms, their coping mechanisms, their help-seeking behavior, their use of services, and their satisfaction with services and clinical outcomes (Canino & Spurlock, 2000; Chung & Lin, 1994). Knowledge that you gain about these and related issues will help you conduct the assessment, formulate a diagnosis, and develop an intervention plan.

You will likely have the difficult task of evaluating whether behaviors that would suggest personality or temperament problems in a member of the majority group reflect similar problems in members of minority groups. For example, when culturally and linguistically diverse examinees remain silent, speak softly, or avoid extended eye contact, are they revealing shyness, weakness, or reluctance to speak, or are they exhibiting politeness and respect? Does expressing emotions in an indirect, understated way suggest denial, lack of affect, lack of awareness of one's feelings, deceptiveness, or resistance, or do such expressions suggest a wish to sustain interpersonal harmony (Morris, 2000; Uba, 1994)? The failure to understand cultural practices can lead to incorrect diagnoses and ineffective interventions.

Gender roles also may differ across cultures, and certain cultures have particularly marked, definitive role expectations for men and women. Role expectations may create complications, for example, in an assessment situation in which a father and an adolescent boy are working with a female professional.

Culture and Communication Styles

Let's now consider how verbal and nonverbal communication styles may lead to difficulties in cross-cultural assessments.

Verbal communication difficulties. You may encounter communication barriers when you work with examinees who are from a minority group (and from the majority group as well), because they may be mystified by medical or psychological terminology. They may view discussing personal or family problems with an outsider as a reflection of their personal inadequacy and as a stigma on the entire family. This is especially true of some Asian American groups. Consequently, be sensitive to any subtle cues that examinees or their parents give you regarding their willingness to talk about personal issues. If you fail to recognize their preferences and mistakenly urge them to be open and direct, they may resent your suggestion and become silent.

Communication difficulties arise when examinees who are from a minority group view examiners as authority figures. In the presence of authority figures, they may become passive and inhibited in their communication and reluctant to ask questions or express disagreement (Kumabe et al., 1985).

Examinees who are from a minority group may respond at their own pace to your interview or test questions (Tharp, 1989). Some Native American children, for example, prefer to wait before responding to questions. If they feel hurried, they may resent your intrusion. Do not perceive their hesitation as refusal to talk to you or as resistance. Rather, respect their need for silence between your question and their answer. In contrast, some Native Hawaiians may interrupt your questions or comments because they want to show their involvement; in such cases, don't interpret their interruptions as a sign of rudeness.

Another source of problems is examiners' misinterpretation of examinees' communication. The following exaggerated hypothetical example illustrates the danger of making interpretations and diagnoses when you are not familiar with the examinee's jargon. (IE stands for examinee, and IR for examiner.)

IE: I was at home and this cat I know came in and asked to borrow some lettuce from me so he could buy some tickets

to the show. (IR notes, "Delusions that cats can talk and that lettuce can be used as money.")

IE: Then, I was shooting the breeze with my chick and the pigs came along and took us to jail. (IR notes, "Fantasies of using a baby chicken to shoot breezes and delusional thinking that pigs can take people to jail.")

IE: I didn't have on my best rags, and they wouldn't let me use a wire to call. (IR notes, "Claims to wear rags of various quality and believes wires can be used to make phone calls. Definite signs of delusions.")

IE: Before the pigs came, I smoked some horse while my chick got high on snow. (IR notes, "Bizarre ideation in thinking that he could smoke a horse and misperceptions that people can use snow to change their mood. Continues to make references to pigs and chicks in his fantasies. Signs of distorted thinking and confusion.")

Diagnosis: Paranoid schizophrenia with delusional material, distorted thinking, and confusion. Psychological treatment needed. Prognosis is guarded.

Here is what the examinee was saying, translated into standard English:

I was at home and a guy I know asked to borrow some money to buy tickets to the show. Then, I was talking to my girlfriend and the police came along and took us to jail. I didn't have on my best clothes, and they wouldn't let me use a phone to make a call. Before the police came, I smoked some heroin while my girlfriend got high on cocaine.

Language may pose a problem in interviewing a family from a minority group, particularly when the family members have different levels of proficiency in their native language and in English. If the parents prefer to speak Spanish and the child prefers to speak English, for example, you may have difficulty knowing which language to use and whether to use an interpreter. When the child's command of English is better than that of the parents, the child may take advantage of the parents' limited language skills to control the flow of information to the parents. In such situations, the child becomes powerful, thus reversing the usual parent-child relationship. Later in the chapter, we discuss working with an interpreter.

Language considerations for African Americans. African American children and their parents may speak a variant of English that linguists call *Black English, nonstandard Black English, Black dialect,* or *Ebonics.* (The term *Ebonics* is a combination of *ebony* and *phonics.*) Black English tends to be used by urban African Americans and by African Americans who remain isolated racially and economically in poor African American communities (Lynch & Hanson, 1992). It is primarily used in informal settings, such as at home and among friends, rather than in business or professional settings.

Black English shares many features with standard English, but it has several distinguishing features in the areas of pronunciation and grammar (see Table 4-3). Features include use of "be" to denote an ongoing action ("he be going to school"), dropping of linking verbs ("you smart"), shortened plurals ("thirty cent"), dropping of some final consonants ("las" instead of "last" or "mas" instead of "mask"), and substitution

Table 4-3
Some Differences Between Black English and Standard English

Black English		Standard English	
Usage	Example	Usage	Example
1. Uses *got*	The girls got a cat.	1. Uses *have*	The girls have a cat.
2. Omits *is* and *are*	The cat in the wagon.	2. Uses *is* and *are*	The cat is in the wagon.
3. Omits the third-person singular ending -*s* from some verbs	The man ask the boy what to wear.	3. Uses the -*s* ending on verbs	The man asks the boy what to wear.
4. Omits the -*ed* ending from verbs	The dog get chase by the cat.	4. Uses the -*ed* ending on verbs	The dog was chased by the cat.
5. Uses *do*	The girl do pull the wagon to the boat.	5. Uses *does*	The girl does pull the wagon to the boat.
6. Uses *be* in place of *am, is,* and *are*	The big ball be rolling down the hill.	6. Uses *am, is,* and *are*	The big ball is rolling down the hill.
7. Uses *he be, we be,* and *they be*	They be going home.	7. Uses *he is, we are,* and *they are*	They are going home.
8. Pronounces *th* at beginning of a word as *d*	Dese boys kick de ball.	8. Pronounces *th* at the beginning of a word as *th*	These boys kick the ball.
9. Pronounces *th* at end of word as *f*	In the baf, he washed his mouf and played wif a toy.	9. Pronounces *th* at the end of a word as *th*	In the bath, he washed his mouth and played with a toy.
10. Drops the final *r* and *g* from words	My fatha and motha were talkin and laughin.	10. Pronounces the final *r* and *g* in words	My father and mother were talking and laughing.

for some pronouns ("that's the person got all the money"). Other markers include substitution of /ks/ for /sk/ in the final position, as in "ax" for "ask," and substitution of the base form for the past, present, or future verb form, as in "he goes" for "he went," "he is going," or "he will go." Black English is a fully formed linguistic system with its own rules of grammar and pronunciation; it has a rich repertoire of forms and usages.

Black English has contributed to the English language in many ways (Emmons, 1996):

> It has enriched the fabric of American English. Black English is in jazz. Among the hundreds of the jazz world's words that have filtered into the American lexicon are "hip," "cool," "gig," "jiving around," "get high" and "gimme five." Black English is in blues and soul, giving America expressive, often sensual, words and phrases like "hot," "baby," "mojo," "fine," "mess with," "thang" (as doin' my), "take it easy," "slick," "rip-off," "cool out," and "bad." Black English is in Negro spirituals ("Dat Ole Man River," "Ah Got Shoes"). It is in gospel ("Ain't No Devil in Hell Gonna Walk on the Jesus in Me") and through these mediums of expression has found home in the vernacular of the black church. (p. B9)

Black English has its roots in the oral traditions of the African ancestors of African Americans. "Black English evolved from West African languages and slave traders who used a form of pidgin English to communicate with African slaves who were allowed neither to speak their tribal languages nor to learn English in a classroom" ("Mainstream English . . . ," 1996, p. M4, with changes in notation). In

many African groups, history and traditions were transmitted orally, and the elder who kept this information was a revered member of the community. African American culture maintains the tradition of orality. To *rap, sound,* or *run it down* is a prized oral skill. Among inner-city African American youths, skill in using language in ritual insults, verbal routines, singing, jokes, and storytelling is a source of prestige. Oral skills are esteemed not just at the street level, but at every level of African American culture.

In school, teachers may tell African American children that their dialect is "wrong" and that standard English dialect is "right." By extension, African American children who typically use Black English may feel that they are inadequate and inferior to other children who speak standard English. These feelings may extend to the psychological evaluation and may lead to reticence and even withdrawal. Regardless of your ethnicity, there may not be much you can do to alleviate such feelings immediately, but children may begin to talk to you if you are supportive and encouraging. African American children who speak both Black English and standard English have a highly developed skill. *Do not view Black English as inferior to standard English.*

Schools have often failed to appreciate that African American children have spoken and written language skills that are extremely useful, such as "keen listening and observational skills, quick recognition of nuanced roles, rapid-fire dialogue, hard-driving argumentation, succinct recapitulation of an event, striking metaphors, and comparative analyses based on unexpected analogies" (Heath, 1989, p. 370). Schools usually make little effort to help African American children use these skills in the classroom.

Some African Americans continue to use Black English because of habit, ease of usage, peer pressure, and group identification and because it provides a sense of protection, belonging, and solidarity. The social distance between African Americans and Euro Americans contributes to the maintenance of African English. Encouraging African American children to speak in their familiar dialect may enable them to speak more freely about themselves and, thus, may give you a better sample of their language skills. Recognize, however, that some African American children and adults are comfortable using either Black English or standard English, depending on the situation. And use of standard English by African Americans may be important for their social and economic mobility. You must attend carefully to the communication of examinees who speak Black English if you are not familiar with the language.

Language considerations for Hispanic Americans.

Linguistically, Hispanic American children and their families are a heterogeneous group, with wide variations in their degree of mastery of English and Spanish. Some Hispanic American children are equally fluent in both languages, whereas others have difficulty in both languages. The complexity of using both languages in the home makes it difficult for some Hispanic American children to become proficient in either language. When Hispanic American children speak Spanish as their primary language, the Euro American examiner may have difficulty talking with them without an interpreter.

Speech patterns of bilingual Hispanic American children can be an intricate mixture of English and Spanish, with words borrowed from English, anglicized words, nonstandard pronunciation, and nonstandard word order.

1. *Borrowing from English.* If their Spanish vocabulary is limited, children may borrow from their English vocabulary to complete expressions begun in Spanish. For example, they may say "Yo estaba leyendo cuando it started to rain" (I was reading when it started to rain).

2. *Anglicizing words.* They may "anglicize certain words or . . . borrow English words to develop specific linguistic patterns (e.g., '*Está reinando*' for 'It's raining' [instead of '*Está lloviendo*'], calling a grocery store a '*groceria*' [instead of '*una tienda de abarrotes*'], or using '*carpeta*' for 'rug' [instead of '*alfombra*'])" (Marin & Marin, 1991, p. 86). English words given Spanish pronunciations and endings are called *pochismos.* Examples of pochismos include the use of the word *huachar* (from the English verb "to watch") instead of the correct Spanish verb *mirar,* and the use of the word *chuzar* (from the English verb "to choose") instead of the correct Spanish word *escoger.*

3. *Nonstandard pronunciation.* They may have difficulties in pronunciation and enunciation in both Spanish and English.

4. *Nonstandard word order.* They may maintain Spanish word order while speaking English.

Language considerations for Asian Americans.

When Euro American clinicians evaluate Asian Americans, misunderstandings may arise because of the ways Asian Americans use language or pronounce English words. For example, some Asian Americans tend to avoid using the word *no* because they consider it rude to do so. "The word 'yes' can mean 'no' or 'perhaps.' A direct 'no' is avoided because it may cause the same individual to lose face. Hesitance, ambiguity, subtlety, and implicity are dominant in Chinese speech" (Giger & Davidhizar, 1991, p. 361).

Asian languages also are context bound. According to Lynch and Hanson (1992),

> Most of the meaningful information is either in the physical context or internalized in the person who receives the information, while relatively little is contained in the verbally transmitted part of the message. . . . The speaker or sender's true intent is thus often camouflaged in the context of the situation. . . . Nonverbal communication thus conveys significantly more information in high-context Asian cultures, wherein silence is particularly valued. (pp. 232, 233)

Language considerations for Native Americans.

There is no universal, traditional Native American language (Everett, Proctor, & Cartmell, 1983). Each tribe is likely to have its own language, and within a tribe different dialects may exist. Like other culturally and linguistically diverse groups, Native Americans differ in their command of the English language: "As with any bilingual group, these abilities range from a very articulate command of English to . . . a limited receptive vocabulary and little or no expressive vocabulary" (Everett et al., 1983, p. 592).

If you speak only English, you may experience difficulties in communicating with Native American children and parents who speak a native language primarily or who have limited knowledge of English. In addition, you will need to consider that Native Americans are more likely than Euro Americans to be hesitant to speak, to speak softly, to give short responses that lack important details, to fear making a mistake, to be nonassertive, and to be reluctant to offer self-disclosures.

Nonverbal communication difficulties.

Nonverbal communications are another potential source of communication difficulties in cross-cultural assessments. Areas of difficulty may include perception and use of personal and interpersonal space (proxemics); body movements (such as facial expressions, posture, and gestures), characteristics of movement, and eye contact (kinesics); and vocal cues used in talking (paralanguage). Misunderstandings of nonverbal communication contribute to the maintenance of stereotypes and judgmental attitudes. Examples of difficulties in nonverbal communication follow.

Proxemics.

Hispanic Americans and African Americans tend to stand closer to the person they are talking with than do Euro Americans. When assessing members of these minority groups, Euro American examiners may back away from the examinee. Such behavior may be misinterpreted as aloof, cold, or haughty; as expressing a desire not to communicate; or as a sign of superiority. Euro American examiners, in turn, may mistakenly view the ethnic examinee's behavior as inappropriately intimate or as a sign of pushiness or aggressiveness (Sue, 1990).

Some minority groups will be sensitive to spatial arrangements during an examination. "Chinese people feel more comfortable in a side-by-side or right-angle arrangement and may feel uncomfortable when placed in a face-to-face situation. Euro Americans prefer to sit face-to-face or at right angles to each other" (Giger & Davidhizar, 1991, p. 363, with changes in notation).

Kinesics.   Cultures may interpret the same gestures in different ways. For example, some cultures interpret the thumbs-up gesture as obscene, and to people from Southeast Asia, the American gesture of waving "bye-bye" means "come here." Cultural upbringing also shapes how people move their bodies. For example, people from Northern Europe tend to hold their torsos rigidly, whereas those from the Caribbean tend to move their bodies more fluidly (Dresser, 1996).

Euro Americans usually view smiling as an indication of positive affect. However, to Asian Americans, smiling may suggest weakness. They tend to consider restraint of feeling to be a sign of maturity and wisdom. Thus, Euro American examiners may assume that Asian American examinees are out of touch with their feelings when, in reality, they are following cultural patterns. Many Native Americans and Japanese avoid eye contact to signal respect or deference. In such cases, it is wrong to assume that avoidance of eye contact indicates "inattentiveness, rudeness, aggressiveness, shyness, or low intelligence" (Sue, 1990, p. 426).

African Americans tend to make greater eye contact when speaking than when listening. The reverse is true of Euro Americans, who tend to make more eye contact when listening than when speaking. For African Americans, attentiveness is signaled by mere physical proximity. When African American listeners do not look at the speaker, do not interpret their behavior as sullen, resistant, or uncooperative. And when Euro American listeners look at the speaker, it is wrong to interpret their behavior as undue scrutiny of the speaker (Sue, 1990).

Japanese people tend to present a blank, nearly motionless facial expression that reveals little of their inner feelings to the Western observer. Westerners, in contrast, tend to keep their forehead and eyebrows constantly in motion as they speak. Thus, "simply because of the greater stillness of the Japanese face there tends to be a large amount of Japanese-Western miscommunication: The Japanese are regarded as noncomprehending or even antagonistic" (Morsbach, 1988, p. 206).

Paralanguage.   Silence, for Asian Americans, is traditionally a sign of respect for elders. When an Asian American speaker becomes silent, it may not be a cue for the listener to begin talking. "Rather, it may indicate a desire to continue speaking after making a particular point. At other times, silence may be a sign of politeness and respect, rather than a lack of desire to continue speaking" (Sue, 1990, p. 426). Native Americans may remain silent in some situations to communicate patience and respect. Thus, when assessing members of minority groups, do not interpret reticence to speak out as a sign of ignorance or lack of motivation. Sometimes, if you break the silence, you may discourage further elaboration.

Asian Americans, Native Americans, and some Hispanic Americans value indirectness in communication. Euphemisms and ambiguity are used so as not to embarrass or hurt the feelings of the other person. Native Americans perceive the asking of direct questions (as occurs when you are taking a social history) as rude or incompetent or an invasion of individual privacy. They prefer that the examiner share personal information about himself or herself (self-disclosure) or deduce the problem by instinct. In contrast, Euro Americans accept direct interrogation and an impersonal style on the part of the examiner (Everett et al., 1983).

Dynamics of Cross-Ethnic and Cross-Cultural Assessment

In cross-ethnic and cross-cultural assessments, your effectiveness will suffer if you display a patronizing attitude, fail to recognize the value of examinees' traditional customs and mores, or are obsessed with the examinees' culture (LaFromboise, Trimble, & Mohatt, 1990). You will be considered patronizing if you expect the worst from examinees or lower your expectations of them. Examinees who are from a cultural or linguistic group different from the examiner's may be especially attentive to any indications of prejudice, superiority, disapproval, or rejection. Trust will be difficult to establish if examinees fear that you are trying to influence their value structure, thereby separating them from their own group and traditions. These individuals want help with their problems, not help in changing cultures. Alienation is the likely result when you focus too much on their customs, mores, and traditions.

Majority-group examiner and minority-group examinee.   Difficulties in the relationship between an examiner from the majority group and an examinee from a minority group stem from several sources. Racial antagonism may prevent examinees and examiners from relating to each other as individuals. Examinees who are from a minority group may view examiners who are from the majority group with suspicion and distrust, as part of the hostile majority world. And, because majority-group examiners have been encouraged through education and training to view prejudice as unacceptable, they may deny or suppress negative reactions toward examinees who are from minority groups. If examiners who are from the majority group begin to feel confused or guilty about their own racial and class identity and allow these feelings to intrude on the relationship or on their decisions, difficulties are likely to arise. For example, examiners who are from the majority group may miss subtle cues given by examinees who are from a minority group, may be too accepting of behaviors, may give credit to borderline or vague responses, or may fail to probe sensitive topics.

Misinterpretations of intercultural communication will occur when examinees who are from a minority group view majority-group examiners as immature, rude, and lacking in finesse because they want to get to the point quickly. Similarly, examiners who are from the majority group should not view minority-group examinees as evasive and afraid to confront their problems because they communicate indirectly.

Examiners who are from the majority group must recognize that minority-group examinees will be judging their behavior (as will many examinees from the majority group). If a majority-group examiner speaks bluntly and directly, some examinees who are from a minority group (such as Asian Americans) may view this behavior as socially disruptive, embarrassing, or even hurtful (Uba, 1994). Examinees who are from a minority group will also be frustrated when the social cues they give are not picked up by majority-group examiners.

Minority-group examiner and majority-group examinee. Examiners who are from a minority group may experience difficulties in their relationships with examinees who are from the majority group because of the sociocultural aspects of minority-majority interpersonal relations. Conflicts may arise if majority-group examinees avoid the race issue, deprecate the examiner, have special admiration for the examiner, or view the examiner as all-forgiving or uncritical. Examiners who are from a minority group, on the other hand, may be unsympathetic or punitive if they are hostile toward the majority group, or they may overcompensate by being too permissive (denying their hostility toward majority-group examinees, overidentifying with the majority group, or being overly liberal in scoring the responses of majority-group examinees). Any of these dynamics can affect the examination process.

Minority-group examiner and examinee from the same minority group. Examiners who are from the same minority group as examinees may be in the best position to obtain reliable and valid information. However, examiners from the middle class may have some difficulties with same-minority examinees who are from a lower socioeconomic class. Difficulties arise in such cases when examiners cannot accept examinees because of their class, become defensive, overidentify with examinees, or attach lower status and priority to working with examinees from their own minority group than to working with examinees from the majority group. Similarly, difficulties arise when examinees perceive exam-

iners from their own minority group as collaborators with the majority community, objects of jealousy because of their success in the majority community, less competent than examiners who are from the majority group, or too removed from their problems.

If minority-group examiners believe that examinees from their own minority group have problems that stem primarily from sociopolitical or economic factors, they may dismiss the examinees' psychological problems and instead deliver lectures about social-class oppression (Hunt, 1987). This is unprofessional and unacceptable. Examiners who are from a minority group must walk a fine line between overidentification and objectivity when evaluating examinees who are from the same minority group.

Minority-group examiner and examinee from a different minority group. Minority-group examiners may experience difficulties in their relationships with examinees who are from a different minority group. There may be problems associated with racial antagonism, depending on how the groups have been getting along in society at large. Examinees may be envious of these examiners, believing, for example, that they have been given special treatment because of their group membership. The examiners might have similar feelings about the examinees. However, because the examiners and examinees are likely to have had similar experiences with racism and discrimination, examiners who are from a minority group may have increased empathy for examinees from any minority group.

Possible distortions in cross-ethnic and cross-cultural assessment. Preoccupation with and heightened sensitivity to ethnic differences may lead to distortions, guardedness, and evasiveness on the part of examinees and to guardedness, failure to probe, defensiveness, and feelings of intimidation on the part of examiners. Because responses given by both examinees and examiners require subtle forms of cognitive activity—such as summarizing one's opinion to oneself, estimating the listener's probable reaction, and then deciding whether to convey the opinion accurately to the listener—there is always the potential for both examinees and examiners to distort opinions, attitudes, and even facts.

Several questions are a matter of special concern in cross-ethnic, cross-cultural, and cross-class assessments: Do some examinees replace genuine feelings with a facade of submissiveness, pleasure, impassivity, or humility? Can examiners be genuine and avoid patronizing? Is any form of social distance between examiners and examinees likely to create difficulties with rapport and communication?

Comment on dynamics of cross-ethnic and cross-cultural assessment. You, as an examiner, are not immune to being racist and harboring stereotypes. *It is your responsibility to ensure that any stereotypical views you have do not adversely affect the assessment.* You should constantly monitor yourself for stereotypical views, lest they interfere with your ability to conduct a nonbiased assessment.

Although we can generalize about ethnic relations and about the examiner-examinee relationship, each assessment involves two unique individuals. It is their specific attitudes, values, experiences, and behavior that will determine whether racism and bias enter the assessment. Even examiners and examinees from the same ethnic or cultural group may be mismatched if they have different values. And, conversely, examiners and examinees from different groups can work cooperatively when they have similar values and speak the same language. Usually, examiners will be effective when they are tolerant and accepting of examinees, despite value differences. Your goal is to establish a professional relationship—characterized by trust and acceptance—with the examinee, whatever his or her ethnic or cultural group. If you cannot establish such a relationship, refer the examinee to another psychologist.

Assessment of Bilingual Examinees

Bilingualism refers to the ability to use two languages. Although generally a second language is learned after the primary one, sometimes two languages are learned simultaneously. Research indicates that children who are fluently bilingual have advantages over their monolingual peers on both verbal and nonverbal tasks (Bialystok, 1992; Diaz & Klinger, 1991). They have better developed selective attention skills and language processing skills, such as more sensitivity to language structure and syntax and greater flexibility in language usage.

The advantages of bilingualism, however, depend in part on whether the child is adding the second language to a well-developed first language and whether both languages continue to be developed. Some Hispanic American children, for example, learn English as a second language and then use it in their schoolwork; they continue, however, to use Spanish at home and in the community, in speaking but seldom in reading. Because of this form of bilingualism, some Hispanic American children fail to develop a sufficient mastery of either language, and learning is more difficult under such conditions.

You can use several informal methods for determining the language preference of a child who speaks more than one language. First, ask the child in which language he or she prefers to be tested. Second, observe which language the child uses in the classroom and at home. Third, ask the teacher and parent to describe the child's language preference, using questions such as those shown in Table 4-4. Finally, ask the teacher to complete the rating scale shown in Table 4-5.

Several formal measures are available to assess bilingual verbal ability; unfortunately, none of those mentioned below has been standardized on a nationally representative sample of individuals with proficiency in each language of the test. One is the Bilingual Verbal Ability Tests (BVAT; Muñoz-Sandoval, Cummings, Alvarado, & Ruef, 1998). This indi-

---

Table 4-4

Interview Questions for Teacher and Parent to Determine Child's Language Preference

Questions for Teacher

1. What language does _____ use in the classroom?
2. In what language can _____ read?
3. In what language does _____ speak with his (her) classmates?
4. In what language does _____ write?
5. Overall, how competent is _____ in English?
6. Overall, how competent is _____ in _____ (language)?

Questions for Parent

1. In what language do you speak with _____?
2. In what language does your husband (wife) speak with _____?
3. In what language do you speak with your husband (wife)?
4. In what language does _____ speak with you?
5. In what language does _____ speak with his (her) father (mother)?
6. (If applicable) In what language does _____ speak with his (her) sisters and brothers?
7. What language does _____ prefer to speak at school?
8. In what language are the television programs _____ watches?
9. In what language do you read stories to _____?
10. In what language does _____ prefer to be tested?

---

vidually administered test is composed of three subtests drawn from the Woodcock-Johnson–Revised Tests of Cognitive Ability—namely, Picture Vocabulary, Oral Vocabulary, and Verbal Analogies. The English version of the test was translated into 15 languages: Arabic, Chinese (simplified and traditional), French, German, Haitian-Creole, Hindi, Italian, Japanese, Korean, Polish, Portuguese, Russian, Spanish, Turkish, and Vietnamese. Each item is first administered in English. Failed items are then readministered in the examinee's other language. The overall score consists of the number of items answered correctly in either language. Raw scores are converted to standard scores, age- and grade-equivalent scores, percentile ranks, a relative proficiency index, and instructional zones (negligible, very limited, limited, fluent, advanced).

There are several technical problems with the test. First, the test was not standardized in each language. Second, data are not presented about the difficulty level of each translated item in each language. Third, each language version does not include all of the items that are in the English version. Fourth, concurrent validity studies are not presented in each language. However, although it is psychometrically imperfect, the BVAT does provide information that can be helpful in classifying an examinee's proficiency in more than one language. It is particularly useful because it includes languages besides Spanish.

Table 4-5
Student Oral Language Observation Matrix (SOLOM) Teacher Observation Checklist

STUDENT ORAL LANGUAGE OBSERVATION MATRIX

Student's name: _____   Date:_____

Grade: _____   Teacher's name: _____

Class: _____   Language observed: _____

Directions:
Based on your observation of the student, put an "X" across the category that best describes the student's abilities.

Note. The SOLOM should be administered only by persons who themselves score at level 4 or above in all categories in the language being assessed.

	1	2	3	4	5
A. Comprehension	Does not understand even simple conversation.	Has great difficulty following what is said. Can comprehend only social conversation spoken slowly and with frequent repetitions.	Understands most of what is said at slower-than-normal speed with repetitions.	Understands nearly everything at normal speed, although occasional repetition may be necessary.	Understands everyday conversation and normal classroom discussions.
B. Fluency	Speech is so halting and fragmentary that conversation is impossible.	Usually hesitant and often silent because of language limitations.	Speech in everyday conversation and classroom discussions is frequently disrupted by a search for the correct expression.	Speech in everyday conversation and classroom discussions is generally fluent with occasional lapses while searching for the correct expression.	Speech in everyday conversation and classroom discussions is fluent and effortless and approximates that of a native speaker.
C. Vocabulary	Vocabulary limitations are so extreme that conversation is impossible.	Misuses words, has limited vocabulary, and has difficulty with comprehension.	Frequently uses wrong words. Conversation is somewhat limited because of inadequate vocabulary.	Occasionally uses inappropriate terms or must rephrase ideas because of language inadequacies.	Extent of vocabulary and usage of idiomatic words approximate those of a native speaker.
D. Pronunciation	Pronunciation problems are so severe that speech is unintelligible.	Hard to understand because of pronunciation problems. Must frequently repeat himself or herself in order to be understood.	Pronunciation problems necessitate concentration on the part of the listener and occasionally lead to misunderstanding.	Always intelligible, although the listener is conscious of an accent and occasional inappropriate intonation patterns.	Pronunciation and intonation approximate those of a native speaker.
E. Grammar	Errors in grammar and word order are so severe that speech is unintelligible.	Makes so many grammar and word errors that comprehension is difficult. Must often rephrase or restrict himself or herself to basic speech patterns.	Makes frequent errors of grammar and word order that occasionally obscure meaning.	Occasionally makes grammatical or word order errors, but these do not obscure meaning.	Grammar and word order approximate those of a native speaker.

Note. A total score of about 20 can be considered proficient. The original form can be downloaded from the following Web site: http://www.helpforschools.com/ELLKBase/forms
Source: Adapted from SOLOM Teacher Observation, developed by San Jose Area Bilingual Consortium.

Other individually administered tests that can be used to assess language proficiency in English and in Spanish include the following:

- The Language Assessment Scales–Oral (LAS–O; Duncan & DeAvila, 1990), a paper-and-pencil multiple-choice oral response test with four levels: preschool age, elementary school age, secondary school age, and adult ages.
- The Language Assessment Scales–Reading and Writing (LAS–R/W; Duncan & DeAvila, 1994), a paper-and-pencil multiple-choice and essay test with three levels (grade 2 through high school).
- The Woodcock-Muñoz Language Survey–Revised (Woodcock, Muñoz-Sandoval, Ruef, & Alvarado, 2005), an individually administered measure of cognitive-academic language proficiency for individuals from age 4 to adult.

After making an informal and formal assessment of language proficiency, classify the child's degree of language proficiency. A useful five-point classification scale follows:

1. Monolingual speaker of a language other than English (speaks the other language exclusively).
2. Predominantly speaks a language other than English (speaks mostly the other language, but also speaks some English).
3. Bilingual (speaks the other language and English with equal ease).
4. Predominantly speaks English (speaks mostly English, but also speaks some in the other language).
5. Monolingual speaker of English (speaks English exclusively).

Interpreters

When you evaluate an examinee or interview a parent who speaks a language you do not speak, you must employ the services of an interpreter. The language spoken by the child or parent can vary depending on, for example, his or her country of origin, ethnicity, economic status, and geographical area. Before you engage an interpreter, ask the child about his or her language preference (see Table 4-1). Also, ask the questions shown in Table 4-4 of the parents and, if possible, the child's teacher as well. *Recognize that, no matter how carefully the interpreter translates, the examination is likely to be ineffective if you and the interpreter are not familiar with the examinee's culture, values, and ideology.*

Ask the interpreter to inform the child and parents about the interpreter's role, that the interpreter is acting as your agent, and that the interpreter will keep all information confidential. Also have the interpreter tell them that you want to get accurate information, to explain the services clearly, and to make them comfortable during the evaluation. Because the use of an interpreter will increase the time needed to complete the evaluation, schedule accordingly, and consider having more than one session if needed.

Even if the family members speak English as a second language, offer them the services of an interpreter, because they may have minimal proficiency in English. Sometimes examinees switch languages during the evaluation (code-switching). For example, examinees may change from their primary language to English to discuss topics that would be upsetting if discussed in their primary language.

Obtain permission from the child and the parents to use an interpreter. Also, *when you write your report or make notes in the examinee's folder or chart, always note that you used an interpreter.* This is especially important if you quote the examinee.

Difficulties involving an interpreter.   Although it may not be intentional, interpreters may delete information or make other changes and embellishments in the translations that distort what you and the examinee say. These distortions may lead to inaccurate information. Also, interpreters who are unfamiliar with testing and standardized directions may unintentionally cue the answer when they translate directions or may relay responses from the child inaccurately. You may have no way of knowing whether the interpreter performed exactly the way you intended him or her to perform. Finally, the use of an interpreter may result in loss of rapport between you and the child and family.

The following are examples of difficulties that can arise in using an interpreter:

1. *Failure to reveal symptoms.* Interpreters may not reveal information that they believe portrays the child or parent in an unfavorable light. Taboo topics for Asian American interpreters, for example, may include sexual matters, financial information, suicidal thoughts, and homicidal thoughts. An interpreter hearing information about these topics may omit details, substitute details, reformulate details, or change the focus of the communication. For example, the interpreter may try to make sense out of disorganized statements made by the examinee and thus prevent you from getting a clear idea of the examinee's mental state.

2. *Mistrust of interpreter.* Some children and parents may be uncomfortable because of the interpreter's age, sex, level of education, relationship to them, or mere presence. They may also distrust the interpreter, fear being judged by the interpreter, fear being misinterpreted, or fear loss of confidentiality.

3. *Preaching to examinees.* Some interpreters, if they believe that the child has strayed from his or her native cultural traditions, may preach to the child and parents about the need to follow traditions.

4. *Lack of equivalent concepts.* Some concepts in English either have no equivalent in other languages or are difficult to translate. Thus, the meaning of important phrases may be lost in translation.

5. *Dialectical and regional differences.* Translations are usually made into a standard language, as translators necessarily have only a limited ability to provide for regional variations. Yet regional variations may be significant. For example,

toston means a half-dollar to a Mexican American child but a squashed section of a fried banana to a Puerto Rican child or Cuban child, and the word for kite is *papagayo* in Venezuela, *cometa* in Spain, and *papalote* in Cuba. Some words differ in meaning not only from one country to another but within a country as well. For example, the word *guila* means sunny in Sonora, Mexico, but in Mexico City it means prostitute.

6. *Mixture of two languages.* The language most familiar to children from some cultural and ethnic groups may be a combination of two languages. For Spanish-speaking children, this combination may be Pocho, pidgin, Spanglish, or Tex-Mex. In such cases, a monolingual translation may be inappropriate. Some examples of words that combine English and Spanish are *raite* (ride), *raiteros* (drivers), *lonche* (lunch), *dompe* (dump), *yonke* (junk), *dame un quebrazo* (give me a break), and *los baggies* (baggy jeans).

7. *Changes in difficulty level.* The level of difficulty of words may change because of translation. For example, *animal domestico,* the Spanish equivalent of the common English word *pet,* is an uncommon phrase in Spanish.

8. *Alteration of meaning.* Translation can alter the meaning of words. For example, seemingly harmless English words may translate into Spanish profanity. *Huevo* is the literal translation of the word *eggs,* but the Spanish term *huevón* has more earthy connotations. The context determines the meaning of the word.

9. *Causing offense with colloquial words.* Interpreters may use colloquial words for more formal words and, in the process, inadvertently offend some examinees. For example, use of the Spanish words *pata* for foot and *espinizo* for back, which are more appropriate for animals than for humans, may offend examinees who prefer the more formal words *pie* and *espalda,* respectively.

Suggestions for working with an interpreter.   Here are some suggestions for working with an interpreter:

1. *Selecting an interpreter.* Select an interpreter who is thoroughly familiar with the examinee's language and, if possible, with the linguistic variations or dialect used by the child's ethnic group. As noted earlier, select an interpreter who also in knowledgeable about the child's culture.

2. *Briefing the interpreter.* Brief the interpreter thoroughly on issues that may affect his or her role. For example, *before* you begin the assessment, discuss with the interpreter (a) the goals of the evaluation, (b) areas you want to cover, (c) the need to address sensitive topics, (d) the level of competence the interpreter has in both languages, (e) the attitude of the interpreter toward the examinee and possible problem areas, (f) the importance of translating your questions and comments and those of the examinee word for word, and (g) the need to maintain confidentiality. Stress that the interpreter should not add words, delete words, or interpret what the examinee says. Also inform the interpreter not to repeat questions unless requested to do so. Stress the importance of establishing rapport, maintaining neutrality, not reacting

judgmentally to what the examinee says or to what you say, transmitting all the information between the parties, and preserving the confidentiality of the proceedings.

You may need to deal with the feelings and reactions of some interpreters, especially when you discuss extremely sensitive issues such as child maltreatment or rape. Also, the gender of the interpreter may be an issue if there are cultural taboos against males and females discussing certain topics. This is an issue that should be discussed before the assessment.

If the interpreter is going to be translating test questions, stress the importance of (a) translating questions and all other communications exactly and not prompting or commenting on the examinee's responses or on your responses, (b) avoiding nonverbal gestures that signal whether the examinee's responses were correct or incorrect, and (c) relaying the examinee's responses precisely. A brief explanation of the reasons for adhering to these guidelines will help the interpreter better understand his or her role.

3. *Discussing technical terms.* Discuss beforehand any technical terms and concepts that may pose a problem for translation. Ideally, the interpreter should be familiar with terms related to psychological disorders and medical disorders. Encourage the interpreter to conduct a sentence-by-sentence interpretation to ensure that each translated phrase is equivalent to the phrase in the original language, to refrain from giving explanations that you did not ask him or her to provide, and to mirror your affective tone as closely as possible. As the examiner, you should use clear, standard, formal English and avoid technical terms and colloquialisms if possible. Even if the interpreter knows the correct translation of your technical term or jargon (e.g., *esquizofrenia* for *schizophrenia*), the examinee may not know that word. Slang words, in particular, are difficult to translate accurately.

4. *Practicing with the interpreter.* Practice with the interpreter *before* the assessment to help the interpreter develop good translating skills.

5. *Selecting a nonfamily member as the interpreter.* Choose an interpreter who is not a family member, a family friend, or someone the family knows, because of possible sensitive subject matter or conflicts of interest.

6. *Involving the interpreter as an assistant.* Engage the interpreter as an assistant, not as a co-examiner. Unless the interpreter is a qualified mental health professional and you give her or him permission to do so, the interpreter should not formulate her or his own questions. If the interpreter does formulate questions, make sure that the interpreter distinguishes between her or his questions and yours.

7. *Positioning yourself and the interpreter.* Face the examinee when you talk to him or her. Position the interpreter at your side, and speak as though the examinee can understand you.

8. *Talking to the interpreter.* Avoid talking to the interpreter about the family in the presence of family members.

9. *Encouraging attention to details.* Encourage the interpreter to tell you about the paralinguistic aspects of the examinee's speech—for example, when cries, laughter, sighs,

stuttering, and melodic voice changes occur. After the session, ask the interpreter to describe the quality of the examinee's vocabulary and language, especially in comparison with that of other children the same age. Although the interpreter's description will not be that of a professional, it may nonetheless be useful.

10. *Speaking and word usage.* Speak in a normal tone of voice; use facial expressions that are not forced or faked; use short, simple sentences; and avoid idioms, colloquialisms, and jargon. Ask the interpreter to alert you to specific translated words that might be too difficult for the examinee to understand. You then can rephrase as needed.

11. *Observing the examinee.* Be attentive to the examinee's reactions, gestures, and facial expressions. If the examinee looks confused or puzzled, try to determine at what point the translation may have gone wrong or whether other factors have interfered with the communication. Do not interrupt the interpreter.

12. *Summarizing and confirming.* Summarize what you have learned at appropriate points, and ask the examinee to confirm your understanding.

13. *Allowing extra time.* As noted previously, allow extra time when you schedule the session, because working with an interpreter will extend the time required to conduct the evaluation.

14. *Reviewing the interpreter's performance.* After you complete the assessment, meet with the interpreter to discuss problems that he or she encountered and to review his or her performance. Include in your report the name and qualifications of the interpreter and any reservations about the reliability and validity of the information you obtained.

15. *Using the interpreter in future sessions.* Assuming that the interpreter performed adequately, make an effort to use the same interpreter in any future sessions with the examinee and in the post-assessment evaluation.

After you complete the assessment, evaluate the adequacy and the quality of the information. Does the information make sense? Do you believe you have obtained all of the relevant information you need? Are you puzzled by any details? Do you think the interpreter omitted some information? Do you believe the interpreter did her or his job well?

In the post-assessment evaluation, also evaluate the family's understanding of the results and the planned intervention program. Do they seem puzzled? If so, why? Ask them to repeat the major findings and recommendations. Don't be afraid to acknowledge candidly that you are not of their culture. Ask how much a certain recommendation would make sense in their culture and ask how they feel about working with a professional of a different culture.

RECOMMENDATIONS

Implementing as many as possible of the following guidelines will help you conduct effective assessments of children who are from a minority group and their families.

LEARN ABOUT THE EXAMINEE'S CULTURE

1. Learn about the child's, family's, and community's cultural values, attitudes, and worldview. For example, learn about the family's structure and roles, including distribution of power and authority; marriage customs; mutual obligations; and how the family handles shame. You can learn about the family's structure by reviewing information about the family's size and composition, ages of family members, and living arrangements; education and employment of family members; and frequency and nature of contact with family members who are living outside the home. Consider whether the family's cultural practices are related to any of the child's symptoms.

2. Learn about the child's and family's ethnic identification. For example, do they consider themselves African American, Black American, or American? Hispanic American, Latino, Mexican American, or American?

3. Learn about the family's specific cultural patterns related to child rearing—for example, the family's attitudes concerning dating among adolescents, age of independence from the family, and the importance of education for males and females.

4. Consider the family's socioeconomic status and how it may affect the family's values, attitudes, and worldview.

5. Learn how the family's community is organized, supported, and developed, including the role of the family in the community, the place of traditional healers, and the role of community leaders.

6. Learn how the sociopolitical system in the United States influences the way the family's minority group is treated.

7. Recognize your ignorance about details of the family's culture, and do not be afraid to let the child and family know that you are *not* aware of some aspects of their value system, worldview, and life style. Not only will you learn, but also they will appreciate your interest and honesty.

8. Recognize that if you are not a member of the minority group, you may be viewed as "the stranger."

LEARN ABOUT THE EXAMINEE'S LANGUAGE

1. Determine the child's and family's preferred language before you begin the evaluation.

2. Ideally, learn the language spoken by the child and family.

3. Do not assume that, because the child and family speak some English, they can fully understand you.

4. Do not assume that, just because you have some speaking knowledge of the family's language, you can ask meaningful questions in that language or fully understand the family's communications.

5. Employ an interpreter, if needed, and recognize the limitations inherent in doing so.

ESTABLISH RAPPORT

1. Show children who are from a minority group and their families that you are sensitive to and respect their culture's perspective and value system, and that you are trying to help them. Convey acceptance of their culture. Allow the

parents and child to consult other family or community members if they ask to do so.

2. Make every effort to encourage the child's and family's motivation and interest.

3. Be prepared to spend more time establishing rapport than you would with children and parents from the majority culture, as examinees who are from a minority group may feel less trusting and particularly vulnerable. You should aim to enlist the child's and family's cooperation.

4. Be diplomatic and tactful. Avoid confrontation, arguments, and kidding, because the child and family may see such actions as disrespectful, rude, or offensive.

5. If taking notes during the evaluation will offend the child or family, write your notes after the evaluation is over. You might also consider using a tape recorder to record your notes. Be sure to get the family's consent before doing so.

IDENTIFY YOUR STEREOTYPES

1. Recognize any stereotypes and prejudices that you have about the family's ethnic group.

2. Take precautions to ensure that your stereotypes and prejudices do not interfere with your work. If you cannot do so, arrange for another psychologist to evaluate the child.

3. Do not assume that the family follows the minority group's traditional healing practices or uses traditional healers. Some families who are from a minority group will be offended if you assume that they believe in traditional healers. Ask them about these matters as needed.

PROMOTE CLEAR COMMUNICATION

1. Speak clearly, and avoid idioms, slang expressions, and statements with implied or double meanings.

2. Ask the parents and the child whom they want at the evaluation. Some families prefer to invite extended family members, whereas others do not.

3. Address all family members present at the evaluation, not just the child and parents.

4. Call children by their proper names. Hispanic Americans, for example, often have two last names, one from each parent. Do not use nicknames unless invited to do so.

5. Monitor your verbal and nonverbal behavior to eliminate words, expressions, and actions that may offend the child and family. Monitoring your nonverbal behavior will not be easy. You must learn whether your behavior changes with members of different minority groups. For example, if you are a examiner who is from the majority group and you work with both minority-group and majority-group examinees, do you place yourself farther away from minority-group examinees than from majority-group examinees, spend less time with them, or make more speech errors with them? If so, you may be revealing signs of anxiety or avoidance behavior. Videotape your evaluations and study the tapes carefully for subtle signs of altered communication with different minority groups. (Of course, you must first obtain permission to videotape an evaluation session. Then erase the tapes after you have

studied them. In exceptional cases when you plan to use the tapes for research purposes, protect them by storing them in a locked cabinet.)

6. Evaluate whether differences between you and the child and family may be hampering the evaluation; if so, try to rectify the problems.

7. Be flexible, and use innovative assessment strategies tailored to the needs of the child's ethnic group.

IDENTIFY FAMILY NEEDS

1. Determine the material resources and physical health of the child and family. For example, do they have adequate food, water, clothing, bedding, shelter, and sanitation and proper immunizations? What unmet needs do the child and family have that could affect the assessment and treatment?

2. Determine the psychological and social needs of the child and family. For example, does the child have adequate time for play? What is the child's level of self-esteem? Has the child established friendships? Does the family have adequate leisure time? Are family members able to practice their religious beliefs? Does the child have adequate schooling? Does the home offer a place to study, free from distractions? Are the parents able to supervise the child? Is the child forced to assume adult responsibilities prematurely? Is the child exposed to violence on the streets?

IDENTIFY FAMILY ATTITUDES
TOWARD HEALTH AND ILLNESS

1. Learn about the child's and family's traditional concepts of illness and healing, traditional rituals, and religious beliefs, and how they differ from those of the majority culture. For example, healing practices that produce bruises on a child may not necessarily indicate child maltreatment, and the shaving of one's head and eyebrows, performed as a sacrifice to wronged ancestors, may not be a sign of mental illness.

2. Learn what the child's and family's expectations are of medical or psychological treatment. For example, when they take medicine, do they expect immediate relief, and if they do not get immediate relief, will they discontinue taking the medicine? Do they believe that only a pill will make them well?

3. Learn what prescribed drugs, over-the-counter drugs, traditional remedies, and illicit drugs the child is taking.

RECOGNIZE THE EXTENT OF
THE FAMILY'S ACCULTURATION

1. Recognize that acculturation will take different forms among different ethnic groups. Learn about the extent to which the child and the parents are acculturated.

2. Expect to find differences among children and families from the same minority group in values and level of acculturation and in the problems they face.

3. Learn about the stresses associated with acculturation, particularly for refugee and immigrant groups. Take time to understand their fears, hopes, and aspirations. The process

of acculturation often carries with it stresses caused by a loss of autonomy and feelings of shame and doubt. Consider such questions as the following: Do family members feel depressed, angry, or guilty about those left behind in their home country? Do they have any symptoms associated with posttraumatic stress disorder? Have traumatic experiences affected the child's development and the child's and family's perceptions of the world and view of the future? If you hold the evaluation after a period of adjustment in the United States, do family members complain that nobody cares about them, express fear of failure or feelings of isolation, or have delayed grief reactions? Do they have conflicts in transition periods, such as when the children enter adolescence? Do other refugee or immigrant families reject them when they try to identify with the new culture? How great are the cultural differences between the United States and the home country? Is there intergenerational conflict between the child and parents because the child is acculturating faster than the adults? Does the child feel alienated—rejected both by his or her culture of origin and by the American culture? Is the child accepted by one culture but not by the other? Or is he or she accepted by both cultures? Does the family need help in interpreting U.S. laws and regulations?

4. Obtain information about how the child and family were functioning before leaving their home country. For example, children and families who had serious problems before their migration may find their unresolved problems exacerbated in the United States.

ACCEPT THE EXAMINEE'S PERSPECTIVES

1. Show a willingness to accept cultural perspectives other than your own, see the strengths and values of the coping mechanisms of ethnic groups other than your own, and appreciate and respect the viewpoint of each ethnic group with which you work. For example, recognize how your own culture—its values, customs, mores, traditions, and standards—differs from other cultures. Be tolerant of family norms that may have developed in response to stress and prejudice. Include extended family members in the intervention if they are highly involved with the child and family. Also consider contacting traditional healers and practitioners as needed, and work with the established power structures within the child's and family's community.

2. Do not violate the child's and family's culture and traditional beliefs during the evaluation or in formulating intervention plans.

3. Build on the child's and family's strengths, use the family's existing support systems, and help the child remain in his or her natural community in the least restrictive environment.

4. Fully support the premise that our society must give each child an equal opportunity to achieve to the limits of his or her capacity.

5. Recognize that members of minority groups (and members of the majority group as well) often face major social issues. Major social issues include changes in women's roles, changes in the concept of the family, substandard schools, unequal pay scales, dilapidated housing, high dropout rates from school, a shortage of mental health services in the community, prejudice and discrimination, inaccessibility of mental health services, and irrelevance of treatments.

6. Recognize that families at a low socioeconomic level can provide a healthy, strong, and nurturing environment for their children; *do not equate low socioeconomic status with dysfunction.*

7. Recognize how the sociopolitical system in the United States treats minority groups and how institutional barriers affect minority groups' use of mental health and medical facilities.

8. Consider each child and family as unique, but use what you know about the child's and family's ethnic background to guide you in the evaluation and in formulating intervention plans.

9. Do not use your knowledge of the family's ethnic background to make sweeping stereotypic generalizations or to probe into cultural practices not relevant to the assessment and interventions.

10. Avoid attributing all the child's and family's problems solely to their minority group status.

11. Have the case reassigned if you find yourself unable to be objective or unwilling to learn about the family's culture.

DEVELOP EFFECTIVE CONSULTATION SKILLS

1. Recognize the limits of your competencies and expertise in working not only with minority groups, but also with all children and their families.

2. View all examinees as being capable of learning, and hold high expectations for them.

3. Work with school personnel and all students in the school to help them understand that all children and their families must be treated as equals, without regard to ethnicity, gender, religion, or disabling condition.

4. Work toward eliminating bias, prejudices, and discrimination in our society.

The above suggestions will help you become a culturally skilled examiner and establish trust with the child and parents. Trust, in turn, will improve the quality of communications. For trust to develop, children and parents must perceive that you have expert knowledge and good intentions and that they can rely on you. *Unless mutual trust develops, the evaluation is doomed to failure.*

You can become more credible in the eyes of families who are from a minority group by conducting several informal evaluations initially and, in some cases, by visiting the child's home. Be sure to obtain the permission of the parents *before* you visit their home, however. Some families who are from a minority group are distrustful of a stranger coming to their home, especially if the person is employed by a city, county, state, or federal agency. Parents who are from a minority group may need time to accept the need for evaluation and treatment. Explain program objectives so that the parents—and the child, where applicable—understand them fully. Repeatedly stress that the welfare of the child is important. Give the parents as much support as they need. Resolve value conflicts to their satisfaction. If the child has a disability, help the parents accept the child's disability and be realistic about it. To orient the examinee's family to the program, recruit parents from the same ethnic group who have children in special programs.

Honesty and reliability can be effective in changing negative opinions about mental health and medical services and about practitioners. By being patient, understanding, competent, and tolerant, you can probably mitigate any hostile feelings that the parents may have and help them see that the child's welfare is the concern of all involved.

Improved intercultural communication will ultimately depend on changes in the sociopolitical system. Until our society eliminates racism and discrimination, there are likely to be vestiges of suspicion and mistrust between people of different ethnicities. As an examiner, you can improve race relations. You can strive to eliminate social inequalities and prejudice from our society by helping children develop pride in their native language and culture, improving families' attitudes toward learning, and helping society and the educational system be more responsive to the attitudes, perceptions, and behaviors of different ethnic groups. These and similar actions will improve the quality of life of the children and families with whom you work.

THINKING THROUGH THE ISSUES

1. With what ethnic or cultural group do you identify?
2. What are your ethnic group's attitudes toward children with behavioral problems, physical disabilities, or medical illnesses?
3. What are your ethnic group's attitudes toward homelessness, divorce, welfare, and other social issues?
4. How does your ethnic or cultural identity relate to your self-view and self-esteem?
5. How do you feel about members of other ethnic or cultural groups?
6. How might your cultural practices and traditions interfere with your ability to understand and relate to examinees from other cultural and ethnic backgrounds?
7. What personal qualities do you have that would be helpful in assessment of culturally and linguistically diverse groups? What personal qualities do you have that would be detrimental?
8. How do you think you can conduct an unbiased assessment?
9. Do you believe that, to be an effective examiner, you must be of the same ethnic group as the examinee? If so, what would you do if you were scheduled to evaluate someone of a different ethnic group?

10. If you were scheduled to be evaluated for your personal problems by someone of an ethnic group different from your own, how would you feel? Would you take any actions to arrange for another professional? If so, why?
11. Do you believe that problems faced by culturally and linguistically diverse examinees are a direct result of an oppressive society? If so, then what role do you think mental health practitioners have in working with culturally and linguistically diverse groups?
12. Have you ever experienced prejudice? If so, what form of prejudice did you experience, and how did you feel during the experience and afterwards?
13. Do the ethnic groups covered in the chapter retain some unique cultural styles, or have they been largely assimilated?
14. What are some benefits and losses associated with assimilation?
15. What aspects of African American, Hispanic American, Native American, and Asian American cultures do you value the most?
16. How might your development have been different if you had been raised in a culture other than your own?
17. How will it be helpful to you as a clinical assessor to know about the culture of other ethnic groups?
18. Can prejudiced examiners be effective clinical assessors? If not, then what should be done about an examiner who harbors prejudice against an examinee's ethnic group? What ethical guidelines can assist you in answering this question?
19. What experiences have you had with different cultures that have influenced your attitudes and behavior toward children and adults of these groups?
20. What were your reactions to the content of this chapter? For example, was any material disturbing or anxiety provoking? Did any of the material stimulate you to want to learn more about a particular ethnic group or groups?

SUMMARY

1. It will not always be easy to evaluate the role that cultural variables play in assessment, in part because members of culturally and linguistically diverse groups differ in their adherence to their group's cultural traditions and practices.
2. Great diversity exists within any cultural group, especially between recent immigrants and those who have had more opportunity to become acculturated into their new society.
3. Even among those who are acculturated, differences exist in patterns of acculturation.
4. Within any cultural group, there are differences in values, motivation, social organization, ways of speaking and thinking, and life styles that vary with education, income, class status, geographic origin, assimilation patterns, religious background, and age.
5. Broad generalizations about cultural practices do not do justice to regional, generational, socioeconomic, and idiosyncratic variations.
6. Knowledge of a child's and family's cultural mores and customs, possible migration experiences, and level of acculturation will help you conduct a more effective assessment.
7. Culture is the human-made part of the environment, consisting of highly variable systems of meaning that are learned and

shared by a people or an identifiable segment of a population. Culture represents designs and ways of life normally transmitted from one generation to another.

8. Race refers to the genetic makeup common to a population.

9. Ethnicity refers to a group's common nationality, culture, or language.

10. Social class refers to group designations within a society, usually based on occupation, education, or both.

11. Personality, temperament, and intelligence, as well as psychological disorders, develop within a cultural context.

12. Cultural variables include ethnic background, language spoken in and outside the home, gender, family interaction patterns, socioeconomic status, neighborhood characteristics, and peer group influences.

13. However much we subscribe to the philosophy that well-normed standardized assessment tools provide the most reliable and valid means of assessment, we also must recognize the cultural diversity of children.

14. Recognizing cultural diversity does not mean that we set aside our nation's laws and customs.

15. Because assessment results have an impact on children's self-esteem and influence their chances of having a successful life, biased tests may be detrimental to all children.

Background Considerations

16. The U.S. Bureau of the Census estimates that there were 70.4 million children under age 18 living in the United States as of June 1, 2000.

17. The ethnic affiliations of the children were as follows: Euro American, 64%; African American, 15%; Hispanic American, 16%; Asian American, 4%; and Native American, less than 1%.

18. It is estimated that by 2050, Hispanic Americans will form 24.3% of the population, up from the current 11.8%, and Asian Americans will make up 9.3%, an increase from the current 3.8%.

19. In the United States, culturally and linguistically diverse groups may face (a) racism and discrimination, (b) poverty, (c) conflicts associated with acculturation and assimilation, especially when children begin to identify more closely with the majority culture and reject their ethnic culture, (d) problems in dealing with medical, educational, social, and law enforcement organizations, and (e) problems in using standard English.

20. Confronting prejudice is a common experience of members of culturally and linguistically diverse groups at all socioeconomic levels in our society.

21. In 2000, Euro Americans families had the lowest percentage of children living below the poverty line (11.2%), followed by Asian Americans (14.3%), Hispanic Americans (27.9%), Native Americans (31.6%), and African Americans (33.1%).

22. Poverty can raise children's and parents' stress levels and place them at increased risk for health problem such as obesity, suicide, and alcoholism.

23. Acculturation is the process of cultural change that occurs in individuals when two cultures meet; it leads individuals to adopt elements of another culture, such as values and social behaviors.

24. The process of acculturation may involve all or some of the following phases: maintaining and practicing mainly the traditions of the culture of origin (traditionalism), partaking of both the old and the new culture (transitional period), trying unsuccessfully to meet the demands of both the old and the new culture (marginality), embracing traditions of the new culture and rejecting practices of the old culture (assimilation), and integrating practices of both the old and the new culture (biculturalism).

25. Variables affecting acculturation include the history of the person's migration experience, temporal and geographic distance from the country of origin and its indigenous culture, place of residence and socioeconomic status in the homeland, type of neighborhood in the United States, ties with immediate and extended family, role of the family's power and authority, language and customs, and individual aspirations.

26. Children (and their families) may face several stresses in dealing with acculturation.

27. Ethnic identity refers to "one's sense of belonging to an ethnic group and the part of one's thinking, perceptions, feelings, and behavior that is due to ethnic group membership." (Rotheram & Phinney, 1986)

28. Stereotypes of children's culturally and linguistically diverse group may impede their identity formation.

29. Ethnic identification becomes particularly complex when individuals have a biracial or multicultural heritage.

Evaluating Bias

30. Considerable research has been conducted on the effects of culture, ethnicity, and language on assessment of intelligence and other cognitive aptitudes, but less research has been conducted on the effect of these variables in personality and clinical assessments.

31. Diagnostic criteria may be susceptible to bias because the criteria may reflect middle-class Euro American values and standards of conduct that are not relevant to other cultural groups.

32. Bias may also affect thresholds for identifying deviance or pathology.

33. Because of the small number of research studies, methodological problems in some of the research, and inconsistent results, we cannot draw firm conclusions about differences among ethnic and cultural groups in the incidence of personality and behavioral disorders.

34. At present, it appears that few differences emerge in relationship to race or ethnicity once the effects of socioeconomic status, sex, and age are controlled.

35. Efforts to ensure that all groups for whom a measure is intended are fairly represented in the standardization sample does not necessarily ensure that a measure is free of bias, nor does the absence of the relevant groups in a standardization sample necessarily indicate that the measure is invalid.

36. Pluralistic norms may serve a limited purpose in some settings, but the reliability and validity of these norms must be established.

37. Several procedures are available for evaluating the presence of cultural bias in psychological measures, but, with a few exceptions, these procedures have not been used in evaluating personality tests, behavioral rating scales, or checklists.

38. Translating a psychological measure from one language to another is difficult because the two languages may not have equivalent concepts, dialectical or regional variations may be difficult to accommodate, and the meanings of words may change in translation.

Ethical and Clinical Guidelines

39. Guidelines regarding the conduct of assessments with culturally and linguistically diverse children are available from several sources.

Practical Considerations in the Conduct of Assessments

40. When you evaluate children and parents who are members of culturally and linguistically diverse groups, be prepared to consider issues related to ethnic and racial identity, acculturation, language, changing family patterns, sex roles, religious and traditional beliefs, customs for dealing with crisis and change, racism, poverty, social class, health care practices, and the interactions among these factors.

41. You will likely have the difficult task of evaluating whether behaviors that would suggest personality or temperament problems in a member of the majority group reflect similar problems in members of minority groups.

42. Gender roles also may differ across cultures, and certain cultures have particularly marked, definitive role expectations for men and women.

43. You may encounter communication barriers when you work with examinees who are from a minority group (and from the majority group as well), because they may be mystified by medical or psychological terminology.

44. Language may pose a problem in interviewing a family from a minority group, particularly when the family members have different levels of proficiency in their native language and in English.

45. Some African American children and their parents speak a variant of English that linguists call Black English, nonstandard Black English, Black dialect, or Ebonics.

46. Black English shares many features with standard English, but it has several distinguishing features in the areas of pronunciation and grammar.

47. Black English has its roots in the oral traditions of the African ancestors of African Americans.

48. Black English should not be viewed as inferior to standard English.

49. Linguistically, Hispanic American children and their families are a heterogeneous group, with wide variations in their degree of mastery of English and Spanish.

50. Speech patterns of bilingual Hispanic American children can be an intricate mixture of English and Spanish, with words borrowed from English, anglicized words, nonstandard pronunciation, and nonstandard word order.

51. When Euro American clinicians evaluate Asian Americans, misunderstandings may arise because of the ways Asian Americans use language or pronounce English words.

52. There is no universal, traditional Native American language. Each tribe is likely to have its own language, and within a tribe different dialects may exist.

53. Nonverbal communications are another potential source of communication difficulties in cross-cultural assessments.

54. Proxemics refers to the perception and use of personal and interpersonal space.

55. Kinesics refers to body movements (such as facial expressions, posture, and gestures), characteristics of movement, and eye contact.

56. Paralanguage refers to the vocal cues used in talking.

57. In cross-ethnic and cross-cultural assessments, examiners' effectiveness will suffer if they display a patronizing attitude, fail to recognize the value of examinees' traditional customs and mores, or are obsessed with the examinees' culture.

58. Misinterpretations of intercultural communication will occur when examinees who are from a minority group view majority-group examiners as immature, rude, and lacking in finesse because they want to get to the point quickly. Similarly, examiners who are from the majority group should not view minority-group examinees as evasive and afraid to confront their problems because they communicate indirectly.

59. Conflicts may arise if majority-group examinees, when they are interviewed by examiners who are from a minority group, avoid the race issue, deprecate the examiner, have special admiration for the examiner, or view the examiner as all-forgiving or uncritical. Examiners who are from a minority group, on the other hand, may be unsympathetic or punitive if they are hostile toward the majority group, or they may overcompensate by being too permissive.

60. Examiners who are from the same minority group as examinees may be in the best position to obtain reliable and valid information. Examiners who are from a minority group must walk a fine line between overidentification and objectivity when evaluating examinees who are from the same minority group.

61. Because of racial antagonism, minority-group examiners may experience difficulties in their relationships with examinees who are from a different minority group.

62. Preoccupation with and heightened sensitivity to ethnic differences may lead to distortions, guardedness, and evasiveness on the part of examinees and to guardedness, failure to probe, defensiveness, and feelings of intimidation on the part of examiners.

63. It is your responsibility to ensure that any stereotypical views you have do not adversely affect the assessment.

64. Examiners will usually be effective when they are tolerant and accepting of examinees, despite value differences. Your goal is to establish a professional relationship, characterized by trust and acceptance.

65. Bilingualism refers to the ability to use two languages.

66. Research indicates that children who are fluently bilingual have advantages over their monolingual peers on both verbal and nonverbal tasks.

67. Before you engage an interpreter, learn about the child's language preference.

68. Recognize that, no matter how carefully the interpreter translates, the evaluation is likely to be ineffective if you and the interpreter are not familiar with the examinee's culture, values, and ideology.

69. When you write your report or make notes in the examinee's folder or chart, always note if you used an interpreter. This is especially important if you quote the examinee.

70. There are several potential difficulties in working with interpreters. Interpreters may fail to reveal symptoms that they believe portray the child or parent in an unfavorable light. Some examinees may be uncomfortable with having an interpreter. Some interpreters will preach to examinees instead of being neutral. Some concepts are difficult to translate. Translations usually are made with limited provision for dialectical or regional variations. The language familiar to children who are from a minority group may be a combination of two languages.

The level of difficulty of words may change because of translation. Translation can alter the meaning of words. Interpreters may use colloquial words for more formal words and, in the process, inadvertently offend some examinees.

71. Select an interpreter who is thoroughly familiar with the examinee's language and, if possible, with the linguistic variations or dialect used by the child's ethnic group.

72. Brief the interpreter thoroughly on issues that may affect his or her role.

73. Discuss beforehand any technical terms and concepts that may pose a problem for translation.

74. Practice with the interpreter *before* the interview to help the interpreter develop good translation skills.

75. Position yourself and the interpreter correctly.

76. Follow other guidelines related to language, observation, summarizing, and reviewing the interpreter's performance.

Recommendations

77. To become a culturally skilled examiner, learn about the examinee's culture and language, establish rapport, identify any stereotypes you may have, promote clear communication, identify family needs, identify family attitudes toward health and illness, recognize the extent of the family's acculturation, accept the examinee's perspectives, and develop effective consultation skills.

78. You can become more credible in the eyes of families who are from a minority group by conducting several informal evaluations initially and, in some cases, by visiting the child's home.

79. Honesty and reliability can be effective in changing negative opinions about mental health and medical services and about practitioners.

80. Improved intercultural communication will ultimately depend on changes in the sociopolitical system.

KEY TERMS, CONCEPTS, AND NAMES

STUDY QUESTIONS

1. Discuss why it is important to consider cultural variables when you evaluate children and families.

2. How do the concepts of culture, race, ethnicity, and social class differ?

3. What is the distribution of culturally and linguistically diverse groups in the United States, as discussed in the text?

4. Describe some of the problems faced by culturally and linguistically diverse groups in the United States.

5. Discuss acculturation. In your discussion, examine factors affecting acculturation, strategies for dealing with acculturation, and stresses associated with acculturation.

6. Discuss ethnic identity and identification.

7. Discuss how cultural or language factors may affect the definition of personality and behavioral constructs.

8. What procedures are available for evaluating the effects of ethnic variables on the validity of psychological assessments?

9. Discuss problems associated with efforts to translate measures from one language to another.

10. Identify the different ethical and practical guidelines relevant to the assessment of ethnic and linguistic minorities.

11. Discuss culture and communication styles. Include in your discussion both verbal and nonverbal communication difficulties. Touch on issues related to proxemics, kinesics, and paralanguage.

12. Discuss the dynamics of cross-ethnic and cross-cultural assessment. Include in your discussion issues related to relationships between a majority-group examiner and a minority-group examinee, between a minority-group examiner and a majority-group examinee, between a minority-group examiner and an examinee who is from the same minority group, and between a minority-group examiner and an examinee who is from a different minority group.

13. Discuss issues involved in working with an interpreter. Include in your discussion difficulties associated with working with an interpreter and suggestions for handling these difficulties.

5

GENERAL INTERVIEWING TECHNIQUES

A question rightly asked is half answered.
—C. G. J. Jacobi, German mathematician (1804–1851)

An answer is invariably the parent of a great family of new questions.
—John Steinbeck, American novelist (1902–1968)

Goals and Objectives

This chapter is designed to enable you to do the following:

- Describe how a clinical assessment interview differs from a conversation, a psychotherapeutic interview, and a survey research interview

- Understand the strengths and weaknesses of the clinical assessment interview

- Compare unstructured, semistructured, and structured clinical assessment interviews

- Develop effective listening skills

- Develop rapport with the interviewee

- Time questions and change topics appropriately

- Formulate appropriate questions

- Avoid ineffective questions

- Use probing techniques

- Use structuring statements

- Encourage appropriate replies

- Deal with difficult situations in the interview

- Recognize your emotions

- Record information and schedule appointments

This section contains three chapters on the clinical assessment interview. The first chapter focuses on general principles of interviewing. The second chapter discusses strategies particularly useful for interviewing children, parents, teachers, and families. The third chapter deals with the post-assessment interview, the reliability and validity of the interview, and other issues related to interviewing. The interviewing guidelines in this section do not cover every possible situation that may arise in the interview. However, mastering the material in this section will prepare you for many different types of interviews. We will use the term *interviewer* instead of *examiner* and *interviewee* instead of *examinee* in this and the next two chapters, because parents and teachers, as well as children, often are interviewed as part of a case study.

The primary goal of the *clinical assessment interview* is to obtain relevant, reliable, and valid information about interviewees and their problems. This includes information about their personalities, temperaments, motor skills, cognitive skills, communication skills, study habits, work habits, interpersonal behaviors, interests, daily living skills and difficulties, and perception of the referral problem. Important sources of information are the *content of the interview* (i.e., what the interviewee tells you) and the *interviewee's style* (i.e., how the interviewee speaks, behaves, and relates to you). The information you obtain will depend on how interviewees perceive you, the atmosphere you establish, your interviewing style, and—with children or special needs clients—your success in gearing the interview to their abilities or developmental levels.

CLINICAL ASSESSMENT INTERVIEWS VERSUS ORDINARY CONVERSATIONS AND OTHER TYPES OF INTERVIEWS

Clinical Assessment Interviews and Ordinary Conversations

There are several key differences between clinical assessment interviews and *ordinary conversations* (see Table 5-1). Ordinary conversation is more spontaneous, less formal, and less structured than clinical assessment interviews and has few of the characteristics associated with formal interviews. *A clinical assessment interview is different from an ordinary conversation in that the interview involves an interpersonal interaction that has a mutually accepted purpose, with formal, clearly defined roles and a set of norms governing the interaction.*

Clinical Assessment Interviews and Psychotherapeutic Interviews

Clinical assessment interviews and *psychotherapeutic interviews* are part of an ongoing assessment process. There is

---

Table 5-1
Key Differences Between Clinical Assessment Interviews and Ordinary Conversations

Clinical assessment interview	Ordinary conversation
1. Usually a formally arranged meeting	1. May occur spontaneously
2. Interviewer usually obliged to accept the interviewee's request for an interview	2. Usually no obligation to enter a conversation
3. Interviewer obliged to stay to the end	3. Parties may end conversation abruptly
4. Has a definite purpose	4. Usually with no specific purpose
5. Interviewer and interviewee have a well-defined and structured relationship in which the interviewer questions and the interviewee answers	5. Usually involves a mutual exchange of ideas
6. Interviewer plans and organizes his or her behavior	6. No planning is necessary
7. Interviewer attempts to direct the interaction and choose the content of the interview	7. Usually flows without specific direction
8. Interviewer must focus on the details of the interviewer-interviewee interaction	8. Little or no attention may be given to the details of the interaction
9. Interviewer does not react emotionally or judgmentally	9. Parties may react emotionally or judgmentally
10. Interviewer clarifies questions and does not presume complete understanding	10. Much may be left unstated or misunderstood
11. Interviewer follows guidelines concerning confidentiality and privileged communication	11. Parties are under no legal or ethical obligation to keep the information discussed confidential

Source: Adapted from Kadushin (1983).

continuity between the two types of interviews, with the goals evolving rather than changing radically from one interview to the other. Still, there are important differences and similarities.

Differences.   Let's look at some of the main differences between clinical assessment interviews and psychotherapeutic interviews:

1. *Goals.* The purpose of the clinical assessment interview is to obtain relevant information in order to make an informed decision about the interviewee—for example, to determine whether there is a problem and what types of treatment, interventions, or services the interviewee may need. The clinical assessment interview is not an open-ended, client-centered counseling session; it is driven by an agenda. The function of the psychotherapeutic interview, in contrast, is to relieve a client's emotional distress, foster insight, and enable changes in behavior and life situations.

2. *Direction and structure.* In the clinical assessment interview, the interviewer may cover a specific set of topics or questions in order to obtain developmental, medical, and social histories; formulate a detailed description of a specific problem; or conduct a mental status evaluation. The interviewer uses probing techniques to obtain detailed and accurate information. In the psychotherapeutic interview, the interviewer uses specialized techniques to achieve therapeutic goals. The focus may be on problem solving, cognitive restructuring, or increasing awareness and expression of feelings.

3. *Contact time.* The length of a clinical assessment interview varies. Often, there is no expectation that the interviewer will see the interviewee again, except for formal testing and possibly a post-assessment interview. Psychotherapeutic interview sessions, in contrast, usually last 50 minutes, and there is an expectation that the therapist will see the client for at least several interviews.

Despite the differences between clinical assessment interviews and psychotherapeutic interviews, they overlap in several ways. For instance, in psychotherapeutic interviews, you should continually assess the interviewee; and in clinical assessment interviews, you should use psychotherapeutic strategies to deal with interviewee reactions (such as emotional distress) during the interview.

Similarities.   Now let's consider some of the similarities between the two types of interviews.

1. *Rapport.* Interviewers and therapists must establish an accepting atmosphere in which interviewees/clients feel comfortable talking about themselves. This requires interviewers and therapists to be respectful, genuine, and empathic.

2. *Skills.* Interviewers and therapists must have a sound knowledge of child development and psychopathology and effective listening skills.

3. *Goals.* Interviewers and therapists must gather information and continuously assess their interviewees' and clients' thinking, affect, perceptions, and attributions.

Clinical Assessment Interviews and Survey Research Interviews

Survey research interviews usually focus on interviewees' opinions or preferences with respect to various topics. To obtain this information, interviewers use techniques similar to those used in clinical assessment interviews. There are, however, major differences between the two types of interviews. In survey research, interviewers usually initiate the interviews in order to obtain interviewees' opinions about particular topics. Interviewees are encouraged to give brief responses or to choose one answer from a list of answers offered by the interviewer (e.g., "disagree," "somewhat agree," or "strongly agree"). What interviewees share in a survey research interview has little or no direct consequence for them personally; responses are used for survey purposes, not for making decisions about the interviewees' personal lives. In contrast, clinical assessment interviews are initiated by interviewees or their families because they are motivated to address problems, relieve symptoms, or make changes. Interviewees are encouraged to provide in-depth responses, and the focus is on personal experiences and behavior. Furthermore, *the consequences of the clinical assessment interview are significant to the interviewee, no matter who initiates the interview*—a diagnosis may be made, an intervention plan formulated, or a recommendation made for placement in a special education program.

STRENGTHS AND WEAKNESSES OF THE CLINICAL ASSESSMENT INTERVIEW

Strengths of the Clinical Assessment Interview

The clinical assessment interview serves several functions for children and their families (Edelbrock & Costello, 1988; Gorden, 1975; Gresham, 1984). It allows the interviewer to do the following:

1. Communicate and clarify the nature and goals of the assessment process to the child and parents
2. Understand the child's and parents' expectations regarding the assessment
3. Obtain information about past and current events in the life of the family
4. Document the context, severity, and chronicity of the child's problem behaviors
5. Use flexible procedures to ask the child and parents questions
6. Resolve ambiguous responses
7. Clarify misunderstandings that the child or parents may have
8. Compare the child's and parents' verbal and nonverbal behaviors
9. Verify previously collected information about the child and family

10. Formulate hypotheses about the child and family that can be tested using other assessment procedures
11. Learn about the child's perception and understanding of his or her problem
12. Learn about the beliefs, values, and expectations held by parents and other adults (e.g., teachers) about the child's behavior
13. Assess the child's and parents' receptivity to various intervention strategies and their willingness to follow recommendations

The interview, as previously noted, is a flexible assessment procedure, useful in generating and explaining hypotheses, as the focus of the discussion can be changed as needed. The interviewee's verbal responses and nonverbal behavior (e.g., posture, gestures, facial expressions, and voice inflection) can serve as valuable guides for understanding and evaluating the interviewee. Sometimes, the interview may be the only direct means of obtaining information from children or parents, particularly those who are illiterate, severely depressed, or unwilling to provide information by other means.

Overall, the interview is one of the most useful techniques for obtaining information, because it allows interviewees to express, in their own terms, their views about themselves and relevant life events. The interview allows great latitude for the interviewee to express concerns, thoughts, feelings, and reactions, with a minimum of structure and redirection on the part of the interviewer.

Weaknesses of the Clinical Assessment Interview

Despite its usefulness, the clinical assessment interview has several weaknesses:

1. Reliability and validity may be difficult to establish (see Chapter 2 for information about reliability and validity).
2. The freedom and versatility offered by the interview can result in lack of comparability across interviews.
3. The information obtained by one interviewer may differ from that obtained by another interviewer.
4. Interviewers may fail to elicit important data.
5. Interviewers may fail to interpret the data accurately.
6. Interviewees may provide inaccurate information (e.g., they may have memory lapses, distort replies, be reluctant to reveal or deliberately conceal information, or be unable to answer the queries).
7. Interviewees, especially young children, may have limited language skills and hence have difficulty describing events or their thoughts and feelings.
8. Interviewees may feel threatened, inadequate, or hurried and thus fail to respond adequately and accurately.
9. Interviewees may be susceptible to subtle, unintended cues from the interviewer that may influence their replies.
10. Interviewees and interviewers may have personal biases that result in selective attention and recall, inaccurate associations, and faulty conclusions.

PURPOSES OF CLINICAL ASSESSMENT INTERVIEWS

The purpose of a clinical assessment interview depends on whether it is an initial interview, a post-assessment interview, or a follow-up interview.

Initial Interview

The *initial interview* is designed to inform the interviewee about the assessment process and to obtain information relevant to diagnosis, treatment, remediation, or placement in special programs. The initial interview may be part of an assessment process that includes standardized psychological testing, or it may be the sole assessment procedure. In a comprehensive assessment, an initial interview usually precedes testing.

During the initial interview, you will form impressions of the interviewee's general attitude, attitude toward answering questions, attitude toward herself or himself, need for reassurance, and ability to establish a relationship with you, the interviewer. You will, of course, form other impressions that will be tested and evaluated as the interview progresses. You will want to obtain as much information as possible during the initial interview, not only because your workload may impose time constraints but also because the interviewee may not be available for further questioning. The goal is to gather information that will help you develop hypotheses, select and administer appropriate tests, arrive at a valid evaluation of the child and her or his family, and design effective interventions.

Post-Assessment Interview

The *post-assessment interview* (also known as the *exit interview*) is designed to discuss the assessment findings and recommendations with the interviewee's parents and, often, the interviewee. Sometimes exit interviews are held with the interviewee's teachers or with the referral source. The post-assessment interview is covered more fully in Chapter 7.

Follow-Up Interview

The *follow-up interview* is designed to assess outcomes of treatment or interventions and to gauge the appropriateness of the assessment findings and recommendations. The treatment or intervention plan will need to be altered if it is not effective. Techniques appropriate for the initial interview and post-assessment interview also are useful for the follow-up interview (see Chapter 7).

DEGREES OF STRUCTURE IN INITIAL CLINICAL ASSESSMENT INTERVIEWS

We now turn to three types of initial clinical assessment interviews—unstructured interviews, semistructured interviews, and structured interviews (Edelbrock & Costello, 1988). In unstructured interviews, the interview process is allowed to unfold without specific guidelines. Semistructured interviews are based on general and flexible guidelines. In structured interviews, the exact order and wording of each question is specified, with little opportunity for follow-up questions not directly related to the specified questions.

Each type of interview can vary in scope and depth. Unstructured interviews may cover one area in depth (e.g., school performance) or touch on several areas superficially (e.g., school, home). Similarly, semistructured interviews may be tailored to a single area (e.g., family relationships) or cover several areas. And structured interviews may differ in the coverage given to a particular area. Let's now look more closely at these three types of initial interviews.

Unstructured Interviews

Unstructured interviews place a premium on allowing interviewees to tell their stories with minimal guidance. "Unstructured" doesn't mean, however, that there is no agenda. You will still need to guide interviewees to talk about issues and concerns relevant to the referral problem, and such guidance requires well-honed clinical skills. Unstructured interviews are more versatile than either semistructured or structured interviews. You are free to follow up leads as needed and to tailor the interview to the specific interviewee. You can ask parents, teachers, friends, and neighbors different questions, depending on their relationship to the child (and the contribution they can make to the assessment task). You also can use unstructured interviews to identify general problem areas, after which you can follow up with a semistructured or structured interview.

Semistructured Interviews

Semistructured interviews also require clinically sophisticated interviewers. Although there are guidelines to follow, these types of interviews allow latitude in phrasing questions, pursuing alternative lines of inquiry, and interpreting responses. They are especially useful when you want to obtain detailed information about specific psychological concerns or physical problems. Appendix B contains several semistructured interviews, including interviews for children, parents, families, and teachers, as well as a mental status evaluation (see Sattler, 1998, for additional semistructured interviews). The semistructured interviews presented in Appendix B orient you to areas that you may want to cover. They are meant to be used as flexible guides, not as rigid rules. Use only those portions you think you need, and feel free to modify the wording and order of questions to fit the situation. Be sure to follow up leads and hypotheses. Each semistructured interview shown in Appendix B will help you target specific areas needing further inquiry.

The Semistructured Clinical Interview for Children and Adolescents (SCICA; McConaughy & Achenbach, 2001) is one example of a standardized semistructured clinical interview for children ages 6 to 18 years. It takes about 60 to 90 minutes to administer. After the interview is completed, the interviewer uses a 4-point scale (no occurrence, very slight or ambiguous occurrence, definite occurrence with mild to moderate intensity, and definite occurrence with severe intensity) to rate the child's reports of various symptoms. Standardized scores for several scales are provided for two age groups—6 to 11 years and 12 to 18 years. The eight syndrome scales are anxious, anxious/depressed, withdrawn/depressed, language/motor problems, aggressive/rule-breaking behavior, attention problems, self-control problems, and somatic complaints (the latter for ages 12 to 18 years only). The six DSM-oriented scales are affective problems, anxiety problems, somatic problems, attention deficit/hyperactivity problems, oppositional defiant problems, and conduct problems. Four additional scales are internalizing, externalizing, total observations, and total self-reports. Scoring can be done by hand or by computer; the scoring program includes a narrative report module.

The norming sample consisted of 381 children ages 6 to 11 years and 305 children ages 12 to 18 years from the United States and Holland who had been referred for mental health problems or special education services. The sample was not representative of children in the United States.

Test-retest reliabilities were based on a sample of 59 children seen by different interviewers over intervals of 5 to 29 days. Test-retest reliabilities for the eight syndrome scales range from .61 to .86 ($Mdn\ r_{tt}$ = .78), while interinterviewer reliabilities range from .60 to .79 ($Mdn\ r_{xx}$ = .74). Test-retest reliabilities for the six DSM-oriented scales range from .66 to .83 ($Mdn\ r_{tt}$ = .72), while interinterviewer reliabilities range from .47 to .85 ($Mdn\ r_{xx}$ = .71). Finally, test-retest reliabilities for the remaining four scales are r_{tt} = .83 for internalizing, r_{tt} = .84 for externalizing, r_{tt} = .76 for total observations, and r_{tt} = .81 for total self-reports; interinterviewer reliabilities are r_{xx} = .82 for internalizing, r_{xx} = .75 for externalizing, r_{xx} = .71 for total observations, and r_{xx} = .71 for total self-reports. The SCICA has acceptable content validity and criterion-related validity.

The SCICA must be used with caution, because the standardization group is not representative of the U.S. population and because reliabilities are somewhat low. In fact, the test manual states that the SCICA is intended to be used in conjunction with other relevant instruments, and "should not be the sole basis for making diagnoses or other important decisions about children and adolescents" (p. iii).

As in all types of interviews, your focus during the semistructured interview must always be on the interviewee. This focus is needed because the interviewee (a) may not want to talk to you, (b) may be hesitant to discuss some topics, (c) may speak so quietly or quickly that you have difficulty understanding him or her, (d) may be upset about a remark made during the interview, (e) may be unable to recall some details because of memory difficulties or other reasons, (f) may be physically sick and unable to concentrate on the questions, or (g) may be recovering from an illness that interferes with the ability to converse. If any of these problems become evident, you must be prepared to deviate from the suggested list of questions as needed to handle the problem. Also deviate from the suggested list of questions when you need to probe, follow up leads, or check some point of interest.

Structured Interviews

Structured interviews are designed to increase the reliability and validity of traditional child diagnostic procedures. Such interviews are usually published for both children and parents. Structured interviews differ in the types of information they provide. Most yield information about the presence, absence, severity, onset, and duration of symptoms, but others yield quantitative scores in symptom areas or global indices of psychopathology. They minimize the effect of interview bias and the necessity for clinical inference in the interview process. Although interviewers must receive specialized training in order to administer structured interviews, even individuals without professional degrees can be given this specialized training.

The following are some structured interviews:

- Child and Adolescent Psychiatric Assessment (CAPA): Version 4.2—Child Version (Angold, Cox, Rutter, & Simonoff, 1996)
- Child Adolescent Schedule (CAS) (Hodges, 1997)
- Diagnostic Interview for Children and Adolescents–IV (DICA–IV) 8.0 (Reich, Welner, Herjanic, & MHS Staff, 1997)
- Diagnostic Interview Schedule for Children (DISC–IV) (Shaffer, 1996)
- Schedule for Affective Disorders and Schizophrenia for School-Age Children (K-SADS–IVR) (Ambrosini & Dixon, 1996)
- Revised Schedule for Affective Disorders and Schizophrenia for School-Age Children: Present and Lifetime Version (K-SADS–PL) (Kaufman, Birmaher, Brent, Rao, & Ryan, 1996)
- Schedule for Affective Disorders and Schizophrenia for School-Age Children: Epidemiological Version 5 (K-SADS–E5) (Orvaschel, 1995)

All of these structured interviews can be used for children with psychological disorders, and most can be used as survey interviews. All of the structured interviews either have separate parent versions or contain parent and child versions within the same interview. Structured interviews are continually being revised to conform to changes in accepted diagnostic systems, such as those reported in the most recent edition of the *Diagnostic and Statistical Manual of Mental Disorders (DSM)*. To incorporate advances in psychology and psychiatry, to conform to the nosology of colleagues, and to facilitate billing, use the latest version of *DSM* and the structured interviews associated with it.

Structured interviews generally use the same questions for each interviewee (unless responses require follow-up questions asked of some but not all interviewees). This standardized procedure is particularly valuable when the primary goal is to make a psychiatric diagnosis or to obtain research data. In addition to assuring that each interviewee is asked the same questions, the standardization provided by structured interviews ensures that no topics are overlooked.

Following are some key points about structured interviews for children and parents that interviewers should be aware of (Hodges, 1993):

1. Children are able to answer questions about their mental status.
2. Asking direct questions about their mental status has no negative effects on children.
3. The reports of the parent and child "cannot be considered interchangeable, nor can the parent report be considered the 'gold standard' to which the child's report is compared" (p. 50).
4. In research studies, diagnostic interviews need to be supplemented with measures that evaluate children's levels of functioning and degrees of impairment.
5. Interviewers, even professionals, need to be trained to use structured interview schedules reliably.
6. Continued research is needed to evaluate the reliability and validity of structured interviews for children.

Potential difficulties with structured interviews. Structured interviews have several disadvantages (Kleinmuntz, 1982). Their rigid format may interfere with the establishment of rapport. Answers may be short and supply minimal information, making it difficult to follow up meaningful leads. Structured interviews primarily indicate whether a disorder is present and are designed to produce diagnoses listed in *DSM* (Mash & Terdal, 1988). They neither address the specific family or individual dynamics that are necessary considerations in any intervention program nor focus on a functional analysis of behavior problems. And, unless they are revised, they become obsolete when the diagnostic system on which they are based is revised.

Reliability also may be a problem with structured interviews (McConaughy, 1996). First, young children may not be reliable informants. Second, reliability fluctuates, depending on the child's diagnosis. Third, a scoring format that merely indicates whether a problem is or is not present may be difficult to use because of subtle gradations of symptoms. Fourth, agreement between the responses of children and parents may be poor. Finally, lengthy interviews may challenge children's attention span, and consequently, the information obtained may not be valid.

The use of a structured interview does not guarantee that the interview will be conducted in a standardized way or that all interviewees will understand the questions in the same way. Let's see why there is inherent variability in the structured interview even when interviewers use a set of standard questions.

1. Interviewers ask questions in different ways and may use somewhat idiosyncratic vocal inflections, intonations, rhythms, pauses, and words and phrases (e.g., "you know," "like," "that's fine"). They may make clarifying remarks (e.g., "Can you repeat what you said?").
2. Interviewers may engage in unique nonverbal behaviors (e.g., clearing the throat, using vocalized pauses such as "hmm" or "uh-huh").
3. Interviewers may follow up responses differently, depending on their interpretation of the interviewees' statements.
4. Interviewees and their parents may not understand the questions or may interpret the same question in different ways. For example, research showed that some children and mothers will have difficulty understanding questions related to obsessive and compulsive symptoms and to delusions (Breslau, 1987).
5. Interviewees' parents' levels of anxiety or distress may be related to the number of symptoms they report. For example, research showed that mothers who were highly anxious or distressed reported that their children had more symptoms than did mothers who were less anxious or distressed (Frick, Silverthorn, & Evans, 1994).
6. Interviewers' and interviewees' language and communication patterns can convey subtle unintended cues about attitudes, prejudices and stereotypes, cultural practices, social and interpersonal patterns of relating, and personal likes and dislikes.

We recommend that you study one or more structured interviews. They are valuable in and of themselves, and they also provide questions that you can incorporate into the traditional unstructured or semistructured assessment interview.

Computer-generated interviews. The ultimate in structured interviewing may be *computer-generated interviewing*. A well-designed interviewing program may lead interviewees to forget that they are interacting with a computer (Nass, Moon, & Carney, 1999); the software is intended to make the interaction mimic a human-human interaction.

Computerized interviewing programs have both advantages and disadvantages (Black & Ponirakis, 2000). The software presents the same questions to all interviewees who are assigned to a particular interview schedule, delivers every question in the same manner, can digitize the voice in a dialect familiar to the child, permits children to hear and see the questions simultaneously, and never fails to ask a question. The computerized interview may make children feel more comfortable in giving answers to sensitive questions because an interviewer is not present, increase the sense of privacy because the responses are given by use of a mouse or touch screen rather than orally, and reduce boredom because the process is novel and interactive. If the computer is programmed to scan responses, it can alert the interviewer if answers require im-

mediate attention—for example, if they reflect a response set (discussed later in the chapter) or an immediate or severe problem. In addition, the computer allows responses to be stored for later analysis and allows interviews to be conducted in any convenient location. Several studies have shown that adolescents are more willing to respond to sensitive questions (e.g., about drug use, sexual contact, family problems, or emotional issues) when questions are administered by a computer than in a questionnaire or face-to-face interview (Millstein & Irwin, 1983; Paperny, Aono, Lehman, Hammas, & Risser, 1990; Romer, Hornik, Stanton, Black, Li, Ricardo, & Feigelman, 1997; Turner, Ku, Rogers, Lindberg, Pleck, & Sonenstein, 1998; Wright, Aquilino, & Supple, 1998).

Disadvantages of computerized interviewing programs include the fact that interviewees unfamiliar with computers may be more anxious when answering questions via a computer than in a face-to-face interview. Computers also are impersonal, will miss subtle verbal and nonverbal cues and reactions that are noticeable to an interviewer, do not use clinical judgment to introduce questions or make inferences about the interviewee's nonverbal behavior, usually do not ask substitute questions or follow up meaningful leads, and may have technical problems in presenting the questions and in storing, retrieving, and analyzing the responses.

To be maximally effective, computer programs must adjust to the age and ability of the interviewee. As the fields of artificial intelligence and expert systems advance, computers are gaining flexibility. Computer interviewing may be the trend of the future. In fact, computers are already being used by some agencies as preliminary assessment tools; the computerized assessment is followed by an interview with an interviewer, who interprets the computer-generated data and explores areas needing further study.

Comparison of Unstructured, Semistructured, and Structured Interviews

All three types of interviews are valuable and play a role in the clinical assessment process. Unstructured interviews are preferred in some types of situations—especially during crises, when the interviewee's concerns must be dealt with or an immediate decision about the interviewee must be made. Semistructured interviews can be tailored to nearly any problem area or situation and can elicit spontaneous information. Structured interviews are valuable when you want to cover several clinical areas systematically. It is best to view unstructured, semistructured, and structured interviews as complementary techniques that can be used independently or together.

The term interview *was derived from the French* entrevoir, *to have a glimpse of, and* s'entrevoir, *to see each other.*
—Arthur M. Wiens, American psychologist (1926–   )

INTRODUCTION TO INTERVIEWING GUIDELINES

Successful interviewing requires the ability to communicate clearly and the ability to understand the communications of interviewees, whether children or adults. Even if your clinical focus is on children, you are likely to interview adults as well, because a thorough assessment of children's problems will require you to interview parents, caregivers, and teachers. Although this section emphasizes interviewing children, much of the material also applies to interviewing adults.

During the interview, you will ask questions, follow up and probe responses, move from topic to topic, encourage replies, answer questions, gauge the pace of the interview, and formulate impressions of the interviewee. Following are important guidelines for conducting the interview, many of which are further described in this chapter (Gratus, 1988, adapted from pp. 91–93).

BEFORE THE INTERVIEW

1. Prepare for the interview by considering the purpose of the interview, the physical setting, and the issues that may arise.
2. Decide whether you want to conduct a structured, semistructured, or unstructured interview or some combination of these different types of interviews.
3. If you decide on a semistructured or unstructured interview, know what information you want to obtain and frame your questions accordingly.
4. Learn as much as you can about the interviewee *before* the interview. Consider how the interviewee's health and situation may affect the interview. The more you know about the interviewee beforehand, the better able you will be to conduct the interview and anticipate problems.
5. Be sure that any equipment you plan to use is in good working order.
6. If necessary, schedule the interview room in advance.
7. Make arrangements to decrease the likelihood of interruptions and distractions during the interview.
8. Consider the interviewee's cognitive and developmental levels and his or her ability to report factual information and feelings in the interview.
9. Greet the interviewee in a friendly, polite, open manner and speak clearly, using a reassuring tone.
10. Be prepared to explain confidentiality, and have the interviewee sign any necessary consent forms.
11. Recognize that you may have difficulty obtaining information when interviewees are anxious, upset, resistant, or unable to concentrate. Adjust your techniques to overcome their problems.
12. Be prepared to explain or expand on the questions you ask. Children, in particular, may not understand every question the first time you ask.
13. Develop the art of good listening. This means concentrating on what interviewees say, showing them that you are doing so, and paying attention to what they convey by their gestures and expressions. Remind yourself to *listen.*
14. Establish rapport and try to put the interviewee at ease.

DURING THE INTERVIEW

1. Answer the interviewee's questions as clearly and directly as possible.
2. Periodically assess how the interview is proceeding, and make adjustments as needed.
3. Do not be frightened of silences. Pauses between questions may indicate that interviewees have more to say. Do not rush them. Give them the chance to answer you completely.
4. Check periodically to see that your understanding of the interviewee's problems is correct by offering a concise summary of the essential details.
5. Toward the end of the interview, summarize the salient aspects of the information you have obtained.
6. Remember to ask open questions, to follow up and clarify ambiguous responses, and to probe carefully.
7. Record the information you obtain accurately, either during the interview or shortly thereafter. This is necessary because memory is unreliable. Keep your notes brief, and try not to lose eye contact with the interviewee for too long if you take notes during the interview.
8. Evaluate the information you obtain and decide whether you will need follow-up interviews. If so, inform the interviewee of this fact.
9. Conclude the interview in the same friendly manner in which it began, and, no matter what the nature of the interview, always try to leave the interviewee with his or her dignity and self-esteem intact.
10. At the end of the interview, give the interviewee an opportunity to ask you any questions that he or she may have.

No matter how well you have planned the interview, each interviewee will present a new challenge. No individual is predictable. Even the most carefully laid plans may need to be changed. You must be flexible and prepared to deal with unanticipated problems. Recognize that there is no single correct way to conduct an interview; alternative ways of asking questions can be equally effective in soliciting information.

Listen carefully to what the interviewee says. Interpret and assess what is significant, but do not accept everything as literal truth; remember, however, that it may be the interviewee's truth (Stevenson, 1960). Let the interviewee's values, culture, attitudes, and developmental level guide your interpretations.

Sometimes the interviewee's words are congruent with her or his emotions and sometimes they are not. *What* interviewees say is important, but *how* they act and speak are equally important. Consequently, you will need to attend to the interviewee's verbal and nonverbal communication. For more information on verbal-nonverbal discrepancies, see Cormier and Cormier (1998).

You will have difficulties as an interviewer if you fail to express interest and warmth, uncover the anxieties of the interviewee, recognize when the anxieties of the interviewee are being exposed too rapidly, or understand the cognitive level and culture of the interviewee. *However, failures are more likely to arise from a negative attitude than from technical difficulties.* Interviewees usually are forgiving of interviewers' mistakes, but not of interviewers' lack of interest or lack of kindness.

To be successful as an interviewer, you must know yourself, trust your ideas, be willing to make mistakes, and, above all, have a genuine desire to help the interviewee (Benjamin, 1981). You must be careful not to present yourself as all-knowing; instead, reveal your humanness to the interviewee. This means being honest with the interviewee and with yourself. Let the interviewee know that you do not have all the answers and that it may be difficult to find solutions.

A good interview takes careful planning, skillful execution, and good organization; it is purposeful and goal-oriented. The success of the interview ultimately rests on your ability to guide the interview successfully. To acquire this skill, you will need practice, which is best acquired by interviewing volunteer children and adults before interviewing actual clients. Videotape and study yourself conducting these volunteer interviews. Ask skilled interviewers to review the videotapes and provide feedback on your interviewing techniques. Role-play various types of interviews. If possible, observe how skilled interviewers conduct interviews, and study their techniques. These activities will help you develop good interviewing skills.

Any interview is affected by interviewer and interviewee characteristics (e.g., physical, cognitive, and affective factors), message components (e.g., language, nonverbal cues, and sensory cues), and interview climate (e.g., physical, social, temporal, and psychological factors). Your task is to be aware of these factors while you conduct the interview and to determine after the interview how these factors may have influenced the information you obtained.

EXTERNAL FACTORS AND ATMOSPHERE

Conduct the interview in a private, quiet room that is free from distractions. Select furniture that is appropriate for the interviewee. For example, use a low chair and table for a young child, and arrange the space so that there is no barrier between you and the child. For an older child or an adult, you can use standard office equipment. You will, of course, need to use suitable furniture for those with special needs, such as interviewees with physical disabilities.

Keep interruptions to a minimum if you cannot avoid them entirely. Because telephone interruptions are particularly troublesome, arrange to have calls answered by the receptionist or sent directly to your voice mail. Another option is simply to unplug your telephone. If you must answer the telephone, inform the caller that you are busy and will call back. Obviously, you should not be glancing at your mail, working on other projects, eating lunch, or frequently looking at your watch during the interview.

Begin the interview at the scheduled time. If you need another session to complete the interview, tell the interviewee. You might say, "Mrs. Smith, we have about 5 minutes left. Because we need more time, let's schedule another meeting for next Tuesday at the same time, if that's convenient for you."

Interview the parent(s) without small children in the room. Small children can be distracting, and you need to have the complete attention of the parent. Ask the parent(s) to arrange for child care, or, as a last resort, arrange for someone to watch the child while you interview the parent.

FORMING IMPRESSIONS

When you and the interviewee first meet, both of you will form initial impressions. These impressions will change as the interview progresses. Be aware of signs of psychological disturbance (e.g., depression, severe anxiety, delusions) and signs of psychological health (e.g., good coping skills, good memory, fluent and expressive language). Also be aware of how the interviewee affects you (e.g., brings out compassion, pity, attraction, irritation, or discomfort). Recognizing these factors will help you regulate the pace of the interview and give you some appreciation of how the interviewee affects others. Your initial impressions will necessarily be subjective, so it is important to try to remain objective and rely on your good listening and observation skills to form accurate impressions of the interviewee.

LISTENING

Good listening skills are difficult to acquire and difficult to implement. Sometimes the interviewer becomes so preoccupied with what should be asked next that he or she fails to listen to what the interviewee is saying. This is especially true of novice interviewers. Effective listening is hampered when the interviewer (a) prematurely evaluates and judges everything the interviewee says, (b) interrupts the interviewee before he or she has enough time to develop an idea, (c) is preoccupied and fails to respond to the interviewee's concerns, or (d) is uncomfortable with silence (Downs, Smeyak, & Martin, 1980).

The following are some steps you can take to improve your listening skills:

1. Make sure that you have no hearing or visual problems that will interfere with your ability to conduct an interview.
2. Attend to your own needs (have lunch or a snack, get a drink of water, go to the restroom) before the interview begins.

3. Maintain interest in and involvement with the interviewee by following the interviewee's communication, paraphrasing the interviewee's communication as needed, reflecting the interviewee's feelings, and probing for important details.
4. Attend to the interviewee's nonverbal communication.
5. Summarize information shared by the interviewee at various points in the interview in order to get feedback from the interviewee and to show the interviewee that you have been listening to her or his communication.

Here are some characteristics of effective listeners and ineffective listeners (adapted from Gratus, 1988).

EFFECTIVE LISTENERS

1. They have sufficient empathy to create comfortable surroundings, which permits the interviewees to give their best.
2. They are so well prepared that they have the freedom and confidence to truly listen to what is being said by the interviewee rather than worry about whether they are asking the right questions.
3. They decide in advance which questions to ask—and when to ask them—so that the interview will be structured to optimize the interviewee's ability to respond and feel at ease.
4. They have cultivated the ability to listen behind the words to catch the slightest nuance of meaning, emphasis, hesitation, uncertainty, omission, or inconsistency.
5. They have the persistence and patience to continue asking questions, even when interviewees omit or avoid giving information; they clearly communicate their expectations for cooperation and are patient but firm in enforcing them.
6. They strive to remain objective when listening; they also recognize that the events and experiences they are hearing about have been subjectively interpreted by the interviewee.
7. They are sparing with words and find ways to communicate their interest nonverbally.

INEFFECTIVE LISTENERS

1. They hear what they want to hear, not what the interviewee is saying.
2. They listen only to those details that interest them and do not pay attention to the rest.
3. They are unable to put themselves in the interviewee's shoes and cannot really understand the feelings the interviewee is expressing.
4. They are too sympathetic to the interviewee's point of view to be able to listen objectively to what the interviewee is saying.
5. They are too involved with their own thoughts and problems to concentrate on those of the interviewee.
6. They are unprepared for the interview, so they are thinking of the next question to ask when they should instead be listening.

7. They are easily distracted by the interviewee's mannerisms, appearance, accent, and so on.
8. They are uncomfortable with silence, lack patience, and will not let the interviewee complete her or his thoughts.

Listening to the Interviewee

Much of the art of interviewing lies in the ability to listen creatively and empathically and to probe skillfully beneath the surface of the communication. *The ability to listen is the key factor in the interview* (Benjamin, 1981). Being a good listener means being free of preoccupations and giving interviewees your full attention. A good listener is attentive not only to *what* the interviewee says but also to *how* he or she says it—that is, to the interviewee's tones, expressions, and gestures, as well as to physiological cues, such as pupil dilation, tremors, and blushing. A good listener is aware of what is *not* said, the feelings or facts lurking behind the interviewee's words. This requires use of the "inner ear" as well as the outer one. A good listener also uses empathic skills to judge when to say something that will relieve the interviewee's discomfort.

Listening to Yourself

Being a good listener also means listening to yourself. Become attuned to your thoughts, feelings, and actions, and learn how to deal with them appropriately during the interview. Often you will need to suppress your reactions so that you can remain objective. If you have videotaped an interview, study the videotape to see how your needs, values, and standards emerged during the interview and how they affected your interview techniques and the hypotheses you formed about the interviewee.

Following are some questions you might ask yourself about your role as an interviewer:

1. Do you recognize how your standards affect the judgments you make? For example, do you think that it is acceptable for an adolescent to be lazy because you were lazy as a 12-year-old? If so, do you say to yourself, "Why can't these parents be like my parents and leave her alone?"
2. Can you determine the basis for your hypotheses? For example, if you hypothesize that a mother is hiding some facts about an issue, is your hypothesis based on something she said, the way she looked when she said it, the way she reacted to your questions, or a combination of these factors?
3. Are you aware of the style or tone of your communications? For example, if you are speaking more rapidly with some interviewees than with others, why are you doing so? Or, if you are speaking in a condescending manner to an interviewee, why are you doing so?
4. Are you aware of your emotional blind spots, such as sensitive words or concepts that may distract you from listening in an unbiased manner? For example, do you flinch

when you hear the term *homosexual*? Do you panic when you hear the word *rape* because you were raped? What can you do about these reactions so that they don't interfere with your ability to listen effectively?

5. If both parents are present in the interview, do you speak differently to one than the other? Do you listen more effectively to the mother or to the father? Why are you doing so?

A good listener is not only popular everywhere, but after a while he knows something.
—Wilson Mizner, American screenwriter (1876–1933)

ANALYTICAL LISTENING

The ability to critically analyze the responses of the interviewee *as* you listen—termed *analytical listening*—is an important interviewing skill. Your questions should be designed to obtain information from the interviewee. As the interviewee gives a response, immediately evaluate it and follow it up with an appropriate comment or question. For example, your evaluation may tell you that the interviewee's response was incomplete, irrelevant, inadequate, minimally appropriate, or appropriate. Based on your evaluation, you decide what to say next. The sequence is

questioning → listening → analyzing → further questioning or clarifying

Purposes of Analytical Listening

Analytical listening serves several purposes (Downs et al., 1980). It will help you understand the interviewee's frame of reference, reduce the interviewee's emotional tension, convey to the interviewee a sense of his or her importance, give the interviewee time to refine his or her thoughts, and relate effectively to the interviewee. Good analytical listening skills include getting the main ideas, facts, and details; understanding the connotative meanings of words; identifying affect and attitudes appropriately; discriminating between fact and imagination; recognizing discrepancies; judging the relevancy of communications; and making valid inferences.

Recognizing Interviewees' Response Sets

Interviewees have certain ways or patterns of answering questions, called *response sets* (or *response styles*). Some response sets simply reflect the interviewee's preferred style of responding, such as giving brief answers, giving elaborate answers, giving answers only when certain of them, or answering only questions that are fully understood. These styles usually do not affect the accuracy of the information.

Other response sets, however, affect the accuracy of the information. Examples include the following:

1. *Acquiescent response style* (usually saying "yes" to yes-no questions)
2. Disagreeing with all or most questions (usually saying "no" to yes-no questions)
3. Choosing the last or first alternative when presented with alternatives
4. Slanting answers in a negative or positive direction
5. Answering in a socially desirable or undesirable manner
6. Giving answers even when uncertain of them in order to please the interviewer
7. Answering questions even when the questions are not understood in order to please the interviewer
8. Answering questions impulsively and then recanting the answers

You will need to be cognizant of the interviewee's response set. When you interview children with developmental disabilities, be particularly alert to response sets that may affect the accuracy of the information. For example, children with developmental disabilities may be deficient in assertiveness skills and thus may be more prone to acquiesce by answering "yes" to yes-no questions (Horton & Kochurka, 1995). When you have a hunch that the interviewee's response set may be affecting the accuracy of her or his replies, introduce questions that will help you determine whether this is so. Here are some suggestions for dealing with two kinds of response sets (Horton & Kochurka, 1995):

1. If the interviewee always answers "yes" to yes-no questions, introduce questions for which you know that "yes" is the wrong answer. For example, ask, "Do both your parents live at home?" when only one parent lives at home, or ask, "Do you have a sister?" when the interviewee has one brother.
2. If the interviewee always selects the last alternative in a series of alternatives, frame questions with an incorrect response as the last alternative. For example, if you know the interviewee is *not* studying biology in school, ask, "Are you studying history, Spanish, or biology this semester?" or after the interviewee says a man touched her but she can't say where and you know she was touched on her buttocks, ask, "Did he touch you on your bottom, your back, or your arm?"

Evaluating Whether You Have Gathered All the Information

You must judge whether you have obtained all the information the interviewee is willing to share with you and whether that amount is sufficient (Gorden, 1975). For example, if you ask an interviewee to tell you about his family and he simply says, "They're okay," you might want to probe further: "Well, tell me about how you get along with them" or "Describe your relationship with your parents." During most interviews, you will need to ask follow-up questions.

The following example illustrates the importance of flexibility in the interview. The interviewer tried to learn about the interviewee's ability to concentrate but appeared to reach a dead end. However, by shifting focus, the interviewer learned some useful information (Mannuzza, Fyer, & Klein, 1993).

IR: What has your concentration been like recently?
IE: I don't understand what you're asking.
IR: Can you read an article in the paper or watch a TV program right through?
IE: I don't read the papers, and my television has been broken for several months.
IR: Do your thoughts drift off so that you don't take things in?
IE: Take things in? Maybe. I'm not sure if I know what you mean.
IR: Well, let's turn to something else. What do you do in your spare time?
IE: I play a lot of baseball.
IR: What position?
IE: Left field.
IR: Do you ever have difficulty focusing on the ball as it's coming toward you?
IE: Not too often.
IR: How often do you drop the ball or let it get past you?
IE: Well, that happens a lot. It's usually because I'm thinking about other things when I'm out in the field.
IR: Do you have any problem keeping your mind on the game or remembering the score from one inning to the next?
IE: Yes. I have to keep on looking at the scoreboard. My teammates always complain that I'm not paying attention. They think that I don't care about the game, but that's not true. (pp. 160–161, with changes in notation)

Interviewees must recognize that you are evaluating their communication and organizing the information into some coherent theme. By conveying an attitude of critical evaluation—interest in precise facts, correct inferences, and an accurate sequence of events—you show interviewees that you want to get beneath the surface of the communication and away from vague, superficial, and incomplete responses.

Staying Attuned

Toward the end of the interview, you can ask about important areas you did not discuss, clarify previously discussed material, make other necessary comments, or invite questions that the interviewee might have. Listening analytically will help you recognize the need for more information. For example, when interviewing parents who are recent immigrants, you may realize that you didn't ask whether the referred child was born in the United States or how old the referred child was when the family arrived in the United States. To know what information is missing, you need to be attuned to what you learned during the interview. Do not wait until the interview is over to evaluate the information, or you will miss a chance to get the important information you are lacking. It is critical that you continuously evaluate the information you obtain.

> *Treat every word as having the potential of unlocking the mystery of the subject's way of viewing the world.*
> —Robert C. Bogdan, American sociologist (1941–   ),
> and Sari K. Biklen, American sociologist (1945–   )

ESTABLISHING RAPPORT

The success of an interview, like that of any other assessment procedure, depends on the rapport you establish with the interviewee. Your aim is to create a comfortable and safe atmosphere that will allow the interviewee to talk openly and without fear of judgment or criticism. *Rapport is based on mutual confidence, respect, and acceptance.* It is your responsibility to engage the interviewee and to encourage him or her to view you as a trustworthy and helping person.

The climate you establish should ensure that the interviewee feels free to give information and express feelings. You must show the interviewee that you are willing to accept whatever information he or she wants to give, within the aims and goals of the interview. Establishing an appropriate climate is not a matter of attending only to the opening minutes of the interview. Because feelings and attitudes can change throughout the interview, you will need to stay keenly aware of how the interviewee responds to you and adjust your techniques accordingly to maintain an open and trusting climate.

Facilitating Rapport

You can facilitate rapport and convey your interest in and respect for the interviewee by doing the following:

1. Make the interview a collaborative effort between you and the interviewee.
2. Give the interviewee your undivided attention.
3. Convey to the interviewee that you want to listen and can be trusted.
4. Give the interviewee reassurance and support.
5. Listen to the interviewee openly and nonjudgmentally.
6. Speak slowly and clearly in a calm, matter-of-fact, friendly, and accepting manner.
7. Interrupt the interviewee only when absolutely necessary.
8. Use a warm and expressive tone.
9. Maintain a natural, relaxed, and attentive posture.
10. Maintain appropriate eye contact.
11. Ask tactful questions.
12. Time questions and comments appropriately.
13. Ask the interviewee which name she or he prefers to use if the interviewee has several names.
14. Ask the interviewee to help you pronounce her or his name if you have difficulty pronouncing it.
15. Dress appropriately, particularly if you know that the interviewee expects a certain level of formality in appearance.

Actions That May Diminish Rapport

The following actions can interfere with establishing rapport. We all engage in these actions at times, but as an interviewer, you should attempt to reduce their occurrence.

1. Don't tell the interviewee about former clients or about the important people who refer cases to you. It is all right, however, to say that you talk to other kids.

2. Don't be flippant or sarcastic about statements made by the interviewee.
3. Avoid vocalized pauses (such as "um") and don't use empty or overworked expressions (such as "you know," "like I said," "well," "all right then," or "whatever").
4. Don't tune in to only the things that interest you.
5. Don't disagree or argue with the interviewee.
6. Don't verbally attack or belittle the interviewee.
7. Don't try to influence the interviewee to accept your values.
8. Don't register shock at life styles that differ from yours.
9. Don't lecture the interviewee about waiting too long to come to see you or being wise to have come now.
10. Don't interrupt the interviewee (unless the interviewee wanders off aimlessly).
11. Don't be distracted by the interviewee's mannerisms, dress, accent, and so forth.
12. Don't concentrate so much on making a good impression that you lose focus on the interviewee.
13. Don't concentrate on the next question you intend to ask to the point that you miss the interviewee's answer to your current question.
14. Don't suggest answers or complete the interviewee's sentence if he or she hesitates.
15. Don't tell the interviewee how others answered a question.
16. Don't engage in nonverbal behaviors that send negative messages (e.g., frowning, poor eye contact, lifting eyebrows critically).
17. Don't tell the interviewee that you can solve all of his or her problems or give the interviewee inappropriate reassurance by saying that there is no cause to worry.
18. Don't superficially listen to the interviewee, wait for the interviewee to finish speaking, and then try to tell the interviewee the way things "really" are.
19. Don't minimize the depth of the interviewee's feelings.
20. Don't tell the interviewee that you also have worries and problems.
21. Don't be judgmental or accusatory.

Because the clinical assessment interview is a formal, professional interaction, the interviewee should not have to deal with your personal concerns. Most of us as interviewers will occasionally be disturbed or moved by some remark made by the interviewee or will let our attention wander to our own lives and situations. When you have such reactions, redirect your attention to the interviewee. Here are some things you can do if you lose your train of thought during the interview (Gratus, 1988):

> Return to the point where things started to go wrong, and no harm or loss of face will come from admitting the problem to the interviewee: "I'm sorry, I seem to have lost my train of thought. Now, where was I? Could we go back to _____?" In fact, the interviewee might even appreciate your admission, because it will make you appear more human and approachable.
>
> You may not wish to go back but to proceed with the interview, in which case you should summarize before asking the

next question. Summing up or paraphrasing has the immediate effect of getting you back into the flow of the interview and at the same time reinforces what the interviewee has already told you. (Adapted from p. 84)

Rapport may be difficult to establish when the interviewee does not want to be interviewed or does not want the information from the interview to be shared with anyone else. In such cases, explain to the interviewee what he or she will gain by cooperating with you.

Getting Started

Interviewees are likely to be anxious to tell you their story as soon as possible. Therefore, it may not be necessary to engage in small talk—about the weather, baseball, or current news—to establish rapport with the interviewee. Sometimes a general opening question such as "How are you today?" may be all that you need to ask. This type of question gives interviewees an opportunity to talk about themselves and helps build rapport. However, it is also good practice to tell interviewees at the beginning of the interview that it is acceptable to say that they do not know the answer to a question.

As soon as possible, focus on topics related to the referral question, to the interviewee's concerns, or to your concerns about what information you need to obtain. Remember, however, that you may have to take a slight detour at times. For example, if the interviewee is anxious and you know about her or his interest in sports or movies, you might want to talk about one of these interests early in the interview. Although such talk seems tangential, it may help the shy, anxious, or inhibited interviewee relax enough to discuss more relevant issues.

Showing Interest

Showing interest in the information the interviewee gives you is crucial in establishing rapport. Interviewees need to sense that you want to understand how they see the world; that you appreciate their experiences; that you share in their struggle to recall, organize, and express their experiences; that you appreciate their difficulties in discussing personal material; and that you want to reflect accurately their opinions, feelings, and beliefs (Gorden, 1975). You can show your interest by the things you say, by the way you say them, and by your actions. You need to be responsive, empathic, and sensitive.

Handling Anxiety

You will need to reassure anxious interviewees. For example, some children or parents may be too embarrassed to discuss their reasons for being at the interview. Older children may wonder what will happen to them because of the assessment. And most parents will be anxious to learn how severe their child's problems are and what can be done about them.

Interviewees may express their anxiety both verbally and nonverbally. Verbal indications of anxiety include sentence corrections, slips of the tongue, repetitions, stuttering, intruding or incoherent sounds, omissions, and frequent use of vocalized pauses. Nonverbal indications of anxiety include sweating, trembling, fidgeting, restlessness, hand clenching, twitching, scowling, and forced smiling.

When you sense that the interviewee's anxiety is interfering with rapport, encourage him or her to talk about it. Following are some possible statements you might use (Kanfer, Eyberg, & Krahn, 1992; Shea, 1988; Stevenson, 1974):

- "Bill, I know that it's difficult to talk at first. I'm wondering what some of your concerns are about being here today."
- "Bill, it's hard to talk about personal feelings. Is there anything I can do to make things easier for you?"
- "This one is tough, huh, Bill?"
- "Something makes it hard for you to talk about this matter; would you tell me what it is that makes it hard?"
- "I know it's difficult to talk to a stranger, and it may take time for you to trust me. That's natural. I don't expect you to say anything that makes you uncomfortable unless you're ready."
- "It's all right if you don't feel like talking about that yet." This statement gives the interviewee permission to wait but also establishes the expectation that the interviewee will be ready to discuss the topic later and that you will inquire about the topic again.

If the interviewee still will not talk with you, you may need to gently point out the responsibilities of the interviewee: "We have to work together; we can't accomplish very much unless you tell me more about yourself." If all else fails and an interviewee is still not ready to discuss sensitive or anxiety-provoking material, return to the topic at a more opportune time. By being attentive to the interviewee's distress, you can help her or him experience what a therapeutic relationship with you or with another psychologist might be like. This knowledge might serve as a valuable introduction to therapeutic interventions, if they are needed.

Young children may not understand that you expect them to share information with you or even that they have a problem. In such cases, be patient and encourage them to talk with you by playing games or doing other activities (see Chapter 6).

If you sense that the interviewee is anxious about some material that he or she has shared with you, you can probably reduce the anxiety by asking "What's it been like for you to share these experiences with me?" You also can compliment the interviewee for sharing. For example, you might say, "You've done an excellent job of sharing difficult material. It's really helping me to understand what you've been experiencing" (Shea, 1988, adapted from p. 47). Phrase your compliment so that it focuses on the interviewee's *sharing,* not on the content of the statement. You do not want to reinforce certain responses or to hint that certain responses are either right or wrong.

Handling Agitation and Crying

Interviewees may become agitated during the interview, especially if they have recently faced a traumatic experience. As they relive the experience, they may cry or express deep personal feelings. Acknowledge their feelings and give them time to work through them; this should help make a difficult situation easier.

An interviewee who is sad and on the verge of tears may feel especially vulnerable. You might say, "You seem sad now" or "Are you trying not to cry?" or "It's all right to cry. We all cry at times. It's our body's way of telling us we're hurting. [Pause] Maybe you can tell me a little more about what is hurting you" (Shea, 1988, p. 259). However, if an adult's crying is excessive, you may have to be more firm and say, for instance, "Mr. Jones, this is obviously very upsetting and would be to most people. Take a moment to collect yourself. It's important for us to talk more about what is bothering you" (Shea, 1988, p. 259, with change in notation). This comment, though firm, still should be said gently. Also, always have a box of tissues within easy reach of the interviewee.

Facilitating Communication

Use language suitable to the age, gender, and education of the interviewee. Be sure that your questions are concrete and easily understood and that you do not unintentionally bias interviewees toward a particular response (Gorden, 1975). You do not want to say, for example, "School isn't that bad, so why don't you like going to school?" Avoid ambiguous words, psychological jargon, and repeating the interviewee's slang or idioms that are unnatural to you. When interviewing children about parts of the body, *always* use their words for the body parts (and become comfortable using these sometimes uncomfortable-to-use words). Recognize when the interviewee's speech is figurative, and do not respond to it as the literal truth. For instance, if an interviewee says, "I feel like my insides are coming out," you do not want to say "Show me where they're coming out." Use of an appropriate vocabulary, especially a developmentally appropriate vocabulary, will also facilitate rapport.

The following techniques will help you convey your interest to the interviewee, encourage the interviewee to elaborate on her or his response, or ease the interviewee's anxiety (Stevenson, 1974).

- Nod your head.
- Give a verbal prompt such as "uh-huh" and lean forward expectantly.
- Repeat, in a questioning manner, the last word or phrase of something the interviewee has said.
- Use gentle urging, such as "What happened then?" or "Go ahead, you're doing fine" or "I'd like to hear more about that."
- Use the name of the interviewee frequently.
- Maintain eye contact.

- Maintain a friendly attitude, gentle speech, and a kind expression.
- Express signs of understanding and empathy by saying, for example, "I can understand how difficult that must have been for you," "That probably made you feel better," "Surely," or "Naturally."

TIMING QUESTIONS APPROPRIATELY

The initial part of the assessment should focus on topics that are not anxiety provoking or sensitive. Premature or poorly timed questions may impede the progress of the assessment and discourage disclosure of vital information. The way the relationship with the interviewee unfolds should guide you in timing questions and discussing sensitive topics. As you and the interviewee develop a more trusting relationship, you can broach topics that you avoided earlier. Time your comments and questions so that they are consistent with the interviewee's flow of thoughts, while moving the assessment toward areas you want to explore.

The following are suggestions on how to pace the assessment properly (Gratus, 1988):

1. Have a good idea of the topics you want to cover.
2. Have a strategy, but be prepared to be flexible.
3. Focus on one subject at a time and then move on.
4. Keep the interviewee interested.
5. Know approximately how much time has elapsed (or remains) in the assessment.

The pace of the assessment should be rapid enough to keep the interest of the interviewee, but slow enough to allow the interviewee to formulate good answers. In addition, the assessment interview should not be too long or have many lapses. For preschool-age children, 20 to 30 minutes may be sufficient; for school-age children, 30 to 45 minutes might be appropriate; and for parents or caregivers, 50 to 75 minutes is suggested. But you are the one who must determine the time needed for each interviewee.

CHANGING TOPICS

Ideally, as noted above, you should proceed in an orderly manner and finish discussing one topic before going on to the next. However, if you find yourself needing to ask about a previous topic, do so. Introduce the question with an appropriate explanation at a convenient time, such as when the interviewee is finished talking about a topic. When you first think about it, you may want to make a note of what you want to ask.

It will take practice and sensitivity to judge when you have exhausted one topic and need to move to another. Continuously evaluate how the interview is progressing and how much shifting you believe the interviewee can tolerate. Some interviewees are disturbed by sudden shifts, whereas others become bored with a planned sequence of topics. As a rule, move on to another topic when the interviewee has adequately answered the previous one. Avoid abrupt shifts that may be puzzling to the interviewee. Transitional statements such as "Let's move on to . . . " or "Now I'd like to discuss . . . " or "We've covered this topic pretty thoroughly; now let's turn to another topic that may relate to your concerns" are useful in moving the assessment forward at a steady pace.

When the interviewee introduces a topic unrelated to the one under discussion, you must decide whether to explore the new topic (and risk losing continuity) or stay with the previous topic (and risk losing additional information). Sometimes the interviewee will change topics to avoid discussing sensitive but relevant material. If this happens, you may want to note that the interviewee evaded the original topic and return to it later.

FORMULATING APPROPRIATE QUESTIONS

Questions form the heart of the interview. Good questions encourage the interviewee to answer freely and honestly about the topic at hand, whereas poor questions inhibit the interviewee or lead to distorted replies (Gratus, 1988). Questions serve many purposes, including (a) drawing out information, (b) amplifying statements, (c) guiding the discussion, (d) bringing out distinctions and similarities, (e) introducing a point needing further discussion, (f) encouraging opinions, (g) encouraging relaxation, and (h) clarifying your understanding.

The way you ask questions is as important as what you ask. Speak clearly and audibly at a moderate pace. When you speak, look at the interviewee. If you find yourself talking too fast, "Stop, take a deep breath and let the interviewee take over the talking again, prompted, of course, by a good question from you" (Gratus, 1988, p. 84). The tone of your voice should convey a sense of assurance and confidence and should vary to suit the topic.

Recognize that the way you ask questions can imply the answers you expect (Foddy, 1993):

- "Are you going to do _____?" implies an expectation.
- "You're not you going to do _____, are you?" implies a negative expectation.
- "You *are* going to do _____, aren't you?" implies a positive expectation—that is, a yes answer.
- "You are going to do _____, *aren't you?*" implies doubt.

The words you stress can determine the meaning of what you say (Foddy, 1993). For example, the meaning of the question "How come you went to that friend's house after school?" depends on which words are stressed. Stressing "how come" conveys surprise or disapproval; stressing "that" implies a particular friend rather than any other friend; stressing "house" conveys a request for an explanation (i.e., of the reason for going to the friend's house rather than to another place); and stressing "after school" implies a request for an explanation (i.e., of the reason for going after school rather than at another time).

When you formulate a question, the interviewee must understand your words in the same way you intend them. The most accurate communication comes about when the speaker (whether interviewee or interviewer) says what she or he *intends to say* and the listener *understands* what the speaker *means to say* (Clark, 1985). However, speakers may mean more than they say, and listeners may read too much into what a speaker says. Speakers will be more accurately understood when their communication is informative, truthful, relevant, unambiguous, and concise. It is only through cooperation between speakers and listeners that speakers' meanings are clearly understood. When a listener misinterprets (or overinterprets) what a speaker says, the meanings attributed to the speaker may be more a function of the listener's interpretation than of the speaker's intention.

> *Men may be read, as well as books, too much.*
> —Alexander Pope, British poet, critic, and essayist (1688–1744)

A Continuum from Open-Ended to Closed-Ended Questions

Questions fall on a continuum with respect to their degree of openness.

1. *Minimally focused questions.* At one end of the continuum are *minimally focused,* or *open-ended, questions;* these have a broad focus ("Tell me about what brings you here today").

2. *Moderately focused questions.* Toward the middle of the continuum are *moderately focused questions;* these focus on a specific topic but give some latitude to the interviewee ("Tell me about how you get along with your mother").

3. *Highly focused questions.* At the other end of the continuum are *highly focused,* or *closed-ended, questions;* these allow little latitude ("What subjects does your son like in school?") and may require a yes-no answer ("Do you like school?") or the selection of one of two alternatives presented ("Do you believe that it would be better for you to remain in your regular class, or would you like to be placed in a special class?"). Closed-ended questions of the latter type are called *bipolar questions.*

Open-ended questions are usually preferable, especially at the start of the assessment, because they give the interviewee some responsibility for sharing her or his concerns and they cannot be answered by a simple yes or no. Open-ended questions give the interviewee the opportunity to describe events in her or his own words and may help you appreciate the interviewee's perspective. One good open-ended question can result in a response you could not obtain with numerous closed-ended questions.

Moderately focused questions are more directive than open-ended questions and are valuable as the assessment proceeds. You will formulate these questions in part in response to the interviewee's answers to your open-ended questions. Moderately focused questions (and closed-ended questions) are more efficient than open-ended questions in eliciting specific information and in speeding up the pace of the assessment. You also can formulate moderately focused questions to obtain clarification of a response previously given by the interviewee.

Bipolar questions are not as constraining as yes-no questions, but they still limit the interviewee's responses. Bipolar questions do not allow the interviewee to express degrees of liking or opinions, can lead to oversimplified responses, and are not suitable for the interviewee who has no opinion at all. However, bipolar questions are useful when you want to find out what the interviewee thinks or feels about specific alternatives or when you need to help a reluctant interviewee express his or her thoughts and feelings. After the interviewee chooses one option, you can then say, "Tell me about your choice."

All three of the above types of questions have their place in the assessment. However, relying on one type or using a type inappropriately or prematurely can bias the assessment. For example, a question like "What's the name of the teacher who showed you pictures of naked children?" is specific and directive and may bias the assessment if used as the initial question in the assessment or to introduce a topic. It assumes that someone—a teacher—showed the child pictures of naked children. In legal settings, questions like this one are called leading questions. Responses to leading questions are often disallowed by the court. However, if the child spontaneously—or in response to an open-ended or moderately focused question—says, "My teacher showed us pictures of naked children," then a follow-up question like "What's the name of the teacher who showed you pictures of naked children?" would be appropriate. Table 5-2 shows the benefits and limitations of open-ended and closed-ended questions. Leading questions are discussed in more detail later in the chapter.

Asking Direct Questions

Phrase questions positively and confidently. For example, say, "Tell me about . . . " or "I would like you to tell me about . . . " rather than "I wonder if you would be willing to tell me about . . . " or "Perhaps you might be willing to tell me about. . . ." Also, state your questions clearly. You do not want to start a question, qualify part of it, then go back and reframe it, and in the process confuse the interviewee. For example, instead of asking "How old was your child when you began to teach him habits of—uh, well, letting him know that he should go to the bathroom when—you know, how to control his bladder?" ask, "When did you begin Eddie's toilet training?" (Darley, 1978, p. 45).

Table 5-2
Benefits and Limitations of Open-Ended and Closed-Ended Questions

Open-ended question (Asks for broad or general information)		Closed-ended question (Asks for specific information)	
Benefits	Limitations	Benefits	Limitations
Helps you discover interviewee's priorities	Consumes time and energy	Saves time and energy	Does not allow you to learn how much information interviewee has
Helps you discover interviewee's frame of reference	Makes it more difficult to control interview	Helps when you have many questions and limited time	Does not allow you to learn how strongly interviewee feels about topics
Allows interviewee to talk through ideas	May elicit long, rambling responses that are difficult to record	Allows you to guide interview	Does not allow you to learn about interviewee's thoughts on a topic
Gives interviewee freedom to structure an answer	Makes it difficult for interviewee to know how much detail you want	Allows you to focus on many specific areas	Thwarts interviewee's need to explain or talk about answers
Encourages catharsis (the relaxation of emotional tension and anxiety through any kind of expressive reaction)		Helps interviewee reconstruct an event	Allows interviewee to falsify answers easily
Reveals interviewee's emotional state		Motivates shy and reluctant interviewees	
Reveals facts about interviewee		Suffices when you need only brief answers without explanations	
Reveals how articulate interviewee is		Is easy for a novice interviewer to use	
Reveals depth of interviewee's knowledge			

Source: Adapted from Downs, Smeyak, and Martin (1980).

The following are useful questions or statements for inquiring about a symptom, problem, or concern.

1. Tell me about _____.
2. How often does it happen?
3. When does it occur?
4. What happens when you feel that way?
5. What is it like to feel that way?
6. What was it like?
7. How old were you the first time you _____?
8. When was the last time you _____?
9. When you _____, how does it affect your school work?
10. Describe what it was like when _____.

Animal, vegetable, or mineral?

That's usually the opening question in the game called "Twenty Questions." Then by narrowing down the scope of your questions, you're supposed to determine the object that someone has in mind.

It isn't guesswork that leads to the right answer. It's using the right questions.

—Research Institute of America

Exercise 5-1
Identifying Types of Questions

Identify each question or statement used by the interviewer as one of the following: embarrassing or sharp question; why question; long, multiple question; double-barreled question; bipolar question; yes-no question; coercive question; leading question; open-ended (and direct) question; random probing question; or highly focused question. Suggested answers follow the questions.

1. Would you rather watch TV or play with your friends?
2. Don't you think that your parents can do anything right?
3. What was her behavior like immediately after the accident?
4. How do you feel about your child's doing things for herself and getting ready to go to a new school?
5. Why don't you listen to your teacher?
6. Tell me about your family.
7. How have you contributed to your child's becoming a delinquent?
8. Although we are here to discuss Tom's reaction to his diabetes, I would like to know what magazines you subscribe to.
9. You know that Mr. Smith is not a nice person. How do you feel about Mr. Smith?
10. Tell me about your neighborhood, then about your family, and then about how you spend your free time.
11. Do you like to read?

AVOIDING CERTAIN TYPES OF QUESTIONS

The major types of questions to avoid are (a) yes-no questions, (b) double-barreled questions, (c) long, multiple questions, (d) leading questions, (e) coercive questions, (f) random probing questions, (g) embarrassing or accusatory questions, and (h) why questions. Let's now consider each of these types of questions and the reasons that they should be avoided.

Avoiding Yes-No Questions

To avoid creating a climate of interrogation, do not formulate questions for which a simple yes or no will suffice, unless you need to ask about a fact (such as whether a child has received help for a particular problem). For example, the questions "Do you like arithmetic?" and "Are your headaches severe?" may bring the conversation to a halt because the interviewee can say "yes" or "no" and then remain silent. In contrast, the question "What do you think about arithmetic?" and the statement "Tell me about your headaches" invite longer replies, giving the interviewee an opportunity to answer more freely and allowing you to obtain more information.

Sometimes children (preschool children in particular) answer questions even if they do not understand them. This is more likely to happen when the question is in a yes-no format ("Was your Dad there?," "Were you in the bedroom when it happened?," "Did it happen at 8 a.m. in the morning?") than in an open-ended format. Thus, avoid yes-no questions if possible; instead use open-ended questions such as "Who else was there?," "Where were you when it happened?," "When did it happen?" (Peterson, Dowden, & Tobin, 1999; Waterman, Blades, & Spencer, 2000). If you must ask yes-no questions, make them as simple and as unambiguous as possible. It is good practice to tell children at the beginning of the interview that it is acceptable to say that they do not know the answer to a question.

Another disadvantage of yes-no questions is that they may require you to ask additional questions (Darley, 1978). For example, "What illnesses has Luanne had?" is a more effective question than "Has Luanne been sick much?" A yes answer to the latter question would require a follow-up question to obtain the needed information. What, when, and how questions are likely to lead to more open and complete replies than yes-no questions. Frame your questions so that there is a good chance of getting the information you want directly. For example, instead of asking "Do you like your teacher?" ask, "What do you think about your teacher?" or "How do you

feel about your teacher?" Using what, when, and how questions is usually a good strategy to encourage the interviewee to describe a problem, symptom, or situation.

Similarly, avoid questions that present only one alternative—for example, "Do you get frustrated when you are tired?"—because these questions, which are restrictive and may be leading, are likely to result in invalid replies. It is better to ask "When do you get frustrated?" or "How do you feel when you are tired?"

Avoiding Double-Barreled Questions

Double-barreled questions detract from the assessment because they confront the interviewee with two questions at once. Here are several examples of double-barreled questions and the dilemmas they cause:

• "How do you feel about your mother and your teacher?" The interviewee might have trouble deciding which part of the question to answer first.
• "What are the advantages and disadvantages of being in Miss Smith's class?" The interviewee might answer only one part of the question.
• "At home, do you do any chores, and do you like doing them?" A "no" response will be difficult to interpret because there is no way of knowing to what part of the question the reply refers.

Avoiding Long, Multiple Questions

Avoid asking three- or four-part questions, as interviewees may answer part of a *long, multiple question* and avoid the rest of the question. Examples of such questions include "Tell me about your parents, your teacher, and your brothers and sisters" and "When did you first notice that you were having trouble with David? Was it before or after you moved to your present neighborhood? And what have you been doing to help David?" Although all the questions in the latter example may be valuable and in the correct sequence, you should ask each separately, giving the interviewee time to respond after each question.

Avoiding Leading, Suggestive, or Coercive Questions

Leading questions (or suggestive or coercive questions) include information about the desired or expected answer. The way leading (or suggestive or coercive) questions are worded biases the interviewee toward answering in a way suggested by the question. Thus they are to be strictly avoided. The *way* you ask questions, as noted earlier, may persuade the interviewee to give the response that you desire. Here are several forms that leading (or suggestive or coercive) questions may take:

1. *Implied expectation.* Examples: "He forced you to do that, didn't he?" directs the interviewee to agree with the re-

sponse expected by the interviewer. This question presents the interviewer's statement as highly probable, thus making it difficult to reject. "What else did she do?" implies that the person did something else.

2. *Identifying the response you expect from the interviewee in your question.* Example: "Don't you think Mr. Smith is a good teacher?" This question puts pressure on the interviewee to conform to the interviewer's authority.

3. *Using introductory statements to cue the interviewee to respond in a certain way.* Example: "It's generally been found that rewarding children for their efforts is helpful in developing good habits. Do you reward Jill often?" This question uses an implied authoritative source to pressure the interviewee to give a certain response.

4. *Persuading the interviewee to agree with your recommendation.* Examples: "To aid Johnny's emotional development, we need to place him in a therapeutic program. Surely you wouldn't want to hold back his progress?" "Miss Jones is an exceptionally fine teacher, and I'm sure you'll give your consent to allow Maria to attend her class for special children." These statements make the interviewee believe that he or she has little choice but to accept the interviewer's recommendations.

5. *Assuming details that were not revealed by the interviewee.* Examples: "When was the first time it happened?" when the interviewee has not mentioned that it happened more than once. "So after that time, after the last time you were touched, whom did you tell?" when the interviewee has never mentioned that he or she told anybody. "That was scary, wasn't it?" when the interviewee has not described any feelings about the incident.

6. *Pressure toward conformity.* Example: "Tom and Mary said that Ms. Jones hit Sara. Didn't you see that too?" This question "uses social comparison (peer pressure) or the force of authority by inducing conflicting tendencies and lowering confidence in an interviewee whose memory does not conform with what is presented to him as others' testimony or opinion" (Endres, 1997, p. 51).

7. *Limiting the number of responses.* Example: "Was it your mother or your father who hit you?" This form of question not only limits that number of responses but also implies that you do not want to hear about anyone else.

8. *Question repetition.* Example: "Are you really sure about your answer to this question? I'll ask you again: Did your mom and dad have a fight last night?" A question repeated immediately following an answer expresses the interviewer's discontent with the first answer and an implied request that the interviewee change her or his answer. However, repeating a question is permissible when the interviewer did not understand the interviewee's answer.

9. *Negative feedback.* Examples: "You really don't mean what you said about your father, do you?" "It is simply not possible that you don't remember what happened last week." Negative feedback implies that what the interviewee said was improbable, incredible, or unacceptable and therefore should be changed.

10. *Threats and promises.* Example: "I will keep asking you until you tell me what your uncle did to you. You must tell me. We can't leave until you do. And you will feel better after telling me." These statements convey to the interviewee that rewards or punishments are contingent on certain answers.

Avoiding Random Probing Questions

Do not use random, hit-or-miss questions (Gilmore, 1973). Using *random probing questions* is like throwing lots of bait in a stream and hoping you will catch a fish. Interviewers tend to use random probing when they do not know what to ask. Here is an example of a random probing question. After a child admits to getting along well in school, the interviewer says, "There must be something that you don't like or that causes you difficulty. How about some of the teachers . . . or other students . . . or recess periods . . . or tests?" It is better to start a new topic than to engage in random probing.

Avoiding Embarrassing or Accusatory Questions

Formulate questions so that they do not embarrass, offend, or put the interviewee on the defensive. For example, instead of asking "How many times have you been expelled from school?" ask, "What difficulties have you had staying in school?" Likewise, for the question "In what school subjects have you received a failing grade?" you might substitute "What school subjects are difficult for you?" Finally, instead of the question "Are you telling me the truth?" you can use "Is it possible that other people believe something different?" In these examples, the rephrased questions are potentially less embarrassing than the original questions because of their softened tone, yet they still might elicit the desired information.

Avoiding Why Questions

As noted earlier, you should generally avoid questions that begin with "Why," particularly when they are directed at the child's actions. Children may react defensively to *why questions,* perceiving them as a request "to account for or justify their behavior rather than to describe what led up to the behavior" (Boggs & Eyberg, 1990, p. 93). The question "Why don't you help around the house?" can be rephrased as "What do you do to help around the house?" followed by "What don't you like to do around the house?" Both children and adults will likely respond better to the alternative wording.

Similarly, a question such as "Why do you drink alcohol?" might cause interviewees to think that you are judging them. Suitable questions are "When do you drink alcohol?" and "How do you feel after you drink?" and "What thoughts do you have when you really want to drink?" Instead of asking "Why are you anxious?" you might ask, "What makes you anxious?" or "What do you do when you are anxious?" or "How long does the anxiety last before it goes away?"

Using too many why questions may interfere with rapport. There are times, however, when carefully worded why questions can be helpful and diagnostic. For example, "Why do you think Daddy said that?" might be useful in a case of alleged child maltreatment.

> *In assessments, as elsewhere, the value of the answer depends on the quality of the question.*
> —John Courtis, British corporate recruitment consultant (20th century)

Exercise 5-2
Rephrasing Questions

Each of the following 15 questions can be improved. Restate each question in a more appropriate form. Suggested answers follow the questions.

1. Do you get along with your brother?
2. Do you like school?
3. Do you argue with your parents often?
4. Is your mother home when you come home from school?
5. Why do you always quit sports?
6. Why have you been sent to the principal's office so many times this year?
7. Why have you been divorced three times?
8. Tell me how you feel about school, your teachers, and your friends.
9. Do you fight with your mother, and how does it make you feel?
10. Kenny is experiencing some learning difficulties, and I believe a special class might be helpful. Surely you wouldn't object to a program that can offer Kenny the extra help he needs?
11. Don't you think Mary tried to be a good friend to you?
12. Many people believe that it is detrimental to punish a child physically. Do you ever punish Bobby physically?
13. Why do you turn to drinking as a way to escape your problems?
14. You've always been treated fairly at school, haven't you?
15. Who could justify a stupid regulation like that?

Suggested Answers

1. How do you and your brother get along?
2. What do you think about school? (Or) How do you feel about school?
3. How do you get along with your parents?
4. Who is home when you come home from school?
5. What sports have you played?
6. How have you been getting along in school?
7. Tell me about your marriages.
8. Tell me how you feel about school. (Then, ask two other separate questions for teachers and friends.)
9. Do you fight with your mother? (If yes) How does it make you feel?
10. What do you think about placing Kenny in a special program?
11. What do you think of what Mary did?

12. How do you discipline Bobby?
13. What do you think are some reasons that you drink alcohol?
14. How do you feel you've been treated at school?
15. What do you think about the regulation?

PROBING EFFECTIVELY

Probing is a key to successful interviewing. You need to probe because interviewees often do not respond fully to your questions. As noted earlier in the chapter, listening analytically can help you identify responses that are inadequate (e.g., incomplete, inconsistent, irrelevant, poorly organized, or ambiguous) or absent altogether.

If you recognize the possible reason for the inadequate response, you may be able to determine the kinds of follow-up questions needed. Inadequate responses can occur for any number of reasons (Downs et al., 1980, adapted from p. 88). For example, the interviewee

1. Does not understand the purpose of the question
2. Does not understand how you might use the information
3. Does not understand the kind of answer you want
4. Is uncertain about how much of an answer to give
5. Does not understand the language in the question
6. Is unwilling to give information that is personal or that may place him or her in a threatening or dangerous position
7. May not know the answer
8. May not remember what happened
9. Finds it difficult to articulate feelings
10. Thinks that you will not accept or understand the answer
11. Does not care about you and therefore chooses not to cooperate fully
12. Does not care about the assessment and therefore chooses not to cooperate fully
13. Fears the results of giving an answer
14. Has competing thoughts, so his or her concentration lags

Probing Techniques

There are many types of probing questions and comments that you can use (see Table 5-3). Let's examine elaboration, clarification, repetition, challenging, silence, neutral phrases, reflective statements, periodic summaries, checking the interviewee's understanding, and miscellaneous probing techniques (Downs et al., 1980).

Elaboration. You will need to ask for *elaboration* when you want the interviewee to provide additional information. Following are examples of comments you might use:

1. "Tell me more about that."
2. "Is there anything else?"
3. "Please go on."
4. "What happened then?"

**Table 5-3
Types of Probing Techniques**

Technique	Purpose	Example
Elaboration	To encourage the interviewee to provide additional information	"Tell me more about your family."
Clarification	To encourage the interviewee to clarify details that are not clear to you	"What do you mean by that?"
Repetition	To encourage the interviewee to respond when he or she has not answered your question	"Tell me again about things that you get angry about."
Challenging	To encourage the interviewee to clarify an incongruity in her or his communication	"Just a few minutes ago you said that you didn't like school, but just now you said that the art teacher was nice. How do you explain these different feelings?"
Silence	To encourage the interviewee to think or reflect about a topic or feeling	Appearing interested in the interviewee or nodding your head
Neutral phrases	To encourage the interviewee to keep talking	"Uh huh," "I see," or "okay"
Reflective statements	To encourage the interviewee to tell you more about a topic	"You seem to be saying that it's very difficult for you to talk with your father."
Periodic summaries	To encourage the interviewee to comment on the adequacy of your understanding and interpretation, to inform the interviewee that what he or she said was what he or she intended to say, to inform the interviewee that you have been listening, to build transitions from one topic to the next and give direction to the interview, to signal that you are at the end of the interview, and to sum up and clarify what you have covered	"Let's see if I understand what is going on at school. . . ."
Checking the interviewee's understanding	To encourage the interviewee to comment on your interpretation of her or his situation	"What do you think about what I just said about your family?"
Miscellaneous probing techniques	To encourage the interviewee to discuss a topic more fully	Echoing the interviewee's last words (e.g., "You are really angry with your mother"), pausing expectantly, or repeating the interviewee's reply and then pausing

5. "Please expand on that."
6. "What happened before the incident?"
7. "What happened after the incident?"
8. "How did you feel about that?"
9. "What were you thinking then?"
10. "Other reasons?"

Clarification.   You will need to ask for *clarification* when you do not understand what the interviewee is saying or when you are puzzled by some details. Because you are responsible for maintaining effective communication, you need to clarify ambiguous communication as it occurs. You do not want to risk getting the meaning wrong by guessing at what the interviewee means. For example, if a girl says, "I study a little every day," find out what she means by "a little." Do not take for granted that your understanding of "a little" is the same as hers.

Here are other examples of how an interviewer might clarify an interviewee's ambiguous statements:

IE: When my son was 12 years old, he had a bad attack of nerves.
IR: What do you mean by a "bad attack of nerves"?

IE: My son is not doing well.
IR: How is he not doing well?

IE: I'm doing okay in my history class.
IR: Tell me more about how you're doing.

Sometimes an interviewer can help the interviewee clarify and describe an indefinite communication (Stevenson, 1960):

IE: When I was younger, I had a nervous breakdown.
IR: Tell me about the nervous breakdown.
IE: I was just nervous then. It was terrible.
IR: Well, tell me exactly how you felt.
IE: I was weak all over, and I couldn't concentrate. I felt panicky and would go to bed for hours at a time, and. . . .

Following are examples of probing comments useful for clarifying communication:

1. "So what you're saying is . . . "
2. "Tell me what you mean by that."
3. "I'm not sure what you mean. Tell me more about that."
4. "Give me some examples."
5. "I seem to have lost your point. I'm not sure what you meant by . . . "
6. "Did that seem to make a difference to you?"
7. "You mentioned that you can't sleep at night. What do you do when you can't sleep at night?"
8. "How did you go about toilet training Sally?"
9. "Which subjects do you like best?"
10. "You mentioned that you like sports. Tell me what kinds of sports you like."
11. "You said that you have trouble making friends. What kind of trouble are you having?"
12. "Horrible? Tell me about how she is horrible."
13. "When did your son do that?"
14. "What is it about talking about _____ that makes you anxious?"
15. "What were you thinking about when you were crying just now?"
16. "Tell me what it is about _____ that makes you angry."

When interviewees tell you about their medical or psychological symptoms, ask them to describe the symptoms in more detail, especially when the symptoms are ambiguous or vague. Examples of ambiguous words often used to refer to symptoms include *spells, blackouts, dizziness, weakness, nervous breakdown, nervousness, tension, anxiety, depression, voices in the head, peculiar thoughts,* and *strange feelings.* Also clarify any terms or phrases that are unfamiliar to you. Finally, ask about terms that may have multiple or unique connotations, such as *touching, stroking, physical contact, punished, caressed, hurt, thing, da da,* and *wee wee.* Your goal is to understand the interviewees' meaning, *not* to change or reject their language.

Repetition. Use *repetition* when the interviewee has not answered your question. You can repeat the question in the same words or with slight modification. Here are two examples in which the interviewer uses repetition:

IR: How are you doing in school?
IE: I'm taking five subjects.
IR: Tell me how you're doing in these subjects.

IR: What games do you like to play?
IE: I like lots of games.
IR: What are the names of some of the games you like?

Challenging. Use *challenging* (also referred to as *confrontation*) to clarify incongruities in the interviewee's communication. For example, if the interviewee makes contradictory statements—"I hate school" and "I really enjoy woodshop"—you might want to call the inconsistency to his or her attention. You might say, "Before, you said that you hate school; now you say you enjoy one of your classes. Can you tell me about what you said?" or "Well, I may have misunderstood what you said about hating school." By exploring inconsistencies, contradictions, or omissions with tact, you may learn that the interviewee had forgotten some important fact, made a mistake, or needed the additional questioning to reveal potentially embarrassing material. Challenging may elicit more complete information or give the interviewee an opportunity to elaborate or change statements. Although challenging is potentially unpleasant to the interviewee (and to the interviewer-in-training), it can sometimes be helpful, especially when the interviewee is unaware of her or his inconsistency.

Challenging marked discrepancies between the verbal and nonverbal communication of the interviewee requires particular skill and sensitivity. Incongruity between verbal and nonverbal behaviors suggests that the interviewee may be experiencing conflict or ambivalent feelings. For example, an interviewee may reveal discomfort by tapping his or her feet and clasping hands while saying extremely pleasant things. Without knowing whether the interviewee is aware of the inconsistency, you must judge whether to call attention to discrepant communication. If you decide to do so, be cautious, because the interviewee may believe that you are being critical. When you challenge the interviewee, do so nonthreateningly and prepare to explore her or his feelings. Do not challenge to punish, accuse, or judge the interviewee. When the relationship is on a firm basis and an accepting climate has been created, the interviewee may accept challenging more readily.

Challenging also can be used with interviewees who are defensive or malingering or who are disengaged from the assessment. In these cases, challenging is designed to get information about their motivation.

The following questions, designed primarily for adolescents and older individuals, give interviewees an opportunity to address ambiguities and incongruities that arise during the assessment (adapted from Rogers, 1988a, pp. 302–303).

INTERVIEWEES WHO ARE DEFENSIVE

If interviewees are unwilling to share relevant material with you because of shyness, lack of trust, guilt, or embarrassment, one of these comments may help them disclose more:

1. "Although you're telling me that everything is going fine, when I hear about [description of current problems] I have some trouble understanding this. Could you help me to understand?"
2. "I know how much you want me to believe that you have your problems well under control, but when I see your [clinical observations of the interviewee] I wonder if this is the case. What do you think?"
3. "Life is not all black and white. Whenever someone tells me only good things, I wonder whether anything is being left out."
4. "According to you, you're having no difficulty handling [describe a specific problem], but according to [a reliable informant], it appears that _____. How do you explain the difference of opinion?"

INTERVIEWEES WHO MAY BE MALINGERING

Interviewees may pretend that they cannot do something or do not know something when they are trying to feign illness, cover up information, or lie. In such cases, the following comments may prove useful:

1. "Some problems you describe are rarely seen in teenagers. I'm worried that you might see things as worse than they are."
2. "Earlier in the evaluation you told me _____; now you're telling me _____. I'm having trouble putting this together."
3. "Although you have told me about [description of current problems], to me you haven't appeared _____."
4. "I haven't been able to understand how things are quite as bad as you tell me they are."
5. "According to you, you have [current problems], but according to [a reliable informant], you are _____. Can you help me understand this?"

INTERVIEWEES WHO ARE DISENGAGED

If interviewees fail to cooperate with you, do not seem to care about their responses, or seem remote, you might try one of the following:

1. "I don't think we got off on the right foot. Can we start over? Tell me in your words what you see as your problems."
2. "It seems as if you're not listening to what I have to say, and I know that you're not particularly pleased about being here. How can we make sure that this isn't a waste of time for you?"
3. "I know you took these [psychological tests] for me, but I get the impression that you didn't pay much attention to how you answered them. What about [specific test items], to which you gave different answers at different times?"

The following excerpt shows how an interviewer talking to a 9-year-old boy called attention to a discrepant communication (Reisman, 1973):

IR: You seem to feel very angry.
IE: (Nods, but says nothing)
IR: Can you tell me about your being angry?
IE: The kids at school make fun of me.
IR: Oh, in what way?
IE: They say I don't try in sports, and that I'm no good in baseball.
IR: And this makes you feel angry with them.
IE: No, I don't care. They're not my friends so I don't care what they say.
IR: (Pause) Well, then I wonder about why you would like help.
IE: (Pause) I'd like to have more friends in school.
IR: (Pause) On the one hand, you're saying you don't care about them, and on the other, you're saying you would like them to be your friends.
IE: (Begins to cry quietly) I do want them to be my friends. (Adapted from pp. 60–61)

Silence.   Use *silence* to allow the interviewee more time to reflect or think. Silence expresses that you are willing to wait for him or her to tell you more about the topic. Occasionally, silence will increase the interviewee's anxiety and lead him or her to talk more. You can accompany your silence with nonverbal cues, such as a nod of your head. Silence is discussed in more detail later in the chapter.

Neutral phrases.   Use *neutral phrases*—such as "uh huh," "I see," or "okay"—to encourage the interviewee to keep talking and to show that you are being attentive.

Reflective statements.   Use *reflective statements,* in which you paraphrase a statement made by the interviewee, to get the interviewee to tell you more about a topic. Useful phrases with which to begin reflective restatements include

1. "You feel that . . . "
2. "It seems to you that . . . "
3. "In other words, . . . "
4. "As you see it, . . . "
5. "What you seem to be saying is that . . . "
6. "You believe . . . "
7. "You think . . . "
8. "I gather that . . . "
9. "It sounds as if . . . "
10. "From what I hear you saying, . . . "
11. "If I'm hearing you correctly, . . . "

Reflection is a useful technique for guiding the interviewee; however, do not restate comments so frequently that you disturb the flow of conversation. Where possible, your restatements should be in your own words. Reflect the content, thoughts, and feelings of the interviewee, but do not parrot.

The following dialogue illustrates the use of a reflective statement in an assessment with a 12-year-old boy:

IE: My teacher doesn't want to help me. In fact, I think she's got something against me.
IR: You feel she doesn't like you.
IE: Well, she's very unfriendly, ever since I got into trouble last year.
IR: She hasn't liked you since last year?
IE: Yes, well, I think so. When I got into trouble last year, she. . . .

Additional uses of reflection.   Reflection also serves other purposes. By occasionally reflecting and paraphrasing the communication of interviewees, you provide them with valuable feedback, let them know that you understand them, and help them verbalize other feelings and concerns more clearly. A statement such as "So you felt that you had no one to turn to" conveys that you are paying attention. Additionally, if your understanding of a statement is inaccurate, interviewees can correct your interpretation. Reflection also can help you when you are not sure what question to ask or in what direction you want the assessment to go. Reflection not only will buy you some time but also may aid interviewees. It changes the focus from questioning and probing to a more personal approach. Finally, you can use reflection when interviewees use jargon or terms you believe they do not understand. By paraphrasing their words, you provide a prompt that may lead them to clarify their comments (Boggs & Eyberg, 1990).

Reflection of both content and nonverbal behavior.   You can reflect both the content of the interviewees' communication and their nonverbal behavior. In reflecting the content of an interviewee's communication, paraphrase the main ideas of the communication without parroting the communication. For example, after an interviewee's lengthy description of a fight at school, you might make the following summary statement: "What you're saying is that you couldn't go back to school after the fight because everybody would look at you."

Interviewees' nonverbal behavior includes affect, gestures, posture, tone of voice, and facial expressions. By reflecting the interviewee's affect, you not only show understanding but also implicitly give him or her permission to experience the emotion. For example, when the interviewee is crying, you might say, "I can see that it makes you sad to talk about this" (Stevenson, 1974). Such remarks may help interviewees experience strong emotions or relive events during the assessment. But you must be cautious; otherwise, interviewees may become more focused on their feelings than on providing the requested information. Supplement your reflection of feelings with nonverbal indications of acceptance, such as smiling or nodding your head.

When an interviewee's nonverbal behavior expresses something that she or he has not yet verbalized, consider making a comment. You might say, for example, "You seem to be fidgety," "You looked frightened when you said that," or "Your fists were clenched when you were talking just now." The interviewee's nonverbal behavior also may be expressing something about you, the interviewer—"You bore me"—or some need—"I have to go to the bathroom." Reflecting nonverbal behavior may be especially useful when there is an impasse during the assessment. However, this technique may make interviewees self-conscious and hinder their communication, so use it with caution.

Exercise 5-3
Interpreting Nonverbal Behaviors

Read each statement and describe what the gestures might mean. Then compare your answers with the suggested interpretations that follow and with those of your classmates. The examples are adapted from Okun (1982).

1. A father walks into your office, takes off his coat, loosens his tie, sits, and puts his feet up on a chair.
2. An adolescent walks into your office, sits erect, and clasps her arms across her chest before saying a word.
3. An adolescent rests her cheek on her hand, strokes her chin, cocks her head slightly to one side, and nods deeply.
4. A father walks into your office, sits as far away as he can, folds his arms, crosses his legs, tilts the chair backward, and looks over your head.
5. A child refuses to talk and avoids eye contact with you.
6. A child gazes at you and stretches out her hands with her palms up.
7. A child quickly covers his mouth with his hand after revealing some sensitive material.
8. An adolescent holds one arm behind her back and clenches her hand tightly while using the other hand to grip her wrist or arm.

9. A mother crosses her legs and moves her foot in a slight kicking motion, while simultaneously drumming her fingers.
10. An adolescent sits forward in his chair, tilting his head and nodding at intervals.

Suggested Interpretations

1. Relaxed, comfortable, confident, feels in control of situation, not taking situation seriously, situation not important, may not care, trying to intimidate
2. Uncomfortable, anxious, hostile and defiant, defensive, upset, it has taken some effort to come to talk with you
3. Listening, thinking, paying attention, eager to please, seductive, reflective, looks interested
4. Uncomfortable, avoidant, resistant, anxious, fearful, defensive, doesn't want to be there, forced to come, feels intimidated
5. Uncooperative, hostile, angry, negative, intimidated, fearful, shy, anxious, doesn't want to be there, forced to come (Conversely, the child may be showing respect. For example, if the child is Native American or Hispanic American, he or she may avoid eye contact but not necessarily refuse to talk.)
6. Helpless, wants help, feels at a loss, shows trust, wants to be comforted
7. Regret, trying to take back what he said, wishes he hadn't said it, perhaps embarrassed, told not to say something and said it, realizes it was inappropriate or dangerous
8. Extremely anxious and tense, making an effort to keep herself where she is
9. Bored, somewhat anxious, impatient, not in agreement, wants to finish
10. Attentive, interested, eager to please, might be listening, wants your trust

---

Rigid versus reflecting interviewer styles. The rigid style of interviewing yields information, but often makes the interviewer appear to be distant and aloof. The reflective style of interviewing, in contrast, not only yields information but also gives interviewees a sense that the interviewer is "with" them and thus facilitates a smooth flow of information.

Let's look at an example of a rigid interviewing style followed by an example of a reflective interviewing style (Shea, 1988, pp. 105–107, with changes in notation).

RIGID STYLE OF INTERVIEWING

IE: The pressures at home have really reached a crisis point. I'm not certain where it will all lead; I only know I'm feeling the heat.
IR: What's your appetite like?
IE: I guess it's okay. . . .
IR: What's your sleep like?
IE: Not too good. I have a hard time falling asleep. My days are such a blur. I never feel balanced, even when I try to fall asleep. I can't concentrate enough to even read.
IR: What about your ability to concentrate?
IE: What do you mean?
IR: Have you noticed any changes in how you study?
IE: Maybe a little.
IR: In what direction?

IE: I guess I can't study as well.

IR: And what about your energy level? How has it been?

IE: Fairly uneven. It's hard to explain; but sometimes I don't feel like doing anything.

REFLECTIVE STYLE OF INTERVIEWING

IE: The pressures at home have really reached a crisis point. I'm not certain where it will all lead; I only know I'm feeling the heat.

IR: Sounds like you've been going through a lot. How has it affected the way you feel in general?

IE: I always feel drained. I'm simply tired. Life seems like one giant chore. And I can't sleep well.

IR: Tell me about the problems you're having with your sleep.

IE: I can't fall asleep. It takes several hours just to get to sleep. I'm wired. I'm wired even in the day. And I'm so agitated I can't concentrate, even enough to read to put myself to sleep.

IR: Once you're asleep, do you stay asleep?

IE: Never; I bet I wake up four or five times a night. And about 5 a.m. I'm awake, as if someone slapped me.

IR: How do you mean?

IE: It's like an alarm went off, and no matter how hard I try, I can't get back to sleep.

IR: What do you do instead?

IE: Worry. . . . I'm not kidding. . . . My mind fills with all sorts of worthless junk.

IR: You mentioned earlier that you have problems with concentration. Tell me a little more about that.

IE: Just simply can't function like I used to. Reading, doing homework, all those things take much longer than usual. It really disturbs me. My system seems out of whack.

IR: Do you think your appetite has been affected as well?

IE: No question. My appetite is way down. Food tastes like paste; really very little taste at all. I've even lost weight.

IR: About how much?

IE: Oh, about five pounds.

IR: Over how long a time?

IE: Maybe over a month or two.

Exercise 5-4
Selecting the Appropriate Reflective Response

This exercise is designed to check on your ability to give appropriate replies. It contains statements made by mothers of disabled children. Each statement is accompanied by two possible interviewer replies. Select the interviewer reply you prefer, and give a justification for your selection. Then compare your choices to those following the items. This exercise was adapted, with permission of the author, from P. J. Winton (1992), *Communicating with Families in Early Intervention: A Training Module,* Frank Porter Graham Child Development Center, pp. 9–10.

1. IE: I try, honestly, to do the physical therapy exercises, but I don't get anywhere. Working hard doesn't seem to make any difference; he's still so far behind.
   IR-1: I guess you're depressed.
   IR-2: You sound frustrated.
2. IE: What can I do? I don't know anything about babies with problems. I know I should do something, but I don't know what.

   IR-1: You sound as if you've given up all hope.
   IR-2: It's hard to know which way to turn.
3. IE: (Showing interviewer a snapshot of her son) You should have seen him at his party. He was really something . . . sitting up like a big boy with all of the other children.
   IR-1: That's cute. You really enjoyed seeing him have so much fun.
   IR-2: That's cute. But don't get your hopes up. You know he's not always going to be able to participate with normal kids.
4. IE: (With head down, speaking in a low tone of voice) I was going out of town, but now my mother-in-law is coming for the weekend.
   IR-1: You don't look too happy about that.
   IR-2: It sounds as if that will be just as enjoyable.
5. IE: Jesse is going to be evaluated at the clinic next week. I'm eager to find out more about his condition, but I know it's going to be a long, hard day.
   IR-1: You're looking forward to getting more information, but you're anxious about the long evaluation process?
   IR-2: It's really going to be great to get more information about Jesse.
6. IE: (Said with tears in her eyes) I'm really glad Jason has gotten into the developmental center.
   IR-1: (Looking briefly at her notes) Oh, I know you're happy about that.
   IR-2: You say you're glad, but you look kind of sad too.
7. IE: (Fidgeting, looking anxious, biting nails, etc., and not talking)
   IR-1: Surely, it can't be that difficult to talk about this; I can't help you unless you talk.
   IR-2: (Silent pause) You seem uncomfortable going on with this discussion.

Suggested Answers

1. IR-2's response is preferable. It reflects the mother's feelings. IR-1's response is an overinterpretation.
2. IR-2's response is preferable. It reflects the mother's confusion. IR-1's response suggests that the mother has given up all hope, an interpretation that may not be accurate.
3. IR-1's response is preferable. It reflects the mother's feelings. IR-2's response puts a damper on the mother's joy; the admonition is not necessary.
4. IR-1's response is preferable. It reflects the mother's nonverbal communication. IR-2's response fails to recognize *how* the response was said.
5. IR-1's response is preferable. It reflects both messages conveyed in the mother's statement. IR-2's response fails to recognize both messages.
6. IR-2's response is preferable. It considers both the mother's verbal behavior and her nonverbal behavior. IR-1's response fails to note the two types of behavior.
7. IR-2's response is preferable. It conveys to the mother that silence is acceptable, and it reflects her feelings. IR-1's response fails to recognize the value of silence or to respect the mother's discomfort with talking.

Periodic summaries. Use *periodic summaries* to (a) convey your understanding of the problem, (b) allow the interviewee to comment on the adequacy of your interpretation, (c) inform the interviewee that you have been listening, (d) build transitions from one topic to the next and give direction to the assessment, (e) signal that you are at the end of the assessment, and (f) sum up and clarify what you have covered (Downs et al., 1980).

You can use different methods to begin a summary, such as "Let's see whether I understand what's going on at home" or "Let me see, as I understand things so far, ... Is that right?" or "If I understand you correctly, you're saying . . . . Have I got it right?" Here is an example of a summary statement to an adolescent: "So, you're concerned about your relationship with your father and how this stress is affecting your school work. I also heard you say that you're trying to find some help for your problem."

Checking the interviewee's understanding. Use a *check of the interviewee's understanding* to learn about the clarity of your communication. Here is an example: "It would help me if you could tell me what I just said about the ways we can help Jim. Then I can be sure that I said what I meant to say." By asking the interviewee to help you, rather than directly asking whether he or she was listening to you or understood what you said, you may reduce pressure on the interviewee.

Miscellaneous probing techniques. Other types of probing questions or techniques can be used to encourage the interviewee to discuss a topic more fully. Examples are echoing the interviewee's last words; pausing expectantly, with a questioning facial expression; and repeating the reply of the interviewee and then pausing. An example of echoing can be found in the following exchange:

IR: How are you getting along in school?
IE: I'm not getting along too well.
IR: Not too well?

Do not confuse echoing with parroting. Echoing is a probing technique in which you rephrase the interviewee's statement in the form of a question to get the interviewee to expand on her or his remark. In contrast, parroting involves merely repeating the interviewee's statement verbatim and, as noted, is *not* a preferred technique.

Guidelines for Probing

Decide on what statements to probe by keeping in mind your assessment goals. For example, if statements made by the interviewee convey two or more possible leads, consider your goals before choosing which lead to follow up.

IE: I'm really mad at my teacher. She never gives us a clear assignment. I'm about ready to explode.
IR-1: How are the assignments unclear?
IR-2: You're really upset about this.

Either response is good. The first response would be appropriate to keep the conversation focused on information. The second response would be useful for exploring the interviewee's feelings. You also have the option of using both responses by first discussing content and then discussing feelings (or vice versa). For example, if you initially asked about how the assignments were unclear but also wanted to explore the interviewee's feelings about the assignments, you could say, "A while ago, you said that you were ready to explode about the way your teacher hands out assignments. Tell me more about the way you feel."

We have seen that probing comments allow you to direct, organize, and focus the assessment. You will want to consider the needs of the interviewee when you use such comments. Some interviewees may need to know your reasons for asking certain questions, see that you are willing to listen when they express feelings, or have help in expressing feelings. Be sensitive to the needs of interviewees as well as to your assessment goals.

The following example illustrates several options for responding to statements made by an 11-year-old girl. Each option is followed by a brief comment. Note that some options are preferable to others.

INTERVIEW SEGMENT

IR: I know you're having problems at home, Sara. Tell me about them.
IE: Yes, I am. I'm planning to leave home and go and live with my aunt. It's impossible to live with my mother.

OPTIONS

IR-1: What kinds of problems are you having? (This is an open-ended question that essentially repeats the original question. It could be useful because it gives the interviewee a chance to be more specific.)

IR-2: So you're having trouble with your mother. I'm interested in hearing about the kinds of problems you're having at home. (This comment is similar to the probing question by IR-1 but contains an introductory comment that shows empathy by paraphrasing the interviewee's words.)

IR-3: Is your aunt's house a better place to live? (This closed-ended question is tangential and a poor choice, especially when you want to find out about the problems the interviewee is facing at home.)

IR-4: In what way is your mother impossible to live with? (This is a focused question asking about the interviewee's feelings about her mother.)

IR-5: It sounds as if you may have reached your limits at home. (This is a reflective comment, but it may be premature, because the interviewer doesn't have enough information to reach this conclusion. It is, nevertheless, a useful option because it may reflect the interviewee's feelings about her situation.)

IR-6: Don't you like it at home? (This closed-ended question is a poor choice. Obviously the interviewee doesn't like it at home. There is little reason to ask this question.)

IR-7: When do you plan to leave home? (This is a closed-ended question that asks for useful information. However, it is premature at this point in the assessment. It assumes that the decision of the interviewee is final, which it may not be. Also, it directs the interviewee away from the original question.)

> *"Then you should say what you mean," the March Hare went on.*
>
> *"I do," Alice hastily replied; "at least—at least I mean what I say—that's the same thing, you know."*
>
> *"Not the same thing a bit!" said the Hatter; "why, you might just as well say that 'I see what I eat' is the same thing as 'I eat what I see!' "*
>
> —Lewis Carroll, English author (1832–1898)

Exercise 5-5
Probing Techniques

This exercise has three parts. The instructions are presented at the beginning of each part.

Part 1. Identifying Probing Techniques

Identify the probing technique used by the interviewer in each of the following interview segments. In segments 3, 4, and 5, identify the probing technique used in the statement followed by an asterisk. Select from the following techniques: repetition, reflective statement, probe for elaboration, use of neutral phrases, clarification probe, and challenging probe. Suggested answers follow the interview segments.

1. IE: The other day at school I got into a fight with my best friend.
   IR: What happened to cause the fight?
2. IE: My mother is always on my back.
   IR: What does she get on your back about?
3. IR: What sports do you enjoy playing?
   IE: We play sports in P.E. at school.
   IR: What sports do you enjoy playing?*
4. IE: I get so uptight when the kids are around the house all day.
   IR: Do they ever go play at a friend's house?
   IE: I'd really rather that they have their friends over at our house, so then I don't have to worry about what they are doing.
   IR: You say that it makes you very uptight when the children are at the house all day, but you prefer to have them at home. Can you tell me more about this?*
5. IE: Sometimes I get so mad.
   IR: Uh huh.
   IE: Well, I get so angry that I can hardly see straight.
   IR: I see.*
6. IE: I tell my father the reasons why I want to do something, and he still says I can't do it.
   IR: So, as you see it, your father doesn't understand your needs because he doesn't let you do what you want.

Suggested Answers

1. Probe for elaboration
2. Clarification probe

3. Repetition
4. Challenging probe
5. Use of neutral phrases
6. Reflective statement

Part 2. Formulating Probing Questions

Following are eight statements that interviewees might make. Read each statement; then formulate two different probing responses you believe are appropriate. Compare your answers with those following the statements. The exercise was adapted from Hepworth and Larsen (1990).

1. My mother doesn't like my friends.
2. The work is too hard in school.
3. Other children pick on him all the time because he is retarded.
4. My husband and I disagree about how to discipline her.
5. I think my brother is a dodo.
6. My 10-year-old has a terrible temper. She'll never change.
7. My mom is 45 years old but still acts like she is 16. She just has no patience.
8. The kids don't appreciate me. I have a full time job and also prepare meals and do the laundry. No one cares.

Suggested Answers

1. a. Tell me more about that.
   b. What reasons does your mother have for not liking your friends?
2. a. In what way is the work too hard?
   b. Give me some examples of how your school work is hard.
3. a. What do they do?
   b. How do you feel when this happens?
   (You might want to ask both questions.)
4. a. In what ways do you disagree?
   b. Tell me about your disagreements.
5. a. I'm not sure what you mean by "dodo." Tell me what that word means.
   b. What is a "dodo"?
6. a. Could you tell me what happens when she loses her temper?
   b. You sound like you don't have much hope she'll ever get control of her temper. What makes you think she'll never change?
   (You might want to ask both questions.)
7. a. Tell me about an instance when she was like that recently.
   b. How does her behavior affect you?
   (You might want to use both responses.)
8. a. You must feel very unappreciated and taken for granted. I'd like to get a picture of exactly what happens between you and the children. Tell me about some recent times when you've had these feelings.
   b. How long have you felt this way?
   (You might want to use both responses.)

Part 3. Evaluating Interviewer Replies

Following is a statement made by an interviewee (a mother) and nine possible replies. Read the interviewee's statement, and then evaluate the nine possible replies offered here. First, decide whether the reply is acceptable or unacceptable. Then, describe the message the reply might send to the interviewee or what the reply represents. Compare your answers with the suggested answers. The exercise was adapted from Sincoff and Goyer (1984).

IE: Yesterday, I really ran into a problem with my son.
IR-1: (Silence)
IR-2: Hmm.
IR-3: Isn't he the one who was arrested six months ago?
IR-4: He's always having problems, isn't he?
IR-5: You ran into a problem with your son?
IR-6: When do you plan to place him in a youth home?
IR-7: How do you know what the problem is?
IR-8: He caused you some difficulty?
IR-9: Your son?

Suggested Answers

IR-1: Acceptable. Silence shows that you want the interviewee to keep talking.
IR-2: Acceptable. This response tells the interviewee that you want her to keep talking.
IR-3: Unacceptable. This is a closed-ended question.
IR-4: Unacceptable. This is a leading question.
IR-5: Acceptable. This comment tells the interviewee that you want her to tell you more.
IR-6: Unacceptable. This is a leading question.
IR-7: Unacceptable. This is a challenge.
IR-8: Acceptable. This comment informs the interviewee that you understand her comment and want to probe the cause of the problem.
IR-9: Acceptable. This comment tells the interviewee that you want her to tell you more about it.

USING STRUCTURING STATEMENTS

Structuring statements guide the interviewee in talking about a topic. Valuable at any time during an interview, they are particularly appropriate to begin or end a phase of the interview, to set an objective, or to provide information about the direction of the assessment. At the beginning of the interview, they may serve to reduce the interviewee's anxiety.

Examples of Structuring Statements Early in the Interview

The following two examples demonstrate different ways to provide structuring statements early in an interview.

1. "The purpose of this assessment is to find ways to help your son Wayne with his temper. I'm interested in anything you can tell me about him." This structuring statement made early in the interview directs parents to discuss their son, acknowledges that parents can give useful information, and enlists their cooperation. It also gives the parents an opportunity to discuss whatever information they believe is relevant.

2. "We have about an hour to talk, so perhaps we could begin with your telling me what brought you to see me today." This structuring statement provides a time frame for the interview, focuses on the perceptions of the interviewee, and invites the interviewee to discuss those perceptions.

Examples of Structuring Statements Later in the Interview

The following three examples illustrate reasons for using structuring statements later in the interview.

1. "Perhaps we can come back to what you're talking about later. But since our time is limited, can you tell me about Jane's . . . ?" This structuring statement can guide a parent to focus on the child's problem rather than on an unrelated problem.
2. "You said that Fred has problems in several different areas. Perhaps we could talk about each in detail. How does that sound to you?" This structuring statement can guide a parent to discuss specific problems.
3. "During the last week . . ." or "Since your headaches began . . ." or "When you were living with your father . . ." These structuring statements can guide the interviewee to discuss the precise time, place, or situation that you are interested in.

DEALING WITH DIFFICULT SITUATIONS

Some interviewees will be more challenging than others. For example, stumbling blocks in the interview will arise when interviewees are uncommunicative, impatient, closed-minded, extremely hyperactive, dogmatic, argumentative, passive-aggressive, excessively anxious, opinionated, hostile, angry, uncooperative, highly agitated, disoriented, extremely depressed, or confused. (Table 5-4 offers information on additional interviewee styles that may create problems during the assessment.) The material in this section will help you deal with these and other difficult assessment situations.

Handling Interviewees Who Try to Take Control

When you lack confidence, feel intimidated by interviewees, or are poorly prepared for the interview, interviewees might try to take control of the interview (Gratus, 1988). They may do this by talking all the time, talking either very quickly or very slowly, talking about irrelevant topics, *not* talking, asking questions instead of answering them, asking to go to the bathroom frequently, or any combination of these and other behaviors. Interviewees may sense that you are not in control during the opening minutes of the interview or, for

Table 5-4
Difficult Interviewee Styles

Interviewee style	Description	Suggestions
Apprehensive	Has unsteady voice, has anxious gestures, constantly shifts body, has frozen facial expressions	Help interviewee see that fears about you are unfounded, give constant reassurance, smile and nod frequently, be calm and relaxed, don't rush questions
Arrogant	Answers each question as concisely and sharply as possible, acts insolent or cute, gives impression that the interview is beneath him or her	Help interviewee see how answering your questions will benefit him or her or someone else who is close to interviewee, probe with increasing directness
Crafty	Acts as if she or he has something to hide, tries to play games with you or outwit you	Let interviewee know that her or his ploy is not working, confront interviewee
Defensive	Says "I don't know," is hesitant, exaggerates, or conceals unfavorable facts	Don't hurry interviewee; praise honest responses; ask simple, narrow questions at first
Disorganized	Seems confused or distracted	Be patient, use short directed questions, summarize frequently
Hostile	Appears angry, will not cooperate, withholds information, presents information hurriedly	Remain calm and interested, reassure interviewee that cooperation can be rewarding, touch on neutral topics at first
Nontalkative	Gives one- or two-word answers, provides little or no elaboration	Help interviewee explore reason for silence; spend more time developing rapport; ask easy questions and open-ended questions; relate anecdotes about similar experiences; convey interest by a nod, an encouraging smile, and an interested voice
Overeager	Talks too much because of a desire to aid you as much as possible	Help interviewee realize that you want an accurate and complete answer, don't be too flattered by interviewee's willingness to talk
Stolid	Appears impassive, unemotional, or slow	Ask questions slowly, be patient, help interviewee dig out facts, use ingenuity and perseverance
Tenacious	Doesn't admit the possibility of error; is bold, aggressive, or stubborn	Use polite, indirect, and tactful approaches; don't lose patience
Too talkative	Says too much; gives roundabout, long-winded answers	Phrase questions in a way that limits the scope of the response, tactfully bring interviewee back to topic

Source: Adapted from Donaghy (1984) and Zima (1983).

that matter, at any time during the evaluation. If you show confidence and appear friendly, helpful, and encouraging, they are less likely to try to assume control. If they still try to control the interview despite all your best efforts, remain calm, detached, and objective; evaluate where the interview has strayed; and refocus on the area of concern. Interviewees also might try to control the interview because they want to avoid certain topics, because they are domineering, or because they have an agenda to cover. In these cases, help the interviewees understand that you need to cover certain topics in order to perform a thorough and meaningful assessment.

Handling Difficult Behavior

Interviewees may behave in ways that make you uncomfortable. Let's now look at some of these ways.

Interviewees who become emotionally upset.
When interviewees become emotionally upset, do not stop their behavior prematurely. They may need time to work through their discomfort. By giving them time, you can learn more about their behavior. Dealing with such situations, of course, requires clinical judgment. You do not want to allow

a situation to arise in which an interviewee becomes too disorganized, frightened, or aggressive. You must develop some tolerance for anxiety-provoking behavior, yet know when to step in to reduce or change the behavior if it becomes too intense or is on the verge of becoming out of control.

When interviewees show strong emotions, remain calm, objective, and detached. You should *not* show excessive sympathy and concern, react critically or judgmentally, or pry too deeply. As a clinical assessment interviewer, you want to obtain information, not uncover traumas. If you believe that uncovering the trauma will be useful, refer the interviewee to another source or address the trauma in a separate therapy session. Often, however, interviewees will feel better simply from talking to someone who cares and is willing to listen to them. Interviewees who break down during the assessment are likely to feel embarrassed and awkward. When this happens, reassure them—through your words, facial expressions, and gestures—that it is acceptable for them to show their feelings and that you are interested in understanding how they feel. However, once they recover their composure, continue the assessment in the direction you had planned.

Occasionally, interviewees may inundate you with their innermost feelings and concerns. When this occurs, you may not grasp everything they say. In such cases, make a mental or written note of the areas to which you might want to return. Keep in mind that, at the end of the interview, it might be appropriate to refer the interviewee to a therapist with whom she or he can further discuss these feelings or problems.

Interviewees who make derogatory remarks about you.   In extreme cases, interviewees may become abusive. They may disparage your training, gender, ethnicity, or other personal qualities. When this happens, consider possible reasons for their comments, such as a thought disorder or simple fright. Although verbally abusive comments may make you anxious and angry, do not respond in kind. You must rise above your personal feelings and help the interviewee calm down and return to the task at hand. To do so, you must remain calm, objective, and detached. At this point you have two options: You can ignore the comments or you can use the opportunity to set limits and boundaries. For example, if an adolescent calls you an "idiot" or a "stupid asshole," you might respond with "I realize you're angry about being here right now. But it's important that we treat each other with respect, which includes not calling each other names. Now, I'd like to hear more about . . . ."

Interviewees who make derogatory remarks about other people.   Occasionally, interviewees may upset you by making racist comments or insulting remarks about members of some group. In such situations, you must control your reactions. Remind yourself that the purpose of interviews is to learn about interviewees, not to instruct them or confront them about your feelings. Although the views expressed by interviewees may conflict with your own values, you want to encourage interviewees to tell you what they feel, think, and

believe. You are not there to change their views, but to learn what their views are and, if possible, how they developed (Bogdan & Biklen, 1982).

Interviewees who are uncooperative.   Interviewees may be uncooperative because they were coerced to come to the assessment; they are shy; they resent you because of your ethnicity, gender, or some other factor; or they are unable to attend to or concentrate on your questions. Uncooperative interviewees may maintain silence, show anger or hostility, give superficial answers, or attempt to end the session early. Remember that interviewees may not understand their role in the interview process. For example, interviewees may appear oppositional when, in reality, they do not have the social orientation or the cognitive maturity to know what is expected of them. Although you should make every effort to establish rapport and reduce interviewees' stress or anger, your efforts may not always be successful.

Interviewees who are violent.   Interviewees sometimes can become violent, particularly in emergency wards of mental hospitals or clinics. (This section is adapted from Shea, 1988.) Usually, the signs of imminent violent behavior are nonverbal, but they also can be verbal.

Interviewees may be exhibiting a sign of potentially violent behavior when they do any of the following:

1. Begin to speak more quickly in a subtly angry tone of voice
2. Make hostile statements such as "You think you're a big shot, don't you?"
3. Pace and refuse to sit down
4. Make rapid and jerking gestures, such as pointing a finger at the interviewer
5. Stare with increased intensity
6. Show signs of paranoia, disorganization, or other psychotic processes
7. Clench fists or grasp an object in a way that causes knuckles to whiten
8. Snarl with lips pulled back, showing front teeth
9. Shake a fist or raise a fist over the head
10. Assume a boxing stance
11. Gesture as if strangling an opponent
12. Pound a fist into the opposite palm
13. Make verbal threats that they are about to strike

Here are some suggestions for preparing for and defusing potentially violent behavior (Shea, 1988):

1. Consider taking precautionary measures, such as having help available and having a buzzer signal for emergencies.
2. Arrange chairs so that you have an unobstructed path to the doorway, especially with an interviewee you do not know.
3. Gently ask the interviewee to return to his or her seat when the interviewee paces: "It might help you to relax if you sit there" or "I'd like you to sit over there so we can talk."

You may quietly add a comment such as "It's difficult to have to keep staring up. I think things will go more smoothly if you sit over there."

4. Compliment the interviewee when he or she says something positive.

5. Change to a more neutral topic if the topic under discussion is too stressful.

6. Avoid the appearance of aggressive actions. You don't want to raise your voice, speed up your movements, make angry remarks, or do anything that may increase the interviewee's level of agitation. Instead, you want to appear calm in order to help an angry or frightened interviewee calm down. Speak in a normal and unhurried voice.

7. Assume a submissive posture: Decrease eye contact, avoid raising your hands in any gesture that may signify attack, avoid placing your hands behind your back (as this may arouse suspicion that a weapon is being hidden), avoid pulling your shoulders back and appearing powerful and confrontational, and remain in front of the interviewee (as an approach from behind or the side may startle him or her).

8. Give the interviewee sufficient space—getting too close may result in your being assaulted.

9. Be prepared to seek help if your actions fail. If you become fearful, consider leaving the room and returning with another staff member or a security guard. You can say, "I want to help you, but I will need some help. Please excuse me for a few minutes."

Confronting violent behavior is a frightening experience. Recognizing signs of possible violence and implementing strategies to prevent it will help you deal more effectively with this most difficult situation. You will need to use your clinical skills to help the interviewee regain a sense of control.

You also should consider your personal safety when you interview children and parents in their homes, particularly if you are in an unfamiliar location or dangerous neighborhood. Consider notifying a friend or colleague of your destination and what time you expect to return, or have a colleague accompany you. Work closely with law enforcement personnel or social services when your visit involves interviewing a family about possible child maltreatment.

Handling Sensitive Topics

You can introduce a potentially sensitive topic by pointing out that the problem is not a unique one. For example, if the referral question or reports from others lead you to suspect that the interviewee has a problem controlling her or his temper, you might say, "Sometimes people have difficulty controlling their tempers. Have you ever lost your temper?" If the answer is affirmative, you might follow it up by asking for examples. You also could ask, "Have you ever done anything you regretted when you lost your temper?"

With a parent who may have difficulty restraining his or her own aggressive behavior, you might say, "Sometimes parents can be pushed to their limit, and they're so upset they just feel like hitting their kid if the kid acts out one more time. Have you ever felt like that yourself?" (Shea, 1988, p. 323, with changes in notation).

If the interviewee is extremely reluctant to talk about a sensitive topic, such as sexual difficulties, you have several options. You can ask an interviewer of the same sex to conduct the assessment, allow the interviewee to write out her or his concerns, or ask a person whom the interviewee trusts to get the needed information.

Handling Inadequate Answers

It will not always be easy to learn why interviewees give inadequate answers or why they do not talk much. For example, interviewees may be shy, embarrassed to talk about themselves, or frightened about the outcome of the assessment; or they may not like the way you are conducting the interview. Try to find out why they are not responding and what you can do to make the situation more comfortable for them. You may have to redouble your efforts to establish rapport—be even more friendly, encouraging, warm, accepting, and nonjudgmental. You want to convey to the interviewee that you both are engaged in a cooperative enterprise from which he or she is likely to benefit.

If the interviewee still fails to respond after your attempts to be supportive, examine your behavior with the aid of the following questions:

1. Do your questions make the interview resemble an interrogation, or are they open-ended questions designed to allow the interviewee to talk freely?

2. Are you asking questions too rapidly?

3. Are your questions too leading?

4. Do you convey the impression that you are in a hurry to complete the assessment?

5. Are you speaking in a dull, plodding manner that bores the interviewee?

6. Are you asking questions that the interviewee has already answered?

7. Did you establish rapport before exploring intimate topics?

8. Does the interviewee understand your questions?

Handling Memory Difficulties

An interviewee may have memory difficulties because the events being discussed occurred in the remote past and were not particularly meaningful, because they are too painful to recall, or because of neurological deficits or acute trauma. Memory lapses also may serve defensive purposes, such as protection against further pain. The pressure to recall may in itself be a barrier to recall. To help interviewees recall information, give them time to think without pressure, switch topics and then come back to the topic later in the assessment, or ask direct questions about the topic to help them structure the sequence of events (Downs et al., 1980). However, do not say anything that might implant false memories.

Handling Silences

Occasionally, conversation will halt. Learn to recognize different silences. A pause may mean one of several things. Maybe the interviewee has finished giving information about the topic, needs time to recall more information or consolidate thoughts, senses that she or he has been misunderstood, recognizes that you have touched on a sensitive area, or does not know what else to say. On the other hand, interviewees may be reluctant to talk because of distrust, dislike, or fear of you; fear of their own emotions; fear of examining themselves too closely; or uncertainty about the confidentiality of the assessment (Stevenson, 1960).

Silence also may be a sign of mourning or deep reflection about some past tragedy; in such cases, do not feel compelled to say something to get the interviewee to talk. An empathic smile or a nod of the head is all that may be needed to show that you understand and are waiting for the interviewee to continue. If you do decide to speak, you might say, "Do you want to just be quiet for a while? That's fine."

Note the interviewee's posture for possible clues about what the silence might mean, but be sure to verify your impressions. For example, crossed arms often suggest resistance, but they may just mean that the interviewee is cold.

Statements to make when silence is extreme.   When progress is stifled or when the interviewee is extremely reluctant to continue, you might try discussing the difficulty. (This discussion of extreme silences pertains particularly to older children and adults. Chapter 6 discusses the implications of silence with younger children.) Following are useful statements to make at these times (Stevenson, 1960):

1. "During the last few minutes, you've become pretty quiet. I'm wondering what you are feeling."
2. "It's hard to go on talking about this, isn't it?"
3. "It seems hard for you to talk about yourself. Is there anything I can do to make it easier for you?"
4. "What are you thinking about right now?"
5. "Something seems to be preventing you from talking. Could you tell me a little about what it is?"
6. "I've been wondering if the difficulty you're having in talking comes from your concern about how I'll react to what you tell me."
7. "We do not seem to have made much progress. Tell me what we can do differently."
8. "We don't seem to be making a lot of progress. What do you think is the reason?"

Statements and questions such as these will likely cause the interviewee to respond with renewed interest. If they do not, think about why the interviewee might still be irritated or

anxious. Do not pressure interviewees to talk, and do not get into an argument about their silence. Instead, sensitively and reassuringly acknowledge their right to be silent, and allow the silence to continue briefly before making one of the statements listed earlier.

Statements to make when silence suggests guilt.   If you believe that the silence may be associated with guilt, you might say, "I can see that this is something that is very difficult for you to talk about, but it's important that we talk about it sometime. Should we do it now or come back to it later?"

Interviewee resistance.   Silence can indicate resistance. When you judge this to be the case, the following techniques may be useful (Shea, 1988):

1. Follow up on topics when interviewees give the slightest hint that they want to discuss them.
2. Temporarily avoid sensitive topics, such as the use of drugs and alcohol, sexual matters, or suicidal thoughts.
3. Choose topics that are neutral ("Tell me about your neighborhood" or "Tell me about your hobbies"), topics that the interviewee may have a strong opinion about ("What are some things your father does that you think are unfair?"), or topics that are meaningful or important to the interviewee ("What important things are happening in your life?").
4. Use phrases with gentle commands. For example, say, "Tell me about . . . " or "Let's discuss . . . " instead of "Can you tell me . . . " or "Would you tell me . . . ." Interviewees might answer the latter phrases with even more silence, frowns, or simply "no."
5. Increase eye contact and positive comments. Accompany comments like "You're doing fine," "Go on," or "That's fine" with positive nonverbal gestures such as head nodding. However, with hostile interviewees, these techniques may not be appropriate because they may be unwarranted or misinterpreted.
6. Avoid long pauses between your questions.
7. Allow interviewees to "save face" by accepting their decision not to talk to you and asking them to complete a form or checklist instead. For example, some interviewees who are not willing to talk to you may be willing to complete a checklist and then discuss their responses with you. In these cases, they may leave the examination convinced that they have won by not talking to you, yet they have provided valuable information.

Appreciating silence.   At first, silences may seem to be interminably long, but in time you will learn to appreciate them. Silences can give you some time to think, reduce the tempo of an assessment that is too intense, or press interviewees to assume responsibility for what they are discussing (Reisman, 1973). You will want to avoid silences, however, when they are causing stress for the interviewee.

Handling Irrelevant Material

Some interviewees have difficulty knowing when to stop talking, and consequently they blurt out much irrelevant information. When this happens, redirect them; otherwise, you will waste time and get useless information. Here are some techniques you can use to redirect interviewees who wander off course (Gratus, 1988; Shea, 1988):

1. Comment on what the interviewee said; then refocus the direction of the interview. Say, for example, "Yes, that's very interesting, and we may come back to it later, but right now I'd like to discuss . . . ." This statement lets interviewees know that they might have a chance to get back to the topic at some later stage and that you're not dismissing them completely. It allows you to regain control.
2. Use narrower questions that require relatively short, specific answers.
3. Avoid positive nonverbal gestures, such as head nodding or any other behaviors that reinforce the behavior of the interviewees.
4. Use structuring statements to introduce topics. Say, for example, "We need to discuss how you're doing at home. This is an important area, so let's focus on it for a few minutes."
5. Use structuring statements to inform interviewees about how you want to conduct the interview, if the above techniques fail. Say, for example, "We have a limited amount of time. Let's focus on one important area at a time, because I need to understand each area as clearly as possible."
6. If necessary, confront interviewees with their behavior. Say, for example, "I notice that when I ask a question, we wander off the topic. What do you think is happening?"
7. Guide interviewees back to the topic as firmly as possible. Say, for example, "Let's focus on how you're doing in school this semester. Please don't discuss other things right now. It's important that I learn about how you're doing in school this semester. If we wander off, I'll bring you back to the topic. Okay? Let's start with how you're getting along with your teacher."

Handling Questions About Your Clinical Competence

Interviewees may occasionally wonder about your competence and may confront you with questions about your ability to help them (Anderson & Stewart, 1983). They may ask you questions about your professional qualifications and credentials—for example, "Are you a student?" or "What kind of professional training have you had?"

Challenges to the interviewer's competence usually arise out of interviewees' concern about whether the interviewer can help them, and out of mistaken notions of what qualities and qualifications a good interviewer should have. Some interviewees rely on advanced degrees, whereas others think that if the interviewer is similar to them in race, culture, gender, or other attributes, he or she will automatically be a better interviewer for them. Interviewers and interviewees alike often make the mistaken assumption that only an interviewer who has successfully negotiated all stages of marriage, parenthood, and life is qualified to assess other people's problems. (Anderson & Stewart, 1983, pp. 149–150, with changes in notation)

Other forms of challenges include "I need a medical doctor, not a psychologist" and "You can't help me because you're [too young, too old, African American, Euro American, Hispanic American, Asian American, Native American, male, female, married, single, childless, too problem-free, too different, too much like me]" (Anderson & Stewart, 1983). These remarks reflect resistance by the interviewees—that is, the interviewees may not be ready to reveal intimate details of their lives to you.

Here are some suggestions on how to deal with challenges to your competence.

1. *Don't be defensive.* Recognize that it is perfectly acceptable for interviewees to wonder about your competence (Anderson & Stewart, 1983). Accept their concerns and, to help yourself become less defensive, focus on the interviewees. Find out exactly what their concerns are. As they see that you are interested, caring, and trustworthy, they may become less challenging. You can accept their concerns with such statements as "That's a good question" or "Your point is a good one, which is one of the reasons we are closely supervised in our work" (Shea, 1988, p. 527). If interviewees are concerned about your professional qualifications, you can briefly explain your background in psychology, counseling, psychiatry, or any other relevant field of training. You can say, "I'm a professional who works with children and their families." If you are licensed or certified, you also can mention this to the interviewee. What you do not want to do is to allow the interviewee to take control of the interview (see earlier part of the chapter). If this happens, the interview process may fail.

2. *Be prepared.* Be aware of your own vulnerabilities and be prepared to deal with them. For example, if you are an interviewer-in-training or look very young, be prepared to discuss these issues with the interviewee (Anderson & Stewart, 1983).

3. *Evaluate the context.* Determine at what point during the interview the interviewee challenged your competence. Was it at the beginning of the session, or was it when a sensitive topic was being raised? Consider what the interviewee's challenge may mean, what you may have done to provoke it, and whether the interviewee was trying to turn the focus away from himself or herself to avoid answering questions.

4. *Answer the question.* Answer directly any questions interviewees have about your professional background and training; do not say, "Why do you ask?" Answering their questions directly in a nondefensive way shows interviewees that you take their concerns seriously and that you are not intimidated (Anderson & Stewart, 1983).

5. *Admit that differences may be a problem and appeal for the interviewee's opinion.* Interviewees may be caught off

guard by an appeal for their opinion: "No, I've never had a child with a drug problem; in fact, I have no children. Do you think that's a problem?" (Anderson & Stewart, 1983, p. 136). The request for feedback about what you might be missing may enlist their cooperation.

6. *Use humor.* If you judge that the interviewee would respond favorably to banter, you might say, if your age is questioned, "I'm only 25, but some days I feel a lot older. Does that qualify?" (Anderson & Stewart, 1983, p. 138, with change in notation). Follow such a remark with an offer to discuss the issue seriously. However, be cautious: "The use of humor demands some skill in knowing when it will be effective and appropriate rather than offensive. . . . A good rule is, 'When in doubt, don't'" (Anderson & Stewart, 1983, p. 138).

7. *Use the team approach.* If you are in training, you can say, for example, "Yes, I'm a first-year psychology graduate student. My work here will be supervised by Dr. Smith, one of the members of the staff." You also can introduce the supervisor to the interviewee, stressing that the supervisor will be reviewing the assessment findings and interpretations.

8. *Admit that you will never know the depth of the interviewee's distress.* When interviewees who have faced a severe crisis say that you cannot understand them, admit that you do not know what they have experienced or are experiencing. However, reassure them that you want to listen to them and to understand how they are feeling. By listening carefully to what they have experienced, you will be establishing rapport.

Handling Self-Disclosure

Interviewees may ask you questions about yourself. Be tactful in responding to such questions. However, don't allow roles to switch to the point where you are doing most of the talking and the interviewee is doing most of the questioning. Although some self-disclosure may be helpful, keep it to a minimum.

Handling Requests for Your Opinion

Interviewees may try to elicit your opinion about some personal matter or may try to get you to side with them. For example, they might ask you whether you support their position. Remain neutral in such situations. Simply reflect what they have told you and ask for further information, as needed.

IE: Mrs. Brown shouldn't have placed me on probation. Don't you agree with me?

IR: You seem to feel that she made the wrong decision. How come?

Occasionally, interviewees become more persistent.

IE: It seems that physical punishment is the only way I can get Darryl to mind. Now what's wrong with hitting him once in a while?

IR: You seem to be uncertain about whether physical punishment is okay.

IE: Well, that's not what I asked you. What do you think of physical punishment?

IR: What would you like me to say?

IE: I want you to agree with me.

IR: I'm not sure how my agreeing with you would help you. Have you found much support from your husband?

IE: Not too much. I don't get much support from anyone.

In the above incident, the interviewer tried to sidetrack the interviewee but was not successful. After the interviewer directly confronted the interviewee's question, the interviewee began talking about her feelings.

REMAINING OBJECTIVE

Distinguishing Between Acceptance and Endorsement

Consider the distinction between accepting the communication of interviewees and endorsing their communication. *Accepting* their communication means that you acknowledge and appreciate their point of view; it does not mean that you agree with or approve of it. *Endorsing* their communication means that you agree that their perspective is accurate. Accept an interviewee's viewpoint but do not endorse it. For example, if an interviewee tells you how angry he is about what another child did, you can acknowledge his feeling by saying "You were hurt when he did that." However, it would be inappropriate to say "That was an awful thing he did to you."

Recognizing Your Emotions and Keeping Them Under Control

Every assessment represents a unique interpersonal encounter. Your ability to conduct an effective interview will be determined not only by your interviewing skills but also by personal factors in your life. You must be sensitive to how you are feeling as the interview begins. Do you have any personal concerns that might interfere with your ability to conduct the interview? Did anything happen shortly before the interview to make you anxious (e.g., a death in the family, too little sleep, recovery from an illness, a harrowing experience on the ward, confrontation with an angry interviewee)? Do you feel tired, rushed, angry, or depressed? You must ensure that these and similar feelings do not interfere with the assessment process.

During the interview, you will react to many things the interviewee says. You may feel, for example, sorrow, disgust, embarrassment, anger, pleasure, or amusement. Recognize these feelings, but keep them under control. Again, you do not want them to interfere with the assessment. You do not have the latitude you have in personal relationships to respond in kind to disagreement or anger. If you express anger or disgust, for example, you might inhibit interviewees from talking further about intimate details of their lives. If something is humorous, you can laugh *with* the interviewee, but never *at* him or her!

If you believe that your feelings hampered the interview, look for the source of the difficulty. For example, were you too sympathetic, indifferent, cold, or overprotective? Were you angry when the interviewee was rude or uncooperative, because of your need to be liked? Were you too reassuring, because the interviewee's problems reminded you of your own problems? Were you too talkative, in an effort to impress the interviewee with your knowledge? *Becoming self-aware is an important part of becoming an effective interviewer.*

RECORDING INFORMATION AND SCHEDULING

Recording Information

You should record what the interviewee says, but not every word unless you use an audio recorder or a video camera. If you take notes, jot down the most important remarks made by the interviewee; you might want to use formal or informal shorthand techniques. You can make note-taking easier by telling the interviewee, "I'm taking notes so that I can remember important things you say, because what you say is important." If your notes are subpoenaed, you may have to make them available to an attorney.

Student clinicians frequently use video or audio recordings during training. Skilled interviewers also use audio recorders, and videotape recording is highly recommended, if not a necessity, in child maltreatment cases. Be sure that you have the *written consent* of adult interviewees to use an audio or video recorder. If the interviewee is a child, written consent of the parent may not be necessary in all circumstances, especially if the parent is suspected of child maltreatment. In child maltreatment cases, some agencies routinely tell children that a video recording is being made; others do not unless the children ask. Realize, however, that the presence of an audio or video recorder may affect an interviewee's comfort level and responses.

If you take notes, do not let note-taking interfere with your listening. Do not hide behind your notes ("Let me see my notes about that matter") or use them in a secretive way. Also, maintain eye contact with the interviewee. If the interviewee speaks too quickly and this interferes with your note-taking, you might say, "Please talk more slowly so that I can write down your important ideas." A remark like this, however, may interfere with the flow of conversation.

Scheduling Appointments

If you have a heavy assessment schedule, take a few minutes between sessions to review, complete, and clarify your notes and to relax. Unless you make a point to take a break, you may be thinking about the previous interview when you should be thinking about the present one.

Second Interviews

Occasionally, you may need more than one session to obtain the needed information. In such cases, schedule additional sessions. Here are some suggestions for ways to begin the second interview (Stevenson, 1960):

1. "How have you been since our last meeting?"
2. "What's been happening since we last met?"
3. "Last time, we had to stop before we covered everything. Perhaps we can pick up where we left off."
4. "You may have thought of some things that you didn't have a chance to say last time. Let's talk about those things now."

If these inquiries are not productive, you can turn to specific areas of the interviewee's history or current situation that you need to inquire about. If you administered psychological tests and the second interview occurs after you have completed the formal testing, you can ask questions related to the testing *and* to case history material. For example, you can ask questions about particular responses to test items, clarify details that came up in the initial interview, and resolve any incongruities in the initial interview, observations, or test findings. Also, if you gave the interviewee a self-monitoring task, you can look over the self-monitoring record and discuss it (see Chapter 9). Finally, you may want to give a brief summary of what you covered or learned during the prior interview.

Exercise 5-6
Selecting the Appropriate Response

This exercise is designed to sharpen your ability to give appropriate responses in an interview. It contains 14 statements made by interviewees, each of which is accompanied by two possible interviewer responses. Select the interviewer response you prefer and justify your selection. Then, compare your choices with the suggested answers.

1. IE: I feel I need affection and can't get any.
   IR-1: Well, we all need affection and you're not alone in this.
   IR-2: What interferes with your getting affection?
2. IE: I'm afraid that I may lose control of myself.
   IR-1: What do you think would happen if you did?
   IR-2: Would that be bad?
3. IE: I was afraid of my parents when I was younger.
   IR-1: What about them made you afraid?
   IR-2: Yes, many young children are afraid of their parents.
4. IE: Doctor, I think that I'm going crazy.
   IR-1: Oh, no, you're not. You don't have any symptoms.
   IR-2: Tell me what you mean by "crazy."
5. IE: My teacher is mean to me.
   IR-1: Can you give me an example of that?
   IR-2: I'm sorry that he is.
6. IE: My headaches are getting worse, and my mother says that she can't stand it much longer.
   IR-1: Does your mother have headaches too?
   IR-2: What can't your mother stand?
7. IE: Yesterday I had a big quarrel with my Dad.
   IR-1: Again?
   IR-2: What happened?

8. IE: I don't think this will help me at all.
    IR-1: Let's talk about that; what do you think is happening?
    IR-2: If you don't cooperate, I'll have to notify the school principal.

9. IE: You look tired.
    IR-1: This headache is killing me.
    IR-2: I've had a touch of sinus congestion, but that won't interfere with our session.

10. IE: I refuse to give in to my mother.
    IR-1: What do you mean by "give in"?
    IR-2: How can you expect your mother to do anything for you if you don't do anything for her?

11. IE: Well, I liked school a lot. I was on the swim team and had lots of friends. I had a good figure then, too. That was before I gained all this weight. My boyfriend liked me better when I was thin. Then, when I was a senior, my mother died from cancer. All of my girlfriends got steady boyfriends. That's when I gained weight. Things just weren't the same.
    IR-1: So things were going pretty well for you until your senior year, when many difficult changes occurred.
    IR-2: Tell me about your mother.

12. IE: My marriage was not exactly good. You see, my husband and I used to get into these huge fights, and he'd get really violent. One time, he shoved me so hard I flew through the sliding glass doors. I had to have all kinds of stitches. It was a real mess.
    IR-1: How long were you and your husband married?
    IR-2: That must have been very frightening for you. What kinds of things did you fight about?

13. IE: I'm not going to be able to finish my senior year in high school.
    IR-1: If you graduate, you'll have a better chance of getting a job.
    IR-2: Tell me about that.

14. IE: (In a hospital) At home, my mom lets me eat whatever I want.
    IR-1: You're unhappy that you can't always eat what you want when you're in the hospital.
    IR-2: Wow! Your mom sure spoils you. She lets you eat anything you want.

Suggested Answers

1. IR-2's response is preferable. It acknowledges the interviewee's statement and also explores possible reasons for not receiving affection. IR-1's response tends to close off the discussion, halting further exploration.

2. IR-1's response is preferable. It gives the interviewee room to comment on a range of possible feelings and actions. IR-2's response is less constructive because it is too specific, pointing to the "badness" of loss of control, even though the interviewer doesn't know what "lose control" means to the interviewee.

3. IR-1's response is preferable. It opens the door to further discussion, whereas IR-2's response tends to close the discussion and provide false reassurance.

4. IR-2's response is preferable. It allows the interviewee to say what he or she means by "crazy." Although it is reassuring, IR-1's response assumes that the interviewer knows what the interviewee means, and this assumption may not be accurate.

5. IR-1's response is preferable. It leads the interviewee to focus on a specific event and to document the statement. IR-2's response, although somewhat sympathetic, tends to close off discussion and imply endorsement of the interviewee's perception. The interviewer could say, "I'm sorry you feel that way. Could you tell me *how* he is mean to you, though?"

6. IR-2's response is preferable. It attempts to clarify what the interviewee meant by saying "can't stand it much longer." IR-1's response is somewhat tangential at this time.

7. IR-2's response is preferable. It asks the interviewee to comment on the quarrel. IR-1's response, which simply recognizes that the quarrel is a recurring event, is not likely to facilitate further discussion.

8. IR-1's response is preferable. It asks the interviewee to explore his or her feelings about the reason for coming to the interview. A punitive response such as the one given by IR-2 should not be used under any circumstances.

9. IR-2's response is preferable. It acknowledges the interviewee's comment but reassures the interviewee that the interviewer is in control. Comments that burden the interviewee with the interviewer's own difficulties, such as IR-1's response, should be avoided.

10. IR-1's response is preferable. It is a clarifying probe. Argumentative comments such as IR-2's response should be avoided.

11. IR-1's response is preferable. It acknowledges the interviewee's statements and allows her to comment further on her difficulties. IR-2's response focuses on one specific area. Although it might be valuable to explore this area at another time during the interview, such a focus is premature.

12. IR-2's response is preferable. It is an empathic response, followed by a request for more information about an important area. IR-1's reply is not as responsive to the interviewee's statements. It is a useful information-gathering probe, but it seems out of place after the interviewee's statements.

13. IR-2's response is preferable. It is a good probing response, which informs the interviewee that the interviewer wants to know about the interviewee's reasons for not going back to school. IR-1's response gives advice—advice the interviewee likely has heard before and knows.

14. IR-1's response is preferable. It is a reflective/interpretive comment, which shows the interviewee that the interviewer understands how the interviewee feels. IR-2's response is somewhat inappropriate because it makes a generalization that may or may not be true.

THINKING THROUGH THE ISSUES

1. How easy might it be for you to forget that you are conducting a clinical assessment interview and fall back into your ordinary mode of conversation?

2. To what extent will the disadvantages associated with the clinical assessment interview affect the information you obtain?

3. When do you think you would use an unstructured interview, a semistructured interview, and a structured interview?

4. How would you prepare for an interview?

5. What do you see as the role of computer-generated interviewing? What are some advantages and disadvantages of comput-

erized interviewing? Will computerized interviewing replace interviewers in clinical assessment? What are the ethical issues involved in using computers for interviewing?

6. During an interview, what clues might guide you in evaluating the extent to which the interviewee is being open and honest?

7. How might an interviewee judge your openness and honesty?

8. Why might you have difficulty establishing rapport in an interview?

9. How will you know when your questions are effective?

10. Which probing techniques do you think you will use most frequently as a clinician? Why did you make these choices?

11. To what extent does the use of probing techniques reflect an invasion of privacy?

12. How can you determine whether silence reflects a mere pause or an impasse in the assessment?

13. How would you deal with interviewees who become emotionally upset?

14. If your emotions interfered with the flow of the interview, what steps would you take to regain control?

15. Imagine that you were an interviewee. How would you know whether the clinician liked you, understood you, and respected you? What would the clinician have to do to convey this information to you?

SUMMARY

1. The primary goal of the clinical assessment interview is to obtain relevant, reliable, and valid information about interviewees and their problems.

2. Information should be obtained about the interviewee's personality, temperament, motor skills, cognitive skills, communication skills, study habits, work habits, interpersonal behavior, interests, daily living skills and difficulties, and perception of the referral problem.

Clinical Assessment Interviews versus Ordinary Conversations and Other Types of Interviews

3. A clinical assessment interview is different from an ordinary conversation in that the interview involves an interpersonal interaction that has a mutually accepted purpose, with formal, clearly defined roles and a set of norms governing the interaction.

4. There is continuity between clinical assessment interviews and psychotherapeutic interviews, with the goals evolving rather than changing radically from one interview to the other.

5. In psychotherapeutic interviews, you should continually assess the interviewee; and in clinical assessment interviews, you should use psychotherapeutic strategies to deal with interviewee reactions (such as emotional distress) during the interview.

6. Survey research interviews usually focus on interviewees' opinions or preferences with respect to various topics.

Strengths and Weaknesses of the Clinical Assessment Interview

7. Overall, the interview is one of the most useful techniques for obtaining information, because it allows interviewees to express, in their own terms, their views about themselves and relevant life events.

8. The interview allows great latitude for the interviewee to express concerns, thoughts, feelings, and reactions, with a minimum of structure and redirection on the part of the interviewer.

9. The interview also has several weaknesses as an assessment tool. Reliability and validity may be difficult to establish, and interviews are susceptible to interinterviewer differences, difficulties in obtaining accurate information, and bias.

Purposes of Clinical Assessment Interviews

10. The purpose of a clinical assessment interview depends on whether it is an initial interview, a post-assessment interview, or a follow-up interview.

11. The initial interview is designed to inform the interviewee about the assessment process and to obtain information relevant to diagnosis, treatment, remediation, or placement in special programs.

12. The post-assessment interview (also known as the exit interview) is designed to discuss the assessment findings and recommendations with the interviewee's parents and, often, the interviewee.

13. The follow-up interview is designed to assess outcomes of treatment or interventions and to gauge the appropriateness of the assessment findings and recommendations.

Degrees of Structure in Initial Clinical Assessment Interviews

14. Types of initial clinical assessment interviews include unstructured interviews, semistructured interviews, and structured interviews.

15. In unstructured interviews, the interview process is allowed to unfold without specific guidelines.

16. Semistructured interviews are based on general and flexible guidelines.

17. The Semistructured Clinical Interview for Children and Adolescents is one example of a standardized clinical interview for children ages 6 to 18 years that takes about 60 to 90 minutes to administer. It has eight syndrome scales, six DSM-oriented scales, and four additional scales. The reliabilities are somewhat low, but validity is satisfactory. It should not be the sole basis in making diagnoses or other important decisions about children and adolescents.

18. In structured interviews, the exact order and wording of each question is specified, with little opportunity for follow-up questions not directly related to the specified questions.

Introduction to Interviewing Guidelines

19. Successful interviewing requires the ability to communicate clearly and the ability to understand the communications of interviewees, whether children or adults.

20. During the interview, you will ask questions, follow up and probe responses, move from topic to topic, encourage replies, answer questions, gauge the pace of the interview, and formulate impressions of the interviewee.

21. No matter how well you have planned the interview, each interviewee will present a new challenge. No individual is predictable.

22. Listen carefully to what the interviewee says.

23. Interpret and assess what is significant, but do not accept everything as literal truth; remember, however, that it may be the interviewee's truth.

24. What interviewees say is important, but how they act and speak are equally important.

25. Interviewing failures are more likely to arise from a negative attitude than from technical difficulties.
26. To be successful as an interviewer, you must know yourself, trust your ideas, be willing to make mistakes, and, above all, have a genuine desire to help the interviewee.
27. A good interview takes careful planning, skillful execution, and good organization; it is purposeful and goal-oriented.
28. The interview is affected by interviewer and interviewee characteristics (e.g., physical, cognitive, and affective factors), message components (e.g., language, nonverbal cues, and sensory cues), and interview climate (e.g., physical, social, temporal, and psychological factors).

External Factors and Atmosphere

29. Conduct the interview in a private, quiet room that is free from distractions.
30. Keep interruptions to a minimum if you cannot avoid them entirely.
31. Begin the interview at the scheduled time.
32. Interview the parent(s) without small children in the room.

Forming Impressions

33. When you and the interviewee first meet, both of you will form initial impressions. These impressions will change as the interview progresses.
34. Be aware of signs of psychological disturbance and signs of psychological health.

Listening

35. The ability to listen is the key factor in the interview.
36. Being a good listener means being free of preoccupations, giving interviewees your full attention, and listening to yourself.

Analytical Listening

37. The ability to critically analyze the responses of the interviewee as you listen—termed analytical listening—is an important interviewing skill.
38. Good analytical listening skills include getting the main ideas, facts, and details; understanding the connotative meanings of words; identifying affect and attitudes appropriately; discriminating between fact and imagination; recognizing discrepancies; judging the relevancy of communications; and making valid inferences.
39. Interviewees have certain ways or patterns of answering questions, called response sets (or response styles).
40. You will need to be cognizant of interviewees' response sets.
41. You must judge whether you have obtained all the information the interviewee is willing to share with you and whether that amount is sufficient.
42. Interviewees must recognize that you are evaluating their communication and organizing the information into some coherent theme.
43. Toward the end of the interview, you can ask about important areas you did not discuss, clarify previously discussed material, make other necessary comments, or invite questions that the interviewee might have.

Establishing Rapport

44. The success of an interview, like that of any other assessment procedure, depends on the rapport you establish with the interviewee.
45. Rapport is based on mutual confidence, respect, and acceptance.

46. Because the clinical assessment interview is a formal, professional interaction, the interviewee should not have to deal with your personal concerns.
47. Rapport may be difficult to establish when the interviewee does not want to be interviewed or does not want the information from the interview shared with anyone else.
48. Showing interest in the information the interviewee gives you is crucial in establishing rapport.
49. Reassure anxious interviewees.
50. Interviewees may express their anxiety both verbally and nonverbally.
51. When you sense that the interviewee's anxiety is interfering with rapport, encourage him or her to talk about it.
52. If the interviewee will not talk with you, you may need to gently point out the responsibilities of the interviewee.
53. Interviewees may become agitated during the interview, especially if they have recently faced a traumatic experience.
54. Acknowledge their feelings and give them time to work through them; this should help make a difficult situation easier.
55. Use language suitable to the age, gender, and education of the interviewee.
56. Several techniques can be used to help you convey your interest to the interviewee, encourage the interviewee to elaborate on her or his response, or ease the interviewee's anxiety.

Timing Questions Appropriately

57. The initial part of the assessment should focus on topics that are not anxiety provoking or sensitive.
58. Premature or poorly timed questions may impede the progress of the assessment and discourage disclosure of vital information.
59. The pace of the assessment should be rapid enough to keep the interest of the interviewee, but slow enough to allow the interviewee to formulate good answers.

Changing Topics

60. Proceed in an orderly manner, and finish discussing one topic before going on to the next.
61. It will take practice and sensitivity to judge when you have exhausted one topic and need to move to another.

Formulating Appropriate Questions

62. Questions form the heart of the interview.
63. The way you ask questions is as important as what you ask. Speak clearly and audibly at a moderate pace.
64. The words you stress can determine the meaning of what you say.
65. When you formulate a question, the interviewee must understand your words in the same way you intend them.
66. Questions fall on a continuum with respect to their degree of openness; they may be minimally focused, moderately focused, or highly focused.
67. Open-ended questions are usually preferable, especially at the start of the assessment, because they give the interviewee some responsibility for sharing her or his concerns.
68. Moderately focused questions are more directive than open-ended questions and are valuable as the assessment proceeds.
69. Bipolar questions are not as constraining as yes-no questions, but they still limit the interviewee's responses.
70. All three of the above types of questions have their place in the assessment.
71. Phrase questions positively and confidently.

Avoiding Certain Types of Questions

72. The major types of questions to avoid are yes-no questions; double-barreled questions; long, multiple questions; leading questions; coercive questions; random probing questions; embarrassing or accusatory questions; and why questions.

Probing Effectively

73. Probing is a key to successful interviewing.
74. If you recognize the possible reason for an inadequate response, you may be able to determine the kinds of follow-up questions needed.
75. Probing techniques include asking questions and making comments designed to elicit elaboration or clarification or check the interviewee's understanding and using repetition, challenging, silence, neutral phrases, reflective statements, periodic summaries, and miscellaneous probing statements.
76. Ask for elaboration when you want the interviewee to provide additional information.
77. Ask for clarification when you do not understand what the interviewee is saying or when you are puzzled by some details.
78. Use repetition when the interviewee has not answered your question.
79. Use challenging (also referred to as confrontation) to clarify incongruities in the interviewee's communication.
80. Use silence to allow the interviewee more time to reflect or think.
81. Use neutral phrases—such as "uh huh," "I see," or "okay"—to encourage the interviewee to keep talking and to show that you are being attentive.
82. Use reflective statements to get the interviewee to tell you more about a topic.
83. Use periodic summaries to convey your understanding of the problem, allow the interviewee to comment on the adequacy of your interpretation, inform the interviewee that you have been listening, build transitions from one topic to the next and give direction to the assessment, signal that you are at the end of the assessment, and sum up and clarify what you have covered.
84. Use a check of the interviewee's understanding to learn about the clarity of your communication.
85. Other types of probing questions or techniques can be used to encourage the interviewee to discuss a topic more fully.
86. Decide on what statements to probe by keeping in mind your assessment goals.

Using Structuring Statements

87. Structuring statements guide the interviewee in talking about a topic.

Dealing with Difficult Situations

88. Some interviewees will be more challenging than others.
89. When you lack confidence, feel intimidated by interviewees, or are poorly prepared for the interview, interviewees might try to take control of the interview.
90. When interviewees become emotionally upset, do not stop their behavior prematurely.
91. When interviewees show strong emotions, remain calm, objective, and detached.
92. When interviewees make derogatory remarks about you, try to determine possible reasons for their comments.
93. When interviewees make derogatory remarks about other people, control your reactions.

94. When interviewees are uncooperative, there may be little that you can do to establish rapport.
95. When interviewees appear to be violent, try to defuse their potentially violent behavior.
96. Consider your personal safety when you interview children and parents in their homes, particularly if you are in an unfamiliar location or dangerous neighborhood.
97. You can introduce a potentially sensitive topic by pointing out that the problem is not a unique one.
98. It will not always be easy to learn why interviewees give inadequate answers or why they do not talk much.
99. Memory difficulties may occur because the events being discussed occurred in the remote past and were not particularly meaningful, because they are too painful to recall, or because of neurological deficits or acute trauma.
100. Learn to recognize different silences, such as extreme silence, silence suggesting guilt, or silence suggesting resistance.
101. When interviewees have difficulty knowing when to stop talking and blurt out much irrelevant material, redirect them; otherwise, you will waste time and get useless information.
102. There are several ways to deal with challenges to your clinical competence: Do not be defensive, be prepared, evaluate the context, answer the question, admit that differences may be a problem, use humor, use the team approach, or admit that you will never know the depth of the interviewee's distress.
103. Interviewees may ask you questions about yourself. Be tactful in responding to such questions.
104. Remain neutral when interviewees try to elicit your opinion about some personal matter or try to get you to side with them.

Remaining Objective

105. Accepting the communication of interviewees means that you acknowledge and appreciate their point of view; it does not mean that you agree with or approve of the communication.
106. Endorsing the communication of interviewees means that you agree that their perspective is accurate.
107. Your ability to conduct an effective interview will be determined not only by your interviewing skills but also by personal factors in your life. You must be sensitive to how you are feeling as the interview begins.
108. Becoming self-aware is an important part of becoming an effective interviewer.

Recording Information and Scheduling

109. You should record what the interviewee says, but not every word unless you use an audio recorder or a video camera. If you take notes, jot down the most important remarks made by the interviewee.
110. If you have a heavy assessment schedule, take a few minutes between sessions to review, complete, and clarify your notes and to relax.

KEY TERMS, CONCEPTS, AND NAMES

Clinical assessment interview (p. 106)
Ordinary conversation (p. 106)
Psychotherapeutic interview (p. 106)
Survey research interview (p. 107)

STUDY QUESTIONS

1. Discuss the similarities and differences between a clinical assessment interview and an ordinary conversation.
2. Discuss the similarities and differences between a clinical assessment interview and a psychotherapeutic interview.
3. Discuss the similarities and differences between a clinical assessment interview and a survey research interview.
4. What are the strengths and weaknesses of the clinical assessment interview?
5. Compare and contrast the initial interview, the post-assessment interview, and the follow-up interview.
6. Compare unstructured, semistructured, and structured interviews. Comment on the advantages and disadvantages of each.
7. Discuss the benefits and limitations of computer-generated interviewing.
8. Pretend that you have been asked to prepare a lecture on 10 important guidelines for conducting clinical assessment interviews, and prepare some remarks.
9. What factors may influence an interview? In your answer, discuss interviewer and interviewee characteristics, components of the message, and the climate of the interview.
10. Characterize an effective listener and an ineffective listener.
11. Discuss the concept of analytical listening. Include in your discussion the various purposes served by analytical reasoning, response sets, and obtaining relevant information.
12. What are some important factors to consider in establishing rapport in an interview?
13. What are some important factors to consider in timing questions?
14. What are some factors to consider in changing topics?
15. What are some factors to consider in formulating appropriate questions?
16. Discuss the major types of questions to avoid in an interview.
17. What are some factors to consider in probing effectively? Include in your discussion several useful probing techniques.
18. Discuss the use of structuring statements and give some examples.
19. How would you go about encouraging appropriate replies?
20. Describe at least four difficult situations that you may encounter in an interview and give suggestions for dealing with them.
21. Distinguish between acceptance and endorsement of an interviewee's communications.
22. Discuss some of the issues involved in recording information and scheduling.

6

INTERVIEWING CHILDREN, PARENTS, TEACHERS, AND FAMILIES

Children live in a world of imagination and feeling. . . .
They invest the most insignificant object with any form they
please, and see in it whatever they wish to see.
　　　　—Adam G. Oehlenschlager, Danish poet and dramatist
　　　　　　　　　　　　　　　　　　　　　　(1779–1850)

Good parents give their children roots and wings. Roots to
know where home is, wings to fly away and exercise what's
been taught them.
　　　　—Jonas Salk, American physician and microbiologist
　　　　　　　　　　　　　　　　　　　　　　(1914–1995)

It is the supreme art of the teacher to awaken joy in creative
expression and knowledge.
　　　　—Albert Einstein, American physicist (1879–1955)

No matter how many communes anybody invents, the family
always creeps back.
　　　　—Margaret Mead, American anthropologist (1901–1978)

Goals and Objectives

This chapter is designed to enable you to do the following:

- Understand techniques useful in interviewing children

- Understand techniques useful in interviewing parents

- Understand techniques useful in interviewing teachers

- Understand techniques useful in interviewing families

General Considerations

Techniques for Interviewing Children

Areas Covered in the Initial Interview with Children

Interviewing Parents

Interviewing Teachers

Interviewing the Family

Thinking Through the Issues

Summary

Key Terms, Concepts, and Names

Study Questions

GENERAL CONSIDERATIONS

Interviews with children will give you information about their problems, their feelings about themselves, and their impressions about their family and situation. You will need to encourage children to reveal their thoughts and feelings to you.

Children are sometimes more difficult to interview than adults because of limitations in language comprehension, language expression, conceptual ability, and memory. They may not know the words to describe their symptoms, particularly the subjective experience associated with their feelings. For example, because of their limited vocabulary, they may have difficulty distinguishing a *throbbing* pain from a *dull* one. They may identify an emotion as a physical sensation: Feelings of anxiety may be described as a stomachache. Poorly worded questions may cause confusion and mislead them.

Interviews with children usually take place because of someone else's concern. Children may not be aware that they have problems. With older children, a sentence or two describing the reason for the interview may help establish rapport and trust. With younger children, you will have to find a way to help them relax. You especially need to gain their trust if they come to the interview under protest. Later in the chapter we provide suggestions for working with reticent children.

Children may give you hints concerning troubling information, such as their having been maltreated. In such cases, convey to them that you are interested in what they might want to tell you. *You want them to know that you can accept them no matter what they tell you.* If you disregard or dismiss their hints about maltreatment or other problems, they probably will not volunteer information about these areas.

When conducting an interview, always consider the child's age, experiences, level of cognitive development, and ability to express himself or herself, as well as the extensiveness of any psychological disturbance. Each of these factors will affect the interview, and some may not become apparent until after the interview has begun. You also want to be aware of the child's attention, concentration, and level of distractibility, as well as any physical impediments that might affect the interview. Several interviewing techniques discussed in the previous chapter also are discussed in this chapter, with particular emphasis on their application to children.

We cannot emphasize enough the importance of considering the child's level of linguistic and conceptual development. Suppose an interviewer asked an 8-year-old girl whether she ever had any delusions. The child, not understanding what the word meant but wanting to please the interviewer, might say, "Yes, all the time." If the interviewer recorded the response and continued the interview, he or she might well reach a tentative diagnosis of a thought disorder. Such a situation can be avoided by telling the child the ground rules, such as "Say 'I don't understand' when you don't understand a word or question and I'll try to explain or ask it better," and by explaining sophisticated vocabulary and concepts.

Children are more dependent on their immediate environments than adults are, as they have less power to shape them. Children have little first-hand knowledge about the opportunities that exist beyond their immediate familial and physical environments. Because of their limited knowledge, they are less able than adults to change their surroundings to reduce stress.

Children also differ from adults in that they are in a process of rapid intellectual, emotional, and behavioral development. They usually are more open than adults to new ways of behaving, thinking, and feeling, and their personality patterns are less rigid or set. They also may be more open in expressing their feelings, thoughts, and concerns.

Memory for Personally Experienced Events

Let's consider how three fundamental memory processes—encoding information, retaining information, and retrieving information—are related to some key findings about children's memory for personally experienced events (Engelberg & Christianson, 2002; Ornstein & Haden, 2002; Pezdek & Taylor, 2002; Saywitz & Lyon, 2002):

1. *Registration in memory.* Effective registration in memory requires the ability to understand events. If events are not understood, they will not be initially encoded and represented in memory. Thus, not everything gets into memory.

2. *Variable memory traces.* Memory traces vary along a continuum from strong to weak. Events that leave strong and coherently organized traces are more easily retrieved than those that leave weak and loosely organized traces. For example, the central details of an event are better recalled than the peripheral details, and distinct events are better retained in memory than ordinary events.

3. *Changes in memory.* The time that elapses between an event and its recall can dramatically alter what children remember. Research shows that the strength of a memory trace decreases over time, that what is remembered may be reinterpreted in light of knowledge accumulated after the event, and that experiences after an event may enhance or interfere with accurate recall. For example, children may adopt into their own memory information about an event that they receive from others, and young children are more suggestible than older children.

4. *Imperfect retrieval from memory.* Not everything in memory can be retrieved at all times. Young children, in particular, have more retrieval problems than older children because their information-processing skills (e.g., speed of encoding) are not as well developed as those of older children. Children also may not want to reveal everything they know to an interviewer because of embarrassment, because they wish to block out memories associated with unbearable psychic pain, or because of other factors. Intervening events may fill

in memory gaps. Finally, the social relationship between children and interviewers may affect children's recall, with a stressful relationship impeding recall and a harmonious relationship facilitating recall.

Strangeness of the Interview Situation

Because the interview setting is unfamiliar and because the interviewer is a stranger, children's behavior in the interview may not be typical of their behavior in other settings (Bierman, 1990). Even so, there is a good chance that you can establish rapport and learn about their feelings, beliefs, and concerns. The first 10 or 15 minutes of the interview may give you useful information about the child's initial reactions to new and potentially stressful situations. Information obtained from children can be followed up in interviews with their parents and teachers.

Interviewer-Initiated Interviews

In school settings, and particularly in juvenile detention settings, you may initiate interviews when neither the children nor the parents have sought help for a problem. In these cases, you must exercise special care on first contact with the children. Inform them simply and directly why you asked them to come to see you. Be prepared to spend additional time establishing rapport. With parents who have not initiated the interview, be prepared to work harder to gain their trust by responding with understanding to their concerns.

Goals of the Initial Interview with Children

The goals of the initial interview with a child will depend on the referral question, as well as on the child's age and communication skills. Generally, the initial interview with a child is designed to do the following:

1. Obtain informed consent to conduct the interview (from older children) or agreement to be at the interview (from younger children)
2. Evaluate the child's understanding of the reason for the interview and her or his feelings about being at the interview
3. Gather information about the child's perception of the situation that led to the interview
4. Identify antecedent and consequent events, including potentially reinforcing events, related to the child's problems
5. Estimate the frequency, magnitude, duration, intensity, and pervasiveness of the child's problems
6. Identify the circumstances in which the problems are most or least likely to occur
7. Identify factors associated with the parents, school, and environment that may contribute to the problems

8. Gather information about the child's perceptions of his or her parents, teachers, peers, and other significant individuals in his or her life
9. Assess the child's strengths, motivations, and resources for change
10. Evaluate the child's ability and willingness to participate in the assessment process
11. Estimate what the child's level of functioning was *before* an injury
12. Discuss the assessment procedures and possible follow-up procedures

TECHNIQUES FOR INTERVIEWING CHILDREN

General Techniques

The most common way to help young children remember, think, and tell you about themselves is to ask them questions. Unskilled use of questions, however, may inhibit their responses. If you use questions extensively and employ relatively few acknowledging or accepting statements (such as "I see," "Oh," or "Really"), children are more likely to give brief replies. Continual questioning also may inhibit children from volunteering information or asking questions themselves.

Recognize that in asking a question, you are making a demand—you are directing the child's attention to memories or ideas that he or she might not have otherwise considered. Children generally need more time than adults to think about the questions and about their answers. If you want to obtain only specific information from children and are confident that they understand the questions, a direct question-and-answer format may be acceptable. However, you should avoid a strict question-and-answer format if you are unsure of exactly what information you want and need; if you want the child to take an active, constructive role in the interview; or if you are unsure whether the child understands your questions. In these cases, use a more conversational style.

You can become a more effective interviewer of children by learning about their current interests. Look at Saturday morning television programs, talk with parents, visit toy stores, look at children's books, and visit day care centers and schools to observe children in their natural environments. Familiarity with children's interests will help you establish rapport with children and understand them better.

Chapter 5 presented general suggestions for conducting interviews. The present chapter focuses on interview strategies that are particularly useful in establishing rapport with and maintaining the cooperation of children. You will need to adjust your interviewing strategy depending on how children respond (Bierman & Schwartz, 1986). Following is an amusing example of how the interviewer heard the adolescent's response but ignored the implications of the response.

IR: Do you have any fears?

IE: I have a terrible fear of deadlines.

IR: Tell me everything about your fear of deadlines. You have until 10:50.

Specific Techniques

Here are 22 techniques that are useful in interviewing children.

1. *Consider the child's age and needs in setting the tempo and length of the interview.* You need to be alert to how tired the child is becoming. Take short breaks of about 5 minutes each during a lengthy interview (e.g., 50 minutes or more). Provide a brief period of free play or nonintense activity at any time, if needed. Leave some time toward the end of the interview to allow the child to regain composure, especially if the child reveals strong feelings during the interview.

2. *Formulate appropriate opening statements.* The opening statement that will help put the child at ease will depend on the child's age, ability level, and behavior and the reason for the referral. After introducing yourself and establishing rapport, you might open with one of the following statements:

- "This is a place where moms and dads and kids come to talk with a helper like me. Sometimes they tell me they wish things could go better at home or at school. I help them figure things out so that they can feel better" (Bierman, 1990, p. 212).
- "Your teacher has told me about some problems you've been having, but I'd like to hear about them from you."
- "I understand that you're having some problems at home."

To an older child, it may be useful to say something like the following:

- "What brings you here today?"
- "We could begin by your letting me know what's bothering you."

To a child in school, an appropriate comment might be

- "I'm Ms. Smith, the school psychologist. I understand from Mr. Jones that you're not doing too well in school. I'd like to hear what you think about how you're doing."

To a child in a juvenile detention center, you might say,

- "I'm Dr. Brown, a staff psychologist here at the center. I'd like to talk to you about why you're here at the center."

3. *Use appropriate language and intonation.* Use simple vocabulary and short sentences tailored to the child's developmental level and cognitive level. For example, instead of saying "What things are reinforcing for you?" say, "What things do you like?" Be sure that the child understands the questions. Use simple terms in exploring the child's feelings. For example, use *sad* instead of *depressed* and *happy* instead of *enthusiastic*. Be friendly, and show interest in the child.

4. *Avoid leading questions.* You especially want to avoid leading the child to give a particular response. For example, in a case of alleged child maltreatment, do not tell the child that the alleged offender is bad or that the child should tell you the bad things the offender has done. Similarly, phrase your questions so that the child does not receive any hint that one response is more acceptable than another. Be sure that the manner and tone of your voice do not reveal any personal biases. Be even more observant about avoiding leading questions with preschool children, because they are more prone to erroneous suggestions than are older children (Ceci, Powell, & Crossman, 1999).

5. *Ask for examples.* Ask the child to give examples of how she or he behaves or how other people behave when they are feeling a certain way (e.g., how they behave when they are sad).

6. *Be open to what the child tells you.* You want to convey to the child that you are open to and accepting of what he or she wants to tell you. This means that you must not ignore information that does not support your expectations or beliefs. You want to take a more active role with children than you would with adults. Gather as complete a story as possible from the child, but do not *interpret* what happened to him or her.

7. *Make descriptive comments.* When you comment on the child's appearance, behavior, or demeanor, you are making a descriptive comment (Kanfer, Eyberg, & Krahn, 1983, 1992). Descriptive comments provide a simple way of giving attention to the child and encouraging the child to continue with appropriate behavior. An added benefit of descriptive comments is that you can use them to maintain communication with the child while you are formulating other questions. Examples of descriptive comments include "I see that you're feeding the doll" and "You look cheerful today." Descriptive comments are nonthreatening, focus the child's attention, and encourage the child to elaborate further (Boggs & Eyberg, 1990).

8. *Use reflection.* Reflective statements rephrase what the child has said or done, retaining the essential meaning of the communication or behavior (Kanfer et al., 1992). These statements provide clarity and help organize the child's behavior. For example, in response to the statement "My brother is a brat," you might say, "So you're saying that your brother doesn't act the way you want him to, is that right?"

9. *Give praise frequently.* Praise and support serve to guide the child to talk about topics that you consider important (Kanfer et al., 1983). Younger children typically will need more praise than older children. Examples of praise are "I'm glad you can tell me about these things" and "Some of these things are hard to talk about, but you're doing fine." *Praise children's efforts, not what they say.* For example, do not reward a child for making responses that she or he thinks you want to hear. Similarly, do not use coercion, pressure, or threats—such as telling the child that she or he cannot play with toys, go to the bathroom, go home, or get to see her or his parents soon—to get the child to respond in the way you would like.

10. *Avoid critical statements.* Criticism is likely to generate anger, hostility, resentment, or frustration—reactions that will interfere with your ability to establish and maintain rapport (Kanfer et al., 1992). Examples of critical statements are "You're not trying very hard" and "Stop tearing the paper." When the child is behaving negatively, focus on more appropriate behavior to turn his or her attention away from the negative behavior. You also can invoke rules that govern the playroom or office. For example, when a child is throwing blocks, say, "Let's throw the ball," or when a child is tearing paper inappropriately, say, "One of the rules is that you can't tear this paper." If you are forewarned that the child is likely to act out in particular ways, you can be prepared; for example, you can give the child some paper to tear and say, "One of the rules is that you can only tear this paper." This may help establish limits and redirect the child's inappropriate behavior. Sometimes you can ignore inappropriate behavior, make a mental note to watch for positive behavior, and reinforce the positive behavior. Here are two examples of how this can be done (Kanfer et al., 1992, adapted from pp. 52–53):

IE: (Climbs on table)
IR: (Ignores climbing)
IE: (Gets off table)
IR: It's safer when you stand on the floor.

IR: Tell me a story about this picture.
IE: I can't think of anything.
IR: (Ignores statement) What is this girl doing?
IE: She's sitting.
IR: She is sitting. I'm glad you told me about part of the picture. What else is going on in the picture?

11. *Use simple questions and concrete referents.* You can increase the child's responsiveness and elicit more coherent and complete responses by simplifying the questions, adding concrete referents, and simplifying the responses required (Bierman, 1983). For example, you can say, "Tell me one thing that you like about your teacher," "What was happening the last time you felt that way?" or "What happened yesterday morning when you woke up?"

Drawing is an especially useful technique to use with children ages 3 to 8 years. Young children are likely to give longer and more descriptive accounts of emotionally laden events when they are asked to draw pictures and talk about the events than when they are asked only to talk about the events (Butler, Gross, & Hayne, 1995; Gross & Hayne, 1998). Drawing appears to facilitate recall by providing children with concrete retrieval cues (i.e., representation on paper) and by allowing children to control the pace of the interview and to focus less on the interviewer and more on the task (i.e., remembering and reporting the event).

Following are techniques that use concrete referents to help children talk about their feelings. These techniques are especially useful with children who are reluctant to talk about themselves.

a. *Ask for affect labels.* Show the child simple line drawings that depict faces expressing emotions such as happiness,

sadness, and anger (Bierman, 1990; see Figure 6-1). First, point to each face and say, "Tell me how this face looks." Then, ask a series of questions such as "How do you look when you go to school?" "How do you look when you go to bed?" and "How do you look when your daddy [mommy] comes home?" After each question, ask the child to point to a face. The pointing technique is especially useful for young children because they do not have to make a verbal response.

If the child is reluctant to tell you about the faces, consider saying "How would a child feel if he [she] had a time out? Point to a picture that shows how he [she] would feel." If the child points correctly, say, "That's right, a child would feel sad [angry] if he [she] was punished. What do you think he [she] did to get punished?" Follow up by asking "Who punished him [her]?" and "What was the punishment?" To learn the child's feelings, for example, about a positive event and about an incident in which he or she was aggressive, you first might say, "How would a child feel if he [she] got a special toy? Point to a picture that shows how he [she] would feel." Follow up with appropriate questions. You then might say, "How would a child feel if he [she] had a fight with another child? Point to a picture that shows how he [she] would feel." Again, follow up with appropriate questions.

A more difficult version of this procedure is to point to each face in turn and say, "Tell me something that makes you feel like this" (Bierman, 1990, p. 213). With children who are willing to talk about their feelings, you can then probe their response to the faces. For example, if a boy says that he is angry when he fights with his brother, you can ask, "What about fighting with your brother makes you angry?" You can follow up with "What do you do when you fight with your brother?" If the child seems threatened by the questions or simply refuses to answer, stop probing. (See Bierman, 1990, for a discussion of other techniques useful in eliciting affect-laden material.)

b. *Use the picture-question technique.* From a magazine, book, or other source, select pictures that you think will engage the child. Show the child the pictures one at time, and ask the child to tell a story about each picture. The picture-question technique, although similar to thematic projective techniques, is not used as a personality or projective test (Bierman, 1990). Rather, it is simply a way to encourage children to talk about their feelings. Showing pictures, as opposed to asking questions, may serve as a less intrusive and

Figure 6-1. Line drawings depicting three emotional expressions.

more concrete way of gathering information about children's feelings.

You may select pictures that relate to specific themes in the child's life. For example, if you want to find out about how a girl feels about a new baby in the family, show her a picture that contains a girl, a mother, and a baby. First ask, "What do you think is happening?" Then say, "How does the girl feel about the baby?" Then ask, "What's going to happen?" If you want to learn about a boy's feelings about his parents' divorce, show him a picture of a boy about his age, a mother, and a father. You might say, "Here are a mom and dad and a boy about your age. The mom and dad are divorced. What do you think happened? . . . What did the mom say? . . . What did the dad say? . . . What did the boy say? . . . How did the mom feel? . . . How did the dad feel? . . . How did the boy feel? . . . What will happen next? . . . Did that ever happen to you? . . . What did you do? . . . How did you feel?" (Bierman, 1983, p. 234, with changes in notation).

Use of the picture-question technique might affect how the child responds to a projective story-telling test, like the Children's Apperception Test, if the test is to be administered later. Therefore, you should weigh the advantages and disadvantages of using the picture-question procedure. To encourage a reluctant child to talk to you, you might want to try other techniques before the picture-question technique, especially if you plan to administer a story-telling test.

c. *Have the child draw pictures of people and then talk about the pictures.* First ask the child to draw a picture of a child and then ask about the picture (Bierman, 1983). Following is a brief list of questions that you might ask as you point to the picture; add additional questions as needed.

- "What an interesting drawing. Now we're going to do something special. Tell me three things that this child likes to do."
- "Tell me three things that this child doesn't like to do."
- "What does this child like about school?"
- "What doesn't this child like about school?"
- "What does this child like about her [his] family?"
- "What doesn't this child like about her [his] family?"
- "What are this child's favorite things to do after school?"
- "What does this child do that gets her [him] into trouble?"
- "What makes this child happy?"
- "What makes this child sad?"
- "What does this child like best about himself [herself]?"
- "What makes this child angry?"
- "What games does this child like to play?"
- "What makes this child frightened?"
- "How do other children feel about this child?"

You can repeat the procedure by asking the child to draw a picture of an adult, substituting "woman" or "man" for "child" in the above questions. The picture-drawing technique allows you to encourage and praise the child for his or her efforts and gives the child a way of expressing hopes, fears, and frustrations (Bierman, 1983).

"You must be Mr. and Mrs. Smith. I'd recognize you anywhere from Henry's drawings."

Courtesy of Jeff Bryson and Jerome M. Sattler.

d. *Have the child draw a picture of the event.* Ask the child to draw a picture of the event that you are concerned about. "Please draw a picture of what happened." Then ask the child to tell you everything he or she can about the picture. Ask clarifying questions as needed.

e. *Use the story-completion technique.* First, ask the child to complete sentence stems that you have constructed about the child's life situation. Here is one way of introducing the task (Bierman & Schwartz, 1986):

> Okay, now I have this story that we're supposed to fill out together. I'll read the story, and then you think of an answer to fill in the blanks, okay? This first story is about the way kids act at school. At school, some kids act really _____. How should I say they act? (Child replies, "mean.") OK, good answer! One mean thing that they do is _____. (Child replies, "fight.") Fight, yeah, that's a mean thing. Another mean thing they do is _____. (p. 271)

As the child becomes more comfortable answering these structured sentence completions, the interviewer can interject probing questions like "Wow, do kids do that in your school, too?" or "Has that ever happened to anyone you know?" Using this flexible story-completion approach, the interviewer can get a basic sense of the social perceptions and reasoning level of the child and, depending on the child's responsiveness, can also pursue themes of personal relevance to the child (Bierman & Schwartz, 1986).

f. *Have the child respond to a hypothetical problem.* Ask the child to respond to a hypothetical problem that addresses relevant issues. Consider this example (Bierman & Schwartz, 1986):

> I know of a girl who has a problem that you might be able to help with. Her parents have been talking about getting a divorce, and she's scared about it. She doesn't really know what it will be like, or how she will feel, or what she can do about it. What do you think I can say to help her? (p. 272, with changes in notation)

This technique may be less anxiety-provoking than open-ended questions would be. It also makes fewer demands on the child's conceptual and verbal skills.

g. *Model the interview after a school-type task.* Sometimes it is helpful to make the interview resemble a more familiar school-type task (Bierman & Schwartz, 1986):

> The interviewer might introduce some papers with a comment such as "There are some questions I need to ask you," and go on to write notes periodically during the interview. This approach enables the interviewer to become an ally of the child—working with the child to obtain the necessary answers. Interviewer comments such as "Oh, here's a tough one—see what you think of this one" can soften the impact of difficult questions, and praise can be directed toward the child's task mastery attempts (e.g., "Neat answer! That one seemed kind of hard to me, but you've clearly thought about it"). Additionally, focusing on the paper enables the interviewer to avoid extended, intensive eye contact with the child. (p. 270, with changes in notation)

12. *Formulate hypothetical questions (using the subjunctive mood) when necessary.* Questions formulated in the subjunctive mood (or hypothetical questions) may encourage a reticent child to speak. Useful leads that employ a subjunctive mood include "Suppose you were . . . ," "Imagine . . . ," "What if you . . . ," and "Let's pretend that . . . ." For example, you might say, "Suppose you were to take a friend to your house. Suppose you were going to show your friend some things there—what kinds of things might your friend see?" Hypothetical questions allow "the child some degree of emotional distance by adding a game-like quality to the question" (Goodman & Sours, 1967, p. 29). For some children, this type of question is preferable to a question such as "What is your family like?"

13. *Be tactful.* Phrase questions tactfully to avoid causing children anxiety or embarrassment. An ineptly worded question may lead to discomfort. For example, after a child complained about a teacher, it would be tactless to ask, "Do you always have trouble with teachers?" You might get a more responsive answer if you asked, "Have you found other teachers as upsetting as this one?" or if you simply acknowledged the child's feelings about his or her teacher. Similarly, instead of asking "Did you quit school?"—which may require an admission of having done so—ask, "What was the last grade you were in?"

14. *Recognize the child's discomfort.* When a child is uncomfortable, it is important to recognize that fact and make the situation as stress-free as possible. Realize that a child may be even more uncomfortable if, for instance, family members are actively responsible for her or his problems. Be ready to change topics if the child becomes too distressed.

15. *Use props, crayons, clay, or toys to help a young child talk.* You will need special skills to help a young child talk. Props can be particularly valuable when the child seems unable to converse freely. Props are commonly used

> to stimulate memory, to supplement language ability, or to facilitate communication in the interview setting. Props can be used to re-create the setting of an event, permitting the child to reen-

act the event itself. A dollhouse and dolls, for instance, can be used to help describe a domestic event that is either too complex or too traumatic to describe in words. Pretending to talk on the telephone may act as a vehicle for talking with the interviewer. It may also help the child feel a sense of control over the interview, since he or she can stop the conversation at any time by hanging up. (Garbarino & Stott, 1989, p. 191, with changes in notation)

Another method for reducing a child's self-consciousness is to allow the child to use crayons or clay while he or she talks to you. Do not allow the use of crayons or clay to become a convenient escape from talking, however. The young child also can be allowed to express himself or herself with toys. Carefully observe the child's play—including motor, language, and fantasy elements.

16. *Use a sentence-completion technique.* A way to elicit information from preteens and adolescents who are hesitant to talk with you is to use a sentence-completion technique. Interpret the results cautiously, however, using the information obtained to establish hypotheses rather than to reach firm conclusions. The technique consists of giving sentence stems orally and then recording the preteen's or adolescent's answers. If the youth's reading and writing skills are sufficiently developed, she or he may be willing to read the sentence stems and write responses. You then can use these responses to probe further about a topic. Table 6-1 shows examples of sentence stems that you can use.

17. *Use fantasy techniques.* For preteens and adolescents who are reluctant to speak with you, consider using fantasy techniques, such as the three wishes technique or the desert island technique (Barker, 1990). As with the sentence-completion technique, results must be interpreted cautiously, with the information obtained used to generate hypotheses rather than to reach firm conclusions.

a. *Three wishes technique.* To use the three wishes technique, say, "If you could have any three wishes, what would they be?" Alternative phrasing is "If you could wish for any three things to happen, what would they be?" Listen carefully to what the preteen or adolescent says. The wishes expressed may give you some indication of feelings about his or her parents, siblings, friends, insecurities, and so forth. You can then follow up on the answers. The three wishes technique may not be appropriate for younger children because they are likely to wish for something concrete, such as a bike, a toy, or something to eat.

b. *Desert island technique.* To use the desert island technique, ask the preteen or adolescent whom she or he would like to be with on a desert island. Say, "Here's a pretend question. Imagine you were shipwrecked on a desert island. There's no one else there, but you've got plenty of food to eat and water to drink. If you could have just one person to be with you on the island—anyone in the whole world—whom would you most want to have?" (Barker, 1990, p. 66, with changes in notation).

After the preteen or adolescent has selected someone, say, "Now if you could have another person—[the person first named] and somebody else—whom would you choose next?"

Table 6-1
Sentence-Completion Technique

SENTENCE COMPLETION

Child's name: _____

Age: _____ Grade: _____ Date: _____

School: _____

Examiner's name: _____

Directions: Say to the child "I'm going to start a sentence. I'd like you to finish it any way you want. Here is an example. If I say 'A car . . . ,' you can say 'is fun to go in,' 'is nice to have,' 'is good when it works,' 'costs a lot of money,' or anything else that you can think of. OK? Let's try the first one."

1. My favorite TV show _____.
2. At night _____.
3. My teacher _____.
4. The scariest thing is when _____.
5. Mothers _____.
6. At school, I usually feel _____.
7. I hate it when _____.
8. When I wake up, I usually _____.
9. I dislike _____.
10. Fathers _____.
11. I am happiest when _____.
12. My favorite subjects are _____.
13. I worry about _____.
14. My friends _____.
15. I need _____.
16. My life would be better if _____.
17. I feel angry when _____.
18. My neighborhood is _____.
19. Animals are _____.
20. It is wrong to _____.
21. The best thing about being me is _____.
22. I like _____.
23. The saddest time is when _____.
24. The best thing about my home is _____.
25. My favorite book is _____.
26. I feel ashamed when _____.
27. My worst subjects are _____.
28. I am proud of _____.
29. If I could change one thing about my family, it would be _____.
30. (If appropriate) My sister(s) _____.
31. (If appropriate) My brother(s) _____.

Then ask, "And if you could have one more—and this would be the last one you could have—whom would you choose for your third person?" You also can ask two or three additional questions, such as "Is there anyone you wouldn't want to have on the island with you?" If the preteen or adolescent says "Yes," ask, "Who would that be?" Follow up with "Tell me the reason for each of your choices."

18. *Help the child express his or her thoughts and feelings.* You can help the child express his or her thoughts and feelings in several ways. First, let the child speak in whatever words he or she chooses. Second, encourage the child to speak freely and openly, and follow up leads that he or she gives you. Third, convey to the child that you are willing to listen to any of his or her feelings and thoughts, even those that the child might think are unacceptable.

The following techniques may help children talk about difficult issues (Yarrow, 1960, adapted from p. 580, with additions from Bierman & Schwartz, 1986, p. 271).

a. *Present two alternatives.* Examples:

- "If your little brother writes on the wall, do you punish him so he won't do it again, or do you make sure your mother finds out about it?"
- "Do you ever wish that you could be someone else, or are you happy being yourself?"
- "Do you ever wish that your dad spent more time with you, or do you think he spends enough time with you?"

You can follow up the child's response to each question. To follow up the first question, you might say, "How would you punish him?" or "What would your mother do when she found out?" A follow-up to the second question might be "Who would you like to be?" or "What makes you happy about yourself?" After any response to the third question, you could ask, "How much time does he spend with you?"

b. *Give children an opportunity to express a positive response before presenting a question that will require a negative response.* Examples:

- "What things do you like best about school?" After the child responds, say, "What things aren't so good about school?"
- "What is one thing that you like best about your sister?" After the child responds, say, "What is something your sister does that you don't like very much?"

You can extend these techniques with specific probing comments.

Follow-up comments that provide concrete structure can help the child expand his or her answers to initial questions. For example, a child might respond to the question "What kinds of things don't you like about school?" with a one-word answer or "I don't know." A structured probe might be "Well, let's just try to think about one thing first. Tell me one thing you don't like at school." If the child simply answers "Math," a structured probing question might be "What happens in math that you don't like very much?" Or, if that does not work, you could offer a choice: "Well, is it more the work you don't like or the teacher?" These focused questions are all preferable to vague questions such as "Can you tell me anything else?" This almost invariably receives a negative response. (Bierman, 1983, p. 235, with changes in notation)

19. *Clarify an episode of misbehavior by recounting it.* When you want to obtain further information from a child about an episode of misbehavior, ask the child to recount the details of the episode, as illustrated in the following dialogue (Karoly, 1981):

> IR: Your teacher tells me that yesterday a bunch of kids in your class "went wild" with paints, throwing them around the room and at other kids.
> IE: Yeah.
> IR: That really happened?
> IE: Yeah. So?
> IR: What led up to it?
> IE: The kids were bored.
> IR: Were you bored?
> IE: Yeah, I guess.
> IR: Did you throw the paints too?
> IE: Yeah.
> IR: Did you enjoy throwing the paints?
> IE: What do you mean?
> IR: Was it a way to be less bored?
> IE: Sure . . . for a while.
> IR: Then what happened?
> IE: We had to clean the place up. It took all afternoon.
> IR: Did you think you would have to clean up?
> IE: I don't know.
> IR: Was it unfair for her to make you clean up?
> IE: The janitor should do it.
> IR: But the kids made the mess.
> IE: Mrs. Masters [the teacher] is supposed to give us stuff to do. (Adapted from p. 102)

In this case, the recounting technique brought to light the child's perception that the teacher is responsible for keeping the students occupied. The interview segment also illustrates that it may take several questions to elicit small bits of information.

20. *Clarify interview procedures for children who are minimally communicative.* Some children may respond to your questions with "Yes," "No," "I don't know," or "I guess." It is best to handle these responses with comments like the following:

- "What I'd like to have you do, rather than just saying 'Yes' or 'No,' is to try to tell me as much as you can about what I ask you."
- "Sometimes it's hard to talk about things. But I'd really like to you try. It will help me get to know you better."

On the rare occasions when a child simply refuses to participate in the initial interview, it probably is best to reschedule the interview, as illustrated in the following case (Reisman, 1973).

> Suzie, a 7-year-old girl, had refused to attend school. When first seen by the interviewer, she was clutching tightly to her mother

and refused to accompany the interviewer to his office. When brought to the office by her mother, she began kicking and biting her mother, crying and screaming because her mother wanted to leave to go to her own appointment. After her mother left, Suzie retreated to a corner, where she wept angrily, hurling curses at the interviewer, demanding to see her mother, and refusing to cooperate. In such cases, it may be best to go along with the child's behavior and allow the behavior to run its course. Arrange to see the child again for another meeting. It may take a few sessions before you obtain the child's trust, acceptance, and cooperation.

21. *Understand and use silence.* Because clinical assessment interviews depend primarily on conversation, children who are silent are a challenge. Children may remain silent because they resent being at the interview, they are frightened, they want to talk but don't know what to say, they prefer to sit quietly and do nothing else, or they need time to collect their thoughts in order to express them (Reisman, 1973). Chapter 5 presents other possible reasons for silence. Determine which possibility is most applicable, because what you decide will have a direct bearing on how you proceed. For some children, silence is comfortable at first but can become stressful. Other children find silence stressful from the beginning but do not know how to break it. Children under 5 or 6 years of age usually have more difficulty with silence than older children do. If silence leads to resistance, it can be detrimental to the interview. Therefore, try to keep silences to a minimum with young children.

There are several ways that you can cope with children's silences. Children who are angry about coming for the interview may be silent initially, but they will likely start to talk to you once they begin to accept you and understand the purpose of the interview. If they wish to remain silent, you should accept their decision. When young children or preteens are silent, point out that they can play with the toys and play materials if they would like. If the silence continues, you can comment from time to time about what they are doing and how much time is left. You also can play with some toys as they play. These activities may serve as a way to break the silence and build rapport.

What you don't want to do is to assume that children's silence (or failure to respond to questions) means that they are ashamed of talking about the topic. Failure to respond may simply mean that they have nothing to say about the question, that the situation is strange, or that other unknown factors are operating.

22. *Handle resistance and anxiety by giving support and reassurance.* Older children may be reluctant to reveal their feelings and thoughts to a stranger, especially when they are concerned about the reason for and outcome of the evaluation. They may show their anxiety through hesitancy in speech, sadness, hostility, or other means (Jennings, 1982).

If you observe that a child is anxious, you may want to help the child express his or her anxiety directly. You could say, "How do you feel about being here today?" or "You look a little nervous about talking to me." Respond to the child's answers with encouragement or support; you might also want to make a statement that asks for further exploration or a comment that acknowledges his or her feelings (Jennings, 1982). Matter-of-factly accepting everything the child says, helping the child understand the reasons for the evaluation, and helping the child work through his or her feelings also may help reduce anxiety. Following are things you might say to reluctant children:

- "Many children feel as you do at the beginning. But in a little while, most feel more relaxed. I hope you will too."
- "I'd like to understand why you don't want to talk."
- "You seem to feel hesitant about talking with me."

If the examinee is an adolescent, you can ask him or her to complete the Personal Data Questionnaire (see Table A-2 in Appendix A) before the interview, and then review it before you meet with her or him. Some adolescents may feel more comfortable and reveal more information on a questionnaire than in an interview. Responses to the Personal Data Questionnaire may give you some useful leads for further inquiry during the interview.

AREAS COVERED IN THE INITIAL INTERVIEW WITH CHILDREN

The typical sequence in an interview with a child is as follows:

1. Introduce yourself to the parent (or caregiver or guardian) and to the child by giving your name and professional title.
2. Greet the child.
3. Open the interview with an introductory statement.
4. Continue the interview as appropriate.
5. Review the referral issues with the child.
6. Describe what will happen to the child after you complete the interview.
7. Express appreciation for the child's effort and cooperation.
8. Close the interview.

Following are typical topics covered in the initial interview with a child:

- Reasons for coming
- Confidentiality and other possible ethical concerns
- School (including the child's perceptions of teachers, peer group, and school environment)
- Home (including the child's perceptions of parents, siblings, and home environment)
- Interests (including leisure time activities, hobbies, recreation, clubs, and sports)
- Friends
- Moods and feelings
- Fears and worries
- Self-concept

- Somatic concerns
- Obsessions and compulsions
- Thought disorders
- Memories or fantasies (the child's own recollections, as well as what his or her parents told the child about his or her infancy and early childhood, including developmental milestones)
- Aspirations (including career possibilities)
- Other information voluntarily supplied by the child

During the initial interview with adolescents, these additional areas could be covered:

- Jobs
- Sexual relations (including sexual identity, peer relationships, and pregnancy—their own or a partner's)
- Eating habits
- Use of alcohol, tobacco, and/or other drugs (including frequency of use and type of drug)

In discussing these areas, attend to the child's (a) ability to relate to you, (b) ability to discuss relevant information, (c) thought processes, (d) language, (e) affect, (f) nonverbal behaviors, and (g) temperament and personality, as well as any indications of possible psychological disturbances. The questions presented in Table B-1 in Appendix B will aid you in obtaining information about the topics noted. The questions in Table B-1 are only sample questions, meant to illustrate the topics most frequently covered in interviews with children; do not use the questions mechanically. Include follow-up and probing questions and reassuring comments as needed. You may need to alter the wording of some questions in Table B-1, depending on the child's age. See Chapter 5 for more information about flexibility in interviewing.

Reinforcers

In some situations (such as when you are planning a therapeutic behavioral intervention), you may want to identify, during the interview, reinforcers important to the children. The positive reinforcement sentence-completion technique shown in Table 6-2 is useful for this purpose.

Children's Environments

If you believe that the physical layout of a child's home may be contributing to the difficulties the child is experiencing, you can ask the child to draw a picture of her or his room and any other relevant rooms in the house. Then ask the child to tell you about each room. This technique also is helpful in establishing rapport and getting children used to the question-and-answer flow of the interview. You should not assume that what the child draws is a valid representation of the home; therefore, you might want to verify details about the home with the parents.

POSITIVE REINFORCEMENT SENTENCE COMPLETION

Child's name: _____

Age: _____ Grade: _____ Date: _____

School: _____

Examiner's name: _____

Directions: Read all the sentence stems to the child, following up on the child's responses as necessary. Then state all the reinforcers named by the child, and ask the child to rank them in order of their importance.

1. My favorite grown-up is _____.
2. My favorite thing to do with him [her] is _____.
3. The best reward anybody can give me is _____.
4. The two things I like best to do are _____.
5. My favorite adult at school is _____.
6. When I do something well, what my mother does is _____
   _____.
7. I feel terrific when _____.
8. When I have money, I like to _____.
9. Something I really want is _____.
10. The person I would like most to reward me is _____.
11. I would like [person's name] to reward me by _____
    _____.
12. The thing I like best to do with my mother is _____.
13. On Saturday or Sunday, my favorite thing to do is _____
    _____.
14. The thing I like to do most is _____.
15. My two favorite TV programs are _____.
16. The thing I like best to do with my father is _____.
17. My favorite music to listen to is _____.

Child's Ranking of Reinforcers

_____

_____

_____

_____

_____

_____

Source: Adapted from Tharp and Wetzel (1969).
From *Assessment of Children: Behavioral, Social, and Clinical Foundations (Fifth Edition)* by Jerome M. Sattler and Robert D. Hoge. Copyright 2006 by Jerome M. Sattler, Publisher, Inc. Permission to photocopy this table is granted to purchasers of this book for personal use only (see copyright page for details).

Mental Status Evaluation

As part of the initial interview with children, you may want to conduct a mental status evaluation. A mental status evaluation may be particularly helpful in cases of brain injury, when children appear confused, or when you want to obtain an overall sense of their general mental functioning. Table B-2 in Appendix B offers a brief mental status examination for older children. This type of evaluation is especially important when children appear to have problems in orientation to time, place, or person or difficulty with memory, attention, or thinking clearly. Interpret all areas in a mental status evaluation within a developmental framework, using age-appropriate norms or age-appropriate expectations.

INTERVIEWING PARENTS

The interview with parents is an important part of the assessment process. Parents have a wealth of knowledge about their children. A well-conducted parent interview will (a) establish rapport and a positive working relationship with the parents, (b) focus the attention of the parents on the issues, (c) provide valuable information about the child and family, (d) help the parents organize and reflect on the information, (e) contribute to the formulation of a diagnosis, (f) provide a basis for decisions about treatment and further investigation, and (g) lay the groundwork for parents to contribute to any intervention efforts (Barkley, 1981; Canino, 1985; La Greca, 1983).

You want the parents to participate actively in the interview. To encourage them to do so, you need to treat them with respect and honesty. Consider their cultural and ethnic backgrounds and practices and use language they understand. Strive to establish a collaborative working relationship with them. Make sure they understand the limits of confidentiality (see Chapter 1).

Parents not only serve as an important source of information but also will play a key role in any proposed intervention. If invasive or demanding questions and unempathic responses during the initial interview cause them to feel threatened, they may prematurely terminate contact with you and find excuses to avoid coming for further help. They may say that they have transportation difficulties, babysitting problems, or problems in scheduling appointments. (In some cases, of course, these will be legitimate concerns.) You want to lessen any anxiety parents have and make every effort to show them that you are interested in them and concerned about what is in the best interest of their child.

Parents provide the most reliable information when they are aware of their child's problems, know who their child is associating with outside the home, know about their child's performance in school, are good observers of behavior, are able to describe their child's problems, and are willing to report the problem behaviors without concealing, minimizing, or exaggerating them. However, not all parents will be reliable or objective informants. Parents may describe a child's preinjury behavior and ability in an overly favorable light. They may selectively disclose historical information or fail to disclose the child's problems. This may happen for several reasons. Developmental milestones are difficult to remember, and relating particular events to particular behavioral responses may be even more difficult. Also, parents may have forgotten important details, have vague recollections, be experiencing emotional distress, or be involved in litigation associated with the child's disability. When possible, it is helpful to interview persons outside the immediate family to document the consistency of the history. Again, recognize that friends and others may not be objective, for some of the same reasons mentioned above. Thus, expect to find some distortions, biases, and memory lapses in the information you collect from parents and others.

Research on the accuracy of parental reports suggests the following (Canino, 1985):

1. Parents recall variables such as the child's weight, height, and health more accurately than information about the child's personality and temperament.
2. Discrete symptoms that the child had (such as nightmares, stuttering, bedwetting, stealing, and temper tantrums) are recalled better than less well-defined symptoms (such as the child's activity level, feeling states, and social relationships).
3. Major events in the family (such as deaths, weddings, moves, financial reversals, and births) and their dates are recalled relatively accurately.
4. Mothers are usually more reliable informants about the child's development than are fathers.

Goals of the Initial Interview with Parents

Following are the main goals of the initial clinical assessment interview with parents (Mash & Terdal, 1981):

1. To gather information about parental concerns and goals
2. To obtain informed consent from the parents to conduct an assessment of the child
3. To discuss the assessment procedures that may be used with the child
4. To assess parental perceptions of the child's strengths and weaknesses
5. To obtain a case history of the child, including the child's medical, developmental, educational, and social histories
6. To identify the child's problem(s) and related antecedent and consequent events
7. To determine how the parents have dealt with the problem(s) in the past (including whether they sought prior treatment and, if so, who provided the treatment and the dates and outcomes of the treatment) and to obtain permission to obtain records from any previous treatment
8. To identify events that reinforced the problem(s) for both the child and the parents
9. To obtain a family history (where relevant)
10. To assess the parents' motivation and resources for change and their expectations for the child's treatment
11. To discuss what follow-up contacts they and their child may need

If you achieve all these goals, you can probably develop some preliminary hypotheses about the child's difficulties, strengths, and weaknesses and about the parents' reactions, concerns, coping abilities, strengths, and weaknesses. You can also construct a picture of the family's life style and its prevailing values, mores, and concerns. In order to achieve these goals, you will need to use the effective interviewing skills described in Chapter 5. These include rapport-building skills, communication skills, and listening skills.

Age of the Child

The age of the child will, in part, determine the content of the interview with the parents. If you are interviewing the parents of a toddler or preschooler, the focus will be on the mother's pregnancy and delivery, the child's early developmental milestones, and the nature of the problem. With parents of elementary school-age children, you also will need to ask about language and motor skills, peer and social relations, and educational progress. With parents of adolescents, you will want to inquire about all of these, as well as about the adolescent's peer group, sexual activity, academic progress, vocational plans, interests, and use of alcohol, tobacco, and/or other drugs.

Concerns of Parents

Parents may be apprehensive about their child's evaluation. Depending on the type and severity of the child's problems, their cultural subgroup and ethnicity, and their religious affiliation, they may be concerned about any of the following issues:

1. *Etiology.* What is the cause of the child's problem? How serious is the child's problem?

2. *Interventions.* What can they do about the child's problem? What treatment is needed, and will the treatment cure the problem? Where can the child get treatment? How long will the treatment last? How much will it cost? Will their insurance cover the cost of treatment (if they are insured)? What special services will their child need? Will they also need to be seen for treatment? What can they do at home to help their child? Where can they get more information about their child's condition? Will the authorities try to remove the child from their home?

3. *Family issues.* Will other children in the family also have these problems? What should they tell their other children about their sibling's condition? How will the other children in the family react if their sibling is seen by a mental health professional? What secrets will the child reveal about the family? Will telling these secrets damage the family in any way?

4. *Parental responsibility.* Are they responsible for their child's problems? Have they exaggerated the problem or put ideas into their child's head? Will other people think that they

are incapable of taking care of their child? Is it one parent's fault more than the other's?

5. *Stigma.* Will their child resent them for taking him or her to a mental health professional? What will it mean that their child has a record of visiting a "shrink"? Will other people think that their family is crazy? What will relatives, neighbors, friends, the child's peers, the peers' parents, and the child's teachers think about the child's going to see a mental health professional?

6. *Results.* Will they receive a report? When will they receive the final results and recommendations? Who will have access to the findings?

Parents may ask you how to prepare their child for the interview. Tell them to be straightforward. Suggest that they tell their child whom the child will be seeing, the reason for the appointment, and what will happen. Explanations should, of course, be consistent with the child's level of comprehension. With children between ages 3 and 6 years, parents should emphasize that there will be toys to play with in the office and that the child will be talking with someone. With children between ages 6 and 10 years, parents should emphasize that the child will be talking with someone and possibly playing some games. With children older than 10 years, parents should emphasize that the interviewer is someone who knows how to help children (or teenagers) and families, that the child (or adolescent) will be talking with that person, and that it often helps to obtain the advice of someone outside the family.

Potential Negative Feelings of Parents

By the time parents seek an evaluation for a school-age child (and sometimes for a preschool child as well), they have already experienced much frustration and anguish. Although they may have seen other professionals, they may still be seeking a magical solution. They may know that their child has a problem but be tired of feeling that they are to blame. If they feel this way, they may displace on you the anger that has developed from prior encounters with medical or mental health professionals. Because parents may feel inadequate—as a result of their inability to work with their child and their impatience and irritability with her or him—they also may have feelings of guilt and a diminished sense of self-esteem.

Parents sometimes deny that there is a problem and react angrily to being interviewed. At a school-initiated interview, for example, they may make the following types of comments:

1. *Comments reflecting anger or denial.* "We didn't know she was having any problems. No one told us before." "We don't see any problems like that at home."

2. *Comments implying blame.* "Do you think it's because my wife works?" "Do you think it's because my husband spends so little time with him?"

3. *Comments reflecting rationalization.* "Perhaps it's because his older brother is like that." "You know, we're divorced. That could be the reason."

4. *Comments reflecting disbelief.* "How can you tell from just a few weeks in class?" "Aren't all children his age like that?"

5. *Comments that point to the school's responsibility.* "If you would give her special help, it would help the problem." "I think he should see a counselor. That will straighten everything out." "You found it. You fix it."

Address any negative feelings the parents have about themselves or others during your initial contact with them; otherwise, their feelings may interfere with the interview. Give them an opportunity to talk about their feelings. Help the parents recognize that you can work together to understand and improve the behavior and functioning of their child. Tell them that you are aware of the discomfort they feel in discussing personal topics and that you welcome their questions. *Keep in mind, however, that the focus of the interview is the child, not the parents.*

Occasionally, you will find that the parents have problems such as depression, stress, marital conflict, or substance abuse. If so, refer them for appropriate treatment services and be sure to give them referral names and telephone numbers. In many clinics, children will not be seen for treatment unless their parents also are involved in treatment.

Background Questionnaire

Another way to obtain information about the child and family is to have the parents complete the Background Questionnaire before the interview (see Table A-1 in Appendix A). The Background Questionnaire is useful in obtaining a detailed account of the child's developmental, social, medical, and educational history, as well as information about the family. You can send the Background Questionnaire to the parents a week or two before the scheduled interview and ask them to send it back a few days before the interview. (If necessary, they can bring it with them to the interview, but it is better to be able to review the questionnaire before the interview.) Be sure to provide your telephone number so that they can contact you if they have questions.

Sometimes you may want to complete the Background Questionnaire jointly with the parents, especially if they have reading or writing difficulties or cannot complete it for some other reason. Filling out the Background Questionnaire together serves as a type of structured interview. Time constraints or agency policy, however, may not allow you to complete the Background Questionnaire in an interview format.

Useful Formats for Interviews with Parents

Three useful formats for interviewing parents are the unstructured (open-ended) interview, the semistructured interview, and the structured interview. When parents are extremely anxious or resistant, it is best to use an open-ended format at the initial stage of the interview before moving on to a semistructured or structured interview. (See Chapter 5 for a discussion of the three types of interviews.)

During any type of interview, when parents have difficulty recalling the child's developmental milestones, you can provide a time frame to help them (Rudel, 1988):

> "Was he walking on his first birthday?" If this fails, you can discuss family history (moves from one place of residence to another, holidays, family celebrations, or visits to relatives) and, by estimating the child's age on these occasions, can relate developmental data to these events. "Was he toilet-trained when you visited your in-laws? Did you have to change diapers en route? Did he speak to your mother when he met her? Do you recall what they said? Was your mother surprised that he was not talking in sentences at that time?" By providing an event-related context, you sometimes can obtain a more reliable estimate of the child's developmental history. (p. 90, with changes in notation)

If parents cannot recall developmental events, this may mean that the child's development was normal; the parents would likely remember unusual or deviant behavior (Rudel, 1988). In rare cases, it could mean that the child was neglected.

Semistructured interview. A semistructured interview is useful in assessing what is important to the parents, what they hope to accomplish from the evaluation, their concerns, and how they view their own role in helping the child. The semistructured interview allows parents the leeway to discuss anything they believe is relevant.

Three common types of semistructured interviews with parents are the developmental history interview, the screening interview with parents of preschool children, and the typical-day interview.

1. *Developmental history interview.* If the parents do not complete a background questionnaire, you will need to obtain a history of the child's development. The history should provide background information, some perspective on the child's current situation, what interventions have been tried and with what success, and clues to what might benefit the child in the future. Following are typical areas covered in a developmental history interview (Nay, 1979):

- *Description of child's birth and events related to the birth* (including mother's health; mother's use of alcohol, tobacco, and/or other drugs during pregnancy; and pregnancy and birth complications)
- *Child's developmental history* (including important developmental milestones such as the age at which the child began sitting, standing, walking, using functional language, and controlling bladder and bowel; self-help skills; and personal-social relationships)
- *Child's medical history* (including types and dates of injuries, accidents, operations, and significant illnesses, as well as prescribed medications)
- *Characteristics of family and family history* (including age, ordinal position, sex, occupation, employment status, and marital status of family members and significant medical, educational, and mental health history of siblings and parents)
- *Child's cognitive level, personality, and temperament* (including the child's reasoning, memory, flexibility, degree of organization, ability to plan, ability to attend and concentrate, and ability to inhibit responses)
- *Child's interpersonal skills* (including child's ability to form friendships and relationships with others, child's play activities, and how other children and adults relate to the child)
- *Child's educational history* (including schools attended, grades, attitude toward schooling, relationships with teachers and peers, and special education services received)
- *Child's sexual behaviors* (including relationships with those of the same and opposite sex)
- *Child's occupational history, if any* (including types and dates of employment, attitude toward work, and occupational goals)
- *Description of presenting problem* (including a detailed description of the problem, antecedent events, consequences, and how the parents have dealt with the problem)
- *Parental expectations* (including the parents' expectations and goals for treatment of their child and, if appropriate, themselves)

Table B-9 in Appendix B provides a semistructured interview for obtaining a detailed case history from parents. The parents are asked to describe the child's problem behavior, home environment, neighborhood, sibling relations, peer relations, relationship with the parents, interests and hobbies, daily activities, cognitive functioning, academic functioning, biological functioning, affective life, and abilities in comparison with those of siblings, as well as their own concerns and related issues.

2. *Screening interview with parents of preschool children.* Table B-11 in Appendix B provides a brief semistructured screening interview for use with parents of preschool children. It focuses on the parents' concerns about their child's development. It is useful when you want an overview of how a preschool child is functioning.

3. *Typical-day interview.* Sometimes you will want to ask a parent or caregiver about how his or her preschool- or elementary school-age child spends a typical day (see the semistructured interview in Table B-12 in Appendix B). This information can help you better understand how the child functions in his or her family and social and interpersonal environments. For preschool-age children who are not attending school, you might ask about any day of the week. For preschoolers who are attending school and for school-age children, you should ask about a typical Saturday or Sunday if you want to know about a full day at home or any weekday if you want to know about a school day. Or, you might ask about both a typical school day and a typical weekend day.

These three types of interviews will not gather biographical information from the parents. You must obtain this information by having the parents complete an information form or questionnaire that asks them to give their name, address, and phone number; the child's teacher's name; and other important identifying information. The Background Questionnaire shown in Table A-1 in Appendix A has a section for obtaining biographical information.

Structured interview. In a structured interview, the questions are designed to cover various areas of psychopathology systematically. Chapter 5 describes several structured interviews. They are useful when you need to arrive at a specific diagnosis.

Major Components of the Initial Interview with Parents

The major components of an initial interview with parents are as follows:

1. *Greet the parents.*
2. *Give your name and professional title.*
3. *Open the interview with an introductory statement.* Useful introductory statements include the following (Lichtenstein & Ireton, 1984):

- "Tell me what brings you here today."
- "How can I help you?"
- "Tell me about your child."
- "Please tell me your concerns about your child."
- "Please tell me what [child's name] has been doing lately."
- "How well do you think your child is doing?"
- "How do you get along with your child?"
- "I understand that your son [daughter] is having some difficulties in school. I'd like to discuss these difficulties with you and see whether we can work together to develop a plan to help him [her]."

4. *Ask parents about items on the Background Questionnaire.* If the parents have completed a Background Questionnaire, you will not have to go over most of the areas covered in a developmental history interview. Nevertheless, allow them to describe in their own words their concerns about their child. Also ask the parents about any items on the Background Questionnaire that need to be clarified—for example, "I see that John is having problems at home. Would you tell me more about these problems?" If the parents have not completed a questionnaire, ask them about the typical areas covered in a developmental history. As previously noted, you might want to use the semistructured interview in Table B-9 in Appendix B.

5. *Review problems.* Review the child's problems as presented by the parents, and ask the parents whether they would like to comment further on any problem.

6. *Describe the assessment procedure.* If psychological tests will be administered to the child, explain the purposes of the tests and why they will be administered. Inform the parents about who will have access to the assessment information and how the information will be used. Discuss confidentiality of the assessment results, including the conditions under which confidentiality will need to be broken. (See Chapter 1 for further discussion of confidentiality.) In some cases, this also would be an appropriate time to offer the parents information on services available through the clinic, school, or hospital. Otherwise, you may want to offer this information in the post-assessment interview.

7. *Arrange for a post-assessment interview.* Arrange to discuss the results of the assessment with the parents. In some cases, the results will be presented to the parents at an interdisciplinary staff conference. In other cases, one staff member may present the overall results of the assessment based on reports provided by all of the professionals involved in the case. In still other cases, only the examiner who conducted the psychological or psychoeducational evaluation will present his or her results to the parents.

8. *Close the interview.* Escort the parents from the room and make appropriate closing remarks, such as "Thank you for coming. In case you have any other questions, here is my phone number."

Guidelines for Interviewing Parents

Following are some guidelines for interviewing parents:

1. Listen carefully to the parents' concerns.
2. Explain what lies ahead, what may be involved in the assessment process, and what interventions are possible.
3. Adopt a calm, nonjudgmental approach to reduce the parents' stress.
4. Reassure parents that the records will be kept confidential, unless the law requires that the records be disclosed or agency policy requires that the records be shared with others (see Chapter 1).
5. Help parents who are having problems in managing their child understand that child rearing is a complex and difficult activity and that a child with special needs may be especially difficult to cope with.
6. Take special care to convey respect for the parents' feelings.
7. Help the parents understand that many children have problems at times and that emotional problems or physical problems may develop in a child because of events beyond the parents' control. Avoid any suggestion that the parents are to blame for their child's difficulties. (This and the following two points may not apply when the parents have maltreated their child or are alleged to have done so.)
8. Emphasize parents' constructive and helpful parenting skills rather than their destructive or harmful approaches.
9. Enlist parents' cooperation in the diagnostic and remediation program; do not be authoritarian.
10. Schedule more than one meeting if parents are uncooperative or if the information provided needs to be clarified.
11. If working with a two-parent family, try to get both parents to come to the interview. Having both parents at the

interview will help you gain a more complete picture of the family.

12. Consider interviewing parents separately, especially in cases of custody evaluations, child maltreatment, or domestic violence or when the parents are hostile to each other.

13. Help the parents clarify vague, ambiguous, or incomplete statements.

14. Encourage the parents to discuss fully their child's problem and how the problem affects the family.

15. Use follow-up and probing questions to learn about the specific conditions that may serve to instigate, maintain, or limit the child's behavior and about the child's and parents' resources and motivation to change.

16. Determine the areas in which the parents agree and disagree about child management.

17. Appropriately and gently guide the parents back to the topic if they give many irrelevant details.

18. Ask the parents to check their recollections against baby books, medical and school records, and other formal and informal records if their memory of important events or of dates is hazy.

19. If you schedule a second interview, ask the parents to keep a record of the occurrences of the problem if you believe that such a record would be helpful. The record should include what happened before the problem behavior occurred, what the child did, and what happened after the problem behavior occurred. You can use the form shown in Table 13-2 in Chapter 13, deleting the term *examiner* and substituting the term *parent*.

> *Before I got married, I had six theories about bringing up children; now I have six children and no theories.*
> —John Wilmot, British poet and satirist (1647–1680)

INTERVIEWING TEACHERS

Teachers are valuable informants, providing information about children's academic skills, behavior at school, and changes in academic performance and behavior. During the initial interview with teachers, you can cover many of the same topics that you cover with parents. The focus, however, is somewhat different. When you interview a teacher, your concern is not only with the teacher's perception of the problem, the antecedents and consequences of the problem behavior, and what the teacher has done to alleviate the problem, but also with how other children and teachers react to the child and how the child performs academically. If the child's problem occurs in a specific situation or setting, learn what the teacher considers appropriate behavior in that situation or setting. For help with interviewing teachers, see Table B-15 in Appendix B.

Courtesy of Herman Zielinski.

You also can ask the teacher to complete the School Referral Questionnaire (see Table A-3 in Appendix A) before the interview, and then review it before you meet with her or him. Like the Background Questionnaire completed by a parent, it may give you some useful leads for further inquiry during the interview.

Areas Covered in the Initial Interview with Teachers

Areas covered in the initial interview with teachers include the teacher's perception of the child's problem behavior, reactions to the child's problem behavior, opinion of the child's relationship with peers, assessment of the child's academic performance, assessment of the child's strengths and weaknesses, view of the child's family, expectations for the child, and suggestions for helping the child.

Questions to Ask in an Initial Interview with Teachers

The following two examples illustrate the types of questions you might ask in an initial interview with a teacher. The examples show how you can use the interview to develop a plan for obtaining further information about the child's problem. (The examples are adapted from Bergan, 1977, pp. 97–99; used with permission of the author.)

CHILD WITH BEHAVIOR PROBLEM

"Tell me about Alice's problem in the classroom."

"What does Alice do when she annoys you?"

"How often during the week does she talk out of turn?"

"You've said that Alice talks without permission. She does this about four times a day. Is that right?"

"What is generally going on right before Alice talks out of turn?"

"What are you usually doing just before Alice talks out of turn?"

"What do you do when Alice talks out of turn?"

"When does she talk out of turn during the day?"

"On what days of the week does she talk out of turn?"

"You've said that Alice usually talks out of turn when your back is turned and you're writing on the blackboard. Is that right?"

"Afterwards, the other kids giggle and laugh and sometimes treat her as though she had really done something great. Is that correct?"

"Will you be able to record when Alice talks out of turn?"

"The record will help us to establish a baseline against which to evaluate the success of our intervention plan."

"Throughout the rest of this week, would you record on this form the number of instances that Alice talks out of turn?"

"If you have the time to do it, you also could make a note of what happens before and after she talks out of turn."

"Do these suggestions meet with your approval?"

"We agreed that you will record the number of instances that Alice talks out of turn during the rest of this week."

"You're going to use this form."

"If you have a chance, please note what happens before and after she talks out of turn."

"Did I summarize our recording plans accurately?"

"Could we meet Monday or Tuesday of next week?"

"Shall we meet in the teacher's lounge or in your classroom?"

"If it's okay, I'll give you a call sometime this week to see how the data collection is going."

CHILD WITH READING PROBLEM

"Tell me about Ted's reading problem."

"Give me some other examples of Ted's reading difficulties."

"About how many errors does Ted make during an oral reading session?"

"You said that Ted continually misreads and omits words during oral reading. Is that correct?"

"How do you introduce oral reading?"

"How do the other children react when Ted makes errors while reading?"

"What is the sequence of steps that you go through in teaching reading in the oral reading groups?"

"You said that when you call on Ted to read, he reads eagerly, and that after he has finished, you always go over all of his mistakes with him. You pronounce the words for him and have him say the words correctly. Is that an accurate review of what happens?"

"If you could record the number of errors that Ted makes during reading for the rest of the week, it would help us to establish a baseline against which we can measure improvement in his reading."

"You could use this form for recording."

"And if you have a chance, note the other children's reactions and your own reactions when Ted makes a mistake."

"Would these plans be okay with you?"

"To summarize, we said that you will use this form to record the number of errors that Ted makes during oral reading for the rest of the week and that, if you have the chance, you'll note your own reactions and those of the other children to Ted's mistakes. Is that right?"

"Could we meet Monday or Tuesday of next week?"

"Shall we meet in the teacher's lounge or in your classroom?"

"If it's okay, I'll give you a call sometime this week to see how the data collection is going."

Working with the Teacher

Allay the teacher's anxiety about his or her responsibility for the child's problem behaviors. Inform the teacher that children's problems likely stem from a variety of factors. Tell the teacher when the assessment results will be ready, and do not leave the impression that immediate changes for the better will occur. If you want to observe the child in the classroom, follow the procedures discussed in Chapters 8 and 9.

Based on your interview with the teacher (and on classroom observations and interviews with the child and parents), you can probably come to some understanding about the following matters:

1. What does the teacher see as the major problem(s)?
2. How effective are the teacher's teaching skills and behavior management skills?
3. Is the child's class placement appropriate?
4. If a placement change is needed for the child, what might be more appropriate?
5. What insights does the teacher have about the child?
6. What techniques have been successful in helping the child?
7. What techniques have not succeeded in helping the child?
8. How do other children contribute to the problem?
9. What stressors exist in the classroom?
10. If stressors are present in the classroom, how can they be diminished?
11. How well does the teacher's account of the child's problem(s) agree with those of the parents and the child?
12. What are the teacher's recommendations for interventions?

Children need models rather than critics.
    —Joseph Joubert, French philosopher (1754–1824)

INTERVIEWING THE FAMILY

Goals of the Initial Family Interview

The goals of the initial family interview are to obtain historical details and information about current family life relevant to the child's problems and to observe patterns of family interaction. The family's strengths and weaknesses also should be noted.

A family interview is valuable for the following reasons (Kinsbourne & Caplan, 1979):

1. It informs the child and the parents that you prefer to be open about the problem and that it is important to include the child in the interview.
2. It allows you to observe how the parents and child interact when discussing the problem and other matters.
3. It allows you to gather information about (a) the child's problem, (b) the family's understanding of the child's problem, (c) family dynamics, communication patterns, and social and cultural values, (d) how well the family accepts the child, (e) what impact the child's difficulties have on the family, on the parents' relationship, and on other family members, and (f) the extent to which the family is using functional or dysfunctional strategies to cope with the child's problems.
4. It will help you clarify the family structure, along with details of the family's makeup, such as names, ages, relationships, and occupations of members. (Alternatively, a parent may supply this information on a questionnaire.)
5. It will help you evaluate the family's motivation to help the child and determine what interventions are possible, given the family's resources.

This interview may be the family's first attempt as a family unit to discuss the perceived problem. Hearing you say to the family, "Let's all go into my office and discuss why you're here today" may be a turning point in the child's life.

Family's Coping Strategies

Let's now consider functional and dysfunctional strategies families may use to cope with their child's psychological or medical problem (DePompei, Blosser, & Zarski, 1989).

FUNCTIONAL FAMILY STRATEGIES

1. *Reacting.* Family members have initial reactions of grief, anger, disappointment, guilt, anxiety, frustration, and a sense of loss.
2. *Mobilizing.* Family members draw on internal and external support systems to respond to the needs of the child.
3. *Recognition.* Family members perceive the strengths and weaknesses of the child in a realistic light.
4. *Understanding.* Family members gain an understanding of what the interventions might accomplish.
5. *Continuing.* Family members continue with other aspects of their lives.

6. *Hoping.* Family members maintain hope for the future for the child and for themselves.
7. *Appreciating.* Family members develop a new appreciation for many aspects of life for themselves and for their child.
8. *Reasoning.* Family members engage in adequate reasoning and do not make faulty assumptions.

DYSFUNCTIONAL FAMILY STRATEGIES

1. *Blaming.* Family members criticize actions of the child, threaten the child, accuse the child of acting to embarrass them, and blame the child for unrelated family problems. Parents also may blame each other, themselves, or someone else for the child's problems.
2. *Taking over, controlling, or employing power.* Family members assume responsibility for the child by speaking for the child and by performing tasks that the child could or should do, by selecting what the child should do rather than allowing the child to choose for himself or herself, by using their authority to direct the behaviors of the child, or by relying heavily on the use of guilt to maintain their position of authority.
3. *Avoiding.* Family members use work, medications, food, and blaming the child to remove themselves from direct involvement in the family; they also fail to accept responsibility for family disharmony.
4. *Denying.* Family members seek to maintain the status quo, failing to recognize that the child's disability or problem has changed the family's patterns of functioning.
5. *Rescuing.* Family members remove the child from situations that the child created so that the child does not have to suffer the consequences of her or his actions.
6. *Faulty reasoning.* Family members engage in rationalizing (e.g., if the child could just come home from the hospital or clinic and return to school or work, everything would return to normal) and assume that the child has behavioral controls that the child does not have.

Families may cope with stress in adaptive or maladaptive ways or with some combination of the two (Turk & Kerns, 1985). A key factor in coping with stress—whether the stress is psychological, environmental, or physical—is how the family was functioning *before* the stress occurred. A family that was functioning well before the stress occurred may continue to function adequately, although with some problems. The family may handle the stress, protect its members, adjust to role changes within the family, and continue to carry out its functions. A family that was not functioning well before the stress may break down in the face of stress; the breakdown, in turn, may lead to maladaptive behavior or illness on the part of its members.

When you interview the family, a sibling may be present. In such cases, you may find that the healthy child who has a sibling with a problem (particularly if it is a psychological or medical disorder) is also under stress. Healthy siblings may dislike their increased responsibilities at home, be unhappy about decreased parental attention and increased parental tension, feel guilt and shame, be upset about having to deal with the negative reactions of those outside the family, resent the sibling with a psychological or medical disorder, and be concerned and worried about the sibling. Be prepared to deal with these and similar issues and reactions.

The family interview, like the interview with the child or with parents alone, may be the first encounter the family has with a mental health professional and may serve as the beginning of a family therapy intervention program.

Necessity for Individual Interviews

The family interview is not a substitute for individual interviews—you should still see the child and the parents separately. You may also have to meet with each parent separately. Parents and children may be more open in an individual interview than in a family interview. Observing how they behave in both an individual and a family interview may be helpful. If you begin the assessment with a family interview, obtain the child's developmental history from the parents during their interview without the child.

Guidelines for Conducting the Family Interview

You want to create a setting in which the family members can risk sharing their feelings and problems and can seek information about the referred child's problems and their own problems as they relate to the child. Help every family member feel at ease and involved. You want family members to interact freely, to contribute ideas about the problem, to describe the conditions that they find most troublesome, and to discuss what changes they would like to see and what might be done to resolve the problem. *Recognize that your questions may result in painful confrontations among family members and may elicit feelings that have not been previously articulated.* When confrontations occur, offer support to the family members who need it.

Before beginning the family interview, consider who referred the family to you, the reason for the referral, and whether the family came voluntarily or under mandate (e.g., at the insistence of the court, the school, or one family member). The following are useful guidelines for conducting the family interview (Kinston & Loader, 1984):

1. Encourage open discussion among the family members.
2. Lower the parents' and child's stress levels as much as possible.
3. Reduce the family's anxiety and fear of negative evaluations.
4. Support any family member who is on the "hot seat."
5. Do not create guilt or loss of face for any family member.
6. Create a safe and supportive atmosphere and a sense of trust so that family members can interact comfortably and naturally.

7. Use praise, approval, and reflection of feeling to foster family members' acceptance of the interview.
8. Help family members see that you are interested in each member's point of view and that you want to understand them. Do not take sides.
9. Help family members clarify their thoughts.
10. Be objective and understanding in your evaluation of family members.
11. Maintain a balance between formality and informality, while promoting informality among the family members.
12. Encourage the children in the family to participate in the discussion.
13. Encourage family members to give specific examples of concerns and problems.
14. Do not provoke family members. Ask, for example, "How do arguments arise?" rather than "Who's the troublemaker in the family?"
15. Be aware of the dynamics among the family members.

If you follow these guidelines, the family members may be more willing to engage in a free discussion of the personal and intimate details of their lives.

Table 6-3 presents some guidelines for observing families. Note, for example, which members talk, in what sequence, at whom each member looks, and who speaks first, interrupts, clarifies, registers surprise, remains silent, disagrees, assumes a leadership role, expresses emotional warmth, and accepts responsibility. In addition, observe whether the child misbehaves and, if so, how the parents discipline the child. Also note how the parents view the child and her or his problems, how the family resolves anger, which members are encouraged to speak, whether members support and cooperate with each other, and whether the members make physical contact.

If you touch on an emotionally charged topic that upsets family members and makes it difficult to continue the interview, consider moving on to a more neutral subject. You can schedule a second session, if needed, to explore sensitive areas. You want to obtain as much information as possible during the initial evaluation, but you do not want to cause undue anxiety. In crises, instead of conducting a standard intake assessment interview, you might need to focus on what can be done immediately about the problem. For more information on crisis interviewing, see Sattler (1998).

During the family interview, when a child seems unable to answer a question and appears uncomfortable, do not prolong the discomfort; instead, take the child off the hook (Karpel & Strauss, 1983). Consider rephrasing the question, switching to another topic, or questioning another family member. You might even consider saying that the question was "too fuzzy," as a way of reassuring the child. Finally, you can "encourage the child to bring up the topic later if he or she gets any new ideas" (Karpel & Strauss, 1983, p. 204).

You want to be aware of how the family members perceive you. For example, note at what points they ask you to give your opinion, to intercede, to solve problems, or to give them support. Key interviewing skills are listening to one

**Table 6-3
Guidelines for Observing the Family**

Early in the Interview
1. How did the family enter the room?
2. Were the family members resistant or cooperative?
3. If the child was resistant, how did the parents deal with him or her?
4. How were the family members dressed?
5. How did they seat themselves?
6. Who replied first to the interviewer's initial comment?
7. What was the tone of voice of each family member?
8. What was the demeanor of each family member (e.g., did they appear anxious, distressed, or comfortable during the early moments of the interview)?

Intrafamily Relations
9. How did the parents treat the referred child?
10. How did the parents treat the other children (if present)?
11. Were all the children treated similarly (if more than one child was present)?
12. How did the children treat their parents?
13. What pairings occurred between family members?
14. Who talked to whom and in what manner?
15. What was the sequence of talking?
16. Were the family members protective of one another?
17. Did one family member speak for another member without taking into account the latter's feelings?
18. Did one family member ask another member about what a third member said in the presence of the third member?
19. Did family members interrupt each other?
20. Did one family member attempt to control, silence, or intimidate other family members?
21. Did two family members engage in nonverbal activities together (e.g., did they cry together, laugh together, roll eyes together, or make certain facial expressions together)?
22. Were there times when there was a chain reaction between pairs of family members that distracted them from their task?

23. Did one family member disregard other members' feelings?
24. Did the family members describe each other in clear terms?
25. Did one family member intercede in a dialogue between two other members? If so, how did the pair accept the intercession?

Affect Displayed by Family Members
26. What type of affect was displayed by the family members during most of the interview (e.g., were the family members anxious, depressed, angry, sullen, calm, happy, upbeat, or hopeful)?
27. What degree of receptivity did the family members show about the problem and its possible resolutions?

Relationship with the Interviewer
28. How did the family members relate to you (e.g., did one member try to get too close to you or were the members distant and aloof from you)?

Background Factors
29. What was happening in the family that might be contributing to the child's problem?
30. Was there someone missing from the interview who might add important information about the problem?
31. Who in the family thought it was a good idea to come to see you, and who did not think so?
32. What did the family expect from the interview?
33. Did the parents share the same view of the child's behavior and problem? If not, how did the parents' views differ?

Causes and Interventions
34. What did the parents think is the cause of the problem?
35. What did the child think is the cause of his or her problem?
36. What can be done to change the situation?
37. What did the parents want to do about the problem?
38. What did the child want to do about the problem?

---

family member while simultaneously observing other family members, being aware of your role in the interactions, and being aware of your reactions to the family members.

Table B-14 in Appendix B provides an example of a semi-structured family interview. It covers the presenting problem and issues related to the family's image, perceptions of its members, organization, communication patterns, relationships, activities, conflicts, and decision-making style.

Strategies for Working with Resistant Families

Interviewing a family that has *not* come to see you voluntarily will require patience. Emphasize your goals. For example, tell the family that you need to obtain information to make the most appropriate recommendations. One way to begin is to say, "The school [or other referral source] has asked me to

meet with you. I understand that Bill is [describe problem]. I'm here to help you and Bill with the problem."

You will also meet some family members who deny their problem or resist your efforts to obtain information. Be patient; show the family that you are a good listener, genuinely interested in its problems, and willing to wait until the reluctant members are willing to participate.

Here are some useful strategies for handling various types of resistance in the family interview (Anderson & Stewart, 1983):

1. *The parents say that the child is the problem, not themselves or the family.* Continue to focus on the child, at least initially. If the child is old enough and mature enough to handle the confrontation, ask the child whether the parents' position is accurate: "Is what they are saying about you really true?"

2. *The family denies there is a problem.* Be supportive of the family so that family members may come to trust you.

Allow the family members to say that they are there because of someone else's referral ("We're doing this only because the doctor told us to come").

3. *One member dominates the discussion.* Attend to the family member who is talking, but move on to other family members. Tell the family member who is talking that what he or she is saying is important, but that you want to hear from everyone.

4. *The child will not talk.* One strategy is to inform the family of the importance of having everyone talk: "I really need to hear what everyone thinks of all this" or "It will help me to understand what's going on in this family if each of you tells me what you think." A second strategy is to give the child permission to be silent: "Henry, it's okay if you don't want to be here and even if you don't want to talk. Maybe if you just listen while your parents and I talk, it will be helpful. If you change your mind and want to join in, let us know." A third strategy is to take the avenue of least resistance and focus on those members who will speak. As the child sees that you are listening and fair, he or she may begin to talk.

5. *The family insists that the focus be only on historical information.* Ask the family why the information is relevant: "Okay, so Helen was 5 when she entered kindergarten and had two teachers. How's that going to help us now?"

6. *The family refuses to focus on historical information.* Provide the family with a rationale for what you want to learn: "I think it's important to get a picture of the family members' health and illnesses, both physical and psychological" or "We don't want to make any assumptions about what the problem is until we look at your history so that we can get a good perspective on what's happening now."

7. *The family cannot find a time for all members to meet.* Be flexible in scheduling appointments, because some families can meet only in the evenings or on weekends. You can give the family members the job of finding available times, you can make a home visit, or you can arrange for transportation.

8. *The family disagrees about the problem.* Find a new definition of the problem that everyone can agree with. Inform the family that everybody's feelings are important and legitimate as they help you explore what the problem might be.

Opening Phase of the Family Interview

Here are some techniques you can use during the opening phase of the family interview.

1. After introducing yourself, you might say, "We are all here today to work out the problems you're having as a family. I'd like to hear from each of you about what is going on." Then you might say, "Who would like to begin the discussion?"
2. Or, looking at no one in particular but addressing the family as a whole, you might say, "Would you like to tell me why you're here today?" or "How can I help you?"

3. Another possibility is to say, "I asked you all to come here today so that I can find out how you all feel about your family." Then pause and see whether anyone begins to speak. If you need to, you can say, "Perhaps you all can tell me what you see as the problems you're having as a family."
4. Encourage reluctant members to speak by emphasizing that what they say could be helpful.
5. Foreclose lengthy or excessive responses with such comments as "We have a lot of ground to cover. Let's hear what Mr. Smith thinks."
6. In working with families that have been coerced to see you because their child has misbehaved, you might say to the family early in the interview, "You know, raising a child is difficult for many families today. How has it been for you?" This comment recognizes that the family is struggling with issues common to many families with children and invites their participation.
7. In cases of a court or school referral, you also might consider saying, "I know that the [court, school, etc.] has asked all of you to come to see me. But I also believe, [say the child's name and look at him or her], that your parents care about what happens to you and that you also care about what happens to you. I'm interested in how I can help all of you [looking at the entire family] get through this." By acknowledging that the parents have complied with an order or referral, these comments may help reduce the family's defensiveness (Oster, Caro, Eagen, & Lillo, 1988).
8. Pay special attention to the way each family member perceives and describes the problem.

Middle Phase of the Family Interview

After each family member has had time to share her or his views about the presenting problems (say, for a total of 15 to 20 minutes), you can turn to a discussion of the family (see questions 15 through 52 in Table B-14 in Appendix B). In addition to what the family members report, be alert to the nonverbal cues that they give (e.g., knowing glances, fidgeting), how they speak to each other (e.g., in friendly tones, hostile tones, or neutrally), power maneuvers (e.g., who tries to control the discussion), provocative behaviors (e.g., who tries to start an argument), and their ability to send and receive messages (e.g., clarity of communication, clarity of responses). Encourage all family members to participate in the discussions.

Family assessment tasks. To study family interaction patterns, you might want to give the family one or more of the tasks described below. The middle phase of the interview may be the most appropriate time to give one of these tasks, but you can do so in any phase of the interview. Tasks 1, 2, and 3 are from Szapocznik and Kurtines (1989, adapted from p. 35), and Task 9 is from Olson and Portner (1983).

TASK 1. PLANNING A MENU

"Suppose all of you had to work out a menu for dinner tonight and would like to have your favorite foods for dinner. But you can only have one main dish, one vegetable, one drink, and one dessert. Discuss this together; however, you must choose one meal you would all enjoy that consists of one main dish, one vegetable, one drink, and one dessert. Go ahead."

TASK 2. COMMENTING ON THINGS OTHERS DO IN THE FAMILY THAT PLEASE OR DISPLEASE THE MEMBERS

"Each of you tell about one thing each person in the family does that pleases you the most and makes you feel good, and one thing each one does that makes you unhappy or mad. Everyone try to give his or her own ideas about this. Go ahead."

TASK 3. DISCUSSING A FAMILY ARGUMENT

"In every family, things happen that create a fuss now and then. Together, discuss an argument you have had—a fight or argument at home. Discuss what started it, who was part of it, what happened, and how it ended. See if you can remember what it was all about. Go ahead."

TASK 4. PLANNING A FAMILY VACATION

"What would your family like to do for a vacation? Discuss this together. However, you must all agree on the final choice. Go ahead."

TASK 5. ALLOCATING LOTTERY WINNINGS

"If a member of your family won $500,000 in a lottery, what would your family do with it? Discuss this together. However, you must all agree on the way the money will be handled. Go ahead."

TASK 6. PLANNING AN ACTIVITY

"Plan something to do together as a family. The plan you come up with should be one with which everyone agrees. Go ahead."

TASK 7. USING DESCRIPTIVE PHRASES TO CHARACTERIZE THE FAMILY

"Come up with as many phrases as you can that describe your family as a group. Select one member to record your answers. All of you must agree with the phrases that describe your family before they are written down. Go ahead."

TASK 8. MAKING UP A STORY

(Select a picture from a magazine or from some other source that you think would be useful for this task.) "Here's a picture. Make up a story about the picture. Select one person to record the story. The story should be one with which you all agree. In the story, tell what is happening in the picture. Include a beginning, a middle, and an end to the story. Go ahead."

TASK 9. DISCUSSING SPECIFIC ISSUES

With a family that is shy or hesitant to discuss issues or with a family that needs more structuring, consider using the following procedure. Say, "I'm going to name some issues, one at a time. I'd like you to tell me whether the issue is or is not a problem in your family. OK? Here's the first one." You can then name each of the following issues or select only the ones you believe are most pertinent for the family: money; communication; express-

ing feelings; physical intimacy; recreation; friends; use of alcohol, tobacco, or other drugs; raising the children; handling parental responsibility; sharing responsibilities for raising the children; jealousy; personal habits; resolving conflicts; taking disagreements seriously; leisure time; vacations; making decisions; time spent away from home; careers; moving to a new place; sharing household duties; putting clothing away; and having time to be alone. Explore any problem area mentioned by the family: "In what way is _____ a problem?" Try to get each member to respond. If there are disagreements, say, "It seems that you have different ideas about whether _____ is a problem. Let's discuss why you have different ideas."

TASK 10. PARTICIPATING IN MISCELLANEOUS ACTIVITIES

Request that a parent ask the child to perform some action, such as writing a sentence, doing an arithmetic problem, or solving a puzzle. Observe how the parent asks the child to perform the task, how the child does it, how other members react as the child performs the task, and how the child presents the finished task. (Also see Chapter 8 for guidelines for observing parent-child interactions.)

Any of these 10 tasks will help you learn about the family's negotiation style; ways of resolving conflicts; pattern of alliances; decision-making style; patterns of parent-child, parent-parent, sibling-sibling, and parent-sibling interactions; roles; communication and language patterns; beliefs and expectations; and affective reactions. Be prepared, though, if a task becomes too stressful, to move on to something less threatening.

Additional areas to probe in a family interview. In addition to asking the questions in Table B-14 in Appendix B and assigning the family assessment tasks, you also might want to explore several aspects of family life. These include the layout of the home; a typical day in the life of the family; rules, regulations, and limit setting within the family; alliances and coalitions within the family; family disagreements; changes that the family members want to make; and previous family crises and how they were resolved. We now consider each of these areas in more detail. (Sample instructions are from Karpel and Strauss, 1983, adapted from pp. 137–147.)

1. *Layout of the home.* After the initial discussion of the problem, a useful way to get family members to talk is to ask them about the layout of the home: "I want to take a little bit of time to pull back from discussing the immediate problem, just to get a better idea about your family. You've mentioned some things already, but maybe one way to start would be for you to give me a description of your home, the layout of the rooms, who sleeps where, and anything you want to tell me about your home." Ask follow-up questions as needed.

2. *A typical day.* A useful probing statement to lead into this subject is "I also want to get a description from all of you of what a typical day consists of for your family. Start from the first thing in the morning, beginning with who gets up first. Go ahead." If the family tells you about an atypical day, redirect them to discuss a typical day, usually a weekday. You also can

ask them how they spend a typical weekend day. You may want to ask about the following aspects of daily life:

- Do any family members have breakfast at home?
- (If yes) Do they eat together?
- Which members, if any, are home during the day or come home for lunch?
- When do different family members arrive home from school or work?
- Who usually prepares dinner?
- Who is usually home for dinner?
- Does the family eat together?
  (If yes, consider the next four questions; if no, go to the fifth question.)
- Do family members have an established seating arrangement at a table for dinner?
- What is the atmosphere around the table at a typical family dinner?
- Are things quiet or noisy at dinner?
- If noisy, is the noise from animated conversations and joking or from petty arguments or major conflicts?
- How does each family member spend the evening?
- When does each family member usually go to bed?

3. *Rules, regulations, and limit setting.* A useful question for introducing this area of family life is "All families have certain rules and regulations for people in the family—chores, curfews, and that kind of thing. What are some of the rules and regulations in your family?" Valuable follow-up questions might cover what happens if chores are not done; how discipline is managed by the parents; whether both parents play active roles in discipline; whether the parents work together, independently, or at cross-purposes in using discipline; what role each parent plays in disciplining the children; and whether the discipline is appropriate for the children's behavior and age.

4. *Alliances and coalitions.* Several different probing statements may easily reveal the family's alliances and coalitions. For example, you might say, "I'd like to get a better idea of who spends time together in your family." After they discuss this, you can say, "I'd like to know who you're most likely to talk to when something is on your mind." You can direct these questions to each member of the family. Other useful questions are "Who sticks up for whom?" and "Who worries about whom in the family?" and "Whom do you worry about the most?"

5. *Family disagreements.* One useful approach (as you look at each family member) is "Every family has things they frequently disagree about, but these things differ from one family to another. I wonder if you could tell me about the kinds of disagreements your family has most often." Another version is "Most families have some kind of disagreement about something or some gripes about something every once in a while. What types of gripes have there been from time to time in your family?" After someone describes an event, obtain more detailed information by asking follow-up questions such as "What was said first?," "What happened next?," "What was everyone doing at the time?," and "How did it end?"

6. *Desired changes.* Useful questions are "Can any of you think of any changes you'd like to see made in your family?," "If you could change anything you wanted about your family or about life in the family, what kinds of changes would you make?," and, directed at the children, "If you had magic powers and could change anything you wanted, what would you change about your family?"

7. *Previous family crises.* A useful statement is "It will help us in dealing with the present problem to learn something about any previous problems that your family has experienced or that any members of the family have gone through. Any past situation that has been especially upsetting to the family or put stress on it would help me better understand your family, as would any previous problems that required professional help." Or you can substitute for the second sentence "Have there ever been times that have been really rough for the family?" Ask follow-up questions as needed. The way the family managed past crises may help you learn about the family's organization, judgment, flexibility, mutual trust, and internal resources.

Closing Phase of the Family Interview

Toward the end of the interview, summarize the salient points, including comments on the family dynamics related to the child's problem. Then ask the family members to respond to your summary. After that, give your initial recommendations and ask the family members what they think about them. Gauge the family's willingness to change and the suitability of its members for treatment.

It also may be useful toward the end of the family interview to ask whether there is anything else you should know about how the family is functioning. Ask about any recent changes, problems, or stressors that the family members think are noteworthy.

What you achieve in the initial family interview will be a function of your interview style and the idiosyncrasies of each family. You may not obtain all the information you want, but do your best to evaluate the family. When you review the information obtained in the family interview, consider such questions as the following:

1. Who referred the family?
2. What is the composition of the family?
3. Who was present at and who was absent from the interview?
4. How does the family provide models for its members; handle its successes and failures; recognize the talents, skills, and interests of its members; and use resources in the community?
5. Overall, what are the strengths and weaknesses of the family?
6. What prior interventions has the family received, and with what result?
7. What are the family's resources?
8. What types of services does the family need?
9. What short-term and long-term goals can be formulated?

For more information about family assessment, see Beavers and Hampson (1990). Also see Sattler (1998) for checklists useful for evaluating families.

Having the Family Prepare for a Second Interview

If you plan to ask the family to return for a second interview, you may want the family to record information about a problem area in the interim. This information may help both you and the family understand the problem better. For example, you might give each member the same task, such as recording disagreements that occur between family members, recording positive statements, or both. When they bring this information to the second session, you can review the types of disagreements that occurred or positive statements that were made and the extent to which the family members agree and disagree about what happened during the week; you will also be able to determine whether there is more agreement between the child and one parent than between the child and the other parent and whether there is more agreement about certain types of behaviors than others (e.g., pleasing versus displeasing behaviors, passive versus active behaviors, cognitive versus affective behaviors). Chapter 8 describes procedures for conducting a home observation.

A family was seated in a restaurant. The waitress took the order of the adults and then turned to their young son. "What will you have, sonny?" she asked. The boy said timidly, "I want a hot dog." Before the waitress could write down the order, the mother interrupted. "No hot dog," she said. "Give him potatoes, beef and some carrots." But the waitress ignored her completely. "Do you want some ketchup or mustard on your hot dog?" she asked of the boy. "Ketchup," he replied with a happy smile on his face. "Coming up," the waitress said, starting for the kitchen. There was a stunned silence upon her departure. Finally, the boy turned to his parents, "Know what?" he said. "She thinks I'm real."

—Bill Adler, American author (1929–   )

THINKING THROUGH THE ISSUES

1. How do interviews with children differ from interviews with adults?
2. What difficulties may arise when you interview young children?
3. Do you think that you can evaluate the psychological framework of a young child?
4. How accurate are the reports of young children?
5. What other types of problems might you encounter in interviewing children, besides those discussed in the text?

6. How would you handle a situation in which the information given by the child and the parents, the child and a teacher, or the parents and a teacher differed?
7. With which type of interview are you likely to be more comfortable—an interview with one individual or an interview with a family? Might you be equally comfortable with both? Explain the basis for your answer.
8. What stresses are you likely to experience during a family interview, and how will these differ from those occurring in individual interviews?
9. What problems do you foresee in handling the group dynamics of the family interview?
10. Does the family interview simply involve interviewing individuals in a group, or does it have its own dynamics? What is the basis for your answer?
11. What do you think you can learn in a family interview that you cannot learn in individual interviews with each family member?
12. How would you deal with a family member who wanted to dominate the family interview?
13. How would you bring a family together for an interview if the members did not want to be together?
14. How have your beliefs about your family changed throughout the years?
15. How have you adopted or assimilated values that differ from those of your family?

SUMMARY

General Considerations

1. Interviews with children will give you information about their problems, their feelings about themselves, and their impressions about their family and situation.
2. Children are sometimes more difficult to interview than adults because of limitations in language comprehension, language expression, conceptual ability, and memory.
3. Keep in mind that children may not be aware that they have problems. When conducting an interview, always consider the child's age, experiences, level of cognitive development, and ability to express himself or herself, as well as the extensiveness of any psychological disturbance.
4. Children are more dependent on their immediate environments than adults are, as they have less power to shape them.
5. Children also differ from adults in that they are in a process of rapid intellectual, emotional, and behavioral development.
6. Information may not be revealed in an interview because it was not entered into memory in the first place, the memory representation was too weak, the status of the representation changed over the course of an extended interval, or other difficulties interfered with retrieval.
7. Because the interview setting is unfamiliar and because the interviewer is a stranger, children's behavior in the interview may not be typical of their behavior in other settings.
8. In school settings, and particularly in juvenile detention settings, you may initiate interviews when neither the children nor the parents have sought help for a problem.
9. The goals of the initial interview with a child will depend on the referral question, as well as on the child's age and communication skills.

Techniques for Interviewing Children

10. The most common way to help young children remember, think, and tell you about themselves is to ask them questions.

11. Recognize that in asking a question, you are making a demand—you are directing the child's attention to memories or ideas that he or she might not have otherwise considered.

12. Children generally need more time than adults to think about questions and about their answers.

13. You can become a more effective interviewer of children by learning about their current interests.

14. The following are 22 useful techniques for interviewing children: Consider the child's age and needs in setting the tempo and length of the interview. Formulate appropriate opening statements. Use appropriate language and intonation. Avoid leading questions. Ask for examples. Be open to what the child tells you. Make descriptive comments. Use reflection. Give praise frequently. Avoid critical statements. Use simple questions and concrete referents. Formulate hypothetical questions (using the subjunctive mood) when necessary. Be tactful. Recognize the child's discomfort. Use props, crayons, clay, or toys to help a young child talk. Use a sentence-completion technique. Use fantasy techniques. Help the child express his or her thoughts and feelings. Clarify an episode of misbehavior by recounting it. Clarify interview procedures for children who are minimally communicative. Understand and use silence. Handle resistance and anxiety by giving support and reassurance.

15. If the examinee is an adolescent, you can ask him or her to complete the Personal Data Questionnaire.

Areas Covered in the Initial Interview with Children

16. The typical sequence in interviewing a child is to introduce yourself to the parent (or caregiver or guardian) and to the child by giving your name and professional title, greet the child, open the interview with an introductory statement, continue the interview as appropriate, review the referral issues with the child, describe what will happen to the child after you complete the interview, express appreciation for the child's effort and cooperation, and close the interview.

17. Typical topics covered in the initial interview with children include reasons for coming to the interview, confidentiality, school, home, interests, friends, moods and feelings, fears and worries, self-concept, somatic concerns, obsessions and compulsions, thought disorders, memories or fantasies, aspirations, and other information voluntarily supplied by the child. In addition, for adolescents, typical areas include jobs, sexual relations, eating habits, and possible use of alcohol, tobacco, and/or other drugs.

18. You may want to ask about reinforcers important to the children if you are planning a therapeutic behavioral intervention.

19. If you believe that the physical layout of a child's home may be contributing to the difficulties the child is experiencing, you can ask the child to draw a picture of her or his room and any other relevant rooms in the house.

20. As part of the initial interview with children, you may want to conduct a mental status evaluation.

Interviewing Parents

21. A well-conducted parent interview will establish rapport and a positive working relationship with the parents, focus the attention of the parents on the issues, provide valuable information about the child and family, help the parents organize and reflect on the information, contribute to the formulation of a diagnosis, provide a basis for decisions about treatment and further investigation, and lay the groundwork for parents to contribute to any intervention efforts.

22. You want the parents to participate actively in the interview.

23. Parents serve as an important source of information and will play a key role in any proposed intervention.

24. Recognize that not all parents will be reliable informants. Expect to find some distortions, biases, and memory lapses in the information you collect from them.

25. If you conduct an appropriate interview with parents, you should be able to develop some preliminary hypotheses about the child's difficulties, strengths, and weaknesses and about the parents' reactions, concerns, coping abilities, strengths, and weaknesses. You can also construct a picture of the family's life style and its prevailing values, mores, and concerns.

26. The age of the child will, in part, determine the content of the interview with the parents.

27. Parents may be apprehensive about their child's evaluation.

28. Depending on the type and severity of their child's problems, their cultural subgroup and ethnicity, and their religious affiliation, parents may be concerned about the etiology of their child's problem, possible interventions, family issues, their responsibility, a possible stigma associated with meeting with a mental health professional, and the results of the assessment.

29. If parents ask you what they should say to their child about coming to see you, advise them to be straightforward with the child.

30. By the time parents seek an evaluation for a school-age child (and sometimes for a preschool child as well), they have already experienced much frustration and anguish. Expect some negative feelings from the parents and deal with these feelings during your initial contact.

31. Another way to obtain information about the child and family is to have the parents complete the Background Questionnaire before the interview.

32. Three useful formats for interviewing parents are the unstructured (open-ended) interview, the semistructured interview, and the structured interview.

33. When parents are extremely anxious or resistant, it is best to use an open-ended format at the initial stage of the interview before moving on to a semistructured or structured interview.

34. A semistructured interview is useful in assessing what is important to the parents, what they hope to accomplish from the evaluation, their concerns, and how they view their own role in helping the child.

35. A structured interview is useful when you want to cover various areas of psychopathology systematically.

36. The major components of the initial interview with parents include greeting the parents, giving your name and professional title, opening the interview with an introductory statement, asking the parents about items on the Background Questionnaire that are of interest (if they have completed the Background Questionnaire) or covering similar content areas, reviewing problems, describing the assessment procedure, arranging for a post-assessment interview, and closing the interview.

37. Following specific guidelines for interviewing parents will allow you to obtain the needed information.

Interviewing Teachers

38. When you interview a teacher, your concern is not only with the teacher's perception of the problem, the antecedents and consequences of the problem behavior, and what the teacher has done to alleviate the problem, but also with how other children and teachers react to the child and how the child performs academically.

39. You also can ask the teacher to complete the School Referral Questionnaire as part of the assessment.

40. Areas covered in the initial interview with teachers include the teacher's perception of the child's problem behavior, reactions to the child's problem behavior, opinion of the child's relationship with peers, assessment of the child's academic performance, assessment of the child's strengths and weaknesses, view of the child's family, expectations for the child, and suggestions for helping the child.

41. Allay the teacher's anxiety about his or her responsibility for the child's problem behaviors.

Interviewing the Family

42. The goals of the initial family interview are to obtain historical details and information about current family life relevant to the child's problems, to observe patterns of family interaction, and to note the family's strengths and weaknesses.

43. This interview may be the family's first attempt as a family unit to discuss the perceived problem.

44. Families may use functional and dysfunctional strategies to cope with their child's psychological or medical problem.

45. The family interview, like the interview with the child or with parents alone, may be the first encounter the family has with a mental health professional and may serve as the beginning of a family therapy intervention program.

46. You can use different strategies during the three phases of the family interview. In the opening phase, encourage the family members to talk about their concerns. During the middle phase, focus on general family dynamics and issues. In the closing phase, summarize the salient points of the interview.

47. There are several family assessment tasks you can use to study family interaction patterns. These include planning a menu, commenting on things others do in the family that please or displease the members, discussing a family argument, planning a family vacation, allocating lottery winnings, planning an activity, using descriptive phrases to characterize the family, making up a story, discussing specific issues, and participating in miscellaneous activities. Any of these tasks will help you learn about the family's negotiation style; ways of resolving conflicts; pattern of alliances; decision-making style; patterns of parent-child, parent-parent, sibling-sibling, and parent-sibling interactions; roles; communication and language patterns; beliefs and expectations; and affective reactions.

48. Other areas of family life that you might want to explore include the layout of the home; a typical day in the life of the family; rules, regulations, and limit setting within the family; alliances and coalitions within the family; family disagreements; changes that the family members want to make; and previous family crises.

49. Toward the end of the interview, summarize the salient points, including comments on the family dynamics related to the child's problem. Then ask the family members to respond to your summary. After that, give your initial recommendations and ask the family members what they think about them. Gauge the family's willingness to change and the suitability of its members for treatment.

50. What you achieve in the initial family interview will be a function of your interview style and the idiosyncrasies of each family.

51. If you plan to ask the family to return for a second interview, you may want the family to record information about a problem area in the interim.

KEY TERMS, CONCEPTS, AND NAMES

Techniques for interviewing children (p. 147)
Descriptive comments (p. 148)
Reflection (p. 148)
Concrete referents (p. 149)
Affect labels (p. 149)
Picture-question technique (p. 149)
Picture-drawing technique (p. 150)
Story-completion technique (p. 150)
Responding to a hypothetical problem (p. 150)
Modeling the interview after a school-type task (p. 151)
Formulating hypothetical questions (p. 151)
Use of props, crayons, clay, or toys (p. 151)
Sentence-completion technique (p. 151)
Fantasy techniques (p. 151)
Three wishes technique (p. 151)
Desert island technique (p. 151)
Handling resistance by giving support and reassurance (p. 153)
Personal Data Questionnaire (p. 154)
Areas covered in the initial interview with children (p. 154)
Reinforcers (p. 154)
Children's environments (p. 154)
Mental status evaluation (p. 155)
Goals of the initial interview with parents (p. 156)
Concerns of parents (p. 156)
Potential negative feelings of parents (p. 157)
Background Questionnaire (p. 157)
Formats for interviews with parents (p. 157)
Developmental history interview (p. 158)
Screening interview with parents of preschool children (p. 158)
Typical-day interview (p. 158)
Major components of initial interview with parents (p. 159)
Guidelines for interviewing parents (p. 159)
School Referral Questionnaire (p. 160)
Areas covered in the initial interview with teachers (p. 160)
Goals of the initial family interview (p. 162)
Functional family strategies (p. 162)
Reacting (p. 162)
Mobilizing (p. 162)
Recognition (p. 162)
Understanding (p. 162)
Continuing (p. 162)
Hoping (p. 162)
Appreciating (p. 162)
Reasoning (p. 162)
Dysfunctional family strategies (p. 162)
Blaming (p. 162)
Taking over (p. 162)
Controlling (p. 162)

STUDY QUESTIONS

1. Discuss some general considerations in interviewing children. In your discussion, include goals of the initial interview and explain why children can be more difficult to interview than adults.
2. Twenty-two specific techniques for interviewing children are discussed in the text. Describe seven of them.
3. What are the typical areas covered in an initial interview with a child?
4. Discuss the mental status evaluation. In your discussion, comment on the areas typically covered in a mental status evaluation and point out some important factors to evaluate in each area.
5. Discuss some important factors to consider in interviewing parents. Include in your discussion some of the goals of the initial interview with parents.
6. What are some typical concerns parents may express in an interview?
7. How can you reduce parental resistance during the initial interview?
8. Discuss how the Background Questionnaire is a useful adjunct to the interview.
9. What are some useful formats for interviewing parents?
10. Describe the major components of the initial interview with parents.
11. Describe several guidelines for interviewing parents.
12. How would you go about interviewing teachers? Include in your discussion the typical areas covered in the initial interview with teachers.
13. Discuss the family interview. Include in your discussion the goals of the family interview, guidelines for conducting the family interview, strategies for working with resistant families, phases of the family interview, and family assessment tasks.
14. Discuss some tasks that you might give the family in preparation for a second family interview.

7

OTHER CONSIDERATIONS RELATED TO THE INTERVIEW

Many individuals have, like uncut diamonds, shining qualities beneath a rough exterior.
            —Juvenal, Roman satirical poet (1st century A.D.)

Goals and Objectives

This chapter is designed to enable you to do the following:

- Close an initial interview

- Evaluate the initial interview

- Describe the major components of a post-assessment interview

- Understand the reactions of parents who learn that their child has special needs

- Discuss the reliability and validity of the interview

This chapter provides guidelines on closing an initial interview, evaluating the initial interview, conducting a post-assessment interview, conducting a follow-up interview, and evaluating the interview findings by considering issues of reliability and validity.

CLOSING THE INITIAL INTERVIEW

The final moments of an interview are as important as any other period in the interview. They give you a chance to summarize what you have learned, obtain feedback from the interviewee about whether you have understood him or her, ask any remaining questions, inform the interviewee about additional assessments that may be needed and about possible interventions, and give the interviewee time to share any final thoughts and feelings.

Do not rush the ending of the interview. Budget your time so that there is enough remaining to go over what you need to cover. You want the interviewee to leave feeling that she or he has made a contribution and that the experience has been worthwhile. Be courteous and friendly; tell the interviewee what will happen next and what you will expect of her or him. A comment such as "Thank you for coming" might be all that you need to say to convey a sense of respect. If you discuss possible interventions and a prognosis, be careful not to create false hopes or expectations. You want to be as realistic as possible, recognizing what the intervention program may or may not accomplish.

The method you use to close the interview is especially important when the interviewee is expressing some deeply felt emotion. Try not to end the interview abruptly; allow enough time for the interviewee to regain composure before he or she leaves. Allow an interviewee who is in the middle of a communication to finish. Gauge the time and, when necessary, provide some indication to the interviewee that the interview will soon be over (say, in 5 to 10 minutes). When the interviewee recognizes that the interview will soon be over, he or she may begin to move away from the subject at hand and regain composure.

What you say, of course, will depend on the interviewee's age and ability and on whether you plan to see the interviewee again. If you do not plan to see the person again but he or she is an adolescent or an adult, you might say, "You have some deep feelings about _____. However, since our time together is about up, I would be glad to give you the names of some professionals you could contact. I'm sure they will be able to help you. I do appreciate your cooperation." If you plan to see the interviewee again, you might say, "I can see that this is extremely important to you, and we need to talk about it some more. But our time is just about up for today. We can continue next time." Then arrange another appointment, while continuing to express support, understanding, and confidence that you can help the interviewee find a solution.

Planning for Enough Time at the Close of the Interview

It is easy to continue an interview to the point where there is little time left to end it appropriately, especially if you are on a tight schedule. Be aware of how much time has passed, what important topics you need to discuss, and how much time the interviewee may need to discuss any remaining concerns. When you are first learning to conduct interviews, keep a clock where you can see it so that you do not lose track of time (however, do not let the clock distract you). Before you begin the interview, make note of the topics you want to discuss, and budget your time so that you can cover them.

Issues to consider near the end of the interview. Here are some issues you will want to consider near the close of the interview:

1. Have you covered everything you wanted to cover?
2. If additional assessments are necessary, does the interviewee understand why?
3. Does the interviewee understand how she or he will obtain the results of the assessment?
4. Have you and the interviewee had the opportunity to correct any misperceptions?
5. Does the interviewee understand how you will use the assessment findings? (For example, will they be used to make recommendations, given to a court, or given to school officials?)
6. Is the interviewee aware of the clinic's, school's, or your policies regarding fees and procedures?

If you find that you cannot recall some important information that has been discussed, you can say, "I know you told me about [describe topic], but I didn't note it fully. Can you tell me more about [the topic]?" You can make this type of statement at any time during the interview.

Give the interviewee the opportunity to ask questions. Use the last minutes of the initial interview to summarize and evaluate what you have learned and to give the interviewee an opportunity to ask any remaining questions that he or she might have.

Recognize the interviewee's concerns. Toward the close of the interview, the interviewee may wonder how the interview went, how serious the problem is, whether you can be of help, what you thought of her or him, whether she or he has told you all you need to know, and what will happen next. Be prepared to deal with these and similar concerns. Here are some useful questions to ask:

- "Is there anything else you would like to tell me?"
- "Is there anything else you think I should know?"
- "I've asked you a lot of questions. Are there any questions that you'd like to ask me?"

Following are some examples of interviewees' concerns and possible interviewer responses. The interviewer's response, of course, depends on the specific situation.

1. IE: Did I say the right things?
   IR-1: You did just fine. There are no right or wrong answers. You told me about yourself, and that was helpful.
   IR-2: Your responses have been helpful, and I believe we can help you.
2. IE: Do you think you can help me?
   IR: Yes, I do, but it will take time to work things out.
3. IE: Well, am I crazy?
   IR-1: (If there is no evidence of psychosis) No, you're not crazy. Sometimes teenagers think that things are not under their control, but this is common.
   IR-2: (If there is evidence of psychosis) You seem to have some problems in your thinking, and that concerns you.
4. IE: Am I going to be sent away?
   IR-1: (If no such plans are being considered) No, you're not going to be "sent away." You'll be going home when we finish.
   IR-2: (If you are not sure whether the child is going to be admitted to an institution) We should wait until all the results are in before we make any decisions. But whatever we decide, we'll let you know, and we'll always try to do what is best for you.
5. IE: So what happens now?
   IR: First, we need to study what we have learned about you and your family. Then, after all the results are in, we'll talk about how to make things better.

The Summary Statement

A summary statement should identify the main points of the problem for the interviewee's confirmation or correction. Following is an example of a summary statement from an interview with a teacher: "You believe that Helen's major problem is her inability to read. Emotionally, you see her as well adjusted. However, her frustration in learning how to read gets her down at times." Toward the close of the initial interview with a parent, you might say something like "We met today so that I could learn about Bill. Do you believe that I have most of the important information?" Or, you could say, "I think we've accomplished a great deal today. The information you have given me is very helpful. I appreciate your cooperation and look forward to seeing you again after we have completed the evaluation." (These statements are not mutually exclusive; they can be used together at the close of the interview.) Toward the end of an interview with a child, you could say, "I know that you're having difficulties in school in reading and math. When we're finished with the evaluation, we'll make plans to help you." If needed, schedule another meeting with the interviewee to discuss the assessment findings and recommendations.

Acknowledge your satisfaction with cooperative interviewees. It may be helpful, especially with children, to acknowledge their openness and willingness to share their problems, concerns, hopes, and expectations. Comments such as the following may be appropriate (Jennings, 1982):

- "I appreciate your sharing your concerns with me."
- "It took a lot of courage to talk to me about yourself, your family, and your school."
- "It took a lot of trust to tell me what you just did, and I'm proud of you for doing that."
- "You took this interview seriously, and that will help me do my best to help you."

Acknowledge your disappointment with uncooperative interviewees. When the interviewee has been uncooperative and you need to schedule another appointment, you might want to express your concern about how the interview went: "We didn't get too much accomplished today. Perhaps next time we can cover more ground."

THE POST-ASSESSMENT INTERVIEW

A post-assessment interview (also called an *interpretive interview*) with children and parents serves several purposes. These include presenting the findings of the assessment, presenting possible interventions, helping children and parents understand the findings and possible interventions, allowing children and parents to express their concerns, and exploring any additional areas of concern. As in the initial interview, use understandable terminology and explanations.

When you plan the post-assessment interview, consider the information you want to discuss with the child and the parents, how much detail you want to give, and the order in which you want to present the information. During the post-assessment interview, leave plenty of time for the child and parents to ask you questions. Encourage them to ask about anything they do not understand, and answer them carefully. In your presentation, be sure to discuss the family's strengths and also its weaknesses. Like the initial interview, the post-assessment interview will be most successful when the child and parents see you as competent, trustworthy, understanding, and interested in helping them. We strongly recommend that you not conduct the post-assessment interview until the psychological report has been completed (see Chapter 25). Although this chapter focuses on post-assessment interviews with children and with parents, the procedures discussed are applicable to any post-assessment interview—with teachers, physicians, attorneys, or other interested parties.

Two cautions about the post-assessment interview are in order. First, if you are presenting the results of examinations performed by other professionals, you might not be able to answer all of the family's questions about these results. Therefore, when needed, arrange to have the other professionals attend the meeting. Second, as a clinical assessor, you will be making important decisions about children's lives. *You should never make a diagnosis, a recommendation concerning a child's treatment or placement, or a decision about whether an alleged event took place unless you are fully qualified to do so.*

Guidelines for the Post-Assessment Interview

A post-assessment interview with a child and parents has five aspects—cognitive, interactive, affective, ethical/religious, and ethnocultural.

1. *Cognitive aspect*—the parents' and child's understanding of the information given to them
2. *Interactive aspect*—the interaction between the interviewer and the parents and child, with the interviewer helping the parents and child understand and accept the results of the evaluation and the treatment recommendations
3. *Affective aspect*—the feelings of the parents and child about the information presented
4. *Ethical/religious aspect*—how the parents' and child's ethical and religious views affect their reactions to the information they receive, their beliefs about their responsibility for the problem, and their willingness to follow the treatment recommendations
5. *Ethnocultural aspect*—how the parents' and child's ethnic background and cultural practices affect their reactions to the information they receive and their willingness to follow the treatment recommendations

The parents and child need time to express their reactions to the information they receive. They may feel enlightened and satisfied by the results or threatened by the results; they may have doubts about the accuracy of the results; or they may experience feelings such as anger, embarrassment, disappointment, or even relief. You will need to deal with any negative reactions.

In discussing the findings, use terms that you feel comfortable with and that children and parents can easily understand. Ask the family members whether they understand what you have said and whether they would like to discuss any matters more fully. Questions such as "Is that clear?" or "Would you like me to go over that again?" or "Do you have any other questions?" are helpful.

Following are examples of ways to discuss technical concepts with older children and parents and other individuals interested in the case.

1. *Statistical significance.* "Test scores can never be perfectly accurate. A statistically significant difference between two test scores is one that is large enough that it likely didn't occur by chance. Thus, there is probably a true difference between the characteristics being measured by the two test scores."

2. *Range of difficulty.* "Most tests go from easy to difficult items. In addition, depending on the examinee's [student's] age, some tests have different beginning points. Some tests also have different ending points depending on how many items the examinee [student] passes or fails. These procedures help make the testing go more smoothly."

3. *Percentile ranks.* "Percentile ranks tell the percentage of children whom we would expect to score lower than this student. The 55th percentile rank means this student scored equal to or higher than 55% of children his [her] age on this test."

As in the initial interview, in the post-assessment interview you will want to (a) listen actively to the child and parents, (b) be aware of their nonverbal behavior (e.g., shaking the head, scowling, frowning, sighing, whistling, raising eyebrows, or crying), (c) treat both the child and the parents with respect and dignity, (d) recognize family values, customs, beliefs, and cultural practices, (e) communicate openly and honestly with the child and parents, (f) build on their strengths, and (g) acknowledge and address their concerns and needs.

To older children and parents, be prepared to offer such comments as the following:

- "This is hard for you to hear."
- "It must be good to hear that the problems were not as bad as you expected."
- "This is a lot of information to understand, and it may be confusing for you."
- "Do you want to get another opinion?"
- "You may be thinking, 'Where do we go from here?'"
- "What would you like to do now?"
- "What do you think about what I've told you?"
- "Is that clear?"
- "Would you like me to go over that again?"
- "Are the results similar to what you expected?" (If not) "In what way are they different?"
- (If the child has been examined before) "How do these findings compare with what you've heard before?"
- "What do you think you should do, based on what I've just told you?"

In addition, to parents only, you might say:

- "It's difficult to learn that your child is having these problems."
- "Perhaps you're wondering what can be done to help your child."

Limit the post-assessment interview to about 1 or 1½ hours. Longer sessions may tax the abilities of the child or parents to comprehend and integrate the information. If needed, schedule a second session. For example, you might discuss the results in one session and the intervention plan in a second session.

Confidentiality. A potentially troubling issue in the post-assessment interview with parents is the confidentiality of the information obtained from the child. Specifically, what role do children have in limiting the information their parents receive? Unfortunately, there are no clear legal guidelines about the extent to which information received from children is confidential; the courts and legislatures are still trying to define the rights of children and their parents. Although parents are responsible for their children, there is an increasing tendency toward protecting the rights of children who appear to be competent to make their own decisions.

Release of information. It is preferable to request children's permission to release information to their parents, but you may not be legally required to do so. Obviously, you should consider a child's age and her or his ability to give the required permission. Any release of information must be in accordance with the laws of your state.

Post-Assessment Interview with Children

Hold the post-assessment interview with the child as soon as possible after the evaluation has been completed—doing so may serve to allay his or her fears about the assessment. For children who can understand the information, knowing the assessment results is beneficial. Children need this information as much as anyone else because they make many important self-appraisals. For example, some children wrongly estimate their abilities, and the information they gain in a post-assessment interview may help build their self-esteem and allow them to correct their self-appraisal.

Post-Assessment Interview with Parents

In the post-assessment interview with the parents, your role is to (a) provide a thorough presentation of the child's problems (description, etiology, severity, and prognosis), (b) plan a specific program geared to the child's needs and capabilities, (c) recognize and deal with the personal problems of the parents as they affect the child or as they are affected by the child's condition, and (d) plan for future meetings as needed. Review the presenting problem, report and explain the assessment findings, and discuss the recommendations in a professional, caring, and thoughtful manner.

Four phases of the post-assessment interview with parents. Four phases characterize the post-assessment interview with parents: establishing rapport, communicating the results, discussing the recommendations, and terminating the interview.

FIRST PHASE: ESTABLISHING RAPPORT

You can do much to establish rapport before the interview even begins by being sure to carry out the first four of the following recommendations.

1. *Arrange to meet with the parents in a private setting, and avoid interruptions.*

2. *Allow enough time for the meeting.*

3. *Make every effort to have both parents at the interview.* This will help you obtain a more objective picture of their reactions and will enable them to share in the decisions that need to be made about their child. It will also relieve one parent of the burden of having to convey to the other parent the results of the evaluation.

4. *Find out whether the parents want to bring other people (such as a relative or an interpreter) to the meeting, and allow them to do so.*

5. *Greet the parents promptly, and provide your name.*

6. *Start the session by saying something positive about the child.*

7. *Show respect and appreciation.* Help the parents feel comfortable during the interview. Encourage them to talk and to ask questions freely. Recognize the frustration and hardship that have brought them to you and that they may still have to face in the future. Convey to them that they have something important to contribute to the discussion. Avoid making them feel defensive, avoid fault finding and accusations, and avoid pity and condescension. Point out how they have been helpful (e.g., bringing their child to the evaluation and participating themselves) and the positive qualities of the family and the child. Your respect for the parents and your appreciation of their problems will go a long way toward facilitating a successful post-assessment interview.

8. *Review what the parents have told you are their primary concerns, what they hope to learn from the evaluation, what they think are the causes of the problem, and what they think should be done about the problem.* If you have not seen the parents before the post-assessment interview, ask them to comment on each of these areas. Encourage the parents to take an active role in the interview.

9. *Never be afraid to say "I don't know."*

SECOND PHASE: COMMUNICATING THE ASSESSMENT RESULTS

1. *Summarize the assessment results and their implications as clearly as possible, in a straightforward, detailed, and unambiguous manner.* Be relaxed and unhurried in your presentation, and speak clearly, gently, and slowly.

2. *Focus the interview on the child.* Explain to the parents which of the child's problems are major and which are minor. This will help keep parents from being overwhelmed by their child's problems. Include information on the child's competencies in addition to limitations. Help the parents understand that children with psychological or medical disorders have the same needs as other children, along with some unique needs of their own. Stress the strengths and potential of the child, keeping in mind, of course, the nature of the child's problems and the limitations associated with them. Inform the parents that your primary concern is the welfare and happiness of the child and that you want to work with them to make things better. This focus might help reduce the personal frustration of the parents. If the parents discuss their personal problems, redirect the discussion to the child's problems. It is

not that the parents' problems are unimportant, but rather that your focus *now* should be on the child. You can refer them to another professional who can address their problems on another occasion.

3. *Be prepared to deal with such parental reactions as anxiety, grief, disbelief, shock, denial, ambivalence, anger, disappointment, guilt, despair—and even relief—if the results suggest that the child has a serious problem.* Some parents may feel cheated because they did not produce a "perfect" child, and others may feel guilty or make self-deprecating remarks. Help the parents express their feelings, and acknowledge the feelings they express. You will need to be especially patient and understanding at these times. If the parents cry, tell them that it is okay and that many parents cry when they are given similar news.

4. *Raise the issue of etiology.* Parents are often concerned about the source of their child's problem, even if they do not ask about it. They may have misperceptions about what caused the child's problem and may feel guilty. Discussing the possible etiology gives you the opportunity to correct their misperceptions and relieve their guilt.

5. *Use the diagnostic findings to help the parents give up erroneous ideas and adopt a more realistic approach to the child's problems.* Give the parents copies of the reports, and discuss the assessment results. Some diagnoses are easier for parents to understand than others. A known genetic disorder such as phenylketonuria (PKU) that has predictable consequences may be easier to discuss than conditions that are not clear-cut, such as attention-deficit/hyperactivity disorder (ADHD). Use labels cautiously whenever there is any doubt about the diagnosis. Help the parents understand that the problems are only one aspect of their child's life, that they need to deal with difficulties rather than avoid them, that they must set realistic expectations for their child, and that they have to shift their focus from searching for the cause of the problems to determining what they can do for the child. Encourage the parents to view their child as a unique individual with rights and potential.

6. *Evaluate how the parents understand the results throughout this second phase.* Occasionally, you may have difficulty helping the parents understand the assessment findings and recommendations. This may happen, for example, because the parents' feelings of guilt interfere with their ability to accept the information or because they are embarrassed to admit that they do not understand the information or are frustrated at not being able to solve the problem themselves and resent your interference. A calm, encouraging, and supportive manner should help parents to accept the results and recommendations more easily. Some parents may consider it impolite to interrupt you, to ask you questions, or to reveal that they did not understand what you said. You cannot be sure from their manner that they understood you. You should check the parents' understanding of their child's disorder by saying something like "Please tell me in your own words what you understand about your child's condition." Use follow-up comments as needed.

Parents who held erroneous beliefs about their child's condition before the interview will probably not change them after one interview. These beliefs may be protecting them from facing unpleasant realities. Therefore, you may need several interviews with the parents.

7. *Be aware of your attitude toward the parents and the child.* You want to be empathic and respectful and show an appreciation of the parents' and child's problems. Do not hide your feelings, because the parents will value them as indications of your concern and your humanity. Keep in mind that your reactions should be professional.

8. *Be aware of potential pitfalls in discussing the results.* You want to be sure to avoid rushing the interview, lecturing the parents, getting sidetracked by tangential issues, offering premature interpretations of the child's behavior or motivation, being vague or too general, being definitive based on limited findings, ignoring parents' views or becoming defensive when they challenge your views, criticizing or blaming the parents, showing pity or sorrow, appearing irritated at questions, or giving too much or too little information.

THIRD PHASE: DISCUSSING THE RECOMMENDATIONS

1. *Try to let the parents formulate a plan of action.* Allow time for the parents to assimilate the findings. Help them plan how much information about the child to give to other individuals, such as siblings, grandparents, friends, and neighbors, and how to share this information with others. Do not try to bring about fundamental changes in the parents' child-rearing or educational philosophy. Instead, focus on the concrete issues at hand.

2. *Present your recommendations, and discuss possible alternative courses of action.* Develop the intervention plans with the parents, and ask for their opinions about any options. If you recommend additional diagnostic procedures, explain to the parents why the procedures are needed. If you recommend a treatment, be prepared to discuss details of the treatment: length, costs, benefits (and drawbacks, if any), and how the treatment will contribute to the child's development. If you (and the school team) recommend placing the child in a special class or other facility, give the parents the opportunity to visit the class or facility and to discuss the placement with the teacher or staff before they make a decision. In any case, present the parents with any and all options that might help their child, deal honestly and nondefensively with any concerns they may have, and let them know that competent professionals are available to work with their child and with them.

3. *Encourage the parents to assume responsibility, not to be dependent.* Some parents may appear attentive but may not actually listen to what you have to say. They may fear the future and resist taking responsibility for addressing their child's problem. They may want to abdicate all their responsibility to you: "We're in your hands, doctor. Anything you say we'll do. You know best." They may attribute magic curative powers to you or view you as all-powerful and

all-knowing. They may prefer that *you* deal with their child's problems. You may feel flattered by their dependence on you, but this is not what they need. They need to assume responsibility and work through their dependency feelings.

4. *Give the parents the opportunity to ask questions about the recommendations.* Evaluate what the parents think and feel about the recommendations. Some parents simply want to hear that everything will work out well without their having to put forth any effort. Others fear that nothing will change and that the problems will continue. Help the parents see that you recognize their concerns, but be realistic.

5. *Carefully consider everything you know about the case before offering an opinion about prognosis, especially when dealing with young children.* Include appropriate precautions about the imprecision of any prognosis. You want to leave the parents with hope, even when their child is severely disabled; however, do not give them false expectations. Parents of a child with a disability need to know that their child will still grow and develop over time, albeit at a slower rate than would a child without disabilities. Focus on the most appropriate means to obtain short-term rehabilitation goals. This will give the parents direction and motivation.

6. *Inform the parents of their legal rights, and be sure they understand them.* Discuss their rights under applicable federal laws and relevant state and local policies (see Sattler, 2001).

7. *Recommend books, pamphlets, or other materials and organizations that will help the parents and child.* Ask the parents whether they are interested in reading about their child's disorder, illness, or condition. Also, ask them whether they are interested in contacting local or national organizations to learn more about their child's problems or in joining a support group or an advocacy group. If they are, provide them with the necessary information.

FINAL PHASE: TERMINATING THE POST-ASSESSMENT INTERVIEW

1. *Evaluate the parents' understanding and feelings about the results and recommendations toward the end of the post-assessment interview.* You could say, for example, "We met today so that we could discuss the results of the evaluation. What is your understanding of the findings? How do you feel about the recommendations?"

2. *Encourage the parents to ask any additional questions, especially if you believe that they still have some concerns about the results or recommendations.* They may ask about how to obtain a second opinion, who will have access to the assessment results, how long treatment may take, what role they will have in the intervention plan, what community resources are available, and the cost of treatment. Answer their questions to the best of your ability, and direct them to other sources of information if necessary.

3. *Inform the parents that you are available for additional meetings.* Make it easy for them to arrange subsequent meetings. You want to have an open-door policy. Encourage them to contact you or other professionals any time they have ques-

tions—even weeks, months, or years after the initial diagnosis has been made.

4. *Convey to the parents your understanding of their difficulty, especially if they are unable to accept the results of the evaluation.* Describe referral services. Should they want other opinions, provide them with the names of other agencies or professionals.

5. *Find out what the parents want to do immediately after the interview is over if they are especially distraught.* Do they want to sit in the waiting room for a while, talk to another professional if one is available, or go home?

6. *Close the interview by giving the parents your business telephone number (if they don't already have it) and by inviting them to call you if they have further questions.* Again, you might want to compliment the parents on their participation in the assessment and encourage them to follow the recommendations. Escort the parents from the room, thank them for their cooperation, and say goodbye.

Evaluation of the post-assessment interview with parents. Questions to consider about the post-assessment interview with parents include the following:

1. How much information did the parents hear and absorb?
2. Did the parents understand the results?
3. Did they accept the results?
4. Did they understand the recommendations?
5. Did they accept the recommendations?
6. What areas of the evaluation and recommendations did they question, if any?
7. What type of interventions did they want?
8. Did they understand their rights under relevant federal and state laws and local policies?
9. Did they want a second evaluation of their child from an independent source?
10. What would they consider indications of successful treatment or remediation?
11. How willing are they to change their own expectations and behavior?
12. Are they willing to involve themselves in parent-training programs or in other skill programs?
13. What are their resources for making changes and for cooperating with the recommendations?
14. What resources do the parents have to hospitalize or institutionalize their child if it should become necessary?

When handled poorly, the initial diagnostic phase will remain as a bitter memory whose details linger in the minds of the parent for many years thereafter. When handled with sensitivity and technical skill, this experience can contribute to a strong foundation for productive family adaptation and for constructive parent-professional collaboration.

—Michael Thomasgard, American developmental behavioral pediatrician (1947–   ), and Jack P. Shonkoff, American developmental behavioral pediatrician (1957–   )

Post-assessment interview with parents as a staff conference. In some settings—such as in schools, mental health clinics, and hospitals—several professionals may evaluate the child and the family. In such settings, having a staff conference—at which each member of the team can make a unique contribution to the presentation—may be helpful, especially when it is important for the parents or child to hear the views of each professional. When the post-assessment interview with parents is in the form of a staff conference, the following guidelines complement those presented previously (Greenbaum, 1982):

1. *Prepare for the conference carefully.* The team leader (sometimes called the case manager) should review all case history information, medical reports, test results, and recommendations.

2. *Set specific goals for the conference.* Before the conference, team members should reach a unified position and the team leader should prepare a list of goals.

3. *Be organized.* The team leader should begin and end the conference on time, follow the agenda, and allow enough time to cover the agenda. Team members should introduce themselves. If each member presents his or her findings, the presentations should be organized and orderly.

4. *Individualize the conference.* Team members should focus on material relevant to the concerns of the child and family.

5. *Appear confident.* Team members should choose their words carefully and maintain their composure.

6. *Don't be defensive.* Team members should recognize that they do not have all the answers. They should not become involved in power struggles with the parents or with each other.

7. *Form an alliance with the parents.* Team members should see the parents as part of the team, help the parents to see themselves as equal participants on the team, and encourage them to work with the team in carrying out the recommendations. Parents should be encouraged to address questions to any team member.

8. *Explore the needs of the parents.* Team members need to understand the feelings and reactions of the parents and be prepared to deviate from the agenda, if necessary, to help the parents work through their special concerns about their child.

9. *Be realistic when presenting information.* Team members should be direct and honest and avoid technical jargon. They should discuss public laws and state and local policies that pertain to the child and family.

10. *Explain the recommended interventions.* Parents should not be pressured to follow a plan they believe is inappropriate for their child.

11. *Make a closing statement.* The team leader should summarize the findings and decisions, arrange for future appointments, and tell the parents how they can reach each member of the team.

Although a staff conference does have some advantages, as noted earlier, it also has a major disadvantage. Sitting at one end of a table watching six or seven professionals give reports is an intimidating experience for many parents. Other alternatives are to have a designated case manager who meets with the parents and summarizes the findings and recommendations of the staff and to have each professional meet individually with the parents.

Overview of the post-assessment interview with parents. The way in which each post-assessment interview unfolds will depend on the needs of the parents and on your theoretical orientation. *Always show warmth, understanding, and respect.* Children and parents appreciate your listening to them and understanding their concerns. Help parents avoid becoming defensive by telling them that you recognize the effort they are making to help their child. The crucial test of the effectiveness of a post-assessment interview is whether the parents act on what they have learned.

In working with families of children with special needs, recognize that the family has considerable influence on the ability of the child to deal with his or her condition and to profit from an intervention program. Help the family members understand what will help the child cope so that they can cooperate in the intervention efforts and support the child at home.

Parents' reactions to the assessment will depend on the entire process—from the beginning of the initial interview to the end of the post-assessment interview. Parents are likely to resent professionals who fail to include them in the decision-making process, view them as objects, talk down to them, or fail to consider their needs (Boyer & Chesteen, 1992). Conversely, parents are likely to appreciate professionals who answer their questions honestly, give understandable explanations, respect their self-determination, solicit their participation, give them support, offer understandable and realistic recommendations, provide information about the best possible care, and are knowledgeable about community resources.

The post-assessment interview with parents requires sensitivity and understanding of their feelings, needs, and desires. It is not a matter of simply reciting results or reading a report. Rather, you should make every effort to enlist the parents' cooperation in working toward an effective intervention plan. You want to establish a collaborative partnership with the parents so that together you can come to a better understanding of the needs of the child and work toward solving the problems.

The post-assessment interview is an important part of the assessment procedure. It can be particularly rewarding because it allows you to present the results in a purposeful way. It also can be frustrating and even heartbreaking. It is important to understand your attitudes toward children with psychological, emotional, or behavioral problems before you begin to work with them and with their parents. By following the guidelines presented in this chapter, you can alleviate some of your anxieties about communicating the assessment results to parents and children.

Thank you for letting me know by your voice and your expression that you cared when you told me the diagnosis.
—Anonymous

THE FOLLOW-UP INTERVIEW

The three interview chapters in this section are focused primarily on the initial clinical assessment interview and the post-assessment interview, but much of the material that you have read regarding the post-assessment interview also applies to the follow-up interview. The follow-up interview is designed to obtain information about how the child and family are functioning and to evaluate the intervention efforts, where applicable. For example, follow-up interviews with parents may focus on the following areas (Krehbiel & Kroth, 1991):

1. Changes in the child's functioning
2. The child's performance at home
3. The child's progress in school (where appropriate)
4. The parents' concerns about whether they are doing the right thing for their child or are expecting too much or too little
5. The family's adjustment to the child's problem
6. The parents' efforts to provide the child with normal experiences
7. Whether the family's needs are being met
8. The family's stress level
9. The family's social, emotional, and community supports
10. The parents' attitudes toward professionals who are working with the child
11. The parents' satisfaction with the intervention program(s)
12. The family's plans for the future

During follow-up interviews, you may need to do one or more of the following (Rollin, 1987):

1. Help the parents and other family members discover any areas of conflict that may interfere with healthy family functioning.
2. Help the parents and other family members see the child's problem(s) as a family issue, not as an issue that belongs to only one or two family members.
3. If the child has a disability, encourage the parents and other family members to use whatever rehabilitation services and assistive devices have been recommended.
4. If the child has a disability, help each family member understand her or his unique role within the family and how she or he can assist.
5. Help the parents and other family members make future plans for the child.
6. Recognize that the parents and other family members may have different attitudes about any recommended interventions; help them work through their differences.

If the parents are taking adequate care of their child, you should acknowledge their progress. Comments such as the following reinforce their efforts (Krehbiel & Kroth, 1991):

- "You've come a long way in learning medical terminology."
- "You have discovered the basis of Paul's refusal to maintain his diet. Tell me how you did that."
- "So things are still frustrating and difficult, but you now have the routine under control."
- "Sometimes parents like to talk with other parents whose children have similar problems. Would you like to do that?" (Adapted from p. 118)

RELIABILITY AND VALIDITY OF INTERVIEWS

Obtaining reliable and valid information from the interviewee is critical in clinical assessment interviewing. Therefore, you must evaluate the interview—as you would any other assessment technique—for reliability and validity. Following are several types of reliability related to interviews (Mash & Terdal, 1981):

- *Intersession reliability* is the degree to which the information obtained from an interviewee on one occasion agrees with the information obtained from the same interviewee on other occasions.
- *Interinterviewee agreement* is the degree to which the information obtained from one interviewee agrees with the information obtained from another interviewee.
- *Internal consistency reliability* is the degree to which the information given by an interviewee is consistent with other information given by the interviewee in the same interview.
- *Interinterviewer reliability,* or *method error,* is the degree to which the information obtained by one interviewer is consistent with that obtained by another interviewer from the same interviewee.

The two major types of validity related to the interview are concurrent validity and predictive validity (Mash & Terdal, 1981):

- *Concurrent validity* is the degree to which the information obtained in the interview corresponds to the information obtained through other methods.
- *Predictive validity* is the degree to which information obtained in the interview predicts the treatment outcome.

You are likely to find that children and parents differ in their reports and that younger children differ from older children in the reliability of their reports. Here are some findings.

1. Children and parents agree *least* often about covert and private symptoms such as anxiety, fear, and obsessions; they agree more often about overt, easily observable behaviors such as behavior problems and conduct problems

(Edelbrock, Costello, Dulcan, Conover, & Kalas, 1986; Thompson, Merritt, Keith, Murphy, & Johndrow, 1993).

2. Older children report more subjective symptoms (e.g., intrusive thoughts and images, feelings of emptiness, concentration difficulties) than their parents, while parents report more objective symptoms (e.g., anxiety, bullying, argumentativeness) than their children (Nader, 1997).

3. Agreement between children and parents is moderate for depressive symptoms (Klein, 1991).

4. Generally, parents are more reliable than children in reporting children's symptoms (Klein, 1991).

5. Adolescents are more reliable than younger school-age children in reporting symptoms (Edelbrock, Costello, Dulcan, Kalas, & Conover, 1985; Schwab-Stone, Fallon, Briggs, & Crowther, 1994; Schwab-Stone, Fisher, Piacentini, Shaffer, Davies, & Briggs, 1993). Younger school-age children have particular difficulties with questions about duration and onset of symptoms, but not with questions about fears.

The last finding indicates that young children's reports of symptoms should be confirmed by other sources. Reports by adolescents are more reliable because their better developed cognitive, memory, and language skills enable them to respond more accurately to questions that require self-awareness, perspective taking, recall, reasoning ability, and expressive skill. But even adolescents' reports may agree poorly with parents' reports (Klein, 1991). Whenever you get conflicting information, you need to inquire further.

You may have difficulty determining the overall reliability and validity of an interview, because interviews yield several types of information, including demographic, developmental, observational, and diagnostic data (Bellack & Hersen, 1980). Ideally, you should have independent estimates of the reliability and validity of each type of information. In addition, interviews are highly dependent on specific interviewer

Courtesy of Brendan Mulcahy.

and interviewee characteristics, the type of interview, and the conditions under which the interview takes place. These factors and their interactions can affect the reliability and validity of the information obtained. Despite these complexities, you need to evaluate the reliability and validity of information obtained in the interview as you would information obtained from other types of assessments.

Interviewee Factors That May Impede Reliability and Validity

A reliable and valid interview is possible only if the interviewee is willing and able to give you accurate information. Consequently, when you evaluate the interviewee's responses, you will need to consider the interviewee's age, intellectual ability, cognitive development, emotional and social development, receptive and expressive language competence, self-awareness, degree of psychological disturbance, and culture and ethnicity.

Some factors that may limit reliability and validity are interviewees' attitudes; understanding of questions; memory; interpretation of events; language; affect; personal likes, dislikes, and values; and behavior. Let's examine these factors in more detail.

1. *Interviewees' attitudes.* Interviewees who are angry or uncooperative, who want to give socially desirable answers, or who want to please you and say things you want to hear likely will not give useful information. The validity of the information also will be compromised if interviewees are under stress, are resistant, lack trust, feel pressured to give certain responses, or fear reprisal or punishment if they are truthful. Those who come for help voluntarily are likely to give more accurate information than are those who are coerced to come (Bellack & Hersen, 1980).

2. *Interviewees' understanding of the questions.* When interviewees fail to understand questions but do not say "I don't understand" or ask you to rephrase the questions, they usually will give misleading information. Such misunderstandings are likely to occur, for example, when interviewees have uncorrected hearing difficulties, have cognitive limitations, have language comprehension difficulties, or are embarrassed to tell you that they do not understand the questions.

3. *Interviewees' memory.* Interviewees may have difficulty recalling information, including important developmental milestones. Sometimes, rather than saying they don't know, they may guess or make up information.

4. *Interviewees' interpretation of events.* Interviewees may distort what happened to them or to others. For example, what interviewees say occurred may not be what actually occurred because people tend to interpret their own behavior in a manner consistent with the image they have of themselves. Interviewees also may exaggerate or minimize the significance of events.

5. *Interviewees' language.* Interviewees may have difficulty finding the correct words to describe their thoughts, feelings, or previous events. They may misuse words and thereby unintentionally give wrong information.

6. *Interviewees' affect.* Interviewees' fears and anxieties may impede their ability to give accurate replies. For example, withdrawal, overtalkativeness, giggling, and loss of voice are possible manifestations of fear or anxiety and possible manifestations of coping and defensive behaviors; these reactions, if present, likely will contribute to the unreliability of the interview.

7. *Interviewees' personal likes, dislikes, and values.* Interviewees may fail to cooperate simply because your ethnic group, economic class, age, or gender differs from theirs. Reactions to the interviewer that are not objective are called *reactive effects.*

8. *Interviewees' behavior.* Interviewees' behavior in the interview—or when they are observed in a playroom or at home—may differ from their usual behavior. For example, they may be more cooperative, use more polished language, or treat people with more respect than they usually do. This change in behavior, arising from the knowledge that they are being evaluated, also is referred to as a reactive effect. Interviewees also may intentionally try to distort their behavior in order to convince you that they have some type of disturbance. Such efforts, which may suggest malingering, are discussed in more detail later in the chapter. Finally, interviewees may be too distraught or preoccupied to talk coherently.

Interviewer Factors That May Impede Reliability and Validity

Factors associated with the interviewer that may affect the reliability and validity of the interview include your techniques and style; personal needs; personal likes, dislikes, and values; understanding of the interviewee; attention to the physical environment; selective perceptions and expectancies; ethnicity; recording techniques; interpretations; and theoretical position. Let's first examine each of these sources and then look at ways to reduce potential impediments.

1. *Interviewer's techniques and style.* You can influence the interviewee's responses by the way in which you word a question, your choice of follow-up responses, the tone of your voice, your facial expressions (particularly those following responses from the interviewee), your posture, and other verbal and nonverbal behaviors. Errors may occur, for example, if you fail to establish rapport, use ambiguous or vague questions, ask more than one question at a time, use complex and abstract words, use biased wording, time questions poorly, ask why questions, ask many leading questions, are insensitive to the interviewee's mood, or fail to monitor your verbal and nonverbal behavior. In addition, you will make errors if you fail to probe adequately or fail to gather enough information to reach valid conclusions. In essence, you do not want your actions to directly or indirectly cause the inter-

viewee to respond in a way that he or she did not intend or distort his or her communication to please you. Sometimes you may not even recognize that you are leading the interviewee to give certain types of responses.

2. *Interviewer's personal needs.* Your personal needs may affect the way you conduct the interview and the topics you approach and avoid. For example, if you have a need to be perceived in a positive light, you may fail to probe for more information so as to avoid seeming to pressure the interviewee; may smile inappropriately; may make inappropriate expressions of sympathy, support, or agreement; or may waste interview time by socializing with the interviewee.

3. *Interviewer's personal likes, dislikes, and values.* Your personal likes, dislikes, and values may influence how you relate to the interviewee. For example, you may unknowingly send signals showing your pleasure to interviewees whom you find attractive (because of their dress, voice quality, ethnic group, or some other characteristic); you may send nonverbal signals of displeasure to interviewees whom you do not find attractive for some reason. Similarly, if you have strong opinions about certain topics (such as abortion, religion, or sexual preference), you may communicate those opinions to the interviewee through your verbal or nonverbal behavior.

You may be susceptible to the interviewee's nonverbal behavior. For example, interviewees who make eye contact, smile, have an attentive posture, or show interest in you may encourage you to probe topics and ask follow-up questions. In contrast, you may be hesitant to probe and ask follow-up questions when interviewees fail to make eye contact, frown, have an inattentive posture, or fail to show interest in you.

Another impediment to validity occurs when you compare your values with those of the interviewee and find the interviewee's values lacking. Your goal as an interviewer is to understand the interviewee's values, not to measure him or her against your personal standards. The way you perceive similarities and differences between you and the interviewee also may affect how you conduct the interview.

You may be attracted by odors some interviewees have and be repelled by others. Nevertheless, you must not let your attitude toward the odors influence either the length or the direction of the interview. Awareness of odors is subtle and often preconscious. By recognizing your preferences for odors, you will be in a better position to guard against allowing these preferences to interfere with the conduct of the interview.

4. *Interviewer's understanding of the interviewee.* You are likely to make errors if you fail to consider the interviewee's age, cognitive level, or culture or if you misunderstand what the interviewee says. These errors may occur, for example, when you have difficulty understanding the interviewee's speech or language, are preoccupied with other thoughts, are distracted, or have hearing difficulties that have not been corrected.

5. *Interviewer's failure to attend to the physical environment or to other situational factors.* If you fail to prepare the

interview room properly—by failing to minimize distractions, keeping the room too hot or too cold, having poor lighting, failing to disconnect the phone, or having uncomfortable seats, for example—the interview may suffer. Other situational factors that may bias the interview include conducting the interview (a) with the child and an alleged abuser in the same room, (b) in a police station or in another stressful environment, or (c) shortly after a traumatic event.

6. *Interviewer's selective perceptions and expectancies.* Selective perceptions and expectancies may shape your questions and probes, what you listen to, and your interpretations. For example, you may fail to ask relevant questions because of preconceived notions, listen only to things that you believe will confirm your expectancies, or interpret marginally aggressive actions as aggressive because of your mindset.

7. *Interviewer's ethnicity.* When your own racial or ethnic group or class status causes you to distort replies or make inaccurate inferences, the validity of the information you obtain is likely to be affected (see Chapter 4). One example: It is wrong to infer that an Asian American or Native American interviewee is evasive because he or she won't look you in the eye; for these interviewees, such behavior is a sign of respect.

8. *Interviewer's recording of data.* You may make recording errors because of careless notations or because you omit, add, or subtly change details. Or you may make recording errors because of your preconceived ideas—you hear what you want to hear or what you expect to hear. These errors may occur either during the interview or after the interview is completed.

9. *Interviewer's interpretation of observations and information.* If you make inferences that are not well supported by your observations or the information you obtain, you may lose objectivity. For example, an interviewee's speech may be characterized as "deliberate" by one interviewer, as "slow and dull" by another interviewer, and as "depressed and despondent" by still another interviewer. To be objective, your notes should reflect the interviewee's behavior—for example, that the interviewee "spoke slowly" or "paused several seconds before responding." Use adjectives that best describe the behavior of the interviewee. Don't draw inferences unless you have sufficient information. Your interpretations are more likely to be misleading when the behavior of the interviewee is ambiguous.

10. *Interviewer's theoretical position.* Errors arise when you interpret all behavior from a preconceived position. Not all of a child's behaviors are likely to be related to an unresolved Oedipus complex, to being an oldest child, or to having an inappropriate reinforcement history.

Improving the Reliability and Validity of the Interview

Here are some strategies for improving the reliability and validity of an interview:

1. *Plan and use guidelines.* Have a plan for the interview. Use semistructured or structured interview schedules as a guide.

2. *Relate to the interviewee.* Word questions so that they do not lead the interviewee toward an answer. Listen carefully to the interviewee, and give the person your undivided interest and attention. Show your acceptance of the interviewee. Maintain an attitude of professional concern. When interviewees are fearful and anxious, try even harder to establish rapport. For example, make frequent supportive comments, show them that you understand their fears and anxieties, and take the pressure off by interjecting light conversation. If you still detect anxiety or defensiveness, stay relaxed and try to get the interviewee to relax by making small talk before broaching or returning to anxiety-laden topics. When interviewees will not cooperate simply because of who you are, you can do nothing to change your status. You can, however, show them that you can be trusted and want to help them.

3. *Develop self-awareness.* Become aware of personal needs that may adversely affect how you conduct the interview, and find ways to suppress them. Recognize your attitudes, values, and objectives and how they relate to interviewees from different ethnic, cultural, or socioeconomic groups. Develop an awareness of your nonverbal and verbal behavior. Be aware not only of the communications of the interviewee and of your reactions to them, but also of your own communications and how the interviewee may perceive them. Minimize selective perceptions, theoretical preconceptions, and expectancies that may distract you from eliciting information and from making appropriate decisions.

4. *Gather additional information.* When you have doubts about the reliability of the information you obtain, ask questions in different ways or at different times, or ask both the interviewee and someone else about the same topics. You can evaluate the validity of the information you obtain by checking baby books, school and medical records, and other formal and informal records, where applicable.

5. *Attend to recordings.* Check your notes for accuracy shortly after the interview is over. If you do not take notes, record (in writing or with a tape recorder) the information you have obtained and your impressions soon after the interview.

6. *Develop hypotheses.* Study all sources of information about the interviewee for corroborating facts. Cross-validate inferences and predictions by trying to find corroborating evidence in two or more sources. Closely review the data before you make inferences. Recognize the limitations of your theoretical approach. Be open to alternative explanations.

You must strive to overcome any conditions that will impede your effectiveness as an interviewer. In case of substantial doubts about your findings, arrange to have the interviewee interviewed by another interviewer, and then compare the results of the two interviews. Your goal is to be vigilant and objective, yet always caring.

ASSESSMENT OF MALINGERING

Another factor that directly affects the reliability and validity of the interview is *malingering* by the interviewee. *Malingering is conscious fabrication or gross exaggeration of physical or psychological symptoms in pursuit of a recognizable goal.* Malingering includes deliberate distortions or misrepresentations of psychological symptoms, attempts to distort or misrepresent a self-report, and outright dishonesty (Rogers, 1988b). Almost any psychological or physical disorder is open to malingering. Malingering is difficult to identify because subjective symptoms are hard to verify.

Degrees of Malingering

There are gradations of malingering (Rogers, 1988a). In *mild malingering,* the distortions or variations present in the interviewee's report have little or no bearing on the diagnosis or disposition. In *moderate malingering,* there is a clear pattern of exaggeration or fabrication of symptoms, making it difficult to arrive at a diagnosis or a disposition. In *severe malingering,* the pattern of fabrication is overwhelming, to the point that the interviewee appears severely psychologically disturbed, displays rare and improbable symptoms, or reports symptoms that remain uncorroborated by clinical observations.

Reasons for Malingering

Interviewees may malinger in an effort to reduce personal accountability, escape the consequences of antisocial or immoral actions, avoid punishment by pretending to be incompetent to stand trial, avoid military service, obtain money for alleged physical or psychological illness, seek a transfer to another setting, or gain admission to a psychiatric hospital.

Age and Malingering

Malingering is more likely to occur in older elementary school–age children and adolescents than in younger children. "Malingering requires considerable skill in role-playing, impression-management, and deception; these skills are simply not available to younger children" (Quinn, 1988, p. 115).

Evaluation of Malingering

Evaluate malingering by considering the interviewee's past and current functioning, test performance (if available), clinical records, and reports from others. Sometimes symptoms may be so exaggerated (e.g., extremely severe confusion, disorientation, and attention-concentration deficits) that they strain credibility. The interviewee who cannot recall even simple word pairs or the day of the week may be malingering, because such memory lapses usually occur only in the most severe cases of amnesia, dementia, or delirium. Other clues to malingering are lack of internal consistency in presented deficits, apparent inconsistencies in performance, implausibility of explanations, evasiveness and uncooperativeness, attempts to avoid examination, and discrepancies between ability to study (or work) and ability to play. When possible, monitor (by observing or recording on videotape) the interviewee's alleged symptoms (for example, fainting spells, sleeplessness, exaggerated startle reactions).

Following are guidelines for evaluating possible malingering (Quinn, 1988):

1. Does the interviewee have the capacity to deceive? Children under 6 years of age usually are not able to lie deliberately and be successful.
2. Does the interviewee have a pattern of persistent lying? If so, the information presented by the interviewee may not be reliable.
3. Does the interviewee have psychological problems that would severely distort communication? If so, the interviewee's behaviors may be a reflection of the psychological problems and not a manifestation of malingering.
4. Are there stressors in the interviewee's environment that may lead to lying? If so, consider these stressors in evaluating the interviewee's behavior.
5. Are the interviewee's symptoms consistent with a well-recognized illness or syndrome? If so, there is less likelihood of malingering.

The following signs should alert you to the possibility that the interviewee might be malingering (Cunnien, 1988). The more signs that are present, the stronger the possibility of malingering. Still, these signs only suggest malingering—they do not prove it.

- Interviewee is involved in a legal action.
- Symptoms worsen when interviewee is observed.
- Symptoms are bizarre or ridiculous.
- Symptoms wax and wane, depending on what is going on in interviewee's environment at the time.
- Symptoms fail to respond to customary treatment.
- Complaints are grossly in excess of physical findings.
- Symptoms cannot be explained by a known mental or physical disorder.
- Interviewee is uncooperative during the examination.
- Symptoms give interviewee some advantage, such as avoidance of school, avoidance of incarceration, financial gain, avoidance of prosecution, or acquisition of drugs.
- Self-report cannot be verified by independent observers.

Ultimately, you can be certain that an interviewee is malingering only when the interviewee voluntarily confesses—convincingly—to the deception or when the interviewee confesses when you confront him or her about an obvious lie. In summary, in assessing malingering, look for incongruities in the interviewee's behavior, observe the interviewee's reaction when confronted with the incongruities, evaluate the interviewee's motivation for the possible deception, and consider both the interviewee's cognitive level *and* moral level of development (Quinn, 1988).

EVALUATING YOUR INTERVIEW TECHNIQUES

This section of the book has presented guidelines to help you become a successful clinical assessment interviewer. However, you should not follow the guidelines rigidly or expect them to cover every possible contingency. Human relationships are variable, and each one is unique, so a "cookbook" of techniques is neither possible nor desirable. You must be the judge of how and when to use a particular procedure.

You should carefully evaluate your interview techniques, particularly when you are first learning to interview or when you have not conducted an interview for some time. You can simply think about the interview and then evaluate your performance in the interview shortly after its completion. Or, you can record some interviews that you conduct on either audiotape or videotape (with proper consent) and then study the recordings. Both audiotapes and videotapes give you the opportunity to study your interview techniques and your diction, speech intensity, and other voice and speech characteristics. Videotapes, in addition, allow you to evaluate your eye contact, posture, gestures, and other nonverbal behaviors. If possible, review your tape recordings with a classmate or, better yet, with someone who has expertise in interviewing.

Questions to Consider in Your Self-Evaluation

You can evaluate your performance during an interview by asking yourself the following questions:

1. How did you feel about the interviewee?
2. How well did you understand the interviewee's verbal communications?
3. Did you formulate clear goals and purposes before beginning the interview?
4. If so, did you keep these goals and purposes in mind during the interview?
5. Did you accomplish your interview goals?
6. How did you react to questions about you posed by the interviewee?
7. What did you learn about your interviewing techniques?
8. Which techniques were most successful?
9. How could you have been a more effective interviewer?
10. What would you do differently if you had another chance to do the interview?
11. How satisfied were you with your overall performance in the interview?

While you are in training, your supervisor can evaluate your interview techniques by rating you on the competencies shown in Table 7-1; these ratings can help you in your own self-evaluation. You may also find it helpful to complete for yourself as many of the items in Table 7-1 as you can after each interview.

As you conduct your self-evaluation (or review your supervisor's evaluation), what themes emerge? What are the strengths and weaknesses of your interviewing style? What can you do to improve your interview techniques? After you conducted several interviews, did any pattern emerge in your interviewing style? Did you improve your skills in subsequent interviews?

If you have a rating of 4 or 5 ("poor demonstration of this skill" or "very poor demonstration of this skill") on any of the items in Table 7-1, determine why and when the difficulty occurred and what you can do to improve your interview techniques. For example, if you daydreamed, try to determine why. During what part of the interview did the daydreaming occur? What content was being covered? Did you have other problems with similar content? Was the content of your daydream related in some way to what the interviewee was saying? Or, if you conveyed your own personal needs to the

Frank and Ernest

© 1991 Thaves / Reprinted with permission. Newspaper dist. by NEA, Inc.

Table 7-1
Interview Techniques Checklist

INTERVIEW TECHNIQUES CHECKLIST

Name of interviewer: _____ Date of interview: _____

Name of interviewee: _____ Rater's name: _____

Rating Key

Excellent demonstration of this skill	Good demonstration of this skill	Adequate demonstration of this skill	Poor demonstration of this skill	Very poor demonstration of this skill	Not applicable
1	2	3	4	5	NA

Skill	Rating
1. Made a smooth transition from opening greeting to next topic	1 2 3 4 5 NA
2. Created a positive interview climate	1 2 3 4 5 NA
3. Showed respect for interviewee	1 2 3 4 5 NA
4. Gave undivided attention to interviewee	1 2 3 4 5 NA
5. Established an environment free from distractions	1 2 3 4 5 NA
6. Used good diction	1 2 3 4 5 NA
7. Spoke in a clear, audible voice with warmth	1 2 3 4 5 NA
8. Spoke in a modulated voice that reflected nuances of feeling	1 2 3 4 5 NA
9. Spoke at a moderate tempo	1 2 3 4 5 NA
10. Used appropriate vocabulary	1 2 3 4 5 NA
11. Formulated general questions	1 2 3 4 5 NA
12. Formulated open-ended questions	1 2 3 4 5 NA
13. Used nonleading questions	1 2 3 4 5 NA
14. Used relatively few yes-no questions	1 2 3 4 5 NA
15. Used few, if any, multiple-choice questions	1 2 3 4 5 NA
16. Used structuring statements	1 2 3 4 5 NA
17. Encouraged replies	1 2 3 4 5 NA
18. Used probes effectively	1 2 3 4 5 NA
19. Allowed interviewee to express feelings and thoughts in her or his own way	1 2 3 4 5 NA
20. Formulated follow-up questions to pursue issues	1 2 3 4 5 NA
21. Was attentive to interviewee's nonverbal behavior	1 2 3 4 5 NA
22. Conveyed a desire to understand interviewee	1 2 3 4 5 NA
23. Conveyed to interviewee an interest in obtaining relevant facts, not in confirming pre-existing hypotheses	1 2 3 4 5 NA
24. Rephrased questions	1 2 3 4 5 NA
25. Used reflection	1 2 3 4 5 NA
26. Used feedback	1 2 3 4 5 NA
27. Handled a minimally communicative interviewee appropriately	1 2 3 4 5 NA
28. Handled interviewee's resistance and anxiety appropriately	1 2 3 4 5 NA
29. Showed sensitivity to interviewee's emotional state	1 2 3 4 5 NA
30. Clarified areas of confusion in interviewee's statements	1 2 3 4 5 NA
31. Intervened when interviewee had difficulty expressing thoughts	1 2 3 4 5 NA
32. Handled rambling communications appropriately	1 2 3 4 5 NA

Table 7-1 (*Continued*)

Skill	Rating					
33. Dealt with difficult behavior appropriately	1	2	3	4	5	NA
34. Used props, crayons, clay, or toys appropriately	1	2	3	4	5	NA
35. Timed questions appropriately	1	2	3	4	5	NA
36. Handled silences appropriately	1	2	3	4	5	NA
37. Used periodic summaries during the interview	1	2	3	4	5	NA
38. Asked questions about all relevant areas without avoiding potentially stressful ones	1	2	3	4	5	NA
39. Provided appropriate support to interviewee to minimize effects of discussing stressful topics	1	2	3	4	5	NA
40. Made clear transitions	1	2	3	4	5	NA
41. Paced the interview	1	2	3	4	5	NA
42. Self-disclosed only when necessary	1	2	3	4	5	NA
43. Evidenced appropriate sensitivity to interviewee's cultural identity	1	2	3	4	5	NA
44. Established and maintained eye contact	1	2	3	4	5	NA
45. Maintained facial expressions relevant to content	1	2	3	4	5	NA
46. Used nonverbal behavior to further the interview	1	2	3	4	5	NA
47. Demonstrated consistency between nonverbal and verbal behavior	1	2	3	4	5	NA
48. Responded in nonjudgmental manner (without moralizing, advising prematurely, persuading, criticizing, or labeling)	1	2	3	4	5	NA
49. Resisted distractions	1	2	3	4	5	NA
50. Avoided overreacting	1	2	3	4	5	NA
51. Avoided arguments	1	2	3	4	5	NA
52. Handled interviewee's questions and concerns appropriately	1	2	3	4	5	NA
53. Allowed interviewee to express remaining thoughts and questions at close of interview	1	2	3	4	5	NA
54. Arranged for post-assessment interview	1	2	3	4	5	NA
55. Used summary statements at the end of the interview as needed	1	2	3	4	5	NA
56. Used closing statements	1	2	3	4	5	NA

Comments: _____

_____

_____

interviewee (such as wanting his or her respect or wanting to be liked), determine whether these messages interfered with the relationship. The interviewee may have felt guilty if she or he did not satisfy your needs. Think about why it was necessary for you to have these needs fulfilled in a professional relationship. Evaluate thoroughly every problem you find with your interview techniques and try to improve them.

Obtaining Feedback from the Interviewee

During your training (and even periodically during your career), you may want to obtain feedback from interviewees

about your performance. If you decide to do so, you can use the checklist shown in Table 7–2. It is designed to be completed by adolescents and adults and contains 18 yes-no questions and space for additional comments.

Recognizing the Interviewee's Limitations

If you were unsuccessful in obtaining information from an interviewee, do not be too hard on yourself. Some children or parents simply will not cooperate or will not disclose information for various reasons. Children with an autistic

Table 7-2
Checklist for an Interviewee's Evaluation of an Interviewer

EVALUATING THE INTERVIEWER

Client's name: _____   Name of interviewer: _____

Date of interview: _____

Directions: Please rate the interviewer on each item. Circle Y for yes, N for No, or ? if you are not sure of your answer. Be sure to respond to each item. Thank you!

Item	Rating			Item	Rating		
1. The interviewer saw me at approximately the scheduled time.	Y	N	?	10. The interviewer asked about my feelings and responded appropriately to them.	Y	N	?
2. The interviewer put me at ease during the interview.	Y	N	?	11. I was able to talk about problems and issues that were important to me.	Y	N	?
3. The interviewer greeted me in a way that made me feel comfortable.	Y	N	?	12. The topics covered by the interviewer were appropriate.	Y	N	?
4. The interviewer appeared interested in me.	Y	N	?	13. The interviewer seemed organized during the interview.	Y	N	?
5. The interviewer appeared to be confident.	Y	N	?	14. The interviewer was thorough in asking me relevant questions.	Y	N	?
6. The interviewer spoke clearly and was easily understood.	Y	N	?	15. The interviewer summarized the problems as he or she saw them.	Y	N	?
7. The interviewer asked questions in a way that allowed me time to think about my answers.	Y	N	?	16. The time spent with the interviewer was adequate for my needs.	Y	N	?
8. The interviewer asked relevant questions about my personal and social life.	Y	N	?	17. I felt nervous during the interview.	Y	N	?
9. The interviewer seemed to understand me.	Y	N	?	18. Overall, I felt satisfied with the interview.	Y	N	?

Any other comments are welcome.

_____

_____

_____

disorder, those with a severe conduct disorder, or those who are severely developmentally disabled, for example, may be uncooperative or unable to provide the desired information. Parents who have been coerced to come to the interview also may be uncooperative. In such cases, note their behavior and schedule another appointment. Your failure to obtain information may be related more to the problems of the interviewee than to your clinical skills. As your clinical skills improve, however, you may become more successful in interviewing challenging children and parents or children and parents who are in difficult situations.

THINKING THROUGH THE ISSUES

1. If you see that you are running out of time in the interview, what is the best strategy to follow? Explain your reasoning.

2. Under what conditions would you want to see an interviewee for a second interview?

3. What problems might arise in bringing an interview to an end?

4. What are the problems involved in explaining the results of clinical or psychoeducational evaluations to children, parents, and others?

5. What steps could you take to prepare for the difficult responsibility of informing children and parents about diagnoses that imply serious pathology?

6. In the post-assessment interview, how would your approach with children differ from your approach with parents?

7. What problems do you think you might have in explaining to children and parents the assessment results obtained by other professionals?

8. Do you think that you will be successful in interviewing all types of clients? If not, what can you do to improve your ability to interview clients of different ages, those from different cultural and linguistic groups, and those with different types of temperaments and psychological disorders?

TOM AND CAROL ARE INTRODUCED TO THE MARVELS OF MODERN COMMUNICATION

Courtesy of Herman Zielinski and Jerome M. Sattler.

9. How do you think you would go about evaluating the reliability and validity of the information you obtained in an interview?
10. Do you believe that you can detect malingering?
11. How effective do you think you can be in evaluating your own interview techniques?
12. How do you think you will feel when someone evaluates your interview techniques?
13. How do you think you will react to constructive criticism?

SUMMARY

Closing the Initial Interview

1. The final moments of an interview are as important as any other period in the interview; they give you a chance to summarize and evaluate what you have learned.
2. Do not rush the ending of the interview.
3. The method you use to close the interview is especially important when the interviewee is expressing some deeply felt emotion.
4. What you say at the conclusion of the initial interview will depend on the interviewee's age and ability and on whether you plan to see the interviewee again.
5. Be aware of how much time has passed, what important topics you need to discuss, and how much time the interviewee may need to discuss any remaining concerns.
6. Use the last minutes of the initial interview to summarize and evaluate what you have learned and to give the interviewee an

opportunity to ask any remaining questions that he or she might have.
7. Be prepared to deal with the interviewee's concerns.
8. A summary statement should identify the main points of the problem for the interviewee's confirmation or correction.
9. It may be helpful, especially with children, to acknowledge their openness and willingness to share their problems, concerns, hopes, and expectations.
10. When the interviewee has been uncooperative and you need to schedule another appointment, you might want to express your concern about how the interview went.

The Post-Assessment Interview

11. A post-assessment interview (also called an interpretive interview) with children and parents serves several purposes, such as presenting the findings of the assessment, presenting possible interventions, helping children and parents understand the findings and interventions, allowing children and parents to express their concerns, and exploring any additional areas of concern.
12. When you plan the post-assessment interview, consider the information you want to discuss with the child and the parents, how much detail you want to give, and the order in which you want to present the information.
13. Recognize that if you are discussing with the parents and child the results of examinations performed by other professionals, you might not be able to answer all of their questions about these results.
14. Remember that, as a clinical assessor, you will be making important decisions about children's lives.
15. You should never make a diagnosis, a recommendation concerning a child's treatment or placement, or a decision about whether an alleged event took place unless you are fully qualified to do so.
16. A post-assessment interview with a child and parents has five aspects—cognitive, interactive, affective, ethical/religious, and ethnocultural.
17. You will need to cope with the reactions of children and parents to the information they receive.
18. In discussing your findings, use terms that you feel comfortable with and that children and parents can easily understand.
19. As in the initial interview, in the post-assessment interview you will want to listen actively to the child and parents; be aware of their nonverbal behavior; treat both the child and the parents with respect and dignity; recognize family values, customs, beliefs, and cultural practices; communicate openly and honestly with the child and parents; build on their strengths; and acknowledge and address their concerns and needs.
20. Limit the post-assessment interview to about 1 or 1½ hours.
21. Although parents are responsible for their children, there is an increasing tendency toward protecting the rights of children who appear to be competent to make their own decisions.
22. Any release of information must be in accordance with the laws of your state.
23. Hold the post-assessment interview with the child as soon as possible after the evaluation has been completed—doing so may serve to allay his or her fears about the assessment.
24. In the post-assessment interview with the parents, your role is to provide a thorough presentation of the child's problems (description, etiology, severity, and prognosis); plan a specific program geared to the child's needs and capabilities; recognize and deal with the personal problems of the parents as they

affect the child or as they are affected by the child's condition; and plan for future meetings as needed.

25. Four phases characterize the post-assessment interview with parents: establishing rapport, communicating the results, discussing the recommendations, and terminating the interview.

26. It is important to evaluate how the post-assessment interview with the parents went.

27. The post-assessment interview with parents may take the form of a staff conference.

28. The way in which each post-assessment interview unfolds will depend on the needs of the parents and on your theoretical orientation. Always show warmth, understanding, and respect.

29. In working with families of children with special needs, recognize that the family has considerable influence on the ability of the child to deal with his or her condition and to profit from an intervention program.

30. Parents' reactions to the assessment will depend on the entire process—from the beginning of the initial interview to the end of the post-assessment interview.

31. The post-assessment interview with parents requires sensitivity and understanding of their feelings, needs, and desires.

32. The post-assessment interview is an important part of the assessment procedure.

The Follow-Up Interview

33. The follow-up interview is designed to obtain information about how the child and family are functioning and to evaluate the intervention efforts, where applicable.

34. If the parents are taking adequate care of their child, you should acknowledge their progress. Your comments can reinforce the parents' efforts in raising a child with special needs.

Reliability and Validity of Interviews

35. You must evaluate the interview—as you would any other assessment technique—for reliability and validity.

36. Types of reliability related to the interview are intersession reliability, interinterviewee agreement, internal consistency reliability, and interinterviewer reliability.

37. Types of validity related to the interview are concurrent and predictive validity.

38. Children and parents are likely to differ in their reports.

39. Adolescents are more reliable than younger school-age children in reporting symptoms.

40. Young children's reports of symptoms should be confirmed by other sources.

41. You may have difficulty determining the overall reliability and validity of an interview, because interviews yield several types of information, including demographic, developmental, observational, and diagnostic data.

42. When you evaluate the interviewee's responses, you will need to consider the interviewee's age, intellectual ability, cognitive development, emotional and social development, receptive and expressive language competence, self-awareness, degree of psychological disturbance, and culture and ethnicity.

43. Some factors that may limit reliability and validity are interviewees' attitudes; understanding of questions; memory; interpretation of events; language; affect; personal likes, dislikes, and values; and behavior.

44. Factors associated with the interviewer that may affect the reliability and validity of the interview include your techniques

and style; personal needs; personal likes, dislikes, and values; understanding of the interviewee; attention to the physical environment; selective perceptions and expectancies; ethnicity; recording techniques; interpretations; and theoretical position.

45. Some strategies for improving the reliability and validity of the interview are to plan and use guidelines, relate to the interviewee, develop self-awareness, gather additional information, attend to recordings, and develop hypotheses.

46. In case of substantial doubts about your findings, arrange to have the interviewee interviewed by another interviewer, and then compare the results of the two interviews.

Assessment of Malingering

47. Malingering is conscious fabrication or gross exaggeration of physical or psychological symptoms in pursuit of a recognizable goal.

48. Malingering ranges from mild to severe.

49. Interviewees may malinger in an effort to reduce personal accountability, escape the consequences of antisocial or immoral actions, avoid punishment by pretending to be incompetent to stand trial, avoid military service, obtain money for alleged physical or psychological illness, seek a transfer to another setting, or gain admission to a psychiatric hospital.

50. Malingering is more likely to occur in older elementary school–age children and adolescents than in younger children.

51. Evaluate malingering by considering the child's past and current functioning, test performance, clinical records, and reports from others.

52. Possible signs of malingering include the following: interviewee is involved in a legal action; symptoms worsen when interviewee is observed; symptoms are bizarre or ridiculous; symptoms wax and wane, depending on what is going on in interviewee's environment at the time; symptoms fail to respond to customary treatment; complaints are grossly in excess of physical findings; symptoms cannot be explained by a known mental or physical disorder; interviewee is uncooperative during the examination; symptoms give interviewee some advantage, such as avoidance of school, avoidance of incarceration, financial gain, avoidance of prosecution, or acquisition of drugs; and self-report cannot be verified by independent observers.

53. Ultimately, you can be certain that an interviewee is malingering only when the interviewee voluntarily confesses—convincingly—to the deception or when the interviewee confesses when you confront him or her about an obvious lie.

Evaluating Your Interview Techniques

54. Do not follow the guidelines presented in the interview section rigidly or expect them to cover every possible contingency.

55. Human relationships are variable, and each one is unique, so a "cookbook" of techniques is neither possible nor desirable.

56. You must be the judge of how and when to use a particular procedure.

57. You should carefully evaluate your interview techniques, particularly when you are first learning to interview or when you have not conducted an interview for some time.

58. During your training (and even periodically during your career), you may want to obtain feedback from interviewees about your performance.

59. If you were unsuccessful in obtaining information from an interviewee, do not be too hard on yourself. Some children or

parents simply will not cooperate or will not disclose information for various reasons.

60. As your clinical skills improve, you may become more successful in interviewing challenging children and parents or children and parents who are in difficult situations.

KEY TERMS, CONCEPTS, AND NAMES

Closing the initial interview (p. 173)
Recognizing the interviewee's concerns (p. 173)
Summary statement (p. 174)
Post-assessment interview (interpretive interview) (p. 174)
Cognitive aspect of the post-assessment interview (p. 175)
Interactive aspect of the post-assessment interview (p. 175)
Affective aspect of the post-assessment interview (p. 175)
Ethical/religious aspect of the post-assessment interview (p. 175)
Ethnocultural aspect of the post-assessment interview (p. 175)
Confidentiality of information (p. 175)
Release of information (p. 176)
Four phases of the post-assessment interview with parents (p. 176)
Evaluation of the post-assessment interview with parents (p. 178)
Post-assessment interview with parents as a staff conference (p. 179)
Follow-up interview (p. 180)
Reliability and validity of interviews (p. 180)
Intersession reliability (p. 180)
Interinterviewee agreement (p. 180)
Internal consistency reliability (p. 180)
Interinterviewer reliability (p. 180)
Concurrent validity (p. 180)
Predictive validity (p. 180)
Malingering (p. 184)

Mild malingering (p. 184)
Moderate malingering (p. 184)
Severe malingering (p. 184)
Evaluating your interview techniques (p. 185)

STUDY QUESTIONS

1. Discuss the closing phase of an initial interview. What factors need to be considered at the close of the interview?
2. Discuss the post-assessment interview. Include in your discussion (a) the purposes of the post-assessment interview, (b) general guidelines, (c) the issue of confidentiality, (d) post-assessment interviews with children, and (e) post-assessment interviews with parents.
3. Discuss the four phases of a post-assessment interview with parents. In your discussion, focus on key points that should be attended to in each phase.
4. What are some important questions to consider in evaluating the post-assessment interview with parents?
5. Discuss the post-assessment interview as a staff conference.
6. Discuss the follow-up interview. Include in your discussion important areas to focus on and how you would acknowledge the progress of the child and parents (if appropriate).
7. Discuss the factors that influence the reliability and validity of an interview. Include in your discussion situational factors, interviewee factors, interviewer factors, and ways to reduce errors.
8. Discuss malingering. Include in your discussion degrees of malingering, reasons for malingering, age and malingering, and evaluation of malingering.
9. What factors should you consider in evaluating your interview techniques?

8

OBSERVATIONAL METHODS, PART I

Observers, then, must be photographers of phenomena; their observations must accurately represent nature. We must observe without any preconceived idea; the observer's mind must be passive, that is, must hold its peace; it listens to nature and writes at nature's dictation.

— Claude Bernard, French physiologist (1813–1878)

Using Observational Methods

Applicability of Observational Methods

Designing an Observational Assessment

Narrative Recording

Interval Recording

Event Recording

Ratings Recording

Evaluations of Recording Methods

Thinking Through the Issues

Summary

Key Terms, Concepts, and Names

Study Questions

Goals and Objectives

This chapter is designed to enable you to do the following:

- Understand four major observational recording methods—narrative, event, interval, and ratings methods

- Compare and contrast these four observational recording methods

- Design an observational assessment

Observing the behavior of children in natural or specially designed settings contributes to a clinical or psychoeducational assessment. Observations add a personalized dimension to the assessment process, particularly when used in conjunction with objective tests, behavior checklists, questionnaires, interviews, personality inventories, projective tests, and other assessment procedures. Behavioral observations serve the following assessment functions:

1. They provide a picture of children's spontaneous behavior in everyday life settings, such as a classroom, playground, or home; in unique settings, such as a hospital ward; or in specially designed settings, such as a clinic playroom.
2. They provide information about children's interpersonal behavior and learning style.
3. They provide a systematic record of children's behaviors and the behaviors of others, which can be used for evaluation, intervention planning, and monitoring changes associated with interventions.
4. They allow for verification of the accuracy of parental and teacher reports about children's behaviors.
5. They allow comparisons between behavior in the test situation and behavior in naturalistic settings.
6. They provide information independent of children's ability or willingness to report information.
7. They provide information about young children and children with developmental disabilities who are difficult to evaluate with other procedures.
8. They permit functional behavioral assessment by providing a means of identifying a target behavior, documenting its antecedents and consequences, and evaluating the effects of interventions.

Observational systems are extremely versatile. They can be designed to quantify many different types of behaviors in almost any setting, and they can be uniquely tailored to the needs of an individual child. To be most useful, the systematic observation of behavior should have a goal, a focus, a limit on the amount of data to be collected, and a standardized recording method that has adequate reliability and validity.

The information you obtain from the observation of behavior will help you evaluate the concerns of the referral source, arrive at a diagnosis, provide feedback and suggestions for achieving behavioral change, and monitor the efficacy of interventions. Although observations give you valuable information about manifest (or observable) behavior, they do not tell you about the child's beliefs, perceptions, feelings, and attitudes about his or her past, present, or future behavior. To obtain this information, you will have to use interviews, self-report inventories, or perhaps projective instruments. Some of these techniques are covered in Chapters 5, 6, 7, and 10.

Let's look at an example of how behavioral observations can assist you in an assessment. Suppose a teacher has referred Bill to you because of his aggressive behavior in class. In addition to carrying out the psychometric assessment and interviews, you decide to visit the classroom a few times to observe Bill and the class. You observe that Bill's aggressive behavior occurs only after other children instigate some hostile act directed at him, such as taking away his pencil or kicking his chair. The psychometric and interview data allow you to rule out psychopathology, brain damage, and familial instability. With this information, you can help the teacher understand Bill's behavior. Perhaps simply moving Bill to a part of the room where the children are more supportive might help; or, you might suggest that Bill (or his peers) participate in a social skills training program.

USING OBSERVATIONAL METHODS

In the *systematic observation of behavior,* you observe a child's behavior in natural or specially designed settings, record or classify each behavior objectively as it occurs or shortly thereafter, ensure that the obtained data are reliable and valid, and convert the data into quantitative information. You may use behavioral observations to obtain global impressions, to rate and record various behaviors, or to focus on specific problem behaviors (such as aggression, inattentiveness, or hyperactivity) that you identified earlier through general observations, interviews, checklists, or reports from others. Ideally, you should compare the child's rate of the behavior of interest to informal norms for how often the behavior occurs naturally in the child's peer group.

Although the scientific principles on which we base systematic behavioral observation should ensure the highest possible degree of accuracy and precision, it is never possible to capture all of the behaviors exhibited by a child during the observation. Thus, you must make decisions about what behavior you want to observe and how you want to record it. The assumption behind the sampling of behavior is that the behaviors recorded over a period of time will constitute a representative sample of behavior.

To be a skilled observer, you must be able to understand behavioral codes, distinguish one behavior from another, sustain attention, attend to detail, react quickly, compute rates of behavior, summarize behavior samples verbally, and recognize how your presence affects the child and others in the setting. *Sensitivity, acuity, and perceptiveness are keys to becoming a skilled observer.* An underlying assumption of all observational methods is that observers can identify important behaviors, note their occurrences, classify them, and judge their strength and degree of deviance. This chapter and the following one cover the principles of behavioral observation and provide exercises to help you develop skills that you can apply to observing a wide range of human behavior in many settings.

Although all assessment procedures require diligence on the part of the clinician, observational assessments require a subtly different type of diligence, because the stimuli are not controlled by the clinician and the scoring procedures are not as exact as those used in standardized tests. As you will read in Chapter 9, several procedures are used to increase observer reliability and validity, including applying well-defined observational codes for operationally defined content categories and following precise methods of recording data.

Defining Observed Behaviors

You must first define the behaviors that you are going to observe—the *target behaviors*—in objective, clear, and complete terms. Your definitions (or those in the coding system that you use) should help you recognize when each behavior is occurring and distinguish the target behaviors from other similar behaviors. You want to record relevant behaviors and exclude irrelevant behaviors. The definitions, sometimes referred to as *operational definitions,* should be as explicit as possible in order to minimize the need to make inferences when you observe behavior. You arrive at an operational definition in part by specifying the precise operations that signal the appearance of the behavior, as well as by specifying the operations that do not reveal the behavior of interest. For example, the operational definition for the behavior "inappropriate gross motor behavior—standing" might include "motor activity that results in the child's leaving his or her seat or standing on one or both legs (on the floor, chair, or desk) in an erect or semi-erect position; this code is not used when the child has permission to leave his or her seat or when the child must move in order to work on a task." (See Table C-1 in Appendix C, category V, for a complete description of the criteria for coding this behavioral category.)

Here are some steps that you can follow in developing an operational definition of a target behavior:

1. Define the target behavior as clearly and precisely as possible.
2. List examples of the target behavior.
3. Revise the definition of the target behavior to include all of the examples.
4. List examples of behaviors that are similar to the target behavior but do not qualify as reflecting the target behavior.
5. Revise the definition so that it does not include the nonqualifying examples.
6. Give the definition to untrained as well as trained observers and see whether they can reliably record the occurrence and nonoccurrence of the target behavior. A videotape of actual behaviors is useful for this step.

Some behaviors are easier to define than others. For example, crying, which can be defined as a vocal noise that is loud enough to be heard and accompanied by tears but not recognizable words, is easier to define than sharing. Behaviors like sharing can be defined by focusing on examples of acts that could constitute sharing, such as giving a toy to another child, allowing another child to sit on the same mat, or giving a piece of candy to another child. Replacing imprecise or vague terms with exact words or descriptions will help you define the behaviors of interest. Your definitions should be precise and clear enough that another observer could replicate your findings.

Here are some examples of precise definitions of behavior in reaction to pain (adapted from Paulsen & Altmaier, 1995, p. 105):

- *Guarding*—displaying abnormally stiff, interrupted, or rigid movements while walking or moving from one position to another
- *Bracing*—maintaining a stationary position in which a fully extended limb supports and maintains an abnormal distribution of weight
- *Rubbing*—touching, rubbing, or holding the affected area
- *Grimacing*—making an obvious facial expression of pain, which may include furrowed brow, narrowed eyes, tightened lips, corners of mouth pulled back, and clenched teeth
- *Verbal complaints*—making any audible language or nonlanguage sounds indicating pain
- *Sighing*—exhaling air in an obviously exaggerated way, usually accompanied by shoulders first rising and then falling; cheeks may be expanded

Conducting Observations in Sequence

In some situations, you may want to begin your observations by using global or general coding categories. This approach would be appropriate, for example, if someone asked you to observe a child who was "having problems" in school. After carefully observing the child's behavior during various classes and times of the day, you might note specific behaviors that you wanted to observe more closely. You would then direct your further observations to the specific behaviors of interest.

When you first observe a child referred for a specified behavior problem, do not focus exclusively on that behavior. At least during your initial observation, observe the child's overall behavior and that of other children and adults in the setting. Doing so is important, because it gives you the opportunity to observe other behaviors that may potentially be important and allows you to evaluate the referred child's behavior in the context of other individuals' behavior in that setting (Nay, 1979).

Timing Observation Periods

Once you have defined the target behaviors you want to observe, select an appropriate observation period—some time when there is a chance that you will observe a representative sample of the behaviors of interest. If the child is participating in a spelling bee in which contestants stand, for example, you will not be able to observe and record episodes of inappropriate out-of-seat behavior. If possible, observe the child at different times during the day and in several settings, such as at home, on the playground, and in school. If you do not obtain a representative sample of behavior, the observational results will not be valid.

Paying Attention to Special Occurrences

Even when you are concentrating on specific behaviors, be attuned to other events happening at the time of the observation. Fire drills, substitute teachers, new aides, special events, upcoming holidays, and other children's misbehavior are examples of events or factors that may have a direct bearing on the referred child's behavior. You will, of course, want to note such events or factors on your observational record.

Preparing for the Unexpected

No matter how carefully you prepare for your observational assessment, observations conducted in naturalistic settings are not under your control. For example, your plan to observe Joyce in a history class with her general education teacher may fall asunder when there is a fire drill, a field trip, an assembly, or a substitute teacher. Similarly, it is possible that on the day you select to visit Dwight's home to observe how he interacts with his parents, his father will be called away. Your scheduled observation of a patient in a hospital ward may be hampered because the patient must be sedated for an unexpected laboratory test. Or, just as you get attuned to listening and observing conversation on the ward, someone may turn on a TV set and people's voices will be drowned out. In naturalistic settings, you are at the mercy of events you cannot control; be aware of these potential difficulties and do not be daunted when you encounter them. Your tolerance for frustration will be tested, along with your flexibility and resourcefulness.

APPLICABILITY OF OBSERVATIONAL METHODS

Observational methods are particularly useful for studying behaviors that are relatively frequent; assessing global behaviors such as aggression, social withdrawal, sociability, and attention; and evaluating a child's progress over time. Systematic observation in a naturalistic setting may *not* be the preferred method for observing behaviors that occur infrequently, covertly, or only in response to specific stimuli or behaviors that are unsafe or unethical. For example, it may not be possible to observe a child stealing or setting fires or a child's responses to stress, outbursts of anger, or reactions to tragedy, for these behaviors may be rare or may occur when no one is watching. In addition, you cannot allow self-injurious behavior, sexual assaults, or other harmful behaviors to occur simply so that you can record their intensity or duration. For example, observing intimate sexual interactions, illicit drug use, or confidential conversations poses significant ethical problems (Thompson, Symons, & Felce, 2001). Self-monitoring techniques (see Chapter 9) are preferred for recording private behaviors (e.g., thoughts or sexual behaviors).

Although you cannot observe psychological processes directly, you can observe behaviors associated with them (Thompson et al., 2001). For example, you cannot observe hallucinations directly, but you can observe a person talking to someone whom no one else sees or picking off a wall insects that no one else can see. You cannot observe delusional thinking directly, but you can observe delusional statements such as "God wants me to punish sinners!" You cannot observe affective states or anxiety directly, but you can observe crying; self-deprecating statements; discouraged, worried, or nervous comments; repeated sighing; hand-wringing; picking of the skin; twirling of the hair; or pacing.

Planned Incident Procedure

A *planned incident procedure* (or controlled observation), which entails observing children in a specially contrived situation or setting, is the method of choice when you want to elicit specific behaviors. It gives you more control over the behaviors of interest. In a natural setting, you must wait for the behavior to occur; in the planned incident procedure, you can create conditions that may evoke the behavior of interest. You can do this by introducing special toys or furniture or by systematically varying how people in the setting react to the child. For example, if you want to study the effects of music or noise on the child's behavior, you can introduce different types of music or noise or different intensities of the same music or noise at specific times into the playroom. Planned incident procedures are also useful when you want to observe how different children react to the same stimulus conditions. Exhibit 8-1 describes a planned incident procedure.

The assumption underlying a planned incident procedure is that a contrived situation can bring out important behaviors more quickly and efficiently than a "natural" situation, saving valuable time. However, one disadvantage of contrived settings is that they do not allow unforeseen, possibly informative events to occur. Another disadvantage is that the participants may not behave spontaneously because they recognize that the situation is contrived. In real-life settings, though, it may be difficult to sample the behaviors of interest, and other conditions may make the recording of the target behaviors difficult. Whichever procedure or procedures you decide to use, recognize that each has advantages and disadvantages and that both planned incident procedures and observations in natural settings can contribute important information to an assessment. They can be used together because they complement each other.

Ecological Assessment

Observational methods are particularly valuable in *ecological assessment,* which focuses on the physical and psychological attributes of the setting in which behavior occurs. Physical attributes of the setting include spatial arrangements,

Exhibit 8-1
Observing Preschool Children's Reactions to Specially Designed Situations

Zahn-Waxler, McKnew, Cummings, Davenport, and Radke-Yarrow (1984) designed a setting for observing preschool children's reactions to specially created incidents. The referred child, a familiar same-age playmate, parents of the two children, and staff members interact in the setting under various conditions intended to induce conflict, distress, frustration, and enjoyment. Aggression, altruism, and other emotions may be revealed.

The room in which the observations are conducted, preferably a living room–kitchenette area, should contain a standard set of toys (e.g., rocking horse, ball, pull toy, toy telephone). The following conditions should be established (adapted from Zahn-Waxler et al., 1984, p. 237):

1. *A novel environment.* Initially, the children play in the novel room, with the mothers watching. (5 minutes)
2. *A background climate of affection and sharing.* Two female adults enter the adjoining kitchen. They greet the mothers and children and then cooperate with each other in a warm and friendly fashion while getting coffee for the mothers and juice for the children and straightening the kitchen. (5 minutes)
3. *A neutral context.* There are no experimental interventions. (5 minutes)
4. *A background climate of hostility, anger, and rejection.* The two women return and have a verbal argument while washing the dishes. Each accuses the other of not doing her share of work around the building. (5 minutes)
5. *A second neutral context.* (5 minutes)
6. *A reconciliation.* The adults return, greet each other with affection, and apologize for their behavior. (2 minutes)
7. *A friend's separation experience.* The mother of the referred child's friend is asked to leave the room. (1 minute)
8. *Separation from the mother.* The referred child's own mother is called from the room as well. (1 minute)
9. *Reunion with the mother.* Both mothers return to the room. (4 minutes)

Mothers should be asked not to initiate activities or to interrupt interactions between the children unless something makes them uncomfortable or appears to be dangerous. The above conditions can be modified to suit the specific room arrangements.

Suggested event observational recording codes are as follows (Zahn-Waxler et al., 1984):

1. *Aggression:* actions that have potential for causing physical or psychological harm

a. Interpersonal physical aggression—hitting, kicking, pushing, or throwing things
b. Object struggle—attempts to grab or take another's possession
c. Undirected aggression—acts against the physical environment (e.g., banging on walls, throwing things on the floor, kicking toys)
d. Intense aggression—acts that are violent or potentially dangerous

2. *Altruism or empathic intervention:* acts of kindness and caring directed toward others
a. Child helps, cooperates, provides comfort, or sympathizes with other person (e.g., pats or hugs a crying person, kisses a hurt, says "It's OK" or "Be careful," provides a bottle)
b. Child shares either objects or self (e.g., invites other to join in particular play activities)

A suggested scale for rating various forms of emotional expressiveness is as follows:

RATING SCALE

1	2	3	4	5
emotion absent	emotion expressed slightly	emotion expressed somewhat	emotion expressed moderately	emotion expressed frequently

Emotion	Rating
a. Positive emotion (laughter, smiling, happiness, excitement expressed facially, vocally, or bodily)	1 2 3 4 5
b. Anger (angry yelling, screaming, angry facial expressions, impassioned threats or complaints)	1 2 3 4 5
c. Distress (crying, crankiness, whining, concerned facial expressions)	1 2 3 4 5
d. Emotionality (combined scores for positive emotion, anger, and distress)	1 2 3 4 5

seating arrangements, lighting, and noise; psychological attributes of the setting include the child's relationships with family members, peers, teachers, or others in the setting. The evaluation of settings is particularly important for answering such questions as "Which classroom is best for Jim, who has a behavior disorder?," "How can the home be modified to improve Helen's behavior?," or "What type of foster home would be best for Jamie?"

Following are examples of questions about a child's behavior problem derived from an ecological perspective. "Does the child engage in the problem behavior . . .

1. with one teacher but not with another?"
2. at school but not at home?"
3. when working independently but not when working in a small group?"

4. with one parent but not with the other?"
5. during the early morning hours but not the evening hours?"
6. with one ward aide but not with others?"

Answers to these and similar questions will help you evaluate the settings that may be associated with the problem behavior (Alessi, 1988). If the child shows problem behaviors in some settings but not others, look for possible explanations. For example, if the problem behaviors occur in only some school settings, is the child encountering different teachers with different expectations or teaching methods in different settings, or do the problem behaviors occur at a particular time of the day?

An ecological assessment may also focus on (a) how changes in one behavior affect other behaviors or (b) how changes in one part of the environment produce changes in other parts of the environment that, in turn, affect the child. You can use a three-component framework, described in Table 8-1, to organize ecological assessment data along the following lines: *setting appearance and contents, setting operation,* and *setting opportunities* (Hiltonsmith & Keller, 1983).

Home Observations

Home observations give you the opportunity to observe family members interacting, environmental stressors, and the physical characteristics of the home. Do not visit a home without gaining the parents' permission beforehand and scheduling the visit with them. In general, you should respect the parents' wishes if they do not want you to visit the home. However, there are exceptions to this guideline. For example, in cases of alleged child maltreatment, Child Protective Services workers may enter a home without the permission of a parent or caregiver to check out the allegation (be familiar with your state laws). In such situations, a law enforcement officer may also be present. Law enforcement personnel can enter a home without the family's permission under various circumstances, such as when they have obtained a warrant or when they have knowledge that a child may be in danger. Case workers in social agencies can make unannounced visits to evaluate foster homes. Parental permission to enter a home is not needed when an agency has a court order to enter the home.

Overall, with a child of any age, you will want to observe whether the parent (a) can relax and be comfortable with her or his child, (b) is accepting and affectionate with the child, (c) is sensitive to the child's needs, wants, and desires, (d) seems able to take the child's perspective, (e) remains alert to issues of safety and protection while allowing the child freedom to explore the environment within the limits of her or his age and ability, and (f) helps the child acquire new skills. Similarly, you will want to observe how the child responds to the parent.

Observing a family at home has several advantages, including the following (Goldenberg, 1983):

1. It gives a picture of how the family functions naturally.
2. It gives a good idea of how each family member functions in his or her everyday role.

Table 8-1
A Framework for Organizing Data on Home and School Settings

Component	Elements
A. *Setting appearance and contents* (observable, physical, and measurable aspects of the setting)	1. *Physical features*—spatial layout, size of room, type and arrangement of furniture, and related features 2. *Ambient features*—noise level, lighting, and temperature 3. *Setting contents*—presence or absence of television sets, books, interactive board games, computers, and similar items
B. *Setting operation* (how the setting works, including interpersonal interactions among people in the setting and in other settings)	1. *Organizational patterns*—who leads and follows and what reinforcers are present in the setting 2. *Communication patterns*—who initiates conversation and to whom the conversation is directed 3. *Ecological patterns*—how the setting is used by the individuals therein
C. *Setting opportunities* (how the setting provides for the needs of the individuals in it)	1. *Nurturance and sustenance*—how basic needs of the individuals are met (e.g., the needs for food, clothing, and shelter) 2. *Cognitive/linguistic stimulation*—the degree to which individuals receive stimulation for cognitive development 3. *Social/emotional stimulation*—the degree to which individuals receive stimulation for social/emotional growth and development

Source: Adapted from Hiltonsmith and Keller (1983).

3. It reduces the chance that a family member will be absent, which is more likely in an office interview.
4. It promotes recognition among family members that the entire family shares responsibility for making changes or improvements.
5. It decreases anxiety among family members because of the familiar surroundings and thus facilitates more open communication among the family members.
6. It decreases the impact of the common "doctor-patient" stereotypes.

Family observations are useful in obtaining information about patterns of interaction among the members of the family, the emotional climate of the home, family conflicts, and patterns of resolution after a conflict. Your observations should help you to answer such questions as the following (Besharov, 1990; Garbarino, Guttman, & Seeley, 1987; Kropenske & Howard, 1994; Polansky, Borgman, & De Saix, 1972):

1. Is the home located in a safe neighborhood?
2. In what condition are the home and home furnishings? For example, are there any observable safety or health hazards within the home (including those associated with the electrical system, gas lines, water supply, and sanitary facilities)? Also, in what condition are beds, chairs, and curtains?
3. Is the food supply adequate, both in quantity and in nutritional content?
4. What play equipment is present?
5. What are the sleeping arrangements?
6. What is the quality of the sleeping areas?
7. If there is a newborn child, what supplies do the parents have for the infant?
8. How are the children dressed and groomed?
9. What educational and recreational equipment and accessories are available?
10. Is there a telephone in the home?
11. Does the family have a car? If so, what condition is it in?
12. Does the family use public transportation?
13. Are inappropriately sexual or violent videos or other materials accessible to the children?
14. How do the children interact with the parents?
15. How do the parents interact with the children?
16. How do the children get along with each other?
17. How do the parents interact with each other?
18. Who is living in the home, and what are their relationships to the children?
19. What are the occupations of the people living in the home?
20. Is there evidence of domestic violence?
21. What type of discipline, if any, do the parents use?

Conditions affecting home observations. Your ability to do a home observation may be influenced by the conditions you meet in the home. You may be fortunate and find parents who are cooperative and grateful for your help. If this is the case, you can spend adequate time with the family and complete your evaluation. On the other hand, you may find hostile parents who resent your presence, or you may find a filthy house and brutalized children. In such cases, you must exercise caution and good judgment, performing only a cursory inspection before you leave quickly and notify the appropriate authorities if you suspect that the children are being abused or neglected. *If you suspect that it is dangerous for you to visit a home because of conditions in the home or neighborhood, do not go to the house unless accompanied by a police officer.*

When evaluating the child's home, remember that poverty will affect the family's material possessions. For example, the fact that the family has no telephone or car or the home lacks toys does not mean that the family is more dysfunctional than a family that can afford those things. *Poverty should not bias your observations about how the family functions.*

When children and parents know that they are being observed, their behavior may change; such changes in behavior are referred to as *reactive effects*. For example, if they feel conspicuous or anxious, they may sweat profusely, stammer, or speak more quickly than usual, or they may appear relaxed, speak more slowly and distinctly than usual, or censor swear words. It is safe to assume that when you observe children and their parents, reactive effects are present. However, the extensiveness of these effects may be difficult to evaluate.

Home visits have some disadvantages (Drotar & Crawford, 1987). First, families may refuse to allow them or may refuse to cooperate during them. Second, as noted above, what you observe may not be a representative sample of the family's behavior. Finally, home visits are more time consuming than office visits. You will have to weigh the advantages of home visits against the disadvantages when deciding whether to arrange for a home visit.

Case illustration. The following case illustrates the advantage of a home visit (adapted from Drotar & Crawford, 1987, p. 344).

Johnny's mother was upset by her 2-year-old's sleep disturbance and behavior problems. She had become increasingly angry and frustrated by his difficult, noncompliant behavior, but during the interview she did not provide specific details concerning her interactions with her son. He was very active but much more competent than his mother had described him. A home visit clarified the nature of their interactions. As Johnny's mother pointed out the places where he had broken knickknacks and otherwise "left the living room in ruins," it became clear that she expected him to curb his age-appropriate curiosity completely. During the home visit, she misinterpreted Johnny's active, curious behavior as deliberate defiance and became angered when he did not immediately follow her commands. She was a single parent managing a job and child care. Johnny, therefore, anxious to have his mother's undivided attention, seemed to engage in negative behavior to get her attention. These observations stimulated a productive dialogue between the psychologist and Johnny's mother that helped her to begin to reappraise Johnny's behavior. She also was able to rearrange the home environment to avoid some of the negative confrontations with Johnny.

Tests and Interviews

When you administer tests and conduct interviews, you also can observe the child's behavior. Many of the principles discussed in this chapter apply to these activities as well.

DESIGNING AN OBSERVATIONAL ASSESSMENT

The key to obtaining meaningful descriptions of behavior is coming up with the right combination of an observational recording method and a coding system. There are several useful recording methods, ranging from those that describe behavioral sequences to those that describe only one or two events. Coding systems specify the categories used in recording the observations. The categories, such as aggressive behavior and passive behavior or on-task behavior and off-task behavior, refer to the behavioral content of the observations. It is best to combine a recording method with a coding system to map the target behaviors. Coding systems not only highlight target behaviors but also may measure several important dimensions of the target behaviors (e.g., the frequency, duration, intensity, and latency of the behaviors), as well as how factors in the setting affect the target behaviors.

The best system for a particular situation will depend on your assessment goals. You may want to use a coding system designed by others, combine or modify features of existing systems, or design your own system. In selecting or designing a coding system, ask yourself what questions you want answered and how the coding system will help you answer these questions. Existing systems differ in the range of behaviors assessed and the level of inference required by the observational categories. If you find a system that is generally useful for your purposes, by all means use it, especially if the system has good definitions of the target behaviors you wish to observe, systematic coding guidelines, good reliability, and good validity. Designing your own observational system can be time consuming. On some occasions, however, you may have to supplement an existing system with additional categories that have special relevance to the referral question. In such instances, you will need to define carefully any coding categories that you add. Although you will usually be interested in behaviors related to the problem, consider other behaviors that might be relevant to the problem or to the situation or setting in which the problem occurs.

Some behaviors occur frequently, others infrequently. Some are of long duration, others of short duration. Some are intense, others mild. Some occur immediately after a request, others are delayed. And some behaviors are consistent during an episode, whereas others are variable. In designing or selecting your recording method, consider the attributes of the target behaviors, because those will determine what methods are most likely to ensure that you will observe the target behaviors.

The observational recording methods particularly useful for clinical and psychoeducational tasks are narrative recording, interval recording, event recording, and ratings recording. The following sections discuss each of these recording methods, providing a description, major uses, design considerations, quantitative data obtained, advantages, disadvantages, examples, and exercises to develop your skill in using the method.

NARRATIVE RECORDING

Narrative recording will help you formulate a comprehensive description of a child's (or a group's) natural behavior. In addition to psychologists and other professionals, others—parents, relatives, or even the child—can record descriptions of behavior. Narrative recordings are referred to as *anecdotal recordings* when they include anything that seems noteworthy to the observer; a specific time frame and specific codes and categories are not needed. A narrative recording produced as behavior occurs is referred to as a *running record.* Narrative recordings describe events without using quantitative recording procedures.

Global, Semi-Global, and Narrow Descriptions of Behavior

Observations in a narrative recording can be global, semi-global, or narrow (Barker & Wright, 1954). *Global descriptions* (also referred to as *molar* or *broad descriptions*) focus on actions that reflect the child's behavior as a whole. They may incorporate various specific behaviors or require inferential judgments. *Semi-global descriptions* contain additional general details of the behaviors of interest. *Narrow descriptions* (also referred to as *molecular* or *fine descriptions*) reflect specific details of the child's behavior or the setting. For example, in each of the following pairs, description (a) is global and description (b) is narrow:

1. (a) Hurrying to school. (b) Tripping when going up the school stairs.
2. (a) Eating. (b) Chewing noisily.
3. (a) Playing at school. (b) Jumping rope.

Here is another example of a child's behavior described globally, semi-globally, and narrowly (Barker & Wright, 1954):

• *Global description.* "George went berry picking for his mother." (This description identifies a complete episode. It tells us what George was observed to do, but relatively little about how George did the activity.)

• *Semi-global description.* "George took a basket from the kitchen table and walked outdoors, where he mounted his bicycle and went to pick berries for his mother." (This description provides more information than the first one, but it still provides limited information about how George's actions were performed.)

• *Narrow description.* "George, with his lips quivering, his brows knit, and the corners of his mouth turned down, took a basket from the kitchen table and, with the fingers of his left hand wound limply around the handle of the basket, his shoulders hunched, his chin sagging against his chest, and his feet dragging, walked outdoors, where he mounted his bicycle and, with his head still bent, went to pick berries for his mother." (This description gives us information about how George's actions were performed. The quivering lips, the knit brows, and the dragging feet suggest that George went to pick the berries unwillingly and unhappily. The information is useful because it tells about the "how" of what George did and gives important information about his disposition.)

A Continuum of Inferential Judgments

Narrative observations fall along a continuum from those requiring minimally inferential judgments to those involving highly inferential judgments. When you record directly observable behavior (e.g., actions, motor activity, and verbalizations), you make minimally inferential judgments; when you record interpretations (e.g., emotions, motives, and reasons) based on behaviors, you make highly inferential judgments. Examples of these two types of statements follow (Alessi, 1980). In each set, description (a) is a behavioral descriptive statement (minimally inferential), whereas description (b) is a behavioral inferential statement (highly inferential).

1. (a) He slams the book on the desk. (b) He is frustrated.
2. (a) She hit Helen three times with a stick. (b) She is angry.
3. (a) He scored 100 percent on his mathematics test. (b) He is gifted in mathematics.
4. (a) She says mostly positive things about herself. (b) She has a good self-concept.

Behavioral descriptive statements describe behaviors that occur, without explanations. *Behavioral inferential statements* go beyond describing behaviors; they reflect attempts to integrate or theorize. In the early stages of your narrative recording, concentrate on making behavioral descriptive statements; keep inferential statements to a minimum. Interpret the observational data you record only after you have had an opportunity to study the observations carefully, and then integrate these observations with information obtained from other sources (e.g., case history, interviews, psychological tests).

Major Uses of Narrative Recording

Narrative observations may help you create an in-depth picture of the behavior of a child, a group, or a teacher. In clinical assessment, narrative recordings are particularly valuable as precursors to more specific and quantifiable observation recording. A running account of a child's behavior may provide leads about behavioral and environmental events worthy of further analysis and suggest hypotheses about factors controlling the target behaviors. Following are examples of situations or settings in which you might use narrative recordings.

Observing a child's social skills and communication skills. Narrative recording can help you to learn about a child's social skills and communication skills (Cohen, Stern, & Balaban, 1997; Gresham, 1983; Mattes & Omark, 1984). Consider the following questions as you observe the child's interactions with others:

1. What are the child's facial expressions, gestures, and actions, as well as the body language and actions of others who communicate with the child?
2. How does the child communicate with others (e.g., rarely initiates verbal interactions, often initiates verbal interactions, uses gestures instead of speech)?
3. How do others respond to the child's communication (e.g., accept the communication, seem puzzled by the communication, withdraw from the child)?
4. Does the child use positive verbalizations, such as *please, thank you,* and *excuse me?*
5. How does the child show interest in other children in the setting (e.g., plays with other children, stares at other children)?
6. How does the child make contact with other children (e.g., confidently, tentatively, aggressively)?
7. What is the quality of the child's behavior with other children (e.g., sharing, friendly, bullying, impatient, aggressive, withdrawn)?
8. How does the child respond when other children initiate interactions (e.g., pleased, displeased, indifferent)?
9. How frequently does the child interact with adults (e.g., frequently, infrequently)?
10. What is the quality of the child's relationship with adults (e.g., matter-of-fact, warmhearted, respectful, disrespectful, reserved, open, whining, belligerent, clinging, hostile)?
11. How does the child gain attention from adults (e.g., politely, through excessive talking, by tattling, by sidling up and touching, by clinging)?
12. Does the child comply with teacher and parent requests to share (e.g., always, frequently, never)?
13. How does the child react to limits set by adults (e.g., accepts limits, defies them, slows but doesn't stop present behavior)?
14. How does the child react to criticism from adults and from other children (e.g., accepts it, cries, pouts)?

Observing a family. Narrative recording can help you evaluate family interactive patterns. When observing a family, you will need not only to listen carefully to what the family members are saying but also to observe their facial expressions, gestures, actions, and body language. Observe the content and style of the communication, such as what is discussed and how it is discussed; the roles assumed by family members, such as leadership and follower roles; the patterns of interaction, such as who communicates with whom; what coalitions exist; and which family members defend, protect, or attack other members. Also observe the affect displayed by the family members, such as the following (Hops, Biglan, Sherman, Arthur, Friedman, & Osteen, 1987):

- Happy affect (happiness, smiling, excitement, humorous tone)
- Caring affect (warmth, affection, supportiveness, liking of another)
- Neutral affect (even-tempered, conversational tone)
- Anxious affect (fear, anxiety, nervousness)
- Whiny affect (whiny voice, worry)
- Dysphoric affect (sadness, depression, fatigue, sullenness, crying)
- Aversive affect (anger, sarcasm toward or ridicule of another, cold detachment)
- Pain affect (any nonverbal expression of pain)

Observing a group.   Narrative recordings are useful when you observe a group. Pay particular attention to the patterns of peer preference or attraction, indifference, antagonism, and influence. The following questions are useful for observing a group of children in a classroom or in other settings:

1. What is the group climate?
2. What patterns of interaction are evident?
3. Who are the leaders and who are the followers?
4. What other roles seem to be represented in the group (e.g., facilitator, troublemaker, conciliator, criticizer)?
5. Which children participate in group activities, and which are on the fringes?
6. What patterns of relationships do you see (e.g., what subgroups are formed)?
7. What is the seating arrangement in the room?
8. Which children are accepted by the group, and which are rejected?
9. How does the group react to newcomers?
10. How does the group react when its leaders are absent?
11. How does the group react to different teachers?
12. How does the group react to new situations?

Observing a teacher and students.   When you visit a classroom, you will want to observe the teacher's method and style of teaching and classroom management, as well as the students' behavior. Be sensitive to both verbal and nonverbal cues, patterns of interaction, group formations, atmosphere in the room, and any other features that will help you understand how the classroom functions. Although you will probably not be able to observe everything alluded to in Table 8-2 during a short observation period, try to answer as many questions as possible.

Observing children in informal interactions.   It is sometimes helpful to observe a child informally in a situation

that combines a natural procedure with a planned incident procedure. For example, after you have finished testing, bring out some toys and ask the child's parent or sibling to play with the child. Leave the situation unstructured. The child's age will govern your observations. The guidelines that follow are applicable for observations conducted in a clinic playroom or in a home and for observing parent-infant interactions (Baird, Haas, McCormick, Carruth, & Turner, 1992; Hirshberg, 1993), parent-toddler interactions (Hirshberg, 1993; Zahn-Waxler, Iannotti, Cummings, & Denham, 1990), and interactions between a parent and a school-age child (Mahoney, Powell, & Finger, 1986; Stein, Gambrill, & Wiltse, 1978).

PARENT-INFANT INTERACTIONS

1. *Social interactions.* Do the parent and infant interact socially? For example, does the parent look and smile at the infant as the infant looks and smiles at the parent? How does the infant respond to physical contact with the parent?

2. *Responsiveness.* Does the parent respond to the infant's interpersonal signals? For example, does the parent take a toy offered by the infant? How does the infant respond to the parent's actions and presence? For example, does the infant take a toy offered by the parent?

3. *Directing.* Does the parent direct the infant in an attempt to determine the pace, content, or form of the infant's behavior? For example, does the parent tell an infant who is playing with beads to "Put them on your arm"? How does the infant respond to the parent's directions?

4. *Intrusiveness.* Does the parent's intrusiveness lead to breaks in the infant's attention? For example, does the parent offer a rattle to an infant who is playing with another toy? How does the infant respond to the parent's intrusions?

5. *Joining.* Does the parent join in the infant's play? For example, does the parent touch an object similar to the one the infant touched? How does the infant respond when the parent joins her or him in play?

6. *Imitation.* Does the parent imitate behaviors initiated by the infant and vice versa? For example, does the parent kiss the infant after the infant kisses the parent or imitate the infant's coos? How does the infant respond to the parent's imitation?

7. *Affect and attitude.* What types of affect do the parent and the infant display? For example, do the parent and infant show (a) pleasure, enjoyment, and a happy mood, (b) warmth, tenderness, and affection, (c) irritability, anger, impatience, or hostility, or (d) approval or disapproval? Does the parent (a) hold and comfort the infant, (b) use affectionate statements such as "You're Mommy's little sweetie," (c) make positive statements such as "That's great!" about the infant's behavior, or (d) display affection in expressions or behavior (e.g., smiling at, holding, or hugging the infant)? How does the infant respond to the parent? Does the infant hug the parent or show other signs of warmth and affection? Is the affect appropriate to the situation?

8. *Safety and protection.* Is the parent alert to the infant's physical safety? Does the parent continuously monitor the

Table 8-2
Questions for Observing a Teacher and Classroom

Description of Classroom

1. What grade are you observing?
2. On what day of the week and at what time are you observing the classroom?
3. How many children, teachers, teacher's aides, and other adults are in the classroom?
4. What are the pertinent classroom environmental variables (e.g., seating arrangements, accessibility for children with disabilities, amount of space, air quality, temperature, lighting, noise level, aromas coming from the cafeteria, activity level, condition of the building and school grounds)?
5. What distractions, if any, are present inside and outside the classroom?
6. What is the atmosphere in the classroom (e.g., organized, disorganized, pleasant, unpleasant, disciplined, undisciplined, quiet, noisy)?
7. What subject matter is being covered (e.g., reading, math, spelling, art, science, music, physical education)?
8. What are the transition routines between subjects and classes (e.g., rules for putting away materials, rules for getting out materials, rules for finishing assignments)?
9. How are the students' contributions—reports, tests, drawings, and other work—organized in the classroom (e.g., displayed in the room, kept in folders near the teacher's desk, kept by each student at his or her desk)?

Teacher Style and Effectiveness

10. What instructional materials does the teacher use (e.g., calculators, tape recorders, computers, multimedia presentations)?
11. What instructional methods are used to facilitate learning (e.g., verbal instructions, written instructions, physical demonstration, pictorial instructions, lectures, cooperative groups, student pairing, learning centers, hands-on activities, individual assignments and activities)?
12. What cuing systems are used (e.g., daily schedule on the bulletin board, lists of tasks on the blackboard, personal contracts, assignment sheets)?
13. What is the quality of the teacher's lectures (e.g., presents clear and concrete messages, delivers lectures with enthusiasm, presents items in sequence and with sufficient repetition, presents material at a satisfactory pace, provides an overview of the content at the beginning of the lesson, reviews objectives of the lesson, outlines the content and signals transitions between parts of the lesson, calls attention to the main ideas of the lesson, summarizes parts of the lesson as they are completed, reviews the main ideas at the end of the lesson)?
14. What are the work expectations (e.g., length of assignments, time allotted for independent work and group work, time allotted to complete assignments and for socializing, use of self-paced materials)?

15. What is the quality of the assignments (e.g., clearly stated, accompanied by objective and well-enforced criteria for completion)?
16. Are the students placed in groups (e.g., low performers in one group, average performers in another group, and high performers in a third group)?
17. What type of assistance does the teacher give the students?
18. Does the teacher provide additional time for students who need help? If so, when is the time available (e.g., before first period, during recess, during lunch, after school, on Saturday)?
19. What assessment takes place (e.g., timed or untimed tests, multiple-choice tests, essay tests, open-book tests, take-home tests, oral presentations)?
20. Is sufficient time allotted for the tests?
21. What grading methods does the teacher use?
22. What kinds of expectations does the teacher communicate to the students about classroom behavior?
23. What kind of questions does the teacher ask (e.g., open-ended, forced-choice)?
24. How effective is classroom management (e.g., type of discipline, enforcement of classroom rules)?
25. How fair and impartial is the teacher?
26. What types of reinforcements and motivational techniques does the teacher use (e.g., praise, tokens for achievement, self-recording or charting of academic progress, time in a game center or on a recreational activity, extra time for lunch or for a break, negative comments, sarcasm, personal ridicule)?
27. Does the teacher meet the needs of children with disabilities? If so, how (e.g., allows them to ask questions when they do not understand, photocopy other students' notes, tape-record lectures, take examinations orally, or obtain time extensions on examinations)?

Student Behavior

28. Do the students ask questions and participate in discussions? If so, how does the teacher respond to their comments and questions (e.g., encourage and accept ideas, discourage ideas)?
29. Do the students seem to be attending to the lectures and involved in the assignments?
30. Do the students help each other?
31. What is the quality of the students' behavior (e.g., ask for help or assistance, volunteer to answer questions, interfere with the work or activity of other students, appear happy and eager to learn, appear frustrated or confused, make positive comments about other students, make negative comments or ridicule other students, participate in teacher-directed activities, interact with teacher, interact with other students)?

Source: Adapted from Boxer, Challen, and McCarthy (1991) and Ylvisaker, Hartwick, and Stevens (1991).

infant and take action to protect her or him when necessary? Is the parent appropriately vigilant and protective, overprotective and highly anxious about the baby's safety, or careless and unaware? Does the infant show excessive caution and timidity or recklessness?

9. *Physiological regulation.* Is the parent alert to the infant's needs for food, warmth, stimulation, elimination, and sleep? For example, does the parent recognize when the infant is hungry or when stimulation should be reduced or increased? How does the infant respond to the parent's attempts at regulation?

10. *Teaching and learning.* Does the parent try to help the infant learn new skills? If so, how does the parent go about teaching the infant those skills? Does the parent show flexibility in helping the infant and in keeping the infant focused on the task? How does the infant respond to the parent's teaching?

11. *Power and control.* How does the parent present herself or himself to the infant? For example, is the parent calm, confident, and in control of herself or himself, of the infant, and of the situation, or does the parent appear passive, overwhelmed, disorganized, confused, tense, or potentially explosive? How does the infant respond to the parent's attempt to control (or failure to control) the situation?

PARENT-TODDLER INTERACTIONS

1. *Attunement to needs.* Is the parent attuned to the toddler's needs? For example, does the parent (a) simplify or provide more information when the toddler apparently does not understand something, (b) show sensitivity to the toddler's visual perspective by moving objects into or out of the toddler's field of vision or by giving information about the location of objects, or (c) indicate awareness of the toddler's wants, needs, or feelings without the toddler's explicitly expressing these? Is the toddler attuned to the parent's needs? Does the toddler push the parent to his or her limits? Does the toddler recognize when the parent is happy, sad, tired, angry, and so forth? How does the toddler react to the parent's mood?

2. *Promotion of prosocial behaviors.* Does the parent verbally encourage prosocial behavior? For example, does the parent say "It's his turn" or something similar when the toddler is playing with another child or share with, help, or show compassion toward the toddler or another child or adult who is present?

3. *Perspective-taking or self-awareness.* Does the parent encourage perspective-taking or self-awareness? For example, does the parent (a) direct the toddler's attention to the feelings of others in the room by making a comment such as "Why is John so sad?," (b) direct the toddler's attention to the toddler's own thoughts by saying "You thought that this was the big block" or something similar, or (c) use another person as a point of reference by saying "It's the one in front of Sarah" or something similar?

4. *Affect and attitude.* What types of affect do the parent and the toddler display? For example, do the parent and toddler show (a) pleasure, enjoyment, and a happy mood, (b) warmth, tenderness, and affection, (c) irritability, anger, impatience, or hostility, or (d) approval or disapproval? Does the parent (a) use affectionate statements such as "You're Daddy's big girl," (b) make positive statements such as "That's great!" about the toddler's behavior, or (c) display affection in expressions or behavior (e.g., smiling at, holding, or hugging the toddler)? Does the toddler hug the parent or show other signs of warmth and affection? Is the affect appropriate to the situation?

5. *Modulated control.* Does the parent modulate his or her behavior? For example, does the parent (a) use qualified commands or questions to direct the toddler's behavior, such as "Would you like to . . . ," "Why don't you . . . ," "How about if we . . . ," or "Maybe you could . . . ," or (b) set limits or establish contingencies by saying "You can have juice as soon as you put your things in this box" or something similar?

6. *Power and control.* How does the parent present himself or herself to the toddler? For example, is the parent calm, confident, and in control of himself or herself, of the toddler, and of the situation, or does the parent appear passive, overwhelmed, disorganized, confused, tense, or potentially explosive? How does the parent manage the challenges the toddler presents during the observation, such as a refusal to clean up, frequent interruptions, or acting-out behavior? Does the parent use unqualified, power-assertive methods such as direct commands, prohibitions, shouting, or physical control methods? How does the toddler respond to the parent's attempt to control (or failure to control) the situation?

7. *Physiological regulation.* Is the parent alert to the toddler's needs for food, warmth, stimulation, elimination, and sleep? For example, does the parent recognize when the toddler is hungry or when stimulation should be reduced or increased? How does the toddler respond to the parent's attempts at regulation and nurturing?

8. *Teaching and learning.* Does the parent try to help the toddler learn new skills? If so, how does the parent go about teaching the toddler those skills? Does the parent show flexibility in helping the toddler and in keeping the toddler focused on the task? How does the toddler respond to the parent's teaching?

INTERACTIONS BETWEEN PARENT AND SCHOOL-AGE CHILD

1. *Affect and attitude.* What types of affect do the parent and the child display? For example, do the parent and child show (a) pleasure, enjoyment, and a happy mood, (b) warmth, tenderness, and affection, (c) irritability, anger, impatience, or hostility, or (d) approval or disapproval? Is the affect appropriate to the situation?

2. *Responsiveness of affect.* How do the parent and child respond to each other's expressions of affect? For example,

does the parent acknowledge and assist the child, if necessary, in the appropriate expression of feelings, such as affection or anger? How does the child respond when the parent is angry, hurt, or disappointed? Do parent and child comfort each other, or are they sarcastic or indifferent to expressions of affect?

3. *Responsiveness to behavior.* Is the parent responsive to the child, and is the child responsive to the parent? For example, does the parent respond to the child's distress, make suggestions to the child, or respond to the child's questions with caring and sensitivity? How does the child respond to the parent's needs and requests?

4. *Stimulation of the child and parent.* Does the parent stimulate the child, and does the child stimulate the parent? For example, does the parent provide toys for the child, play with the child, make physical contact with the child, talk to the child, or encourage the child? Does the child introduce new ideas to the parent? How does the parent respond to new ideas presented by the child (e.g., welcomes them, denies them, becomes angry)?

5. *Power and control.* Does the parent control the child's behavior, does the child control the parent's behavior, or is there flexibility in the interaction? For example, does the parent (a) protect the child, (b) control the child's play and behavior by ordering, demanding compliance, or making threats, (c) restrict the child's activities, or (d) criticize or punish the child? Does the child demand certain things from the parent or criticize the parent? How does the parent deal with issues of child management? For example:

- What behaviors evoke praise or punishment from the parent?
- How much time elapses before the parent responds to the child's behavior?
- What behavior does the parent ignore?
- What rewards or punishments does the parent use (e.g., a hug or a positive statement, physical punishment or a demeaning statement)?
- How realistic is any promised punishment (e.g., "You can't go out for the next two months!")?
- How consistent is the parent in following through on promised rewards or punishments?
- Does the parent make threatening statements (e.g., "If you aren't good, I'll leave you" or "I won't love you anymore if you do that again")?
- Does the parent tell the child why the child is being punished?
- Does the parent deliver punishments and rewards uniformly to all the children involved in the behavior?
- Do verbal communications accompany punishments or rewards?
- In two-parent families, do both parents administer the punishments and rewards, and do the parents agree or disagree about the punishments and rewards?
- Does the parent bribe the child (e.g., "If you leave me alone, I'll give you candy later on")?

- Does the parent set limits for the child (e.g., "You may go as far as the street corner, but you cannot cross the street")?
- Does the parent appear to respect the child's viewpoint?

How to Design a Narrative Recording

In designing a narrative recording, you must decide on (a) the number of times you will observe the child, (b) the length of each observation period, (c) the time periods during which you will conduct the observations, (d) the type of narrative recording you will use, (e) the target behaviors you will observe, and (f) the method of recording data.

Frequency, length, and timing of observations. The child's age, the setting, and the reason for the assessment will influence the number of times you will need to observe the child, the length of each observation period, and when you should conduct the observations. An observation period may last from 10 to 30 minutes or longer. Time your observations so that they will yield representative data; if possible, observe the child more than once and at different times during the day. To find out when the target behavior is most likely to occur, consult with the referral source (e.g., the classroom teacher) about when and where the target behavior occurs most frequently, and observe at those times.

Type of narrative recording. For clinical and psychoeducational assessment, anecdotal recordings are preferred. Usually, there are no restrictions on what you observe. In addition to the behavior of the referred child, fully describe the setting (e.g., the scene, the people in the setting, and the ongoing action). Report everything that the referred child says and does, everything that other people say and do to the referred child, and what other people say and do that you think is relevant. Use everyday descriptive language in all of your narratives. The narrative should read like a newspaper article, telling when and how the behavior of concern occurred and what features of the environment altered or influenced the behavior.

Target behaviors. If you are conducting a preliminary observation, include general impressions of the child and the setting in your narrative recording. When you have identified the target behaviors, begin to concentrate on them along with their antecedent and consequent events.

Method of recording data. You may write your narrative recording, enter it into a portable computer, or record your comments on audiotape. You may use narrative recording with other recording methods, such as videotaping. If you plan to videotape a child or to record his or her comments on tape, be sure to obtain parental permission and explain how the audiotape or videotape will be used. If the behaviors of interest occur frequently, an anecdotal record form (see Table 8-3) is useful for recording specific observations at specified times.

Table 8-3
Anecdotal Record Form

Western Michigan University
CLASSROOM OBSERVATION RECORD PROTOCOL

Student: _____Mary_____   Comparison: _____C.J._____   Observer: _____School Psychologist (L.C.)_____

Age: _____6-10_____   Age: _____6-7_____   Other Observer: _____Social Worker_____

Grade: _____2nd_____   Class Size: _____26_____

School: _____Westwood_____   Class Type: _____Regular ed._____

Teacher: _____Mrs. Kaput_____   Time Stop: _____10:23_____

Date: _____4 / 3 / 05_____   Time Start: _____10:13_____
     month day year   Total Time: _____:10_____

Reason for observation (What question do we want to answer?):
To explore reported discrepancy between Mary's behavior and that of her classroom peers.

Classroom activity and explicit rules in effect at time of observation:
Activity: Math. See notes below for details. Rules: 1. Follow teacher's directions; 2. work quietly; 3. complete work.

Description of observation techniques (interval or time sample and length):
30-second interval for Mary and comparison, 2-minute time sample for class scan check.

Behavior codes:	Grouping codes:	Teacher/peer reaction codes:	Participants' codes:
T = on-task	L = large group	AA = attention to all	Ma = Mary
V = verbal off-task	S = small group	A+ = positive attention to student	Te = teacher
M = motor off-task	O = one to one	A− = negative attention to student	
P = passive off-task	I = independent act	Ao = no attention to student	
=	F = free time	An = neutral attention to student	
=	=	=	

	Time	Student	Comparison	Class scan check	Anecdotal notes on behavior	Grouping	Teacher reaction	Peer reaction
1.	10:13	P	T		Ma not responding to teacher	L	An	Ao
2.		M	T		Standing up—other sitting	L	Ao	A+
3.	10:14	M	T		Te leads Ma back to desk	L	An	Ao
4.		M	T	80%	Standing up	L	Ao	A+
5.	10:15	P	T		Sitting staring at others	L	Ao	A+
6.		T	M		Looking at teacher	S	Ao	Ao
7.	10:16	T	M	76%	Sitting quietly and listening	S	Ao	Ao
8.		T	T		Working at desk	S	Ao	Ao
9.	10:17	P	T		Looking out window	L	Ao	Ao
10.		T	T	83%	Copying math problems	L	Ao	Ao
11.	10:18	P	T		Staring at board	L	Ao	Ao
12.		M	T		On floor getting pencil	L	Ao	Ao
13.	10:19	M	T	80%	On floor getting pencil	L	Ao	A+
14.		M	M		On floor poking other	L	Ao	A+
15.	10:20	P	T		In seat staring	L	Ao	Ao
16		P	T	88%	In seat staring	L	Ao	Ao
17.	10:21	T	T		Writing math	S	An	Ao
18.		T	T		Writing math	S	Ao	Ao
19.	10:22	M	T	80%	Walking around classroom	S	Ao	A+
20.		T	T		Writing math	S	Ao	Ao
Summary:		35% (7/20)	85% (17/20)	81%		L = 13; S = 7	Ao = 17; An = 3	Ao = 14; A+ = 6

Reliability = 83%

(Continued)

Table 8-3 (*Continued*)

Note. The top part of the protocol contains spaces to record identifying information, as on any test protocol. Also included is space for noting the reason for referral, classroom activity and rules in effect during the observation period, and a description of the recording procedure used (e.g., 30-second interval). The middle section of the protocol contains a coding system for noting various behaviors, situations, and teacher reactions during the observation session. The bottom half of the protocol contains 20 blank lines, each one representing either an interval for observation or a time sample frame. Each blank line has a space to record the behavior of the referred and comparison students, the percentage of students in the class who are performing a given behavior (class scan check), anecdotal notes on the incident, the grouping situation at that time, and the teacher's and peers' reactions to the incident.

The recorded data are summarized at the bottom. In the sample case, the referred student was on-task during only 7 of the 20 intervals observed, whereas the comparison student was on-task during 17 of the same 20 intervals. Furthermore, the referred student's off-task behavior was sometimes motor and sometimes passive. By contrast, the comparison student's off-task behavior was entirely motor. The teacher gave no attention to the referred student during 17 of 20 intervals observed, and neutral attention during the other three intervals. However, peers attended to the off-task behavior on 6 occasions.

Source: Reprinted and adapted with permission of the publisher and author from G. J. Alessi, "Behavioral Observation for the School Psychologist: Responsive-Discrepancy Model," *School Psychology Review,* 1980, *9*, pp. 36–37. © National Association of School Psychologists.

Guidelines for Making a Narrative Recording

You may find the following suggestions for making a narrative recording helpful.

1. In advance, identify the referred child, as well as other children and adults in the setting that you intend to observe.
2. Note the setting and the time of day.
3. Describe the referred child's behavior, that of other children and adults in the setting, and the factors (including the setting) that affect the behavior of the referred child and others.
4. Record the referred child's and others' verbal and nonverbal behavior.
5. Record the event (or anecdote) as soon as possible after you complete your observation.
6. Record important verbalizations as precisely as possible; quote the referred child and others directly whenever possible.
7. In your written description, preserve the sequence of the behaviors observed.
8. Be as objective, accurate, and complete as possible in your written description.
9. Use everyday language in your written description.
10. Describe, rather than interpret, the referred child's behavior and the behavior of others.
11. Record the reactions of others to the referred child's behavior.
12. Recognize that your initial impressions of the referred child and others in the setting may change during the observation.
13. Consider how your presence in the setting may have affected the referred child's behavior and that of others.
14. Always consider your role in the assessment process, particularly how you are reacting and feeling.
15. Do not allow your interest in specific behaviors to keep you from recording general impressions.
16. If you do find it necessary to interpret the referred child's behavior, consider possible reasons for the behavior.
17. Finally, integrate all sources of behavioral information, including observations and interpretations, into a unified and coherent picture of the referred child's behavior.

Quantitative Data in Narrative Recordings

Although narrative recordings do not involve quantitative recording procedures, you can use your record to obtain quantitative data. For example, you may note the number of times the child performed a particular action or the number of times the child spoke. In addition, you can code the qualitative information into various categories and then quantify the coding (see, for example, Barker & Wright, 1954).

Advantages and Disadvantages of Narrative Recording

Narrative recording provides a record of a child's behavior and of your general impressions. It maintains the original sequence of events and provides a means of gathering information and discovering critical behaviors. It also allows you to assess progress, provides a record of continuing difficulties, requires little equipment, and serves as a valuable precursor to more systematic observational procedures.

Narrative recording, however, is not well suited for obtaining quantitative data. The recording is difficult to validate and may not fully describe some types of critical behaviors. The findings also may have limited generalizability and may vary from observer to observer.

Illustrations of Narrative Recording

The example below is a narrative record of a 4½-year-old boy at preschool (adapted from Cohen & Stern, 1970, p. 34). The record captures the child's mood and contains many qualifying details.

> Winky points to the window and, with radiant face, calls in delight, "It's snowing cherry blossoms! First they are white, then green, then red, red, red! I want to paint!" He goes to the easel and quickly snatches up a smock. Sliding in beside Wayne, he whispers to him, "Wayne, you want blue? I give it to you, okay? You give me red because I'm going to make cherries, lots of red cherries!"
>
> After the boys exchange paint jars, Winky sits erect and, with a sigh of contentment, starts quickly but with clean strokes to ease his brush against the edge of the jar. He makes dots all around the outer part of the paper. His tongue licks his upper lip, his eyes shine, his body is still but his manner is intense. The red dots are big, well-rounded, full of color, and clearly separated. While working, Winky sings to himself, "Red cherries, big, round red cherries!" The first picture completed, he calls the teacher to hang it up to dry. The next picture starts as the first did, with dots at the outside edge, but soon filling the entire paper. He uses green too, but the colors do not overlap.
>
> Still singing his little phrase, Winky paints a third and fourth picture, concentrating intently on his work.
>
> The other children pick up his song, and Wayne starts to paint blue dots on his paper. Waving his brush, Winky asks, "Wayne, want to try my cherries?" Swiftly and jubilantly he swishes his brush across Wayne's chin. Laughing, he paints dots on his own hands. "My hands are full of cherries," he shouts. He runs into the adjoining room, calling excitedly to the children, "My hands are full of cherries!" He strides into the bathroom to wash his hands. Susie follows him in, calling, "Let's see, Winky." "Ha, I ate them all," he gloats as he shows his washed hands with a sweeping movement. He grabs a toy bottle from the shelf, fills it with water, and asks the teacher to put the nipple on. He lies down then on a mattress and sucks the bottle, his face softly smiling, his eyes big and gazing into space, his whole body relaxed.

The next example is a 4-minute narrative record of a 7-year, 4-month-old boy, beginning when he awoke on the morning of a school day (adapted from Barker & Wright, 1966, pp. 15–17). Notice that the recording describes the mother's statements, as well as her voice quality, and the child's facial expressions, glances, and actions, together with the quality of his behavior.

7:00   Mrs. Birch said with pleasant casualness, "Raymond, wake up." With a little more urgency in her voice, she spoke again: "Son, are you going to school today?"
Raymond didn't respond immediately.
He screwed up his face and whimpered a little.
He lay still.
His mother repeated, "Raymond, wake up." This was said pleasantly; the mother was apparently in good spirits and was willing to put up with her son's reluctance.
Raymond whimpered again and kicked his feet rapidly in protest.
He squirmed around and rolled over crossways on the bed.
His mother removed the covers.
He again kicked his feet in protest.
He sat up and rubbed his eyes.
He glanced at me and smiled.
I smiled in return as I continued making notes.

7:01   Raymond picked up a sock and began tugging and pulling it on his left foot. As his mother watched him, she said kiddingly, "Can't you get your peepers open?"
Raymond stopped putting on his sock long enough to rub his eyes again. He appeared to be very sleepy.
He said "Mommie" plaintively and continued mumbling in an unintelligible way something about his undershirt.

7:02   His mother asked, "Do you want to put this undershirt on, or do you want to wear the one you have on?"
Raymond sleepily mumbled something in reply.
Raymond struggled out of the T-shirt that he had on.
He put on the clean striped T-shirt more easily.

7:03   He pulled on his right sock.
He picked up his left tennis shoe and put it on.
He laced his left shoe with deliberation, looking intently at the shoe as he worked steadily until he had it all laced.

7:04   He put on his right shoe.
He laced up his right shoe. Again he worked intently, looking at the shoe as he laced it.
His mother called, "Raymond, do you want an egg for breakfast?" in a pleasant, inquiring tone.
Raymond responded very sleepily, "No."
Raymond climbed back into bed.

Exercises 8-1
Narrative Recording Exercises

Exercise 1

With a co-observer, make an anecdotal recording of one child on a playground for 5 minutes. (If the playground is associated with a school, obtain permission from the administration before engaging in this activity.) Do not record the child's name or any other information that could identify the child.

Compare your record with that of your co-observer. How similar are the two recordings? What did your co-observer include that you did not, and vice versa? Consider the following questions in evaluating your narrative recording:

1. How detailed is your recording of the child's behavior? Does the recording conjure up a visual picture of the behavior?
2. What behaviors might you have missed?
3. Why did you record some behaviors and not others?
4. How did the setting influence the child's behavior?
5. To what extent did the child's behavior represent that of his or her peer group?
6. What biases, if any, may have affected your observations?
7. Did you observe primarily specific details or general behaviors?
8. What hypotheses did you develop about potential problem behaviors?
9. What specific behaviors would you like to observe at another time?
10. How might your presence have altered the child's behavior?
11. What could you have done to minimize this influence?
12. How did your narrative recording contribute to your understanding of the child?
13. Which statements in your recording reflect a high, medium, and low level of inference?

To answer the last question, construct a form with two columns, one headed "Statement" and one headed "Inference

Level (high, medium, low)." Select 30 statements from your report—10 from the beginning, 10 from the middle, and 10 from the end. Statements may be complete sentences or sentence fragments. Thus, one sentence in your recording may generate more than one statement. Number each statement, and place the numbered statements in the first column. Decide whether each statement reflects a high, medium, or low level of inference. The chart below illustrates how the form might look if you were to evaluate the first part of the narrative running record shown on page 207.

Statement	Inference Level (high, medium, low)
1. Mrs. Birch said with pleasant casualness,	Medium
2. "Raymond, wake up."	Low
3. With a little more urgency in her voice, she spoke again:	Medium
4. "Son, are you going to school today?"	Low
5. Raymond didn't respond immediately.	Low
6. He screwed up his face	Low
7. and whimpered a little.	Low
8. He lay still.	Low

To get feedback about whether your ratings of inference level agree with those of another rater (not feedback about the accuracy of your anecdotal recording), ask a colleague to rate each statement also. (You may find it helpful to photocopy the form after you list the statements but before you classify them.) Determine the level of agreement of your ratings of inference level by calculating the percentage agreement (number of agreements divided by number of statements, which in this case is 30).

Write a one- or two-paragraph summary of your narrative recording. Include information about (a) the child (age, gender, and other relevant characteristics), (b) the physical setting in which the observation took place, (c) how long you observed the child, (d) what you observed, (e) the level of agreement with your co-observer, and (f) the implications of the findings (e.g., whether the behaviors were appropriate or inappropriate under the circumstances).

Exercise 2
With a co-observer, observe a group of children on a playground. Make a running record of the group's behavior for 5 minutes. Follow the guidelines given in Exercise 1 for evaluating a recording, but substitute *group* for *child* as the focus of your observation.

Exercise 3
Compare the recordings obtained in Exercises 1 and 2. What are the differences between observing one child and observing a group? What information do you gain (or lose) with each type of recording? Summarize your analysis in one or two paragraphs.

Exercise 4
Narrative recordings can also be made of specific types of behavior in various settings. Study the attachment behavior of 1- or 2-year-olds by observing them when they are left at a day care center or at a church or synagogue nursery during a religious service. (Obtain approval from the center, church, or synagogue administration before engaging in this activity.)

With a co-observer, make an anecdotal record of (a) one child's behavior when her or his parent leaves, (b) the parent's re-action, (c) the caregiver's behavior, (d) the child's response to the caregiver, and (e) the child's behavior after the parent has left the room. Conduct the observation for at least a 30-minute period. If time permits, observe the attachment behavior of one or two other children, one at a time. Be sure that you and your co-observer agree on the child to be observed and the observation method to be used. Arrive early. Use the guidelines in Exercise 1 to evaluate your recording.

INTERVAL RECORDING

Interval recording (sometimes referred to as *time sampling, interval sampling,* or *interval time sampling*) focuses on selected aspects of behavior as they occur within specified intervals. The term *sampling* conveys the basic idea of interval recording—you sample behavior rather than recording every behavior as it occurs during the observation period. The observation period is divided into brief segments—intervals of about 5 to 30 seconds, depending on the length of the observation—during which you note whether a behavior occurs. You tally the presence or absence of the target behavior in each interval. Interval recording is especially suitable for controlled observations and laboratory studies. Some practitioners distinguish between time sampling and interval recording. In this case, *time sampling* implies that brief observations are made either at specified times during the day or at random times, rather than during a discrete observational period—of, say, 15 or 30 minutes—divided into a specified number of intervals. (Such time sampling requires that the target behavior occur moderately frequently or very frequently.)

There are several interval recording procedures.

1. *Partial-interval time sampling.* You record (score) a behavior *only once,* regardless of how long it lasts or how many times it occurs in a given interval. This commonly used interval recording method is particularly useful for behaviors that occur fleetingly, such as smiling. It reveals the consistency of behavior. (See Table 8-4.)

2. *Whole-interval time sampling.* You score a behavior *only when it occurs at the beginning of the interval and lasts throughout the interval.* This method is particularly useful when you want to know which behaviors (such as out-of-seat behavior) the child performs continuously during an interval.

3. *Point time interval sampling.* You score a behavior *only when it occurs at a specific time (or times) during the interval.* For example, you might record a specific behavior only if it occurs during the first 10 seconds of each minute, not when it occurs during the remaining 50 seconds. This procedure allows you to observe behavior for brief periods at different times during an observation period. When you use this procedure with groups of children, you can set up a rotational system for observing each child in turn. This variant is useful with behaviors that occur at moderate rates (e.g., tics, hand movements, thumbsucking, stereotypic behaviors, facial expressions).

Table 8-4
Example of a Three-Minute Partial-Interval Time Sample Recording

Referred (R): _____Jim_____

Comparison (C): _____Ted_____

Date: _____March 2, 2005_____

Class: _____Mrs. Jones_____

Time: _11:00 to 11:03 a.m._

Behaviors	Total		1	2	3	4	5	6	7	8	9	10	11	12
Passive off-task	5	R	X	O	O	O	O	O	X	X	X	O	O	X
	1	C	O	O	O	O	O	O	X	O	O	O	O	O
Disruptive off-task	1	R	O	O	O	X	O	O	O	O	O	O	O	O
	0	C	O	O	O	O	O	O	O	O	O	O	O	O
On-task	6	R	O	X	X	O	X	X	O	O	O	X	X	O
	11	C	X	X	X	X	X	X	O	X	X	X	X	X

Note. R = referred child, C = comparison child, X = behavior observed, O = behavior not observed.

Each numbered interval consists of a 10-second observation period followed by a 5-second pause for recording data. Three types of behavior were recorded: passive off-task behavior, disruptive off-task behavior, and on-task behavior. Jim engaged in off-task behavior in 6 of the 12 intervals; 5 of the off-task behaviors were passive. Thus, in 50% of the intervals he showed some kind of off-task behavior. In contrast, Ted had only 1 interval with off-task behavior (passive).

4. *Momentary time interval sampling.* You score a behavior *only if it occurs at the moment the interval ends.* For example, if the interval is 30 seconds, you score only behaviors observed at the end of the 30-second interval. You can use this procedure for observing groups of children. For example, with five children, you can set up a 50-second observation cycle, observing a different one of the five children at the end of each 10-second interval within the 50-second cycle. This variant is useful with behaviors that occur at moderate but steady rates (e.g., tics, hand movements, thumb-sucking, stereotypic behaviors, facial expressions). A 30-second interval is sufficient for observing most behaviors (Kearns, Edwards, & Tingstrom, 1990).

5. *Variable interoccasion interval time sampling.* You score a behavior *only if it occurs during preselected random time intervals.* For example, instead of always recording behaviors during the first minute of each 5-minute observation period (a fixed interval), you might randomly designate any 1-minute period between the 1st and the 5th minutes. For a 25-minute observation period, a random 1-minute observation schedule might be as follows: 4th minute, 1st minute, 5th minute, 3rd minute, and 2nd minute of the respective 5-minute observation periods. This method is useful when you want to obtain a sample of behavior over an extended period of time and rule out temporal effects.

Major Uses of Interval Recording

Interval recording is useful for recording behaviors that are overt, do not always have a clearcut beginning and end, and

occur with moderate frequency, such as once every 10 to 15 seconds. In addition to the examples already mentioned, other behaviors that can be recorded with the interval method include reading, working, sitting, touching objects, roughhousing, pushing other children, conversing appropriately, shouting, screaming, hitting, playing with toys, making excessive noise, lying down, mouthing objects, self-stimulation, sleeping, and arguing. Interval recording is not suitable for recording the exact frequency of behavior, the duration of behavior, or covert behaviors such as subtle body movements.

How to Design an Interval Recording

In designing an interval recording, you must decide on (a) the number of times you will observe the child, (b) the total length of the observation period, (c) the time periods during which you will conduct the observations, (d) the type of interval recording to be used, (e) the length of each observation interval, (f) the length of the recording interval (an interval devoted only to recording data), if needed, (g) the target behaviors you will observe, and (h) the method of recording data.

Frequency, length, and timing of observations.

The child's age, the setting, and the reason for the assessment will influence the number of times you will need to observe the child, the total length of the observation period, and when you should conduct the observations. An observation period may last from 10 to 30 minutes or longer. Time your observations so that you can observe a representative sample of the target behaviors. Try to observe the child more than once and at different times during the day.

Type of interval recording. Select the type of interval recording best suited to the information that you need.

Length of each observation interval. The length of the observation interval will depend on the target behaviors. Gear the interval length to the onset and termination of the behaviors under observation. An appropriate interval length will minimize distortion of the behavioral sequences and frequencies. Short intervals are preferable for behaviors that last a short time, such as making excessive noise, pushing other children, mouthing objects, and self-stimulation. Long intervals are useful for behaviors that last a long time, such as arguing excessively or sleeping in the classroom.

Length of the recording interval. Include a recording interval whenever the scoring will interfere with the ongoing observations. The length of the recording interval will depend on the number of behaviors you want to record.

Target behaviors. Select target behaviors based on prior narrative recordings, interview information, referral questions, or the child's test behavior. When you use a pre-designed observational coding system (see Chapter 9), the coding system will specify the target behaviors.

Method of recording data. You can record data with pencil and paper or with an electronic recording device. Table

8-5 shows a general recording form that you can use with various recording methods and coding systems.

Another approach is to use a system that allows you to graph the data automatically as you record them. When you finish your observations, you have a picture of the child's behavior that you can share immediately with the referral source. Table 8-6 shows a self-graphing data recording form in which the time intervals are measured in minutes. You also can graph the collected data across days, as shown in Table 8-7.

When you use interval recording, you may record the score for the behavior(s) either during the interval or immediately afterward. If you record during the interval, there will be no break between intervals; the observation intervals will be successive. If you record after the interval, the observation intervals will alternate with intervals for recording behavior. For example, the observation period might consist of a series of 10-second observation intervals, each followed by a 5-second recording interval. A typical sequence would be as follows:

1. Observation interval (10 seconds)
2. Recording interval (5 seconds)
3. Observation interval (10 seconds)
4. Recording interval (5 seconds)
   (Sequence repeats)

The second approach is usually a necessity when you are recording several behaviors during an interval, for you must look away from the child to make notations. The length of the

---

Table 8-5
General Recording Protocol

Western Michigan University
CLASSROOM OBSERVATION RECORD PROTOCOL

Referred (R): _____ Sue _____	Comparison (C): _____ Andrea _____	Observer: _____ Psychologist _____
Age: _____ 8-6 _____	Age: _____ 8-5 _____	Other Observer: _____ Paraprofessional _____
Grade: _____ 3rd _____		Class Size: _____ 31 _____
School: _____ Pine Elementary _____		Class Type: _____ Regular ed. _____
Teacher: _____ Mrs. Graves _____		Time Stop: _____ 11:16 _____
Date: _____ 10 / 6 / 04 _____		Time Start: _____ 11:12 _____
month day year		Total Time: _____ :04 _____

Reason for observation (What question do we want to answer?):
To observe whether Sue's behavior during reading differs from that of another child.

Classroom activity and explicit rules in effect at time of observation:
Activity: Reading. Rules: 1. Work quietly; 2. sit at desks; 3. raise hand for help.

Grouping situation (G):	*Teacher (T)/peer (P) reaction codes:*	*Observation recording method (circle one):*
(circle one)	AA = attention to all	(a) interval size _15"_.
L = large group ⓘ = independent act	A+ = positive attention to student	(b) time sample: size _____.
S = small group F = free time	A− = negative attention to student	(c) event count
O = one to one	Ao = no attention to student	(d) duration
	An = neutral attention to student	(e) latency

(Continued)

Table 8-5 (Continued)

Behaviors*	Tot.		1 — 15	30	45	60	2 — 15	30	45	60	3 — 15	30	45	60	4 — 15	30	45	60
Verbal off-task	8	R	X	O	O	X	X	O	O	X	X	O	O	X	X	O	X	
	2	C	O	X	O	O	X	O	O	O	O	O	O	O	O	O	O	
		T	Ao	Ao		Ao	An			Ao	Ao			Ao	An		Ao	
		P																
		G																
1		Sc																
Motor off-task	4	R	X	O	X	O	O	O	O	O	O	X	X	O	O	O	O	
	1	C	O	O	O	O	O	O	O	O	O	O	O	X	O	O	O	
		T	Ao		Ao							Ao	An	Ao				
		P																
		G																
2		Sc																
Passive off-task	1	R	O	O	O	O	O	X	O	O	O	O	O	O	O	O	O	
	1	C	O	O	O	O	O	O	X	O	O	O	O	O	O	O	O	
		T						Ao	An									
		P																
		G																
3		Sc																
On-task	3	R	O	X	O	O	O	O	X	O	O	O	O	O	O	X	O	
	11	C	X	O	X	X	O	X	O	X	X	X	X	O	X	X	X	
		T	Ao	An	An	An	Ao		Ao		Ao	An	Ao		Ao	An	Ao	
		P																
		G																
4		Sc																
Out of seat (duration)	53"	R	14"	8"	22"	9"												
	6"	C	6"															
		T	A–	A–	An	A–												
		P																
		G																
5		Sc																

Were reliability data collected? (Yes) No.   If yes, interobserver % agreements = _83%_. Sc = Scan check.
*Include specific behavior definitions on back, as well as comments (strengths, contextual observations, etc.).

Note. The form includes spaces for identifying information and spaces down the left side for writing in the behaviors being observed. Across the page are numbered columns of boxes. Each number can refer to successive (a) intervals, (b) behavior counts, (c) duration measures, or (d) latency measures. For interval and behavior measures, data would be recorded with an X (target behavior occurred) or an O (target behavior did not occur) in each block. For duration and latency measures, the actual elapsed time would be entered in the successive boxes (e.g., 14"/8"/22"/9").

Each space for writing in a behavior category has six rows of boxes after it: R = referred student, C = comparison student, T = teacher's reaction, P = peer reaction, G = group reaction, and Sc = Scan check. (Scan check refers to the percentage of children in the class who are performing the behavior.) Two spaces are provided for summarizing the data recorded in the blocks across the first two rows.

The duration recording is entered in the same boxes as the interval data, but it does not refer to any specific intervals. In this example, there were four occasions during the session when the referred child was out of her seat and one occasion when the comparison child was out of her seat. The duration recording was made independently of the interval recording.

Source: Reprinted and adapted with permission of the publisher and author from G. J. Alessi, "Behavioral Observation for the School Psychologist: Responsive-Discrepancy Model," *School Psychology Review*, 1980, *9*, pp. 36–37. © National Association of School Psychologists.

observation interval—as well as the length of the recording interval, if used—should remain fixed across all observations to ensure uniformity of the observations.

To observe the referred child, the teacher, and the class, you might use a sequential procedure in which you observe first the child, then the teacher, and then the class. You could divide a 60-second observation period in the following way:

1. Observe child (seconds 1–10)
2. Observe teacher (seconds 11–20)
3. Observe class (seconds 21–30)
4. Observe child (seconds 31–40)
5. Observe teacher (seconds 41–50)
6. Observe class (seconds 51–60)
   (Sequence repeats)

Table 8-6
Self-Graphing Data Recording Form

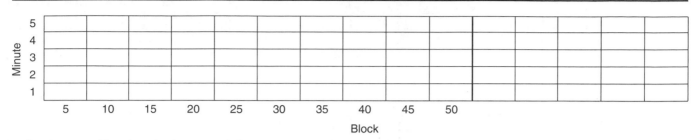

Minute	5	10	15	20	25	30	35	40	45	50					

Block

a. Graph paper with series of columns, each five blocks high. Double heavy line marks off 10 columns, for a 50-minute period.

Minute															
5	O	O	O												
4	O	O	O												
3	O	O													
2	X	X													
1	X	X	X												

5   10   15   20   25   30   35   40   45   50

Block

b. Chart after 13 minutes of monitoring student's behavior. First two columns are completed, and the third is partially completed. If the student behaves appropriately during the next (14th) minute, the observer will mark an X in the third column just above the other X. If the student misbehaves, the observer will mark an O in that column just under the other two Os.

Minute															
5	O	O	O	O	O	O	O	O	O	O					
4	O	O	O	O	O	O	X	O	X	X					
3	O	O	O	X	O	X	X	X	X	X					
2	X	X	X	X	X	X	X	X	X	X					
1	X	X	X	X	X	X	X	X	X	X					

5   10   15   20   25   30   35   40   45   50

Block

c. Chart after the observer has completed the 50-minute period.

Note. To create a self-graphing data recording system, begin with a piece of graph paper. Mark two heavy lines across the paper so that 5 blocks are between the lines. You have now a series of columns, all 5 blocks high. Each block will represent an interval (e.g., 1 minute) of observation time. Mark off the number of 5-block columns needed for the scheduled observation periods: For a 50-minute period you would need 10 columns of 5 blocks, for a 30-minute period you would need 6 columns, for a 45-minute period you would need 9 columns, and for a 5-minute period you would need only one column. For now, let's assume you have scheduled a 50-minute period for your observations, as shown in (a). You have marked off 10 columns on your paper, each 5 blocks high, for a total of 50 blocks: one block for each minute scheduled.

For each interval (minute) in which the target behavior occurs, you will place an X in a box. For each interval in which the target behavior does not occur, you will place an O in a box. Start with the left column and work toward the right. In each column, work from the

bottom up with the Xs and from the top down with the Os. When the Xs and Os meet in the middle, the column is filled. Move to the next column to the right and continue: Xs from the bottom up, Os from the top down, until they meet. As you move across the row of 5-block columns, the data recorded will automatically form a graph. With this method, trends in data across the session can be easily identified and shared with school personnel, referral sources, or parents. Focusing on the Xs in (c) shows that the amount of the referred child's on-task behavior is steadily increasing during the observation session (i.e., there are fewer Xs in the first columns and more Xs in the later columns).

Source: Reprinted and adapted with permission of the publisher and author from G. J. Alessi, "Behavioral Observation for the School Psychologist: Responsive-Discrepancy Model," *School Psychology Review,* 1980, *9,* pp. 39–40. © National Association of School Psychologists.

If necessary, you can intersperse recording intervals with observation periods. The following sequence consists of 7-second observation intervals and 3-second recording intervals:

1. Observe child (seconds 1–7)
2. Record behavior (seconds 8–10)
3. Observe teacher (seconds 11–17)

Table 8-7
Automatic Graphing Data Collection Form

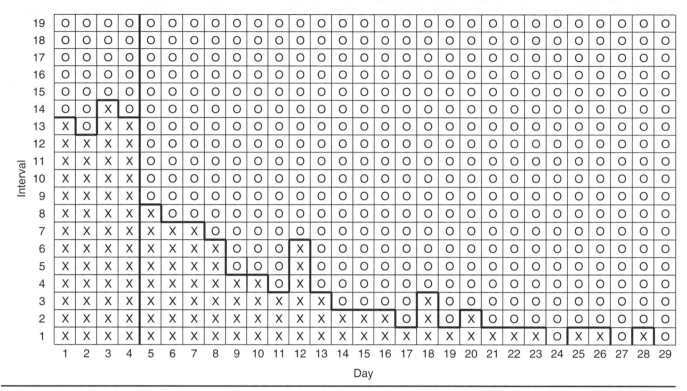

Note. Days 1 through 29 are across the bottom, and intervals 1 through 19 are up the left side. For a given day, the intervals in which the behavior of interest (in this case, talking out) occurred are indicated by Xs; the intervals in which the behavior did not occur are indicated by Os. By reading from left to right and focusing on the Xs, you can see the clear decline over the 29-day period in the number of intervals in which the target behavior occurred (more Xs earlier in the 30-day period than later in the period). The heavy line between days 4 and 5 indicates the beginning of an intervention plan. Note the immediate decline in the behavior just after the intervention was implemented, which suggests that the intervention was successful.

Source: Reprinted and adapted with permission of the publisher and author from G. J. Alessi, "Behavioral Observation for the School Psychologist: Responsive-Discrepancy Model," *School Psychology Review,* 1980, *9,* p. 41. © National Association of School Psychologists.

4. Record behavior (seconds 18–20)
5. Observe class (seconds 21–27)
6. Record behavior (seconds 28–30)
   (Sequence repeats)

Sequential observation procedures permit flexibility in recording the behavior of individuals and groups. You also can use them with different behavioral coding systems to fit particular assessment needs.

If you use a recording interval, you need to have something to tell you when an interval begins and ends, such as a silent cuing device that signals the onset and termination of the observation and recording intervals. Although you can use various electronic devices, a simple method is to record on an audio cassette tape words that signal the observation and recording intervals and to listen to the tape via an earphone while observing. For 10-second observation intervals and 5-second recording intervals, you could use the following sequence: At the beginning of the observation (0 seconds), the word "First" signals the beginning of the first observation interval; at 10 seconds, the word "Record" instructs you to record your observations; at 15 seconds, the word "Second" signals the beginning of the second observation period; at 25 seconds, the word "Record" instructs you to record your observations for the second interval; at 30 seconds, the word "Third" signals the beginning of the third observation period; at 40 seconds, the word "Record" instructs you to record your observations for the third interval; and so on. You can use a similar cuing system when you have only observation intervals. Whatever the cuing system, it should not interfere with the ongoing observations. A cuing system will help to ensure that you and any other observers score the same numbered interval, which will result in greater interobserver agreement.

Quantitative Data in Interval Recording

The primary piece of quantitative data obtained in interval recording is the number of intervals in which the target behaviors did occur. Note that the frequency count reflects the number of *intervals* in which the behavior occurred, not the number of times the target behavior occurred. Event recording (discussed below) focuses on the number of times a target behavior occurs.

If you want information on the intensity of a behavior, you can build an intensity dimension into the behavioral code. For example, if you want to record the intensity of hyperactive behavior, you can include codes representing different degrees of intensity (e.g., mildly hyperactive, moderately hyperactive, and extremely hyperactive).

Advantages and Disadvantages of Interval Recording

Interval recording helps to define important time-behavior relations. It facilitates checking for interobserver reliability and helps to ensure that the predefined behaviors are observed under the same conditions each time. It uses time efficiently and focuses the observer's attention on the child's behavior by structuring the observations. The method also permits the recording of virtually any observable behavior, allows for the collection of a large number of observations in a short period of time, and requires minimal and inexpensive equipment.

Interval recording, however, provides a somewhat artificial view of a behavior sequence, because the time interval—not the behavior—dictates the recording framework. It allows important behaviors related to a problem to be overlooked and fails to provide information about the quality of the behavior (e.g., how the behavior was performed) or about the situation (e.g., whether the child was agitated, paying attention, or sleeping while in his or her seat) unless such information is specifically coded into the recording system. It does not reveal the actual frequency or duration of a behavior (e.g., one continuous 60-second period of off-task behavior would be recorded as four separate events in a 10-second observation/5-second recording interval system). It also may overestimate the frequency of low-rate behaviors or behaviors of short duration and underestimate the frequency of high-rate behaviors. Finally, observers must undergo considerable training to learn the recording system.

Illustrations of Interval Recording

Two examples of interval recording follow.

EXAMPLE 1. PARTIAL-INTERVAL TIME SAMPLING

This example illustrates how an observer used interval recording in a classroom to observe the on-task and off-task behaviors of children with mental retardation (adapted from Whitman, Scibak, Butler, Richter, & Johnson, 1982, pp. 557–558). In addition to the data on on-task and off-task behaviors, the observer obtained data on the number of problems each child completed and solved. Chapter 9 discusses the interobserver reliability referred to in the illustration.

Students and Setting

Three students with attentional problems from a class for children identified as having mental retardation were the focus of the observation. The three children could follow simple instructions and were achieving at a first-grade level. When assigned an academic task to complete, they were generally off-task, frequently glancing up from assigned work, turning to watch other children, and playing with objects on their desks.

A fourth child was selected as a comparison student. Her teacher reported that she did not have attentional problems.

The observation took place in the classroom during math and writing periods. There were 13 students in the class. The daily curriculum was aimed at developing basic math, writing, and reading skills. Special materials constructed for the observation period consisted of worksheets of simple one-digit math problems and spelling exercises. During each math period, 140 addition and subtraction problems were given to each child, considerably more than any of them had time to complete. The spelling exercises required children to copy three- and four-letter words. During each period, the students were asked to copy two pages of spelling words, each page containing 16 words.

Coding Categories

For children's behavior to be considered on-task, their buttocks had to be touching the seat of the chair, their eyes had to be oriented toward the task materials, and they had to be handling the task materials. Two of the three referred children were observed simultaneously on an alternating basis—that is, every 5 minutes a different pair of children was observed. Thus, during each 30-minute period, each child was observed for a total of 20 minutes. These observations were made once a week. The comparison child was observed separately, once a week for 20 minutes.

A partial-interval rating system was used, with 10-second observation intervals. Any break in eye contact or manual contact with the task materials or incorrect posture resulted in that child's being scored as off-task during the given interval. Other responses recorded included the percentage of arithmetic problems completed correctly and the percentage of words copied correctly by each child.

Interobserver reliability was determined twice during each period by use of a second observer. Interobserver reliability for both occurrence and nonoccurrence of on-task behavior was computed on an interval-by-interval basis. The number of agreements across the two observers was divided by the number of agreements plus disagreements, and the result was multiplied by 100. Thus, the reliability of the performance measures was expressed as percentage agreement.

EXAMPLE 2. MOMENTARY TIME INTERVAL SAMPLING

The second example shows how momentary time interval sampling can be used to evaluate the behavior of children in a classroom (Slate & Saudargas, 1987).

Procedure

A 20-minute observation period was divided into 15-second intervals. At the end of every 15-second interval, an observer recorded the occurrence of one of six target behaviors.

Target Behaviors

The six target behaviors were as follows: *schoolwork* (student is doing assigned work, head and eyes are oriented toward the work materials or oriented toward the teacher during a lecture or discussion), *looking around* (student's eyes are oriented away from the classroom activity), *out-of-seat* (student is out of her or his seat for any reason), *social interaction–child* (verbal or nonverbal interactions are taking place between target student and any other student while target student is seated), *social interaction–teacher* (target student and teacher are interacting verbally or nonverbally while target student is seated), and *other activity* (student is engaged in an activity not defined as schoolwork, such as preparing to begin work or doing math during reading time). Only one behavior was coded in any one interval, because the six behaviors were mutually exclusive.

Exercises 8-2
Interval Recording Exercises

Exercise 1
With a co-observer, observe one child on a playground for 5 minutes. Select a child who appears to be playing with another child. Use a partial-interval time sampling procedure, with 10 seconds for the observation interval and 5 seconds for the recording interval. Use a tape recorder, preferably with earphones, to signal the beginning of the observation and recording intervals. Use a two-category coding system: (a) aggressive behavior (as defined in Exhibit 8-1) and (b) nonaggressive behavior. Mark an X for aggressive behavior and an O for nonaggressive behavior, using the recording protocol shown in Table 8-6.

After you complete your recording, determine the level of interobserver agreement by calculating the following interobserver agreement indices: (a) percentage agreement for occurrence of target behavior, (b) percentage agreement for nonoccurrence of target behavior, (c) percentage agreement for both categories, and (d) kappa. Formulas for obtaining these indices are covered in Chapter 9.

Consider the following questions in evaluating your interval recording:

1. How clearly was each behavior observed?
2. To what extent might the time of day have affected the child's behavior?
3. To what extent did the setting affect the child's behavior?
4. Were the observational categories useful?
5. How could the observational categories be improved?
6. To what extent was the child's behavior similar to that of other children of the same age level?
7. Did the coding categories reveal information that might have been missed if only a narrative recording had been used?
8. What biases, if any, may have affected your observations?
9. How might your presence have altered the child's behavior?
10. What could you have done to minimize your influence?
11. How did your interval recording contribute to your understanding of the child?

Write a one- or two-paragraph summary of your observations. Include information about (a) the child (age, gender, and other relevant characteristics), (b) the physical setting in which the observation took place, (c) the length of time you observed the child, (d) the number of intervals in which the target behavior occurred, (e) the level of agreement with your co-observer, (f) any difficulty in determining when the target behavior began and ended, (g) whether the definition of the target behavior was satisfactory and suggestions for improving the definition, and (h) the implications of the findings (e.g., whether the behavior was appropriate or inappropriate).

Exercise 2
Follow the steps described in Exercise 1. Using a whole-interval time sampling procedure, observe a different child on the playground. Again, choose one who appears to be playing with another child.

Exercise 3
Compare the recordings obtained in Exercises 1 and 2. What are the differences between a partial-interval and a whole-interval time sampling procedure? Which one gives you a more accurate picture of the child's behavior? Why? Write a one- or two-paragraph analysis of your findings.

EVENT RECORDING

In *event recording* (also called *event sampling*), you record each instance of a specific behavior or event as it occurs during the observation period. Like interval recording, event recording samples behavior. However, whereas the unit of measure in interval recording is the time interval imposed on the target behavior, the unit of measure in event recording is the behavior. In other words, you wait for the preselected behavior (the event) to occur and then record it. Like interval recording, event recording is especially useful for controlled observations and laboratory studies.

Major Uses of Event Recording

Event recording provides a continuous temporal record of observed behaviors and thus is particularly appropriate for measuring discrete responses that have clearly defined beginnings and ends. Examples are spelling a word correctly, completing a problem, making a social response (e.g., saying "hello" or sharing a toy), pulling clothing, acting aggressively, getting out of a seat, using profanity, going to the bathroom, eating, asking a question, suffering a seizure, making a speech error, or arriving late to class. Behaviors that leave *permanent products* (such as number of words spelled correctly, number of problems completed, or number of drawings) are especially easy to measure by event recording. Additionally, if you use permanent products as measures of behavior, you do not need to be present when the behavior occurs. The teacher or parent can collect the permanent products for you.

Event recording is less suitable for high-rate behaviors or for behaviors that vary in duration. For example, hand clapping is a behavior that may occur so frequently that separating each occurrence becomes difficult. Other behaviors that may occur too frequently for event recording include rocking movements; rapid jerks of the head, hands, or legs; running; and tapping objects. Responses that may extend over different periods and that will be difficult to record by event recording include thumbsucking, reading, listening, and behaving aggressively.

How to Design an Event Recording

In designing an event recording, you must decide on (a) the number of times you will observe the child, (b) the total length of the observation period, (c) the time periods during which you will conduct the observations, (d) the target behaviors you will observe, and (e) the method of recording data.

Frequency, length, and timing of observations. The child's age, the setting, and the reason for the assessment will influence the number of times you will need to observe the child, the total length of the observation period, and when you should conduct the observations. An observation period may last from 10 to 30 minutes or longer. Time your observations so that you can observe a representative sample of the target behavior. If possible, observe the child more than once and at different times during the day.

Target behaviors. As in interval recording, base the selection of target behaviors on prior narrative recordings, interview information, referral questions, or the child's test behavior. If you use a predesigned coding system, the system will specify target behaviors (see Chapter 9). Remember to select behaviors that have an easily discernible beginning and ending.

Method of recording data. You can record responses in various ways, such as by using a checklist, a wrist counter, a hand counter, an electromechanical counter, or another mechanical device or by transferring small objects from one of your pockets to another. You can also use bar code technology. Each target behavior is assigned a bar code label. Then, when the target behavior is displayed, the corresponding bar code is scanned. A bar coding system may be inappropriate for high-rate behaviors.

For paper-and-pencil recordings, you can use various methods to make tallies. One is the traditional stroke method:

$$| \quad || \quad ||| \quad |||| \quad \text{卌}$$

Another is the dot-and-line method, which is often used when the recording form offers limited space:

Table 8-8 illustrates these methods for making tallies.

You can also use the general recording protocol shown in Table 8-5 for event recording. For behaviors that occur frequently, a combination of event recording and 1-minute interval recording may be the best choice (see Table 8-9; Alessi, 1980).

To record the duration of a behavior, you can use a stopwatch, a wristwatch with a second hand, a kitchen timer, a wall clock, or some other timing device. If you want to record the exact time a behavior occurred, you may want to use a hand-held computer. There are also some counters that will

Table 8-8
Two Paper-and-Pencil Methods for Recording Frequency of Behavior

Behavior	Method		Frequency of behavior
	Dot and line	Stroke	
Aggression	(dot-and-line figure)	卌 ||||	9
Cooperation	(dot-and-line figure)	||||	4
Crying	(dot-and-line figure)	||	2

Note. In the dot-and-line method, each dot represents one count and each line represents one count.

record both the frequency of an event and its duration. For example, on a counter panel that has several keys, one key can be assigned to each behavior. Then you simply hold the key down for the duration of the behavior, and the panel records the frequency and duration of the behavior.

Quantitative Data in Event Recording

The primary piece of quantitative data obtained in event recording is the *frequency count*—the number of occurrences of a behavior in a given time period. For example, an event recording might yield the information that "Chris used 10 profane words during a 20-minute observation period." In addition to the frequency of the behavior, you can measure several other behavioral dimensions in event recording, including the rate of the behavior, duration of the behavior, intensity of the behavior, and latency of the behavior. Let's consider each of these dimensions.

Rate of behavior. You obtain the rate at which a behavior occurs during the observation period by dividing the number of behaviors by the length of the observation period:

$$\text{Rate of behavior} = \frac{n}{t}$$

where n = number of behaviors
t = length of observation period

For example, if Jessica were observed to be out of her seat 40 times during a 10-minute observation period, her rate of out-of-seat behavior would be as follows:

$$\text{Rate of behavior} = \frac{n}{t} = \frac{40}{10} = \frac{4}{1}$$

$$= 4 \text{ occurrences per minute}$$

Table 8-9
Comparison of Event and Interval Records of Observation Conducted in 1-Minute Intervals

Behaviors	Tot.		1	2	3	4	5	6	7	8	9	10	11	12	13	14	15
Record of talk-outs by event	76	R	⊔⊔	⊠	⊓⊔	⊠	⊔⊔	⊔∴	⊓		∙∙	∙∙ / ∙∙	⊔∙	∙∙	∙∙	∙	∙
	9	C		∙∙ / ∙∙	∙	∙		∙						∙∙			
1		T															
Record of talk-outs by interval	14	R	X	X	X	X	X	X	X	O	X	X	X	X	X	X	X
	4	C	O	X	O	X	O	X	O	O	O	O	O	X	O	O	O
2		T															

Note. The top part of the form shows event data for talking-out behavior within each interval. The bottom part shows the same data as scored by the interval-only method. The comparison shows that the interval record is not as sensitive to the dynamics of the high rate of behavior as the event-within-interval record is. The event record (top) shows a sudden decrease in rate of talking out after minute 7. The interval record is insensitive to this change. Likewise, the discrepancy between the two students' data is greater as measured by the event record; it is underestimated by the interval record. R = referred student, C = comparison student, T = teacher.

Source: Reprinted and adapted with permission of the publisher and author from G. J. Alessi, "Behavioral Observation for the School Psychologist: Responsive-Discrepancy Model," *School Psychology Review,* 1980, *9,* p. 39. © National Association of School Psychologists.

Rate of behavior is a useful index for noting changes in a child's behavior, especially across observation periods of differing length.

Duration of behavior. You obtain the duration of behavior by noting how long each occurrence of the behavior lasts—the period between the beginning and the end of the behavior. You might use a duration measure, for example, to determine the duration of temper tantrums, crying episodes, arguments, verbal tirades, sustained conversations, on-task behavior, out-of-seat behavior, cooperative behavior, thumb-sucking, off-task responding, or delays in returning home from school.

In addition to the duration measure, there are two other measures of the duration of behavior (Cone & Foster, 1982). One is the percentage of time the behavior occurs, and the other is the average duration of the behavior. The percentage of time the behavior occurs is computed by dividing the total duration of the behavior by the length of the observation period:

$$\text{Percentage of time behavior occurs} = \frac{d}{t} \times 100$$

where d = total duration of behavior (time spent responding)

t = length of observation period

The average duration of the behavior is computed by dividing the total duration of the behavior by the number of episodes of the behavior:

$$\text{Average duration of behavior} = \frac{d}{e}$$

where d = total duration of behavior (time spent responding)

e = number of episodes (or occurrences) of behavior

Suppose a child has two 3-minute tantrums (two episodes) during a 30-minute observation period on day 1 and six 1-minute tantrums (six episodes) during a 60-minute observation period on day 2. The total duration of the tantrums is 6 minutes on both days, but the response patterns differ.

Using the formula for the percentage of time spent having tantrums, we have

Day 1:

$$\text{Percentage of time having tantrums} = \frac{d}{t} \times 100 = \frac{6 \text{ min}}{30 \text{ min}} \times 100$$

$$= 20\% \text{ of session}$$

Day 2:

$$\text{Percentage of time having tantrums} = \frac{d}{t} \times 100 = \frac{6 \text{ min}}{60 \text{ min}} \times 100$$

$$= 10\% \text{ of session}$$

Using the formula for the average duration of each episode, we have

Day 1:

$$\text{Average duration of behavior} = \frac{d}{e} = \frac{6 \text{ min}}{2}$$

$$= 3 \text{ minutes per response}$$

Day 2:

$$\text{Average duration of behavior} = \frac{d}{e} = \frac{6 \text{ min}}{6}$$

$$= 1 \text{ minute per response}$$

The behavior occurred 20% of the time on day 1 and 10% of the time on day 2, and the average duration of an incident was 3 minutes per response on day 1 and 1 minute per response on day 2.

The first measure is preferable when you are interested in how much time a child spends in a particular activity relative to other activities (e.g., "academic engaged time") but care little about the duration of each instance of the behavior. This method masks the duration per response. The second method is useful when you are interested in the average duration of a response, such as when you are assessing the average duration of an appropriate behavior. This method ignores the length of the time interval over which the data are collected. If you prefer, you can report both measures.

Intensity of behavior. You obtain the intensity of behavior by dividing the behavior into degrees of intensity, as in ratings recording. For example, if you want to record intensities of aggressive behavior, categorize behaviors as slightly aggressive, moderately aggressive, and severely aggressive. If you are observing a student whose teacher has reported that he turns in all assignments but complains, you can create four categories, such as "(1) hands in assignment on time with no complaints; (2) hands in assignment on time and complains; (3) hands in assignment late with no complaints; (4) hands in assignment late and complains" (Cone & Foster, 1982). Record a separate frequency count for each category.

Latency of behavior. You obtain the latency of behavior by noting the amount of time that elapses between a given cue and the onset of the behavior; this tells you how long it took the child to begin the behavior. The cue might be the initiation of a request or an event *known* to produce or facilitate the occurrence of a behavior, such as the ringing of a bell to signal the end of a class period. Latency is usually measured with a stopwatch, used to determine the time from the cue to the onset of the behavior. Latency measures are useful when you need to determine the time it takes a child to begin working after instructions have been given, to begin complying with a request (e.g., to sit down, stand up, put away objects, or begin an assignment), or to stand up after an alarm rings (Sulzer-Azaroff & Reese, 1982). Latency measures are particularly useful when you are concerned about the child's ability to follow directions (Alessi, 1988).

Advantages and Disadvantages of Event Recording

Event recording is useful for measuring low-rate behaviors, facilitates the study of many different behaviors or events, and uses time and personnel efficiently, especially when persons who are ordinarily in the setting can make the observations. It can accommodate many different recording methods and provides information about changes in behavior over time and in the amount of behavior performed.

Event recording, however, provides a somewhat artificial view of a behavior sequence by separating the present event from conditions in the past that may have led up to the event. It does not reveal sequences or temporal patterns, unless the time of the response is recorded. It breaks up the continuity of behavior by using limited categories and is not suited to recording behaviors that are not discrete. It presents difficulties in establishing reliability across multiple observers. It requires observers to maintain an optimal level of attention over long periods of time, because few cues are used and responses may be relatively infrequent. It also is difficult to quantify the *how* and *why* associated with the event, even if these characteristics also are recorded. Finally, it makes comparison across periods difficult when the length of the observation period is not constant.

Illustrations of Event Recording

Table 8-10 illustrates how you can use event recording to compare two children's inappropriate talking.

In the example that follows, event recording and a duration measure were used in combination to examine one child's out-of-seat behavior (Whitman et al., 1982). Notice that interobserver reliability was determined.

Table 8-10
Example of Event Recording of Inappropriate Talking

Referred child: Jim   Comparison: March 1, 2004
Comparison child: Ted   Class: Mrs. Jones

Day	9:00 to 9:30 a.m.	11:00 to 11:30 a.m.	2:00 to 2:30 p.m.	Total (Jim/Ted)
Monday	4/1	3/0	2/0	9/1
Tuesday	3/0	2/0	0/0	5/0
Wednesday	4/1	4/1	1/0	9/2
Thursday	2/0	2/0	1/1	5/1
Friday	1/0	1/0	0/1	2/1
Total	14/2	12/1	4/2	30/5

Note. This table summarizes observational records for two children: Jim, the referred child, and Ted, the comparison child. The entries indicate the number of times Jim or Ted spoke with another child inappropriately. Numbers for Jim are to the left of the slash, and numbers for Ted are to the right of the slash. The record indicates that during the 7½ hours of observations, Jim talked inappropriately six times more frequently than Ted did. His inappropriate behavior occurred most frequently on Monday and Wednesday and at 9:00–9:30 and 11:00–11:30 a.m. The inappropriate behavior seldom occurred on Friday or at 2:00–2:30 p.m. Further investigation would be needed to determine what factors in the child's environment lead to increases and decreases in the inappropriate behavior. In addition, further observation should be made to determine the stability of the observed behavior pattern.

EVENT AND DURATION RECORDING: OBSERVING OUT-OF-SEAT BEHAVIOR

Linda is a 9-year-old girl who attended a primary-level special class for children with mental retardation in a public school system. Her teacher said that Linda functioned educationally at approximately the first-grade level and spent most of the day out of her seat. This behavior interfered with classroom work and distracted other children. Observations were made Monday through Friday from 9:00 a.m. to 9:20 a.m. during the math period in the child's classroom. The observation was designed so as not to interfere with regular classroom routines.

The observers sat against a wall in the classroom, approximately 10 feet from Linda. The target behavior was Linda's out-of-seat behavior. This behavior was recorded when the child's buttocks were not in contact with the chair seat. An event recording system was used to count out-of-seat behavior as defined. In addition, the total duration of each occurrence of the target behavior was recorded using a stopwatch that was started and stopped at the beginning and end of the target behavior. Interobserver reliability was assessed by checking, a minimum of two times per period, whether the two observers were rating Linda's behavior the same way (simultaneously but independently). Interobserver agreement was calculated by (a) dividing the number of out-of-seat responses scored by the observer with the lower number of responses by the number of out-of-seat responses scored by the observer with the greater number of responses and then (b) multiplying by 100. Interobserver agreement with regard to duration was calculated in a similar manner.

Exercises 8-3
Event Recording Exercises

Exercise 1

With a co-observer, observe one child on a playground for 5 minutes. Using an event recording procedure, record each time the child engages in play (as a general category) with another child. Play with another child includes parallel, cooperative, and uncooperative play (see Table F-2 in Appendix F for definitions), but not solitary play. Use the dot-and-line method to record the target behavior.

After you have completed your recording, determine the level of interobserver agreement by calculating percentage agreement (see the section on procedures for assessing reliability in Chapter 9). Also calculate the rate of the target behavior.

Consider the following questions in evaluating your event recording:

1. How clearly was the target behavior observed?
2. Did the target behavior occur with sufficient frequency to be observed?
3. To what extent might the time of day have affected the child's behavior?
4. To what extent did the setting affect the child's behavior?
5. How could the definition of the target behavior be improved?
6. What could be done to improve the representativeness of the observations?
7. To what extent was the child's behavior similar to that of his or her peers?
8. What biases, if any, may have affected your observation?
9. How might your presence have altered the child's behavior?
10. What could you have done to minimize your influence?

11. How did your event recording contribute to your understanding of the child?

Write a one- or two-paragraph summary of your observations. Include information about (a) the child (age, gender, and other relevant characteristics), (b) the physical setting in which the observation took place, (c) the length of time you observed the child, (d) the frequency of the target behavior, (e) the level of agreement with your co-observer, (f) any difficulty in determining when the target behavior began and ended, (g) whether the definition of the target behavior was satisfactory and suggestions for improving the definition, and (h) the implications of the findings (e.g., whether the behavior was appropriate or inappropriate).

Exercise 2

Follow the same general procedure described in Exercise 1. Now, however, observe three target behaviors: (a) solitary play, (b) parallel play, and (c) group play (see Table F-2 in Appendix F for definitions). Calculate the level of interobserver agreement separately for each of the three target behaviors. Calculate the rate of behavior separately for each target behavior. Follow the guidelines in Exercise 1.

Exercise 3

Follow the same general procedure described in Exercise 1. Now, however, observe four subtypes of play—functional play, constructive play, dramatic play, and games-with-rules play (see Table F-2 in Appendix F for definitions)—that fall within each type of play (solitary play, parallel play, and group play). Calculate the level of interobserver agreement separately for each of the 12 target behaviors. Calculate the rate of behavior separately for each target behavior. Follow the guidelines in Exercise 1.

Exercise 4

Compare the recordings obtained in Exercises 1, 2, and 3. What are the differences between observing play as a general category, as in Exercise 1; observing the three different types of play, as in Exercise 2; and observing the 12 subtypes of play, as in Exercise 3? What purposes does each type of recording serve? What information do you gain (or lose) with each type of recording? Which type of recording is more reliable, and why? Write up your analysis in a one- or two-paragraph report.

Exercise 5

With a co-observer, observe a child in a preschool for a 30-minute period. (Obtain permission from the school administration before beginning this activity.) Select a child who appears to be engaging in inappropriate behavior (a target behavior), such as fighting, temper tantrums, disruptive behavior, or uncooperative behavior. Record each time the inappropriate behavior occurs, using the dot-and-line method.

Observe whether the child's inappropriate behavior receives attention from an adult in the room (a target behavior). This information will provide some indication of the consequences of the behavior. Record each time the child receives attention, using the dot-and-line method. Your recording form should have spaces for recording the frequency of the child's inappropriate behavior and the frequency of the adult's attention.

Calculate the level of interobserver agreement separately for the two target behaviors. Calculate the rate of behavior separately for the two target behaviors. Follow the guidelines in Exercise 1.

Exercise 6

Follow the same general procedure described in Exercise 1. Now, however, record the *duration* of the child's play with another child. Use a stopwatch or other device to record the elapsed time. Calculate the level of interobserver agreement, the average duration of the behavior, and the percentage of time spent on the behavior.

RATINGS RECORDING

With ratings recording, you rate behavior on a scale or checklist, usually at the end of the observation period. The scale is designed so that you can indicate the degree to which you have observed the attribute (e.g., cooperativeness, aggression) or perceived the attribute to be present in the child. Thus, you must not only observe the child but also evaluate the degree to which the attribute being rated is present. The rating produces an ordinal score (see Chapter 2). Rating scales usually involve a greater degree of observer subjectivity than do other behavioral recording methods.

Major Uses of Ratings Recording

Ratings recording is useful for evaluating the more global aspects of behavior and for quantifying impressions (e.g., whether the examinee was motivated or hostile, whether the results were reliable). Rating scales are useful for assessing behaviors or products that are difficult to measure precisely. For example, you can use a rating scale that ranges from very poor (1) to excellent (7) to rate the legibility of handwriting, the quality of arts and crafts products, the neatness of a room, or performance style during physical exercises or other activities. For judgments about the intensity of a behavior, ratings from not intense (1) to extremely intense (5) are useful. Because rating scales are easy to standardize, they can be used for many purposes in numerous settings.

You can compare results of ratings recording with results obtained from more specific observational procedures, such as interval or event recording. These comparisons will reveal the consistency of the results across methods. Ratings recording is valuable in some assessment situations because it is less costly in time and personnel than are other methods. Ratings recording also allows you to (a) consider more subtle and unique clues, (b) overcome the fragmentation associated with behavioral counts, and (c) evaluate some quality in the child's behavior that may be inaccessible with more detailed and objective coding systems. The quantitative dimension associated with ratings recording is sometimes referred to as "behavior as a whole."

How to Design a Ratings Recording

In designing a ratings recording, you must decide on (a) the number of times you will observe the child, (b) the total length of the observation period, (c) the time periods during which you will conduct the observations, (d) the target behaviors you will observe, and (e) the method of recording data.

Frequency, length, and timing of observations. As with other recording methods, the child's age, the setting, and the reason for the assessment will influence the number of times you will need to observe the child, the length of the observation period, and when you should conduct the observations. An observation period may last from 10 to 30 minutes or longer. Time the observation period so that you obtain a representative sample of behavior. If possible, observe the child more than once and at different times during the day.

Target behaviors. As in interval and event recording, base your selection of target behaviors on prior information from narrative recordings, interviews, referral questions, and test results.

Method of recording data. Your ratings will usually be recorded on a 5-point scale. The points or numbers represent a behavioral continuum that should be defined as precisely as possible. Following are some typical formats for rating scales:

EXAMPLE 1

How cooperative is Jose? Circle one.

5	4	3	2	1
highly cooperative	moderately cooperative	neither cooperative nor uncooperative	moderately uncooperative	highly uncooperative

EXAMPLE 2

To what extent does Helena share toys? Circle one.

5	4	3	2	1
always	frequently	sometimes	seldom	never

EXAMPLE 3

How self-reliant is Matilda? Circle one.

1	2	3	4	5
very dependent	usually dependent	somewhat self-reliant and somewhat dependent	usually self-reliant	very self-reliant

EXAMPLE 4

To what extent is Frank visually attentive or alert? Circle one.

5 Eyes closed all the time
4 Eyes open about one-quarter of the time
3 Eyes open about half the time
2 Eyes open about three-quarters of the time
1 Eyes open most or all of the time

EXAMPLE 5

How anxious was Barbara? Place an X on the line that best reflects your rating.

anxious ___:___:___:___:___ not anxious

You can design a ratings recording to measure selected antecedents and consequences associated with the target behavior. For example, you might ask, "When situation Z occurs, how often does Mike do X?" or "After Mike does X, how often does [other person] react by doing Y?" Examples 6 and 7 below show rating scales for these types of ratings.

EXAMPLE 6

After Justin throws a temper tantrum, how often do his peers react by laughing? Circle one.

5	4	3	2	1
always	frequently	sometimes	seldom	never

EXAMPLE 7

How does Helen's behavior this week compare with her behavior 4 weeks ago? Circle one.

1	2	3	4	5
much worse	worse	no different	better	much better

EXAMPLE 8

How frequently does Veronica engage in positive behavior? Circle one.

5	4	3	2	1
always	freqently	occasionally	rarely	never

EXAMPLE 9

How confident are you that your ratings are accurate? Circle one.

5	4	3	2	1
definitely confident	moderately confident	confident	not very confident	definitely not confident

Notice that, in Example 5, verbal descriptions are given only for the endpoints of the continuum and no numbers are used, whereas in the other examples each point on the continuum has a number coupled with a verbal description. You can, however, also convert each entry on the scale in Example 5 to a number (e.g., 5, 4, 3, 2, 1).

Quantitative Data in Ratings Recording

The prime source of data in ratings recording is the value (number or score) on the rating scale. A major difficulty associated with ratings is that the assumptions underlying the scale values are not always clear; observers may therefore differ in their interpretation of the scale positions. For example, does *almost always* mean 99% to 100% of the time or 90% to 100% of the time? Does *often* mean the same on a 5-point scale as it does on a 7-point scale? Providing detailed examples of behaviors associated with each scale point will help you to apply consistent standards in interpreting scale values and will enhance interobserver reliability. Always make your ratings shortly after the completion of the observation period. If you wait too long, you may forget what you saw or your impression may become distorted.

You may improve a rating scale designed to obtain an estimate of frequency of occurrence by anchoring the frequency descriptions to percentages of time. Here is an example:

5 Almost always (86% to 100% of the time)
4 Frequently (66% to 85% of the time)
3 Occasionally (36% to 65% of the time)
2 Rarely (16% to 35% of the time)
1 Almost never (0% to 15% of the time)

Note that even though these percentages more precisely define the frequency descriptions ("almost always" to "almost never"), raters still must estimate how often the behaviors in question occurred.

Advantages and Disadvantages of Ratings Recording

The ratings recording method provides a common frame of reference for comparing individuals. It is well suited to recording many different behaviors and is useful for rating the behaviors of many individuals or an entire group. It also is useful for recording qualitative aspects of behavior. Finally, it generates data in a form suitable for statistical analyses, is time efficient, and is a convenient method for recording the perceptions of multiple observers.

Ratings recording, however, may yield low interobserver reliability for several reasons. First, the scale values may be based on unclear assumptions. Second, the terms may be complex or ambiguous. Third, the scale positions may be interpreted differently by different observers. Fourth, observers may use the center of the rating scale and avoid extreme positions (central tendency error). Finally, ratings recording may generate halo effects or permit a time delay between the behavioral observations and the observer's ratings of the behavior. Ratings recording also is not suited to recording important quantitative information, such as the frequency, duration, or latency of behavior, or to recording antecedent and consequent events (unless a method for doing so is built into the design of the ratings recording).

Illustration of Ratings Recording

Table 8-11 shows a behavioral rating scale for assessing the presence of distress behaviors (reactions to pain and anxiety) in children undergoing a painful medical procedure—bone marrow aspiration treatment for cancer. Observers can complete the scale at various times during the procedure. The observers do not participate in the treatment procedure; they position themselves so that they are unobtrusive but have a clear view of the child lying on the treatment table. Observers also can use this scale for rating children's reactions to other painful medical procedures.

Table 8-11
Behavioral Checklist

BEHAVIOR CHECKLIST

Child's name: _____

Age: _____ Grade: _____ Date: _____

Hospital: _____

Examiner's name: _____

Directions: Rate each behavior using the following 5-point scale.

1	2	3	4	5
very mild	mild	neutral	intense	extremely intense

Circle one number for each behavior.

Behavior			Rating		
1. Muscle tension	1	2	3	4	5
2. Screaming	1	2	3	4	5
3. Crying	1	2	3	4	5
4. Restraint used	1	2	3	4	5
5. Pain verbalized	1	2	3	4	5
6. Anxiety verbalized	1	2	3	4	5
7. Verbal stalling	1	2	3	4	5
8. Physical resistance	1	2	3	4	5

Note. Behaviors are defined as follows: (1) *Muscle tension*—contraction of any observable body part (e.g., shuts eyes tight, clenches jaw, stiffens body, clenches fists, or grits teeth); (2) *Screaming*—raises voice or yells with sounds or words; (3) *Crying*—displays tears or sobs; (4) *Restraint used*—is held down by someone or has heavy tape placed across legs onto table; (5) *Pain verbalized*—says "ow" or "ouch" or comments about hurting (e.g., "You're hurting me"); (6) *Anxiety verbalized*—says "I'm scared" or "I'm afraid"; (7) *Verbal stalling*—verbally expresses desire to delay ("Stop," "I'm not ready," "I want to tell you something," etc.); (8) *Physical resistance*—moves around, will not stay in position, or tries to climb off table.

See Katz, Kellerman, and Siegel (1980) for additional items.
Source: Adapted from LeBaron and Zeltzer (1984).
From *Assessment of Children: Behavioral, Social, and Clinical Foundations (Fifth Edition)* by Jerome M. Sattler and Robert D. Hoge. Copyright 2006 by Jerome M. Sattler, Publisher, Inc. Permission to photocopy this table is granted to purchasers of this book for personal use only (see copyright page for details).

Exercises 8-4
Ratings Recording Exercises

Exercise 1

With a co-observer, observe one child on a playground for a period of 5 minutes. After you observe the child, complete the following five rating scales.

RATING SCALES

Directions: Place an X in the appropriate space.

1. cooperative ____:____:____:____:____:____ uncooperative

2. sad ____:____:____:____:____:____ happy
3. active ____:____:____:____:____:____ inactive
4. coordinated ____:____:____:____:____:____ uncoordinated
5. aggressive ____:____:____:____:____:____ passive

After you complete the scales, convert each rating to a number, assigning the number 1 to ratings in the left-most column and the number 5 to ratings in the right-most column. Determine the level of interobserver agreement by calculating (a) the percentage agreement (i.e., how many ratings were the same across the five scales; see Chapter 9) and (b) the product-moment correlation (see Chapter 2).

Consider the following questions in evaluating your ratings recordings.

1. How did the rating scales guide your observations?
2. What additional scales would have been useful?
3. To what extent might the time of day have affected the child's behavior?
4. To what extent did the setting affect the child's behavior?
5. To what extent were the dimensions covered in the scales representative of the child's general behavior?
6. What could be done to improve the representativeness of the observations?
7. To what extent was the child's behavior similar to that of her or his peers?
8. Did the scales reveal information that might have been missed with a narrative recording?
9. What biases, if any, may have affected your observations?
10. How might your presence have altered the child's behavior?
11. What could you have done to minimize your influence?
12. How did your ratings recording contribute to your understanding of the child?

Write a one- or two-paragraph summary of your observations. Include information about (a) the child (age, gender, and other relevant characteristics), (b) the physical setting in which the observation took place, (c) the length of time you observed the child, (d) the ratings you made, (e) the level of agreement with your co-observer, (f) the difficulties you had in using the rating scales and suggestions for improving the scales, and (g) the implications of the findings (e.g., whether the behaviors were appropriate or inappropriate).

Exercise 2

Design your own ratings recording procedure for observing children in some setting. Develop five rating scales, different from those used in Exercise 1. With a co-observer, observe one child or a group of children, depending on the specific procedure developed, for a period of 5 minutes. Follow the procedures in Exercise 1 for evaluating your recording.

EVALUATIONS OF RECORDING METHODS

Interval, event, and ratings recording methods may not provide the breadth of information that narrative recordings do, but they allow you to (a) systematically evaluate specific behaviors of interest, (b) sample many children and various situations, (c) compare children and develop norms, and (d) generalize findings, all within a reasonable period. With both interval and event recording, it is relatively easy to tally behaviors, particularly when they are clearly defined and observable. Both methods provide information about behavior during one time period and about changes in the child's behavior from one time period to another. Table 8-12 summarizes the four types of recording methods.

Table 8-12
Observational Recording Methods

Recording method	Types	Applications	Data	Advantages	Disadvantages
Narrative recording: Behavior is comprehensively described.	*Anecdotal recording:* Anything that appears noteworthy is recorded. *Running record:* Observer describes behaviors as they occur.	Is useful as a precursor to more specific and quantifiable observations Helps in the development of hypotheses about factors controlling target behaviors Provides an in-depth picture of behavior	Does not yield specific quantitative data, although the record can be analyzed for various occurrences of behavior	Provides a record of child's behavior and general impressions Maintains original sequence of events Facilitates discovering critical behaviors and noting continuing difficulties Requires a minimum of equipment	Is not well suited to obtaining quantifiable data Is costly in terms of time and person power Is difficult to validate May be insensitive to critical behaviors Produces findings with limited generalizability
Interval recording: Observation period is divided into brief segments or intervals; observer notes whether a behavior occurs in each interval.	*Partial-interval time sampling:* Behavior is scored only once during an interval, regardless of duration or frequency of occurrence. *Whole-interval time sampling:* Behavior is scored only when it lasts from the beginning to the end of the interval. *Point time interval sampling:* Behavior is scored only when it occurs at a designated time during the interval. *Momentary time interval sampling:* Behavior is scored only when it occurs at the end of the interval. *Variable inter-occasion interval time sampling:* Behavior is scored only when it occurs during designated random time intervals.	Is useful for behaviors that are overt or easily observable, that are not clearly discrete, and that occur with reasonable frequency (for example, reading, working, roughhousing, smiling, playing with toys)	Yields number of intervals in which target behaviors did or did not occur	Defines important time-behavior relationships Facilitates checking interobserver reliability Is an economical way to standardize observation conditions Enhances attention to specific behaviors Allows for flexibility in recording large numbers of behaviors	Provides a somewhat artificial view of behavior sequence May lead observer to overlook important behaviors Usually tells little about quality of behaviors or situation Provides numbers that are usually not related to frequency of behaviors Is not sensitive to very low frequency behaviors or, in the case of point time sampling, behaviors of short duration

(*Continued*)

Table 8-12 (*Continued*)

Recording method	Types	Applications	Data	Advantages	Disadvantages
Event recording: Each instance of a specific behavior (event) is observed and recorded.	*Rate:* Observer waits for preselected behavior to occur and then records its occurrence. *Duration:* Observer determines the amount of time that elapses between the beginning and the end of behavior. *Intensity:* Behavior is divided into various degrees of intensity, and behavior of each degree is recorded separately. *Latency:* Observer determines the amount of time that elapses between the initiation of a request or the occurrence of a cue and the onset of behavior.	Is useful for behaviors that have clearly defined beginnings and ends, such as spelling words correctly, making rocking movements, asking questions, and making speech errors	Yields number of occurrences of behavior– frequency count Also, in some cases, yields rate of behavior, duration of behavior (time), intensity of behavior (if built into code), or latency of behavior (time)	Facilitates detection of low-frequency behaviors Facilitates study of many different behaviors in an economical and flexible manner Provides information about the frequency with which behavior occurs and about changes in behavior over time	Provides artificial view of behavior sequence and breaks up continuity of behavior Is not suited to recording nondiscrete behaviors Presents difficulties in establishing reliability Limits quanti-fication of the how and why associated with behavior Makes comparison across sessions difficult when the length of the observation period is not constant
Ratings recording: Behavior is observed and then rated on various scales.	*Five-point scales Seven-point scales Other dimensional scales*	Is useful for evaluating more global aspects of behavior and for quantifying impressions	Yields value (number or score) on rating scale	Allows for the recording of many different behaviors in an efficient manner Allows for the rating of many individuals in a group and the group as a whole Permits rating of subtle aspects of behavior Facilitates statistical analyses	Yields scale values, which may be based on unclear assumptions May have low reliability Does not allow for recording of important quantitative dimensions Usually does not allow for recording of antecedent and consequent events

Narrative recording is more useful than the other recording methods for preserving the sequence of interactions observed so that relationships among behaviors can be measured adequately. For example, with a narrative recording you are in a better position to answer questions such as "If this happens, what is likely to happen next?"

Interval recording is useful when you want to obtain information about behavior across time intervals (or temporal patterns of behavioral occurrences). Interval recording can answer questions such as "Did Tom's off-task behavior occur throughout the observation period or only during part of the observation period?" You can enhance your interval recording by making the length of the interval as close as possible to the duration of the behavior. Generally, interval recording provides a sample of behavior adequate for many clinical and psychoeducational purposes, particularly when your concern is the presence or absence of behavior. You have a reasonable chance of recording even infrequent momentary behaviors with interval recording if observation periods are sufficiently long.

Event recording is more useful than interval recording when you want a measure of the number of times a behavior occurs. You will want this information (rather than the number of scored intervals) when your goal is to bring about either an increase or a decrease in certain behaviors or when the frequency of an event or behavior is of interest. Event recording, however, is not as useful as interval recording for behaviors that do not have a discrete beginning and end or that occur rarely, such as temper tantrums.

Ratings recordings may be especially useful because they provide information about the intensity of a behavior. They also are more useful than the other recording methods in quantifying global impressions of behavior.

THINKING THROUGH THE ISSUES

1. Why is it important to observe a child at school, at home, or at free play when you perform a clinical assessment? Discuss your answer.
2. What can you do to ensure that your observations are reliable and valid?
3. When would it be valuable to use four different recording methods (e.g., narrative, interval, event, and ratings) to observe a child, a family, or a class?
4. What are the basic requirements for an effective recording system?
5. What stresses might you face when you visit a child's home?
6. What conditions in a child's home would affect you, and how might you react to these conditions?

SUMMARY

1. Observing the behavior of children in natural or specially designed settings contributes to a clinical or psychoeducational assessment.
2. Behavioral observations provide a picture of children's spontaneous behavior in everyday life settings, unique settings, or specially designed settings; provide information about children's interpersonal behavior and learning style; provide a systematic record of children's behaviors and the behaviors of others, which can be used for evaluation, intervention planning, and monitoring changes; allow for verification of the accuracy of parental and teacher reports about children's behavior; allow comparisons between behavior in the test situation and behavior in naturalistic settings; provide information independent of children's ability or willingness to report information; provide information about young children and children with develop-

mental disabilities who are difficult to evaluate with other procedures; and permit functional behavioral assessment by providing a means of identifying a target behavior, documenting its antecedents and consequences, and evaluating the effects of interventions.

3. To be most useful, the systematic observation of behavior should have a goal, a focus, a limit on the amount of data collected, and a standardized recording method that has adequate reliability and validity.

Using Observational Methods

4. In the systematic observation of behavior, you observe a child's behavior in natural or specially designed settings, record or classify each behavior objectively as it occurs or shortly thereafter, ensure that the obtained data are reliable and valid, and convert the data into quantitative information.
5. It is never possible to capture all of the behaviors exhibited by a child during the observation.
6. The assumption behind the sampling of behavior is that the behaviors recorded over a period of time will constitute a representative sample of behavior.
7. Sensitivity, acuity, and perceptiveness are keys to becoming a skilled observer.
8. In observational assessments, the stimuli are not controlled by the clinician and the scoring procedures are not as exact as those used in standardized tests.
9. In designing an observation, first define the behaviors that you are going to observe—the target behaviors—in objective, clear, and complete terms.
10. Your definitions (or those in the coding system that you use) should help you recognize when each behavior is occurring and distinguish the target behaviors from other similar behaviors.
11. When you first observe a child referred for a specified behavior problem, do not focus exclusively on that behavior.
12. Once you have defined the target behaviors you want to observe, select an appropriate observation period—some time when there is a chance that you will observe a representative sample of the behaviors of interest.
13. If possible, observe the child at different times during the day and in several settings.
14. Even when you are concentrating on specific behaviors, be attuned to other events happening at the time of the observation.
15. No matter how carefully you prepare for your observational assessment, observations conducted in naturalistic settings are not under your control.

Applicability of Observational Methods

16. Observational methods are particularly useful for studying behaviors that are relatively frequent; assessing global behaviors such as aggression, social withdrawal, sociability, and attention; and evaluating a child's progress over time.
17. Systematic observation in a naturalistic setting may *not* be the preferred method for observing behaviors that occur infrequently, covertly, or only in response to specific stimuli.
18. You cannot allow self-injurious behavior, sexual assaults, or other harmful behaviors to occur simply so that you can record their intensity or duration.
19. Observing intimate sexual interactions, illicit drug use, or confidential conversations poses significant ethical problems.
20. Self-monitoring techniques are preferred for recording private behaviors.

21. Although you cannot observe psychological processes directly, you can observe behaviors associated with them.

22. A planned incident procedure (or controlled observation), which entails observing children in a specially contrived situation or setting, is the method of choice when you want to elicit specific behaviors.

23. Observational methods are particularly valuable in ecological assessment, which focuses on the physical and psychological attributes of the setting in which behavior occurs.

24. Physical attributes of the setting include spatial arrangements, seating arrangements, lighting, and noise; psychological attributes of the setting include the child's relationships with family members, peers, teachers, or others in the setting.

25. An ecological assessment may also focus on (a) how changes in one behavior affect other behaviors or (b) how changes in one part of the environment produce changes in other parts of the environment that, in turn, affect the child.

26. Observing a family at home has several advantages. It gives a picture of how the family functions naturally; gives a good idea of how each family member functions in his or her everyday role; reduces the chance that a family member will be absent, which is more likely in an office interview; promotes recognition among family members that the entire family shares responsibility for making changes or improvements; decreases anxiety among family members because of the familiar surroundings and thus facilitates more open communication among the family members; and decreases the impact of the common "doctor-patient" stereotypes.

27. Family observations are useful in obtaining information about patterns of interaction among the members of the family, the emotional climate of the home, family conflicts, and patterns of resolution after a conflict.

28. Your ability to do a home observation may be influenced by the conditions you meet in the home.

29. When children and parents know that they are being observed, their behavior may change; such changes in behavior are referred to as reactive effects.

30. When you administer tests and conduct interviews, you also can observe the child's behavior. Many of the principles discussed in this chapter apply to these activities as well.

Designing an Observational Assessment

31. The key to obtaining meaningful descriptions of behavior is coming up with the right combination of an observational recording method and a coding system.

32. Coding systems not only highlight target behaviors but also may measure several important dimensions of the target behaviors (e.g., the frequency, duration, intensity, and latency of the behaviors), as well as how factors in the setting affect the behaviors.

33. The observational recording methods particularly useful for clinical and psychoeducational tasks are narrative recording, interval recording, event recording, and ratings recording.

Narrative Recording

34. Narrative recording will help you formulate a comprehensive description of a child's (or a group's) natural behavior.

35. Narrative recordings are referred to as anecdotal recordings when they include anything that seems noteworthy to the observer; a specific time frame and specific codes and categories are not needed.

36. A narrative recording produced as behavior occurs is referred to as a running record.

37. Narrative recordings describe events without using quantitative recording procedures.

38. Observations in a narrative recording can be global, semi-global, or narrow.

39. Global descriptions (also referred to as molar or broad descriptions) focus on actions that reflect the child's behavior as a whole.

40. Semi-global descriptions contain additional general details of the behaviors of interest.

41. Narrow descriptions (also referred to as molecular or fine descriptions) reflect specific details of the child's behavior or the setting.

42. Narrative observations fall along a continuum from those requiring minimally inferential judgments to those involving highly inferential judgments.

43. When you record directly observable behavior (e.g., actions, motor activity, and verbalizations), you make minimally inferential judgments.

44. When you record interpretations based on behaviors, you make highly inferential judgments.

45. Behavioral descriptive statements describe behaviors as they occur, without explanations.

46. Behavioral inferential statements go beyond describing behaviors; they reflect attempts to integrate or theorize.

47. Narrative observations may help you create an in-depth picture of the behavior of a child, a group, or a teacher.

48. In clinical assessment, narrative recordings are particularly valuable as precursors to more specific and quantifiable observations. A running account of a child's behavior may provide leads about behavioral and environmental events worthy of further analysis and suggest hypotheses about factors controlling the target behaviors.

49. Narrative recording can help you to learn about a child's social skills and communication skills, help you evaluate family interactive patterns, and help you learn about a group.

50. When observing a family, you will need not only to listen carefully to what the family members are saying but also to observe their facial expressions, gestures, actions, and body language.

51. In observing a group, pay particular attention to the patterns of peer preference or attraction, indifference, antagonism, and influence.

52. When you visit a classroom, you will want to observe the teacher's method and style of teaching and classroom management.

53. It is sometimes helpful to observe a child informally in a situation that combines a natural procedure with a planned incident procedure.

54. In designing a narrative recording (or an interval, event, or ratings recording), you must decide on (a) the number of times you will observe the child, (b) the length of each observation period, (c) the time periods during which you will conduct the observations, (d) the type of narrative recording you will use, (e) the target behaviors you will observe, and (f) the method of recording data.

55. The child's age, the setting, and the reason for the assessment will influence the number of times you will need to observe the child, the length of each observation period, and when you should conduct the observations. (This also holds for interval, event, or ratings recording.)

56. For clinical and psychoeducational assessment, anecdotal recordings are preferred.

57. If you are conducting a preliminary observation, include general impressions of the child and the setting in your narrative recording.

58. You may write your narrative recording, enter it into a portable computer, or record your comments on audiotape.

59. Although narrative recordings do not involve quantitative recording procedures, you can use your record to obtain quantitative data.

60. Narrative recording provides a record of a child's behavior and of your general impressions. It maintains the original sequence of events and provides a means of gathering information and discovering critical behaviors. It also allows you to assess progress, provides a record of continuing difficulties, requires little equipment, and serves as a valuable precursor to more systematic observational procedures.

61. Narrative recording, however, is not well suited for obtaining quantifiable data. The recording is difficult to validate and may not fully describe some types of critical behaviors. The findings also may have limited generalizability and may vary from observer to observer.

Interval Recording

62. Interval recording (sometimes referred to as time sampling, interval sampling, or interval time sampling) focuses on selected aspects of behavior as they occur within specified intervals of time. The term *sampling* conveys the basic idea of interval recording—you sample behavior rather than recording every behavior as it occurs during the observation period.

63. Interval recording procedures include partial-interval time sampling, whole-interval time sampling, point time interval sampling, momentary time interval sampling, and variable interoccasion interval time sampling.

64. Interval recording is useful for recording behaviors that are overt, do not always have a clearcut beginning and end, and occur with moderate frequency, such as once every 10 to 15 seconds.

65. The child's age, the setting, and the reason for the assessment will influence the number of times you will need to observe the child, the total length of the observation period, and when you should conduct the observations.

66. Select the type of interval recording best suited to the information that you need.

67. The length of the observation interval will depend on the target behaviors.

68. The length of the recording interval will depend on the number of behaviors you want to record.

69. Select target behaviors based on prior narrative recordings, interview information, referral questions, or the child's test behavior.

70. You can record data with pencil and paper or with an electronic recording device.

71. The primary piece of quantitative data obtained in interval recording is the number of intervals in which the target behaviors did occur.

72. Interval recording helps to define important time-behavior relations. It facilitates checking for interobserver reliability and helps to ensure that the predefined behaviors are observed under the same conditions each time. It uses time efficiently and focuses the observer's attention on the child's behavior by structuring the observations. The method also permits the recording of virtually any observable behavior, allows for the collection of a large number of observations in a short period of time, and requires minimal and inexpensive equipment.

73. Interval recording, however, provides a somewhat artificial view of a behavior sequence, because the time interval—not the behavior—dictates the recording framework. It allows important behaviors related to a problem to be overlooked and fails to provide information about the quality of the behavior (e.g., how the behavior was performed) or about the situation (e.g., whether the child was agitated, paying attention, or sleeping while in his or her seat) unless such information is specifically coded into the recording system. It does not reveal the actual frequency or duration of a behavior (e.g., one continuous 60-second period of off-task behavior would be recorded as four separate events in a 10-second observation/5-second recording interval system). It also may overestimate the frequency of low-rate behaviors or behaviors of short duration and underestimate the frequency of high-rate behaviors. Finally, observers must undergo considerable training to learn the recording system.

Event Recording

74. In event recording (also called event sampling), you record each instance of a specific behavior or event as it occurs during the observation period.

75. Event recording provides a continuous temporal record of observed behaviors and thus is particularly appropriate for measuring discrete responses that have clearly defined beginnings and ends.

76. Event recording is less suitable for high-rate behaviors or for behaviors that vary in duration.

77. Select target behaviors based on prior narrative recordings, interview information, referral questions, or the child's test behavior.

78. You can record responses in various ways, such as by using a checklist, a wrist counter, a hand counter, an electromechanical counter, or another mechanical device or by transferring small objects from one of your pockets to another.

79. The primary piece of quantitative data obtained in event recording is the frequency count—the number of occurrences of a behavior in a given time period.

80. Event recording is useful for measuring low-rate behaviors, facilitates the study of many different behaviors or events, and uses time and personnel efficiently, especially when persons who are ordinarily in the setting can make the observations. It can accommodate many different recording methods and provides information about changes in behavior over time and in the amount of behavior performed.

81. Event recording, however, provides a somewhat artificial view of a behavior sequence by separating the present event from conditions in the past that may have led up to the event. It does not reveal sequences or temporal patterns, unless the time of the response is recorded. It breaks up the continuity of behavior by using limited categories and is not suited to recording behaviors that are not discrete. It presents difficulties in establishing reliability across multiple observers. It requires observers to maintain an optimal level of attention over long periods of time, because few cues are used and responses may be relatively infrequent. It also is difficult to quantify the how and why associated with the event, even if these characteristics also are recorded. Finally, it makes comparison across periods difficult when the length of the observation period is not constant.

Ratings Recording

82. With ratings recording, you rate behavior on a scale or checklist, usually at the end of the observation period.

83. Ratings recording is useful for evaluating the more global aspects of behavior and for quantifying impressions (e.g., whether the examinee was motivated or hostile, whether the results were reliable).

84. You can compare results of ratings recording with results obtained from more specific observational procedures, such as interval or event recording.

85. Your ratings will usually be recorded on a 5-point scale.

86. The prime source of data in ratings recording is the value (number or score) on the rating scale.

87. The ratings recording method provides a common frame of reference for comparing individuals. It is well suited to recording many different behaviors and is useful for rating the behaviors of many individuals or an entire group. It also is useful for recording qualitative aspects of behavior. Finally, it generates data in a form suitable for statistical analyses, is time efficient, and is a convenient method for recording the perceptions of multiple observers.

88. Ratings recording, however, may yield low interobserver reliability for several reasons. First, the scale values may be based on unclear assumptions. Second, the terms may be complex or ambiguous. Third, the scale positions may be interpreted differently by different observers. Fourth, observers may use the center of the rating scale and avoid extreme positions (central tendency error). Fifth, ratings recording may generate halo effects or permit a time delay between the behavioral observations and the observer's ratings of the behavior. Ratings recording also is not suited to recording important quantitative information, such as the frequency, duration, or latency of behavior, or to recording antecedent and consequent events (unless a method for doing so is built into the design of the ratings recording).

Evaluation of Recording Methods

89. Interval, event, and ratings recording methods may not provide the breadth of information that narrative recordings do, but they allow you to (a) systematically evaluate specific behaviors of interest, (b) sample many children and various situations, (c) compare children and develop norms, and (d) generalize findings, all within a reasonable period.

90. Narrative recording is more useful than the other recording methods for preserving the sequence of interactions observed so that relationships among behaviors can be measured adequately.

91. Interval recording is useful when you want to obtain information about behavior across time intervals (or temporal patterns of behavioral occurrences).

92. Event recording is more useful than interval recording when you want a measure of the number of times a behavior occurs.

93. Ratings recordings may be especially useful because they provide information about the intensity of a behavior.

KEY TERMS, CONCEPTS, AND NAMES

STUDY QUESTIONS

1. What purposes does the direct observation of behavior serve?

2. Discuss an ecological assessment. Include in your discussion the assets and limitations of this type of assessment.

3. What are some of the key areas to consider in designing a systematic observation of behavior?

4. Discuss the narrative recording method. Include in your discussion types of narrative recordings, different levels of description, inferential judgments, major uses of the method, design considerations, and the advantages and disadvantages of the method.

5. Discuss the interval recording method. Include in your discussion the five different types of interval recording methods, major uses of the method, design considerations, quantitative data, and the advantages and disadvantages of the method.

6. Discuss the event recording method. Include in your discussion a description of the method, major uses of the method, design considerations, quantitative data, and the advantages and disadvantages of the method.

7. Discuss ratings recording. Include in your discussion a description of the method, major uses of the method, quantitative data, and the advantages and disadvantages of the method.

8. Which type of recording method would be preferable for observing each of the following, and why: (a) use of slang words, (b) tics, (c) quality of a story, and (d) the event preceding an aggressive behavior (antecedent event)?

9. Compare and contrast narrative recording, interval recording, event recording, and ratings recording.

9

OBSERVATIONAL METHODS, PART II

I assume that some people may find themselves tempera-
mentally more suited to systematic observation than others.
But I also assume that anybody can be trained to be a better
questioner, a more careful methodologist, a more nuanced
paraphraser, a more patient observer, a more subtle student
of everyday life, a more complicated person capable of reg-
istering more of the complications in the world.
— Karl E. Weick, American psychologist (1936–   )

Observational Coding Systems

Reliability

Validity

Procedures for Reducing Errors in Observations

Observations of Infants

Cautions on the Use of Observations

Self-Monitoring Assessment

Reporting Behavioral Observations

Case Study

Thinking Through the Issues

Summary

Key Terms, Concepts, and Names

Study Questions

Goals and Objectives

This chapter is designed to enable you to do the following:

- Become familiar with coding systems

- Learn how to evaluate the reliability of observational methods

- Learn how to evaluate the validity of observational methods

- Understand self-monitoring assessment

- Prepare reports based on observational assessments

This chapter continues the book's coverage of systematic behavioral observation. It will (a) familiarize you with several observational coding systems, (b) provide you with the tools with which to evaluate the reliability and validity of your observations, (c) help you reduce errors associated with behavioral observations, (d) help you use self-monitoring procedures, and (e) teach you how to report your observational findings.

OBSERVATIONAL CODING SYSTEMS

Observational coding systems are used to categorize behavioral observations. They usually consist of two or more categories that cover a range of behaviors, although, on occasion, a single category may be appropriate. Even when you are considering just one target behavior, you must also consider those times when it does *not* occur. Thus, though your focus is on one behavior, you can think of a one-category coding system used in interval or event recording as having two categories—the *presence* of the behavior and the *absence* of the behavior.

Before you use a coding system, carefully evaluate the following (Nay, 1979): (a) its rationale, (b) the setting(s) in which it is applicable, (c) definitions of the coding categories, (d) the description of how behavior is sampled, (e) rules governing observers' use of rating scales, such as a hierarchy of codes, (f) reliability, including overall reliability and the reliability of each coding category, (g) validity, and (h) positive and negative features (including potential problem areas).

How to Select an Observational Coding System

In selecting an observational coding system, consider the following:

1. What questions do you want to answer with your observational assessment?
2. What existing system best meets the assessment, treatment, or research goals?
3. Are you interested in investigating global areas of behavior or just a few specific behaviors?
4. How many behaviors do you want to observe?
5. What aspects of the situation merit attention?
6. Are the behaviors you want to observe easily identified?

Select the simplest possible coding system that will answer your questions. If your purpose is to obtain a general description of behavior, select a system that uses global categories. If you are interested in only a few behaviors related to the referral question, select a system that uses specific categories related to these behaviors. If you want to examine the relationship between a behavior and its environmental determinants, use a multidimensional system that includes codes for relevant antecedent and consequent events. Finally, if you want to record sequential observational data, use a sequential observational procedure (see Bakeman & Gottman, 1986).

When you want to measure a few behaviors, you should have little difficulty in selecting an adequate recording system. Avoid selecting a coding system that requires you to make multiple decisions and to use multiple categories, at least during your initial training period, because such systems are difficult to use. Memorize the coding system *before* you begin the formal observation, but keep the code definitions handy in case you need to refresh your memory.

Observational coding systems have been developed to evaluate individual children, groups of children, and classes. Observational codes also can cover environmental responses to children's behavior. Table 9-1 lists several observational coding systems; recognize, however, that these are only a sample of the hundreds of systems that have been developed for different purposes. Later in this section, Tables 9-2, 9-3, and 9-4 illustrate coding systems for observing children, teachers, and classes, respectively. The systems illustrated require immediate, not retrospective, observation; observers must observe and record behavior as the behavior occurs, while keeping inferences to a minimum.

Use of Computers in Observational Recording

Computerized observational systems, which use a laptop computer, hand-held computer, or bar-code scanner, are valuable for collecting real-time observational data (see Kahng & Iwata, 2000, for a review of 15 computerized systems). Various systems are capable of (a) recording many different responses, (b) recording responses for different groups, (c) recording and calculating response frequency, duration of behavior, interval responses, latency of behavior, interresponse time, and discrete trials, (d) calculating measures of central tendency (mean and median), variability (range and frequency distribution), statistical significance, and reliability (interobserver agreement—overall occurrence, occurrence, and nonoccurrence—and kappa), and (e) graphing the data.

Coding Systems for Observing Children's Behavior

Table 9-2 shows several coding systems for observing children's behavior.

1. The *two-category coding system* provides broad information about on-task and off-task behavior. It is particularly useful when the general climate of a classroom or other facility is the focus of assessment. You may have to make some inferences about which of the two categories in the system applies to a particular observed behavior.
2. The *three-category coding system* is a refinement of the two-category system. It is useful for assessing passive and disruptive dimensions of inappropriate behavior. These two dimensions are similar to the internalizing (passive) and externalizing (disruptive) dimensions of child behavior found on many behavioral checklists. (See Chapter 10

Table 9-1
Examples of Observational Coding Systems

Authors	Title	Description
Atkins, Pelham, & Licht (1988)	Classroom Observations of Conduct and Attention Deficit Disorders (COCADD)	A 32-item behavioral observational coding system that includes five domains (positive, physical-social orientation, vocal activities, nonvocal activities, and play activities) organized into seven composite variables for classroom observations (overactive, distracted, verbal disruptive, off-task verbal, verbal aggressive, physical aggressive, and stealing/cheating) and five composite variables for playground observations (verbal disruptive, verbal aggressive, physical aggressive, stealing/cheating, and highly active play).
Atwater, Carta, & Schwartz (1989)	Assessment Code Checklist for Evaluation of Survival Skills (ACCESS)	An observation system designed to provide information about teacher-student interactions during independent work time, group instruction, and other classroom activities.
Bradley (1994)	HOME Inventory	A home observational schedule useful for observing homes of normal children. Separate scales are available for infants, preschool children, and elementary school-age children. For example, for preschool children there are eight subscales—Learning Stimulation, Language Stimulation, Physical Environment, Warmth and Affection, Academic Stimulation, Modeling, Variety in Experience, and Acceptance. There also is a HOME Inventory for children with disabilities.
Bramlett & Barnett (1993)	Preschool Observation Code (POC)	A 20-item behavioral observational code—with nine state categories, five event categories, and six teacher-child interaction categories—designed to record preschool children's behavior.
Dadds, Schwartz, & Sanders (1987)	Family Observation Schedule (FOS)	A 20-item behavioral observational code—including 13 categories of parent behaviors and 7 categories of child behaviors—useful for observing family interaction patterns.
Dumas (1987)	INTERACT	A computer-based 38-item coding system—with 10 natural behavior codes, five positive behavior codes, five aversive behavior codes, eight response codes, and ten setting codes—designed to measure family interactions in natural settings.
Favazza & Odom (1993)	Code for Active Student Participation and Engagement–Revised (CASPER)	An observation system designed to provide information about classroom ecology of infant and toddler programs.
Forbes, Vuchinich, & Kneedler (2001)	Family Problem Solving Code (FAMPROS)	A six-category system, with 25 codes, designed to measure a family's problem-solving style.
Gilbert & Christensen (1988)	Family Alliances Coding System (FACS)	A 20-item behavioral observational code—with six positive valence codes, three neutral valence codes, eight negative valence codes, and three affect codes—designed to measure the interactional behaviors by which family members express their alliance relations with one another.
Greenwood, Carta, & Dawson (2000)	Ecobehavioral Assessment Systems Software (EBASS)	A family of computerized observational instruments designed to be used in assessing educational environments for children with and without developmental disabilities.
Guida (1987)	Naturalistic Observation of Academic Anxiety (NOAA)	A five-item behavioral observational code for recording anxiety in a classroom.
Harms & Clifford (1998)	Early Childhood Environment Rating Scale (ECERS)	An objective rating scale for measuring the quality of the childcare environment, with 43 individual scales grouped into six areas.
Hops, Biglan, Sherman, Arthur, Friedman, & Osteen (1987)	Living in Family Environments (LIFE)	A 38-category home behavioral observational code, including seven context codes, eight affect codes, and 23 content codes.

(Continued)

Table 9-1 (*Continued*)

Authors	Title	Description
Iverson & Segal (1992)	Behavior Observation Record (BOR)	A 35-item time/event sampling behavioral observational code designed to assess social behaviors and the quality or effectiveness of these behaviors on a playground. The items are grouped into four categories of social behaviors: child alone, child approaching others, child being approached, and child interacting with others.
Landesman (1987)	Home Observation Code (Modified)	A 79-item behavioral observational code, with items grouped into eight areas, designed for use in residential settings for individuals with mental retardation.
LePage & Mogge (2001)	Behavioral Observation System (BOS)	A 34-item inventory of behaviors grouped into four scales. The system is designed to measure psychopathology in inpatient settings.
Mash & Barkley (1986)	Response-Class Matrix (RCM)	A 13-item behavioral observational code—with six child behaviors and seven maternal behaviors—designed to measure parent-child interactions in a clinic, laboratory, playroom, or home setting.
Mayes (1991)	Mayes Hyperactivity Observation System (MHOS)	A seven-item behavioral observational code designed to measure hyperactivity under standardized free-play conditions.
Pianta, Smith, & Reeve (1991)	Global Ratings of Mother-Child Interaction	An eight-item behavioral observational rating scale—including five child scales and three adult scales—designed to measure interactions between child and mother.
Saudargas & Lentz (1986)	State-Event Classroom Observation System (SECOS)	An 11-item classroom observational code with eight state behaviors and 11 event behaviors, of which five are for students and six are for the teacher.
Shapiro (1996)	Behavior Observation of Students in Schools (B.O.S.S.)	A six-category classroom code, five of which are for students and one of which is for teachers.
Smith & Hardman (2003)	Classroom Interaction Scale (CIS)	A computerized system for recording interactions between teachers and students. The system allows an observer to log the frequency and duration of several different types of discourse, including question, answer, explain, refocus, read, write, and direct.
Stern, MacKain, Raduns, Hopper, Kaminsky, Evans, Shilling, Giraldo, Kaplan, Nachman, Trad, Polan, Barnard, & Spieker (1992)	Kiddie-Infant Descriptive Instrument for Emotional States (KIDIES)	A nine-item behavioral observational rating system designed to evaluate affective states in infants and preschool children.
Tapp & Walden (2000)	PROCORDER	A computer-based system for observing social interaction processes. The system provides event data and interval data.
Tarbell, Cohen, & Marsh (1992)	Toddler-Preschooler Postoperative Pain Scale (TPPPS)	A seven-item behavioral observational code, divided among three pain behavior categories: vocal pain, facial pain, and bodily pain. It is designed to measure postoperative pain in children aged 1 through 5 years.
Wistedt, Rasmussen, Pedersen, Malm, Traskman-Bendz, Wakelin, & Bech (1990)	Social Dysfunction and Aggression Scale (SDAS)	An 11-item behavioral observational code designed for observing individuals in inpatient settings who may display socially disturbed or aggressive behavior.

Note. See references for complete citation. Also see Kerig and Lindahl (2001) for a discussion of family observational coding systems and Thompson, Felce, and Symons (2000) for behavioral observation systems useful for individuals with developmental disabilities.

Table 9-2
Four Examples of Coding Systems for Observing Children's Behavior

Coding system	Examples
I. Two Categories	
1. On-Task Behavior (behavior appropriate for the situation)	Putting hand up when he or she wants to say something, listening while teacher is talking, working quietly at desk, asking teacher for permission to leave desk, volunteering information, answering questions, following teacher's directions
2. Off-Task Behavior (behavior inappropriate for the situation)	a. Passive inappropriate actions (for example, staring into space, lacking perseverance, looking around room, working on wrong assignment) b. Active inappropriate actions (for example, talking to classmates, making noise, hitting, fighting, banging, being out of seat without permission, physical destructiveness, stealing, threatening others, setting fires)
II. Three Categories	
1. On-Task Behavior	See examples under I.1.
2. Passive Off-Task Behavior (passive behavior that is inappropriate but does not disrupt others)	See examples under I.2.a.
3. Disruptive Off-Task Behavior (inappropriate disruptive behavior)	See examples under I.2.b.
III. Four Categories	
1. On-Task Behavior	See examples under I.1.
2. Verbal Off-Task Behavior	Talking out, teasing
3. Motor Off-Task Behavior	Being out of seat, hitting others, throwing objects, playing with objects
4. Passive Off-Task Behavior	Daydreaming, sleeping, sulking
IV. Ten Categories	
1. Interference	Interrupting teacher or another student
2. Off-Task	Engaging in other than assigned work
3. Noncompliance	Failing to follow teacher's instructions
4. Minor Motor Movements	Moving buttocks, rocking
5. Gross Motor Movements	Leaving seat, standing without permission
6. Out-of-Chair Behavior	Remaining out of chair for a period of time
7. Physical Aggression	Kicking, hitting
8. Threat or Verbal Aggression	Making threatening gestures, bullying
9. Solicitation of Teacher	Raising hand, calling out to teacher
10. On-Task	Engaging in on-task behavior

Note. The 10-category system is from Abikoff and Gittelman (1985) and can be found in Table C-1 in Appendix C.

for coverage of behavioral checklists.) You can use this three-category coding system for individuals as well as for an entire class.

3. The *four-category coding system* is useful when you need information about whether disruptive off-task behavior is verbal, motor, or passive. You can use this four-category coding system for observing individual children in a classroom.

4. The *ten-category system* is a more extensive system for observing classroom behavior, with nine of the ten categories referring to inappropriate behavior. This system provides detailed information about a child's actions. Table C-1 in Appendix C shows the complete system with recording instructions; it is called the Classroom Observation Code: A Modification of the Stony Brook Code. The system is especially useful for recording children's hyperactive behavior.

Here is an example of a three-category system that is useful for observing children's social behavior (adapted from Whalen, Henker, Swanson, Granger, Kliewer, & Spencer, 1987, p. 189):

1. *Appropriate social behavior* (e.g., conversing, initiating social contact, participating in an ongoing game)
2. *Negative social behavior* (e.g., rule-breaking, noncompliance, disruption, teasing, verbal or physical aggression)
3. *Nonsocial behavior* (e.g., solitary play, daydreaming, bystanding)

The categories are mutually exclusive and allow for the monitoring of appropriate and inappropriate interpersonal behavior and social and nonsocial interpersonal behavior.

Appendix F shows two other coding systems. Table F-1 in Appendix F is a coding system for observing children's play, with three global categories and four subcategories. And Table F-2 in Appendix F is a 28-item behavioral observational system for observing the social competence of preschool children; it classifies behavior according to such dimensions as interest, apathy, cooperation, and anger.

Coding Systems for Observing Teachers' Behavior

Observational coding systems also are useful for studying the behavior of classroom teachers. Assessing a teacher's behavior is important, because the teacher's behavior may affect the referred child's behavior and the classroom climate. The two-, three-, and six-category systems shown in Table 9-3 provide a record of the teacher's interactions with a specific child or with the class as a whole.

Coding Systems for Observing Students, Teachers, and Classes

The separate coding systems designed for students and teachers can be combined to form a more complete coding system, and additional categories for entire classes can be added. Table 9-4 illustrates one such combined coding system, which emphasizes appropriate as well as inappropriate behaviors. Eleven student behavior codes (six on-task behaviors, four off-task behaviors, and one neutral behavior) are included, along with four teacher codes and two class codes.

Example of a Recording Method and Coding System Combined

Exhibit 9-1 describes an event recording method combined with a three-category coding system that can be used in observing aggressive behavior on a playground. Exhibit 9-2 describes an interval recording method combined with a staff-resident interaction coding system that can be used to

---

Table 9-3
Examples of Coding Systems for Observing Teachers' Behavior

Coding system	Examples
I. Two Categories	
1. Verbal Approval Responses (comments that follow an on-task behavior)	"Bob, your spelling has improved considerably."
2. Verbal Disapproval Responses (comments that follow an off-task behavior)	"Class, stop making noise."
II. Three Categories	
1. Praise (verbalization indicating that the teacher was pleased with a student's behavior)	"John, your reading was excellent."
2. Prompts (verbalization conveying additional information or directing a student's attention to the task)	"The first step in solving the problem is to divide the sales price by the number of items purchased."
3. Criticism (verbalization indicating that the teacher was displeased with a student's behavior)	"Mary, do not talk during the reading assignment."
III. Six Categories	
1. Academic Approval	"Your score was much improved."
2. Academic Disapproval	"Your study habits are not satisfactory."
3. Social Approval	"I am pleased with your ability to work with Helen."
4. Social Disapproval	"Your relationship with your teammates is poor."
5. Inappropriate Approval or Disapproval	Informing child that behavior was satisfactory or unsatisfactory when there was no evidence that it was
6. No Approval or Disapproval	Absence of behaviors that could be recorded as approval or disapproval

Table 9-4
Coding System for Observing Students and Teachers in the Classroom

Student Code Summaries

Attending (AT)	The student must be (a) looking at the teacher when the teacher is talking, (b) looking at the materials in the classroom that have to do with the lesson, or (c) engaged in other attending behavior appropriate to the academic situation.
Working (WK)	The student is working on academic material, either in a group or individually, and is not talking.
Volunteering (VO)	By verbal or nonverbal means, the student responds to teacher requests by volunteering academic information.
Reading Aloud (RA)	The student is reading aloud, either individually or as part of a group recitation.
Appropriate Behavior (AB)	This is a broad category used to code appropriate behavior not otherwise specifically defined, including asking or answering questions, raising hand for help, and acquiring or distributing materials.
Interaction with Peer about Academic Materials (IP+)	The student is interacting with a peer or peers about academic materials (e.g., talking, handling materials, working with others on materials) and is not violating classroom rules.
Interaction with Peer about Nonacademic Materials (IP−)	The student is interacting with a peer or peers about academic materials inappropriate for the period in which the observation occurs (unless this has been approved by the teacher) or about nonacademic materials. The interaction may be verbal or nonverbal.
Don't Know (DK)	The child indicates, in either a verbal or a nonverbal manner, that he or she does not know the answer.
Inappropriate Locale (IL)	The child, without the teacher's approval, is in a classroom area that is not appropriate for the academic activity that is occurring at the time.
Looking Around (LA)	The child is looking away from the academic task at hand.
Inappropriate Behavior (IB)	This is a second broad category, used to code inappropriate behaviors not otherwise defined. Behaviors include calling out an answer when a question is directed to another student and interrupting the teacher or another student who is talking.

Teacher Code Summaries

Approval (AP)	The teacher gives a clear verbal or nonverbal signal of approval to the student or to the group of which the student is a member.
Disapproval (DI)	The teacher gives a clear verbal or nonverbal signal of disapproval to the student or to the group of which the student is a member.
No Response (NR)	The teacher does not respond to the student, either as part of the group or individually.
Verbal Interactions (VI)	The teacher directs verbalizations that are not approval or disapproval to the child or her or his group. Verbalizations may relate to instruction or management.

Class Code Summaries

Appropriate Behavior (AB)	The entire class (all students) is engaged in activities that are considered appropriate to the situation, as defined by the teacher's rules and the activity at hand.
Inappropriate Behavior (IB)	At least one student in the class is engaged in behaviors not considered appropriate according to the teacher's rules and the activity at hand.

Source: Adapted from Greenwood, Hops, Walker, Guild, Stokes, Young, Keleman, and Willardson (1979).

Exhibit 9-1
Naturalistic Observation on a Playground: Recording Aggressiveness and Related Behaviors

---

Coding Categories

Three classes of problem behaviors were observed:

1. *Aggression:* Striking, slapping, tripping, kicking, pushing, or pulling others; "karate" moves ending within 1 foot of another person; doing anything that ends with another child's falling to the ground.
2. *Property abuse:* Taking another person's property without permission; throwing school books, lunches, or anyone else's property; throwing any object at passing or parked cars; digging holes in the ground with one's feet or hands; breaking pencils or pens or other objects.
3. *Rule violations:* Resisting or talking back to an aide; climbing more than 1 foot off the ground on a playground structure not meant for climbing; jumping off a playground structure that is more than 3 feet off the ground.

The Playground Observation System

To adapt to the existing geography (e.g., building corners and edges of playground equipment), the playground was divided into three roughly equivalent "pie slices," which were the responsibility of separate observers. These slices were then halved (again, as defined by other permanent structures), and each half was monitored for alternate 15-second periods. Thus, an observer attended to only one-sixth of the playground at a time, and only half the playground was observed at any given moment.

Three observers stood in the middle of the playground facing their areas. A tape recording instructed them to start watching the left-hand portion of their section, at which time they began recording incidents with the aid of hand counters. After 15 seconds, the tape cued a "switch" to the remaining portion of the observer's area. This continued for 2 minutes, when a "stop" signaled that the cumulative frequency of incidents observed was to be entered on the data sheets. The entire process occurred in 10 iterations (i.e., observe left for 15 seconds, observe right for 15 seconds, then observe left again, then right again, and so on, recording the totals every 2 minutes), from 8:20 to 8:40 a.m.

A given inappropriate incident (e.g., one child's kicking another child) was counted only once per 15-second interval. However, more than one incident was scored if one child displayed several types of aggression toward another (e.g., one child's hitting and kicking another was counted as two incidents). If two children assaulted a third individual or one child assaulted a third individual or one child assaulted two peers, two incidents were scored. The 15-second intervals were arbitrarily considered to be independent; thus, if two children were observed to be wrestling with each other for two intervals, four incidents were recorded.

Reliability

Reliability was determined by interobserver checks conducted on various days.

Source: Adapted from Murphy, Hutchison, and Bailey (1983).

---

study efforts at rehabilitation of individuals with mental retardation. The detailed coding system in Exhibit 9-2 allows analysis of various staff-resident interactions, whereas the playground coding system in Exhibit 9-1 focuses on aggressive behaviors only. The playground coding system could, of course, be expanded to include other behavioral categories.

Designing or Selecting a Recording and Coding System

Keep the following in mind when you are designing or selecting a recording and coding instrument and conducting a behavioral observational assessment:

1. Design or select a coding system that reflects the behaviors of concern.
2. Use categories sparingly; do not overload the coding system.
3. Use categories that are easily identifiable and clearly defined.
4. Select the recording method that best fits the coding system.
5. Select an interval length obat matches the duration of the target behavior.
6. Select a length of time for the observations that is sufficient to reveal the most salient features of the target behavior without taxing your ability to record accurately.
7. Schedule the observation period so that it coincides with the times of day when the target behavior is most likely to occur.
8. Conduct observations across multiple settings and on multiple occasions, if possible.
9. Design or select an appropriate recording sheet, with clearly labeled precoded categories and spaces for your entries.
10. Conduct a general observation prior to formulating your specific observational strategy.
11. Design or select a final assessment strategy likely to detect the target behaviors of interest, given their typical rate and duration.

RELIABILITY

The data you obtain from behavioral observations, like the data you obtain from any other assessment procedure, must be reliable and valid. Establishing interobserver agreement

Exhibit 9-2
Naturalistic Observation in an Institution for Children with Mental Retardation: Recording Staff and Residents' Efforts at Rehabilitation

Coding Categories

Behaviors of both staff and residents were recorded. The following coding categories were used for staff and resident behaviors:

STAFF BEHAVIORS

1. *No interaction*—no physical or verbal interaction between the staff member and any resident.
2. *Verbal instruction*—through standard language (i.e., either vocal or manual communication), staff instructs the resident to perform some activity and offers no physical assistance.
3. *Nonverbal instruction*—through a nonverbal gesture (not including manual communication), staff instructs the resident to perform some activity and offers no physical assistance.
4. *Verbal instruction with physical assistance*—through standard language (i.e., either vocal or manual communication), staff instructs the resident to perform some activity and provides physical assistance (e.g., guides resident through a self-dressing task with verbal aid).
5. *Nonverbal instruction with physical assistance*—through a nonverbal gesture (not including manual communication), staff instructs the resident to perform some activity and provides physical assistance (e.g., points to the door and guides resident to move toward the door).
6. *Physical assistance*—without prior verbal or nonverbal instruction, staff physically assists resident (e.g., staff helps resident put on his or her shoes).
7. *Social*—staff claps for, praises, hugs, etc., resident.
8. *Custodial guidance*—staff physically assists resident in a custodial manner in a non-task situation (e.g., ties shoes of resident in order to allow resident to move along quickly with other residents).

RESIDENT BEHAVIORS

1. *On-task*—resident emits a verbal or motor response to a question, command, instruction, or nonverbal cue (e.g., a gesture by the staff) or complies without making an overt response when no overt response is necessary or appropriate (e.g. looking at pictures in a book).
2. *Off-task*—in the presence of a cue for responding, resident either does not respond, responds inappropriately, or does not look at relevant task stimuli.
3. *No programming*—nothing is being asked of the resident, being demonstrated to the resident, or being provided for the resident to do.
4. *Self-aggressive*—resident intentionally strikes, bites, slaps, hits, or kicks own body or brings his or her body forcefully into contact with other objects.

5. *Other aggressive*—resident intentionally strikes at, throws objects at, verbally threatens, or in some other way threatens to harm another resident or a staff member.
6. *Self-stimulatory*—resident engages in solitary activity but actively manipulates some object(s) or is engaged in solitary, asocial, repetitive behavior (e.g., rocking, headweaving).

Recording Procedure

For 16 days, four observers each recorded for 250 minutes per day. Each person observed in one of five locations for about 50 minutes. Then the observer walked to another location and recorded for another 50 minutes. This procedure was followed from about 9:30 to 11:20 a.m.and from 1:00 to 3:50 p.m. each day, until each observer had recorded in the five locations. Sites were rotated so that no observer was in a site more than once per day and so that each site was observed by each person about the same amount of time. Data were recorded at 6-second intervals, with the intervals being signaled through earplugs by a portable tape recorder. At the end of each interval, the observer marked any response category that had occurred within the 6-second interval.

Other than simply marking what had just occurred, observers were to observe three recording rules:

(a) After observation of a staff member, observers were required to record something. If none of the seven response categories occurred, the observer marked the no interaction category.
(b) After each observation of a resident, observers were to record on-task, off-task, or no programming only if it had just occurred.
(c) If more than one resident or staff response occurred in the same interval, both could be marked (e.g., self-stimulatory and off-task responding).

Reliability

Interobserver agreement was assessed each day by randomly assigning a second observer to the various recording sites. This produced about 40 hours of reliability assessment. Observations were coordinated by using a y-plug from the tape recorder that allowed each observer to hear the beginning of each successive interval. Because each observer marked something at the end of each 6-second interval and because the observers were 3 meters apart, the observations were quite independent. Interobserver agreement was calculated by dividing the number of intervals in which both observers agreed by the total number of intervals.

Source: Adapted from Repp and Barton (1980).

will ensure that your observations are replicable and consistent (reliable), which in turn will help establish their accuracy (validity). In the observation of behavior, reliability and validity are influenced by several factors, including the observer; the setting; the coding system; the child, parent, teacher, other target person, or group; and the interactions among these sources. Any of these can be a source of error, as shown in Table 9-5. Although most of Table 9-5 requires no explanation, some types of observer errors warrant further comment.

Table 9-5
Sources and Types of Errors in Observations of Behavior

Source of error	Type of error
Personal qualities of the observer	*Central tendency*—Observer uses the middle category of a rating scale more frequently than the end categories and, in the process, tends to underestimate intense behaviors and overestimate weak behaviors.
	Leniency or generosity—Observer makes overly positive judgments about the referred child.
	Primacy effect—Observer allows first impressions to have a distorting effect on later impressions or judgments.
	Halo effect—Observer makes judgments based on a general impression of the referred child or the child's most salient characteristic.
	Personal theory—Observer fits the observations to his or her personal theoretical assumptions.
	Personal values—Observer fits the observations to his or her personal expectations, values, and interests.
	Overestimation of traits or behaviors that are barely self-acknowledged—Observer overestimates in the referred child traits and behaviors that observer barely acknowledges in himself or herself.
	Logical error—Observer makes similar judgments about traits that seem to be logically related.
	Contrast error—On specific traits, observer judges the referred child to be more different from himself or herself than the child actually is.
	Proximity error—Observer judges specific traits as similar because the format of the observation places them close together in time or space.
	Personal effects—Without observer's knowing it, his or her personal characteristics (such as age, sex, race, and status) affect the referred child's behavior.
	Observer drift—Over time, observer changes the criterion (or threshold) for judging the presence or absence of a behavior because of fatigue, additional information, or other variables.
	Omission—Observer fails to score behavior that has occurred.
	Commission—Observer miscodes behavior.
	Expectancy effects—Observer's expectations influence what he or she records; or, observer expects something to happen and communicates these expectations to the child.
	Observer reactivity—Observer changes recording of behavior when he or she is aware of being observed.
	Nonverbal cues—Observer unintentionally cues the child nonverbally and by so doing reinforces certain behaviors.
Setting, codes, scales, and instruments	*Unrepresentative behavioral setting*—Observer selects only one setting or only one time period and thereby fails to sample representative behaviors adequately.
	Coding complexity—Observer cannot use codes accurately because (a) the system has too many categories, (b) the observer must score too many categories on a given occasion, and/or (c) the observer must score too many children on a given occasion.
	Influence of extraneous cues—Certain events in the environment influence observer to score the occurrence of a behavior when the behavior is not occurring.
	Rating scales—Observer inappropriately uses broad-category rating scales to classify behaviors and thereby loses fine distinctions.
	Mechanical instruments—Observer fails to check the accuracy of mechanical devices used for recording data (for example, stopwatch or counter).
The referred child (or children)	*Child reactivity*—Referred child changes his or her behavior or attitude or adopts a role because he or she is aware of being observed and of having behavior measured.
	Response to cues—Referred child responds in a manner that conforms to cues from the observer.
	Behavior drift—Child's behavior continues, but in a form that drifts outside the range of definitions being used.
The sample (usually large samples or groups)	*Unrepresentative sample*—Observer fails to obtain a representative sample of the population.
	Sample instability—Observer fails to recognize population changes over time, making it difficult to compare results of present sample with those of previous samples.
	Unrepresentative data—Observer fails to recognize geographical and regional differences in behavior between samples.

Source: Adapted from Fassnacht (1982).

Errors committed by the observer in the course of an observational assessment are referred to as *observer bias*. The term encompasses anything an observer does that distorts the recording of behavior, such as allowing expectations to influence his or her observations, using certain categories or scale positions to excess and neglecting others, showing leniency by not recognizing the severity of an observed behavior, allowing his or her attention to wander, or allowing the recording to be influenced by extraneous cues. Observers are susceptible to the influence of halo effects, prior information about the child, qualities of the setting, and expectations of others. A behavior that does not clearly fit a particular category is more likely to be affected by observer bias than is a behavior that fits a category clearly.

The following examples illustrate observer bias:

- Observers' expectations that a referred child will act aggressively influence them to record marginally aggressive acts as aggressive, whereas other observers without this expectation would record the same acts as nonaggressive.
- An extraneous cue, such as the teacher's praising a referred child for completing a previous assignment, leads observers to record on-task behavior in the observation interval, even though the referred child is not working on the current class assignment.
- Observers change the way they observe when they know that they are being observed by a supervisor or when they are told that their records will be compared with those of another observer. This tendency to be more careful, vigilant, and attentive to details when they know they are being evaluated is referred to as *observer reactivity*. Interestingly, when observers know they are being observed, their accuracy tends to increase (Foster & Cone, 1986).

When observation continues over a long period, observers may show signs of forgetfulness, fatigue, and decreased motivation. For example, an observer may begin with one standard for scoring aggression, but over time change that standard. This *observer drift* may occur even when observers use specific definitions of behavior.

Reliability may be more difficult to achieve with global categories; global categories, such as *off-task behavior* or *inappropriate behavior,* require a higher level of inference than do specific categories, such as *hitting* or *out-of-seat behavior.* And although you should attempt to define target behaviors precisely, some behaviors may be difficult to categorize. For example, how will you distinguish between merely staring into space and thinking about a problem? Using observational codes often requires careful judgment.

The timing of a sequence of events is not as simple as it appears. For example, when exactly does a child's refusal to eat begin and end? The time unit selected by the observer may not always correspond exactly to the behavioral event.

You may not always be able to see or hear the child you are observing. For example, the child may wander out of view, turn his or her face away from you, whisper when you are trying to record what he or she is saying, or suddenly leave the room to go to the bathroom.

Chapter 2 discusses general procedures for evaluating reliability. We now consider reliability procedures specific to observational methods. Three useful estimates of the reliability of observational coding are interobserver reliability, test-retest reliability, and internal consistency reliability. *Interobserver reliability is the most important form of reliability for behavioral observations. Without interobserver reliability, the other forms of reliability have little meaning.*

Interobserver Reliability

Estimates of interobserver reliability (also called *interobserver agreement*) are usually based on scores of two or more observers who record the same information while *simultaneously* and *independently* observing the same child or group (Nay, 1979). The data may be in the form of categorical judgments or interval scale ratings. Interobserver agreement can be affected by several factors, including the type of data collected (e.g., narrative, interval, event, ratings), the complexity of the coding system, the clarity of the behavioral definitions, and the length of the observation period.

Once observational data have been collected by two or more observers, it is important to select and compute an appropriate statistical index of agreement. Several procedures are available for measuring interobserver reliability, including correlational coefficients (such as the product-moment correlation coefficient, or phi coefficient, and the intraclass correlation coefficient) and percentage agreement indices (such as kappa and uncorrected percentage agreement). These procedures measure different aspects of interobserver agreement and may yield different reliability estimates for the same set of data. A computerized system for computing interobserver reliability, called The Observer, offers a flexible procedure for obtaining reliability data (Jansen, Wiertz, Meyer, & Noldus, 2003).

Product-moment correlation coefficient. If you are interested in the pattern of agreement among the observers' ratings, irrespective of the actual level of agreement (i.e., irrespective of whether the observers use the same absolute ratings), and you are using an interval scale of measurement, then the *product-moment correlation coefficient* is a satisfactory measure of reliability. The product-moment correlation coefficient is sufficient when you simply want to establish whether one measure is linearly related to another measure. It does not tell you the extent to which the observers used exactly the same ratings. As an index of the agreement between observers, the product-moment correlation coefficient is usually not the method of choice, except with rating scale data. The *phi coefficient* is a particular version of the product-moment correlation coefficient used when the data are dichotomous—that is, in the form of 1s and 0s. The phi coefficient is applicable to a 2 × 2 table only. Table 2-4 in Chapter 2 shows the formulas for computing the product-moment correlation coefficient and the phi coefficient.

Intraclass correlation coefficient. When both the pattern of agreement and the level of agreement are important and you have used an interval scale of measurement, you can use the *intraclass correlation coefficient* as a measure of reliability (McGraw & Wong, 1996; Shrout & Fleiss, 1979; Wong & McGraw, 1999). This correlation coefficient is useful when you have several sets of scores on one variable and no way of ordering the scores within a set. A computer program is available for computing four different intraclass correlation coefficient estimates (Strube, 1985).

Kappa. When the data form an ordinal scale and you are interested in correcting for chance agreement, *kappa* (κ) is a useful index of agreement (Cohen, 1960, 1968). Kappa considers both the occurrence and the nonoccurrence of behavior, corrected for chance agreement among observers. It is appropriate in situations in which there are no independent criteria or bases for independent expert evaluation. Kappa measures the degree of consensus among observers; it evaluates precision, but not whether the observations are valid. Kappa is one of the preferred measures of interrater reliability and can be used for multiple observers and multiple categories. Exhibit 9-3 shows procedures for computing kappa. A computer program is available for computing kappa for multiple observers, multiple categories, and missing data (Oud & Sattler, 1984).

Kappa should not be used when the observed behaviors occur infrequently, because kappa has high variability in such situations (Shrout, Spitzer, & Fleiss, 1987). For example, kappa should not be used when there is a shift from high levels of the problem behavior (such as hitting) during a preintervention baseline period to low levels of the problem behavior (little or no hitting) during or after treatment. Kappa values of .75 or higher indicate excellent agreement, values of .40 to .74 indicate fair to good agreement, and values below .40 indicate poor agreement.

Percentage agreement. When you want a measure of the percentage agreement among two or more observers but are not concerned with correcting for chance agreement, you can use an uncorrected percentage agreement index. *Uncorrected percentage agreement,* which is simply the percentage of cases in which two or more observers agree, is likely to be an overestimate of agreement when chance agreement is high. Although percentage agreement is not synonymous with reliability, it is useful as a preliminary check of the adequacy of your observational recordings, because it is easy to compute and interpret and is sensitive to bias and systematic errors. In the material that follows, we will refer to uncorrected percentage agreement as *percentage agreement.*

Interval recording percentage agreement estimate. With interval recording, you can use several percentage agreement measures for determining interobserver agreement. Three such measures are overall agreement, agreement on the occurrence of the behavior, and agreement on the nonoccurrence of the behavior. The key difference among the three measures is the specific interval used to determine the level of interobserver agreement. Let's use the data in Figure 9-1 to calculate these three interobserver percentage agreement measures.

Exhibit 9-3
Procedures for Computing Kappa (κ)

Kappa (κ) is a useful statistic for measuring interobserver reliability (or interobserver agreement) for categorical data. Kappa indicates the proportion of agreements, corrected for chance agreements. Like correlation coefficients, kappa ranges from +1.00 to −1.00. When kappa is positive, the proportion of observed agreement is *more than* would be expected by chance. When kappa is equal to zero, the proportion of observed agreement *equals* what would be expected by chance. When kappa is negative, the proportion of observed agreement is *less than* what would be expected by chance.

Suppose two observers scored one child over 100 intervals for the occurrence or nonoccurrence of a behavior. Observer 1 scored the occurrence of the behavior in 90 intervals, and Observer 2 scored the occurrence of the behavior in 80 intervals. In this situation, there must be some agreement, because both observers scored more than 50 intervals. The figure shows that, for the two observers, the lowest possible number of overlapping occurrence intervals (that is, intervals scored identically by the two observers) is 70. This minimum overlap of 70 intervals occurs when 10 of the occurrence intervals scored by Observer 2 correspond to the 10 nonoccurrence intervals scored by Observer 1. In this case, the correction for chance agreement in the kappa formula is 72%. The procedure for obtaining the chance correction is discussed below.

Kappa can be used for multiple categories and multiple raters. Formulas are presented below for computing kappa for (a) two observers and multiple categories and (b) the special case of two observers and two categories (2 × 2 contingency table). Formulas for computing kappa for multiple categories as well as for multiple raters are found in Conger (1980) and Uebersax (1982). Uebersax presents a generalized kappa formula that is also appropriate for handling missing data.

Exhibit 9-3 *(Continued)*

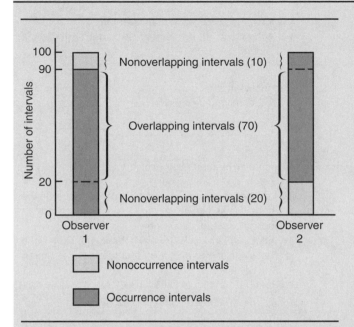

Nonoverlapping intervals (10)

Overlapping intervals (70)

Nonoverlapping intervals (20)

Observer 1   Observer 2

☐ Nonoccurrence intervals

▨ Occurrence intervals

Kappa for Two Observers and Multiple Categories

To introduce the general kappa formula for two observers and multiple categories, let us set up a 3 × 3 contingency table representing two observers and three recording categories. The designations for the contingency table are as follows:

Observer 2

		C_1	C_2	C_3	
	C_1	n_{11}	n_{12}	n_{13}	n_{1+}
Observer 1	C_2	n_{21}	n_{22}	n_{23}	n_{2+}
	C_3	n_{31}	n_{32}	n_{33}	n_{3+}
		n_{+1}	n_{+2}	n_{+3}	N

Each cell is designated by two subscripts. The first subscript refers to the row, the second to the column. Thus, n_{23} designates the cell in the second row, third column. The rows and columns correspond to the three different observation categories (C_1, C_2, C_3). The marginal totals for Observer 1 are designated by n_{1+}, n_{2+}, and n_{3+}, and those for Observer 2 are designated by n_{+1}, n_{+2}, and n_{+3}.

The general formula for kappa is

$$\kappa = \frac{p_o - p_c}{1 - p_c}$$

where p_o = the observed proportion of agreement
  p_c = the proportion of agreement expected by chance alone

The computational formulas for p_o and p_c are

$$p_o = \frac{\sum_{i=1}^{C} n_{ii}}{N}$$

$$= \frac{n_{11} + n_{22} + n_{33} + \cdots + n_{ii}}{N}$$

$$p_c = \frac{\sum_{i=1}^{C} (n_{i+})(n_{+i})}{N^2}$$

$$= \frac{(n_{1+} \times n_{+1}) + (n_{2+} \times n_{+2}) + (n_{3+} \times n_{+3}) + \cdots + (n_{i+} \times n_{+i})}{N^2}$$

where n_{ii} = total number of agreements for the ith category (main diagonal)
  n_{i+} = marginal total for Observer 1 on the ith category
  n_{+i} = marginal total for Observer 2 on the ith category
  N = total number of observation periods (for example, intervals)

Let us apply this formula to some hypothetical data obtained by two observers who scored the same child over 10 intervals, using three observation categories. The three codes used by the two observers were verbal off-task (VO), motor off-task (MO), and on-task (OT). The data were as follows:

Interval	Observer 1	Observer 2
1	VO	MO
2	VO	VO
3	MO	MO
4	OT	OT
5	OT	OT
6	VO	VO
7	MO	MO
8	MO	VO
9	MO	MO
10	VO	VO

Placing these scores in a 3 × 3 contingency table gives us the following:

		Observer 2			
		VO	MO	OT	
	VO	3	1	0	4
Observer 1	MO	1	3	0	4
	OT	0	0	2	2
		4	4	2	10

(Continued)

Exhibit 9-3 *(Continued)*

To calculate kappa, we first obtain p_o and p_c:

$$p_o = \frac{n_{11} + n_{22} + n_{33} + \cdots + n_{ii}}{N}$$

$$= \frac{3 + 3 + 2}{10} = \frac{8}{10} = .80$$

$$p_c = \frac{(n_{1+} \times n_{+1}) + (n_{2+} \times n_{+2}) + (n_{3+} \times n_{+3}) + \cdots + (n_{i+} \times n_{+i})}{N^2}$$

$$= \frac{(4 \times 4) + (4 \times 4) + (2 \times 2)}{10^2} = \frac{16 + 16 + 4}{100}$$

$$= \frac{36}{100} = .36$$

Then we put the values of p_o and p_c into the formula for kappa:

$$\kappa = \frac{.80 - .36}{1 - .36} = \frac{.44}{.64} = .69$$

If a straight percentage agreement had been used, the level would have been 80% (or the value of p_o). Kappa gives us a coefficient of .69, a somewhat lower level of agreement. A kappa of .70 is considered to indicate an acceptable level of agreement.

Kappa for a 2 × 2 Contingency Table

We now consider kappa for the special case of binary ratings, with two observers and two observation categories (e.g., occurrence/nonoccurrence) in a 2 × 2 contingency table.

		Observer 2		
		O	NO	Total
	O	a	b	$a + b$
Observer 1	NO	c	d	$c + d$
	Total	$a + c$	$b + d$	N

The general formula for kappa, as we have seen, is

$$\kappa = \frac{p_o - p_c}{1 - p_c}$$

In a 2 × 2 contingency table, p_o is computed by dividing the sum of the two cells in which both observers agree by the total number of observation periods or intervals (N); p_c is computed by adding the products of the marginal frequencies and then dividing this value by the total number of observation periods or intervals squared.

Thus,

$$p_o = \frac{a + d}{N}$$

$$p_c = \frac{(a + b)(b + d) + (a + c)(c + d)}{N^2}$$

where p_o = observed proportion of agreement
p_c = proportion of agreement expected by chance alone
N = total number of observation periods

A computationally more convenient formula for computing kappa in a 2 × 2 contingency table is

$$\kappa = \frac{2(ab - bc)}{(a + b)(b + d) + (a + c)(c + d)}$$

where a = number of intervals in which Observer 1 and Observer 2 scored the behavior as occurring
b = number of intervals in which Observer 1 scored the behavior as occurring and Observer 2 scored the behavior as not occurring
c = number of intervals in which Observer 1 scored the behavior as not occurring and Observer 2 scored the behavior as occurring
d = number of intervals in which Observer 1 and Observer 2 scored the behavior as not occurring

The data for two observers who scored one child over 100 intervals are summarized as follows:

		Observer 2		
		O	NO	Total
	O	20	6	26
Observer 1	NO	2	72	74
	Total	22	78	100

$$\kappa = \frac{2(ab - bc)}{(a + b)(b + d) + (a + c)(c + d)}$$

$$= \frac{2[(20 \times 72) - (6 \times 2)]}{(26 \times 78) + (22 \times 74)} = \frac{2(1440 - 12)}{2028 + 1628}$$

$$= \frac{2(1428)}{3656} = \frac{2856}{3656} = .78$$

For the above data, p_o, the observed proportion of agreement, is

$$p_o = \frac{a + d}{N} = \frac{20 + 72}{100} = \frac{92}{100} = 92\%$$

and p_c, the proportion of agreement expected by chance alone, is

$$p_c = \frac{(a + b)(a + c) + (c + d)(b + d)}{N^2}$$

$$= \frac{(26 \times 22) + (74 \times 78)}{100^2}$$

$$= \frac{6344}{10,000} = 63\%$$

Again, a kappa of .78 is a more conservative estimate of interobserver agreement than the 92% agreement rate, which is uncorrected for chance.

	1	2	3	4	5	6	7	8	9	10
Observer 1	X	O	X	O	X	O	O	X	O	X
Observer 2	X	O	X	X	X	O	O	O	X	X

Note: X indicates occurrence of behavior; O indicates nonoccurrence of behavior

Figure 9-1. Raw data for three interobserver percentage agreement measures.

Overall agreement. Overall agreement considers the total number of intervals and the occurrence or nonoccurrence of a behavior in each interval. Agreement occurs when both observers score either the occurrence or the nonoccurrence of a behavior in a given interval. The procedure for calculating overall agreement as follows:

1. Considering all intervals, make two counts—one of the number of intervals in which the observers agreed on the occurrence or nonoccurrence of a behavior and one of the number of intervals in which they disagreed.
2. Divide the number of agreements by the total number of agreements plus disagreements and multiply by 100. The result is the percentage of interobserver agreement for the total number of intervals.

The formula for overall interobserver percentage agreement is as follows:

$$\%A_{\text{IR tot}} = \frac{A_{\text{tot}}}{A_{\text{tot}} + D} \times 100$$

where $\%A_{\text{IR tot}}$ = interval recording percentage agreement for the total number of intervals

A_{tot} = number of intervals in which Observer 1 and Observer 2 agreed on whether the behavior occurred or did not occur

D = number of intervals in which Observer 1 and Observer 2 disagreed on whether the behavior occurred or did not occur

Example: The two observers in Figure 9-1 agreed that the target behavior occurred or did not occur in intervals 1, 2, 3, 5, 6, 7, and 10 (seven agreements), but disagreed about intervals 4, 8, and 9 (three disagreements). Therefore, there was a 70% rate of agreement in scoring the target behavior over the total number of intervals recorded:

$$\%A_{\text{IR tot}} = \frac{A_{\text{tot}}}{A_{\text{tot}} + D} \times 100$$

$$= \frac{7}{7 + 3} \times 100$$

$$= \frac{7}{10} \times 100 = 70\%$$

Agreement on occurrence of behavior. A measure of agreement on the occurrence of a behavior considers only those intervals in which at least one of the two observers recorded the occurrence of a behavior. Agreement occurs when both observers score the occurrence of a behavior in a given interval. The calculation is similar to the one used for total observations, except that you use only a portion of the intervals.

1. Considering only those intervals in which at least one of the two observers recorded the occurrence of a behavior, make two counts—one of the number of intervals in which the observers agreed on the occurrence of a behavior and one of the number of intervals in which the observers disagreed.
2. Divide the number of agreements by the total number of agreements plus disagreements and multiply by 100. The result is the percentage of interobserver agreement for those intervals in which at least one observer scored the behavior as occurring.

The formula for interobserver percentage agreement for behavior occurrence is a variant of the one used for overall percentage agreement:

$$\%A_{\text{IR occ}} = \frac{A_{\text{occ}}}{A_{\text{occ}} + D} \times 100$$

where $\%A_{\text{IR occ}}$ = interval recording percentage agreement for intervals in which occurrence of behavior is scored

A_{occ} = number of intervals in which both observers agreed that the behavior did occur

D = number of intervals in which the observers disagreed on whether the behavior occurred

Example: The two observers in Figure 9-1 agreed that the target behavior occurred in intervals 1, 3, 5, and 10 (four agreements), but only one of the observers scored an occurrence of the behavior in intervals 4, 8, and 9 (three disagreements). Thus, there was a 57% rate of agreement in scoring the target behavior as occurring:

$$\%A_{\text{IR occ}} = \frac{A_{\text{occ}}}{A_{\text{occ}} + D} \times 100$$

$$= \frac{4}{4 + 3} \times 100$$

$$= \frac{4}{7} \times 100 = 57\%$$

If neither observer records any occurrence of a target behavior, you cannot calculate a reliability index for the observation.

Agreement on nonoccurrence of behavior. A measure of agreement on the nonoccurrence of a behavior considers only those intervals in which either one or both observers recorded the nonoccurrence of a behavior. Agreement occurs when both observers score the nonoccurrence of a behavior in a given interval. The calculation is similar to the one described above.

1. Considering only those intervals in which at least one of the two observers recorded the nonoccurrence of a behavior, make two counts—one of the number of intervals in which the observers agreed on the nonoccurrence of a behavior and one of the number of intervals in which the observers disagreed.
2. Divide the number of agreements by the total number of agreements plus disagreements and multiply by 100. The result is the percentage of interobserver agreement for those intervals in which the observers scored the behavior as not occurring.

The formula for interobserver percentage agreement for behavior nonoccurrence is another variant of the one used for overall percentage agreement:

$$\%A_{\text{IR non}} = \frac{A_{\text{non}}}{A_{\text{non}} + D} \times 100$$

where $\%A_{\text{IR non}}$ = interval recording percentage agreement for intervals in which nonoccurrence of behavior is scored

A_{non} = number of intervals in which both observers agreed that the behavior did not occur

D = number of intervals in which the observers disagreed on whether the behavior did not occur

Example: The two observers in Figure 9-1 agreed that the target behavior did not occur in intervals 2, 6, and 7 (three agreements). In intervals 4, 8, and 9, however, only one of the observers scored the nonoccurrence of the behavior (three disagreements). Thus, there was a 50% rate of agreement in scoring the target behavior as not occurring:

$$\%A_{\text{IR non}} = \frac{A_{\text{non}}}{A_{\text{non}} + D} \times 100$$

$$= \frac{3}{3 + 3} \times 100$$

$$= \frac{3}{6} \times 100 = 50\%$$

If neither observer records any nonoccurrence of a target behavior, you cannot calculate an agreement index for the observation.

Comment on interval recording percentage agreement estimates. When observers score the occurrence of a behavior in only a small proportion of intervals, compute inter-observer percentage agreement only for those intervals in which the observers scored occurrence of the behavior; the use of total intervals might cause some distortion of the rate of agreement. For example, suppose that, in a 100-interval observation period, one observer scored occurrence of the target behavior in three intervals and the other observer scored occurrence of the behavior in one of those three intervals. The observers' rate of agreement in scoring occurrence of the behavior is 33%. Use of the total intervals would result in an agreement rate of 98%. The 33% agreement figure more accurately represents the observers' ability to identify the target behavior when it occurs.

When observers score occurrence of a behavior in a large proportion of the intervals, you might want to study the rate of agreement of nonoccurrence of the behavior. In this case, you would use the third method discussed above.

When you use more than one category in an observation system, as is common, you must decide whether to evaluate interobserver agreement for the total observations, for the separate categories, or for both. We recommended that you compute interobserver agreement for each category as well as for the total observations. This will give you valuable information about where potential difficulties may lie, such as with the coding system or with the observers. *Consider a percentage agreement of 80% or above as satisfactory.*

Event recording percentage agreement estimate. With event recording, you can estimate interobserver percentage agreement by dividing the number of occurrences of the event reported by the observer recording the lower frequency f_l by the number of occurrences of the event reported by the other observer f_h. The percentage agreement formula for event recording is as follows:

$$\%A_{\text{ER}} = \frac{f_l}{f_h} \times 100$$

Example: Two observers recorded out-of-seat behavior, the target event. During a 20-minute observation period, one observer recorded 5 occurrences of the behavior and the other observer recorded 8 occurrences. Substitute into the formula as follows:

$$\%A_{\text{ER}} = \frac{f_l}{f_h} \times 100$$

$$= \frac{5}{8} \times 100 = 62.5\%$$

There was 62.5% agreement between the two observers on the number of occurrences of the target behavior. This level of agreement does not mean that the observers recorded the same instances of the target behavior, however. It could be that there were 13 occurrences of the target behavior, 5 of which were recorded by one observer and 8 of which were recorded by the other. The level of agreement simply indicates that the ratio of number of events reported by the two observers was 5/8. Unless the observational recording procedure used specific intervals or times, there is no way of knowing whether the two observers recorded the same events.

Duration recording percentage agreement estimate.

The interobserver percentage agreement estimate for duration recording is similar to the one used for event recording. The percentage agreement formula for duration recording is as follows:

$$\%A_{DR} = \frac{t_1}{t_h} \times 100$$

Example: Two observers recorded the target event of a child's staring out the window. One observer timed an episode at 360 seconds; the other, at 365 seconds. Substitute into the formula as follows:

$$\%A_{DR} = \frac{t_1}{t_h} \times 100$$

$$= \frac{360}{365} \times 100 = 98\%$$

Thus, there was 98% agreement between the two observers on the duration of the behavior of staring out the window. This level of agreement does not mean that the observers recorded the duration of the same target behavior, however. It could be that the child stared out the window for a total of 400 seconds and the two observers recorded different times when the behavior occurred.

Ratings recording percentage agreement estimate.

With ratings recording, you can estimate interobserver percentage agreement by determining whether the two observers gave the same rating on each scale. The percentage agreement formula for ratings recording is as follows:

$$\%A_{RR} = \frac{A_{rr}}{A_{rr} + D} \times 100$$

where　$\%A_{RR}$ = ratings recording percentage agreement for the total number of rating scales

　　　　A_{rr} = number of scales in which both observers agreed on the rating

　　　　D = number of scales in which the observers disagreed on the rating

Example: After a 30-minute observation period, two observers completed ten 5-point rating scales. They agreed on ratings for eight of the 10 scales. Substitute into the formula as follows:

$$\%A_{RR} = \frac{A_{rr}}{A_{rr} + D} \times 100$$

$$= \frac{8}{8 + 2} \times 100 = \frac{8}{10} \times 100 = 80\%$$

Thus, there was 80% agreement between the two observers in their ratings.

In ratings recording, the more points there are on a scale, the finer the discrimination an observer must make in rating a behavior; thus, for example, a 7-point scale requires finer discriminations than a 3-point or 5-point scale. Hence, the more categories you have in a rating scale, the lower the interobserver percentage agreement is likely to be. Normally, percentage agreement considers only the absolute level of agreement; that is, you count an agreement only when both observers give exactly the same rating. This method of calculating agreement does not consider the pattern of ratings—for example, if one observer is consistently one scale position above (or below) the other observer, you still count a disagreement for each scale. An alternative approach is to count an agreement when the two observers are no more than one scale position apart. This is a less stringent method but still provides information about the pattern of observer agreement. In ratings recording, you also may want to compute a product-moment correlation coefficient (or intraclass correlation coefficient) to determine the pattern of agreement between the two observers.

Comment on interobserver reliability.

Do not confuse percentage agreement indices with product-moment correlation coefficients—they do not mean the same thing (Moore, 1987). For example, a percentage agreement of 60% does not express the same degree of interobserver reliability as $r = .60$. In fact, when the phenomenon of interest occurs in about 50% of the observations, a percentage agreement of 50% yields $r = .00$, a percentage agreement of 75% yields $r = .50$, and a percentage agreement of 95% yields $r = .90$. When the phenomenon of interest occurs rarely or frequently, the range of correlation coefficients associated with each percentage agreement rate is considerable. Depending on whether the phenomenon occurs rarely, about half the time, or frequently, a percentage agreement of 50% yields interobserver reliability correlation coefficients ranging from $r = -.12$ to $r = .02$, a percentage agreement of 75% yields interobserver reliability correlation coefficients ranging from $r = .23$ to $r = .50$, and a percentage agreement of 90% yields interobserver reliability correlation coefficients ranging from $r = .76$ to $r = .90$.

Obtaining satisfactory interobserver reliability does not ensure that data are meaningful or accurate. High reliabilities may be associated with observation codes that are relatively insensitive to the occurrence of important or meaningful behaviors. Or behaviors may occur at levels beyond those included in the observation codes. Thus, high agreement between observers is no guarantee that the observational system provides accurate measurements of behaviors related to a problem. And after the observations are completed, inferences must be made and conclusions drawn. This is by no means a foolproof process. Different observers may draw different conclusions from the same set of observations.

Test-Retest Reliability

The consistency of behavior over time and situations is another measure of the reliability of behavioral observations. You should strive to sample the target behaviors more than once and in more than one setting. You can use the interval recording percentage agreement formulas to evaluate test-retest reliability. You can also use various correlational procedures, depending on the scaling of the data. For example, you can assess intraindividual stability by correlating the frequency of each targeted behavior observed on one occasion with the frequency of each targeted behavior observed by the same observer on another occasion. The product-moment correlation coefficient that you obtain does not allow you to evaluate which of the behaviors show more or less stability, because you compute the correlation across all categories. By scanning the changes from the first to the second observation period for each category, however, you can obtain some idea of which categories show the most change.

Instability in behaviors may result from changes in the child, the setting, the observer, the definitions of the behaviors used by the observer, or the methods used for the observation. Determine which factor or combination of factors is responsible for the instability by carefully studying all sources of data and the procedures you used in the observational assessment.

Internal Consistency Reliability

Internal consistency reliability reflects how consistent the components of an assessment instrument are in measuring the same characteristics. One way of obtaining internal consistency estimates is to divide the observation measure into two equal parts (e.g., odd- and even-numbered items). Chapter 2 describes formulas for measuring internal consistency reliability. You also can use factor analysis, discriminant function analysis, and various correlational procedures (depending on the scaling of the data) to evaluate the consistency of items in observational coding systems.

VALIDITY

Chapter 2 discusses general procedures for evaluating validity. In this section we cover validity procedures specific to observational methods. Ensuring the validity of behavioral observations is often problematic, because it is difficult to obtain an adequate and representative sample of behavior in a short time. Acquiring an adequate and representative sample of behavior would require sampling in many different types of situations, and this is rarely practical. Validation criteria include ratings from others familiar with the child and observations in controlled experimental situations. But these criteria are not absolute and do not offer proof of validity. A further difficulty arises when two indices purporting to measure the same behavior are not in agreement (e.g., differences in event and ratings recording). Because behavior is variable, it is possible that both measures are accurate, even though the measures show poor agreement.

Here are some examples of how you might establish the validity of an observational coding system designed to evaluate hyperactivity. For *content validity,* you could ask, "Do the behaviors coded (e.g., fidgeting, out-of-chair movements) reflect the nature and degree of hyperactivity displayed during the observation?" For *construct validity,* you could ask, "Do the behaviors coded constitute a satisfactory and functional definition of hyperactivity?" For *criterion-related concurrent validity,* you could ask, "Do the behaviors coded accurately reflect the child's reactions in other situations?" For *criterion-related predictive validity,* you could ask, "Do the behaviors coded predict other important criteria?" If your answers to the above questions are yes, you can be fairly certain that you are measuring hyperactivity.

Representativeness and Generalizability of Findings

Two major factors affecting the validity of an observational assessment are the *representativeness* and the *generalizability* of the findings. For example, to what degree does the behavior observed during the time-sampling procedure reflect behavior in the total time period and behavior in other situations to which you want to generalize the findings? Or, to what degree is the narrative recording, event recording, or ratings recording representative of the referred child's behavior in similar settings? Consider these questions each time you evaluate your observational assessment.

Reactivity

A child's behavior under observation may be affected by the child's awareness that someone is observing him or her, by the child's prior interactions with the observer, or by the observer's personal characteristics. We refer to this effect as *reactivity,* or the *guinea pig effect.* Reactivity, in this sense, refers to changes in the behavior of the observed child that are related to the presence of the observer. Ordinarily, these changes are unwanted, because they distort the child's usual pattern of behavior, which is of major interest to the observer. For example, a child who is usually aggressive may avoid aggressive behavior when an observer is present. (Similarly, parents, teachers, or teacher aides may refrain from engaging in socially undesirable behaviors, such as emotional abuse or excessive punishment, when they are aware of being observed.) Whether the child is conscious of being observed depends on several factors, including the child's age, degree of sophistication, familiarity with the observer, and previous experience with being observed; the setting; the number of children in the setting; the number of children being observed; and the conspicuousness of the observer.

To minimize reactivity, conduct your observations as unobtrusively as possible. Recognize that what you observe may not necessarily be typical of the child's behavior. Reactivity presents a significant threat to the validity of the observational assessment. In some cases, it may be better to have an observer whom the child knows, whereas in other cases it may be better to have someone unfamiliar to the child. If you have a choice in selecting the observer, your knowledge of the case should guide your selection.

Reactive effects may be indicated by (a) atypical changes in the child's behavior, (b) increased variability in the child's behavior, (c) the child's own admission that his or her behavior changed as a result of being observed, (d) reports from others that the child's behavior changed when the child was being observed, and (e) discrepancies between different measures of the same behavior (Haynes & Horn, 1982). Although these indices do not prove that reactive effects are present, they suggest that such effects may be operating.

Harris and Lahey (1982) believe that reactivity is often so powerful that it clouds the observational data. "Unless it has been well-documented that reactivity is not a factor in a given situation, observational data may be taken as a demonstration that a particular behavior is in a [child's] repertoire, but not that it is performed in the absence of observation" (p. 536).

Not everyone agrees, however, that reactivity is necessarily detrimental to observational assessment. Cone and Foster (1982), for example, noted that reactivity may pose problems for some research and clinical objectives but not for others.

> The important issue seems to be not whether observed individuals react differently under conditions of known observation but rather whether data collected under such conditions are less useful than those collected surreptitiously.
>
> In this vein it is conceivable that reactive data may have even greater utility or social validity than nonreactive data in some circumstances. This could occur when you wish to generalize to situations involving similar levels of obtrusive observation. For example, in assessing the adequacy of vocal presentations before audiences, it is probably the case that data obtained from conditions in which the client is aware of being observed will correlate more highly with subsequent real-life presentations. . . . As Barker and Wright (1954) pointed out long ago, interaction between an observer and a person observed is important in its own right, not just a potential confounding element to be uniformly eliminated or controlled. (p. 343, with changes in notation)

Reactivity also is useful because it may suggest possible interventions (Galen Alessi, personal communication, March 2000). For example, a child who reacts positively to the mere presence of an observer clearly can control some negative behavior.

PROCEDURES FOR REDUCING ERRORS IN OBSERVATIONS

Reducing Errors in Reliability

You can use several procedures to reduce errors that compromise reliability. A first step is to familiarize yourself with the errors listed in Table 9-5 and then try to avoid or limit them when you perform behavioral observations. You can reduce

or eliminate many of these errors simply by practicing your observational skills. To eliminate others, you may need to further refine your recording procedures and rating scales.

You can increase reliability by (a) using clear and precise definitions of behaviors, (b) following systematic and precise rules governing the observations, (c) becoming well trained in observational procedures, and (d) using observation periods that are not excessively long. Although observer drift is difficult to control, you can reduce it by frequently checking your recordings, becoming thoroughly familiar with the recording system beforehand, and making periodic calibrations during the observation session to check the consistency of your observations (e.g., determining whether you are using the recording system in the same way as other observers and whether your understanding of the definitions has changed during the course of the observation).

You also can increase reliability by reviewing your decision criteria—such as when to report that a behavior did or did not occur—and then comparing your decision criteria with those of other observers. Signal detection approaches can be useful in achieving these goals (Lord, 1985). These approaches focus on an observer's ability to detect stimuli, considering the observer's response style (e.g., whether the observer uses liberal or conservative decision criteria). In some cases, using global categories to classify behavior (such as *sociable* vs. *unsociable* or *sensitive* vs. *insensitive*) may be unwise, because global categories—which require more inferences than narrow categories (such as *out of seat* vs. *in seat*)—are more susceptible to observer bias. Global categories have their place, but narrow categories may give you more precision.

Comparing Observation Results with a Criterion

During your training, regularly compare your results with those of a highly trained observer or with standard criterion recordings. The agreement between an observer's recordings and standard criterion recordings is referred to as *criterion-related agreement*. Even trained observers should periodically compare their results with those of another observer or standard criterion recordings to evaluate the reliability of their observations.

Another method of checking the reliability of your ratings is to videotape the behavior of a child (or class). (Always obtain parental permission before making a videotape recording.) After recording your observations in the setting in which the behaviors occur, rate the child's behavior again from the videotape. The level of agreement between the two recordings is a measure of the reliability of your ratings. This method is generally used for training purposes only, and it may overestimate reliability because your memory of the first observation may affect your second observation.

If possible, also compare your observations of the videotape with the observations of an expert and those of one or two peers. Thoroughly discuss any disagreements, and compute estimates of interobserver agreement. Low interobserver percentage agreement may mean that categories are not clearly defined, that one (or more) of the observers does not understand the observational codes, or that other factors are interfering with agreement. You may be able to increase interobserver reliability by practicing observational assessment in environments similar to those in which you will work, whether during site visits or from videotaped recordings.

An acceptable level of interobserver agreement does not rule out observer error, however. You can have a high level of interobserver agreement and still have observer bias and observer drift if both observers have a similar bias or make similar errors. This especially may happen when you compare two of your own recordings.

Reducing Reactivity

Although reactivity may be useful in limited cases, you will most often want to minimize it. To this end, here are some suggestions (Nay, 1979):

1. *Limit your stimulus value—become as neutral a stimulus as possible.* Do not dress or act in a manner that attracts attention. Avoid making eye contact with or interacting with the referred child or any other children during the observation period. To provide a rationale for your presence in the classroom, the teacher might say to the class, "Ms. A is here today to see what we do." At the beginning of each school year, make a few short visits to each class so that the children become accustomed to seeing you.

2. *Position yourself so that you are away from the ordinary paths of movement in the classroom and yet still have an unobstructed view of the child and setting.* A good position in the classroom is often to the rear or side of the room. You want to have as clear a view as possible of everything occurring in the classroom.

3. *Shift your attention from one child to another.* By so doing, you will avoid calling attention to any individual child.

4. *Follow all rules, regulations, and informal policies of the school, institution, or family.* Before going into a classroom, institution, or home, review your specific procedures with the teacher, administrative personnel, or the parents.

5. *Enter the setting when your entrance will least disrupt the ongoing behavior.* For classroom observations, enter the classroom before class begins or at break time. If possible, try to be in the setting for a period of time *before* beginning the formal observation. If the teacher, family, or children become used to your presence, their behavior may be more natural, and less reactive, when the formal observation begins.

6. *Use distance observation.* In some settings, you can observe the referred child from a room with a one-way mirror, from a classroom that overlooks the playground, or from a video monitor.

These suggestions will help you become a more natural part of the setting and diminish the child's awareness of your presence. Awareness by itself does not necessarily affect the child's behavior—but if and when it does, the validity of the observation is jeopardized. The reason for the assessment may determine how much influence your presence will have on the child's behavior. A child who knows that the results of the assessment will be used to determine her or his class placement (or some other outcome) may be more affected by your presence than a child who believes that the results will have little or no bearing on her or his status.

If you conduct the observations *prior* to interviewing or testing a child, the child is less likely to feel concerned about your being in the classroom. Additionally, when you do work with the child, the child may have a sense of familiarity with you from the beginning: "Oh, you're the lady who was in my class the other day."

Establishing Informal Norms

Developing informal norms will help you place the child's behavior in a meaningful context. In a group setting, you might observe the behavior of the referred child and that of one or more peers (Alessi, 1980). The behavior of the child's peers can then serve as a norm (sometimes referred to as a "micro-norm") against which you can compare the behavior of the referred child. The peers should be children of the same age and sex as the referred child, who have not been identified as experiencing behavior problems and who are as representative of the total peer group as possible. From this pool, you can randomly select one or more children for comparison.

Another procedure is to establish local norms for the entire class, using the scan check method. The scan check method involves scanning the entire class for, say, 2 seconds every 2 minutes (for a period of 8 to 10 minutes) and recording how many students are engaging in the target behavior. Still another procedure for establishing informal norms is to compare the child's present behavior with his or her past behavior, thereby using the child as his or her own norm, or standard.

Obtaining a peer or class rating permits you to measure the difference between the frequency with which the referred child engages in a particular behavior and the frequency with which the peer or class does. You can compute a discrepancy ratio to summarize the results of peer or class comparisons. A *discrepancy ratio* is the difference between the median level of the referred child's behavior and the median level of the peer's (or class's) behavior. You could describe the referred child who is off-task six times per minute while his or her peers are off-task three times per minute as "off-task twice as often as his or her peers."

Here is an example of how you can obtain informal norms (Alessi, 1980). Assume that a teacher referred Robert for his talking-out and out-of-seat behaviors in class. You observe Robert along with Todd, who has not been identified as talking out or being out of seat excessively and is considered an "average" child in this regard. Every few minutes, you also scan the class and note how many of the children are talking out or are out of their seats. You obtain the following results:

	Instances of talking-out behavior	Instances of out-of-seat behavior
Robert	20	10
Todd	2	1
Class (%) (6 scans)	3% (1/30)	6% (2/30)

These data suggest that Robert engages in more inappropriate behavior than does either the comparison child or the class as a whole. If you accept these data as reflecting approximate norms for these behaviors in this class, you can conclude that Robert's behaviors deviate from the norm. In this example, both a comparison child and local class norms provide standards for interpreting the behavior of the referred child. Without these standards, it would be difficult to know whether Robert's behavior was deviant.

Some Potential Problems and Suggested Solutions

Following are some potential problems associated with classroom observation and suggested solutions (Alessi, 1980, 1988).

Problem 1. The observation occurs during a part of the day in which the child does not exhibit the problem behavior.

Suggestion: Confer with the teacher before you schedule your observations. For example, ask the teacher the following questions: "When does this behavior occur most often? At what times? Which day or days of the week? During which subjects? When might I have the best chance of witnessing the behavior? When is the behavior at its worst?" Then arrange your schedule to observe the child at a prime time. Whenever possible, spread your observations over three or four 10-minute sessions, rather than one 30-to-40-minute session, and across a week or two. Also, find out what, if anything, might be different about the day or the part of the day when you made your observation. The fact that the referred child's inappropriate behavior did not occur during the observation is a positive sign because it indicates that the behavior may be under some voluntary control.

Problem 2. The comparison child whom you select or who is selected for you also has a behavioral problem.

Suggestion: You can control this potential difficulty by consulting with the teacher about selecting an "average" child or by selecting a different comparison child for each 10-minute observation period.

Problem 3. The critical behaviors that you need to observe are poorly defined.

Suggestion: Further discussion with the teacher about the child's problems may eliminate this potential source of difficulty. For example, suppose a teacher has referred a child for talking-out behavior, but on the few occasions on which the child talks out, the talking is laced with profanity. Discussion with the teacher

may clarify that the teacher is more concerned with the content of the child's outbursts than their frequency. Learning of the teacher's true concern puts you in a better position to develop more appropriate interventions.

Problem 4. The child has been referred for reasons other than those given, either because the teacher does not want to state the primary reason for the referral or because the teacher has a hidden agenda. For example, the teacher may want the child removed from the classroom for behavior problems but refer the child for poor academic performance.

Suggestion: This may be the most difficult problem to solve. Its solution depends on the teacher's willingness to discuss his or her feelings about the referred child openly with you. Teachers may not be aware of their own hidden agendas. Good consultation and interviewing skills (see Chapters 5 to 7) are especially important in this situation. Determining the teacher's standards can also be valuable. Some teachers have rigid standards; others have lenient standards. For example, some teachers want children to be perfectly behaved, whereas others accept less perfect behavior without becoming too concerned.

Problem 5. The level of the child's problem behavior differs from task to task within the same class.

Suggestion: Examine the way each task is taught. It may be that different teaching practices are used for each task. Also consider the possibility that the child's ability varies from task to task, and that the child acts out when frustrated.

Problem 6. The interval recording method does not capture the changes in behavior.

Suggestion: Check to see how frequently the behavior is occurring and what kind of interval was selected for recording the behavior. For example, suppose the behavior occurs steadily about six times a minute, but the interval selected is a 1-minute interval. You will not be able to detect a change to one occurrence per minute because you record only one instance per interval. The solution is to use an interval short enough to match the frequency with which the behavior occurs.

General Guidelines for Obtaining Reliable and Valid Observations

The following general guidelines will assist you in conducting reliable and valid behavioral observations:

1. Understand thoroughly the recording techniques, rating scales, checklists, mechanical instruments, and/or computer program used for the observations. Be sure that the critical behaviors are highly specific and clearly defined.
2. Before beginning the observations, check the accuracy of all mechanical instruments used for data collection.
3. Use a timer that is silent. If your timing device beeps, modify it so that it does not beep while you conduct the observation.
4. Train yourself to be a critical observer of behavior.
5. Draw samples of behavior from various situations and at different times during the day, particularly when you are observing groups of children or developing norms.

6. Discover what biases, faults, and weaknesses you may have that influence your observation of behavior. Develop self-understanding and critical self-evaluation skills.

7. Do not accept previous reports about the referred child's behavior uncritically; make every effort to be as objective as possible.

8. While you are recording data, suppress assumptions and speculations about the meaning and implications of the child's behavior.

9. Consider whether reactivity affected your findings and conclusions.

10. Consider what factors precipitate and maintain the child's behavior and how other individuals in the child's setting respond to the behavior.

11. Compare your observations periodically with those of an independent observer who is using the same scoring system.

12. Recalibrate your recordings regularly by checking them against standard protocols.

13. Keep abreast of observation research and theory.

You cannot avoid having beliefs and expectations; what you can and must avoid is prejudging what you observe. Your observations will be affected by the child's behavior; the reasons for the referral; your willingness to record a behavior as occurring or not occurring (i.e., your decision criteria); your familiarity with the behavioral observational coding system; the amount of time you spend observing; your experience with children with special needs (these include children with physical disabilities, mental health problems, or behavioral problems, or children who are gifted); and your familiarity with the referred child. Similar factors may also affect a co-observer's recordings. An understanding of these factors will help you obtain more reliable and valid recordings.

OBSERVATIONS OF INFANTS

Observing an infant in her or his natural environment (e.g., at home) and seeing how the infant interacts with the parents will be a useful part of a formal assessment. The guidelines in Table 9-6 will help you observe several facets of an infant's behavior: interactions with play materials and involvement in play, affect in play, attention span in play, temperament and motivation, auditory responsiveness, expressive language, motor behavior, eating patterns, and general behavior.

Although most of the information needed to classify an infant's temperament will come from a caregiver, observations are useful. The following nine dimensions may be used for classifying an infant's temperament (Laucht, Esser, & Schmidt, 1993; Medoff-Cooper, Carey, & McDevitt, 1993; Chess & Thomas, 1986; Willis & Walker, 1989).

1. *Activity level* refers to the amount of physical motion displayed by the infant during sleeping, eating, playing, dressing, bathing, and so forth. An active infant is charac-

terized by much movement and fitful sleep; the caregiver is likely to feel that he or she cannot leave the infant alone for even a few seconds for fear that the infant will move or fall. Note whether the infant appears to have a normal activity level or is hyperactive or hypoactive.

2. *Rhythmicity* refers to the regularity of the infant's physiological functions, such as hunger, sleep, and elimination. A rhythmic infant has regular feeding times, sleeping times, and times for bowel movements. Note whether the infant has predictable rhythmicity or is dysrhythmic.

3. *Approach or withdrawal* refers to the nature of the infant's initial responses to new stimuli, including people, situations, places, foods, toys, and procedures. An infant with an approach tendency approaches people eagerly and reacts well to new people and new surroundings. Note whether the infant has a tendency to approach or shows resistance to change.

4. *Adaptability* refers to the ease or difficulty with which the infant's reactions to stimuli can be modified in an appropriate way. An adaptable infant adjusts easily to unexpected company, new people, new foods, and unfamiliar settings. Note whether the infant appears to be adaptable or is slow to adapt.

5. *Threshold of responsiveness* refers to the amount of stimulation, such as sound or light, necessary to evoke discernable responses in the infant. An infant with a good threshold of responsiveness adjusts well to noises, textures of clothing, heat, cold, and environmental sounds, such as the ring of a telephone or a siren. Note whether the infant appears to be normally responsive or is hypersensitive or hyposensitive.

6. *Intensity of reaction* refers to the energy level of the infant's responses. Note whether the infant displays a high level of intensity (e.g., displays pleasure or displeasure vigorously), a moderate level of intensity (e.g., displays pleasure or displeasure moderately), or a low level of intensity (e.g., displays pleasure or displeasure minimally).

7. *Quality of mood* refers to whether the infant's behavior tends to be pleasant, joyful, and friendly or unpleasant, peevish, and unfriendly. An infant with a joyful mood is happy and content overall and displays this mood in varied situations. Note whether the infant's mood is happy or dysphoric.

8. *Distractibility* refers to the ability of extraneous environmental stimuli to interfere with or alter the direction of the infant's ongoing behavior. An infant who is not distractible can continue with current activities, such as eating, despite some noise or people entering the room. Note whether the infant is minimally, moderately, or highly distractible.

9. *Attention span and persistence* refer to how long the infant pursues particular activities and the extent to which he or she continues activities in the face of obstacles. An infant with a good attention span and persistence can stay with an activity for a period—when the infant drops a toy, for instance, he or she looks for the toy and then persists at

Table 9-6
Guidelines for Observing Infants

Guideline 1. Observe the infant's interactions with play materials and involvement in play.
Note, for example:

- How does the infant examine, touch, and manipulate objects (e.g., actively, passively)?
- What objects hold special interest for the infant (e.g., those that make sounds; those made of wood, plastic, or cloth; those that can be used as containers)?
- How does the infant play with toys that can be used in several ways (e.g., small boxes with tops; nesting toys; cubes and containers with lids, including pots and pans)?
- How does the infant approach new situations or objects (e.g., with anticipation, fearfully)?
- How much encouragement does the infant require to become involved in play (e.g., little encouragement, much encouragement)?
- How does the infant show interest in a toy (e.g., looks at the toy, makes grasping movements toward the toy)?
- How does the infant's interest vary with different activities?
- How intense is the infant's play?
- How much time does it take the infant to become involved in playing with a toy?
- How does the infant's behavior change when he or she is given time to explore an object or use materials?
- How often does the infant achieve goals in play?
- What does the infant do after being interrupted in an activity (e.g., goes back to the activity, goes to a new activity)?

Guideline 2. Observe the infant's affect in play.
Note, for example:

- What emotions does the infant show during play (e.g., happiness, anger, tension, irritability, sadness)?
- How does the infant express likes and dislikes (e.g., smiles, whines, laughs, cries)?
- How does the infant react when he or she is given a new object, discovers a new way to use a toy, or is given just enough help to succeed in an activity?
- What activities frustrate the infant?
- What does the infant do when frustrated (e.g., cries, reacts stoically, looks for caregiver)?

Guideline 3. Observe the infant's attention span in play.
Note, for example:

- What activities hold the infant's attention the longest?
- How does the infant explore objects (e.g., attends briefly, attends for a long period of time, turns object frequently)?
- How long does the infant play with an object?
- What toys does the infant select (e.g., those that keep him or her involved and interested for a reasonable time, those that are nearest)?

Guideline 4. Observe the infant's temperament and motivation.
Note, for example:

- What is the infant's temperament (e.g., active or passive, content or fussy, relaxed or tense, engaged or unfocused, sleepy or alert, cuddly or rigid, easy to comfort or difficult to comfort)?
- What distresses the infant, and how does the infant show distress (e.g., frowns, turns away, makes sounds, kicks)?

- What cues does the infant give that she or he is overstimulated, bored, frustrated, happy, or involved?
- How consistent is the infant's tempo across several activities?
- How does the infant's tempo compare with that of the infant's parent(s)?
- How persistent is the infant in pursuing a goal in play in the face of obstacles?
- How interested is the infant in activities?
- What changes in temperament does the infant show during the observation?

Guideline 5. Observe the infant's auditory responsiveness.
Note, for example:

- How does the infant respond to the spoken language of others (e.g., becomes attentive, animated, quiet; looks up when someone calls his or her name; looks at a ball when it is mentioned; touches his or her nose when it is named)?
- What is required to get the infant's attention (e.g., clapping hands, talking loudly, using dramatic gestures)?
- How does the infant attend to language when there is background noise?

Guideline 6. Observe the infant's expressive language.
Note, for example:

- What sounds does the infant make?
- Does the infant babble or use jargon (e.g., as if participating in others' conversation) or make playful sounds (without seeming to participate in others' conversation)?
- What vocalizations does the infant make in various situations (e.g., when excited, when a parent is on the telephone, when a parent watches, when engaged in solitary play)?
- How does the infant react to his or her own vocalizing (e.g., becomes more animated, shows no particular reaction)?
- What does the infant do when making certain sounds (e.g., looks consistently at the same object when making a specific sound, such as "baba" for blanket or "ga" for cracker; makes sounds without specific referents)?
- How does the infant express wants or needs (e.g., makes sounds, kicks feet, points, crawls somewhere)?
- How does the infant communicate without using vocal language?
- How does the infant react when he or she continues making a certain sound and does not get a response?

Guideline 7. Observe the infant's motor behavior.
Note, for example:

- What fine- and gross-motor behaviors does the infant show (e.g., ability to handle objects of different sizes and shapes, ability to throw a ball, ability to move)?
- What is the quality of the infant's motor behaviors (e.g., normal motor development, delayed motor development, disturbed motor development)?
- How does the infant react when staying in one place for long periods?
- How does the infant's motor behavior change in different situations?
- How does the infant show newly acquired or emerging skills (e.g., persists in repeating skills, performs skill only once or a few times)?
- What does the infant do when encouraged to perform a motor movement for which he or she is not developmentally ready?

(Continued)

Table 9-6 (*Continued*)

Guideline 8. Observe the infant's eating patterns.
Note, for example:

- What cues does the infant give indicating a readiness to eat (e.g., reaches for bottle, spoon, or food; opens mouth eagerly)?
- How is the infant fed (e.g., breast fed, bottle fed, breast and bottle fed, fed with solid food and finger foods)?
- How does the infant feed himself or herself (e.g., with fingers, with utensils)?
- What foods does the infant eat (e.g., liquids, solids, soft foods, chewable foods)?
- How does the infant react to being fed (e.g., sucks, swallows, or chews food eagerly; pushes food or bottle away; holds food in mouth without chewing or swallowing; vocalizes to avoid eating; becomes easily distracted from feeding)?

Guideline 9. Observe the infant's general behavior.
Note, for example:

- What are the infant's best-developed skills?
- How does the infant's behavior vary in different activities (e.g., when engaged in play, in social behavior, in language, in motor activities)?
- How does the infant react to people (e.g., familiar adults, children, strangers)?
- What atypical behaviors does the infant display (e.g., fails to cuddle, cries excessively, rocks constantly, bangs head)?
- In what situations are the atypical behaviors displayed (e.g., with mother, with father, with both parents, with babysitter, with stranger present along with caregiver, with siblings, with other relative)?
- How does the infant indicate readiness for some independence (e.g., plays alone, sits on floor alone)?

Note. Record specific instances of each behavior, where appropriate, and the conditions under which the behavior occurred.

---

trying to retrieve it. Note whether the infant shows a good, moderate, or poor attention span.

These nine dimensions, in turn, lead to three temperamental types (Willis & Walker, 1989, p. 35, with changes in notation):

1. The *easy infant* is one who is mild, predominantly positive in mood, approachable, adaptable, and rhythmic.
2. The *difficult infant* is one who is predominantly negative and intense in mood, not very adaptable, and dysrhythmic.
3. The *slow-to-warm-up infant* is one who is low in activity and adaptability, withdrawn, and variable in rhythm.

CAUTIONS ON THE USE OF OBSERVATIONS

Observational methods, like other assessment procedures, have their strengths and weaknesses.

STRENGTHS

1. Observation of behavior can yield a representative picture of the typical behavior of a child; can help in the formulation of hypotheses about important dimensions of temperament, personality, and interpersonal relations; and can provide information about the development and adjustment of the child to his or her physical and social surroundings.
2. Observed behavior may differ from that reported by teachers and parents and by children themselves.
3. Observation of behavior provides information that cannot be gained in other ways from uncooperative children.
4. Observation of behavior can yield a more finely differentiated picture of the child's reactions than can broader

measures such as test scores or numbers of right and wrong responses.

5. Observation of behavior may yield valid data.
6. Observation of behavior can be tailored to the specific concerns of the referral source.
7. Important psychological concepts, such as attitude, role, and motivation, make most sense when anchored at a behavioral level with observations.
8. Observation of behavior is important in evaluating and monitoring the progress of treatment and remediation programs.
9. Exact descriptions of behavior patterns aid in developing treatment and remediation programs and provide a basis for making decisions about a child—such as whether the child should be admitted into a treatment program, special home, hospital, or juvenile detention center.

WEAKNESSES

1. The observer may view an unrepresentative sample of the child's behavioral repertoire.
2. The observer may influence the child's behavior in uncontrollable ways.
3. Observation rooms with one-way screens are not a natural environment in which to observe behavior.
4. Situational constraints may preclude observations that could contribute to an understanding of the child.
5. Societal norms impose constraints on observations, placing great emphasis on the privacy of the child's and family's personal life.
6. Children may feel anxious when they are being observed.
7. Classroom observations may make teachers feel intruded on and insecure, even though it is the child who is primarily being observed.
8. There are no generally accepted systems of observation.

9. Certain observational systems are tied to narrowly focused theories.
10. Achieving interobserver reliability is a problem.
11. Observation of behavior is a costly method of data collection in terms of personnel, time, and materials.
12. Inferential statistics are difficult to apply to data obtained in observations, particularly because observational methods must necessarily sample behaviors, times, and situations.

The strengths of naturalistic observation also contribute to its weakness as a scientific procedure: It is difficult to standardize naturally occurring stimulus conditions, and human observers are fallible. These weaknesses must be considered when you conduct observations and evaluate the results.

Although it may be tempting to observe just a single behavior or a few behaviors, consider the disadvantages. First, you may preconsciously identify behaviors according to how easily you can observe and record them. Second, the observation of a few behaviors may complicate detection of other behaviors—either positive or negative—that reveal important information about a child. If you still decide to focus on a single behavior, remain aware of the child's other behaviors as well.

Consider any possible unintended harmful consequences associated with your behavioral observations, and be sure to take appropriate steps to avoid such outcomes. For example, going into a work setting to observe an adolescent who has been in an inpatient unit could cause the adolescent to be identified, labeled, and ostracized. In such cases, you may need to observe the adolescent from a distant location.

SELF-MONITORING ASSESSMENT

You can obtain valuable information about a particular behavior by asking a child to conduct a self-monitoring assessment. (Here we use the term *behavior* to include the child's actions, thoughts, and feelings.) In a *self-monitoring assessment,* the child observes and records specific overt or covert aspects of her or his behavior and, sometimes, the circumstances associated with the behavior over a specified period. To perform a self-monitoring assessment, the child must discriminate the presence or absence of a particular response (e.g., a thought, an action performed by the child himself or herself, or an action performed by another) and record the response in a behavioral log or diary or use a golf counter, wrist counter, mechanical device, or hand-held computer. The appropriate procedure depends on how easy the target behavior is to detect, the response frequency, the age and intellectual ability of the child, and how easy the procedure is to use. The goal is to have the child make a systematic record of the behaviors of interest, gain awareness of her or his behavior, and participate in resolving the problem.

Recording their own behavior may help children become better observers of their behavior. The recordings also may help them discriminate changes in their problem behaviors and see how their problem behaviors change over time and across situations. Self-monitoring also enables children with problems to recognize that they are not helpless, but can do something to change their own behavior.

A child's self-monitoring of the frequency of symptoms, changes in symptoms, activity level, mood ratings, and situational contexts will give you information about antecedent and consequent events associated with the child's symptoms. With this information, you are in a better position to formulate hypotheses about the relationship between environmental or situational variables and the child's problem. For example, you may find a relationship between particular settings and the child's problem (e.g., the problem appears at school but not at home) or a relationship between stressful events and problem expression (e.g., the problem appears before a test but not before a picnic).

Self-monitoring assessment has several advantages (Bornstein, Hamilton, & Bornstein, 1986; Tunks & Billissimo, 1991):

1. It minimizes the use of retrospective reporting, thereby diminishing the chance of memory errors or other distortions.
2. It can aid the child in answering questions about his or her behavior.
3. It may sensitize the child to his or her problem behavior and to the situations in which the problem behavior occurs.
4. It provides a relatively objective picture of the child's behavior, because it tends to minimize the child's reactions to being observed by someone else, such as defensiveness and the withholding of information, thereby reducing (but not eliminating) reactive effects.
5. It provides information about the child's behavior in different settings and over a period of time.
6. It is helpful in obtaining information about private behavior (e.g., covert thoughts or feelings, levels of anxious or depressed feelings) or behaviors that are relatively rare (e.g., a self-inflicted wound, a panic attack, a seizure, a migraine headache, or an eating binge).
7. It provides a baseline of the frequency, intensity, duration, latency, and other characteristics of the presenting problem before an intervention is begun.
8. It can be done anywhere and is cost effective.
9. It often has good reliability and validity, depending on the task and the child's ability.

Setting Up a Self-Monitoring Assessment

Setting up a self-monitoring assessment involves selecting the appropriate target behaviors, identifying the variables that may relate to those behaviors, and choosing a recording procedure that is easy to use and provides adequate and accurate information. Here are some factors to consider in setting up a self-monitoring assessment:

1. Frequency of the behavior (e.g., five times a day)
2. Onset of the behavior (e.g., at the beginning of the class)
3. Quality of the behavior (e.g., depressive behavior)

4. Intensity of the behavior (e.g., crying ranging from mild to severe)

5. Duration of the behavior (e.g., 3 minutes)

6. Latency of the behavior (e.g., 1 hour after instructions are given)

7. Situation in which the behavior occurs (e.g., on the playground)

8. Antecedent events associated with the behavior (e.g., not chosen to be on a team)

9. Consequent events associated with the behavior (e.g., sent to the assistant-principal's office)

Following are examples of self-monitoring strategies that can be used for specific types of problems in children (Peterson & Tremblay, 1999; Shapiro & Cole, 1999):

1. *Self-monitoring of on-task behavior.* The child reports instances of paying attention to teacher or parent, cleaning up after an activity, or working on an activity.

2. *Self-monitoring of academic skills.* The child records the number of problems completed on a worksheet, the number of correct answers to math problems, the number of words written in an essay, or the number of words spelled correctly.

3. *Self-monitoring of study methods and goals.* The child sets goals and then determines whether he or she makes progress toward the goals and reaches them.

4. *Self-monitoring of social anxiety* (primarily for older children). The child records the frequency and duration of contacts with others, the number of social interactions, or the rate of speech difficulty.

5. *Self-monitoring of asthma.* The child takes readings of breathing capacity, records when medication is taken, and records the severity of the asthma attacks.

6. *Self-monitoring of other behavioral and nonacademic problems.* The child records disruptive behaviors, compliance with teacher's daily expectations (e.g., bringing necessary materials to class, writing homework assignments in a notebook, completing class assignments, completing homework, completing classroom chores), social skills, stereotypical behaviors (e.g., number of hairs pulled out), or inappropriate verbalizations.

Implementing a Self-Monitoring Assessment

In implementing a self-monitoring assessment, consider the child's age, motivation, and cognitive level and how these factors may affect her or his ability to do the recording. The child should understand fully how to use the recording procedure and how to recognize the target behaviors. Here are some guidelines (Korotitsch & Nelson-Gray, 1999; Mace & Kratochwill, 1988).

1. *If the self-monitoring form requires reading ability, be sure that the child can read at the required level.*

2. *Focus on a single target behavior.*

3. *Select a positive target behavior rather than a negative one, if possible.*

4. *Give the child a clear and simple definition of the behavior to be monitored and recorded.* The child needs to know as clearly as possible what the target behavior is that he or she is to record and must be able to distinguish the target behavior from other similar behaviors. Define the behavior clearly and use illustrations as needed; you can write, use pictures, or invent other methods to present the definitions, depending on the child's level of functioning. When appropriate, include the definition on the recording form.

5. *Provide clear and simple instructions on how to perform the self-monitoring task.* Inform the child about how to monitor the behavior. For example, give the following instructions to a child who needs to record the number of math problems completed correctly: "First, set the timer for 25 minutes [demonstrate]. Second, do as many math problems on the worksheet as you can until the timer rings. Third, when the timer rings, stop working, shut off the timer, and mark your answers as right or wrong, using the answer key. Fourth, count the number of problems you completed correctly. Fifth, write the number in the box next to today's date on the record form."

6. *Instruct the child to record the target behavior as soon as possible after its occurrence.*

7. *Demonstrate the self-monitoring procedure, using the actual recording form or recording device.* Model the recording procedure for the child. Discuss with the child any potential problems. With some children, you may want to use mechanical recording means—such as counters or tokens and plastic boxes—instead of written records of behavior or computer recording. Label each step as you complete it.

8. *Ask the child to role-play the self-monitoring procedure, including defining the target behavior.*

9. *Ask the child if he or she has any questions about the procedure.*

10. *Conduct several trials to see whether the child understands and can carry out the procedure adequately.*

11. *Conduct accuracy checks randomly and inform the child that you will be doing so.*

12. *Arrange for the child to receive reinforcements contingent on recording accurate data.*

Self-monitoring assessment may make a child anxious, particularly when the child records failures or lack of progress. Consequently, you will need to monitor whether the procedure induces anxiety. If you find that it does, alter it as needed. Or, you might reassure the child that this is an important first step in reducing the anxiety-provoking problem. For self-monitoring to be effective, the child's parents, teachers, and siblings and other significant persons in the child's environment must support the procedure and encourage the child to record the needed information.

The following case illustrates the use of a self-monitoring procedure to assess a problem behavior (adapted from Evans & Sullivan, 1993, pp. 79–80).

Paul, a 12-year-old boy, was referred because of excessive thumbsucking. His dentist had informed his parents that this behavior was having a destructive effect on his teeth. Paul and his parents said that his friends had begun to tease him more frequently about sucking his thumb. As part of the evaluation, the psychologist wanted to assess the frequency of thumbsucking and the antecedent events for this behavior. Paul was instructed to record the number of times he sucked his thumb before school, in the morning in school, during the afternoon in school, and after school. In addition, Paul recorded where he was and what he was doing when he sucked his thumb. To estimate the accuracy of Paul's self-recordings, his father recorded the number of times Paul sucked his thumb when Paul was at home.

Examples of Self-Monitoring Assessment Forms

Table 9-7 shows a self-monitoring form that you can give to older children to record stressful situations and other events. Table 9-8 contains a daily exercise log. Table 9-9 shows a self-monitoring form that can be used by school-age children to record whether they are attending to school work when a tone sounds. The students are given an audio device with earphones. When they hear a tone, they record whether or not they were attending to school work. The tones are presented randomly at intervals ranging from 15 to 90 seconds, with a tone emitted about every 30 seconds. The form can be used for several different types of behaviors in addition to attending.

Table 9-10 illustrates a diary form that can be used by older students to record events associated with problem behaviors. You can modify it to obtain the information you want the child to record. For example, the form might include a section covering positive behaviors, a section covering both negative and positive behaviors, or an instruction to record a particular behavior, such as the number of pages the child read in class or the number of times his or her attention wandered from the assigned task.

Table 9-11 shows a different type of form for recording the number of times a target behavior occurs. The target behavior can be any off-task behavior (e.g., being out of seat, touching others' property, making inappropriate sounds, interrupting, hitting, or pushing others) or on-task behavior (paying attention

---

Table 9-7
Self-Monitoring Form for Recording Stressful Situations

SELF-MONITORING QUESTIONNAIRE

Name: _____

Directions: Complete the following items for each situation that made you unhappy.

Date	Describe situation	What happened before?	What happened after?	Who else was there?	What were you feeling and thinking?	Stress rating[a]

[a]Rate how much stress you were feeling on a scale from 1 to 10, with 1 = the least intense stress and 10 = the most intense stress.
Note. This form can be expanded to include 7 days.
From *Assessment of Children: Behavioral, Social, and Clinical Foundations (Fifth Edition)* by Jerome M. Sattler and Robert D. Hoge. Copyright 2006 by Jerome M. Sattler, Publisher, Inc. Permission to photocopy this table is granted to purchasers of this book for personal use only (see copyright page for details).

Table 9-8
Self-Monitoring Form for Recording Daily Exercise

EXERCISE LOG

Name: _____

Directions: Complete the following items about your daily exercise.

Date	What kinds of exercise did you do?	What time of day did you exercise?	How many minutes did you exercise?	Who else was there?	How much did you exert yourself?[a]	How much did you enjoy yourself?[b]	What problems did you have while exercising?

[a]Use a scale from 1 to 10, with 1 = No exertion and 10 = Completely exhausted.
[b]Use a scale from 1 to 10, with 1 = Did not enjoy at all and 10 = Really enjoyed.
Note. This form can be expanded to include 7 days.
From *Assessment of Children: Behavioral, Social, and Clinical Foundations (Fifth Edition)* by Jerome M. Sattler and Robert D. Hoge. Copyright 2006 by Jerome M. Sattler, Publisher, Inc. Permission to photocopy this table is granted to purchasers of this book for personal use only (see copyright page for details).

Table 9-9
Self-Monitoring Form for Recording Attention

RECORDING FORM

Name: _____ Date: _____

Directions: Circle **Yes** each time you were paying attention to the teacher when you heard the tone, and circle **No** if you weren't paying attention to the teacher when you heard the tone.

1. Yes No	6. Yes No	11. Yes No	16. Yes No
2. Yes No	7. Yes No	12. Yes No	17. Yes No
3. Yes No	8. Yes No	13. Yes No	18. Yes No
4. Yes No	9. Yes No	14. Yes No	19. Yes No
5. Yes No	10. Yes No	15. Yes No	20. Yes No

From *Assessment of Children: Behavioral, Social, and Clinical Foundations (Fifth Edition)* by Jerome M. Sattler and Robert D. Hoge. Copyright 2006 by Jerome M. Sattler, Publisher, Inc. Permission to photocopy this table is granted to purchasers of this book for personal use only (see copyright page for details).

to the teacher, working on the current lesson, raising a hand to ask a question, being quiet unless called on).

Table 9-12 presents a form for recording intensity of reaction. Children are asked to note the time at which the recording was made and the intensity of the feeling at that time. The hours shown are from 6 a.m. to 12 midnight. A 5-point scale is used to record the intensity of the feeling; the intensity dimension can be changed to accommodate different feelings (or behaviors). Table 9-13 shows a form to use with children who have trouble remembering their homework assignments.

Two additional tables are useful with younger children. Table 9-14 shows pairs of faces (smiling and sad) that can be used to record whether children thought they were on-task or off-task. Table 9-15 shows a series of five faces, ranging from smiling to neutral to sad, that provide a finer scale for children to use in recording their thoughts about their behavior. In using any of these tables, present the task clearly to the children. For example, children can be asked to record such things as the following when they hear a tone or bell: Was I paying attention? Was I doing what I was supposed to be doing? Was I working hard? Was I in my seat? If the child

---

Table 9-10
Student's Diary Form for Describing a Target Behavior

STUDENT DIARY

Name: _____   Date: _____

1. Did you have any problems today? (Circle one) Yes   No
   If you circled Yes, please complete the following items.
2. Describe the problem.

_____
_____

3. What happened before the problem began?

_____
_____

4. What happened after the problem began?

_____
_____

5. What did you do about the problem?

_____
_____

6. What did your teacher do about the problem?

_____
_____

7. What did the other students in the class do about the problem?

_____
_____

8. Why do you think the problem happened?

_____
_____

9. Describe anything else about the problem that you think is important.

_____
_____

From *Assessment of Children: Behavioral, Social, and Clinical Foundations (Fifth Edition)* by Jerome M. Sattler and Robert D. Hoge. Copyright 2006 by Jerome M. Sattler, Publisher, Inc. Permission to photocopy this table is granted to purchasers of this book for personal use only (see copyright page for details).

---

cannot read, an adult will need to read the directions to the child; in addition, the child may need several practice sessions to understand the task.

Use of Computers in Self-Monitoring

Hand-held computers are another means for recording data. They can (a) prompt children to record responses at prescribed times during the day, (b) record responses at the actual time the responses are taking place, (c) check children's accuracy by examining inconsistencies and invalid responses, (d) summarize data in graphic or table form, which can then be downloaded to a desk-top computer, and (e) help children set goals and monitor their progress (Farrell, 1991; Haynes, 1998; Richard & Bobicz, 2003).

Problems in Self-Monitoring Assessment

Limitations associated with self-monitoring assessment include reactive effects and difficulty in keeping accurate records. Let's examine each of these in more detail.

Reactive effects.   Reactive effects are possible with self-monitoring assessment because the children know that someone will be looking at their recording sheet and because their own attention has been drawn to selected behaviors. If children change their behavior because of reactive effects, the changes may distort or modify the behaviors being studied. Reactive effects may be beneficial, though, in intervention programs if they reduce the frequency of negative behaviors or increase the frequency of positive behaviors. You need to

---

Table 9-11
Self-Monitoring Form for Recording Target Behavior

RECORDING FORM

Name: _____ Date: _____

Behavior to record: Out of seat

Directions: Fill in one circle each time you were out of your seat when you were not supposed to be out of your seat.

Morning ○○○○○○○○○○○○○○○○○○○○○○○○○○○○○○○

Afternoon ○○○○○○○○○○○○○○○○○○○○○○○○○○○○○○○

Note. The target behavior can be changed as needed. The form also can be changed to show specific time periods if needed.
From *Assessment of Children: Behavioral, Social, and Clinical Foundations (Fifth Edition)* by Jerome M. Sattler and Robert D. Hoge. Copyright 2006 by Jerome M. Sattler, Publisher, Inc. Permission to photocopy this table is granted to purchasers of this book for personal use only (see copyright page for details).

Table 9-12
Self-Monitoring Form for Recording Intensity of Reaction

RECORDING FORM FOR FEELINGS

Name: _____

Directions: Three times each day—once in the morning, once in the afternoon, and once at night—complete the sadness graph. In the column that indicates the time when you record your answer, put an X in the square opposite the number that says how you feel. Use the following scale:

1 = I do not feel sad.
2 = I feel a little sad.
3 = I feel somewhat sad.
4 = I feel very sad.
5 = I feel extremely sad.

Day: _____ Date: _____

5																			
4																			
3																			
2																			
1																			

6	7	8	9	10	11	12	1	2	3	4	5	6	7	8	9	10	11	12
A.M.						P.M.												

Note. This form can be used for any type of emotion or pain. Adapted from Allen and Matthews (1998).
From *Assessment of Children: Behavioral, Social, and Clinical Foundations (Fifth Edition)* by Jerome M. Sattler and Robert D. Hoge. Copyright 2006 by Jerome M. Sattler, Publisher, Inc. Permission to photocopy this table is granted to purchasers of this book for personal use only (see copyright page for details).

Table 9-13
Self-Monitoring Form for Recording Homework Assignments

RECORDING FORM FOR HOMEWORK

Name: _____   Date: _____

Class: _____   Teacher: _____

Directions: Circle Y ("yes"), N ("no"), or NA ("not applicable") after each question.

Questions	Circle One		
1. Did you read the homework assignment sheet in class?	Y	N	NA
2. Did you put the homework assignment sheet in your notebook or write the homework assignment in your notebook in class?	Y	N	NA
3. Did you ask questions when you did not understand the homework assignment?	Y	N	NA
4. Did you take home the homework assignment sheet or your notes about the homework assignment?	Y	N	NA
5. Did you take home the books you needed to do the homework?	Y	N	NA
6. Did you complete the homework at home?	Y	N	NA
If you said "no" to question 6, leave questions 7 and 8 blank. If you said "yes" to question 6, go to question 7.			
7. If you completed the homework, did you bring it to class?	Y	N	NA
If you said "no" to question 7, leave question 8 blank. If you said "yes" to question 7, answer question 8 if you have a work folder in class.			
8. If you brought the homework to class, did you file it in your work folder?	Y	N	NA

Source: Adapted from Trapani and Gettinger (1996).
From *Assessment of Children: Behavioral, Social, and Clinical Foundations (Fifth Edition)* by Jerome M. Sattler and Robert D. Hoge. Copyright 2006 by Jerome M. Sattler, Publisher, Inc. Permission to photocopy this table is granted to purchasers of this book for personal use only (see copyright page for details).

monitor reactive effects to learn whether they are interfering with the assessment.

Accuracy effects. The accuracy of self-monitoring recordings may be affected by the following factors:

1. The child's age
2. The degree and type of psychopathology
3. The child's degree of cooperativeness and interest
4. The child's willingness to be objective and record negative behavior as well as positive behavior
5. The type of behavior targeted (e.g., verbal or nonverbal, private or public, appropriate or inappropriate)
6. The difficulty in discriminating on-task and off-task behavior
7. The length of time it takes to record the behavior
8. The degree of effort required to record the behavior (e.g., the number of behaviors to be monitored and what needs to be done to record the behavior)
9. The other behaviors occurring at the same time as the target behavior
10. The setting in which the recording takes place (e.g., home, school, playground)
11. The response of others in the setting (e.g., teachers, other students, parents, siblings, other relatives)
12. The type of recording device (e.g., paper and pencil, mechanical device, computer)
13. The presence of observers who also may be recording the child's behavior

Children who are not well motivated, for example, may not make daily recordings. In such cases, they should be encouraged to turn in their recordings every day and be rewarded for their efforts. Sometimes children will be well motivated initially but will lose interest. In such cases, you might want to change the cuing device (Shapiro, 1984). Sometimes children become so absorbed in their work that they forget to monitor their behavior.

Children are more likely to misreport behaviors that run counter to parents' or teachers' standards than behaviors that conform to those standards. For example, eating forbidden foods is more likely *not* to be reported than eating acceptable foods. Children also may be embarrassed to report inappropriate behavior and may "fake good."

Encourage children to be honest in their reports. Emphasize that they do not have to impress you with positive reports

Table 9-14
Self-Monitoring Form for Younger Children for Recording Behavior in Two Categories

RECORDING FORM

Name: _____ Date: _____

Directions:

If you were paying attention to your school work or teacher when the tone sounded, put an X on this face:

If you were *not* paying attention to your school work or teacher when the tone sounded, put an X on this face:

1.
2.
3.
4.
5.
6.
7.
8.
9.
10.

Note. This form can be used for any off-task behavior.
From *Assessment of Children: Behavioral, Social, and Clinical Foundations (Fifth Edition)* by Jerome M. Sattler and Robert D. Hoge. Copyright 2006 by Jerome M. Sattler, Publisher, Inc. Permission to photocopy this table is granted to purchasers of this book for personal use only (see copyright page for details).

Table 9-15
Self-Monitoring Form for Younger Children for Recording Behavior in Five Categories

RECORDING FORM

Name: _____ Date: _____

Directions: Put an X on the face that shows what you were doing when the tone sounded. Here is what the faces mean.

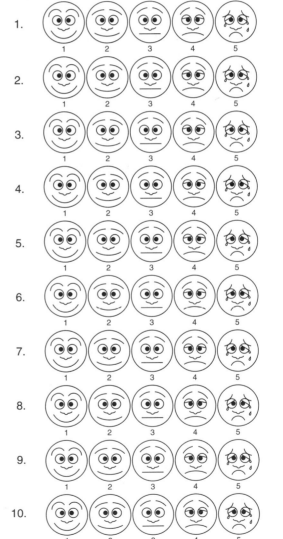

1	2	3	4	5
I was fully paying attention.	I was almost paying attention.	I was paying some attention.	I was paying just a little attention.	I was not paying attention at all.

1. 1 2 3 4 5
2. 1 2 3 4 5
3. 1 2 3 4 5
4. 1 2 3 4 5
5. 1 2 3 4 5
6. 1 2 3 4 5
7. 1 2 3 4 5
8. 1 2 3 4 5
9. 1 2 3 4 5
10. 1 2 3 4 5

From *Assessment of Children: Behavioral, Social, and Clinical Foundations (Fifth Edition)* by Jerome M. Sattler and Robert D. Hoge. Copyright 2006 by Jerome M. Sattler, Publisher, Inc. Permission to photocopy this table is granted to purchasers of this book for personal use only (see copyright page for details).

and that, by being honest, they allow you to help them better. Reassure them that they will not be punished for reporting negative behavior and that you simply want to get a better idea of how they behave in one or more settings. However, you should caution children that if you observe any behavior that may be dangerous to them, you must report it to their parents or to the authorities.

Children under 5 or 6 years of age will likely have difficulty making self-monitoring recordings (Shapiro, 1984). Therefore, limit the target behaviors to one or two behaviors and use a simple and clear recording procedure. Also use visual or verbal-auditory cues whenever possible to prompt the self-observation and recording. Finally, you may want to give children appropriate rewards or establish a token economy for accurate recordings.

Even with older children, the procedure must be simple and readily comprehensible. You can enhance children's accuracy by giving immediate feedback about how their recording agreed with that of an external judge, carefully defining the target behaviors, providing examples, selecting behaviors that are readily discriminable, modeling the process, giving several trials, keeping the procedure short (e.g., less than 5 minutes), and having them record the behavior immediately after it occurs rather than waiting until the end of the day.

When children are completing a self-monitoring assessment for specific symptoms, prompts from parents or teachers at the appointed or critical times usually increase the children's compliance with the procedure. However, children may sometimes be engaged in activities that interfere with the self-monitoring. In such cases, accept the fact that the procedure will be less than perfect because of natural events that happen in the children's lives. You may want to evaluate the accuracy of the children's recordings by having an observer also record the children's behavior or by examining byproducts associated with the behavior of interest (e.g., the number of problems completed on an assignment sheet).

Comment on Self-Monitoring Assessment

In establishing a self-monitoring assessment, tailor the techniques and instructions to the comprehension level of the child. Role-play the self-monitoring procedure before you end the instruction session. Obviously, self-monitoring assessment, like any self-report measure, is open to distortion if a child wants to deny problems, exaggerate symptoms to gain attention, or withhold sensitive information. Make every effort to enlist the child's cooperation and interest in the procedure. Help the child understand the purpose and value of the activity. The keys to successful self-monitoring assessment are to clearly define the behavior of interest, ensure that the child understands the procedures, make the recording procedure uncomplicated, enlist the child's cooperation and the cooperation of significant others, and minimize interference from others.

The cues used in a self-monitoring assessment should be randomly distributed to avoid the negative effects of a fixed interval (Shapiro & Cole, 1994). With a fixed interval, children may stop working until they hear the cue. For many behaviors, the cues should be given 10 to 90 seconds apart. To increase children's motivation, the cues can be an interesting sound, such as a bell, whistle, funny noise, or beep.

When self-monitoring assessment is part of an intervention program, you may use the data as an index of change, to evaluate improvement in self-regulation, to evaluate the effectiveness of the intervention plan, and to justify changes in

MR. WOODHEAD © 2003 by John P. Wood

the plan. Self-monitoring assessment also may help children focus on the behavior of interest and may help them understand the relationship among situational events, the occurrence of the behavior, and possible consequences associated with the behavior. For more information about self-monitoring, see issue Number 4 of *Psychological Assessment* (1999, Volume 11) and Shapiro and Cole (1994).

REPORTING BEHAVIORAL OBSERVATIONS

Following is a list of topics generally included in a report of observational findings. Not all of the information will apply to every situation, of course.

1. *Personal data.* Note the child's age, sex, physical characteristics, and other relevant characteristics.

2. *Setting data.* Note the date, time, place, length of observation, setting (including type of room and people present during the observation), recording method, and coding system (or behaviors observed).

3. *Reliability.* Discuss the reliability of the findings, and describe the method used to assess reliability, if appropriate.

4. *Validity.* Discuss the validity of the findings, and describe the method used to assess validity, if appropriate.

5. *Intensity.* Discuss how much the problem behavior interfered with the child's other activities.

6. *Severity.* Discuss the extent to which the problem behavior reflects psychopathology.

7. *Duration.* Note the length of the episodes of the problem behavior.

8. *Frequency.* Note how often the problem behavior occurred.

9. *Generality.* Note the number of situations in which the problem behavior occurred.

10. *Norms.* Note how often the comparison child and/or the referred child's peer group (or class) engaged in the same behavior.

11. *Antecedents of the problem behavior.* Note what the child was doing before the problem behavior occurred and what was happening in the setting at that time.

12. *Consequences of the problem behavior.* Note what happened to the child after he or she engaged in the problem behavior (e.g., the child obtained relief by escaping or avoiding a task, in which case the target behavior provided negative reinforcement; the child obtained a reward for the problem behavior, in which case the target behavior provided positive reinforcement; or the child was disciplined for the problem behavior). Also note how much the problem behavior disrupted the activities of the other children and the responses of the teacher, parents, or other children.

13. *Peer group acceptance.* Note whether other children accepted the problem behavior.

14. *Adult acceptance.* Note whether adults accepted the problem behavior.

15. *Agreement with referral source.* Note whether the problem behavior was consistent with the referral source's description.

16. *Additional problem behaviors.* Note whether the child exhibited any other problems.

17. *Positive behaviors.* Note the behaviors that may be useful for designing interventions.

18. *Observational difficulties.* Note the difficulties encountered in conducting the observation (e.g., problems in determining onset or termination of response, counting number of responses, defining target responses).

19. *Implications of the findings.* Discuss the actions that should be taken as a result of the findings (e.g., whether the child would benefit from being transferred to another setting).

In describing the results of a systematic behavioral observation, you should evaluate how the setting, the people in the setting, and the environment as a whole may have affected the child's behavior. For example, if there were other people in the setting, how did they affect the child? If the child's behavior changed with changes in the setting, did other children's behavior change as well?

When you write about people at a facility, refer to them the way the facility does, as *clients, patients, members,* or *students.* Describe the examinee consistently throughout the report. Generally, it is good practice to refer to the examinee by her or his name. (If you are conducting a systematic behavioral observation for a practice class assignment and there is no referred child, select a child for the practice observation and make up a name for that child that you can use in the report.). If you present in the report information that comes from an agency brochure, agency staff member, or another source, give the origin of the information. Otherwise, readers may think that the information was based on your observations.

A statement such as "Twelve percent of the time the teacher's comments were approving" is incomplete if it is not accompanied by another statement indicating what the teacher was doing the rest of the time. Including too many numbers can cloud the meaning of an observational report; instead, report averages and general findings.

Do not include in the report comments about what you were thinking as you were recording the information. The main focus should be on what you observed.

If you introduce a paragraph with a statement such as "Five methods were used . . . . The first was . . . ," you should go on to describe the first method and then each of the other four methods, prefacing each description with a similar introductory phrase (e.g., "The second was . . . .").

Help the reader understand the reason for your conclusions. For example, the statement (made about a duration count) that "Fred's play with other children was infrequent, at the rate of only once every 36 seconds" may leave the reader wondering why the rate of once every 36 seconds was considered infrequent. Was this rate different from that of the other children playing?

Clearly describe the categories you used to observe behavior. The following sentence, for example, gives incomplete information: "The observers recorded the number of times Bill engaged in the following behaviors: attending, working, inappropriate locale, and don't know." Instead of "inappropriate locale," give the complete name of the behavior category: "goes to an inappropriate locale." Instead of "don't know," use "says 'I don't know'."

Never give statistics without explanation. If you say, for example, that there was 40% agreement on the five rating scales, explain to the reader what this level of agreement means. When you report a percentage agreement or a reliability coefficient obtained for a systematic behavioral observation, follow it with a statement about whether the percentage agreement or reliability coefficient is satisfactory. Consider reliability in an all-or-none fashion—that is, report that it was or was not satisfactory rather than reporting that it was marginally satisfactory.

If reliability was low, discuss the reasons. Also discuss the implications of all reliability indices. For example, does the low reliability of an observational method influence the results of the entire systematic behavioral observation or just selected parts? Also, if reliability was not satisfactory, indicate that the findings must be viewed with caution or that they are not representative of the behaviors under observation.

Do not minimize the importance of low interrater reliability just because a behavior was infrequent. For example, if you have poor interrater agreement when the behavior occurred once only (i.e., one rater recorded it and the other one did not), do not write, "The percentage agreement for aggression was 0%. However, this figure is misleading because the behavior was seen only once." The 0% agreement is *not* misleading; it reflects what the observers actually recorded. If your findings differ from those of your co-observer, explain the possible reasons for the differences. You could write, "The percentage agreement for aggression was 0%. The child was observed to be aggressive on one occasion by one of the observers but not by the other one. This might mean that the child's aggressive acts were surreptitious, that the observers did not agree on what constituted aggression, or that the aggressive acts were not clearcut and therefore were difficult to interpret."

When you report the reliability of a ratings observation, provide the percentage agreement as well as the absolute values of the ratings (e.g., 4.3 or 2.8) and indicate what the values imply (e.g., extremely aggressive behavior or somewhat passive behavior). For example, does the percent agreement, correlation coefficient, or kappa indicate satisfactory or unsatisfactory observer agreement? Were the ratings reliable or unreliable? And, as noted previously, if the ratings were unreliable, discuss what may have led to the poor reliability.

CASE STUDY

Exhibit 9-4, a psychological evaluation of an adolescent with mental retardation observed at a vocational training center, is a case study of systematic behavioral observation. In practice, you would typically choose one or two observational procedures, based on the reason for referral, previous psychometric assessment findings, and the frequency, duration, and type of behavior under observation. Because the purpose of this case study is to demonstrate the various observational approaches discussed in this chapter, it applies five observational techniques and shows the kinds of results each renders. The report presents a description of the adolescent, a detailed description of the observational methods used (including target behaviors and rating scales), and a statement about reliability and validity. The observational findings section integrates the findings from the five techiniques used. The report concludes with a short summary, which highlights the observational findings.

THINKING THROUGH THE ISSUES

1. What are the basic requirements for an effective recording system?
2. Develop a recording system for some setting with which you are familiar, and include both positive and negative behaviors.
3. Reactivity is said to be the bane of observational recording. Do you agree or disagree? Why?
4. How could you use behavioral observations to confirm hypotheses generated from a child's performance on an individual intelligence test?
5. What special problems arise in observing infants and young children?
6. How useful is self-monitoring assessment? Describe several situations in which you believe self-monitoring might be helpful.

SUMMARY

Observational Coding Systems

1. Observational coding systems are used to categorize behavioral observations. They usually consist of two or more categories that cover a range of behaviors, although, on occasion, a single category may be appropriate.
2. Before you use a coding system, carefully evaluate (a) its rationale, (b) the setting(s) in which it is applicable, (c) definitions of the coding categories, (d) the description of how behavior is sampled, (e) rules governing observers' use of rating scales, such as a hierarchy of codes, (f) reliability, including overall reliability and the reliability of each coding category, (g) validity, and (h) positive and negative features (including potential problem areas).
3. Select the simplest possible coding system that will answer your questions.
4. Observational coding systems have been developed to evaluate individual children, groups of children, and classes.
5. Computerized systems, which use a laptop computer, handheld computer, or bar-code scanner, are valuable for collecting real-time observational data.
6. Observational coding systems also are useful for studying the behavior of classroom teachers.

Exhibit 9-4
Psychological Evaluation: Behavioral Observation

Name: Andy Lopez
Date of birth: June 1, 1988
Chronological age: 16-11
Observer: Todd Johnson

Date of observation: May 1, 2005
Date of report: May 6, 2005
Co-observer: Jill Cole

Reason for Referral

Andy was observed at Path Services in order to evaluate his progress in a special training program for mentally retarded adolescents. The observation was conducted to fulfill a requirement for a graduate psychological assessment course at Blank State University.

Description of Client Observed and Setting

Andy was observed for a 1-hour period in a class at Path Services, a vocational training and placement center for mentally retarded individuals. The observation was conducted on May 1, 2005 from 8:30 a.m. to 9:30 a.m.

Andy is a black-haired, olive-complected male. He is 16 years 11 months of age, 5 feet 10 inches tall, and weighs 200 pounds. He wore a blue work shirt, blue work pants, and black calf-high work boots. He was neatly groomed. Andy was observed during a class lecture on window washing and a window-washing activity.

Observational Methods

Narrative, running record, event, interval, and rating observation techniques were used. For the purpose of assessing reliability, two observers simultaneously but independently observed Andy's behavior. During the 10-minute narrative recording, the entire class was observed. For the 5-minute running record, Andy's behavior was observed and recorded.

During the 10-minute event recording, the observers recorded the number of times Andy engaged in the following behaviors: touching his boot with his hand, tapping his foot on the floor, touching his face or head with his hand, yawning, and raising his hand or motioning with it to gain another person's attention.

For the interval recording, Andy was observed over the course of three time periods. The first, which lasted for 6 minutes and 40 seconds, consisted of 16 15-second observation intervals interspersed with 10-second recording intervals. During this time, the observers recorded whether Andy engaged in any of the following nine behaviors: attending, working, volunteering, reading aloud, displaying other appropriate behavior, interacting with a peer about academic materials, interacting with a peer about nonacademic materials, looking around, and displaying other inappropriate behavior.

The second and third interval recordings each lasted for 4 minutes, and consisted of 16 10-second observation intervals interspersed with 5-second recording intervals. The target behaviors for the second interval recording involved the following behaviors on the part of the teacher with respect to Andy or the entire class: expressing approval, expressing disapproval, offering no response, and engaging in verbal interaction. The target behaviors for the third interval recording were appropriate behavior and inappropriate behavior of the class as a whole.

Andy was observed for approximately 45 minutes while the observers made narrative, running record, event, and interval recordings. An additional 10 minutes of observation time was used for narrative recording of the teacher's behavior in relation to Andy. After all of the observations were finished, the observers completed eight seven-point rating scales: on-task (always-never), verbal off-task (always-never), motor off-task (always-never), passive off-task (always-never), verbalization (clear-unclear), teacher verbal approval responses (frequent-absent), teacher verbal disapproval responses (frequent-absent), and class-appropriate behavior (always-never).

Several interobserver agreement indices were calculated from the event, interval, and rating observational data. These included overall percentage of agreement, percentages of agreement on occurrence and nonoccurrence of the behaviors, and kappa. Six reliability indices for the occurrence of particular behaviors could not be calculated because both observers agreed that the behavior had not occurred. Fifty-three of the 63 reliability indices calculated were satisfactory (at least 90% agreement). The 10 unsatisfactory indices were primarily in areas in which the behavior assessed was not discrete or the observers could not observe Andy, the teacher, or the class because their view was restricted. Overall, interrater reliability appears to be satisfactory. The results also appear to be valid.

Observational Findings

Andy predominantly engaged in appropriate class behavior. He did, however, occasionally exhibit inappropriate verbal and passive off-task behaviors. During the first 15 minutes of the lecture on window washing, Andy appeared tired, distracted, and restless. He sat in a slouched position, with his buttocks on the edge of the chair, legs outstretched, and upper back against the top of the chairback. He frequently closed his eyes or rubbed them in what looked like an attempt to wake up and coughed 11 times during the 10-minute event recording. When Andy heard noises or voices outside the classroom or when someone entered or left, he always turned around to look and he often waved. Andy occasionally bent over to untie and retie his boot laces. He frequently rubbed his head or the skin around his mouth and nose; during event recording, he did this at a rate of once every 40 seconds.

Andy demonstrated that his full attention was not on the teacher by asking "Do we have to go outside and clean up?" approximately 2 minutes after the teacher spoke to the class about that same issue. Andy failed to sign in when he entered the room, and the teacher had to tell him to do so approximately 10 minutes into the class period. Upon approaching the sign-in sheet, Andy searched in his pockets for a pen. When he realized he did not have one, he turned toward his classmates and asked in a fairly loud voice if anybody had a pen that he could borrow. On three

Exhibit 9-4 *(Continued)*

occasions during the first 5 minutes of the lecture, Andy spoke to another class member. Despite Andy's inappropriate behavior, he was not disruptive to the others in the classroom.

As the lecture progressed, Andy's boredom and restlessness decreased, and his attentiveness increased. Despite his seeming distractedness, he answered many of the teacher's questions appropriately. First, he eagerly and quickly sat up straight, raised his hand, and then waited for the teacher to call on him. However, on two occasions he shouted out an answer before being called on by the teacher. For example, after a majority of the class members unsuccessfully guessed answers to a question, Andy answered with conviction, "I know what it is—water is minerals." However, at other times his behavior was quite appropriate, and he gave accurate answers after waiting to be recognized by the teacher. In response to the teacher's question about what supplies the window washer needs, Andy quickly said, "squeegee, bucket, spray bottle, and rags." When the teacher subsequently asked what the bucket was used for and why the rags were folded, Andy promptly supplied the correct reasons. When he was not called on, Andy tended to look disappointed.

Andy exhibited the same eagerness during the window-washing activity. He pulled his chair close to the demonstration window, attended to the teacher, and enthusiastically volunteered to perform the task. Andy apparently understood the teacher's instructions, as he washed the window accordingly. He worked diligently and responded well to the teacher's questions. When Andy was done, for example, the teacher said, "Now what are you going to do?" Andy quickly and correctly replied, "Look for streaks." When Andy found spots on the window, he asked the teacher, "Want me to get paper towels?" When the teacher indicated yes, Andy promptly retrieved paper towels from the front of the classroom and wiped the spots off the window. Andy meticulously inspected the window and enthusiastically asked, "How does it look, Tim?" The teacher responded, "Good, I think," and Andy smiled. Andy's verbalizations were always clear and grammatically correct. Although he usually sat off to the side, rather than among his classmates, he appeared to be friendly with them.

The teacher interacted with the students throughout the observation period. Interaction was predominantly verbal—it included lecturing, asking questions, explaining how to wash the window, and commenting on the students' demonstrations. Most of the interaction was instructional; thus, approval and disapproval were infrequent. When approval was given, it was more frequently nonverbal (e.g., a smile or a nod of the head) than verbal. Andy received nonverbal approval on two occasions and verbal approval on one occasion. He appeared content when he was given either verbal or nonverbal approval. When the teacher expressed disapproval, it was in a firm but gentle manner. Andy did not receive disapproval for any of his actions. Overall, the teacher was patient and had good rapport with the students. Andy and his classmates, for the most part, were cooperative, respectful, and well behaved.

Summary and Impressions

This observation was conducted on the morning of May 1, 2005 at Path Services in order to fulfill a course requirement. Andy is a 16-year, 11-month-old male. At the beginning of the class on window-washing procedures, Andy appeared to be restless, distracted, and tired. When the teacher began to ask questions, however, Andy became more involved. His attention increased as he eagerly, correctly, and appropriately answered many of the teacher's questions. Andy's verbalizations were always clear and coherent, and he was eager and enthusiastic as he washed windows. He followed instructions and worked diligently and consistently. Andy's distractibility seemed to be caused by an over-alertness to the things happening in his environment. He appeared to be outgoing and amiable. Andy was attracted to both mental and physical stimulation. He seemed to enjoy the recognition he received through successful participation in the class activity.

(Signature)_____

Todd Johnson, B.A., Observer

Source: Adapted from Repp and Barton (1980).

7. The separate coding systems designed for students and teachers can be combined to form a more complete coding system, and additional categories for entire classes can be added.

Reliability

8. The data you obtain from behavioral observations, like the data you obtain from any other assessment procedure, must be reliable and valid.

9. In the observation of behavior, reliability and validity are influenced by several factors, including the observer; the setting; the coding system; the child, parent, teacher, other target person, or group; and the interactions among these sources.

10. Observer bias refers to errors committed by the observer in the course of an observational assessment.

11. When observation continues over a long period, observers may show signs of observer drift, such as forgetfulness, fatigue, and decreased motivation.

12. Reliability may be more difficult to achieve with global categories.

13. Estimates of interobserver reliability (also called interobserver agreement) are usually based on scores of two or more observers who record the same information while simultaneously and independently observing the same child or group.

14. If you are interested in the pattern of agreement among the observers' ratings, irrespective of the actual level of agreement, and you are using an interval scale of measurement, then the product-moment correlation coefficient is a satisfactory measure of reliability.

15. When both the pattern of agreement and the level of agreement are important and you have used an interval scale of measurement,

you can use the intraclass correlation coefficient as a measure of reliability.

16. When the data form an ordinal scale and you are interested in correcting for chance agreement, kappa (κ) is a useful index of agreement.

17. When you want a measure of the percentage agreement among two or more observers but are not concerned with correcting for chance agreement, you can use an uncorrected percentage agreement index.

18. With interval recording, you can use several percentage agreement methods for determining interobserver agreement.

19. When observers score the occurrence of a behavior in only a small proportion of intervals, compute interobserver percentage agreement only for those intervals in which the observers scored occurrence of the behavior; the use of total intervals might cause some distortion of the rate of agreement.

20. With event recording, you can estimate interobserver percentage agreement by dividing the number of occurrences of the event reported by the observer recording the lower frequency by the number of occurrences of the event reported by the other observer.

21. The interobserver percentage agreement estimate for duration recording is similar to the one used for event recording.

22. With ratings recording, you can estimate interobserver percentage agreement by determining whether the two observers gave the same rating on each scale.

23. Obtaining satisfactory interobserver reliability does not ensure that data are meaningful or accurate. High reliabilities may be associated with observation codes that are relatively insensitive to the occurrence of important or meaningful behaviors.

24. The consistency of behavior over time and situations is another measure of the reliability of behavioral observations.

25. You should strive to sample the target behaviors more than once and in more than one setting.

26. Internal consistency reliability reflects how consistent the components of an assessment instrument are in measuring the same characteristics.

Validity

27. Ensuring the validity of behavioral observations is often problematic, because it is difficult to obtain an adequate and representative sample of behavior in a short time.

28. Two major factors affecting the validity of the observational assessment are the representativeness and the generalizability of the findings.

29. A child's behavior under observation may be affected by the child's awareness that someone is observing him or her, by the child's prior interactions with the observer, or by the observer's personal characteristics. We refer to this effect as reactivity, or the guinea pig effect.

30. To minimize reactivity, conduct your observations as unobtrusively as possible.

31. Reactive effects may be indicated by (a) atypical changes in the child's behavior, (b) increased variability in the child's behavior, (c) the child's own admission that his or her behavior changed as a result of being observed, (d) reports from others that the child's behavior changed when the child was being observed, and (e) discrepancies between different measures of the child's same behavior.

32. Reactivity also is useful because it may suggest possible interventions.

Procedures for Reducing Errors in Observations

33. You can increase reliability by (a) using clear and precise definitions of behaviors, (b) following systematic and precise rules governing the observations, (c) becoming well trained in observational procedures, and (d) using observation periods that are not excessively long.

34. Although observer drift is difficult to control, you can reduce it by frequently checking your recordings, becoming thoroughly familiar with the recording system beforehand, and making periodic calibrations during the observation session to check the consistency of your observations.

35. You also can increase reliability by reviewing your decision criteria—such as when to report that a behavior did or did not occur—and then comparing your decision criteria with those of other observers.

36. During your training, regularly compare your results with those of a highly trained observer or with standard criterion recordings.

37. The agreement between an observer's recordings and standard criterion recordings is referred to as criterion-related agreement.

38. Another method of checking the reliability of your ratings is to videotape the behavior of a child (or class) and then rate the child's behavior again from the videotape.

39. An acceptable level of interobserver agreement does not rule out observer error. You can have a high level of interobserver agreement and still have observer bias and observer drift if both observers have a similar bias or make similar errors.

40. To reduce reactivity, (a) limit your stimulus value by becoming as neutral a stimulus as possible, (b) position yourself so that you are away from the ordinary paths of movement in the classroom and yet still have an unobstructed view of the child and setting, (c) shift your attention from one child to another, (d) follow all rules, regulations, and informal policies of the school, institution, or family, (e) enter the setting when your entrance will least disrupt the ongoing behavior, and (f) use distance observation.

41. If you conduct the observations prior to interviewing or testing a child, the child is less likely to feel concerned about your being in the classroom.

42. Developing informal norms will help you place the child's behavior in a meaningful context.

43. Another procedure is to establish local norms for the entire class, using the scan check method.

44. Obtaining a peer or class rating permits you to measure the difference between the frequency with which the referred child engages in a particular behavior and the frequency with which the peer or class does.

45. A discrepancy ratio is the difference between the median level of the referred child's behavior and the median level of the peer's (or class's) behavior.

46. You cannot avoid having beliefs and expectations; what you can and must avoid is prejudging what you observe.

Observations of Infants

47. Observing an infant in her or his natural environment (e.g., at home) and seeing how the infant interacts with the parents will be a useful part of a formal assessment.

48. The following nine dimensions may be used for classifying an infant's temperament: activity level, rhythmicity, approach or withdrawal, adaptability, threshold of responsiveness, intensity of reaction, quality of mood, distractibility, and attention span and persistence.

49. The nine dimensions lead to three temperamental types: easy infant, difficult infant, and slow-to-warm-up infant.

Cautions on the Use of Observations

50. The strengths of naturalistic observation also contribute to its weakness as a scientific procedure: It is difficult to standardize naturally occurring stimulus conditions, and human observers are fallible.

51. Consider any possible unintended harmful consequences associated with your behavioral observations, and be sure to take appropriate steps to avoid such outcomes.

Self-Monitoring Assessment

52. You can obtain valuable information about a particular behavior by asking a child to conduct a self-monitoring assessment. We use the term *behavior* to include the child's actions, thoughts, and feelings.

53. In a self-monitoring assessment, the child observes and records specific overt or covert aspects of her or his behavior and, sometimes, the circumstances associated with the behavior over a specified period.

54. To perform a self-monitoring assessment, the child must discriminate the presence or absence of a particular response (e.g., a thought, an action performed by the child himself or herself, or an action performed by another) and record the response in a behavioral log or diary or use a golf counter, wrist counter, mechanical device, or hand-held computer.

55. The appropriate procedure depends on how easy the target behavior is to detect, the response frequency, the age and intellectual ability of the child, and how easy the procedure is to use.

56. The goal is to have the child make a systematic record of the behaviors of interest, gain awareness of her or his behavior, and participate in resolving the problem.

57. Recording their own behavior may help children become better observers of their behavior.

58. The recordings also may help them discriminate changes in their problem behaviors and see how their problem behaviors change over time and across situations.

59. Self-monitoring also enables children with problems to recognize that they are not helpless, but can do something to change their own behavior.

60. A child's self-monitoring of the frequency of symptoms, changes in symptoms, activity level, mood ratings, and situational contexts will give you information about antecedent and consequent events associated with the child's symptoms.

61. Setting up a self-monitoring assessment involves selecting the appropriate target behaviors, identifying the variables that may relate to those behaviors, and choosing a recording procedure that is easy to use and provides adequate and accurate information.

62. In implementing a self-monitoring assessment, consider the child's age, motivation, and cognitive level and how these factors may affect his or her ability to do the recording.

63. The child should understand fully how to use the recording procedure and how to recognize the target behaviors.

64. Self-monitoring assessment may make a child anxious.

65. For self-monitoring to be effective, the child's parents, teachers, and siblings and other significant persons in the child's environment must be supportive of the procedure and encourage the child to record the needed information.

66. Hand-held computers are another means for recording data.

67. Limitations associated with self-monitoring assessment include reactive effects and difficulty in keeping accurate records.

68. Reactive effects are possible with self-monitoring assessment because the children know that someone will be looking at their recording sheet and because their own attention has been drawn to selected behaviors.

69. Children who are not well motivated may not make daily recordings. In such cases, they should be encouraged to turn in their recordings every day and be rewarded for their efforts.

70. Children are more likely to misreport behaviors that run counter to parents' or teachers' standards than behaviors that conform to those standards.

71. Children under 5 or 6 years of age will likely have difficulty making self-monitoring recordings.

72. When children are completing a self-monitoring assessment for specific symptoms, prompts from parents or teachers at the appointed or critical times usually increase the children's compliance with the procedure.

73. In establishing a self-monitoring assessment, tailor the techniques and instructions to the comprehension level of the child.

74. The cues used in a self-monitoring assessment should be randomly distributed to avoid the negative effects of a fixed interval.

75. When self-monitoring assessment is part of an intervention program, you may use the data as an index of change, to evaluate improvement in self-regulation, to evaluate the effectiveness of the intervention plan, and to justify changes in the plan.

Reporting Behavioral Observations

76. In describing the results of a systematic behavioral observation, you should evaluate how the setting, the people in the setting, and the environment as a whole may have affected the child's behavior.

77. When you write about people at a facility, refer to them the way the facility does, as *clients, patients, members,* or *students.*

78. Do not include in the report comments about what you were thinking as you were recording the information.

79. Help the reader understand the reason for your conclusions.

80. Clearly describe the categories you used to observe behavior.

81. When you report a percentage agreement or a reliability coefficient obtained for a systematic behavioral observation, follow it with a statement about whether the percentage agreement or reliability coefficient is satisfactory.

82. If reliability was low, discuss the reasons.

83. Do not minimize the importance of low interrater reliability just because a behavior was infrequent.

84. When you report the reliability of a ratings observation, provide the percentage agreement as well as the absolute values of the ratings (e.g., 4.3 or 2.8) and indicate what the values imply (e.g., extremely aggressive behavior or somewhat passive behavior).

KEY TERMS, CONCEPTS, AND NAMES

Observational coding systems (p. 230)
Reliability (p. 236)
Observer bias (p. 239)
Observer reactivity (p. 239)
Interobserver reliability (p. 239)
Interobserver agreement (p. 239)
Product-moment correlation coefficient (p. 239)
Phi coefficient (p. 239)

STUDY QUESTIONS

1. What factors should you consider when designing or selecting an observational coding system?
2. Discuss factors that may affect the reliability of behavioral observations.
3. Discuss the following measures of interobserver agreement: product-moment correlation coefficient, intraclass correlation coefficient, kappa, and percentage agreement.
4. What factors may affect the test-retest reliability and internal consistency of behavioral observations?
5. Discuss factors affecting the validity of behavioral observations.
6. Discuss reactivity in observational recordings. Explain why reactivity may not necessarily be detrimental, and suggest ways to reduce reactivity.
7. How would you go about reducing the number of errors that occur in your behavioral observations?
8. Discuss the strengths and limitations of observational methods.
9. Discuss special problems in observing infants.
10. Discuss self-monitoring observational procedures, including their strengths and weaknesses.
11. Present 10 guidelines for reporting behavioral observations in psychological reports.

BROAD MEASURES OF BEHAVIORAL, SOCIAL, AND EMOTIONAL FUNCTIONING AND OF PARENTING AND FAMILY VARIABLES

. . . the character which shapes our conduct is a definite and durable "something," and therefore it is reasonable to measure it.

—Sir Francis Galton, English scientist (1822–1911)

Goals and Objectives

This chapter is designed to enable you to do the following:

- Understand issues related to the evaluation of behavioral, social, and emotional competencies in children

- Become familiar with a range of standardized instruments useful in assessing behavioral, social, and emotional functioning in children and parenting and family variables

This chapter covers measures designed to enable a broad assessment of behavioral, social, and emotional competencies in children and adolescents, as well as assessment of parenting and family variables. The measures covered in Chapter 14, in contrast, are designed to assess more specific areas of clinical functioning, such as antisocial behavior, anxiety, or depression. The measures discussed in this chapter are useful in identifying children with special needs and making decisions about appropriate interventions for such children, in conducting follow-up evaluations, and in evaluating parenting and family variables. Assessing behavioral, social, and emotional functioning is important, because nearly 20% of children and adolescents in the United States show symptoms of psychological disorder in any given year. Unfortunately, most symptoms go unidentified and the disorders untreated (U.S. Department of Health and Human Services, 1999).

BACKGROUND CONSIDERATIONS

The chapter considers both objective and projective measures of behavioral, social, and emotional competencies of children and adolescents. The objective measures contain clear and structured items, require specific responses, and use precise scoring procedures. The resulting scores can be quantified, normed, and profiled. The "objectivity" in objective measures lies in the test material (e.g., uniform instructions, item content, response format), the statistical underpinnings of the test (e.g., standardized norms), and examiner procedures (e.g., rigorous scoring methods).

Projective measures, in contrast, contain ambiguous stimuli, such as inkblots or pictures of situations or people, onto which an examinee projects covert aspects of his or her personality. The examinee's responses are then evaluated by the examiner using his or her clinical expertise or one or more interpretive systems associated with the specific projective measure. Projective measures may provide quantifiable scores, depending on the method used to interpret the responses. Projective techniques are more open ended than objective measures, and their scoring and interpretation usually require a high level of clinical judgment.

Measures of behavioral, social, and emotional competencies and the scores derived from them reflect the complex interaction of several elements:

- The characteristics of the scale or checklist used (e.g., content, wording of items, reading level required, completion time, standardization sample, date of standardization)
- The child's age, sex, ethnicity, type of disturbance, reading ability, response style, and degree of openness
- The informant's or rater's expectancies, recall ability, openness, comprehension of items, accuracy of observations, and response style
- The examiner's sex, ethnicity, traits, and ability to establish rapport

- The setting (e.g., school, home, playground, hospital, clinic, prison)
- The reasons for the evaluation (e.g., screening, diagnosis, placement, intervention, program evaluation)

In different personality tests and behavior rating and checklist measures, scales with similar names may or may not assess the same behaviors; scales with different names may cover similar behaviors. For example, some scales measure only hyperactive behavior, whereas others include hyperactive behavior as part of a conduct problem factor (Hoge & Andrews, 1992). You will need to study each measure carefully in order to determine precisely what it is intended to measure.

Some instruments are designed to assess normal personality traits, while others are clinical tools designed to assess psychopathological conditions. The latter types of instruments may use various diagnostic systems, such as *DSM-IV–TR* or empirically derived personality dimensions (see Chapter 1).

The results from personality tests, behavior rating and checklist measures, and observational methods (see Chapters 8 and 9) may not always be congruent, because the measures are based on different behavior samples. Personality tests and behavior rating and checklist measures usually sample behaviors that have existed for a long time, whereas observational methods focus on present behaviors. These three types of measures are each valid for different purposes. Because each type of measure provides a different perspective on problem behaviors, we recommend that, if possible, personality tests, behavior rating and checklist measures, and observational methods all be used in an assessment.

PERSONALITY TESTS

Personality tests are primarily self-report measures; that is, the individual responds to specific items using fixed response categories (e.g., "true" or "false"). Most personality tests use a paper-and-pencil format, although computerized response formats are also available. Some personality tests are designed for identifying pathological states, others focus on normal personality traits, while still others provide information about both normal and abnormal dimensions of personality. This chapter covers five personality tests:

- Adolescent Psychopathology Scale (APS)
- Adolescent Psychopathology Scale–Short Form (APS–SF)
- Millon Adolescent Clinical Inventory (MACI)
- Minnesota Multiphasic Personality Inventory–Adolescent (MMPI–A)
- Personality Inventory for Youth (PIY)

Because personality tests are based on the individual's responses to fixed questions, the validity of test scores may be affected by the readability of the items. Examinees may be unable to read items or may misinterpret or misunderstand them. Therefore, it is critical that the examinee have the reading level required for the specific personality test.

Another factor that can compromise the validity of personality tests is response bias (or response set). One type of response bias is associated with the examinee's intentions. Examinees may slant their replies to create a certain impression. For example, some examinees want to present a favorable impression (*faking-good response set*); others, an unfavorable impression (*faking-bad response set*); still others, a specific impression of themselves (e.g., self-assertive, extroverted). The faking-good response set may be used in an employment interview, where the examinee wants to appear in the best possible light. The examinee responds to questions dishonestly in order to improve the chances of getting a job offer. The faking-bad response set may be used when the examinee wants to obtain special services (such as exemption from academic expectations) or financial gain, to remain in a setting rather than be discharged, or to get attention or sympathy.

Another type of response bias arises from the characteristic way individuals respond to items, regardless of content. An examinee with an *acquiescence response set* has a tendency to agree with each item; an examinee with a *deviance response set* has a tendency to respond in a deviant, unfavorable, uncommon, or unusual way. An examinee with a *social desirability response set* has a tendency to answer items in what he or she perceives as the "right," "appropriate," or most socially accepted way, regardless of whether the answers describe what the examinee actually thinks, believes, or does. Examinees typically give socially desirable answers in an attempt to look good, more acceptable, less deviant, or less idiosyncratic. The faking-good and social desirability response sets may lead to similarly biased responses. However, the faking-good response set is an intentional attempt to create a favorable impression, while the social desirability response set is a more passive attempt to please the examiner by responding in a way that society generally approves.

Test makers usually try to control for response bias by using a combination of positively worded items, negatively worded items, and neutrally worded items. Ideally, personality tests should contain scales to detect biased responding. For example, the Personality Inventory for Youth (PIY; Lachar & Gruber, 1995a, 1995b) has (a) a Dissimulation Scale (which identifies profiles reflecting faking-bad or malingering types of response sets), (b) a Defensiveness Scale (which detects efforts to engage in minimization or denial), and (c) an Inconsistency Scale (which detects random response strategies). Validity scales in personality tests are an important aid to interpretation.

To determine whether an examinee's responses reflect an underlying response style, you should routinely consider the following questions:

- Did the examinee answer all items either "yes," "no," "agree," or "disagree"?

- Was there any indication of a faking-good or faking-bad response set (e.g., did the examinee always respond "yes" to either positive or negative items)?
- Was there a consistent pattern of responding (e.g., did the examinee alternate "yes" and "no" responses)?
- Were there indications that the examinee was indifferent or careless in completing the test?

ADOLESCENT PSYCHOPATHOLOGY SCALE AND ADOLESCENT PSYCHOPATHOLOGY SCALE–SHORT FORM

The 346-item Adolescent Psychopathology Scale (APS; Reynolds, 1998a, 1998b) and the 115-item Adolescent Psychopathology Scale–Short Form (APS–SF; Reynolds, 2000) are two separate but related measures. The APS is a comprehensive measure of 25 *DSM-IV–TR* disorders and other social and emotional problems, whereas the APS–SF is a brief form that assesses 12 critical areas of adolescent social and emotional competencies.

The APS is a self-report measure of adolescent psychopathology, personality, and psychosocial problems, developed for adolescents ages 12 to 19 years. It requires a third-grade reading level and takes about 45 to 60 minutes to complete. It has 40 scales: (a) 20 clinical and 5 personality scales that evaluate symptoms associated with *DSM-IV–TR* disorders, (b) 11 psychosocial problem content scales that assess psychological problems, and (c) 4 response style scales that provide information on truthfulness, consistency, infrequency, and critical item endorsement (e.g., veracity of responses, random responding, or unusual or bizarre behaviors). The scales in the APS are grouped into three broad factors that provide scores for internalizing, externalizing, and personality problem domains (see Table 10-1).

The APS–SF is useful when you need a brief form. Designed for ages 12 to 19 years, it measures 12 clinical disorders, has two validity scales that provide information on defensiveness and consistency in responding, and takes about 15 to 20 minutes to complete. The APS–SF includes an Academic Problems scale and an Anger/Violence Proneness scale that are not included on the APS, and it also has modified APS scales. Table 10-2 lists the 14 APS–SF scales and the corresponding APS scales.

Scores

Item response formats (both rating scale and time period) on both forms vary, depending on the disorder. For example, the Conduct Disorder scale uses a true/false response format for rating problem behaviors over the past 6 months, whereas the Major Depression scale uses a 3-point response format for

Table 10-1
Domains and Scales on the Adolescent Psychopathology Scale

Domain	Scales
Clinical Disorders	Attention-Deficit/Hyperactivity Disorder
	Conduct Disorder
	Oppositional Defiant Disorder
	Adjustment Disorder
	Substance Abuse Disorder
	Anorexia Nervosa
	Bulimia Nervosa
	Sleep Disorder
	Somatization Disorder
	Panic Disorder
	Obsessive-Compulsive Disorder
	Generalized Anxiety Disorder
	Social Phobia
	Separation Anxiety Disorder
	Posttraumatic Stress Disorder
	Major Depression
	Dysthymic Disorder
	Mania
	Depersonalization Disorder
	Schizophrenia
Personality Disorders	Avoidant Personality Disorder
	Obsessive-Compulsive Personality Disorder
	Borderline Personality Disorder
	Schizotypal Personality Disorder
	Paranoid Personality Disorder
Psychosocial Problem Content	Self-Concept Scale
	Psychosocial Substance Use Difficulties
	Introversion Scale
	Alienation-Boredom Scale
	Anger Scale
	Aggression Scale
	Interpersonal Problem Scale
	Emotional Lability Scale
	Disorientation Scale
	Suicide Scale
	Social Adaptation Scale
Response Style Indicators	Lie Response Scale
	Consistency Response Scale
	Infrequency Response Scale
	Critical Item Endorsement
Factor Score	Internalizing Disorder Factor Score Scale
	Externalizing Disorder Factor Score Scale
	Personality Disorder Factor Score Scale

rating symptoms of depression over the past 2 weeks: 0 (almost never), 1 (sometimes), 2 (nearly every day). The APS can be scored only by a computer program, which provides raw scores and T scores ($M = 50$, $SD = 10$) for all scales.

Table 10-2
Correspondence of Scales on the Adolescent Psychopathology Scale–Short Form (APS–SF) with Those on the Adolescent Psychopathology Scale (APS)

Scale	APS–SF	APS
Conduct Disorder	X	X
Oppositional Defiant Disorder	X	X
Substance Abuse Disorder	X	X
Anger/Violence Proneness	X	—
Anger/Aggression	—	X
Academic Problems	X	—
Attention-Deficit/Hyperactivity Disorder	—	X
Generalized Anxiety Disorder	X	X
Posttraumatic Stress Disorder	X	X
Major Depression	X	X
Eating Disturbance	X	—
Anorexia Nervosa/Bulimia Nervosa	—	X
Suicide Scale	X	X
Self-Concept Scale	X	X
Interpersonal Problems	X	X
Defensiveness	X	—
Lie Response Scale	—	X
Consistency Response	X	X

Standardization

The APS and the APS–SF were standardized on a stratified sample of 1,827 adolescents, drawn from eight states between 1989 and 1991, that closely matched the 1990 U.S. Census data for age, gender, and ethnicity. In addition, there was a clinical sample of 506 adolescents from 31 psychiatric inpatient and outpatient settings in 22 states that represented a range of *DSM-IV–TR* disorders. An additional sample of 1,007 adolescents from school settings was used in reliability and validity studies.

Reliability

Internal consistency reliabilities for the APS in the school-based standardization sample range from .69 to .95 (*Mdn* r_{xx} = .83) for the Clinical Disorder, Personality Disorder, and Psychosocial Problem Content scales. Median internal consistency reliabilities are .95 for the Internalizing Disorder factor, .86 for the Externalizing Disorder factor, and .86 for the Personality Disorder factor.

In the clinical sample, internal consistency reliabilities for the APS range from .70 to .95 (*Mdn* r_{xx} = .84) for the Clinical Disorder, Personality Disorder, and Psychosocial Problem Content scales. Median internal consistency reliabilities are .95 for the Internalizing Disorder factor, .82 for the Externalizing Disorder factor, and .88 for the Personality Disorder factor.

Test-retest reliabilities, obtained on a sample of 64 adolescents in a school setting over a 2-week retest interval, range from .76 to .89 (*Mdn* r_{tt} = .84) for the Clinical Disorder, Personality Disorder, and Psychosocial Problem Content scales. Median test-retest reliabilities are .82, .85, and .81 for the Internalizing Disorder factor, Externalizing Disorder factor, and Personality Disorder factor, respectively.

In the school-based standardization sample, internal consistency reliabilities for the APS–SF range from .80 to .91 (*Mdn* r_{xx} = .84) for the 12 clinical scales. In the clinical sample, internal consistency reliabilities for the 12 clinical scales range from .82 to .91 (*Mdn* r_{xx} = .86). Test-retest reliabilities, obtained on a sample of 64 adolescents in a school setting over a 2-week retest interval, range from .76 to .91 (*Mdn* r_{tt} = .84) for the 12 clinical scales.

Validity

The content validity of the APS and the APS–SF is supported by strong correlations of items with the total scale and by findings from factor analyses. Construct validity and criterion-related validity are supported by a factor analysis indicating that APS and APS–SF scales correspond satisfactorily to the relevant *DSM-IV–TR* disorders and by the finding that scores correlate satisfactorily with scores from parallel self-report and clinical measures, including the Minnesota Multiphasic Personality Inventory. Discriminant validity is good, as demonstrated by (a) low correlations between the APS scales and measures of social desirability and cognitive ability and (b) significant differences in scores between the standardization and the clinical samples on all APS scales except the Consistency Response scale.

Comment on the APS and the APS–SF

The APS allows a comprehensive assessment of many *DSM-IV–TR* clinical and personality disorders, including disorders not evaluated by other measures. Reliability and content, construct, and criterion-related validity are satisfactory. The computer program not only scores the test but also provides a detailed psychological report. The APS–SF also has satisfactory reliability and validity, and it allows the assessment of important domains of adolescent psychopathology. It serves as an alternative to the APS when time is limited. The Academic Problems and Anger/Violence Proneness scales make the APS–SF particularly useful in school settings.

MILLON ADOLESCENT CLINICAL INVENTORY

The Millon Adolescent Clinical Inventory (MACI; Millon, 1993) is a replacement for the Millon Adolescent Personality Inventory. The MACI is a 160-item self-report scale designed for measuring adolescent personality characteristics and clinical syndromes in youths from ages 13 to 19 years. It requires a sixth-grade reading level, takes about 30 minutes to complete, and contains 3 domains, 27 scales, and 4 validity scales (see Table 10-3). The MACI is based on Millon's theory of personality, which proposes that both normal and abnormal personality styles can be derived by combining three polarities: pleasure-pain, active-passive, and self-other.

Table 10-3
Domains and Scales on the Millon Adolescent Clinical Inventory

Domain	Scales
Personality Patterns	Introversive
	Inhibited
	Doleful
	Submissive
	Dramatizing
	Egotistic
	Unruly
	Forceful
	Conforming
	Oppositional
	Self-Demeaning
	Borderline Tendency
Expressed Concerns	Identity Diffusion
	Self-Devaluation
	Bodily Disapproval
	Sexual Discomfort
	Peer Insecurity
	Social Insensitivity
	Family Discord
	Childhood Abuse
Clinical Syndromes	Eating Dysfunctions
	Substance-Abuse Proneness
	Delinquency Predisposition
	Impulsive Propensity
	Anxious Feelings
	Depressive Affect
	Suicidal Tendency
Modifying Indices	Disclosure
	Desirability
	Debasement
Other	Reliability

Scores

The MACI uses a true/false answer format. Although a hand-scoring template is provided with the scale, the scoring procedure is complex, and thus computer-based scoring is recommended. (The test publisher offers a computerized scoring service, or users can purchase scoring software to install on their own computers.) A standard score is provided for each of the scales and subscales reflecting the relative standing of the examinee's raw score based on gender and age group (13 to 15 years or 16 to 19 years).

Standardization

The standardization sample consisted of 579 youths (313 males, 266 females) between the ages of 13 and 19 years. Seventy-nine percent of the sample was Euro American, 7% African American, 6% Hispanic American, and 8% Other. The sample does not match U.S. Census data.

Reliability

Internal consistency reliabilities for 29 of the 31 scales (no internal consistency reliabilities for the Disclosure and Reliability scales) range from .69 to .91 ($Mdn\ r_{xx} = .83$). Test-retest reliabilities, based on a sample of 47 youths retested over a 3- to 7-day interval, range from .57 to .92 ($Mdn\ r_{tt} = .82$).

Validity

Construct validity is supported through correlations between MACI scales and parallel scales on the Beck Depression Inventory, the Beck Hopelessness Scale, the Beck Anxiety Inventory, the Eating Disorders Inventory–2, and the Problem Oriented Screening Instrument. Clinicians were asked to rate the 333 clients in the two cross-validation samples on the Personality Patterns, Expressed Concerns, and Clinical Syndromes scales. For one sample, 14 of 25 correlations were statistically significant, and for the other sample, 20 of 24 correlations were statistically significant.

Comment on the MACI

The MACI is based on considerable research with the Millon Adolescent Personality Inventory. The scales are theoretically derived and clinically meaningful. Reliability and validity are minimally satisfactory. In addition, the standardization sample is small and probably not representative of the U.S. population. Therefore, the MACI must be used with caution.

MINNESOTA MULTIPHASIC PERSONALITY INVENTORY–ADOLESCENT

The Minnesota Multiphasic Personality Inventory–Adolescent (MMPI–A; Butcher, Williams, Graham, Archer, Tellegen, Ben-Porath, & Kaemmer, 1992), designed to be used with adolescents ages 14 to 18 years, draws on the long history of the MMPI, which was developed in the 1940s by Hathaway and McKinley. Most of the 478 items on the MMPI–A were drawn from the MMPI. The MMPI–A has 10 basic scales, 7 validity scales, and 15 content scales (see Table 10-4) and takes about 45 to 60 minutes to complete. The reading level varies by item, with a seventh-grade reading level recommended; however, many items require a higher reading level (Archer, 1992).

Table 10-4
Scales on the Minnesota Multiphasic Personality Inventory–Adolescent

Type of scale	Scales
Basic	Hypochondriasis Depression Hysteria Psychopathic Deviate Masculinity-Femininity Paranoia Psychasthenia Schizophrenia Hypomania Social Introversion
Validity	Variable Response Inconsistency True Response Inconsistency Infrequency 1 Infrequency 2 Infrequency Lie Defensiveness
Content	Anxiety Obsessiveness Depression Health Concerns Alienation Bizarre Mentation Anger Cynicism Conduct Problems Low Self-Esteem Low Aspiration Social Discomfort Family Problems School Problems Negative Treatment Indicators

Scores

The MMPI–A uses a true/false response format. It can be scored by hand; by the test publisher, who will provide several score and interpretive reports; or by computer software available from other sources (Archer, 1999). Raw scores are transformed to T scores ($M = 50$, $SD = 10$).

Standardization

The standardization sample consisted of 805 males and 815 females drawn from eight states between 1985 and 1989, with 85% of the sample from the Midwest and the East Coast. Most of the adolescents (95%) were between the ages of 14 and 17 years, and the sample was matched to the 1980 U.S. Census data. The ethnic distribution was 76% Euro American, 12% African American, and 12% Other. Over 60% of the sample came from families in which the parents had some college education. Norms are provided separately for males and females. A clinical sample of 713 adolescents from treatment settings in Minnesota, tested between 1985 and 1988, was used for additional norms.

Reliability

Internal consistency reliabilities in the school-based standardization sample range from .40 to .89 ($Mdn\ r_{xx} = .67$) for the basic scales and from .55 to .83 ($Mdn\ r_{xx} = .75$) for the content scales. Internal consistency reliabilities in the clinical sample range from .35 to .91 ($Mdn\ r_{xx} = .66$) for the basic scales and from .63 to .89 ($Mdn\ r_{xx} = .78$) for the content scales. Test-retest reliabilities, assessed on 154 adolescents in a school setting over a 1-week retest interval, range from .65 to .84 ($Mdn\ r_{tt} = .80$) for the basic scales and from .62 to .82 ($Mdn\ r_{tt} = .72$) for the content scales.

Validity

Construct validity is limited. A factor analysis of the basic scales conducted separately for males and females in the school sample yielded four factors, with most scales loading on the first factor and interpretability of the factors limited. The factors did not differentiate between internalizing and externalizing problems. This difficulty may be due in part to the overlap in item content across the basic MMPI–A scales. Correlations between the basic scales and the Child Behavior Checklist and clinical information derived from records were low, with most in the .10 to .29 range.

Comment on the MMPI–A

The MMPI–A is a downward extension and revision of the MMPI, although much of the content of the original MMPI developed for adults in the 1940s remains in this revision. The MMPI–A has a limited age range, requires a somewhat high reading level, has moderate reliability and limited validity, and is difficult to interpret. If you do use the MMPI–A, consult books by Archer (1992), Butcher and Williams (1992), and Williams, Butcher, Ben-Porath, and Graham (1992) for help with interpretation.

PERSONALITY INVENTORY FOR YOUTH

The Personality Inventory for Youth (PIY; Lachar & Gruber, 1995a, 1995b), a 270-item self-report measure of psychopathology, is a companion measure to the Personality Inventory for Children–Second Edition (PIC–2) discussed later. It is appropriate for use with children and adolescents in grades 4 to 12, requires a third-grade reading level, and takes about 30 to 60 minutes to complete. The PIY has nine clinical scales (with each further divided into two or three subscales), four validity scales, and 87 critical items to help in the assessment of psychopathology (see Table 10-5).

Scores

The PIY uses a true/false response format. It can be hand scored by the examiner or computer scored by the test publisher. Raw scores are converted to T scores ($M = 50$, $SD = 10$). Norms are provided for males and females.

Standardization

The PIY was standardized in 1991 and 1992 on a stratified sample of 2,327 students from grades 4 to 12. The sample was matched to the 1987 U.S. Census data and drawn from five states. In addition, there was a clinical standardization sample of 1,178 adolescents.

Reliability

Internal consistency reliabilities for the nine clinical scales range from .71 to .90 ($Mdn\ r_{xx} = .82$) in the school-based sample and from .74 to .92 ($Mdn\ r_{xx} = .85$) in the clinical sample. Internal consistency reliabilities for the subscales range from .40 to .79 ($Mdn\ r_{xx} = .70$) in the school-based sample and from .44 to .84 ($Mdn\ r_{xx} = .73$) in the clinical sample. Test-retest reliabilities for the clinical scales range from .81 to .91 ($Mdn\ r_{tt} = .85$) in a school-based sample of 129 adolescents retested over a 7- to 10-day interval and from .76 to .91 ($Mdn\ r_{tt} = .82$) in a clinical sample of 86 adolescents retested over a 7-day interval.

Table 10-5
Scales and Subscales on the Personality Inventory for Youth

Scale	Subscales
Cognitive Impairment	Poor Achievement and Memory Inadequate Abilities Learning Problems
Impulsivity and Distractibility	Brashness Distractibility Impulsivity
Delinquency	Antisocial Behavior Dyscontrol Noncompliance
Family Dysfunction	Parent-Child Conflict Parent Maladjustment Marital Discord
Reality Distortion	Feelings of Alienation Hallucinations and Delusions
Somatic Concern	Psychosomatic Syndrome Muscular Tension and Anxiety Preoccupation with Disease
Psychological Discomfort	Fear and Worry Depression Sleep Disturbance
Social Withdrawal	Social Introversion Isolation
Social Skills Deficits	Limited Peer Status Conflict with Peers
Validity	—
Inconsistency	—
Dissimulation	—
Defensiveness	—

Validity

Construct validity is satisfactory to good, as demonstrated by low to moderate correlations between the PIY and the MMPI in a group of 152 adolescents from the clinical sample. Moderate correlations with other measures of adjustment in a clinical sample of 50 females and 29 males provide additional evidence of criterion-related validity.

Comment on the PIY

The PIY evaluates a number of domains, such as Family Dysfunction, Delinquency, and Social Withdrawal, useful in un-

derstanding the problems of adolescents. It is limited in its evaluation of specific disorders, such as depression and anxiety, because of the small number of items in these areas and low to moderate reliability of the subscales. Because the PIY scales were developed by factor-analytic procedures, the content of each scale and subscale needs to be carefully examined to determine whether elevated scores are associated with the scale description. Overall, reliability and validity are satisfactory.

BEHAVIOR RATING AND CHECKLIST MEASURES

Standardized behavior rating and checklist measures usually assess overt displays of behavioral maladjustment, although some assess positive behavioral competencies as well. Behavior rating and checklist measures are generally completed by an individual familiar with the examinee, such as a parent, teacher, caregiver, or clinician, but some are self-report measures. Self-report measures sometimes bear a close resemblance to personality tests, although personality tests usually focus on underlying personality traits rather than on patterns of overt behavior.

Behavior rating and checklist measures require informants to make judgments about a child's functioning. Because judgments are subject to bias and distortion, informants' credibility must be carefully examined. If there are doubts about an informant's credibility, the validity of the results must be questioned. In the process of completing behavior rating and checklist measures, informants may reveal their own attitudes toward the child and toward the topics covered by the measure. Depending on the problem being evaluated, informants may or may not have had the opportunity to observe the behavior or know how the child is feeling.

When multiple informants are used, it is important to consider the consistency of ratings across informants. Differences among informants' ratings may mean one or more of the following:

- The child changes her or his behavior depending on the situation or setting.
- One or more of the informants is unreliable.
- The informants have different response styles (e.g., one informant is reluctant to report minor deviations, while another is willing to report the slightest deviation as a problem; one informant tends to use extremely high and low ratings, while another sticks closely to average ratings).
- One or more of the informants is experiencing high stress levels.
- The type of problem manifested by the child is difficult to observe (e.g., symptoms of an internalizing disorder are more difficult to observe than symptoms of an externalizing disorder).
- Other, unknown factors are contributing to the unreliability of the ratings.

Informants differ as to their familiarity with the child, sensitivity to and tolerance for behavior problems, personality, expectations, comfort with various test formats, and willingness to use certain rating scale positions. In addition, informants may use different frames of reference or interpret similar behaviors in different ways, depending on whether the child is a clinic patient or is attending a public school. The child's race, socioeconomic status, appearance, and degree of psychopathology also may influence informants' judgments of the child's behavior.

Because parents and teachers are likely to see different aspects of a child, information from both sources is needed to obtain a comprehensive picture of the child. Parents are better able to rate behaviors that occur primarily at home (eating, sleeping, sibling relations, family relations, acting out), whereas teachers are more qualified to rate behaviors that occur primarily at school (academic performance, peer relations, attention, following directions). Teacher ratings have the advantage of being based on observations made in a relatively consistent setting and on direct comparisons with other children who are usually at the same developmental level as the referred child. However, teachers may have to rely on a limited sample of behavior when they are asked to rate a child during the first few months of the school year or when they are asked to rate behaviors that occur outside the classroom.

Rating adolescent behaviors is particularly difficult for teachers, because they have limited contact with junior and senior high school students outside the formal classroom setting. Parent ratings have the advantage of being based on observations of the child's behavior in different settings and over a long period. However, parents, too, usually have fewer opportunities to observe behavior as children grow older and become more independent.

The reliability and validity of ratings may be affected by the specificity of the rating task. For example, items that require rating of specific behaviors (e.g., "Has the child fought with another child on at least three occasions during the last month?") may yield more reliable results than items requiring global judgments (e.g., "Is the child aggressive?").

As with the personality tests, several diagnostic systems are represented in the behavior rating and checklist measures discussed below. Two dimensions appear with some frequency. One is an internalizing dimension, represented by scales such as Anxiety, Depression, Sleep Disturbance, Somatic Concerns, Thought Disorders, and Withdrawal. The other is an externalizing dimension, represented by scales such as Aggressive Behavior (Covert), Aggressive Behavior (Overt Physical), Aggressive Behavior (Overt Verbal), Attention Problems, Delinquency, Hyperactivity, Impulse Control, and Oppositional/Defiant. As noted earlier, although dimensions in different measures may have the same name, they may be defined differently. Table 10-6 provides an overview of the 18 behavior rating and checklist measures covered in this section.

Table 10-6
Ages and Informant Types for 17 Children's Behavior Rating and Checklist Measures

Behavioral rating and checklist measures of children	Ages (in years)	Informant
Behavior Assessment System for Children–Second Edition (BASC–2)	2 to 25	Teacher, parent, self
Behavior Dimensions Scale–School Version (BDS–S)	5 to 15	Teacher
Behavior Dimensions Scale–Home Version (BDS–H)	3 to 18	Parent
Child Behavior Checklist for Ages 6–18 (CBCL/6–18)	6 to 18	Parent
Teacher's Report Form (TRF)	6 to 18	Teacher
Youth Self-Report (YSR)	11 to 18	Self
Child Behavior Checklist for Ages 1½–5 (CBCL/1½–5)	1½ to 5	Parent
Caregiver–Teacher Report Form (C–TRF)	1½ to 5	Teacher, day-care provider
Connors' Rating Scales–Revised (CRS–R)	3 to 17	Parent, teacher, self
Devereux Scales of Mental Disorders (DSMD)	5 to 18	Parent, teacher
Eyberg Child Behavior Inventory (ECBI)	2 to 16	Parent
Sutter-Eyberg Student Behavior Inventory–Revised (SESBI–R)	2 to 16	Teacher
Jesness Inventory–Revised (JI–R)	8 to adult	Self
Personality Inventory for Children–Second Edition (PIC–2)	5 to 19	Parent
Revised Behavior Problem Checklist (RBPC)	5 to 18	Parent, teacher
Reynolds Adolescent Adjustment Screening Inventory (RAASI)	12 to 19	Self
Student Behavior Survey (SBS)	5 to 18	Teacher

BEHAVIOR ASSESSMENT SYSTEM FOR CHILDREN–SECOND EDITION

The Behavior Assessment System for Children–Second Edition (BASC–2; Reynolds & Kamphaus, 2004) is a measure of adaptive behavior and problem behavior in children and adolescents. The BASC–2 contains Teacher Rating Scales, Parent Rating Scales, and a Self-Report of Personality. The BASC–2 also includes a structured developmental history and a behavioral observation system; however, these two sections are not covered in this review.

Both the Teacher Rating Scales and the Parent Rating Scales have three forms that cover the same ages: preschool (2 to 5 years), child (6 to 11 years), and adolescent (12 to 21 years). In the Teacher Rating Scales, the preschool form has 100 items, the child form has 139 items, and the adolescent form has 139 items. In the Parent Rating Scales, the preschool form has 134 items, the child form has 160 items, and the adolescent form has 150 items.

The Self-Report of Personality also has three forms: child (8 to 11 years), with 139 items; adolescent (12 to 21 years), with 176 items; and young adult (18 to 25 years, attending a post-secondary school), with 185 items. Each form takes about 20 to 30 minutes to complete and requires about a third-grade reading level.

The BASC–2 has primary scales, content scales, and composite scales (see Table 10-7), as well as several indexes that measure response sets. For example, the Teacher Rating Scales, Parent Rating Scales, and Self-Report of Personality have an F Index to measure a preponderance of negative answers (faking bad). The Self-Report of Personality also has an L Index that measures a preponderance of positive statements (faking good) and a V Index that measures responses that are nonsensical or highly implausible. Finally, the BASC–2 scoring software provides a Consistency Index that measures differing responses to items usually answered similarly and a Response Pattern Index that measures the number of times a response differs from the response to the previous item.

Scores

The Teacher Rating Scales and the Parent Rating Scales both use a 4-point response format: 0 (never), 1 (sometimes), 2 (often), 3 (almost always); the Self-Report of Personality uses a true/false response format for some items and a 4-point response format for other items: 0 (never), 1 (sometimes), 2 (often), 3 (almost always). The BASC–2 provides T scores ($M = 50$, $SD = 10$) and percentile ranks. Scoring can be accomplished with self-scoring carbonless answer sheets or by computer.

Standardization

The manual provides norms for a general population sample and for a clinical sample. The norm group for the Teacher Rating Scales consisted of teachers of 1,050 children ages 2 to 5 years, 1,800 children ages 6 to 11 years, and 1,800 children ages 12 to 18 years. The norm group for the Parent Rating Scales consisted of parents of 1,200 children ages 2 to 5 years, 1,800 children ages 6 to 11 years, and 1,800 adolescents ages 12 to 18 years. The norm group for the Self-Report of Personality consisted of 1,500 children ages 8 to 11 years, 1,900 adolescents ages 15 to 18 years, and 706 young adults ages 18 to 25 years. Except for the young adult sample, all samples closely match the 2001 U.S. Census data with regard to age, gender, and ethnicity; for the young adult sample, the manual provides no information about ethnicity or educational level of the mother.

The clinical standardization sample consisted of children receiving mental health or special education services from schools and clinics. The sample for the Teacher Rating Scales contained 317 children ages 4 to 5 years, 673 children ages 6 to 11 years, and 789 adolescents ages 12 to 18 years. The sample for the Parent Rating Scales contained 300 children ages 4 to 5 years, 799 children ages 6 to 11 years, and 876 adolescents ages 12 to 18 years. The sample for the Self-Report of Personality contained 577 children ages 6 to 11 years and 950 adolescents ages 12 to 18 years. Learning disability and ADHD were the most common diagnoses.

Reliability

Internal consistency reliabilities for the standardization group range from .75 to .97 ($Mdn\ r_{xx} = .88$) for the Teacher Rating Scales, from .70 to .88 ($Mdn\ r_{xx} = .84$) for the Parent Rating Scales, and from .67 to .90 ($Mdn\ r_{xx} = .81$) for the Self-Report of Personality. Similar internal consistency reliabilities were reported for the clinical samples.

For the Teacher Rating Scales, test-retest reliabilities range from .65 to .92 ($Mdn\ r_{tt} = .83$) for a sample of 240 teachers retested over 8 to 65 days. For the Parent Rating Scales, test-retest reliabilities range from .65 to .89 ($Mdn\ r_{tt} = .79$) for a sample of 252 parents retested over 9 to 70 days. For the Self-Report of Personality, test-retest reliabilities range from .63 to .97 ($Mdn\ r_{tt} = .75$) for a sample of 240 children and adolescents retested over intervals ranging from 13 to 66 days.

Interrater reliabilities range from .23 to .71 ($Mdn\ r_{rr} = .56$) for the Teacher Rating Scales, based on a sample of 170 children rated by two teachers, and from .56 to .90 ($Mdn\ r_{rr} = .76$) for the Parent Rating Scales, based on a sample of 134 children rated by two parents or caregivers.

Validity

The content, construct, and criterion-related validities of the BASC–2 scales are satisfactory. The content of the BASC–2 is related to standard diagnostic systems, factor analyses support the grouping of scales into composites, and correlations with parallel measures of behavior are satisfactory.

Table 10-7
Scales and Composites of the Behavior Assessment System for Children–Second Edition

Teacher Rating Scales: scales and composites	Ages covered (in years)	Parent Rating Scales: scales and composites	Ages covered (in years)	Self-Report of Personality: scales and composites	Ages covered (in years)
Primary Scale					
Adaptability	2 to 21	Activities of Daily Living	2 to 21	Alcohol Abuse	18 to 25
Aggression	2 to 21	Adaptability	2 to 21	Anxiety	8 to 25
Anxiety	2 to 21	Aggression	2 to 21	Attention Problems	8 to 25
Attention Problems	2 to 21	Anxiety	2 to 21	Attitude to School	8 to 21
Attitude to Teachers	2 to 21	Attention Problems	2 to 21	Attitude to Teachers	8 to 21
Atypicality	2 to 21	Attitude to Teachers	2 to 21	Atypicality	8 to 25
Conduct Problems	6 to 21	Atypicality	2 to 21	Depression	8 to 25
Depression	2 to 21	Conduct Problems	6 to 21	Hyperactivity	8 to 25
Functional Communication	2 to 21	Depression	2 to 21	Interpersonal Relations	8 to 25
Hyperactivity	2 to 21	Functional Communication	2 to 21	Locus of Control	8 to 25
Leadership	6 to 21	Hyperactivity	2 to 21	Relations with Parents	8 to 25
Learning Problems	6 to 21	Leadership	6 to 21	School Adjustment	18 to 25
Social Skills	2 to 21	Social Skills	2 to 21	Self-Esteem	8 to 25
Somatization	2 to 21	Somatization	2 to 21	Self-Reliance	8 to 25
Study Skills	6 to 21	Withdrawal	2 to 21	Sensation Seeking	12 to 25
Withdrawal	2 to 21			Sense of Inadequacy	8 to 25
				Social Stress	8 to 25
				Somatization	12 to 25
Content Scale					
Anger Control	2 to 21	Anger Control	2 to 21	Anger Control	12 to 25
Bullying	2 to 21	Bullying	2 to 21	Ego Strength	12 to 25
Developmental Social Dis.	2 to 21	Developmental Social Dis.	2 to 21	Mania	12 to 25
Emotional Self-Control	2 to 21	Emotional Self-Control	2 to 21	Test Anxiety	12 to 25
Executive Functioning	2 to 21	Executive Functioning	2 to 21		
Negative Emotionality	2 to 21	Negative Emotionality	2 to 21		
Resiliency	2 to 21	Resiliency	2 to 21		
Composite					
Adaptive Skills	2 to 21	Adaptive Skills	2 to 21	Emotional Symptom Ind.	8 to 25
Behavioral Symptom Index	2 to 21	Behavioral Symptom Index	2 to 21	Inattention/Hyperactivity	8 to 25
Externalizing Problems	2 to 21	Externalizing Problems	2 to 21	Internalizing Problems	8 to 25
Internalizing Problems	2 to 21	Internalizing Problems	2 to 21	Personal Adjustment	8 to 25
School Problems	6 to 21			School Problems	8 to 21

Note. Abbreviations: Development Social Dis. = Developmental Social Disorder, Emotional Symptom Ind. = Emotional Symptom Index.
Source: Adapted from Reynolds and Kamphaus (2004).

Comment on the BASC–2

The BASC–2 is one of the few measures that permits an integrative approach to the assessment of children and adolescents across multiple informants. Reliability and validity are satisfactory. However, the failure to have similar scales in all three measures hinders comparisons across the three measures. Because little information is provided about the norm group for 18- to 25-year-olds for the Self-Report of Personality, it must be used cautiously at these ages.

BEHAVIOR DIMENSIONS SCALE–SCHOOL VERSION AND BEHAVIOR DIMENSIONS SCALE–HOME VERSION

The Behavior Dimensions Scale–School Version (BDS–S; McCarney, 1995b) and the Behavior Dimensions Scale–Home Version (BDS–H; McCarney, 1995a) are designed to measure several behavior disorders. Both scales yield subscores reflecting seven *DSM-IV* diagnostic categories: ADHD-Inattentive, ADHD-Hyperactive-Impulsive, Oppositional-Defiant, Conduct Disorder, Avoidant Personality, Generalized Anxiety, and Major Depressive Episode. The school version, completed by a teacher, contains 99 items, is appropriate to use with children ages 5 to 15 years, and takes about 30 minutes to complete. The home version, completed by a parent or guardian, contains 108 items, is appropriate to use with children ages 3 to 18 years, and takes about 30 minutes to complete. An Intervention Manual providing specific intervention guidelines for the disorders is also available (McCarney & McCain, 1995).

Scores

The BDS–S and the BDS–H use a 5-point scale that reflects the frequency with which behaviors are observed: 0 (does not engage in the behavior), 1 (one to several times per month), 2 (one to several times per week), 3 (one to several times per day), 4 (one to several times per hour). Raw scores are converted to standard scores ($M = 10$, $SD = 3$) and percentile ranks. Scoring can be accomplished with a template or by using a computer program.

Standardization

The standardization sample for the BDS–S was composed of 4,760 children ages 5 to 15 years, rated by 2,241 teachers. Norms are presented separately by gender and six age groups. The standardization sample for the BDS–H was composed of 3,427 children ages 3 to 18 years, rated by 3,232 parents. Normative groups for both measures are representative of the 1992 U.S. Census data with respect to gender, race, geographic area, and parents' occupations.

Reliability

Internal consistency reliabilities for the seven BDS–S subscores range from .82 to .97 (*Mdn* r_{xx} = .91). Test-retest reliabilities for the BDS–S subscores, based on a sample of 229 children retested over a 30-day interval, range from .75 to .92 (*Mdn* r_{tt} = .82). Interrater reliabilities for the BDS–S, based on 97 cases, range from .77 to .80 (*Mdn* r_{rr} = .79).

Internal consistency reliabilities for the seven BDS–H subscores range from .74 to .96 (*Mdn* r_{xx} = .89). Test-retest reliabilities for the BDS–H subscores, based on a sample of 258 children retested over a 30-day interval, range from .78 to .91 (*Mdn* r_{tt} = .85).

Validity

The construct validity of both the BDS–S and the BDS–H is satisfactory, as demonstrated by significant correlations with parallel scores from the Child Behavior Checklist, the Revised Behavior Problem Checklist, and the Burks Behavior Rating Scale. The criterion-related validity of the measures is also satisfactory, as demonstrated by subscores that significantly discriminated between children who had been clinically diagnosed with a behavior disorder and normal children.

Comment on the BDS–S and the BDS–H

The BDS–S and the BDS–H are easy to administer and score and yield clinically relevant information about *DSM-IV* diagnostic categories. Reliability and validity are adequate for both measures. The Behavior Dimensions Intervention Manual is useful in providing concrete intervention guidelines.

CHILD BEHAVIOR CHECKLIST FOR AGES 6–18, TEACHER'S REPORT FORM, YOUTH SELF-REPORT, CHILD BEHAVIOR CHECKLIST FOR AGES 1½–5, AND CAREGIVER–TEACHER REPORT FORM

The Child Behavior Checklist for Ages 6–18 (CBCL/6–18; Achenbach & Rescorla, 2001), Teacher's Report Form (TRF; Achenbach & Rescorla, 2001), Youth Self-Report (YSR; Achenbach & Rescorla, 2001), Child Behavior Checklist for Ages 1½ to 5 (CBCL/1½–5; Achenbach & Rescorla, 2000), and Caregiver–Teacher Report Form (C–TRF; Achenbach & Rescorla, 2000) measure internalizing-externalizing problems in children and adolescents and provide *DSM*-oriented scales.

The CBCL/6–18, with 112 items in eight scales, is designed to be completed by parents of children ages 6 to 18 years. The TRF, with 112 items in eight scales, is designed to be completed by teachers of children ages 6 to 18 years. The YSR, with 112 items in eight scales, is designed to be completed by adolescents ages 11 to 18 years; it requires a fifth-grade reading level. The CBCL/1½–5, with 100 items in seven scales, is designed to be completed by parents of children ages 1½ to 5 years. The C–TRF, with 100 items in six scales, is designed to be completed by day-care providers and preschool teachers who see the child in a group of at least four children. Table 10-8 shows the scales in each measure. All scales were developed on the basis of factor analysis. Scores for Total Problems, Internalizing, Externalizing, and *DSM*-oriented scales are also obtained on each measure. The latter, based on *DSM-IV,* were formed by judgments provided by experienced clinicians. Finally, the CBCL/6–18 and the YSR have three additional competence scales: Activities, Social, and School.

Scores

Items are scored on a 3-point scale: 0 (not true), 1 (somewhat true or sometimes true), 2 (very true or often true). Scoring

templates, scannable answer sheets, and computer scoring are available. Computer scoring produces a profile of the scores. T scores ($M = 50$, $SD = 10$) and percentile ranks are provided for all scales.

Standardization

The standardization sample for the CBCL/6–18 consisted of parents who rated 1,753 children ages 6 to 18 years (912 males, 841 females). Norms are presented separately by gender and for two age groups (6 to 11 years and 12 to 18 years). The sample is considered representative of the 1999 U.S. Census data with respect to SES, ethnicity, and geographic region.

The standardization sample for the TRF consisted of teachers who rated 2,319 children ages 6 to 18 years (1,113 males, 1,206 females). Norms are presented separately by

Table 10-8
Scales and Ages on the Child Behavior Checklist for Ages 6–18 (CBCL/6–18), Teacher's Report Form (TRF), Youth Self-Report (YSR), Child Behavior Checklist for Ages 1½–5 (CBCL/1½–5), and Caregiver–Teacher Report Form (C–TRF)

Scales	Form				
	CBCL/6–18	TRF	YSR	CBCL/1½–5	C–TRF
Syndrome Scales					
Internalizing Scales					
Emotionally Reactive	—	—	—	X	X
Anxious/Depressed	X	X	X	X	X
Withdrawn/Depressed	X	X	X	—	—
Somatic Complaints	X	X	X	X	X
Social Problems	X	X	X	—	—
Thought Problems	X	X	X	—	—
Attention Problems	X	X	X	—	—
Withdrawn	—	—	—	X	X
Sleep Problems	—	—	—	X	—
Externalizing Scales					
Attention Problems	—	—	—	X	X
Rule-Breaking Behavior	X	X	X	—	—
Aggressive Behavior	X	X	X	X	X
***DSM*-Oriented Scales**					
Affective Problems	X	X	X	X	X
Anxiety Problems	X	X	X	X	X
Pervasive Developmental Problems	—	—	—	X	X
Attention-Deficit/Hyperactivity Problems	X	X	X	X	X
Oppositional Defiant Problems	X	X	X	X	X
Somatic Problems	X	X	X	—	—
Conduct Problems	X	X	X	—	—

gender and for two age groups (6 to 11 years, 12 to 18 years). The manual says that the sample is representative of the 1999 U.S. Census data with regard to SES, ethnicity, and geographic region, even though 1,333 cases were from a 1989 norm sample.

The standardization sample for the YSR consisted of 1,057 adolescents ages 11 to 18 years (550 males, 507 females) who completed the inventory. Norms are presented separately by gender. The sample is considered representative of the 1999 U.S. Census data with respect to SES, ethnicity, and geographic region.

The standardization sample for the CBCL/1½–5 consisted of parents who rated 700 children ages 1½ to 5 years (362 boys, 338 girls). One set of norms is presented for both sexes together. The sample is considered representative of the 1999 U.S. Census data with respect to SES, ethnicity, and geographic region.

The standardization sample for the C–TRF consisted of caregivers who rated 1,192 children ages 1½ to 5 years (588 boys, 604 girls). Norms are presented separately for boys and girls. The manual says that the sample is considered representative of the 1999 U.S. Census data with respect to SES, ethnicity, and geographic region, even though 989 cases were from a 1997 norm sample.

Reliability

Internal consistency reliabilities for the CBCL/6–18 are .97 for Total Problems, .90 for Internalizing, and .94 for Externalizing, and range from .78 to .94 ($Mdn\ r_{xx} = .83$) for the scales. Internal consistency reliabilities for the DSM-oriented scales range from .72 to .91 ($Mdn\ r_{xx} = .83$). All internal consistency reliabilities are based on a sample size of 3,210.

Test-retest reliabilities for the CBCL/6–18 for 73 children and adolescents retested over an 8-day interval are .94 for Total Problems, .91 for Internalizing, and .92 for Externalizing, and range from .82 to .92 ($Mdn\ r_{tt} = .90$) for the scales. Test-retest reliabilities for the DSM-oriented scales range from .80 to .93 ($Mdn\ r_{tt} = .87$).

Interrater reliabilities for 297 mothers and fathers who completed the CBCL/6–18 are .80 for Total Problems, .72 for Internalizing, and .85 for Externalizing. Reliabilities for the scales range from .65 to .85 ($Mdn\ r_{rr} = .74$). Interrater reliabilities for the DSM-oriented scales range from .63 to .88 ($Mdn\ r_{rr} = .70$).

Internal consistency reliabilities for the TRF are .97 for Total Problems, .90 for Internalizing, and .95 for Externalizing, and range from .72 to .95 ($Mdn\ r_{xx} = .89$) for the scales. Internal consistency reliabilities for the DSM-oriented scales range from .73 to .94 ($Mdn\ r_{xx} = .90$). All internal consistency analyses are based on a sample size of 3,086.

Test-retest reliabilities for the TRF for 44 teachers retested over a 16-day interval are .95 for Total Problems, .86 for Internalizing, and .89 for Externalizing, and range from .60 to .96 ($Mdn\ r_{tt} = .88$) for the scales. Test-retest reliabilities for the DSM-oriented scales range from .62 to .95 ($Mdn\ r_{tt} = .82$).

Interrater reliabilities for 88 pairs of teachers who completed the TRF are .55 for Total Problems, .58 for Internalizing, and .69 for Externalizing, and range from .28 to .69 ($Mdn\ r_{rr} = .59$) for the scales. Interrater reliabilities for the DSM-oriented scales range from .20 to .76 ($Mdn\ r_{rr} = .60$).

Internal consistency reliabilities for the YSR are .95 for Total Problems, .90 for Internalizing, and .90 for Externalizing, and range from .71 to .86 ($Mdn\ r_{xx} = .79$) for the scales. Internal consistency reliabilities for the DSM-oriented scales range from .67 to .83 ($Mdn\ r_{xx} = .76$). All internal consistency analyses are based on a sample size of 1,938.

Test-retest reliabilities for the YSR for 89 adolescents retested over an 8-day interval are .87 for Total Problems, .80 for Internalizing, and .89 for Externalizing, and range from .67 to .88 ($Mdn\ r_{tt} = .77$) for the scales. Test-retest reliabilities for the DSM-oriented scales range from .68 to .86 ($Mdn\ r_{tt} = .81$).

Internal consistency reliabilities for the CBCL/1½–5 are .95 for Total Problems, .89 for Internalizing, and .92 for Externalizing, and range from .66 to .92 ($Mdn\ r_{xx} = .75$) for the scales. Internal consistency reliabilities for the DSM-oriented scales range from .63 to .86 ($Mdn\ r_{xx} = .78$).

Test-retest reliabilities for the CBCL/1½–5 for 68 parents retested over an 8-day interval are .90 for Total Problems, .90 for Internalizing, and .87 for Externalizing, and range from .68 to .92 ($Mdn\ r_{tt} = .84$) for the scales. Test-retest reliabilities for the DSM-oriented scales range from .74 to .87 ($Mdn\ r_{tt} = .82$).

Interrater reliabilities for 72 mothers and fathers who completed the CBCL/1½–5 are .65 for Total Problems, .59 for Internalizing, and .67 for Externalizing, and range from .48 to .67 ($Mdn\ r_{rr} = .64$) for the scales. Interrater reliabilities for the DSM-oriented scales range from .51 to .67 ($Mdn\ r_{rr} = .65$).

Internal consistency reliabilities for the C–TRF are .97 for Total Problems, .89 for Internalizing, and .96 for Externalizing, and range from .52 to .96 ($Mdn\ r_{xx} = .80$) for the scales. Internal consistency reliabilities for the DSM-oriented scales range from .68 to .93 ($Mdn\ r_{xx} = .79$).

Test-retest reliabilities for the C–TRF for 59 caretakers retested over an 8-day interval are .88 for Total Problems, .77 for Internalizing, and .89 for Externalizing, and range from .74 to .91 ($Mdn\ r_{tt} = .80$) for the scales. Test-retest reliabilities for the DSM-oriented scales range from .57 to .87 ($Mdn\ r_{tt} = .79$).

Interrater reliabilities for 226 caregivers and teachers who completed the C–TRF are .50 for Total Problems, .30 for Internalizing, and .58 for Externalizing, and range from .28 to .58 ($Mdn\ r_{rr} = .30$) for the scales. Interrater reliabilities for the DSM-oriented scales range from .21 to .52 ($Mdn\ r_{rr} = .42$).

Validity

The content, construct, and criterion-related validity of the CBCL/6–18, TRF, YSR, CBCL/1½–5, and C–TRF are satisfactory. The content of these scales is related to standard diagnostic systems, factor analyses support the grouping of scales into their components, and correlations with parallel measures of behavior are satisfactory. The validity of the current versions is based on both studies with the earlier versions of the scales (see Vignoe & Achenbach, 1999 for a bibliography of this research) and studies with the present versions.

Comment on the CBCL/6–18, TRF, YSR, CBCL/1½–5, and C–TRF

A strength of the five instruments is that they support cross-informant assessment of children and adolescents. The CBCL/1½–5 and the C–TRF are important additions that expand the age range covered by these instruments. Reliabilities for the Total Problem scores and Internalizing and Externalizing dimensions are good. However, several of the syndrome scales have relatively low reliabilities and therefore should not be used for decision making. Content, construct, and criterion-related validity are satisfactory. It would have been preferable for all norm groups to be based solely on a 1999–2000 sample rather than a combination of cases from 1989, 1997, and 1999–2000.

CONNERS' RATING SCALES–REVISED

Conners' Rating Scales–Revised (CRS–R; Conners, 1997) provides for cross-informant assessment of behavior problems in children and adolescents, with a primary emphasis on externalizing problems. The parent and teacher versions are designed for rating children ages 3 to 17 years, whereas the self-report versions are designed to be completed by adolescents ages 12 to 17 years. The CRS–R has several forms (also see Table 10-9):

- Conners' Parent Rating Scale–Revised: Long Form (80 items)
- Conners' Parent Rating Scale–Revised: Short Form (27 items)
- Conners' Teacher Rating Scale–Revised: Long Form (59 items)
- Conners' Teacher Rating Scale–Revised: Short Form (28 items)
- Conners–Wells' Adolescent Self-Report Scale: Long Form (87 items)
- Conners–Wells' Adolescent Self-Report Scale: Short Form (27 items)

Note that Conners' Global Index, a subscale of Conners' Parent Rating Scale–Revised: Long Form, is the same as the well-known 10-item Conners' Hyperactivity Scale. The 10-item scale is useful when a child's behavior has to be rated frequently, as in the case of assessing day-to-day behavior changes. The 10-item form takes about 5 to 10 minutes to complete, whereas the longer forms take about 15 to 20 minutes to complete.

Table 10-9
Scales and Subscales on Conners' Rating Scales–Revised

Scale	Subscales
Conners' Parent Rating Scale–Revised: Long Form (CPRS–R: L)	Oppositional Cognitive Problems Hyperactivity Anxious-Shy Perfectionism Social Problems Psychosomatic Conners' Global Index 　Restless-Impulsive 　Emotional Lability ADHD Index *DSM-IV* Symptom Subscale 　*DSM-IV* Inattentive 　*DSM-IV* Hyperactivity-Impulsive
Conners' Parent Rating Scale–Revised: Short Form (CPRS–R: S)	Oppositional Cognitive Problems Hyperactivity ADHD Index
Conners' Teacher Rating Scale–Revised: Long Form (CTRS–R: L)	Oppositional Cognitive Problems Hyperactivity Anxious-Shy Perfectionism Social Problems Conners' Global Index 　Restless-Impulsive 　Emotional Lability ADHD Index *DSM-IV* Symptom Subscale 　*DSM-IV* Inattentive 　*DSM-IV* Hyperactivity-Impulsive
Conners' Teacher Rating Scale–Revised: Short Form (CTRS–R: S)	Oppositional Cognitive Problems Hyperactivity ADHD Index
Conners–Wells' Adolescent Self-Report Scale: Long Form (CASS: L)	Family Problems Emotional Problems Conduct Problems Cognitive Problems Anger Control Problems Hyperactivity ADHD Index *DSM-IV* Symptom Subscale 　*DSM-IV* Inattentive 　*DSM-IV* Hyperactivity-Impulsive
Conners–Wells' Adolescent Self-Report Scale: Short Form (CASS: S)	Conduct Problems Cognitive Problems Anger Control Problems Hyperactive-Impulsive ADHD Index

Scores

All versions of the CRS–R use a 4-point rating scale: 0 (not true at all), 1 (just a little true), 2 (pretty much true), 3 (very much true). Scoring is accomplished with an answer sheet, which can be self-scored or can be faxed to the publisher for computer scoring and interpretation. Alternatively, the examinee (parent, teacher, or adolescent) can complete the CRS–R on a computer that scores the responses and provides an interpretive report. Raw scores are converted to T scores ($M = 50$, $SD = 10$).

Standardization

The standardization sample consisted of over 8,000 individuals, drawn from 45 states in the United States and from 10 Canadian provinces between 1993 and 1996. Norms are provided separately for males and females by age levels. The sample does not match 1997 U.S. Census data. For example, there is a higher proportion of Euro American children in the standardization sample than in the general population. In addition, there are substantial differences in ethnic composition across the samples used for the various forms.

Reliability

Internal consistency reliabilities for the Parent and Teacher Forms are acceptable, ranging from .73 to .96 ($Mdn\ r_{xx} = .90$). Internal consistency reliabilities for the Adolescent Self-Report Form are also acceptable, ranging from .75 to .92 ($Mdn\ r_{xx} = .84$).

Test-retest reliabilities for the Parent and Teacher Forms with a sample of 49 children and adolescents over a 6- to 8-week retest interval are variable. They range from .47 to .85 ($Mdn\ r_{tt} = .70$) for the Parent Long Form, .62 to .85 ($Mdn\ r_{tt} = .73$) for the Parent Short Form, .47 to .86 ($Mdn\ r_{tt} = .72$) for the Teacher Long Form, and .72 to .92 ($Mdn\ r_{tt} = .83$) for the Teacher Short Form. Test-retest reliabilities with a sample of 50 children and adolescents retested over a 6- to 8-week interval range from .73 to .89 ($Mdn\ r_{tt} = .83$) for the Adolescent Self-Report Long Form and from .72 to .87 ($Mdn\ r_{tt} = .83$) for the Adolescent Self-Report Short Form.

Validity

Construct validity is satisfactory, based on the results of a factor analysis used to construct the scales. Construct validity is also supported by correlations between parallel scores from the measures. For example, high correlations (range of .95 to .99) were obtained between long and short forms of the various scales. However, these reflect relations among scores from the same family of measures. The manual also reports that factor scores significantly discriminate between clinical and nonclinical groups. On the other hand, there is limited information about the relation between CRS–R scores and criteria

relating to adjustment or responsiveness to treatment. We do not know, for example, whether the measures are sensitive to changes in attention-deficit/hyperactivity following treatment.

Comment on the CRS–R

The CRS–R scales are a significant improvement over previous versions. A useful addition is the Self-Report Form. However, the standardization samples are small (i.e., below 100) for many age and gender groups. The CRS–R scales show good reliability and adequate validity, with the informant versions particularly effective for evaluating externalizing problems, such as those associated with ADHD. The Self-Report Form is useful for measuring general distress, but it is limited in its coverage of specific social and emotional problems. Finally, the standardization sample fails to match U.S. Census data.

DEVEREUX SCALES OF MENTAL DISORDERS

The Devereux Scales of Mental Disorders (DSMD; Naglieri, LeBuffe, & Pfeiffer, 1994) is a behavior rating scale for children ages 5 to 12 years (111 items) and adolescents ages 13 to 18 years (110 items) that can be completed by a parent or teacher in about 15 minutes. The DSMD has six scales, five of which are common to both age groups (see Table 10-10).

Scores

Items on the DSMD are scored on a 5-point scale based on the frequency of occurrence of the behavior over the past 4

Table 10-10
Scales and Composites on the Devereux Scales of Mental Disorders

Scale or composite	Child version	Adolescent version
Scale		
Conduct	X	X
Attention	X	—
Delinquency	—	X
Anxiety	X	X
Depression	X	X
Autism	X	X
Acute Problems	X	X
Composite		
Externalizing	X	X
Internalizing	X	X
Critical Pathology	X	X

weeks: 0 (never), 1 (rarely), 2 (occasionally), 3 (frequently), 4 (very frequently). Raw scores are converted to T scores ($M = 50$, $SD = 10$) and percentile ranks. Standard scores are provided for each scale and for three composites: Externalizing (Conduct and Attention/Delinquency), Internalizing (Anxiety and Depression), and Critical Pathology (Autism and Acute Problems).

Standardization

The DSMD was standardized on 2,042 children ages 5 to 12 years and 1,111 adolescents ages 13 to 18 years. The standardization sample was collected in 1991 from 17 states and closely matched the 1990 U.S. Census data. Norms for child and adolescent versions are provided separately by gender, based on teacher and parent ratings.

Reliability

Internal consistency reliabilities for the six DSMD scales range from .70 to .99 ($Mdn\ r_{xx} = .87$) for parents and from .76 to .98 ($Mdn\ r_{xx} = .91$) for teachers. Test-retest reliability was assessed on 30 children and adolescents rated by teachers and on 18 children and adolescents rated by staff in a clinical setting over a 1-day retest interval. Test-retest reliabilities range from .75 to .95 ($Mdn\ r_{tt} = .81$) for teacher ratings and from .41 to .79 ($Mdn\ r_{tt} = .75$) for staff ratings. Test-retest reliabilities for 99 children and 35 adolescents from several public schools retested over a 1-week interval range from .32 to .89 ($Mdn\ r_{tt} = .87$) for the children and from .40 to .83 ($Mdn\ r_{tt} = .61$) for the adolescents. Interrater reliabilities based on 45 children and seven sets of teacher and teachers' aide ratings range from .44 to .66 ($Mdn\ r_{rr} = .54$).

Validity

The DSMD was developed on the basis of factor analysis. However, the placement of items appears to be somewhat peculiar. For example, items dealing with excessive eating are placed on the same factor as items dealing with having hallucinations and torturing animals. Construct validity, in the form of contrasted groups, is acceptable, as demonstrated by several studies of clinical and nonclinical samples that show significant differences between groups on all DSMD scales. The manual provides no evidence of criterion-related validity. As with other instruments, parents and teachers differed significantly in their ratings of children and adolescents.

Comment on the DSMD

The DSMD is a parent and teacher rating scale that has satisfactory reliability, but evidence of validity is limited. Some items include content that is difficult for parents and teachers to evaluate. Although the manual states that the DSMD is de-

signed to reflect symptoms of disorders in *DSM-IV*, the scale fails to do so.

EYBERG CHILD BEHAVIOR INVENTORY AND SUTTER-EYBERG STUDENT BEHAVIOR INVENTORY–REVISED

The Eyberg Child Behavior Inventory (ECBI; Eyberg & Pincus, 1999) and the Sutter-Eyberg Student Behavior Inventory–Revised (SESBI–R; Eyberg & Pincus, 1999) provide for cross-informant assessment of conduct problems (or disruptive behaviors) in children ages 2 to 16 years. The ECBI is completed by a parent, and the SESBI–R is completed by a teacher. The ECBI contains 36 items, and the SESBI–R contains 38 items. Both inventories have two scales, Intensity and Problem, and can be completed in about 10 minutes. The Intensity scale reflects the frequency with which the behaviors occur, and the Problem scale reflects the frequency with which the parent or teacher indicates that the behavior is a problem.

Scores

Two rating scales are used for each item. The first is a 7-point scale used to indicate the frequency with which the behavior occurs: 1 (never), 2–3 (seldom), 4 (sometimes), 5–6 (often), 7 (always). The second scale requires a yes or no response to the question "Is this a problem for you?" Scores are calculated by hand, and raw scores are converted to T scores ($M = 50$, $SD = 10$).

Standardization

The standardization sample for the ECBI consisted of 798 children ages 2 to 16 years. The ethnic distribution of the sample matches the 1992 U.S. Census data. About half the sample was male and half female. The manual indicates that the sample is representative in terms of socioeconomic status and urban/rural residence, although it does not cite any formal comparisons with census data. The standardization sample for the SESBI–R is not clearly described in the manual.

Reliability

Internal consistency reliabilities for the ECBI are .95 for the Intensity scale and .93 for the Problem scale ($N = 798$ children between the ages of 2 and 16 years). Test-retest reliabilities over a 3-week interval are .86 for the Intensity scale and .88 for the Problem scale. Test-retest reliabilities over a 10-month interval are .75 for the Intensity scale and for the Problem scale. Unfortunately, the numbers of children retested in these analyses are not provided in the manual. Interrater reliabilities based on correlations between ratings by fathers and mothers are .69 for the Intensity scale and .61 for the Problem scale ($N = 44$).

Internal consistency reliabilities for the SESBI–R are .98 for the Intensity scale and .96 for the Problem scale ($N = 415$). Test-retest reliabilities are .87 for the Intensity scale and .93 for the Problem scale. Again, the manual does not indicate numbers of children or time intervals for the test-retest reliabilities.

Validity

Construct validity is supported both by the fact that ECBI scores relate significantly to parallel scores from observational and rating measures and by the fact that they do not relate to scores with which they should theoretically not be related. Criterion-related validity is supported both by significant correlations between ECBI scores and scores from the Child Behavior Checklist and Parenting Stress Index and by significant differences between scores for clinical and nonclinical groups of children. Studies also demonstrate that ECBI scores are sensitive to treatment effects.

The construct validity of the SESBI–R is satisfactory, as demonstrated by significant correlations with scores from observational measures. Criterion-related validity is also supported by evidence that the SESBI–R discriminates between clinical and nonclinical groups of children and correlates significantly with the Child Behavior Checklist. Criterion-related (predictive) validity is supported by significant correlations between children's scores on the SESBI–R and indices of behavioral adjustment collected 1 and 2 years later.

Comment on the ECBI and the SESBI–R

Both the ECBI and the SESBI–R are easily administered and scored measures of behavioral pathology. The standardization sample of the ECBI is adequate, but the standardization sample of the SESBI–R is not given. Both inventories have adequate reliability and validity. However, the SESBI–R should be used with caution because little is known about the standardization group.

JESNESS INVENTORY–REVISED

The Jesness Inventory–Revised (JI–R; Jesness, 2003) is a 160-item self-report measure for youths and adults ages 8 years to 35+ years. It requires a fourth-grade reading level and can be completed in about 20 to 30 minutes. The JI–R was originally designed to assess conduct disorders in juvenile offenders but now assesses a broad range of psychological disorders. It has 11 personality scales, 9 subtypes, 2 *DSM-IV* scales, and 2 validity scales (see Table 10-11).

Table 10-11
Areas and Scales on the Jesness Inventory–Revised

Area	Scales
Personality	Social Maladjustment Value Orientation Immaturity Autism Alienation Manifest Aggression Withdrawal-Depression Social Anxiety Repression Denial Asocial Index
Subtype	Undersocialized, Active/Unsocialized, Aggressive Undersocialized, Passive/Unsocialized, Passive Conformist/Immature Conformist Group-oriented/Cultural Conformist Pragmatist/Manipulator Autonomy-oriented/Neurotic, Acting-out Introspective/Neurotic, Anxious Inhibited/Situational Emotional Reaction Adaptive/Cultural Identifier
Conduct Disorder	—
Oppositional Defiant Disorder	—
Lie	—
Random Response	—

Scores

The JI–R uses a true/false format. Scoring templates, scannable answer sheets, and computer scoring are available. T scores ($M = 50$, $SD = 10$) are provided.

Standardization

The nondelinquent standardization group consisted of 1,973 children ages 8 to 17 years (987 males and 986 females) and 1,448 adults (355 males and 1,093 females). The delinquent standardization group consisted of 660 children ages 12 to 17 years (572 males and 88 females) and 299 adults (197 males and 102 females). The genders and the ethnic and educational backgrounds of the samples are reported. However, the nondelinquent sample is not representative of the U.S. population, and no information is presented about whether the delinquent sample is representative of the delinquent population.

Reliability

Internal consistency reliabilities for 10 of the 11 personality scales (the manual contains no data on the Asocial Index) range from .52 to .90 ($Mdn\ r_{xx}$ = .78) in the nondelinquent youth sample and from .60 to .90 ($Mdn\ r_{xx}$ = .75) in the delinquent youth sample. Internal consistency reliabilities for the nine subtypes range from .58 to .92 ($Mdn\ r_{xx}$ = .82) in the nondelinquent youth sample and from .74 to .93 ($Mdn\ r_{xx}$ = .82) in the delinquent youth sample. No test-retest reliability coefficients are reported for this revision.

Validity

The construct validity of the JI–R receives limited support from the fact that the test correlates significantly with the State-Trait Anger Inventory. Criterion-related validity is satisfactory, as the JI–R significantly discriminates between delinquent and nondelinquent youths. In addition, the manual cites validity studies with the previous edition of the scale to support the validity of the present revision.

Comment on the JI–R

The JI–R is easy to administer and score and yields clinically meaningful scores. While considerable reliability and validity research has been reported for the original version, psychometric support for the revised version is limited. Additional research on test-retest reliability, construct validity, and criterion-related validity is needed.

PERSONALITY INVENTORY FOR CHILDREN–SECOND EDITION

The Personality Inventory for Children–Second Edition (PIC–2; Wirt, Lachar, Seat, & Broen, 2001) is a survey of children's behavior that can be completed by a parent or other caregiver. It is a revision of a scale originally published in 1977. The PIC–2 is designed to provide information on children and adolescents from ages 5 to 19 years. The standard form contains 275 items and takes about 40 minutes to complete. The brief form (called the Behavioral Summary) contains 96 items and takes about 15 minutes to complete. Items cover behavioral, emotional, cognitive, and interpersonal adjustment.

The PIC–2 has nine adjustment scales, 21 adjustment subscales, and three validity scales (see Table 10-12). Parents or caregivers complete the PIC–2 using an answer sheet provided by the test publisher. The survey can be scored by hand or mailed to the test publisher for computer scoring. The PIC–2 also can be administered and scored on a personal computer. The manual provides interpretive guidelines for all scales and subscales. There is a Spanish-language version of the PIC–2.

Table 10-12
Scales and Subscales on the Personality Inventory for Children–Second Edition

Scale	Subscales
Adjustment Scale	
Cognitive Impairment	Inadequate Abilities Poor Achievement Developmental Delay
Impulsivity and Distractibility	Disruptive Behavior Fearlessness
Delinquency	Antisocial Behavior Dyscontrol Noncompliance
Family Dysfunction	Conflict Among Members Parent Maladjustment
Reality Distortion	Developmental Deviation Hallucinations and Delusions
Somatic Concern	Psychosomatic Preoccupation Muscular Tension and Anxiety
Psychological Discomfort	Fear and Worry Depression Sleep Disturbance/ Preoccupation with Death
Social Withdrawal	Social Introversion Isolation
Social Skill Deficits	Limited Peer Status Conflict with Peers
Response Validity Scale	
Inconsistency	—
Dissimulation	—
Defensiveness	—

Scores

Items are scored true/false. Raw scores for all scales and subscales are converted into T scores (M = 50, SD = 10). The standard form has no composite scores or total score. The Behavioral Summary has scores for eight scales, as well as three composite scores and a total score (see Table 10-13). The PIC–2 has one set of norms that includes both males and females.

Standardization

The standardization sample consisted of 2,306 examinees who were administered the PIC–2 from 1995 to 2000. The sample was generally representative of the 1997 U.S. Census data. Stratification variables were gender, age, ethnic background, geographic region, parents' education (as an index of SES), and guardianship status. Examinees were mothers

Table 10-13
Composites and Adjustment Scales on the Behavioral Summary for the Personal Inventory for Children–Second Edition

Composite	Scales
Externalizing Composite	Impulsivity and Distractibility–Short Delinquency–Short
Internalizing Composite	Family Dysfunction–Short Reality Distortion–Short Somatic Concern–Short Psychological Discomfort–Short
Social Adjustment Composite	Social Withdrawal–Short Social Skill Deficits–Short
Total	—

(82%), fathers (15%), and other caregivers (3%) whose children were in 23 schools in 12 states.

The referred sample consisted of 1,551 cases from 39 cities in 17 states. This sample was not representative of the 1997 U.S. Census data. For example, 68% of the sample was male and 32% was female, and 65% of the sample was from the South (whereas 35.1% of the 1997 U.S. population was from the South). No information is provided about parents' educational level. The manual states that the imbalances in gender are consistent with clinical referral patterns; however, no statistics or references are provided to support this statement. Furthermore, it is highly unlikely that 65% of referred children in the United States are from the South.

Reliability

Internal consistency reliabilities for the nine adjustment scales range from .75 to .91 (Mdn r_{xx} = .84) in the standardization sample and from .81 to .95 (Mdn r_{xx} = .89) in the referred sample. Internal consistency reliabilities for the 21 adjustment subscales range from .49 to .86 (Mdn r_{xx} = .74) in the standardization sample and from .68 to .92 (Mdn r_{xx} = .80) in the referred sample.

Internal consistency reliabilities for the eight Behavioral Summary adjustment scales range from .63 to .82 (Mdn r_{xx} = .72) in the standardization sample and from .73 to .89 (Mdn r_{xx} = .82) in the referred sample. Internal consistency reliabilities for the Behavioral Summary composite scores and total score range from .78 to .93 (Mdn r_{xx} = .86) in the standardization sample and from .86 to .95 (Mdn r_{xx} = .92) in the referred sample.

A sample of the standardization group (N = 110) and a sample of the referred group (N = 38) were retested after 1 week. Test-retest reliabilities for the nine adjustment scales range from .66 to .90 (Mdn r_{tt} = .82) in the standardization sample and from .88 to .94 (Mdn r_{tt} = .90) in the referred sample.

Test-retest reliabilities for the 21 adjustment subscales range from .63 to .87 (Mdn r_{rr} = .79) in the standardization sample and from .76 to .95 (Mdn r_{xx} = .88) in the referred sample.

Test-retest reliabilities for the eight Behavioral Summary adjustment scales range from .58 to .85 (Mdn r_{tt} = .78) in the standardization sample and from .85 to .89 (Mdn r_{tt} = .87) in the referred sample. Test-retest reliabilities for the Behavioral Summary composite scores and total score range from .71 to .85 (Mdn r_{tt} = .82) in the standardization sample and are all at .89 in the referred sample.

Interrater reliabilities for the nine adjustment scales range from .54 to .90 (Mdn r_{rr} = .80) in the standardization sample for mothers and fathers who rated 60 children and from .67 to .88 (Mdn r_{rr} = .73) in the referred sample for mothers and fathers who rated 65 children. Interrater reliabilities for the 21 adjustment subscales range from .49 to .89 (Mdn r_{rr} = .80) in the standardization sample and from .56 to .93 (Mdn r_{rr} = .71) in the referred sample.

Interrater reliabilities for the eight Behavioral Summary adjustment scales range from .54 to .82 (Mdn r_{xx} = .72) in the standardization sample and from .61 to .82 (Mdn r_{xx} = .65) in the referred sample. Interrater reliabilities for the Behavioral Summary composite scores and total score range from .71 to .86 (Mdn r_{xx} = .79) in the standardization sample and from .68 to .78 (Mdn r_{xx} = .71) in the referred sample.

Validity

Construct validity is supported to the extent that items generally correlate more highly with their home scale than with other scales. In addition, the PIC–2 correlates more highly with similar measures than with different measures. However, support for construct validity is limited in the sense that a factor analysis of the scales with the referred sample resulted in five factors rather than the nine factors that represent the PIC–2 scales. The manual does not report a factor analysis for the standardization sample. The PIC–2 also discriminates between different types of clinical groups.

Comment on the PIC–2

The PIC–2 has several strengths. First, it covers a range of psychological and adjustment problems. Second, the validity scales are potentially useful. Third, the interpretive guidelines are useful. However, reliability and validity are variable. Additional research is needed to evaluate the PIC–2 more fully.

REVISED BEHAVIOR PROBLEM CHECKLIST

The 89-item Revised Behavior Problem Checklist (RBPC; Quay & Peterson, 1996) is an updated and expanded version of the Behavior Problem Checklist (BPC) and is designed to be used by parents and teachers of children and adolescents ages 5 to 18 years. It has six scales (Conduct Disorder, Socialized Aggression, Attention Problems–Immaturity, Anxiety–Withdrawal, Psychotic Behavior, and Motor Tension–Excess) and takes about 15 to 20 minutes to complete.

Scores

Items are rated on a 3-point scale: 0 (not a problem), 1 (mild problem), 2 (severe problem). Raw scores are converted to T scores ($M = 50$, $SD = 10$).

Standardization

The standardization sample consisted of 972 students in kindergarten to eighth grade from schools in three states, plus 270 seriously emotionally disturbed students in kindergarten to twelfth grade from a school district in Florida. For the regular education sample, norms are provided by grade and gender, with relatively small sample sizes (e.g., 53 and 69 for the seventh- and eighth-grade norm groups, respectively). Similarly, there are low numbers of students with emotional disturbance in the older age group (29 males and 22 females in the seventh through twelfth grades). The standardization sample is described as a "convenience" sample and was not matched to U.S. Census data. Although no information is provided about when the standardization data were collected, they appear to have been collected in the early and mid 1980s. The school sample was estimated to be approximately 90% Euro American.

Reliability

Internal consistency reliabilities range from .68 to .95 (*Mdn* $r_{xx} = .89$) for the six scales in a sample of 294 children in regular education. Interrater reliabilities for a sample of 172 developmentally delayed children rated by their teachers range from .53 to .85 (*Mdn* $r_{rr} = .58$). Interrater reliabilities for 70 children rated by their mothers and fathers range from .55 to .93 (*Mdn* $r_{rr} = .72$). Test-retest reliabilities for 149 children in grades 1 to 6 rated by their teachers over a 2-month interval range from .49 to .83 (*Mdn* $r_{rr} = .66$).

Validity

Construct validity is satisfactory, as demonstrated by high correlations (range of .63 to .97) between the RBPC and similar scales. Construct validity is also supported by acceptable correlations between the RBPC and behavioral observations and between the RBPC and peer nominations with respect to aggression, withdrawal, and likability in a sample of 34 children. Discriminant validity is satisfactory, as shown by significant differences between clinical and normal samples for males and females.

Comment on the RBPC

The RBPC is a major revision of the BPC, the latter being one of the first contemporary standardized rating scales for the assessment of behavior problems in children. The RBPC evaluates problems of children and adolescents, although it does not provide specific diagnostic formulations and focuses primarily on externalizing problems, such as conduct disorder, aggression, attention, and motor excesses. Reliability and validity are adequate; however, caution should be used in the interpretation of standard scores, because the sample is not representative of the U.S. population. In addition, the norms are based on small sample sizes for some groups. Finally, although the RBPC is presented as a parent and teacher rating scale, norms are provided for teachers only.

REYNOLDS ADOLESCENT ADJUSTMENT SCREENING INVENTORY

The Reynolds Adolescent Adjustment Screening Inventory (RAASI; Reynolds, 2001) is a 32-item rapid-screening self-report measure of adjustment designed to be used by adolescents ages 12 to 19 years. It provides scores for two externalizing problems and two internalizing problems, as well as a score for total adjustment. The RAASI requires a third-grade reading level and takes about 5 minutes to complete. It has five scales: Antisocial Behavior, Anger Control Problems, Emotional Distress, Positive Self, and Adjustment Total.

Scores

The RAASI items use a 3-point scale: 1 (never or almost never), 2 (sometimes), 3 (nearly all the time). The test has a self-scoring carbonless answer sheet. Raw scores are converted into T scores ($M = 50$, $SD = 10$) and percentile ranks. Norms are provided for the total sample and for gender and age groups (ages 12 to 14 years and ages 15 to 19 years).

Standardization

The RAASI was standardized on a stratified sample of 1,827 adolescents ages 12 to 19 years. The sample was drawn from eight states between 1989 and 1991 and closely matched the 1990 U.S. Census data for age, gender, and ethnicity. In addition, there was a clinical sample of 506 adolescents from 31 psychiatric inpatient and outpatient settings in 22 states, representing a wide range of *DSM-IV–TR* disorders. An additional 1,007 adolescents from school settings were used in the RAASI reliability and validity studies.

Reliability

Internal consistency reliabilities for the first four scales range from .71 to .91 (*Mdn* $r_{xx} = .82$) in the school-based sample and from .68 to .91 (*Mdn* $r_{xx} = .83$) in the clinical sample. The internal consistency reliability for the Adjustment Total scale is .91 in both the school-based and the clinical sample. Test-retest reliabilities in a sample of 64 adolescents in a school setting who were retested over a 2-week interval range from .83 to .89 (*Mdn* r_{tt} = .85) for the first four scales. For the Adjustment Total scale, the test-retest reliability is .89.

Validity

Construct validity is satisfactory, as demonstrated by a factor analysis that supports the internalizing and externalizing dimensions of the RAASI. Construct validity is also supported by acceptable correlations between the RAASI and the APS Clinical Disorder Scales, the MMPI, and various other self-report and clinical interview measures. Discriminant validity is supported by low correlations between the RAASI and measures of intelligence, achievement, and social desirability, as well as by significant differences between the school and clinical samples.

Comment on the RAASI

The RAASI has satisfactory reliability and validity and is useful as a screening measure of adjustment problems in adolescents. It can be administered individually or in a group and followed up with more in-depth measures as warranted.

STUDENT BEHAVIOR SURVEY

The Student Behavior Survey (SBS; Lachar, Wingenfeld, Kline, & Gruber, 2000) is a 102-item survey of student behavior designed to be completed by teachers. The SBS focuses on students ages 5 to 18 years and takes about 15 minutes to complete. Items cover student achievement, academic and social skills, parent cooperation, and emotional and behavioral adjustment. The SBS contains three sections, with a total of 14 scales (see Table 10-14). To complete the SBS, teachers use an answer sheet provided by the test publisher. Scoring can be done by hand. The manual provides interpretive guidelines for each scale. The SBS is designed to be used as a screening measure, not for making diagnostic decisions.

Scores

Items on 13 of the scales are scored on a 4-point scale: 1 (never), 2 (seldom), 3 (sometimes), 4 (usually). Items on the Academic Performance Scale are scored on a 5-point scale: 1 (deficient), 2 (below average), 3 (average), 4 (above average), 5 (superior). Raw scores are converted into *T* scores (*M* = 50, *SD* = 10) for all of the scales. There are no composite scores and there is no total score. Norms are provided separately for males and females for two age groups (5 to 11 years and 12 to 18 years).

Table 10-14
Sections and Scales on the Student Behavior Survey

Section	Scales
Academic Resources	Academic Performance Academic Habits Social Skills Parent Participation
Adjustment Problems	Health Concerns Emotional Distress Unusual Behavior Social Problems Verbal Aggression Physical Aggression Behavior Problems
Disruptive Behavior	Attention-Deficit/Hyperactivity Oppositional Defiant Conduct Problems

Standardization

The SBS was standardized from 1994 to 1999 on a regular education sample and on a clinically and educationally referred sample. The regular education sample consisted of 2,612 students who were generally representative of the 1998 U.S. Census data. Stratification variables were gender, age, ethnic background, geographic region, and parents' education (as an index of SES). However, parents whose educational level was higher than average were overrepresented in the regular education sample (35.2% had 4 or more years of college, compared to 26.9% in the general population). Teachers participating in the standardization were from 22 schools in 11 states.

The clinically and educationally referred sample consisted of 1,315 students from 41 cities in 17 states. This sample was not representative of the 1998 U.S. Census data. For example, 72.4% of the sample was male and 27.6% was female, 11.1% of the sample was age 13 years and 10.5% of the sample was age 14 years (compared to 8.2% and 7.0%, respectively, of the general population), 21.5% of the sample was African American (compared to 14.8% of the general population), and 76.1% of the sample was from the South (compared to 35.1% of the general population). In addition, no information is provided about parents' educational levels. The manual states that the imbalances in gender and age in the clinically and educationally referred sample "reflect the nature of referral patterns for behavioral and psychological assessment and treatment in school-age children" (p. 29). However, no statistics or references are provided to support this statement. Furthermore, it is highly unlikely that 76% of clinically and educationally referred children in the United States are in the South.

Reliability

In the regular education sample, internal consistency reliabilities range from .86 to .95 ($Mdn\ r_{xx}$ = .90). In the clinically and educationally referred sample, they range from .85 to .95 ($Mdn\ r_{xx}$ = .91).

Test-retest reliabilities for four samples retested over 28.5 weeks, 11.4 weeks, 1.7 weeks, and 2.1 weeks (N of 49, 56, 52, and 31, respectively) range from .29 to .97 ($Mdn\ r_{tt}$ = .81). The manual does not indicate whether the test-retest samples were from the regular education group or from the clinically and educationally referred group.

Interrater reliabilities range from .44 to .91 ($Mdn\ r_{rr}$ = .76) for two teachers who rated 30 regular education students and from .56 to .83 ($Mdn\ r_{rr}$ = .74) for two teachers who rated 30 special education students.

Validity

Construct validity is satisfactory, as items generally correlate more highly with their home scale than with other scales. Construct validity is also supported by a factor analysis that yielded three factors with the clinically and educationally referred sample. The manual, however, does not report a factor analysis for the regular education sample. Convergent validity and discriminant validity are satisfactory, as the SBS correlates more highly with similar measures than with different measures. The SBS also discriminates between different types of clinical groups.

Comment on the SBS

The SBS has satisfactory reliability and validity, although further psychometric data would be helpful. Despite minor reservations about the instrument, we believe that it can be used effectively as a screening measure of student behavior.

PROJECTIVE TECHNIQUES

Projective techniques are designed to assess personality dynamics. These techniques emerged from psychodynamic theories of personality, and in most cases interpretation of responses continues to reflect a psychodynamic orientation. The assumption is that responses to ambiguous stimuli can reveal underlying dynamics of personality, including cognitions and emotions not normally expressed through conscious activities.

There has been vigorous debate about the strengths and weaknesses of projective techniques (Anastasi & Urbina, 1997; Garb, Wood, Lilienfeld, & Nezworski, 2002; Gittelman-Klein, 1988; Kleiger, 2001; Knauss, 2001). Proponents of their use assert that such techniques have several strengths. First, projective techniques allow access to personality states and processes not normally tapped by more objective measures. In particular, they allow suppressed and repressed content to emerge. Second, because the stimuli are ambiguous and the purpose of the test is obscure, deliberate faking is less likely. Third, because the administration procedures are less structured, these techniques provide an opportunity to establish rapport with a child. Finally, they allow clinicians to apply their knowledge and experience to an analysis of a child's personality dynamics.

Detractors point out that, because administration and scoring are usually not standardized, clinicians vary in their interpretations of responses to projective techniques, and the same clinician may change her or his interpretations from situation to situation. Therefore, the interrater reliability of projective measures tends to be low. In addition, internal consistency and test-retest reliability are generally low, and validity tends to be inadequate. Finally, scoring is complicated by the absence of adequate norms for most projective tests.

Projective tests perhaps should be treated as sources of hypotheses for clinicians rather than as psychometric measures. "Thus, they may serve as supplementary qualitative interviewing aids in the hands of a skilled clinician. Their value as clinical tools is proportional to the skill of the clinician and hence cannot be assessed independently of the individual clinician using them. Attempts to evaluate them in terms of the usual psychometric procedures may thus be inappropriate" (Anastasi & Urbina, 1997, p. 441). *We therefore recommend that important decisions about individuals never be made solely on the basis of their performance on projective measures.*

Projective tests are generally based on one of three formats. One format involves asking a child to draw a picture of an object or person. A second format entails presenting pictorial stimuli to a child and asking the child to tell a story. A third format involves presenting a child with inkblots to interpret. In this section we review three tests—the Draw-A-Person Test, the Children's Apperception Test, and the Rorschach Inkblot Test—that make use, respectively, of these three formats. We also review the Roberts–2, although it is considered a test of social cognition rather than a projective technique.

DRAW-A-PERSON TEST

The procedure underlying the Draw-A-Person Test (DAP) is simple. A child is given a blank sheet of paper and asked to draw a person. If the child draws a stick figure, he or she is given another sheet of paper and asked to draw a whole person. After the child completes one figure, he or she may be asked to draw a person of the opposite sex. Once the drawings are complete, the child is asked to tell a story about the persons drawn. The assumption is that the quality and content of the drawings will yield information about the child's self-perceptions and perceptions of his or her family, as well as the emotions associated with these perceptions. The approach to interpreting the drawings is usually purely clinical and holistic. That is, the examiner uses his or her clinical experiences to draw inferences about the child's personality from features of the drawings and the child's responses to queries.

Scores

Some efforts have been made to develop standardized guides for interpreting the DAP. An example is the Koppitz (1968, 1984) system. This system identifies features of drawings that can serve as diagnostic indicators of such emotional states as anger, anxiety, fear, and pleasure. Scoring focuses on how the child draws the picture, who the child draws, and what the child is trying to express through the drawing.

Standardization

Norms are not available for the DAP.

Reliability

Reliability of the DAP is difficult to evaluate because of the variety of scoring procedures used. A review of interrater reliabilities based on 12 studies using several scoring procedures yielded estimates ranging from .75 to .97 ($Mdn\ r_{rr} = .88$), while test-retest reliabilities from eight studies ranged from .68 to .94 ($Mdn\ r_{tt} = .79$; Cummings, 1986).

Validity

Reviews indicate that the validity of the DAP is weak (Cummings, 1986; Kamphaus & Pleiss, 1991).

Comment on the DAP

Reviews have concluded that the methodology of much of the research on the DAP is weak and relatively little support is available for its reliability or validity (Cummings, 1986; Kamphaus & Pleiss, 1991; Kleiger, 2001; Smith & Dumont, 1995). The DAP should be regarded as a purely clinical tool.

CHILDREN'S APPERCEPTION TEST

The Children's Apperception Test (CAT; Bellak & Bellak, 1949) is an adaptation of the Thematic Apperception Test and is designed to be used with children ages 3 to 10 years. It consists of 10 cards, each containing a drawing of an animal in a "human" situation. An alternative form of the measure, the Children's Apperception Test–Human (CAT–H; Bellak & Bellak, 1965), consists of drawings portraying humans. The latter is used with children ages 10 years and older. Children are asked to make up a story about each picture. The scoring of both instruments depends on clinical interpretations, although general scoring guides are available (Bellak & Abrams, 1997; Chandler & Johnson, 1991).

Scores

Standard scoring procedures are not provided in the CAT manual.

Standardization

Norms are not provided in the manual.

Reliability

Reliability data are not provided in the manual.

Validity

Validity data are not provided in the manual.

Comment on the CAT and the CAT–H

The CAT and the CAT–H must be considered as clinical techniques for investigating a child's personality and emotional dynamics. The absence of standardized administration and scoring procedures, normative data, and psychometric analyses makes it difficult to evaluate the psychometric properties of these measures.

ROBERTS–2

The Roberts–2 (Roberts & Gruber, 2005), a revised version of the Roberts Apperception Test for Children, is a standardized test for evaluating children's social perception on the basis of the stories they tell about stimulus pictures. The test authors state that Roberts–2 is not a projective test. Designed for children ages 6 to 18 years, the test has an objective scoring system, updated norms, and new stimulus pictures. The 16 drawings in the Roberts–2 have various positive and negative themes, dealing with such issues as parent-child affection and parent-child disagreement. Each card has one drawing, and the 16 drawings show children and adults in various situations, such as a child standing near a man who is sitting on a chair holding a paper, a woman "upset" because a child is smearing the wall, and a child holding a chair upside down. The child is asked to tell a story about each picture. The test has three parallel versions—one with Euro American figures, one with African American figures, and one with Hispanic American figures.

The Roberts–2 has seven sections and 28 scales, with between 2 and 6 scales in each section (see Table 10-15). The two Theme Overview Scales measure a child's ability to see the major theme in each picture and to tell a complete story. The six Available Resources Scales measure a child's resources for dealing with problematic feelings and situations. The five Problem Identification Scales measure a child's ability to identify and differentiate problems. The five Resolution Scales measure a child's ability to develop a positive outcome for each story. The four Emotion Scales measure a child's ability to portray in his or her stories themes of anxiety, aggression, depression, and rejection depicted in the pictures. The four Outcome Scales measure whether a child provides unresolved, nonadaptive, maladaptive, or unrealistic outcomes for the stories she or he tells. The two Unusual or Atypical Responses Scales measure the presence in the child's stories of any unusual themes or themes that fail to conform to social norms or lawful behavior.

Scores

Each story is scored on all 28 scales. The presence of a specific theme corresponds to a score of 1, and the absence of a specific theme corresponds to a score of 0. Raw scores are converted to T scores ($M = 50$, $SD = 10$). Norms are presented for four age groups: 6 to 7 years, 8 to 9 years, 10 to 13 years, and 14 to 18 years. The standard score distributions are variable among for the four age groups and among the 28 scales. For example, at ages 6 to 7 years, the standard scores on the two Theme Overview Scales range from 20 to 66 for Popular Pull and from 44 to 85 for Complete Meaning. At ages 10 to 13 years, the standard scores range from 20 to 58 for Popular Pull and from 39 to 63 for Complete Meaning.

Standardization

The standardization sample consisted of 1,060 children and adolescents ages 6 to 18 years, selected from schools and community organizations. The sample closely matched the 2004 U.S. Census data for gender, ethnicity, geographic region, and parents' educational level. The clinical sample consisted of 595 children and adolescents ages 6 to 18 years who were attending clinics or who were students in special education classes. The clinical sample drew subjects from several different clinical settings and reflected a variety of clinical problems. As is the case with research and validation samples for all clinical tests, the clinical sample was not designed to be representative of the general population.

Reliability

No internal consistency reliabilities are presented in the manual, which notes that this form of reliability is not applicable

Table 10-15
Sections and Scales on the Roberts–2

Section	Scales
Theme Overview Scales	Popular Pull Complete Meaning
Available Resources Scales	Support Self–Feeling Support Self–Advocacy Support Other–Feeling Support Other–Help Reliance on Other Limit Setting
Problem Identification Scales	Problem Identification 1–Recognition Problem Identification 2–Description Problem Identification 3–Clarification Problem Identification 4–Definition Problem Identification 5–Explanation
Resolution Scales	Resolution 1–Simple Closure or Easy Outcome Resolution 2–Easy and Realistically Positive Outcome Resolution 3–Process Described in Constructive Resolution Resolution 4–Process Described in Constructive Resolution of Feelings and Situation Resolution 5–Elaborated Process with Possible Insight
Emotion Scales	Anxiety Aggression Depression Rejection
Outcome Scales	Unresolved Outcome Nonadaptive Outcome Maladaptive Outcome Unrealistic Outcome
Unusual or Atypical Responses	Unusual–Refusal, No Score, Antisocial Atypical Categories

Source: Material from the *Roberts–2* copyright © 2005 by Western Psychological Services. Adapted and reprinted by permission of the publisher, Western Psychological Services, 12031 Wilshire Boulevard, Los Angeles, California 90025, U.S.A. (www.wpspublish.com). Not to be reprinted in whole or in part for any additional purpose without the express, written permission of the publisher. All rights reserved.

to this kind of test. Test-retest reliabilities for 30 nonreferred children who were retested over an interval of 5 to 9 days (Mdn = 7 days; personal communication, Chris Gruber, June 2005) range from .24 (Rejection) to .92 (Support Self–Feeling; $Mdn\ r_{tt}$ = .70). Test-retest reliabilities for a clinical sample of 30 children who were retested over an interval of 5 to 9 days (Mdn = 7 days; personal communication, Chris Gruber, June 2005) range from .17 (Anxiety) to .88 (Depression; $Mdn\ r_{tt}$ = .76). Because of the low frequency of cases, no test-retest reliabilities were computed in the nonreferred sample for the Problem Identification 5, Resolution 5, Maladaptive Outcome, and Unrealistic Outcome Scales. Similarly, no test-retest reliabilities were computed in the clinical sample for the Problem Identification 4, Problem Identification 5, Resolution 3, Resolution 4, and Resolution 5 Scales. Absent this information, a limitation that is specified in the manual in both the technical and the clinical interpretation sections, these latter scales must be interpreted with particular caution.

Interrater reliabilities are based on a comparison of the ratings of one of the test authors (Roberts) with the ratings of 10 professionals who each rated five nonreferred and five referred protocols. For the nonreferred group, interrater reliabilities range from .43 to 1.00 ($Mdn\ r_{rr}$ = .92). For the referred group, interrater reliabilities range from .49 to 1.00 ($Mdn\ r_{rr}$ = .89). However, no interrater reliabilities are reported in the nonreferred group for five scales (Popular Pull, Nonadaptive Outcome, Maladaptive Outcome, Unrealistic Outcome, and Atypical Categories) and in the referred group for three scales (Problem Identification 5, Resolution 3, and Resolution 5), because all protocols received either a maximum score (16) or a minimum score (0) on these scales. No interrater reliabilities are reported among the 10 raters.

Validity

The validity of the Roberts–2 is supported by analyses showing that scores reflect increased emotional maturity with increasing age and significant differences in scale scores between clinical and nonclinical groups of children. However, the manual does not report results of any construct or criterion-related validity studies.

Comment on the Roberts–2

Its updated pictorial materials and more representative normative sample make the Roberts–2 an improvement over the prior edition. However, it must be used with caution as a psychometric measure of children's social cognition. Test-retest reliabilities are based on a small sample of children (less than 3% of the standardization sample), most reliability coefficients are below .80 (and several are below .70), and no separate test-rest reliabilities are reported for the four age groups or for some of the scales. The evidence of validity also is sparse. Finally, the standard score distributions vary, not only

among the four age groups but also among the scales in each age group. We acknowledge the authors' efforts to move use of this test onto a less projective and more objective plane and their commitment in producing far more extensive materials related to standardization and validation. We conclude, however, that the Roberts–2 should be seen as a "work in progress," and recommend that it be used only as a clinical measure of social cognition until further information is available about the reliability and validity of the scale.

EXNER'S COMPREHENSIVE SYSTEM FOR THE RORSCHACH INKBLOT TEST

The Rorschach Inkblot Test (Rorschach, 1942) consists of 10 cards, each containing a symmetrical inkblot. Five of the cards are printed in black and white, and five are in color. The examinee is asked to "free associate" to each card and then is asked about his or her responses. Because the Comprehensive System (Exner, 1993, 1995; Exner & Weiner, 1995) is the most popular system for scoring the Rorschach, the remainder of this section focuses on it. Based on an analysis of the structural features and content of each Rorschach response (e.g., presence of movement, use of colors), it yields information about patterns of developmental psychopathology (e.g., depression, anxiety-withdrawal, schizophrenia).

Scores

The Comprehensive System provides standardized administration and scoring procedures. Standardized codes are used to identify personality traits and dispositions. Scoring and interpretation are complex, but computerized procedures are available.

Standardization

The standardization sample for the Comprehensive System consisted of 1,390 children ages 5 to 16 years divided into 12 age groups. The sample is reported to be representative of the 1970 U.S. Census data in terms of race and socioeconomic status.

Reliability

Test-retest reliabilities over a 9-month interval range from .06 to .88 ($Mdn\ r_{tt}$ =.47) for a sample of twenty 7-year-olds and from .16 to .89 ($Mdn\ r_{tt}$ = .76) for a sample of twenty 15-year-olds. Test-retest reliabilities over a 2-year interval range from .08 to .86 ($Mdn\ r_{tt}$ = .51) for a sample of thirty 6-year-olds and from .09 to .58 ($Mdn\ r_{tt}$ = .58) for a sample of twenty-five 9-year-olds. Exner and Weiner (1995) attribute the relatively low test-retest reliabilities to the fact that personality traits are still developing through childhood. They suggest that children's Rorschach scores be treated as reflecting personality states rather than traits.

Validity

Research on the validity of the Comprehensive System has yielded mixed results with children (Garb et al., 2002; Garb, Wood, Nezworski, Grove, & Stejskal, 2001; Wood, Nezworski, Lilienfeld, & Garb, 2003; Wood, Nezworski, & Stejskal, 1996). Although studies support the construct validity of the major scoring dimensions of the Comprehensive System, support is weaker for the measurement of psychological problems such as anxiety or depressive disorder or for predictions of future performance and adjustment. Special caution is advised in using the Comprehensive System for diagnosing psychopathology or for detecting child physical and sexual abuse (Garb et al., 2002).

Comment on the Comprehensive System

The Comprehensive System has an improved (although outdated) standardization group and administration guidelines. Scoring and interpretation have also been improved with the development of computer-based report programs. Reliability is not satisfactory. The validity of the major scoring dimensions is satisfactory, but the validity for individual clinical syndromes is not satisfactory. Therefore, the Comprehensive System for the Rorschach must be used cautiously with children.

MEASURES OF PARENTING AND FAMILY VARIABLES

Chapter 1 discusses several issues related to parenting and family variables. These issues include the structure and dynamics of the family, the role of parenting in child development, how psychological problems develop in children (including the role of poor parenting behaviors), the factors that place children at risk for developing psychological, physical, or adaptive difficulties, and the factors that protect children and help them cope with stress.

Methods of assessing parenting behavior are similar to those of assessing children's behavior. Interviews are useful for obtaining information from parents (see Chapters 5, 6, and 7), and behavioral observations are useful in assessing parenting behavior. Observations can be conducted in a natural setting, such as the home, or in a structured laboratory setting where the parent and child interact under standard conditions (see Chapters 8 and 9). Questionnaires and rating and checklist measures administered to the parent and to the child (where possible) are also useful for collecting information (see Tables A-1 and A-2 in Appendix A). Finally, standardized measures of parenting behavior are valuable.

Following is a discussion of five such measures: Parent-Child Relationship Inventory, Parenting Satisfaction Scale, Parenting Stress Index–Third Edition, Parenting Stress Index–Short Form, and Stress Index for Parents of Adolescents.

PARENT-CHILD RELATIONSHIP INVENTORY

The Parent-Child Relationship Inventory (PCRI; Gerard, 1994) is a 78-item self-report questionnaire designed to measure a parent's attitudes toward parenting. It requires a fourth-grade reading level and takes about 15 minutes to complete. It has seven content scales (Parental Support, Satisfaction with Parenting, Involvement, Communication, Limit Setting, Autonomy, and Role Orientation) and two validity scales (Social Desirability and Inconsistency).

Scores

The PCRI uses a 4-point response format: 1 (strongly agree), 2 (agree), 3 (disagree), 4 (strongly disagree). Raw scores are converted to T scores ($M = 50$, $SD = 10$) and percentile ranks. Scoring can be accomplished with a self-scoring form or by computer.

Standardization

The standardization sample consisted of 1,100 mothers and fathers recruited from schools and day-care centers from the four geographical regions of the United States (Northeast, South, Midwest, and West). The sample was weighted toward the middle of the SES continuum but was representative of the 1991 U.S. Census data in terms of parents' age, educational level, and ethnic background. Separate norms are presented for mothers and fathers.

Reliability

Internal consistency reliabilities for the seven content scales range from .70 to .88 ($Mdn\ r_{xx} = .80$). Test-retest reliabilities are also satisfactory, although they are lower for a 5-month interval than for a 1-week interval. Test-retest reliabilities based on ratings by 22 parents over a 1-week interval range from .68 to .93 ($Mdn\ r_{tt} = .81$). Test-retest reliabilities based on ratings by 82 parents over a 5-month interval range from .44 to .71 ($Mdn\ r_{tt} = .51$).

Validity

The construct validity of the seven content scales is supported by factor analyses. The criterion-related validity of the PCRI is supported by several analyses. First, parents in custody mediation sessions obtained scores that were significantly below the mean of the normative group. Second, PCRI scores for the same sample significantly correlated with scores on the Personality Inventory for Children. Third, in another sample, correlations between PCRI subscales and a measure of preferred disciplinary practices were consistent with expectations. Finally, a sample of adolescent mothers participating in a program for young, unmarried mothers displayed PCRI scores that were significantly below those of the normative group.

Comment on the PCRI

The PCRI is useful for obtaining information about parents' perceptions of their children and their attitudes toward child rearing. The content scales reflect the dimensions identified by professionals in the field of parenting as important to the socialization of the child. Reliability and validity are adequate, although additional evaluations of construct validity are needed. No information is presented about the psychometric properties of the two validity scales.

PARENTING SATISFACTION SCALE

The Parenting Satisfaction Scale (PSS; Guidubaldi & Cleminshaw, 1994) is a 45-item self-report measure completed by parents. Designed to identify parents' attitudes toward parenting and the parent-child relationship, it requires an upper elementary school reading level and takes about 20 minutes to complete. Scoring is based on three domains: Satisfaction with the Spouse/Ex-Spouse Parenting Performance, Satisfaction with the Parent-Child Relationship, and Satisfaction with Parenting Performance. A scoring template is provided.

Scores

The PSS uses a 4-point response scale: 1 (strongly agree), 2 (agree), 3 (disagree), 4 (strongly disagree). T scores ($M = 50$, $SD = 10$) and percentile ranks are provided.

Standardization

The standardization sample consisted of 644 parents of school-age children in the first, third, and fifth grades. Parents in the sample were from both two-parent families ($N = 341$) and single-parent families ($N = 303$). The majority of the respondents were mothers (89%), whose children were about equally divided between males and females.

Reliability

Internal consistency reliabilities for the three subscales are .95 (Satisfaction with Spouse/Ex-Spouse Parenting Perfor-

mance), .89 (Satisfaction with the Parent-Child Relationship), and .82 (Satisfaction with Parenting Performance). In a 2-year follow-up with 137 parents, test-retest reliabilities for the three subscales are .81 (Satisfaction with Spouse/Ex-Spouse Parenting Performance), .59 (Satisfaction with the Parent-Child Relationship), and .64 (Satisfaction with Parenting Performance).

Validity

Construct validity and criterion-related validity of the PSS are satisfactory, as demonstrated by significant correlations between the PSS and measures of children's social, emotional, and academic competencies, family health, and family environment. Correlations between these measures were similar in a 2-year follow-up. In addition, PSS scores correlate significantly with measures of mothers' satisfaction in spousal and employee roles and life satisfaction in general.

Comment on the PSS

The PSS is an easily administered and scored measure of parents' attitudes toward parenting and the parent-child relationship. The instrument displays adequate reliability and validity.

PARENTING STRESS INDEX–THIRD EDITION AND PARENTING STRESS INDEX–SHORT FORM

The Parenting Stress Index–Third Edition (PSI–3; Abidin, 1995) and the Parenting Stress Index–Short Form (PSI–SF; Abidin, 1995) are two separate but related measures of parent-child problem areas. The PSI–3 is a comprehensive self-report measure of problems in 13 areas for parents of children between 1 month and 12 years of age (see Table 10-16). (A separate measure, the Stress Index for Parents of Adolescents, is described on pages 297–298.) The PSI–3 contains 120 items, requires a fifth-grade reading level, and takes about 20 to 30 minutes to complete. The PSI–3 yields a Total Stress score reflecting parent-child systems that are under stress and at risk for the development of dysfunctional parenting behaviors or behavior problems in the child, a Life Stress score reflecting stressful situational circumstances that are often beyond the control of parents (e.g., a death in family, becoming unemployed), 13 subscale scores divided into a Child Domain and a Parent Domain, and a Defensive Responding validity score.

The PSI–SF, based on the PSI–3, contains 36 items and takes about 10 minutes to complete. It yields a Total Stress score and three scale scores: Parental Distress, Parent-Child Dysfunctional Interaction, and Difficult Child.

Table 10-16
Domains and Scales on the Parenting Stress Index–Third Edition

Domain	Scales
Child	Distractibility/Hyperactivity Adaptability Reinforces Parent Demandingness Mood Acceptability
Parent	Competence Isolation Attachment Health Role Restriction Depression Spouse

Scores

Both the PSI–3 and the PSI–SF use a 5-point scale for most items: 1 (strongly agree), 2 (agree), 3 (not sure), 4 (disagree), 5 (strongly disagree). However, several items on the PSI–3 use other 5-point scales or 4-point scales, and two items on the PSI–SF use other 5-point scales. The PSI–3 and the PSI–SF can be scored either with a template or by computer. Scores are expressed as percentile ranks for both measures.

Standardization

The standardization sample for the PSI–3 consisted of 2,633 mothers ranging in age from 16 to 61 years. Norms are presented separately by age of child. The ethnic composition of the parent sample was 76% Euro American, 11% African American, 10% Hispanic American, and 2% Asian American. There was no separate standardization sample for the PSI–SF. Although the norms are based on the sample of mothers, means and standard deviations are also presented for a sample of 200 fathers and 223 Hispanic American parents.

Reliability

Internal consistency reliabilities for the Child Domain and the Parent Domain scales of the PSI–3 range from .57 to .92 (*Mdn* r_{xx} = .76) for a sample of 435 mothers and fathers. No test-retest reliability studies were conducted for the PSI–3. However, test-retest reliabilities for prior editions range from .65 to .96 (*Mdn* r_{tt} = .71) over retest intervals of 3 weeks to 1 year.

Internal consistency reliabilities for the three subscales of the PSI–SF are .87 for Parental Distress, .80 for Parent-Child Dysfunctional Interaction, and .85 for Difficult Child. Test-

retest reliabilities, based on 270 cases and a retest interval of 6 months, are .84 for Total Stress, .85 for Parental Distress, .68 for Parent-Child Dysfunctional Interaction, and .78 for Difficult Child.

Validity

Factor analysis supports the construct validity of the two-factor scoring system (Child Domain and Parent Domain) of the PSI–3. Criterion-related validity is satisfactory, as demonstrated by significant correlations between the PSI–3 and the Child Abuse Potential Inventory and the Inventory of Parenting Experiences Scale, and by significant correlations between the PSI–3 and measures of child adjustment. Finally, treatment validity is supported by the fact that parents scoring high on the PSI–3 were less likely to complete treatment programs than those with lower scores. The criterion-related validity of the PSF–SF is satisfactory, as demonstrated by high correlations between the PSI–SF Total Stress scale and that of the PSI–3 (r = .94), between the PSI–SF Parental Distress scale and the PSI–3 Parent Domain (r = .92), and between the PSI–SF Difficult Child scale and the PSI–3 Child Domain (r = .87).

Comment on the PSI–3 and the PSI–SF

The PSI–3 is a carefully developed and well-researched measure of parenting stress and parent-child problems. The instrument yields clinically and theoretically meaningful scores and has adequate psychometric properties. However, additional reliability and validity studies are needed for the PSI–SF.

STRESS INDEX FOR PARENTS OF ADOLESCENTS

The Stress Index for Parents of Adolescents (SIPA; Sheras, Abidin, & Konold, 1998), which is related to the Parenting Stress Index, is a parent self-report measure for identifying areas of stress in parent-adolescent relationships. It requires a fifth-grade reading level and takes about 20 minutes to complete. The 112-item scale yields a Total Stress score reflecting the overall level of stress being experienced by the parent in the parent-adolescent relationship, a Life Stressors score reflecting the total of all stressful events experienced in the past year, three domain scores, and eight subscale scores (see Table 10-17).

Scores

Items are scored on a 5-point scale: 1 (strongly agree), 2 (agree), 3 (not sure), 4 (disagree), 5 (strongly disagree). A

Table 10-17
Domains and Subscales on the Stress Index for Parents of Adolescents

Domain	Subscales
Adolescent Domain	Moodiness/Emotional Lability Social Isolation/Withdrawal Delinquency/Antisocial Failure to Achieve or Persevere
Parent Domain	Life Restrictions Relationship with Spouse/Partner Social Alienation Incompetence/Guilt
Adolescent–Parent Relationship Domain	—

scoring template is provided. Scores are expressed as T scores ($M = 50$, $SD = 10$) and percentile ranks.

Standardization

The standardization sample consisted of 778 parents of adolescents ages 11 to 19 years. Parents ranged in age from 23 to 70 years. The sample is considered representative of the 1997 U.S. Census data. One set of norms is provided.

Reliability

The internal consistency reliability of the Total Stress score is .97. Scores for the subscales range from .81 to .95 ($Mdn \, r_{xx} = .90$). Test-retest reliability, based on 46 cases and a 4-week retest interval, is .93 for Total Stress, and ranges from .74 to .92 ($Mdn \, r_{tt} = .85$) for the three domains.

Validity

The criterion-related validity of the SIPA is satisfactory, as demonstrated by significant correlations between it and measures of parental relationships, parental coping, family cohesion, and adolescent social and emotional competence. Scores on the measure also discriminated between clinical groups of parents. For example, parents with a history of psychiatric treatment or parents whose children had been diagnosed with behavioral disorders had higher scores than parents of children with no behavioral problems.

Comment on the SIPA

The SIPA is a carefully constructed measure that provides useful information about areas of stress in parent-child rela-

tionships. The SIPA generally has satisfactory reliability and validity, but additional information is needed about construct validity.

THINKING THROUGH THE ISSUES

1. For what types of problems are parents or teachers a preferred source of information, and for what types of problems are children or adolescents better reporters?
2. How does the reading level required to complete a self-report measure influence the selection of such a measure?
3. How do measures of behavioral, social, and emotional competencies differ from measures of intelligence, achievement, and language?
4. What are the similarities and differences among personality tests, behavior rating and checklist measures, projective techniques, and behavioral observations?

SUMMARY

1. A variety of measures have been designed to enable a broad assessment of behavioral, social, and emotional competencies in children and adolescents, as well as assessment of parenting and family variables. These measures are useful in identifying children with special needs and making decisions about appropriate interventions for such children, conducting follow-up evaluations, and evaluating parenting and family variables.
2. Assessing behavioral, social, and emotional functioning is important, because nearly 20% of children and adolescents in the United States show symptoms of psychological disorder in any given year. Unfortunately, most symptoms go unidentified and the disorders untreated.

Background Considerations

3. There are both objective and projective measures of behavioral, social, and emotional competencies of children and adolescents.
4. The objective measures contain clear and structured items, require specific responses, and use precise scoring procedures. The resulting scores can be quantified, normed, and profiled.
5. Projective measures, in contrast, contain ambiguous stimuli, such as inkblots or pictures of situations or people, onto which an examinee projects covert aspects of his or her personality.
6. Measures of behavioral, social, and emotional competencies and the scores derived from them reflect the complex interaction of several elements, including the characteristics of the scale or checklist used, the child, the informant or rater, the examiner, and the setting, as well as the reasons for the evaluation.
7. In different personality tests and behavior rating and checklist measures, scales with similar names may or may not assess the same behaviors; scales with different names may cover similar behaviors.
8. Some instruments are designed to assess normal personality traits, while others are clinical tools designed to assess psychopathological conditions.

9. The results from personality tests, behavior rating and checklist measures, and observational methods may not always be congruent, because the measures are based on different behavior samples.

10. Personality tests and behavior rating and checklist measures usually sample behaviors that have existed for a long time, whereas observational methods focus on present behaviors.

11. Because each type of measure provides a different perspective on problem behaviors, we recommend that, if possible, personality tests, behavior rating and checklist measures, and observational methods all be used in an assessment.

Personality Tests

12. Personality tests are primarily self-report measures; that is, the individual responds to specific items using fixed response categories (e.g., "true" or "false").

13. Some personality tests are designed for identifying pathological states, others focus on normal personality traits, while still others provide information about both normal and abnormal dimensions of personality.

14. Because personality tests are based on the individual's responses to fixed questions, the validity of test scores may be affected by the readability of the items.

15. Examinees may be unable to read items or may misinterpret or misunderstand them.

16. Another factor that can compromise the validity of personality tests is response bias (or response sets).

17. Forms of response bias include a faking-good response set, a faking-bad response set, an acquiescence response set, a deviance response set, and a social desirability response set.

18. Test makers usually try to control for response sets by using a combination of positively worded items, negatively worded items, and neutrally worded items.

19. You should routinely consider whether an examinee's responses reflect response bias.

Adolescent Psychopathology Scale and Adolescent Psychopathology Scale–Short Form

20. The APS is a comprehensive measure of 25 *DSM–IV–TR* disorders and other social and emotional problems, whereas the APS–SF is a brief form that assesses 12 critical areas of adolescent social and emotional competencies. The APS covers ages 12 to 19 years, requires a third-grade reading level, and takes about 45 to 60 minutes to complete. Reliability and validity are satisfactory.

Millon Adolescent Clinical Inventory

21. The MACI is a self-report measure designed for measuring adolescent personality characteristics and clinical syndromes in youths from ages 13 to 19 years. It requires a sixth-grade reading level, takes about 30 minutes to complete, and contains 3 domains, 27 scales, and 4 validity scales. Reliability and validity are minimally satisfactory, and the standardization sample does not match U.S. Census data.

Minnesota Multiphasic Personality Inventory–Adolescent

22. The MMPI–A, designed to be used with adolescents ages 14 to 18 years, draws on the long history of the MMPI, which was developed in the 1940s by Hathaway and McKinley. Most of the 478 items on the MMPI–A were drawn from the MMPI. The MMPI–A has 10 basic scales, 7 validity scales, and 15 content scales and takes about 45 to 60 minutes to complete. The test has moderate reliability and limited validity.

Personality Inventory for Youth

23. The PIY is a self-report measure of psychopathology for use with children and adolescents in grades 4 to 12. It requires a third-grade reading level and takes about 30 to 60 minutes to complete. It has nine clinical scales, each with two or three subscales, and four validity scales. The PIY has satisfactory reliability and validity.

Behavior Rating and Checklist Measures

24. Standardized behavior rating and checklist measures usually assess overt displays of behavioral maladjustment, although some assess positive behavioral competencies as well.

25. Behavior rating and checklist measures are generally completed by an individual familiar with the examinee, such as a parent, teacher, caregiver, or clinician, but some are self-report measures.

26. Behavior rating and checklist measures require informants to make judgments about a child's functioning.

27. Because judgments are subject to bias and distortion, informants' credibility must be carefully examined.

28. When multiple informants are used, it is important to consider the consistency of ratings across informants.

29. Informants differ as to their familiarity with the child, sensitivity to and tolerance for behavior problems, personality, expectations, comfort with various test formats, and willingness to use certain rating scale positions.

30. Informants may use different frames of reference or interpret similar behaviors in different ways, depending on whether the child is a clinic patient or is attending a public school.

31. The child's race, socioeconomic status, appearance, and degree of psychopathology also may influence informants' judgments of the child's behavior.

32. Because parents and teachers are likely to see different aspects of a child, information from both sources is needed to obtain a comprehensive picture of the child.

33. Rating adolescent behaviors is particularly difficult for teachers, because they have limited contact with junior and senior high school students outside the formal classroom setting.

34. The reliability and validity of ratings may be affected by the specificity of the rating task.

35. An internalizing dimension and an externalizing dimension appear with some frequency on behavior rating and checklist measures.

Behavior Assessment System for Children– Second Edition

36. The BASC–2 is a measure of adaptive behavior and problem behavior in children and adolescents ages 2 to 25 years. It contains Teacher Rating Scales, Parent Rating Scales, a Self-Report of Personality, a structured developmental history, and a behavioral observation system. Reliability and validity are satisfactory. However, the failure to have similar scales in all three measures hinders comparisons across the three measures. Because little information is provided about the norm group

for 18- to 25-year-olds for the Self-Report of Personality, it must be used cautiously at these ages.

Behavior Dimensions Scale–School Version and Behavior Dimensions Scale–Home Version

37. The BDS–S and BDS–H are designed to measure several behavior disorders, including ADHD, opposition defiant disorder, conduct disorder, avoidant personality, generalized anxiety, and major depressive episode. The school version, completed by a teacher, contains 99 items, is appropriate to use with children ages 5 to 15 years, and takes about 30 minutes to complete. The home version, completed by a parent or guardian, contains 108 items, is appropriate to use with children ages 3 to 18 years, and takes about 30 minutes to complete. Both versions have adequate reliability and validity.

Child Behavior Checklist for Ages 6–18, Teacher's Report Form, Youth Self-Report, Child Behavior Checklist for Ages 1½–5, and Caregiver–Teacher Report Form

38. The CBCL/6–18, TRF, YSR, CBCL/1½–5, and C–TRF measure internalizing-externalizing problems in children and adolescents and provide *DSM*–oriented scales. Reliabilities for the Total Problem scores and Internalizing and Externalizing dimensions are good. However, several of the syndrome scales have relatively low reliabilities and therefore should not be used for decision making. Content, construct, and criterion-related validity are satisfactory.

Conners' Rating Scales–Revised

39. The CRS–R provides for cross-informant assessment of behavior problems in children and adolescents, with a primary emphasis on externalizing problems. The parent and teacher versions are designed for rating children ages 3 to 17 years, whereas the self-report versions are designed to be completed by adolescents ages 12 to 17 years. The standardization samples are small for many age and gender groups. The CRS–R has good reliability and adequate validity, with the informant versions particularly effective for evaluating externalizing problems, such as those associated with ADHD. The Self-Report Form is useful for measuring general distress, but it is limited in its coverage of specific social and emotional problems. Finally, the standardization sample fails to match U.S. Census data.

Devereux Scales of Mental Disorders

40. The DSMD is a behavior rating scale for children ages 5 to 12 years and adolescents ages 13 to 18 years that can be completed by a parent or teacher in about 15 minutes. The DSMD has six scales, five of which are common to both age groups. It has satisfactory reliability but limited validity.

Eyberg Child Behavior Inventory and Sutter-Eyberg Student Behavior Inventory–Revised

41. The ECBI and SESBI–R provide for cross-informant (parent and teacher) measurement of conduct problems in children ages 2 to 16 years. Both inventories take about 10 minutes to complete. The standardization sample of the ECBI is adequate, but the standardization sample of the SESBI–R is not given. Both inventories have adequate reliability and validity. However, the SESBI–R should be used with caution because little is known about the standardization group.

Jesness Inventory–Revised

42. The JI–R is a 160-item self-report measure for youths and adults ages 8 years to 35+ years. It requires a fourth-grade reading level and can be completed in about 20 to 30 minutes. It has 11 personality scales, 9 subtypes, 2 *DSM-IV* scales, and 2 validity scales. Reliability is variable, criterion-related validity is satisfactory, but construct validity receives only limited support. Additional research on test-retest reliability, construct validity, and criterion-related validity is needed.

Personality Inventory for Children–Second Edition

43. The PIC–2 is a survey of children's behavior that can be completed by a parent or other caregiver. It is designed to provide information on children and adolescents from ages 5 to 19 years. The standard form contains 275 items and takes about 40 minutes to complete; the brief form contains 96 items and takes about 15 minutes to complete. Items cover behavioral, emotional, cognitive, and interpersonal adjustment. It has nine adjustment scales, 21 adjustment subscales, and three validity scales. The PIC–2 covers a range of psychological and adjustment problems, the validity scales are potentially useful, and the interpretive guidelines are useful. However, reliability and validity are variable. Additional research is needed to evaluate the PIC–2 more fully.

Revised Behavior Problem Checklist

44. The RBPC is an updated and expanded version of the BPC. It is designed to be used by parents and teachers of children and adolescents ages 5 to 18 years. It has six scales and takes about 15 to 20 minutes to complete. Reliability and validity are adequate. Caution should be used in the interpretation of standard scores, because the sample is not representative of the U.S. population. In addition, the norms are based on small sample sizes for some groups. Finally, although the RBPC is presented as a parent and teacher rating scale, norms are provided for teachers only.

Reynolds Adolescent Adjustment Screening Inventory

45. The RAASI is a rapid-screening self-report measure of adjustment designed to be used by adolescents ages 12 to 19 years. It provides scores for two externalizing problems and two internalizing problems, as well as a score for total adjustment. The RAASI requires a third-grade reading level and takes about 5 minutes to complete. It has satisfactory reliability and validity and is useful as a screening measure of adjustment problems in adolescents.

Student Behavior Survey

46. The SBS is a 102-item survey of student behavior designed to be completed by teachers. It focuses on students ages 5 to 18 years and takes about 15 minutes to complete. Items cover student achievement, academic and social skills, parent cooperation, and emotional and behavioral adjustment. The SBS contains three sections, with a total of 14 scales. The SBS has satisfactory reliability and validity, although further psycho-

metric data would be helpful. Despite minor reservations about the instrument, we believe that it can be used effectively as a screening measure of student behavior.

Projective Techniques

47. Projective techniques are designed to measure personality dynamics. These techniques emerged from psychodynamic theories of personality, and in most cases interpretation of responses continues to reflect a psychodynamic orientation.

48. The assumption is that responses to ambiguous stimuli can reveal underlying dynamics of personality, including cognitions and emotions not normally expressed through conscious activities.

49. Proponents of projective techniques assert that they allow access to personality states and processes not normally tapped by more objective measures, limit deliberate faking, provide an opportunity to establish rapport with a child, and allow clinicians to apply their knowledge and experience to an analysis of a child's personality dynamics.

50. Detractors point out that interrater reliability, internal consistency, and test-retest reliability are generally low and norms and validity tend to be inadequate.

51. Projective tests perhaps should be treated as sources of hypotheses for clinicians rather than as psychometric measures.

52. We recommend that important decisions about individuals never be made solely on the basis of their performance on projective measures.

53. Projective tests are generally based on one of three formats. One involves asking a child to draw a picture of an object or person, a second entails presenting pictorial stimuli to a child and asking a child to tell a story, and a third involves presenting a child with inkblots to interpret.

Draw-A-Person Test

54. The DAP test requires a child to draw a picture of a person and sometimes a second picture of a person of the opposite sex. Once the drawings are completed, the child is asked to tell a story about the persons drawn. The approach to interpreting the drawings is usually purely clinical and holistic. Reliability and validity are weak. The DAP should be regarded as a purely clinical tool.

Children's Apperception Test

55. The CAT is designed to be used with children ages 3 to 10 years. It consists of 10 cards, each containing a drawing of an animal in a "human" situation. An alternative form of the measure, the CAT–H, is designed for children ages 10 years and older; it consists of drawings portraying humans. Standard psychometric data are not provided in the manual. The CAT and CAT–H should be regarded as clinical techniques, given the absence of psychometric data.

Roberts–2

56. The Roberts–2 is a standardized test for evaluating children's social perception; the test authors state that it is not a projective test. Although its updated pictorial materials, standardized scoring procedures, and more representative normative sample make the Roberts–2 an improvement over the prior edition, it must be used with caution as a psychometric measure of chil-

dren's social cognition because of its limited reliability and validity. It is recommended only as a clinical measure of social cognition.

Exner's Comprehensive System for the Rorschach Inkblot Test

57. The Rorschach Inkblot Test consists of 10 cards, each containing a symmetrical inkblot. Five of the cards are printed in black and white and five are in color. The examinee is asked to "free associate" to each card and then is asked about his or her responses. The Comprehensive System is the most popular system for scoring the Rorschach. It has an improved (although outdated) standardization group. Administration and scoring are standardized, although the scoring and interpretation procedures are complex. Reliability is not satisfactory. The validity of the major scoring dimensions is satisfactory, but the validity for individual clinical syndromes is not satisfactory. Therefore, the Comprehensive System for the Rorschach must be used cautiously with children.

Measures of Parenting and Family Variables

58. Methods of assessing parenting behavior are similar to those of assessing children's behavior and include interviews, observations, questionnaires and rating and checklist measures, and standardized measures.

Parent-Child Relationship Inventory

59. The PCRI is a 78-item self-report questionnaire designed to measure a parent's attitudes toward parenting. It requires a fourth-grade reading level and takes about 15 minutes to complete. It has seven content and two validity scales. Reliability and validity are adequate, although additional studies of construct validity are needed.

Parenting Satisfaction Scale

60. The PSS is a 45-item self-report measure completed by parents. Designed to identify parents' attitudes toward parenting and the parent-child relationship, it requires an upper elementary school reading level and takes about 20 minutes to complete. Scoring is based on three domains. Reliability and validity are adequate.

Parenting Stress Index–Third Edition and Parenting Stress Index–Short Form

61. The PSI–3 and the PSI–SF are two separate but related measures of parent-child problem areas. The PSI–3 is a comprehensive self-report measure of problems in 13 areas for parents of children between 1 month and 12 years of age. The PSI–3 contains 120 items, requires a fifth-grade reading level, and takes about 20 to 30 minutes to complete. The PSI–3 yields a Total Stress score, a Life Stress score, and 13 scale scores. The PSI–SF yields a Total Stress score and three scale scores. The PSI–3 has adequate reliability and validity, but less psychometric support is available for the PSI–SF.

Stress Index for Parents of Adolescents

62. The SIPA is a parent self-report measure designed to identify areas of stress in parent-adolescent relationships. It requires a fifth-grade reading level and takes about 20 minutes to

complete. The SIPA yields a Total Stress score, a Life Stressors score, and scale scores in three domains. The SIPA generally has satisfactory reliability and validity, but additional information is needed about construct validity.

KEY TERMS, CONCEPTS, AND NAMES

Objective measures (p. 270)
Projective measures (p. 270)
Personality tests (p. 270)
Response bias (p. 271)
Response sets (p. 271)
Faking-good response set (p. 271)
Faking-bad response set (p. 271)
Acquiescence response set (p. 271)
Deviance response set (p. 271)
Social desirability response set (p. 271)
Adolescent Psychopathology Scale (p. 271)
Adolescent Psychopathology Scale–Short Form (p. 271)
Millon Adolescent Clinical Inventory (p. 273)
Minnesota Multiphasic Personality Inventory–Adolescent (p. 274)
Personality Inventory for Youth (p. 275)
Behavior rating and checklist measures (p. 276)
Behavior Assessment System for Children–Second Edition (p. 278)
Behavior Dimensions Scale–School Version (p. 280)
Behavior Dimensions Scale–Home Version (p. 280)
Child Behavior Checklist for Ages 6–18 (p. 280)
Teacher's Report Form (p. 280)
Youth Self-Report (p. 280)
Child Behavior Checklist for Ages 1½–5 (p. 280)
Caregiver–Teacher Report Form (p. 280)
Conners' Rating Scales–Revised (p. 283)
Devereux Scales of Mental Disorders (p. 284)
Eyberg Child Behavior Inventory (p. 285)
Sutter-Eyberg Behavior Inventory–Revised (p. 285)
Jesness Inventory–Revised (p. 286)
Personality Inventory for Children–Second Edition (p. 287)
Revised Behavior Problem Checklist (p. 288)
Reynolds Adolescent Adjustment Screening Inventory (p. 289)
Student Behavior Survey (p. 290)
Projective techniques (p. 291)
Draw-A-Person Test (p. 291)
Children's Apperception Test (p. 292)
Roberts–2 (p. 292)
Exner's Comprehensive System for the Rorschach Inkblot Test (p. 294)
Measures of Parenting and Family Variables (p. 295)
Parent-Child Relationship Inventory (p. 295)
Parenting Satisfaction Scale (p. 296)
Parenting Stress Index–Third Edition (p. 296)
Parenting Stress Index–Short Form (p. 296)
Stress Index for Parents of Adolescents (p. 297)

STUDY QUESTIONS

1. Discuss the differences between objective measures and projective measures.
2. What are some difficulties in using personality tests?
3. Discuss each of the following personality tests. Include in your discussion a description of the test, scales, scores, standardization, reliability, and validity, and provide an overall evaluation of the test.

    Adolescent Psychopathology Scale
    Adolescent Psychopathology Scale–Short Form
    Millon Adolescent Clinical Inventory
    Minnesota Multiphasic Personality Inventory–Adolescent
    Personality Inventory for Youth

4. Discuss each of the following behavior rating and checklist measures. Include in your discussion a description of the measure, scales, scores, standardization, reliability, and validity, and provide an overall evaluation of the measure.

    Behavior Assessment System for Children–Second Edition
    Behavior Dimensions Scale–School Version
    Behavior Dimensions Scale–Home Version
    Child Behavior Checklist for Ages 6–18
    Teacher's Report Form
    Youth Self-Report
    Child Behavior Checklist for Ages 1½–5
    Caregiver–Teacher Report Form
    Conners' Rating Scales–Revised
    Devereux Scales of Mental Disorders
    Eyberg Child Behavior Inventory
    Sutter-Eyberg Behavior Inventory–Revised
    Jesness Inventory–Revised
    Personality Inventory for Children–Second Edition
    Revised Behavior Problem Checklist
    Reynolds Adolescent Adjustment Screening Inventory
    Student Behavior Survey

5. Discuss the strengths and weaknesses of projective and story-telling techniques.
6. Discuss each of the following projective and story-telling techniques. Include in your discussion a description of the measure, scales, scores, standardization, reliability, and validity, and provide an overall evaluation of the technique.

    Draw-A-Person Test
    Children's Apperception Test
    Roberts–2
    Exner's Comprehensive System for the Rorschach Inkblot Test

7. Discuss each of the following measures of parenting. Include in your discussion a description of the measure, scales, scores, standardization, reliability, and validity, and provide an overall evaluation of the measure.

    Parent-Child Relationship Inventory
    Parenting Satisfaction Scale
    Parenting Stress Index–Third Edition
    Parenting Stress Index–Short Form
    Stress Index for Parents of Adolescents

11

ADAPTIVE BEHAVIOR

Talents are best nurtured in solitude. Character is best formed in the stormy billows of the world.
—Johann Wolfgang Goethe,
German poet and dramatist (1749–1832)

Definition of Adaptive Behavior

Assessment Considerations

Vineland Adaptive Behavior Scales, Second Edition

AAMR Adaptive Behavior Scale–School: Second Edition

AAMR Adaptive Behavior Scale–Residential and Community: Second Edition

Scales of Independent Behavior–Revised

Adaptive Behavior Assessment System–Second Edition

Battelle Developmental Inventory, 2nd Edition

Thinking Through the Issues

Summary

Key Terms, Concepts, and Names

Study Questions

Goals and Objectives

This chapter is designed to enable you to do the following:

- Understand the concept of adaptive behavior

- Describe and evaluate individual measures of adaptive behavior

Adaptive behavior scales can help you make diagnoses, formulate discharge plans, and develop interventions. They play an important role in the assessment of children with developmental disabilities—and children with mental retardation, in particular. Before we review the major instruments designed to assess adaptive behavior in children and adults, we will look at the definition of adaptive behavior and some assessment considerations involved in the measurement of adaptive behavior.

DEFINITION OF ADAPTIVE BEHAVIOR

The American Association on Mental Retardation (AAMR, 2002) defines *adaptive behavior* as "the collection of conceptual, social, and practical skills that have been learned by people in order to function in everyday lives" (p. 73). *Conceptual skills* include skills in receptive and expressive language, reading and writing, basic arithmetical concepts, handling money, and directing self. *Social skills* include skills in establishing friendships, interacting with others, social reasoning, and social comprehension. *Practical skills* include skills in dressing, bathing, preparing food, washing dishes, basic housekeeping activities, taking medicine, using a telephone, and using a computer. (See Chapter 18 for a discussion of adaptive behavior in relation to mental retardation.)

Adaptive behavior is best understood as the degree to which individuals are able to function and maintain themselves independently and meet cultural expectations for personal and social responsibility at various ages. During infancy and early childhood, adaptive behavior involves the development of sensorimotor skills, communication skills, self-help skills, and socialization skills. During childhood and early adolescence, adaptive behavior involves the application of basic academic skills in daily life activities, appropriate reasoning and judgment in interacting with the environment, and social skills. And during late adolescence and adult life, adaptive behavior includes carrying out vocational and social responsibilities and behaviors. Adaptive behavior thus reflects a person's competence in meeting his or her own needs and satisfying the social demands of his or her environment.

Adaptive behavior involves the child's physical skills, cognitive ability, affect, motivation, culture, socioeconomic status, family (including the expectations of parents, siblings, and extended family), and environment. It represents the interaction of personal, cognitive, social, and situational variables.

Adaptive behavior is difficult to measure, for several reasons. First, adaptive behavior is not independent of intelligence. A reasonable estimate of the correlation between adaptive behavior and intelligence would be between .30 and .50 (Editorial Board, 1996; Harrison & Oakland, 2003). Both adaptive behavior and intelligence enable an individual to meet the physical and social demands of her or his environment. Second, behaviors accepted as adaptive at one age may not be acceptable at another age. For example, adaptive behavior reflects maturation during preschool years, academic performance during school years, and social and economic independence during early adulthood. Third, what constitutes adaptive behavior is variable, not absolute, and depends on the demands of a given environment. For example, a child may show acceptable adaptive behavior at school or when living in a small town but not at home or when living in a metropolitan area.

ASSESSMENT CONSIDERATIONS

The measurement of adaptive behavior usually depends on information obtained from a parent, teacher, or other informant. Informants may differ as to their familiarity with the child, ability to provide reliable and valid information about the child, sensitivity to and tolerance for behavior problems, personality, expectations, tendency to agree or disagree with items, preference for using extreme or intermediate positions on rating scales, and frame of reference used to evaluate the child. Difficulties in any of these areas can invalidate measurement results.

Ratings of adaptive behavior also differ depending on the extent of the informant's opportunities to observe the child's behavior. If a behavior is present in the child's repertoire but not observed by the informant, the child may not receive credit for that behavior.

Not only do informants' ratings differ among themselves; they also differ from children's self-ratings. An analysis of 269 studies that compared informants' ratings on behavioral

SCHOOLIES © 2000 by John P. Wood

Okay, I found the web site and downloaded the software that will teach us how to tie our own shoes . . .

checklists with those of other informants and with children's self-ratings found the following relationships (Achenbach, 1993):

- A mean *r* of .60 between informants who occupied similar roles in relation to the child (e.g., both informants were caregivers, both informants were teachers, or both informants were mental health workers)
- A mean *r* of .28 between informants who occupied different roles in relation to the child (e.g., parents and teachers, parents and mental health workers)
- A mean *r* of .22 between children's self-ratings and ratings by others (e.g., children and parents, children and teachers, children and mental health workers)

The relatively low correlations between parent and teacher ratings of adaptive behavior suggest that there is considerable situational specificity in children's adaptive behavior. In other words, behavioral checklists yield relatively independent information about children's adaptive behavior in home and school settings. One implication of the low correlations between parent and teacher ratings of adaptive behavior is that proposed interventions may be inappropriate when information on adaptive behavior comes from a single source or setting. A second implication is that carrying out a complete assessment of adaptive behavior requires obtaining information from a parent *and* a teacher (or aide), as well as conducting systematic behavioral observations (see Chapters 8 and 9). In addition, where feasible, ratings should be obtained from the children themselves. A third implication is that children may need different interventions in different settings.

Informal Assessment

There are several informal ways of obtaining additional information about adaptive behavior.

1. *Interviews and case history.* Interviews with the parents, other family members, and teachers, in addition to the case history, are valuable sources of information about a child's adaptive behavior.

2. *Daily diary or checklist.* It will be useful if the parents keep a daily diary or checklist (or both) for a week at a time, observing their child's daily activities and performance and noting skills needing development. Role playing and practice keeping a diary or using a checklist can help parents learn good observation and recording skills. Also obtain from the child, parents, and teacher a list of the life skills needed by the child.

3. *Teacher-parent communication.* Ask the teacher and parents to communicate daily in writing about the child's behavior and school performance, especially when interventions are being implemented, and get a copy of their communications.

4. *Observation in simulated home settings at school.* Ask the teacher whether you can make a part of the classroom approximate part of the home setting. For example, the area might contain eating utensils, toys, clothing, and other stimuli similar to those found at home. Then use role playing or free play procedures to observe how the child functions in that setting.

5. *Task analysis.* Select a skill that the child needs to learn and divide it into its component parts. For example, washing hands can be subdivided into 22 specific steps (see Table 11-1). To evaluate a child's ability to wash her hands, you might say, "Bridgette, show me how you would wash your hands" and then observe how adequately she performs the task. Assess the number of steps in the task that Bridgette performed independently. Depending on where she had difficulty, you could determine the appropriate entry level skill with which to begin instruction. For more information about task analysis see Alberto and Troutman (2003) and Van Etten, Arkell, and Van Etten (1980).

6. *Systematic observation and controlled teaching trials.* The goal of systematic observation and controlled teaching trials is to determine which elements of a child's behavior interfere with instruction, how interference from these elements can be reduced, and what motivates the child to attend and respond. Ideally, you should observe the child in the settings in which he or she is expected to function (e.g., school, home, bus, job).

Strain, Sainto, and Maheady (1984) provide suggestions on how you might implement systematic observation and controlled teaching trials. First, determine which behavior

---

Table 11-1
Task Analysis for Washing Hands

Component Skills

1. Walks to front of sink (bar of soap is in dish on sink).
2. Directs hand toward water faucet handle (cold, then hot).
3. Touches water faucet handle.
4. Grasps water faucet handle.
5. Turns on water.
6. Adjusts for adequate temperature (not too hot or too cold).
7. Wets hands under running water.
8. Removes hands from water.
9. Directs hand toward soap dish.
10. Touches soap.
11. Picks up soap.
12. Rubs soap between hands.
13. Puts soap back into soap dish.
14. Rubs palms of hands together to create lather.
15. Rubs back of right hand.
16. Rubs back of left hand.
17. Places hands under running water.
18. Rinses all soap off hands.
19. Turns off running water.
20. Picks up towel.
21. Dries hands.
22. Puts down towel.

Source: Adapted from Van Etten, Arkell, and Van Etten (1980), p. 178.

patterns interfere with instruction—such as self-stimulating behavior, attention difficulties, or destructive behavior—and the conditions under which they occur. Second, determine the motivational mechanism that supports the inappropriate behavior—such as desire to obtain positive reinforcement, terminate an unpleasant task, or obtain sensory feedback. (See Chapter 13 on functional behavioral assessment.) Then use this information to develop interventions.

7. *Evaluation of life skills.* Compare the life skills that the child needs with those that he or she possesses. Develop a program to teach the child the skills that he or she does not have.

8. *Informal checklist.* Table 11-2 provides an informal checklist to help you evaluate the three skill areas delineated in the AAMR definition of adaptive behavior. You must consider the child's age in evaluating the skills needed in each adaptive area.

Table 11-2
Informal Checklist of Adaptive Behavior

INFORMAL CHECKLIST OF ADAPTIVE BEHAVIOR

Name: _____   Date: _____

Age: _____   Sex: _____   Name of rater: _____

Key: **Y** (Yes) = Examinee can perform skill at a level appropriate for his or her age.
N (No) = Examinee cannot perform skill at a level appropriate for his or her age.
DK (Don't Know) = Don't know whether examinee can perform skill at a level appropriate for his or her age.
NR (Not Relevant) = Examinee is not expected to be able to perform this skill at his or her current age level.

Area	Check One
Conceptual Skills (Ability to learn at school and to express information through symbolic behaviors)	
1. Comprehends a request.	☐ Y ☐ N ☐ DK ☐ NR
2. Identifies emotions.	☐ Y ☐ N ☐ DK ☐ NR
3. Spells.	☐ Y ☐ N ☐ DK ☐ NR
4. Writes a letter.	☐ Y ☐ N ☐ DK ☐ NR
5. Reads.	☐ Y ☐ N ☐ DK ☐ NR
6. Knows basic math.	☐ Y ☐ N ☐ DK ☐ NR
7. Identifies coins.	☐ Y ☐ N ☐ DK ☐ NR
8. Makes change.	☐ Y ☐ N ☐ DK ☐ NR
Other _____	☐ Y ☐ N ☐ DK ☐ NR
Social Skills (Ability to engage in socially appropriate behavior)	
9. Has friends.	☐ Y ☐ N ☐ DK ☐ NR
10. Takes turns in interactions.	☐ Y ☐ N ☐ DK ☐ NR
11. Demonstrates honesty, trustworthiness, and appropriate play.	☐ Y ☐ N ☐ DK ☐ NR
12. Follows rules.	☐ Y ☐ N ☐ DK ☐ NR
13. Obeys laws.	☐ Y ☐ N ☐ DK ☐ NR
14. Avoids being a victim of fraud.	☐ Y ☐ N ☐ DK ☐ NR
15. Demonstrates appropriate assertiveness and self-advocacy.	☐ Y ☐ N ☐ DK ☐ NR
16. Assumes responsibility.	☐ Y ☐ N ☐ DK ☐ NR
Other _____	☐ Y ☐ N ☐ DK ☐ NR
Practical Skills (Ability to take care of oneself)	
17. Dresses self.	☐ Y ☐ N ☐ DK ☐ NR
18. Uses utensils properly.	☐ Y ☐ N ☐ DK ☐ NR
19. Uses toilet appropriately.	☐ Y ☐ N ☐ DK ☐ NR
20. Uses telephone.	☐ Y ☐ N ☐ DK ☐ NR
21. Prepares meals.	☐ Y ☐ N ☐ DK ☐ NR
22. Uses public transportation.	☐ Y ☐ N ☐ DK ☐ NR
23. Takes medicine by himself or herself.	☐ Y ☐ N ☐ DK ☐ NR
24. Has appropriate work skills.	☐ Y ☐ N ☐ DK ☐ NR
Other _____	☐ Y ☐ N ☐ DK ☐ NR

Psychometric Concerns

In evaluating measures of adaptive behavior, use the same criteria you would for any psychometric measure. Essentially, you will want to consider (a) the representativeness of the norm group, (b) the measure's reliability, validity, scope, structure, and clinical utility, and (c) the reliability and validity of the informants' ratings and the children's self-ratings. Like all assessment measures, different adaptive behavior measures may give different results. Results vary because of differences in response formats, content and technical adequacy, standardization groups, when the standardization was conducted, and raters.

Additional psychometric concerns associated with the assessment of adaptive behavior follow (Jenkinson, 1996):

1. How do the reliability and validity of part scores compare with the reliability and validity of global scores?
2. What do scores on measures of adaptive behavior tell us about the supports the person needs?
3. How much do scores on measures of adaptive behavior reflect how the person functions in a specific environment?
4. How much do scores on measures of adaptive behavior generalize to different environments?
5. How should measures of adaptive behavior be used if they have negatively skewed distributions (i.e., scores drop off sharply at the positive end of the distribution and cluster at the negative end of the distribution)?

VINELAND ADAPTIVE BEHAVIOR SCALES, SECOND EDITION

The Vineland Adaptive Behavior Scales, Second Edition (Vineland–II; Sparrow, Cicchetti, & Balla, 2005), first published as the Vineland Social Maturity Scale by Doll in 1953, assesses adaptive behavior skills of infants, children, and adults from birth to 90 years of age. It requires that an informant (parent, caregiver, or teacher) familiar with the behavior of the referred individual answer behavior-oriented questions posed by an examiner or complete a questionnaire. The Vineland–II has four forms: Survey Interview Form, Parent/Caregiver Rating Form, Expanded Interview Form, and Teacher Rating Form. The Survey Interview Form and the Parent/Caregiver Rating Form were published in 2005; the Expanded Interview Form and the Teacher Rating Form will be published in 2006. This review covers the Survey Interview Form and the Parent/Caregiver Rating Form because the Expanded Interview Form and the Teacher Rating Form were under development when this book was published. Information about the Expanded Interview Form and the Teacher Rating Form was obtained from the publisher's (American Guidance Services) Web site.

The Vineland–II is based on a definition of adaptive behavior that focuses on the ability of the individual to perform daily activities required for personal and social sufficiency. The Survey Interview Form and the Parent/Caregiver Rating Form measure adaptive behavior in four domains at ages birth to 6 years (Communication, Daily Living Skills, Socialization, and Motor Skills) and in three domains at ages 7 years to 90 years (Communication, Daily Living Skills, and Socialization). An optional Maladaptive Behavior Domain, with Internalizing and Externalizing subscales, is included for ages 3 years to 90 years on the Survey Interview Form, the Parent/Caregiver Rating Form, and the Expanded Interview Form, but not on the Teacher Rating Form.

Each domain evaluates various adaptive skills (see Table 11-3).

- The Communication Domain evaluates receptive, expressive, and written communication skills.
- The Daily Living Skills Domain evaluates personal living habits, domestic task performance, and behavior in the community.
- The Socialization Domain evaluates interpersonal relations, play and leisure, and coping skills such as responsibility and sensitivity to others.
- The Motor Skills Domain evaluates gross- and fine-motor coordination for children under the age of 6 years.
- The Maladaptive Behavior Domain evaluates internalizing and externalizing behaviors that may interfere with adaptive behavior.

The Communication, Daily Living Skills, and Socialization Domains of the Vineland–II generally correspond with the AAMR's definitions of conceptual skills, practical skills, and social skills presented earlier in the chapter. However, the Vineland–II assesses additional skills (e.g., fine- and gross-motor skills) as well as maladaptive behavior.

Table 11-3
Domains and Subdomains on the Vineland Adaptive Behavior Scales, Second Edition (Survey Forms)

Domain	Subdomain
Communication	Receptive Expressive Written
Daily Living Skills	Personal Domestic Community
Socialization	Interpersonal Relationships Play and Leisure Time Coping Skills
Motor Skills	Gross Fine
Maladaptive Behavior	—

Source: Adapted from Sparrow, Cicchetti, and Balla (2005).

The Survey Interview Form and the Parent/Caregiver Rating Form each contain 383 items. The optional Maladaptive Behavior Domain contains an additional 50 items. In format, the Survey Interview Form is a semistructured interview that a clinician can use to interview a parent or caregiver, whereas the Parent/Caregiver Rating Form is a rating scale that can be completed by a parent or caregiver. Item content and scoring are the same for both forms. The Survey Interview Form requires about 20 to 60 minutes to complete, whereas the Parent/Caregiver Rating Form takes about 30 to 60 minutes to complete.

The Expanded Interview Form covers birth to 90 years, uses a semistructured interview format, and provides a more comprehensive assessment of adaptive behavior than the Survey Interview Form. It can be used to follow up information obtained on the Survey Interview Form. The Teacher Rating Form covers ages 3 years to 21 years, uses a questionnaire format, and assesses the adaptive behavior of a student in a classroom.

Scores

Items are scored using four categories: 2 (usually), 1 (sometimes, partially), 0 (never), DK (don't know). Raw scores are converted to standard scores ($M = 100$, $SD = 15$) and percentile ranks for the four domains and for the Adaptive Behavior Composite. The Adaptive Behavior Composite is based on four domains at ages birth to 6 years and on three domains at ages 7 years to 90 years. The subdomain raw scores are converted to v scores (a standard score with $M = 15$, $SD = 3$) and to age-equivalent scores.

The Vineland–II manual provides confidence intervals and percentile ranks for the subdomain scores, domain scores, and Adaptive Behavior Composite scores and has tables showing significant differences for pairwise comparisons of the domain scores. Standard scores for the subdomains, domains, and Adaptive Behavior Composite are classified as Low, Below Average, Average, Above Average, or High (see Table C.4 in the Vineland–II manual).

Standard scores for the subdomains, domains, and Adaptive Behavior Composite should be interpreted with caution. First, the ranges of v scores for the subdomains differ by age. For example, at age 2-0 to 2-1, the Expressive subdomain has a range of v scores from 1 to 24. However, the range of v scores is only 1 to 16 at 16 years of age. At 3 years of age, the lowest v score for the Written subdomain is 10, whereas at 16 years of age it is 4.

Second, the possible range of standard scores for the domains is 20 to 160, but this range is not available at all ages. For example, at the lowest age level of the scale (0-0-0 to 0-11-30), the highest standard score is 143 for the Communication and Daily Living Skills Domains, 152 for the Socialization Domain, and 144 for the Motor Skills Domain, whereas the lowest standard scores are 22 for the Communication Domain, 36 for the Daily Living Skills Domain, 21 for

the Socialization Domain, and 22 for the Motor Skills Domain. At age levels 7-0 to 9-11, the highest standard score is 160 for the Communication and Socialization Domains and 155 for the Daily Living Skills Domain.

Third, the range of Adaptive Behavior Composite scores is 20 to 160, but this range is not available at all ages. For example, at 2 years of age, the range is 24 to 160, whereas at 16 years of age, the range is 20 to 141. Therefore, a child who performs at the highest level of the scale at both 2 years and 16 years of age has not lost 19 points. This is purely an artifact of the instrument—the highest Adaptive Behavior Composite possible at 16 years of age is 141. The skewed and uneven distribution of scaled scores means that, when individuals have above-average adaptive behavior skills, it will be difficult to evaluate them over time or to evaluate their differential performance in the skill areas.

Finally, the gradients of raw scores to age-equivalent scores show dramatic differences. For example, a raw score of 39 on the Receptive subdomain reflects an age-equivalent score of 11, whereas a raw score of 40 reflects an age-equivalent score of 18. Thus, a change of 1 raw-score point yields a change of 7 years in age-equivalent scores. At the early ages, a change of 1 raw-score point (e.g., from 33 to 34) represents a change in age-equivalent scores of 7 months (4-11 to 5-6). You must be thoroughly familiar with these differences if you use the age-equivalent scores. (See Sattler, 2001, for a discussion of problems associated with the use of age-equivalent scores.)

Standardization

The standardization samples for the Vineland–II consisted of 3,695 individuals from birth to age 90 years. The samples were stratified by gender, race/ethnicity, community size, geographic region, and SES, as described by the 2001 U.S. Census.

Reliability

Internal consistency reliabilities for the four domains (Communication, Daily Living Skills, Socialization, and Motor Skills) range from .70 to .95 ($Mdn\ r_{xx} = .91$). Internal consistency reliabilities for the Adaptive Behavior Composite range from .86 to .98 ($Mdn\ r_{xx} = .97$). Internal consistency reliabilities for the Maladaptive Behavior Domain range from .85 to .91 ($Mdn\ r_{xx} = .89$).

Test-retest reliabilities for a sample of 414 individuals retested over 13 to 34 days range from .74 to .95 ($Mdn\ r_{tt} = .86$) for the four domains. The median test-retest reliability for the Adaptive Behavior Composite is .94. Test-retest reliabilities for the Maladaptive Behavior Domain based on a sample of 389 individuals retested over 14 to 30 days range from .83 to .93 ($Mdn\ r_{tt} = .90$).

Interrater reliabilities for the Survey Interview Form based on 112 respondents range from .58 to .82 ($Mdn\ r_{rr} = .67$) for the four domains. The median interrater reliability for the Adaptive Behavior Composite is .73. Interrater reliabilities for the Maladaptive Behavior Index of the Survey Interview Form range from .40 to .83 ($Mdn\ r_{tt} = .55$) for a sample of 129 individuals. Interrater reliabilities for the Parent/Caregiver Rating Form based on 152 individuals range from .61 to .82 ($Mdn\ r_{tt} = .73$). The median interrater reliability for the Adaptive Behavior Composite is .78. Interrater reliabilities for the Maladaptive Behavior Index of the Parent/Caregiver Rating Form range from .59 to .81 ($Mdn\ r_{rr} = .67$), based on a sample of 154 individuals.

Validity

The Vineland–II has satisfactory construct, content, and criterion-related validity. For example, the content is consistent with definitions of adaptive behavior, the scores increase with age, a factor analysis generally supports the various domains, and the forms have satisfactory correlations with other measures of adaptive behavior.

Comment on the Vineland–II

The Vineland–II is a useful tool for the assessment of adaptive behavior. The revision provides updated content, increased coverage of the early years of development and later adult years, a new rating form, and increased sensitivity to measuring adaptive behavior in individuals with limited adaptive behavior skills. Because the Survey Interview Form allows for open-ended questions, learning to administer it takes time. The publisher offers a helpful training tape.

The interrater reliabilities are lower than preferred, which may in part be associated with difficulties in framing questions, eliciting appropriate responses, and scoring responses. Some items require knowledge that informants may not possess. For example, in the Communication Domain, informants must tell whether a child says at least 50 recognizable words, uses negatives in sentences, and identifies all printed letters of alphabet. However, the Vineland–II interrater reliabilities are similar to those reported by other adaptive behavior scales. As noted previously, because the range of standard scores is not the same at all ages or across all domains, you must know the available standard-score ranges if you are to make appropriate interpretations.

AAMR ADAPTIVE BEHAVIOR SCALE–SCHOOL: SECOND EDITION

The AAMR Adaptive Behavior Scale–School: Second Edition (ABS–S:2; Lambert, Nihira, & Leland, 1993) is designed to measure children's personal and community independence and social skills and adjustment (see Table 11-4). It is to be used in assessing children ages 3 to 21 years who may have

Table 11-4
Domains and Subdomains on the AAMR Adaptive Behavior Scale–School: Second Edition

Domain	Subdomains
Part I	
Independent Functioning	Eating
	Toilet Use
	Cleanliness
	Appearance
	Care of Clothing
	Dressing and Undressing
	Travel
	Other Independent Functioning
Physical Development	Sensory Development
	Motor Development
Economic Activity	Money Handling and Budgeting
	Shopping Skills
Language Development	Expression
	Verbal Comprehension
	Social Language Development
Numbers and Time	—
Prevocational/Vocational Activity	—
Self-Direction	Initiative
	Perseverance
	Leisure Time
Responsibility	—
Socialization	—
	—
Part II	
Social Behavior	—
Conformity	—
Trustworthiness	—
Stereotyped and Hyperactive Behavior	—
Self-Abusive Behavior	—
Social Engagement	—
Disturbing Interpersonal Behavior	—

Source: Adapted from Lambert, Nihira, and Leland (1993).

mental retardation. The 1993 version is a revision of a scale first published in 1975.

Part I of the ABS–S:2 covers nine behavioral domains and 18 subdomains and has three factors (listed below). It is organized along developmental lines and measures behaviors and habits needed to maintain personal independence in daily living. Part II covers seven domains and has two factors (also listed below). It focuses primarily on maladaptive behavior related to personality and behavior disorders.

The three factors in Part I and the two factors in Part II are as follows:

PART I

1. *Personal Self-Sufficiency.* Items are from the Independent Functioning and Physical Development domains.

2. *Community Self-Sufficiency.* Items are from the Independent Functioning, Economic Activity, Language Development, Numbers and Time, and Prevocational/Vocational Activity domains.

3. *Personal-Social Responsibility.* Items are from the Prevocational/Vocational Activity, Self-Direction, Responsibility, and Socialization domains.

PART II

4. *Social Adjustment.* Items are from the Social Behavior, Conformity, and Trustworthiness domains.

5. *Personal Adjustment.* Items are from the Stereotyped and Hyperactive Behavior and Self-Abusive Behavior domains.

The ABS–S:2 takes approximately 15 to 30 minutes to administer, and someone with minimal training can administer it. Two methods can be used to administer the scale. In the *first-person assessment method,* an informant who is familiar with the referred individual completes the scale by himself or herself. In the *interview method,* the examiner completes the scale based on information provided by an informant.

Be sure that informants evaluating the adaptive behavior levels of deaf-blind children give credit for any alternative methods of communication the children use—such as sign language, Braille, or finger spelling—when they score language development items on the scale. If they do not give credit for alternative forms of communication, they will penalize children with severe sensory impairments for their inability to use normal modes of communication. These same considerations apply when the examiner completes the scale.

Scores

In Part I, items are scored in one of two ways. Some items have statements arranged in order of increasing difficulty, and the score corresponds to the statement that describes the most difficult or highest level the person can usually manage (e.g., 3, 2, 1, or 0). Other items are scored yes or no. In Part II, items are scored using four categories: N (never occurs), O (occasionally occurs), F (frequently occurs), Other (specific example is recorded).

Raw scores are converted into standard scores for the 16 domains ($M = 10$, $SD = 3$) and for the five factors ($M = 100$, $SD = 15$). Percentile ranks are available for both parts, but test-age equivalents are available only for Part I, because the maladaptive behaviors covered in Part II are not age related.

The range of scaled scores on the domains in Parts I and II is not uniform throughout the ages covered by the scale. For example, in Part I, Socialization has a scaled-score range of 1 to 16 for 3-year-olds, whereas Numbers and Time has a scaled-score range of 7 to 17. In Part II, Social Behavior has a scaled-score range of 1 to 16 for 3-year-olds, whereas Self-Abusive Behavior has a scaled-score range of 1 to 11. In fact, there is no age at which all the domains in Parts I and II have scaled scores that range from 1 to 20.

The range of scaled scores on the factors also is not uniform throughout the ages covered by the scale. For example, Personal Self-Sufficiency has a scaled-score range of 60 to 141 for 3-year-olds, but a scaled-score range of 60 to 102 for 17-year-olds. In Part II, Social Adjustment has a scaled-score range of 59 to 126 for 3-year-olds, but a scaled-score range of 59 to 120 for 17-year-olds.

The range of test-age equivalents for the nine domains and three factors in Part I also is not uniform throughout the ages covered by the scale. For example, Independent Functioning has an age-equivalent score range of <3-0 to >16-0, whereas Responsibility has a range of <3-0 to 8-6. Community Self-Sufficiency has an age-equivalent score range of <3-0 to >15-9, whereas Personal-Social Responsibility has a range of <3-0 to 12-9.

Table C-1 in the ABS–S:2 manual shows that the distribution of age equivalents for raw scores is not uniform. In fact, in some cases the distribution shows large gaps. For example, in Independent Functioning a change of 1 raw-score point from 82 to 83 represents a change in test-age equivalents of 3 months (5-6 to 5-9), whereas in Physical Development a change of 1 raw-score point from 19 to 20 represents a change in test-age equivalents of 24 months (5-6 to 7-6). Thus, the distribution of item gradients (in this case, conversion of raw scores to test-age equivalents) is not smooth.

Standardization

The ABS–S:2 was standardized on 2,074 individuals with mental retardation and 1,254 individuals without mental retardation. The samples came from 40 states and were stratified on the basis of race/ethnic group status, gender, residence, and geographic region. The sample distribution was similar to that of the school-age population, but the comparison U.S. Census year is not given in the manual.

Reliability

Average internal consistency reliabilities in the sample with mental retardation are as follows: In Part I, they range from .82 to .98 (*Mdn* r_{xx} = .93) for the domains and from .97 to .98

(*Mdn* r_{xx} = .98) for the factors. In Part II, they range from .84 to .94 (*Mdn* r_{xx} = .90) for the domains and from .93 to .97 (*Mdn* r_{xx} = .95) for the factors.

Average internal consistency reliabilities in the sample without mental retardation in Part I range from .82 to .92 (*Mdn* r_{xx} = .88) for the domains and from .88 to .93 (*Mdn* r_{xx} = .93) for the factors. In Part II, they range from .87 to .97 (*Mdn* r_{xx} = .88) for the domains and from .92 to .96 (*Mdn* r_{xx} = .94) for the factors.

Test-retest reliabilities in Part I for a sample of 45 adolescents with emotional disturbance retested over 2 weeks range from .42 to .79 (*Mdn* r_{tt} = .61) for the domains and from .61 to .72 (*Mdn* r_{tt} = .66) for the factors. Interrater reliabilities for two professionals completing 15 protocols are .97 and above for the domains and factors in each part.

Validity

Content validity is satisfactory for Part I, as noted by acceptable correlations between items and the total score. However, in Part II, correlations between items and the total score are less satisfactory. Criterion-related validity is acceptable for Part I, as noted by satisfactory correlations with other measures of adaptive behavior, including the Vineland Adaptive Behavior Scales and the Adaptive Behavior Inventory. Construct validity is satisfactory. Correlations between Part I and the WISC–R range from .28 to .59 (*Mdn* r_{xx} = .41) for the domains and from .41 to .61 (*Mdn* r_{xx} = .59) for the factors. Correlations between Part II and the WISC–R are not significant or are very low (–.14 to –.18). As noted earlier, the manual specifies that the ABS–S:2 has three factors in Part I and two factors in Part II, derived from a factor analysis. However, an independent factor analysis reported only two factors in the ABS–S:2 (Stinett, Fuqua, & Coombs, 1999). Discriminant validity is satisfactory, as the ABS–S:2 discriminates between children with mental retardation and those without mental retardation.

Comment on the ABS–S:2

The ABS–S:2 is a useful measure of adaptive behavior for children who are being assessed for possible mental retardation. Both parts of the scale provide information useful for assessing behavior and for monitoring progress. Reliability and validity are satisfactory. However, because the range of standard scores is not uniform, it will be difficult to evaluate differential performance among the domains. In retest situations, you should study the available scaled-score ranges in order to make appropriate interpretations of score changes. Gradients of raw scores to test-age equivalents also show dramatic differences on Part I. You must be thoroughly familiar with these differences if you use test-age equivalents. (See Sattler, 2001, for a discussion of problems associated with the use of test-age equivalents.) Because the range of test-age equivalents is restricted in several domains, you must use caution in making comparisons among the domains and factors when you use these scores. Part II must be used cautiously, because items are given equal weighting regardless of the severity of the behavior (e.g., the item involving stamping one's feet receives the same weight as the item involving choking others; Perry & Factor, 1989).

AAMR ADAPTIVE BEHAVIOR SCALE–RESIDENTIAL AND COMMUNITY: SECOND EDITION

The AAMR Adaptive Behavior Scale–Residential and Community: Second Edition (ABS–RC:2; Nihira, Leland, & Lambert, 1993) is designed to measure personal independence and responsibility in daily living and social behavior in adults ages 18 to 79 years (see Table 11-5). It is to be used in assessing people who may have mental retardation. The 1993 version is a revision of the scale first published in 1969.

Part I of the ABS–RC:2 covers 10 behavioral domains and 21 subdomains and has three factors (listed below). It measures behaviors and habits needed to maintain personal independence in daily living. Part II covers eight domains and has two factors (also listed below). It focuses primarily on maladaptive behavior related to personality and behavior disorders.

The three factors in Part I and the two factors in Part II are as follows:

PART I

1. *Personal Self-Sufficiency.* Items are from the Independent Functioning and Physical Development domains.

2. *Community Self-Sufficiency.* Items are from the Independent Functioning, Economic Activity, Language Development, Numbers and Time, and Domestic Activity domains.

3. *Personal-Social Responsibility.* Items are from the Prevocational/Vocational Activity, Self-Direction, Responsibility, and Socialization domains.

PART II

4. *Social Adjustment.* Items are from the Social Behavior, Conformity, and Trustworthiness domains.

5. *Personal Adjustment.* Items are from the Stereotyped and Hyperactive Behavior, Sexual Behavior, and Self-Abusive Behavior domains.

The ABS–RC:2 takes approximately 15 to 30 minutes to administer, and someone with minimal training can administer it. Two methods can be used to administer the scale. In the *first-person assessment method,* an informant who is familiar with the referred individual completes the scale by himself or herself. In the *interview method,* the examiner completes the scale based on information provided by an informant.

Be sure that informants evaluating the adaptive behavior levels of severely disabled individuals give credit for any alternative method of communication the individuals use—such as sign language, Braille, or fingerspelling—when you

Table 11-5
Domains and Subdomains on the AAMR Adaptive Behavior Scale–Residential and Community: Second Edition

Domain	Subdomains
Part I	
Independent Functioning	Eating
	Toilet Use
	Cleanliness
	Appearance
	Care of Clothing
	Dressing and Undressing
	Travel
	Other Independent Functioning
Physical Development	Sensory Development
	Motor Development
Economic Activity	Money Handling and Budgeting
	Shopping Skills
Language Development	Expression
	Verbal Comprehension
	Social Language Development
Numbers and Time	—
Domestic Activity	Cleaning
	Kitchen
	Other Domestic Duties
Prevocational/ Vocational Activity	—
Self-Direction	Initiative
	Perseverance
	Leisure Time
Responsibility	—
Socialization	—
Part II	
Social Behavior	—
Conformity	—
Trustworthiness	—
Stereotyped and Hyperactive Behavior	—
Sexual Behavior	—
Self-Abusive Behavior	—
Social Engagement	—
Disturbing Interpersonal Behavior	—

Source: Adapted from Nihira, Leland, and Lambert (1993).

score language development items on the scale. If they do not give credit for alternative forms of communication, they will penalize individuals with severe sensory impairments for their inability to use typical modes of communication. These same considerations apply when examiners complete the scale.

Scores

In Part I, items are scored in one of two ways. Some items have statements arranged in order of increasing difficulty, and the score corresponds to the statement that describes the most difficult or highest level the person can usually manage (e.g., 3, 2, 1, 0). Other items are scored yes or no. In Part II, items are scored using four categories: N (never occurs), O (occasionally occurs), F (frequently occurs), Other (specific example is recorded).

Raw scores are converted into standard scores for the 18 domains ($M = 10$, $SD = 3$) and for the five factors ($M = 100$, $SD = 15$). Percentile ranks are available for both parts, but test-age equivalents are available only for Part I, because the maladaptive behaviors covered in Part II are not age related.

The range of scaled scores on the domains in Parts I and II is not uniform throughout the ages covered by the scale. For example, in Part I, Independent Functioning has a scaled-score range of 1 to 19 for 18-year-olds, whereas Responsibility has a scaled-score range of 5 to 15. In Part II, Stereotyped and Hyperactive Behavior has a scaled-score range of 1 to 16 for 18-year-olds, whereas Sexual Behavior has a scaled-score range of 1 to 12. In fact, on Part II, the longest scaled-score range is only 1 to 16.

The range of scaled scores on the factors also is not uniform throughout the ages covered by the scale. For example, Personal Self-Sufficiency has a scaled-score range of 60 to 144 for 18-year-olds, but a scaled-score range of 63 to 142 for 60-year-olds. In Part II, Personal Adjustment has a scaled-score range of 56 to 122 for 18-year-olds, but a scaled-score range of 58 to 125 for 60-year-olds.

Table B-1 in the ABS–RC:2 manual shows test-age equivalents for the 10 domains and three factors on Part I. Although the ABS–RC:2 is designed for adults, the manual provides the same test-age equivalents (ranging from 3-0 to 16-0) that are in the ABS–S:2 manual. The manual provides no rationale for presenting test-age equivalents for adults. *We recommend that they not be used on the ABS–RC:2.*

Standardization

The ABS–RC:2 was standardized on 4,103 individuals with developmental disabilities who resided in their community or in residential facilities. The sample came from 46 states and was stratified on the basis of race/ethnicity, gender, and urban/rural status. The distribution of the sample was similar to that of the adult population, but the comparison U.S. Census year is not provided in the manual.

Reliability

Average internal consistency reliabilities in Part I range from .82 to .98 (Mdn r_{xx} = .94) for the domains and from .97 to .99 (Mdn r_{xx} = .98) for the factors. In Part II, they range from .81 to .94 (Mdn r_{xx} = .87) for the domains and from .96 to .97 (Mdn r_{xx} = .96) for the factors.

Test-retest reliabilities for a sample of 45 individuals ages 24 to 65 retested over 2 weeks are satisfactory. On Part I, they range from .88 to .99 (Mdn r_{tt} = .96) for the domains and from .93 to .98 (Mdn r_{tt} = .94) for the factors. On Part II, they range from .96 to .99 (Mdn r_{tt} = .96) for the domains and from .85 to .98 (Mdn r_{tt} = .92) for the factors.

Interrater reliabilities for two graduate students completing 16 protocols are .96 and above for the domains and factors in Parts I and II except for Prevocational/Vocational Activity, which has a reliability coefficient of .83.

Validity

Content validity is satisfactory for Part I, as noted by acceptable correlations between items and the total score. However, in Part II, correlations between items and the total score are less satisfactory. Criterion-related validity is acceptable for Part I, as noted by satisfactory correlations with other measures of adaptive behavior, including the Vineland Adaptive Behavior Scales and the Adaptive Behavior Inventory. Construct validity is satisfactory. Correlations between Part I and the WAIS–R range from .27 to .73 (Mdn r_{xx} = .51) for the domains and from .49 to .72 (Mdn r_{xx} = .62) for the factors. Correlations between Part II and the WAIS–R are not significant or are very low (–.09 to .15). As noted earlier, the ABS–RC:2 has three factors in Part I and two factors in Part II, derived from a factor analysis. Discriminant validity is satisfactory, as the ABS–RC:2 discriminates between adults with mental retardation and those without mental retardation.

Comment on the ABS–RC:2

The ABS–RC:2 is a useful measure of adaptive behavior for adults who are being assessed for possible mental retardation. Both parts of the scale provide information useful for assessing behavior and for monitoring progress. Reliability and validity are satisfactory. However, because the range of standard scores is not uniform, it will be difficult to evaluate differential performance among the domains. In retest situations, it will be important that you study the available scaled-score ranges in order to make appropriate interpretations of score changes. *Use of test-age equivalents is not recommended for any clinical or diagnostic purpose.*

SCALES OF INDEPENDENT BEHAVIOR–REVISED

The Scales of Independent Behavior–Revised (SIB–R; Bruininks, Woodcock, Weatherman, & Hill, 1996) is an individually administered measure of skills needed to function independently in home, social, and community settings. The SIB–R covers an age span from infancy to mature adult (age 80 years and older). The SIB–R has the following composition (see Table 11-6):

- The Full Scale contains 14 subscales organized into four adaptive behavior clusters (Motor Skills, Social Interaction and Communication Skills, Personal Living Skills, and Community Living Skills).
- The Problem Behavior Scale contains eight problem area scales organized into three maladaptive behavior clusters (Internalized Maladaptive Behavior, Asocial Maladaptive Behavior, and Externalized Maladaptive Behavior).

Table 11-6
Clusters and Skills/Areas on the Scales of Independent Behavior–Revised

Cluster	Skills/Areas
Adaptive Behavior Skills (Full Scale)	
Motor Skills	Gross Motor Fine Motor
Social Interaction and Communication Skills	Social Interaction Language Comprehension Language Expression
Personal Living Skills	Eating and Meal Preparation Toileting Dressing Personal Self-Care Domestic Skills
Community Living Skills	Time and Punctuality Money and Value Work Skills Home/Community Orientation
Maladaptive Behavior Areas (Problem Behavior Scale)	
Internalized Maladaptive Behavior	Hurtful to Self Unusual or Repetitive Habits Withdrawal or Inattentive Behavior
Asocial Maladaptive Behavior	Socially Offensive Behavior Uncooperative Behavior
Externalized Maladaptive Behavior	Hurtful to Others Destructive to Property Disruptive Behavior

- The Short Form contains 40 items that can be administered to persons at any developmental level.
- The Early Development Scale contains 40 items designed for children from infancy through about 6 years of age or for older individuals with a developmental level of 8 years of age or below.

The SIB–R Full Scale takes approximately 60 minutes to administer, and the Short Form and the Early Development Form each take about 15 to 20 minutes to administer. Although an informant usually completes the scale, in some cases the individual herself or himself can provide the information needed to complete the scale.

Scores

The adaptive behavior items are scored on a 4-point scale: 0 (never or rarely performs the task or activity), 1 (does the task but not well or about one-quarter of the time), 2 (does the task fairly well or about three-quarters of the time), 3 (does the task very well or always or almost always). Raw scores are converted into standard scores ($M = 100$, $SD = 15$), percentile ranks, stanines, normal-curve equivalents, or age-equivalent scores. The standard score for the Full Scale is called "Broad Independence," and the standard score for the Problem Behavior Scale is called "General Maladaptive Index." The manual for the SIB–R includes instructional range scores, a Support Score based on an individual's adaptive behavior and problem behavior scores, and an adjusted behavior score associated with the Woodcock-Johnson–R Broad Cognitive Ability cluster score. Because the Woodcock-Johnson has been revised, this comparison procedure does not use the latest norms available on the Woodcock-Johnson.

The problem behavior items are scored on two 5-point scales. The five ratings on the frequency scale are 1 (less than once a month), 2 (one to three times a month), 3 (one to six times a week), 4 (one to 10 times a day), and 5 (one or more times an hour). The five ratings on the severity scale are 0 (not serious), 1 (slightly serious), 2 (moderately serious), 3 (very serious), and 4 (extremely serious).

Standardization

The norm sample for the SIB–R consisted of 2,182 individuals ages 3 months to 60 to 90 years. Individuals were chosen to conform to the 1990 U.S. Census data on gender, race, Hispanic origin, occupational status, occupational level, geographic region, and type of community. Of the 2,182 individuals in the sample, 1,817 were between 3 months and 19 years of age, and 365 were between 20 and 90 years of age. The SIB–R manual does not give the numbers of people at the individual ages from 20 to 90 years.

The distribution of the norm group does not match the distribution in the four nationwide census regions. For example,

in the 1990 U.S. Census data, the Northwest region comprised 20.4% of the population and the Midwest region comprised 24.0% of the population. In the norm group, these two regions comprised 12.2% and 50.5%, respectively. Thus, there are disparities of 8.3% and 26.5%, respectively, between the norm group and the U.S. Census data for these two regions. Disparities are 11.7% for the South region and 6.4% for the West region.

Reliability

Median corrected split-half reliabilities for all age levels range from .70 to .88 ($Mdn\ r_{xx} = .81$) for the 14 adaptive subscales and from .88 to .94 ($Mdn\ r_{xx} = .90$) for the four cluster scores on the Full Scale. The median corrected split-half reliabilities are .98 for Broad Independence and .76 for the Short Form. Standard errors of measurement are reported in W scale units, not in the more popular standard score distribution with $M = 100$ and $SD = 15$. Further, median corrected split-half reliabilities are not presented for the Problem Behavior Scale.

Test-retest reliability was assessed on a sample of 31 children without disabilities, ages 6 to 13 years, who were retested within 4 weeks. Median stability coefficients are $r_{tt} = .93$ for the 14 adaptive subscales, $r_{tt} = .96$ for the four clusters, $r_{tt} = .98$ for Broad Independence, $r_{tt} = .83$ for the General Maladaptive Index, and $r_{tt} = .96$ for the Support Score. Other test-retest studies reported in the SIB–R manual for the Maladaptive Behavior Index and Early Development Form generally show test-retest reliability coefficients in the .70s and .80s.

Interrater reliabilities are reported in the manual for four different samples. They range from the .70s to the .90s for the 14 adaptive subscales for two samples, from the .80s to the .90s for the four adaptive clusters and Broad Independence for three samples, in the .90s for the Support Score for two samples, and from the .60s to the .80s for the Maladaptive Behavior Index for four samples. The interrater reliability is .91 for the Broad Independence–Early Development Form for one sample of preschool children.

Validity

The SIB–R manual reports several indices of construct validity. First, correlations between SIB–R adaptive behavior scores and chronological age were high (ranging from .54 to .73 for the four clusters and Broad Independence). Second, based on the prior version of the scale, adaptive behavior scores were lower for individuals with disabilities than for those without disabilities. Third, the pattern of subscale intercorrelations provides support for construct validity. Criterion-related validity is satisfactory, as seen, for example, by a .82 correlation between Broad Independence and the Woodcock-Johnson Broad Cognitive Ability Scale in a sample of 312 individuals without disabilities. Finally, the manual presents other evidence of construct validity and criterion validity based on the former version of the scale.

Comment on the SIB–R

The SIB–R is useful in assessing adaptive behavior over a wide age range. However, the manual and scale have several limitations. First, the numerous scores complicate use of the scale. Second, the procedure that compares the scale with the Woodcock-Johnson Broad Cognitive Ability cluster score is out of date. Third, the distribution of the norm sample by region does not match U.S. Census data. Fourth, additional test-retest reliability studies are needed over the entire age span covered by the scale for both individuals with disabilities and those without disabilities. Fifth, the manual does not provide a factor analysis of the SIB–R or criterion-related validity studies using the SIB–R. Sixth, the SIB–R does not measure all of the skill areas proposed by the AAMR. Finally, research is needed to evaluate the usefulness of the support scores and other special scores provided in the manual.

ADAPTIVE BEHAVIOR ASSESSMENT SYSTEM–SECOND EDITION

The Adaptive Behavior Assessment System–Second Edition (ABAS–II; Harrison & Oakland, 2000, 2003) is designed to measure adaptive behavior skills of infants, children, and adults from birth to age 89 years (see Table 11-7). This revision retains the features of the original ABAS, but adds two new forms, introduces additional items to reflect 2002 AAMR guidelines, and extends the normative and psychometric data. There are now five forms, each of which takes about 15 to 20 minutes to complete:

- The Parent/Primary Caregiver Form covers children ages birth to 5 years, contains 241 items, and can be completed by parents or other primary caregivers.
- The Teacher/Daycare Provider Form covers children ages 2 to 5 years, contains 216 items, and can be completed by teachers or other preschool providers.
- The Teacher Form covers children ages 5 to 21 years, contains 193 items, and can be completed by a teacher or teacher's aide.
- The Parent Form covers ages 5 to 21 years, contains 232 items, and can be completed by a parent or other primary caregiver.
- The Adult Form covers ages 16 to 89 years and contains 239 items. This form can be completed by the referred individual, a family member, or another adult familiar with the referred individual.

According to the ABAS–II manual, the forms require at least a fifth-grade reading level. However, our analysis indicates that the forms generally require a seventh-grade reading level and include items that range from a third-grade to a

Table 11-7
Adaptive Domains and Skill Areas on the Adaptive Behavior Assessment System–Second Edition

Adaptive domain	Skill areas
Conceptual	Communication Functional Pre-Academics[a]/Academics[b] Self-Direction
Social	Leisure Social
Practical	Self-Care Home Living[c]/School Living[d] Community Use[e] Health and Safety Work[f]

Note. The Parent/Primary Caregiver and Teacher/Daycare Provider Forms have a Motor Skills area, the scaled score for which is included in the General Adaptive Composite (GAC) but not in any of the adaptive domains.
[a] For ages 1 to 5 years.
[b] For ages 5 to 89 years.
[c] Not administered to children under 1 year of age; is on the Parent/Primary Caregiver, Parent, and Adult Forms.
[d] Is on the Teacher/Daycare Provider and Teacher Forms.
[e] Not administered to children under 1 year of age; not included on the Teacher/Daycare Provider Form.
[f] For ages 16 to 89 years.
Source: Adapted from Harrison and Oakland (2003).

tenth-grade reading level. The higher reading level should not pose a problem for teachers, but it may be a problem for some informants and adult clients. Items may be read to respondents who are unable to read them.

Several items appear to require a high level of comprehension. For example, not all informants will know what a noun and a verb are, what irregular plural nouns are, what "personal identification" means, and what "routing household task" means. Some items appear to be abstract, such as "Follows safety rules for fire or weather alarms at home," "Maintains safety of bike or car," "Makes plans for home projects in logical steps," and "Places reasonable demands on friends." And some items require information that a parent might not have. For example, one item asks whether the child follows a daily work schedule without reminders from a supervisor, and another item asks whether the child behaves safely at work so that no one will be harmed.

Scores

Each item is rated on a 4-point scale: 0 (is not able), 1 (never when needed), 2 (sometimes when needed), 3 (always when needed). Each item offers the respondent the option of guessing, but there is no scale number representing "Don't know" or "Does not apply." Raw scores are converted into standard scores for the 10 skill areas ($M = 10$, $SD = 3$) and the four composite scores (Conceptual, Social, Practical, and General Adaptive) ($M = 100$, $SD = 15$) and into test-age equivalents. The ABAS–II manual provides confidence intervals and percentile ranks for the four composite scores and has tables showing significant differences for pairwise comparisons of the composite scores. The following classifications are used for the four composite scores: Extremely Low, Borderline, Below Average, Average, Above Average, Superior, and Very Superior.

Caution must be exercised in interpreting the standard scores. First, the range of scaled scores for the 10 skill areas differs by age. For example, on the Teacher Form, at age 2-0 to 2-2, each skill area has a possible range of 1 to 19 points. However, the range of scaled scores is only 1 to 11 or 1 to 12 at age 16 years. Similarly, the range of General Adaptive Composite (GAC) scores is 40 to 130 at 5 years of age but only 40 to 120 at 8 years of age. The three adaptive domains also have variable ranges throughout the age levels covered by the scale. On the Teacher Form, for example, the Practical Adaptive Domain has a range of 41 to 130, whereas the Social Adaptive Domain has a range of 55 to 130.

Thus, the standard scores are not normally distributed and the range of scaled scores is not the same at all ages. Therefore, you must know the available scaled-score ranges if you are to use the scores to make interpretations. For example, a child who obtains a GAC score of 130 at the age of 5 years and a GAC score of 120 at the age of 8 years has not lost 10 points. This is purely an artifact of the instrument—the highest GAC score possible at the age of 8 years is 120. The skewed and uneven distribution of scaled scores means that, when individuals have above-average adaptive behavior skills, it will be difficult to evaluate them over time or to evaluate their differential performance in the skill areas.

Two other cautions are merited. First, the ABAS–II has a limited ceiling (scores run two standard deviations or less above the mean). However, this should not be a problem in evaluating most children with developmental disabilities. Second, the gradients of raw scores to test-age equivalents show dramatic differences on the Teacher Form. For example, a raw score of 45 on Health and Safety reflects test-age equivalents of 8-0 to 8-3, whereas a raw score of 46 reflects test-age equivalents of 11-4 to 11-7. In this example, a change of 1 raw-score point yielded a change of over 3 years in test-age equivalents. You must be thoroughly familiar with these differences if you use the test-age equivalents. (See Sattler, 2001, for a discussion of problems associated with the use of test-age equivalents.) Similarly, because the range of test-age equivalents is restricted in some skill areas, you must use caution in making comparisons among the skill areas when using test-age equivalents. For example, on the Teacher Form, test-age equivalents on Communication range from 5-4 to 21-11, whereas on Health and Safety they range from 5-4 to 11-7, on Self-Care, from 5-4 to 12-4, and on School Living, from 5-4 to 12-8.

Standardization

The standardization samples for the Parent/Primary Caregiver and Teacher/Daycare Provider Forms consisted of 2,100 individuals. These samples were stratified by gender, race/ethnicity, and educational level in accordance with 2000 U.S. Census data. The standardization samples for the Teacher, Parent, and Adult Forms comprised 5,270 individuals stratified by gender, race/ethnicity, and educational level in accordance with 1999 U.S. Census data.

Reliability

On the Teacher/Daycare Provider Form, average internal consistency reliabilities range from .82 to .93 ($Mdn\ r_{xx} = .91$) for the nine skill areas. The median domain composite internal consistency reliability is .94, while the average GAC internal consistency reliability is .98. For the individual ages, the internal consistency reliabilities range from .72 to .95 ($Mdn\ r_{xx} = .90$) for the nine skill areas. Test-retest reliabilities based on a sample of 115 children evaluated over 13 days range from .77 to .86 ($Mdn\ r_{tt} = .82$) for the nine skill areas and from .87 to .88 ($Mdn\ r_{tt} = .87$) for the three domain composites. The test-retest reliability for the GAC is .91. Interrater reliabilities on a sample of 42 children rated by two informants range from .44 to .82 ($Mdn\ r_{rr} = .53$) for the nine skill areas and from .62 to .83 ($Mdn\ r_{rr} = .65$) for the three domain composites. The interrater reliability for the GAC is .74.

On the Parent/Primary Caregiver Form, average internal consistency reliabilities range from .81 to .90 ($Mdn\ r_{xx} = .86$) for the 10 skill areas. The median domain composite internal consistency reliability is .92, while the average GAC internal consistency reliability is .97. For the individual ages, the internal consistency reliabilities range from .48 to .94 ($Mdn\ r_{xx} = .86$). Test-retest reliabilities based on a sample of 207 children evaluated over 12 days range from .75 to .85 ($Mdn\ r_{tt} = .76$) for the 10 skill areas and from .83 to .86 ($Mdn\ r_{tt} = .85$) for the three domain composites. The test-retest reliability for the GAC is .88. Interrater reliabilities on a sample of 56 children rated by two informants range from .50 to .82 ($Mdn\ r_{rr} = .67$) for the 10 skill areas and from .69 to .83 ($Mdn\ r_{rr} = .74$) for the three domain composites. The interrater reliability for the GAC is .91.

On the Teacher Form, average internal consistency reliabilities range from .89 to .96 ($Mdn\ r_{xx} = .94$) for the 10 skill areas. The median domain composite internal consistency reliability is .97, while the average GAC internal consistency reliability is .99. For the individual ages, the internal consistency reliabilities range from .79 to .98 ($Mdn\ r_{xx} = .91$). Test-retest reliabilities based on a sample of 143 children evaluated over 11 days range from .88 to .97 ($Mdn\ r_{tt} = .92$) for nine skill areas (Work not included) and from .96 to .97 ($Mdn\ r_{tt} = .96$) for the three domain composites. The test-retest reliability for the GAC is .97. Interrater reliabilities on a sample of 84 children rated by two informants range from .77 to .86

($Mdn\ r_{rr}$ = .84) for the nine skill areas and from .84 to .93 ($Mdn\ r_{rr}$ = .85) for the three domain composites. The inter-rater reliability for the GAC is .94.

On the Parent Form, average internal consistency reliabilities range from .86 to .93 ($Mdn\ r_{xx}$ = .92) for the 10 skill areas. The median domain composite internal consistency reliability is .96, while the average GAC internal consistency reliability is .98. For the individual ages, the internal consistency reliabilities range from .79 to .96 ($Mdn\ r_{xx}$ = .94). Test-retest reliabilities based on a sample of 104 children evaluated over 11 days range from .80 to .92 ($Mdn\ r_{tt}$ = .88) for nine skill areas (Work not included) and from .89 to .94 ($Mdn\ r_{tt}$ = .92) for the three domain composites. The test-retest reliability for the GAC is .96. Interrater reliabilities on a sample of 75 children rated by two informants range from .63 to .87 ($Mdn\ r_{rr}$ = .73) for the nine skill areas and from .77 to .91 ($Mdn\ r_{rr}$ = .85) for the three domain composites. The inter-rater reliability for the GAC is .83.

On the Adult Form (Self Report), average internal consistency reliabilities range from .88 to .94 ($Mdn\ r_{xx}$ = .92) for the 10 skill areas. The median domain composite internal consistency reliability is .97, while the average GAC internal consistency reliability is .99. For the individual ages, the internal consistency reliabilities range from .82 to .97 ($Mdn\ r_{xx}$ = .92). Test-retest reliabilities based on a sample of 66 adults evaluated over 11 days range from .92 to .97 ($Mdn\ r_{tt}$ = .94) for the 10 skill areas and from .95 to .99 ($Mdn\ r_{tt}$ = .96) for the three domain composites. The test-retest reliability for the GAC is .99.

On the Adult Form (Rated by Others), average internal consistency reliabilities range from .93 to .97 ($Mdn\ r_{xx}$ = .95) for the 10 skill areas. The median domain composite internal consistency reliability is .98, while the average GAC internal consistency reliability is .99. For the individual ages, the internal consistency reliabilities range from .82 to .99 ($Mdn\ r_{xx}$ = .94). Test-retest reliabilities based on a sample of 52 adults evaluated over 11 days range from .80 to .95 ($Mdn\ r_{tt}$ = .89) for the 10 skill areas and from .91 to .95 ($Mdn\ r_{tt}$ = .92) for the three domain composites. The test-retest reliability for the GAC is .94. Interrater reliabilities on a sample of 52 adults rated by two informants range from .66 to .84 ($Mdn\ r_{rr}$ = .75) for the 10 skill areas and from .81 to .83 ($Mdn\ r_{rr}$ = .82) for the three domain composites. The interrater reliability for the GAC is .86.

The consistency between Teacher/Daycare Provider and Parent/Primary Caregiver ratings was studied in a sample of 130 children. Interrater reliabilities range from .39 to .64 ($Mdn\ r_{rr}$ = .44) for the nine skill areas and from .56 to .70 ($Mdn\ r_{rr}$ = .60) for the three domain composites. The inter-rater reliability for the GAC is .68. The consistency between Teacher and Parent ratings was studied in a sample of 30 children. Interrater reliabilities range from .51 to .84 ($Mdn\ r_{rr}$ = .67) for nine skill areas (Work not included) and from .73 to .85 ($Mdn\ r_{rr}$ = .73) for the three domain composites. The interrater reliability for the GAC is .81.

Validity

The various forms of the ABAS–II generally have satisfactory content, construct, and criterion-related validity. Criterion-related validity is supported through analyses showing significant correlations between ABAS–II scores and scores from the Vineland Adaptive Behavior Scales–Classroom Edition, Scales of Independent Behavior–Revised, and the Behavior Assessment Scale for Children. ABAS–II scores significantly discriminated between clinical and nonclinical samples. Results of factor analytic studies show that both a single-factor solution and a three-factor solution are possible, depending on the form of the analysis. However, the ABAS–II manual fails to present any factor loadings by age, thus making the factor analysis difficult to interpret.

Comment on the ABAS–II

The ABAS–II is a valid and reliable instrument for assessing adaptive behavior of children and adults. The manual is well done, with clear guidelines regarding administration and scoring and thorough discussions of reliability and validity. Modifications in the structure of the scale made to reflect changes in current AAMR guidelines are desirable, as is the downward extension of the instrument to include preschool children. Although the interrater reliabilities are lower than preferred, and may in part be associated with the fact that some items require knowledge that informants may not possess, the interrater reliabilities are similar to those reported by other behavior scales. The instrument should be used with caution because of several psychometric issues.

BATTELLE DEVELOPMENTAL INVENTORY, 2ND EDITION

The Battelle Developmental Inventory, 2nd Edition (BDI–2; Newborg, 2005) is designed to measure developmental skills in children from birth to 7-11 years. The BDI–2 has 450 items grouped into five domains: Adaptive, Personal-Social, Communication, Motor, and Cognitive. Within each domain, items are clustered into subdomains, which represent specific skill areas (see Table 11-8). A Screening Test is composed of 100 of the 450 items. The BDI–2 takes about 60 to 90 minutes to administer; the Screening Test takes about 10 to 30 minutes to administer. Typically, administering the scale to younger children (under 2 years of age) takes less time than administering it to older children.

Following is a description of each domain.

- The Adaptive Domain has 60 items that measure the child's ability to become self-sufficient and to assume personal responsibility.
- The Personal-Social Domain has 100 items that measure the child's ability to engage in meaningful social interactions

Table 11-8
Domains and Subdomains on the Battelle Developmental Inventory, 2nd Edition

Domain	Subdomains
Adaptive	Self-Care Personal Responsibility
Personal-Social	Adult Interaction Peer Interaction Self-Concept and Social Role
Communication	Receptive Communication Expressive Communication
Motor	Gross Motor Fine Motor Perceptual Motor
Cognitive	Attention and Memory Reasoning and Academic Skills Perception and Concepts

Source: Adapted from Newborg (2005).

with adults and peers and to develop his or her own self-concept and sense of social role.

- The Communication Domain has 85 items that measure the child's receptive and expressive communication skills.
- The Motor Domain has 100 items that measure the child's gross-motor development, fine-motor development, and perceptual motor development.
- The Cognitive Domain has 105 items that measure the child's intellectual ability, including attention and memory, reasoning and academic skills, and perception and concepts.

The information needed to score each item is obtained by one of three methods: (a) a structured test format, (b) interviews with parents, or (c) observations of the child in a natural setting. Items can be modified for use with children with disabilities. Several items require parents or caregivers to judge how often the child uses parts of speech or talks to them about various topics, and these may be difficult for them to judge accurately. For example, some items require them to state how often the child asks questions that begin "why" and "how" or "who" and "where." Other items require them to state how often the child talks to them about other people or how often the child uses words first before using nonverbal communication.

Scores

Most items are rated on a 3-point scale: 2 (behavior meeting the specified criterion), 1 (behavior attempted but not meeting

the specified criterion), 0 (behavior that fails to meet the specified criterion or is not attempted). Four items are rated on a 2-point scale: 2 (present), 0 (absent). Raw score totals are converted into standard scores ($M = 10$, $SD = 3$) and into age-equivalent scores for the subdomains. The subdomain standard scores are summed and converted into Developmental Quotients (DQs) for the five domains and for the Total BDI–2 ($M = 100$, $SD = 15$). Percentile ranks, NCE (normal-curve equivalent) scores, z scores, and T scores also are provided for the subdomains, domains, and Total BDI–2 scores. A computer program is available for scoring.

At all age levels, the range of DQs is 55 to 145 for the five domains and 45 to 155 for the Total BDI–2, except at ages 6-0 to 7-11 years, where the total BDI–2 range is 50 to 150. The range of standard scores for the subdomains is 1 to 19 at almost all ages, except for the subdomains that do not have items covering birth to 1-11 years or covering 6-0 to 7-11 years. Four subdomains cover birth to 7-11 years (Self-Concept and Social Role, Receptive Communication, Expressive Communication, Perception and Concepts), five subdomains cover ages 0-0 to 5-11 years (Self-Care, Adult Interaction, Gross Motor, Fine Motor, Attention and Memory), three subdomains cover ages 2-0 to 7-11 (Personal Responsibility, Perceptual Motor, Reasoning and Academic Skills), and one subdomain covers ages 2-0 to 5-11 years (Peer Interaction). Subdomains do not cover the entire range from birth to 7-11 years because some skills usually are not developed before the age of 2 years and other skills are generally fully developed by the age of 5-11 years. Therefore, you should not directly compare age-equivalent scores across all subdomains, particularly at the lower and upper age levels.

Standardization

The standardization sample consisted of 2,500 children stratified by age, geographical region, race, socioeconomic status, and sex in accordance with 2001 U.S. Census data.

Reliability

The average internal consistency reliability for the Total BDI–2 is .99, with a range of .98 to .99 for the 16 age groups. The average internal consistency reliabilities for the five domains range from .90 to .96 (Mdn r_{xx} = .93), with a range of .79 to .98 (Mdn r_{xx} = .88) for the 16 age groups. Average internal consistency reliabilities for the 13 subdomains range from .85 to .95 (Mdn r_{xx} = .89). The average internal consistency reliability for the Total Screening score is .91, with a range of .78 to .94 over the 16 age groups. The 7-6 years to 7-11 years age group had the lowest internal consistency reliability coefficient.

Test-retest reliabilities are reported for two samples of children re-evaluated over an interval of 2 to 25 days (Mdn = 8 days). Test-retest reliabilities based on a sample of 126

2-year-olds range from .87 to .90 (*Mdn r_{tt}* = .89) for the five domains and from .77 to .90 (*Mdn r_{tt}* = .80) for the 13 subdomains. The test-retest reliability is .93 for the Total BDI–2. Test-retest reliabilities based on a sample of 126 4-year-olds range from .87 to .92 (*Mdn r_{tt}* = .90) for the five domains and from .74 to .91 (*Mdn r_{tt}* = .86) for the 13 subdomains. The test-retest reliability is .94 for the Total BDI–2. The manual does not report test-retest reliabilities for the Total Screening score.

Out of a total of 450 items, interrater reliabilities are reported for only 17 items in the Fine Motor and Perceptual Motor subdomains. Two raters scored the 17 items for 120 children, and their scores were compared with the scores of the original examiner. These reliability coefficients are r_{rr} = .97 and r_{rr} = .99.

Validity

The BDI–2 has satisfactory content, construct, and criterion-related validity. Experts judged the item content to be relevant. Criterion-related validity is supported through analyses showing significant correlations between the BDI–2 and several other developmental measures, including the Bayley Scales of Infant Development–Second Edition, the Denver Developmental Screening Test–Second Edition, the Preschool Language Test–Fourth Edition, and the Vineland Social-Emotional Early Childhood Scales. Acceptable correlations were also reported between the BDI–2 and the Comprehensive Test of Phonological Processing, the Wechsler Preschool and Primary Scale of Intelligence–Third Edition, and the Woodcock-Johnson III Tests of Achievement. The BDI–2 also differentiates children without developmental difficulties from children with developmental difficulties, including those with an autistic disorder, cognitive delays, developmental delays, motor delays, prematurity, and speech and language delays.

Construct validity is supported by the fact that older children pass a greater percentage of items than younger children; by intercorrelations among subdomain, domain, and Total BDI–2 scores; and by factor analysis. The manual does not report any validity studies for the Total Screening score.

Comment on the BDI–2

The BDI–2 is a reliable and valid instrument for assessing developmental skills in young children. Useful features include the mixture of structured test items with interview and observational data. However, more information is needed about interrater reliability for the Total BDI–2, domain, and subdomain scores, and about the test-retest reliability, interrater reliability, and validity of the Total Screening score. The manual is well done, with clear guidelines regarding administration and scoring. The instrument is a valuable addition to the field of developmental assessment.

THINKING THROUGH THE ISSUES

1. What are some differences and similarities between adaptive behavior and intelligence?
2. What are some differences and similarities among the following three children: (a) a child with an IQ of 65 and an Adaptive Behavior Composite of 65, (b) a child with an IQ of 65 and an Adaptive Behavior Composite of 90, and (c) a child with an IQ of 90 and an Adaptive Behavior Composite of 65?
3. What uses, if any, might adaptive behavior scales have for individuals other than those with mental retardation?

SUMMARY

1. Adaptive behavior scales can help you make diagnoses, formulate discharge plans, and develop interventions.
2. Adaptive behavior scales play an important role in the assessment of children with developmental disabilities—and children with mental retardation, in particular.

Definition of Adaptive Behavior

3. The American Association on Mental Retardation defines adaptive behavior as "the collection of conceptual, social, and practical skills that have been learned by people in order to function in everyday lives" (AAMR, 2002, p. 73).
4. Adaptive behavior is best understood as the degree to which individuals are able to function and maintain themselves independently and meet cultural expectations for personal and social responsibility at various ages.
5. During infancy and early childhood, adaptive behavior involves the development of sensorimotor skills, communication skills, self-help skills, and socialization skills.
6. During childhood and early adolescence, adaptive behavior involves the application of basic academic skills in daily life activities, appropriate reasoning and judgment in interacting with the environment, and social skills.
7. During late adolescence and adult life, adaptive behavior includes carrying out vocational and social responsibilities and behaviors.
8. Adaptive behavior involves the child's physical skills, cognitive ability, affect, motivation, culture, socioeconomic status, family (including the expectations of parents, siblings, and extended family), and environment.
9. Adaptive behavior is difficult to measure, because it is not independent of intelligence, because behaviors accepted as adaptive at one age may not be acceptable at another age, and because what constitutes adaptive behavior is variable, not absolute, and depends on the demands of a given environment.

Assessment Considerations

10. The measurement of adaptive behavior usually depends on information obtained from a parent, teacher, or other informant.
11. Informants may differ as to their familiarity with the child, ability to provide reliable and valid information about the child, sensitivity to and tolerance for behavior problems, personality, expectations, tendency to agree or disagree with items, preference for using extreme or intermediate positions on rating scales, and frame of reference used to evaluate the child.

12. Ratings of adaptive behavior also differ depending on the extent of the informant's opportunities to observe the child's behavior.

13. Not only do informants' ratings differ among themselves; they also differ from children's self-ratings.

14. Informants who occupy similar roles in relation to the child have higher levels of agreement ($M\ r = .60$) than those who occupy different roles ($M\ r = .28$).

15. The relatively low correlations between parent and teacher ratings of adaptive behavior suggest that there is considerable situational specificity in children's adaptive behavior.

16. There are several informal ways of obtaining additional information about children's adaptive behavior, including interviews and case history, daily diaries, information obtained from teacher-parent communications, observations in simulated home settings at school, task analysis, systematic observation and controlled teaching trials, and evaluation of life skills.

17. In evaluating measures of adaptive behavior, use the same criteria you would for any psychometric measure.

Vineland Adaptive Behavior Scales, Second Edition

18. The Vineland Adaptive Behavior Scales, Second Edition assesses adaptive behavior skills of infants, children, and adults from birth to 90 years of age. Standardization, reliability, and validity are satisfactory. Caution must be exercised in interpreting standard scores for the subdomains, domains, and Adaptive Behavior Composite and in interpreting age-equivalent scores.

AAMR Adaptive Behavior Scale–School: Second Edition

19. The ABS–S:2 is an adaptive behavior scale designed to measure children's personal and community independence and social skills and adjustment. It is to be used in assessing children ages 3 to 21 years who may have mental retardation. Standardization, reliability, and validity are satisfactory. The nonuniform range of standard scores makes it difficult to evaluate differential performance among the domains. Caution must be used in comparing test-age equivalents among the domains.

AAMR Adaptive Behavior Scale–Residential and Community: Second Edition

20. The ABS–RC:2 is an adaptive behavior scale designed to measure personal independence and responsibility in daily living and social behavior in adults ages 18 to 79 years. It is to be used in assessing individuals who may have mental retardation. Standardization, reliability, and validity are satisfactory. The nonuniform range of standard scores makes it difficult to evaluate differential performance among the domains.

Scales of Independent Behavior–Revised

21. The SIB–R is an individually administered measure of skills needed to function independently in home, social, and community settings. It covers an age span from infancy to mature adult (age 80 years and older). The distribution of the standardization sample by region does not match U.S. Census data. Reliability and validity are satisfactory. The numerous scores provided complicate the use of the scale. Additional reliability and validity studies are needed.

Adaptive Behavior Assessment System–Second Edition

22. The ABAS–II has five forms designed to measure the adaptive behavior skills of infants, children, and adults from birth to age 89 years. Standardization, reliability, and validity are satisfactory. However, the instrument should be used with caution because of several psychometric issues.

Battelle Developmental Inventory, 2nd Edition

23. The BDI–2 is designed to measure developmental skills in children from birth to 7-11 years. The BDI–2 has 450 items grouped into five domains: Adaptive, Personal-Social, Communication, Motor, and Cognitive. Within each domain, items are clustered into subdomains, which represent specific skill areas. A Screening Test is composed of 100 items. The BDI–2 takes about 60 to 90 minutes to administer; the Screening Test takes about 10 to 30 minutes to administer. Reliability and validity are generally satisfactory; however, additional information is needed about interrater reliability and about the validity of the Total Screening score. The instrument is a valuable addition to the field of developmental assessment.

KEY TERMS, CONCEPTS, AND NAMES

Adaptive behavior (p. 304)
Assessment considerations (p. 304)
Informal assessments (p. 305)
Psychometric concerns (p. 307)
Vineland Adaptive Behavior Scales, Second Edition (p. 307)
AAMR Adaptive Behavior Scale–School: Second Edition (p. 309)
AAMR Adaptive Behavior Scale–Residential and Community: Second Edition (p. 311)
Scales of Independent Behavior–Revised (p. 313)
Adaptive Behavior Assessment System–Second Edition (p. 315)
Battelle Developmental Inventory, 2nd Edition (p. 317)

STUDY QUESTIONS

1. Define adaptive behavior and discuss the AAMR definition and the difficulties in measuring adaptive behavior.

2. Discuss assessment considerations involved in the measurement of adaptive behavior.

3. Describe each of the following measures of adaptive behavior and discuss scoring, standardization, reliability, validity, and strengths and weaknesses for each:

> Vineland Adaptive Behavior Scales, Second Edition
> AAMR Adaptive Behavior Scale–School: Second Edition
> AAMR Adaptive Behavior Scale–Residential and Community: Second Edition
> Scales of Independent Behavior–Revised
> Adaptive Behavior Assessment System–Second Edition
> Battelle Developmental Inventory, 2nd Edition

4. Imagine you were going to create a new measure of adaptive behavior for infants, children, and adults to age 90 years. Given the knowledge that you have acquired from this chapter, what type of information would you include in the measure and why? Discuss whether any measure of adaptive behavior can meet the rigorous psychometric requirements of a norm-referenced measure.

12

VISUAL-MOTOR PERCEPTION AND MOTOR PROFICIENCY

What should be remembered is that many less than perfect measures have proven to be useful in psychology.
—Edward Zigler, American psychologist and director of the Bush Center in Child Development and Social Policy, Yale University (1927–)

Goals and Objectives

This chapter is designed to enable you to do the following:

- Describe and evaluate three individually administered measures of visual-motor ability

- Describe and evaluate an individually administered measure of motor proficiency

The expressive and receptive functions measured by tests of visual-motor perception and integration and motor proficiency are important links in the processing of information. Measuring expressive and receptive functions is useful in evaluating children with possible learning disabilities or neurological deficits. Tests of visual-motor integration and fine- and gross-motor ability are helpful in determining the intactness of the child's sensory and motor modalities and in developing remediation programs. The guidelines that follow are designed to help you observe children's performance, test limits, and interpret their performance on these tests. Other parts of the chapter review the major visual-motor tests.

GUIDELINES FOR ADMINISTERING AND INTERPRETING VISUAL-MOTOR TESTS

Observation Guidelines

Observations provide qualitative information that complements the information you obtain from formal scoring systems. Answers to the following questions will help you evaluate a child's style of responding, reaction to frustration, ability to correct errors, planning and organizational ability, and motivation, as well as other characteristics related to his or her performance on visual-motor tests.

1. How does the child approach the task (e.g., with extreme care and deliberation or impulsively and haphazardly)?
2. What is the child's affect?
3. What is the child's understanding of the task?
4. How well does the child follow directions?
5. How does the child hold the pencil?
6. In which hand does the child hold the pencil?
7. Does the child show signs of tremor or other motor difficulties? If so, what are the signs?
8. Does the child trace any designs with a finger before she or he draws them? If so, which designs?
9. Does the child count the dots, loops, or sides of a figure before drawing any designs? If so, which designs?
10. Does the child glance at a design briefly and then draw it from memory? If so, how often does he or she do this?
11. Does the child rotate the card or his or her paper (or both)? If so, what is rotated and on which designs?
12. Does the child have difficulty drawing the designs? If so, what are the difficulties and what parts of the designs are difficult for the child to draw (e.g., curves, angles, overlapping parts, open figures)?
13. What part of a design does the child draw first?
14. In what direction does the child copy the designs (e.g., from top down, from bottom up, from inside out, from outside in)?
15. Does the child change direction of movement from design to design? If so, what is the change?
16. Does the child sketch the designs? If so, which designs?
17. How much space does the child use to draw the designs (e.g., are the child's drawings approximately the same size as the originals or greatly reduced or expanded)?
18. How are the designs arranged on the page (e.g., are they organized or random, and is there sufficient space between the designs)?
19. How accurate are the child's drawings (highly accurate, somewhat accurate, highly inaccurate)?
20. How does the child react to failure or frustration (e.g., withdraws, gets angry, becomes agitated, blames himself or herself)?
21. Does the child show signs of fatigue? If so, what signs does the child show and when do these signs become evident (e.g., at the beginning, middle, or end of the test)?
22. Does the child recognize her or his errors? If so, which errors does the child recognize? How does the child handle errors? What does the child say about poorly executed drawings?
23. Does the child make comments about each design? If so, what are the comments?
24. Does the child need encouragement to complete the drawings? If so, how much encouragement is needed and how does the child respond to encouragement?
25. How long does the child take to copy each design? Does the child take an excessively long or unusually short amount of time to draw any of the designs?
26. How long does the child take to complete the test?
27. What is the child's overall reaction to the task (e.g., satisfaction or dissatisfaction)?
28. Is there anything unusual or atypical about how the child responds to or carries out the task? If so, what is unusual or atypical?

Testing-of-Limits

Testing-of-limits can help you pinpoint whether a child's problem is perceptual or motor or involves perceptual-motor integration; develop and test hypotheses about the child's performance; and develop recommendations. In testing-of-limits, you can ask the child to compare his or her drawing with the model drawing. You can say, "Look at your drawing and at the one on the card. How are they alike?" Then ask, "How are they different?" Then ask the child to draw one or more of the designs again. You might say, "Draw this design again. Do your very best." Note whether the child recognizes any differences between her or his drawing and the model drawing and whether the child draws the figures correctly the second time. Some children are aware of their errors and can correct them, others are aware of their errors but cannot correct them, and still others are not aware of their errors.

Interpretation Guidelines

Copying designs requires fine-motor development, perceptual discrimination ability, the ability to integrate perceptual and motor processes, and the ability to shift attention between the original design and the design being drawn. Inadequate visual-motor performance may result from misperception (receptive difficulties), difficulties with execution (expressive difficulties), or integrative or central processing difficulties (problems with memory storage or retrieval).

Sometimes it is possible to discern whether the difficulty lies in expressive functions or in receptive functions.

- If the child struggles to reproduce the designs, the difficulty is likely to be in expressive functions.
- If the child draws the designs quickly and easily but makes errors that he or she does not recognize, the difficulty may be partly in receptive functions and not entirely in expressive functions.
- If the child cannot see his or her errors, the trouble may lie in receptive functions.
- If the child can acknowledge his or her errors but cannot correct them, the difficulty may be in expressive functions.

Poor perceptual-motor functioning may be associated with several factors. These include carelessness; developmental immaturity; emotional problems; environmental stresses; fatigue; fear of completing a difficult task; impulsiveness; inadequate motivation; lack of interest; limited experiences with visual and motor tasks; mental retardation; motor problems; physically disabling conditions, such as low birth weight, cerebral palsy, or sickle cell anemia; physiological limitations associated with illness, injury, fatigue, or muscular weakness; poor attention to detail; poor organization; social or cultural deprivation; and visual problems.

There are no specific pathognomonic signs (i.e., signs indicative of a disease process) in the results of visual-motor tests that are definitively associated with brain injury, mental retardation, or any other physical or psychological disorder. *We therefore recommend that you never use visual-motor tests alone to make a diagnosis of brain injury, mental retardation, or other conditions.* These tests are tools for evaluating visual-motor ability; they are not designed to be the basis for definitive diagnoses. However, when visual-motor tests are used in conjunction with a battery of neuropsychological tests, they do add useful information (see Chapter 24).

Following are some examples of problems on visual-motor tests that may indicate poor visual-motor ability (Marley, 1982). (The examples are children's renderings of the Bender-Gestalt designs in Figure 12-1.) You will need to evaluate these indications in the context of medical, developmental, educational, psychological, and neuropsychological information in order to develop hypotheses to account for a child's performance.

1. *Sequence confusion:* changing direction three or more times. A directional change occurs when the order in which the child draws the designs differs from the expected or logical progression. Example:

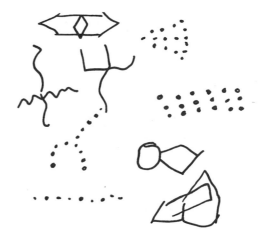

2. *Collision:* crowding the designs or allowing the end of one design to touch or overlap a part of another design. Example:

3. *Superimposition of design:* drawing one or more designs directly on top of another design. Example:

4. *Workover:* reinforcing a line or lines in a part of a design or throughout the whole design. Example:

5. *Irregular line quality:* drawing irregular lines or exhibiting tremor during the drawing of lines. Example:

6. *Difficulty with angles:* increasing, decreasing, distorting, or omitting the angles on any figure in a design. Example:

7. *Perseveration:* repeating a part of a design or the whole design. Example:

8. *Line extension:* extending a line or adding lines that were not present in the stimulus figure. Example:

9. *Contamination:* combining parts of two different figures. Example:

10. *Rotation:* rotating a figure 45° or more from its standard position. Example:

11. *Omission:* leaving a gap in a figure, reproducing only part of a figure, separating or fragmenting parts of a design, or omitting elements of a design. Example:

12. *Retrogression:* substituting solid lines or loops for circles; substituting dashes for dots, dots for circles, or circles for dots; and/or filling in circles. Example:

13. *Bizarre doodling:* adding peculiar elements that have no relationship to the stimulus design. Example:

14. *Scribbling:* drawing primitive lines that have no relationship to the stimulus design. Example:

BENDER VISUAL MOTOR GESTALT TEST

The Bender Visual Motor Gestalt Test (Bender-Gestalt; Bender, 1938) was developed by Lauretta Bender in 1938 to measure perceptual motor skills, neurological maturation, and organic brain deficits in both children and adults. It was derived from Gestalt configurations devised by Max Wertheimer in 1923 to demonstrate the perceptual principles of Gestalt psychology.

The Bender-Gestalt is an individually administered paper-and-pencil test. It uses nine geometric figures drawn in black (see Figure 12-1) on 4-by-6-inch white cards. The designs are presented one at a time, and the child is instructed to copy them on a blank sheet of paper. The test serves as a good icebreaker at the beginning of an evaluation—the task is innocuous, nonthreatening, interesting, and usually appealing to children.

Suggestions for Administration

Give the child a No. 2 pencil with an eraser. Place a single sheet of unlined, blank, 8½-by-11-inch paper on the table, aligned vertically in front of the child. Also have available extra sheets of paper (equal to the number of cards) and an extra pencil (in case the child breaks one). Next, place the stack of nine Bender-Gestalt cards face down on the table in the correct position (card A on the top and card 8 on the bottom) and say the following: "Now I would like you to draw some designs. There are nine cards here, and each card has a drawing on it." Point to the stack of cards. "I want you to copy each drawing. Make each drawing the best you can." Turn over the first card. "Now go ahead and make one just like it."

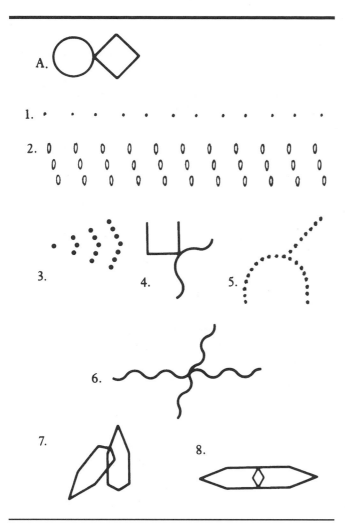

Figure 12-1. Designs on the Bender Visual Motor Gestalt Test.

Variations in Administration

Other ways to administer the Bender-Gestalt include an immediate memory procedure, a recall procedure, and a group-test procedure.

In the *immediate memory procedure,* show each card for 5 seconds and then remove the card and ask the child to draw the design from memory. To start out, say, "I am going to show some cards with designs on them. After I show you each card, I will take the card away. Then I want you to draw the design from memory. Do not begin to draw the design until I say, 'Go ahead and draw the design.' Here is the first card. Look at the design." Show the card for 5 seconds, take the card away, and say, "Go ahead and draw the design." Introduce each of the following cards by saying "Here is the next card. Look at the design." Use the same procedure as for the first card.

In the *recall procedure,* have the child draw the nine designs following the standard procedure. Then remove the child's drawings and give the child a fresh sheet of paper. Ask the child to draw as many of the designs as he or she can remember: "Now, draw as many of the designs as you can remember. Go ahead."

For the *group-test procedure,* you need to do one of the following:

- Make enlarged copies of the designs and present the enlarged cards at the front of the room.
- Reproduce the designs in a booklet, with a blank space under each design. Instruct the children to copy each design in the blank space under the design.
- Show the designs on an overhead projector or on a slide projector.
- Present individual decks of Bender-Gestalt cards to the children.

The most successful method with large numbers of children is the enlarged card method. The projector method requires special equipment and leaves the room in semi-darkness. Although individual decks have been used successfully with hyperactive or immature children who require extra attention, only two or three children should be tested at the same time with this method. Overall, studies indicate that group administration of the Bender-Gestalt yields reliable results, comparable to those obtained with individual administration (Koppitz, 1975).

Developmental Bender Test Scoring System

The Developmental Bender Test Scoring System (Koppitz, 1964, 1975) is an objective scoring system for evaluating the Bender-Gestalt drawings of preadolescent children. It has two parts: developmental scoring and an optional scoring of emotional indicators. The first part, which has the most relevance for the evaluation of visual-motor perception, has 30 items. Each item is scored 1 or 0 points (see Table 12-1).

If the child raises any questions, give a noncommittal reply such as "Make it look as much like the picture on the card as you can," "Do it the way you think best," or "Do the best job you can."

Present each card individually, beginning with card A and following with cards 1 through 8 in numerical order. Be sure to orient the cards correctly. The cards are numbered sequentially in approximate order of difficulty. Permit the child to erase, but do not allow the use of any mechanical aids such as a ruler, because the child is required to draw freehand. Record the starting and ending time for each design.

The nine designs take approximately 5 minutes to complete. Observe the child as he or she draws each design (refer to the list of questions earlier in the chapter). If the child rotates any cards, note the letter or number of each rotated card and the amount and direction of the rotation. Obviously, you should not administer visual-motor tests to children with severe visual impairments, unless their vision has been sufficiently corrected with glasses, or to children with severe motor impairments.

Table 12-1
Developmental Bender Test Scoring System

Figure	Error	Description of error
A	Distortion of shape	(a) Square, circle, or both excessively flattened or misshapen, with one axis of circle or square being twice as long as the other one; (b) disproportionate sizing of square and circle, with one being twice as large as the other one.
	Rotation	(a) Rotation of figure or any part of it by 45° or more; (b) rotation of stimulus card, even if figure is then copied correctly as shown on the rotated card.
	Integration	Failure to join circle and square, with curve and adjacent corner of square being more than ⅛ inch apart (applies also to overlap).
1	Distortion of shape	Five or more dots converted into circles.
	Rotation	(a) Rotation of figure by 45° or more; (b) rotation of stimulus card, even if figure is then copied correctly as shown on the rotated card.
	Perseveration	More than 15 dots in a row.
2	Rotation	(a) Rotation of figure by 45° or more; (b) rotation of stimulus card, even if figure is then copied correctly as shown on the rotated card.
	Integration	(a) Omission of one or two rows of circles; (b) use of row of dots for Figure 1 as third row for Figure 2; (c) four or more circles in the majority of columns; (d) addition of row of circles.
	Perseveration	More than 14 columns of circles in a row.
3	Distortion of shape	Five or more dots converted into circles.
	Rotation	(a) Rotation of axis of figure by 45° or more; (b) rotation of stimulus card, even if figure is then copied correctly as shown on the rotated card.
	Integration	(a) Shape of design lost, as noted by failure to increase number of dots in each successive row, unrecognizable or reversed shape of arrow head, conglomeration of dots, or single row of dots; (b) continuous line instead of row of dots.
4	Rotation	(a) Rotation of figure or part of it by 45° or more; (b) rotation of stimulus card, even if figure is then copied correctly as shown on the rotated card.
	Integration	(a) Curve and adjacent corner more than ⅛ inch apart (applies also to overlap); (b) curve touching both corners.
5	Distortion of shape	Five or more dots converted into circles.
	Rotation	Rotation of total figure by 45° or more.
	Integration	(a) Shape of design lost, as noted by conglomeration of dots, straight line, or circle of dots instead of an arc; (b) continuous line instead of dots in either arc, extension, or both.
6	Distortion of shape	(a) Substitution of three or more distinct angles for curves; (b) no curve at all in one or both lines.
	Integration	(a) Two lines not crossing or crossing at the extreme end of one or both lines; (b) two wavy lines interwoven.
	Perseveration	Six or more complete sinusoidal curves in either direction.
7	Distortion of shape	(a) Disproportionate sizing of two hexagons, with one being at least twice as large as the other one; (b) hexagons excessively misshapen, as noted by extra or missing angles in one or both.
	Rotation	(a) Rotation of figure or any part of it by 45° or more; (b) rotation of stimulus card, even if figure is then copied correctly as shown on the rotated card.
	Integration	Lack of overlap or excessive overlap of hexagons.
8	Distortion of shape	Hexagon or diamond excessively misshapen, as noted by extra angles, missing angles, or omission of diamond.
	Rotation	(a) Rotation of figure by 45° or more; (b) rotation of stimulus card, even if figure is then copied correctly as shown on the rotated card.

Source: Adapted from Koppitz (1975).

Four categories are used to classify errors: distortion of shape, rotation, integration, and perseveration. On a scoring sheet, record 1 point for each error made by the child. Then sum the points to obtain a total error score, and convert this score to a percentile rank. Percentile norms are available for children ages 5-0 to 11-11 years (Koppitz, 1975). Table F-3 in Appendix F shows standard scores ($M = 100$, $SD = 15$), based on the Koppitz data, for the total error raw score. These scores are most suitable for children ages 5-0 through 8-0 years and should not be used for children above age 11-11 years. Because the norms are over 30 years old, they should be used cautiously; we do not know whether they are valid for the current population.

Error classifications. Let's look at the four types of errors in the Developmental Bender Test Scoring System in more detail.

1. The *distortion of shape* error involves destruction of the Gestalt. For example, a figure may be misshapen, the parts of a figure may be sized disproportionately, circles or dashes may be substituted for dots, distinct angles may be substituted for curves, curves or angles may be missing, or extra angles may be included. This error is scored for Figures A (two possibilities), 1, 3, 5, 6 (two possibilities), 7 (two possibilities), and 8, for a possible total error score of 10 points.

2. The *rotation* error involves rotating a figure or any part thereof by 45° or more. An error is considered to have occurred even if the child correctly copies the design in the rotated position. This error is scored for Figures A, 1, 2, 3, 4, 5, 7, and 8, for a possible total error score of 8 points.

3. The *integration* error involves failure to connect the two parts of a figure properly, either by leaving more than ⅛ inch between the parts or by causing them to overlap; failure to cross two lines or crossing them in an incorrect place; or omission or addition of rows of dots or loss of the overall shape in the case of figures composed of dots or circles. This error is scored for Figures A, 2, 3 (two possibilities), 4, 5 (two possibilities), 6, and 7, for a possible total error score of 9 points.

4. The *perseveration* error involves increase, continuation, or prolongation of the number of units in a design. This error is scored for Figure 1 (more than 15 dots in a row), Figure 2 (more than 14 columns of circles), and Figure 6 (six or more complete curves in either direction), for a possible total of 3 points. The above type of perseveration is referred to as *within-card perseveration*. A second, much rarer type of perseveration, called *card-to-card perseveration*, occurs when a preceding design or parts of it influence succeeding designs. Card-to-card perseveration is not scored in the Developmental Bender Test Scoring System.

Emotional indicators. The 12 emotional indicators in the Developmental Bender Test Scoring System are based on a qualitative analysis of a child's drawings and purport to measure the child's emotional stability. Because little is known about the validity of these indicators, they are not further discussed in this chapter and *are not recommended for use*.

Standardization. The 1975 Developmental Bender Test Scoring System norms are based on a sample of 975 elementary school children, ages 5-0 to 11-11 years, living in rural areas, small towns, suburbs, and large metropolitan centers in the West, South, and Northeast. The composition of the sample was 86% Euro American, 8.5% African American, 4.5% Hispanic American, and 1% Asian American. The sample was not representative of the country, as its geographic distribution was highly skewed in favor of the Northeast. The socioeconomic characteristics of the sample were not reported.

Reliability. Test-retest reliabilities for the Developmental Bender Test Scoring System total score range from .50 to .90 (*Mdn* r_{tt} = .77), with intervals ranging from the same day to 8 months for samples of 19 to 193 children in kindergarten to sixth grade (Koppitz, 1975). Although these reliabilities are not sufficiently high to warrant the making of diagnostic decisions, they are adequate for formulating hypotheses about a child's visual-motor ability.

Interrater reliabilities are satisfactory, ranging from .79 to .99 (*Mdn* r = .91; Koppitz, 1975). Other studies report high interrater reliabilities (r ranges from .93 to .97; Bolen, Hewett, Hall, & Mitchell, 1992; McIntosh, Belter, Saylor, & Finch, 1988; Neale & McKay, 1985).

The test-retest reliabilities of the four separate error scores (distortion, rotation, integration, and perseveration) are lower than those of the total score (r_{tt} = .83 for total score, r_{tt} = .29 to .62 for error scores; Wallbrown & Fremont, 1980) and are not sufficiently high to justify using these error scores to make diagnostic decisions. Therefore, the total score, and not the error scores, should be used in interpreting the Bender-Gestalt.

Validity. The Developmental Bender Test Scoring System has acceptable construct validity for children ages 5 to 8 years. Copying errors decrease steadily between these ages, suggesting that the test is sensitive to maturational changes. Koppitz (1964) found that, for children over 8 years of age, the Developmental Bender Test Scoring System distinguishes only those with below-average perceptual-motor development from those with normal development, because most children obtain near-perfect performance after 8 years of age. Another study, however, found that errors continued to decrease until 11-5 years of age (Mazzeschi & Lis, 1999).

Concurrent validity of the Developmental Bender Test Scoring System is satisfactory. Correlations between the Developmental Bender Test Scoring System and the Frostig Developmental Test of Visual Perception range from .39 to .56 (*Mdn r* = .47), and correlations with the Developmental Test of Visual-Motor Integration range from .51 to .77 (*Mdn r* = .65; Breen, 1982; Breen, Carlson, & Lehman, 1985; DeMers, Wright, & Dappen, 1981; Krauft & Krauft, 1972; Lehman & Breen, 1982; Porter & Binder, 1981; Shapiro & Simpson, 1994; Skeen, Strong, & Book, 1982; Spirito, 1980; Wesson & Kispert, 1986; Wright & DeMers, 1982).

Correlations between the Developmental Bender Test Scoring System and several intelligence tests range from –.19 to –.66 (*Mdn r* = –.48; Koppitz, 1975). (The negative correlations occur because the Developmental Bender Test Scoring System yields error scores—higher error scores are associated with lower intelligence test scores.) Other studies also report low to moderate correlations between the Developmental Bender Test Scoring System and measures of intelligence (Aylward & Schmidt, 1986; Breen et al., 1985; Nielson & Sapp, 1991; Shapiro & Simpson, 1994; Yousefi, Shahim, Razavieh, Mehryar, Hosseini, & Alborzi, 1992). Studies also indicate that the Developmental Bender Test Scoring System has low to moderate correlations with measures of reading and arithmetic and school grades for elementary school children (Blaha, Fawaz, & Wallbrown, 1979; Brannigan, Aabye, Baker, & Ryan, 1995; Caskey & Larson, 1980; Fuller & Vance, 1993; Fuller & Wallbrown, 1983; Koppitz, 1975; Lesiak, 1984; Nielson & Sapp, 1991; Smith & Smith, 1988; Vance, Fuller, & Lester, 1986).

Other Scoring Systems

Hutt (1969), Mercer and Lewis (1978), Pascal and Suttell (1951), and Watkins (1976) provided alternative scoring systems for the Bender-Gestalt. However, these systems are not reviewed in this chapter.

Comment on the Bender-Gestalt

The Bender-Gestalt is useful for developing hypotheses about a child's perceptual-motor ability, but not for making definitive diagnoses. It provides indices of perceptual-motor development, particularly in children between 5 and 8 years of age,

You see—at this age they can't copy a diamond properly.

From *OF CHILDREN, 3rd edition,* by G. R. Lefrancois © 1980. Reprinted with permission of Wadsworth, a division of Thomson Learning. Fax 800 730-2215.

and of perceptual-motor deficits in older children and adults. However, the norms for the Developmental Bender Test Scoring System, which are out of date and not representative of the United States, should be used cautiously and primarily for children between 5 and 8 years of age, and little is known about the validity of the emotional indicators.

BENDER-GESTALT II

The Bender-Gestalt II (Brannigan & Decker, 2003) is a revised and improved version of the Bender-Gestalt. It has extended lower and upper score ranges, an expanded and updated normative sample (ages 4 to 85+ years), more items, an improved scoring system, and both a Copy phase and a Recall phase. Supplemental tests of motor and perceptual skills are also included, but because the psychometric basis of these measures is not described in the manual, they are not reviewed in this chapter.

The Bender-Gestalt II consists of 16 stimulus cards (nine from the original edition and seven new ones), each containing a line drawing. The child is asked to copy each design on a blank sheet of paper (Copy phase) and then to draw the designs from memory after he or she has finished copying them all (Recall phase). Children from 4-0 to 7-11 years of age are administered 13 items, whereas children from 8-0 to 16-11 years of age (and adults) are administered 16 items. Like the Bender-Gestalt, the Bender-Gestalt II serves as a good ice-breaker at the beginning of an evaluation—the task is innocuous, nonthreatening, interesting, and usually appealing to both children and adults.

The Global Scoring System developed by Brannigan and Brunner (1989, 1996, 2002) is used to score the Bender-Gestalt II. Separate total scores are calculated for the Copy phase and the Recall phase. Because the Bender-Gestalt II retains all of the original Bender-Gestalt items, the scoring system previously discussed in the chapter also can be used on the overlapping nine cards.

Scores

With the Global Scoring System, the following 5-point rating scale is used to score each item: 0 (no resemblance, random drawing, scribbling, lack of design), 1 (slight or vague resemblance), 2 (some or moderate resemblance), 3 (strong or close resemblance, accurate reproduction), 4 (nearly perfect).

The manual provides scoring examples for each point on the rating scale for each card. Raw scores are converted to standard scores ($M = 100$, $SD = 15$) and to percentile ranks.

The range of standard scores for the Copy phase of the Bender-Gestalt II differs at different ages (see Table 12-2). The highest standard score is 160, but this score is available only at ages 4-0 to 8-3 years. Beginning at age 8-4 years, the highest scaled score available drops by anywhere from 1 to 25 points. By age 17-0 years, the highest standard score is 135. Similarly, the lowest standard score is 40, but this score is first available at age 6-4 years. In fact, the lowest standard score available at age 4-0 years is 84. Similar considerations hold for the range of scores available for the Recall phase, although the highest standard scores are considerably higher (i.e., the ceiling is better) than they are for the Copy phase (e.g., 160 is available at all ages from 5-0 to 16-11 years). However, the lower limits for the Recall phase scores are not nearly as low (i.e., the floor is more limited) as they are for the Copy phase (e.g., at age 5-0 years, 85 vs. 65; at age 10-0 years, 70 vs. 40; at age 17-0 years, 67 vs. 40).

Standardization

The standardization sample for the Bender-Gestalt II consisted of 4,000 individuals, ages 4 to 85+ years. The sample was divided into 21 age groups. There were at least 100 individuals in each age group, with a range of 100 to 400 individuals. Norms are presented separately for each age group. The sample matches 2000 U.S. Census data on age, gender, race/ethnicity, geographic region, and socioeconomic status.

Reliability

Internal consistency reliabilities for the Copy phase at ages 4 to 16 years range from .86 to .94 ($Mdn\ r_{xx} = .90$), with a Mdn SEM = 4.79. Test-retest reliabilities, based on intervals of approximately 2 to 3 weeks for the Copy scores, were $r_{tt} = .77$ at ages 4 to 7 years and $r_{tt} = .76$ at ages 8 to 16 years. Test-

**Table 12-2
Range of Bender-Gestalt II Standard Scores**

Age	Copy	Recall
4-0	84–160	—
5-0	65–160	85–160
6-0	45–160	79–160
7-0	40–160	74–160
8-0	46–160	73–160
9-0	42–157	71–160
10-0	40–153	70–160
11-0	40–149	69–160
12-0	40–146	68–160
13-0	40–143	67–160
14-0	40–141	66–160
15-0	40–138	66–160
16-0	40–137	66–160
17-0	40–135	67–157

Note. At age 4, ages represent 1-month intervals (e.g., 4-0 represents 4-0 to 4-1). At age 17, ages represent 3-year intervals (e.g., 17-0 represents 17-0 to 19-11). All other ages represent 3-month intervals (e.g., 5-0 represents 5-0 to 5-3; 16-0 represents 16-0 to 16-3).
Source: Adapted from Brannigan and Decker (2003).

retest reliabilities for the Recall scores were $r_{tt} = .80$ at ages 4 to 7 years and $r_{tt} = .77$ at ages 8 to 16 years. Interrater reliabilities based on five examiners who scored 30 cases range from .83 to .94 ($M\ r_{rr} = .90$) for the Copy phase and from .94 to .97 ($M\ r_{rr} = .96$) for the Recall phase.

Validity

Construct validity is supported by significant correlations between the Bender-Gestalt II and the Bender-Gestalt ($r = .70$) and the Beery-Buktenica Developmental Test of Visual-Motor Integration–Fourth Edition ($r = .55$). A factor analysis indicates that a single factor underlies the test. In addition, scores increase from 4 to 16 years of age, gradually plateau, and then decline after the age of 59 years.

Criterion-related validity is supported by significant correlations between the Bender-Gestalt II and the Woodcock-Johnson III Tests of Achievement (rs range from .22 to .44, $Mdn\ r = .38$) and the Total Achievement score of the Wechsler Individual Achievement Test–2 ($r = .37$). Significant correlations are also reported between the Bender-Gestalt II and the Stanford-Binet–V ($r = .51$ with the Nonverbal IQ, $r = .47$

with the Verbal IQ, and $r = .51$ with the Full Scale IQ) and the WISC–III ($r = .62$ with the Performance IQ, $r = .31$ with the Verbal IQ, and $r = .51$ with the Full Scale IQ). Finally, criterion-related validity is further supported by studies showing that children with exceptionalities obtain lower scores on the Bender-Gestalt II than do children without exceptionalities.

Comment on the Bender-Gestalt II

The Bender-Gestalt II has an improved normative sample, new items, a new scoring system, and both a Copy phase and a Recall phase. Reliability and validity are adequate. The Bender-Gestalt II appears useful as a measure of visual-motor perception. However, at ages above 12-8 years, the norms for the Copy phase are skewed in that standard scores range four standard deviations below the mean but only three standard deviations (or less) above the mean. Thus, you must be careful in interpreting retest scores. For example, a change in standard scores from 157 at age 9-0 years to 143 at age 13-0 years does not reflect a decline in visual-motor abilities. At both ages, these are the highest possible standard scores available on the test. Even for children between 4-0 and 12-0 years of age, you must be careful in interpreting retest scores at the upper ranges of the test (e.g., 160 is the highest score at age 4-0 years, whereas 146 is the highest score at age 12-0 years).

You also must be careful when you compare standard scores on the Copy and Recall phases. The different ranges of standard scores mean that they cannot be directly compared in many cases. For example, a 10-0-year-old who has a raw score of 0 receives a standard score of 40 on the Copy phase but a standard score of 70 on the Recall phase. The highest raw score a 16-year-old can obtain is 48, which translates to a standard score of 137 on the Copy phase but a standard score of 160 on the Recall phase. Finally, since the test is new, additional research is needed to evaluate its properties.

Exercise 12-1
Evaluating Statements Made on the Basis
of Bender-Gestalt

Critically evaluate each statement, and then compare your evaluations with those in the Comments section.

1. "She drew quickly and carefully during the Bender-Gestalt test, but rarely inspected the cards. She positioned her face very close to each card and was very precise in counting the dots."
2. "The Bender-Gestalt determines whether or not the person is suffering from distortion in the visual-motor process."
3. "Her small Bender-Gestalt drawings suggest that she was anxious during the test session."
4. "Her completion of the designs in less than 3 minutes may indicate an impulsive style."
5. "All of the errors Tom made on the Bender-Gestalt are significant indicators of brain injury."

6. "Two figures collided, which possibly indicates some peripheral neurological impairment."
7. "The Bender-Gestalt results suggest good reading ability."
8. "Karla's generally quiet behavior during testing was supported by indications of passivity in her Bender-Gestalt drawings."
9. "Her variable use of space on the Bender-Gestalt—constricting and expanding in the same protocol—may indicate ambivalent modes of approach-avoidance behavior and wide mood fluctuations."
10. "Maria had a much better ability to copy designs on the Bender-Gestalt at 5 years of age than she has at 11 years of age (160 vs. 115)."

Comments

1. This description is contradictory and confusing. If she rarely inspected the cards, how could she have been very precise in counting the dots?
2. This is an awkward way of describing the abilities required by the Bender-Gestalt. A description of the given child's performance on the Bender-Gestalt would be more relevant: "On the Bender-Gestalt, which is a measure of visual-motor ability, the child's performance was in the normal range (at the 55th percentile)."
3. Small Bender-Gestalt drawings may have nothing to do with anxiety. Small drawings may simply reflect the examinee's response style.
4. Drawing or copying rapidly may be an indication of impulsivity, but it is not necessarily one. The quality of an examinee's performance is also important in determining impulsivity. Before suggesting impulsivity, you should look for corroborating signs.
5. This statement is misleading. Errors on the Bender-Gestalt may have no relationship to brain injury. They may be indicators of maturational difficulties, developmental delays, perceptual difficulties, integration difficulties, and so forth. Do not suggest a possible brain disorder exclusively on the basis of Bender-Gestalt errors. A diagnosis of brain injury should be arrived at by considering the neurological evaluation and clinical history, as well as a neuropsychological evaluation where appropriate (see Chapters 23 and 24).
6. Do not interpret collision as indicating "peripheral neurological impairment." This interpretation is not supported by research. Collision may be due to poor planning, carelessness, impulsiveness, or other factors; it may have nothing to do with peripheral neurological impairment. A statement indicating possible neurological impairment should never be made solely on the basis of Bender-Gestalt performance.
7. Results from the Bender-Gestalt should not be used to assess reading ability. Reading ability should be evaluated with valid measures of reading.
8. There is little, if any, research to indicate that the Bender-Gestalt provides valid indices of passivity in children. Therefore, a statement like this is not justified.
9. "Variable use of space" may indicate organizational difficulties, lack of efficiency in judgment or planning, or some other type of difficulty and may have little to do with personality or mood. Therefore, a statement like this is not justified.
10. This interpretation is incorrect because both 115 and 160 are the highest scores that can be obtained on the Bender-Gestalt at these ages. *Suggestion:* "Maria had excellent visual-motor ability at the age of 5 years and at the age of 11 years."

BEERY VMI–FIFTH EDITION, VISUAL PERCEPTION–FIFTH EDITION, AND MOTOR COORDINATION–FIFTH EDITION

The Beery VMI–Fifth Edition (also referred to as the Beery-Buktenica Developmental Test of Visual-Motor Integration–Fifth Edition; Beery & Beery, 2004) is a test of perceptual-motor ability for children ages 2 to 18 years. There are 30 items arranged in order of increasing difficulty. The first six items are administered to children who are under the age of 5 years or who have difficulty copying designs. The first three items require children to draw spontaneously, scribble, or imitate the scribbles of the examiner. Items 4, 5, and 6 require them to imitate the examiner's drawing of vertical, horizontal, and circular lines. Young children begin with items 4, 5, and 6. If they fail these, items 1, 2, and 3 may be administered, depending on the child's ability to perform each task.

The remaining 24 items require children to copy designs printed in a test booklet. The child draws each design in a square directly below the model. No erasing or rotating of the booklet is permitted. The test is discontinued after three consecutive failures. The Beery VMI–Fifth Edition can be administered either individually or to a group in about 15 minutes. There is also a short form of the Beery VMI–Fifth Edition consisting of 21 items for children ages 2 to 7 years. However, because the psychometric basis of the short form is not described in the manual, it is not reviewed here.

There are two supplemental tests, Visual Perception–Fifth Edition and Motor Coordination–Fifth Edition, each of which has 30 items. The three tests are administered in the following order: Beery VMI–Fifth Edition, Visual Perception–Fifth Edition, and Motor Coordination–Fifth Edition.

The first three items of Visual Perception–Fifth Edition require children to identify parts of their own bodies. The remaining 27 items require children to find a design that matches a key design. The test has a time limit of 3 minutes. There is no short form for Visual-Perception–Fifth Edition.

The first three items of Motor Coordination–Fifth Edition require the child to climb into a chair, hold a pencil, and hold paper with one hand while scribbling with the other. The remaining 27 items require the child to draw a line or lines between a black dot and a grey dot. The test has a time limit of 5 minutes. There is no short form for Motor Coordination–Fifth Edition.

Scores

Each design is scored 1 or 0. To obtain a score of 1, the child's drawing must meet several criteria for that design (e.g., correct number of parts, correct orientation, both acute angles 60° or less). Raw scores are converted into standard scores ($M = 100$, $SD = 15$), percentile ranks, and age-equivalent scores. Norms for the Beery VMI–Fifth Edition are in 1-month intervals from ages 2-0 to 17-11 years, whereas norms for Visual Perception and Motor Coordination–Fifth Edition are in 3-month intervals for these ages.

The range of standard scores for the Beery VMI–Fifth Edition differs at different ages (see Table 12-3). The highest standard score is 155, but this score is available only at ages 2-0 to 8-9. Beginning at age 8-10, the highest scaled score available drops by 1 or 2 points at each age group. By age 18-0, the highest standard score is 105. Similarly, the lowest standard score is 45, but this score is first available at age 6-0. In fact, the lowest standard score available at age 2-0 is 80. Similar considerations hold for the range of scores available for Visual Perception–Fifth Edition and Motor Coordination–Fifth Edition.

Standardization

The standardization sample consisted of 2,512 children stratified by gender, ethnicity, region, geographical residence, and socioeconomic status, based on 2002 U.S. Census data.

Reliability

For the 24 items that are directly copied, internal consistency reliabilities range from .79 to .89 ($M\ r_{xx} = .82$) for the Beery

---

Table 12-3
Range of Beery VMI–Fifth Edition Standard Scores

Age	Beery VMI	Visual Perception	Motor Coordination
2-0	80–155	85–155	79–155
3-0	64–155	55–155	45–155
4-0	53–155	45–155	45–155
5-0	47–155	45–155	45–155
6-0	45–155	45–155	45–155
7-0	45–155	45–155	45–155
8-0	45–155	45–152	45–148
9-0	45–154	45–144	45–142
10-0	45–148	45–137	45–137
11-0	45–142	45–128	45–129
12-0	45–134	45–122	45–122
13-0	45–127	45–117	45–117
14-0	45–123	45–112	45–112
15-0	45–118	45–108	45–107
16-0	45–113	45–104	45–104
17-0	45–108	45–101	45–101
18-0	45–105	45–99	45–99

Note. For the VMI, ages represent 1-month intervals (e.g., 2-0 represents 2-0 to 2-1, 18-0 represents 18-0 to 18-1). For Visual Perception and Motor Coordination, ages represent 3-month intervals (e.g., 2-0 represents 2-0 to 2-3, 18-0 represents 18-0 to 18-3).
Source: Adapted from Beery and Beery (2004).

VMI–Fifth Edition, from .74 to .87 ($M\ r_{xx}$ = .81) for Visual Perception–Fifth Edition, and from .71 to .89 ($M\ r_{xx}$ = .82) for Motor Coordination–Fifth Edition. SEMs range from 4 to 6 points for the Beery VMI–Fifth Edition, and all SEMs are 6 points for Visual Perception–Fifth Edition and Motor Coordination–Fifth Edition. Test-retest reliabilities with a sample of 115 children between the ages of 5 and 11 years in regular schools, who were administered the test twice over a 10-day period, were .89 for the Beery VMI–Fifth Edition, .85 for Visual Perception–Fifth Edition, and .86 for Motor Coordination–Fifth Edition. Interrater reliabilities, assessed by having two raters score 100 protocols, were r_{xx} = .92 for the Beery VMI–Fifth Edition, .98 for Visual Perception–Fifth Edition, and .93 for Motor Coordination–Fifth Edition.

Validity

The content validity and construct validity of the Beery VMI–Fifth Edition are satisfactory. The items represent the domain of interest, and an increase in raw scores with age reflects the developmental changes associated with perceptual-motor development. However, other types of construct validity and conconcurrent validity were established through studies of the Fourth Edition. Although the results from the Fourth Edition likely pertain to the Fifth Edition because the two editions are similar, it would be preferable to have studies of the Fifth Edition.

A brief review of Fourth Edition validity studies follows. Correlations between the Beery VMI–Fourth Edition and other tests of perceptual-motor ability are satisfactory. Construct validity is supported by acceptable correlations with intelligence test scores and achievement test scores. For example, in a sample of 17 children between the ages of 6 and 12 years who had learning disabilities, correlations between the Beery VMI–Fourth Edition and the WISC–R were .48 with the Verbal Scale IQ, .66 with the Performance Scale IQ, and .62 with the Full Scale IQ. For Visual Perception–Fourth Edition, correlations were .43 with the Verbal Scale IQ, .58 with the Performance Scale IQ, and .54 with the Full Scale IQ. For Motor Coordination–Fourth Edition, correlations were .41 with the Verbal Scale IQ, .55 with the Performance Scale IQ, and .51 with the Full Scale IQ. In a sample of 44 fourth- and fifth-grade students from regular classrooms, correlations between the Beery VMI–Fourth Edition and the California Test of Basic Skills were .58 with Reading, .68 with Language, .42 with Mathematics, and .63 with Overall Total.

Comment on the Beery VMI–Fifth Edition, Visual Perception–Fifth Edition, and Motor Coordination–Fifth Edition

The Beery VMI–Fifth Edition is a useful measure of perceptual-motor ability. The designs early in the series are especially helpful with young children. Although a high level of interrater reliability is reported in the manual, several subjective scoring

judgments are required, a protractor is needed for accurate scoring, and the sample drawings provided in the manual for scoring the designs are smaller than would be ideal.

At ages above 12-6 years, the norms are skewed in that standard scores range three standard deviations below the mean but only two standard deviations (or less) above the mean. Thus, you must be careful in interpreting the norms, and retest scores in particular, especially for adolescents with above-average perceptual-motor ability. For example, a change in standard scores from 142 at age 11 years to 127 at age 13 years does not reflect a decline in perceptual-motor abilities. At both ages, these are the highest possible standard scores available on the test. In addition, validity studies of the Beery VMI–Fifth Edition are needed.

Visual Perception–Fifth Edition and Motor Coordination–Fifth Edition are narrow tests of visual perception and motor coordination. Visual Perception–Fifth Edition uses only geometric designs and does not measure perceptual abilities involving common objects. Motor Coordination–Fifth Edition is primarily a test of fine-motor control involving a pencil. Gross-motor coordination and other types of fine-motor coordination are not measured. In addition, at ages above 10-11 years, the norms for Visual Perception–Fifth Edition and Motor Coordination–Fifth Edition are skewed in that standard scores range three standard deviations below the mean but only two standard deviations (or less) above the mean. Thus, you must be careful in interpreting retest scores. It is important to consider these limitations in evaluating children's visual perceptual and motor skills.

BRUININKS-OSERETSKY TEST OF MOTOR PROFICIENCY

The Bruininks-Oseretsky Test of Motor Proficiency (Bruininks, 1978) is an individually administered test of gross- and fine-motor functioning for children ages 4-6 to 14-6 years. The test contains 46 items grouped into eight subtests (see Table 12-4); four measure gross-motor skills (subtests 1, 2, 3, and 4), three measure fine-motor skills (subtests 6, 7, and 8), and one measures both gross- and fine-motor skills (subtest 5). A short form of 14 items serves as a brief survey of motor proficiency. The complete test takes between 45 and 60 minutes to administer.

The Bruininks-Oseretsky, based on the Oseretsky Tests of Motor Proficiency (Doll, 1946), has about 40% of the items from the original test and about 60% new items. The Bruininks-Oseretsky reflects advances in content, structure, and technical qualities over the former version of the test.

Scores

The test provides subtest scores (M = 15, SD = 5), a Gross Motor Composite score, a Fine Motor Composite score, and a Battery Composite score (M = 50, SD = 10 for all composite scores). In addition to standard scores, the manual pro-

Table 12-4
Subtests in the Bruininks-Oseretsky Test of Motor Proficiency

Test	Skill Assessed
1. Running Speed and Agility (one item)	Running speed
2. Balance (eight items)	Static balance and maintaining balance while executing various walking movements
3. Bilateral Coordination (eight items)	Sequential and simultaneous coordination of upper with lower limbs and of upper limbs only
4. Strength (three items)	Arm and shoulder strength, abdominal strength, and leg strength
5. Upper Limb Coordination (nine items)	Visual tracking with movements of arms and hands and precise movements of arms, hands, and fingers
6. Response Speed (one item)	Ability to respond quickly to a moving visual stimulus
7. Visual-Motor Control (eight items)	Ability to coordinate precise hand and visual movements
8. Upper Limb Speed and Dexterity (eight items)	Hand and finger dexterity, hand speed, and arm speed

vides percentile ranks, stanines, and age-equivalent scores for the subtests.

Standardization

The Bruininks-Oseretsky was standardized on 765 boys and girls selected from several schools, day-care centers, nursery schools, and kindergartens in the United States and Canada. A stratified sampling procedure, based on 1970 U.S. Census data, was used to select the children. Stratification variables included age, sex, race, community size, and geographic region.

Reliability

Test-retest reliabilities over a period of 7 to 12 days for the Battery Composite were $r_{tt} = .89$ for a sample of 63 second-graders and for a sample of 63 sixth-graders. For the Fine Motor Composite, they were $r_{tt} = .88$ and $r_{tt} = .68$ for the second- and sixth-graders, respectively; and for the Gross Motor Composite, they were $r_{tt} = .77$ and $r_{tt} = .85$ for the second- and sixth-graders, respectively. Average subtest test-retest reliabilities range from .56 to .86 (Mdn $r_{tt} = .74$). These reliabilities indicate that caution is needed in using subtest scores diagnostically. Average standard errors of measurement are 4.0 for the Battery Composite, 4.6 for the Gross Motor Composite, and 4.7 for the Fine Motor Composite.

Validity

Construct validity is satisfactory. For example, correlations between subtest scores and chronological age in the standardization sample range from .57 to .86 (Mdn $r = .78$). These correlations indicate a close relationship between subtest scores and chronological age. Subtest scores show the expected increase from one age group to the next. And correla-

tions between items and their respective subtest scores are closer than between items and total test scores.

A factor analysis performed on the standardization sample provides limited support for the individual subtests as distinct entities. The manual reports five factors, with one factor (general motor ability) accounting for approximately 70% of the total variance. Thus, only 30% of the variance was associated with the individual subtests. Most of the items measuring

GUILFORD PONDERS WHETHER TIM'S MOTOR SKILLS ARE 'GROSS' OR 'FINE'

Courtesy of Herman Zielinski.

fine-motor ability (14 out of 17) loaded on the general motor ability factor. While the gross-motor subtests clustered on identifiable factors, the fine-motor factors did not.

The 14-item short form may not be reliable for children under 9 years of age and may provide scores that are not comparable to those of the full scale (Moore, Reeve, & Boan, 1986; Verderber & Payne, 1987). More research is needed on the validity of the short form.

Comment on the Bruininks-Oseretsky Test of Motor Proficiency

The Bruininks-Oseretsky Test is useful as a clinical aid in assessing gross- and fine-motor skills. However, it should not be used as a psychometric measure of gross- and fine-motor skills, because the norms are out of date, the structure of the test is not supported by factor analysis, and reliability coefficients are lower than desirable.

THINKING THROUGH THE ISSUES

1. When would you include a visual-motor test or a test of fine- and gross-motor proficiency in an assessment battery?
2. How are tests of visual-motor perception different from tests of cognitive ability?
3. If a child made an error on a visual-motor test, how might you investigate the source of the error?

SUMMARY

1. The expressive and receptive functions measured by tests of visual-motor perception and integration and motor proficiency are important links in the processing of information.
2. Measuring expressive and receptive functions is useful in evaluating children with possible learning disabilities or neurological deficits.
3. Tests of visual-motor integration and fine- and gross-motor ability are helpful in determining the intactness of the child's sensory and motor modalities and in developing remediation programs.

Guidelines for Administering and Interpreting Visual-Motor Tests

4. The information obtained from observing a child's performance on visual-motor tests complements the information obtained from formal scoring systems.
5. Testing-of-limits procedures can help you pinpoint whether a child's problem is perceptual or motor or involves perceptual-motor integration; develop and test hypotheses about the child's performance; and develop recommendations.
6. Copying designs requires fine-motor development, perceptual discrimination ability, the ability to integrate perceptual and motor processes, and the ability to shift attention between the original design and the design being drawn.

7. Inadequate visual-motor performance may result from misperception (receptive difficulties), difficulties with execution (expressive difficulties), or integrative or central processing difficulties (problems with memory storage or retrieval).
8. Factors that may lead to poor perceptual-motor functioning include emotional problems; environmental stresses; impulsiveness; inadequate motivation; limited experiences with visual and motor tasks; mental retardation; physically disabling conditions, such as low birth weight, cerebral palsy, or sickle cell anemia; physiological limitations associated with illness, injury, fatigue, or muscular weakness; social or cultural deprivation; and visual problems.
9. We recommend that you never use measures of visual-motor perception alone to make a diagnosis of brain injury, mental retardation, or other conditions.

Bender Visual Motor Gestalt Test

10. The Bender Visual Motor Gestalt Test was developed by Lauretta Bender in 1938 to measure perceptual motor skills, neurological maturation, and organic brain deficits in both children and adults.
11. It was derived from Gestalt configurations devised by Max Wertheimer in 1923 to demonstrate the perceptual principles of Gestalt psychology.
12. The Bender-Gestalt is an individually administered paper-and-pencil test that uses nine geometric figures drawn in black on 4-by-6-inch white cards.
13. Other procedures developed for the Bender-Gestalt include the immediate memory procedure, recall procedure, and the group-test procedure.
14. The most successful method for administering the Bender-Gestalt to large numbers of children is the enlarged card method.
15. The Developmental Bender Test Scoring System is an objective scoring system for evaluating the Bender-Gestalt drawings of preadolescent children. It is composed of two parts: developmental scoring and an optional scoring of emotional indicators.
16. The Developmental Bender Test Scoring System uses four categories to classify errors: distortion of shape, rotation, integration, and perseveration.
17. The 12 emotional indicators in the Developmental Bender Test Scoring System are not recommended for use.
18. Test-retest reliabilities for the Developmental Bender Test Scoring System total score are not sufficiently high to warrant the making of diagnostic decisions. However, they are adequate for formulating hypotheses about a child's visual-motor ability.
19. Interrater reliabilities for the Developmental Bender Test Scoring System are satisfactory.
20. Because the test-retest reliabilities of the four separate error scores are not sufficiently high to justify using these error scores to make diagnostic decisions, your focus in interpreting the Bender-Gestalt should be on the total score, not on the individual error scores.
21. When the Developmental Bender Test Scoring System is used as a measure of visual-motor development in children ages 5 to 8 years, it has acceptable validity.
22. Concurrent validity of the Developmental Bender Test Scoring System is satisfactory.

23. Correlations between the Developmental Bender Test Scoring System and several intelligence tests range from –.19 to –.66 (*Mdn r* = –.48).
24. Studies indicate that the Developmental Bender Test Scoring System has low to moderate correlations with measures of reading and arithmetic and school grades for elementary school children.
25. Other scoring systems are available for the Bender-Gestalt but are not reviewed in this chapter.
26. The norms for the Developmental Bender Test Scoring System, which are out of date and not representative of the United States, should be used cautiously and primarily for children between 5 and 8 years of age.

Bender-Gestalt II

27. The Bender-Gestalt II is a revised and improved version of the Bender-Gestalt. It has extended lower and upper score ranges, an expanded and updated normative sample (ages 4 to 85+ years), more items, an improved scoring system, and both a Copy phase and a Recall phase. Supplemental tests of motor and perceptual skills are also included, but because the psychometric basis of these measures is not described in the manual, they are not reviewed in this chapter.
28. The Bender-Gestalt II consists of 16 stimulus cards (nine from the original edition and seven new ones), each containing a line drawing.
29. Reliability and validity are adequate.
30. Caution is needed in interpreting retest scores and in comparing Copy and Recall scores.
31. Because the test is new, additional research is needed to evaluate its properties.

Beery VMI–Fifth Edition, Visual Perception–Fifth Edition, and Motor Coordination–Fifth Edition

32. The Beery VMI–Fifth Edition, Visual Perception–Fifth Edition, and Motor Coordination–Fifth Edition are useful tests of perceptual-motor ability, visual perception, and motor coordination, respectively, for children ages 2 to 18 years. However, at ages above 12-6 years, the norms are skewed; thus, retest scores for children above this age should be interpreted with caution. In addition, Visual Perception–Fifth Edition and Motor Coordination–Fifth Edition are narrow tests of visual perception and motor coordination.

Bruininks-Oseretsky Test of Motor Proficiency

33. The Bruininks-Oseretsky Test of Motor Proficiency is useful as a clinical aid in assessing gross- and fine-motor skills, but not as a psychometric measure of skills, because the norms are out of date, the structure of the test is not supported by factor analysis, and reliability coefficients are lower than desirable.

KEY TERMS, CONCEPTS, AND NAMES

Observing performance (p. 322)
Testing-of-limits (p. 322)
Bender Visual Motor Gestalt Test (p. 324)
Bender-Gestalt immediate memory procedure (p. 325)
Bender-Gestalt recall procedure (p. 325)
Bender-Gestalt group-test procedure (p. 325)
Developmental Bender Test Scoring System (p. 325)
Distortion of shape on the Bender-Gestalt (p. 327)
Rotation on the Bender-Gestalt (p. 327)
Integration on the Bender-Gestalt (p. 327)
Perseveration on the Bender-Gestalt (p. 327)
Bender-Gestalt II (p. 328)
Beery VMI–Fifth Edition (p. 331)
Visual Perception–Fifth Edition (p. 331)
Motor Coordination–Fifth Edition (p. 331)
Bruininks-Oseretsky Test of Motor Proficiency (p. 332)

STUDY QUESTIONS

1. Discuss issues in observing performance on visual-motor tests.
2. Discuss issues in the testing-of-limits on visual-motor tests.
3. Discuss the strengths and limitations of the Bender-Gestalt. Include in your discussion the Developmental Bender Test Scoring System.
4. Discuss the strengths and limitations of the Bender-Gestalt II.
5. Discuss the strengths and limitations of the Beery VMI–Fifth Edition.
6. Discuss the strengths and limitations of the Bruininks-Oseretsky Test of Motor Proficiency.

13

FUNCTIONAL BEHAVIORAL ASSESSMENT

It is the close observation of little things which is the secret of success in business, in art, in science, and in every pursuit in life.
—Samuel Smiles, Scottish political reformer (1812–1904)

The unfortunate thing about this world is that good habits are so much easier to give up than bad ones.
—W. Somerset Maugham, British novelist (1874–1965)

Goals and Objectives

This chapter is designed to enable you to do the following:

- Understand when and how to conduct a functional behavioral assessment

- Understand how to design interventions stemming from a functional behavioral assessment

When Is a Functional Behavioral Assessment Needed?

Functions of Challenging Behavior

Guidelines for Conducting a Functional Behavioral Assessment

Assessing Behavior Through Observations and Interviews

Describing the Problem Behavior

Formulating Hypotheses to Account for the Problem Behavior

Behavioral Intervention Plans

Thinking Through the Issues

Summary

Key Terms, Concepts, and Names

Study Question

A *functional behavioral assessment* is designed to help you arrive at an understanding of a student's problem behavior and develop a behavioral intervention plan. To conduct a functional behavioral assessment, you will need to consider (a) the type of problem behavior, (b) conditions under which the problem behavior occurs (including the events that trigger the problem behavior), (c) probable reasons for or causes of the problem behavior (including biological, social, cognitive, affective, and environmental factors), and (d) the functions that the problem behavior might serve.

WHEN IS A FUNCTIONAL BEHAVIORAL ASSESSMENT NEEDED?

A functional behavioral assessment can be used to evaluate any problem behavior in any setting, such as destructive, aggressive, noncompliant, or disruptive behaviors directed toward self, others, or objects. A functional behavioral assessment is also useful when a student is rejected by peers, is in need of a more restricted placement because of behavioral concerns, is in an intervention program that involves excessively intrusive procedures (e.g., restraints or isolation), or is not responsive to current interventions. In school settings, it is better to conduct a functional behavioral assessment when the student first displays a potentially serious problem behavior, rather than waiting until she or he is removed from the setting in which the problem behavior occurred.

IDEA 2004 (Sec. 615) requires that a functional behavioral assessment be performed when a child with a disability violates a code of student conduct and either (a) a change in placement is being considered for the child (i.e., an interim alternative educational setting, another setting, or suspension) or (b) the local education agency, the parent, and relevant members of the IEP team determine that the behavior was a manifestation of the child's disability. In the latter case, a behavioral intervention plan also must be implemented.

Several members of the interdisciplinary team contribute to a functional behavioral assessment. Psychologists, counselors, and behavior specialists (who also may be psychologists or counselors) have special skills in assessing behavior and in dealing with challenging behavior. Social workers have special skills in family relations. Nurses have special skills in assessing children with physical illnesses and evaluating the effects of medication. General education teachers have special skills in teaching and classroom management. Special education teachers have expertise in working with students with disabilities. And speech and language pathologists have special skills with regard to communication.

The motivation underlying human behavior is complex, varied, and sometimes difficult to ascertain. However, identifying the functions of behavior provides straightforward explanations of how a particular behavior "works" for an individual in a given context. By examining the outcomes or consequences of human behavior, including challenging behavior, we can describe two main functions: (a) to get something (e.g., social attention, a tangible object) (positive reinforcement) or (b) to escape or avoid something (e.g., an undesired activity or person) (negative reinforcement).

Examples of behavioral functions are observed daily in classrooms. For example, students learn to raise their hand in class to gain access to adult social attention or extra assistance on a difficult task or to indicate that they are finished with a task. Similarly, students learn to use their words to tell another student to leave them alone or stop teasing. Unfortunately, some students use socially inappropriate behaviors to achieve the same outcomes. Some students push other students to gain access to the first place in line, close their textbooks to get the teacher to assist them with difficult work, or display noncompliant behavior with their teachers to enhance their social status with peers. Finally, some students disrupt lessons so that the teacher will ask them to leave the classroom, and yet other students display self-injurious or aggressive behavior to avoid having to comply with adult requests. In each of these examples, both appropriate and inappropriate behaviors are maintained because the outcomes (consequences) provide opportunities for the student to gain or get something (positive reinforcement) or to escape something (negative reinforcement).

Three additional considerations help in determining the function of behavior. First, more than one behavior may serve the same or a similar function for a student. For example, a student might talk out, leave the classroom, or touch other people's property to gain teacher attention. Second, the same behavior might serve different functions in different contexts. For example, a student might use profanity to gain peer attention in the hallway, but also use the same behavior to be removed from a difficult lesson. Third, students usually do not display individual behaviors, but strings or chains of behavior that are occasioned by social interactions. For example, the first talkout displayed by a student might function to gain adult attention, but as the interaction escalates, talkouts might function to escape the confrontation. (pp. 3–4, with changes in notation)

Later in this chapter you will read about factors in the student or in the environment that might be associated with a problem behavior. Always consider the interaction of all relevant factors in accounting for a problem behavior. Key issues related to the school environment are (a) whether the student misbehaves in order to escape from ineffective instruction or from the frustration arising from his or her inability to cope with the learning environment or (b) whether the student's misbehavior increases peer rejection, which in turn leads to continued student misbehavior.

FUNCTIONS OF CHALLENGING BEHAVIOR

Before you conduct a functional behavioral assessment, it is important to understand why children exhibit challenging behavior (OSEP Technical Assistance Center, 2001).

GUIDELINES FOR CONDUCTING A FUNCTIONAL BEHAVIORAL ASSESSMENT

It is useful to follow seven steps in conducting a functional behavioral assessment in a school setting (Miller, Tansy, & Hughes, 1998).

Step 1. *Describe problem behavior.* Describe the problem behavior in observable and measurable terms.

Step 2. *Perform the assessment.* Review the student's records (e.g., results from prior psychological or psychoeducational evaluations, teachers' comments on report cards, disciplinary records, anecdotal home notes, medical reports, descriptions of prior interventions and their results). Then conduct systematic behavioral observations (see Chapters 8 and 9) and interview the student, teacher, parents, and other individuals as needed (see Chapters 5, 6, and 7). Finally, conduct other formal and informal assessments as necessary.

Step 3. *Evaluate assessment results.* Identify patterns in the results that may indicate the purpose or cause of the problem behavior.

Step 4. *Develop hypotheses.* Develop plausible hypotheses to account for the problem behavior. Try to explain the relationship between the problem behavior and the situations in which the problem behavior occurs. The hypotheses should contain a description of the problem behavior, possible antecedents, possible consequences, and possible *setting events* (any events that predispose the student to engage in the problem behavior, such as not taking medication or arguing with parents before school).

Step 5. *Formulate an intervention plan.* Propose a behavioral intervention plan to improve the problem behavior. In school settings, work with the IEP team.

Step 6. *Start the intervention.* Start the behavioral intervention plan as soon possible.

Step 7. *Evaluate the effectiveness of the intervention plan.* After the intervention plan starts, evaluate its effectiveness periodically by interviewing the student, teachers, and parents, observing the student, and administering other assessment procedures as needed. Make any necessary modifications and evaluate the effectiveness of the modifications periodically.

ASSESSING BEHAVIOR THROUGH OBSERVATIONS AND INTERVIEWS

Observations

After defining the problem behavior, you will want to observe the student in several different settings (e.g., classroom, gym, cafeteria, playground), during different types of activities (e.g., lectures, study periods, group activities, sports), and at different times during the day (e.g., morning, afternoon; Gable, Quinn, Rutherford, & Howell, 1998). Design the behavioral observation using the procedures described in Chapters 8 and 9.

Observation may have either an *interindividual focus,* in which a child's performance is compared with that of a norm group or a peer, or an *intraindividual focus,* in which a child's own performance is compared across different environments and across different tasks (Alessi, 1988). When a teacher refers a student for a problem behavior, you will want to de-

termine whether the student's behavior is considerably different from that of his or her classroom peers. If you determine that the behavior is considerably different, you then will want to identify the factors that influence the student's problem behaviors: (a) settings, (b) tasks, (c) reward contingencies (e.g., positive reinforcement, such as attention, extra playtime, access to toys, and watching TV), and (d) relief contingencies (e.g., negative reinforcement, such as escaping from tasks and responsibilities). In essence, an interindividual focus is used for screening, while an intraindividual focus is used for a more comprehensive individual assessment.

A functional behavioral assessment may also involve manipulating environmental events (e.g., type of activity, consequences) and then observing the effects of the manipulations; this approach is referred to as a *functional analysis.* For example, to support the hypothesis that the student engages in off-task behavior when she or he is in a group, you might ask the teacher to have the student engage in a solitary activity, in addition to being in a group. There are ethical issues, however, associated with manipulating environmental events. For example, if you hypothesize that off-task behavior occurs when the student faces difficult material, is it ethical to arrange for the student to be given difficult material in order to see whether the behavior occurs under this condition? Doing so might increase the student's anxiety level. In such situations, consider whether you should use another method to support or explore your hypothesis. However, if the teacher is fairly certain that the student can do the task and simply does not want to do it, there should be no breach of ethics in presenting the task.

Interview Questions

The following questions may be useful in interviewing a student about a problem behavior (Gable et al., 1998; also see the semistructured interview questions for a child or adolescent of school age in Table B-1 in Appendix B):

1. Tell me what happened.
2. (If needed) Where did it happen?
3. (If needed) When did it happen?
4. How often does [name of problem behavior] occur?
5. How long does [name of problem behavior] last?
6. What do you think makes you [description of problem behavior]?
7. What were you thinking just before you [description of problem behavior]?
8. How did you feel just before you [description of problem behavior]?
9. What was happening to you before [name of problem behavior] began?
10. When you [description of problem behavior], what usually happens afterward?
11. What changes could be made so that [name of problem behavior] wouldn't happen again?

The following questions are useful for interviewing a teacher or a parent about the student's problem behavior:

1. Tell me about [name of child]'s problem behavior.
2. When does the problem behavior typically occur?

(Ask questions 3 to 6 as needed.)

3. (If the problem behavior is associated with activities that the child is asked to do) Does it happen when [name of child] is asked to clean [his/her] room, pick up toys, do homework, complete tasks in school, or do something else?
4. (If the problem behavior is associated with activities that the child is asked to stop doing) Does it happen when [name of child] is asked to stop watching TV, stop talking in class, stop teasing peers, stop playing video games, or stop doing something else?
5. (If the problem behavior is associated with the child's pressuring someone else to do something that person doesn't want to do) Does it happen when [name of child] is trying to get you to play games, buy toys or clothes, give [him/her] money, drive [him/her] someplace, or do something else?
6. (If the problem behavior is associated with the child's pressuring someone else to stop doing something that person wants to do) Does it happen when [name of child] is trying to get you to stop watching TV, stop talking on the phone, stop enforcing a rule, or stop doing something else?
7. When does the problem behavior typically *not* occur?
8. Where does the problem behavior typically occur?
9. When is the problem behavior the worst?
10. How often does the problem behavior occur?
11. How long does the problem behavior last?
12. If there are other students or adults present, how do they react to [name of child]'s problem behavior?
13. What do you think triggers the problem behavior?
14. Is anything happening at home that might help us understand [name of child]'s problem behavior?
15. What do you do when the problem behavior occurs?
16. How does [name of child] react to what you do?
17. If there are other children or adults present, how do they react to what you do?
18. What happens to the task or project that is going on when [name of child] engages in the problem behavior?
19. Why do you think [name of child] acts this way? (If needed) What does [name of child] get out of it or avoid?
20. Tell me what you have done in the past that has helped reduce the problem behavior.
21. Tell me what you have done in the past that has not been successful in reducing the problem behavior.
22. What are [name of child]'s strengths or positive attributes?
23. What are [name of child]'s weaknesses or negative attributes?
24. What are [name of child]'s academic grades?
25. What are [name of child]'s citizenship grades?
26. What do you think needs to be done to help [name of child]?
27. Tell me anything else that you believe may be important in understanding or in helping [name of child].

In interviewing a student's teacher and parents about the student's problem behavior, you also can use the interview questions shown in Tables B-15 and B-9, respectively, in Appendix B. Three questionnaires also will be useful in obtaining information that will help you assess the problem behavior. These are the Background Questionnaire (Table A-1 in Appendix A), the Personal Data Questionnaire (Table A-2 in Appendix A), and the School Referral Questionnaire (Table A-3 in Appendix A). Finally, you can review the student's school and medical records to obtain relevant information.

DESCRIBING THE PROBLEM BEHAVIOR

Table 13-1 shows a form for recording behavior, antecedents, consequences, and interventions. Answering the questions in Table 13-1 will help you describe the problem behavior. The questions focus on events that occur during, before, and after the problem behavior. Table 13-2 shows a brief form for recording antecedents (A), behavior (B), and consequences (C).

Let's look in more detail at some of the issues covered in the questions in Table 13-1.

1. *Note the type of problem behavior, such as the following:* assaulting others; banging head; being physically aggressive: being truant; biting; crying; defying authority; destroying property; disrupting class; engaging in inappropriate sexual behavior; engaging in self-injurious behavior; engaging in self-stimulating behavior; failing to complete assignments; failing to follow directions; failing to remain in seat; fighting; grabbing, pushing, or pulling others; hurting self; kicking; loud talking; marking up walls; refusing to follow instructions; refusing to work; running away; screaming or yelling; showing noncompliant behavior; showing psychotic symptoms; stealing; talking out of turn; teasing; threatening others physically; threatening others verbally; throwing temper tantrums; throwing things; using drugs or alcohol; using inappropriate language; violating school rules; violating weapons prohibitions.

2. *Note where the problem behavior occurs, such as the following:* auditorium, bus, bus stop, cafeteria, classroom, computer room, hallway, gym, library, locker room, playground, restroom, special classrooms, study hall, walkways, workshop.

3. *Note when the problem behavior occurs,* relative to such factors as (a) *subject being taught* (e.g., history, English, math, physical education, science, social studies), (b) *time of day* (e.g., before school, in the morning, at noon, in the afternoon), (c) *instructional activity* (e.g., individual assignments,

Table 13-1
Functional Behavioral Assessment Recording Form

FUNCTIONAL BEHAVIORAL ASSESSMENT RECORDING FORM

Name of student:_____ Date:_____

Sex: _____ Age: _____ School: _____

Date of birth: _____ Examiner: _____

Problem Behavior

1. What is the problem behavior? _____
_____

2. When does it begin? _____
_____

3. When does it stop? _____
_____

4. Does it escalate gradually or quickly? _____
_____

5. How intense is the problem behavior?_____
_____

6. How often does the problem behavior occur? _____
_____

7. How long does the problem behavior last? _____
_____

8. When did the problem behavior first start? _____
_____

9. Has the frequency of the problem behavior increased or decreased recently?_____
_____

10. When was the last time the problem behavior occurred? _____
_____

11. Have there been any significant medical problems that may have affected the problem behavior? _____
_____

12. What individual characteristics of the student may have affected the problem behavior? _____
_____

13. What events in the life of the student might have affected his or her behavior? _____
_____

Events Before the Problem Behavior (Antecedent Events)

1. What usually happens before the problem behavior begins? _____
_____

2. Where does the problem behavior usually take place? _____
_____

3. What are the setting characteristics where the problem behavior takes place? _____
_____

4. At what times of day does the problem behavior usually occur?_____
_____

5. Who usually is present when the problem behavior takes place? _____
_____

Table 13-1 (*Continued*)

6. When the problem behavior takes place, is anyone absent who is usually in the setting? _____

7. What classroom activities usually take place prior to the problem behavior? _____

8. What is the pace of the classroom activity before the problem behavior takes place? _____

9. What is the student's affect before the problem behavior takes place? _____

10. What is happening in the student's home and life in general on days when the problem behavior occurs? _____

Events After the Problem Behavior (Consequent Events)

1. How does the teacher react to the problem behavior? _____

2. How do other students react to the problem behavior? _____

3. How does the administrator react to the problem behavior? _____

4. What are the consequences associated with the problem behavior? _____

5. How do others usually respond to the problem behavior? _____

6. What functions are served by the problem behavior? _____

7. How much time elapses between when the student engages in the problem behavior and when others respond? _____

8. How does the student usually react after the problem behavior takes place? _____

9. What actions seem to decrease the problem behavior once it begins? _____

10. How long does it usually take to get the student back to the scheduled activity? _____

11. How do the intensity, duration, and frequency of the problem behavior interfere with the student's learning? _____

Interventions

1. Are crisis intervention procedures needed to ensure safety and deescalation of the student's behavior, and, if so, what procedures should be used? _____

2. What potential cognitive and motivational resources does the student have for coping with the problem behavior? _____

3. What are the student's attitudes about the class, the teacher, and the school? _____

4. What are the student's attitudes about his or her parents, siblings, and other relatives? _____

5. What are the teachers', parents', and other concerned individuals' levels of understanding of the problem behavior? _____

Table 13-1 (Continued)

6. What are the student's, family's, school's, and community's strengths and resources for change? _____
_____

7. What are some positive strategies for diminishing the problem behavior and promoting skills the student needs to function more effectively? _____
_____

8. What are some positive strategies for changing the environment to prevent the problem behavior from occurring? _____
_____

9. What other factors should be considered in designing the behavioral intervention plan? _____
_____

10. What strategies should be used to facilitate the transfer of behavior changes across environments? _____
_____

11. What previous interventions, if any, were attempted and with what success? _____
_____

12. How should the intervention strategies be structured? _____
_____

small-group work, lecture, independent work), and (d) *nonacademic activity* (e.g., changing classes, eating lunch, playing games on the playground, watching other children play on the playground).

4. *Note characteristics of the setting and events related to the problem behavior, such as the following:* length of activity; nature of the materials being used; lighting; noise level; number of other students and adults present; presence of a teacher's aide, substitute teacher, staff member, or other person; seating arrangements; temperature.

5. *Note situations or personal events that might induce the problem behavior, including actions of others that increase, decrease, or trigger the problem behavior, such as the following:* arguing with parents before school; arguing with a peer; being asked to perform a task; being given a warning; being required to perform a disliked activity, a difficult assignment, a long assignment, or a boring assignment; being teased, intimidated, or harassed by a peer; being told to do something; a change from one assignment to another; a change of routine; engaging in horseplay; fatigue; family stress; fear of failure; fear of ridicule by a teacher or peers; hunger; illness; not knowing what is required on an assignment; not taking medications; receiving test results; rejection by peers; a reprimand by the teacher; social conflict; transition from one class period to another class period; taking a test.

6. *Note the consequences associated with the problem behavior, such as the following:* additional writing assignments, alternative educational placement, being given an alternative activity, being removed from task, being sent to office or sent home for the remainder of the day, cool off at desk or other area, in-school suspension, loss of privileges, lunch detention, out-of-school suspension, planned ignoring, physical re-

straint, referral to counselor, reprimand, structured warning, student-teacher conference, time-out, telephone call or note to parents.

FORMULATING HYPOTHESES TO ACCOUNT FOR THE PROBLEM BEHAVIOR

Hypotheses serve to summarize assessment results, offer explanations for the student's problem behavior, and guide the development of the behavioral intervention plan (Knoster & Llewellyn, 1998a). To develop hypotheses to account for the problem behavior, review the antecedents of the behavior, the behavior itself, and consequences associated with the behavior, as well as background factors, functions or purposes served by the behavior, reactions of students and others to the problem behavior, others' understanding of the problem behavior, and attitudes of the student, family, school, and community toward the problem behavior, as well as their resources for coping with it.

1. *Note the relevant student background factors associated with the problem behavior, such as the following:* academic history, age, cultural background, ethnicity, health history (including prescribed medications), interpersonal relations, personal appearance (including height, weight, physical anomalies), physiological factors (e.g., sleep patterns, physical pain, hunger), previous responses to interventions and their effectiveness, psychological/emotional history, sex, socioeconomic status.

2. *Note the relevant environmental background factors associated with the problem behavior, such as the following:*

Table 13-2
Functional Behavioral Assessment Brief Recording Form

FUNCTIONAL BEHAVIORAL ASSESSMENT BRIEF RECORDING FORM

Name of student:_____   Date:_____

Sex:_____   Age:_____   School:_____

Date of birth:_____   Examiner:_____

A—Antecedents (Describe what happened before the problem behavior occurred)	B—Behavior (Describe what the child did)	C—Consequences (Describe what happened after the problem behavior occurred)

From *Assessment of Children: Behavioral, Social, and Clinical Foundations (Fifth Edition)* by Jerome M. Sattler and Robert D. Hoge. Copyright 2006 by Jerome M. Sattler, Publisher, Inc. Permission to photocopy this table is granted to purchasers of this book for personal use only (see copyright page for details).

(a) *community characteristics* (e.g., income level, presence of violence, prevalence of gangs and drug and alcohol abuse, ethnic tensions), (b) *environmental events* (e.g., death or illness in the family, divorce, moving, natural disaster, traumatic event in or out of school), (c) *family attributes* (e.g., how the family has dealt with the problem, family structure, family disciplinary practices, parental expectations, parent/child relationships, child maltreatment, domestic vio-

lence), (d) *societal factors* (e.g., approval of violence and violence-related behaviors), (e) *peer group factors* (e.g., type of peer group, gender and age of peer group members), and (f) *school factors* (e.g., poorly trained teachers; ineffective instruction; large classes; ineffective administration; limited support services, facilities, and supplies).

3. *Note the functions or purposes—including escape, attention or control, and self-regulation—that are served by the*

problem behavior, such as the following: avoid a demand or request; avoid an activity; avoid failure; avoid a person; avoid responsibility; communicate that the work is too hard or too demanding; decrease sensory input; escape the classroom or setting; escape the school; express anger, frustration, justice, or revenge; gain acceptance or affiliation with a group; gain access to an activity; gain adult or peer attention; gain control over others; gain desired activity or object; gain increased sensory input; maintain control; obtain assistance with a task; obtain physical attention; obtain something desirable; obtain sensory stimulation; obtain a tangible item; obtain verbal attention; protect self; reduce anxiety; release anxiety; signal hunger, thirst, or pain.

4. *Note how the student reacts to the problem behavior, such as the following:* apologetic, anxious, confused, defiant, depressed, happy, remorseful, unable to concentrate on school work.

5. *Note how others react to the problem behavior, such as the following:* are unable to concentrate on school work; become angry, confused, or frightened by the problem behavior; ignore the problem behavior; model the problem behavior; reinforce the problem behavior; want retribution.

6. *Note the teachers', parents', and other concerned individuals' levels of understanding of the problem behavior, such as the following:* show little or no understanding, show some understanding, show in-depth understanding of the problem behavior and offer reasonable explanations of the problem behavior.

7. *Note the student's attitudes about the learning environment, such as the following:* attitude toward school, awareness of the amount of time spent studying, awareness of the amount of help received from others, awareness of the difficulty level of the material, opinion about classroom rules, understanding of teacher expectations.

8. *Note the student's attitudes about his or her parents, siblings, and peers, such as the following:* has positive, negative, or indifferent attitudes; believes that parents' expectations are too high, too low, or just right; feels superior, inferior, or neutral toward peers.

9. *Note the cognitive and motivational resources that the student has for coping with the problem behavior, such as the following:* has the ability to monitor his or her behavior, has the ability to perform the desirable behavior, knows the consequences of engaging in the problem behavior, knows the consequences of engaging in the desirable behavior, knows what behaviors are expected of him or her, knows where and when he or she engages in the problem behavior, knows which behaviors are undesirable, is motivated to behave in an appropriate manner, understands why the behavior occurs, understands that some behaviors are appropriate in one situation but not in another (e.g., shouting at a sporting event but not during a spelling bee).

10. *Note the student's, family's, school's, and community's strengths and resources for change, such as the following:* availability of counseling services in the school; availability of economic resources in the family; availability of mental health resources, sports facilities, and other support facilities in the community; degree to which the student's physical health, mental health, cognitive ability, personality, and temperament can assist in the intervention plan; willingness of the family to support the intervention program.

Following are four examples of hypotheses developed on the basis of a functional behavioral assessment.

EXAMPLE 1—SELENA

When Selena is not engaged with others or with activities for 15 minutes or longer (especially during lunch or free time), or when she does not get to sleep before 10:00 p.m. the previous evening or does not feel well, she screams, slaps her face, and pulls her hair to gain access to teacher attention. (Knoster & Llewellyn, 1998a, p. 4, with changes in notation)

EXAMPLE 2—DAVID

When David is presented with academic work (in large- or small-group settings) requiring writing, multiple worksheets, or work that he perceives to be too difficult, he mumbles derogatory comments about the teacher, refuses to complete his work, destroys his assignment sheet, and/or pushes/kicks his desk or chair over in order to escape demonstrating academic failure in front of his peers. (Knoster & Llewellyn, 1998a, p. 4, with changes in notation)

EXAMPLE 3—JUAN

When Juan is unclear about what is expected of him on an assignment or what is going to happen next in the daily schedule, or when unexpected changes in his typical routine or transition activities occur, Juan will make loud guttural sounds, grind his teeth, and scratch, bite, or hit others in order to gain teacher attention in the form of reassurance or clarification as to what is to occur next. (Knoster & Llewellyn, 1998a, p. 4, with changes in notation)

EXAMPLE 4—KAREN

Karen enjoys interacting with others and keeping busy with activities. She seems happiest when she is interacting one-to-one with an adult (e.g., teacher) or participating in adult-led activities. She will occasionally sit alone for 15 minutes when listening to music of her choice, although she seems to grow bored in such situations. Karen currently has limited means of formal communication. While she enjoys interacting with others, she has never been observed to independently initiate appropriate interactions with her teacher or other students. Her independent initiation skills are very limited. Karen has limited access to nondisabled peers during her day at school (e.g., afternoon recess) and has a history of colds and viral infections which, in turn, adversely affect her sleep patterns. Karen's self-injury appears to signal her desire for social interaction, something to do, teacher assistance, or comfort when she is tired and/or not feeling well. Given her current situation, Karen's self-injury appears to be her most viable means to communicate these basic needs. (Knoster & Llewellyn, 1998b, p. 7)

Now let's look at some examples of hypotheses and possible interventions based on functional behavioral assessments.

EXAMPLE 1—MATT

Matt's problem behavior takes place when he is asked to write, read, or use higher-order thinking skills. He talks with peers when he is not supposed to, leaves his seat without permission, yells, and refuses to do assigned activities in order to get out of tasks that are challenging and frustrating. He should be required to complete writing, reading, and higher-order thinking assignments (escape responses should be blocked). Then he should be rewarded (e.g., complimented by his teacher, given passes, or given free time on the computer) when the required task is completed. (Lohrmann-O'Rourke, Knoster, & Llewellyn, 1999, p. 40, with changes in notation)

EXAMPLE 2—HENRY

In the cafeteria, between classes, before and after school, or in the locker room, Henry teases other students, curses them, pushes them, hits them, or puts them in a headlock in order to draw attention from other peers and also to gain control over situations in which he feels inferior. He needs to be disciplined for his problem behavior (e.g., given time-outs, kept after school, or sent to the principal's office) and rewarded (e.g., complimented by the teacher, given passes or free time on the computer, or appointed to assist the teacher or be a peer tutor to a younger child) when he performs acceptable behaviors. (Lohrmann-O'Rourke, Knoster, & Llewellyn, 1999)

EXAMPLE 3—JACOB

When other children play with Jacob's toys, he bangs his head, whines, and throws things. When he does this, the children return his toys. Jacob needs to be taught to ask children to return his toys when they take them (e.g., teach him sign language). When he exhibits aggressive behavior, he should not get his toys back. (Miltenberger, 1997)

EXAMPLE 4—JAMIE

Jamie, who does not talk, becomes aggressive whenever she is asked to sit and complete a sorting task. Her nonverbal actions suggest that she does not like the sorting task. When she becomes aggressive, the staff moves her to a chair in the corner of the room. Her actions appear to be getting her relief because she is removed from a disliked task. Jamie should be taught a means to signal when she thinks the tasks are too hard or when she dislikes them. If the sorting task is deemed to be useful, it might be changed in some way (e.g., made easier or more difficult) to better meet her needs. If, in spite of these changes, she is still aggressive, she should not be allowed to escape from the task. (Snell, 1988)

BEHAVIORAL INTERVENTION PLANS

The information you obtain from a functional behavioral assessment will help you design a behavioral intervention plan (Miltenberger, 1997). Behavioral intervention plans are intended to help the student develop more appropriate behaviors and to reduce the frequency and severity of the problem behavior. The key is to replace undesirable behavior with desir-

able behavior that serves the same function for the student (OSEP Technical Assistance Center, 2001). This may be done in part by arranging the setting and antecedent events so that the *replacement behaviors* (appropriate behaviors) are more likely to be encouraged and by arranging consequent events so that the replacement behaviors are more likely to be reinforced and the problem behavior is less likely to be reinforced.

In designing the behavioral intervention plan, you need to consider the following issues:

1. Alternative desirable behaviors that are in the student's repertoire
2. Reinforcers and punishers, including items, activities, and the reactions of others
3. Environmental changes needed to prevent the problem behavior from occurring and to promote positive behaviors
4. Ways to make changes in the antecedent variables
5. Skills needed by the student to replace problem behaviors

Developing the Behavioral Intervention Plan

The behavioral intervention plan should be practical, workable, and reasonable, and it should help the student benefit from classroom instruction. Thus, the plan should be tailored to the student's needs, be designed so that it is consistent with the student's skill level and resources, and have a high level of acceptance by those responsible for carrying it out. The plan generally should include incremental improvement goals designed to reduce the problem behavior, rather than one large-scale improvement goal. Let's look at what is involved in developing a behavioral intervention plan (Gable et al., 1998).

1. *Include in the plan positive strategies for diminishing the problem behavior and increasing appropriate replacement behaviors, such as the following:*

- Arrange for easier access to desired items or activities.
- Arrange for the student to receive counseling.
- Clarify rules and expected behavior for the whole class.
- Have the student use self-monitoring forms under the guidance of a counselor or psychologist (see Chapter 9).
- Include a written behavioral contract.
- Modify assignments to match the student's skills (e.g., easier assignments, small units of work, fewer problems).
- Modify instructional procedures (e.g., more detailed instructions, simplified instructions, step-by-step instructions).
- Provide clearer directions.
- Provide extra assistance.
- Use reinforcers such as verbal praise, positive social reinforcement, a point system, tangible reinforcements, or additional privileges more effectively.

- Provide student with skill training, including training in more appropriate ways to obtain desired goals (acceptable replacement behaviors).
- Remove unintended consequences that may be reinforcing the problem behavior (e.g., prevent the student from escaping or avoiding required classroom tasks through misbehavior).
- Set clear limits.
- Suggest to teachers ways to maximize reinforcements for positive behavior and minimize reinforcements for negative behavior.
- Teach adaptive social skills.
- Teach replacement behaviors that are not in the student's repertoire.
- Use adult or peer role models and tutors.

2. *Include in the plan positive strategies for changing the environment in order to prevent the problem behavior from occurring, such as the following:*

- Allow legitimate movement.
- Change seating arrangements.
- Increase distance between desks.
- Increase ratio of adults to students.
- Provide choices related to assignments.
- Make changes in the student's class schedule—change classes or teachers or reschedule classes.
- Remove distracting materials from the classroom.
- Seat student near teacher or near a positive peer model.
- Use resource rooms.

3. *Include in the plan consequences that might prevent the problem behavior from recurring* (see the previous section on "Describing the Problem Behavior").

4. *Consider other elements that should be included in the behavioral intervention plan, such as the following:*

- Availability of crisis management procedures to ensure safety and deescalation of the student's problem behavior (e.g., fully available, partially available, not available)
- Capability of student to perform the behaviors recommended in the intervention plan (e.g., fully capable, moderately capable, minimally capable)
- Effectiveness of the behavioral intervention plan with more than one problem behavior (e.g., highly effective, moderately effective, minimally effective)
- Extent to which interventions allow behavior changes to transfer across environments (e.g., fully allow for transfer, moderately allow for transfer, minimally allow for transfer)
- Presence of safeguards to ensure that the student will receive reinforcement for positive behavior and not for the problem behavior (e.g., safeguards fully in place, moderately in place, minimally in place)
- Usefulness of other reinforcing behaviors or items (e.g., objects, free time, computer time, privilege of assisting teacher)

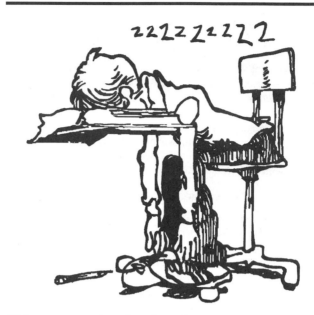

This was not quite what the school psychologist had in mind as an intervention for Timmy's out-of-seat behavior.

Courtesy of Daniel Miller.

5. *Include in the plan information about how the intervention strategies should be structured, such as the following:*

- Individual roles and responsibilities of staff members for the interventions
- Setting in which the interventions should take place
- Time and duration of the interventions

Monitoring the Behavioral Intervention Plan

In monitoring the behavioral intervention plan, you should review the student's progress periodically at specified times. Consider such questions as the following (Tilly, Knoster, Kovaleski, Bambara, Dunlap, & Kincaid, 1998):

1. Is the plan being implemented as proposed?
2. Which short- and long-term goals have been reached, if any?
3. What information is helpful in the teacher's anecdotal notes and checklists and any self-monitoring forms completed by the student?
4. Is the student acquiring new skills?
5. Is the student using the new skills in different situations?
6. Has the problem behavior decreased to an acceptable rate?
7. What barriers hinder the student's learning?
8. Is the student's academic performance improving?

9. Does the student understand the consequences of her or his actions?
10. Is the student able to control her or his behavior?
11. Are the student, teachers, and parents satisfied with the plan and its outcomes?
12. Do the student, teachers, and parents have any suggestions for improving the plan?
13. What modifications, if any, in the plan are needed to improve its effectiveness?

A behavioral intervention plan should foster interdisciplinary cooperation and efforts among teachers, related service providers, administrators, family members, and outside agency personnel (as appropriate). Conducting a functional behavioral assessment and implementing a behavioral intervention plan may require considerable time and effort on the part of the professionals involved. However, dealing effectively with problem behaviors in their early stages of development can deliver significant benefits by reducing the severity of future problems (McComas, Hoch, & Mace, 2000).

Examples of Behavioral Intervention Plans

Two examples of behavioral intervention plans follow. Note that the consequences that maintained the problem behavior in Example 1 (Repp, 1999) differ from those in Example 2.

EXAMPLE 1

Assessment

Setting: Henry's problem behavior occurs during a large-group instructional session.
Setting event: Henry did not take his medication.
Antecedents: The teacher attends to peers, Henry needs to wait his turn, and he has few turns.
Problem behavior: He lies down on the floor, shouts, and kicks his feet.
Consequences: The teacher reprimands Henry, and his peers laugh at him.
Function: Henry obtains attention from others.
Setting where problem behavior does not occur: The problem behavior does not take place during small-group instruction, during which the teacher gives Henry attention and each student has several turns.

Intervention

Change setting: Use small-group instruction or one-on-one instruction when possible.
Change setting event: Ensure that Henry takes his medication.
Change antecedents: Ask teacher to try to give both Henry and his peers attention during large-group instruction.
Replacement behaviors: The teacher (a) has the group respond in unison, (b) has students raise their hands, (c) has

students follow instructions, and (d) has students wait their turn.
Change consequences: The teacher praises Henry (and other students) for listening and waiting.
Function of replacement behavior: Henry obtains attention for enacting the replacement behaviors.

EXAMPLE 2

Assessment

Setting: Amanda's problem behavior occurs when she is working individually on assignments in class.
Setting event: Amanda arrived at school hungry.
Antecedents: The assignments require that Amanda work quietly and independently.
Problem behavior: She slams materials and makes noises (e.g., bird calls) about 10 to 15 times in a 45-minute class period. This behavior interferes with other students' learning.
Consequences: The teacher checks Amanda's work, reminds her to be quiet, and, if the behavior does not improve, sends her to time-out.
Function: Amanda escapes doing the task.
Setting where problem behavior does not occur: The problem does not occur during music or during cooperative learning activities.

Intervention

Change setting: Use peer learning activities when possible.
Change setting event: To try to ensure that Amanda does not come to school hungry, offer to enroll her in the school breakfast program.
Change antecedents: Ask the teacher to try to use more group learning activities in the classroom.
Replacement behaviors: The teacher encourages Amanda to (a) use a keyboard for typing when she works on lengthy written assignments, (b) raise her hand when she needs help, when she is ready to have her work checked, and when she needs a break, and (c) join the band to develop friendships.
Change consequences: The teacher gives Amanda attention whenever she raises her hand, even if it is to say, "I'll be there in a minute." The teacher also ignores all the noises Amanda makes and instructs other students to do the same, minimizes the use of time-outs, and allows Amanda to earn homework passes for the assignments she completes.
Function of replacement behavior: Amanda achieves success, obtains attention from the teacher, and discontinues the disruptive behaviors.

Exhibit 13-1 shows an in-depth behavioral intervention plan for a 10-year-old girl who was uncooperative and engaged in disruptive behavior. For more information about functional behavioral assessment, see O'Neill, Horner, Albin, Sprague, Storey, and Newton (1997); Repp and Horner (1999); and Sturmey (1996).

Exhibit 13-1
Behavioral Intervention Plan

Behavioral Intervention Plan

Name of student: Marisa Springfield

Sex: Female

Date of birth: April 12, 1995   Age: 10-0

Date: April 15, 2005

Grade: 4th

School: Harper Elementary

Behaviors in Need of Change

1. Leaves assigned area without permission
2. Refuses to go to designated area
3. Disruptive behavior, such as slamming lockers, screaming, and banging desks

Perceived Functions of Behaviors

1. Attention
2. To gain control or power
3. To avoid nonpreferred activities
4. To express anger or frustration

Target Replacement Behaviors

1. Remain in assigned area unless given permission to leave
2. Go to designated area when directed to do so
3. Use an appropriate voice to communicate to others when upset
4. Respect property

Strategies to Prevent the Problem Behavior(s)

1. Pre-kindergarten helper

To provide Marisa with additional attention in a positive way, the following are recommended:

   a. When Marisa comes to school each morning, she will assist the pre-kindergarten teacher.
   b. Marisa's time in the pre-kindergarten classroom should be 10 to 15 minutes daily. Marisa can help set up the class, assist children with the morning transition, and do other jobs as requested by the teacher.
   c. Marisa's morning job in the pre-kindergarten classroom is not contingent upon her behavior. Therefore, it is not something she must earn. However, Marisa's classroom teacher and the pre-kindergarten teacher should communicate frequently to monitor Marisa's ability to handle the responsibilities of the job.
   d. Both the classroom teacher and the pre-kindergarten teacher should provide Marisa with verbal praise for a job well done.

2. Library assistant

To provide Marisa with opportunities for additional attention, the following are recommended:

   a. Marisa should report to the library at the end of every day to assist the librarian.
   b. Marisa should spend 10 to 15 minutes helping put books away, cleaning up the library, and assisting with other duties as assigned.

   c. Marisa's time in the library is not contingent upon her behavior. If, however, Marisa is having a problem at the time she is to report to the library, she should not go until she is calm and has completed what she needed to do in class.
   d. The librarian and the classroom teacher should maintain communication to make sure that the job is working well for everyone. They should also provide Marisa with verbal praise for doing her job well.

3. Morning snack break

To provide Marisa with a break from the classroom, as well as an opportunity for adult attention and time to discuss any concerns she may have, the following are recommended:

   a. Marisa should be given the opportunity daily at 11:30 a.m. to eat a snack in the guidance office or school office.
   b. This snack time is not contingent upon good behavior, nor is it mandatory. Marisa may choose not to go if she wishes.
   c. This snack time should last about 10 minutes, and it is a good time to play games or talk if Marisa wants to.
   d. Verbal praise should be provided for any appropriate behaviors that Marisa demonstrates while in the office.

4. Increased opportunities for choice

To meet Marisa's need for control, the following are recommended:

   a. Provide Marisa with daily opportunities to make choices. Opportunities for choice may include which work to do first, whether to do odd or even problems, where to sit in a group, whom to pick first for a group, and when in the period to complete an assignment.
   b. Provide verbal praise for good choices made.

5. Skill-building sessions

To provide Marisa with social skills and anger management training and to help her develop coping skills, the following are recommended:

   a. Marisa will have two sessions weekly with the school guidance counselor.
   b. Sessions will last 20–30 minutes each. The tentative schedule for Marisa is Tuesdays 11:10–11:30 a.m. and Thursdays 1:15–1:45 p.m.
   c. The guidance counselor initially will work on establishing rapport with Marisa. Once Marisa feels comfortable with the guidance counselor, they will work on anger identification and management skills, social skills, and coping skills (to assist with handling disappointment, noise in the cafeteria, etc.). There will also be ongoing work to assist Marisa in learning how to communicate her feelings appropriately when there is a problem.

(Continued)

Exhibit 13-1
(*Continued*)

6. *Daily reinforcement system*

To provide Marisa with the incentive to remain in class, as well as feedback regarding her behavior, the following are recommended:

a. Marisa will be provided with a daily sheet and will be awarded a sticker or stamp or initial every time she goes to and remains in the assigned area for an entire class period.

b. Marisa will be provided with a list of reinforcers she can buy with her stickers. *The reinforcer list will be developed with Marisa* and will include things like lunch with a chosen adult, pencils and other school supplies, and having her fingernails painted.

c. Marisa will choose when and how to spend her stickers.

d. Marisa's daily sheet will go home every afternoon for her mother to review and sign. Marisa will earn a bonus sticker for returning the sheet to school with her mother's signature on it.

e. Verbal praise should be provided when Marisa earns stickers. Positive daily sheets should be shared with administrators to provide her with positive attention from them.

Strategies to Deal with the Problem Behavior(s)

1. Leaves assigned area without permission or refuses to go to designated area

To correct Marisa's leaving an area without permission or refusing to go to a designated area, the following are recommended:

a. Always use a calm, matter-of-fact tone of voice when giving Marisa directions.

b. State directions positively. Tell Marisa exactly what she needs to do (e.g., "Go to reading").

c. Only one person should deal with Marisa, to minimize the amount of attention she receives for her behavior. If the person who originally gave the direction is unable to stay with Marisa, another person should be called to step in.

d. Marisa should be told that a staff member will talk to her only after she follows directions. No other verbal interactions should occur until she follows directions. This is not the time to play games or have fun with Marisa. Positive attention should occur only when Marisa is doing well.

e. When Marisa finally follows directions, the staff member should review with her better choices she can make in the future if a similar situation arises. No further mention of the incident should be made, to avoid reinforcing the behavior accidentally. Get Marisa back on task as quickly as possible.

2. *Disruptive behavior*

To address the occurrence of disruptive behavior, the following are recommended:

a. Give Marisa clear and concise directions, using a calm tone of voice.

b. Do not address specific behaviors. Simply tell her what she needs to do.

c. Keep verbal interactions to a minimum. Let Marisa know you will talk to her when she is calm and following directions.

d. Only one staff member should be involved, if possible, to minimize the attention Marisa receives for negative behavior.

e. If Marisa becomes a danger to herself or others, staff may, as a last resort, physically intervene to keep her and others safe.

f. Once calm, Marisa may need 20–30 minutes of quiet time out of the classroom to get herself together.

g. Follow-up problem solving should occur after her quiet time to determine her ability to get back to work.

h. The goal is to get Marisa back on task and in a regular routine as quickly as possible with as little attention as possible. It is important to remember that attention and time out of class are reinforcing to Marisa, and we do not want to reinforce her challenging behaviors—we want to reinforce positive behaviors.

THINKING THROUGH THE ISSUES

1. How does a functional behavioral assessment differ from a psychological or psychoeducational assessment?

2. In what ways can a functional behavioral assessment be useful for conditions other than behavioral problems?

SUMMARY

1. A functional behavioral assessment is designed to help you arrive at an understanding of a student's problem behavior and develop a behavioral intervention plan.

2. To conduct a functional behavioral assessment, you will need to consider (a) the type of problem behavior, (b) conditions under which the problem behavior occurs (including the events that trigger the problem behavior), (c) probable reasons for or causes of the problem behavior (including biological, social, cognitive, affective, and environmental factors), and (d) the functions that the problem behavior might serve.

When Is a Functional Behavioral Assessment Needed?

3. A functional behavioral assessment can be used to evaluate any problem in any setting, such as destructive, aggressive, noncompliant, or disruptive behaviors directed toward self, others, or objects.

4. A functional behavioral assessment is also useful when a child is rejected by peers, is in need of a more restricted placement because of behavioral concerns, is in an intervention program that involves excessively intrusive procedures (e.g., restraints or isolation), or is not responsive to current interventions.

5. IDEA 2004 (Sec. 615) requires that a functional behavioral assessment be performed when a child with a disability violates a

code of student conduct and either (a) a change in placement is being considered for the child or (b) the local education agency, the parent, and relevant members of the IEP team determine that the behavior was a manifestation of the child's disability. In the latter case, a behavioral intervention plan also must be implemented.

6. Several members of the interdisciplinary team contribute to a functional behavioral assessment, including psychologists, social workers, nurses, general education teachers, special education teachers, and speech and language pathologists.

Functions of Challenging Behavior

7. Two main functions of challenging behavior are to get something (positive reinforcement) and to escape or avoid something (negative reinforcement).
8. More than one behavior may serve the same or a similar function for a student.
9. The same behavior might serve different functions in different contexts.
10. Students usually do not display individual behaviors, but strings or chains of behavior that are occasioned by social interactions.

Guidelines for Conducting a Functional Behavioral Assessment

11. The following seven steps are useful in conducting a functional behavioral assessment in a school setting: (1) describe the problem behavior, (2) perform the assessment, (3) evaluate the assessment results, (4) develop hypotheses, (5) formulate an intervention plan, (6) start the intervention, and (7) evaluate the effectiveness of the intervention plan.

Assessing Behavior Through Observations and Interviews

12. After defining the problem behavior, you will want to observe the student in several different settings, during different types of activities, and at different times during the day.
13. Observation may have either an *interindividual focus,* in which a child's performance is compared with that of a norm group or a peer, or an *intraindividual focus,* in which a child's own performance is compared across different environments and across different tasks.
14. A functional behavioral assessment may also involve manipulating environmental events (e.g., type of activity, consequences) and then observing the effects of the manipulations; this approach is referred to as a functional analysis.
15. The student and his or her teachers and parents should be interviewed about the problem behavior.

Describing the Problem Behavior

16. In describing the student's problem behavior, focus on events that occur during, before, and after the problem behavior.

Formulating Hypotheses to Account for the Problem Behavior

17. Hypotheses serve to summarize assessment results, offer explanations for the student's problem behavior, and guide the development of the behavioral intervention plan.

18. To develop hypotheses to account for the problem behavior, review the antecedents of the behavior, the behavior itself, and consequences associated with the behavior, as well as background factors, functions or purposes served by the behavior, reactions of students and others to the problem behavior, others' understanding of the problem behavior, and attitudes of the student, family, school, and community toward the problem behavior, as well as their resources for coping with it.

Behavioral Intervention Plans

19. Information obtained from a functional behavioral assessment will help you design a behavioral intervention plan that includes (a) alternative desirable behaviors that are in the student's repertoire, (b) reinforcers and punishers, including items, activities, and the reactions of others, (c) environmental changes needed to prevent the problem behavior from occurring and to promote positive behaviors, (d) ways to make changes in the antecedent variables, and (e) skills needed by the student to replace problem behaviors.
20. In developing a behavioral intervention plan, also consider (a) positive strategies for diminishing the problem behavior and increasing appropriate replacement behaviors, (b) positive strategies for changing the environment in order to prevent the problem behavior from occurring, (c) consequences that might prevent the problem behavior from recurring, (d) other elements that should be included, and (e) information about how the intervention strategies should be structured.
21. A behavioral intervention plan should foster interdisciplinary cooperation and efforts among teachers, related service providers, administrators, families, and outside agency personnel.
22. Be sure to monitor the behavioral intervention plan.

KEY TERMS, CONCEPTS, AND NAMES

Functional behavioral assessment (p. 337)
Challenging behavior (p. 337)
Conducting a functional behavioral assessment (p. 337)
Observations (p. 338)
Interindividual focus (p. 338)
Intraindividual focus (p. 338)
Functional analysis (p. 338)
Interview questions (p. 338)
Describing the problem behavior (p. 339)
Formulating hypotheses (p. 342)
Behavioral intervention plans (p. 345)
Replacement behaviors (p. 345)

STUDY QUESTION

Describe functional behavioral assessment. Include in your discussion guidelines for conducting a functional behavioral assessment, assessing behavior through observations and interviews, describing the problem behavior, formulating hypotheses to account for the problem behavior, and developing a behavioral intervention plan.

14

ANTISOCIAL BEHAVIOR DISORDERS, ANXIETY DISORDERS, DEPRESSIVE DISORDERS, SUICIDE RISK, AND SUBSTANCE ABUSE DISORDERS

I've never forgotten this child, because when I asked her to tell me about her picture, she said: "I'm screaming and no one hears me."

—Eliana Gil, Ph.D., American art and play therapist

Antisocial Behavior Disorders

Aggression Questionnaire

Beck Disruptive Behavior Inventory for Youth and Beck Anger Inventory for Youth

Anxiety Disorders

Beck Anxiety Inventory for Youth

Depressive Disorders

Beck Depression Inventory for Youth

Children's Depression Inventory and Children's Depression Inventory–Short Form

Reynolds Child Depression Scale and Reynolds Adolescent Depression Scale–Second Edition

Suicide Risk

Substance Abuse Disorders

Thinking Through the Issues

Summary

Key Terms, Concepts, and Names

Goals and Objectives

This chapter is designed to enable you to do the following:

- Become familiar with how psychological problems develop in children

- Understand various approaches to the treatment of psychological problems in children

- Become familiar with measures of antisocial behaviors, anxiety disorders, depressive disorders, suicide risk, and substance abuse disorders

This section of the text will introduce you to the theory and practice of assessing children with various kinds of special needs. The first chapter in the section covers antisocial behavior disorders, anxiety disorders, depressive disorders, suicide risk, and substance abuse disorders. Subsequent chapters discuss attention-deficit/hyperactivity disorder, learning disabilities, mental retardation, giftedness, visual impairments, hearing impairments, autistic disorder, and brain injuries.

ANTISOCIAL BEHAVIOR DISORDERS

Antisocial behavior disorders (or externalizing or disruptive behavior disorders) are characterized by behaviors that violate social norms and seriously impair a child's functioning in the home, community, and school (Johnson, McCaskill, & Werba, 2001; Quay & Hogan, 1999; Rutter, Giller, & Hagell, 1998). The two *DSM-IV–TR* diagnostic categories covering antisocial behavior disorders are conduct disorder and oppositional defiant disorder.

Conduct Disorder

Children with a conduct disorder have a pattern of antisocial behavior, rule breaking, or aggressive behavior. The condition represents "a repetitive and persistent pattern of behavior in which the basic rights of others or major age-appropriate societal norms or rules are violated" (American Psychiatric Association, 2000, p. 93). The following types of behaviors are associated with conduct disorders:

1. *Aggressive conduct* that causes or threatens physical harm to other people or animals (e.g., bullying, threatening, or intimidating others; initiating physical fights; using a weapon; displaying physical cruelty to people or animals; stealing while confronting a victim; forcing someone into sexual activity)
2. *Nonaggressive conduct* that causes property loss or damage (e.g., deliberately setting fires; deliberately destroying others' property by other means)
3. *Deceitfulness or theft* (e.g., breaking into someone else's residence or car; lying to obtain goods or favors or to avoid obligations; stealing items of nontrivial value without confronting a victim)
4. *Serious violation of rules* (e.g., staying out at night despite parental prohibitions; running away from home overnight; missing school)

DSM-IV–TR describes other characteristics of children and adolescents who have a conduct disorder, such as little empathy and concern for the feelings, wishes, and well-being of others; minimal feelings of guilt or remorse; poor tolerance for frustration; irritability, temper outbursts, and recklessness;

early onset of sexual behavior, drinking, smoking, or use of illegal substances; school suspension or expulsion; adjustment problems at work; legal difficulties; sexually transmitted diseases; unplanned pregnancy; promiscuity; and physical injury from accidents or fights. Thus, children with a conduct disorder may have impairments in their social, academic, and occupational functioning.

DSM-IV–TR makes a distinction between childhood-onset conduct disorder (symptoms appearing before age 10 years) and adolescent-onset conduct disorder (symptoms appearing after age 10 years). Childhood-onset disorder is generally regarded as having a poorer prognosis because it is likely to be more persistent and to develop into adult antisocial personality disorder.

The nature and severity of conduct disorder may vary with gender:

> Conduct disorder, especially the Childhood-Onset Type, is more common in males. Gender differences are also found in specific types of conduct problems. Males with a diagnosis of conduct disorder frequently exhibit fighting, stealing, vandalism, and school discipline problems. Females with a diagnosis of conduct disorder are more likely to exhibit lying, truancy, running away, substance use, and prostitution. Whereas confrontational aggression is more often displayed in males, females tend to use more nonconfrontational behaviors. (American Psychiatric Association, 2000, p. 97)

Oppositional Defiant Disorder

Children with an oppositional defiant disorder have a recurrent pattern of negativistic, defiant, disobedient, and hostile behavior toward authority figures (American Psychiatric Association, 2000). Typical behaviors include arguing with adults, actively defying or refusing to comply with the requests or rules of adults, deliberately doing things that annoy other people, blaming others for one's own mistakes or misbehavior, being touchy or easily annoyed by others, being angry and resentful, or being spiteful or vindictive. Children with this pattern of behavior also may have impairments in social, academic, or occupational functioning (Ledingham, 1999). Unlike children with a conduct disorder, children with an oppositional defiant disorder do not engage in behavior that seriously violates others' rights or violates age-appropriate social norms and rules. Thus, they usually do *not* show aggressive behavior toward people or animals, destroy property, steal, or deceive people.

The features associated with oppositional defiant disorder depend on a child's age and gender (American Psychiatric Association, 2000). Oppositional symptoms may begin in the preschool years and tend to increase with age. The disorder is more prevalent in males than females during early childhood, but rates become more equal after puberty. Males may display more confrontational behavior and females more passive forms of resistance.

Other Aspects of Antisocial Behavior Disorders

Age of onset of symptoms. The symptoms of oppositional defiant disorder usually appear between ages 3 and 8 years, whereas the symptoms of conduct disorder typically appear between ages 8 and 13 years. Specific symptoms of oppositional defiant disorder and conduct disorder, as noted in the reports of parents, typically appear at the following ages (Lahey & Loeber, 1994):

- *Oppositional defiant disorder:* acts stubborn (3 years), defies adults (5 years), has temper tantrums (5 years), is irritable (6 years), argues (6 years), blames others (6½ years), annoys others (7 years), is spiteful (7½ years), and is angry (8 years)
- *Conduct disorder:* lies (8 years), fights (8½ years), bullies (9 years), sets fires (9 years), uses weapon (9½ years), vandalizes (10 years), is cruel to animals (10½ years), engages in physical cruelty (11½ years), steals (12 years), runs away from home (12 years), is truant (12½ years), mugs (12½ years), breaks and enters (12½ years), and forces sex (13 years)

Contextual variations. Because antisocial behaviors are defined as behaviors that violate social norms, contextual variations in those norms may affect the diagnosis. While acts of physical violence and other criminal activities are universally condemned, other forms of behavior may be more difficult to evaluate. For example, some forms of physical aggression may be functional in contexts where aggression is critical to survival. Similarly, levels of oppositional defiant behaviors considered dysfunctional in some home or school settings might not be considered problematic by parents or teachers with a more accommodating attitude. For example, some parents encourage their child to challenge them and others and to engage in verbal arguments.

Incidence of antisocial behaviors. The incidence of antisocial behaviors varies with the way in which the construct is defined, the specific behaviors in question, and the child's stage of development. *DSM-IV-TR* estimates that rates of conduct disorder range from 6% to 16% for males and from 2% to 9% for females. Estimates of the rate of oppositional defiant disorder are between 2% and 16%. Conduct and oppositional disorders often co-occur with attention-deficit/hyperactivity disorder (American Psychiatric Association, 2000).

Commission of a crime. The commission of a crime constitutes an important form of antisocial behavior. As noted in Chapter 1, relatively few youths commit criminal actions, and an even smaller percentage commit serious crimes. Still, FBI data indicate that nearly one and a half million youths under the age of 18 were arrested in 2002 (Office of Juvenile Justice & Delinquency Prevention, 2004).

Violent aggressive acts such as assaults or murder constitute a special category of antisocial behaviors. These actions often cause significant harm to the victims and have serious consequences for youths perpetrating them. Estimating the prevalence of violent aggressive actions is difficult, because none of the available measures, including official arrest statistics, victim report data, and self-report indices, are perfect measures of the actual incidence of violent acts (Loeber, Farrington, & Waschbusch, 1998; Snyder & Sickmund, 1999). FBI data show a significant increase in arrests of young people for violent crime between 1980 and 1994 (Office of Juvenile Justice & Delinquency Prevention, 2004). The incidence of arrest reached a peak in 1994, but, as noted in Chapter 1, the rates of both general and violent crime on the part of juveniles have been declining since 1994. For example, FBI data indicate that arrests of juveniles for violent crimes declined 44% between 1994 and 2001.

School violence. School violence constitutes another concern. Here, too, it is difficult to obtain reliable estimates of incidence, because school policies on the treatment of aggressive actions and procedures for reporting incidents vary widely across jurisdictions (Dolmage, 1996; Furlong & Morrison, 2000; U.S. Department of Education, 1999). Analyses by the National Center for Education Statistics (2004) indicate that, in 2003, 5% of students ages 12 to 18 years reported being the victim of some type of nonfatal crime while in school and 1% reported being the victim of a violent incident. Seven percent of students ages 12 to 18 years reported being bullied in school in 2003. The rate of violent incidents in school declined between 1992 and 2002, however, and between 1993 and 2003 the number of students in grades 9 to 12 who reported being in a fight on school property declined from 16% to 13%. It is estimated that the odds of a child dying in school through homicide are exceptionally low. Thus, media reports on tragic cases such as the 1999 school shooting at Columbine High School in Littleton, Colorado, where multiple victims were shot, may lead the public to accept an exaggerated picture of the risk of violent actions in school settings (Borum, 2000; Dolmage, 1996).

In light of the well-publicized incidents of school shootings in the 1990s, threats of school violence have received considerable attention. The U.S. Secret Service National Threat Assessment Center studied 37 incidents of targeted school violence. The cases spanned a period from 1974 to 2000 and took place in 37 communities. Incidents were *not* included if the shootings were clearly related to gang or drug activity or if they were the result of an interpersonal or relationship dispute and just happened to occur at school. The study's 10 key findings concerning targeted school violence are as follows (Fein, Vossekuil, Pollack, Borum, Modzelski, & Reddy, 2002; adapted from pp. 18–25):

1. Incidents of targeted violence at school rarely are sudden, impulsive acts.

2. Prior to most incidents, other people knew about the attacker's idea and/or plan to attack.

3. Most attackers did not threaten their targets directly prior to carrying out the attack.

4. There is no accurate or useful "profile" of students who engage in targeted school violence.

5. Most attackers engaged in some behavior, prior to the incident, that caused others concern or indicated a need for help.

6. Most attackers had difficulty coping with significant losses or personal failures. Many had considered or attempted suicide.

7. Many attackers felt bullied, persecuted, or injured by others prior to the attack.

8. Most attackers had access to and had used weapons prior to the attack.

9. In many cases, other students were involved in the attack in some capacity.

10. Despite prompt law enforcement responses, most attacks were stopped by means other than law enforcement intervention and most ended quickly.

Etiology of Conduct Disorder

Biological, behavioral, and familial factors have been proposed to account for the development of conduct disorder; however, there is no firm evidence to support any one etiological theory (American Psychiatric Association, 2000; Frick, 1998; Johnson et al., 2001; Quay & Hogan, 1999). Here are some examples of these etiological factors:

- *Biological factors* include children's genetic makeup and constitutional factors.
- *Behavioral factors* include difficult infant temperament, sensation seeking, learning deficits, academic under-achievement, immaturities in moral reasoning, maladaptive peer relationships, association with a delinquent peer group, and poor interpersonal problem-solving skills.
- *Familial factors* include parental marital conflict and divorce, depression, substance abuse, antisocial behavior, social isolation, rejection of child, failure to supervise the child properly, harsh or inconsistent discipline, ineffective communication with the child, and failure to become involved in the child's activities.

The following model is useful for understanding how children develop a conduct disorder (Conduct Problems Prevention Research Group, 1992; Johnson et al., 2001; Shaw & Bell, 1993). At each developmental stage, genetic factors either may be involved in the children's behavior problems or may exacerbate problems related to parental attachment and neglect. *Thus, parents may be victims of a child's behavior problems as well as contribute to the child's problems.* The developmental model emphasizes that there is an interaction between genetic and familial/environmental conditions that places children at risk for developing a conduct disorder.

Infancy.   From birth to 24 months, infants who later develop a conduct disorder may be neglected by caregivers who are indifferent to them and who fail to comfort them. When this happens, infants may become demanding, which, in turn, may make caregivers even more nonresponsive. By 24 months, infants who are insecure may become more bold, noncompliant, and negative. Caregivers, in turn, are likely to continue to be indifferent to them and to try to control the infants' behavior. Caregivers might prefer not to interact at all with infants who show unpleasant behavior (Shaw & Bell, 1993).

Preschool years.   By 2 years of age, "the basic pattern of interaction and emotional attachment between the parent and child has been formed. The child has developed an internal working model of expected responsiveness from the caregiver, and she or he has developed her or his own expectations and standards of appropriate responsiveness concerning the child's most common reactions to her or his interventions" (Shaw & Bell, 1993, p. 512, with changes in notation). Caregivers begin to demand more things from the toddler. When physical contact has been negative and infrequent in the first 2 years, this situation is likely to continue during the next 2 years. In such cases, there is little opportunity for the caregiver to negotiate goals and plans with the child. When the relationship is secure, these negotiations can take place successfully. Children as young as 2 and 3 years of age may show irritability, inattentiveness, and impulsivity and have discipline problems. When there is a coercive caregiver-child relationship, the caregiver may provide only low levels of stimulation and support, so the child fails to develop needed emotional control, social skills, and academic readiness (Conduct Problems Prevention Research Group, 1992).

The conflict between preschool children and their caregivers has ramifications for the development of later antisocial behavior (Shaw & Bell, 1993). The children may not internalize parental or societal standards. Parents may give rewards infrequently and, when they do give them, use them as a means of controlling the child's behavior. Children may comply only because of perceived threats to their freedom or to their physical safety. They develop an extrinsic motivation system, doing things because they have to—they do not independently pursue complex and challenging activities.

Middle-childhood years.   Between 6 and 12 years of age, children who develop a conduct disorder may show deficiencies in critical social-cognitive skills (Conduct Problems Prevention Research Group, 1992). Compared with their peers, they may be less likely to attend to relevant social cues, to interpret peers' intentions accurately, and to assume a friendly attitude toward others. They may hold negative values and beliefs regarding authority figures such as parents, teachers, and police. These children may have limited skills in solving social problems, and, instead of using competent verbally assertive social strategies, they may respond aggressively in social situations. Aggression may become their preferred way of interacting with others.

The following picture emerges during the middle-childhood years for children who develop a conduct disorder (Conduct Problems Prevention Research Group, 1992):

> During the grade school years, negative school and social experiences further exacerbate the adjustment difficulties of children with conduct problems. Children who are aggressive and disruptive with peers quickly become rejected by their peers. . . . Because of their noncompliant and disruptive behavior, high-risk children develop poor relations with their teachers and are less supported and nurtured in the school setting. . . . Parents' negative encounters with teachers, coupled with continued and escalating aversive interactions with their children in the home, lead some parents to reject their own highly aggressive children and show less interest in them as they enter adolescence. Several consequences follow from this spiraling pattern of aversive behavior, rejection, and reactivity. One is that high-risk children perform more poorly in school and become alienated from the goals and values of [school]. . . . A second consequence is that some of these children become depressed and develop negative self-concepts in the cognitive, social, and behavioral domains. A third consequence is that rejected, aggressive children drift into deviant peer groups in early adolescence. (p. 513)

Adolescent years. Adolescents need to establish a strong bond, consisting of attachment, commitment, and positive beliefs, with the family and other social institutions to prevent deviant behavior and delinquency from developing (Catalano & Hawkins, 1996). The following picture emerges during adolescence of children with a conduct disorder (Conduct Problems Prevention Research Group, 1992):

> By early adolescence, alienation from the mainstream culture and association with deviant peers may play a particularly critical role in promoting adolescent delinquency. . . . It is the deviant peer group in adolescence that appears to be a major training ground for delinquency and substance abuse. . . . Parents of high-risk adolescents are relatively unlikely to monitor their children's activities adequately . . . and teachers at this level cannot consistently monitor contact with adolescents. . . . In fact, dropping out of school seems to be predictable from deviant peer group membership in middle school. (p. 513)

Also keep in mind the resilience and protective factors discussed in Chapter 1. These factors help to reduce the occurrence of conduct disorder.

Treatment of Conduct Disorder

Children with conduct disorder are difficult to treat (Johnson et al., 2001; Quay & Hogan, 1999; Rutter et al., 1998). Treatment approaches include the use of pharmacological agents, behavioral approaches, parent-training approaches, cognitive-behavioral approaches, and multimodal approaches.

Pharmacological agents include mood stabilizers (such as lithium), stimulants (such as Ritalin), and neuroleptics (such as thioridazine, chlorpromazine, and haloperidol; Waslick, Werry, & Greenhill, 1999). Some success has been achieved, but research on long-term outcomes is needed. Neuroleptics have several side effects, including impairment of adaptive behavior, increased disturbances in mood and behavior, weight gain, drowsiness, gastrointestinal problems, and movement disorders that may not abate following drug withdrawal. Medication alone will rarely suffice in the treatment of children with conduct disorder (Lewis, 1991; Waslick et al., 1999).

Behavioral approaches use contingency management programs that aim to increase children's coping behaviors and improve their self-esteem and positive behaviors (e.g., interactions with peers, cooperative behaviors, and respectful comments to adults), increase their frustration tolerance, and reduce their aggressive behavior (Frick & McCoy, 2001; Kazdin, 1998; Quay & Hogan, 1999). Contingency management programs monitor children's progress toward these goals and use a system of positive and negative consequences to encourage behavioral change.

Parent-training approaches are used to teach parents and children better ways to communicate and to respond to each other's needs and ways to improve family management practices in order to alter maladaptive family patterns. These programs developed from social learning approaches emphasizing that what is taught in the home greatly influences behavior.

Cognitive-behavioral approaches are used to help children overcome deficits in social, cognitive, and social problem-solving skills (Frick & McCoy, 2001). For example, children with conduct disorder are taught to inhibit impulsive and aggressive responses, to overcome hostile perceptions in interpersonal situations, to inhibit anger, and to use nonaggressive alternatives in resolving interpersonal conflicts.

Multimodal intervention programs might use coordinated strategies to address parenting problems in the home, improve the youth's school performance and adjustment, and divert the youth from an antisocial peer group (Henggeler, Schoenwald, Rowland, & Cunningham, 2002; Hoge, 2001). The Multisystemic Therapy program developed in South Carolina is an example of this approach (Henggeler et al., 2002).

The first strategic developmental point for preventive intervention is at school entry. At this point in development,

> high-risk children need help in learning to control anger, in developing social-cognitive skills, and in generating more socially acceptable and effective alternatives to aggression and oppositional behavior. Many high-risk children need concentrated assistance in getting ready for the academic tasks of school. Their parents need to acquire more consistent, more positive, and less punitive discipline methods. Parents also need to learn how to provide support for their children's cognitive growth. Many parents need support in learning to relate to teachers and to provide support at home for the goals of the school for their children. Third, teachers may need help in preparing their classrooms for these high-risk children, especially classrooms with a high concentration of high-risk children. Finally, a case management

approach may be necessary to assist highly stressed and disorganized families in providing a more stable and supportive atmosphere for child rearing.

A second logical point for intervention is at the transition into middle school. High-risk children are clearly identifiable at this age. The key issues for these children seem to be the control of aggressive behavior, the acquisition and use of prosocial skills for integrating themselves into the mainstream peer culture, and concentrated assistance with academic skills. They may also profit from individual competency-enhancing experiences to maintain or restore self-esteem and positive affect. Parents of these preadolescents need to establish effective and nonpunitive disciplinary control of their children and to maintain or regain an active interest in their activities so that reasonable monitoring of adolescent behavior can occur. Furthermore, some effective partnership between parents and the schools must take place if the monitoring of homework, school attendance, and resistance to deviant peer group involvement is to take place. (Conduct Problems Prevention Research Group, 1992, p. 514, with changes in notation)

Juvenile offenders.   Interventions for children already in conflict with the law are of special concern. While a punitive strategy remains popular, punishment usually is not effective in reducing the incidence of reoffending (Andrews & Bonta, 1998; Lipsey & Wilson, 1998). Rather, the most effective programs for reducing the probability of recidivism emphasize an assessment and treatment of the needs of youth, including associated risk factors (Hoge, 2001; Hoge & Andrews, 1996; Lipsey & Wilson, 1998). Early prevention programs, particularly those directed toward high-risk youth, are also an effective means for reducing the onset of youthful criminal activity (Brewer, Hawkins, Catalano, & Neckerman, 1995). The Primary Mental Health Project (Cowen, Hightower, Pedro-Carroll, Work, Wyman, & Haffey, 1996) and the Anti-Bullying program (Olweus, 1991, 1994) are examples of successful early prevention programs.

The following is an example of a comprehensive strategy for addressing the problem of serious and violent juvenile offenders (Wilson & Howell, 1993):

1. Strengthen the family in its primary responsibility to instill moral values and provide guidance and support to children.
2. Support core social institutions (schools, religious institutions, and community organizations) in their roles in developing capable, mature, and responsible youth.
3. Promote delinquency prevention as the most cost-effective approach to dealing with juvenile delinquency. When children engage in acting-out behavior, the family and community, in concert with child welfare services, must take primary responsibility for responding with appropriate treatment and support services. Communities must take the lead in designing and building comprehensive prevention approaches that address known risk factors and target youth at risk of delinquency.
4. Intervene immediately and effectively when delinquent behavior occurs to prevent delinquent offenders from be-

coming chronic offenders or committing progressively more serious and violent crimes. Initial intervention attempts should be centered on the family and other core social institutions.
5. Identify and control the small group of serious, violent, and chronic juvenile offenders who have failed to respond to community-based treatment and rehabilitation services offered by the juvenile justice system.

Targeted school violence.   Schools should have policies and procedures in place to handle targeted school violence. The following guidelines are useful in establishing a threat management program (O'Toole, 2000):

1. *No threat should be ignored.* "Plausible or not, every threat must be taken seriously, investigated, and responded to. A clear, vigorous response is essential for three reasons: first and most important, to make sure that students, teachers, and staff *are* safe (that is, that a threat will not be carried out); second, to assure that they will *feel* safe; and third, to assure that the person making the threat will be supervised and given the treatment that is appropriate and necessary to avoid future danger to others or himself" (O'Toole, 2000, p. 25).
2. *Make sure that threat management policies are in writing and include clear guidelines about how to handle potentially violent situations.* The guidelines should include a safety plan in the event that a violent act occurs.
3. *Inform students and parents of school policies.* At the beginning of each year, the school should inform all students and parents about what is expected of them. Students should be told that they are expected to inform school authorities any time they know of a threat. Parents should be told that if their child makes a threat of any kind, they will be contacted and asked to provide information to evaluate the threat. When new students enter the school, they and their parents should be similarly informed.
4. *Designate a school threat assessment coordinator.* A threat assessment coordinator should be appointed at each school to oversee that school's response to threats. This individual should be knowledgeable about the school's policies on targeted school violence, be able to assess the seriousness of the threat of targeted violence (or refer to another member of the staff who has this skill), and be capable of working with law enforcement personnel. Whoever initially learns of a threat should refer the threat to the threat assessment coordinator. The threat assessment coordinator should (a) be given the authority to make decisions on how to respond to the threat, (b) establish a close working relationship with local law enforcement personnel, and (c) have several responsibilities, including developing a threat management system, maintaining consistency in the school's threat response procedures, arranging for an initial assessment to determine the level of threat, making a decision about what to do in case of an attack, arranging for an evaluation of the student or students who made the threat, monitoring all interventions, and acting as a liaison with outside experts.

5. *Form a multidisciplinary team.* The school should form a multidisciplinary team, including, at a minimum, the threat assessment coordinator, a law enforcement representative, and a school administrator. The team should regularly review the school's threat management program, consult with outside experts as needed, and provide recommendations and advice to the school administration.

6. *Evaluate the threat or the student's intent in each case.* Schools "should not deal with threats by simply kicking the problem out the door. Expelling or suspending a student for making a threat must not be a substitute for careful threat assessment and a considered policy of intervention. Disciplinary action alone, unaccompanied by any effort to evaluate the threat or the student's intent, may actually exacerbate the danger . . ." (O'Toole, 2000, p. 26). Because suspended or even expelled students eventually come back to school, it is important to be prepared for their reentry.

7. *Provide training to school administrators and staff in the fundamentals of threat assessment, adolescent development and violence, and other mental health issues.*

8. *Educate and sensitize students about cues indicating potential violence.* "Students are often in the best position to see and hear signs or cues of potential violence, and training should stress that ignoring those cues or remaining silent can be dangerous for themselves as well as others" (O'Toole, 2000, p. 32). Schools should strive to develop an atmosphere in which students feel free to report information to adults. Students need to understand and believe that everyone is responsible for safety in the school.

9. *Provide intervention services to the threatener.* Counseling should be offered to students who have made threats. For example, efforts should be directed to understanding why the student made the threat in the first place (e.g., uncovering unmet needs) and helping the student work through conflict areas.

To ensure a safe school environment, it may be necessary to use preventive strategies such as metal detectors and security guards. These strategies, however, may also have a negative impact on the school environment. Instead, it may be possible to achieve long-term positive benefits by implementing the following strategies, which focus on systemic changes in the school structure and environment:

1. Foster conditions that maintain high morale and strong commitment on the part of all staff members.
2. Decrease school and class size so that teachers and other school professionals have an opportunity to know their students.
3. Maintain contact and communication with parents.
4. Ensure that special services are available to address academic, social, and emotional problems of students.
5. Identify youths at high risk for antisocial behaviors and offer appropriate interventions.
6. Provide extracurricular activities for students, particularly for after school hours.

7. Teach conflict resolution skills to students and staff members.
8. Establish a firm policy regarding antisocial actions, but ensure that programming is available for suspended students, whether through special classes or special schools.

Assessing Antisocial Behavior Disorders

The three measures covered in this part of the chapter are useful in assessing antisocial behavior disorders, as are some of the broad-based personality tests and behavior checklists discussed in Chapter 10 (see Table 14-1). Two other measures

Table 14-1
Antisocial Dimensions and Factor Scores from Several Personality Tests and Behavior Checklists

Instrument	Dimensions or factor scores
Adolescent Psychopathology Scale	Conduct Disorder Oppositional Defiant Disorder Adjustment Disorder Anger Scale Aggression Scale
Behavior Assessment System for Children–Second Edition	Aggression Conduct Problems
Child Behavior Checklist, Teacher's Report Form, and Youth Self-Report	Social Problems Delinquent Behavior Aggressive Behavior
Conners' Rating Scales–Revised	Oppositional Conduct Problems Anger Control Problems
Devereux Scales of Mental Disorders	Conduct Problem Delinquency
Millon Adolescent Clinical Inventory	Delinquent Predisposition
Minnesota Multiphasic Personality Inventory–Adolescent	Psychopathic Deviate Anger Conduct Problems
Personality Inventory for Children–Second Edition	Delinquency
Personality Inventory for Youth	Delinquency
Student Behavior Survey	Verbal Aggression Physical Aggression Behavior Problems
Revised Behavior Problem Checklist	Conduct Disorder Socialized Aggression

Note: Instruments are described in Chapter 10.

provide information about antisocial behavior disorders, although they do not have a representative national sample. One is the How I Think Questionnaire (HITQ; Barriga, Gibbs, Potter, & Liau, 2001), which is a self-report measure for adolescents ages 12 to 18 years covering such areas as disrespect for rules, laws, or authorities; physical aggression; and lying and stealing. The other measure is the Youth Level of Service/ Case Management Inventory (YLS/CMI; Hoge, Andrews, & Leschied, 2002), which is a structured inventory for evaluating risk and need factors associated with criminal activity in adolescents ages 12 to 18 years. In addition, Table B-1 in Appendix B provides a semistructured interview that can be used for a child who may have an antisocial behavior disorder.

AGGRESSION QUESTIONNAIRE

The Aggression Questionnaire (AQ; Buss & Warren, 2000), a 34-item self-report measure assessing anger and aggression in children ages 9 years and older and in adults, is an updated version of the Buss-Durkee Hostility Inventory (Buss & Durkee, 1957). The AQ requires a third-grade reading level and takes about 10 minutes to complete. In addition to a total aggression score, it has five subscale scores (Physical Aggression, Verbal Aggression, Anger, Hostility, and Indirect Aggression) and a validity index (Inconsistent Responding).

Scores

The AQ uses a 5-point response scale: 1 (not at all like me), 2 (a little like me), 3 (somewhat like me), 4 (very much like me), 5 (completely like me). Raw scores are converted to T scores ($M = 50$, $SD = 10$) and percentile ranks.

Standardization

The standardization sample consisted of 2,138 individuals, ages 9 to 88 years. The manual states that the sample is generally representative of the U.S. population, particularly for children under the age of 19 years. Separate norms are presented by gender for ages 9 to 18 years.

Reliability

Internal consistency reliabilities for a sample of 2,038 children between ages 9 and 18 years range from .90 to .94 (Mdn $r_{xx} = .92$) for the total score and from .71 to .88 (Mdn $r_{xx} = .78$) for the five subscales. Test-retest reliabilities are reported for a small group of adults, but not for children.

Validity

Considerable evidence for the validity of the AQ is presented for both children and adults. Construct and criterion-related validities are supported by research showing that the total score correlates significantly with several other self-report and observer rating measures. However, construct validity is not robust, because the AQ does not reliably discriminate offenders from nonoffenders or predict violent actions.

Comment on the AQ

The AQ was developed on the basis of an explicit theory of aggression and represents the culmination of several years of research. Reliability and construct and criterion-related validity are satisfactory, but the instrument's test-retest reliability and predictive validity for children need to be investigated further, because no data are presented for these indices.

BECK DISRUPTIVE BEHAVIOR INVENTORY FOR YOUTH AND BECK ANGER INVENTORY FOR YOUTH

The Beck Disruptive Behavior Inventory for Youth (BDBI–Y) and the Beck Anger Inventory for Youth (BANI–Y; Beck, Beck, & Jolly, 2001) are two of the five instruments in the Beck Youth Inventories. (The others are the Beck Anxiety Inventory for Youth, Beck Depression Inventory for Youth, and Beck Self-Concept Inventory for Youth.) Each instrument is administered, scored, and interpreted separately; requires a second-grade reading level; and takes about 5 to 10 minutes to complete. Items on the BDBI–Y measure symptoms of conduct disorder and oppositional defiant disorder—aggression toward people and animals, destruction of property, deceitfulness or theft, serious violation of rules, arguing with and defying adults, deliberately annoying others, blaming others, being annoyed by others, and being spiteful and vindictive. Items on the BANI–Y measure affect and cognitions related to anger, including perceptions of mistreatment, negative thoughts about others, and feelings of anger.

Scores

Items on both measures use a 4-point response format: 0 (never), 1 (sometimes), 2 (often), 3 (always). Raw scores are converted to T scores ($M = 50$, $SD = 10$) and percentile ranks.

Standardization

The standardization sample for both measures consisted of the same 800 children (397 boys, 403 girls), ages 7 to 14 years. A stratified sampling procedure was used to ensure that the sample was representative of 1999 U.S. Census data with respect to race/ethnicity and education level. Approximately 200 children were included in each of four groups: females, ages 7 to 10 years and 11 to 14 years; males, ages 7 to 10 years and 11 to 14 years. Percentile ranks are also presented for a clinical sample of 107 children.

Reliability

Internal consistency reliabilities range from .86 to .90 (Mdn r_{xx} = .87) for the BDBI–Y and from .87 to .92 (Mdn r_{xx} = .90) for the BANI–Y. Test-retest reliabilities, based on 105 children over a 7-day period, range from .88 to .92 (Mdn r_{tt} = .89) for the BDBI–Y and from .74 to .87 (Mdn r_{tt} = .84) for the BANI–Y.

Validity

Validity is supported through significant correlations between the BDBI–Y and the BANI–Y and four scales from the Conners–Wells Adolescent Self-Report Scale: Short Form: conduct problems, cognitive problems, hyperactive-impulsive, and AD/HD index. Validity is also supported through analyses that indicated significantly lower BDBI–Y and BANI–Y scores for nonclinical samples than for clinical samples.

Comment on the BDBI–Y and the BANI–Y

The BDBI–Y and the BANI–Y are carefully developed measures with good reliability, validity, and standardization. The scales are easy to administer and score and are particularly useful in evaluating conduct disorder and oppositional defiant disorder.

ANXIETY DISORDERS

Fear, which is a natural response to stimuli perceived as threatening, has cognitive, affective, physiological, and behavioral components. Fear responses have an adaptive function in that they prepare the individual to confront potentially harmful situations. However, when fear responses are based on inaccurate or irrational appraisals of threats and when they interfere with a child's functioning, the responses constitute an *anxiety disorder.*

Diagnosis of Anxiety Disorders

DSM–IV–TR describes the following nine types of anxiety disorders (American Psychiatric Association, 2000):

1. *Separation anxiety disorder* is characterized by excessive anxiety concerning separation from the home or from those to whom the child is attached, anxiety beyond that expected for the child's developmental level, and anxiety that causes clinically significant distress or impairment in social, academic, occupational, or other important areas of functioning.

2. *Panic disorder* is characterized by a sudden onset of fear or terror triggered by a nonthreatening event. Symptoms include shortness of breath, heart palpitations, chest pain or discomfort, and a fear of losing control; a persistent concern about the consequences of the panic attack or having another panic attack is sometimes present.

3. *Agoraphobia* is characterized by anxiety about being in places or situations from which escape might be difficult or embarrassing.

4. *Specific phobia* is characterized by "clinically significant anxiety provoked by exposure to a specific feared object or situation, often leading to avoidance behavior" (p. 429).

5. *Social phobia* is characterized by "clinically significant anxiety provoked by exposure to certain types of social or performance situations, often leading to avoidance behavior" (p. 429).

6. *Obsessive-compulsive disorder* is characterized by "current obsessions or compulsions that are severe enough to be time consuming . . . or cause marked distress or significant impairment" (p. 456). *Obsessions* are persistent ideas or thoughts that an individual recognizes as irrational but can't get rid of. *Compulsions* are irrational and repetitive impulses to perform some act.

7. *Posttraumatic stress disorder (PTSD)* is characterized by "the reexperiencing of an extremely traumatic event accompanied by symptoms of increased arousal and by avoidance of stimuli associated with the trauma" (p. 429).

8. *Acute stress disorder* is characterized by symptoms similar to those of posttraumatic stress disorder and covers the period immediately following an extremely traumatic event.

9. *Generalized anxiety disorder* is characterized by "at least 6 months of persistent and excessive anxiety and worry" (p. 429).

From a developmental perspective, the major types of fears and anxiety during normal childhood development and the adult years are as follows (Reed, Carter, & Miller, 1992):

1. *Birth to 6 months:* fears of excessive or unexpected sensory stimuli, loss of support, and loud noises

2. *6 to 9 months:* fears of strangers and novel stimuli, such as masks and heights

3. *1 year:* fears of separation, injury, or toilets

4. *2 years:* fears of monsters, imaginary creatures, loss of a loved object or person, and robbers

5. *3 years:* fears of dogs, large animals, and being alone

6. *4 to 5 years:* fears of the dark, separation from parents, and abandonment

7. *6 to 12 years:* fears of school (including fears of taking tests and getting poor grades), injury, natural events, parental punishment, and rejection by peers

8. *13 to 18 years:* fears of injury (especially injuries that may disfigure the body), anxiety about feelings of social alienation and rejection, and fear of the macabre

9. *19 years and older:* fears of injury and natural events and anxiety about sexual issues (including personal adequacy,

sexually transmitted diseases, pregnancy, having a defective child, and abortion), economic issues, moral issues, and religious issues

Let's look at three of the nine types of anxiety disorders in more detail. We discuss separation anxiety disorder because it is most prominent in childhood, obsessive-compulsive disorder because its onset is usually between ages 6 and 15 years for males (but ages 20 to 29 years for females), and posttraumatic stress disorder because it can occur at any age. Other anxiety disorders also may begin in childhood, but because of space limitations they are not discussed further.

Separation anxiety disorder. Separation anxiety disorder refers to developmentally inappropriate and excessive anxiety concerning separation from home or from those to whom the child is attached. Symptoms of separation anxiety disorder include excessive distress about being harmed when separated from attachment figures, worry that something will happen to attachment figures, school refusal, reluctance to sleep alone or to sleep away from home without an attachment figure, repeated nightmares involving themes of separation, and physical complaints and signs of distress in anticipation of separation or at the time of separation (American Psychiatric Association, 2000). The prevalence of separation anxiety disorder is estimated to be about 4% in children and young adults (American Psychiatric Association, 2000). The onset of separation anxiety disorder typically occurs during the early and middle-school years and before adolescence; symptoms vary with age. Note that "separation anxiety is a normal developmental phenomenon from approximately age 7 months to the early preschool years" (Bernstein & Borchardt, 1991, p. 520).

Separation anxiety disorder "most often occurs following a major stressor, such as the start of school, death of a parent, or a move to a new school or neighborhood. . . . The onset of [separation anxiety disorder] has been tied to developmental transition periods, such as entering kindergarten or making the change from elementary school to junior high school" (Albano, Chorpita, & Barlow, 1996, p. 217). Note that school refusal is a symptom of several possible disorders, including separation anxiety disorder and social phobia.

Obsessive-compulsive disorder. Common *obsessions* among children primarily center on (a) dirt, germs, or environmental toxins and (b) concerns that something terrible is going to happen, such as a fire or the death or illness of oneself or a loved one (Rapoport, Swedo, & Leonard, 1992). Common *compulsions* primarily center on (a) excessive or ritualized handwashing, showering, bathing, toothbrushing, or grooming, (b) repeating rituals (such as going in or out of the door or getting up from or sitting down in a chair), (c) excessive checking (such as repeatedly checking doors, locks, stoves, appliances, emergency brakes on cars, and homework), and (d) miscellaneous rituals involving writing, moving, or speaking.

Posttraumatic stress disorder. Posttraumatic stress disorder (PTSD) is a clinical label for a traumatic reaction following any event or crisis involving actual or threatened death or serious injury, such as a natural or human-induced disaster, accident, suicide attempt, or violent crime involving child abuse (American Psychiatric Association, 2000; Eth, 1990). The traumatic reactions may affect children's cognitions, affect, and behavior. Even infants and toddlers may develop PTSD with symptoms similar to those of older children and adults, but with unique symptoms as well (see discussion below; Drell, Siegel, & Gaensbauer, 1993). *DSM-IV–TR* describes three phases of PTSD: (a) *acute,* if the duration of symptoms is less than 3 months, (b) *chronic,* if the duration of symptoms is 3 months or more, and (c) *delayed onset,* if the onset of symptoms is at least 6 months after the stressor.

Following are the symptoms associated with PTSD in children:

* *Reexperiencing the trauma* involves "recurrent, intrusive, and markedly dysphoric memories [*dysphoric* refers to an emotional state characterized by anxiety, depression, and restlessness] and dreams of the trauma . . . and traumatic play, which reenacts elements of the event in a repetitive, stereotyped, and joyless fashion" (Eth, 1990, p. 264).
* *Psychic numbing* is characterized by inability to remember parts of the event, erosion of interest in life, loss of interest in school, constricted affect, interpersonal detachment, pessimism about the future, and suppression of thoughts, feelings, and actions associated with the event (Eth, 1990).
* *Pathologic psychophysiologic arousal* includes disorganized or agitated behavior, regressive behavior (in young children, this may be seen in loss of acquired skills such as expressive language and toileting skills), irritability, hypervigilance, exaggerated startle reactions, poor concentration, sleep disturbances, and night terrors (American Psychiatric Association, 2000; Eth, 1990).
* *Interpersonal difficulties* may include feelings of humiliation, feelings of being singled out, inability to trust people, fearfulness of strangers, oversensitivity, and withdrawal (Dunne-Maxim, Dunne, & Hauser, 1987).

From a developmental standpoint, posttraumatic stress disorder has the following features (Eth, 1990, pp. 270–272, with changes in notation):

1. *Preschool children* may have changes in personality, play, and fears that reflect the traumatic event. They may be particularly helpless when confronted with great danger and become withdrawn, subdued, or even mute and prone to regression.
2. *School-age children* may exhibit a wider range of cognitive, behavioral, and emotional responses to psychic trauma than do preschool children. They may no longer be bound to the passive role of spectators but may become participants in the traumatic event, if only in fantasy. They may display a diversity of behavioral alterations in the af-

termath of trauma, ranging from actively confronting the traumatic event to withdrawal.

3. *Adolescents* may have symptoms that resemble those of adults, ranging from extremely agitated and disorganized states to withdrawal. Reactions to trauma can be life threatening to adolescents because of the combination of poor impulse control and bad judgment and access to automobiles and weapons.

Incidence of Anxiety Disorders

The overall prevalence rate for all anxiety disorders in children and adolescents is 2% to 9% (Anderson, 1994). Girls have higher rates of specific phobias and generalized anxiety disorder than boys. Children exhibiting an anxiety disorder in one area are likely to experience anxiety in other areas as well; nearly 50% of children exhibiting one anxiety disorder also display features of another anxiety disorder. For example, children with separation anxiety disorder often display specific phobias. Anxiety disorders often co-occur with conduct disorders, attention-deficit/hyperactivity disorders, or depression. About one-third to one-half of children with anxiety disorder also have a diagnosis of depression (Frick, Strauss, Lahey, & Christ, 1992). The incidence of obsessive-compulsive disorder in children is estimated at 1% to 2.3% (American Psychiatric Association, 2000).

Etiology of Anxiety Disorders

Biological theories explain the etiology of anxiety disorders by emphasizing the role of genetic factors in creating a vulnerability to maladaptive reactions to threatening situations or by locating the causes of the disorder in physiological or neurophysiological processes (e.g., a highly reactive autonomic nervous system; Herbert, 1994). Still other lines of research are focusing on the role of neurotransmitter substances such as benzodiazepines and on serotonin processes. Although ongoing research in this area is exciting, research findings are as yet inconclusive.

Psychoanalytic theory, learning theory, and psychosocial theory all offer psychological explanations of anxiety disorders (Herbert, 1994). Psychoanalytic theory emphasizes the breakdown of defense mechanisms in response to unacceptable thoughts or impulses. Learning theory explains anxiety reactions in terms of either (a) classical conditioning (whereby a fear response becomes conditioned to a previously neutral object or situation) or (b) cognitive schemas that interfere with rational interpretations of stimuli. Finally, psychosocial theory stresses the learning processes that occur through family and parenting dynamics (e.g., children learn maladaptive responses to stimuli by modeling the reactions of others in the environment, and such responses are then reinforced).

Treatment of Anxiety Disorders

Several methods of treating anxiety disorders are available (Albano, Causey, & Carter, 2001; Ollendick & King, 1998). Pharmacological treatments include the use of anti-anxiety and antidepressant medications. However, the efficacy of these medications for children is not well supported (Hagopian & Ollendick, 1993). Where used, medications should be combined with psychological therapies (American Academy of Child and Adolescent Psychiatry, 1997).

Behavior therapies such as systematic desensitization, flooding, contingency management, and modeling have been used successfully in treating anxiety disorders in children. Behavior therapies are based on learning theory and are designed to replace maladaptive anxiety responses to a precipitating stimulus with more functional reactions. Systematic desensitization, for example, involves exposing the child to gradually increasing levels of a fear-invoking stimulus while providing the child with a way to cope with his or her fear at each stage of exposure.

Cognitive behavioral therapies designed to alter the child's cognitions relating to a feared stimulus have also proven successful in the treatment of anxiety disorders. The child is taught to monitor cognitions and emotions associated with the stimulus and to cope with his or her reactions in a more competent manner. Techniques may involve self-talk, relaxation, and self-reinforcement.

When an anxiety disorder has developed in the family context, interventions may involve both the child and the parents. This may be required when the disorder was created by the parent, a parent's actions are somehow perpetuating the condition, and/or a parent has encouraged the child to become highly dependent on him or her. Even more generally, though, the involvement of parents in the treatment of anxiety disorders seems to enhance the effectiveness of treatment (Ollendick & King, 1998).

Although anxiety disorders present special challenges because they are often resistant to change, here are some helpful guidelines for parents:

1. Ensure that your child receives thorough psychological and medical examinations to identify the causes of anxiety, especially when the child shows irrational fears or obsessive/compulsive behaviors.
2. Cooperate fully with the therapeutic plan suggested by the professional and work closely with teachers and other school personnel as needed.
3. Be patient with your child. Coping with these disorders sometimes requires prolonged periods of treatment.
4. Monitor your own behavior, and especially look for anything in your relationship with your child that may reinforce or otherwise perpetuate your child's anxious behaviors.
5. When your child or members of your family confront a traumatic event, ensure that they receive appropriate supports and interventions.

Assessing Anxiety Disorders

We now cover a standardized measure for assessing anxiety. In addition, several personality tests and checklists described in Chapter 10 assess anxiety disorders; these tests and checklists are listed in Table 14-2. See Eth (2001) for more information about the assessment and treatment of children with PTSD. Finally, Table B-1 in Appendix B provides a semistructured interview for children who may have an anxiety disorder.

Table 14-2
Anxiety Symptom Dimensions and Factor Scores from Several Personality Tests and Behavior Checklists

Instrument	Dimensions or factor scores
Adolescent Psychopathology Scale	Panic Disorder Obsessive Compulsive Disorder Generalized Anxiety Disorder Social Phobia Separation Anxiety Disorder Posttraumatic Stress Disorder
Behavior Assessment System for Children–Second Edition	Anxiety
Child Behavior Checklist, Teacher's Report Form, and Youth Self-Report	Anxious/Depressed
Conners' Rating Scales–Revised	Anxious-Shy
Devereux Scales of Mental Disorders	Anxiety
Millon Adolescent Clinical Inventory	Anxious Feelings
Minnesota Multiphasic Personality Inventory–Adolescent	Anxiety Obsessiveness Social Discomfort
Personality Inventory for Children–Second Edition	Somatic Concern (Muscular Tension and Anxiety) Psychological Discomfort (Fear and Worry)
Personality Inventory for Youth	Somatic Concern (Muscular Tension and Anxiety) Psychological Discomfort (Fear and Worry)
Revised Behavior Problem Checklist	Anxiety-Withdrawal Motor Tension–Excess

Note: Instruments are described in Chapter 10.

BECK ANXIETY INVENTORY FOR YOUTH

The Beck Anxiety Inventory for Youth (BAI–Y), part of the Beck Youth Inventories, is a 20-item self-report measure designed to assess anxiety disorders in children ages 7 to 14 years (Beck et al., 2001). The BAI–Y yields a single score reflecting the severity of anxiety disorder. It requires a second-grade reading level and takes about 5 to 10 minutes to complete.

Scores

Items use a 4-point response format based on the presence of the symptom during the previous 2-week period: 0 (never), 1 (sometimes), 2 (often), 3 (always). Raw scores are converted to T scores ($M = 50$, $SD = 10$) and percentile ranks.

Standardization

The standardization group consisted of 800 children ages 7 to 14 years (397 boys, 403 girls). A stratified sampling procedure was used to ensure that the sample was representative of 1999 U.S. Census data with respect to race/ethnicity and education level. Approximately 200 children were included in each of four norm groups: females, ages 7 to 10 years and 11 to 14 years; males, ages 7 to 10 years and 11 to 14 years. Percentile ranks are also presented for a clinical sample of 107 children, ages 7 to 10 years (75 boys, 32 girls).

Reliability

Internal consistency reliabilities range from .89 to .91 (*Mdn* r_{xx} = .89). Test-retest reliabilities for 105 children, based on a median retest interval of 7 days, range from .64 to .88 (*Mdn* r_{tt} = .80).

Validity

The construct validity of the BAI–Y total score is supported by a significant correlation with the total score of the Revised Children's Manifest Anxiety Scale and by results showing that a sample of children in special education had significantly higher BAI–Y scores than did a nonclinical sample. However, a nonclinical sample was not significantly different from a psychiatric outpatient sample.

Comment on the BAI–Y

The BAI–Y is a carefully developed measure that has good reliability, but more information is needed about its validity. Norm groups have been carefully formed, and the scale is easy to administer and score. The instrument appears to be useful for screening for anxiety disorders in children.

DEPRESSIVE DISORDERS

Depression can refer to a symptom such as sad affect, a common experience of everyday life, or to a syndrome made up of a group of symptoms (Kazdin, 1990). Although fluctuations in emotional mood are normal in children and adults, elevated levels of depression, particularly if they persist over time, may seriously interfere with a youth's adjustment. *DSM-IV–TR* cites the following symptoms associated with a major depressive episode:

1. Irritable or depressed mood most of the day and nearly every day
2. Markedly diminished interest or pleasure in all or almost all activities most of the day and nearly every day
3. Failure to make expected weight gain, significant weight loss when not dieting, weight gain, or decrease or increase in appetite nearly every day
4. Insomnia or hypersomnia nearly every day
5. Psychomotor agitation or retardation nearly every day
6. Fatigue or loss of energy nearly every day
7. Feeling of worthlessness or excessive or inappropriate guilt nearly every day
8. Diminished ability to think or concentrate or indecisiveness nearly every day
9. Recurrent thoughts of death, recurrent suicidal ideation without a specific plan, or a suicide attempt or a specific plan for committing suicide

From a developmental perspective, symptoms of depression include the following (Edwards & Starr, 1996; Gotlib & Hammen, 1992; Kazdin, 1990; Kazdin & Marciano, 1998; Milling, 2001; Reynolds & Johnston, 1994; Schachter & Romano, 1993; Sheras, 2001):

1. *Infants and preschool children.* Although infants during the first year of life may not have "depression" in the clinical sense, they do experience depressive symptoms. These include sleep disturbances, increased clinging, aggressive behavior, crying, sadness, apprehension, decreased contact with parents or caregivers, stupor, loss of appetite, and refusal to eat.

2. *Children in middle childhood.* Besides the symptoms noted for infants, children between ages 6 and 12 years may show loss of weight, temper tantrums, concentration difficulties, and sleeplessness.

3. *Adolescents.* Besides the symptoms noted for infants and children in middle childhood, symptoms include loss of feelings of pleasure and interest, low self-esteem, excessive fatigue and loss of energy, inability to tolerate routines, over-involvement with pets, aggressive behavior, somatic complaints, restlessness, loneliness, irritability, running away, stealing, guilt feelings, feelings of worthlessness, weight loss or gain, and suicidal preoccupations.

Because many of these symptoms occur in children who are developing normally, a depressive disorder should be considered primarily when the symptoms reflect a change in a child's behavior maintained over time and are detrimental to the child's functioning. Additionally, children may have psychotic depression or melancholic depression, both of which are subtypes of the kind of depression found in adults. Children initially diagnosed as depressed sometimes develop a bipolar reaction—that is, both depression and mania (Gotlib & Hammen, 1992).

Depressive disorders in children often coexist with other disorders (Gotlib & Hammen, 1992; Sheras, 2001), including conduct or oppositional defiant disorders, anxiety disorders, and, less often, attention-deficit/hyperactivity disorder. In older children, depressive disorders often coexist with eating disorders or with drug or alcohol abuse. Children with depressive disorders frequently have academic difficulties and low achievement in school, as well as interpersonal difficulties, particularly with their parents. Depression, then, often disrupts children's cognitive, academic, and interpersonal functioning.

Incidence of Depressive Disorders

Estimates of the incidence of depressive disorders vary with the diagnostic criteria and the measures used. Estimates for major depressive disorders in adolescents (12 to 19 years) vary from 5% to 28% (Sheras, 2001). Occurrence rates are higher for girls than for boys.

Etiology of Depressive Disorders

The etiology of depression is uncertain, but both biological and psychosocial theories have merit (Kazdin, 1990; Milling, 2001; Sheras, 2001). Biological theories point to deficits in or imbalance of neurotransmittors (substances found in the brain) and genetic transmission (e.g., a family history of depression). Psychosocial theories propose that depression results from limited rewards or life satisfactions, parental resentment or rejection of the child, deficits in self-regulatory skills for coping with stress, negative thinking about oneself, failure of one's behavior to influence events in one's life, deficits in interpersonal problem-solving skills, and reactions to major and minor forms of stress (e.g., illness, death of a parent, minor daily hassles, remarriage of a parent, child maltreatment, and pregnancy). Furthermore, psychosocial theories focusing on cognitive processes postulate that cognitive schemas distort perceptions of reality and that it is these distortions that underlie depressive episodes (Abramson, Metalsky, & Alloy, 1989; Beck, Rush, Shaw, & Emery, 1979). For example, a tendency to overemphasize the importance of negative events may contribute to a general attitude of hopelessness, which, in turn, creates a depressive mood.

Treatment of Depressive Disorders

Psychopharmacological approaches to the treatment of depression include medications such as imipramine, nortriptyline, and amitriptyline. Imipramine is the most popular antidepressant because its use with children has been approved by the U.S. Food and Drug Administration (for the treatment of enuresis). The efficacy of psychopharmacological treatments with children has not been well established (Milling, 2001; Sheras, 2001), and there is an increased risk of suicidal thinking and behavior with the use of these agents (U.S. Food and Drug Administration, 2004).

Useful psychological interventions include cognitive-behavior modification (e.g., self-monitoring, cognitive restructuring, and attribution retraining) and psychodynamic therapies (e.g., play therapy). Drug treatments may be combined with psychological interventions.

The following suggestions may be helpful for parents of a child with a depressive disorder (Oster & Montgomery, 1995):

1. Treat your child as you normally would.
2. Encourage your child to share her or his thoughts and feelings.
3. Show that you care about and value your child.
4. Share with your child unpleasant experiences that you had that ended positively, to provide a basis for hope.
5. Offer your child praise and compliments.
6. Do not criticize or blame your child for her or his bad feelings.
7. Acknowledge your child's pain and suffering. It is easy to become impatient and angry with someone who is depressed. Make it clear that you are genuinely concerned about her or his feelings.
8. Take seriously any talk or threats of suicide that your child makes or any attempts that your child makes to hurt herself or himself.

Interventions will be complicated if the parents also are depressed or have other forms of psychological disturbance (Reynolds, 1992). Depressed parents, for example, may reinforce their children's depressive cognitions and behaviors.

Assessing Depressive Disorders

We now review three behaviorally based checklists designed to be completed by a child or by a knowledgeable informant (e.g., parent, teacher, clinician). In addition, some of the broad-based behavioral checklists and projective techniques discussed in Chapter 10 may be useful is assessing depression (see Table 14-3 for a list of these behavioral checklists). Finally, Table B-3 in Appendix B provides a semistructured interview for children who may have a depressive disorder.

BECK DEPRESSION INVENTORY FOR YOUTH

The Beck Depression Inventory for Youth (BDI–Y), part of the Beck Youth Inventories (Beck et al., 2001), is a 20-item self-report measure based on *DSM-IV* symptoms. It is designed to provide an index of depressive disorder independent

Table 14-3
Depressive Symptom Dimensions and Factor Scores from Several Personality Tests and Behavior Checklists

Instrument	Dimensions or factor scores
Adolescent Psychopathology Scale	Major Depression Dysthymic Disorder
Behavior Assessment System for Children–Second Edition	Depression
Child Behavior Checklist, Teacher's Report Form, and Youth Self-Report	Anxious/Depressed
Conners' Rating Scales–Revised	Emotional Lability
Devereux Scales of Mental Disorders	Depression
Millon Adolescent Clinical Inventory	Depressive Affect
Minnesota Multiphasic Personality Inventory–Adolescent	Depression
Personality Inventory for Children–Second Edition	Psychological Discomfort (Depression)
Personality Inventory for Youth	Psychological Discomfort (Depression)
Student Behavior Survey	Emotional Distress
Revised Behavior Problem Checklist	Emotional Distress

Note: Instruments are described in Chapter 10.

of other diagnoses, including anxiety, for children ages 7 to 14 years. The instrument yields a single score reflecting the severity of depressive disorder, requires a second-grade reading level, and takes about 5 to 10 minutes to complete.

Scores

Items use a 4-point response format based on the presence of the symptom during the previous 2-week period: 0 (never), 1 (sometimes), 2 (often), 3 (always). Raw scores are converted to T scores ($M = 50$, $SD = 10$) and percentile ranks.

Standardization

The standardization group consisted of 800 children (403 girls and 397 boys), ages 7 to 14 years. A stratified sampling procedure was used to ensure that the sample was representative of 1999 U.S. Census data with respect to race/ethnicity and educational level. Approximately 200 children were in four groups: females, ages 7 to 10 years and 11 to 14 years; males, ages 7 to 10 years and 11 to 14 years. Norms are also provided for a clinical sample of 107 children drawn from outpatient mental health services.

Reliability

Internal consistency reliabilities range from .90 to .92 (*Mdn r_{xx}* = .91). Test-retest reliabilities for 105 children over a median retest interval of 7 days range from .79 to .92 (*Mdn r_{tt}* = .87).

Validity

The construct validity of the BDI–Y is supported by significant correlations with the Total Scale, Negative Mood, and Negative Self-Esteem scores from the Children's Depression Inventory and through analyses showing that a sample of children in special education had higher scores than children in regular classes. However, scores did not significantly differentiate between a psychiatric outpatient clinic sample and a normal sample.

Comment on the BDI–Y

The BDI–Y is a carefully developed measure showing good reliability and minimally adequate construct validity. It has a satisfactory norm group, is easy to administer and score, and may be useful for screening symptoms of depression in children.

CHILDREN'S DEPRESSION INVENTORY AND CHILDREN'S DEPRESSION INVENTORY–SHORT FORM

The Children's Depression Inventory (CDI; Kovacs, 2001) is a 27-item self-report measure designed to assess cognitive, affective, and behavioral symptoms of depression in children ages 7 to 17 years. The Children's Depression Inventory–Short Form (CDI–S; Kovacs, 2001) is a 10-item version of the CDI. The CDI has five scales: Negative Mood, Interpersonal Problems, Ineffectiveness, Anhedonia (impaired ability to experience pleasure), and Negative Self-Esteem. The CDI–S has no individual scales. Both measures require a first-grade reading level. It takes about 15 minutes to complete the CDI and under 10 minutes to complete the CDI–S.

Scores

On each item of the CDI and the CDI–S, the child selects one of three statements that best reflects his or her depressive symptoms (e.g., "I do not feel alone," "I feel alone many times," "I feel alone all the time"). The statements are keyed 0, 1, 2, with higher scores indicating increasing severity. A scoring template is provided, and computer-based scoring

and interpretation programs are available. Raw scores are converted to *T* scores (*M* = 50, *SD* = 10) and percentile ranks.

Standardization

The standardization sample consisted of 1,266 Florida public school students (592 boys, 674 girls), ages 7 to 17 years, who were administered the test in the 1980s, as far as we can determine. The ethnic composition was 77% Euro American and 23% African American, Native American, and Hispanic American. No other information is provided about the standardization sample. Norms are provided separately by gender and for two age groups: 7 to 12 years and 13 to 17 years.

Reliability

The internal consistency reliability of the total CDI is r_{xx} = .86, and the internal consistency reliabilities for the five scales range from .59 to .68 (*Mdn r_{xx}* = .63). The internal consistency reliability for the CDI–S is r_{xx} =. 80. Test-retest reliabilities are not reported in the manual.

Validity

Support for the construct validity of the CDI and the CDI–S is mixed, but generally adequate. Because factor analysis indicates that a single factor accounts for most of the variance, there is little support for the construct validity of the five scales. The ability of the CDI and the CDI–S to discriminate among clinical groups, based on the severity and nature of the depressive disorder, and between clinical and normal groups is equivocal, with some comparisons being significant and others not. However, criterion validity is satisfactory, as noted by significant correlations between the CDI and measures of depression, self-esteem, and social adjustment. The CDI is also sensitive to treatment effects.

Comment on the CDI and the CDI–S

The CDI is a carefully developed measure of depression that has attracted considerable research attention. It is easy to administer and score, and it has satisfactory reliability for the total score and inadequate internal consistency reliability for the scales. The norms are not based on a national sample and are outdated, and no test-retest reliabilities are reported. Construct and criterion-related validity receive mixed support. Both the CDI and CDI–S should be used with caution.

REYNOLDS CHILD DEPRESSION SCALE AND REYNOLDS ADOLESCENT DEPRESSION SCALE–SECOND EDITION

The Reynolds Child Depression Scale (RCDS; Reynolds, 1989) and the Reynolds Adolescent Depression Scale–Second

Edition (RADS–2; Reynolds, 2002) are companion scales for measuring depressive symptoms in children. The RCDS is designed for children ages 8 to 12 years. Items are presented orally to children under age 10 years and in written form to children over age 10 years. The RADS–2 is used with children ages 11 to 20 years and requires a third-grade reading level. Both scales contain 30 items, yield a total score indicating overall level of depression, and with four exceptions have the same items. The RADS–2 also has four subscales reflecting underlying dimensions of adolescent depression: Dysphoric Mood, Anhedonia/Negative Affect, Negative Self-Evaluation, and Somatic Complaints. The RADS–2 takes about 5 to 10 minutes to complete; the RCDS takes about 10 minutes to complete.

Scores

Items on both scales use a 4-point scale—1 (almost never), 2 (sometimes), 3 (a lot of the time), 4 (all the time)—with the exception of one item on the RCDS that uses a response format with five faces displaying a range of emotions. Raw scores for the RCDS are expressed as percentile ranks and may be computed separately for girls and boys. The total score and subscale scores for the RADS–2 are expressed as T scores ($M = 50$, $SD = 10$) and percentile ranks. Norms for the RADS–2 are provided for the total sample and by gender and age group (11 to 13 years, 14 to 16 years, 17 to 20 years). Scoring templates are provided for both scales, and computer scoring is available for the RADS–2.

Standardization

The standardization group for the RCDS consisted of 1,620 children (751 boys, 842 girls). Although the sample is not completely representative of 2000 U.S. Census data, its ethnic and socioeconomic composition is satisfactory. The RADS–2 was standardized on 3,300 adolescents (1,650 boys, 1,650 girls) and was generally representative of 2000 U.S. Census data.

Reliability

The internal consistency reliability for the total group is $r_{xx} = .90$ for the RCDS. Similar internal consistency values were obtained for age, gender, and ethnic group. A test-retest reliability coefficient of $r_{tt} = .82$ was reported over a 2-week interval for a sample of 24 children. Reliability coefficients for a sample of 220 children tested over a 4-week interval range from .81 to .92 (Mdn $r_{tt} = .85$).

The internal consistency reliability for the total group is $r_{xx} = .92$ for the RADS–2. For the four subscales, internal consistency reliabilities range from .80 to .87 (Mdn $r_{xx} = .86$). Similar internal consistency reliability coefficients were obtained for gender and age level for the total group and sub-

scales. Test-retest stability over a 2-week interval for a nonclinical sample of 1,750 children was $r_{tt} = .85$ for the RADS–2 total score and ranged from .77 to .84 (Mdn $r_{tt} = .82$) for the subscales.

Validity

The RCDS has satisfactory construct, criterion-related, and treatment validity. For example, the total score's significant relationship to the Children's Depression Inventory and to the Children's Depression Rating Scale–Revised supports construct validity. Criterion-related validity is supported by acceptable correlations with measures of anxiety, self-esteem, and academic achievement.

The RADS–2 also has satisfactory construct validity, as noted by significant correlations of the total score and four subscale scores with parallel self-report and interview measures of depression. In addition, factor analyses support the construct validity of the four subscales. Finally, the total score and the clinical cutoff score distinguish normal and clinical groups.

Comment on the RCDS and the RADS–2

Both the RCDS and the RADS–2 are carefully developed instruments with adequate reliability and validity, although a more fully representative sample would be preferred for the RCDS. Both measures may be useful as screening tools in the identification of children with a depressive disorder.

SUICIDE RISK

The suicide of a child is one of the most devastating events that a family can experience. Emotions associated with the suicide of a child are often complicated by feelings of guilt for not recognizing warning signs and preventing the tragedy. However, the causes of suicide and suicide attempts (*parasuicide*) are often complex and difficult to detect, and this complicates assessing *suicide risk*. Although suicide and depression are often related, they also can occur separately.

Diagnosis of Suicide Risk

The situational and psychological factors associated with suicide and parasuicide are listed on the checklist in Table 14-4. However, those who complete suicide may exhibit a different constellation of factors from those who attempt suicide but do not complete it (Goldman & Beardslee, 1999; Sheras, 2001). For example, individuals who attempt suicide but who do not complete it are more likely to be female, to be teenage parents, and to have made previous suicide attempts than are those who complete suicide attempts. Suicide completers, on the other hand, are more likely to be male and to suffer from

Table 14-4
Checklist for Risk Factors for Child or Adolescent Suicide

Historical-Situational Risk Factors

☐ 1. Chronic and debilitating illness
☐ 2. Chronic preoccupation with death and related themes
☐ 3. Fantasies about being immune to death
☐ 4. Romanticizing and glorifying death
☐ 5. Inadequate coping mechanisms
☐ 6. Repeated failures in school
☐ 7. Family pressures to achieve
☐ 8. Poor peer relations
☐ 9. Dysfunctional family (including severe marital discord) and/or parents with severe emotional distress (e.g., psychosis, suicidality, chronic depression)
☐ 10. Severe life stressor (e.g., death of a family member or friend, parental divorce, termination of a significant relationship, family economic hardship, suspension from school, being forced to leave home, failure to get into college)
☐ 11. Physical, emotional, or sexual abuse or neglect
☐ 12. Family history of suicide
☐ 13. Engaging in deliberately dangerous behaviors
☐ 14. Previous suicide attempts
☐ 15. Peer suicides
☐ 16. Awareness of media attention given to suicide

Psychological Risk Factors

☐ 17. Depression (including flat affect, loss of interest in everyday activities, limited energy, feelings of sadness, worry, poor attention and concentration, difficulty sleeping, excessive feelings of guilt, excessive crying, changes in appetite or weight)
☐ 18. Feelings of hopelessness (e.g., saying he or she wants to die)
☐ 19. Feelings of helplessness
☐ 20. Feelings of not being in control of his or her life
☐ 21. Severe anxiety, tension, or irritability
☐ 22. Low self-esteem and poor self-image
☐ 23. Psychosis (especially mood disorders)
☐ 24. Changes in temperament and behavior (e.g., sudden displays of disruptive behavior and abrupt changes in school performance and attendance)
☐ 25. Eating disorders (e.g., bulimia nervosa or anorexia nervosa)
☐ 26. Substance abuse (including alcohol and drug abuse)
☐ 27. Withdrawal from family and friends
☐ 28. Suicidal plan[a]
☐ 29. Final arrangements (e.g., saying goodbye with finality, giving away favored possessions, putting affairs in order, appearing unusually calm and contented)

[a] A suicidal plan would consider availability and lethality of means of suicide and would suggest intent. The most common means, in decreasing order of lethality, are gunshot, carbon monoxide, hanging, drowning, suffocation with plastic bag, impact associated with jumping from a high place, fire, poison, drugs, gas, and cutting wrists.
Source: Adapted from DeSpelder and Strickland (1992) and Fremouw, De Perczel, and Ellis (1990).

depressive and substance abuse disorders. Self-mutilation, more common in females than in males, is often associated with parasuicide.

Incidence of Suicide and Parasuicide

In 2002, suicide was the third leading cause of death for youths ages 15 to 19 years, with a rate of 7.4 per 100,000 (Child Trends Data Bank, 2003a, b). This figure represents a decline of about 4% since 1994, when the rate was 11.1 per 100,000. The suicide rate for male youths was about 5 times higher than for female youths (12.2 per 100,000 vs. 2.4 per 100,000). American Indian male youths had the highest rate (22.7 per 100,000) followed by Euro American male youths (13.4 per 100,000), Hispanic American male youths (9.1 per 100,000), African American male youths (6.9 per 100,000), and Asian American male youths (5.7 per 100,000). Suicide by firearms was the most common method.

Estimating the incidence of attempted suicides is more difficult, because many attempts never come to the attention of mental health practitioners. However, we can assume that the number of parasuicides exceeds the number of completed attempts. In 2003, 17% of youths ages 15 to 19 years thought seriously about committing suicide, with the percentage of female youths more than twice as high as male youths (12% vs. 5%, respectively). There is considerable variability in the severity of the means used to attempt suicide, ranging from the consumption of nonlethal doses of medicines to use of a weapon.

Treatment to Diminish Suicide Risk

The treatments for children with depressive disorder covered previously in the chapter also may be appropriate for youths who are at risk for suicide. Where suicide risk is acute, hospitalization and medication may be indicated until the acute phase has passed. Because youths in correctional custody settings are at particular risk for suicide, careful assessment of their risk level is needed. They also should be placed in a protective environment until the risk has been reduced.

Parents who suspect that their child may be contemplating suicide may benefit from the following advice (Suicide Awareness Voices of Education, 2003, p. 3, with changes in notation):

1. Educate yourself on childhood and adolescent depressive illnesses and suicide.
2. Tell your child that he or she will feel better, that suicidal thoughts are only temporary, and that there are people who want to help him or her.
3. Always take suicide threats seriously and respond immediately by notifying a knowledgeable professional.
4. Know that early intervention is the key to successful treatment for children who suffer from depressive illnesses.

Assessing Suicide Risk

Assessments of suicide risk should explore the seriousness of the threat, the nature of suicidal ideations associated with the threat, and the motivating or precipitating factors associated with the threat. Table B-4 in Appendix B provides a semi-structured interview for an older child or adolescent who may be suicidal. The behavioral rating checklists described earlier for depressive disorders are also useful in assessing suicide risk.

SUBSTANCE ABUSE DISORDERS

Use of alcohol and other drugs is generally not a problem among children younger than 10 years of age, but may be during the adolescent years. The use of these substances by children not only is illegal, but also may be associated with risky behaviors such as careless use of automobiles, sexual assaults (e.g., date rapes), and other illegal activities (American Psychiatric Association, 2000). When excessive, drug use may lead to impairments in health, school work, employment, and social relationships. Finally, a physical or psychological dependence on a substance may develop and be linked with addiction problems in later life, although occasional use of these substances does not necessarily constitute abuse (Brown, Aarons, & Abrantes, 2001).

Diagnosis of Substance Abuse Disorders

DSM-IV–TR recognizes a distinction between substance abuse and substance dependence. *Substance abuse* applies to cases in which the use of alcohol or other drugs is associated with impairment in emotional or behavioral functioning but with no signs of substance dependence. *Substance dependence* is defined as cognitive, behavioral, and physiological symptoms indicating that an individual continues use of the substance despite significant substance-related problems. Symptoms are described for specific diagnostic categories (e.g., alcohol use disorders, cannabis-related disorders, inhalant-related disorders). However, the symptoms in *DSM-IV–TR* are presented for adults and consequently may not be relevant for adolescents. Conditions co-occurring with substance abuse include conduct disorder, oppositional defiant disorder, and depressive disorder. More research is needed on the diagnosis and development of substance abuse and dependence disorders in children (Martin & Winters, 1998).

The major substances implicated in substance abuse and substance dependence include alcohol, sedative-hypnotics (e.g., Quaalude), stimulants (e.g., cocaine), marijuana, opiates (e.g., heroin), hallucinogens (e.g., LSD), and inhalants (e.g., gasoline). The following have been identified as indicators of drug use in children (Brown et al., 2001, p. 763, with changes in notation):

PHYSICAL CHANGES

1. Bloodshot eyes; extremely large or small pupils; watery eyes, with blank stares or nystagmus (involuntary oscillation of eyeball)
2. Deterioration in physical appearance, rapid weight loss, unexplained injury (e.g., cuts, bruises), unusual breath or body odors

EMOTIONAL CHANGES

1. Extremes of energy and lethargy, insomnia and excessive sleep or fatigue, dramatic appetite fluctuation
2. Marked or rapid changes in school grades, social activities, or peer groups; irresponsibility with money
3. Clinically significant levels of depression or anxiety

HEALTH CHANGES

1. Chronic coughing, sniffing, black phlegm
2. Evidence of intravenous drug use (needle tracks) or inhalation (perforated nasal septum)
3. Skin boils or sores; nasal bleeding

Incidence of Substance Abuse Disorders

Table 14-5 summarizes some of the data reported by the *Monitoring the Future* survey, which is an annual national survey sponsored by the National Institute on Drug Abuse and conducted by the University of Michigan (Johnston, O'Malley, Bachman, & Schulenberg, 2005). The table shows the proportion of 8th, 10th, and 12th grade students who used drugs or alcohol and who had been drunk in the prior 12 months and the proportion of students who tried drugs or alcohol sometime during their lifetime. The table shows data only for drugs or alcohol used by at least 10% of the students in one or more of the three grades in the prior 12 months. Highlights of the table are that at least 15% of 8th grade students, 31% of 10th grade students, and 39% of 12th grade students used an illicit drug in 2004. Alcohol is the most frequent substance used by adolescents in 2004 or tried sometime in their lifetime and 52% of 12th grade students had been drunk in 2004. Drug and alcohol use shows dramatic increases from 8th to 12th grades. For example, the proportion of 12th graders using any type of drug was 2.5 times greater than that of 8th graders. Similarly, the use of alcohol by 12th graders was about 2 times greater than that of 8th graders. Similar increases are also evident for the other drugs shown in Table 14-5.

In another survey conducted in 2003 (Substance Abuse and Mental Health Service Administration, 2004), youths age 12 to 17 years who perceived that their parents would strongly disapprove of their trying marijuana or hashish were about 5 times less likely to have tried these substances in the past month (5.4% tried) than youths whose parents would not strongly disapprove (28.7% tried). In addition, the majority of youths indicated that their parents would strongly disapprove of their use of marijuana during the past month (about 90% disapproval).

Table 14-5
Drug and Alcohol Use by Adolescents in 2004 and in Their Lifetime

Use	Past Year			Lifetime[a]		
	8th grade	10th grade	12th grade	8th grade	10th grade	12th grade
Any illicit drug	15%	31%	39%	22%	40%	51%
Marijuana/hashish	12%	27%	34%	16%	35%	46%
Amphetamines	5%	8%	10%	8%	12%	15%
Alcohol	37%	58%	71%	44%	64%	77%
Flavored alcoholic beverage	—	—	56%	—	—	—
Been drunk	14%	35%	52%	20%	42%	60%

[a]"Lifetime" refers to the proportion of students who tried drugs or alcohol sometime during their lifetime.
Source: Johnston et al. (2005).

Etiology of Substance Abuse Disorders

Biological theories stress the role of genetic factors in affecting temperamental factors and physiological mechanisms that are, in turn, linked with substance abuse. For example, some individuals may have a genetic predisposition to develop an addiction to alcohol. Behavioral theories explain addictions in terms of learning theory principles that emphasize the reinforcement value of the substance. Family system theories locate the causes of addiction in family dynamics, stressing the role of parental modeling, supervision, and family conflicts. Sociological theories emphasize the relationship of socioeconomic status and cultural norms to substance abuse. Finally, the multiple risk models of substance abuse disorders focus on a broad range of interacting biological, psychological, and social factors as determinants of abuse (Petraitis, Flay, & Miller, 1995).

Treatment of Substance Abuse Disorders

Primary prevention programs teach children about the risks associated with substance use and provide skills for resisting drug and alcohol experimentation. While these programs offer some potential for a long-term solution to the problem of substance abuse, their efficacy has not yet been established (Brown et al., 2001).

Psychological treatments of substance abuse disorders focus on resolution of emotional problems linked with the abuse, on skill development, and on cognitive modification (Jenson, Howard, & Yaffee, 1995). Self-help programs popular with adults—such as Alcoholics Anonymous—are often used with adolescents. Multimodal treatments may employ several therapeutic techniques that address a range of problems associated with the abuse. Long-term residential treatment programs emphasizing group therapy (e.g., the Therapeutic Community Program; Graham & Wexler, 1997) make use of this approach. Unfortunately, the failure rate in the treatment of childhood substance abuse is generally high, and research supporting the efficacy of any specific treatment modality for children is scant (Brown et al., 2001).

Interventions should focus on a youth's broad social environment, because substance abuse often relates to family dynamics and usually occurs within a peer group. Since relapse is common among adolescents with a substance abuse disorder, interventions need to continue for as long as risk of relapse exists.

You can help parents in dealing with their child's use of alcohol or other drugs by providing them with the following suggestions:

1. Maintain good communication with your child.
2. Insist on meeting your child's friends and becoming acquainted with them.
3. Set clear rules about curfew in cooperation with your child and enforce the rules consistently.
4. Set clear rules for your child about attendance at parties, including those held at your home and elsewhere.
5. Be alert to signs of alcohol and drug use (see guidelines described earlier in this chapter).
6. Seek immediate professional help for your child when he or she shows indications of substance abuse.
7. Cooperate fully with any treatment program. Remember that relapse is common, and be prepared to respond to any relapses by continuing treatment.
8. Monitor your own use of alcohol and other drugs; remember, you are an important role model for your child.

Assessing Substance Abuse Disorders

The assessment of substance abuse disorders involves determining the extent and nature of the substance abuse. We recommend a broad approach to assessment, because substance abuse has complex causes and affects many aspects of a youth's functioning (Brown et al., 2001).

1. Initially focus on issues the adolescent is most concerned about, including problem behaviors and current difficulties.
2. Inquire about substance use.
3. Find out when symptoms and problem behaviors started and construct a time line.
4. Gather information from a parent (or other caregiver) about the child's sequence of difficulties, symptoms, and drug use.
5. Use biochemical verification to evaluate drug use (e.g., toxicology screen of blood, urine, hair samples).
6. Assess symptoms on several occasions to determine symptom stability.

Three semistructured interviews in Appendix B can assist you in evaluating adolescents with substance abuse problems. Table B-1 covers general areas of development, Table B-5 focuses on problems with alcohol, and Table B-6 focuses on drug abuse problems.

THINKING THROUGH THE ISSUES

1. What are some diagnostic issues associated with the disorders discussed in this chapter?
2. Are there any elements common to the treatment of the disorders discussed in this chapter?
3. Where are the greatest areas of need in the development of assessments for the disorders discussed in the chapter?

SUMMARY

Antisocial Behavior Disorders

1. Antisocial behavior disorders (or externalizing or disruptive behavior disorders) are characterized by behaviors that violate social norms and seriously impair a child's functioning in the home, community, and school.
2. The two DSM-IV–TR diagnostic categories covering antisocial behavior disorders are conduct disorder and oppositional defiant disorder.
3. Children with a conduct disorder have a pattern of antisocial behavior, rule breaking, or aggressive behavior. The condition represents "a repetitive and persistent pattern of behavior in which the basic rights of others or major age-appropriate societal norms or rules are violated" (American Psychiatric Association, 2000, p. 93).
4. The types of behaviors that are associated with conduct disorders are aggressive conduct that causes or threatens physical harm to other people or animals, nonaggressive conduct that causes property loss or damage, deceitfulness or theft, and serious violation of rules.

5. Childhood-onset disorder (before age 10 years) is generally regarded as having a poorer prognosis than adolescent-onset disorder (after age 10 years), because it is likely to be more persistent and to develop into adult antisocial personality disorder.
6. Conduct disorder is more common in males than in females.
7. Children with an oppositional defiant disorder have a recurrent pattern of negativistic, defiant, disobedient, and hostile behavior toward authority figures.
8. Oppositional defiant disorder is more prevalent in males than females during early childhood, but rates become more equal after puberty.
9. The symptoms of oppositional defiant disorder usually appear between ages 3 and 8 years, whereas the symptoms of conduct disorder typically appear between ages 8 and 13 years.
10. Because antisocial behaviors are defined as behaviors that violate social norms, contextual variations in those norms may affect the diagnosis.
11. Levels of oppositional defiant behaviors considered dysfunctional in some home or school settings might not be considered problematic by parents or teachers with a more accommodating attitude.
12. DSM-IV–TR estimates that rates of conduct disorder range from 6% to 16% for males and from 2% to 9% for females.
13. Estimates of the rate of oppositional defiant disorder are between 2% and 16%.
14. Conduct and oppositional disorders often co-occur with attention-deficit/hyperactivity disorder.
15. The commission of a crime constitutes an important form of antisocial behavior.
16. Violent aggressive acts such as assaults or murder constitute a special category of antisocial behaviors.
17. In 2003, 5% of students ages 12 to 18 years reported being the victim of some type of nonfatal crime while in school and 1% reported being the victim of a violent incident.
18. Biological, behavioral, and familial factors have been proposed to account for the development of conduct disorder; however, there is no firm evidence to support any one etiological theory.
19. From birth to 24 months, infants who later develop a conduct disorder may be neglected by caregivers who are indifferent to them and who fail to comfort them.
20. When there is a coercive caregiver-child relationship, the caregiver may provide only low levels of stimulation and support, so the child fails to develop needed emotional control, social skills, and academic readiness.
21. Between 6 and 12 years of age, children who develop a conduct disorder may show deficiencies in critical social-cognitive skills.
22. Children with conduct disorder are difficult to treat. Treatment approaches include the use of pharmacological agents, behavioral approaches, parent-training approaches, cognitive-behavioral approaches, and multimodal approaches.
23. Interventions for children already in conflict with the law are of special concern. While a punitive strategy remains popular, punishment usually is not effective in reducing the incidence of reoffending.
24. The most effective programs for reducing the probability of recidivism emphasize an assessment of the needs of youth, including associated risk factors.
25. Schools should have policies and procedures in place to handle targeted school violence.

26. To ensure a safe school environment, it may be necessary to use preventive strategies such as metal detectors and security guards. These strategies, however, may also have a negative impact on the school environment.

Aggression Questionnaire

27. The AQ, a 34-item self-report measure assessing anger and aggression in children ages 9 years and older and in adults, is an updated version of the Buss-Durkee Hostility Inventory. The AQ requires a third-grade reading level and takes about 10 minutes to complete. In addition to a total aggression score, it has five subscale scores. Reliability and construct and criterion-related validity are satisfactory, but the instrument's test-retest reliability and predictive validity for children need to be investigated further.

Beck Disruptive Behavior Inventory for Youth and Beck Anger Inventory for Youth

28. The BDBI–Y and the BANI–Y are two of the five instruments in the Beck Youth Inventories. Each instrument is administered, scored, and interpreted separately; requires a second-grade reading level; and takes about 5 to 10 minutes to complete. The BDBI–Y measures symptoms of conduct disorder and oppositional defiant disorder. The BANI–Y measures affect and cognitions related to anger. Reliability and validity are satisfactory.

Anxiety Disorders

29. Fear, which is a natural response to stimuli perceived as threatening, has cognitive, affective, physiological, and behavioral components.
30. *DSM-IV–TR* describes the following nine types of anxiety disorders: separation anxiety disorder, panic disorder, agoraphobia, specific phobia, social phobia, obsessive-compulsive disorder, posttraumatic stress disorder, acute stress disorder, and generalized anxiety disorder.
31. Separation anxiety disorder refers to developmentally inappropriate and excessive anxiety concerning separation from home or from those to whom the child is attached.
32. Common obsessions among children primarily center on (a) dirt, germs, or environmental toxins and (b) concerns that something terrible is going to happen.
33. Common compulsions among children primarily center on (a) excessive or ritualized handwashing, showering, bathing, toothbrushing, or grooming, (b) repeating rituals, (c) excessive checking, and (d) miscellaneous rituals involving writing, moving, or speaking.
34. Posttraumatic stress disorder (PTSD) is a clinical label for a traumatic reaction following any event or crisis involving actual or threatened death or serious injury, such as a natural or human-induced disaster, accident, suicide attempt, or violent crime involving child abuse.
35. The traumatic reactions may affect children's cognitions, affect, and behavior.
36. *DSM-IV–TR* describes three phases of PTSD: acute, chronic, and delayed onset.
37. The overall prevalence rate for all anxiety disorders in children and adolescents is 2% to 9%.
38. Girls have higher rates of specific phobias and generalized anxiety disorder than boys.

39. Children exhibiting an anxiety disorder in one area are likely to experience anxiety in other areas as well.
40. Biological theories explain the etiology of anxiety disorders by emphasizing the role of genetic factors in creating a vulnerability to maladaptive reactions to threatening situations or by locating the causes of the disorder in physiological or neurophysiological processes.
41. Psychoanalytic theory, learning theory, and psychosocial theory all offer psychological explanations of anxiety disorders.
42. Treatments for anxiety disorders may involve pharmacological treatments, behavior therapies, and cognitive behavioral therapies. Interventions may also involve the family.

Beck Anxiety Inventory for Youth

43. The BAI–Y is a 20-item self-report measure designed to assess anxiety disorders in children ages 7 to 14 years. The BAI–Y yields a single score reflecting the severity of anxiety disorder. It requires a second-grade reading level and takes about 5 to 10 minutes to complete. It has good reliability, but more information is needed about its validity.

Depressive Disorders

44. Depression can refer to a symptom such as sad affect, a common experience of everyday life, or to a syndrome made up of a group of symptoms.
45. *DSM-IV–TR* cites nine symptoms associated with a major depressive episode. They are irritable or depressed mood most of the day and nearly every day; markedly diminished interest or pleasure in all or almost all activities most of the day and nearly every day; failure to make expected weight gain, significant weight loss when not dieting, weight gain, or decrease or increase in appetite nearly every day; insomnia or hypersomnia nearly every day; psychomotor agitation or retardation nearly every day; fatigue or loss of energy nearly every day; feeling of worthlessness or excessive or inappropriate guilt nearly every day; diminished ability to think or concentrate or indecisiveness nearly every day; and recurrent thoughts of death, recurrent suicidal ideation without a specific plan, or a suicide attempt or a specific plan for committing suicide.
46. A depressive disorder should be considered primarily when the symptoms reflect a change in a child's behavior maintained over time and are detrimental to the child's functioning.
47. Depressive disorders in children often coexist with other disorders, including conduct or oppositional defiant disorders, anxiety disorders, and, less often, attention-deficit/hyperactivity disorder.
48. Estimates of the incidence of depressive disorders vary with the diagnostic criteria and the measures used.
49. Estimates for major depressive disorders in adolescents (12 to 19 years) vary from 5% to 28%.
50. Occurrence rates for major depressive disorder are higher for girls than for boys.
51. The etiology of depression is uncertain, but both biological and psychosocial theories have merit.
52. Biological theories point to deficits in or imbalance of neurotransmittors.
53. Psychosocial theories propose that depression results from limited rewards or life satisfactions, parental resentment or rejection of the child, deficits in self-regulatory skills for coping

with stress, negative thinking about oneself, failure of one's behavior to influence events in one's life, deficits in interpersonal problem-solving skills, and reactions to major and minor forms of stress.

54. Psychopharmacological approaches to the treatment of depression include medications such as imipramine, nortriptyline, and amitriptyline.

55. Useful psychological interventions include cognitive-behavior modification (e.g., self-monitoring, cognitive restructuring, and attribution retraining) and psychodynamic therapies (e.g., play therapy).

56. Drug treatments may be combined with psychological interventions.

57. Interventions will be complicated if the parents also are depressed or have other forms of psychological disturbance.

Beck Depression Inventory for Youth

58. The BDI–Y is a 20-item self-report measure based on *DSM-IV* symptoms. It is designed to provide an index of depressive disorder independent of other diagnoses, including anxiety, for children ages 7 to 14 years. The instrument yields a single score reflecting the severity of depressive disorder, requires a second-grade reading level, and takes about 5 to 10 minutes to complete. It has good reliability and minimally adequate construct validity.

Children's Depression Inventory and Children's Depression Inventory–Short Form

59. The CDI is a 27-item self-report measure designed to assess cognitive, affective, and behavioral symptoms of depression in children ages 7 to 17 years. The CDI–S is a 10-item version of the CDI. The CDI has five scales, whereas the CDI–S has no individual scales. Both measures require a first-grade reading level. It takes about 15 minutes to complete the CDI and under 10 minutes to complete the CDI–S. The CDI has satisfactory reliability for the total score and inadequate internal consistency reliability for the scales. The norms are not based on a national sample and are outdated, and no test-retest reliabilities are reported. Validity receives mixed support. Both the CDI and CDI–S should be used with caution.

Reynolds Child Depression Scale and Reynolds Adolescent Depression Scale–Second Edition

60. The RCDS and the RADS–2 are companion scales for measuring depressive symptoms in children. The RCDS is designed for children ages 8 to 12 years. The RADS–2 is used with children ages 11 to 20 years and requires a third-grade reading level. Both scales contain 30 items, yield a total score indicating overall level of depression, and with four exceptions have the same items. The RADS–2 also has four subscales reflecting underlying dimensions of adolescent depression. The RADS–2 takes about 5 to 10 minutes to complete; the RCDS takes about 10 minutes to complete. Both measures have adequate reliability and validity.

Suicide Risk

61. The suicide of a child is one of the most devastating events that a family can experience.

62. Emotions associated with the suicide of a child are often complicated by feelings of guilt for not recognizing warning signs and preventing the tragedy. However, the causes of suicide and

suicide attempts (parasuicide) are often complex and difficult to detect, and this complicates assessing suicide risk.

63. Both situational and psychological factors are associated with suicide and parasuicide.

64. In 2002, suicide was the third leading cause of death for youths ages 15 to 19 years, with a rate of 7.4 per 100,000.

65. This figure represents a decline of about 4% since 1994 when the rate was 11.1 per 100,000.

66. The suicide rate for male youths was about 5 times higher than for female youths (12.2 per 100,000 vs. 2.4 per 100,000).

67. American Indian male youths had the highest rate of suicide (22.7 per 100,000) followed by Euro American male youths (13.4 per 100,000), Hispanic American male youths (9.1 per 100,000), African American male youths (6.9 per 100,000), and Asian American male youths (5.7 per 100,000).

68. Suicide by firearms was the most common method.

69. Estimating the incidence of attempted suicides is more difficult, because many attempts never come to the attention of mental health practitioners.

70. In 2003, 17% of youths ages 15 to 19 years thought seriously about committing suicide, with the percentage of female youths more than twice as high as male youths (12% vs. 5%, respectively).

71. There is considerable variability in the severity of the means used to attempt suicide, ranging from the consumption of non-lethal doses of medicines to use of a weapon.

72. The treatments described for children with depressive disorder also may be appropriate for youths who are at risk for suicide.

73. Where suicide risk is acute, hospitalization and medication may be indicated until the acute phase has passed.

74. Assessments of suicide risk should explore the seriousness of the threat, the nature of suicidal ideations associated with the threat, and the motivating or precipitating factors associated with the threat.

Substance Abuse Disorders

75. Use of alcohol and other drugs is generally not a problem among children younger than 10 years of age, but may be during the adolescent years.

76. The use of alcohol and other drugs by children not only is illegal, but also may be associated with risky behaviors such as careless use of automobiles, sexual assaults, and other illegal activities.

77. When excessive, drug use may lead to impairments in health, school work, employment, and social relationships.

78. A physical or psychological dependence on a substance may develop and be linked with addiction problems in later life, although occasional use of these substances does not necessarily constitute abuse.

79. *DSM-IV–TR* recognizes a distinction between substance abuse and substance dependence.

80. Substance abuse applies to cases in which the use of alcohol or other drugs is associated with impairment in emotional or behavioral functioning but with no signs of substance dependence.

81. Substance dependence is defined as cognitive, behavioral, and physiological symptoms indicating that an individual continues use of the substance despite significant substance-related problems.

82. Conditions co-occurring with substance abuse include conduct disorder, oppositional defiant disorder, and depressive disorder.

83. The major substances implicated in substance abuse and substance dependence include alcohol, sedative-hypnotics, stimulants, marijuana, opiates, hallucinogens, and inhalants.

84. At least 15% of 8th grade students, 31% of 10th grade students, and 39% of 12th grade students used an illicit drug in 2004.

85. Alcohol is the most frequent substance used by adolescents in 2004 or sometime in their lifetime and 52% of 12th grade students had been drunk in 2004.

86. Drug and alcohol use shows dramatic increases from 8th to 12th grades.

87. Youths age 12 to 17 years who perceived that their parents would strongly disapprove of their trying marijuana or hashish were about 5 times less likely to have tried these substances in the past month (5.4% tried) than youths whose parents would not strongly disapprove (28.7% tried).

88. The majority of youths indicated that their parents would strongly disapprove of their use of marijuana during the past month (about 90% disapproval).

89. Biological theories stress the role of genetic factors in affecting temperamental factors and physiological mechanisms that are, in turn, linked with substance abuse.

90. Behavioral theories explain addictions in terms of learning theory principles that emphasize the reinforcement value of the substance.

91. Family system theories locate the causes of addiction in family dynamics, stressing the role of parental modeling, supervision, and family conflicts.

92. Sociological theories emphasize the relationship of socioeconomic status and cultural norms to substance abuse.

93. Multiple risk models of substance abuse disorders focus on a broad range of interacting biological, psychological, and social factors as determinants of abuse.

94. Primary prevention programs teach children about the risks associated with substance use and provide skills for resisting drug and alcohol experimentation.

95. Psychological treatments of substance abuse disorders focus on resolution of emotional problems linked with the abuse, on skill development, and on cognitive modification.

96. Self-help programs popular with adults—such as Alcoholics Anonymous—are often used with adolescents.

97. Multimodal treatments may employ several therapeutic techniques that address a range of problems associated with the abuse.

98. Unfortunately, the failure rate in the treatment of childhood substance abuse is generally high, and research supporting the efficacy of any specific treatment modality for children is scant.

99. Interventions should focus on a youth's broad social environment, because substance abuse often relates to family dynamics and usually occurs within a peer group.

100. The assessment of substance abuse disorders involves determining the extent and nature of the substance abuse.

101. We recommend a broad approach to assessment, because substance abuse has complex causes and affects many aspects of a youth's functioning.

KEY TERMS, CONCEPTS, AND NAMES

Antisocial behavior (p. 352)
Conduct disorder (p. 352)
Childhood-onset conduct disorder (p. 352)
Adolescent-onset conduct disorder (p. 352)
Oppositional defiant disorder (p. 352)
Aggression Questionnaire (AQ) (p. 358)
Beck Disruptive Behavior Inventory for Youth (BDBI–Y) (p. 358)
Beck Anger Inventory for Youth (BANI–Y) (p. 358)
Anxiety disorders (p. 359)
Separation anxiety disorder (p. 359)
Panic disorder (p. 359)
Agoraphobia (p. 359)
Specific phobia (p. 359)
Social phobia (p. 359)
Obsessive-compulsive disorder (p. 359)
Posttraumatic stress disorder (p. 359)
Acute stress disorder (p. 359)
Generalized anxiety disorder (p. 359)
Psychic numbing (p. 360)
Pathologic psychophysiologic arousal (p. 360)
Beck Anxiety Inventory for Youth (BAI–Y) (p. 362)
Depressive disorders (p. 363)
Beck Depression Inventory for Youth (BDI–Y) (p. 364)
Children's Depression Inventory (CDI) (p. 365)
Children's Depression Inventory–Short Form (CDI–S) (p. 365)
Reynolds Child Depression Scale (RCDS) (p. 365)
Reynolds Adolescent Depression Scale–Second Edition (RADS–2) (p. 365)
Parasuicide (p. 366)
Suicide risk (p. 366)
Substance abuse disorders (p. 368)
Substance abuse (p. 368)
Substance dependence (p. 368)

STUDY QUESTIONS

1. Discuss issues in the diagnosis of antisocial behavior disorders.
2. Describe the developmental course of conduct disorder.
3. Contrast alternative approaches to the treatment of antisocial behavior disorders.
4. Discuss ways of addressing the problem of school violence.
5. Review the different forms of anxiety disorders.
6. Describe the different approaches to the treatment of anxiety disorders.
7. Discuss the symptoms of depressive disorder.
8. Discuss the factors associated with suicide risk.
9. Describe the indicators of childhood drug use.
10. Discuss each of the following measures. Include in your discussion a description of the measure, scales, scores, standardization, reliability, and validity, and provide an overall evaluation of the measure.

    Aggression Questionnaire
    Beck Anger Inventory for Youth
    Beck Anxiety Inventory for Youth
    Beck Depression Inventory for Youth
    Beck Disruptive Behavior Inventory for Youth
    Children's Depression Inventory
    Children's Depression Inventory–Short Form
    Reynolds Adolescent Depression Scale–Second Edition
    Reynolds Child Depression Scale

15

ATTENTION-DEFICIT/HYPERACTIVITY DISORDER

by Jerome M. Sattler, Lisa Weyandt, and John O. Willis

In all our efforts to provide "advantages" we have actually produced the busiest, most competitive, highly pressured and over-organized generation of youngsters in our history—and possibly the unhappiest. We seem hell-bent on eliminating much of childhood.

—Eda J. Le Shan, American educator and author (1922–)

Goals and Objectives

This chapter is designed to enable you to do the following:

- Learn about the behavioral and other deficits exhibited by children who have attention-deficit/hyperactivity disorder

- Become familiar with methods for assessing children who may have attention-deficit/hyperactivity disorder

- Learn about interventions for children with attention-deficit/hyperactivity disorder

Attention-deficit/hyperactivity disorder (ADHD) is a neurobehavioral syndrome marked by inattention, hyperactivity, and impulsivity (American Psychiatric Association, 2000). Historically, the disorder has been referred to as minimal brain damage, minimal brain dysfunction, hyperkinetic reaction of childhood, and attention deficit disorder with or without hyperactivity. A diagnosis of ADHD is made when a child displays the required number of symptoms of the disorder (6 of 9 symptoms of inattention, 6 of 9 symptoms of hyperactivity-impulsivity, or 6 of 9 symptoms of both) and these symptoms

- are present before age 7 years, for at least 6 months, and to a degree that is maladaptive and inconsistent with an individual's developmental level;
- occur in two or more settings; and
- significantly affect the child's social or academic functioning.

The three types of ADHD cited in *DSM-IV–TR* are (a) attention-deficit/hyperactivity disorder: combined type, (b) attention-deficit/hyperactivity disorder: predominantly inattentive type, and (c) attention-deficit/hyperactivity disorder: predominantly hyperactive-impulsive type. Confusingly, the *DSM-IV–TR* codes for combined type and the predominantly hyperactive-impulsive type are the same (314.01), while the code for predominantly inattentive type is 314.00. There is also a code for "attention-deficit/hyperactivity disorder not otherwise specified" (314.9) for symptoms that do not meet the criteria for any of the three primary types of ADHD. The three major symptoms of ADHD are inattention, hyperactivity, and impulsivity.

INATTENTION

1. Often fails to give close attention to details or makes careless mistakes in schoolwork, work, or other activities
2. Often has difficulty sustaining attention in tasks or play activities
3. Often does not seem to listen when spoken to directly
4. Often does not follow through on instructions and fails to finish schoolwork, chores, or duties in the workplace
5. Often has difficulty organizing tasks and activities
6. Often avoids, dislikes, or is reluctant to engage in tasks that require sustained mental effort (e.g., schoolwork or homework)
7. Often loses things needed to perform tasks or activities (e.g., toys, school assignments, pencils, or books)
8. Often is easily distracted by extraneous stimuli
9. Often is forgetful in daily activities

HYPERACTIVITY

1. Often fidgets with hands or feet or squirms in seat
2. Often inappropriately leaves seat in classroom or in other situations
3. Often runs about or climbs excessively
4. Often has difficulty playing or engaging in leisure activities quietly

5. Often is "on the go" or acts as if "driven by a motor"
6. Often talks excessively

IMPULSIVITY

1. Often blurts out answers before questions have been completed
2. Often has difficulty awaiting his or her turn
3. Often interrupts or intrudes on others

The ADHD population is heterogeneous, displaying a diversity of associated behavior problems in addition to underlying attention problems. About 44% of children with ADHD have at least one co-occurring disorder, about 33% have two co-occurring disorders, and about 10% have three co-occurring disorders (Root & Resnick, 2003). Following are disorders that tend to co-occur with ADHD, also referred to as *comorbid disorders,* and estimates of their prevalence (Agency for Health Care Policy and Research, 1999; American Psychiatric Association, 2000; Friedman, Chhabildas, Budhiraja, Willcutt, & Pennington, 2003; Green, Wong, Atkins, Taylor, & Feinlieb, 1999; Shelton & Barkley, 1994):

- Learning disorders (25–50%)
- Oppositional defiant disorder (25–33%)
- Conduct disorder (26%)
- Depressive disorder (18%)
- Anxiety disorder (26%)

Other disorders that may co-occur with ADHD are mood disorder, communication disorder, and Tourette's disorder. Children with ADHD also may display aggressive behavior, low self-esteem, lability of mood (i.e., quickly shifting from one emotion to another), low tolerance for frustration, and temper outbursts.

ADHD often becomes most evident when children enter elementary school, where the demands of the classroom require sustained attention and in-seat, independent work. Overactivity is a common hallmark of ADHD in early childhood, but overactivity decreases with age and may be replaced with feelings of restlessness in adolescence (Weyandt, Iwaszuk, Fulton, Ollerton, Beatty, Fouts, Schepman, & Greenlaw, 2003). Boys with ADHD tend to display more aggressive and oppositional behaviors than do girls, whereas girls with ADHD tend to have more internalizing problems and greater intellectual impairments than do boys (Gaub & Carlson, 1997; Gershon, 2002).

During adolescence and adulthood, children with a dual diagnosis of ADHD and conduct disorder are likely to have more problems than those who have either diagnosis alone. For example, those with this dual diagnosis have increased risk for antisocial behaviors, substance abuse, peer rejection, depression, personality disorders, and difficulties in processing social information (Abikoff & Klein, 1992; Barkley, Fischer, Smallish, & Fletcher, 2004; Dalsgaard, Mortensen, Frydenberg, & Thomsen, 2002; Fischer, Barkley, Smallish & Fletcher, 2002; Moffit, 1990; Paternite, Loney, Salisbury, & Whaley, 1999). Their parents may face increased parenting stress, frustration, and despair. Children with both ADHD and a learning disability usually have more problems controlling impulses, working independently, and functioning adequately in a classroom than do children who have a learning disability only (Robins, 1992). ADHD symptoms tend to be exacerbated in children who have chronic illnesses, who have intermittent hearing losses associated with otitis media, who take drugs (e.g., Phenobarbital or decongestants), or who have disorders of the central nervous system (e.g., seizure disorder, autistic disorder, fetal alcohol syndrome, Tourette's disorder, or brain injury).

Approximately 3% to 7% of the school-age population has ADHD, with estimates of male-to-female ratios ranging from 2:1 to 9:1 (American Psychiatric Association, 2000). ADHD is the most frequent reason for referral to child mental health clinics (Barkley, 1998).

Children with ADHD, in addition to having problems with inattention, hyperactivity, and impulsivity, may have cognitive deficits; social and adaptive functioning deficits; motivational and emotional deficits; and motor, physical, and health deficits (Barkley & Murphy, 1998; Weyandt & Willis, 1994; Whalen, 1989). Examples of these deficits follow.

COGNITIVE DEFICITS

1. Information-processing deficits involving task analysis, strategic planning, and executive behavior (e.g., using time inefficiently, underestimating the amount of work and time needed to complete assignments, failing to pace work evenly throughout the time allotted for assignments, failing to begin assignments in a timely manner, failing to analyze written or spoken material thoroughly, failing to use appropriate rehearsal strategies, failing to use appropriate problem-solving or recall strategies)
2. Mild deficits in intelligence test scores (e.g., verbal IQs in the 90s, lower-than-average immediate memory scores)
3. Learning disabilities (e.g., problems in reading, mathematics, spelling, written expression, or oral language and below-average achievement test scores in these and related areas)
4. Memory difficulties (e.g., difficulty memorizing rote information, forgetting to write down homework assignments, neglecting to bring home materials needed to complete homework assignments, forgetting to check assignment books when doing homework, forgetting to bring completed homework to school)
5. Impaired behavioral and verbal creativity (e.g., impaired flexibility and originality)

SOCIAL AND ADAPTIVE FUNCTIONING DEFICITS

1. Difficulties with social and adaptive functioning (e.g., poor self-help skills, difficulty assuming personal responsibility and independence, limited insight into his or her problems, externalizing blame and becoming defensive when criticized, difficulty behaving in a socially acceptable manner, alienating friends through aggressive or unintentionally rough play, unwillingness to take turns,

inflexibility, tantrums, silliness inappropriate to the child's age and the situation, bossiness, impulsivity, laziness)
2. Difficulties adhering to rules and instructions (e.g., frequent arguments with parents, chronic lateness and poor time management, failing to comply with instructions)

MOTIVATIONAL AND EMOTIONAL DEFICITS

1. Motivational difficulties (e.g., limited interest in achievement, difficulty getting work done on time)
2. Limited persistence (e.g., tendency to give up easily and not to persist on a difficult task)
3. Emotional reactivity (e.g., difficulty modulating emotional responses, occasionally exploding in anger when encountering a disappointment, becoming disproportionately happy when something pleasant happens)

MOTOR, PHYSICAL, AND HEALTH DEFICITS

1. Poor fine-motor and gross-motor coordination (e.g., difficulty drawing designs, poor handwriting)
2. Minor physical anomalies (e.g., enlarged head circumference, index finger longer than middle finger)
3. General health problems and possible delay in growth during childhood (e.g., small stature, more illnesses than peers, sleep problems)
4. Proneness to accidental injuries (e.g., falling more frequently than peers, greater than average risk of automobile accidents as an adolescent and young adult)

Deficits in self-regulation may underlie the difficulty children with ADHD have with organization and planning, with the mobilization and maintenance of effortful attention, and with the inhibition of inappropriate responding (Barkley, 1997). Consequently, children with ADHD may show considerable variability across situations depending, in part, on the task requirements, the quantity and type of environmental distracters, and the environmental supports available.

Parents of children with ADHD tend to be more depressed and to have lower self-esteem than parents of normally functioning children; they may believe that they have diminished parenting skills, may feel stigmatized or guilty, and may enjoy less marital satisfaction than parents of normal children (Blakemore, Shindler, & Conte, 1993; Norvilitis, Scime, & Lee, 2002). No listing of symptoms of ADHD can capture the hardships faced by the parents of children with ADHD. Here is a description by one mother (Richard, 1993):

> I'm the mother of nine-year-old twin boys who have (finally) been diagnosed with ADD [attention-deficit disorder] through our school. It has been a rough nine years. They were out of their cribs before they could even crawl. They could open any childproof lock ever made and slept less than any human beings I have ever known. No baby-sitter has ever been willing to come more than twice. No child care center or after-school program has even been willing to keep them, so I quit my part-time teaching job and have stayed home with them since they were three. My husband has to work a second job, so most of the supervision of the boys falls on me. I almost never have any relief. Their grandparents work full-time and live in another state. Over the

last few years my health has begun to fail. Although my doctor cannot find anything wrong with me, I am constantly catching colds [and am] exhausted, and have frequent headaches. I'm losing weight. I sleep very poorly. Are there other mothers of children with ADD who feel this way? Is there anything I can do about it? (p. 10)

ETIOLOGY

Given the heterogeneity of its symptoms, ADHD probably has no single cause; multiple factors likely contribute to its development and expression. Although the precise causes and mechanisms of ADHD are unknown, research suggests that genetic, neurological, and prenatal factors underlie the disorder (Barkley, 2004; Barkley & Murphy, 1998). For example, ADHD tends to run in families and is more likely to occur in identical twins than in fraternal twins (Stevenson, Pennington, Gilger, DeFries, & Gillis, 1993; Willcutt, Pennington, & DeFries, 2000). The precise mode of inheritance of ADHD, however, has yet to be identified.

The brain structures of individuals with and without ADHD differ anatomically (Mostofsky, Cooper, Kates, Denckla, & Kaufmann, 2002; Semrud-Clikeman, Filipek, Biederman, Steingard, Kennedy, Renshaw, & Bekken, 1994). In addition, individuals with ADHD may have an imbalance of or deficiency in one or more neurotransmitters (e.g., dopamine), in several areas of the brain, particularly the frontal lobes and connections to subcortical structures (DiMaio, Grizenko, & Joober, 2003; Durston, Tottenham, Thomas, Davidson, Eigsti, Yang, Ulug, & Casey, 2003; Faraone, Doyle, Mick, & Biederman, 2001; Hechtman, 1994; Smith, Daly, Fischer, Yiannoutsos, Bauer, Barkley, & Navia, 2003). Finally, the difficulty experienced by individuals with ADHD in performing neuropsychological tasks suggests deficits in cortical functioning (Barkley, 2004; Barkley, Grodzinsky, & DuPaul, 1992; Weyandt, 2004).

Exposure of the fetus to nicotine, alcohol, and other drugs and maternal psychosocial stress during pregnancy have been associated with increased risk of ADHD (Barkley, 1998; Linnet, Dalsgaard, Obel, Wisborg, Henriksen, Rodriguez, Kotimaa, Moilanen, Thomsen, Olsen, & Jarvelin, 2003; Mick, Biederman, Faraone, Sayer, & Kleinman, 2002; Weyandt, 2001). Contrary to some hypotheses, food additives, sugar, and fluorescent lighting have not been found to cause ADHD (Barkley, 1998). Prenatal and postnatal exposure to toxic substances such as lead, methylmercury, and pesticides has been associated with a spectrum of neurodevelopmental deficits (e.g., problems in memory, attention, and learning), but it is not known whether exposure to these substances affects the developing brain in such a way as to contribute to ADHD (Stein, Schettler, Wallinga, & Valenti, 2002).

Advances in brain-imaging technology and genetic research should help to clarify the etiology of ADHD. Whatever the etiology, problems with self-regulation comprise the core of ADHD; these problems, in turn, may express them-

selves as behavioral deficits in executive functions, working memory, internalized speech, and behavioral inhibition (Barkley, 1998). We also need to consider that poor classroom organization, limited parental education, and ineffective parenting styles may cause ADHD-like behaviors in children who do not have the disorder or may exacerbate symptoms of ADHD in children who do have the disorder.

ASSESSMENT

As is true of all childhood disorders, the assessment of ADHD requires a comprehensive and thorough evaluation. You will want to assess the following:

- Presence of symptoms (e.g., inattention, hyperactivity, impulsivity)
- Number, type, severity, and duration of symptoms
- Situations in which symptoms are displayed
- Verbal abilities, nonverbal abilities, short- and long-term memory abilities, and other cognitive abilities
- Presence of any co-occurring disorders
- Social competence and adaptive behavior
- Educational and instructional needs

The assessment should include a review of the child's cumulative school records and relevant medical information (including a current medical evaluation, in part to rule out other medical conditions that may mimic ADHD and require treatment); interviews with parents, teachers, and the child; observations of the child's behavior in the classroom and on the playground; administration of rating scales to parents, teachers, and older children who can read; and administration of a battery of psychological tests to the child. Schedule the assessment so that it does not follow a stressful situation (e.g., a classroom test), and be prepared to use two or more sessions. Do not rely on the results of group intelligence or achievement tests, because these results may not be valid—they may underestimate the child's ability level. This is especially true if the tests were administered without accommodations (e.g., without extending the time limit).

Interviews

Interviews with the child's parents and teachers, as well as with the child, will form a key part of the assessment. Parents and teachers are the most familiar with the child's behavior under sustained conditions.

Parent interview. An interview with at least one parent (preferably both parents) is critical for obtaining information about the child's prenatal and postnatal development; medical, social, and academic history; medications taken currently and previously; the parent's view of the child's problems (including the age at which the problems began and the pervasiveness of the problems); parenting styles and disciplinary techniques; environmental factors that may contribute to the child's problems; and resources available to the family. Parents often report concerns with behavior the child exhibited prior to starting school, including a difficult temperament, irregular sleeping and feeding routines, proneness to accidents as a toddler, and excessive motor activity (Sanson, Smart, Prior, & Oberklaid, 1993). As noted earlier, the *DSM-IV–TR* stipulates that the symptoms must be present before 7 years of age. Table B-10 in Appendix B and the Background Questionnaire in Table A-1 in Appendix A are useful for obtaining case history information from a parent. Parents might also be asked to complete one or more rating scales, as discussed later in the chapter.

Teacher interview. Teachers can offer valuable information about when symptoms occur, the specific behaviors that interfere with the child's school functioning, the severity of symptoms, the factors that may exacerbate the problem behavior, the child's academic strengths and weaknesses, the child's social skill strengths and weaknesses, and the quality of the child's peer relationships. Teachers might be asked to complete the School Referral Questionnaire (see Table A-3 in Appendix A) and one of the rating scales discussed later in the chapter. Ratings from several teachers may help determine whether the child's behavior varies with different teachers or when working on different academic subjects.

Child interview. Although children often provide valuable information about themselves, they occasionally provide information of questionable validity (Smith, Pelham, Gnagy,

Molina, & Evans, 2000). They also may not perceive their behaviors as bothersome to others (Kaidar, Wiener, & Tannock, 2003). The questions in Table B-1 in Appendix B may help in obtaining information from children. Children who can read and write also may be asked to complete the Personal Data Questionnaire (see Table A-2 in Appendix A).

Behavioral Observations

Observation of the child's behaviors will give you information about the antecedents and consequences of the behaviors; intensity, duration, and rate of the behaviors; and factors that may be contributing to and sustaining the behaviors. Conduct the observations in multiple settings (recall that the *DSM-IV–TR* criteria require that symptoms be present in two or more settings) and at different times of the day.

Observation of the following behaviors during an assessment indicates possible ADHD (Schworm & Birnbaum, 1989). Note, however, that children with ADHD may not show any of these behaviors during the assessment and that children without ADHD may display some of them, especially preschool children.

INATTENTION

1. Playing with his or her own clothing, such as fiddling with shirt collars, threads, zippers, buttons, pockets, pants, or socks
2. Touching nearby objects, such as playing with a pencil or the edges of a paper or trailing hands along the desk or table top
3. Attending to an irrelevant part of a visual task, such as pointing to or commenting on an irrelevant part of the stimulus
4. Insisting on turning the pages of the test easel and paying more attention to page-turning than to the test questions
5. Attending to an irrelevant part of the environment, such as looking out the window or around the room, or simply gazing or staring during a task
6. Attending to background noises or sounds outside the room, such as footsteps, voices, or buzzers
7. Stopping in the middle of a timed task to talk, scratch, or do something else

HYPERACTIVITY

1. Excessive verbalizations that may or may not be related to a task
2. Movements of the lower extremities, such as swinging, tapping, or shaking of legs and feet
3. Movements of the upper extremities, such as shaking hands, tapping or drumming fingers, playing with hands, or twirling thumbs
4. Whole-body movements, such as rocking movements or frequent changes in seating position or posture
5. Odd noises, such as humming, clicking teeth, or whistling, during a task
6. Grabbing and handling materials

SCHOOLIES

I wanted to talk about your son's inability to stay on-task.

IMPULSIVITY

1. Quickly responding with an incorrect answer, without first scanning or surveying choices, or responding randomly
2. Unsystematic searching, such as looking in the middle of the stimulus first without scanning or surveying in a left-to-right direction
3. Responding before directions are given or completed
4. Failing to look at possible alternatives or stopping searching prematurely

Following are three formal classroom observation systems for children who may have ADHD:

- Classroom Observation Code (Abikoff & Gittleman, 1985; see Table C-1 in Appendix C)
- Revised ADHD Behavior Coding System (DuPaul & Stoner, 2003)
- ADHD School Observation Code (Gadow, Sprafkin, & Nolan, 1996)

If you want to observe a child's behavior while he or she works on a school-related assignment in a clinic playroom, you can use the Structured Observation of Academic and Play Settings (SOAPS; Roberts, Milich, & Loney, 1984; see Table C-2 in Appendix C). This procedure is particularly useful in evaluating the effects of medication on a child's attention.

If a child is given an assignment during an observation period, inspect the quality of the completed assignment. Although a child may be on task, she or he may not complete the task accurately (DuPaul & Stoner, 2003). When you observe a child, note any symptoms associated with ADHD, including whether the child remains focused on a task, responds to distractions, makes repetitive purposeless motions (e.g., playing with things on the desk), leaves his or her seat without per-

mission, vocalizes, or engages in aggressive or noncompliant behavior.

Rating Scales

Both broadband and narrowband rating scales administered to parents, teachers, and children can help to identify appropriate and inappropriate behaviors, including those specifically related to ADHD. *Broadband rating scales* survey a wide spectrum of symptoms and behaviors (e.g., externalizing and internalizing disorders), whereas *narrowband rating scales* survey behaviors associated with a specific disorder (e.g., ADHD or depression only). The following broadband rating scales reviewed in Chapter 10 are useful in the assessment of ADHD:

- Conners' Rating Scales–Revised (Conners, 1997)
- Child Behavior Checklist for Ages 6–18 (Achenbach & Rescorla, 2001), Teacher's Report Form (Achenbach & Rescorla, 2001), Youth Self-Report Form (Achenbach & Rescorla, 2001), Child Behavior Checklist for Ages 1½–5 (Achenbach & Rescorla, 2000), and Caregiver–Teacher Report Form (Achenbach & Rescorla, 2000)
- Behavior Assessment System for Children–Second Edition (Reynolds & Kamphaus, 2004)
- Personality Inventory for Children–Second Edition (Wirt et al., 2001)

The following narrowband rating scales are useful in the assessment of ADHD (see Collett, Ohan, & Myers, 2003, for a review of several of these rating scales). Note that purchasers of this book have permission to reproduce the ADHD Questionnaire in Appendix C and that the four NICHQ Vanderbilt Assessment Scales listed below can be downloaded

MR. WOODHEAD © 1998 by John P. Wood

You just can't seem to sit still today. What's the problem?

Well, people keep calling me.

And my pager is set on "Vibrate."

from http://www.utmem.edu/pediatrics/general/clinical/behavior/index.php.

- ACTeRS Parent Form (Ullman, Sleator, Sprague, & Metri Tech Staff, 1996) and ACTeRS Teacher Form–Second Edition (Ullman, Sleator, & Sprague, 1991)
- ADHD Questionnaire (see Table C-3 in Appendix C)
- ADHD Rating Scale–IV: Home Version and ADHD Rating Scale–IV: School Version (DuPaul, Power, Anastopolous, & Reid, 1998)
- ADHD Symptom Checklist–4 (Gadow & Sprafkin, 1997)
- Attention-Deficit/Hyperactivity Test (Gilliam, 1995)
- Attention Deficit Disorder Evaluation Scale–Second Edition (McCarney, 1989)
- BASC Monitor (Kamphaus & Reynolds, 1998)
- Brown Attention-Deficit Disorder Scales (Brown, 2001)
- Early Childhood Deficit Disorders Evaluation Scale–School Version (McCarney, 1995b) and Early Childhood Deficit Disorders Evaluation Scale–Home Version (McCarney, 1995a)
- NICHQ Vanderbilt Assessment Scale–PARENT Informant, NICHQ Vanderbilt Assessment Scale–TEACHER Informant, NICHQ Vanderbilt Assessment Scale Follow-Up–PARENT Informant, and NICHQ Vanderbilt Assessment Scale Follow-Up–TEACHER Informant (American Academy of Pediatrics and National Initiative for Children's Healthcare Quality, 2002)
- Scales for Diagnosing Attention-Deficit/Hyperactivity Disorder (Ryser & McConnell, 2002)

Following are narrowband rating scales, several of which were reviewed in Chapter 14, that are useful in the assessment of disorders that may occur with ADHD:

- Aggression Questionnaire (Buss & Warren, 2000)
- Beck Disruptive Behavior Inventory for Youth (Beck et al., 2001)
- Beck Anger Inventory for Youth (Beck et al., 2001)
- Beck Anxiety Inventory for Youth (Beck et al., 2001)
- Revised Children's Manifest Anxiety Scale (Reynolds & Richmond, 1985)
- Multidimensional Anxiety Scale for Children (March, 1997)
- Beck Depression Inventory for Youth (Beck et al., 2001)
- Children's Depression Inventory (Kovacs, 2001)
- Reynolds Child Depression Scale (Reynolds, 1989)
- Reynolds Adolescent Depression Scale–Second Edition (Reynolds, 2002)

Psychological Tests

Intelligence tests, achievement tests, memory tests, and neuropsychological tests are useful in the assessment of ADHD. Sattler (2001) provides information about intelligence and achievement tests, Chapter 24 in this book provides information about neuropsychological tests, and Appendix D provides several informal procedures useful in assessing achievement skills and attitudes toward academic subjects.

Achievement tests must be considered and chosen carefully. Those with brief items and short subtests may allow a child with a short attention span to show his or her strongest abilities but may fail to reveal genuine difficulties with normal tasks of age-appropriate length and complexity. Multiple-choice tests may penalize impulsive children but may give higher scores to children who struggle with sustained paper-and-pencil work.

Some examiners like to include a computerized continuous performance test such as the Gordon Diagnostic System (GDS; Gordon, 1988), Conners' Continuous Performance Test II (CPT II; Conners & MHS Staff, 2000), Intermediate Visual and Auditory Continuous Performance Test (IVA; Sanford & Turner, 1995), or Test of Variables of Attention (T.O.V.A; Greenberg, 1990) in the assessment. These tests measure sustained attention and/or impulsivity in a specific context. Most involve presenting a visual or auditory stimulus to the child at variable intervals for approximately 15 to 20 minutes. The child's task is to indicate (usually by pressing a button) when the stimulus is presented. A record is kept of the number of times the child correctly identifies the stimulus, fails to identify the stimulus, or identifies the stimulus incorrectly.

Scores on continuous performance tests indicate how the child's attention and impulsivity compare to those of a norm group of the child's age and sex. Continuous performance tests should never be used independently to make a diagnosis of ADHD. It is questionable whether continuous performance tests provide additional useful diagnostic information about ADHD. One problem is that a child's continuous performance test profile could look like an ADHD profile simply because the child was taking cold medication, was suffering from anxiety, was fatigued, was bored with the task, or was experiencing other problems that interfered with his or her concentration. Additional reliability and validity studies are needed to evaluate the contribution of continuous performance tests to the assessment of ADHD.

Intelligence tests also are not sufficiently sensitive to be used exclusively in making a diagnosis of ADHD or in discriminating among various subtypes of ADHD (Schwean & Saklofske, 1998). For example, scores on specific intelligence tests—such as on the Wechsler Working Memory and Processing Speed Index—are not useful for identifying ADHD (Anastopolous, Spisto, & Maher, 1994; Cohen, Becker, & Campbell, 1990; Mayes, Calhoun, & Crowell, 1998; Reinecke, Beebe, & Stein, 1999; Riccio, Cohen, Hall, & Ross, 1997; Semrud-Clikeman, Hynd, Lorys, & Lahey, 1993; Weyandt, Mitzlaff, & Thomas, 2002). Although children with ADHD may have variable scores on an individual intelligence test, no pattern of scores on a Wechsler test or on any other intelligence test is diagnostic of ADHD. However, patterns of strengths and weaknesses revealed by intelligence tests are useful in evaluating children's cognitive abilities. Children with ADHD usually obtain IQs in the Average range, although their IQs tend to be 7 to 14 points lower than those of their peers; however, children of different IQ levels also can have ADHD (Faraone, Biederman, Lehman, Spencer, Norman, Seidman, Kraus, Perrin, Chen, & Tsuang, 1993; Fischer, Barkley, Fletcher, & Smallish, 1990; Tripp, Ryan, & Peace, 2002; Whalen, 1989).

Comment on Assessment

Arriving at a diagnosis of ADHD is not easy, because restlessness, inattention, and overactive behavior are common in children between the ages of 2 and 12 years. Additionally, parents may find it difficult to judge whether their child's symptoms "have persisted for at least 6 months to a degree that is maladaptive and inconsistent with developmental level," as the *DSM-IV–TR* requires (American Psychiatric Association, 2000, p. 92). Some "problem" children are never referred for hyperactive behavior because their parents are tolerant of their behavior, their teachers do not perceive their behavior as a problem, or the parents and teachers provide environments that are structured to manage problem behavior. Conversely, normal but active children are sometimes referred for an evaluation because their parents or teachers are less tolerant, the parents have inadequate parenting skills, or the teachers have ineffective classroom management skills. In addition, the source of information (e.g., parent, child, teacher, clinician) and the method of data collection (e.g., direct observations, teacher ratings, parent ratings) can affect the diagnostic process (Barkley, 1998; Gomez, Burns, Walsh, & De Moura, 2003). Rating scales, for example, are a less labor-intensive assessment method than direct observations and are based on a large sample of behavior, but they usually do not provide for a functional analysis of the variables that interact with the child's behavior (see Chapter 13). Consequently, a comprehensive assessment of ADHD requires the use of both rating scales and direct observations. Finally, some medications prescribed for other conditions may mask ADHD symptoms, so the symptoms may not be apparent until the medication is discontinued.

The following comparisons illustrate just how subjective the labeling of behavior can be.

If an adult is reinforced for behaving appropriately we call it *recognition.*
If a child is reinforced for behaving appropriately we call it *bribery.*

If an adult laughs we call it *socializing.*
If a child laughs we call it *misbehaving.*

If an adult writes in a book we call it *doodling.*
If a child writes in a book we call it *destroying property.*

If an adult sticks to something we call it *perseverance.*
If a child sticks to something we call it *stubbornness.*

If an adult seeks help we call it *consulting.*
If a child seeks help we call it *whining.*

If an adult is not paying attention we call it *preoccupation.*
If a child is not paying attention we call it *distractibility.*

If an adult forgets something we call it *absentmindedness.*
If a child forgets something we call it *attention deficit.*

If an adult tells his side of a story we call it *clarification.*
If a child tells his side of a story we call it *talking back.*

If an adult raises his voice in anger we call it *maintaining control.*
If a child raises his voice in anger we call it *a temper tantrum.*

If an adult hits a child we call it *discipline.*
If a child hits a child we call it *fighting.*

If an adult behaves in an unusual way we call him *unique.*
If a child behaves in an unusual way we refer him for a psychological evaluation.

—Author Unknown

The major difficulties of children with ADHD may be reflected in their performance in some, but not all, situations and on some, but not all, psychological tests. Novel, structured, one-on-one situations (as in an individual assessment) or situations that are highly stimulating and that provide frequent feedback about performance (e.g., video games) may not elicit the same degree of ADHD symptomatology as the child's classroom.

The questions in Table 25-1 in Chapter 25 will help you evaluate the results of your psychological evaluation. After you have finished your evaluation, completing Table C-4 in Appendix C will help you arrive at a *DSM-IV–TR* diagnosis.

INTERVENTIONS

Pharmacological, behavioral, cognitive-behavioral, instructional, and familial interventions are used in the treatment of children with ADHD.

Pharmacological Interventions

Children with ADHD are often prescribed stimulant medications. Stimulant medications may be short-acting (e.g., taken every 4 hours or when medication is needed), (b) intermediate-acting (e.g., taken twice a day), or (c) long-acting (e.g., taken in the morning). Short-acting stimulants are helpful when it is preferable for the medication to take effect rapidly but not last a long time; long-acting stimulants are helpful for children whose activities require sustained attention beyond school hours (e.g., homework, family activities, club meetings, team sports). Approximately 80% of hyperactive children respond positively to stimulant medication (American Academy of Pediatrics, 2001).

Examples of each type of stimulant medication follow (American Academy of Pediatrics, 2001; Davis, 2005).

- *Short-acting stimulant medications:* Ritalin, Methylin, Focaline (methylphenidates); Dexedrine, Dextrostat, Adderall (amphetamines)
- *Intermediate-acting stimulant medications:* Ritalin SR, Ritalin LA, Metadate ER, Methylin ER (methylphenidates); Dexedrine spansule (amphetamine)

- *Long-acting stimulant medications:* Adderall XR (amphetamine); Concerta, Metadate CD (methylphenidates)

Strattera (atomoxetine), a nonstimulant, nonantidepressant long-acting medication, also improves ADHD symptomatology (Biederman, Spencer, & Wilens, 2004). Strattera is given in a single dose, usually in the morning, but should not be given if the child shows symptoms of jaundice.

Both stimulant and nonstimulant medications may have side effects that range from mild to severe. Examples of side effects are insomnia, appetite suppression, sleep disturbance, weight loss, headaches, irritability, stomachache, nausea, dizziness, fatigue, mood swings, social withdrawal, and increased activity or bad mood as the medication wears off; less common side effects are dry mouth, dizziness, and transient tics (American Academy of Pediatrics, 2001). Nutritional counseling is helpful in addressing appetite suppression (e.g., encouraging supplementary calorie consumption during breakfast and evening snacks when medication levels are low). Most side effects can be relieved by adjusting the dosage or the schedule of medication or by using a different medication.

Antidepressants also have been used with some success, particularly when children with ADHD have coexisting depression (Spencer, Biederman, Wilens, Harding, O'Donnell, & Griffin, 1996). However, antidepressant medications also have their side effects (e.g., fatigue, constipation, dry mouth, blurred vision) and may increase the risk of suicidal thinking and behavior in children with depression and other psychiatric illnesses (Davis, 2005). Antidepressants also are not as effective as stimulant medications in improving attention and concentration. Finally, other medications, such as Clinidine, an antihypertensive medication, are also sometimes used for the treatment of ADHD.

Although exactly how stimulant medications improve symptoms of ADHD is not known, these medications are thought to restore central nervous system arousal levels and inhibitory levels to normal, thereby giving children with ADHD better attention and self-control. Thus—in what is commonly, but mistakenly, called a "paradoxical effect"—stimulant medication *decreases* behavioral excesses or disruptive behaviors by increasing the ability to sustain focus. Many children with ADHD who take stimulant medication show dramatic behavioral changes, with noticeable improvement in motor behavior, attention, and impulse control; in addition, they may show, to a lesser degree, better compliance and more positive social behaviors because their impulsivity is reduced (Crenshaw, Kavale, Forness, & Reeve, 1999). However, pharmacological intervention usually does not correct social or academic deficits.

The use of medication for children with ADHD is controversial. Some parents refuse to consider medication, and courts have held that a school district may *not* require a child to take medication as a condition for attending school or for receiving services. Some states have passed or are considering legislation restricting the ability of school personnel to discuss medication with parents. Consequently, it is important to stay conversant with your state laws and regulations.

Behavioral Interventions

The use of stimulant medication does not eliminate the need for other types of interventions. For example, behavioral interventions can enhance the effectiveness of medication and are often effective alone, although the combination of stimulant medications and behavioral interventions seems most promising (Farmer, Compton, Burns, & Robertson, 2002). Following are examples of behavioral interventions.

1. *Positive reinforcement* (e.g., verbal praise, eye contact) is used to increase appropriate behavior. Brief verbal praise immediately following a child's performance of desirable behaviors is more effective in changing behavior than is lengthy, delayed verbal feedback (Abramowitz, O'Leary, & Futtersak, 1988). Positive reinforcement should be used whenever possible to increase desirable behavior.
2. *Withdrawal of reinforcement* (e.g., time out or a response-cost program, which incorporates a loss of points or privileges if a child displays inappropriate behavior) is used to reduce the frequency of inappropriate behavior. Withdrawal of reinforcement should be used sparingly.
3. A *point system* (token reinforcement) is used to reduce inappropriate behaviors; it is especially effective when used in conjunction with a response-cost program.
4. *Contracts* between teacher and student or between parent and child are useful for stipulating desired and expected behaviors at school and/or at home, as well as the consequences of not performing the desired behaviors (DuPaul & Stoner, 2003). For example, the teacher might complete a daily student rating card that included specific behavioral goals (e.g., attended class, completed assigned work). The student would take the rating card home each day, give it to the parent for review and signature, and return it to the teacher the next day. The parent and child would be encouraged to work together to create a list of reinforcers that the parent could use when the child reached the behavioral goals. The following Web site contains instructions and forms for establishing a school-home daily report card: http://www.utmem.edu/pediatrics/general/clinical/behavior/index.php.

Cognitive-Behavioral Interventions

Cognitive-behavioral interventions are based on the premise that a child's behavior is mediated by cognitions (see Chapter 1). The aim of such interventions is to increase the child's ability to think before acting or to delay gratification. An example is the child's use of self-directed speech and problem-solving skills to guide his or her behavior. However, studies indicate that cognitive-behavioral interventions for the treatment of ADHD are not effective when used independently of other types of interventions (Gittelman & Abikoff, 1989; Pelham, Wheeler, & Chronis, 1998). More promising are self-monitoring programs, which train children and adolescents to monitor their own behavior and keep track of the frequency of inappropriate and appropriate behaviors (see Chapter 9). In school-based programs, behavior management and instructional interventions are more effective in changing behavior than are cognitive-behavioral interventions (DuPaul & Eckert, 1997; Shapiro, DuPaul & Bradley-Klug, 1998).

Instructional Interventions

Table 15-1 provides suggestions that teachers can use to help children with ADHD function better in school. The suggestions are grouped under rearranging classroom layout, modifying teaching techniques, increasing student motivation, implementing organizational strategies, using alternative testing procedures, and offering counseling and special programs.

Family Interventions

Parent training programs can help parents increase a child's compliant behavior and reduce the child's noncompliant behavior (Barkley, 2000). Parents need to understand what factors lead to noncompliant behavior, how to attend to and reinforce acceptable behavior in and out of the home, and how to use time-outs. They should use positive reinforcement for positive behavior, follow through with punishment for negative behavior, set up a system to give rewards for good behavior, simplify and shorten directions for activities and chores, set clear and consistent rules, establish achievable expectations, help the child develop his or her natural talents, and keep a routine schedule of daily activities and home life. Parents also need to receive appropriate support and education about ADHD and about the developmental needs of their child. Parents with a child who has ADHD may benefit from participating in a local support group or joining a national organization such as Children and Adults with ADD (CHADD).

Good communication between parents and teachers may help to improve the behavior and academic performance of children with ADHD. Teachers and parents should be encouraged to use the same (or similar) behavior management programs and to keep each other informed about the child's progress. Communication between home and school may be daily or less frequent, depending on the specific needs of the child.

Alternative Treatments

"Unconventional" treatments for ADHD have little scientific support. Controversial alternative treatments include dietary interventions (e.g., using foods that are additive-free, using megavitamins and mineral supplements, treating alleged candida yeast infections), anti-motion sickness medicines, EEG biofeedback, applied kinesiology (manipulation of bones in the body), optometric-vision training (exercises to improve eye tracking), and auditory training (enhancing the ability to hear certain frequencies of sound).

Comment on Interventions

The most effective treatment for ADHD is multi-faceted and tailored to the individual needs of the child (DuPaul & Stoner, 2003). Depending on the situation, a child or adolescent with ADHD may require medication, behavior management, social skills training, and/or special accommodations in school. A combination of medication and psychosocial treatment should be considered for children with more severe forms of ADHD, for children who also have significant problems with aggression or who have severe problems in school,

Table 15-1
Strategies to Help a Teacher Work with a Child with ADHD

Rearranging Classroom Layout

- Seat the student toward the front of the classroom, preferably with quiet students, in order to reduce distractions, to better monitor the student's behavior, and to apply behavior management techniques. You may need to experiment to find the best seating arrangement. You might want to offer the student a study carrel (a small enclosure for individual study) if carrels are available. It is best to allow other children to use carrels as well so that the child with ADHD is not singled out.
- The currently popular classroom arrangement of desks in groups of four, five, or six facing each other in "pods" may not be ideal for children with ADHD. The traditional rows of desks or a large, U-shaped arrangement may work better for some children with ADHD.

Modifying Teaching Techniques

- Use directed teaching with individual attention to increase the student's scholastic ability and improve school behavior. Implement these techniques by using highly structured, step-by-step methods, with ample opportunities for practice, targeting of goals, and regular monitoring of performance. Try to ensure that the student understands information presented orally and in print. Maintain appropriate eye contact with the student and sometimes physical proximity, especially when giving instructions.
- Use multi-sensory approaches and stimulating tasks to help the student learn the material. Supplement traditional lectures with visual aids (diagrams, illustrations, graphic organizers), video clips, demonstrations, and small-group activities; use physical movement and hands-on activities and computers, calculators, and tape recorders. Teach children to actively visualize information while listening and reading.
- Modify work demands to increase the student's success rate. For example, (a) assign fewer problems for in-class and homework assignments, (b) allow the student to turn in at least half of an assignment if he or she meets a specified criterion, such as 90% accuracy on the completed part, and (c) divide tasks into manageable segments, set task priorities, establish fixed work periods, intersperse high-interest activities with regular work activities to maintain motivation, use novel tasks, alternate activities involving sitting and moving, promote consistent study habits, and promote a sense of responsibility for completing tasks.
- Modify instructions to improve the student's attention. Use short and simple instructions, slow the rate at which instruction are presented, demonstrate and model what is to be done, alert the student to critical information by using key phrases (e.g., "this is important" and "listen carefully"), encourage the student to ask for the instructions to be repeated if he or she doesn't understand them, and confirm that the student understands the instructions before proceeding to the task.
- Before the start of the activity, remind the student, if needed, about expected behaviors that are part of an activity.
- Establish peer tutoring programs to facilitate the student's learning. Pair the student with a student who does not have ADHD but does have well-developed social, behavioral, or academic skills and who will not exploit the child with ADHD.

Increasing Student Motivation

- Increase the student's motivation by modeling enthusiasm and interest in the lesson and by encouraging the student to pay attention in class, interact appropriately with other students, and show good behavior in school.
- Reinforce attending behavior by setting an egg timer, alarm clock, or tape recorder to make a sound at random intervals. Give the student reinforcement—such as verbal praise, points, tokens, free choice of an activity, or access to a classroom computer—if the student is attending when the sound occurs or if the student completes a difficult project.

Implementing Organizational Strategies

- Suggest organizational strategies to help the student complete his or her assignments and better control his or her behavior. For example, encourage the student to use assignment logs; memory and study strategies; a notebook with dividers to separate sections for lecture notes, assignments, appointments, phone numbers, and so forth; color-coded folders to organize assignments for reading, mathematics, social studies, science, and other subjects; highlighters and colored pens; concrete aids (e.g., a checklist of the day's activities placed on the desk); and self-monitoring procedures (see Chapter 9).
- Ensure that the student knows the homework assignments before leaving school. Give the student a homework assignment sheet, post assignments in the classroom and have the student copy them in his or her notebooks, post assignments on a classroom Web site or on the school's Web site, have the student complete at least one item of each homework task before leaving school, or encourage the student to e-mail the list of assignments to his or her home (if the school offers e-mail service to students).
- Establish firm class routines to help the student organize his or her day and know what is going on in class. Give the student a schedule indicating what will be done during each class period. Schedule academic subjects in the morning and nonacademic subjects in the afternoon, because the attention span of students with ADHD tends to worsen over the course of the day. Explain in advance when any change in the routine will be needed. Make the transition from one activity to another in a brief and well-organized manner.
- Have clear rules and guidelines for appropriate behavior. Remind students of the classroom rules, teach these rules as needed, and provide examples of students who are following the rules.

Using Alternative Testing Procedures

- Use alternative ways to test the student's mastery of the material. For example, allow the student to complete a project or make a poster instead of taking a test, take a multiple-choice test instead of a short-answer test, answer questions orally instead of in writing, take tests without the usual time limits, use special software, or take tests in a quiet room.

Table 15-1 (*Continued*)

Offering Counseling and Special Programs

• Encourage the student to seek counseling or to enroll in a special program (e.g., a social skills training program, an anger management and conflict management training program, an organizational skills training group, a study skills training program, or a coaching program) if the student

appears likely to benefit from one or more of these services. In a coaching program, an adult coach helps the student with ADHD develop better time-management and study skills and organize assignments into meaningful, manageable tasks (Dawson & Guare, 1998).

Source: Barkley (1998); Busch (1993); DuPaul, Ervin, Hook, and McGoey (1998); DuPaul and Hennington (1993); DuPaul and Stoner (2003); Lerner (1997); Rich and Taylor (1993); Rief (1993, 2003); Scruggs and Mastropieri (1992); Weyandt, Stein, Rice, and Wermus (1994). From *Assessment of Children: Behavioral, Social, and Clinical Foundations (Fifth Edition)* by Jerome M. Sattler and Robert D. Hoge. Copyright 2006 by Jerome M. Sattler, Publisher, Inc. Permission to photocopy this table is granted to purchasers of this book for personal use only (see copyright page for details).

when there is a severe family disruption caused by ADHD symptoms, when the severe problems occur during the day and in the evening, when there is a need for rapid response, for all three types of ADHD (especially the combined type), for all age groups except preschool, or for children with a co-occurring externalizing disorder (e.g. conduct disorder), mental retardation, or central nervous system problems. In contrast, psychosocial treatment should be considered for children with milder forms of ADHD, for preschool children with ADHD, for children with a co-occurring internalizing disorder (e.g., anxiety), for children with co-occurring social skill deficits, and when the family prefers psychosocial treatment (Conners, March, Frances, Wells, & Ross, 2001).

Teachers and parents may need information about ADHD, as well as additional training in behavior management, and parents may also need to learn effective parenting skills. Unfortunately, in some cases, one or more teachers or family members may not "believe in" ADHD, may refuse to cooperate with any treatment, and may criticize and interfere with the efforts of other family members or teachers who are trying to work with the child. Ongoing consultation by a psychologist may be essential in such cases.

The principal aim in treating children with ADHD (and similar problems) is to help them focus and sustain their at-

tention and keep impulsive responding to a minimum so that they can learn and realize their potential. A structured and predictable environment, clear and consistent expectations, and immediate feedback are helpful. Psychosocial interventions for children with ADHD should also address their unique interpersonal problems and adjustment difficulties. Finally, long-term interventions may be more effective than short-term ones (Barkley, 2002). The prognosis is better when children with ADHD have average to above-average intelligence; a supportive, nurturing family; nonaggressive behavior; and a good relationship with their peers (Barkley, 1998).

In schools, a case manager—a school psychologist, school counselor, school social worker, school nurse, or trained teacher—might be designated to follow the student's progress. The case manager's duties would include troubleshooting, providing counseling and support, checking schoolwork, serving as a liaison between the teaching staff and the parents, and overseeing and helping carry out behavioral interventions.

THINKING THROUGH THE ISSUES

1. Do you know a child with attention-deficit/hyperactivity disorder? What have you observed?
2. Do you know of any families that have a child with attention-deficit/hyperactivity disorder? If so, what has it been like for the family to raise the child?
3. What are the pros and cons of using medication for children with ADHD?
4. Why do you think some parents seek unconventional or alternative treatments for their child with ADHD?

Courtesy of Jerome M. Sattler and Jeff Bryson.

SUMMARY

1. Attention-deficit/hyperactivity disorder (ADHD) is a neurobehavioral syndrome marked by inattention, hyperactivity, and impulsivity.
2. A diagnosis of ADHD is made when a child displays the required number of symptoms of the disorder and these symptoms are present before age 7 years, for at least 6 months, and to

a degree that is maladaptive and inconsistent with an individual's developmental level; occur in two or more settings; and significantly affect the child's social or academic functioning.

3. The three types of ADHD cited in *DSM-IV–TR* are (a) attention-deficit/hyperactivity disorder: combined type, (b) attention-deficit/hyperactivity disorder: predominantly inattentive type, and (c) attention-deficit/hyperactivity disorder: predominantly hyperactive-impulsive type.

4. The three major symptoms of ADHD are inattention, hyperactivity, and impulsivity.

5. The ADHD population is heterogeneous, displaying a diversity of associated behavior problems, in addition to underlying attention problems.

6. About 44% of children with ADHD have at least one co-occurring disorder, about 33% have two co-occurring disorders, and about 10% have three co-occurring disorders.

7. The disorders that tend to co-occur with ADHD are learning disorders (25–50%), oppositional defiant disorder (25–33%), conduct disorder (26%), depressive disorder (18%), and anxiety disorder (26%).

8. Children with ADHD also may display aggressive behavior, low self-esteem, lability of mood, low tolerance for frustration, and temper outbursts.

9. ADHD often becomes most evident when children enter elementary school, where the demands of the classroom require sustained attention and in-seat, independent work.

10. Overactivity is a common hallmark of ADHD in early childhood, but overactivity decreases with age and may be replaced with feeling of restlessness in adolescence.

11. Boys with ADHD tend to display more aggressive and oppositional behaviors than girls, whereas girls with ADHD tend to have more internalizing problems and greater intellectual impairments than boys.

12. During adolescence and adulthood, children with a dual diagnosis of ADHD and conduct disorder are likely to have more problems than those who have either diagnosis alone.

13. Children with both ADHD and a learning disability usually have more problems controlling impulses, working independently, and functioning adequately in a classroom than do children who have a learning disability only.

14. ADHD symptoms tend to be exacerbated in children who have chronic illnesses, who have intermittent hearing losses associated with otitis media, who take drugs, or who have disorders of the central nervous system.

15. Approximately 3% to 7% of the school-age population has ADHD, with estimates of male-to-female ratios ranging from 2:1 to 9:1.

16. ADHD is the most frequent reason for referral to child mental health clinics.

17. Children with ADHD, in addition to having problems with inattention, hyperactivity, and impulsivity, may have neuropsychological deficits; cognitive deficits; social and adaptive functioning deficits; motivational and emotional deficits; and motor, physical, and health deficits.

18. Deficits in self-regulation may underlie the difficulty children with ADHD have with organization and planning, with the mobilization and maintenance of effortful attention, and with the inhibition of inappropriate responding.

19. Consequently, children with ADHD may show considerable variability across situations depending, in part, on the task requirements, the quantity and type of environmental distracters, and the environmental supports available.

20. Parents of children with ADHD tend to be more depressed and to have lower self-esteem than parents of normally functioning children; they may believe that they have diminished parenting skills, may feel stigmatized or guilty, and may enjoy less marital satisfaction than parents of normal children.

Etiology

21. Given the heterogeneity of its symptoms, ADHD probably has no single cause; multiple factors likely contribute to its development and expression.

22. Although the precise causes and mechanisms of ADHD are unknown, research suggests that genetic, neurological, and prenatal factors underlie the disorder.

23. The brain structures of individuals with and without ADHD differ anatomically.

24. In addition, individuals with ADHD may have an imbalance of or deficiency in one or more neurotransmitters (e.g., dopamine) in several areas of the brain, particularly the frontal lobes and connections to subcortical structures.

25. Finally, the difficulty experienced by individuals with ADHD in performing neuropsychological tasks suggests deficits in cortical functioning.

26. Exposure of the fetus to nicotine, alcohol, and other drugs and maternal psychosocial stress during pregnancy have been associated with increased risk of ADHD.

27. Contrary to some hypotheses, food additives, sugar, and fluorescent lighting have not been found to cause ADHD.

28. Prenatal and postnatal exposure to toxic substances such as lead, methylmercury, and pesticides has been associated with a spectrum of neurodevelopmental deficits (e.g., problems in memory, attention, and learning), but it is not known whether exposure to these substances affects the developing brain in such a way as to contribute to ADHD.

29. Advances in brain-imaging technology and genetic research should help to clarify the etiology of ADHD.

30. Whatever the etiology, problems with self-regulation comprise the core of ADHD; these problems, in turn, may express themselves as behavioral deficits in executive functions, working memory, internalized speech, and behavioral inhibition.

31. We also need to consider that poor classroom organization, limited parental education, and ineffective parenting styles may cause ADHD-like behaviors in children who do not have the disorder or may exacerbate symptoms of ADHD.

Assessment

32. As is true of all childhood disorders, the assessment of ADHD requires a comprehensive and thorough evaluation.

33. You will want to assess the presence of symptoms; number, type, severity, and duration of symptoms; situations in which symptoms are displayed; verbal abilities, nonverbal abilities, short- and long-term memory abilities, and other cognitive abilities; presence of any co-occurring disorders; social competence and adaptive behavior; and educational and instructional needs.

34. Interviews with the child's parents and teachers, as well as with the child, will form a key part of the assessment.

35. An interview with at least one parent (preferably both parents) is critical for obtaining information about the child's prenatal and postnatal development; medical, social, and academic history; medications taken currently and previously; the parent's view of the child's problems (including the age at which the problems began and the pervasiveness of the problems); par-

enting styles and disciplinary techniques; environmental factors that may contribute to the child's problems; and resources available to the family.

36. Teachers can offer valuable information about when symptoms occur, the specific behaviors that interfere with the child's school functioning, the severity of symptoms, the factors that may exacerbate the problem behavior, the child's academic strengths and weaknesses, the child's social skill strengths and weaknesses, and the quality of the child's peer relationships.

37. Although children often provide valuable information about themselves, they occasionally provide information of questionable validity.

38. Observation of the child's behaviors will give you information about the antecedents and consequences of the behaviors; intensity, duration, and rate of the behaviors; and factors that may be contributing to and sustaining the behaviors.

39. Conduct the observations in multiple settings and at different times of the day.

40. If you want to observe a child's behavior while he or she works on a school-related assignment in a clinic playroom, you can use the Structured Observation of Academic and Play Settings (SOAPS).

41. If a child is given an assignment during an observation period, inspect the quality of the completed assignment.

42. When you observe a child, note any symptoms associated with ADHD, including whether the child remains focused on a task, responds to distractions, makes repetitive purposeless motions, leaves his or her seat without permission, vocalizes, or engages in aggressive or noncompliant behavior.

43. Both broadband and narrowband rating scales administered to parents, teachers, and children can help to identify appropriate and inappropriate behaviors, including those specifically related to ADHD.

44. Broadband rating scales survey a wide spectrum of symptoms and behaviors (e.g., externalizing and internalizing disorders), whereas narrowband rating scales survey behaviors associated with a specific disorder (e.g., ADHD or depression only).

45. Intelligence tests, achievement tests, memory tests, and neuropsychological tests are useful in the assessment of ADHD.

46. Some examiners like to include a computerized continuous performance test in the assessment.

47. Continuous performance tests should never be used independently to make a diagnosis of ADHD.

48. Additional reliability and validity studies are needed to evaluate the contribution of continuous performance tests to the assessment of ADHD.

49. Intelligence tests also are not sufficiently sensitive to be used exclusively in making a diagnosis of ADHD or in discriminating among various subtypes of ADHD.

50. However, patterns of strengths and weaknesses revealed by intelligence tests are useful in evaluating children's cognitive abilities.

51. Arriving at a diagnosis of ADHD is not easy, because restlessness, inattention, and overactive behavior are common in children between the ages of 2 and 12 years.

52. A comprehensive assessment of ADHD requires the use of both rating scales and direct observations.

53. The major difficulties of children with ADHD may be reflected in their performance in some, but not all, situations and on some, but not all, psychological tests.

54. Novel, structured, one-on-one situations (as in an individual assessment) or situations that are highly stimulating and that

provide frequent feedback about performance (e.g., video games) may not elicit the same degree of ADHD symptomatology as the child's classroom.

Interventions

55. Pharmacological, behavioral, cognitive-behavioral, instructional, and familial interventions are used in the treatment of children with ADHD.

56. Children with ADHD are often prescribed stimulant medications.

57. Stimulant medications may be short-acting (e.g., taken every 4 hours or when medication is needed), (b) intermediate-acting (e.g., taken twice a day), or (c) long-acting (e.g., taken in the morning).

58. Short-acting stimulants are helpful when it is preferable for the medication to take effect rapidly but not last a long time; long-acting stimulants are helpful for children whose activities require sustained attention beyond school hours (e.g., homework, family activities, club meetings, team sports).

59. Approximately 80% of hyperactive children respond positively to stimulant medication.

60. Examples of short-acting stimulant medications are Ritalin, Methylin, and Focaline (methylphenidates); Dexedrine, Dextrostat, and Adderall (amphetamines).

61. Examples of intermediate-acting stimulant medications are Ritalin SR, Ritalin LA, Metadate ER, and Methylin ER (methylphenidates); and Dexedrine spansule (amphetamine).

62. Examples of long-acting stimulant medications are Adderall XR (amphetamine); Concerta and Metadate CD (methylphenidates).

63. Strattera (atomoxetine), a nonstimulant, nonantidepressant long-acting medication, also improves ADHD symptomatology.

64. Both stimulant and nonstimulant medications may have side effects that range from mild to severe.

65. Examples of side effects are insomnia, appetite suppression, sleep disturbance, weight loss, headaches, irritability, stomachache, nausea, dizziness, fatigue, mood swings, social withdrawal, and increased activity or bad mood as the medication wears off; less common side effects are dry mouth, dizziness, and transient tics.

66. Most side effects can be relieved by adjusting the dosage or the schedule of medication or by using a different medication.

67. Antidepressants also have been used with some success, particularly when children with ADHD have coexisting depression.

68. Antidepressant medications also have their side effects (e.g., fatigue, constipation, dry mouth, blurred vision) and may increase the risk of suicidal thinking and behavior in children with depression and other psychiatric illnesses.

69. Antidepressants are not as effective as stimulant medications in improving attention and concentration.

70. Although exactly how stimulant medications improve symptoms of ADHD is not known, these medications are thought to restore central nervous system arousal levels and inhibitory levels to normal, thereby giving children with ADHD better attention and self-control.

71. Many children with ADHD who take stimulant medication show dramatic behavioral changes, with noticeable improvement in motor behavior, attention, and impulse control; in addition, they may show, to a lesser degree, better compliance and more positive social behaviors because their impulsivity is reduced.

72. However, pharmacological intervention usually does not correct social or academic deficits.

73. Behavioral interventions can enhance the effectiveness of medication and are often effective alone, although the combination of stimulant medications and behavioral interventions seems most promising.

74. Examples of behavioral interventions are positive reinforcement, withdrawal of reinforcement, a point system, and contracts between teacher and student or between parent and child that stipulate the desired and expected behaviors at school and/or at home.

75. Cognitive-behavioral interventions are based on the premise that a child's behavior is mediated by cognitions. The aim of such interventions is to increase the child's ability to think before acting or to delay gratification. However, studies indicate that cognitive-behavioral interventions for the treatment of AHDH are not effective when used independently of other types of interventions. More promising are self-monitoring programs, which train children and adolescents to monitor their own behavior and keep track of the frequency of inappropriate and appropriate behaviors.

76. In school-based programs, behavior management and instructional interventions are more effective in changing behavior than are cognitive-behavioral interventions.

77. Teachers can help children with ADHD by rearranging classroom layout, modifying teaching techniques, increasing student motivation, implementing organizational strategies, using alternative testing procedures, and offering counseling and special programs.

78. Parent training programs can help parents increase a child's compliant behavior and reduce the child's noncompliant behavior.

79. Parents need to understand what factors lead to noncompliant behavior, how to attend to and reinforce acceptable behavior in and out of the home, and how to use time-outs.

80. They should use positive reinforcement for positive behavior, follow through with punishment for negative behavior, set up a system to give rewards for good behavior, simplify and shorten directions for activities and chores, set clear and consistent rules, establish achievable expectations, help the child develop his or her natural talents, and keep a routine schedule of daily activities and home life.

81. Parents also need to receive appropriate support and education about ADHD and about the developmental needs of their child.

82. Parents with a child who has ADHD may benefit from participating in a local support group or joining a national organization such as Children and Adults with ADD (CHADD).

83. Good communication between parents and teachers may help to improve the behavior and academic performance of children with ADHD.

84. "Unconventional" treatments for ADHD have little scientific support.

85. Controversial alternative treatments include dietary interventions, anti-motion sickness medicines, EEG biofeedback, applied kinesiology, optometric-vision training, and auditory training.

86. The most effective treatment for ADHD is multi-faceted and tailored to the individual needs of the child.

87. Depending on the situation, a child or adolescent with ADHD may require medication, behavior management, social skills training, and/or special accommodations in school.

88. A combination of medication and psychosocial treatment should be considered for children who have a severe form of ADHD, for children who also have significant problems with aggression or in school, when there is severe family disruption, when severe problems occur during the day and in the evening, when there is a need for a rapid response, for all three types of ADHD, for all age groups except preschool, or for children with a co-occurring externalizing disorder, mental retardation, or central nervous system problems.

89. In contrast, psychosocial treatment should be considered for children with milder forms of ADHD, for preschool children with ADHD, for children with a co-occurring internalizing disorder (e.g., anxiety), for children with co-occurring social skill deficits, and when the family prefers psychosocial treatment.

90. Teachers and parents may need information about ADHD, as well as additional training in behavior management, and parents may also need to learn effective parenting skills.

91. The principal aim in treating children with ADHD (and similar problems) is to help them focus and sustain their attention and keep impulsive responding to a minimum so that they can learn and realize their potential. A structured and predictable environment, clear and consistent expectations, and immediate feedback are helpful.

92. Psychosocial interventions for children with ADHD should also address their unique interpersonal problems and adjustment difficulties.

93. Finally, long-term interventions may be more effective than short-term ones.

94. The prognosis is better when children with ADHD have average to above-average intelligence; a supportive, nurturing family; nonaggressive behavior; and a good relationship with their peers.

95. In schools, a case manager—a school psychologist, school counselor, school social worker, school nurse, or trained teacher—might be designated to follow the student's progress.

KEY TERMS, CONCEPTS, AND NAMES

Attention-deficit/hyperactivity disorder (ADHD) (p. 375)

Attention-deficit/hyperactivity disorder: combined type (p. 375)

Attention-deficit/hyperactivity disorder: predominantly inattentive type (p. 375)

Attention-deficit/hyperactivity disorder: predominantly hyperactive-impulsive type (p. 375)

Inattention (p. 375)

Hyperactivity (p. 375)

Impulsivity (p. 375)

Co-occurring disorder (p. 375)

Comorbid disorder (p. 375)

Cognitive deficits (p. 376)

Social and adaptive functioning deficits (p. 376)

Motivational and emotional deficits (p. 376)

Motor, physical, and health deficits (p. 376)

Deficits in self-regulation (p. 376)

Etiology of ADHD (p. 377)

Assessment of ADHD (p. 377)

Parent interview (p. 377)

Teacher interview (p. 378)

Child interview (p. 378)

Behavioral observations (p. 378)

Formal classroom observation systems for children who may have ADHD (p. 379)

Structured Observation of Academic and Play Settings (SOAPS) (p. 379)

Broadband rating scales (p. 379)

Narrowband rating scales (p. 379)

Psychological tests (p. 380)

Computerized continuous performance test (p. 380)

Pharmacological interventions (p. 381)

Short-acting stimulant medications (p. 381)

Intermediate-acting stimulant medications (p. 381)

Long-acting stimulant medications (p. 382)

Antidepressants (p. 382)

Paradoxical effect (p. 382)

Behavioral interventions (p. 382)

Positive reinforcement (p. 382)

Withdrawal of reinforcement (p. 382)

Point system (p. 382)

Contracts between teacher and student or between parent and child (p. 382)

Cognitive-behavioral interventions (p. 382)

Instructional interventions (p. 383)

Family interventions (p. 383)

Parent training programs (p. 383)

Home-school communication (p. 383)

Alternative treatments (p. 383)

STUDY QUESTIONS

1. Describe attention-deficit/hyperactivity disorder and discuss its etiology.
2. Discuss the assessment of attention-deficit/hyperactivity disorder.
3. Discuss interventions for attention-deficit/hyperactivity disorder. Compare and contrast pharmacological interventions, behavioral interventions, cognitive-behavioral interventions, instructional interventions, and family interventions.

16

SPECIFIC LEARNING DISABILITIES: BACKGROUND CONSIDERATIONS

by Jerome M. Sattler and Barbara Lowenthal

The most turbulent, the most restless child has, amidst all his faults, something true, ingenious and natural, which is of infinite value, and merits every respect.
—Felix-Antoine-Philibert Dupanloup, French bishop and educator (1802–1878)

What Are the Signs of Learning Disability?

Definitions of Learning Disability

Etiology of Learning Disabilities

Precursors of Learning Disabilities at Preschool Age

School-Age Children with Learning Disabilities

The Process of Reading

Communication Disorders

Reading Disorder

Mathematics Disorder

Disorder of Written Expression

Nonverbal Learning Disability

Thinking Through the Issues

Summary

Key Terms, Concepts, and Names

Study Questions

Goals and Objectives

This chapter is designed to enable you to do the following:

- Become familiar with several definitions of learning disability

- Become familiar with theories of the etiology of learning disabilities

- Understand information-processing models of learning disabilities

- Understand the major forms of learning disabilities

Approximately 10% to 15% of children in the United States have some form of learning disability, although prevalence rates are difficult to establish because reporting sources use different definitions and diagnostic criteria (Silver, 1991). The major types of learning disability are reading disorder, mathematics disorder, and disorder of written expression (including spelling). Other types of learning disability are communication disorder and nonverbal learning disability. The reported prevalence rate of learning disability is higher for boys than for girls by a ratio of about 3 to 1 (DeFries, 1989).

WHAT ARE THE SIGNS OF LEARNING DISABILITY?

Following are signs that suggest a possible learning disability (National Information Center for Children and Youth with Disabilities, 2004):

- Has trouble learning the alphabet, rhyming words, or connecting letters to their sounds
- Makes mistakes when reading aloud
- Repeats words and pauses often when reading aloud
- Has trouble understanding what he or she reads
- Has trouble with spelling
- Has messy handwriting
- Holds a pencil awkwardly
- Has difficulty expressing ideas in writing
- Learned to talk late
- Has a limited vocabulary
- Has trouble remembering the sounds that letters represent
- Has trouble hearing slight differences between words
- Has trouble understanding jokes, comic strips, metaphorical language, and sarcasm
- Has trouble following directions
- Mispronounces words
- Incorrectly uses a word that sounds similar to the correct word
- Has trouble organizing what he or she wants to say
- Has difficulty retelling a story in order
- Has trouble thinking of the word that he or she needs for writing or conversation
- Has difficulty following social rules of conversation, such as taking turns
- IIas difficulty knowing where to begin a task
- Confuses math symbols
- Misreads numbers
- Becomes lost in the middle of mathematical calculations
- Reverses numbers

DEFINITIONS OF LEARNING DISABILITY

There are several definitions of learning disability. (Note that the terms *learning disability* and *specific learning disability* are sometimes used interchangeably.)

IDEA 2004

The Individuals with Disabilities Education Improvement Act (IDEA 2004) defines specific learning disability in the following way:

SEC. 602. DEFINITIONS.
(30) SPECIFIC LEARNING DISABILITY—
(A) IN GENERAL—The term "specific learning disability" means a disorder in 1 or more of the basic psychological processes involved in understanding or in using language, spoken or written, which disorder may manifest itself in the imperfect ability to listen, think, speak, read, write, spell, or do mathematical calculations.
(B) DISORDERS INCLUDED—Such term includes such conditions as perceptual disabilities, brain injury, minimal brain dysfunction, dyslexia, and developmental aphasia.
(C) DISORDERS NOT INCLUDED—Such term does not include a learning problem that is primarily the result of visual, hearing, or motor disabilities, of mental retardation, of emotional disturbance, or of environmental, cultural, or economic disadvantage.

The definition of specific learning disability in IDEA 2004 needs further refinement, for the following reasons.

1. Several terms in the federal definition—including "disorder," "basic psychological processes," and "imperfect ability"—are vague, subjective, and open to interpretation. For example, what criteria do we use to classify a child's performance as "disordered" or "imperfect"? What are "basic psychological processes" and how should they be measured?
2. The disorders included in the definition are rather general and need to be more specific. Do all perceptual disabilities and brain injuries constitute learning disabilities? Under what conditions does a child with minimal brain dysfunction also have a learning disability?
3. In dealing with children with multiple problems, it is often difficult to decide which condition is primary and which is secondary. For instance, are the emotional problems of some children with learning disabilities a result of prolonged poor achievement, or are children with emotional problems at greater risk for developing learning disabilities?
4. The exclusionary criteria in the federal definition of learning disability make it difficult to classify children with sensory problems, emotional problems, or environmental disadvantages as learning disabled. Neither the definition of learning disability nor the accompanying provisions of IDEA provide any operational criteria for identifying children who have sensory problems, emotional problems, or environmental disadvantages. What degree of sensory loss, for example, is required to exclude a child? Similarly, what criteria are used to identify children as having an emotional disturbance or cultural disadvantage?

Furthermore, the exclusionary criteria—such as cultural or economic disadvantage and emotional disturbance—are criteria that influence the development of learning disabilities because they shape "the central nervous system and the child's cognitive and linguistic repertoire" (Lyon, Fletcher, Shaywitz, Shaywitz, Torgesen, Wood, Schulte, & Olson, 2001, p. 268). The exclusionary criteria may lead to the mistaken belief that a child cannot have a specific learning disability together with a visual, hearing, or motor disability; an emotional disturbance; or an environmental, cultural, or economic disadvantage. Consequently, it is poor policy to have an exclusionary element as part of the definition of learning disability.

5. The federal definition does not discuss the heterogeneity of the condition or appropriate interventions.
6. The federal definition does not explain that learning disabilities may exist concurrently with other conditions.
7. The federal definition implies but does not explain the causes of learning disability.

National Joint Committee on Learning Disabilities

Another definition of learning disability, approved in 1989 by the National Joint Committee on Learning Disabilities, is generally consistent with IDEA 2004. The National Joint Committee on Learning Disabilities, however, does not use the term "basic psychological processes" and it specifies difficulties in reasoning, in addition to the possible academic and spoken language problems listed in IDEA 2004. This definition recognizes the heterogeneity of the condition (National Joint Committee on Learning Disabilities, 1991):

> *Learning disabilities* is a general term that refers to a heterogeneous group of disorders manifested by significant difficulties in the acquisition and use of listening, speaking, reading, writing, reasoning, or mathematical abilities. These disorders are intrinsic to the individual, presumed to be due to central nervous system dysfunction, and may occur across the life span. Problems in self-regulatory behaviors, social perception, and social interaction may exist with learning disabilities but do not by themselves constitute a learning disability. Although learning disabilities may occur concomitantly with other handicapping conditions (for example, sensory impairment, mental retardation, serious emotional disturbance), or with extrinsic influences (such as cultural differences, insufficient or inappropriate instruction), they are not the result of those conditions or influences. (p. 19)

This definition also is somewhat vague and ambiguous, fails to operationalize the procedures needed for the determination of a learning disability, and lacks empirical validation (Lyon, 1996a).

Learning Disabilities Association of Canada

The Learning Disabilities Association of Canada (2002) adopted a national definition of learning disabilities that is more comprehensive than the other definitions in this section. First, it emphasizes disorders in either verbal or nonverbal areas. Second, it indicates that a learning disability label applies only to individuals who have average thinking and/or reasoning abilities. Third, it emphasizes that learning disabilities may also involve problems in organization, interpersonal relations, and perspective taking. Finally, it stresses the need for early identification and intervention.

> "Learning Disabilities" refer to a number of disorders which may affect the acquisition, organization, retention, understanding or use of verbal or nonverbal information. These disorders affect learning in individuals who otherwise demonstrate at least average abilities essential for thinking and/or reasoning. As such, learning disabilities are distinct from global intellectual deficiency.
>
> Learning disabilities result from impairments in one or more processes related to perceiving, thinking, remembering or learning. These include, but are not limited to: language processing; phonological processing; visual spatial processing; processing speed; memory and attention; and executive functions (e.g. planning and decision-making).
>
> Learning disabilities range in severity and may interfere with the acquisition and use of one or more of the following:
>
> - oral language (e.g. listening, speaking, understanding);
> - reading (e.g. decoding, phonetic knowledge, word recognition, comprehension);
> - written language (e.g. spelling and written expression); and mathematics (e.g. computation, problem solving).
>
> Learning disabilities may also involve difficulties with organizational skills, social perception, social interaction and perspective taking.
>
> Learning disabilities are lifelong. The way in which they are expressed may vary over an individual's lifetime, depending on the interaction between the demands of the environment and the individual's strengths and needs. Learning disabilities are suggested by unexpected academic under-achievement or achievement which is maintained only by unusually high levels of effort and support.
>
> Learning disabilities are due to genetic and/or neurobiological factors or injury that alters brain functioning in a manner which affects one or more processes related to learning. These disorders are not due primarily to hearing and/or vision problems, socio-economic factors, cultural or linguistic differences, lack of motivation or ineffective teaching, although these factors may further complicate the challenges faced by individuals with learning disabilities. Learning disabilities may co-exist with various conditions including attentional, behavioral and emotional disorders, sensory impairments or other medical conditions.
>
> For success, individuals with learning disabilities require early identification and timely specialized assessments and interventions involving home, school, community and workplace settings. The interventions need to be appropriate for each individual's learning disability subtype and, at a minimum, include the provision of:
>
> - specific skill instruction;
> - accommodations;
> - compensatory strategies; and
> - self-advocacy skills.

DSM-IV–TR

DSM-IV–TR provides the following guidelines for defining *learning disorders* (American Psychiatric Association, 2000):

> Learning Disorders are diagnosed when the individual's achievement on individually administered, standardized tests in reading, mathematics, or written expression is substantially below that expected for age, schooling, and level of intelligence. The learning problems significantly interfere with academic achievement or activities of daily living that require reading, mathematical, or writing skills. A variety of statistical approaches can be used to establish that a discrepancy is significant. *Substantially below* is usually defined as a discrepancy of more than 2 standard deviations between achievement and IQ. A smaller discrepancy between achievement and IQ (i.e., between 1 and 2 standard deviations) is sometimes used, especially in cases where an individual's performance on an IQ test may have been compromised by an associated disorder in cognitive processing, a co-occurring mental disorder or general medical condition, or the individual's ethnic or cultural background. If a sensory deficit is present, the learning difficulties must be in excess of those usually associated with the deficit. Learning Disorders may persist into adulthood. (pp. 49–50)

DSM-IV–TR guidelines generally follow those of IDEA 2004.

Comment on Definitions of Learning Disability

Although the definition of learning disability continues to be elusive and children with this label represent an extraordinarily heterogeneous population, *the common characteristic usually shared by children with learning disabilities is academic underachievement.* Our real task is to determine which children need assistance, regardless of legal definitions that specify what constitutes a learning disability. Children with learning disabilities are especially vulnerable to the development of severe academic and perhaps social-emotional difficulties if they fall behind academically and are unable to catch up with their peers.

ETIOLOGY OF LEARNING DISABILITIES

Learning disabilities likely have multiple etiologies—including genetic, biological, and environmental bases—that presumably produce an altered or dysfunctional central nervous system (Bigler, Lajiness-O'Neill, & Howes, 1998).

Genetic Basis

Learning disabilities can occur across generations of families. Phonological processing problems, in particular, can be heritable (Lyon, 1996b; Olson, 1999). *Phonological processing* (or *phonological awareness*) refers to the ability to detect the sounds of speech and how they relate to print, including sequences of sounds within words, awareness of word boundaries, blending, segmentation, deletion, and rhyming.

The risk of dyslexia is estimated to be eight times greater for children of parents with reading disorders than for children of parents without reading disorders (Wadsworth, Olson, Pennington, & DeFries, 2000). The severity of the learning disorders is greater when both parents are affected (DeFries & Alarcon, 1996; Pennington, 1999). In addition, the reading skills of identical twins are similar even if they have been raised separately (DeFries, Gillis, & Wadsworth, 1993; Wadsworth et al., 2000). Finally, multiple genes appear to be involved in the transmission of learning disabilities (Olson, 1999; Raskind, 2001).

Biological Basis

Hypotheses postulating biological bases for learning disabilities receive support from studies using computed tomography (CT), magnetic resonance imaging (MRI), computerized EEG, and positron emission tomography (PET; see Chapter 24 for descriptions of these procedures). Research shows that there are anatomical and electrophysiological differences between the brains of children with learning disabilities and the brains of children without them (Ackerman, McPherson, Oglesby, & Dykman, 1998; Filipek, 1995; Shaywitz & Shaywitz, 2003). For example, in comparison with children without learning disabilities, children with learning disabilities have different patterns of brain activation while reading and a disruption in the neural systems for reading in the parietotemporal and occipitotemporal areas of the brain (Shaywitz, Shaywitz, Pugh, Mench, Fulbright, Skudlarski, Constable, Marchione, Fletcher, Lyon & Gore, 2002). In addition, PET scans show that adults with learning disabilities have more irregularities in cerebral blood flow and glucose metabolism than do those without learning disabilities (Shaywitz et al., 2002). (Most PET scans are conducted with adults instead of with children because the procedure is invasive and involves exposure to radioactive materials.)

Environmental Basis

Several environmental factors may be involved in the development of learning disabilities. First, children with learning disabilities may use ineffective learning strategies in analyzing problems, relating the nature of the problem to previous experience, developing a strategic plan for operating on the information, and monitoring and adjusting performance (Lyon & Moats, 1988). Second, learning disabilities may be pedagogically induced, especially among children from minority linguistic and cultural groups (National Reading Panel, 2000). Other factors may include parental attitudes toward learning, parents' child-management techniques, family verbal interaction patterns, early reading experiences, children's temperament, children's level of motivation, and the family's socioeconomic status (Hart & Risley, 1995; Whitehurst & Fischel, 1994). However, children at all socioeconomic levels may have learning disabilities (Fletcher, Lyon, Barnes, Stuebing, Francis, Olson, Shaywitz, & Shaywitz, 2002).

PRECURSORS OF LEARNING DISABILITIES AT PRESCHOOL AGE

Precursors of learning disabilities at preschool age include specific delays or deviances in one or more of the following domains (Cook, Tessier, & Klein, 2004; Pisecco, Baker, Silva, & Brooke, 2001):

"Your feelings of insecurity seem to have started when Mary Lou Gurnblatt said, 'Maybe I don't have a learning disability—maybe you have a teaching disability.'"

Courtesy of Tony Saltzmann.

• *Motor.* Preschool children may have difficulties or delays in both gross- and fine-motor development. They may have difficulty with walking, jumping, hopping, running, skipping, throwing, catching, assembling puzzles, building with blocks, doing art projects, and using scissors.

• *Behavioral.* Preschool children may show hyperactivity, impulsivity, inattention, and distractibility. They may not listen, often lose things, need much supervision, continually shift from one activity to another, and fail to finish what they start.

• *Cognitive/executive.* Preschool children may be disorganized. They may have difficulty in planning ahead, show confusion about the sequence of routine activities, and lose clothes, toys, and school materials.

• *Memory.* Preschool children may have memory difficulties or difficulty in acquiring facts, accumulating general knowledge, and learning word sounds.

• *Communication.* Preschool children may show speech and language delays. They may have difficulties in learning listening and speaking skills and age-appropriate vocabulary and may have problems with syntax, articulation, and pragmatics.

• *Perceptual.* Preschool children may have visual or auditory processing difficulties. They may be able to see and hear, but they may not be able to interpret the sensations appropriately. Those with *auditory processing difficulties* may not recognize sounds in the environment or be able to differentiate sounds in words, whereas those with *visual processing problems* may not be able to sort objects by size, color, or shape or to interpret pictures accurately.

• *Social-emotional.* Preschool children may have difficulties in regulating emotions and in developing friendships.

Although some of these same problems may be exhibited by preschool children without learning disabilities, the problems should be evaluated when a child has several of them over a long period.

SCHOOL-AGE CHILDREN WITH LEARNING DISABILITIES

School-age children with learning disabilities have deficient academic skills. They also may have deficits in information-processing abilities, neuropsychological skills, and social-behavioral adjustment (Hallahan & Mercer, 2002). Research indicates that approximately 75% of children with learning disabilities have social-skill deficits. These deficits may be associated with prolonged failure in school, which leads to a diminished self-concept, low achievement expectations, and feelings of helplessness (Kavale & Forness, 1996; Lerner, 2003). The presence of a learning disability, however, should not in itself be taken as evidence of poor social adjustment. Factors such as the nature of the learning disability, the child's self-concept, the quality of the parent-child relationship, and family functioning should be considered. Children with learning disabilities also may have symptoms of attention-deficit/hyperactivity disorder. Estimates of the percentage of children with reading disabilities who also have ADHD range from 10% to 45% (Aaron, Joshi, Palmer, Smith, & Kirby, 2002).

School-age children with learning disabilities may encounter some of the following problems. (Again, note that children without learning disabilities also may have some of these problems.)

• *Cognitive/academic.* School-age children may have difficulty with verbal material, including poor phonological awareness and poor reading recognition (e.g., confusion in identifying or printing certain letters and numerals). They may frequently lose their place when reading printed materials and may read slowly or with limited fluency. They also may have poor reading comprehension, deficient oral vocabulary, below-average grammatical understanding, poor verbal expression, limited pragmatic skills, poor listening, limited written expression, and poor mathematical skills.

• *Information-processing/executive.* School-age children may have poor cognitive strategies, inadequate study skills, difficulty recognizing whether tasks have been performed correctly, difficulty identifying critical information needed to solve problems, difficulty recognizing whether more information is needed to solve problems, and other difficulties with self-monitoring skills and self-regulation skills. In addition, they may have poor independent work habits, poor organizational and planning skills (including carelessness in paperwork and a disorganized approach to tasks that involve a sequence of actions), a tendency to be slow to complete work, and difficulty working under time constraints. Finally, they may have poor retrieval of encoded information.

• *Perceptual.* School-age children may have difficulty memorizing auditory or visual stimuli, poor visual organization, poor spatial perception, poor revisualization, difficulty in perceiving figure-ground relationships, difficulty in temporal sequencing, difficulty in interpreting facial expressions and body language, limited attention span, visual and audi-tory perceptual difficulties, difficulties with cross-modal sensory integration (such as problems integrating visual and auditory information presented simultaneously), speech articulation problems, delayed development of consistent hand preference, and poor fine-motor coordination (including poor writing and/or drawing).

• *Social-behavioral.* School-age children may show immaturity, distractibility, disruptiveness, impulsiveness, destructiveness, hyperactivity, disorganization, irritability, mischievousness, acting-out behavior, difficulty with conflict management, poor self-image, low self-esteem, minimal confidence in their ability to influence learning outcomes, low expectations for future achievement, anxiety, depression, a tendency to relate better to younger children, and difficulty in making friends.

Because children with learning disabilities are such a heterogeneous group, it is unlikely that any one child will exhibit all or most of these problems. Behavioral problems, if present, may stem from learning problems, learning problems may stem from behavioral problems, and both learning and behavioral problems may stem from a common etiology.

A Four-Stage Information-Processing Model

The following four-stage information-processing model is helpful in the study of children with learning disabilities. It emphasizes the importance of memory in the intervening stages between the reception of information and the output of a response (also see Figure 16-1; Deshler, Ellis, & Lenz, 1996).

Stage 1: Short-term sensory storage, or sensory register. An intact representation of the incoming information is briefly stored (e.g., the contents of a sentence that is read or the directions given by the teacher for an assignment).

Stage 2: Perceptual encoding, or short-term memory or working memory storage. The intact representation of the information is encoded into a more durable representation, probably a name code, which can be held in short-term memory storage. This is a temporary holding area where information is maintained for immediate use or for transfer to long-term memory storage. Working memory storage has at least two core areas. One is the *verbal communications area,* useful for storing speech-based phonological information, and the other is the *visual-spatial information area,* useful for storing mental images (Swanson & Sáez, 2003). Mental operations or calculations can be performed on information in working memory storage (e.g., verbal rehearsal can be used to remember a phone number or to perform a mental arithmetic task, or visual-spatial information can be used to generate and manipulate mental images). Tasks performed in working memory may also require the retrieval of information from long-term memory. The more automatic the retrieval, the more easily the task can be performed.

Stage 3: Central processing, or long-term memory storage. The encoded information is manipulated, and decisions are made about it (e.g., the encoded stimulus may be compared with other stimuli held in short-term memory, or associates of the encoded stimulus may be retrieved from long-term memory). Long-term memory has a large capacity and is relatively permanent. Memory in long-term storage can be classified as episodic or semantic. *Episodic memory* refers to representations of personal experience (e.g., the name of your first teacher), while *semantic memory* refers to facts, concepts, or generalizations interconnected in some manner (e.g., what we celebrate on the Fourth of July).

Stage 4: Response selection mechanisms. Relevant information is retrieved, and a response program or a processing strategy is selected, based on decisions made in the prior stage (e.g., a decision might be made to answer a question in a certain way).

Various processes such as selective attention, coding, organization, rehearsal, and retrieval help to regulate the flow of information through the four stages. These processes direct a child toward sources of relevant information, arrange material to be remembered in meaningful chunks, store information in short-term memory, and mediate the transfer of information to long-term memory. In summary, the stages of the model are discrete, incoming stimuli are transformed, and the transformed (or recoded) stimuli serve as input to subsequent stages.

Deficits Associated with Learning Disabilities

Children with learning disabilities may have inadequate executive control functions, which lead them to have difficulty on tasks requiring active information processing and verbal working memory (Torgesen, 1981; Webster, Plante, & Couvillion, 1997). Thus, they typically fail to use mnemonic aids such as labeling, verbal rehearsal, clustering, chunking, and selective attention to help themselves remember important information. In addition, they have difficulties in generalizing and flexibly deploying other strategies needed to understand, remember, and solve problems. If they have a reading disorder, they may be unable to detect inadequacies, confusion, and inconsistencies in the material they read; to identify the critical content of what they read; and to encode phonological information in long-term memory (Siegler, 1998).

The major problem of children with learning disabilities may be not so much an inability to attend selectively to materials as difficulty in analyzing a task and selecting the proper strategies to accomplish it. Difficulty in applying efficient task strategies is not unique to children with learning disabilities, however; children with mental retardation and young nondisabled children also have such difficulties. From an information-processing perspective, learning disabilities may be viewed as a deficiency in the executive or regulatory system (Borkowski & Burke, 1996).

Several explanations have been offered to account for the difficulty children with learning disabilities have in using active, organized strategies (Mastropieri & Scruggs, 1998; Swanson & Sáez, 2003; Torgesen, 2002). One hypothesis is that such children have deficits in memory and attention that underlie their verbal language processing difficulties, and particular difficulties in holding on to relevant information in the face of interference or distraction. A second hypothesis is that their strategies develop more slowly than those of children without learning disabilities; this is referred to as a *developmental-lag hypothesis.* A third hypothesis is that children with learning disabilities come to school unprepared to assume the role of active, organized learners—they may never have been successfully taught how to participate actively in the teaching-learning and studying processes.

The effects of early academic failure in school also must be considered. Because early failure affects motivation and self-confidence, children who fail may not put forth the effort required for success in school. Motivational difficulties can limit the development of strategies needed to accomplish more complex tasks. Children with learning disabilities can be taught to use more efficient learning strategies. Both effective learners and poor learners may have the necessary knowledge and learning strategies at their disposal, but poor learners fail to use them effectively whereas effective learners use the organization present in the material to help them learn it (Torgesen, 2000).

Learning Disabilities and Mental Retardation

Children with learning disabilities, as well as those with mental retardation, have deficiencies in academic skills and information processing, including limitations in strategic behavior and in working memory (Torgesen, 2002). However,

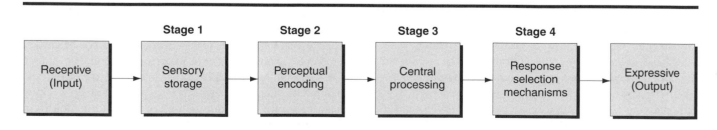

Figure 16-1. Diagram of a four-stage information-processing model.

the deficiencies of children with learning disabilities differ from those of children with mental retardation. For example, children with learning disabilities may have more narrowly focused limitations, such as limitations in the processing of phonological information. In contrast, children with mental retardation may have a pervasive deficiency that affects their ability to perform a broad range of complex tasks. In addition, children with learning disabilities usually can learn appropriate compensatory strategies (such as how to study) more quickly than can children with mental retardation.

Learning Disabilities and Nonnative English Speakers

When the children being assessed for learning disabilities are nonnative English speakers, you will need to consider several factors (Limbos & Giva, 2001; Salend & Salinas, 2003):

• *Experiential background.* Consider their length of residence in the United States, quality of instruction in school, school attendance record, health history, and family history.
• *Peer comparisons of language ability.* Compare their language abilities with those of peers who have similar linguistic/cultural backgrounds and similar amounts of exposure to second language instruction.
• *Sibling comparisons of language ability.* Compare their language abilities with those of their siblings when they were of the same age.
• *Typical difficulties in learning a second language.* Compare their learning difficulties with those of other nonnative English-speaking children who have learning problems.
• *Assessment focus.* Compare their linguistic proficiency and academic achievements in their primary language and in English.
• *Assessment battery.* Use standardized tests as one component of the assessment process, along with informal measures such as checklists, language samples, interviews, questionnaires, observations, portfolios, their journals, work samples, and curriculum-based measures.

The *objectives* of your assessment are to obtain information about academic functioning and to distinguish between learning problems that are primarily the result of language differences and those that are primarily the result of learning disabilities. You can then develop interventions based on the assessment findings.

Distinguishing between a learning disorder and a language difference is not easy, because children who are learning a second language often have difficulties with language processing similar to those of children who have a learning disorder (Salend & Salinas, 2003). Ideally, children should show a learning disorder both in their native language and in their second language before being diagnosed as having a learning disability (McLean, Worley, & Bailey, 2004; Salvia & Ysseldyke, 2001). However, this is not possible if children have not been exposed to academic materials both in their native language and in English.

Children who come from cultural and linguistic backgrounds that differ from those of the majority group may perform poorly in school because of experiential differences, family expectations, limited English proficiency, stresses associated with acculturation and discrimination, and/or cognitive styles and learning strategies that differ from those of the majority group. Learning a new language also may hinder their academic performance. Consequently, a minority child whose achievement is below average may not have a learning disability per se; rather, her or his achievement level may be related to cultural and linguistic factors. When this is the case, it is improper to label the child as having a learning disability. Chapter 4 discusses other issues and challenges involved in working with culturally and linguistically different children.

Learning Disabilities and Childhood Maltreatment

Being maltreated as a child may contribute to the development of learning problems and behavior problems (Barnett, 1997; Cicchetti & Toth, 1998; Kinard, 1999; Shonk & Cicchetti, 2000; Stanton-Chapman, Chapman, Bainbridge, & Scott, 2002). For example, if children have been physically abused, they may have lower self-esteem and take longer to accomplish cognitive problem-solving tasks than their nonabused peers. Some also may have sustained brain injury as a result of the abuse. Those who were neglected may be more noncompliant, dependent, and withdrawn and have more difficulties in academic achievement. And those who were emotionally abused may be less persistent in their school work than their nonabused peers. Overall, compared to peers who were not maltreated, maltreated youngsters tend to be more impulsive, less flexible, and more impatient and to make more nonrelevant responses to questions.

THE PROCESS OF READING

Every language has a basic set of elementary sounds called *phonemes* (Harris & Coltheart, 1986); spoken words are formed by combining these sounds into meaningful wholes. The way written words are formed, in contrast, differs greatly across languages. The main kinds of writing systems are those in which individual characters generally stand for whole words (referred to as *pictographic writing systems* or *logographic writing systems*) and those in which individual characters or combinations of characters stand for individual sounds within a word (referred to as *syllabic writing systems* or *alphabetic writing systems*).

Alphabetic System

Three thousand years ago, the Greeks established the first fully phonetic alphabet system that included vowels. The alphabetic system used in English is based on the Greek system and includes the following features (adapted from Harris & Coltheart, 1986, pp. 22–24):

• *Mapping of letters onto phonemes.* In the English writing system, a letter may stand for a phoneme or, as is often the case, a sequence of two or more letters may represent a phoneme. For example, the word *thick* has five letters but only three phonemes; the word *thatcher* has eight letters for its four phonemes. A useful concept here is the *grapheme,* which is a written representation of a phoneme. The word *thatcher,* for example, is composed of four graphemes: <th>, <a>, <tch>, and <er>. In English, there is by definition a one-to-one relationship between graphemes and phonemes, but not always between letters and phonemes.

• *Homophones.* Homophones are words that differ in spelling and meaning but have the same pronunciation, such as *knows* and *nose* or *eye* and *I.* In English, homophones occur because one phoneme can be written in various ways— *f* and *ph,* for example.

• *Regularity of spelling-to-sound correspondences.* Although the alphabetic system in English maps each grapheme in the written form of a word onto a single phoneme in the spoken form, the correspondences between graphemes and phonemes are not uniform across all words. For example, in *splint, hint, mint,* and many other words, the grapheme *i* (in *int*) corresponds to a short i sound, but there is one word, *pint,* for which this is not true. A table that specified what phoneme normally corresponded to each grapheme in English would need to include a set of words that disobeyed these normal correspondences. Such words are known as exception words, or irregular words; examples are *sew, yacht, gauge,* and *colonel.*

Phonological Awareness

Early phonological awareness skills—such as sensitivity to rhyme and the ability to break words into their constituent sounds and blend sounds into words—are especially helpful to young children who are beginning to read (Jenkins & O'Connor, 2002). Phonological sensitivity begins with sensitivity to large units of sound such as words or syllables and progresses to sensitivity to small units of sound, or phonemes (Whitehurst & Lonigan, 1998).

Examples of such skills are as follows (Rubba, 2003):

• Awareness that sentences and phrases can be divided into single words (e.g., "How are you?" can be divided up into *how, are,* and *you*)

• Awareness that some words share sounds or sound sequences (e.g., the words *had* and *fat* have the same middle sound)

• Awareness that a word can be broken down into component syllables (e.g., *tomorrow* has three parts: *to, ma, row*)

• Awareness that a syllable can be broken down into onsets and rimes (e.g., *black* has the onset *bl* and the rime *aek*)

Other phonological awareness skills are referred to as *phonemic awareness skills.* These are skills that pertain to individual sounds (or phonemes) that build words. Phonemic awareness skills include the following (Rubba, 2003):

• Awareness that a single sound in a word can be changed, thereby producing a new word (e.g., removing *t* from *tan* and replacing it with *c* to make *can*)

• Awareness that a word can be broken down into single sounds (phonemes) and that the number of phonemes in a word can be counted (e.g., recognizing that the word *boot* has three sounds /b/, /u/, /t/)

• Awareness of the individual sounds in a word together with the ability to identify them (referred to as *segmentation;* e.g., being able to pronounce each sound of *boot* separately and in any order: the last sound in *boot* is /t/, the first is /b/, and the middle is /u/)

• Awareness that the single sounds in a word can be moved around to create a new word (referred to as *manipulation;* e.g., being able to produce the word *lap* given the word *pal*)

• Awareness that single sounds can be put together to form one or more words (referred to as *blending;* e.g., when given separate sounds such as /ae/, /t/, /p/, being able to use them to form *tap, apt,* or *pat*)

Phonological awareness helps young children learn how spellings relate to sounds, permitting them to decode words when they are learning to read. Even at later stages of reading, phonological decoding skills (i.e., the ability to detect and interpret the phonemes that comprise words, including different sound segments) contribute to fluent reading, aid in the recognition of new and infrequently seen words, and foster the recognition of meaningful word clauses. Phonological information may help children recall words they have already read and thus increase comprehension by aiding word integration.

Phonological awareness and word awareness are probably closely related to the early stages of reading. It is important to note that pure phonological awareness does not involve knowledge of letters. It is important for children initially to have knowledge of word sounds and sound structure apart from knowledge of letters (Rubba, 2003). Deficient phonological development will impede the learning of phonological decoding skills and phonics-code acquisition (i.e., acquisition of the sound-symbol system of language) in general, while deficient semantic or syntactic development (i.e., failure to understand grammatical structures) will impede the learning of the skills needed to identify whole words. The ability to retain phonological material in working memory directly influences vocabulary acquisition and reading comprehension (Gathercole & Adams, 1993). Impaired phonological memory skills in early childhood are linked with poor "language development in middle childhood and may even play a causal role in specific developmental language impairments" (Gathercole & Adams, 1993, p. 770). Thus, skills in phonological awareness and memory are good predictors of success in early reading (Gresham, 2002), including word attack skills, reading comprehension skills, spelling skills, and written expression skills (Greene, 1996).

Word Features

Five types of word features are important in the acquisition of decoding ability (Mather & Goldstein, 2001; Vellutino & Shub, 1982):

1. *Phonological features* are the particular sound characteristics of a word, defined by the unique ordering of vowel and consonant sounds (i.e., phonemes) in a given word.
2. *Graphic features* refer to the particular visual patterns of a word formed by the unique array of letters that comprise the word (*bad* vs. *dad* or *hot* vs. *not*)—that is, how the word looks. In learning to read, children must store graphic (or featural) information in order to distinguish accurately among printed words.
3. *Orthographic features* refer to the internal structure of a word—that is, the spelling rules that determine a word's structure. Orthographic features include structural regularities, such as sequential dependencies (*sta* is acceptable whereas *xtz* is unacceptable), and letter-sound correspondences (*at* in *fat, cat,* and *rat*). The child who discovers the regularities and redundancies of orthography is developing efficient processing strategies for making fine distinctions among visually similar words (e.g., *fat/rat, was/saw*) and reducing the amount of visual information that must be processed.
4. *Syntactic features* refer to the more abstract qualities of a word—those features a word has in common with other words by virtue of rules of grammar. Syntactic classes include nouns, verbs, adjectives, and adverbs. Children use syntactic clues to determine whether words make sense in a given location. Implicit knowledge of such markers helps make words memorable.
5. *Semantic features* refer to the particular concept or entity symbolized by a word. Semantic features are dynamic—they change as a result of a child's experience. It is these properties that make a word a linguistic unit that can be easily remembered. For example, seeing the word *ball* in close proximity to a picture of a ball helps establish a linguistic unit.

A Progression of Reading Skills

Children usually learn to read aloud by one of two methods. In the *whole-word procedure* (or *whole-language procedure*), children learn to read by direct recognition of a word as a whole. When they see a familiar word, they normally recognize it by its shape and then pronounce it. For example, they might be shown the word *cat* and be told that this word (letter string) says "cat." In the *phonics procedure,* children learn to read by sounding out letter by letter. This method is used for unfamiliar words and requires recognition of individual letters and knowledge of the sounds they make. For example, they learn that the *c* in the word *cat* is pronounced /k/, *a* is pronounced /a/, and *t* is pronounced /t/.

Learning to read likely involves the successive acquisition and integration of several hierarchically organized skills, as noted in the following four-phase model (Ehri, 1998; Moats, 1998).

Phase 1: Prealphabetic phase, or sight-vocabulary phase. Children form connections between selected visual attributes of words and their pronunciations or meanings and then store these associations in memory. At this time, the connections are enhanced by paired-associated learning or by visual-cue reading, but not by letter-sound relations. Children remember visual cues that accompany print but not the written words themselves. They develop a limited vocabulary of whole words through cues such as pictures and logos. Activities carried out orally at this stage include rhyming; counting, adding, and deleting syllables; matching beginning sounds in words; substituting sounds; and identifying sounds that exist in selected words. Activities carried out through print include alphabet matching, letter naming, and following print with the finger while someone reads aloud. One aim at this phase is for children to develop awareness of the alphabetic principle that letters roughly represent segments of one's own speech.

Phase 2: Partial alphabetic phase, or discrimination-net phase. Children "remember how to read sight words by forming partial alphabetic connections between only some of the letters in written words and sounds detected in their pronunciations" (Ehri, 1998, p. 19). They develop an understanding that letters represent phonemes or sounds (Moats, 1998). First and final letters are often the cues that are remembered. Children need to know the relevant letter-sound correspondences and how to segment initial and final sounds in words. When asked to read single words aloud, children seem to select words in their vocabulary that most resemble the items they see. Children in this phase cannot read novel or unfamiliar words aloud.

Phase 3: Full alphabetic phase, or phonological-recoding phase. Children "remember how to read sight words by forming complete connections between letters seen in the written form of words and phonemes detected in their pronunciations" (Ehri, 1998, p. 21). Children now "understand how most graphemes symbolize phonemes in the conventional spelling system . . . and spellings become . . . bonded to pronunciations of words in memory" (Ehri, 1998, p. 21). Children now have the ability to decode new words by blending letters into a pronunciation and recognizing phonograms, or chunks of words (e.g., *ack, ele*) and endings of words as units (e.g., *er, ed;* Moats, 1998).

Phase 4: Consolidated alphabetic phase, or orthographic phase. Children develop skills in using orthographic (i.e., visual) recoding principles—recognizing words on the basis of the way they are spelled rather than the way they sound—and they develop fluency in reading (Moats, 1998). They are able to read homophonic words and exception words. Children learn to recognize the same letter patterns in different words. For example, the multiletter unit -est will be stored as a consolidated unit as a result of reading words with this suffix. When children at this stage encounter a word with the suffix -est (e.g. newest), they connect two units—new and est—to read the word.

Good readers not only have progressed through these phases of reading skills but also use metacognitive strategies (Erickson, Stahl, & Rinehart, 1985; Jenkins & O'Connor, 2002). For example, they are aware of the purposes for reading; they adjust their performance to different purposes and tasks; they monitor ongoing comprehension and correct comprehension failures when they occur; they have a clear notion of what good reading entails; they accurately estimate the likelihood of their own comprehension; they judge the importance of different idea units to the meaning of a text as a whole; and they can detect ambiguous, inconsistent, or otherwise anomalous information.

The following whimsical sentences illustrate why English is difficult to master (Anonymous).

Our Incredible English Language

We polish the Polish furniture.
He could lead if he would get the lead out.
A farm can produce produce.
The dump was so full it had to refuse refuse.
The soldier decided to desert in the desert.
The present is a good time to present the present.
At the Army base, a bass was painted on the head of a bass drum.
The dove dove into the bushes.
I did not object to the object.
The insurance for the invalid was invalid.
The bandage was wound around the wound.
There was a row among the oarsmen about how to row.
They were too close to the door to close it.
The buck does funny things when the does are present.
They sent a sewer down to stitch the tear in the sewer line.
To help with planting, the farmer taught his sow to sow.
The wind was too strong to wind the sail.
After a number of Novocain injections, my jaw got number.
I shed a tear when I saw the tear in my clothes.
I had to subject the subject to a series of tests.
How can I intimate this to my most intimate friend?
I spent last evening evening out a pile of dirt.
The melting ice became more minute minute by minute.

COMMUNICATION DISORDERS

Communication disorders can impede reading and written expression, including spelling. Three broad types are identified in *DSM-IV–TR:* expressive language disorder, mixed receptive-expressive language disorder, and phonological disorder (American Psychiatric Association, 2000). As you read this section, keep in mind that the three types of communication disorders listed in *DSM-IV–TR* have not been extensively validated as independent disorders (Lyon, 1996a, 1996b). Also, note that *DSM-IV–TR* does not have a separate classification for receptive language disorders, because children with receptive disorders usually have expressive disorders as well.

Expressive Language Disorder

DSM-IV–TR defines *expressive language disorder* as follows (American Psychiatric Association, 2000):

> The essential feature of Expressive Language Disorder is an impairment in expressive language development as demonstrated by scores on standardized individually administered measures of expressive language development substantially below those obtained from standardized measures of both nonverbal intellectual capacity and receptive language development. . . . When standardized instruments are not available or appropriate, the diagnosis may be based on a thorough functional assessment of the individual's language ability. The difficulties may occur in communication involving both verbal language and sign language. The language difficulties interfere with academic or occupational achievement or with social communication. . . . (p. 58)

Children with expressive language disorder may have one or more of the following difficulties (Baker & Cantwell, 1989; Damico, 1991):

- *Problems with vocabulary,* such as (a) persistent use of only a core set of words (e.g., "you know," "thing"), (b) word-finding difficulties and substitution errors (e.g., *chair* for *table*), (c) substitution of functional descriptions for nouns (e.g., "thing you drink out of" for *glass*), and (d) overgeneralization (e.g., *thing* or *tool* for *hammer*).

- *Problems with expressive grammar,* such as (a) simplification or omission of grammatical structures (e.g., "Daddy go," "Me eat"), (b) limited varieties of grammatical structures (e.g., verbs limited to present tense), (c) inappropriate word order (e.g., "Sock Daddy has"), and (d) inappropriate combinations of grammatical forms (e.g., "He were gone," "The ball flown through the air").

- *Problems with pragmatic use of language,* such as (a) tangential or inappropriate responses, (b) failure to provide significant information to listeners, (c) limitations in the range of speech content, (d) difficulty in maintaining or changing topics, (e) difficulty in initiating interactions, (f) lack of assertiveness in conversation, (g) failure to ask relevant questions, (h) repetitions or unusual pauses in conversation, (i) false starts and self-interruptions, (j) difficulty in taking turns during conversation, (k) difficulty in using gestures and facial expressions, (l) difficulty in making eye contact, and (m) difficulty in telling a story (e.g., poor sequencing, excessive pauses, vague cohesion, obscuring main points).

Mixed Receptive-Expressive Language Disorder

DSM-IV–TR defines *mixed receptive-expressive language disorder* as follows (American Psychiatric Association, 2000):

> The essential feature of Mixed Receptive-Expressive Language Disorder is an impairment in both receptive and expressive language development as demonstrated by scores on standardized individually administered measures of both receptive and expressive language development that are substantially below those obtained from standardized measures of nonverbal intellectual capacity. . . . When standardized instruments are not available or appropriate, the diagnosis may be based on a thorough functional assessment of the individual's language ability. The difficulties may occur in communication involving both verbal language and sign language. The language difficulties interfere with academic or occupational achievement or with social communication. . . . (p. 62)

Children with mixed receptive-expressive language disorder may have one or more of the following difficulties (Baker & Cantwell, 1989):

- *Problems with vocabulary,* such as interpreting *elbow* as *knee, down* as *up, this* as *here,* or *glasses* only as eyeglasses (rather than as either eyeglasses or drinking glasses, depending on context).
- *Problems in comprehending grammatical units,* such as interpreting *pencils* as *pencil* or *had* as *has* or failing to recognize differences among *large, larger,* and *largest.*
- *Problems in comprehending word-ordering rules (syntax),* such as failing to distinguish between "The rat chased the mouse" and "The rat was chased by the mouse" or misinterpreting "Is this yours?" as "This is yours."
- *Problems in recognizing multiple meanings,* such as failing to understand that "smoking grass" can refer to a smoldering lawn or inhaling marijuana or that "The fly flew through the air" can refer to an insect or a fishing lure.
- *Problems in comprehending the meaning of subtle aspects of language usage,* such as difficulty understanding facial expressions, intonation patterns, tone of voice, sarcasm, innuendo, puns, metaphors, and figures of speech. A concrete example is not knowing whether the statement "Can you get the can opener?" is a question or an imperative.

Phonological Disorder

DSM-IV–TR defines *phonological disorder* as follows (American Psychiatric Association, 2000):

> The essential feature of Phonological Disorder is a failure to use developmentally expected speech sounds that are appropriate for the individual's age and dialect. . . . This may involve errors in sound production, use, representation, or organization such as, but not limited to, substitutions of one sound for another (use of /t/ for target /k/ sound) or omission of sounds (e.g., final consonants). The difficulties in speech sound production interfere with

"No, Timmy, not 'I sawed the chair.' It's 'I saw the chair' or 'I have seen the chair.'"

Courtesy of Glenn Bernhardt.

> academic or occupational achievement or with social communication. . . . (p. 65)

Thus, children with phonological disorder may have (a) difficulty manipulating the sounds of oral language, including diminished sensitivity to large units of sound (such as words or syllables) or to small units of sound (phonemes), (b) difficulty with immediate recall of verbal information (e.g., repeating words or digits), and (c) difficulty in quickly naming items in a group of letters, numbers, or colors (Lonigan, Burgess, Anthony, & Barker, 1998; Whitehurst & Lonigan, 1998).

READING DISORDER

DSM-IV–TR defines *reading disorder* as follows (American Psychiatric Association, 2000):

> The essential feature of Reading Disorder is reading achievement (i.e., reading accuracy, speed, or comprehension as measured by individually administered standardized tests) that falls substantially below that expected given the individual's chronological age, measured intelligence, and age-appropriate education. . . . The disturbance in reading significantly interferes with academic achievement or with activities of daily living that require reading skills. . . . If a sensory deficit is present, the reading difficulties are in excess of those usually associated with it. . . . In individuals with Reading Disorder (which has also been called "dyslexia"), oral reading is characterized by distortions, substitutions, or omissions; both oral and silent reading are characterized by slowness and errors in comprehension. (pp. 51–52)

Children with reading disorder may have one or more of the following difficulties:

- *Problems with attention and concentration,* such as difficulty in focusing on printed material and retaining the material in short-term memory.
- *Problems in phonological awareness,* such as difficulty in segmenting words into their constituent syllables and phonemes, recognizing rhyme, blending phonemic elements, deleting and substituting phonemes, and appreciating puns.
- *Problems in orthographic awareness,* such as difficulty in recognizing how words look, recognizing letters, and recognizing letter clusters.
- *Problems in word awareness,* such as difficulty in segmenting sentences or phrases into words, separating words from their referents, appreciating jokes involving lexical ambiguity, matching words with other words, recognizing synonyms and antonyms, and making substitutions.
- *Problems in semantic or syntactic awareness* (i.e., awareness of grammatical structures), such as difficulty in detecting the structural ambiguity in sentences, correcting word order violations, and completing sentences when words are missing.
- *Problems in rapid decoding,* such as difficulty in recognizing words quickly and automatically and processing information rapidly.
- *Problems in verbal comprehension,* such as difficulty in understanding words and word order. A child may have difficulty with *literal comprehension* (understanding the information that is explicitly contained in a reading selection); with *inferential comprehension* (using the information contained in a selection to formulate inferences and hypotheses, including cause-and-effect relationships, comparisons, and sequences); or with *critical comprehension* (evaluating the quality of a selection, including its adequacy, worth, appropriateness, and desirability).
- *Problems in pragmatic awareness* (i.e., awareness of the way verbal and nonverbal language is used), such as difficulty in detecting inconsistencies between sentences, recognizing message inadequacy, understanding and repairing communication failures, and recognizing the overall message.

Reading disorder is a type of learning disability in which children fail to master basic processes such as letter recognition and sound blending, despite adequate intelligence and educational opportunities. Reading disorder is usually not diagnosed in children who are of below-average intelligence (unless their reading ability is well below the level expected for their below-average level of intelligence), who have had poor educational experiences, or who have not attended school. Children with these characteristics or experiences may be poor readers, but they are not usually considered to have a reading disorder. Children with reading disorder may have *developmental dyslexia,* which refers to difficulty learning to read, or *acquired dyslexia,* which refers to loss of reading ability that has already been acquired, usually as a result of a traumatic brain injury or a disease that affects the brain (see Chapters 23 and 24).

The International Dyslexia Association (2002) defines *dyslexia* in the following way:

> Dyslexia is a specific learning disability that is neurological in origin. It is characterized by difficulties with accurate and/or fluent word recognition and by poor spelling and decoding abilities. These difficulties typically result from a deficit in the phonological component of language that is often unexpected in relation to other cognitive abilities and the provision of effective classroom instruction. Secondary consequences may include problems in reading comprehension and reduced reading experience that can impede growth of vocabulary and background knowledge.

Reading disorder is the most common type of learning disability—approximately 80% of children in learning disability programs have a diagnosis of reading disorder (Aaron, 1997). Like obesity, reading disorder is best thought of as occurring on a continuum that extends from mild to severe, with somewhat arbitrary divisions (Stanovich, 1988). Unlike obesity, however, which has one critical dimension (weight), dyslexia may involve difficulties in at least two important dimensions: *phonological decoding* (i.e., the ability to read words phonetically) and *orthographic decoding* (i.e., the ability to recognize letter sequences or words based on their visual features). Some children have phonological decoding deficits, others have orthographic coding deficits, and still others have deficits in both dimensions. Finally, some children with reading disorder have no deficits in either dimension, but have deficits in comprehension.

Reading disorder is most likely to be associated with difficulties in the phonological decoding of written language, particularly phoneme segmentation (Pennington & Welsh, 1995). These difficulties, as noted earlier in the chapter, may be related to genetic factors, sociocultural factors, or both. For example, genetic factors may alter the neurological structures that underlie phonological processing; or, minimal sociocultural stimulation and failure to provide reading materials may lead to problems in phoneme segmentation skills. Children who have phonological difficulty usually have "slow reading speed, errors in oral reading, poor spelling, errors of syntax in written language, and excessive dependence on context for reading" (Aaron & Simurdak, 1991, p. 525). Instead of focusing on the meaning of what they are reading, they spend a great amount of energy on word recognition (Jenkins & O'Connor, 2002).

Poor readers may have difficulty in recognizing whole words (e.g., *south* is read as "sug," *circuit* as "kircute," *bowl* as "bowel," *sour* as "sowl"), in reading quickly because of a need to sound out even simple words (e.g., *cat, go*) to obtain their pronunciation and meaning, in reading multisyllabic words (e.g., *bicycle, hamburger*), in reading words that have irregular spelling-to-sound patterns (e.g., *laugh, come*), in reading words that have homophones (e.g., *sail/sale*), in sounding out words (e.g., *circuit* is read as "circle," *bowl* as "barrel," *children* as "child," *high* as "height"), and in using phonic analysis and synthesis skills (e.g., reading nonwords such as *dek, lem,* and *git;* Hallahan & Kauffman, 2003).

Subtypes of Reading Disorder

Although there is little consensus about whether reading disorder can usefully be divided into specific subtypes, use of the following three subtypes may have some merit:

*   *Phonological dyslexia* (or auditory type of disorder) is characterized by a deficiency in phonological decoding, or print-to-sound conversion; the greatest percentage of children with dyslexia have this type of disorder. Children with this type of disorder are unable to decode written words using phonic or sound principles. They have difficulty segmenting individual sounds within words and blending separate speech sounds to produce words, and they prefer the whole-word method in reading. Examples of errors they make are reading "cat" as "car" and pronouncing "comet" as "planet." They tend to read irregular words, such as *yacht* and *depot,* just as well (or as poorly) as words with standard print-to-sound correspondence. They read relatively quickly and produce many errors.
*   *Orthographic dyslexia* (or visual type of disorder) is characterized by a deficiency in whole-word recognition. Children with this type of disorder have difficulties in visualizing letters and word shapes. They are unable to develop a sight vocabulary. They prefer the phonological decoding, or alphabetic, method of reading. Because they are unable to read orthographically irregular words (e.g., *yacht*), their rate of reading is much slower than that of people with phonological dyslexia. However, they commit relatively few errors. Errors in or omissions of short function words (e.g., *the, an*) are common, because so much effort is needed to decode long content words that shorter words that convey less meaning may be ignored or misread.
*   *Disorder of rapid naming* (or disorder of symbol processing or fluency) is characterized by difficulty reading text quickly, accurately, and with proper expression (National Reading Panel, 2000).

Unfortunately, there is no one-to-one relationship between specific intervention techniques and specific types of reading disorder. In addition, many children do not fall clearly into one subtype of reading disorder, and some children have deficiencies in all of the above areas. Children in the latter group are the most severely impaired and the most resistant to intervention (Wolf, 2002).

Hyperlexia

Children who have a precocious ability to recognize written words, beyond what would be expected at their general level of intellectual development, are said to be hyperlexic. Although the cause of hyperlexia is unknown, hyperlexic children may have accelerated neurological development that results in a precocious ability to recognize written words as linguistic symbols. Hyperlexic children, however, also may demonstrate a delay or disability in receptive or expressive language development, including language comprehension. It is important that parents and teachers not develop unrealistic expectations of these children's educational abilities. Although they have superior word-naming ability, many do not have commensurate reading comprehension ability.

Neurological Correlates of Reading Disorder

Research on neurological correlates of reading disorders provides us with the following information (Hotz, 1998):

> First, reading depends on two separate but equally important neural systems involving sound and pictures. The brain engages in complex firing patterns that translate written characters into the phonological building blocks of spoken language. The prior neural connections in the brain also help to link a memorized picture of a complete written word to its meaning. This link helps to bypass the need to sound out the word and thereby facilitates the process of recalling words.
>
> Second, if a child is to read well, his or her brain must translate symbols into their proper sound in a few thousandths of a second. Most children can translate symbols to sounds in less than 40 milliseconds, but children with a language impairment may need up to 500 milliseconds—fast enough to speak fluently, but too slow to read well.
>
> Third, minor differences in how the brain handles the visual processing of images, color, fast motion, and contrast can impede reading. Again, the speed of visual processing may be crucial.
>
> Finally, everyone has some trouble adjusting to the written word because it makes such taxing demands on so many different parts of the brain. (pp. A38–A39, with changes in notation)

MATHEMATICS DISORDER

DSM-IV–TR defines *mathematics disorder* as follows (American Psychiatric Association, 2000):

> The essential feature of Mathematics Disorder is mathematical ability (as measured by individually administered standardized tests of mathematical calculation or reasoning) that falls substantially below that expected for the individual's chronological age, measured intelligence, and age-appropriate education. . . . The disturbance in mathematics significantly interferes with academic achievement or with activities of daily living that require mathematical skills. . . . If a sensory deficit is present, the difficulties in mathematical ability are in excess of those usually associated with it. . . . (p. 53)

Children with mathematics disorder (also called *dyscalculia*) may have one or more of the following difficulties (American Psychiatric Association, 2000; Rourke & Tsatsanis, 1996):

- *Problems in mastering basic mathematical skills,* such as difficulty in following sequences of mathematical steps, counting objects, and learning multiplication tables.
- *Problems in understanding mathematical terminology,* such as difficulty in understanding or naming mathematical terms, operations, or concepts and difficulty in encoding written problems into mathematical symbols.
- *Problems involving perceptual or spatial processing,* such as difficulty in recognizing or reading numerical symbols or mathematical signs, clustering objects into groups, aligning numbers in columns, and using a number line.
- *Problems with attention,* such as difficulty in copying numbers or figures correctly, adding "carried" numbers, and observing operational signs.
- *Problems in shifting,* such as difficulty in shifting from one mathematical operation to another.
- *Problems in writing,* such as difficulty in writing numbers clearly or writing in a straight line.
- *Problems in verbal memory,* such as difficulty in remembering facts, steps, and procedures necessary to solve mathematical problems.

Mathematics disorder is a heterogeneous condition that may occur in conjunction with reading disorder or with another learning disorder (Fletcher et al., 2002). The core deficits of children with both mathematics and reading disorders may be problems in both short- and long-term memory, including working memory, and not just difficulties with mathematical facts and procedures and retrieval of verbal information (Geary, Hamson, & Hoard, 2000). Support for this hypothesis comes from research indicating that children with poor mathematics achievement tend to be poor readers, that the letter recognition ability of kindergarten children correlates equally well with later reading achievement and later mathematics achievement, that the ability of kindergarten children to count dots also correlates equally well with later reading achievement and later mathematics achievement, and that early cognitive and neuropsychological predictors of reading and mathematics achievement are strikingly similar (Share, Moffitt, & Silva, 1988). Still, some children have difficulties in mathematics but adequate reading skills, and other children have adequate mathematical skills but difficulties in reading.

For children who have difficulties only with mathematics, the primary problem may be the use of immature problem-solving strategies (Geary et al., 2000). At early ages, they may make errors in simple arithmetic procedures, such as counting, carrying, and borrowing. At later ages, they may have difficulties in learning the rules needed to solve complex multiplication and division problems (Geary, 1994).

Like reading disorder, mathematics disorder ranges from mild to severe. Some children have good conceptual understanding of mathematics but poor understanding of the rote aspects, such as mathematics facts, placement of numbers, and attention to signs. Other children have difficulty at the conceptual level but not at the rote level. And still other chil-

dren have difficulty with the expressive language skills used to talk about mathematics (e.g., for the number 372, they say, "three seven hundred two") but no difficulty with calculation. Finally, others have difficulty with calculation (e.g., they may say that $4 \times 5 = 50$ or $56 \div 7 = 6$) but no difficulty in recognizing Arabic numerals.

The cognitive requirements of mathematics change with time. Computation-focused activities are stressed during the early school years, followed by an emphasis on conceptual and abstract mathematical concepts in later years. The incidence of mathematics disorder is approximately 6% of the school-age population of children who are of average intelligence and socioeconomic status and without sensory deficits (Lyon, 1996b). Overall, there are at least two different groups of children with mathematics disorders: those who have only a mathematics disorder and those who have both a mathematics disorder and a reading disorder (Fletcher et al., 2002).

DISORDER OF WRITTEN EXPRESSION

DSM-IV–TR defines *disorder of written expression* as follows (American Psychiatric Association, 2000):

> The essential feature of Disorder of Written Expression is writing skills (as measured by an individually administered standardized test of functional assessment of writing skills) that fall substantially below those expected given the individual's chronological age, measured intelligence, and age-appropriate education. . . . The disturbance in written expression significantly interferes with academic achievement or with activities of daily living that require writing skills. . . . If a sensory deficit is present, the difficulties in writing skills are in excess of those usually associated with it. . . . There is generally a combination of difficulties in the individual's ability to compose written texts evidenced by grammatical or punctuation errors within sentences, poor paragraph organization, multiple spelling errors, and excessively poor handwriting. This diagnosis is generally not given if there are only spelling errors or poor handwriting in the absence of other impairment in written expression. . . . Tasks in which the child is asked to copy, write to dictation, and write spontaneously may all be necessary to establish the presence and extent of this disorder. (pp. 54–55)

Children with a disorder of written expression may have the following difficulties (Berninger, Mizokawa, & Bragg, 1991):

- *Problems in the early stages of learning to write,* such as difficulty in producing letters of the alphabet rapidly and automatically, retrieving letters from long-term memory, obtaining sufficient finger dexterity and fine-motor coordination, and integrating visual and motor skills.
- *Problems in the later stages of learning to write,* such as difficulty in connecting orthographic codes (words, letters, and letter clusters) with the corresponding phonological codes (phonetic/semantic, phonemic, and syllabic/rhyme, respectively), constructing meaningful sentences and paragraphs, planning, and making revisions.

Disorder of written expression is commonly found in combination with reading disorder, mathematics disorder, or pervasive oral language disorders. Children with oral language difficulties also may have problems translating their thoughts into written language (Fletcher et al., 2002). As noted above, early writing skills are primarily related to fine-motor coordination and word-level skills such as decoding and spelling, whereas later writing skills require the generation of ideas and ability to organize. If language is not well established and if its use has not been fully automatized, the process of composing and producing written text likely will be difficult. Finally, acquiring writing skills may be related to the type of instruction received (Graham, Harris, & Larsen, 2001).

Writing may be especially taxing for children with attention and concentration problems, including those with attention-deficit/hyperactivity disorder. For children who have a short attention span or poor organizational skills, writing is tedious, as they have difficulty paying attention to several issues at once—for example, content, grammar, style, spelling, and punctuation.

Spelling Difficulties

As noted earlier, children with a disorder of written expression may also have spelling difficulties. Learning to spell involves five stages (Lerner, 2003; Moats, 2001; Treiman, 1998; Treiman & Bourassa, 2000; Vaughn, Bos, & Schumn, 2000):

Stage 1: Prephonetic writing. Children combine strings of unrelated letters to represent words. They draw, scribble, and learn to form letters.

Stage 2: Mastering the names of some letters and learning beginning phonics. Children learn a few letters to represent sounds. They master a limited number of phonemes that correspond to letters and may invert letters when they spell.

Stage 3: Acquiring word patterns. Children try to represent all the sounds of a word. Their spelling shows correspondence between letters and sounds and becomes more like conventional spelling. Although their spelling often lacks precision, children at this stage spell some sight words accurately.

Stage 4: Spelling multisyllabic words. Children begin to spell multisyllabic words but may still have difficulty with some multisyllabic words, such as spelling "bottom" as "bottim."

Stage 5: Mature spelling. Children acquire multiple strategies for spelling words correctly. They learn irregular spellings and comprehend the structure of words, which helps them spell prefixes, contractions, and compound words. They also learn to correct their spelling errors.

Children who have a reading disorder often have difficulty with spelling, although the processes involved in reading and spelling are different. Spelling requires knowledge of sound-symbol correspondence (phonological skills), as well as lin-

guistic competence (such as an understanding that the way words are spelled may depend on how they are used). Reading, as discussed previously, involves phonological decoding and whole-word reading ability. Children whose spelling is phonetically inaccurate often have problems with phonological processing, while those whose spelling is phonetically accurate but still poor may have difficulties in handwriting, syntax or grammar, and knowledge of the orthographic rules that guide written expression (Lyon, 1996a). Some children memorize the spelling of individual words but have difficulty spelling the words correctly when they are used in sentences. Others may be stuck at a particular stage of learning to spell and unable to make progress beyond that stage (Moats, 2001).

Achieving skill in spelling requires knowledge of the correct spelling of irregular words. Children can usually master spelling by focusing on the sound elements or the meaning and structure of the word. Children who have both reading and writing difficulties tend to have a more generalized language disability than those who have either a reading disorder or a disorder of written expression alone (Harris, 1995a). Children who are good readers but poor spellers tend to have more difficulty manipulating sounds than do good readers who also are good spellers (Goswami, 1992).

Handwriting Difficulties

As noted earlier, children with a disorder of written expression may also have difficulty with handwriting. Learning to write involves four stages (Mather & Gregg, 2003):

Stage 1: Imitation (preschool and kindergarten). Children pretend to write by imitating what other people do.

Stage 2: Graphic presentation (first and second grades). Children learn to form letters and place them on lines.

Stage 3: Progressive incorporation (third grade). Children write letters with less effort.

Stage 4: Automatization (fourth to seventh grades). Children write more rapidly and efficiently.

Children with good penmanship form letters in cursive or manuscript style that are recognizable out of context, of good proportion, consistent in size, and appropriately capitalized. Slant is generally consistent, rhythm is easy and flowing, and pressure is even (not too heavy or too light). They write in reasonably straight lines with uncrowded letters, words, and lines and have relatively balanced margins. Finally, a page of their writing does not contain excessive strikeovers (Phelps, Stempel, & Speck, 1985).

NONVERBAL LEARNING DISABILITY

Nonverbal learning disability is a subtype of learning disability. Children with nonverbal learning disability typically exhibit the following strengths and limitations (Nonverbal Learning Disorders Association, n.d.):

STRENGTHS

- Good verbal expressive ability
- Good vocabulary ability
- Good receptive language ability
- Good auditory perceptual ability
- Good rote verbal memory ability
- Good reading ability
- Good spelling ability

LIMITATIONS

- Tactile-perceptual deficits
- Psychomotor coordination deficits
- Deficiencies in visual-spatial-organizational abilities
- Deficits in nonverbal problem solving, concept formation, and hypothesis testing
- Difficulty dealing with negative feedback in novel or complex situations
- Difficulties in dealing with cause and effect relationships
- Difficulties in the appreciation of incongruities
- Fear of unfamiliar situations
- Difficulty with mathematical reasoning
- Poor psycholinguistic pragmatics (interpreting messages literally, responding to one or two words in a sentence rather than to the entire sentence, using circumlocutions, and failing to take turns appropriately)
- Poor speech prosody (intonation, rhythm, and vocal stress in speech)
- Misspellings that are almost exclusively phonetically accurate
- Difficulties in perceiving gestures, facial expressions, and other nonverbal social cues
- Deficits in social perception, social judgment, and social interaction skills
- Marked tendency for social withdrawal and isolation as age increases

Children with nonverbal learning disabilities may have a dysfunction in the right cerebral hemisphere (Rourke & Conway, 1997; Spreen, 2001).

The following suggestions are for parents of children with nonverbal learning disabilities (Boyse, 2004). The parents should be encouraged to do the following:

- Keep the environment predictable and familiar.
- Provide structure and routine.
- Prepare the child for changes, giving logical explanations when possible.
- Pay attention to sensory input from the environment, like noise, temperature, and smells.
- Help the child learn coping skills for dealing with anxiety.
- Be logical, organized, clear, concise, and concrete.
- Avoid jargon, double meanings, sarcasm, nicknames, and teasing.
- State expectations clearly.
- Be specific about cause and effect relationships.
- Work with the child's school to modify homework assignments, testing procedures, and physical education.

- Have the child use the computer at school and at home for schoolwork.
- Help the child learn organizational and time management skills.
- Make use of the child's verbal skills to help him or her with social interactions.
- Teach the child about nonverbal communication (facial expressions, gestures).
- Help the child learn to tell whether he or she is communicating well by observing other people's reactions.
- Arrange for the child to have a playmate who shares the child's interests.
- Enroll the child in a small-group social skills training program.
- Encourage the child to develop interests that will build his or her self-esteem.

THINKING THROUGH THE ISSUES

1. What role do psychological factors have in the etiology of learning disabilities?
2. Can learning disabilities be easily overcome? Explain your answer.
3. Do genetic factors, biological factors, or environmental factors play the most important role in the etiology of learning disabilities? Explain your answer.
4. Is phonological processing an important skill in learning how to read? Discuss your answer.

SUMMARY

1. Approximately 10% to 15% of children in the United States have some form of learning disability.
2. The major types of learning disability are reading disorder, mathematics disorder, and disorder of written expression (including spelling). Other types of learning disability are communication disorder and nonverbal learning disability.

What Are the Signs of Learning Disability?

3. Signs suggestive of learning disability include difficulty with reading, spelling, handwriting, language, comprehension, organization, and mathematics.

Definitions of Learning Disability

4. IDEA 2004 defines specific learning disability as "a disorder in 1 or more of the basic psychological processes involved in understanding or in using language, spoken or written, which disorder may manifest itself in the imperfect ability to listen, think, speak, read, write, spell, or do mathematical calculations."
5. The definition of learning disability in IDEA 2004 has been criticized because it includes several ambiguous terms; the disorders in the definition are rather general and need to be more specific; distinguishing between primary and secondary causes is difficult; the exclusionary criteria may prevent children with sensory problems, emotional problems, or environmental disadvantages from being identified as learning disabled; it does

not discuss the heterogeneity of the condition or appropriate interventions; it does not explain that learning disabilities may exist concurrently with other conditions; and it does not explain the causes of learning disability.

6. The National Joint Committee on Learning Disabilities defines learning disabilities in a way that is generally consistent with IDEA 2004.

7. The Learning Disabilities Association of Canada's definition of learning disabilities is more comprehensive than other definitions. It emphasizes that learning disorders can be in either verbal or nonverbal areas; that the learning disability label applies only to individuals who have average thinking and/or reasoning abilities; that learning disabilities may also involve problems in organization, interpersonal relations, and perspective taking; and that early identification and intervention are needed.

8. *DSM-IV-TR* guidelines for defining learning disorders generally follow those of IDEA 2004.

Etiology of Learning Disabilities

9. Learning disabilities likely have multiple etiologies—including genetic, biological, and environmental bases—that presumably produce an altered or dysfunctional central nervous system.

10. A genetic basis for learning disabilities is plausible because learning disabilities can occur across generations of families and phonological processing problems, in particular, can be heritable.

11. *Phonological processing* refers to the ability to detect the sounds of speech and how they relate to print, including sequences of sounds within words, awareness of word boundaries, blending, segmentation, deletion, and rhyming.

12. The risk of dyslexia is estimated to be eight times greater for children of parents with reading disorders than for children of parents without reading disorders.

13. A biological basis for learning disabilities is plausible because there are anatomical and electrophysiological differences between the brains of children with learning disabilities and the brains of children without them.

14. Environmental factors that may be involved in the development of learning disabilities include children's learning strategies, teachers' styles of teaching, parental attitudes toward learning, parents' child-management techniques, family verbal interaction patterns, early reading experiences, children's temperament, children's level of motivation, and the family's socioeconomic status.

Precursors of Learning Disabilities at Preschool Age

15. Precursors of learning disabilities at preschool age include specific delays or deviances in one or more of the following domains: motor, behavioral, cognitive/executive, memory, communication, perceptual, and social-emotional.

School-Age Children with Learning Disabilities

16. School-age children with learning disabilities have deficient academic skills. They also may have deficits in information-processing abilities, neuropsychological skills, and social-behavioral adjustment.

17. Children with learning disabilities are a heterogeneous group.

18. A four-stage information-processing model—encompassing short-term sensory storage, perceptual encoding, central processing, and response selection mechanisms—is helpful in the study of children with learning disabilities.

19. Various processes such as selective attention, coding, organization, rehearsal, and retrieval help to regulate the flow of information through the four stages.

20. Children with learning disabilities have inadequate executive control functions, which lead them to have difficulty on tasks requiring active information processing and verbal working memory.

21. Children with learning disabilities typically fail to use mnemonic aids such as labeling, verbal rehearsal, clustering, chunking, and selective attention to help them remember important information.

22. The major problem of children with learning disabilities may be not so much an inability to attend selectively to materials as difficulty in analyzing a task and selecting the proper strategies to accomplish it.

23. Children with learning disabilities may have deficits in memory and attention that underlie their verbal language processing difficulties, they may develop strategies more slowly than children without learning disabilities, and they may come to school unprepared to assume the role of an active, organized learner.

24. Motivational difficulties can limit the development of strategies needed to accomplish more complex tasks.

25. Children with learning disabilities can be taught to use more efficient learning strategies.

26. Children with learning disabilities have deficiencies in academic skills and information processing that differ from those of children with mental retardation.

27. When the children being assessed for learning disabilities are nonnative English speakers, you will need to consider their experiential background; the language ability of their peers, siblings, and other nonnative English speakers; their linguistic proficiency and academic achievements in their primary language and in English; and the assessment battery you want to use.

28. Distinguishing between a learning disorder and a language difference is not easy, because children who are learning a second language often have difficulties with language processing similar to those of children who have a learning disorder.

29. Ideally, children should show a learning disorder both in their native language and in their second language before being diagnosed as having a learning disability.

30. Children who come from cultural and linguistic backgrounds that differ from those of the majority group may perform poorly in school because of experiential differences, family expectations, limited English proficiency, stresses associated with acculturation and discrimination, and/or cognitive styles and learning strategies that differ from those of the majority group.

31. Consequently, a minority child whose achievement is below average may not have a learning disability per se; rather, her or his achievement level may be related to cultural and linguistic factors.

32. Being maltreated as a child may contribute to the development of learning problems and behavior problems.

The Process of Reading

33. Every language has a basic set of elementary sounds called phonemes; spoken words are formed by combining these sounds into meaningful wholes.

34. Early phonological awareness skills—such as sensitivity to rhyme and the ability to break words into their constituent sounds and blend sounds into words—are especially helpful to young children who are beginning to read.

35. Phonemic awareness skills are skills that pertain to individual sounds or phonemes.
36. Phonological awareness helps young children learn how spellings relate to sounds, permitting them to decode words when they are learning to read.
37. Phonological awareness and word awareness are probably closely related to the early stages of reading.
38. Word features important in the acquisition of decoding ability include phonological, graphic, orthographic, syntactic, and semantic features.
39. Children usually learn to read aloud by either the whole-word procedure or the phonics procedure.
40. The four phases in learning to read are the prealphabetic phase, or sight-vocabulary phase; the partial alphabetic phase, or discrimination-net phase; the full alphabetic phase, or phonological-recoding phase; and the consolidated alphabetic phase, or orthographic phase.
41. Good readers not only have progressed through these phases of reading skills but also use metacognitive strategies.

Communication Disorders

42. Communication disorders include expressive language disorder, mixed receptive-expressive language disorder, and phonological disorder.
43. Children with expressive language disorder may have problems with vocabulary, expressive grammar, and pragmatic use of language.
44. Children with mixed receptive-expressive language disorder may have problems with vocabulary, comprehending grammatical units, comprehending word-ordering rules (syntax), recognizing multiple meanings, and comprehending the meaning of subtle aspects of language usage.
45. Children with phonological disorder may have difficulty manipulating the sounds of oral language, difficulty with immediate recall of verbal information, and difficulty in quickly naming items in a group of letters, numbers, or colors.

Reading Disorder

46. Children with reading disorder may have problems with attention and concentration, phonological awareness, orthographic awareness, word awareness, semantic or syntactic awareness, rapid decoding, verbal comprehension, and pragmatic awareness.
47. Reading disorder is a type of learning disability in which children fail to master basic processes such as letter recognition and sound blending, despite adequate intelligence and educational opportunities.
48. Children with reading disorder may have *developmental dyslexia,* which refers to difficulty learning to read, or *acquired dyslexia,* which refers to loss of reading ability that has already been acquired, usually as a result of a traumatic brain injury or a disease that affects the brain.
49. Reading disorder is the most common type of learning disability—approximately 80% of children in learning disability programs have a diagnosis of reading disorder.
50. Dyslexia may involve difficulties in at least two important dimensions: phonological decoding (i.e., the ability to read words phonetically) and orthographic decoding (i.e., the ability to recognize letter sequences or words based on their visual features).

51. Reading disorder is most likely to be associated with difficulties in the phonological decoding of written language, particularly in phoneme segmentation.
52. Three subtypes of reading disorder are phonological dyslexia, orthographic dyslexia, and disorder of rapid naming.
53. Children who have a precocious ability to recognize written words, beyond what would be expected at their general level of intellectual development, are said to be hyperlexic.
54. Research on neurological correlates of reading disorders indicates that reading depends on two separate but equally important neural systems involving sound and pictures.
55. For a child to read well, the brain must translate symbols into their proper sound in a few thousandths of a second.
56. Minor differences in how the brain handles the visual processing of images, color, fast motion, and contrast can impede reading.
57. Everyone has some trouble adjusting to the written word because it makes such taxing demands on so many different parts of the brain.

Mathematics Disorder

58. Children with mathematics disorder (also called dyscalculia) may have problems in mastering basic mathematical skills, understanding mathematical terminology, perceptual or spatial processing, attention, shifting from one operation to another, writing numbers, and verbal memory.
59. Mathematics disorder is a heterogeneous condition that may occur in conjunction with reading disorder or with another learning disorder.
60. The core deficits of children with both mathematics and reading disorders may be problems in both short- and long-term memory—not just difficulties with mathematical facts and procedures and retrieval of verbal information.
61. For children who have difficulties only with mathematics, the primary problem may be the use of immature problem-solving strategies.
62. Like reading disorder, mathematics disorder ranges from mild to severe.
63. The cognitive requirements of mathematics change with time. Computation-focused activities are stressed during the early school years, followed by an emphasis on conceptual and abstract mathematical concepts in later years.

Disorder of Written Expression

64. A disorder of written expression significantly interferes with children's academic achievement or with activities of daily living that require writing skills.
65. Children with a disorder of written expression may have problems in the early stages of learning to write (including difficulty in producing letters of the alphabet rapidly and automatically, retrieving letters from long-term memory, obtaining sufficient finger dexterity and fine-motor coordination, and integrating visual and motor skills) and in the later stages of learning to write (including difficulty in connecting orthographic codes with the corresponding phonological codes, constructing meaningful sentences and paragraphs, planning, and making revisions).
66. Disorder of written expression is commonly found in combination with reading disorder, mathematics disorder, or pervasive oral language disorders.

67. Children with oral language difficulties also may have problems translating their thoughts into written language.

68. Early writing skills are primarily related to fine-motor coordination and word-level skills such as decoding and spelling, whereas later writing skills require the generation of ideas and ability to organize.

69. Writing may be especially taxing for children with attention and concentration problems, including those with attention-deficit/hyperactivity disorder.

70. Learning to spell involves five stages: prephonetic writing, mastering the names of some letters and learning beginning phonics, acquiring word patterns, spelling multisyllabic words, and mature spelling.

71. Children who have a reading disorder often have difficulty with spelling, although the processes involved in reading and spelling are different.

72. Spelling requires knowledge of sound-symbol correspondence (phonological skills), as well as linguistic competence (such as an understanding that the way words are spelled may depend on how they are used).

73. Reading involves phonological decoding and whole-word reading ability.

74. Achieving skill in spelling requires knowledge of the correct spelling of irregular words.

75. Learning to write involves four stages: imitation, graphic presentation, progressive incorporation, and automatization.

76. Children with good penmanship form letters in cursive or manuscript style that are recognizable out of context, of good proportion, consistent in size, and appropriately capitalized.

Nonverbal Learning Disability

77. Children with nonverbal learning disabilities have the following strengths: good verbal expressive ability, good vocabulary ability, good receptive language ability, good auditory perceptual ability, good rote verbal memory ability, good reading ability, and good spelling ability.

78. Children with nonverbal learning disabilities have the following limitations: tactile-perceptual deficits; psychomotor coordination deficits; deficiencies in visual-spatial-organizational abilities; deficits in nonverbal problem solving, concept formation, and hypothesis testing; difficulty dealing with negative feedback in novel or complex situations; difficulties in dealing with cause and effect relationships; difficulties in the appreciation of incongruities; fear of unfamiliar situations; difficulty with mathematical reasoning; poor psycholinguistic pragmatics; poor speech prosody; misspellings almost exclusively of the phonetically accurate variety; difficulties in perceiving gestures, facial expressions, and other nonverbal social cues; deficits in social perception, social judgment, and social interaction skills; and marked tendency for social withdrawal and isolation as age increases.

79. Children with nonverbal learning disabilities may have a dysfunction in the right cerebral hemisphere.

80. Parents of children with nonverbal learning disabilities should be encouraged to do the following: keep the environment predictable and familiar; provide structure and routine; prepare the child for changes, giving logical explanations when possible; pay attention to sensory input from the environment, like noise, temperature, and smells; help the child learn coping skills for dealing with anxiety; be logical, organized, clear, concise, and concrete; avoid jargon, double meanings, sarcasm, nicknames, and teasing; state expectations clearly; be specific about cause and effect relationships; work with the child's school to modify homework assignments, testing procedures, and physical education; have the child use the computer at school and at home for schoolwork; help the child learn organizational and time management skills; make use of the child's verbal skills to help him or her with social interactions; teach the child about nonverbal communication; help the child learn to tell whether he or she is communicating well by observing other people's reactions; arrange for the child to have a playmate who shares the child's interests; enroll the child in a small-group social skills training program; and encourage the child to develop interests that will build his or her self-esteem.

KEY TERMS, CONCEPTS, AND NAMES

Learning disability (p. 391)
Specific learning disability (p. 391)
Individuals with Disabilities Education Improvement Act (IDEA) 2004 (p. 391)
National Joint Committee on Learning Disabilities (p. 392)
Learning Disabilities Association of Canada (p. 392)
DSM-IV–TR (p. 393)
Etiology of learning disabilities (p. 393)
Genetic basis of learning disabilities (p. 393)
Phonological processing (or phonological awareness) (p. 393)
Biological basis of learning disabilities (p. 394)
Environmental basis of learning disabilities (p. 394)
Precursors of learning disabilities at preschool age (p. 394)
School-age children with learning disabilities (p. 395)
A four-stage information-processing model of learning disabilities (p. 395)
Short-term sensory storage, or sensory register (p. 395)
Perceptual encoding, or short-term memory or working memory storage (p. 395)
Central processing, or long-term memory storage (p. 396)
Response selection mechanisms (p. 396)
Deficits associated with learning disabilities (p. 396)
Developmental-lag hypothesis (p. 396)
Learning disabilities and mental retardation (p. 396)
Learning disabilities and nonnative English speakers (p. 397)
Learning disabilities and childhood maltreatment (p. 397)
The process of reading (p. 397)
Phonemes (p. 397)
Pictographic writing systems (p. 397)
Logographic writing systems (p. 397)
Syllabic writing systems (p. 397)
Alphabetic writing systems (p. 397)
Mapping of letters to phonemes (p. 398)
Homophones (p. 398)
Regularity of spelling-to-sound correspondences (p. 398)
Phonological awareness (p. 398)
Phonemic awareness skills (p. 398)
Segmentation (p. 398)
Manipulation (p. 398)
Blending (p. 398)

Word features (p. 399)
Phonological features (p. 399)
Graphic features (p. 399)
Orthographic features (p. 399)
Syntactic features (p. 399)
Semantic features (p. 399)
Whole-word procedure or whole-language procedure (p. 399)
Phonics procedure (p. 399)
Prealphabetic phase, or sight-vocabulary phase (p. 399)
Partial alphabetic phase, or discrimination-net phase (p. 399)
Full alphabetic phase, or phonological-recoding phase (p. 399)
Consolidated alphabetic phase, or orthographic phase (p. 399)
Communication disorders (p. 400)
Expressive language disorder (p. 400)
Mixed receptive-expressive language disorder (p. 401)
Phonological disorder (p. 401)
Reading disorder (p. 401)
Literal comprehension (p. 402)
Inferential comprehension (p. 402)
Critical comprehension (p. 402)
Developmental dyslexia (p. 402)
Acquired dyslexia (p. 402)
Dyslexia (p. 402)
Phonological decoding (p. 402)
Orthographic decoding (p. 402)
Phonological dyslexia (p. 403)
Orthographic dyslexia (p. 403)
Disorder of rapid naming (p. 403)
Hyperlexia (p. 403)
Neurological correlates of reading disorder (p. 403)
Mathematics disorder (dyscalculia) (p. 403)
Disorder of written expression (p. 404)
Spelling difficulties (p. 405)
Stage of prephonetic writing (p. 405)
Stage of mastering the names of some letters and learning beginning phonics (p. 405)
Stage of acquiring word patterns (p. 405)
Stage of spelling multisyllabic words (p. 405)

Stage of mature spelling (p. 405)
Handwriting difficulties (p. 405)
Stage of imitation (p. 405)
Stage of graphic presentation (p. 405)
Stage of progressive incorporation (p. 405)
Stage of automatization (p. 405)
Nonverbal learning disability (p. 405)

STUDY QUESTIONS

1. Discuss definitions of learning disabilities. Include in your discussion the definition included in IDEA 2004, definitions proposed by the National Joint Committee on Learning Disabilities and the Learning Disabilities Association of Canada, and the definition in *DSM-IV–TR*. Critically evaluate the strengths and weaknesses of each definition.

2. Discuss theories of the etiology of learning disabilities, including genetic, biological, and environmental bases.

3. Discuss the precursors of learning disabilities at preschool age.

4. Discuss learning disabilities in school-age children. Include in your discussion the four-stage information-processing model, deficits associated with learning disabilities, learning disabilities and mental retardation, learning disabilities in nonnative English speakers, and learning disabilities and child maltreatment.

5. Describe the process of reading. Include in your discussion the alphabet system, abilities involved in reading, word features, and the progression of reading skills.

6. Discuss communication disorders. Include in your discussion expressive language disorder, mixed receptive-expressive disorder, and phonological disorder.

7. Discuss reading disorder. Include in your discussion subtypes of reading disorder, hyperlexia, and neurological correlates of reading disorder.

8. Discuss mathematics disorder.

9. Discuss disorder of written expression. Include in your discussion spelling difficulties and handwriting difficulties.

10. Discuss nonverbal learning disability.

17

SPECIFIC LEARNING DISABILITIES: ASSESSMENT AND INTERVENTION

by Jerome M. Sattler and Barbara Lowenthal

What makes the desert beautiful is that somewhere it hides a well.

—Antoine-Marie-Roger de Saint-Exupery,
French poet and author (1900–1944)

IDEA 2004

Response to Intervention

Discrepancy Model

Assessment

Interventions for Learning Disabilities

Prognosis for Children with Learning Disabilities

Thinking Through the Issues

Summary

Key Terms, Concepts, and Names

Study Questions

Goals and Objectives

This chapter is designed to enable you to do the following:

- Understand the procedures for conducting formal and informal assessments of learning disabilities

- Become familiar with the research findings concerning intelligence tests and learning disabilities

- Understand interventions for children with learning disabilities

Learning disabilities may hinder children's educational progress and adversely affect their self-esteem, social status, interpersonal relations, and occupational choices. Early identification and effective interventions are needed to help children with learning disabilities succeed, both academically and socially, in and out of the classroom.

The assessment of learning disabilities serves several purposes:

- It identifies the child's areas of impaired functioning and areas of strength, including those associated with reading (e.g., word-level reading, comprehension, and fluency), oral language (e.g., oral vocabulary, listening comprehension, and oral expression), mathematics (e.g., computation fluency, concepts, and reasoning), and written expression (e.g., expression, writing fluency, spelling, and handwriting).
- It identifies patterns of academic strengths and weaknesses.
- It estimates the child's general level of intelligence, which suggests whether the child has the potential to achieve at a higher level.
- It establishes whether the child has deficits in basic psychological processes.
- It provides explanations for the child's poor achievement.
- It is helpful in developing interventions.

IDEA 2004

As noted in Chapter 1, IDEA 2004 provides the following guidelines for assessing children with a specific learning disability.

> (6) SPECIFIC LEARNING DISABILITIES—
> (A) IN GENERAL—Notwithstanding section 607(b), when determining whether a child has a specific learning disability as defined in section 602, a local educational agency shall not be required to take into consideration whether a child has a severe discrepancy between achievement and intellectual ability in oral expression, listening comprehension, written expression, basic reading skill, reading comprehension, mathematical calculation, or mathematical reasoning.
> (B) ADDITIONAL AUTHORITY—In determining whether a child has a specific learning disability, a local educational agency may use a process that determines if the child responds to scientific, research-based intervention as a part of the evaluation procedures described in paragraphs (2) and (3).

The assessment guidelines in IDEA 2004 need further refinement, for the following reasons.

1. The law does not define how a severe discrepancy between achievement and intellectual ability should be determined.
2. The law does not provide any guidance as to what constitutes "scientific, research-based intervention as a part of the evaluation procedures . . . ."

Let's now consider the two principal methods for identifying learning disability: response to intervention and the discrepancy model.

RESPONSE TO INTERVENTION

Establishing whether a child has a learning disability is not a simple task. You need to consider all relevant factors, including the child's age, behavior, sensory functioning, health history, educational history, family history, and cultural background, as well as the type of learning difficulties the child is experiencing. As noted above, IDEA 2004 states that a specific learning disability diagnosis may be determined in part by how a child responds to a scientific, research-based intervention; this approach to diagnosis is referred to as *response to intervention* (RTI). In an RTI assessment, children are given standard instruction in a regular classroom, their progress is monitored, those who are making poor progress are given specialized intensive and systematic instruction, and their progress is again monitored (Fuchs, Mock, Morgan, & Young, 2003).

Advantages and Disadvantages of RTI

RTI has the following potential advantages and disadvantages (Gresham, 2002; Marston, 2002; O'Connor, Fulmer, Harty, & Bell, 2001; O'Connor, Notari-Syverson, & Vadasy, 1996; Vaughn & Fuchs, 2003; Vellutino, Scanlon, & Lyon, 2000; Vellutino, Scanlon, Spay, Small, Pratt, Chen, & Denckla, 1996).

ADVANTAGES

1. *Children who are at risk can be identified.* All children in kindergarten to third grade can be screened to see whether they are at risk for learning problems. Children at risk are then given systematic and direct instruction. When their progress is assessed, children who are no longer at risk are given no further specialized assistance. Children who are still at risk are evaluated for special education.

2. *Identification and assistance can begin early.* Children who are not performing at grade level are identified early in their education and provided with assistance.

3. *Bias in teacher referrals may be reduced.* Compared to the traditional discrepancy model, RTI may more accurately identify children who need special education, regardless of their cultural or linguistic background, classroom behavior, and gender. However, research to determine whether RTI does in fact reduce bias in teacher referrals is still needed.

4. *Assessment is connected to instruction.* RTI uses instructionally relevant tasks (Speece, Case, & Malloy, 2003). Curriculum-based measurement (CBM) helps to monitor progress of at-risk children, and the results of weekly assessments can be used to develop and revise instructional plans (Fuchs & Fuchs, 1998).

5. *The number of children labeled as learning disabled may be reduced.* Intensive instruction in small groups may help young, at-risk readers (O'Connor, 2000; O'Connor & Jenkins, 1999). Children who benefit from such instruction may, therefore, not need to be referred for special education assessment. Fewer referrals in turn might reduce the number of children labeled as having a specific learning disability (Donovan & Cross, 2002). Again, research is needed to determine whether implementation of RTI reduces rates of identification of learning disabilities.

DISADVANTAGES

1. *Validated measurements are needed to quantify responsiveness to interventions.* Valid RTI procedures are available for reading, especially in kindergarten to third grade, but more work is needed to validate RTI procedures for mathematics, written expression (including spelling), and oral language in all grades (Deshler, 2002; Rooney, 2002; Vaughn & Fuchs, 2003).

2. *Many questions remain unanswered.* What learning deficits qualify for intervention? What are the standards for determining which interventions are effective (e.g., sample size, ages of participants, type of disability, robustness of findings)? What interventions are appropriate at each grade and for each type of disability? What is an acceptable level of improvement? How do we effectively monitor children's progress (e.g., frequency, types of tests)? Should monitoring procedures be the same for children in all grades? How long must an intervention be continued before we can determine whether a child is benefiting from it? What will happen if parents request an individual assessment and invoke timelines in state regulations (McBride, Dumont, & Willis, 2004)? What will be the role of independent evaluations (McBride et al., 2004)? How much will it cost to implement an RTI assessment? How intense should the intervention be? Who should conduct the RTI assessment (e.g., special educators, school psychologists, or paraprofessionals)? How will these individuals be trained? Will RTI be useful for culturally and linguistically diverse children? Will RTI be useful for children with mental retardation, severe sensory disorders, severe emotional problems, autistic disorder, neurological disorders, or other developmental disabilities?

Methods Used in RTI

Two methods used in RTI are the problem-solving approach and the standard protocol approach (Marston, 2002; Torgesen, Alexander, Wagner, Rashotte, Voellor, & Conway, 2001; Vellutino et al., 2000). An example of the *problem-solving approach,* using four levels, follows.

Level 1. On the basis of achievement test scores and the scores of other children, the teacher identifies at-risk children.

Level 2. The teacher consults informally with other general education teachers and special education teachers (as needed) about instructional modifications that will best meet the needs of the at-risk children. These modifications are then implemented and their effects monitored. CBM is the preferred method of monitoring progress.

Level 3. If the interventions are not successful, the school support team—composed of a special educator, a psychologist, and a social worker—considers the possible causes of the problems observed in the at-risk children, selects more intensive interventions, implements the modified intervention plan, and evaluates the children's progress.

Level 4. If the additional interventions are not successful, the school support team will likely recommend, with parent consent, that at-risk children be assessed for eligibility for special education. The assessment uses multiple sources of information, including (a) a review of the child's prior response to interventions, (b) information (both informal and formal) about the child's adaptive behavior in school and at home, (c) observation of the child at school, (d) the child's performance on norm-referenced measures and on informal measures of learning rate, problem solving, and ability to generalize, and (e) information about how the child's cultural, linguistic, and economic backgrounds are related to her or his level of achievement.

The *standard protocol approach* involves intensive tutoring using a standard validated protocol, or method of teaching. All children who have similar difficulties are given the same intensive instruction. The advantages of the standard protocol approach include uniform implementation, one standard instructional approach, and simple evaluative procedures (Fuchs et al., 2003). Limitations of the standard protocol approach are that one tutoring approach may not be suitable for all children with the same problem, schools may not have the funds to implement intensive tutoring sessions, and children who are low functioning or children with mental or neurological disorders may need other types of instruction. However, research suggests that standard protocol approaches do improve academic performance (Jitendra, Edwards, Starosta, Sacks, Jacobson, & Choutka, 2004; Torgesen et al., 2001; Torgesen, Wagner, Rashotte, Rose, Lindamood, Conway, & Garvan, 1999; Vellutino et al., 2000; Vellutino et al., 1996).

With the problem-solving approach, classroom teachers implement the instructional program after consulting with other school personnel, whereas with the standard protocol approach, trained tutors are the instructors (Fuchs et al., 2003). The problem-solving approach also may use different remediation procedures for different children, depending on the teachers and school, whereas the standard protocol approach uses one standard remediation procedure.

Both approaches require several decisions, including decisions on (a) the timing of the assessment (pre- and post-treatment, weekly, daily, etc.), (b) the method for measuring responsiveness, (c) the type of norms (national norms, local norms, or norms for at-risk children), and (d) the method for training teachers or tutors (Speece, Case, & Malloy, 2003).

We need more research about the effectiveness of both approaches with children and about the preferred methods of teaching reading, mathematics, and written expression (including spelling) to children of all grades (Fuchs, 2003; Fuchs et al., 2003; Vaughn & Fuchs, 2003).

DISCREPANCY MODEL

The discrepancy model requires that, in order for children to be classified as having learning disabilities, a severe discrepancy be found between *ability,* usually defined by an intelligence test score, and *achievement,* usually defined by a reading, mathematics, or written expression test score or by an overall achievement test score. A discrepancy of 1 to 1½ standard deviations between the scores generally qualifies as severe. However, this is a rule of thumb, because IDEA 2004 does not provide any guidelines for determining what constitutes a severe discrepancy.

A severe discrepancy is best identified by comparing scores on two appropriate tests, using a regression equation to determine expected scores on the second test (see Sattler, 2001). The equation takes into account *regression-to-the-mean effects,* which occur when the correlation between two measures is less than perfect. The regression-to-the-mean effect predicts that children who score above the mean on the first measure will tend to score somewhat lower on the second measure, whereas those who score below the mean on the first measure will tend to score somewhat higher on the second measure. Calculating a regression equation requires knowledge of the correlation between the two tests. Ideally, the correlation should be based on a large representative sample. Table F-4 in Appendix F provides expected scores on academic achievement tests, as predicted from intelligence test scores, for correlations between .30 and .80. A criterion level is set for a severe discrepancy, such as a difference of 1 standard deviation between the academic achievement test score and the intelligence test score. The criterion level may be set at different points, depending on the preference of those who establish the guidelines.

In some school districts, children may be identified as having learning disabilities when there is a discrepancy between verbal and performance (or nonverbal) abilities, as noted by scores on an intelligence test. *We strongly recommend never diagnosing a learning disability on the basis of a discrepancy between any two WISC–IV Indexes, such as Verbal Comprehension and Perceptual Reasoning, or between any two indexes on other individually administered intelligence tests.* Such a discrepancy may not indicate a learning disability, and conversely, a learning disability may be present even if there is no significant difference between the Verbal Comprehension Index and the Perceptual Reasoning Index or between any two indexes on other individually administered intelligence tests. It is extremely poor practice to rely *exclusively* on patterns of scores on an intelligence test to arrive at a diagnosis of learning disability. Furthermore, the use of two scores on an intelligence test to classify a child as having a learning disability would violate the guidelines of IDEA 2004, because the severe discrepancy would not be arrived at by using a measure of achievement and a measure of intelligence.

Advantages and Disadvantages of the Discrepancy Model

Discrepancy procedures have their advantages and disadvantages (Ashton, 1996; Scruggs, 1987).

ADVANTAGES

1. *Reliability and validity are known to be adequate.* Discrepancy formulas rely on reliable and valid assessment instruments.

2. *A rationale is provided for dispensing services.* Discrepancy formulas provide the basis for obtaining services for children who need them, even when we do not know the specific causes of a learning disability.

3. *The focus is on the core area.* Discrepancy formulas help professionals focus on academic achievement as an integral part of the assessment process.

4. *The identification procedure is characterized by objectivity.* Discrepancy formulas provide a consistent, objective, and accountable identification procedure. Doing away with discrepancy formulas might reintroduce subjectivity into the classification process. We need to distinguish between general and specific learning difficulties and to evaluate whether some specific learning difficulties are more serious than others (Ashton, 1996).

5. *Special education services are provided to those most likely to benefit from them.* Because funding is limited, the discrepancy model does serve a useful purpose in channeling special education services to those most likely to benefit from them.

DISADVANTAGES

1. *Clinicians using the same discrepancy formula, but different tests, may arrive at different classifications.* This happens because tests differ in their content, format, and psychometric properties (including degree of reliability and validity), and consequently may yield different scores. This is especially true when reading tests are used, because a reading test may be a measure of word recognition only, word comprehension only, or both word recognition and comprehension.

2. *Using discrepancy formulas without regard for the absolute level of the child's performance may result in serious misinterpretations and misclassifications.* A discrepancy formula should never be applied without considering the child's actual scores—that is, the level at which the child is functioning. For example, consider the case of a child who obtains a Full Scale IQ of 150 on the WISC–IV and standard scores of 132 on the WRAT–3 Reading, Spelling, and Arithmetic subtests. This child is clearly superior in the achievement

areas measured by both tests. To identify this child as learning disabled because of these discrepant scores would be inappropriate. This child is functioning in the 99th percentile on both tests! A learning disability label indicates that a child needs special help to remediate a disability—clearly not the case in this example. Furthermore, we are not in favor of schools' providing remedial services when children are functioning at or above grade level.

3. *Discrepancy formulas are based on the assumption that the tests used to evaluate a child's intelligence and achievement measure independent constructs, when in fact achievement and intelligence tests measure similar constructs (e.g., vocabulary, mathematics, factual information).* Furthermore, the same processing difficulties that cause a child to have low achievement test scores may impair the child's intelligence test scores. We also need to consider which Index to use when there is a large discrepancy between the Verbal Comprehension Index and the Perceptual Reasoning Index of the WISC–IV, for example. In cases in which children have no physical impairments (e.g., visual, auditory, or motor), choosing the Verbal Comprehension Index for one child and the Perceptual Reasoning Index for another child would mean that different measures were used to determine a discrepancy. Decisions concerning eligibility will change depending on whether the Full Scale, Verbal Comprehension Index, or Perceptual Reasoning Index is used. Choosing either the Verbal Comprehension Index or the Perceptual Reasoning Index alone is fraught with danger. Unless there is some compelling reason to use the Verbal Comprehension Index only or the Perceptual Reasoning Index only (e.g., the child has a hearing deficit or a visual deficit or a severe language problem), *we recommend that you not use one part of an intelligence test alone to measure a child's intelligence level.*

4. *Discrepancy formulas fail to identify children with learning disabilities who show no discrepancy between achievement and intelligence test scores.* Lower SES children tend to obtain lower scores on intelligence tests than do higher SES children (Siegel, 1999). Therefore, the discrepancy between IQ test scores and achievement test scores may be smaller in lower SES children, and thus they may be denied services. We know little about the distribution of discrepancies in the general population, which makes the use of any discrepancy procedure problematic.

5. *Discrepancy formulas have never been empirically validated.* The discrepancy criterion tacitly assumes that children with average or above-average IQs who are poor readers are cognitively and neurologically different from poor readers with low IQs, can reliably be differentiated from nondisabled readers and "slow learning" children or children who do not have discrepancies between achievement and intelligence, and can improve their reading skills if assessed and taught properly. However, research to support these assumptions is needed (Lyon, 1996a).

6. *The discrepancy formula approach prevents children from receiving services during their early school years.* Because children's achievement abilities cannot be reliably measured before the age of 9 years, children ages 6 to 8 years do not receive services, although services are needed at those ages (Lyon, Fletcher, Shaywitz, Shaywitz, Torgesen, Wood, Schulte, & Olson, 2001).

Comment on RTI and the Discrepancy Model

Research to determine the best methods for identifying children with learning disabilities is still needed. Some writers (e.g., Fletcher et al., 2002; Lyon, 1996a; Speece et al., 2003; Torgesen et al., 2001) believe that RTI is more effective than the discrepancy model in identifying children with specific learning disabilities; however, the evidence is not compelling. We may find that, although it has limitations, the discrepancy model is useful when applied in conjunction with other assessment procedures (Kavale, 2002; Scruggs & Mastropieri, 2002). It may be that the discrepancy model is useful in documenting underachievement, not learning disabilities per se. We believe, along with others (e.g., Kaufman & Kaufman, 2001), that intelligence is one factor that should be considered in the identification of learning disabilities. Perhaps RTI is best used in the prereferral process, prior to a psychological evaluation (Kavale, Kaufman, Naglieri, & Hale, 2005).

Substituting listening comprehension for intelligence in discrepancy formulas might be part of a more useful approach (Badian, 1999; Stanovich, 1991). Children showing a significant discrepancy between listening comprehension and reading comprehension would likely be diagnosed as having a decoding problem. However, listening comprehension measures also have limitations. First, they may not be suitable for children whose primary language is not English. Second, phonological memory or attention difficulties may interfere with tasks involving listening comprehension, as well as with tasks involving reading comprehension. Finally, children may have difficulty comprehending oral language as well as written language; IDEA 2004 recognizes a deficit in listening comprehension as a form of learning disability. Although children who have poor ability in both listening and reading may not be considered dyslexic (because they do not have *unexpectedly* low achievement), we believe that it is premature to preclude them from receiving a diagnosis of learning disability.

We believe that any procedure for identifying children as having learning disabilities must take into account other factors in addition to low achievement and inability to respond to interventions. Among such factors are a low level of intelligence, poor health, physical disabilities, limited motivation, boredom, absenteeism, emotional problems, a mismatch between the child's skills and the curriculum, cultural factors, and poor teaching. We also need to remember that low scores on an achievement test may simply represent the lower end of a distribution of scores and may not reflect a unique disability. Therefore, the designation "learning disability" should be used only to indicate underachievement related to specific processing deficits whose presumed origin is neurological dysfunction. *A formula that uses only two test scores or only the results of an intervention procedure cannot substitute for skilled clinical judgment and a synthesis of all relevant information available about a child.*

Efforts should be directed to developing a comprehensive and useful classification system, together with appropriate techniques for identification. Finally, all children who are not functioning at grade level should be given remedial instruction, regardless of whether they satisfy the RTI or the discrepancy criterion or any other criterion. This recommendation is reinforced by the provisions of the federal No Child Left Behind legislation.

ASSESSMENT

In assessing a child for a possible learning disability, you will want to obtain information about the following areas: (a) academic, intellectual, perceptual, motor, and behavioral functioning, (b) health history, (c) developmental history, developmental delays, and prenatal and perinatal complications, (d) personality, temperament, affect, motivation, and interpersonal relations, (e) family history of learning problems, and (f) cultural factors, peer group factors, pedagogical factors, and school factors. You will also want to develop interventions based on the assessment results, the child's resources, and the resources of the family, school, and community.

Assessment Battery

The most important tools in the assessment of children who may have learning disabilities are your good clinical skills, in conjunction with reliable and valid achievement tests, intelligence tests, and other relevant formal and informal tests and procedures. The tests should assess major content areas such as reading, mathematics, and written language (including spelling). Although there is no one standard battery for the assessment of learning disability, many of the tests reviewed in *Assessment of Children: Cognitive Applications* (Sattler, 2001) are useful. In addition to interviewing the parents, ask them to complete the Background Questionnaire (Table A-1 in Appendix A). Ask adolescent examinees to complete the Personal Data Questionnaire (Table A-2 in Appendix A).

Learning Disabilities and the WISC–IV

Because the WISC–IV is a relatively new instrument (Wechsler, 2004), little information is available about how children with learning disabilities perform on the test. Previous work on the WISC–III indicated that various WISC–III patterns do not provide a basis for differentiating children with learning disabilities from children who do not have learning disabilities, from children with behavior problems, or from children with mental retardation (see Sattler, 2001, for a review). The failure to find a unique Wechsler test pattern for children with learning disabilities is not surprising. Children with learning disabilities are too heterogeneous a group for one type of Wechsler test profile to be typical of a majority of its members. However, the WISC–IV or another standardized intelligence test can be used to assess children's level and type of intellectual functioning.

Informal Assessment

Because well-normed standardized tests are not available for assessing all types of school readiness, written and oral expression skills, and listening comprehension skills, several additional sources of information are useful. These include informal tests; curriculum-based measures; children's portfolios; interviews with the child, teacher, and parents; behavioral observations; visual-motor tests; behavior checklists; and personality tests. Children's portfolios contain a collection of their work over time, including audiotapes or videotapes demonstrating their performance in language and oral reading; any stories, letters, and essays that they have written; completed math worksheets and informal tests of math proficiency; and weekly spelling tests (Hallahan, Kauffman, & Lloyd, 1999).

You will need to evaluate a child's behavior at home and at school, the types of errors the child makes on both formal and informal tests (including classroom tests), and the factors that facilitate the child's learning. As always, the selection of tests should be based partly on the referral question. Observe the child to see whether he or she has any visual processing problems (Center for Technology in Education, 1997). Note how long it takes the child to understand, respond to, and cognitively process visual materials; whether the child scans materials in a sequential or a random pattern; and whether the child has difficulties viewing a computer screen, locating keys on a keyboard, and/or using a mouse.

Also observe the child's organizational skills. Check the top and inside of the child's desk and locker to see how well they are organized. Are materials well organized and can the child easily locate them?

Inspect the child's written assignments. Check the quality of the handwriting, neatness, margins, alignment of numbers in arithmetic problems, and spacing.

In addition to conducting an interview and observing the child, ask the teacher to complete the School Referral Questionnaire (Table A-3 in Appendix A). This essentially is a checklist describing the child's academic skills, deficits, progress, and classroom behavior, as well as any interventions that have been attempted and their degree of success. The assessment of behavior is important in cases of suspected learning disability, because children with learning disabilities also may have behavioral problems (Bender & Smith, 1990; Lerner, 2003).

Following are some guidelines for assessing young school-age children who may have reading difficulties (Jenkins & O'Connor, 2002).

1. Assess letter naming and phonemic awareness at the start of the school year.
2. Use measures that can be administered in 5 minutes or less (e.g., letters named in 1 minute; sound segments identified in 10 spoken words).
3. Conduct follow-up assessments monthly (or more frequently if needed) of children who do not know the names of the letters.
4. Conduct follow-up assessments monthly (or more frequently if needed) of children who cannot segment sounds (i.e., differentiate the first sound from other sounds) or blend sounds (i.e., combine separate phonemes into a whole word). Increase the difficulty level when a child masters easy levels.
5. Observe children as they attempt to write or spell words, in order to gain information about their understanding of the alphabetic principle.
6. Provide remediation to children who have not mastered letter and phonemic knowledge.

Informal assessment of reading skills. In an informal assessment of reading skills, consider such factors as the child's level of phonemic awareness; ability to identify letters; understanding of letter-sound correspondences of vowels, consonants, and blends; level of comprehension of material read aloud and material read silently; level of listening comprehension; ability to read fluently (including speed of reading words and nonwords); use of inflection during oral reading; ability to use the linguistic context to identify words in sentences; level of vocabulary; and use of reading strategies.

Recording oral reading errors. Table 17-1 shows a useful way for recording oral reading errors. After recording the errors, evaluate the types of errors the child made and how the errors affected the child's reading. Following are some questions to consider: What types of errors occurred most frequently? Did the child's omissions change the meaning of the text or interfere with his or her ability to respond to comprehension questions? Did the child consistently omit any

Table 17-1
Recording Word-Recognition Miscues and Errors

Miscue	Explanation	Marking
External assistance	Underline any word with which the child receives help	time
Functional attribute	Above the word in question, write the words the child uses to describe the word instead of actually reading it	*sit on* chair
Hesitation	Place a check mark over any word the child hesitates on	time✓
Insertion	Insert a caret mark to show any word the child inserts in the reading	*new* time ^ to
Losing place	Write "lp" over the word where the child loses her or his place	lp time
Mispronunciation	Above any mispronounced word, write the way the child pronounces it	*door* dog
Omission	Circle any word the child omits in reading	time (to)
Phonemic substitution	Above the word in question, write the word the child uses instead	*stool* spool
Refusal to pronounce	Write "rp" above any word the child refuses to pronounce	rp time
Repetition	Draw a left-facing arrow above any word the child repeats	← time
Self-correction	Draw a wavy line below any word the child mispronounces but then says correctly	time
Semantic substitution	Above the word in question, write the word the child uses instead	*leap* jump
Synonym substitution	Above the word in question, write the word the child uses instead	*big* large
Transpose	Use a curvy line to indicate words the child reads in the wrong order	time to go
Verb substitution	Above the word in question, write the word the child uses instead	*beat* heart
Visual misidentification	Above the word in question, write the word the child uses instead	*ball* balloon

specific types of words? Did the child spontaneously correct errors? If so, how often and under what circumstances? What types of substitutions were most common? Did the child's insertions change the meaning of the text? Was there a pattern to the insertions? Did the child consistently mispronounce a particular type of word, such as names or multisyllabic words? Were any reading errors associated with the dialect the child speaks?

Phonological awareness. Measures of phonological awareness are good predictors of the speed with which children will acquire reading fluency in the early grades (Jenkins & O'Connor, 2002). A child's degree of phonological awareness can be assessed via the following tasks:

1. *Phonological Memory Test.* This test, which is shown in Table D-3 in Appendix D, consists of 30 words. The child is asked to repeat each word after the examiner says the word. The test is designed for use with preschool children, although children of any age can be given the test.

2. *Phonological Oddity Task.* This task, which is shown in Table D-4 in Appendix D, involves three tests. Each test contains two sample items and eight sets of four words. In Test 1, three words in each set of four begin with the same sound (e.g., *n, b,* or *g*) and the fourth word is different. In Test 2, the common sound is the middle sound; in Test 3, the common sound is the ending sound. In each test, the child is asked to name the one word in each set that has a different sound.

3. *Strip Initial Consonant Task.* This task, which is shown in Table D-2 in Appendix D, involves two practice words and nine test trials. The child is asked to say the new word that results when the first sound is taken away.

4. *Yopp-Singer Test of Phoneme Segmentation.* This test, which is shown in Table D-7 in Appendix D, consists of 22 items. The child is asked to articulate separately, in order, the sounds of each word.

5. *Auditory Analysis Test.* This test, which is shown in Table D-6 in Appendix D, consists of two practice words and 40 test words. The child is asked to say the word that results after a specified syllable or phoneme is removed (e.g., "Say *smile* without the /s/").

6. *Comprehensive Test of Phonological Processing* (Wagner, Torgesen, & Rashotte, 1999). This test is a useful standardized measure of phonological awareness. However, several indices of reliability are below .90. Validity is satisfactory.

Word reading. To assess word-level reading ability, randomly select words from a basal curriculum reader and have the child read the words aloud. Record the number of words the child reads correctly and incorrectly in 1 minute. To assess sentence-reading ability, randomly select passages from a basal curriculum reader and have the child read the passages aloud. Record the number of sentences the child reads correctly and incorrectly in 1 minute.

To evaluate second- and third-grade children's ability to read regular words, irregular words, and nonsense words, you might use lists like the ones shown in Table D-5 in Appendix D; the lists are also useful for evaluating children in other grades who are having problems in reading. A child's ability to read these words may help you to determine whether the child uses a memory-based reading strategy, a phonics strategy, or no strategy. Children who use a *memory-based strategy* read irregular words better than they read nonsense words. Because they attempt to memorize associations between printed words and their pronunciations, they have sight-word recognition skills. Children who use a *phonics strategy* read nonsense words better than they read irregular words. They laboriously plod through the task of sounding out grapheme by grapheme, unable to use vocabulary knowledge to solve the problem of a word's identity. And some children may not have one dominant strategy or may not use any strategy.

Word prediction abilities (or cloze procedures). Informal tests of word prediction abilities, such as *cloze procedures,* allow you to study the way a child uses semantic and syntactic cues to identify words. Table D-1 in Appendix D shows a cloze procedure that requires the child to complete sentences.

Informal assessment of written expression. Start a story (or give a topic sentence) and have the child complete the story in writing. Allow 3 minutes. Record the number of words used in the writing sample and the number and percentage of words spelled correctly.

The following guidelines will help you evaluate children's written expressions (State of Iowa, Department of Public Instruction, 1981):

1. *Written assignments.* Evaluate the child's classroom writing assignments, especially successive drafts of the same paper. Verify, if possible, the conditions under which each draft was written—such as how much help the child received and whether the child used grammar-check and spell-check programs.

2. *Comparison with peer group.* Evaluate the child's written sample by comparing it with samples written by a random sample of children in his or her class.

3. *Copying.* Evaluate how the child copies letters, words, sentences, and short paragraphs presented in cursive and printed form in near-point positions (in materials placed on the child's desk) and far-point positions (written on the blackboard).

4. *Writing.* Evaluate how the child writes letters, words, or sentences (using both uppercase and lowercase cursive or print or both).

5. *Description of pictures.* Evaluate the child's written descriptions of 10 different pictures.

6. *Behavior.* Evaluate the child's behavior during classroom writing assignments.

In observing how the child writes and in reviewing the child's written work, note any specific handwriting difficulties, such as failure to connect parts of letters, distortion or unequal spacing of letters, unequal size of letters, letters wavering on a line, heavy or light use of pencil, tense grip, grasping pencil improperly (e.g., in the fist), progressive deterioration of letters, letters copied out of sequence, letters omitted or inserted, and words combined inappropriately. Table D-8 in Appendix D has guidelines for evaluating the content, grammar, and mechanics of a child's writing sample.

To assess spelling, randomly select words from a basic spelling curriculum, say the words one at a time, and have the child spell them aloud. Record the number and percentage of words spelled correctly and incorrectly in 2 minutes.

Two tables in Appendix D are useful for evaluating spelling ability. Table D-9 presents two informal tests of spelling—List 1 is appropriate for second- and third-grade children, and List 2 is appropriate for third- to sixth-grade children. Table D-10 identifies the critical elements tested by the words in the two lists. In addition, Table 17-2 gives guidelines for classifying spelling errors.

Table 17-2
A System for Classifying Spelling Errors

Type of error	Test word	Response
1. Omission of a silent letter—a silent consonant or vowel is omitted from the test word.	Weather Remain	Wether Reman
2. Omission of a sounded letter—a letter that is sounded in the ordinary pronunciation of the test word is omitted.	Request Pleasure	Requst Plasure
3. Omission of a double letter—one of a pair of successive, identical letters is omitted from the test word.	Sudden Address	Suden Adress
4. Addition—a letter or letters are added to the test word.	Until Basket	Untill Baskest
5. Transposition or reversal—the correct sequence of the letters of the test word is disturbed.	Saw Test	Was Tset
6. Phonetic substitution for a vowel sound—a vowel or a vowel and a consonant are substituted for a vowel of the test word.	Prison Calendar	Prisin Calender
7. Phonetic substitution for a consonant sound—a consonant that is an alternative sound for a consonant of the test word is substituted.	Second Vacation	Cecond Vakation
8. Phonetic substitution for a syllable—a similar-sounding syllable is substituted for a syllable of the test word or a single letter is substituted for a syllable.	Purchased Neighborhood	Purchest Naborhood
9. Phonetic substitution for a word—an actual word that is generally similar in sound to the test word is substituted.	Very Chamber	Weary Painter
10. Nonphonetic substitution for a vowel—a vowel or a vowel and a consonant are substituted for a vowel of the test word.	Station Struck	Stition Strick
11. Nonphonetic substitution for a consonant—a consonant or a vowel and a consonant are substituted for a consonant of the test word.	Washing Importance	Watching Inportance
12. Semantic substitution—a synonym or word from a similar category is substituted for the test word.	Jolt Pencil	Shock Pen
13. Letter misorientation—one or more letters of the test word are reversed.	Job Hop	Jod Hog
14. Unrecognizable or incomplete—the spelled word is unrecognizable as the test word.	Cotton Liberty	Cano Libt

Source: Adapted from Spache (1981).

The following case illustrates an informal assessment of a fifth-grader's written expression (State of Iowa, Department of Public Instruction, 1981).

This assessment is based on five classroom writing assignments that Mary completed since the beginning of the school year. Her work was compared with that of a random sample of five other classmates. Mary was also administered the Capitalization and Punctuation subtests of the Brigance Diagnostic Inventory of Basic Skills and asked to copy short paragraphs using cursive style.

Mary made numerous spelling and writing errors on each of the five written assignments. High-frequency words were misspelled, sentences were incomplete, and capitalization and punctuation errors were frequent. She mixed cursive and printing style, her letter formation was awkward and frequently illegible, and her spacing between words was variable. Mary's sentences were simple ones, with limited use of adjectives and adverbs. In contrast, her classmates in their written samples consistently used cursive style; made fewer capitalization, punctuation, and spelling errors; demonstrated more accurate letter formation and more consistency in spacing; used adjectives and adverbs more frequently; demonstrated the use of paragraph development; and used compound sentences, questions, quotations, and complex sentences.

On the two Brigance subtests, Mary showed moderate understanding of the correct use of capitalization (Capitalization subtest = 80% accuracy) and some understanding of the correct use of punctuation (Punctuation subtest = 70% accuracy). However, she usually does not apply her knowledge of capitalization and punctuation consistently when she is writing.

Mary's copying was laborious. She copied some words letter by letter, mixing cursive and printing styles. For the most part she used printing. After questioning, Mary said that she did not like to use cursive writing ("I don't know how to make all the letters"). The general appearance of her writing (legibility, spacing, and letter formation) improved significantly when she used printing only. She is the only child in her class who does not use cursive style.

In summary, Mary's written samples indicate problems in spelling, capitalization, punctuation, and paragraph development. Her use of complex language structures in writing is considerably below that of her classmates. She appears to have a severe disability in written expression.

Informal assessment of mathematics ability.   Select one problem (or more, depending on the curriculum) from each basic arithmetic area (e.g., addition, subtraction, multiplication, division, fractions, decimals) appropriate to the child's grade level and have the child solve the problems. Record the number and percentage of problems solved correctly and the amount of time it took to solve the problems.

Whether you use an informal or a formal test in your evaluation, note the child's knowledge of mathematical operations and the types of errors the child makes. Examples of errors include answering randomly, confusing place values when writing numbers, exhibiting directional confusion by adding columns from left to right, not attending to details, not carrying the right number, not lining up answers correctly, not using an appropriate amount of working space on the sheet, not writing clearly, not understanding the written instructions, giving the same answer to different problems, having difficulty shifting from addition to subtraction problems, inverting numbers, making computational errors, misreading numbers, reversing numbers, and using wrong mathematical operations. Table D-11 in Appendix D has a list of mathematics problems that can be used in an informal assessment, and Table 17-3 shows examples of errors children may make in multiplication and division.

An assessment of mathematical skills should include assessment of computational skills, knowledge of the language of mathematics (e.g., special words such as *together* and *less,* symbols, and operation signs), and the ability to solve mathematics application problems presented orally and in writing (see Sattler, 2001, for a description of standardized mathematics achievement tests). After administering a mathematics test, you can use testing-of-limits by, for example, having the child redo problems in which she or he misread the operation signs (e.g., adding instead of subtracting or multiplying instead of dividing), use a calculator to solve failed items, or use paper and pencil to solve problems presented orally.

Table 17-3
Examples of Multiplication and Division Errors

Multiplication errors	*Division errors*
1. Does not know multiplication facts	1. Omits remainder from quotient
2. Does not complete problem	2. Estimates quotient incorrectly
3. Does not regroup	3. Fails to bring down all numbers
4. Does not align properly	4. Fails to recognize that difference is greater than divisor
5. Shifts multipliers	5. Fails to record part of quotient
6. Does not add in regrouped number	6. Fails to use complete divisor
7. Guesses	7. Records quotient digits in wrong place
8. Regroups with wrong number	8. Divides into remainder
9. Multiplies vertically	9. Brings down wrong number
10. Adds instead of multiplies	10. Omits part of remainder from quotient
11. Is careless	11. Guesses
12. Multiplies left to right	12. Is careless
Addition Step	**Multiplication Step**
13. Does not know addition facts	13. Does not know multiplication facts
14. Fails to add and regroup	14. Fails to regroup
15. Is careless	15. Is careless
16. Adds wrong partial product	**Subtraction Step**
	16. Does not know subtraction facts
	17. Fails to regroup
	18. Subtracts up

Source: Adapted from Miller and Milam (1987).

Informal assessment of meaningful memory.
Table D-12 in Appendix D has three stories for evaluating a child's ability to remember the meaning of a paragraph. The stories are divided into 44, 34, and 37 logical units.

Informal assessment of metacognition.
Ask a school-age child to write down as many as seven different methods that could help him or her remember to bring his or her completed homework assignment to school the next morning. This procedure might give you information about the child's ability to generate strategies for remembering an assignment.

Informal assessment of social and environmental influences.
Interviews with the child, parents, and teachers (see Chapters 5, 6, and 7), together with questionnaires or checklists they complete (see Tables B-1, B-9, and B-15 in Appendix B), will help you evaluate social and environmental influences that may relate to the child's learning problems. Consider demographic characteristics (e.g., socioeconomic class, size of family, birth order, ethnicity), cultural values, degree of acculturation, family interaction patterns, parental attitudes toward learning, child management practices in the family, peer pressures related to schooling, changes in choices of peer groups, whether conditions in the home are conducive to studying, and the settings in which the child's problems typically occur.

Informal assessment of personality, temperament, and attitudes toward school.
Interviews with the child, parents, and teachers can give you information about the child's personality and temperament (see Tables B-1, B-9, and B-15 in Appendix B). It is also useful to inquire about the child's attitude toward reading and writing (see Table D-13 in Appendix D) and to administer a specialized sentence-completion technique to learn about the child's thoughts and feelings about reading, mathematics, and writing (see Table D-14 in Appendix D). If you use the sentence-completion technique, give the sentences orally and follow up with questions based on the child's answers. Information about the child's personality and temperament also can be obtained from formal methods of personality assessment, such as structured interviews, behavior checklists, rating scales, story completion techniques, and personality tests (see Chapter 10 for descriptions of personality tests).

Comment

A thorough assessment should provide you with information about a child's developmental history and family background; medical history; educational history, including current educational performance; level of intelligence; language abilities; mathematical abilities; written expression abilities; motor abilities; and behavioral and social skills. Table 25-1 in Chapter 25 is a list of questions and topics that will help you evaluate the information you obtain from the assessment.

Always try to account for any inconsistencies between the results obtained from formal assessment procedures and those obtained from informal ones.

Reading, mathematics, and written expression are complex cognitive activities influenced by *biological factors* (including intellectual ability, auditory and visual processing, and memory), *affective and nonintellectual factors* (including motivation, self-concept, and the degree of confidence children have in their ability to influence learning outcomes), and *environmental factors* (including language and cultural experiences, level of achievement, and teaching environment). When you evaluate a child for a suspected learning disability, consider all of these factors. Unfortunately, the diagnosis of learning disability remains problematic because of the ambiguity of the federal definition (and other definitions as well), variability in the interpretation of the federal definition at state and local levels, the broadness of the concept, its co-occurrence with other disabilities, and limitations of current assessment tools.

Despite these difficulties, the techniques available for the assessment of learning disabilities provide valuable information about important areas of academic, cognitive, and social-behavioral functioning. There is much wisdom in Christensen's (1992) observation that "the way ahead does not lie in the continued search for the 'true' child with a learning disability, but rather in a search for specific instructional solutions to reading failure and other learning difficulties,

Courtesy of Herman Zielinski.

regardless of whether the child is developmentally delayed, economically disadvantaged, from a racial or cultural minority, or a Euro American, middle-class male" (p. 278, with changes in notation).

INTERVENTIONS FOR LEARNING DISABILITIES

The three major types of interventions for learning disabilities are the cognitive, the linguistic, and the cognitive-behavioral instructional methods. These methods are not mutually exclusive, and children with learning disabilities may benefit from exposure to all three. All three intervention methods have in common long duration and intensity; they provide for more systematic teaching and practice and more repetitions than regular teaching does. Cognitive methods emphasize instruction in strategy, linguistic methods emphasize direct instruction in phonological awareness and other skills related to reading and writing, and cognitive-behavioral methods emphasize both. However, all three methods may combine two or more strategies as needed.

Before we consider the three intervention methods, note that in some cases children may have low scores on achievement tests because of poor instruction in phonics, in mathematics, or in written expression. The challenge then is to improve teacher preparation. The examples in Table 17-4 show some reading and mathematics instructional techniques that might be recommended for use in general education classrooms. In addition, Table 17-5 shows interventions useful for young children with reading difficulties.

Cognitive Methods

Metacognition refers to awareness of one's own cognitive processes and of one's own self-regulation, or what may be termed "knowing about knowing." Use of metacognitive strategies, such as those shown in Table 17-6, may help children become more effective learners. If you want to learn about a child's reading study skills, you might use Table D-15 in Appendix D. And if you want to learn about a child's thoughts about his or her note-taking ability, use Table D-16 in Appendix D.

Linguistic Methods

Children with a reading disorder may benefit from instruction in phonemic awareness and phonics, fluency (guided oral reading and independent silent reading), and comprehension (vocabulary instruction and text comprehension instruction). Children with a disorder of written expression may benefit from help with fine-motor coordination, visual processing,

---

Table 17-4
Examples of Reading and Mathematics Instructional Techniques for Use in the General Education Classroom

General Reading Weakness
- Whole-group reading/language arts instruction
- Small-group reading instruction using materials at the student's level

Decoding Skills Weaknesses
- Small-group phonemic awareness instruction
- Small-group or individualized multisensory code-based instruction (instruction based on visual and auditory presentation stressing phonics)
- Synthetic phonics instruction (part-to-whole)
- Analytic phonics instruction (whole-to-part)
- Small-group or individualized literature-based instruction that includes semantic and syntactic cues
- Daily fluency practice using decodable texts as well as rich and interesting texts at the student's independent reading level
- Daily opportunities to write, using skills emphasized in lessons

Comprehension Weaknesses
- Using for instruction texts of interest to students
- Small-group instruction in active reading and comprehension strategies—including semantic, graphophonic, and syntactic cue systems
- Vocabulary building
- Daily opportunities to write, using higher-order thinking skills

Mathematics Weaknesses
- Making appropriate technology available, as needed (e.g., calculators, computers)
- Providing regular opportunities for both guided and independent practice
- Classroom instruction that incorporates real-world examples as well as the student's personal experiences and language
- Use of manipulative materials to foster the development of abstract concepts
- Individual or small-group direct instruction to re-teach weak skills

Source: Adapted from the Connecticut State Department of Education (1999).

---

organization and attention, written expression and the mechanics of writing, and/or spelling. Interventions include environmental modifications, task modifications, instructional modifications, and assistive technology modifications (see Table 17-7).

Phonemic awareness and phonics. *Phonemic awareness* refers to the ability to determine the separate sounds of spoken words, and *phonics* refers to the ability to relate printed letters (graphemes) to the sounds (phonemes) in language. Examples of instructional approaches to the teaching of phonics follow (National Reading Panel, 2000):

1. *Analogy phonics.* Children are taught to read unfamiliar words by using parts of words they already know—recognizing "that the rime segment of an unfamiliar word is identical to that of a familiar word, and then blending the known rime with the new word onset" (National Reading Panel, 2000, p. 8). For example, children would be taught to read *brick* by recognizing that *-ick* is contained in the word *tick* or to read *stump* by analogy to *lump.*

2. *Analytic phonics.* Children are taught to identify whole word units and link the specific letters in the word with their respective sounds. For example, children would be asked to break the word *stop* into sounds and then blend the sounds into the whole word.

3. *Embedded phonics.* Phonics skills are taught indirectly, by embedding phonics in instruction in text reading.

4. *Phonics through spelling.* Children are taught "to segment words into phonemes and to select letters for those phonemes" (National Reading Panel, 2000, p. 8). In a spelling lesson, for example, children would be taught to divide the word *fish* into phonemes and then select letters for the phonemes: *f/i/sh.*

5. *Synthetic phonics.* Children are taught "to convert letters into sounds (phonemes) and then blend the sounds to form recognizable words" (National Reading Panel, 2000, p. 8). For example, children would be asked to analyze the sounds in the word *baking.*

One phonologically mediated reading intervention program that improved reading fluency also brought about constructive changes in brain organization (Shaywitz, Shaywitz, Blachman, Pugh, Fulbright, Skudlarski, Mench, Constable, Holahan, Marchione, Fletcher, Lyon, & Gore, 2004). Another program designed to remediate language-processing deficits resulted not only in improved reading but also in improved brain functioning in regions associated with phonological processing and in other regions as well (Temple, Deutsch, Poldrack, Miller, Tallal, Merzenich, & Gabrieli, 2003).

Fluency. Fluency is a critical factor in becoming an effective reader. Examples of instructional approaches designed to enhance fluency are guided oral reading, paired reading, and independent silent reading. In *guided oral reading,* children read passages orally and receive systematic help from a teacher, peer, or parent. In *paired reading,* an adult reads text aloud with the child. In *independent silent reading,* children read silently with little or no feedback. Research shows that guided oral reading, but not independent silent reading, increases word recognition, fluency, and comprehension (National Reading Panel, 2000).

Comprehension. Comprehension is based in part on a good vocabulary and proper use of reading comprehension strategies. Research shows that comprehension is improved by using appropriate vocabulary instruction and by teaching reading comprehension strategies (National Reading Panel,

---

Table 17-5
Examples of Interventions for Young Children with Reading Disorders

Fostering Phonemic Awareness

- Teach phonemic awareness early—in preschool, kindergarten, and first grade.
- With novices, begin instruction using larger (easier) linguistic units (e.g., words, syllables) and progress to smaller units (i.e., phonemes), but be sure that children can segment words into phonemes by the end of kindergarten.
- Teach phonemic awareness in conjunction with letter sounds.
- Encourage spelling/writing early in literacy instruction, because practicing these skills prompts children to notice the segmental features of language.
- Emphasize the sounds in spoken words when teaching phonics.
- Assess children's phonemic awareness regularly until children attain proficiency, and do not allow any child to lag behind in developing this skill.
- Provide children with whatever additional help they need to become sensitive to the segmental features of spoken language.

Promoting Alphabetic Reading

- Teach grapheme-phoneme conversions explicitly right from the start.
- Teach and assess graphophonemic relations directly and systematically, not with worksheets.
- To bolster word-level reading skill, encourage spelling/writing, right from the start.
- Teach sounding-out, right from the start.
- Provide beginning readers with ample opportunity to practice reading words that are consistent with their phonics instruction.
- As children become proficient at decoding short words, teach strategies for reading multisyllabic words.
- Find ways to provide more instruction in decoding for those who need it.

Building Fluency

- Find ways to make text reading easier for children with reading disability, using various forms of assisted reading (audiotapes, computer programs, choral reading, and partner reading).
- Experiment with texts of various levels of difficulty.
- Motivate children to read more by taking into account their interests, the variety of reading materials available to them, and the personal, linguistic, and cultural relevance of texts. Consult with the school librarian or someone knowledgeable about children and literature.
- Help children to identify areas of interest and teach children to explore those interests through reading.
- Experiment with supplements to text reading (such as word and subword study), word lists, and the proportion of time devoted to text- and word-level practice.
- Measure children's text fluency regularly to inform instructional decision making.

Source: Adapted from Jenkins and O'Connor (2002).

Table 17-6
Examples of Metacognitive Strategies for Children with Reading Disorders

Strategy	Example
Activating background knowledge—understanding that comprehension of the material will be affected by prior knowledge of the material and how the text is organized	"What do I know about this topic?"
Creating analogies after reading a passage	"How is the character in the first paragraph similar to the one in the second paragraph?" "How is the material I am reading similar to what I learned the other day about the topic?"
Evaluating the difficulty level of the material and understanding that some parts of the text are more difficult to read than other parts	"I'll need to spend more time with this material to master it than I usually do." "I'll have to read this part more slowly than the first part."
Evaluating the importance of material, knowing that information in a text may vary in importance	"What are the most important points in the paragraph that I should remember?"
Evaluating what has been learned	"I'm going to quiz myself when I finish reading this section."
Facilitating recall—taking good notes and underlining words that will be helpful in learning the material	"Did I underline the key ideas and terms?"
Imagining occasionally what the characters, objects, and settings in the story look like or imagining what it would be like to be in the story	"I wonder what the main character looks like?"
Linking new information from the passage with other material in the passage and with background knowledge	"How does this paragraph fit in with the whole passage?" "How does this passage relate to what I already know?"
Monitoring comprehension and reading progress	"What should I remember about the paragraph?" "What should I remember about the full passage?"
Monitoring and evaluating note-taking ability	"Do my notes have all the essential information?" "Do my notes have any unnecessary material?"
Organizing information into patterns	"What ideas in the passage seem to go together?"
Paraphrasing and summarizing the material	"What are the main ideas of the paragraph?" "What are the main ideas of each heading in the chapter?" "What are the main points of the passage?"
Planning—estimating how much time it will take to do the assignment	"How much time should I spend on the assignment tonight?"
Predicting—stopping while reading and trying to guess what will happen next	"What do I think is going to happen to the main character after the first paragraph?"
Recognizing discrepancies in the material, such as between a heading of a section and the contents in the section	"I only found two descriptions of countries when the heading indicated that there were three."
Recognizing environmental conditions—understanding when the environment is distracting	"I'll have to move to another location because I can't read too well with so much noise."
Recognizing incomplete mastery—recognizing when one does not fully understand or recall the material	"Do I need to reread part of the story?" "Do I need to pay more attention to details?" "Does the passage have too many words I don't know?" "Do I need to read it more slowly?" "I'll have to go back to find the names of the first four presidents."

(Continued)

Table 17-6 (*Continued*)	
Strategy	*Example*
Self-appraisal—evaluating one's attitude and feelings	"Will I try harder to do well on this assignment than on the last one?" "How does what happened today at school affect how I will study tonight?" "Will I let the problems that I am having at home affect how I study tonight?"
Using graphic organizers—making tables, lists, charts, webs, or diagrams of material	 Shared characteristics Things unique to baseball Things unique to football

Note. The examples illustrate what a child engaging in metacognition might say to himself or herself.
Source: Bender (2001); Billingsley and Wildman (1990); Deshler, Ellis, and Lenz (1996); John Willis (personal communication, April 2005); and Vaughn, Bos, and Schumn (2000).

2000). The metacognitive strategies shown in Table 17-6 are useful in improving comprehension.

Cognitive-Behavioral Methods

Cognitive-behavioral interventions are designed to improve the social and behavioral adjustment of children with learning disabilities, particularly children who have negative attitudes, mental blocks, insecurity, anxiety, depression, poor motivation, learned helplessness, and low expectations for academic success (Casey, Levy, Brown, & Brooks-Gunn, 1992; Deshler et al., 1996). The goals are to help them become less frustrated at school and at home, recognize their strengths and weaknesses, develop reasonable expectations, and use their strengths to compensate for their weaknesses. Teaching such children motivational strategies as well as metacognitive strategies can help them become more effective learners (see Table 17-8). They must come to believe that effort, ability, and choice of strategy—not just luck—are responsible for their success.

Comment on Interventions

There are several treatment options for children with learning disorders. For example, the methods covered in this section may be used individually or in combination. Regardless of the method or methods selected, use of the techniques shown in Table 17-9 should be considered in order to help children with learning disabilities become more effective learners (Hallahan & Kauffman, 2003; Mather & Goldstein, 2001; Mercer & Mercer, 2005).

Finally, knowledge about how children normally learn language may provide clues to helping children who have difficulty learning language. Research shows that 20-month-old children all learn language in a similar way, regardless of what language they are learning (Bornstein, Cote, Maital, Painter, Park, Pascual, Pêcheux, Ruel, Venuti, & Vyt, 2004). Toddlers learn nouns first, followed by verbs and then adjectives. On average, children of this age know about 300 nouns (e.g., names of animals, toys, body parts), 100 verbs (e.g., *run, walk, clap*), and 20 pronouns (e.g., *me, he, she*). Perhaps children learn nouns first because they refer to concrete things that the children can see and touch. Verbs and adjectives are more abstract and may be more difficult to grasp. Therefore, it might be preferable to emphasize concrete words in teaching children with language difficulties.

Preparation for the World of College and Work

Older adolescents with learning disabilities may need help in finding colleges and universities that meet their needs and have appropriate support services, and then they may need assistance in filling out applications. Adolescents entering the work force may need guidance in finding job training, reading want ads, filling out job applications, interviewing, following directions on the job, learning job skills, taking criticism, finishing work on time, paying attention on the job, working carefully, learning about their legal rights on the job, and learning how to advocate for necessary job accommodations.

Table 17-7
Examples of Interventions for Children with Disorders of Written Expression

Environmental Modifications

- Use direct lighting (e.g., seat child away from windows to avoid glare; place the child's seat with back to window to take advantage of natural lighting; reduce amount of fluorescent lighting; increase natural lighting).
- Reduce glare by using black print on cream-colored paper, rather than black print on white paper.
- Minimize visual distractions (such as bright pictures or objects) around material to be copied or around the posted directions.
- Seat the child close to the chalkboard (or dry erase board) and the teacher, and keep the chalkboard clean.
- To highlight information on the board, use different colors of chalk (or markers), draw lines beneath specific information, and use arrows to connect information.

Task Modifications

- Encourage the child to practice letter formation with different writing implements (e.g., pencil, pen, felt-tipped pens of different types, markers, crayons, chalk, paint).
- Give the child a slanted writing surface such as an easel or a sling board, if needed, to help with fine-motor control.
- Use fill-in-the-blank tests, multiple-choice tests, or true-false tests to reduce writing demands; also allow the child to demonstrate mastery of the material orally.
- Allow the child to highlight words or phrases on worksheets instead of copying the words.
- Use large, bold type, paper with triple-spaced lines, paper with wide margins, and extra spacing between letters, words, and graphics.
- To help the child stay within a defined writing space, use handwriting guides or templates, instruct the child to use every other line (if paper with triple lines is not used), or provide a writing space of a different color or shade on the paper.
- Encourage the child to use his or her preferred method of writing (manuscript or cursive) and writing implements that are easy to grasp.
- To help the child align numbers, have the child use graph paper, writing one number in each block.
- Permit the child to begin each assignment early, shorten the length of assignments, reduce the number of assignments, allow additional time for the child to complete the assignments, as needed, and permit the child to complete homework during study hall periods.
- To help the child form letters, use raised-line paper, sandpaper letters, or stencils as guides.
- To help the child organize thoughts and information, use graphic organizers and outlining techniques.
- Provide the child with both written and oral directions for an assignment (and a tape recording of directions and assignments if needed), and ask the child to repeat the directions orally.
- Have the child make an assignment calendar book organized by subject.
- Have available a telephone hotline and/or Web site that the child can use to review each day's assignment, if needed.

Instructional Modifications

- Use a multisensory approach to teach letter formation. Have the child talk about the mechanics of writing as he or she writes, have the child write in the air, have the child use dot-to-dot techniques, or have the child write words in sand.
- Encourage the child to leave a space between letters (and between words) about the size of his or her letter "o."
- Encourage the child to examine the items in his or her notebooks, folders, and desk daily and to remove unneeded items. Check to see whether this has been done. Provide help as needed.
- Encourage the child to ask questions about unclear directions.
- Give the child a list of materials needed for each activity, ask the child review the list before starting an activity, and assign a peer to check on whether the child has the proper materials for the activity.
- Teach the child organizational strategies, including making a daily "to do" list and prioritizing assignments.
- Encourage parents to help their child use organizational strategies at home.
- With the child, develop a checklist of the steps needed to complete each assignment.
- Develop short, clear objectives for the written assignments, use a specific routine or sequence of tasks to structure the writing process, and gear the written assignments to the child's level of readiness.
- Allow the child to draw a line through errors instead of erasing them.
- Brainstorm ideas for essay topics and journal entries with the child before he or she begins an assignment.
- Give the child opportunities to read and write daily, especially writing about everyday activities.
- Review and post the rules of punctuation and capitalization.
- Give the child a checklist to help him or her edit drafts.
- Use oral, pictorial, and written cues to help enrich the child's knowledge of word use and word order.
- Encourage the child to use a dictionary and a thesaurus, and show him or her how to use these resources if necessary.
- Encourage the child to make cards (or a personal spelling notebook) with words that he or she frequently misspells and to review these words daily.
- Analyze the child's writing samples for content, organization, and spelling errors. Give the child prompt feedback about his or her work, with appropriate reinforcements, and teach the child how to reduce errors.
- Show the child how to check drafts of his or her written assignments and how to proofread.
- Encourage the child to practice visualizing how words are spelled.
- Develop with the child mnemonic strategies to assist in spelling.
- Grade the content of the child's written assignment and not his or her handwriting, spelling (unless spelling is the focus of the assignment), or organization.

Assistive Technology Modifications

- Use software to help the child learn to write more effectively. For example, use software with spelling and grammar checking features, outline/graphic organizer features, voice feedback, word prediction features, and templates to structure different writing tasks.

Source: Adapted from Center for Technology and Education (1997).

Table 17-8
Examples of Motivational Strategies for Children with Learning Disabilities

Strategy	Example
Establishing a purpose	"I need to learn this material because someday I may become a teacher."
Knowing one's attitudes	"I feel much better about going to school because my close friend didn't move to another city."
Knowing what you gain from doing well	"My parents will be happy if I get a good grade."
Monitoring progress toward goals	"I have completed about 50% of the assignment and still need about 3 hours more to finish it."
Setting goals	"I want to do the entire assignment tonight."
Using self-affirmation statements	"I want to try harder on this assignment than on the last one."
Using self-coping statements	"I know how to use a dictionary to find out about the words I don't know."
Using self-reinforcement	"I felt good when I completed this assignment."

Source: Deshler, Ellis, and Lenz (1996).

Table 17-9
Examples of Interventions for Children with Learning Disabilities

Example	Description
Adequate time	Give children more time to think and respond to the lesson.
Alternative presentations	Provide extensive verbal explanations of visual materials. Provide visual aids to supplement verbal presentations.
Computer-assisted instruction	Use computer software as a teaching tool. Use word processing software to help children with their writing assignments.
Cooperative learning	Have children work together on a project.
Critical thinking	Encourage children to predict, question, clarify, and summarize the material. Begin with easy material.
Goal setting	Set objectives at the beginning of the lesson; also help children set their own objectives.
Mastery notebooks	Help children create personal notebooks detailing phonics and syllabication rules, steps in mathematics calculations, spelling rules, and other frequently used information.
Metacognitive strategy instruction	Encourage children to think about, preplan, and monitor their academic work, including what worked and what did not work.
Peer tutoring	Have one child act as a teacher and provide instruction to another child.
Reciprocal teaching	Teachers and children may take turns leading discussions about an assignment.
Specific praise	Give children positive and specific feedback about their performance.
Task analysis	Divide the learning task into sequential, small steps and then teach each step until the child masters the task.

Role-playing, tutorials, supervised job training, and other similar interventions may improve their chances of success in the world of work. IDEA 2004 requires that schools provide children with disabilities with effective transition services between educational settings or from school to post-school settings.

PROGNOSIS FOR CHILDREN WITH LEARNING DISABILITIES

Although learning disabilities often persist into adulthood, most individuals with learning disabilities function well in society (Deshler, 2002; Goldberg, Higgins, Raskind, & Herman, 2003; Goldstein, Murray, & Edgar, 1998; Hallahan & Kauffman, 2003; Morrison & Cosden, 1997; Raskind, Goldberg, Higgins, & Herman, 1999; Reiff, Gerber, & Ginsberg, 1997; Witte, Philips, & Kakela, 1998). In estimating the prognosis of any child or young adult with a learning disability, you will need to consider the following factors: ability to engage in creative problem solving, abilities required in different careers, ability to set reasonable goals, access to appropriate interventions, age at which the learning disability was recognized, attitude toward life challenges, available support systems, awareness of limitations and strengths, coping skills, cognitive ability, family's attitude toward the learning disability, interventions attempted and responses to the interventions, motivation, peer group's attitude toward the learning disability and toward achievement, perseverance, presence of co-occurring disorders, self-concept, severity of the learning disability, teachers' attitudes toward the learning disability, and type of learning disability.

THINKING THROUGH THE ISSUES

1. Do you think learning disabilities can be easily overcome? Explain your answer.
2. Explain why researchers have been unable to isolate patterns in intelligence test scores that differentiate individuals with learning disabilities from other individuals.
3. Why do you think that some children benefit from interventions and others do not?

SUMMARY

1. Learning disabilities may hinder children's educational progress and adversely affect their self-esteem, social status, interpersonal relations, and occupational choices.
2. Early identification and effective interventions are needed to help children with learning disabilities succeed, both academically and socially, in and out of the classroom.
3. The assessment of learning disabilities serves several purposes: (a) identifying the child's areas of impaired functioning and areas of strength, including those associated with reading (e.g., word-level reading, comprehension, and fluency), oral language (e.g., oral vocabulary, listening comprehension, and oral expression), mathematics (e.g., computation fluency, concepts, and reasoning), and written expression (e.g., expression, writing fluency, spelling, and handwriting), (b) identifying patterns of academic strengths and weaknesses, (c) estimating the child's general level of intelligence, which suggests whether the child has the potential to achieve at a higher level, (d) establishing whether the child has deficits in basic psychological processes, (e) providing explanations for the child's poor achievement, and (f) helping in the development of interventions.

IDEA 2004

4. IDEA 2004 regulations indicate that a local educational agency shall not be required to take into consideration whether a child has a severe discrepancy between achievement and intellectual ability in oral expression, listening comprehension, written expression, basic reading skill, reading comprehension, mathematical calculation, or mathematical reasoning. A local educational agency may use a process that determines whether the child responds to scientific, research-based intervention as a part of the evaluation.
5. IDEA 2004 does not define how a severe discrepancy between achievement and intellectual ability should be determined or provide any guidance as to what constitutes "scientific, research-based intervention as a part of the evaluation procedures. . . ."

Response to Intervention

6. Establishing whether a child has a learning disability is not a simple task. You need to consider all relevant factors, including the child's age, behavior, sensory functioning, health history, educational history, family history, and cultural background, as well as the type of learning difficulties the child is experiencing.
7. IDEA 2004 states that a specific learning disability diagnosis may in part be determined by how a child responds to a scientific, research-based intervention; this approach to diagnosis is referred to as response to intervention (RTI).

8. In an RTI assessment, children are given standard instruction in a regular classroom, their progress is monitored, those who are making poor progress are given specialized intensive and systematic instruction, and their progress is again monitored.
9. RTI may help to identify children at risk, provide for early identification and assistance, reduce bias in teacher referrals, connect assessment to instruction, and reduce the number of children labeled as learning disabled.
10. RTI needs better validated measurements, and proponents of RTI need to define standard instruction, monitoring progress, intensiveness of instruction, and systematic instruction; need to specify how long instruction should last before one concludes that a child is not benefiting from it; and need to consider whether professionals or nonprofessionals will be trained to conduct the procedure and whether the procedure will apply to all children with disabilities.
11. Two methods used in RTI are the problem-solving approach and the standard protocol approach.
12. With the problem-solving approach, classroom teachers implement the instructional program after consulting with other school personnel, whereas with the standard protocol approach, trained tutors are the instructors.

Discrepancy Model

13. The discrepancy model requires that, in order for children to be classified as having learning disabilities, a severe discrepancy be found between *ability,* usually defined by an intelligence test score, and *achievement,* usually defined by a reading, mathematics, or written expression test score or by an overall achievement test score.
14. A discrepancy of 1 to 1½ standard deviations between two test scores generally qualifies as severe. However, this is a rule of thumb, because IDEA 2004 does not provide any guidelines for determining what constitutes a severe discrepancy.
15. We strongly recommend never diagnosing a learning disability on the basis of a discrepancy between any two WISC–IV Indexes, such as Verbal Comprehension and Perceptual Reasoning, or between any two indexes on other individually administered intelligence tests.
16. Advantages of the discrepancy model include that reliability and validity are adequate, a rationale is provided for dispensing services, the focus is on the core area, identification procedures are characterized by objectivity, and special education services are provided to those most likely to benefit from them.
17. Disadvantages of the discrepancy model include the fact that clinicians using the same discrepancy formula, but different tests, are likely to arrive at different classifications; using discrepancy formulas without regard for the absolute level of the child's performance may result in serious misinterpretations and misclassifications; discrepancy formulas are based on the assumption that the tests used to evaluate a child's intelligence and achievement measure independent constructs, when in fact achievement and intelligence tests measure similar constructs; discrepancy formulas fail to identify children with learning disabilities who show no discrepancy between achievement and intelligence test scores; discrepancy formulas have never been empirically validated; and the discrepancy formula approach prevents children from receiving services during their early school years.
18. Research to determine the best methods for identifying children with learning disabilities is still needed.

19. Substituting listening comprehension for intelligence in discrepancy formulas might be part of a more useful approach.

20. We believe that any procedure for identifying children as having learning disabilities must take into account other factors, in addition to low achievement and inability to respond to interventions.

21. Among such factors are a low level of intelligence, poor health, physical disabilities, limited motivation, boredom, absenteeism, emotional problems, a mismatch between the child's skills and the curriculum, cultural factors, and poor teaching.

22. We also need to remember that low scores on an achievement test may simply represent the lower end of a distribution of scores and may not reflect a unique disability.

23. A formula that uses only two test scores or only the results of an intervention procedure cannot substitute for skilled clinical judgment and a synthesis of all relevant information about a child.

24. Efforts should be directed toward developing a comprehensive and useful classification system, together with appropriate techniques for identification.

25. All children who are not functioning at grade level should be given remedial instruction, regardless of whether they satisfy the RTI or the discrepancy criterion or any other criterion.

Assessment

26. In assessing a child for a possible learning disability, you will want to obtain information about the following areas: (a) academic, intellectual, perceptual, motor, and behavioral functioning, (b) health history, (c) developmental history, developmental delays, and prenatal and perinatal complications, (d) personality, temperament, affect, motivation, and interpersonal relations, (e) family history of learning problems, and (f) cultural factors, peer group factors, pedagogical factors, and school factors.

27. You will also want to develop interventions based on the assessment results, the child's resources, and the resources of the family, school, and community.

28. The most important tools in the assessment of children who may have learning disabilities are your good clinical skills, in conjunction with reliable and valid achievement tests, intelligence tests, and other relevant formal and informal tests and procedures.

29. Because the WISC–IV is a relatively new instrument, little information is available about how children with learning disabilities perform on the test.

30. Because well-normed standardized tests are not available for assessing all types of school readiness, written and oral expression skills, and listening comprehension skills, several additional sources of information are useful. These include informal tests; curriculum-based measures; children's portfolios; interviews with the child, teacher, and parents; behavioral observations; visual-motor tests; behavior checklists; and personality tests.

31. You will need to evaluate a child's behavior at home and at school, the types of errors the child makes on both formal and informal tests (including classroom tests), and the factors that facilitate the child's learning.

32. In addition to conducting an interview and observing the child, ask the teacher to complete the School Referral Questionnaire. This essentially is a checklist describing the child's academic skills, deficits, progress, and classroom behavior, as well as any interventions that have been attempted and their degree of success.

33. Guidelines for assessing school-age children who may have reading difficulties include assessing letter naming and phonemic awareness at the start of the school year; using measures that can be administered in 5 minutes or less; conducting monthly follow-up assessments of children who do not know the names of the letters or who cannot segment or blend sounds; observing children as they attempt to write or spell words, to gain information about their understanding of the alphabetic principle; and providing remediation to children who have not mastered letter and phonemic knowledge.

34. In an informal assessment of reading skills, consider such factors as the child's level of phonemic awareness; ability to identify letters; understanding of letter-sound correspondences of vowels, consonants, and blends; level of comprehension of material read aloud and material read silently; level of listening comprehension; ability to read fluently (including speed of reading words and nonwords); use of inflection during oral reading; ability to use the linguistic context to identify words in sentences; level of vocabulary; and use of reading strategies.

35. In observing how the child writes and in reviewing the child's written work, note any specific handwriting difficulties, such as failure to connect parts of letters, distortion or unequal spacing of letters, unequal size of letters, letters wavering on a line, heavy or light use of pencil, tense grip, grasping pencil improperly (e.g., in the fist), progressive deterioration of letters, letters copied out of sequence, letters omitted or inserted, and words combined inappropriately.

36. In a formal or an informal assessment of mathematics ability, note the child's knowledge of mathematical operations and the types of errors the child makes.

37. A thorough assessment should provide you with information about a child's developmental history and family background; medical history; educational history, including current educational performance; level of intelligence; language abilities; mathematical abilities; written expression abilities; motor abilities; and behavioral and social skills.

Interventions for Learning Disabilities

38. The three major types of interventions for learning disabilities are the cognitive, the linguistic, and the cognitive-behavioral instructional methods.

39. Metacognition refers to awareness of one's own cognitive processes and of one's own self-regulation, or what may be termed "knowing about knowing."

40. Children with a reading disorder may benefit from instruction in phonemic awareness and phonics, fluency (guided oral reading and independent silent reading), and comprehension (vocabulary instruction and text comprehension instruction).

41. Phonemic awareness refers to the ability to determine the separate sounds of spoken words, and phonics refers to the ability to relate printed letters (graphemes) to the sounds (phonemes) in language.

42. Fluency is a critical factor in becoming an effective reader.

43. Three instructional approaches designed to enhance fluency are guided oral reading, paired reading, and independent silent reading.

44. In guided oral reading, children read passages orally and receive systematic help from a teacher, peer, or parent.

45. In paired reading, an adult reads aloud with the child.
46. In independent silent reading, children read silently with little or no feedback.
47. Research shows that guided oral reading, but not independent silent reading, increases word recognition, fluency, and comprehension.
48. Comprehension is based in part on a good vocabulary and proper use of reading comprehension strategies.
49. Research shows that comprehension is improved by using appropriate vocabulary instruction and by teaching reading comprehension strategies.
50. Cognitive-behavioral interventions are designed to improve the social and behavioral adjustment of children with learning disabilities, particularly children who have negative attitudes, mental blocks, insecurity, anxiety, depression, poor motivation, learned helplessness, and low expectations for academic success.
51. Older adolescents with learning disabilities may need help in finding colleges and universities that meet their needs and have appropriate support services, and then they may need assistance in filling out applications.

Prognosis for Children with Learning Disabilities

52. Although learning disabilities often persist into adulthood, most individuals with learning disabilities function well in society.
53. In estimating the prognosis for any child or young adult with a learning disability, you will need to consider the following factors: ability to engage in creative problem solving, abilities required in different careers, ability to set reasonable goals, access to appropriate interventions, age at which the learning disability was recognized, attitude toward life challenges, available support systems, awareness of limitations and strengths, coping skills, cognitive ability, family's attitude toward the learning disability, interventions attempted and responses to the interventions, motivation, peer group's attitude toward the learning disability and toward achievement, perseverance, presence of co-occurring disorders, self-concept, severity of the learning disability, teachers' attitudes toward the learning disability, and type of learning disability.

KEY TERMS, CONCEPTS, AND NAMES

STUDY QUESTIONS

1. Discuss the guidelines provided in IDEA 2004 for the assessment of children with specific learning disabilities.
2. Discuss response to intervention (RTI) as a way of evaluating a child for a possible learning disability.
3. Discuss the discrepancy model as a way of evaluating a child for a possible learning disability.
4. Discuss the assessment of learning disabilities. Include in your discussion a typical assessment battery, the WISC–IV, and informal assessment of reading skills, written expression, mathematics ability, meaningful memory, social and environmental influences, personality, temperament, and attitudes toward school.
5. Discuss interventions for learning disabilities. Include in your discussion cognitive methods, linguistic methods, and cognitive-behavioral methods.
6. Discuss the prognosis for children with learning disabilities.

18

MENTAL RETARDATION

Some measure of genius is the rightful inheritance of every man.

—Alfred North Whitehead, British philosopher, physicist, and mathematician (1861–1947)

Goals and Objectives

This chapter is designed to enable you to do the following:

• Understand mental retardation

• Understand how to assess children with mental retardation

• Understand appropriate outcomes and instructional strategies for students with mental retardation

The term *mental retardation* applies to a heterogeneous group of conditions characterized by low scores on a standardized measure of intelligence, together with deficits in adaptive behavior. Two leading professional organizations offer somewhat different definitions of mental retardation. The American Association on Mental Retardation (AAMR, 2002) defines mental retardation as follows:

> Mental retardation is a disability characterized by significant limitations both in intellectual functioning and in adaptive behavior as expressed in conceptual, social, and practical adaptive skills. The disability originates before age 18. (p. 8)

Note that the current AAMR classification system does not use categories—such as mild, moderate, severe, and profound—to classify degrees of mental retardation.

The AAMR (2002) operationally defines significant limitations in adaptive behavior in terms of performance on a standardized measure of adaptive behavior: Either the individual's score on one of the three skills areas (conceptual, social, or practical) measured by the instrument or the individual's overall score must be at least two standard deviations below the mean. However, the AAMR does not provide the basis for the requirement that performance in only *one* skill area (not two or all three) be at least two standard deviations below the mean. In addition, the two different ways of establishing significant limitations (skill area vs. overall score) do not seem to be comparable. Finally, deficits in one skill area may not have the same practical consequences as deficits in another skill area. (See Chapter 11 for a discussion of adaptive behavior.)

The AAMR cautions that the definition of mental retardation must be applied with five assumptions in mind (AAMR, 2002, adapted from pp. 8–9):

1. Limitations in present functioning must be considered within the context of community environments typical of the individual's age, peers, and culture.
2. Valid assessment considers cultural and linguistic diversity, as well as differences in communication and behavioral factors.
3. Limitations may coexist with strengths; people with mental retardation may have gifts as well as limitations.
4. An important purpose of describing limitations is to develop a profile of needed supports.
5. The life functioning of the person with mental retardation will generally improve with appropriate supports over a sustained period.

The American Psychiatric Association (2000), in *DSM-IV–TR,* defines mental retardation as

> significantly subaverage intellectual functioning . . . that is accompanied by significant limitations in adaptive functioning in at least two of the following skill areas: communication, self-care, home living, social/interpersonal skills, use of community resources, self-direction, functional academic skills, work, leisure, health, and safety. . . . The onset must occur before age 18 years. (p. 41)

The *DSM-IV–TR* specifies four degrees of severity of mental retardation (also see Table 18-1):

- *Mild mental retardation* (IQ level of 50–55 to approximately 70)
- *Moderate mental retardation* (IQ level of 35–40 to 50–55)
- *Severe mental retardation* (IQ level of 20–25 to 35–40)
- *Profound mental retardation* (IQ level below 20 or 25)

One of these four degrees of severity must be included in a *DSM-IV–TR* diagnosis of mental retardation, except when there is a strong presumption of mental retardation but the child's intelligence is untestable by standard tests. In the latter case, *DSM-IV–TR* states that the diagnosis should be "Mental Retardation, Severity Unspecified."

The two definitions of mental retardation overlap considerably. In fact, *DSM-IV–TR* follows the 1983 AAMR formulation (Grossman, 1983). Both approaches emphasize the importance of evaluating intelligence as well as adaptive behavior. We recommend that intelligence be evaluated with an individually administered intelligence test and that adaptive behavior be evaluated with a standardized adaptive behavior scale. Furthermore, we favor using the four-level classifica-

Table 18-1
Classification of Mental Retardation

Level of mental retardation	Approximate range in standard deviations	Range in IQ for any test with SD = 15	Approximate mental age at adulthood	Approximate % of persons with mental retardation at this level
Mild	−2.01 to −3.00	50–55 to 70	8-3 to 10-9	85.0
Moderate	−3.01 to −4.00	35–40 to 50–55	5-7 to 8-2	10.0
Severe	−4.01 to −5.00	20–25 to 35–40	3-2 to 5-6	3.5
Profound	<−5.00	<20 to 25	<3-2	1.5

tion scheme specified in *DSM-IV–TR,* because it focuses on the degree of severity of the condition and is useful for administrative and research purposes.

Neither the AAMR nor the *DSM-IV–TR* definition makes any reference to etiology, and both definitions avoid the implication that mental retardation is irreversible. In addition, both definitions have several implications.

1. Assessment must focus on a description of *present* intelligence and behavior. (Prediction of future intelligence and behavior is a separate process that is fraught with difficulties.)
2. The phrases "significant limitations in intellectual functioning and adaptive behavior" and "significantly subaverage in intellectual functioning" refer to performance that is approximately two or more standard deviations below the population mean on a standardized measure of intelligence and a standardized measure of adaptive behavior (although clinical judgment also can be used to assess adaptive behavior).
3. "Intellectual functioning" refers to performance on a standardized intelligence test that measures, as far as is possible, general cognitive ability rather than one limited facet

of ability, such as receptive vocabulary or spatial-analytic skills.
4. Two criteria—level of intelligence and level of adaptive behavior—are considered jointly in arriving at a diagnosis. Consequently, a diagnosis of mental retardation should be made only when an individual has deficits in both intellectual functioning *and* adaptive behavior functioning.
5. A diagnosis of mental retardation does not rule out the coexistence of other disorders, such as mental illness or attention-deficit/hyperactivity disorder.
6. A diagnosis of mental retardation is inappropriate when an individual is adequately meeting the demands of his or her environment.

Table 18-2 shows a classification system for adaptive behavior that parallels the classification system for measured intelligence in *DSM-IV–TR.* The system coordinates developmental stages and levels of intellectual disability, emphasizing sensorimotor skills, language and communication, learning, degree of self-sufficiency, and vocational skills. A child's adaptive behavior classification may differ from her or his intelligence classification. For instance, a child may

---

Table 18-2
Levels of Adaptive Behavior for Persons with Mental Retardation

Level	Preschool age: birth to 5 years	School age: 6 to 21 years	Adult: over 21 years
Mild retardation (IQs = 50–55 to 70)	Can develop social and communication skills; motor coordination is slightly impaired; often not diagnosed until school age.	Can learn up to about the sixth-grade level by late teens; needs special education, particularly at secondary-school age levels; can learn appropriate social skills.	Can achieve social and vocational skills with proper education and training; frequently needs guidance when under serious social or economic stress.
Moderate retardation (IQs = 35–40 to 50–55)	Can talk or learn to communicate; poor social awareness; fair motor development; may profit from training in self-help; can be managed with moderate supervision.	Can learn up to about the fourth-grade level by late teens if given special education; may learn to travel alone in familiar places.	Can contribute to self-support by performing unskilled or semiskilled work under sheltered conditions; needs supervision and guidance when under mild social or economic stress.
Severe retardation (IQs = 20–25 to 35–40)	Poor motor development; minimal speech; generally unable to profit from training in self-help skills; few or no communication skills.	Can learn to speak or communicate; can learn simple health habits; cannot learn functional academic skills; can profit from habit training.	Can contribute partially to self-support under complete supervision; can develop self-protection skills to a minimal useful level in a controlled environment.
Profound retardation (IQs < 20 to 25)	Extremely limited in motor development and in all cognitive areas; likely needs nursing care.	Some motor development; limited communication skills; cannot profit from training in self-help skills; cannot learn functional academic skills; needs total care.	Can achieve some motor and speech development; totally incapable of self-maintenance; needs complete care and supervision.

Note. States may differ in their definitions of these levels.

receive a classification of mild mental retardation with regard to adaptive behavior, but a classification of moderate mental retardation on a standardized intelligence measure.

Intelligence tests are more precisely constructed than are measures of adaptive behavior. The WISC–IV, WPPSI–III, WAIS–III, and Stanford-Binet Intelligence Scale–V are well-normed instruments for the assessment of intelligence, with excellent reliability and validity. In contrast, there are few nationally standardized instruments for the assessment of adaptive behavior that meet acceptable psychometric standards. Instruments such as the AAMR Adaptive Behavior Scale, the Vineland Adaptive Behavior Scales–Second Edition, and the Adaptive Behavior Assessment System–Second Edition (see Chapter 11) can be helpful in assessing adaptive behavior, but they are highly dependent on the reliability of the informant (e.g., parent, teacher, primary caregiver). The informant's ability to observe and reliably report on a child's skills, behavior, and temperament will determine the accuracy of the adaptive behavior ratings. It is critical to consider interrater reliability when scoring these instruments. A diagnosis of mental retardation rests in part on clinical judgment (e.g., the clinician must evaluate the reliability of the informant's report and the reliability of the child's responses to questions on intelligence tests); the clinician must therefore consider all relevant factors in arriving at a diagnosis.

Children with mental retardation have difficulties in both intellectual and adaptive areas. They have a slow rate of cognitive development, limited expressive and receptive language abilities, limited adaptive skills, limited experiential background, short attention span, distractibility, and a concrete and literal style in approaching tasks (Cobb, 1989). They tend to have more consistent scores on tests of intellectual functioning than do their nondisabled peers (Silverstein, 1982). They are likely to reach developmental milestones (e.g., sitting, crawling, walking, talking) later than other children, and they may have problems with motor coordination, remembering things, understanding how to pay for things, understanding social rules, seeing the consequences of their actions, solving problems, thinking logically, and learning complex job skills (National Dissemination Center for Children with Disabilities, 2005).

ETIOLOGY OF MENTAL RETARDATION

Mental retardation can be a primary diagnosis, can occur as part of a syndrome (e.g., fetal alcohol syndrome or fragile X syndrome; see below), or can co-occur with other developmental disabilities (autism, attention-deficit/hyperactivity disorder), neurological disorders (epilepsy, cerebral palsy), or psychiatric disorders (conduct disorder, anxiety disorder). Mental retardation can result from a diverse set of predisposing factors, including genetic (or hereditary) disorders, chromosomal deviations, cranial malformations, other congenital factors, perinatal factors, and postnatal factors. Following are examples of disorders that can lead to mental retardation. Most of the information in this section was obtained from the Genetics Home Reference Web site of the U.S. National Library of Medicine (http://ghr.nlm.nih.gov/).

GENETIC DISORDERS

- *Fragile X syndrome* is a sex-linked genetic disorder that results from a physical abnormality of the X chromosome. The syndrome is characterized by mental retardation, psychomotor retardation, short stature, microcephaly, eye defects, and small testes in males. It occurs in about 1 in 4,000 to 6,000 male births and in about 1 in 8,000 to 9,000 female births.

- *Galactosemia* is a recessive genetic disorder that causes the body to be unable to metabolize galactose (a major sugar) into glucose. It is characterized by liver and kidney dysfunction, cataracts, and mental retardation. It occurs in about 1 in 30,000 births.

- *Lesch-Nyhan syndrome* is a sex-linked genetic disorder that results in overproduction of uric acid. Because it is inherited by means of an X-linked recessive pattern, it is more common in males. It is characterized by pain and swelling of the joints; irritability; muscle weakness; uncontrolled spastic muscle movements; neurological problems leading to uncontrolled urges to cause injury to oneself (e.g., biting, head banging) and others, use of obscene language, and inability to control impulses; and moderate mental retardation. It occurs in only about 1 in 380,000 births.

- *Neurofibromatosis 1* is a dominant genetic disorder that causes noncancerous tumors (called neurofibromas) to grow along the nerves of the skin, brain, and other parts of the body. It is characterized by multiple café-au-lait spots (flat, round spots on the skin that are the color of coffee with milk), visual problems, high blood pressure, and curvature of the spine. Symptoms appear in early childhood. About 4% to 8% of children with this condition have mental retardation, and about 50% have learning disabilities. It occurs in about 1 in 3,000 births.

- *Phenylketonuria (PKU)* is a recessive genetic disorder that causes the body to be unable to metabolize the protein phenylalanine (an amino acid); this results in harmful levels of phenylalanine in the blood. It is characterized by severe mental retardation, convulsions, behavioral problems, skin rash, and a musty odor of the body and urine. A diet low in phenylalanine keeps symptoms from appearing. It occurs in about 1 in 10,000 births.

- *Rett syndrome* is caused by a genetic mutation that affects brain development, primarily in girls. It is characterized by language, learning, and coordination difficulties; mental retardation; and autistic-like behavior (e.g., repeated hand wringing or washing motions). It occurs in about 1 in 10,000 to 15,000 female births.

- *Rubinstein-Taybi syndrome* results from a gene mutation that causes a fetus to receive only one half of the protein needed for normal fetal development. The condition is characterized by short stature, broad thumbs and first toes, distinctive facial features, mental retardation, and an increased risk of cancer. It occurs in about 1 in 125,000 births.
- *Tay-Sachs disease* is a recessive genetic disorder that causes a buildup of toxic fatty substances in the nerve cells. It is characterized by severe mental retardation, vision and hearing loss, seizures, paralysis, and death in early childhood. It occurs in only about 1 in 300,000 births.
- *Tuberous sclerosis* is a dominant genetic disorder that results in small noncancerous growths on the skin, surfaces of the brain, and other body tissues. It is characterized by progressive intellectual deterioration and seizures—and, in some cases, hyperactivity, autistic-like behavior, aggression, kidney problems, or heart defects. Symptoms vary depending on the location of the growths. It occurs in about 1 in 6,000 births.

CHROMOSOMAL DEVIATIONS

- *Angelman syndrome* is a chromosomal disorder that results from loss of a gene on chromosome 15. It is characterized by mental retardation, severe speech impairment, and movement and balance problems. It occurs in about 1 in 10,000 to 20,000 births.
- *Cri-du-chat syndrome* (so named because an affected infant's cry sounds like the cry of a cat) is a chromosomal disorder that results when a particular piece of chromosome 15 is missing. It is characterized by mental retardation, small head, low birth weight, and weak muscle tone in infancy. It occurs in about 1 in 20,000 to 50,000 births.
- *Down syndrome,* also called *trisomy 21,* is a chromosomal disorder that results from an extra chromosome 21. It is characterized by a flat skull; thickened skin on the eyelids; stubby fingers; a short, stocky body; reduced brain volume (mass); and increased risk of heart defects, digestive problems, hearing loss, other physical problems, and mental retardation. It occurs in about 1 in 800 births.
- *Edwards syndrome,* also called *trisomy 18,* is a chromosomal disorder that results from an extra chromosome 18. It is characterized by low birth weight; a small, abnormally shaped head; small jaw and mouth; clenched fist with overlapping fingers; mental retardation; heart defects; and other physical defects. It occurs in about 1 in 5,000 to 6,000 births.
- *Klinefelter's syndrome* is a chromosomal disorder in males (sometimes referred to as *XXY males*) that results from an extra X chromosome. It is characterized by reduced facial and body hair, infertility, difficulty with speech and language, the acquisition of female secondary sex characteristics, and mild levels of intellectual retardation. It occurs in about 1 in 500 to 1,000 births.
- *Patau syndrome* is a chromosomal disorder that results from an extra chromosome 13. It is characterized by severe mental retardation, small eyes, cleft lip, weak muscle tone, heart defects, skeletal abnormalities, and other medical problems; children rarely live past infancy. It occurs in about 1 in 10,000 births.
- *Prader-Willi syndrome* is a chromosomal disorder that results from partial deletion of chromosome 15. It is characterized by weak muscle tone, feeding difficulties, poor growth, obesity, short stature, mental retardation or learning disabilities, and behavioral problems. It occurs in about 1 in 10,000 to 22,000 births.

CRANIAL MALFORMATIONS

- *Hydrocephalus* can result from a chromosomal disorder, can be a congenital disorder resulting from a maternal infection such as syphilis or toxoplasmosis, or can be inherited. An abnormal accumulation of cerebrospinal fluid within the cavities (ventricles) of the brain causes the ventricles to enlarge and pressure inside the head to increase. Hydrocephalus is characterized by malformations of the brain and spinal cord, harelip, cleft palate, and—if the condition is not recognized and treated—mental retardation. It occurs in about 2 in 1,000 births. Treatment consists of draining off the fluid to decrease cranial pressure.
- *Microcephalus* results from genetic factors or from any condition that arrests brain development, such as congenital rubella, fetal alcohol syndrome, or exposure to environmental toxins (e.g., radiation). It is characterized by a small, conical skull; a curved spine; impairments in cognitive, motor, and speech functions; stunted growth; diminished weight; and severe or profound mental retardation.

OTHER CONGENITAL FACTORS

- *Congenital hypothyroidism* (*cretinism*) results from a partial or complete loss of thyroid function. It is characterized by mental retardation and stunted growth. In about 15% to 20% of cases, the condition is inherited. It occurs in about 1 in 3,000 to 4,000 births and affects more than twice as many females as males.
- *Congenital toxoplasmosis* is a parasitic infection transmitted by pregnant women to developing fetuses. It is characterized by blindness, central nervous system damage, jaundice, hydrocephalus, and mental retardation. About 400 to 4,000 newborns in the United States had the disease in 2000.
- *Fetal alcohol syndrome* (*FAS*) results from maternal alcohol abuse during pregnancy. It is characterized by abnormal facial features, growth deficiency, visual and hearing problems, hyperactivity, and central nervous system problems (e.g., microcephalus, delayed development, memory and attention problems, communication problems, and

mental retardation). It occurs in about 1 in 650 to 5,000 births.

- *Human immunodeficiency virus type I (HIV-1) infection* is caused by a virus and can lead to acquired immune deficiency syndrome (*AIDS*). The syndrome drastically increases an individual's susceptibility to other illnesses that may be fatal. Children with AIDS are at risk for developmental problems (e.g., failure to thrive), medical problems (e.g., chronic diarrhea, weight loss, swelling of glands, seizures, unusual sores, dry cough, numbness or pain in the hands and feet), and psychological problems (e.g., depression, anxiety, agitated behavior, loss of interest in people, language and memory problems, attentional problems, mental retardation). Congenital HIV occurs in about 1 in 500,000 births.

- *Rh incompatibilities* arise when a pregnant woman has Rh negative blood and her fetus has Rh positive blood. When blood from the fetus mixes in the placenta with the mother's blood, the mother's body produces antibodies that destroy the red blood cells of the fetus in any subsequent pregnancy. The condition may lead to abortion of the fetus or stillbirth or to jaundice, deafness, and mental retardation. It occurs in about 1 in 1,000 births.

- *Rubella,* or German measles, is caused by a virus that may be transmitted by a pregnant woman to her fetus. If transmission occurs during the first three months of pregnancy, the newborn may suffer congenital anomalies, deafness, cataracts, cardiac malformation, learning disabilities, and mental retardation. Nine cases in newborns were reported in the United States in 2000.

- *Syphilis* is caused by a bacterium that may be transmitted by a pregnant woman to her fetus, leading to damage of the central nervous system. When it does not cause stillbirth or early neonatal death, syphilis leads to meningitis, seizures, hydrocephalus, enlargement of the liver and spleen, bone changes, and mental retardation. There were 412 cases reported in newborns in the United States in 2002.

PERINATAL FACTORS

- *Cytomegalovirus (CMV)* is a systemic illness that may be transmitted perinatally, as the baby passes through an infected mother's birth canal, or postnatally, through contact with infected urine, saliva, breast milk, feces, tears, or blood. In its most severe form, it is characterized by central nervous system infection involving the cerebral cortex, brain stem, cochlear nuclei, cranial nerves, and inner ear. Some children with the illness are completely asymptomatic; others have mental retardation.

- *Extreme prematurity* refers to a birth weight of 1 to 1.5 pounds. It is accompanied by mental retardation, cerebral palsy, attention deficits, and other neurological and medical complications, such as blindness or deafness.

- *Hypoxic-ischemic encephalopathy* results when oxygen cannot reach the tissues of the body during delivery. In its most severe form, it is characterized by mental retardation, lack of muscle tone, seizures, and motor disabilities.

- *Neural tube defect* is caused by the failure of the neural folds in the embryo to fuse and form a neural tube. The defect contributes to hearing loss, heart defects, mental retardation, speech and language disorders, and attention-deficit/hyperactivity disorder.

- *Placental dysfunction* refers to improper functioning of the placenta, an organ that develops in mothers during pregnancy. The placenta may fail to supply adequate oxygen, nutrients, and antibodies to the fetus, or it may fail to adequately remove waste products. When this happens, mental retardation may result.

- *Teratogens* are agents in the environment of a developing embryo and fetus that can cause structural and functional abnormalities. Examples include alcohol (see discussion above of FAS), radiation, pathogens causing intrauterine infection, drugs and environmental chemicals, and untreated maternal metabolic imbalances (see discussion above of PKU).

POSTNATAL FACTORS

- *Brain tumors* can interfere with neurological processes and, in some cases, can lead to mental retardation, along with motor and sensory disturbances.

- *Head injuries* caused by trauma, including automobile accidents and child maltreatment (e.g., violent shaking), can result in mental retardation and other neurological malfunctions.

- *Malnutrition,* especially during the first 6 months of life, can hinder the development of brain cells, contributing to mental retardation.

- *Meningitis,* an acute inflammation of the membranes that cover the brain and spinal cord, can result in drowsiness, confusion, irritability, sensory impairments, and mental retardation.

- *Severe abuse and neglect,* including depriving a child of social, linguistic, or cognitive stimulation, can lead to mental retardation.

- *Toxins,* such as lead and mercury, can damage the central nervous system and lead to seizures, cerebral palsy, and mental retardation.

Distribution in the Population

Approximately 1% of the population could be classified as mentally retarded. Of people with mental retardation, approximately 85% need limited supports, 10% need moderate supports, 3% to 4% need extensive supports, and the remaining 1% to 2% may also have physical or emotional problems that require ongoing medical attention (American Psychiatric Association, 2000). During the 2000–2001 school year, 612,978 children and young adults between 6 and 21 years of age received a diagnosis of mental retardation and were enrolled in special education programs under the Individuals with Disabilities Act (U.S. Department of Education, 2002). The group with mental retardation constituted about 10.61% of the total special education school population. Among those with a diagnosis of mental retardation, the ratio of boys to girls is about 6:1 (Singh, Oswald, & Ellis, 1998).

Categorization by Origin

Individuals with mental retardation can be grouped into two broad categories: those with mental retardation with a familial origin and those with mental retardation caused by brain injury (Hodapp & Dykens, 2003; Hodapp & Zigler, 1999).

Familial origin. The intelligence levels of most individuals with IQs from about 50 to 69 are probably associated with normal polygenic variation—that is, with the combined action of many genes. Thus, such individuals are said to have retardation with a familial origin. Performance in this range, however, also can be associated with (a) pathological factors that interfere with brain functioning (such as brain damage that has yet to be discovered) or (b) the combined effect of below-average heredity and a markedly below-average environment. In most cases, however, there is no demonstrable organic etiology (Zigler & Hodapp, 1986). Rates are somewhat higher within minority groups and low socioeconomic groups. Children with familial mental retardation are more responsive to social reinforcement than are their nondisabled peers, perform better on tasks when the reward is tangible, and are outer-directed—that is, they are sensitive to cues provided by adults and are highly imitative (Zigler & Balla, 1981).

Brain injury origin. Children with mental retardation caused by brain injury usually have severe and diffuse brain damage or malformations commonly originating during the prenatal period. They typically show a severe lag in behavioral development, sometimes accompanied by an abnormal appearance, with IQs usually below 50. Identification of the more severe forms of retardation is relatively easy because the child clearly fails to reach normal motor and language developmental milestones. Adults with severe forms of mental retardation will require supervision and life-long care. Rates of mental retardation from brain injury are about equal across all ethnic groups and socioeconomic levels; the intellectual level of siblings of children with brain injury is usually average. Chapter 23 discusses brain injury in more detail.

Prevention

Several methods have helped to reduce the occurrence of mental retardation.

1. *Screening.* Hospitals routinely screen newborns for biochemical and other inherited conditions that may produce mental retardation and other disabilities. In most states, conditions routinely screened for by a blood test include phenylketonuria, congenital hypothyroidism, and galactosemia. *Amniocentesis,* a surgical procedure in which a small sample of amniotic fluid is drawn out of the uterus through a needle inserted in the abdomen of the mother, is useful for identifying Down syndrome and other genetic disorders in the early stages of pregnancy. The work of the Human Genome Project may suggest new ways to screen for mental retardation and to design gene therapies that can substitute normal genes for defective ones.

2. *Phenylalanine-restricted diet.* Although metabolic control of PKU can be difficult to achieve because of the difficulty in following a phenylalanine-restricted diet, women with PKU must maintain strict metabolic control both before and during their pregnancies to prevent damage to their fetuses. Children with PKU are placed on a phenylalanine-restricted diet. They cannot have meat, milk, or many other foods that contain protein, although they can eat some low-protein foods such as fruits, vegetables, and restricted amounts of certain grain cereals. To supplement these, they must eat specially processed phenylalanine-free food. Individuals with PKU need to maintain metabolic control throughout their life spans (National Institutes of Health, 2000).

3. *Immunization.* Immunizing children is an effective way to prevent diseases that can impair mental functioning.

4. *Education.* Educating the public about the effects of using alcohol, tobacco, or other drugs during pregnancy can be an effective public health measure. Public health measures designed to reduce unintended pregnancies and child abuse and neglect and to increase use of seat belts and infant seats in automobiles (see below) are also helpful.

5. *Reducing exposure to lead and mercury.* Reducing children's exposure to lead and mercury is important. Although this has in part been accomplished by laws prohibiting the sale of lead-based paint, people must be encouraged to reduce their consumption of foods with high levels of mercury and to dispose of products containing mercury properly.

6. *Constructing safer automobiles.* Safer cars with front, side, and head air bags, seat belts, and anchors for infant car seats provide the occupants better protection against head injury.

7. *Governmental policies.* Federal, state, and local governments need to reduce poverty and homelessness; to provide information to the public about prevention of mental retardation, including educational programs focusing on quality of family life and effective parenting; and to develop universal health-care programs.

RELATIONSHIP BETWEEN MEASURED INTELLIGENCE AND ADAPTIVE BEHAVIOR

Earlier in the chapter we noted that a diagnosis of mental retardation requires that a child be below the population average by approximately two standard deviations on a measure of intelligence and a measure of adaptive behavior. Because intelligence and adaptive behavior are not perfectly correlated, children who fall below −2 *SD* on an intelligence test may have adaptive behavior scores that do not fall below −2 *SD*. Thus, the number of children classified as having mental retardation will be *lower* when both criteria are used than when a single criterion is applied.

As you can see in Table 18-3, hypothetical prevalence rates decrease markedly as one moves from a correlation of 1.00 (reflecting the hypothetical case in which all children whose intelligence test scores fell in the mental retardation range also had adaptive behavior scores in this range) to a correlation of .00 (reflecting the hypothetical case in which there was no relationship between children's scores on an intelligence test and their scores on an adaptive behavior measure). If the two measures were perfectly correlated, every child who fell below the cutoff on one measure would also fall below the cutoff on the other measure, which would lead to the largest possible number of identifications. If the two measures were not perfectly correlated, some children who fell below the cutoff on one measure would be above the cutoff on the other measure, which would lead to a smaller number of identifications. Nationwide estimated prevalence rates, using −2 *SD* as the cutoff score on each measure, range from 140,000 to over 6,384,000, depending on the correlation assumed between the two measures.

It is estimated that the relationship between measured intelligence and adaptive behavior is about .30 to .50 (Editorial Board, 1996; Harrison & Oakland, 2000). Correlations between the two variables tend to be higher in individuals with severe mental retardation than in individuals with average intellectual ability.

Table 18-3
Hypothetical Prevalence Rates of Mental Retardation

Correlation	Hypothetical prevalence rate per 1,000	Hypothetical prevalence nationwide
.00	.5	140,000
.20	1.4	392,000
.40	2.9	1,102,000
.60	5.5	1,540,000
.80	9.8	2,744,000
1.00	22.8	6,384,000

Note. These data are based on an assumed population of 280,000,000 and a cutoff of −2 standard deviations for estimates of the correlation between measured intelligence and adaptive behavior in the population.
Source: Adapted from Silverstein (1973).

UNDERSTANDING MENTAL RETARDATION

Mental retardation is not a disease. It is a symptom of a variety of conditions that interfere with normal brain development, and intellectual impairment may be a functional expression of these conditions. As with children who do not have mental retardation, there is considerable variability in the personalities and behavior of children with mental retardation. They may exhibit symptoms of mental illness and have emotional disorders similar to those found in children without mental retardation (Bütz, Bowling, & Bliss, 2000). Noncognitive factors, such as low motivation and poor self-concept, sometimes further reduce the cognitive performance of children with mental retardation.

The label of "mental retardation" should not prevent us from seeing that children with mental retardation differ among themselves, as do all children. Mental retardation is complex, and making generalizations about the cognitive processes and personalities of children with mental retardation is as difficult as doing so for any other group of children. However, the behavior of children with mental retardation is similar in many ways to that of children without it, especially younger children of like chronological age.

Chronological age (CA) affects many traits and should be considered in evaluating and making recommendations for individuals with mental retardation. Although chronological age per se may have little impact on intelligence test performance, it does relate to how cognitively demanding one's social behaviors and interests are, to the life experiences one accumulates, and to the way others relate to the individual with mental retardation. The intellectual deficiencies of children with mental retardation are more closely related to higher-order cognitive processes (such as efficient problem-solving strategies, generalization, and abstraction) than to subordinate processes (such as attention, rehearsal, ability to inhibit responses, and discrimination of the elements of a problem).

ASSESSMENT

The assessment of mental retardation requires the use of a reliable, valid, and comprehensive individual measure of intellectual functioning and a reliable, valid, and comprehensive measure of adaptive behavior. The evaluation must be comprehensive because mental retardation may exist concurrently with other disabling conditions (Editorial Board, 1996). You will need to select an appropriate assessment battery and carefully review the child's case history, medical reports, teacher reports and school grades, and any other relevant information. Your selection of instruments should take into account the child's language, sensory, or motor abilities. It is important to select instruments with sufficient "floor" that the child is able to pass at least a few items on the test. A total score based on a raw score of zero means that there will be little actual test performance to observe and is therefore likely to be difficult to interpret. After you complete the assessment, answer the questions in Table 25-1 in Chapter 25. The answers will guide you as you prepare your report on the assessment.

Establishing Rapport

Conduct the assessment in a location where the child is comfortable. However, recognize that rapport may be difficult to establish because children with mental retardation may have limited verbal abilities, may fear strangers, or may distrust their own ability to communicate effectively (Ollendick, Oswald, & Ollendick, 1993). Adjust your assessment techniques as needed. For example, if you see signs of fatigue—such as changes in attentiveness, restlessness, fidgeting, drooping of head, or yawning—take a break; if necessary, schedule several short sessions. Some children with mental retardation may be hesitant to ask for breaks in the assessment session. If they are uncooperative during the assessment, evaluate the possible reasons for the behavior. As with all children, developing a warm, accepting relationship will help to reduce unacceptable behavior.

Interviewing

During the interview with the child, you may need to simplify questions, provide examples, ask structured questions, use frequent prompts, and repeat or rephrase your questions. These strategies will take time and practice to develop. Children with mental retardation may be more likely than their nondisabled peers to acquiesce; thus, do not rely primarily on yes-no questions in an interview. In fact, uncritical acceptance of their responses to yes-no questions may lead you to draw invalid inferences. Because they also may have memory difficulties, they may not recall when their problems began and other important details of their lives. To help improve their recall, link problems to events such as birthdays, holidays, school projects, or summer vacations. See Chapters 5, 6, and 7 for more information about interviewing.

The semistructured developmental history interview shown in Table B-10 in Appendix B is useful for obtaining information from parents about their children's language and speech comprehension and production; nonverbal communication; responses to sensory stimuli; movement, gait, and posture; social and emotional responses; resistance to change; play; immaturity; special skills; self-care; sleeping patterns; school activities; and domestic and practical skills.

Interpreting Intelligence Test Results

As early as the first decade of the twentieth century, the National Education Association described the proper use of intelligence tests in the study of children with mental retardation. The policy formulated by a committee of the as-

sociation concerning the use of tests is as appropriate today as it was when it was first issued (Bruner, Barnes, & Dearborn, 1909): "Tests of mental deficiency are chiefly useful in the hands of the skilled examiner. No sets of tests have been devised that will give a categorical answer as to the mental status of any individual. In nearly every instance in which they are used, tests need to be interpreted" (p. 905, with changes in notation). The committee noted that the tests proposed by DeSanctis and by Binet and Simon were of considerable value as tests of general capacity.

Conducting Observations

You will want to observe the child in more than one setting (e.g. at home and at school) and obtain information from different informants about how the child behaves in various settings. You should not rely exclusively on parents or teachers, because they may fail to observe important behaviors or environmental contingencies. Observations in multiple settings are important, because the contextual variables that affect behavior may differ in different environments (Moore, Feist-Price, & Alston, 2002).

The school environment is suitable for assessing some, but not all, of the learning needs of children with severe disabilities. On the one hand, you can observe how a child functions in the cafeteria, locates the bathroom, interacts with schoolmates, places forms on a formboard, or performs other school-related activities. On the other hand, you usually will not be able to evaluate how adequately the child uses the bathtub, the refrigerator, or a stove and how the child spends leisure time unless you use a simulated home environment in the classroom (see below). Chapters 8 and 9 contain more information about conducting systematic behavioral observations.

Assessing Adaptive Behavior

To assess adaptive behavior, you can use the adaptive behavior scales and informal measures discussed in Chapter 11. You can also obtain information about adaptive behavior from interviews with the parents, other family members, and teachers and from the child's case history.

Assessing Maladaptive Behavior

Several formal procedures are useful for the assessment of maladaptive behaviors in children and adults with mental retardation. They include the (a) Reiss Screen for Maladaptive Behavior (Reiss, 1988), (b) Aberrant Behavior Checklist (Aman, Singh, Stewart, & Field, 1985), (c) Diagnostic Assessment for the Severely Handicapped–II (Matson, 1994), (d) Psychopathology Inventory for Mentally Retarded Adults (Matson, 1988), (e) Reiss Scales for Children's Dual Diagnosis (Reiss & Valenti-Hein, 1994), (f) Nisonger Child Behavior Rating Form (Tasse, Aman, Hammer, & Rojahn, 1996), and (g) Questions About Behavioral Function (Paclawskyj, Matson, Rush, Smalls, & Vollmer, 2000). These checklists complement intelligence tests, adaptive behavior scales, interviews, and observations.

Distinguishing Mental Retardation from Developmental Delay

When you suspect that a child may have intellectual disabilities, consider a possible diagnosis of *developmental delay,* especially with infants or preschool children. Make a diagnosis of mental retardation *only* when the child shows significantly below average general intellectual functioning in conjunction with significant deficits in adaptive behavior, and you are confident that the assessment results are valid.

It is important to distinguish between mental retardation and developmental delay during infancy and the preschool years for the following reasons. First, although an infant or young child may meet the criteria for a diagnosis of mental retardation, the measure of intelligence may not be valid, because intelligence test scores of infants reflect primarily developmental progress. With infants and young children, it is important to conduct repeated assessments to check for changes in the rate of development in order to arrive at a valid diagnosis. Second, other conditions in infancy and the preschool years may mimic mental retardation. For example, temporary conditions such as post-traumatic stress disorder may reduce a young child's ability to communicate, thus making the assessment of intellectual ability difficult. Third, there may be home circumstances, such as child abuse and neglect, that impair a child's adaptive functioning. Providing a more nurturing environment can improve the child's adaptive and cognitive functioning. Thus, a diagnosis of developmental delay holds hope that the child's deficiencies may decrease.

Diagnosing Severe or Profound Mental Retardation

Children with severe or profound mental retardation may be especially difficult to evaluate because of self-stimulating behavior, self-injurious behavior, limited attention span, destructive behavior, temper tantrums, seizures, noncompliance with requests, or inability to understand the test questions. These children often have accompanying physical defects (e.g., impaired vision, hearing, and motor coordination), difficulty in attaining an upright posture, undeveloped speech, poor feeding and toileting skills, and difficulty in guarding against physical dangers (Kim & Arnold, 2002). Children with profound mental retardation, in particular, have a high incidence of motor, sensory, and physical disabilities and need comprehensive supports. They tend to have higher needs for support because of seizures, enuresis, communication difficulties, *pica* (a strong craving to eat nonnutritive substances, such as paint, gravel, or hair), self-biting, fecal smearing, mutism, *echopraxia* (a tendency toward automatic imitation of the movements and gestures of others), abnormal EEGs, *encopresis* (involuntary defecation not due to a local organic defect or illness), difficulty in self-recognition, inadequate socialization skills, and high pain thresholds (Kim & Arnold, 2002; Switzky, Haywood, & Rotatori, 1982).

Traditional assessment approaches may not be useful with children with severe or profound mental retardation. Standardized norm-referenced tests are of limited use because (a) the instructions may be too difficult for a child to understand, (b) the administrative procedures may be too inflexible to permit a child to display his or her knowledge by unconventional means, and (c) the items may be too difficult to allow the child to demonstrate his or her knowledge. Extrapolated scores are not appropriate for individual diagnosis because their reliability and validity cannot be established. Norm-referenced tests are also relatively insensitive to the developmental changes that occur in children with severe or profound mental retardation (Kim & Arnold, 2002). To maintain their relative standing on an intelligence test, children with severe or profound mental retardation would need to develop their abilities as rapidly as children without mental retardation. Thus, it is better to use raw scores rather than standard scores for estimating the progress of children with severe or profound disabilities.

Curriculum-based assessment, which usually follows standard curriculum guidelines, was once thought to be inappropriate for children with extensive support needs, because such children were rarely candidates for instruction in the school's standard curriculum. However, the No Child Left Behind Act of 2001 requires that all children participate in annual state assessments. The curriculum content for students with disabilities should be similar to that of their nondisabled peers, but modified to allow them to work at their own pace. They should also receive additional instruction as needed.

The use of normal developmental scales with children who have extensive disabilities is also problematic. Because the development of children with significant cognitive challenges does not proceed like that of normal young children, these scales do not to take into account the types of opportunities to develop concepts that are available to children with disabilities.

Although norm-referenced tests, curriculum-based assessment measures, and development-based tests and scales have shortcomings for the assessment of children with significant cognitive disabilities, they do play a role. Developmental-age scores from these scales provide indices of a child's approximate developmental level. Individual items provide information about what the child can and cannot accomplish on the tests.

INTERVENTIONS

After a diagnosis of mental retardation is made, you will need to determine the level of support that the individual may need.

Following are four support levels (AAMR, 2002, adapted from p. 152):

Level 1. Intermittent. Supports are provided on an as-needed basis (e.g., during transitions and crises).

Level 2. Limited. Supports are provided more consistently than at level 1 (e.g., during training for employment or transitions from school to work).

Level 3. Extensive. Supports are provided at least daily in one or more environments and are not time limited (e.g., long-term home living support).

Level 4. Pervasive. Supports are provided consistently across many or all environments, at high intensity, and may be of a life-sustaining nature (e.g., full-time medical care).

Services for children with mental retardation may begin immediately after the child's birth or during the preschool years and continue throughout the developmental period. Early intervention services mandated by IDEA 2004 include psychological and social work services, speech and language services, occupational and physical therapy services, medical and dental care services, special education programs, in-home living assistance programs, and transportation services. These services may help children with mental retardation lead more normal lives during their developmental period and when they reach adulthood (Parsons, Reid, Green, Browning, & Hensley, 2003). Table 18-4 lists some areas of support that such services may focus on.

Following are useful suggestions for parents of children with mental retardation (National Dissemination Center for Children with Disabilities, 2005, p. 6, with changes in notation):

1. Learn about mental retardation. The more you know, the more you can help yourself and your child.
2. Encourage independence in your child. For example, help your child learn daily care skills, such as dressing, feeding himself or herself, using the bathroom, and grooming.
3. Give your child chores, keeping in mind your child's age, attention span, and abilities.
4. Find out what skills your child is learning at school, and find ways for your child to apply those skills at home.
5. Find opportunities in your community for social activities, such as scouts, recreation center activities, and sports. These will help your child build social skills as well as have fun.
6. Talk to other parents whose children have mental retardation.
7. Meet with your child's teachers, work with them to develop an educational plan to address your child's needs, keep in touch with them, and offer them support.

Here are some recommendations made to professionals by parents of children with mental retardation (Westling, 1996):

1. Provide individually determined meaningful instruction, services, and supports appropriate for the child's age and disability, in general education, in tutorial sessions, or in special classes, as needed. These might include home-based early intervention services for infants and toddlers and preschool and after-school programs for older children.
2. Include in the curriculum socialization and friendship development.
3. Provide opportunities for parents to participate in school activities, especially in planning activities involving their child.
4. Make parent education programs available in different formats, such as printed material, workshops, and small-group meetings. Include medical or developmental information as needed.
5. Provide other forms of support for parents, such as emotional support and information about respite care, parent and advocacy groups, and public and private community agencies.
6. Provide family-focused services, including family planning and help in obtaining financial aid and better housing, if needed.
7. Designate a staff person to be responsible for helping the family coordinate services and deal with community agencies.
8. Encourage agencies to collaborate with each other when children move from one program or school to another.
9. Encourage professionals, parents, and advocates to work together to increase funding for both individuals with disabilities and their families.
10. Formulate and carry out transition services for adolescents who are leaving school and entering adulthood. These services include providing information about residential placement, if appropriate; discussing employment opportunities; and offering training that focuses on the needs of young adults, which might include developing functional skills, social and interpersonal skills, vocational skills, leisure skills, and domestic living skills.
11. Give parents information during the developmental period about (a) possible positive life styles for their child, (b) their child's potentials, and (c) their child's possibilities when she or he reaches maturity.

Therapeutic interventions for children with mental retardation include environmental changes, behavioral treatments, individual psychotherapy, group psychotherapy, family therapy, and pharmacotherapy (under a health care provider's guidance). In designing therapeutic interventions, consider the child's levels of cognitive, social, and physical functioning. For example, therapeutic sessions may need to be short and frequent, and therapeutic interventions may need to incorporate extensive structure, reassurance, problem solving, and constructive feedback (Bregman, 1991; Bütz et al., 2000).

Interventions usually will not lead to significant improvements in the intelligence test scores of children with mental retardation. For example, an examination of the Milwaukee Project (an environmental enrichment project designed to

Table 18-4
Support Areas and Goals for Individuals with Mental Retardation

Support area	Goals
Human development activities	• To develop eye-hand coordination skills, fine-motor skills, and gross-motor skills • To provide opportunities to use words and images to represent the world and reason logically about concrete events • To trust, engage in autonomous activities, and take initiative
Teaching and education activities	• To interact with trainers, teachers, and fellow trainees and students • To participate in making decisions on training and educational activities • To develop problem-solving strategies • To use technical equipment • To read signs, count change, and engage in other functional activities • To develop self-determination skills
Home living activities	• To use the restroom • To launder and take care of clothes • To prepare food • To develop housekeeping skills • To dress • To bathe, maintain personal hygiene, and develop grooming skills • To operate home appliances and other equipment • To participate in leisure activities within the home
Community living activities	• To use public transportation • To participate in recreational and leisure activities • To visit friends and family • To go shopping and purchase goods • To interact with community members • To use public buildings and settings
Employment activities	• To learn specific job skills • To interact with co-workers and supervisors • To complete work-related tasks with speed and quality • To adjust to changes in job assignments • To access and obtain crisis intervention assistance
Health and safety activities	• To obtain medical services • To take medication • To avoid health and safety hazards • To communicate with health care providers • To access emergency services • To maintain a nutritious diet • To maintain physical health • To maintain mental health and emotional well-being
Behavioral activities	• To develop specific skills or behaviors • To make appropriate decisions • To access and obtain mental health services • To access and obtain substance abuse services • To incorporate personal preferences into daily activities • To maintain socially appropriate behavior in public • To control anger and aggression
Social activities	• To socialize within the family • To participate in recreational and leisure activities • To make appropriate sexual decisions • To socialize outside of the family • To make and keep friends • To communicate with others about personal needs

(Continued)

Table 18-4 (*Continued*)

Support area	Goals
Social activities (*continued*)	• To engage in loving and intimate relationships • To offer assistance to others
Protection and advocacy activities	• To advocate for self and others • To manage money and personal finances • To protect self from exploitation • To exercise legal rights and responsibilities • To locate and participate in self-advocacy and support organizations • To obtain legal services • To use a bank, including writing checks and making deposits

Source: Adapted from American Association on Mental Retardation (2002).

prevent mental retardation with a familial origin in high-risk children between 6 months and 6 years of age) failed to produce evidence that early intervention for children at risk for mental retardation results in meaningful and lasting changes in intelligence (Gilhousen, Allen, Lasater, Farrell, & Reynolds, 1990). These and similar results, however, do not mean that interventions are not needed. The interventions discussed previously focus on enhancing children's life skills and not just on raising their intelligence test scores.

All children need the opportunity to access the general curriculum, regardless of their IQ and level of adaptive behavior. This principle also is embedded in the No Child Left Behind Act of 2001. Test scores should not be used to deny children with mental retardation access to programs that may help them learn valuable skills. Many children whose test scores fall into the mentally retarded range can develop into self-sufficient and productive adults. They need education and training regimens that encourage the full realization of their potentials. In fact, with proper training, children with Down syndrome continue to develop their language expression skills during adolescence and young adulthood (Chapman, Hesketh, & Kistler, 2002). All children with mental retardation need help in bolstering their self-esteem and expectancy of success (Zigler, 1995). The use of adaptive technology, computer-assisted instruction, and inclusive classrooms can help them become more productive citizens. Children with mental retardation have the best prognosis when their level of mental retardation is mild and they have no major physical disabilities, have a positive self-image, and have support from their parents, family, and community (O'Brien, 2001).

People with mental retardation need to be integrated into society, to have their individuality recognized, and to be given opportunities for growth and development. Following are some strategies to help meet these goals:

1. Emphasize the similarities, rather than the differences, between people with and without mental retardation.
2. Recognize that people with mental retardation can improve their level of functioning.
3. De-emphasize labeling.
4. Increase respect for individuality.
5. Expand legal rights for people with mental retardation.
6. Increase society's tolerance for individual differences.
7. Recognize that some mental retardation arises out of conditions in society.
8. Emphasize prevention.
9. Plan and coordinate services.

CONCLUDING COMMENT

Research on intelligence and mental retardation has changed our view of people with mental retardation (Detterman, Gabriel, & Ruthsatz, 2000):

> People with mental retardation are now regarded as people who can learn and accomplish. This is quite a radical change to occur in less than 100 years. . . . Over the next century, there is reason to hope that the connection between intelligence and mental retardation will be more fully, and perhaps even completely, explicated. Advances in genetics, brain imaging and recording, and neuroscience may allow the connection of behavioral data collected over the last 50 years with underlying biological processes. (p. 155, with changes in notation)

Intelligence tests currently are used in ways that were never anticipated by the early psychologists and test developers. Government agencies and the court system in particular rely on intelligence test data. For example, the Social Security Administration uses intelligence test results to determine whether individuals are eligible for disability benefits. In criminal cases, intelligence tests are used to determine whether individuals are competent to stand trial (i.e., whether they have diminished capacity) and even, in cases involving capital punishment, to determine whether a defendant can be sentenced to death. The U.S. Supreme Court in 2002 ruled, in a 6 to 3 opinion, that executing people who are mentally retarded is unconstitutional (*Atkins v. Virginia,* 2002). Thus, the assessment of individuals referred for evaluation of mental retardation has extremely far-reaching consequences.

THINKING THROUGH THE ISSUES

1. What data obtained from a psychological evaluation would you consider in formulating a response to a parent who asked, "Is my child going to be mentally retarded forever?"

2. How might the following three children differ in their ability to function in school and in society: (a) a child with a WISC–IV IQ of 60 and a Vineland Adaptive Behavior Scale Composite score of 90, (b) a child with a WISC–IV Full Scale IQ of 90 and a Vineland Adaptive Behavior Scale Composite score of 60, and (c) a child with a WISC–IV Full Scale IQ of 60 and a Vineland Adaptive Behavior Scale Composite score of 60?

3. Why should you *not* expect to see similar WISC–IV patterns in different children who are classified as mentally retarded?

4. Of what value are informal assessment procedures with children who have severe disabilities? Why do you suppose we don't have better tests to assess low-incidence disabling conditions?

SUMMARY

1. The term *mental retardation* applies to a heterogeneous group of conditions characterized by low scores on a standardized measure of intelligence, together with deficits in adaptive behavior.

2. The American Association on Mental Retardation defines mental retardation as follows: "Mental retardation is a disability characterized by significant limitations both in intellectual functioning and in adaptive behavior as expressed in conceptual, social, and practical adaptive skills. The disability originates before age 18" (p. 8).

3. The AAMR operationally defines significant limitations in adaptive behavior in terms of performance on a standardized measure of adaptive behavior: Either the individual's score on one of the three skills areas (conceptual, social, or practical) measured by the instrument or the individual's overall score must be at least two standard deviations below the mean.

4. The definition of mental retardation must be applied with five assumptions in mind: Limitations in present functioning must be considered within the context of community environments typical of the individual's age, peers, and culture. Valid assessment considers cultural and linguistic diversity, as well as differences in communication and behavioral factors. Limitations may coexist with strengths; people with mental retardation may have gifts as well as limitations. An important purpose of describing limitations is to develop a profile of needed supports. The life functioning of the person with mental retardation will generally improve with appropriate supports over a sustained period.

5. The American Psychiatric Association, in *DSM-IV–TR,* defines mental retardation as "significantly subaverage intellectual functioning . . . that is accompanied by significant limitations in adaptive functioning in at least two of the following skill areas: communication, self-care, home living, social/interpersonal skills, use of community resources, self-direction, functional academic skills, work, leisure, health, and safety. . . . The onset must occur before age 18 years" (2000, p. 41).

6. The *DSM-IV–TR* also specifies four degrees of severity: (a) mild mental retardation (IQ level of 50–55 to approximately 70), (b) moderate mental retardation (IQ level of 35–40 to 50–55), (c) severe mental retardation (IQ level of 20–25 to 35–40), and (d) profound mental retardation (IQ level below 20 or 25).

7. The two definitions of mental retardation overlap considerably and both emphasize the importance of evaluating intelligence as well as adaptive behavior.

8. Neither the AAMR nor the *DSM-IV–TR* definition makes any reference to etiology, and both definitions avoid the implication that mental retardation is irreversible.

9. Both definitions imply that (a) assessment must focus on a description of present intelligence and behavior, (b) "significant limitations in adaptive behavior" and "significantly subaverage intellectual functioning" refer to performance that is approximately two or more standard deviations below the population mean on a standardized measure of intelligence and a standardized measure of adaptive behavior, (c) "intellectual functioning" refers to performance on a standardized intelligence test that measures, as far as is possible, general cognitive ability rather than one limited facet of ability, (d) two criteria—level of intelligence and level of adaptive behavior—are considered jointly in arriving at a diagnosis, (e) a diagnosis of mental retardation does not rule out the coexistence of other disorders, and (f) a diagnosis of mental retardation is inappropriate when an individual is adequately meeting the demands of his or her environment.

10. Intelligence tests are more precisely constructed than are measures of adaptive behavior.

11. Children with mental retardation have a slow rate of cognitive development, limited expressive and receptive language abilities, limited adaptive skills, limited experiential background, short attention span, distractibility, and a concrete and literal style in approaching tasks.

Etiology of Mental Retardation

12. Mental retardation can be a primary diagnosis, can occur as part of a syndrome, or can co-occur with other developmental disabilities, neurological disorders, or psychiatric disorders.

13. Mental retardation can result from a diverse set of predisposing factors, including genetic disorders, chromosomal deviations, cranial malformations, other congenital factors, prematurity and perinatal factors, and postnatal factors.

14. Examples of genetic disorders that can lead to mental retardation include fragile X syndrome, galactosemia, Lesch-Nyhan syndrome, neurofibromatosis 1, phenylketonuria (PKU), Rett syndrome, Rubinstein-Taybi syndrome, Tay-Sachs disease, and tuberous sclerosis.

15. Examples of chromosomal deviations that can lead to mental retardation include Angelman syndrome, cri-du-chat syndrome, Down syndrome (trisomy 21), Edwards syndrome (trisomy 18), Klinefelter's syndrome (XXY males), Patau syndrome, and Prader-Willi syndrome.

16. Examples of cranial malformations that can lead to mental retardation are hydrocephalus and microcephalus.

17. Examples of other congenital factors that can lead to mental retardation include congenital hypothyroidism (cretinism), congenital toxoplasmosis, fetal alcohol syndrome (FAS), human immunodeficiency virus type I (HIV-I) infection and AIDS, Rh incompatibilities, rubella, and syphilis.

18. Examples of perinatal factors that can lead to mental retardation are cytomegalovirus (CMV), extreme prematurity, hypoxic-ischemic encephalopathy, neural tube defect, placental dysfunction, and teratogens.

19. Examples of postnatal factors that can lead to mental retardation include brain tumors, head injuries, malnutrition, meningitis, severe abuse and neglect, and toxins.

20. Approximately 1% of the population could be classified as mentally retarded.

21. Of people with mental retardation, approximately 85% need limited supports, 10% need moderate supports, 3% to 4% need extensive supports, and the remaining 1% to 2% may also have physical or emotional problems that require ongoing medical attention.

22. During the 2000–2001 school year, 612,978 children and young adults between 6 and 21 years of age received a diagnosis of mental retardation and were enrolled in special education programs under the Individuals with Disabilities Act.

23. The group with mental retardation constituted about 10.61% of the total special education school population.

24. Individuals with mental retardation can be grouped into two broad categories: those with mental retardation with a familial origin and those with mental retardation caused by brain injury.

25. Several methods have helped to reduce the occurrence of mental retardation. They include screening, putting individuals with PKU on a phenylalanine-restricted diet, immunizing children, educating the public, reducing children's exposure to lead and mercury, constructing safer automobiles, and instituting governmental policies designed to reduce poverty and homelessness, provide information to the public about prevention of mental retardation (including educational programs focusing on quality of family life and effective parenting), and develop universal health-care programs.

Relationship Between Measured Intelligence and Adaptive Behavior

26. Because intelligence and adaptive behavior are not perfectly correlated, children who fall below –2 *SD* on an intelligence test may have adaptive behavior scores that do not fall below –2 *SD*.

27. It is estimated that the relationship between measured intelligence and adaptive behavior is about .30 to .50, but it tends to be higher in individuals with severe mental retardation than in individuals with average intellectual ability.

Understanding Mental Retardation

28. Mental retardation is not a disease. It is a symptom of a variety of conditions that interfere with normal brain development, and intellectual impairment may be a functional expression of these conditions.

29. There is considerable variability in the personalities and behavior of children with mental retardation.

30. The label of "mental retardation" should not prevent us from seeing that children with mental retardation differ among themselves, as do all children.

31. Chronological age (CA) affects many traits and should be considered in evaluating and making recommendations for individuals with mental retardation.

Assessment

32. The assessment of mental retardation requires the use of a reliable, valid, and comprehensive individual measure of intellectual functioning and a reliable, valid, and comprehensive measure of adaptive behavior.

33. The evaluation must be comprehensive because mental retardation may exist concurrently with other disabling conditions.

34. Conduct the assessment in a location where the child is comfortable. However, recognize that rapport may be difficult to establish because children with mental retardation may have limited verbal abilities, may fear strangers, or may distrust their own ability to communicate effectively.

35. During the interview with the child, you may need to simplify questions, provide examples, ask structured questions, use frequent prompts, and repeat or rephrase your questions.

36. In the early part of the twentieth century, the National Education Association stated, "Tests of mental deficiency are chiefly useful in the hands of the skilled examiner. No sets of tests have been devised that will give a categorical answer as to the mental status of any individual. In nearly every instance in which they are used, tests need to be interpreted" (Bruner, Barnes, & Dearborn, 1909, p. 905, with changes in notation).

37. You will want to observe the child in more than one setting and obtain information from different informants about how the child behaves in various settings.

38. The school environment is suitable for assessing some, but not all, of the learning needs of children with severe disabilities.

39. To assess adaptive behavior, you can use adaptive behavior scales and informal measures and obtain information from interviews with the parents, other family members, and teachers and from the child's case history.

40. Several formal procedures are useful for the assessment of maladaptive behaviors in children and adults with mental retardation.

41. When you suspect that a child may have intellectual disabilities, consider a possible diagnosis of developmental delay, especially with infants or preschool children.

42. Make a diagnosis of mental retardation only when the child shows significantly below average general intellectual functioning in conjunction with significant deficits in adaptive behavior.

43. Children with severe or profound mental retardation may be especially difficult to evaluate because of self-stimulating behavior, self-injurious behavior, limited attention span, destructive behavior, temper tantrums, seizures, noncompliance with requests, or inability to understand the test questions.

44. Traditional assessment approaches may not be useful with children with severe or profound mental retardation.

45. The curriculum content for students with disabilities should be similar to that of their nondisabled peers, but modified to allow them to work at their own pace.

46. The use of normal developmental scales with children who have extensive disabilities is problematic.

Interventions

47. After a diagnosis of mental retardation is made, you will need to determine the level of support that the individual may need.

48. Four support levels offered by the AAMR are intermittent, limited, extensive, and pervasive.

49. Services for children with mental retardation may begin immediately after the child's birth or during the preschool years and continue throughout the developmental period.

50. Early intervention services mandated by IDEA 2004 include psychological and social work services, speech and language services, occupational and physical therapy services, medical

and dental care services, special education programs, in-home living assistance programs, and transportation services.

51. These services may help children with mental retardation lead more normal lives during their developmental period and when they reach adulthood.

52. Suggestions for parents of children with mental retardation include the following: Learn about mental retardation. Encourage independence in your child. Give your child chores, keeping in mind your child's age, attention span, and abilities. Find out what skills your child is learning at school, and find ways for your child to apply those skills at home. Find opportunities in your community for social activities, such as scouts, recreation center activities, and sports. Talk to other parents whose children have mental retardation. Meet with your child's teachers, work with them to develop an educational plan to address your child's needs, keep in touch with them, and offer them support.

53. Therapeutic interventions for children with mental retardation include environmental changes, behavioral treatments, individual psychotherapy, group psychotherapy, family therapy, and pharmacotherapy.

54. Interventions usually will not lead to significant improvements in the intelligence test scores of children with mental retardation.

55. All children need the opportunity to access the general curriculum, regardless of their IQ and level of adaptive behavior.

56. Children with mental retardation have the best prognosis when their level of mental retardation is mild and they have no major physical disabilities, have a positive self-image, and have support from their parents, family, and community.

57. People with mental retardation need to be integrated into society, to have their individuality recognized, and to be given opportunities for growth and development.

Concluding Comment

58. Intelligence tests currently are used in ways that were never anticipated by the early psychologists and test developers.

59. The Social Security Administration uses intelligence test results to determine whether individuals are eligible for disability benefits.

60. In criminal cases, intelligence tests are used to determine whether individuals are competent to stand trial and even, in cases involving capital punishment, to determine whether a defendant can be sentenced to death.

61. The U.S. Supreme Court in 2002 ruled, in a 6 to 3 opinion, that executing people who are mentally retarded is unconstitutional (*Atkins v. Virginia*, 2002).

62. Thus, the assessment of individuals referred for evaluation of mental retardation has extremely far-reaching consequences.

KEY TERMS, CONCEPTS, AND NAMES

STUDY QUESTIONS

1. Define mental retardation and discuss the implications of the AAMR and *DSM-IV–TR* definitions and related classification issues.

2. Discuss the etiology of mental retardation.

3. Discuss the distribution of mental retardation in the population.

4. Discuss the categorization of mental retardation based on whether it is of familial origin or based on brain injury.

5. Discuss several methods that have been successful in reducing mental retardation.

6. How are prevalence rates for mental retardation a function of the relationship between measured intelligence and adaptive behavior?

7. Discuss some general considerations in understanding mental retardation.

8. Discuss the assessment of mental retardation.

9. How do you distinguish between mental retardation and developmental delay?

10. Discuss the assessment of children with severe or profound mental retardation, and in your discussion address problems with standardized tests and scales.

11. Discuss interventions for individuals with mental retardation.

19

GIFTEDNESS

A great society not only searches out excellence but rewards it when it is found.

—Anonymous

Great achievers have high IQs, but high IQ does not guarantee creative achievement.
—Hans J. Eysenck, British behavioral psychologist (1916–1997)

Goals and Objectives

This chapter is designed to enable you to do the following:

- Become familiar with methods for assessing gifted children

- Understand how creativity is defined and measured

Children are generally referred to as gifted and talented if they are outstanding in an area—for example, have an extremely high IQ (above 130, which represents the 99th percentile rank), display unusual artistic or musical talent, or achieve high scores on tests of creativity. Such children require educational programs and services beyond those normally provided by the regular program if they are to maximize their potential.

Gifted and talented children include those with demonstrated achievement or potential ability in any of the following areas: general intellectual ability, specific academic aptitude, creative or productive thinking, leadership ability, or visual and performing arts (Gifted and Talented Children's Education Act of 1981, Section 572). Approximately 3% to 5% of children in the United States have one or more of these special abilities or talents.

Table 19-1 gives expected prevalence rates, based solely on IQ, for scores at 0 to 6 standard deviations above the mean. The table shows, for example, that approximately 2 in 100 individuals have IQs of 130 or above, whereas approximately 3 in 100,000 individuals have IQs of 160 or higher.

INTELLECTUAL AND PERSONALITY CHARACTERISTICS OF GIFTED CHILDREN

The intellectual and personality characteristics of gifted children are shown in Table 19-2 (Coleman & Cross, 2002; Silverman, 1997). Table 19-2 also serves as a checklist that parents and teachers can use to identify gifted children. Factors that influence the development of gifted intellectual performance include genetics, ability to master symbol systems, opportunities to develop talent, parental encouragement of talent and approval of intellectual activities, and positive peer influences for intellectual activities (Feldhusen, 1998; Gallagher, 1991; Mönks & Mason, 2000).

Gifted children usually will not display all of the characteristics shown in Table 19-2. In addition, some gifted children may display these characteristics at different ages than other gifted children or may have different clusters of these characteristics (Baska, 1989). Finally, these characteristics are not exclusive to gifted children; rather, gifted children simply tend have more of these characteristics than children who are not gifted.

Gifted children also may have temperament and personality difficulties (Kansas State Department of Education, n.d.). They may be impatient, strong-willed, stubborn, nonconforming, bossy, bored with peers, intolerant of others, neglectful of duties during periods of intense concentration, frustrated with inactivity, or disorganized and scattered. They may resist routine activities, question teaching procedures, use words to manipulate others, and take on the role of "class clown" in order to get attention. Note that not all gifted children will show these difficulties and other children may have these difficulties as well.

Studies conducted in the 1980s and 1990s on the psychological characteristics of gifted children indicate the following (Robinson & Clinkenbeard, 1998):

Gifted elementary or secondary age children . . . show some advantages over other students particularly in quantity, speed, and complexity of cognition. They know more about metacognition and can use strategies better in new contexts, but they may not use a wider variety of metacognitive strategies than other students. . . . both creativity and motivation probably influence the results of research on cognitive and metacognitive characteristics. . . .

Gifted students . . . tend to have better psychosocial adjustment than other students. They are at least as popular, though they may have different friendship styles. Their self-concepts, while heavily weighted with their academic abilities, are generally high, and they tend to score at normal or above levels on personality measures. They tend to be more internally motivated and have more positive attributions for success and failures; however, they may have more trouble coping when they do encounter failures.

These positive findings may not be true for various subgroups of the gifted. Sex differences have been found such that through adolescence, females tend to decrease and males tend to increase on several positive emotional characteristics. In addition, these psychological advantages may start to disappear as the level of giftedness increases. Students who are extremely far from the norm intellectually seem to have more trouble fitting in socially and emotionally as well. Gifted students who are underachievers may demonstrate considerably different psychological profiles. Finally, students from cultural or ethnic groups where the identification of giftedness has not been traditional have not been thoroughly investigated. (pp. 125, 129–130)

Table 19-1
Expected Probability of Occurrence of IQs at or Above Each Standard Deviation (*SD* = 15) Above the Mean

Standard deviations above the mean	IQ	Approximate expected occurrence
0	100	50 in 100
1	115	16 in 100
2	130	2 in 100
3	145	1 in 1,000
4	160	3 in 100,000
5	175	3 in 10,000,000
6	190	1 in 1,000,000,000

Table 19-2
Teacher and Parent Recommendation Form for Children Who Are Gifted and Talented

TEACHER AND PARENT RECOMMENDATION FORM
FOR CHILDREN WHO ARE GIFTED AND TALENTED

Child's name: _____ Date: _____ Grade: _____

School: _____ Name of person filling out form: _____

Directions: Please circle the number that represents your rating of each characteristic.

Rating scale:	1	2	3	4	5
	Never	Almost never	Sometimes	Often	Always

Characteristics	Rating (Circle one number)				

Learning Characteristics

1. Has outstanding memory.	1	2	3	4	5
2. Has excellent reasoning ability.	1	2	3	4	5
3. Is intellectually curious.	1	2	3	4	5
4. Learns things rapidly.	1	2	3	4	5
5. Is a keen and alert observer.	1	2	3	4	5
6. Is good with abstract concepts.	1	2	3	4	5
7. Shows complex thought processes.	1	2	3	4	5
8. Has an advanced vocabulary.	1	2	3	4	5
9. Achieves well above grade level in several academic areas.	1	2	3	4	5
10. Has an unusual interest in an area such as art, computers, mathematics, or music.	1	2	3	4	5

Motivational Characteristics

11. Is persistent when faced with difficult tasks.	1	2	3	4	5
12. Is resourceful in finding answers to questions.	1	2	3	4	5
13. Becomes absorbed in tasks when he or she is interested in the tasks.	1	2	3	4	5
14. Requires little external motivation to follow through in work that initially excites him or her.	1	2	3	4	5
15. Likes to organize things.	1	2	3	4	5
16. Strives toward perfection.	1	2	3	4	5
17. Enjoys intellectual pursuits.	1	2	3	4	5
18. Is concerned about social and moral issues.	1	2	3	4	5

Leadership Characteristics

19. Is self-confident with other children and adults.	1	2	3	4	5
20. Enjoys taking on responsibility.	1	2	3	4	5
21. Expresses self well.	1	2	3	4	5

Creativity Characteristics

22. Shows emotional sensitivity.	1	2	3	4	5
23. Is nonconforming (or an independent thinker).	1	2	3	4	5
24. Is curious about many things.	1	2	3	4	5
25. Generates a large number of ideas and solutions to problems.	1	2	3	4	5
26. Is imaginative.	1	2	3	4	5
27. Asks many questions.	1	2	3	4	5
28. Has a sense of humor and can laugh at himself or herself.	1	2	3	4	5
29. Is a high risk taker and adventurous.	1	2	3	4	5

GIFTED CHILDREN WHO ARE UNDERACHIEVING

Intellectual giftedness does not ensure success in school (Colangelo & Assouline, 2000; Rimm, 1997). The academic success of gifted children is determined by the same environmental forces that affect the success of all children—namely, motivation, interests, self-concept, family and home, teachers and school, peers, and society. If the needs of gifted children are not recognized and met, these children may not achieve their potential.

Gifted children may underachieve and rebel when (a) they experience excessive parental pressure to succeed in school, (b) they attend schools that do not value high achievement in children, pressure children to achieve excessively high goals, or provide curricula that do not challenge children, or (c) they experience peer pressure to conform to the average, "play it cool" by not studying, or not put out much effort to learn the course material.

Underachieving gifted children may exhibit one or more of the following characteristics (Clark, 1988; Colangelo & Assouline, 2000; Peters, Grager-Loidl, & Supplee, 2000; Rimm, 1997): low self-esteem, low sense of personal control over their lives or inability to assume responsibility for their actions, feelings of being rejected by their family, marked hostility toward adult authority, resistance to guidance from teachers and parents, feelings of victimization, dislike of school and teachers, rebelliousness, weak motivation for academic achievement, poor study habits, limited intellectual adaptiveness, limited persistence in completing classroom assignments, limited leadership qualities, immaturity, poor personal adjustment, few hobbies, phobia about tests, low aspirations, poor planning for the future, goals that do not match their interests or abilities, and preference for unchallenging careers. The characteristics most frequently found among underachieving students who are gifted are *low self-esteem* and *a low sense of personal control over their own lives* (Rimm, 1997).

Underachieving students who are gifted may have complex behavior patterns that are not easily amenable to intervention, especially if their behavior patterns have been established over a long period of childhood (Gallagher, 1997; Peterson & Colangelo, 1996). When teachers and parents see a longstanding pattern of underachievement, they may assume that a student who was once gifted is no longer gifted. To reverse longstanding patterns of underachievement, the following six steps are recommended (Rimm, 1997):

1. Assess the child.
2. Obtain information from the parents and teachers about the child.
3. Change the expectations of the child, parents, teachers, peers, and siblings about the child's ability to succeed in school.
4. Provide role models for the child.
5. Correct skill deficiencies.
6. Modify reinforcements used at home and at school.

GIFTED CHILDREN WHO HAVE LEARNING DISABILITIES

Some gifted children have specific learning disabilities that interfere with their ability to learn in school (Brody & Mills, 1997; McCoach, Kehle, Bray, & Siegle, 2001; Moon & Hall, 1998; Peterson & Colangelo, 1996; Weinfeld, 2003). Those with a specific learning disability may have one or more of the following characteristics associated with academic performance and personality: reading difficulties (including problems with phonics); written language difficulties (including poor penmanship, poor spelling, and reversal of letters); difficulty in keeping numbers in order (including difficulty in making numeric transpositions); short-term memory difficulties; listening difficulties; feelings of frustration, unhappiness, and isolation; poor social skills; hostility toward teachers; attention difficulties; and difficulties with organization. In addition, they may be immature, self-critical, stubborn, inflexible, or passionate about some topics and indifferent to others; they may use humor to divert attention from school failure; and they may find clever ways to avoid school tasks.

In the early grades, gifted children with a learning disability usually are able to compensate for their disability and show only minor problems, such as failing to do their written assignments (McEachern & Bornot, 2001). However, in the secondary grades, they may no longer be able to compensate for their disability as the task demands increase.

Gifted children with a learning disability may show an uneven pattern of strengths and weaknesses on psychoeducational tests. For example, they may obtain high scores on vocabulary tests and give fluent and in-depth definitions of words, but obtain low scores on arithmetic or spelling tests. Their learning disabilities may conceal their advanced abilities and, contrariwise, their advanced abilities may conceal their learning disabilities. *What is especially important is that gifted children not be labeled as "unmotivated" or "inattentive" when it is their learning disability that is interfering with their ability to master the school curriculum.*

Following is a case of a child who is gifted and has a learning disability:

Paul, aged 13 years 2 months, was referred because of a severe spelling disability (1st percentile on the Stanford Achievement Test). His teachers indicated that his specific deficits in spelling and writing were interfering with his academic performance. His test scores in other areas indicated average to above-average reading skills (44th to 88th percentiles) and average to above-average arithmetic skills (54th to 94th percentiles). Reading comprehension scores were better than word recognition scores. On the WISC–IV, Paul obtained a Full Scale IQ of 134 with no noticeable differences between the four individual scales. The results suggested that Paul is a gifted youngster with a specific learning disability in the area of written expression.

Table 19-3 describes a continuum of services for gifted students with learning disabilities. These services range from inclusion in full-time general education classes to inclusion in full-time special education classes.

GIFTED CHILDREN WHO HAVE EMOTIONAL PROBLEMS

The incidence of emotional problems is likely to be about the same among gifted children as it is among children who are not gifted (Pendarvis, Howley, & Howley, 1990; Schneider, Clegg, Byrne, Ledingham, & Crombie, 1989). However, when gifted children challenge authority, respond in unconventional ways, or have limited tolerance for frustration, they may be classified by teachers as emotionally disturbed. Some gifted children may be at risk for emotional problems because

of other children's jealousy, fear, or negative attitudes or because of an absence of appropriate school programs or lack of intellectual peers. It is not high intelligence per se, but rather its consequences, that may have a negative effect on some gifted children (Grossberg & Cornell, 1988).

PRESCHOOL GIFTED CHILDREN

The intellectual and personality characteristics of preschool gifted children are shown in Table 19-4 (Roedell, 1980b; Silverman, 1997). Table 19-4 also serves as a checklist that parents and teachers can use to identify preschool gifted children. Preschool gifted children tend to be more precocious in memory than in general intelligence, reading achievement, or spatial reasoning.

Let's look at a case of a remarkably gifted preschool girl (Roedell, 1980a):

This preschool girl obtained an estimated Stanford-Binet Intelligence Scale: Form L-M IQ of 177. Her highest performance was

Table 19-3
Continuum of Alternative Service Options for Learning Disabled Gifted Students

Service options	Type of student	Description
A. General education with no special education services or modifications	Gifted students with learning disabilities who require no special supports	Standard general education curriculum
B. General education with supplemental aids and materials	Gifted students with very mild learning disabilities	Standard general education curriculum
C. General education with special education consultation services	Gifted students with very mild learning disabilities, with special education less than 10% of school day	Standard general education curriculum
D. General education with special education services	Gifted students with mild learning disabilities, with special education contact time up to 49% of school day	Blended program services—gifted education or special education resource room service combined with general education or both gifted and special education resource room service combined with general education
E. Special education for at-risk gifted students	Gifted students with mild to moderate learning disabilities, with special education contact time 50% or more of school day	Designed for gifted students who are academically at risk because of low socioeconomic status or culturally or ethnically diverse backgrounds. Teachers need training in both gifted education and special education. Curriculum designed to provide academic support combined with gifted education enrichment.
F. Special education for academically handicapped students	Gifted students with moderate to severe learning disabilities, with special education contact time approaching entire school day	Designed for learning disabled gifted students. There should be a student-teacher ratio of about 8 to 1 and an educational assistant. Teachers need certification in special education and extensive training in gifted education. Curriculum designed to address the social-emotional, gifted, and remedial needs of students.

Source: Adapted from Nielsen (2002), p. 102.

Table 19-4
Parent and Teacher Recommendation Form for Preschool Children Who Are Gifted and Talented

PARENT AND TEACHER RECOMMENDATION FORM
FOR PRESCHOOL CHILDREN WHO ARE GIFTED AND TALENTED

Child's name: _____ Date:_____

Age: _____ Name of person filling out form: _____

Directions: Please circle the number that represents your rating of each characteristic.

Rating scale:	1	2	3
	Not true	Somewhat true	Very true

Characteristics	Rating (Circle one number)		

Developmental Characteristics

1. Showed unusual alertness in infancy.	1	2	3
2. Showed advanced progression through the early developmental milestones.	1	2	3
3. Understood directions, such as right and left, at an early age.	1	2	3
4. Showed early interest in time.	1	2	3
5. Learned to read before age 5 years.	1	2	3

Learning Characteristics

6. Has outstanding memory and carries out complex instructions to do several things in succession.	1	2	3
7. Has a long attention span.	1	2	3
8. Has an advanced vocabulary.	1	2	3
9. Uses metaphors or analogies.	1	2	3
10. Makes up songs or stories spontaneously.	1	2	3
11. Makes interesting shapes or patterns with blocks, board shapes, or other materials.	1	2	3
12. Puts together difficult puzzles.	1	2	3
13. Understands abstract or complex concepts.	1	2	3
14. Masters a new skill, concept, song, or rhyme with unusual speed.	1	2	3
15. Uses language to exchange ideas.	1	2	3
16. Takes apart and reassembles things with unusual skill.	1	2	3
17. Remembers and makes mental connections between past and present experiences.	1	2	3

Personality Characteristics

18. Demonstrates a preference for novelty.	1	2	3
19. Shows curiosity and asks many questions.	1	2	3
20. Modifies language when talking to less mature children.	1	2	3
21. Has a sense of humor.	1	2	3
22. Becomes absorbed in one kind of activity.	1	2	3
23. Displays great interest or skill in ordering or grouping objects.	1	2	3
24. Shows sensitivity to the needs or feelings of other children or adults.	1	2	3
25. Shows unusual attentiveness to features of the home or preschool environment.	1	2	3
26. Uses verbal skills to handle conflict or to influence other children's behavior.	1	2	3
27. Prefers to play with older children or with adults.	1	2	3

Source: Adapted from Roedell (1980b) and Silverman (1997).

on verbal reasoning items; she showed less extraordinary spatial reasoning skills. Although she was not remarkably proficient in map-making or design-copying, she read at the fourth grade level by the age of 4 years. Her favorite books then were the *Little House* series by Laura Ingalls Wilder. She also enjoyed making up elaborate fantasy dramas involving several characters and complicated plots. Her daily language skills were also excellent.

The academic abilities of preschool gifted children show diverse skill patterns (Roedell, 1980a). However, the early acquisition of advanced academic skills may not be related to level of intelligence. Some preschool children with IQs above 160 have not mastered reading or arithmetic, whereas others with IQs of 116 are fluent readers by the age of 3 years. Preschool gifted children may show highly differentiated abilities in various cognitive areas, such as highly developed spatial reasoning ability and vocabulary, exceptional memory ability, unusual mathematical skills, or unusual early reading skills. Young children who are exceptionally adept in one area are not necessarily advanced in other areas, as "intraindividual differences among abilities are the rule, not the exception" (Robinson, 1981, p. 72). For example, children with extraordinary spatial reasoning ability may have only moderately advanced verbal skills; those who have remarkable memory skills may be ordinary in other respects. It is highly unlikely, however, that children who are extraordinary in one area of mental functioning will be average or below average in all other areas of functioning.

The following sketch describes some personality and adjustment patterns of preschool gifted children (Roedell, 1980a):

> Preschool gifted children show a wide range of personality characteristics and levels of social maturity. While children with moderately advanced intellectual abilities often show good overall adjustment, children with extremely advanced intellectual skills may have more difficulty. Adjustment problems may, in some cases, result from the uneven development that occurs when intellectual capabilities far outstrip the child's levels of physical or social development. Children with advanced intellectual skills sometimes tend to show advanced understanding of social situations and to be better able to judge other people's feelings. Intellectually advanced preschool children, however, may need guided social experience to help them make use of their advanced social understanding. (p. 26, with changes in notation)

In identifying the abilities of preschool gifted children, you may need to use tests that did not include their age range in the standardization group. For example, if a young child obtains scores at the highest level on one or more of the WPPSI–III subtests, you can administer similar WISC–IV subtests, though the WISC–IV was not standardized on preschool children. In such cases, you can use test-age equivalents to estimate the child's performance. For example, the test-age equivalent for a 4-year-old who obtains a raw score of 30 on the WISC–IV Block Design subtest is 9-10 (9 years 10 months).

In addition to the WPPSI–III and WISC–IV, you can use other tests to obtain test-age equivalents for children younger than age 4 years (e.g., Stanford-Binet: V). The test-age equivalents that accompany each subtest are helpful for this purpose. Do not use group tests of general intelligence with preschool children; children at these ages usually are not sufficiently attentive, compliant, and persistent in a group situation.

TERMAN'S AND LOVELL AND SHIELDS'S STUDIES OF GIFTED INDIVIDUALS

An extensive longitudinal study by Terman (1925; Terman & Oden, 1959) followed a sample of 1,528 children who were gifted (857 males and 671 females), from the time they were approximately 11 years old through adulthood. The children's IQs on the Stanford-Binet Intelligence Scale: 1916 Form ranged from 135 to 200, and their IQs on group tests were 135 and above. In comparison with a control group of children, the gifted children were physically healthier; superior in reading, arithmetical reasoning, and information, but not in computation and spelling; more interested in abstract subjects (literature, debating, dramatics, and history); and less interested in practical subjects (penmanship, manual training, drawing, and painting). Teachers rated this sample of gifted children as above the mean of the control group on intellectual, volitional, emotional, aesthetic, moral, physical, and social traits. In only one area—mechanical ingenuity—were the children who were gifted rated slightly below the children in the control group.

On follow-up in middle age (Terman & Oden, 1959), members of the group who were gifted were found to have more education, higher incomes, more desirable and prestigious occupations, more entries in *Who's Who*, better physical and mental health, a lower suicide rate, a lower mortality rate, a lower divorce rate, and brighter spouses and children than a random sample of the population. This sample of children who were gifted "evolved into productive professionals with good mental health and stable interpersonal relationships" (Subotnik, Karp, & Morgan, 1989, p. 143). The follow-up study demonstrates that measured intelligence does relate to accomplishments outside of school. As Brody and Brody (1976) observed, "It is doubtful that the attempt to select children scoring in the top 1% of any other single characteristic would be as predictive of future accomplishment" (p. 109).

A similar but less extensive study was carried out in England with a sample of 55 English boys and girls, ages 8 to 12 years, who had WISC Verbal Scale IQs above 140 (Lovell & Shields, 1967). Teachers rated the children outstandingly high in general intelligence and desire to know; very high in originality, desire to excel, truthfulness, common sense, will power, perseverance, and conscientiousness; rather high in prudence and forethought, self-confidence, and sense of humor; and close to average in freedom from vanity and egotism. There were few sex differences. The mean ratings given by the British teachers to their sample of children were close to those given by the American teachers to the children in

Terman's sample over 40 years earlier. The ordering of the traits in the two studies was highly correlated ($r = .90$). Thus, despite changes over time and differences between countries in education and in life generally, teachers in the United States in the 1920s and in England in the 1960s rated children who were gifted in similar ways. The results also indicated that tests of creativity did not measure any intellectual functions independent of those measured by the WISC or by tests of logical thought.

PROMOTING PSYCHOSOCIAL ADJUSTMENT IN GIFTED CHILDREN

The following 12 guidelines will assist you in promoting the psychosocial adjustment of gifted children (Blackburn & Erickson, 1986; Robinson & Noble, 1991). In using these guidelines, recognize that there is a wide range of individual differences among gifted children and among their families. Table 19-5 presents guidelines for parents of gifted children.

1. Establish a good working relationship with the parents, who themselves may be bright, verbal, highly child-centered, and effective advocates for their children.
2. Reach out to parents of children who are culturally and linguistically diverse. These parents may be less sophisticated than parents from the majority group in working with the school system.
3. Help families who have less than optimal functioning cope with their gifted children.
4. Encourage children to express their potential in any area.
5. Give young children academic challenges so that they develop a strong sense that achievement comes with effort.
6. Encourage children to pursue traditional as well as nontraditional goals and select from a range of available options.
7. Help children develop healthy, realistic self-esteem, based on a clear understanding of their strengths and weaknesses.
8. Help children become internally motivated and set realistic goals.
9. Help children learn to accept their mistakes, to reduce their fear of failure (if present), and to recognize that they can learn from their errors.
10. Help children learn to accept help from others.
11. Help children learn how to help others.
12. Help children develop a sense of humor about themselves and events outside their control.

EDUCATING GIFTED CHILDREN

Gifted children need instructional programs commensurate with their abilities. Ideally, the programs should enable them to operate cognitively and affectively at complex levels of thought and feeling and to learn critical thinking skills, creative thinking skills, research methodology skills, problem-solving skills, decision-making skills, and leadership skills. Children can develop these skills if they are given opportunities to engage in activities stressing divergent production, talk to intellectual peers, understand human value systems, see interrelationships among bodies of knowledge, study subjects in their areas of strength and interest as well as in new areas, and apply their abilities to problems in the world of work and in the community (Feldhusen, 1998; VanTassel, 1979).

Programs offered by schools to enhance the unique needs of gifted children may take various forms, as noted in the following examples (Pendarvis et al., 1990; Kansas State Department of Education, n.d.):

1. *General classroom enrichment.* Enriched programs are offered in general classes. In addition, an area of the classroom may be set aside for independent student activity. Emphasis should be on both content (e.g., facts) and process (e.g., ways in which information is acquired and how to conduct research).
2. *Accelerated curriculum.* An accelerated curriculum—that is, a faster paced presentation of standard material—is provided in a general education classroom, in a resource room, or in a special class.
3. *Curriculum compacting.* Students are assessed to determine their level of proficiency in an academic subject and then a plan is developed to help them master the remaining material.
4. *Self-designed or independent study courses and other enrichment opportunities.* Special courses, together with a study plan, can be designed by the student and supervised by the teacher. Students also can take after-school or weekend enrichment classes or attend specialized summer school classes.
5. *Pull-out groups.* Students are pulled out of the general education classroom and given specialized instruction.
6. *Subject acceleration.* Students are permitted to attend classes at more advanced grade levels (e.g., a first-grade student is permitted to take mathematics instruction with the third graders, or high-school students are permitted to take classes at institutions of higher learning).
7. *Receiving credit by examinations.* Students are permitted to obtain course credit by taking examinations without attending classes.
8. *Grade skipping.* Students are permitted to skip a grade.
9. *Early admission.* Students are permitted to enter school at an earlier age than the regulations require.
10. *Honors classes.* Special classes are offered that cover content at a more rapid pace and with greater depth than general education classes.
11. *Magnet schools.* Specialized schools offer advanced courses and programs in specific areas such as science, performing arts, languages, or computer science.
12. *Advanced placement (AP) programs.* These programs allow students to take college-level courses and examinations while in high school.

Table 19-5
Tips for Parents of Children Who Are Gifted

Teaching Your Child to Be a Productive and Positive Member of Society

1. Teach your child to accept students with diverse abilities. Everyone has value.
2. Involve your child in nonacademic activities that shape a child's life.
3. Teach your child to help others and make a positive contribution to the world.
4. Teach your child to respect other cultures, religions, and life styles.
5. Teach your child to respect teachers or other adults.
6. Teach your child that first impressions are important.
7. Model respect for others, honest communication, and personal accountability.
8. Discuss current events.
9. Encourage independence through responsible behavior.
10. Show your child how to effect change through positive action.

Nurturing Special Interests and Talents

1. Nurture your child's passions, strengths, interests, and creative forms of expression.
2. Make music and art a part of your life and your child's life.
3. Find a healthy balance between school and outside activities.

Nurturing a Positive Parent and Child Relationship

1. Value your child's individuality; even children who are gifted can be very different from one another.
2. Teach your child to be his or her best and not to make comparisons.
3. Know your child's friends.
4. Encourage open, two-way communication and really listen.
5. Know the difference between encouragement and support and "pushing."
6. Don't over-schedule your child.
7. Don't expect adult behavior from a child.
8. Never underestimate your child's potential for growth, but be reasonable.
9. Encourage your child to work hard and play hard.
10. Encourage a love of reading.
11. Connect your child to your family heritage.
12. Allow your child to fail and teach him or her that much can be learned through mistakes. Model "safe risk-taking."

13. Tolerate "safe" rebellion.
14. Offer choices rather than ultimatums.
15. Set clear and consistent expectations and consequences.
16. Always try to maintain a sense of humor.

Monitoring Your Child's Education

1. Know your child's teachers and whether they have high expectations and are willing to modify instruction for bright learners.
2. Volunteer for school activities unrelated to your child's specific needs.
3. Help organize curriculum-related field trips, guest speakers, and topic displays.
4. Offer supportive assistance to the teacher.
5. Participate on school committees involving gifted children.
6. Keep a home file of school documents and a portfolio of your child's work.
7. At home, help your child develop good study habits and time management skills.
8. Teach your child that on Monday through Friday, school receives top priority.
9. Teach your child how to "play the game" and work within the system without giving up creativity and individuality.
10. Ask for the school's assistance in career guidance and post-secondary planning for your high school student.
11. Start saving early for post-secondary education.

Navigating Your Child Through Life

1. Don't be intimidated by having a child who is gifted. You still need to be in charge.
2. Remember that a child who is gifted is often his or her own worst critic.
3. Let your child know that sometimes life is difficult and looking for help is okay.
4. Teach your child to seek more than one solution.
5. Teach your child that some failure is inevitable and acceptable.
6. Teach your child to challenge himself or herself.
7. Teach your child that alone time is not lonely time.
8. Teach your child that quality, not quantity, counts.
9. Enjoy your child who is gifted.

Note. Many of these suggestions pertain to children at all levels of ability.
Source: Adapted from Kansas State Department of Education (n.d.).
From *Assessment of Children: Behavioral, Social, and Clinical Foundations (Fifth Edition)* by Jerome M. Sattler and Robert D. Hoge. Copyright 2006 by Jerome M. Sattler, Publisher, Inc. Permission to photocopy this table is granted to purchasers of this book for personal use only (see copyright page for details).

---

13. *Internship, apprenticeship, or mentorship programs.* These programs expose students to specialized training and experiences in a career, interest, talent, or content area that usually is not available in the general school setting.

14. *International baccalaureate.* A program based in Switzerland offers advanced curricula options for gifted and talented students.

Gifted children who receive inappropriate placements may experience frustration and disappointment. A special placement should not be made without the approval of the child, the child's family, and the teacher.

The child and her or his family should be apprised of the special placement and why it is recommended. Keeping gifted children in regular classes with an unmodified curriculum may be acceptable if the children are not bored and can work on individual projects or do other activities to enhance their skills. This, however, should be a last resort, considered only when (a) the school district does not have the resources to offer special classes or other educational opportunities for the gifted and talented or (b) there are personal or family reasons for keeping a gifted child in a regular classroom (e.g., difficulty in getting the child to a special school or a need for the child to leave school at a certain time). However, we are doing a disservice to gifted children if we let them become bored and turned off by an unchallenging curriculum. As a nation, we cannot afford to lose our brightest and most talented youngsters because of inadequate school curricula (Robinson, Zigler, & Gallagher, 2000).

The simplest way to educate academically advanced children is to place them in existing classes at more advanced grade levels, based on the principle of *placement according to competence* (Robinson, 1980). Following this procedure ensures that gifted children receive an appropriate education. Correct placement also may enhance their zest for learning, reduce boredom in school, and enhance feelings of self-worth and accomplishment. Arguments that acceleration is harmful to children have proven to be without empirical foundation (Feldhusen, Proctor, & Black, 2002). The following case illustrates the application of the placement principle to a mathematically gifted adolescent (Robinson, 1980):

> A month after his tenth birthday, CB took the SAT in a regular administration and scored 600 Verbal and 680 Mathematical; a year later he raised these scores to 710 and 750, respectively. His IQ was estimated to be about 200. A Chinese-American youngster whose father is a professor of physics and whose mother has a master's degree in psychology, CB has two younger siblings who are also bright. He attended a private school in Baltimore, where he was given special educational opportunities. Although CB had only taken first-year high-school algebra (as a fifth grader), he had acquired by age 11 the subject matter of algebra II, algebra III, and plane geometry. Trigonometry took him a few weeks to learn, as did analytic geometry. At age 12, while his father was doing research using the linear accelerator at Stanford University, CB completed his high school career in Palo Alto while simultaneously taking a demanding calculus course at Stanford. When he was still 12 years old, CB entered Johns Hopkins with sophomore standing. He had been accepted at Harvard and Cal Tech as well. He received his baccalaureate at age 15, with a major in physics. (pp. 11–12, with changes in notation)

CREATIVITY

Creativity is a loosely defined, broad, complex, and multifaceted concept; it involves the *creative process,* defined as the production of novel and original content, and the *creative product,* defined as what stems from the creative process. Some creative productions improve on or extend existing ideas, whereas other creative productions move a field to a

completely new direction (Lubart, 2003). The relationship between creativity and intelligence is complicated by problems of measurement and definition. A reasonable hypothesis is that creativity is minimal at low levels of intelligence, whereas all levels of creativity are found at high levels of intelligence; however, only some children with IQs above 120 perform in a creative manner (Amabile, 1983; Runco, 1992). Intelligence appears to be a component of creativity—a necessary but not sufficient contributing factor. Some minimum level of intelligence is probably required for creative peformance. Most traditional intelligence tests do not assess creativity.

Individuals who are creative have been found to have both positive and negative traits (Csikszentmihalyi & Wolfe, 2000; Davis, 1997; Lubart, 2003; Welsh, 1975). On the positive side, they may be original, attracted to complexity, able to engage in divergent thinking, tolerant of ambiguity, open-minded, able to evaluate and revise their ideas, intuitive, independent, adventurous, spontaneous, energetic, curious, flexible, willing to take risks, willing to grow, or artistic. They may also show perseverance and have a sense of humor. On the negative side, they may be unstable, irresponsible, careless, disorderly, rebellious, uncontrolled, self-seeking, tactless, temperamental, emotional, unwilling to follow rules, uncooperative, impulsive, argumentative, and overactive physically and mentally.

Creative individuals know in what situations it is best to use their talents and when they need to apply their talents. It may take several years of study to acquire the knowledge needed to develop special talents (Eysenck, 1994). Because of the highly specialized knowledge and the amount of factual information needed to make a creative contribution, it would be difficult for any person in the 21st century to be creative in more than one field.

SUGGESTIONS FOR MAINTAINING AND ENHANCING CREATIVITY IN CHILDREN

The following suggestions are useful for encouraging creativity in children (Amabile, 1983):

AT SCHOOL

1. Teachers should create a stimulating learning environment.
2. Teachers should teach children to scan the environment for cues that might be relevant to problem solving.
3. Schools should provide children with special teachers, special materials, and the time and freedom to develop their talents when they show special aptitudes.
4. Schools should try to diminish peer pressures toward conformity by teaching highly talented children in special classes.
5. Teachers should allow some time in the classroom for individualized and self-directed learning in an informal atmosphere.

AT HOME

1. Parents should endorse appropriate socialization experiences by providing their children with nurturance and affectional bonds and displaying low levels of authoritarianism.

2. Parents should show respect for and confidence in their children, providing secure affection but allowing their children some independence from parental evaluation.

3. Parents should expose their children to models of creative achievement and encourage their children to go beyond the observed modeled behavior.

4. Parents should expose their children to cultural diversity throughout their development—through travel and other means—so as to enrich and elevate their capacity for creative behavior.

5. Parents should help their children appreciate the enjoyable aspects of their work, the inherent satisfaction in engaging in work activities, and the pleasure of watching their own work unfold; by so doing, parents may foster an appropriate work ethic.

6. Parents should help their children eliminate the strict dichotomy between work and play.

7. Parents should allow their children the freedom to choose which problems to approach, which materials and methods to use, and which subgoals to establish.

8. Parents should give their children as much latitude as possible in choosing their activities.

9. Parents should teach their children to be self-observant and to engage in self-evaluation in order to limit their dependence on external evaluation.

10. Parents should help their children develop high levels of self-determination and self-control.

AT SCHOOL AND AT HOME

1. Teachers and parents should be enthusiastic and supportive, and nurture creative processes in children who are nonconforming and unpredictable.

2. Teachers and parents should train children to identify and use the positive aspects of their own work and the work of others.

3. Teachers and parents should tailor reinforcements to the individual child's levels of interest and ability.

4. Teachers and parents should use tangible rewards sparingly, especially if they are given explicitly as payment for some activity; however, unusually high rewards, given as bonuses for performance, may enhance creativity.

5. Teachers and parents should stimulate interest level, particularly when a high level of intrinsic interest is not present initially. In such cases, it may be necessary to offer a reward to encourage the child to engage in the activity. As interest develops, rewards can be withdrawn or made less salient.

6. Teachers and parents should teach children to resist peer pressure to conform.

7. Teachers and parents should find alternative ways of educating children if formal education provides no opportunities for independent projects and leads to overreliance on established ways of thinking.

IDENTIFYING AND ASSESSING GIFTEDNESS AND CREATIVITY

Identifying and assessing giftedness are complicated because the concept is defined differently in different situations (Feldhusen & Jarwan, 2000; Hoge, 1988). Sometimes it is defined solely on the basis of intellectual aptitudes; other definitions include elements of creativity, task commitment, personality, and motivation. Assessment procedures will depend on the goals of the program.

The most effective means of identification combines the results of several kinds of measures—such as group intelligence tests, individual intelligence tests, achievement tests, and other tests—with information from teacher nominations, parent nominations, peer nominations, and self-nominations; school grades; ratings of creative products and accomplishments; and direct observations of children's behavior. The single best method available for identifying children with superior cognitive abilities is a standardized, individually administered, multidimensional test of intelligence, such as a Wechsler test or the Stanford-Binet: V. In practice, schools may give a group intelligence test (such as the Raven Progressive Matrices), rather than individual intelligence tests, to identify children eligible for a gifted program, because group tests are less costly to administer. Schools also are likely to evaluate achievement through group achievement tests.

Because giftedness is not a unitary concept, students should not be selected for a gifted program solely on the basis of high scores on a test that measures only one specific ability, such as receptive vocabulary or perceptual reasoning. A multidimensional cognitive ability test should be used as one component of the identification process.

Creativity is difficult to identify for the following reasons (Boden, 1994):

> Creativity is a puzzle, a paradox, some say a mystery. Inventors, scientists, and artists rarely know how their original ideas arise. They mention intuition, but cannot say how it works. Most psychologists cannot tell us much about it, either. What's more, many people assume that there will never be a scientific theory of creativity—for how could science possibly explain fundamental novelties? As if all this were not daunting enough, the apparent unpredictability of creativity seems to outlaw any systematic explanation, whether scientific or historical. (p. 75)

Still, psychologists and educators attempt to measure and assess creativity. Representative procedures used to measure creativity include the following: (a) Torrance Tests of Creativity (Torrance, 1966), (b) Wallach and Kogan tests, which include such tests as Instances, Alternate Uses, Pattern Meanings, and Line Meanings (Wallach & Kogan, 1965), (c) attitude and interest inventories, (d) personality inventories, (e) biographical inventories, (f) ratings of creativity by teachers, peers, supervisors, and parents, and (g) evaluations of actual achievements, such as publications, patent awards, and awards given by organizations.

The simplest and most straightforward method for identifying creativity is the last one listed above: *an inventory of creative achievements and activities* (Hocevar, 1981). Examples of creative achievements and activities include placing first, second, or third in a science contest; exhibiting or performing a work of art; publishing poems, stories, or articles in a newspaper; inventing a patentable or useful device; and

acting in plays. Table 19-6 shows a checklist for rating creative traits in children.

Measures of ideational fluency, which are included in the Torrance tests and the Wallach and Kogan tests, also are useful in identifying creativity (see Chapter 24, Table 24-15, for measures of ideational fluency). Ideational fluency tests, which involve coming up with imaginative verbal or nonverbal responses or productive ideas, measure divergent thinking (Eysenck, 1994). Divergent-thinking problems—for example, "What are some uses for a rock?"—have several possible

---

Table 19-6
Checklist for Identifying Children Who Are Creative

CHECKLIST FOR IDENTIFYING CHILDREN WHO ARE CREATIVE

Child's name: _____   Rater: _____

Sex: _____   Grade:_____   Class: _____   Date:_____

Rating scale:	1	2	3	4	5
	Not present	Minimally present	Somewhat present	Moderately present	Strongly present

Characteristic	Rating (Circle one number)	Characteristic	Rating (Circle one number)
1. Ability to concentrate	1 2 3 4 5	19. Imagination, insight	1 2 3 4 5
2. Ability to defer judgment	1 2 3 4 5	20. Independence	1 2 3 4 5
3. Ability to see that solutions generate new problems	1 2 3 4 5	21. Internal locus of control and evaluation	1 2 3 4 5
4. Above-average IQ	1 2 3 4 5	22. Inventiveness	1 2 3 4 5
5. Adaptability	1 2 3 4 5	23. Lack of tolerance for boredom	1 2 3 4 5
6. Aesthetic appreciation	1 2 3 4 5	24. Need for supportive climate	1 2 3 4 5
7. Attraction to the complex and mysterious	1 2 3 4 5	25. Nonconformism	1 2 3 4 5
8. Commitment to a task	1 2 3 4 5	26. Openness to experience	1 2 3 4 5
9. Curiosity	1 2 3 4 5	27. Playfulness	1 2 3 4 5
10. Delight in beauty of theory	1 2 3 4 5	28. Self-confidence	1 2 3 4 5
11. Delight in invention for its own sake	1 2 3 4 5	29. Sense of identity as originator	1 2 3 4 5
12. Desire to share products and ideas	1 2 3 4 5	30. Sense of mission	1 2 3 4 5
13. Eagerness to resolve disorder	1 2 3 4 5	31. Sensitivity	1 2 3 4 5
14. Extensive knowledge background	1 2 3 4 5	32. Spontaneity	1 2 3 4 5
15. Flexibility	1 2 3 4 5	33. Tolerance for ambiguity and conflict	1 2 3 4 5
16. Good memory, attention to detail	1 2 3 4 5	34. Willingness to face social ostracism	1 2 3 4 5
17. High energy level, enthusiasm	1 2 3 4 5	35. Willingness to daydream and fantasize	1 2 3 4 5
18. Humor (perhaps bizarre)	1 2 3 4 5	36. Willingness to take risks	1 2 3 4 5

Source: Characteristics obtained from Ford and Ford (1981).
From *Assessment of Children: Behavioral, Social, and Clinical Foundations (Fifth Edition)* by Jerome M. Sattler and Robert D. Hoge. Copyright 2006 by Jerome M. Sattler, Publisher, Inc. Permission to photocopy this table is granted to purchasers of this book for personal use only (see copyright page for details).

answers. Scoring for divergent-thinking problems can be both quantitative (the number of responses, also referred to as *ideational fluency*) and qualitative (the unusualness or usefulness of the responses). In contrast, convergent-thinking problems—for example, "What number comes after 1, 4, 7, 10, 13?"—usually have only one correct answer and can be scored only quantitatively.

Tests designed to measure creativity have several potential shortcomings (Cohen, 2003; Eysenck, 1994). They may be influenced by extraneous factors such as boredom or the type of classroom instruction received by the child; fail to measure the quality of the responses; have limited construct validity, failing to predict creative production; fail to measure motivation or task commitment; have subjective scoring procedures that rely on arbitrary criteria rather than meaningful criteria such as novelty, appropriateness, or satisfyingness; fail to correlate with other measures of creativity; or restrict the meaning of originality because of the heavy influence of verbal fluency on originality scores.

What little common variance tests of creativity have with each other may be accounted for by *g,* the general intelligence factor. Some tests of creativity measure cognitive abilities not reliably distinguished from intelligence, whereas others measure attributes different from those measured on intelligence tests. Although many creativity tests do measure abilities and dispositions probably important for creative performance, it is inappropriate to label the results of creativity tests "as directly indicative of some global quality that can be called creativity . . . such judgments can ultimately only be subjective" (Amabile, 1983, p. 26).

GIFTED AND TALENTED EVALUATION SCALES

The Gifted and Talented Evaluation Scales (GATES; Gilliam, Carpenter, & Christensen, 1996) for identifying gifted and talented students are appropriate for parent and teacher ratings of children 5 to 18 years. The GATES has five scales: Intellectual Ability, Academic Skills, Creativity, Leadership, and Artistic Talent. Each scale takes about 5 to 10 minutes to complete.

Scores

Items on the GATES are scored on a 9-point scale ranging from below average to above average. Raw scores are converted to standard scores ($M = 100$, $SD = 15$) and percentile ranks.

Standardization

The GATES was standardized on 1,083 children ages 5 to 18 years, identified by teachers as gifted and talented. The sample matched the 1990 U.S. Census norms for ethnicity, race, geographic region, SES, and type of school attended. Norms are not presented separately by age or gender.

Reliability

Internal consistency reliabilities for the five GATES scales based on samples of gifted and talented students ($N = 400$) and average students ($N = 210$) range from .95 to .97 ($Mdn\ r_{xx} = .96$). Test-retest reliabilities over a 1-week interval for the five scales range from .70 to .87 ($Mdn\ r_{tt} = .78$) for a sample of gifted and talented students ($N = 17$), from .69 to .87 ($Mdn\ r_{tt} = .80$) for a sample of average students ($N = 33$), and from .93 to .98 ($Mdn\ r_{tt} = .95$) for a sample of students with disabilities ($N = 14$).

Validity

The construct validity of the GATES is supported by significant correlations between scale scores and parallel scores from three alternative measures of gifted and talented potential: the Renzulli-Hartman Scale, the Creativity Assessment Packet, and the Comprehensive Scales of Student Abilities. Construct validity is also supported in analyses showing that GATES scores significantly discriminate between groups of gifted and average students identified within school systems.

Comment on the GATES

The GATES is an easily administered and scored screening instrument for identifying gifted and talented students. It has good reliability and adequate validity and is useful as part of a comprehensive assessment of gifted and talented students. However, it would benefit from having norms based on age and gender.

THINKING THROUGH THE ISSUES

1. Develop a procedure that you believe would be useful in identifying gifted children, and compare it to the procedures used in your school district. How would your procedure be useful in identifying gifted children who also are underachievers, physically or neurologically handicapped, or culturally different?

2. How can we increase children's creativity at home and at school?

SUMMARY

1. Children are generally referred to as gifted and talented if they are outstanding in an area—for example, have an extremely high IQ (above 130, which represents the 99th percentile rank), display unusual artistic or musical talent, or achieve high scores on tests of creativity.

2. Gifted and talented children include those with demonstrated achievement or potential ability in any of the following areas: general intellectual ability, specific academic aptitude, creative or productive thinking, leadership ability, or visual and performing arts.

Intellectual and Personality Characteristics of Gifted Children

3. "Gifted elementary or secondary age children . . . show some advantages over other students particularly in quantity, speed, and complexity of cognition. They know more about metacognition and can use strategies better in new contexts, but they may not use a wider variety of metacognitive strategies than other students. . . . Gifted students . . . tend to have better psychosocial adjustment than other students" (Robinson & Clinkenbeard, 1998, pp. 129–130).

Gifted Children Who Are Underachieving

4. Intellectual giftedness does not ensure success in school.
5. The academic success of gifted children is determined by the same environmental forces that affect the success of all children—namely, motivation, interests, self-concept, family and home, teachers and school, peers, and society.
6. The characteristics most frequently found among underachieving students who are gifted are low self-esteem and a low sense of personal control over their own lives.
7. Underachieving students who are gifted may have complex behavior patterns that are not easily amenable to intervention, especially if their behavior patterns have been established over a long period of childhood.
8. To reverse longstanding patterns of underachievement, (a) assess the child, (b) obtain information from the parents and teachers about the child, (c) change the expectations of the child, parents, teachers, peers, and siblings about the child's ability to succeed in school, (d) provide role models for the child, (e) correct skill deficiencies, and (f) modify reinforcements used at home and at school.

Gifted Children Who Have Learning Disabilities

9. Some gifted children have specific learning disabilities that interfere with their ability to learn in school.
10. In the early grades, gifted children with a learning disability usually are able to compensate for their disability and show only minor problems, such as failing to do their written assignments. However, in the secondary grades, they may no longer be able to compensate for their disability as the task demands increase.
11. Gifted children with a learning disability may show an uneven pattern of strengths and weaknesses on psychoeducational tests.
12. What is especially important is that gifted children not be labeled as "unmotivated" or "inattentive" when it is their learning disability that is interfering with their ability to master the school curriculum.

Gifted Children Who Have Emotional Problems

13. The incidence of emotional problems is likely to be about the same among gifted children and children who are not gifted.

14. When gifted children challenge authority, respond in unconventional ways, or have limited tolerance for frustration, they may be classified by teachers as emotionally disturbed.

Preschool Gifted Children

15. Preschool gifted children tend to be more precocious in memory than in general intelligence, reading achievement, or spatial reasoning.
16. The academic abilities of preschool gifted children show diverse skill patterns. However, the early acquisition of advanced academic skills may not be related to level of intelligence. Some preschool children with IQs above 160 have not mastered reading or arithmetic, whereas others with IQs of 116 are fluent readers by the age of 3 years.
17. Preschool gifted children show a wide range of personality characteristics and levels of social maturity.
18. In identifying the abilities of preschool gifted children, you may need to use tests that did not include their age range in the standardization group.

Terman's and Lovell and Shields's Studies of Gifted Individuals

19. An extensive longitudinal study by Terman followed a sample of 1,528 children who were gifted (857 males and 671 females), from the time they were approximately 11 years old through adulthood. The children's IQs on the Stanford-Binet Intelligence Scale: 1916 Form ranged from 135 to 200, and their IQs on group tests were 135 and above.
20. In comparison with a control group of children, the children who were gifted were physically healthier; superior in reading, arithmetical reasoning, and information, but not in computation and spelling; more interested in abstract subjects (literature, debating, dramatics, and history); and less interested in practical subjects (penmanship, manual training, drawing, and painting).
21. Teachers rated this sample of gifted children as above the mean of the control group on intellectual, volitional, emotional, aesthetic, moral, physical, and social traits. In only one area—mechanical ingenuity—were the children who were gifted rated slightly below the children in the control group.
22. A similar but less extensive study that was carried out in England showed similar findings.

Promoting Psychosocial Adjustment in Gifted Children

23. The 12 guidelines presented in this section of the text will assist you in promoting the psychosocial adjustment of gifted children.

Educating Gifted Children

24. Gifted children need instructional programs commensurate with their abilities.
25. Ideally, the programs should enable them to operate cognitively and affectively at complex levels of thought and feeling and to learn critical thinking skills, creative thinking skills, research methodology skills, problem-solving skills, decision-making skills, and leadership skills.
26. Programs that schools can offer include general classroom enrichment; accelerated curriculum; curriculum compacting; self-designed or independent study courses and other enrichment

opportunities; pull-out groups; subject acceleration; receiving credit by examinations; grade skipping; early admission; honors classes; magnet schools; AP programs; internship, apprenticeship, or mentorship programs; and international baccalaureate.

27. Gifted children who receive inappropriate placements may experience frustration and disappointment.

28. The simplest way to educate academically advanced children is to place them in existing classes at more advanced grade levels, based on the principle of placement according to competence.

Creativity

29. Creativity is a loosely defined, broad, complex, and multifaceted concept; it involves the creative process, defined as the production of novel and original content, and the creative product, defined as what stems from the creative process.

30. A reasonable hypothesis is that creativity is minimal at low levels of intelligence, whereas all levels of creativity are found at high levels of intelligence; however, only some children with IQs above 120 perform in a creative manner.

31. Individuals who are creative have been found to have both positive and negative traits.

32. Creative individuals know in what situations it is best to use their talents and when they need to apply their talents.

Suggestions for Maintaining and Enhancing Creativity in Children

33. Creativity in children can be enhanced many ways, including creating a stimulating teaching environment, using effective teaching methods, diminishing peer influences for conformity, and allowing self-directed learning.

34. At home, creativity can be enhanced by endorsing appropriate socialization experiences, showing respect for children, exposing children to models of creativity and cultural diversity, helping children develop an appropriate work ethic, allowing children to select problems to work on, giving children choices, teaching children to be self-observant, and helping children develop high levels of self-determination.

35. At school and at home, teachers and parents should be enthusiastic and supportive, train children to identify and use the positive aspects of their own work and the work of others, tailor reinforcements to the individual child's levels of interest and ability, use tangible rewards sparingly, stimulate interest level, teach the children to resist peer pressure to conform, and find alternative ways of educating the children if formal education provides no opportunities for independent projects.

Identifying and Assessing Giftedness and Creativity

36. Identifying and assessing giftedness are complicated because the concept is defined differently in different situations.

37. Sometimes it is defined solely on the basis intellectual aptitudes; other definitions include elements of creativity, task commitment, personality, and motivation.

38. The most effective means of identification combines the results of several kinds of measures—such as group intelligence tests, individual intelligence tests, achievement tests, other tests—with information from teacher nominations, parent nominations, peer nominations, and self-nominations; school grades; ratings of creative products and accomplishments; and direct observations of the child's behavior.

39. The single best method available for identifying children with superior cognitive abilities is a standardized, individually administered, multidimensional test of intelligence.

40. In practice, schools may give a group intelligence test, rather than individual intelligence tests, to identify children eligible for a gifted program, because group tests are less costly to administer.

41. Because giftedness is not a unitary concept, students should not be selected for a gifted program solely on the basis of high scores on a test that measures only one specific ability, such as receptive vocabulary or perceptual reasoning ability.

42. Creativity is difficult to identify.

43. Representative procedures used to measure creativity include the following: (a) Torrance Tests of Creativity, (b) Wallach and Kogan tests, which include such tests as Instances, Alternate Uses, Pattern Meanings, and Line Meanings, (c) attitude and interest inventories, (d) personality inventories, (e) biographical inventories, (f) ratings of creativity by teachers, peers, supervisors, and parents, and (g) evaluations of actual achievements, such as publications, patent awards, and awards given by organizations.

44. The simplest and most straightforward method for identifying creativity is the last one listed above: an inventory of creative achievements and activities.

45. Measures of ideational fluency, which are included in the Torrance tests and the Wallach and Kogan tests, also are useful in identifying creativity.

46. Tests designed to measure creativity have several potential shortcomings. They may be influenced by extraneous factors such as boredom or the type of classroom instruction received by the child; fail to measure the quality of the responses; have limited construct validity, failing to predict creative production; fail to measure motivation or task commitment; have subjective scoring procedures that rely on arbitrary criteria rather than meaningful criteria such as novelty, appropriateness, or satisfyingness; fail to correlate with other measures of creativity; or restrict the meaning of originality because of the heavy influence of verbal fluency on originality scores.

47. What little common variance tests of creativity have with each other may be accounted for by *g*, the general intelligence factor.

Gifted and Talented Evaluation Scales

48. The GATES is an easily administered and scored screening instrument for identifying gifted and talented students. It has good reliability and adequate validity and is useful as part of a comprehensive assessment of gifted and talented students. However, it would benefit from having norms based on age and gender.

KEY TERMS, CONCEPTS, AND NAMES

Gifted and talented children (p. 449)
Intellectual and personality characteristics of gifted children (p. 449)
Gifted children who are underachieving (p. 451)
Gifted children who have learning disabilities (p. 451)
Gifted children who have emotional problems (p. 452)
Preschool gifted children (p. 452)

STUDY QUESTIONS

1. Discuss the definition of gifted and talented children, and then describe the intellectual and personality characteristics of gifted children.

2. Discuss children who are gifted and underachieving, children who are gifted and have learning disabilities, and children who are gifted and have emotional problems.
3. Discuss preschool gifted children.
4. Discuss Terman's and Lovell and Shields's studies of the gifted.
5. Explain how you would go about promoting psychosocial adjustment in gifted children.
6. Discuss educating gifted children.
7. Define creativity, and then discuss the positive and negative traits associated with individuals who are creative.
8. How would you go about maintaining and enhancing creativity in children?
9. How would you go about identifying and assessing gifted and creative children?

20

VISUAL IMPAIRMENTS

by Jerome M. Sattler and Carol Anne Evans

Have you ever been at sea in a dense fog, when it seemed as if a tangible white darkness shut you in, and the great ship, tense and anxious, groped her way toward the shore with plummet and sounding-line, and you waited with beating heart for something to happen? I was like that ship before my education began, only I was without compass or sounding-line, and had no way of knowing how near the harbour was.

—Helen Keller, American author, lecturer, and blind and deaf activist (1880–1968)

Goals and Objectives

This chapter is designed to enable you to do the following:

- Understand how to evaluate children with visual impairments
- Understand how to develop interventions for children with visual impairments

Children with visual impairments have conditions that range from limited vision to no vision at all. In this chapter we use the phrase "children with visual impairments" to refer to those who are blind and those who have low vision of varying degrees. Any type of serious vision loss can affect children's ability to process information. Vision helps in (a) identifying the qualities, attributes, colors, shapes, and other features of objects, (b) acquiring concepts related to space, distance, relationships, sizes, and other attributes of spatial relations, and (c) integrating disparate elements into a more coherent whole, or gestalt. Key variables in understanding visual impairments are the type, severity, etiology, and age of onset of the visual impairment. Several disorders that affect vision are congenital; others are acquired through an accident, injury, or illness. Congenital etiologies account for over 50% of visual impairments in children, and impairments with congenital etiologies frequently are associated with developmental disabilities, such as cerebral palsy (Flanagan, Jackson, & Hill, 2003; Freedman, Feinstein, & Berger, 1988). However, about 90% of children with visual impairments retain some vision (Kelley, Sanspree, & Davidson, 2000).

Children who have recently lost all or part of their vision will need to adjust to their visual loss and learn to use adaptive strategies and compensatory devices. For many of the conditions causing low vision there are no medical or surgical treatments; rather, visual functioning may be improved by optical aids and teaching of visual efficiency skills. Children with the same etiology may have varied functional vision depending on their visual experiences, intervention history, and level of cognitive development.

In the 2000–2001 school year, the percentage of children aged 6 to 21 years served under the Individuals with Disabilities Education Act (IDEA) because of visual impairments was .45% (25,975; U.S. Department of Education, 2002). This number is probably an underestimate because children with multiple disabilities including a visual impairment may be classified under a disability category other than visual impairment.

IDEA 2004 (Sec. 614, 3B, iii) emphasizes teaching Braille to blind or visually impaired children unless it is not appropriate to do so. The nationwide shortage of credentialed teachers of the visually impaired who are qualified to teach Braille means that this provision may be difficult to implement. Technologies for accessing print, including video magnification and auditory materials, blur the distinction between those who should use Braille and those who should use print. Some children with visual impairments may use both Braille and print, choosing one or the other for different tasks and under different circumstances. For example, Braille is used on elevator buttons, automatic teller buttons, room numbers, and other items. Whether they select Braille or print as their primary reading medium, children with visual impairments often will benefit from the use of auditory materials. Auditory materials should supplement, not substitute for, the reading of Braille or print, because Braille and print provide students with a better appreciation of the structure of language (Martelle, 1999).

IDEA 2004 (Sec. 674) also requires that a National Instructional Materials Access Center be established and supported by the American Printing House for the Blind (a) to provide access to printed materials useful for visually impaired or blind children, (b) to receive and maintain a catalog of print instructional materials, and (c) to develop procedures to protect against copyright infringement, with respect to the print instructional materials provided under the law. Implementing these and other provisions of IDEA 2004, as well as providing adequate funding, will assure that children with visual impairments receive the services they need to enhance their well being and to become productive members of society.

CLUES TO POTENTIAL VISUAL DIFFICULTIES

Of all the organs, the eye is the most fully developed at birth. Following are signs of potential visual difficulties that can be observed in infants and older children (Orel-Bixler, 2003):

INFANTS

1. Lack of eye contact by 3 months
2. Lack of visual fixation or following by 3 months
3. Lack of accurate reaching for objects by 6 months
4. Persistent failure of the eyes to move in concert or sustained crossing of one eye after about 4 months
5. Frequent horizontal or vertical jerky eye movements (nystagmus)
6. Lack of a clear black pupil (haziness of the cornea, a whitish appearance inside the pupil, or a significant asymmetry in the "red eye" effect in a flash photograph)
7. Persistent tearing when the infant is not crying
8. Significant sensitivity to bright light (photophobia)
9. Persistent redness of the normally white conjunctiva
10. Drooping of an eyelid sufficient to obscure the pupil
11. Any asymmetry of pupil size
12. Any obvious abnormalities of the shape or structure of the eyes

OLDER CHILDREN

1. Rubs eyes excessively
2. Shuts or covers one eye, tilts head, or thrusts head forward
3. Has difficulty reading or doing close visual work
4. Blinks excessively or is irritable when doing close visual work
5. Complains of tiredness, dizziness, headaches, or nausea following close visual work
6. Moves head excessively when reading
7. Holds books too close to or too far from eyes
8. Is inconsistent in reading print at different distances (e.g., is able to read a book but not material written on the blackboard or vice versa)
9. Is unable to see distant objects or near objects clearly
10. Squints or frowns when using eyes

11. Loses place while reading, skips words or lines of print, or keeps place with finger
12. Has poor sitting posture while reading (e.g., places face too close to a book)
13. Walks overcautiously or runs into objects not directly in line of vision
14. Has difficulty judging distances
15. Has crossed eyes
16. Has jerky eye movements
17. Has red-rimmed, encrusted, or swollen eyelids
18. Has inflamed or watery eyes
19. Has recurring sties
20. Reports that eyes itch, burn, or feel scratchy
21. Reports that he or she cannot see well
22. Reports blurred or double vision
23. Reports spots before eyes
24. Reports that lights bother him or her when reading
25. Reports that eyes are tired after reading
26. Attends to the left side of space and neglects the right (or vice versa)

If any of these signs are present in an infant or a child, he or she should be referred for a visual examination to an optometrist or ophthalmologist. We recommend that formal screening of visual acuity occur by the age of 5 years, or before children enter school. School screenings are not sufficient because they usually address only distance acuity and fail to evaluate near vision, binocular coordination, eye movement skills, focusing skills, peripheral awareness, eye/hand coordination, and other aspects of vision.

STRUCTURE OF THE EYE

The structure of the eye can be likened to that of a simple camera. An opening at the front allows light to enter. The light travels through the cornea, the aqueous humor, the lens, and the vitreous body until it reaches the retina. Let's review the main structures of the eye.

1. The *cornea* is the dome-shaped transparent portion of the front of the eye that allows light into the eye.
2. The *aqueous humor* is the clear, watery fluid that fills the anterior chamber between the cornea and the iris and the lens.
3. The *iris* is the colored part of the eye in front of the lens. It controls the size of the pupil and thereby the amount of light that enters the eye.
4. The *pupil* is the opening in the iris, analogous to the shutter of a camera. It dilates (opens wider) in dim light to allow more light to enter the eye and constricts (reduces in size) in bright light to limit the amount of light entering the eye.
5. The *lens,* or *crystalline lens,* is the clear biconvex body that focuses light on the retina and accommodates (changes shape when pulled by tiny muscles) to allow focusing on both distant and near targets.
6. The *vitreous humor* is the clear, gelatinous mass that fills the posterior chamber of the eye between the lens and the retina.
7. The *retina* is the part of the eye, analogous to the film in a camera, that turns light into electrical signals.
8. The *cones* are the cells located in the center of the retina (in areas known as the macula and the fovea) that are most sensitive in bright light. They are responsible for sharp central vision (such as that used for reading and close work) and for color vision.
9. The *rods* are the cells located in the periphery of the retina that are most sensitive in low light. They are responsible for sensing motion, for perceiving objects in the periphery of the visual field, and for helping us avoid bumping into obstacles in the environment.

DISORDERS THAT AFFECT VISION

Vision can be impaired by refractive errors, central visual field defects, peripheral visual field defects, whole visual field defects, and other conditions. Let's look at each of these errors and defects.

Refractive Errors

The following three conditions result from refractive errors (errors in the way light travels to the retina, caused by irregularities in one of the structures of the eye). Refractive errors are usually correctable to normal with corrective lenses (i.e., glasses or contact lenses).

- In *astigmatism,* irregular curvature of the cornea or lens causes distorted or blurred vision.
- In *hyperopia,* or farsightedness, the eyeball is too short or the shape of the lens or cornea is such that the focal point for light entering the eye is behind the retina rather than directly on it. The individual can see objects that are distant, but has difficulty focusing on near targets.
- In *myopia,* or nearsightedness, the eyeball is too long or the shape of the lens or cornea is such that the focal point for light entering the eye is in front of the retina rather than directly on it. The individual can see objects that are near, but has difficulty focusing on distant targets.

Central Visual Field Defects

The central portion of the retina (the macula and the fovea) contains mostly cones, specialized light-sensitive cells (called photoreceptors) that provide sharp central vision and color vision. Three conditions that result in vision loss in the central visual field are achromatopsia, diabetic retinopathy, and juvenile macular degeneration.

- *Achromatopsia* is a genetically transmitted disorder that impairs the cones at the center of the retina, causing color blindness, poor visual acuity, and extreme sensitivity to bright light. Devices that reduce the intensity of visual stimulation (e.g., visors and sunglasses) can increase comfort and improve visual function.

- *Diabetic retinopathy* is an acquired disease, associated with diabetes, that affects the retina. Symptoms include blurred vision and, in advanced cases, bleeding from blood vessels in the back of the eye. The condition eventually can lead to blindness. Laser surgery can sometimes prevent and/or reduce loss of vision or slow its progression.

- *Juvenile macular degeneration* (Stargardt's disease) is a genetically transmitted disorder, affecting the cones at the center of the retina, that becomes evident during mid- to late childhood. The photoreceptors of the macula malfunction and eventually die, causing gradual decline and loss of central vision but leaving peripheral vision intact. Currently, there is no cure for the condition, but visual function can be improved through the use of optical aids and teaching more effective use of low vision abilities, and degeneration may be slowed down by protecting the eye from bright light (Hammer, 2002).

Peripheral Visual Field Defects

The peripheral portion of the retina contains mostly rods, photoreceptors that provide peripheral vision and the ability to see objects in dim light. Glaucoma and retinitis pigmentosa are two progressive disorders that result in loss of vision in the peripheral portion of the visual field, causing mobility problems; in their initial stages, they leave central vision intact.

- *Glaucoma* is a progressive condition in which the pressure inside the eye increases because of excessive production of or inability to drain aqueous humor (fluid), causing damage to the optic nerve. Glaucoma may be congenital (caused by a recessive gene) or acquired (caused by any of several illnesses). Some types of glaucoma can be treated and controlled with surgery or medication, but not cured. People with glaucoma are at risk for blindness.

- *Retinitis pigmentosa* is a genetically transmitted, progressive disorder resulting in degeneration and atrophy of the rods at the periphery of the retina. First comes loss of night vision. Following are several stages of "tunnel vision" as peripheral field vision decreases. Eventually the entire retina becomes involved and the individual becomes blind. The rate of progression is variable, with some individuals progressing to near total blindness in childhood and others retaining a relatively functional central field of vision into their retirement years. Research is exploring ways of slowing the progress of the disease.

Whole Visual Field Defects

The following are examples of disorders that can cause general visual loss across the whole visual field.

- *Albinism* is an inherited condition in which there a deficiency of pigmentation in the skin, hair, or eyes (i.e., little or no melanin is formed). Lack of pigmentation in the iris and retina causes extreme sensitivity to bright light and significant reduction in visual acuity. Albinism varies in severity; in some individuals it is restricted to the eyes, and pigmentation in the skin and hair is relatively normal. Visual function may be improved by reducing illumination.

- *Aniridia* is a congenital absence of the iris that prevents regulation of the amount of light entering the eye, causing extreme sensitivity to bright light and a significant reduction in visual acuity. Children with aniridia are at risk for developing glaucoma. As in albinism, visual function may be improved by reducing illumination through the use of visors, tinted lenses, and soft contact lenses with a dark periphery that act as artificial irises.

- *Cataracts* are congenital or acquired opacities of the lens that prevent light and images from entering the eye. Most cataracts can be removed surgically. Following removal of the cataracts, intraocular lenses may be implanted and lenses prescribed for reading and/or distance vision.

- *Retinoblastoma* is a rare, but life-threatening, malignant tumor of the retina that may be transmitted genetically or may result from a spontaneous mutation. Most cases are diagnosed before the age of 4 years. Large tumors are treated by enucleation (removal) of the more severely affected eye if the cancer is present in both eyes; smaller tumors may be treated by radiation, cryotherapy (freezing), laser therapy, or chemotherapy. Visual functioning in the remaining eye may be improved through the use of low-vision devices. Those who have had retinoblastoma in childhood are at higher than normal risk of secondary cancers later in life (Finger, 1998).

- *Retinopathy of prematurity* is a disorder in which blood vessels in the back of the eye develop abnormally in premature infants. In severe cases, the blood vessels may bleed and lead to a detached retina, causing vision loss. "The main risk factor for developing retinopathy of prematurity is extreme prematurity; high oxygen levels in the blood from the treatment of breathing problems may increase the risk" (Berkow, 1997, p. 1207). Treatments include freezing the peripheral portions of the retina and use of lasers.

Other Conditions That May Affect Vision

Following are examples of other conditions that may affect vision.

- *Amblyopia,* or "lazy eye," is a disorder characterized by blurry vision that is not correctable with glasses in an eye that is otherwise normal. The disorder results from either no transmission or poor transmission of the visual image to the brain for a sustained period during childhood. It usually affects one eye only. If the condition persists, the weaker eye may become severely impaired. Early detection and treatment are essential. Treatment options include covering the stronger eye for periods of time with a patch to force the weak eye to develop good vision (or using eye drops in the stronger eye to blur vision), having the child wear glasses or contact lenses, and surgery.

- *Cortical visual impairment* refers to damage to the visual cortex or posterior visual pathways of the brain. The damage can occur in conjunction with neurological insults, such as *hypoxia* (insufficient oxygen) or *anoxia* (no oxygen) during birth, premature birth, cerebral palsy (sometimes caused by *in utero* stroke), infections of the central nervous system (meningitis, encephalitis), or traumatic brain injury (near drowning, a motor vehicle accident, a gunshot wound, etc.). Some children with cortical visual impairment benefit from stimulation activities to increase their visual awareness.

- *Fetal alcohol syndrome* is associated with several neurological and learning deficits, which sometimes include vision loss. Treatment consists of vision stimulation, use of optical aids, and teaching more effective use of low-vision abilities.

- *Optic nerve atrophy* (a wasting away of the axons) is a permanent visual impairment caused by damage to the optic nerve. Conditions that may lead to optic nerve atrophy include tumors of the visual pathways, inadequate blood or oxygen supply at birth, trauma, hydrocephalus, or rare degenerative diseases; optic nerve atrophy can also result from a genetic abnormality. Although there is no cure, visual functioning can be improved by increasing the size, contrast, and lighting of material, presenting materials in the child's visual field, and developing the child's depth perception through fine- and gross-motor activities.

- *Optic nerve hypoplasia* refers to the underdevelopment of the optic nerve during the early prenatal developmental period. It can result in mild to serious visual impairment in the form of decreased visual acuity and visual field, in addition to abnormal sensitivity to light and nystagmus. The condition also may be associated with midline brain defects and endocrine deficits. In most cases there is no known cause or cure. However, visual functioning can be enhanced by use of high levels of illumination and enlarged print with high contrast magnification.

- *Toxoplasmosis* is caused by a parasite contracted by the mother and passed to the developing fetus. It can result in vision loss, hearing loss, hydrocephalus, or mental retardation. Treatment consists of using various drugs, including corticosteroids used to reduce inflammation of the heart, lungs, or eyes. Primary prevention techniques are important to reduce the spread of the parasite (e.g., meats should be cooked thoroughly, hands and cooking utensils should be washed thoroughly after raw meat is prepared, fruit and vegetables should be washed thoroughly to remove all traces of soil, expectant mothers should not handle cat litter).

Many eye conditions (as well as disorders of the central nervous system) may be accompanied by *nystagmus*—rapid, involuntary, repeated oscillations of one or both eyes in any or all fields of vision. The eyes may move together or separately, reducing the ability to maintain steady fixation on a visual target. Individuals with nystagmus may require more time to complete visual tasks. To increase their ability to focus, they may turn their heads and tilt their faces to find a gaze position (called the null point) that reduces movements.

CLARITY OF VISION

Although their visual acuity or their visual field may be diminished, children with visual impairments usually have some useful vision. Children with mild or moderate visual loss still may use vision as their primary learning channel. Some rely solely on their low residual vision, with varying results. Children with severe to profound visual loss, however, need tactile and auditory sensory input to obtain information, in addition to using whatever residual vision is available to them.

Clarity of vision is defined in terms of *visual acuity.* Berkow (1997) explains the system for expressing visual acuity as follows: "As acuity decreases, vision becomes progressively blurred. Acuity is usually measured on a scale that compares a person's vision at 20 feet with that of someone who has full acuity. Thus, a person who has 20/20 vision sees objects 20 feet away with complete clarity, but a person who has 20/200 vision sees at 20 feet what a person with full acuity sees at 200 feet" (p. 1027).

Visual acuity is measured on a continuum from normal vision to blindness.

1. Normal vision is acuity of 20/20.
2. Mild low vision is acuity of 20/70.
3. Moderate low vision is acuity of 20/200.
4. Severe low vision is acuity of 20/400.
5. Profound low vision is acuity lower than 20/400.
6. Total blindness refers to no light perception at all.

Visual acuity that is too limited to be described by the fraction 20/400 but that is still not total blindness is designated by one of the following terms:

1. CF (counts fingers)—has the ability to count fingers at a specified distance
2. HM (hand motion)—has the ability to see hand motion at a specified distance
3. LP (light perception)—has the ability to detect light
4. LP&P (light perception and projection)—has the ability to detect the direction from which light is coming

Individuals with profound vision loss can still perceive some objects in the environment and have some vision for use in daily living and travel. For example, a person who has profound low vision and is considered functionally blind may use Braille for reading and writing and mobility devices for travel in the environment, but he or she may be able to maintain orientation in travel through a corridor when there are windows on one side. The medical report of a person with no light perception may indicate that vision is *NLP* or *nil.*

Blindness refers to vision loss that is total or sight that is so impaired that the individual primarily uses senses other than vision for obtaining information and for interacting with the environment. Blindness occurs when "(a) light can't reach the retina, (b) light rays don't focus properly on the retina, (c) the retina can't sense light rays normally, (d) the nerve impulses from the retina aren't transmitted to the brain normally, or (e) the brain can't interpret information sent by the eye" (Berkow, 1997, p. 1028, with changes in notation). People who are blind may still be able to distinguish shapes and shadows, but not normal visual detail. Reading is accomplished by using Braille supplemented with auditory materials (e.g., recorded speech or speech synthesized by a computer). Travel in the environment is managed by the use of a long cane or guide dog. Children who are blind need training by credentialed teachers of the visually impaired and by orientation and mobility specialists to master these specialized aids and skills.

Legal blindness is defined as corrected distance visual acuity of less than 20/200 in the better eye or a visual field of 20° or less (a normal field is close to 180°) in the better eye. This is the definition used to determine eligibility for certain government benefits. Children who are referred to as "legally" blind still have useful vision. Because the term "legal blindness" does not mean total blindness, it can be misleading for understanding how a child sees. If you use the term, also report the child's level of useful visual function.

DEVELOPMENTAL CONSIDERATIONS

Children who become blind before they are 5 years old have more developmental challenges than those who become blind after 5 years. For example, without help, children who are born blind will be hampered in exploring their environment and may have difficulty learning concepts, as vision helps in learning about the world.

Children who become blind after infancy face the struggles associated with having to expend extra energy to accomplish routine tasks. They will need help in travel and written communication and usually will not be invited to participate fully in many recreational activities, thus remaining dependent on their parents (Freedman et al., 1988). Physical movement may be somewhat restricted, sensory input is reduced, and cues from nonverbal visual communication are not available. However, children who become blind after the age of 5 years may recall the shapes and colors of objects in their environment, and these memories may assist them in their interactions with others and in their schooling (Bradley-Johnson, 1994).

Children with normal vision usually learn the meaning of words in the context of their visual experience, while children who are blind usually learn the meaning of words, particularly those relating to objects outside of their immediate experience, through verbal explanations. Although the language ability of children with visual impairments may develop relatively normally (Hodapp, 1998), children who are blind may have difficulty understanding words that depend on visual experiences (Elbers & Van Loon-Vervoorn, 1999). Therefore, children who are blind should receive special instruction to help them understand words and concepts. One way to do this is by placing blind children in physical contact with objects that stimulate their remaining senses, such as hearing, taste, and touch. An example would be having the child explore the main parts of a car while the teacher labels each part verbally (e.g., tires, steering wheel, brake pedal).

Children with congenital blindness develop concepts of space in a sequence similar to that of sighted children, but at a slower rate; those born prematurely who are congenitally blind are at higher risk for spatial impairments (Stuart, 1995). Spatial understanding is essential to blind children's emerging skills in learning Braille and in learning orientation and mobility. Knowledge of spatial concepts will facilitate their ability to understand directions given by others and cross safely at light-controlled intersections (Hill, Guth, & Hill, 1985). Overall, children who are totally blind have more developmental variability and are more likely to show regressions in development than those with even a small degree of vision.

Children with severe visual impairments are at more risk for impaired social functioning than their peers who are normally sighted. They have difficulty acquiring meaningful physical gestures and facial expressions, using assertiveness skills, using visual cues to assist them in interpersonal relations, receiving adequate feedback about their actions, and receiving positive feedback from others (Sisson & Van Hasselt, 1987). They also have difficulty joining in sports and other activities that help form social bonds. In addition, they may have more behavioral problems than children with normal sight. Blind children with multiple handicaps often have mental health problems (Hodapp, 1998). Children who are suddenly blinded by trauma or who have progressive vision loss will require considerable support as they adjust to these changes (as they would with other life-changing events and processes).

Children who are congenitally blind may show behaviors similar to those seen in autistic disorder. These include echolalia, pronoun reversal, late emergence of pretend play activities, difficulty with abstract language, idiosyncratic vocabulary, difficulty conversing, perseveration, stereotypic behavior or mannerisms, and poor posture (Jamieson, 2004). We do not know, however, whether children with congenital blindness have a genuine autistic disorder or whether the autistic-like behaviors are a result of blindness. Blindness, as we have seen, often interferes with socialization experiences, and the autistic-like symptoms may in part reflect difficulty relating to others.

Just as there is enormous variability among children with normal vision, there is similar variability among children with severe visual impairments. Severe visual impairment or blindness does not exclude the presence of giftedness or mental retardation or the presence of learning, physical, mental, or developmental disabilities.

ASSESSMENT CONSIDERATIONS

Verbal tests usually are used to assess children with visual impairments. However, if a child has useful functional vision, you also can use visual or performance tests in the assessment. You will have to judge when you can use visual stimuli in your assessment and when modifications are needed. Children with mild or moderate low vision often can see the test materials with the aid of some means of magnification. A functional visual examination conducted by a teacher of the visually impaired or a vision specialist will help you decide what test materials you might want to use.

You might begin by using the standard test materials in the usual way. If the child has difficulty seeing the test materials, modify the materials as needed. Recognize that any modifications in the test stimuli or other test procedures represent a violation of standard procedures, must be reported, and may affect the validity of the test results. The critical consideration is the extent to which the modifications give additional cues to the child. If the modifications do not give the child additional cues, there is less chance that modifying the procedures will invalidate the results. If you do modify the procedures, note in the report precisely what you did. For example, you might write, "These results should be interpreted with caution because students with visual impairments were specifically excluded from the standardization sample, and certain accommodations were made to allow the student to take the test. These accommodations consisted of _____."

Background Factors

Before you evaluate a child who has a visual impairment or is suspected of having a visual impairment, consider the following factors:

1. Type of loss
2. Degree of loss
3. Age of onset
4. Severity and course of disorder
5. Etiology
6. Use of assistive visual devices
7. Ability to benefit from assistive visual devices
8. Stability of visual loss
9. Age at identification of visual impairment
10. Degree of residual vision
11. Education history
12. Functional vision (see below)
13. Co-occurring disorders

14. Information about the sensory channels and media that best help the child learn (e.g., print, Braille, or auditory media)
15. Other health-related information

Interview Guidelines

In addition to conducting a developmental history interview (see Table B-10 in Appendix B) and having the parents complete the Background Questionnaire (see Table A-1 in Appendix A), ask the parents the following questions.

1. When did you first suspect that [child's name] had a visual problem?
2. What led you to believe that [child's name] had a visual problem?
3. How have [child's name]'s visual difficulties affected his [her] ability to get around?
4. What professional did you see first to help you determine whether [child's name] had a visual problem?
5. What other professionals have you consulted?
6. How long did it take to confirm your suspicions that [child's name] had a visual problem?
7. What interventions did [child's name] receive when the visual loss was diagnosed?
8. (If interventions were used) How have the interventions helped [child's name]?
9. What other concerns do you have about [child's name]'s development?

In reviewing the child's case history, note references to any of the clues to potential visual difficulties covered earlier in the chapter. Also, ask the child's teacher to complete the School Referral Questionnaire in Table A-3 in Appendix A. Adolescents can complete the Personal Data Questionnaire in Table A-2 in Appendix A.

Observation Guidelines

Although optometrists and ophthalmologists are the specialists in determining visual loss, and although teachers of the visually impaired and vision specialists perform functional vision assessments, you, as a psychologist, will be making observations, both formal and informal, of the child's visual abilities. Observations of the child's use of vision in everyday settings—such as the classroom, hallways, lunchroom, and playground—will give you information about the child's *functional vision,* as will evaluations from a teacher of the visually impaired or a vision specialist. Consider the following questions, as applicable (Bishop, 1996). Note that many of these questions may be answered by referring to reports written by a teacher of the visually impaired or an orientation and mobility specialist if either has conducted an assessment.

TASK PERFORMANCE

1. How well does the child reach for objects?
2. How well does the child pick up objects?

3. How well does the child locate objects?
4. How well does the child place objects in a specific location?
5. How well does the child find food on a table or tray?
6. How well does the child use utensils?
7. How well does the child imitate gestures?
8. How well does the child write letters, numbers, words, and sentences and draw shapes and designs?
9. How well does the child identify details in a picture?
10. How well does the child use a computer or typewriter?
11. How well does the child color within lines, fill in missing parts, trace, cut, string beads, and draw from memory?
12. How does the child's reading fluency compare to that of the norm group?
13. How does the length of time the child spends on reading passages compare to times for the norm group?
14. How well does the child use a zipper, tie shoes, and button clothes?
15. How well does the child use a screwdriver, use a hammer, and thread a needle (depending on the age of the child)?
16. How well does the child find locations, such as the classroom, main office, restroom, and cafeteria?
17. How well does the child walk on the sidewalk, cross streets, read street signs, and avoid obstacles?
18. How does the child compare with her or his sighted peers in terms of time required to complete tasks?
19. Which activities does the child participate in during physical education and at recess?
20. Which activities does the child avoid?

QUALITATIVE FEATURES

1. What is the child's apparent level of visual discomfort while reading?
2. What does the child say about her or his ability to read and level of comfort while reading?
3. Which activities does the child prefer?
4. Does the child use low-vision aids in class?
5. If low-vision aids are used, what aids are used, and when does the child use them? Does the teacher need to tell the child to use them?
6. What is the quality of the child's social relationships?
7. What materials can the child read?
8. How do lighting and quality of materials affect the child's performance?

Suggestions for Test Administration

The following suggestions can help you evaluate children with visual impairments.

1. Before you administer any tests, review any medical evaluations and functional vision evaluations, and ask the child's teacher and parents about how to make the environment visually comfortable for the child (e.g., need for increased or decreased lighting, what the child's po-

sition should be relative to the window) and how to present the materials (e.g., using enlarged print, the child's prescribed optical magnifier, or video magnification in the form of a closed-circuit television device). Note that enlarged print takes more time to read than ordinary print (Bradley-Johnson, 1994).
2. Ask the parents and teacher for suggestions about interacting with the child, including the child's preferred manner of navigating in the environment. To walk beside you to your office, a child who is familiar with the school may need no more assistance than the sound of your voice as you engage in conversation. The child who is blind but uses a cane effectively will be able to walk along with you to your office with just some verbal direction about upcoming turns in the corridor. Blind children who have not yet mastered techniques for using a cane may appreciate an offer of assistance, particularly when in unfamiliar environments such as a clinic. Do this by offering your upper arm, elbow, or wrist (depending on the height of the child), but not by taking the child's arm. You should be about a half-step ahead. Hesitate briefly at obstacles, giving a verbal direction (e.g., say, "Stairs going up" before going up the stairs). When entering a narrow space, say so, and extend your arm behind you as a signal to the child to walk behind, rather than next to you. You can offer your hand to a young child who is blind.
3. Be sure that the child is wearing his or her prescribed glasses or contact lenses, that they are clean, and that the child uses his or her prescribed low-vision device.
4. Inform the child about the general layout of the room and about other details, such as the presence of a tape recorder if you are using one.
5. If your stopwatch or other equipment makes any sound, let the child know what to expect.
6. Allow the child to explore your office, provide verbal descriptions as needed, and guide him or her to a chair. If necessary, place the child's hand on the top of the back of the chair to orient the child to its location.
7. In the examination room, reduce glare, use a supplementary light source if needed (such as a high-intensity or full-spectrum compact fluorescent lamp), eliminate flickering light, and offer the use of a book stand to free the child's hands and to reduce the child's fatigue while reading (Bradley-Johnson, 1994). Also, use a contrasting background (e.g., dark for light materials and light for dark materials) behind all testing materials. Children with visual impairments can usually see things better when there is a good contrast between the testing materials and the table or blackboard.
8. Speak in a normal tone of voice to the child. (It is all too easy to slip into using a louder voice.)
9. Feel free to use common expressions that might seem awkward at first, such as asking a child who is blind whether he or she has *seen* a specific event. The English language is filled with these terms, and you are likely to

be more sensitive to them than the children you are evaluating. Moreover, children who are blind commonly use the terms *see* and *look* themselves.

10. Use specific language when directing older children who are blind. Say, for example, "From where you are standing now, the chair is about three feet straight ahead," instead of saying "The chair is right over there."

11. Encourage the child to let you know of his or her concerns and to ask you any questions at any time.

12. As you administer the tests, talk about what you are doing.

13. Use Lego® blocks for counting tasks, a Braille ruler for measuring tasks, and a Braille teaching clock for clock-reading tasks.

14. Give the child every opportunity to know what is going on during the evaluation and to explore the materials.

15. If you are testing a blind child with Brailled stimuli and do not know Braille, ask someone proficient in Braille, such as a teacher of the visually impaired, to assist you.

16. If a test requires interpretation of pictures (e.g., some academic tests of writing) and the child's vision is insufficient for the task, do not verbally describe the pictures, as doing so changes the fundamental intent of the items; instead, substitute some other test of writing skills.

Use of Standardized Tests

Although cognitive tests designed especially for children with visual impairments would be useful, there currently are no nationally standardized tests available for use with this population. Therefore, you will need to select from the more general instruments currently available. Tests that place heavy emphasis on visual activities, especially those with verbal subtests having visual components, may not be the best choice for children who are blind or who have severe to profound low vision.

The ability of children to answer verbal items on cognitive ability tests may be limited if the information depends in part on visual experiences ("What should you do if you see a child hit another child on the playground?" or "What does the phrase 'room with a view' mean?"). This consideration pertains primarily to children who are congenitally blind, although it may also apply to those severely visually impaired children who have not had life experiences similar to those of sighted children.

Carefully evaluate the requirements for performing timed tests before you use them, because these tests may lead to lower scores for children with visual impairments (Groenveld & Jan, 1992). *In the psychological or psychoeducational report, always report the modifications you use.*

You should be able to administer the verbal portions and some nonverbal portions of intelligence tests—such as the WISC–IV, WPPSI–III, WAIS–III, Stanford-Binet: V, and Differential Ability Scales (DAS)—to children with visual impairments, depending on their degree of useful vision (see

Sattler, 2001). On any test that has separate scores for verbal and performance items, you can, for example, administer only the verbal subtests if the child is blind or severely visually impaired.

The visual materials on the WISC–IV may be useful for children with low vision because they are large, bold, bright, and of high contrast. It is also helpful that the early items of the WISC–IV Block Design subtest do not have time bonuses; although they have time limits, there is an optional untimed scoring procedure for Block Design. The verbal portions of the Stanford-Binet: V are useful, but the nonverbal portions require adequate vision.

The DAS also has some useful features. The Pattern Construction subtest has an optional un-timed scoring procedure that eliminates time bonuses but retains time limits. Also, the pieces used for items 3 through 6 of the subtest are flat rather than cube-shaped, making the surface easier to recognize. However, the other school-age spatial subtest—Recall of Designs—requires the child to draw from memory copies of relatively small geometric designs. If you want to administer this subtest, consider enlarging the stimuli. Finally, the Speed of Information Processing subtest is supplementary and not part of the core cognitive subtests. Disadvantages of the DAS for children with visual impairments are that the verbal subtests for preschool children use pictures and objects and there are not enough subtests at this level that tap verbal ability.

Some examiners simply do not give performance or visual spatial subtests to students with low vision. Omitting such items, however, deprives you of important information about children who use their vision to learn. Therefore, we recommend that performance-type tests be administered to children with low vision, and the results used for qualitative purposes only and for recommending appropriate modifications of classroom materials and instructional methods.

Following are examples of qualitative information that you might include in psychological reports on children who have visual impairments:

• Samantha correctly completed some of the more difficult items on the WISC–IV Block Design subtest, but she required about 50% more time than fully sighted children of her age usually do. These results suggest that she is able to do some types of visual work accurately when given adequate time to complete the work. Therefore, when she is given visual tasks to perform, she should be given extra time if necessary.

• Although Lynne's performance on the WISC–IV Symbol Search and Coding subtests was accurate, she worked slowly on these subtests of processing speed. This is likely a result of the nystagmus (rapid involuntary movement of the eyes) and photophobia (extreme response to light) associated with albinism. Lynne requires extended time to perform visual tasks accurately.

• Despite his severe visual field loss, Chandler completed all the WISC–IV Block Design items within the time limits. Chandler has been fascinated with puzzles since early childhood and spends much of his recreational time doing them.

- Joel persisted in calling the sample item on the WISC–IV Picture Completion a banana because of its color and was unable to identify correctly any of the pictures on the subtest. He also was unable to identify objects on my desk by sight, but was able to identify them by touch. This suggests a severe limitation in functional vision and indicates that touch is his primary learning channel.

- Rosalie had difficulty seeing the details of some pictures on the WISC–IV Picture Concepts subtest when wearing her glasses, but she was able to see the details when she used a video magnifier. This suggests that using a video magnifier would help her when reading.

INTERVENTIONS

Interventions for children with visual impairments should be designed to help them meet developmental challenges and achieve competence in academic, social, linguistic, and personal areas. To meet these goals, the children will need instruction in (a) compensatory skills needed to access the core curriculum, (b) orientation and mobility skills, (c) use of assistive devices, (d) social interaction skills, (e) personal and home care skills, (f) independent living skills, (g) recreation and leisure skills, and (h) career education (Hatlen, 1996).

The ideal learning environment (Jamieson, 2004) would be one rich in varied and consistent experiences, including (a) experiences with concrete objects to help the child gain knowledge about the world around him and to aid in the development of meaningful concepts, (b) opportunities to learn by doing, (c) unified lessons that give an idea of the whole task and not just a portion of the task, and (d) opportunities to explore objects systematically by using all available senses (e.g., pairing vision with tactile exploration).

Decisions on how to teach reading to a child with a visual impairment should be based on a careful case study. The need to teach Braille is clear for children with severe to profound low vision or blindness. For children with less severe losses, the decision is more complicated. You should consider (a) the type and severity of the vision loss, (b) the portions of the retina and visual field affected, (c) the prognosis with respect to further deterioration of vision, and (d) the length of time the child can comfortably read print. Some children with moderate to severe low vision who are not taught Braille may have difficulty learning to read because they cannot easily distinguish some letters and are confused by the vast number of type styles.

Children with visual impairments but no other significant disabilities should achieve at levels comparable to those of sighted children with similar advantages, provided they receive appropriate interventions. Early intervention should be geared toward educating parents about helping their children become more aware of their environment by using their senses of hearing and touch. Programs for school-age children should include high-quality academic teaching, preferably by a credentialed teacher of the visually impaired; travel instruction provided by a credentialed orientation and mobility specialist; provision of materials in appropriate formats, including auditory materials as needed; direct experiences geared to the children's remaining senses; instruction in assistive technologies; and assistance for family members in learning how to provide proper support for the children.

Assistive devices for children with visual impairments include the following.

ENHANCEMENT OF PRINT

1. *Large print* facilitates reading for children with some useful vision.
2. *Colored overlays* help to reduce glare for children with some useful vision.
3. *Optical aids* include portable magnifiers used to improve ability to read print and see small objects and portable telescopes used to locate distant targets (e.g., scan a shopping center to find a particular store).
4. *Video magnifiers* are closed-circuit televisions with adjustable print size, color combinations, brightness, and contrast.
5. *Screen magnification software* enlarges on-screen text and graphics for word processing and other applications.

AUDITORY ACCESS

1. *Cassette and CD players* allow the user to play (and in some cases record) reading materials and music.
2. *Speech synthesizers* consist of hardware (either an external unit that connects to a computer or an internal chip or circuit card) that enables the computer to produce speech output.
3. *Speech output software* (often integrated into a specific application, such as a word-processing program) translates standard text into a phonetic code that can be "spoken" by a speech synthesizer.
4. *Screenreaders* work in conjunction with other applications to convert text on screen into speech output.
5. *Scanners* convert printed text into a form appropriate for input into speech synthesizers or computer sound cards.

BRAILLE ACCESS

1. A *Braille slate* is a hinged device made of metal or plastic; a *stylus* is used to punch dots into paper inserted between the parts of the slate. The slate and stylus are analogous to the sighted person's paper and pencil.
2. A *Braille writer* is a nine-key machine that enables users to write Braille text on inserted paper. It is analogous to a manual typewriter.
3. *Braille keyboard conversion software* converts nine specified keys on a standard keyboard into a Braille keyboard.
4. *Braille keyboard labels* are labels with Braille letters that can be placed on individual computer or typewriter keys. Alternatively, Braille dots can be glued directly on keys.

5. *Tactile locators* are stickers or other materials that can be placed in strategic spots on a keyboard to identify important keys and facilitate positioning for touch typing.

6. A *"refreshable"* or *"paperless" Braille display* consists of a hardware template (either a separate component or part of an integrated system) that displays Braille as it is being written. As each letter is typed, round-tip plastic pins corresponding to Braille dots pop up on the template to form Braille letters. The Braille display is refreshable because it can be altered as the text is changed and advanced letter by letter or line by line.

7. *Braille software translators* enable users to print high-quality Braille documents from a computer. Software converts the screen display to Braille before it is sent to the Braille embosser to be printed. Reading systems perform optical character recognition to convert printed text into computer files.

8. *Braille embossers* emboss documents in Braille. Braille embossers typically have blunt pins that punch dots into special heavy (100-pound weight) paper.

For further information, consult the following sources:

- American Foundation for the Blind. http://www.afb.org.
- American Printing House for the Blind. http://www.aph.org.
- Goodman, S. A., & Wittenstein, S. H. (Eds.). (2003). *Collaborative assessment: Working with students who are blind or visually impaired, including those with additional disabilities.* New York: AFB Press.

Courtesy of Herman Zielinski and Carol Evans.

- Hatlen, P. (1996). *The Core Curriculum for Blind and Visually Impaired Students, Including Those with Additional Disabilities.* Retrieved from http://www.afb.org/section.asp?Documentid=1349.
- Texas School for the Blind and Visually Impaired. http://www.tsbvi.edu/.
- Tuttle, D. W. (2004). *Self-esteem and adjusting with blindness: The process of responding to life's demands* (3rd ed.). Springfield, IL: Charles C Thomas.

THINKING THROUGH THE ISSUES

1. How would your life be different if you were born totally blind?
2. What adjustment would you have to make in your life if you became blind at 5 or more years of age?
3. Which condition do you believe has a more profound effect on a child's ability to function—a visual impairment or a hearing impairment? What is the basis for your answer?
4. Read each verbal item on your favorite cognitive ability test. Which items appear to depend on visual experience? How might a child who is totally congenitally blind learn that information?

SUMMARY

1. Children with visual impairments have conditions that range from limited vision to no vision at all.
2. Key variables in understanding visual impairments are the type, severity, etiology, and age of onset of the visual impairment.
3. Congenital etiologies account for over 50% of visual impairments in children, and impairments with congenital etiologies frequently are associated with developmental disabilities, such as cerebral palsy.
4. Children who have recently lost all or part of their vision will need to adjust to their visual loss and learn to use adaptive strategies and compensatory devices.
5. In the 2000–2001 school year, the percentage of children aged 6 to 21 years served under the IDEA because of visual impairments was .45% (25,975).
6. IDEA 2004 (Sec. 614, 3B, iii) emphasizes teaching Braille to blind or visually impaired children unless it is not appropriate to do so.
7. IDEA 2004 (Sec. 674) also requires that a National Instructional Materials Access Center be established and supported by the American Printing House for the Blind (a) to provide access to printed materials useful for visually impaired or blind children, (b) to receive and maintain a catalog of print instructional materials, and (c) to develop procedures to protect against copyright infringement, with respect to the print instructional materials provided under the law.
8. Implementing these and other provisions of IDEA 2004, as well as providing adequate funding, will assure that children with visual impairments receive the services they need to enhance their well being and to become productive members of society.

Clues to Potential Visual Difficulties

9. Of all the organs, the eye is the most fully developed at birth.
10. Signs of potential visual difficulties can be seen in infants and children.

11. If any of these signs are present in an infant or a child, he or she should be referred for a visual examination to an optometrist or ophthalmologist.

Structure of the Eye

12. The structure of the eye can be likened to that of a simple camera. An opening at the front allows light to enter. The light travels through the cornea, the aqueous humor, the lens, and the vitreous body until it reaches the retina.
13. The main structures of the eye are the cornea, aqueous humor, iris, pupil, lens (or crystalline lens), vitreous humor, retina, cones, and rods.

Disorders That Affect Vision

14. Vision can be impaired by refractive errors, central visual field defects, peripheral visual field defects, whole visual field defects, and other conditions.
15. Three conditions that result from refractive errors are myopia (or nearsightedness), hyperopia (or farsightedness), and astigmatism (irregular curvature of the cornea or lens).
16. Three conditions that result in vision loss in the central visual field are juvenile macular degeneration, diabetic retinopathy, and achromatopsia.
17. Retinitis pigmentosa and glaucoma are two progressive disorders that result in loss of vision in the peripheral portion of the visual field, causing mobility problems; in their initial stages, they leave central vision intact.
18. Disorders that cause visual loss across the whole visual field include retinopathy of prematurity, cataracts, aniridia, albinism, and retinoblastoma.
19. Other conditions that may affect vision include cortical visual impairment, fetal alcohol syndrome, optic nerve atrophy, optic nerve hypoplasia, toxoplasmosis, and amblyopia.
20. Many eye conditions (as well as disorders of the central nervous system) may be accompanied by nystagmus—rapid, involuntary, repeated oscillations of one or both eyes in any or all fields of vision.

Clarity of Vision

21. Although their visual acuity or their visual field may be diminished, children with visual impairments usually have some useful vision.
22. Children with mild or moderate visual loss still may use vision as their primary learning channel.
23. Children with severe to profound visual loss need tactile and auditory sensory input to obtain information, in addition to using whatever residual vision is available to them.
24. Clarity of vision is defined in terms of visual acuity.
25. A person who has 20/20 vision sees objects 20 feet away with complete clarity, but a person who has 20/200 vision sees at 20 feet what a person with full acuity sees at 200 feet.
26. Visual acuity is measured on a continuum from normal vision to blindness.
27. Individuals with profound vision loss can still perceive some objects in the environment and have some vision for use in daily living and travel.
28. Blindness refers to vision loss that is total or sight that is so impaired that the individual primarily uses senses other than vision for obtaining information and for interacting with the environment.

29. Legal blindness is defined as corrected distance visual acuity of less than 20/200 in the better eye or a visual field of 20° or less (a normal field is close to 180°) in the better eye.

Developmental Considerations

30. Children who become blind before 5 years old have more developmental challenges than those who become blind after 5 years.
31. Children who become blind after infancy face the struggles associated with having to expend extra energy to accomplish routine tasks.
32. Children with normal vision usually learn the meaning of words in the context of their visual experience, while children who are blind usually learn the meaning of words, particularly those relating to objects outside of their immediate experience, through verbal explanations.
33. Children with congenital blindness develop concepts of space in a sequence similar to that of sighted children, but at a slower rate; those born prematurely who are congenitally blind are at higher risk for spatial impairments.
34. Children with severe visual impairments are at more risk for impaired social functioning than their peers who are normally sighted.
35. Children who are congenitally blind may show behaviors similar to those seen in autistic disorder. We do not know, however, whether children with congenital blindness have a genuine autistic disorder or whether the autistic-like behaviors are a result of blindness. Blindness often interferes with socialization experiences, and the autistic-like symptoms may in part reflect difficulty relating to others.
36. Just as there is enormous variability among children with normal vision, there is similar variability among children with severe visual impairments.

Assessment Considerations

37. Verbal tests usually are used to assess children with visual impairments.
38. When possible, you will also want to use visual or performance tests to assess children with some functional vision.
39. You will have to judge when you can use visual stimuli in your assessment and when modifications are needed.
40. Children with mild or moderate low vision often can see the test materials with the aid of some means of magnification.
41. Recognize that any modifications in the test stimuli or other test procedures represent a violation of standard procedures, must be reported, and may affect the validity of the test results.
42. Before you evaluate a child who has a visual impairment or is suspected of having a visual impairment, consider the type of loss, degree of loss, age of onset, etiology, use of assistive visual devices, ability to benefit from assistive visual devices, stability of visual loss, age at identification of visual impairment, degree of residual vision, education history, functional vision, co-occurring disabilities, information about the sensory channels and media that best help the child learn, and other health-related information.
43. Although optometrists and ophthalmologists are the specialists in determining visual loss, and although teachers of the visually impaired and vision specialists perform functional vision assessments, you, as a psychologist, will be making observations, both formal and informal, of the child's visual abilities.

44. Observations of the child's use of vision in everyday settings—such as the classroom, hallways, lunchroom, and playground—will give you information about the child's functional vision.

45. Although cognitive tests designed especially for children with visual impairments would be useful, there currently are no nationally standardized tests available for use with this population.

46. The ability of children to answer verbal items on cognitive ability tests may be limited if the information depends in part on visual experiences.

47. Carefully evaluate the requirements for performing timed tests before you use them, because these tests may lead to lower scores for children with visual impairments.

48. In the psychological or psychoeducational report, always report the modifications you use.

49. You should be able to administer the verbal portions and some nonverbal portions of intelligence tests to children with visual impairments, depending on their degree of useful vision.

50. We recommend that performance-type tests be administered to children with low vision, and the results used for qualitative purposes only and for recommending appropriate modifications of classroom materials and instructional methods.

Interventions

51. Interventions for children with visual impairments should be designed to help them meet developmental challenges and achieve competence in academic, social, linguistic, and personal areas.

52. To meet these goals, children with visual impairments will need instruction in (a) compensatory skills needed to access the core curriculum, (b) orientation and mobility skills, (c) use of assistive devices, (d) social interaction skills, (e) personal and home care skills, (f) independent living skills, (g) recreation and leisure skills, and (h) career education.

53. The ideal learning environment would be one rich in varied and consistent experiences, including experiences with concrete objects, opportunities to learn by doing, unified lessons that give the child an idea of the whole task and not just a portion of the task, and opportunities to explore objects systematically by using all available senses.

54. Decisions on how to teach reading to a child with a visual impairment should be based on a careful case study.

55. Children with visual impairments but no other significant disabilities should achieve at levels comparable to those of sighted children with similar advantages, provided they receive appropriate interventions.

56. Programs should include high-quality academic teaching, preferably by a credentialed teacher of the visually impaired; travel instruction provided by a credentialed orientation and mobility specialist; provision of materials in appropriate formats, including auditory materials as needed; direct experiences geared to the children's remaining senses; instruction in assistive technologies; and assistance for family members.

57. Assistive devices can help children with visual impairments.

KEY TERMS, CONCEPTS, AND NAMES

Speech output software (p. 473)
Screenreaders (p. 473)
Scanners (p. 473)
Braille access (p. 473)
Braille slate and stylus (p. 473)
Braille writer (p. 473)
Braille keyboard conversion software (p. 473)
Braille keyboard labels (p. 473)
Tactile locators (p. 474)
"Refreshable" or "paperless" Braille display (p. 474)
Braille software translators (p. 474)
Braille embossers (p. 474)

STUDY QUESTION

Discuss children with visual impairments. Include in your discussion IDEA 2004, clues to potential visual difficulties, disorders that affect vision, clarity of vision, developmental considerations, assessment considerations, and interventions.

21

HEARING IMPAIRMENTS

by Jerome M. Sattler, Steven T. Hardy-Braz, and John O. Willis

[Sign language] is, in the hand of its masters, a most beautiful and expressive language, for which, in their intercourse with each other and as a means of easily and quickly reaching the minds of the deaf, neither nature nor art has given them a satisfactory substitute.

It is impossible for those who do not understand it to comprehend its possibilities with the deaf, its powerful influence on the moral and social happiness of those deprived of hearing, and its wonderful power of carrying thought to intellects which would otherwise be in perpetual darkness. Nor can they appreciate the hold it has upon the deaf. So long as there are two deaf people upon the face of the earth and they get together, so long will signs be in use.

—J. Schuyler Long, American writer and principal
of the Iowa School for the Deaf (1869–1933)

Goals and Objectives

This chapter is designed to enable you to do the following:

- Understand how to assess children with hearing impairments

- Understand how to design interventions for children with hearing impairments

Inability to hear clearly can adversely affect children's language development, speech intelligibility, socialization, and academic performance. Acquiring fluency in a spoken language is a major developmental task facing children with hearing impairments. In this chapter we use the phrase "children with hearing impairments" to refer to children with hearing losses ranging from mild to profound. The term *deaf* is used only for a child who has a hearing impairment so severe that it prevents successful processing of linguistic information through audition.

Hearing impairments affect not only children's ability to hear, but also their behavior, self-concept, identity, and social and emotional development. Some children who have severe hearing losses tend to be somewhat more impulsive, dependent, and rigid and less able to accept personal responsibility than children with normal hearing (Keane, 1987). Children with hearing impairments also may have conduct problems and anxiety disorders (Hodapp, 1998). Those with multiple disabilities usually have more academic difficulties than those with hearing impairments only.

Deafness is an invisible, as well as a low-incidence, disability; it usually represents a static and irreversible condition (Danek, 1988). About 96% of children who have been identified for educational programs or services because of hearing impairments are born into families in which both parents can hear (Mitchell & Karchmer, 2004). The remaining 4% have one or two parents who are deaf. Thus, many children with hearing impairments are raised almost entirely around people who can hear.

Parents are often unprepared to recognize a hearing impairment in their infant. At first, they may believe that their child is slow, mentally retarded, or learning disabled, or they may simply be aware that "something is not quite right." There may be a considerable delay between when the parents first suspect some difficulty and when a conclusive diagnosis is reached. However, the national movement to have newborns tested routinely for hearing loss has been extremely successful; almost 90% of babies born in 2004 were tested (National Center for Hearing Assessment and Management, 2005). Because the false positive rate can be extremely high (as a consequence of debris in the infant's external ear canal or fluid in the middle ear), repeated hearing screenings at planned intervals are recommended (Shoup, Owen, Jackson, & Laptook, 2005).

If you suspect that a child has an undiagnosed hearing loss, refer the child to an audiologist for a hearing evaluation. In the 2000–2001 school year, the percentage of children aged 6 to 21 years served under the Individuals with Disabilities Education Act (IDEA) because of hearing impairments was 1.23% (70,767; U.S. Department of Education, 2002). This number is probably an underestimate because children with multiple disabilities, including a hearing impairment, may be classified under a disability category other than hearing impairment.

IDEA 2004 covers hearing impairment as a disability (Sec. 602). The law emphasizes that Individualized Education Programs (IEPs) must "consider the communication needs of the child, and in the case of a child who is deaf or hard of hearing, consider the child's language and communication needs, opportunities for direct communications with peers and professional personnel in the child's language and communication mode, academic level, and full range of needs, including opportunities for direct instruction in the child's language and communication mode" (Sec. 614, 3, iv). IDEA 2004 also requires schools to consider whether the child needs assistive technology devices and services (Sec. 612, 3, v) and to prepare personnel to assist children with hearing impairments (Sec. 662, 2, E). Finally, the law authorizes states to provide technical assistance and in-service training to schools and agencies serving deaf-blind children and their families and to address the post-secondary needs of individuals who are deaf or hard of hearing (Sec. 663, c, A, B, and C). Implementing these and other provisions of IDEA 2004, as well as providing adequate funding, will assure that children with hearing impairments receive the services they need to enhance their well-being and to become productive members of society.

CLUES TO POTENTIAL HEARING DIFFICULTIES

The following behavioral, speech, and specific language signs may suggest a hearing difficulty.

BEHAVIORAL SIGNS

1. Lack of normal response to sound
2. Lack of interest in general conversation
3. Inattentiveness
4. Difficulty following oral directions
5. Failure to respond when spoken to
6. Frequent requests to have the speaker repeat what was said
7. Mistakes in carrying out spoken instructions
8. Intent observation of the speaker's lips (lipreading, speechreading) rather than looking at the speaker's eyes in face-to-face encounters
9. Leaning forward to hear the speaker
10. Habitually turning one ear toward the speaker
11. Cupping hand behind ear
12. Frequent earaches, discharges from ears, discomfort of the ears, or hearing strange ringing or buzzing noises
13. Turning up the volume of the radio, television, or stereo system or sitting closer to the sound source
14. Difficulty understanding voices on the telephone
15. Difficulty understanding poor-quality sound (e.g., public address systems, two-way radios)
16. Unexplained irritability
17. Pulling on or scratching at the ears

SPEECH SIGNS

1. Unusual voice quality (e.g., monotonous or high pitched)
2. Abnormally loud or soft speech
3. Faulty pronunciation
4. Poor articulation

SPECIFIC LANGUAGE SIGNS

1. Difficulty discriminating consonant sounds (e.g., the child hears *bet* for *bed, tab* for *tap*)
2. Difficulty discriminating and learning short vowel sounds *a, e, i, o,* and *u*
3. Difficulty hearing quiet sounds (e.g., *s, sh, f, t,* and *k*)
4. Difficulty sounding out a word, sound by sound (e.g., the child has difficulty saying /k/ . . . /a/ . . . /t/ for *cat*)
5. Difficulty relating printed letters such as *f, pl,* and *ide* to their sounds
6. Difficulty separating blended sounds (e.g., the child has difficulty determining that *fl* has the sounds /f/ . . . /l/)
7. Better spelling and reading of sight words (words read by the whole-word or look-say method) than of phonetic words (words read by learning the sounds that letters and their combinations make)
8. Difficulty rhyming or recognizing rhymes
9. Omission of suffixes (e.g., *ed* or *s*)

STRUCTURE OF THE EAR

Let's review the three main structures of the ear.

1. The *outer ear* is made up of the external part of the ear (the *pinna,* or *auricle*) and the *ear canal.* "The pinna consists of cartilage covered by skin and is shaped to capture sound waves and funnel them through the ear canal to the eardrum (tympanic membrane), a thin membrane that separates the outer ear from the middle ear" (Berkow, 1997, p. 1244).
2. The *middle ear* consists of the *eardrum* and a chamber containing three tiny bones—*hammer (malleus), anvil (incus),* and *stirrup (stapes)*—that connect the eardrum to the inner ear. The middle ear transmits vibrations to the inner ear. The eustachian tube connects the middle ear with the back of the nose and maintains proper air pressure in the middle ear.
3. The *inner ear* consists of two chambers—the *cochlea,* which is the organ of hearing, and the *vestibular labyrinth* or *vestibular system,* which is the organ of balance. Both chambers are filled with fluid.

When sound waves strike the eardrum, it vibrates. The vibrations pass through the bones to the middle ear and then to the inner ear. The vibrations then disseminate into the cochlea, where they are converted into electrical impulses, which are transmitted to the brain via the eighth cranial nerve (the vestibulochlear, or auditory, nerve).

DISORDERS THAT AFFECT HEARING

There are two major classifications of hearing impairments. When a hearing impairment is caused by conditions present at birth (congenital) or occurs before speech and language are developed, it is referred to as a *prelingual hearing impair-*

ment. Children with prelingual hearing impairments have great difficulty acquiring speech. When a hearing impairment is caused by later disease or trauma, after speech and language have been developed, it is referred to as a *postlingual hearing impairment.* Children with postlingual hearing impairments have difficulty acquiring or maintaining additional spoken language proficiency, but not as much difficulty as children who are prelingually deaf.

Congenital disorders account for about 50% of early childhood hearing impairments with known etiology (Marschark, 1993). Following are examples of conditions or agents that may lead to a hearing impairment in infancy or in later life, as well as to other disabilities.

INFANCY

- *Asphyxia* is a lack of oxygen or excess of carbon dioxide in the body. It may lead to unconsciousness, seizures, damage to various sensory systems including the auditory system, and death.
- *Cleft palate* is a genetic defect associated with multiple factors that may result in a conductive hearing loss (discussed later in the chapter).
- *Cytomegalovirus* (CMV) is a virus that may be transmitted prenatally, as the baby passes through an infected birth canal, or postnatally, through infected urine, saliva, breast milk, feces, tears, or blood. Although some carriers of the virus are asymptomatic, in its most severe form CMV causes global central nervous system infection involving the cerebral cortex, brainstem, cochlear nuclei, cranial nerves, and inner ear.
- *Down syndrome* is a chromosomal abnormality that may lead to a conductive hearing loss resulting from narrow ear canals and frequent middle ear infections.
- *Herpes simplex virus* is a virus that may be transmitted to the fetus during the birth process if the mother is actively infected. It may cause a severe generalized disease in the neonate, with high risk of mortality and devastating consequences, including brain infections, respiratory difficulties, convulsions, hepatitis, and hearing impairment.
- *Hyperbilirubinemia,* also known as elevated bilirubin, is a condition that occurs when the blood contains an excessive amount of bilirubin (formed from the metabolism of red blood cells). High levels of bilirubin can cause jaundice, and excessively high levels can lead to a grave form of jaundice in newborns *(kernicterus),* causing brain and spinal cord damage and hearing impairment. Initial treatment of hyperbilirubinemia is by light (photo) therapy; transfusions may be needed in severe cases.
- *Meningitis* is a brain infection involving acute inflammation of the membranes that cover the brain and spinal cord. It is characterized by drowsiness, confusion, irritability, and sensory impairments, including hearing impairment.
- *Premature birth* is defined as birth before 36 weeks' gestation. *Low birth weight* is defined as a birth weight of less than 3 pounds 8 ounces, or 2,500 grams. The condition may result in a hearing impairment and/or other impairments.

- *Rh incompatibility* is a condition that arises when the mother has Rh negative blood and the fetus has Rh positive blood. When blood from the fetus mixes in the placenta with the mother's blood, antibodies may be produced that will destroy the red blood cells of the fetus in any subsequent pregnancy. If this condition is not treated, it can cause such pathologies as abortion, stillbirth, jaundice, deafness, and mental retardation.
- *Rubella,* or German measles, is an infectious disease that, if contracted by the mother during the first three months of pregnancy, has a high risk of causing congenital anomalies, including deafness, deaf-blindness, visual impairments, cardiac malformation, and mental retardation. On reaching adulthood, children with congenital rubella syndrome may have diabetes, glaucoma, pathology of the endocrine system, and central nervous system infections.
- *Syphilis* is a sexually transmitted bacterial infection that can be passed from an infected mother to her unborn child. It can cause central nervous system abnormalities, including hearing loss, vestibular dysfunction, and damage to the heart. Mental retardation also may result, depending on the severity of the neurologic damage.
- *Toxoplasmosis* is caused by a parasite contracted by the mother and passed to the developing fetus. It can result in vision loss, hearing loss, hydrocephalus, or mental retardation. Treatment consists of various drugs, including corticosteroids used to reduce inflammation of the heart, lungs, or eyes. Primary prevention techniques are important to reduce the spread of the parasite (e.g., meats should be cooked thoroughly, hands and cooking utensils should be washed thoroughly after raw meat is prepared, fruit and vegetables should be washed thoroughly to remove all traces of soil, expectant mothers should not handle cat litter).
- *Treacher-Collins syndrome* is a genetic defect that may result in a conductive or mixed hearing loss associated with physical defects and abnormalities of the ears.
- *Usher syndrome* and *CHARGE syndrome* are genetic defects that may result in hearing loss and progressive vision loss.
- *Waardenburg syndrome* is a genetic defect that may result in hearing loss and changes in skin and hair pigmentation.

LATER LIFE

- Severe blow to the head
- Exposure to very loud noise (or sustained exposure to loud noise) that results in acoustic trauma
- Childhood diseases such as measles, mumps, and chicken pox
- Inner ear infections (otitis media)
- Perforated eardrum
- Sudden pressure changes from flying, diving, or strenuous exercise
- Brain tumors
- Demyelinating diseases (diseases that destroy the myelin sheath covering the nerves)
- Viral infections of the inner ear

- Other infections accompanied by high fever
- Reactions to certain prescription medications

Adequate prenatal care and efficient obstetrical procedures, as well as early treatment of ear infections and high fevers, may prevent some auditory problems from developing.

ACUITY OF HEARING

Hearing ability is measured on a continuum ranging from very acute perception, such as that of a gifted conductor who can detect a single out-of-tune instrument in an orchestra, to total deafness, such as that of an individual who can detect sound only tactilely, in the form of strong vibrations. Hearing impairment may be either unilateral (in just one ear) or bilateral (in both ears).

Hearing ability is evaluated on two dimensions: ability to perceive sounds of different frequencies and different intensities. *Sound frequency,* or the pitch of sound, is measured in units called hertz (Hz), or cycles per second. Hearing loss can be confined to low or to high frequencies, or it can be present across all frequencies. *Sound intensity,* or the loudness of sound, is measured in units called decibels (dB). A decibel is $\frac{1}{10}$ of a bel—hence the prefix *deci.* The bel is a logarithmic unit; a sound that is 10 decibels louder than another represents a 10-fold increase in sound intensity and a doubling of perceived loudness. Thus, 20 dB is 10 times the intensity of 10 dB and appears twice as loud, while 30 dB is 100 times the intensity of 10 dB and appears four times as loud. Typical average decibel levels are 30 dB for a whisper, 60 dB for normal conversation, 100 dB for a chainsaw, 120 dB for a jet plane taking off, and 150 dB for rock music at close range.

Audiologists use the following classification scheme to evaluate hearing ability. It is based on the extent to which the individual needs a higher-than-average intensity of sound to hear.

1. *Normal range* is a loss of 0–15 dB. A child with a loss of less than 15 dB is not considered to have a hearing impairment.
2. *Slight hearing loss* is a loss of 16–25 dB. Children with a loss of less than 25 dB are the least hard of hearing. They hear vowel sounds clearly, but they may miss unvoiced consonant sounds (e.g., /t/ is unvoiced; /d/ is voiced). You should have no difficulty evaluating these children.
3. *Mild hearing loss* is a loss of 26–40 dB. A mild hearing loss may not be recognized unless a child develops communication problems, in which case the child may be referred for an audiological evaluation. Children with mild hearing loss may miss soft or whispered speech, and they may have mild speech problems. You should have little difficulty evaluating these children unless they exhibit communication problems. Nevertheless, you should be aware of any testing conditions (e.g., noisy environments) that may impede the child's ability to perceive information accurately.

4. *Moderate hearing loss* is a loss of 41–70 dB. Children with moderate hearing loss may have difficulty hearing most speech sounds at normal conversational levels when there is background noise. They usually have moderate speech problems. You may have difficulty evaluating these children—you may have to speak loudly and use special communication procedures (discussed later in the chapter).

5. *Severe hearing loss* is a loss of 71–90 dB. Children with severe hearing loss hear only the loudest speech sounds; they cannot detect any speech sounds at normal conversational levels. If they have oral speech, their articulation, vocabulary, and voice quality differ from those of children with normal hearing; these speech problems are usually severe, especially if the hearing loss is prelingual. You will need to use special communication procedures to evaluate most, if not all, children in this group.

6. *Profound hearing loss* is a loss of 91 dB or greater. Children with profound hearing loss usually hear no speech or other sounds. Many have speech that is inarticulate. This degree of hearing loss has a profound impact on communication. You may often need to use special communication procedures to evaluate children in this group.

There are four main types of hearing loss.

1. In *conductive hearing loss,* sound levels are reduced, making it difficult to hear faint sounds. Causes include diseases or obstructions in the outer or middle ear, such as a buildup of fluid in the middle ear, wax in the ear canal, puncture of the eardrum, or injuries to the bones or membranes, that impede sound conduction. Medical or surgical intervention, as well as hearing aids, may be helpful.

2. *Sensorineural hearing loss* also reduces sound levels, making it difficult not only to hear faint sounds, but also to hear clearly and to understand speech. Causes include damage to the inner ear or auditory nerve associated with birth injuries, toxic drugs, exposure to loud noises, infection or other diseases, genetic disorders, head trauma, tumors, or aging. About 90% of all people with hearing impairments suffer from sensorineural hearing loss. Sensorineural hearing loss is treated with hearing aids or cochlear implants.

3. In a *mixed hearing loss,* there are elements of both conductive and sensorineural loss. The outer or middle ear and the inner ear are involved in the hearing loss. A mixed loss can develop when a person with a sensorineural loss later develops a conductive loss. Interventions that apply to conductive losses and sensorineural losses also apply to mixed losses.

4. A *central hearing loss* (also referred to as a *central auditory processing disorder*) produces difficulties in hearing when there is background noise, in localizing sounds, in following directions, and in attending. Causes include damage to or impairment of the nerves of the central nervous system, either in the pathway to the brain or in the brain itself, associated with tumors or a genetic abnormality; often the cause is unknown. Interventions include

training in auditory and phonological awareness skills, language processing skills, and functional organization and study skills.

When a child is evaluated for a hearing loss, her or his hearing ability should be assessed with *and* without an assistive listening device (discussed later in the chapter). A child may have a severe hearing loss when unaided, but only a moderate loss when wearing a hearing aid. However, a child with a mild to moderate hearing loss when aided still may not have fluent speech or speech perception.

Children with hearing impairments are a heterogenous group. Two children with the same degree of loss may have different abilities to hear sound or produce speech and may benefit differently from assistive listening devices. The distinction between deaf and hard of hearing may be difficult to specify. Because eligibility criteria are not consistent across states, what one state considers to be "deaf" might be considered "hard of hearing" in another state (Bienenstock & Vernon, 1994).

DEVELOPMENTAL CONSIDERATIONS

The study of children with hearing impairments gives us insights into the process of cognitive development (Mayberry, 1992): "Children who are deaf have taught us that the human mind is characterized by enormous linguistic creativity. When language is unavailable, the child invents the beginnings of one (home sign). When a group of people is cut off from acoustic language, they evolve a visual language (sign)" (pp. 65–66, with changes in notation).

Infants born with hearing impairments follow a normal pattern of vocalization until about 7 months of age (Marschark, 1993). After this age, the rate of development of spoken productions is often reduced. The frequent failure of such infants to learn to speak clearly is not the result of a vocal problem; it is because they can hear speech only faintly, if at all.

Research reviewed by Hodapp (1998) indicates that "Deaf children with higher levels of language perform better on high-level cognitive tasks than do deaf children with lower language skills. . . . [And] the language of children who are deaf develops best when their parents are [American Sign Language] ASL signers who are deaf. These children develop language from their earliest years, in a natural way" (p. 168).

Children with hearing impairments also may have difficulties with balance, equilibrium, and other motor skills related to the vestibular system. Thus, delays in early developmental milestones (e.g., walking) may also be observed.

ASSESSMENT CONSIDERATIONS

Evaluating children with hearing impairments may be more fatiguing, demand greater attention and concentration, and require more time and flexibility than evaluating children with normal hearing. Both you and the children may be self-conscious because observation plays such an important role in these assessments—you may feel as though you are being intrusive, and the children may feel as though they are under a microscope. With proper preparation, however, you should be able to meet the challenges of evaluating children with hearing impairments. It is critical that you make the child understand the test instructions without giving leading cues in the process. If you routinely evaluate children with hearing impairments, learn sign language and other means of communicating with them. *If you believe that you are not qualified to evaluate children with hearing impairments, refer them to a more qualified professional.*

Although children with hearing impairments may give the impression of being able to understand your questions, they may be feigning comprehension in order to obtain your approval or to avoid being embarrassed. In turn, you may have difficulty understanding their answers, particularly if they have accents or speech or motor difficulties. Do *not* interpret the difficulties that children with hearing impairments have with expressive language, receptive language, or both as indications of limited intelligence.

Because sight is the chief means by which children who have hearing impairments receive information, they are particularly likely to seek to gain understanding from visual cues—such as facial expressions and hand movements. Recognize that any movements you make, including eye movements, may cue a child. Facial expressions, rather than the tone of your voice, will convey your mood. For example, children may quickly notice if you frown or grimace in impatience and may interpret such gestures unfavorably. Smile to reward their efforts, but not to reward their responses. Avoid smiling when they say something that is not comprehensible; you do not want to encourage them to think that they are communicating effectively. Being aware of your facial expressions and gestures is especially important when you administer multiple-choice tests or subtests or other tests that require you to point. You must avoid looking at the correct response—or at any response, for that matter.

Particularly if their primary language involves signing, children with hearing impairments may have a poorer command of standard English grammar, use different idioms, or use more concrete expressions than children with normal hearing. These difficulties can affect rapport. If children with hearing impairments are uncooperative, they may sign too rapidly, look away from you, turn off their assistive listening device, close their eyes, or seem to have only selective understanding of what you say. They also may have difficulty handling silence, as they may view silence as a breakdown in communication rather than a simple pause. If rapport problems develop, handle them with the same techniques you would use with other children.

Background Factors

In your evaluation of a child who has a hearing impairment or who is suspected of having a hearing impairment, consider the following background factors:

1. Type of loss
2. Degree of loss in each ear
3. Range of frequencies affected in each ear
4. Age of onset
5. Etiology
6. Use of assistive listening devices (including availability)
7. Ability to benefit from assistive listening devices
8. Stability of hearing loss
9. Age at identification of hearing problem
10. Educational history
11. Communication ability
12. Communication preference (e.g., signing, speech and signing, or speech only)
13. Visual acuity
14. Ability to use fine-motor skills for fingerspelling or Cued Speech (see the description later in the chapter of this system of handshapes and placements that, when combined with information provided by movements of the mouth and face, renders English as a visual, rather than a spoken, language)
15. Degree of residual hearing
16. Auditory processing capability
17. Co-occurring disabilities
18. Communication patterns within the family, school, and other environments, including use of spoken language and sign language (including home signs—i.e., signs used in the home only)

Let's look at some of these factors in more detail.

1. *Etiology of hearing loss.* Some etiologies lead not only to a hearing loss but also to other adverse effects. For example, 17% of children who are born deaf as a result of genetic transmission also have an additional disability (Braden, 1994). If the hearing loss is a result of a neurological disorder (such as those resulting from meningitis or cytomegalovirus), the child may suffer from concomitant dysfunctions that have to be considered in selecting appropriate assessment procedures.

2. *Degree of hearing loss.* Children with mild to moderate hearing loss may be able to be evaluated orally if they have an assistive listening device. Some children with mild to moderate hearing loss prefer using sign language. Children with severe hearing loss will need to be administered tests in their primary mode of communication.

3. *Onset of hearing loss.* Children who heard oral language before their hearing loss was sustained may understand verbal communication better than those who sustained the hearing loss earlier. Onset of deafness prior to the age of 5 years is likely to have a negative effect on the development of language, particularly of spoken language.

4. *Stability of hearing loss.* The ability to hear may fluctuate from day to day, month to month, or year to year. For example, some etiologies result in a decline in residual hearing ability, and illnesses, ear infections, ear wax, episodic tinnitus (i.e., ringing or buzzing), and other conditions can affect a child's hearing in various ways.

5. *Degree of residual hearing.* Ask the parents, an audiologist, or a speech and language therapist whether the child's hearing loss affects his or her ability to understand speech sounds. Find out the methods by which the child receives information (receptive skills) and communicates information (expressive skills). It is also helpful to observe the child in a classroom and in other settings to learn about his or her receptive and expressive skills.

Interview Guidelines

In addition to conducting a developmental history interview (see Table B-10 in Appendix B) and having the parents complete the Background Questionnaire (see Table A-1 in Appendix A), ask the parents the following questions.

1. When did you first suspect that [child's name] had a hearing problem?
2. What led you to believe that [child's name] had a hearing problem?
3. How have [child's name]'s hearing difficulties affected his [her] ability to understand speech?
4. How do you and others communicate with [child's name]?
5. What professional did you see first to help you determine whether [child's name] had a hearing problem?
6. What other professionals have you consulted?
7. How long did it take to confirm your suspicions that [child's name] had a hearing problem?
8. What interventions did [child's name] receive when the hearing loss was diagnosed?
9. (If interventions were used) How have the interventions helped [child's name]?
10. What other concerns do you have about [child's name]'s development?
11. Do you have any other evaluations not in the file that you can give me?

You can also ask the following questions, if needed, of parents of young children of specific ages or when you inquire about the child's development.

3-Month-Olds
- Does your child startle or cry at loud noises?
- Does your child respond to sounds or your voice?

6-Month-Olds
- Does your child like toys that make sound?
- Does your child turn to locate where a sound is coming from?

9-Month-Olds
- Does your child turn and look when you call his or her name?
- Does your child respond to "no" or changes in the tone of your voice?

12-Month-Olds
- Does your child babble and make sounds?
- Does your child understand the names of some simple items such as "cup" or "shoe"?

15-Month-Olds
- Does your child respond to simple directions?
- Does your child say some simple words?

In reviewing a child's case history, note references to any of the clues to potential hearing difficulties covered earlier in the chapter. Also ask the child's teacher to complete the School Referral Questionnaire in Table A-3 in Appendix A. Adolescents can complete the Personal Data Questionnaire in Table A-2 in Appendix A.

Observation Guidelines

Although audiologists and speech-language pathologists are the specialists in determining the communication skills of children with hearing impairments, you, as a psychologist, will be making observations, both formal and informal, of a child's communication skills. Record where your observations occurred (e.g., your office, a classroom, the playground, the child's home, a job or social setting), because the child's communication skills may differ across settings. Also note how the child and the other individuals in each setting communicated with one another (i.e., spoken language or sign language or a combination of both). Assess the child's skills in reading and writing, speech (intelligibility and pleasantness), and speech reading. Notice the extent to which the child was able to understand conversation during the evaluation.

Consider the following questions:

SPEECH

1. Are the volume and pitch of the child's voice appropriate to the situation?
2. Is the child's pronunciation intelligible, consistent, and age appropriate?
3. Is the child's speech fluent, or are there unusual pauses?
4. Does the child grope for words?
5. Does the child turn to you in an effort to hear you better?
6. Does the child confuse similar-sounding words?
7. Does the child respond once to a sound and not respond again?
8. Does the child understand your speech?

SIGNING

1. Are the size and rate of the child's signs appropriate to the situation?
2. Is the child's signing fluent, or are there unusual pauses?
3. Does the child confuse similar-looking signs?
4. Does the child understand your signs?
5. Does the child use fingerspelling?
6. (If yes) Is it used accurately?
7. Does the child understand your fingerspelling?

GENERAL

1. Are the child's replies timely, or are there unusual delays?
2. Does the child ask you to repeat what you have just said?
3. If the child does not speak or sign, how does he or she communicate (e.g., pointing, gesturing, shifting eye gaze)?
4. How does the child react when you do not understand him or her?
5. How does the child behave when he or she is frustrated (e.g., withdraws, acts out, tries a new approach such as drawing)?
6. How well does the child understand questions that are out of context or that are unexpected?

Suggestions for Test Administration

The following suggestions are designed to help you administer tests to children with hearing impairments (Braden & Hannah, 1998):

PREFERRED MODE OF COMMUNICATION

1. Determine the child's preferred mode of communication.
2. Administer the tests in the child's preferred communication modality or language.
3. Arrange for a psychologist who knows how to communicate in the child's preferred communication modality or language to administer the tests if you cannot do so.

INTERPRETER

1. Use a qualified interpreter who can communicate in the child's preferred communication modality or language if you cannot obtain the services of a psychologist who can do so. (See the Web site of the Registry of Interpreters for the Deaf at www.rid.org for more information about interpreters who work with individuals with hearing impairments.)
2. Do not use a parent, another family member, or the child's teacher or aide as the interpreter, because the child may not discuss his or her feelings openly in the presence of a family member or teacher. Confidentiality issues arise if you use a volunteer interpreter who is not a registered interpreter.
3. Maintain eye contact and speak directly to the child (not to the interpreter), using a normal conversational tone and pace.
4. Do not speak to the interpreter about the child as if the child were not there.
5. Sit across from the child, with the interpreter slightly to your rear and to one side, within the child's line of sight.
6. Do not speak at the same time as the interpreter.
7. Coordinate your activities with the interpreter so that the child can look at any demonstration you may give, either before or after looking at the interpreter. Remember that the child will not be able to attend simultaneously to the interpreter's signs *and* your demonstrations. Realize that when instructions on language-reduced tests are signed, children with hearing impairments may be at a disadvantage. These children must process the instructions visually and then shift their attention to the test items, whereas children with normal hearing can view the test materials while the instructions are being given.
8. Use an interpreter while evaluating the child even if you administer nonverbal tests in which gestures and demonstrations are used.
9. Prepare and train the interpreter prior to the evaluation. Make sure that the interpreter has the necessary skills to assist with the assessment.
10. After the evaluation, discuss with the interpreter any issues pertaining to the translation of the test stimuli or the interpretation of the child's responses.
11. Recognize that English and ASL (or other spoken and native languages) have different structures. For example, in English the word *right* has two meanings—the opposite of wrong and the opposite of left. In ASL there is no sign with these two meanings; instead, they are expressed by two different signs. Also, ASL may combine into a single sign complex meanings that can only be expressed in English with a sequence of words. For example, one sign in ASL can express the sentence "I ask her," which in English requires three words.
12. Be aware that some test items may be difficult to administer in ASL. Test items that require recall of numbers and letters (e.g., Letter–Number Sequencing on the WISC–IV and WAIS–III) are one example. Because some letters and numbers are signed in similar ways (e.g., the letter F and the numeral 9, the letter D and the numeral 1, the letter W and the numeral 6), items using these letters or numbers together in noncontextual strings (e.g., 6D9W1) may not be administered clearly in sign language. In assessing a child using ASL, consider the accuracy of handshape responses in light of the task stimuli (letters, numbers, or both). For example, if the stimuli are numbers only, you do not have to question whether the child means 6 or W. Another example is a test item that asks the child to point to his or her nose or eye. Because the signs for these terms demonstrate the item, the task in ASL is different from the task in spoken English.
13. Recognize that using an interpreter will increase the time needed to conduct the evaluation.

CONDITION OF THE ROOM

1. Illuminate the room adequately, so that your face and hands (and those of the interpreter, if there is one) can be clearly seen.
2. Sit close to the child.
3. If the child's hearing acuity is better in one ear than in the other, sit on the side of the better ear.
4. Do not sit with the sun or a bright light behind you, because this can create shadows and eyestrain for the child.

5. Make sure that lights do not shine in the child's eyes or create a glare on the materials.
6. Keep the room free of noise and visual distractions.

FACIAL EXPRESSIONS AND SPEECH

1. Look at the child when you speak to him or her and be sure that the child, in turn, is watching you (or the interpreter, if there is one).
2. Maintain a pleasant facial expression.
3. Speak clearly, distinctly, and naturally, at a reduced rate, without exaggerating or distorting your lip movements, particularly if the child has some hearing ability or speech-reading ability.
4. Use short, simple sentences.
5. Emphasize key words in your phrases.
6. If you need to repeat yourself, rephrase if at all possible.
7. Do not turn away from the child in the middle of a sentence.
8. Be sure that no obstructions block the child's view of your lips.
9. Do not chew gum, smoke a cigarette, put your hand on your chin, cover your mouth, or do anything else that might impede speech reading.

ADDITIONAL ADMINISTRATIVE SUGGESTIONS

1. Check to see that the child who regularly uses an assistive listening device has it turned on, that it is working, and that she or he brings extra hearing-aid batteries to the examination.
2. Touch the child gently on the arm or wave your hand in the child's line of vision if the child is looking away, unless the child has sufficient residual or aided hearing for you simply to say the child's name.
3. Rephrase misunderstood concepts into simpler, more visible forms rather than repeating them in the same way.
4. Consider presenting some questions in written form if the child can read.
5. Provide supplementary examples/demonstrations of similar test items. For example, you might demonstrate the task requirements with items below the starting point items.
6. Observe the child's nonverbal behavior.
7. Give credit to a pantomimed response only when you have no doubt about the accuracy of the response.
8. Do not accept a nod or a smile when you are trying to determine whether the child understands the task; instead, ask the child to tell you in her or his own words.
9. Take breaks as needed.
10. State in your report how communication was established, what means were used to check the child's comprehension of instructions and test items, whether you used an interpreter, and, if so, the qualifications of the interpreter.
11. Check with the child's audiologist, teacher of the deaf, or speech/language pathologist to find out if you can administer tests that require the child to listen to audiotapes or compact discs.

Use of Standardized Tests

We recommend that when you evaluate a child with a hearing impairment, you select only the most appropriate tests and use at least one well-standardized nonverbal measure of cognitive ability. Use verbal tests or portions of tests cautiously when trying to estimate the cognitive ability of children with hearing impairments. Verbal ability measures are certainly important, but they may not accurately reflect intelligence in children with hearing impairments. Traditionally, verbal cognitive tests have been viewed as giving an inaccurate picture of the mental ability of children with hearing impairments; instead, they have been assumed to measure the extent of the children's verbal or English language achievement. This may be true in many cases, especially when children have not been exposed to signing or other methods of communication.

Sullivan and Montoya (1997), however, maintain that verbal cognitive tests *should* be used to estimate the intelligence level of children with hearing impairments:

> The historic taboo against the use of verbal intelligence tests with children who are hearing impaired needs to be reexamined for several reasons. The majority of children with hearing impairments are educated in settings where they must compete with hearing peers in academic subjects that are language based. The Wechsler Verbal Scale IQ is a better predictor than the Performance Scale IQ of reading and math achievement among children with hearing impairments. Finally, in order for children and youth with a hearing impairment to obtain higher paying jobs in adulthood, they need numeracy skills, English literacy skills, and face-to-face communication skills with hearing peers. (p. 320, with changes in notation)

Children with hearing impairments sometimes obtain significantly different scores on verbal and nonverbal intelligence tests. The verbal score may reflect degree and type of hearing loss, age of onset of hearing loss, experience and instruction with oral language, or related factors, rather than level of intelligence per se. Also, the high correlation between the Wechsler Verbal Scale and achievement tests may simply indicate that both measures depend on language skills.

The language-reduced tests you select for children with hearing impairments should not depend on oral directions, unless the tests are administered in the child's preferred mode of communication. Timed tests may be less valid for children with hearing impairments because the added stress of being timed may interfere with their performance more than it does with the performance of children with normal hearing. Representative nonverbal tests include the Perceptual Reasoning subtests of the WISC–IV and the Performance Scale subtests of the WPPSI–III and WAIS–III; the nonverbal subtests of the Stanford-Binet: V; the Leiter International Performance Scale–Revised (Leiter–R); the Universal Nonverbal Test of Intelligence (UNIT); the Spatial, Nonverbal, and Nonverbal

Reasoning clusters of the DAS; the nonverbal subtests of the K-ABC–II; Raven's Progressive Matrices; the Comprehensive Test of Nonverbal Intelligence; and the Test of Nonverbal Intelligence–Third Edition. These tests differ with respect to reliability, validity, norming samples, date of publication, and types of cognitive ability measured; it is important to select the most valid one(s) to obtain a measure of the cognitive ability of children with hearing impairments (see Sattler, 2001). Note that the WISC–IV Administrative Manual and the Stanford-Binet: V Manual have guidelines for administering the tests to children with hearing impairments.

Research is needed about the reliability and validity of any test used to estimate the cognitive ability and achievement level of children with hearing impairments. At present, we know little about the reliability and validity of the WISC–IV and WPPSI–III with children with hearing impairments. If you use the WISC–IV, we recommend that you consider the Perceptual Reasoning Index as the best estimate of such children's cognitive ability and the Verbal Comprehension Index as an estimate of their English language learning. You need, also, to be alert to the possibility that a child with a hearing impairment might also have a specific learning disability in addition to the hearing loss. A weakness in, for example, visual perception, visual memory, sequencing, eye-hand coordination, or some other ability not related to the hearing loss might co-exist with the hearing loss and might require additional educational interventions.

Research on the WISC–III is helpful in understanding how children with hearing impairments perform on Verbal and Performance subtests. In three studies that reported WISC–III Verbal Scale IQs, Performance Scale IQs, and Full Scale IQs for samples of children who are deaf, Performance Scale IQs were higher than Verbal IQs by from 21 to 25 points (VS IQ = 81.63 vs. PS IQ = 102.32; VS IQ = 75.35 vs. PS IQ = 100.63; VS IQ = 81.10 vs. PS IQ = 105.80; Braden, Kostrubala, & Reed, 1994; Sullivan & Montoya, 1997; Wechsler, 1991). In reviewing these studies, Braden and Hannah (1998) noted that other than the lower Verbal than Performance Scale IQs, there is no characteristic Wechsler profile for children who are deaf. Factor analysis supports a language comprehension factor and a visual-spatial organization factor on the WISC–III (Sullivan & Montoya, 1997). Correlations between the WISC–III and achievement tests with samples of children who are deaf are moderately high; rs range from .43 to .81 for the Full Scale, from –.04 to .64 for the Performance Scale, and from .48 to .85 for the Verbal Scale (Braden et al., 1994; Maller & Braden, 1993; Slate & Fawcett, 1995). Even though correlations between the WISC–III Verbal Scale and achievement tests are satisfactory, items on the WISC–III Verbal Scale have a different rank order of difficulty for children with hearing impairments than they do for children with normal hearing (Maller, 1996).

A review of 324 studies of the intelligence test scores of individuals with hearing impairments found a mean nonverbal IQ of 97.14 (Braden, 1994). A study of 39 children with hearing impairments, but with no co-occurring disorders, indi-

cated that their UNIT Full Scale IQs (M = 102.58, SD = 16.52) were similar to those of a matched group of children with normal hearing (M = 100.56, SD = 16.05; Krivitski, McIntosh, & Finch, 2004). Thus, individuals with hearing impairments have nonverbal IQs similar to those of individuals with normal hearing. However, the academic achievement test scores of individuals with hearing impairments are well below those reported for individuals without hearing impairments (Braden, 1994). The reading skills of prelingually deaf children, in particular, may be as much as 50% or more below those of children with normal hearing (Morgan & Vernon, 1994).

Modifying Standard Procedures

Test administration procedures can be modified for children with hearing impairments by omitting verbal tests, adding printed or signed words, and using pantomime, demonstration, and manual communication. To obtain additional information, you can test limits, reinforce responses, use test-type items for practice, drop time limits, or demonstrate task strategies. Sattler and Dumont (2004; see Table C-7 in Appendix C, pp. 380–390) present special instructions for administering the WISC–IV Perceptual Reasoning subtests and the WPPSI–III and WAIS–III Performance Scale subtests to children with hearing impairments. Some of the supplementary measures in the WISC–IV Integrated, such as the multiple-choice versions of the verbal subtests, may be helpful. *Obviously, when standard procedures are modified, standardized norms can be used only as a rough guide, and the results should be used only qualitatively or as an approximation of the child's level of cognitive ability. Any modifications that you use need to be noted in the report.*

If you use pantomime, recognize that children may not interpret your actions as you intend. Pantomime and visual aids are inferior administration procedures for the majority of standardized tests. The UNIT and the Leiter–R, however, are exceptions, because both of these tests have been standardized, for the most part, using pantomime procedures (see Sattler, 2001). Unless you are administering tests that have been standardized using pantomime procedures, use pantomime and visual aids only when you cannot communicate fluently in sign language, Cued Speech, or written language or when the children are not versed in sign language or other special communication modalities. Pantomime and visual aids are preferable to an oral-only administration. Pantomime, however, may inadvertently mimic actual ASL signs, which is extremely confusing for the child.

Following are examples of qualitative information that you might include in psychological reports on children with hearing impairments.

- Henry obtained a Verbal Comprehension Index of 78. In Henry's case, this score, which is at the 8th percentile rank, should be considered as a measure of his facility with spoken English. However, his three other Index scores were all in the average range. For example, he obtained a

Perceptual Reasoning Index of 100 (50th percentile rank), a Working Memory Index of 98 (45th percentile rank), and a Processing Speed Index of 93 (32nd percentile rank). We recommend that his Perceptual Reasoning Index of 100 be used as the best estimate of his intellectual ability.

- Using sign language, Marie obtained a scaled score of 4 (2nd percentile rank) on the WISC–IV Vocabulary subtest, which required her to explain the meanings of words. However, her performance was closer to average (scaled score of 9, percentile rank of 37) on the WISC–IV Integrated Multiple-Choice Vocabulary, where she had to select the best of several printed definitions for each word. These results suggest that her English vocabulary knowledge is average and that she may need to develop her sign language skills.

- Esmerelda was tested with the WISC–IV using special administrative procedures, in addition to those described in the WISC–IV Manual. She obtained a Perceptual Reasoning Index of 108 (61st percentile rank) and a Processing Speed Index of 91 (37th percentile rank). Both of these scores are in the Average range. Although nonstandardized methods of administration were used, including some additional practice items, nothing was done that materially altered the difficulty of the items. Therefore, it appears that these two scores give reasonably accurate estimates of Esmerelda's current level of nonverbal cognitive functioning as measured by the WISC–IV.

- Arturo's WISC–IV Verbal Comprehension score was 67 (1st percentile rank), and his Perceptual Reasoning score was 86 (18th percentile rank). However, Arturo appeared to have difficulty understanding the signed instructions and the demonstrations for the Perceptual Reasoning subtests. On the Leiter International Performance Scale–Revised, a nonverbal test standardized with pantomime instructions, Arturo's Full Scale IQ score was 101 (53rd percentile rank). Although his difficulties with oral and sign language are likely to impair his performance in school and in other settings, Arturo's intelligence is in the average range on a nonverbal test.

INTERVENTIONS

Interventions for children with hearing impairments should be designed to help them meet developmental challenges and achieve competence in academic, social, linguistic, and personal areas. To meet these goals, the children will need (a) help in obtaining any needed assistive devices, including cochlear implants, (b) speech, language, and auditory training, (c) instruction in sign language, (d) extensive early language experiences, (e) a diversity of experiences that will allow them to actively explore and interact with their environment and with people (both hearing and deaf), (f) opportunities to foster social interactions that can enhance their self-concept, achievement motivation, and moral develop-

ment, and (g) schools that provide the services of an interpreter if needed, favorable seating in class to facilitate lip reading, captioned films and videos, assistance of a note-taker, instruction for teachers in alternative communication methods, specialized academic instruction, especially in reading, and counseling. Family members also may need help in learning how to work with children who have hearing impairments.

Several types of technological devices and assistive language communication modalities have been designed to help children with hearing impairments.

COMPUTER-ASSISTED DEVICES

1. In *computer-assisted note-taking,* a note-taker types into a computer what the teacher says to the class, which is then displayed on the computer monitor.
2. *Speech recognition software* converts spoken language to written text and displays it on a computer monitor.

TELEPHONE COMMUNICATION SYSTEMS

1. *Telecommunication devices for the deaf (TDDs* or *TTYs)* are electronic devices that allow users to converse by typing. They come with several options, including printers, large-print displays, and announcers.
2. *Amplified telephones* enhance the clarity and loudness of spoken words. One type has a built-in sound equalizer that selectively increases the volume of high-frequency sounds. Or, a regular telephone can be fitted with an in-line amplifier that receives the incoming signals intended for the handset, increases the volume of these signals, and sends the boosted signals out to the handset.

ENVIRONMENTAL ALERT DEVICES

1. *Visual alert signalers and remote receivers* use an electrical connection to alert people to signals from doorbells, telephones, or smoke detectors. The signal from the doorbell or other source may trigger a flashing light, a loud horn, or vibrations.
2. *Wake-up alarm systems* use visual, auditory, and/or tactile stimulation to wake people. A device connected to a lamp, horn, or bed shaker activates flashing, honking, or gentle shaking.
3. *Hearing ear dogs* are trained to alert their owners to significant sounds.
4. *Car alert systems* emit a high-pitched sound that supplements a person's residual ability to detect unusual or sudden noises.
5. *Visual beep indicator programs* add visual indicators to audible computer beeps that signal an error or another message. These programs are particularly helpful to computer users with little or no residual hearing ability.

IMPLANTS

1. *Cochlear implants,* surgically inserted in the inner ear, transmit electronic signals to the auditory nerve in the

inner ear. They are used primarily for individuals with severe to profound nerve deafness who cannot be helped by conventional hearing aids. Cochlear implants facilitate hearing but cannot restore normal hearing, and their effectiveness varies with the recipient.

2. *Auditory brainstem implants* use the same technology as cochlear implants, but they are placed on the area of the brainstem that ordinarily receives neural impulses from the cochlea through the auditory nerve.

ASSISTIVE LISTENING DEVICES (ALDS)

1. *Infrared systems* use invisible light beams to transmit sounds to users wearing receivers. The receiver must be directly within sight of the transmitter of the light beam. Infrared systems are usable in several situations where poor acoustics, distance, or background noise can affect hearing (in classrooms, on tours, in restaurants, at parties, at movies). The transmitters connect directly to television sets, audio output jacks, or microphones. The infrared system does not work well outdoors because of interference from sunlight.

2. *FM systems* transmit sounds via radio waves. The speaker wears a compact transmitter and microphone, while the listener uses a portable receiver with headphones or earphones. FM systems are useful in classrooms and work well both indoors and outdoors.

3. With *loop systems,* the primary speaker uses a special microphone and amplifier, and the amplified speech signals are transmitted through a loop wire in a telecoil circuit placed within the listener's hearing aid.

4. Hearing aids are small electronic devices that amplify sounds. Several different types are available. In-the-ear hearing aids fit completely in the outer ear and are held in a hard plastic case. Behind-the-ear hearing aids consist of a plastic case that holds the components and a plastic earmold that fits inside the outer ear. In-the-canal hearing aids are customized to fit in the ear canal. Body aids consist of a microphone, receiver, and an amplifier circuit attached to a belt or pocket and connected to the ear by a wire.

OTHER TECHNOLOGIES

1. *Text messaging devices,* such as smart phones, pagers, personal digital assistants (PDAs), and other handheld devices, can be used to send short messages of up to about 200 characters to other similar devices. A PDA is a lightweight, handheld computer that has no keyboard, relying instead on special hardware and pen-based computer software to enable the recognition of handwritten input, which is entered on the surface of a liquid crystal display screen.

2. With *instant messaging,* two or more people can exchange messages via the Internet in real time when both are logged on to their instant messaging services.

3. *E-mail,* with its now-familiar advantages (worldwide reach, ability to edit and cut and paste text and include graphics and sound in messages), has made it possible for those with hearing impairments to send or receive a lengthy communication instantaneously.

ASSISTIVE LANGUAGE COMMUNICATION MODALITIES

1. *Oral communication methods* (or auditory-oral methods) emphasize the use of residual hearing, speech development, and speech reading. Children can use hearing aids, cochlear implants, or FM systems to amplify sounds. Children should be given intensive speech therapy to help them learn to speak English or other spoken languages. The primarily auditory approach stresses residual hearing and the development of discrimination and sound perception ability. The *Cued Speech* approach combines an auditory emphasis with visual cues to help children with hearing impairments discriminate among words that look or sound the same. The cues are eight hand shapes, which are used in four positions near the face to supplement spoken language. Each hand shape represents a group of consonant sounds, and the positions represent vowel sounds.

2. There are several *artificial manual sign methods* with which children with hearing impairments can communicate; they differ primarily in the language used as a base. Signed English, Seeing Essential English, and Signing Exact English are all forms of a signed system based on the English language and used most often in educational settings. When they are faithful to spoken English, signed systems tend to be much slower than natural speech or ASL.

3. A *native manual sign language* such as ASL is a recognized language with its own grammar and syntax. ASL is widely used in the deaf community in the United States, while other sign languages are used in some other countries. Movement, handshapes, facial expressions, and location of signs are all used to convey complex grammatical structures. Children born to parents who are deaf usually can hear, but their first language may be a native sign language such as ASL. Fingerspelling, representing each letter of the alphabet with a handshape, can be used to supplement a native manual sign language.

4. *Closed-captioning decoders* allow a person to view the dialogue and sound effects of any television program whose sounds have been encoded into text. The text appears at the bottom of the screen, much like the subtitles on foreign movies.

Several methods combine two of the above assistive language communication modalities. The Rochester method involves the simultaneous use of fingerspelling and speech. In the Total Communication philosophy (also referred to as Simultaneous Communication), which is commonly used in programs for children who are deaf, speech is used in conjunction with English-based signs, signs used in English order, or ASL. Children using ASL or any other method of communication must still learn to read and write in English, because ASL and English have different grammatical and phonological structures (Hodapp, 1998).

THINKING THROUGH THE ISSUES

1. How would your life be different if you were born totally deaf?
2. What adjustment would you have to make in your life if you became deaf at 5 or more years of age?
3. When would you use a verbal cognitive test with children with hearing impairments?
4. What challenges do teachers encounter when they have a child with a hearing impairment in their class?
5. When might be the best time for children with hearing impairments to learn ASL?
6. On the issue of cochlear implants, how might the views of hearing parents of a child with a hearing impairment differ from those of the deaf community?

SUMMARY

1. Inability to hear clearly can adversely affect children's language development, speech intelligibility, socialization, and academic performance.
2. Acquiring fluency in a spoken language is a major developmental task facing children with hearing impairments.
3. The phrase "children with hearing impairments" refers to children with hearing losses ranging from mild to profound.
4. The term *deaf* is used only for a child who has a hearing impairment so severe that it prevents successful processing of linguistic information through audition.
5. Hearing impairments affect not only children's ability to hear, but also their behavior, self-concept, identity, and social and emotional development.
6. Deafness is an invisible, as well as a low-incidence, disability; it usually represents a static and irreversible condition.
7. About 90% of children who have been identified for educational programs or services because of hearing impairments are born into families in which both parents can hear.
8. Parents are often unprepared to recognize a hearing impairment in their infant.
9. If you suspect that a child has an undiagnosed hearing loss, refer the child to an audiologist for a hearing evaluation.
10. In the 2000–2001 school year, the percentage of children aged 6 to 21 years served under the IDEA because of hearing impairments was 1.23% (70,767).
11. IDEA 2004 covers hearing impairment as a disability. The law (a) emphasizes that IEPs must consider the communication needs of children with hearing impairments, (b) requires schools to consider whether the child needs assistive technology devices and services and to prepare personnel to assist children with hearing impairments, and (c) authorizes states to provide technical assistance and in-service training to schools and agencies serving deaf-blind children and their families and to address the post-secondary needs of individuals who are deaf or hard of hearing.
12. Implementing the provisions of IDEA 2004, as well as providing adequate funding, will assure that children with hearing impairments receive the services they need to enhance their well-being and to become productive members of society.

Clues to Potential Hearing Difficulties

13. Several behavioral, speech, and specific language signs may suggest a hearing difficulty.

Structure of the Ear

14. The ear has three main structures: outer ear, middle ear, and inner ear.
15. When sound waves strike the eardrum, it vibrates. The vibrations pass through the bones to the middle ear and then to the inner ear. The vibrations then disseminate into the cochlea, where they are converted into electrical impulses, which are transmitted to the brain via the eighth cranial nerve (the vestibulochlear, or auditory, nerve).

Disorders That Affect Hearing

16. When a hearing impairment is present at birth (congenital) or occurs before speech and language are developed, it is termed a prelingual hearing impairment.
17. When a hearing impairment is caused by later disease or trauma, after speech and language have been developed, it is termed a postlingual hearing impairment.
18. Congenital disorders account for about 50% of early childhood hearing impairments with known etiology.
19. The following are examples of conditions or agents that may lead to a hearing impairment in infancy: asphyxia, cleft palate, cytomegalovirus (CMV), Down syndrome, Herpes simplex virus, hyperbilirubinemia, meningitis, premature birth, Rh incompatibility, rubella, syphilis, toxoplasmosis, Treacher-Collins syndrome, Usher syndrome, CHARGE syndrome, and Waardenburg syndrome.
20. The following are examples of conditions that may lead to a hearing impairment later in life: severe blow to the head; exposure to very loud noise (or sustained exposure to loud noise) that results in acoustic trauma; childhood diseases such as measles, mumps, and chicken pox; inner ear infections (otitis media); perforated eardrum; sudden pressure changes from flying, diving, or strenuous exercise; brain tumors; demyelinating diseases; viral infections of the inner ear; other infections accompanied by high fever; and reactions to certain prescription medications.
21. Adequate prenatal care and efficient obstetrical procedures, as well as early treatment of ear infections and high fevers, may prevent some auditory problems from developing.

Acuity of Hearing

22. Hearing ability is measured on a continuum ranging from very acute perception, such as that of a gifted conductor who can detect an out-of-tune instrument in an orchestra, to total deafness, such as that of an individual who can detect sound only tactilely, in the form of strong vibrations.
23. Hearing ability is evaluated on two dimensions: ability to perceive sounds of different frequencies and different intensities.
24. Sound frequency, or the pitch of sound, is measured in units called hertz (Hz), or cycles per second.
25. Sound intensity, or the loudness of sound, is measured in units called decibels (dB).
26. Audiologists use the following classification scheme to evaluate hearing ability: normal range, loss of 0–15 dB; slight hearing loss, loss of 16–25 dB; mild hearing loss, loss of 26–40 dB; moderate hearing loss, loss of 41–70 dB; severe hearing loss, loss of 71–90 dB; and profound hearing loss, loss of 91 dB or greater.
27. Hearing loss falls into four types.
28. A conductive hearing loss may be caused by diseases or obstructions in the outer or middle ear that impede sound conduction.

29. A sensorineural hearing loss may be caused by damage to the inner ear or auditory nerve.
30. A mixed hearing loss represents a combination of conductive and sensorineural loss.
31. A central hearing loss may be caused by damage to or impairment of the nerves of the central nervous system, either in the pathway to the brain or in the brain itself.
32. When a child is evaluated for a hearing loss, her or his hearing ability should be assessed with *and* without an assistive listening device.
33. Children with hearing impairments are a heterogenous group.

Developmental Considerations

34. "When a group of people is cut off from acoustic language, they evolve a visual language (sign)" (Mayberry, 1992, pp. 65–66, with changes in notation).
35. "Deaf children with higher levels of language perform better on high-level cognitive tasks than do deaf children with lower language skills . . . " (Hodapp, 1998, p. 168).
36. "[And] the language of children who are deaf develops best when their parents are ASL signers who are deaf. These children develop language from their earliest years, in a natural way" (Hodapp, 1998, p. 168)
37. Children with hearing impairments also may have difficulties with balance, equilibrium, and other motor skills related to the vestibular system. Thus, delays in early developmental milestones (e.g., walking) may also be observed.

Assessment Considerations

38. Evaluating children with hearing impairments may be more fatiguing, demand greater attention and concentration, and require more time and flexibility than evaluating children with normal hearing.
39. It is critical that you make the child understand the test instructions without giving leading cues in the process.
40. If you routinely evaluate children with hearing impairments, learn sign language and other means of communicating with them.
41. If you believe that you are not qualified to evaluate children with hearing impairments, refer them to a more qualified professional.
42. Although children with hearing impairments may give the impression of being able to understand your questions, they may be feigning comprehension in order to obtain your approval.
43. Do *not* interpret the difficulties that children with hearing impairments have with expressive language, receptive language, or both as indications of limited intelligence.
44. Because sight is the chief means by which children who have hearing impairments receive information, they are particularly likely to seek to gain understanding from visual cues—such as facial expressions and hand movements.
45. Recognize that any movements you make, including eye movements, may cue a child.
46. Particularly if their primary language involves signing, children with hearing impairments may have a poorer command of standard English grammar, use different idioms, or use more concrete expressions than children with normal hearing.
47. In your evaluation of a child who has a hearing impairment or who is suspected of having a hearing impairment, consider such factors as the etiology, degree, onset, and stability of the hearing loss and the degree of residual hearing.

48. In addition to conducting a developmental history interview and having the parents complete the Background Questionnaire, ask the parents questions pertaining to a possible hearing impairment.
49. Although audiologists and speech-language pathologists are the specialists in determining the communication skills of children with hearing impairments, you, as a psychologist, will be making observations, both formal and informal, of a child's communication skills.
50. When you administer tests to children with hearing impairments, determine their preferred mode of communication, work with an interpreter if needed, check the condition of the room, attend to your facial expressions and speech, and use other appropriate techniques depending on the needs of the child.
51. We recommend that when you evaluate a child with a hearing impairment, you select only the most appropriate tests and use at least one well-standardized nonverbal measure of cognitive ability.
52. Use verbal tests or verbal portions of tests cautiously when trying to estimate the cognitive ability of children with hearing impairments.
53. Sullivan and Montoya (1997) maintain that verbal cognitive tests *should* be used to estimate the intelligence level of children with hearing impairments.
54. The language-reduced tests you select for children with hearing impairments should not depend on oral directions, unless the tests are administered in the child's preferred mode of communication.
55. Research is needed about the reliability and validity of any test used to estimate the cognitive ability and achievement level of children with hearing impairments.
56. There is no characteristic Wechsler profile for children who are deaf.
57. A review of 324 studies of the intelligence test scores of individuals with hearing impairments found a mean nonverbal IQ of 97.14.
58. Test administration procedures can be modified for children with hearing impairments by omitting verbal tests, adding printed or signed words, and using pantomime, demonstration, and manual communication.
59. Obviously, when standard procedures are modified, standardized norms can be used only as a rough guide, and the results should be used only qualitatively or as an approximation of the child's level of cognitive ability. Any modifications that you use need to be noted in the report.
60. If you use pantomime, recognize that children may not interpret your actions as you intend.
61. Pantomime and visual aids are inferior administration procedures for the majority of standardized tests.

Interventions

62. Interventions for children with hearing impairments should be designed to help them meet developmental challenges and achieve competence in academic, social, linguistic, and personal areas.
63. To meet these goals, the children will need (a) help in obtaining any needed assistive devices, including cochlear implants, (b) speech, language, and auditory training, (c) instruction in sign language, (d) extensive early language experiences, (e) a diversity of experiences that will allow them to actively explore and interact with their environment and with people (both hearing and deaf), (f) opportunities to foster social interactions

that can enhance their self-concept, achievement motivation, and moral development, and (g) schools that provide the services of an interpreter if needed, favorable seating in class to facilitate lip reading, captioned films and videos, assistance of a note-taker, instruction for teachers in alternative communication methods, and counseling.

64. Technological devices and assistive language communication modalities include computer-assisted devices, telephone communication systems, environmental alert devices, implants, assistive listening devices (ALDs), and oral and sign methods of communication.

KEY TERMS, CONCEPTS, AND NAMES

Hearing impairment (p. 479)
Deaf (p. 479)
IDEA 2004 (p. 479)
Clues to potential hearing difficulties (p. 479)
Structure of the ear (p. 480)
Outer ear (p. 480)
Pinna, or auricle (p. 480)
Ear canal (p. 480)
Middle ear (p. 480)
Eardrum (p. 480)
Hammer (malleus) (p. 480)
Anvil (incus) (p. 480)
Stirrup (stapes) (p. 480)
Inner ear (p. 480)
Cochlea (p. 480)
Vestibular labyrinth (p. 480)
Vestibular system (p. 480)
Disorders that affect hearing (p. 480)
Prelingual hearing impairment (p. 480)
Postlingual hearing impairment (p. 480)
Asphyxia (p. 480)
Cleft palate (p. 480)
Cytomegalovirus (CMV) (p. 480)
Down syndrome (p. 480)
Herpes simplex virus (p. 480)
Hyperbilirubinemia (p. 480)
Kernicterus (p. 480)
Meningitis (p. 480)
Premature birth (p. 480)
Low birth weight (p. 480)
Rh incompatibility (p. 481)
Rubella (p. 481)
Syphilis (p. 481)
Toxoplasmosis (p. 481)
Treacher-Collins syndrome (p. 481)
Usher syndrome (p. 481)
CHARGE syndrome (p. 481)
Waardenburg syndrome (p. 481)
Acuity of hearing (p. 481)
Sound frequency (p. 481)
Sound intensity (p. 481)
Normal range (p. 481)
Slight hearing loss range (p. 481)
Mild hearing loss range (p. 481)
Moderate hearing loss range (p. 482)
Severe hearing loss range (p. 482)
Profound hearing loss range (p. 482)
Conductive hearing loss (p. 482)

Sensorineural hearing loss (p. 482)
Mixed hearing loss (p. 482)
Central hearing loss (central auditory processing disorder) (p. 482)
Developmental considerations (p. 482)
American Sign Language (ASL) (p. 482)
Assessment considerations (p. 482)
Background factors (p. 483)
Etiology of hearing loss (p. 483)
Degree of hearing loss (p. 483)
Onset of hearing loss (p. 483)
Stability of hearing loss (p. 483)
Degree of residual hearing (p. 484)
Interview guidelines (p. 484)
Observation guidelines (p. 484)
Suggestions for test administration (p. 485)
Preferred communication (p. 485)
Interpreter (p. 485)
Condition of room (p. 485)
Facial expressions and speech (p. 486)
Additional administrative suggestions (p. 486)
Use of standardized tests (p. 486)
Modifying standard procedures (p. 487)
Interventions (p. 488)
Computer-assisted devices (p. 488)
Computer-assisted note-taking (p. 488)
Speech recognition software (p. 488)
Telephone communication systems (p. 488)
Telecommunication devices for the deaf (TDDs or TTYs) (p. 488)
Amplified telephones (p. 488)
Environmental alert devices (p. 488)
Visual alert signalers and remote receivers (p. 488)
Wake-up alarm systems (p. 488)
Hearing ear dogs (p. 488)
Car alert systems (p. 488)
Visual beep indicator programs (p. 488)
Implants (p. 488)
Cochlear implants (p. 488)
Auditory brainstem implants (p. 489)
Assistive listening devices (ALDs) (p. 489)
Infrared systems (p. 489)
FM systems (p. 489)
Loop systems (p. 489)
Hearing aids (p. 489)
Other technologies (p. 489)
Text messaging devices (p. 489)
Instant messaging (p. 489)
E-mail (p. 489)
Assistive language communication modalities (p. 489)
Oral communication methods (p. 489)
Cued Speech (p. 489)
Artificial manual sign methods of communication (p. 489)
Native manual sign languages (p. 489)
Closed-captioning decoders (p. 489)

STUDY QUESTION

Discuss children with hearing impairments. Include in your discussion IDEA 2004, clues to potential hearing difficulties, the structure of the ear, disorders that affect hearing, acuity of hearing, developmental considerations, assessment considerations, and interventions (including technological devices and assistive language communication modalities).

22

AUTISTIC DISORDER

Children are ever the future of a society. Every child who does not function at a level commensurate with his or her possibilities, every child who is destined to make fewer contributions to society than society needs, and every child who does not take his or her place as a productive adult diminishes the power of that society's future.

—Frances Degen Horowitz, American psychologist (1932–   )
and Marion O'Brien, American psychologist (1943–   )

Goals and Objectives

This chapter is designed to enable you to do the following:

- Become familiar with the symptoms of autistic disorder

- Understand how to assess children who may have autistic disorder

- Understand interventions with children who have autistic disorder

This chapter focuses on autistic disorder, one of the five pervasive developmental disorders described in *DSM-IV–TR* (American Psychiatric Association, 2000). The chapter also briefly discusses the other four disorders: Rett's disorder, childhood disintegrative disorder, Asperger's disorder, and pervasive developmental disorder not otherwise specified. These disorders are sometimes referred to as autism spectrum disorders.

PERVASIVE DEVELOPMENTAL DISORDERS

Autistic Disorder

Autistic disorder is a lifelong neurodevelopmental disorder that is evenly distributed across socioeconomic and educational levels. Although there are no biological markers or laboratory tests that reliably diagnose the disorder, genetic factors play a dominant role in its etiology (see below; Jordan, 1999; Kabot, Masi, & Segal, 2003; Pericak-Vance, 2003). In addition, there is no widely accepted theory that explains the characteristic symptoms of autistic disorder (such as difficulties in development and use of language, imitation, affective expression, sharing, attention, and social comprehension), which can vary from mild to severe. A few children with autistic disorder have special skills, such as the ability to dismantle and reassemble a complicated mechanical apparatus or the ability to memorize mathematical tables, bus schedules, and calendars.

The prevalence of autistic disorder historically has been estimated to be about 1 in 2,000 children, with a male-to-female ratio of about 3.7 to 1 (American Psychiatric Association, 2000; Fombonne, 1998). However, the incidence of autistic disorder has been rising precipitously and mysteriously; recent prevalence estimates have ranged from 1 in 160 to 1 in 200 children (Begley, 2003; Gillberg & Billstedt, 2000). We do not know whether the increased prevalence rates result from changes in diagnostic criteria, prior misclassifications of autistic disorder as mental retardation, heightened public awareness, better training of health professionals in recognizing the disorder, or an actual increase in the disorder itself. In the 2000–2001 school year, the percentage of children ages 6 through 21 years with autistic disorder served under IDEA was 1.36% ($N = 78,749$; U.S. Department of Education, 2002), an increase of 417% since the 1993–1994 school year.

Rett's Disorder

Rett's disorder involves the loss of several functions after the first 5 months of normal development (American Psychiatric Association, 2000). The primary symptoms include (a) deceleration of head growth between 5 and 48 months, (b) loss of previously acquired purposeful hand skills between 5 and 30 months, with subsequent development of stereotyped hand movements, (c) loss of social engagement, (d) poorly coordinated gait or trunk movements, (e) severely impaired expressive and receptive language, and (f) severe psychomotor retardation. Rett's disorder occurs only in females. The prognosis for children with Rett's disorder is much worse than that for children with autistic disorder (Willemsen-Swinkels & Buitelaar, 2002).

Childhood Disintegrative Disorder

Childhood disintegrative disorder involves the loss, after the age of 2 years (but before the age of 10 years), of previously acquired skills in expressive or receptive language, social or adaptive behavior, bowel or bladder control, play, and motor coordination. Symptoms include qualitative impairments in social interaction and communication and restricted, repetitive, and stereotyped patterns of behavior, interests, and activities. Childhood disintegrative disorder is a relatively uncommon condition.

Asperger's Disorder

Children with a diagnosis of *Asperger's disorder* (also referred to as Asperger's syndrome) function at the higher levels of the autistic continuum. The essential features of Asperger's disorder are severe and sustained impairment in social interactions and development of restricted, repetitive patterns of behavior and interests (American Psychiatric Association, 2000; see Table E-8 in Appendix E). Some children with Asperger's disorder also are clumsy, lack an appreciation of humor, and use language in a stilted and stereotyped manner. The disorder occurs in both males and females, with males outnumbering females by a ratio of about 10 to 1 (McGough, 2003).

Children with Asperger's disorder show many similarities to children with autistic disorder; the distinctions between the two conditions are a matter of degree. However, a key difference is that, although children with Asperger's disorder may have all-absorbing circumscribed interests, they do not have the speech delay or cognitive delay present in children with autistic disorder. Some researchers believe that Asperger's disorder is not distinct from high-grade autistic disorder (Jordan, 1999; Langstrom, 2002; Macintosh & Dissanayake, 2004; Tidmarsh & Volkmar, 2003), and even the existence of the disorder is controversial. However, the prognosis is better for children with Asperger's disorder than for children with autistic disorder. It may be best to view Asperger's disorder as a case of high-functioning or mild autism in a child with normal or near-normal intelligence (Mayes & Calhoun, 2004). Both Asperger's disorder and autistic disorder likely have the same underlying basis and a common etiology (Willemsen-Swinkels & Buitelaar, 2002).

Pervasive Developmental Disorder Not Otherwise Specified

Pervasive developmental disorder not otherwise specified is the diagnostic classification used for children who have severe and pervasive impairment in social interaction, verbal communication, and nonverbal communication or who display stereotyped behaviors, interests, and activities, but not to the extent needed to fully meet the criteria for any of the other types of pervasive developmental disorders or any other *DSM–IV–TR* classification. Children with this disorder usually do not show facial expressions that convey subtle emotions; they do show emotions such as joy, fear, or anger, but usually only when they are experiencing intense or extreme levels of these emotions.

SYMPTOMS OF AUTISTIC DISORDER

Symptoms of autistic disorder vary as a function of level of cognitive development and age (Mayes & Calhoun, 2004). As level of intelligence increases, symptoms tend to decrease; in addition, children with higher IQs usually are identified as having an autistic disorder at a later age than children with lower IQs (Mayes & Calhoun, 2004). Table 22-1 shows developmental indicators that suggest an autistic disorder in children from birth through 3 years of age and at any age.

About 31% to 55% of children with autistic disorder show symptoms of the disorder in the first year of life, and about 75% to 95% show symptoms by the end of the second year of life (Young, Brewer, & Pattison, 2003). The most common early symptoms are language and speech problems, failure to respond to one's name, failure to engage in imitation play behavior, and failure to switch the gaze to follow pointing. After 2 years of age other behaviors can be observed, such as stereotyped and repetitive language or idiosyncratic language, difficulty in establishing peer relationships, and ritualistic behaviors. (Very young children often do not have the opportunity to demonstrate these behaviors.) In addition, about 20% to 47% show regression or loss of skills at 16 to 24 months of age (Klinger, Dawson, & Renner, 2003).

A diagnosis of autistic disorder is arrived at when a child has impairments in each of three areas: social interaction, communication, and behavior. A delay or abnormal functioning in at least one of these areas must occur before the age of 3 years (American Psychiatric Association, 2000; see Table E-6 in Appendix E). Specific impairments in each of these areas are discussed below (American Psychiatric Association, 2000; Filipek, Accardo, Baranek, Cook, Dawson, Gordon, Gravel, Johnson, Kallen, Levy, Minshew, Prizant, Rapin, Rogers, Stone, Teplin, Tuchman, & Volkmar, 1999; Prior & Ozonoff, 1998; Trevarthen, Aitken, Papoudi, & Robarts, 1998).

IMPAIRMENTS IN SOCIAL INTERACTION

1. *Marked impairment in the use of nonverbal behaviors.* Children with autistic disorder are impaired in their ability to perceive and process social and emotional cues from people and the environment. These impairments may be associated with their difficulty in maintaining attention, their difficulty in selecting the salient attributes of stimuli to be processed, and their susceptibility to distraction by irrelevant stimuli. As infants, they may not lift their arms or change posture in

---

Table 22-1
Possible Developmental Indicators of Autistic Disorder

DURING EARLY INFANCY
- Does not lift arms or change posture in anticipation of being held.
- Does not cuddle.
- Is stiff and resistant to contact.
- Body is passive and floppy.
- Does not gaze into a parent's face.
- Appears to be deaf.

BY THE END OF 7 MONTHS
- Does not participate in vocal turn-taking (baby makes a sound, adult makes a sound, and so forth).
- Does not smile when parents smile.
- Does not make eye contact with parents during an interaction.
- Does not respond to peek-a-boo games.
- Has little interest in the human voice.

BY THE END OF 12 MONTHS
- Does not babble or coo.
- Does not gesture (point, wave, grasp, etc.).
- Does not engage in give-and-take lap play or initiate actions during play (e.g., clapping when mother claps).
- Does not show affection toward people.
- Does not enjoy imitating people in play.

BY THE END OF 18 MONTHS
- Does not say any single words unprompted.
- Does not engage in simple pretend play (e.g., talking on a toy phone).
- Does not want to play close to a parent; prefers to play alone.

BY THE END OF 24 MONTHS
- Does not say two-word phrases on his or her own (as opposed to repeating what someone says).
- Does not show interest in other children; prefers solitary or ritualistic play.
- Does not engage in pretend play.

BY THE END OF 36 MONTHS
- Does not show affection toward adults or other children.
- Does not have a special friend.
- Does not use four- to five-word sentences.
- Does not imitate adults and playmates.
- Does not play make-believe with dolls and animals.
- Does not express affection openly.

AT ANY AGE
- Shows a loss of language skills.
- Shows a loss of social skills.

---

anticipation of being held, they may not cuddle, they may be stiff and resistant to contact, their bodies may be passive and floppy, and they may be either "good" babies or difficult-to-manage babies. As development proceeds, they may engage in unacceptable self-stimulatory or self-injurious behavior (e.g., rocking, head banging, biting their hands, punching themselves, screaming, temper tantrums, aggressive behavior, hyperactive behavior, stealing, unmannerly eating, and inappropriate toileting).

2. *Failure to develop peer relationships.* Preschool- and school-age children with autistic disorder have extreme difficulty in interacting with their peers, particularly in spontaneous interactions. If they do make friends, the focus may be on participating in only one activity with them. They may gravitate to adults or to older children.

3. *Lack of social and emotional reciprocity and of spontaneous efforts to share enjoyment or interests with others.* One of the distinguishing features of autistic disorder is a lack of reciprocal social interaction, which stems in part from difficulty in empathizing with others—children with autistic disorder lack insight into the thoughts, feelings, plans, and wishes of others. Even at 7 months of age, children with autistic disorder may not smile when parents smile, participate in turn-taking games, make eye contact with parents during an interaction, respond to peek-a-boo games, show interest in the human voice, or show interest in receiving affection. At 1 year of age, children with autistic disorder may not initiate actions during play or engage in the give-and-take lap play typically seen in infants at this age. Although most infants who later develop an autistic disorder tend to display a lack of normal emotional attachment to parents, some do display secure attachments (Rutgers, Bakermans-Kranenburg, van IJzendoorn, & van Berckelaer-Onnes, 2004). However, later in life even these children are likely to exhibit avoidant behavior (e.g., make minimal mutual eye contact with family members and peers, pay minimal attention to people and events), have difficultly recognizing emotions at a level commensurate with their level of intelligence, and have difficulty developing emotional attachments to others. Although, in middle childhood, children with autistic disorder may (depending on the severity of their condition) develop greater awareness of others and become more affectionate and friendly with family members, social difficulties are likely to continue. They may still have problems playing group games, forming close peer relationships, and understanding the complexity of social relationships.

IMPAIRMENTS IN COMMUNICATION

1. *Delay in or lack of development of spoken language, which is not compensated for by other modes of communication.* Children with autistic disorder usually do not develop communicative language. If they have not acquired language by 6 years of age, it is rare for them to do so. As infants and toddlers, they often do not babble, attend to human speech, show comprehension of language, speak their first words when they are expected to, or imitate sounds and speech. They may use another person's hand to indicate a desired object (i.e., "hand-over-hand pointing").

2. *Marked impairment in the ability to initiate or sustain conversation with others.* Preschool- and school-age children with autistic disorder may have difficulty in following a conversation, may interpret messages literally, may have difficulty in taking turns in conversation, and may have problems maintaining conversational topics; they may have particular difficulty in following other people's points of view. Essentially, they fail to use language to communicate socially. Part of their difficulty is in forming a coherent functional picture of the world.

3. *Stereotyped and repetitive language or idiosyncratic language.* Language difficulties include interpreting language in an overly concrete and literal way, *pronominal reversal* (reversal of pronouns, such as referring to oneself as "he" and to others as "I"), deviant or monotonous *prosodic features* (features of speech such as intonation, stress, and rhythm), difficulty in understanding *metaphorical language* (figures of speech in which a word or phrase that ordinarily designates one thing is used to designate another), ritualistic and inflexible language, and insensitivity to a listener's responses (Prior & Ozonoff, 1998). At 14 months of age, children with autistic disorder may regress after initial speech development (e.g., lose words), show both *immediate* and *delayed echolalia* (inappropriate repetition of speech previously uttered by another speaker), repeat rhymes or jingles without any apparent communicative function, or make no attempt to speak.

IMPAIRMENTS IN BEHAVIOR

1. *Lack of varied, spontaneous make-believe play or social imitative play appropriate to developmental level.* Children with autistic disorder may show little interest in using toys in pretend play, but may use toys in a mechanical fashion or invent a fantasy world that becomes a focus of repetitive play (Filipek et al., 1999).

2. *Stereotyped and restricted patterns of interest.* Children with autistic disorder may ask the same question repeatedly if they speak, may engage in highly repetitive perseverative play, or may be preoccupied with unusual interests. They may appear to be oblivious to or avoid most environmental stimuli (responding to only a subset of environmental cues), have limited curiosity, have little desire to obtain information, fail to ask "wh" questions (what, when, where, and why), and perform better in scholastic areas requiring primarily rote, mechanical, or procedural abilities than in areas requiring abstract, conceptual, or interpretive abilities (e.g., a child may be better at reading single words and nonwords and at spelling than at reading for comprehension or expressing ideas in writing).

3. *Inflexible adherence to specific nonfunctional routines or rituals.* Some children with autistic disorder "are so preoccupied with 'sameness' in their home and school environments or with routines, that little can be changed without prompting a tantrum or other emotional disturbance" (Filipek et al., 1999, p. 446).

4. *Stereotyped and repetitive motor movements.* At 1 year of age, children with autistic disorder may display stereotypic motor movements, such as hand clapping, arm flapping, aimless running, rocking, spinning, or toe-walking.

5. *Persistent preoccupation with parts of objects or things that move.* At 1 year of age, children with autistic disorder

may show abnormal sensitivity to sounds, light, or touch. As preschoolers, they may engage in repetitive actions involving particular objects and may be obsessed with sensory effects. For example, they may open and close doors, drawers, or flip-top trash cans; turn light switches on and off; flick strings, elastic bands, measuring tapes, or electric cords; transfer water back and forth from one vessel to another; or spin objects for long periods of time.

ETIOLOGY OF AUTISTIC DISORDER

Autistic disorder has a strong genetic component (M.I.N.D. Institute, 2002). For example, if one sibling has autistic disorder, the other sibling is 45 to 90 times more likely to have the disorder than is someone in the general population. Similarly, the concordance rate for identical twins is 36% to 91% above the concordance rate for fraternal twins, which is less than 1%. Autistic disorder may have prenatal, perinatal, or postnatal origins. There is "overwhelming evidence that abnormalities of brain structure and function underlie the autistic syndrome" (Willemsen-Swinkels & Buitelaar, 2002, p. 828). Other explanations for autistic disorder include "viral exposures, vaccination, immunologic factors, autoimmune disorders, gastrointestinal disorders, prenatal exposure to thalidomide, anticonvulsants, and food allergies. The interaction between a genetic predisposition and early environmental insults has also been suggested" (M.I.N.D. Institute, 2002, p. 11). Recent research, for example, suggests that children with autistic disorder may have a dysfunctional immune system (leading to abnormal responses to pathogens and other agents in the environment) and an unusual constellation of proteins in the blood (e.g., higher concentrations of white blood cells and natural killer cells; Maugh, 2005). In addition, there is wide concern that thimerosal, a preservative in vaccines that contains about 50% mercury, is toxic and can damage newborns (Centers for Disease Control and Prevention, 2004). Although the evidence to support this explanation remains scant, research is continuing. Because of the uncertainty about thimerosal, some parents are perplexed about whether their children should receive the measles-mumps-rubella (MMR) vaccination.

It also has been hypothesized that autistic disorder is due to early developmental failures of the mirror neuron system located in the frontal cortex (Nishitani, Avikainen, & Hari, 2004; Williams, Whiten, Suddendorf, & Perrett, 2001). The mirror neuron system is important for imitation learning and for some aspects of social cognition, especially for understanding the intentions of other people. Mirror neurons are activated when individuals view the actions and intentions of others (e.g., obtain information from observing the face, limbs, and whole body of others) and then perform similar actions themselves. The failure of the mirror neuron system may be due to genetic or other endogenous factors, external factors, or the interaction of the two.

CO-OCCURRING DISORDERS

The estimated prevalence rates of co-occurrence of autistic disorder with other disorders are difficult to establish, as noted in the following wide estimated ranges (Klinger et al., 2003):

- 40% to 69% for autistic disorder and mental retardation
- 4% to 58% for autistic disorder and depression
- 7% to 84% for autistic disorder and anxiety disorders
- 30% for autistic disorder and tic disorders
- 11% to 39% for autistic disorder and seizure disorders

PROGNOSIS

The prognosis for children with autistic disorder is poor (Klinger et al., 2003). Academic achievement is likely to lag, and children may have difficulty acquiring independent living skills. However, the prognosis is more favorable for children who receive intensive early interventions. The most favorable prognostic signs are an IQ above 70 and the presence of some communicative speech before the age of 5 years.

ASSESSMENT OF AUTISTIC DISORDER

The evaluation of children for autistic disorder is similar to evaluations for other exceptionalities. The assessment should include interviewing the child, parents, and teachers (see Chapters 5, 6, and 7); observing the child (see Chapters 8 and 9); administering a battery of psychological tests (see Chapters 10, 11, 12, 14, and 24); having the parents complete the Background Questionnaire (see Table A-1 in Appendix A); and having teachers complete the Teacher Referral Form (see Table A-3 in Appendix A). Depending on the child's age, the test battery might include a developmental scale or an intelligence test, an achievement test, a perceptual-motor test, and a language test. Receptive language tests with multiple-choice picture responses, such as the Peabody Picture Vocabulary Test–Third Edition (PPVT–III) and the Listening Comprehension Scale of the Oral and Written Language Scales (OWLS) or subtests from the Comprehensive Assessment of Spoken Language (CASL; see Sattler, 2001), may be valuable. Similarly, multiple-choice achievement tests, such as the Bracken Basic Concept Scale–Revised (BBCS–R), the Peabody Individual Achievement Test–Revised Normative Update (PIAT–R/NU), or various group achievement tests may be valuable (see Sattler, 2001). Items from paper-and-pencil, multiple-choice group tests can be enlarged on a photocopier and presented one at a time if necessary. Also consider administering a nonverbal test of intelligence that has minimal verbal instructions, such as the Leiter International Performance Scale–Revised (Leiter–R) or the Universal Nonverbal Intelligence Test (UNIT; see Sattler, 2001), or one or more of the special instruments discussed later in this chapter.

Interviewing

The inherent disabilities of children with autistic disorder—such as their difficulty establishing social relationships, their impaired communication skills, and their unusual responses to sensory stimuli—may tax your skills as an examiner. As many as 50% of individuals with autistic disorder remain mute or nonverbal (Wetherby & Prizant, 1992). In addition, children with autistic disorder may show little or no desire to interact with you, and your normal methods of encouragement, such as smiling, may be ineffective. If the child can speak and attend to your questions, use the semistructured interview shown in Table B-1 in Appendix B. For guides to interviewing parents, see Tables B-9, B-10, B-11, B-12, and B-13 in Appendix B.

Before you interview a child who may have autistic disorder, find out as much as possible about the child's communication skills from his or her parents and teachers; also observe how the child talks and behaves in the classroom. Consider the following questions:

1. Can the child follow simple directions?
2. Can the child answer "yes" or "no"?
3. Does the child understand gestures or signing?
4. Can the child read?
5. Can the child speak?
6. Does the child have any idiosyncrasies, such as using code words or phrases ("bye-bye" for "no" or "look, look" for a favorite toy)?
7. Does the child have sufficient attention to answer questions?

In interviewing a child with autistic disorder, talk slowly and simply, use short sentences, be concrete, omit unnecessary words and complex grammatical forms, and repeat sentences or rephrase them to make them simpler, if necessary. Make sure that you have the child's visual attention when you speak; visual cues will help the child attend to and process your speech.

Under no condition should you use facilitated communication to interview a child with autistic disorder. In facilitated communication, a facilitator guides an individual's hand, wrist, or arm across a keyboard or keyboard facsimile to help the individual type a message or point to letters. The theoretical justification for facilitated communication is the belief that people with autistic disorder do not have cognitive impairments but instead have motor apraxia, or the "neurologically determined inability to voluntarily initiate behavior or movement" (Mulick, Jacobson, & Kobe, 1993, p. 277). Motor apraxia supposedly prevents individuals with autistic disorder from communicating via speech or writing without the aid of a facilitator (Biklen, Morton, Gold, Berrigan, & Swaminathan, 1992). Thus, according to Biklen et al. (1992), the use of facilitated communication enables children with autistic disorder to show their advanced communication skills and general knowledge. However, there is no scientific support for this view, as investigations of facilitated communication show that the procedure is invalid (Jacobson, Mulick, & Schwartz, 1995). In fact, Shane (1993) concluded that *facilitated communication appears to be a pseudoscientific procedure and a hoax.*

Facilitated communication raises numerous questions (Sattler, 1998). First of all, why is facilitated communication necessary with children with autistic disorder or other severe communication disorders who have the motor skills needed to type or point? Why can't the children simply type out their responses or point to letters without help if they can spell, however poorly? Why can't they use reliable and valid augmentative communication procedures that do not require a facilitator? And if they can't spell on their own, how can they spell when a facilitator merely guides their hand?

If you are reviewing a report based on information obtained by means of facilitated communication, ignore the information. The information is likely contaminated and probably reflects the facilitator's communications rather than those of the child. Facilitated communication is not a harmless tool creating the illusion of intelligence and normalcy in individuals with autistic disorder or with other severe developmental disabilities. *It is a dangerous, ineffective procedure that is inadvertently being used to disrupt families, ruin reputations, and waste the time, energy, and money of all those involved in helping communicatively handicapped individuals.* "If the rhetoric and media hype boosting 'facilitated communication' without research accountability continues, it may succeed in setting autism back 40 years" (Schopler, 1992, p. 6). The American Psychological Association (APA) at its Spring 1995 council meeting approved the following resolution: "Therefore, be it resolved that APA adopts the position that facilitated communication is a controversial and unproved communicative procedure with no scientifically demonstrated support for its efficacy." For more information about facilitated communication, see Sattler (1998).

Observations

When you observe children who may have autistic disorder, note how they make eye contact, interact with toys, interact with parents, and interact with you, and observe their speech patterns, affect, motor patterns, and activity level. In each case, consider the type of behavior displayed, the situations in which the behavior is displayed, the quality of the behavior displayed, the antecedents and consequences of the behavior, and the appropriateness of the behavior. Ask yourself the following questions as you are observing:

1. Does the child make spontaneous eye contact, make eye contact when requested to do so, or make no eye contact?
2. Is the child's play behavior appropriate? Does the child have restricted repertoires of play behavior, show long delays in approaching toys, or show repetitive manipulations of toys?
3. Does the child avoid looking at parents, refuse to cooperate with parents, initiate affectionate contact with parents (such as sitting on a parent's lap or hugging or kissing a parent), or refuse to respond to a parent's request for a hug?

4. Is the child cooperative or uncooperative with you? Is the child aloof, or does he or she engage in some activity?

5. Does the child have speech? If so, is it age-appropriate, or is it limited, peculiar, or unrecognizable?

6. What are the child's facial expressions, postures, and mannerisms?

7. What type of affect does the child display?

8. Does the child appear to be driven or apathetic? Is it difficult to get the child to respond to your requests? Does the child engage in self-stimulating activities? Is it possible to redirect the child from one activity to another one?

You can use the procedures described in Chapters 8 and 9 in your observations. Table 9-6 in Chapter 9 (pp. 251–252), for example, has detailed guidelines for observing infants. In addition, you might want to use the following procedure to observe children with autistic disorder in a playroom or similar setting (Adrien, Ornitz, Barthelemy, Sauvage, & LeLord, 1987):

> Present the child with the following toys, each for a 2-minute period: a toy that produces musical sounds when a handle is turned, a toy helicopter, a toy that produces music when a string is pulled, a flashlight, a telephone that rings when dialed, a textured ball, a spinning top, 10 blocks, a doll, a toy cup, a toy pot, and a toy stove. Other toys can be used as appropriate. Except during the sixth period, allow the child to play by himself or herself. During the sixth period, actively interact with the child and attempt to engage in ball play. Use a whole-interval procedure.

See Chapter 8 for information about how to record the behaviors you observe during each period; also see the recording form in Table E-1 in Appendix E.

Cognitive Functioning

In the past, IQs obtained from children with autistic disorder were often considered to be invalid. The hope was that with the right intervention, intellectual ability would develop to a normal level. Unfortunately, interventions with children with autistic disorder usually do not result in significantly improved levels of intellectual performance.

Research on the intellectual functioning of children with autistic disorder indicates the following (Freeman, Rahbar, Ritvo, Bice, Yakota, & Ritvo, 1991; Geurts, Verte, Oosterlaan, Roeyers, & Sergeant, 2004; Harris, Handleman, & Burton, 1990; Klinger et al., 2003; Lord & Schopler, 1989; National Institute of Mental Health, 1997; Prior & Ozonoff, 1998; Sattler, 1992; Siegel, Minshew, & Goldstein, 1996; Trevarthen et al., 1998; Venter, Lord, & Schopler, 1992):

- As noted earlier, about 40% to 69% of children with autistic disorder fall into the mentally retarded range.

- Their IQs have the same properties as the IQs obtained by other children. For example, IQs show moderate stability throughout childhood and adolescence (test-retest correlations for periods of 2 to 15 years range from .63 to .90), especially if the children are tested after 5 years of age, and IQs are a reasonable predictor of later educational attainment.

- Their mean scores on 11 Wechsler Scale subtests range from a high of 9.61 on Block Design to a low of 3.57 on Comprehension (see Table 22-2).

- There are no profiles on intelligence tests that can reliably distinguish children with an autistic disorder from children with other kinds of psychological disorders.

- The IQs of children with autistic disorder fail to change markedly even after their social responsiveness improves. Poor motivation does not account for their below-average performance on intelligence tests.

- Those who were untestable on an intelligence test when they were young later performed in much the same manner as severely retarded children.

- Those who appear to be untestable on an intelligence test may respond to items that are for younger age levels.

- Those who have adequate conversational speech or adequate social relationships obtain higher IQs than do those with inadequate conversational speech or social relationships.

- Skills that are relatively poorly developed include language, imitation, abstract or conceptual reasoning, sequencing, organization, planning, and flexibility; seeing relations between pieces of information, identifying central patterns or themes, distinguishing relevant from irrelevant information, and deriving meaning from the bigger picture; and appreciating subtleties of thought. Even high-functioning children with autistic disorder have profound difficulties with executive function tasks (e.g., inhibition, working memory, planning, cognitive flexibility, and verbal fluency).

Table 22-2
Mean Scaled Scores of Children with Autistic Disorder on 11 Wechsler Subtests

Scale and subtest	N	Mean	Rank
Verbal Scale			
Information	207	5.48	7
Similarities	278	6.14	5
Arithmetic	278	5.39	8
Vocabulary	278	4.68	10
Comprehension	278	3.57	11
Digit Span	254	7.28	3
Performance Scale			
Picture Arrangement	278	5.80	6
Picture Completion	278	6.78	4
Object Assembly	278	8.53	2
Block Design	278	9.61	1
Coding	223	5.04	9

Source: Adapted from Happé (1994).

- Skills that are relatively well developed are visual-spatial processing, eye-hand coordination (e.g., ability to solve tasks that involve manipulating concrete materials), attention to detail, and rote memory (e.g., ability to solve tasks in which the stimulus materials themselves suggest what is required).
- Children with autistic disorder have selective memory deficits, rather than widespread and all-encompassing ones.
- They likely have a specific cognitive defect involving the use of language, given that they have relatively good visual-spatial and memory skills but poor sequencing and language skills.

Special Instruments

Following are brief descriptions of 10 instruments or checklists specifically designed to evaluate children with autistic disorder.

1. The Gilliam Autism Rating Scale (GARS; Gilliam, 1995a) is a 56-item scale that is completed by a parent, teacher, or other professional about an individual between the ages of 3 and 22 years. It yields four subscores: Stereotyped Behaviors, Communication, Social Interaction, and Developmental Disturbances. It was standardized on 1,092 individuals and has adequate reliability and validity. The norms, however, are not differentiated by age or gender.

2. The Autism Diagnostic Observation Schedule–WPS (ADOS–WPS; Lord, Rutter, DiLavore, & Risi, 1999) is a highly structured observation instrument for assessment of social interactions, communication, play, and imaginative use of materials in individuals with autistic disorder or related disorders. It consists of four modules designed for children of different ages and language levels.

3. The Childhood Autism Rating Scale (CARS; Schopler, Reichler, DeVellis, & Daly, 1980) evaluates 15 dimensions of behavior related to autistic disorder (see Table E-2 in Appendix E). The examiner uses a 4-point scale to rate each behavior. See Schopler, Reichler, and Renner (1993) for a more current version of the CARS.

4. The Screening Tool for Autism in Two-Year-Olds (STAT; Stone, 1998) contains 12 activities involving play (both pretend play and reciprocal social play), motor imitation, and nonverbal and verbal communication development.

5. The Autism Screening Instrument for Educational Planning (ASIEP; Krug, Arick, & Almond, 1980) has five parts: Autism Behavior Checklist, Sample of Vocal Behavior, Interaction Assessment, Educational Assessment of Functional Skills, and Prognosis of Learning Rate. Scores and percentile ranks are provided for each part.

6. The Autism Diagnostic Interview–Revised (ADI–R; Rutter, LeCouteur, & Lord, 1994) is a semistructured interview that contains five sections: opening questions, communication, social development and play, repetitive and restricted behaviors, and general behavior problems. Behaviors are coded on a severity scale that ranges from 0 to 3.

7. The Social Communication Questionnaire (SCQ; Rutter, Bailey, & Lord, 2004), previously known as the Autism Screening Questionnaire, is a brief questionnaire used to evaluate the communication skills and social functioning of children who may have an autism spectrum disorder. It is completed by a parent or primary caregiver.

8. The Modified Checklist of Autism in Toddlers (M-CHAT; Robins, Fein, Barton, & Green, 2001) is a 23-item screening measure designed to evaluate the presence of autistic disorder in children 18 months of age (see Table E-3 in Appendix E). It is completed by a parent.

9. The Autistic Disorder Questionnaire (see Table E-4 in Appendix E) has 24 items that satisfy the following *DSM-IV–TR* criteria for autistic disorder: items 1 and 2, criterion A1(a); items 3 and 4, criterion A1(b); items 5 and 6, criterion A1(c); items 7 and 8, criterion A1(d); items 9 and 10, criterion A2(a); items 11 and 12, criterion A2(b); items 13 and 14, criterion A2(c); items 15 and 16, criterion A2(d); items 17 and 18, criterion A3(a); items 19 and 20, criterion A3(b); items 21 and 22, criterion A3(c); and items 23 and 24, criterion A3(d).

10. The Asperger's Disorder Questionnaire (see Table E-7 in Appendix E) has 23 items that satisfy the following *DSM-IV–TR* criteria for Asperger's disorder: items 1 and 2, criterion A1; items 3 and 4, criterion A2; items 5 and 6, criterion A3; items 7 and 8, criterion A4; items 9 and 10, criterion B1; items 11 and 12, criterion B2; items 13 and 14, criterion B3; items 15 and 16, criterion B4; items 17 to 19, criterion C; item 20, criterion D (reverse scoring); and items 21 to 23, criterion E (reverse scoring). Also note that the first eight criteria for Asperger's disorder (A1 through B4) are exactly the same as 8 of the 12 criteria for autistic disorder (A1a through A1d and A3a through A3d).

There are also several other scales that may be useful in evaluating Asperger's disorder. They are the Asperger's Syndrome Diagnostic Scale (Myles, Bock, & Simpson, 2001), the Autism Spectrum Screening Questionnaire (Ehlers, Gillberg, & Wing, 1999), the Australian Scale for Asperger's Syndrome (Attwood, 1998), the Autism Screening Questionnaire (Berument, Rutter, Lord, Pickles, & Bailey, 1999), the Gilliam Asperger's Disorder Scale (Gilliam, 2001), the Childhood Asperger Syndrome Test (Scott, Baron-Cohen, Bolton, & Brayne, 2002), and the Autism-Spectrum Quotient (Baron-Cohen, Wheelright, Skinner, Martin & Clubley, 2001).

Evaluating Assessment Information

Answering the questions in Table 22-3 will help you evaluate the information you obtain from parents and teachers (and the child, where possible). Table E-5 in Appendix E shows

Table 22-3
Guidelines for Evaluating a Child for Possible Autistic Disorder

Developmental History

1. Were there any prenatal or perinatal difficulties? If so, what were they?
2. Were there any suspicions of sensory deficits, such as deafness or blindness? If so, what were the suspicions based on?
3. Did the child reach developmental language milestones, such as babbling by 12 months, gesturing (pointing, waving bye-bye) by 12 months, using single words by 16 months, and using two-word spontaneous phrases by 24 months?

Social Behavior as an Infant

1. Was the infant responsive to people?
2. How did the infant react when he or she was held (e.g., was the infant overly rigid or flaccid, resistant to being held, indifferent to being held)?
3. Did the infant make eye contact with others?
4. Was the infant content to be alone, or did he or she cry or demand attention?
5. Did the infant reciprocate in lap play (engage in give-and-take play)?

Social Behavior as a Toddler or Older Child

1. Does the child seem to tune out the parents?
2. Does the child seem to be in her or his own world?
3. Does the child make eye contact with the parents?
4. Do the parents think that their child is truly "attached" to them?
5. Is the child affectionate with the parents?
6. Does the child seek out the parents if she or he is hurt or frightened?
7. What is the child's interest in other children (i.e., does the child want to be with other children or does the child prefer to play alone)?
8. Does the child interact with other children? If so, what is the quality of the child's interactions?
9. Does the child appear to be isolated from her or his surroundings? If so, in what way?
10. Does the child smile when expected to?

Speech Development and Communication

1. Does the child have speech? If not, has the child ever spoken in the past? If so, when and for how long?
2. If the child speaks, what is the quality of the speech (e.g., does the child display echolalia, pronominal reversals, or extreme literalness in comprehension and expression)?
3. Does the child respond to his or her name?
4. Was there a loss of language at any age? If so, at what age?
5. Does the child point or wave bye-bye?
6. Does the child understand what other people say? If so, how does the child show his or her understanding?
7. Does the child indicate his or her own wishes? If so, how does the child do this?
8. In the parents' estimation, what is the extent of the child's language abilities?

Self-Stimulation or Self-Injury

1. Does the child engage in self-stimulation? If so, what kind of self-stimulation?
2. Does the child engage in self-injurious behavior? If so, what kind of self-injurious behavior?
3. If the child currently does not engage in self-stimulation or self-injurious behavior, has she or he ever done so? If so, when did the behavior occur, and what kind of behavior was it?

Affect

1. Does the child have any irrational fears? If so, what are they?
2. Does the child have appropriate fears (e.g., fear of moving vehicles on a busy street)?
3. Does the child seem to laugh or cry at unusual times or for no apparent reason? If so, at what times?
4. Does the child show rapid, sometimes inexplicable mood swings? If so, what kind of mood swings and when do they happen?

Perception

1. Does the child have an empty gaze?
2. Does the child have a strange gaze (e.g., looks through you as if you were a pane of glass, stares directly into your face)?
3. Is the child interested in only certain parts of objects? If so, what parts?
4. Is the child exceptionally interested in things that move? If so, what things?
5. Does the child seem not to listen when spoken to?
6. Does the child have strange reactions to sight or sound (e.g., squeals with excitement at the sight or sound of a wheel spinning or a toy truck, displays fear or avoidance of noisy or moving objects such as water)? If so, what kind of reactions?
7. How does the child react to cold?

Insistence on Maintenance of Sameness

1. Does the child become upset if the environment is altered (e.g., if the furniture is rearranged)?
2. Does the child become upset at changes in routine?
3. Does the child have any compulsive rituals? If so, what are they?
4. Does the child have any unusual food demands (e.g., eats only one or two foods, demands to eat out of a particular bowl, refuses to eat crackers or cookies if they are broken)? If so, what are they?
5. Is the child unusually attached to an object (e.g., always demands to carry a certain object, refuses to relinquish an outgrown garment)? If so, what is the object, and how long has the attachment existed?

Isolated Skills

1. Does the child show particular skill at a certain task? If so, what is the skill?
2. Is the child a whiz at assembling puzzles? If so, what kind of puzzles?
3. Does the child demonstrate unusual ability in music? If so, what kind of ability?
4. Does the child have an exceptional memory in one or more areas? If so, in what areas?

Behavior and Behavior Problems

1. What is the child's behavior at home?
2. What is the child's behavior at school?
3. Does the child show stereotyped behavior or have behavior problems (e.g., has severe tantrums, is hyperactive, is uncooperative, is aggressive, toe-walks, lines things up frequently, is oversensitive to certain textures or sounds, performs odd movements)?
4. Is the child toilet trained? If so, at what age was the child toilet trained?
5. Does the child eat without assistance?
6. Does the child dress herself or himself?

Source: Adapted from Filipek et al. (1999); Gillberg, Nordin, and Ehlers (1996); and Schreibman (1988).

some signs that may be obtained from a case history suggesting that the child is at risk for having autistic disorder. Table E-6 in Appendix E is a checklist for autistic disorder, based on *DSM-IV–TR*.

INTERVENTIONS FOR AUTISTIC DISORDER

There are no cures for autistic disorder; the focus of any intervention is on reducing symptoms and encouraging desirable behaviors. Interventions should begin early in life, and parents should be actively involved in the treatment process. Intense interventions in some cases can help children with autistic disorder to perform at normal levels and to appear normal to all but the most expert observers. As Gabovitch and Wiseman (2005) noted:

> With proper intervention, a child can overcome a wide range of developmental problems. Intensive, well-designed, and timely intervention can improve the prospects—and the quality of life— for many children who are considered at risk for cognitive, social, or emotional impairment. In some cases, effective intervention can improve conditions once thought to be virtually untreatable, such as autism. Well-implemented programs can brighten a child's future and the impact a developmental disorder has on the family. They can lead a child to greater independence, enable that child to be included in the community, and offer a more productive and fulfilling life. (p. 145)

Effective early intervention programs have the following attributes (Klinger et al., 2003, p. 443, with changes in notation):

1. A curriculum focusing on attention and compliance, motor imitation, behavioral imitation, communication, appropriate use of toys, and social skills
2. Highly structured teaching environments with a low student-to-staff ratio
3. Systematic strategies for generalizing newly acquired skills to a wide range of situations
4. Maintenance of predictability and routine in the daily schedule
5. A functional approach to problem behaviors
6. A focus on skills needed for successful transition from the early intervention program to the regular preschool or kindergarten classroom
7. A high level of family involvement

At all ages, behavioral techniques are used to reduce maladaptive behaviors, such as self-stimulation (e.g., rocking and twirling) and self-injurious behaviors (e.g., head banging and biting hands or wrists), and to teach more appropriate behavioral skills (e.g., sitting and establishing eye contact). If the self-injurious behaviors are life-threatening, physical restraints also may be needed.

Cognitive approaches are used to develop meaningful experiences, generalization skills, and cognitive flexibility.

Social-learning approaches are used to develop social communication skills and interpersonal skills through structured activities with peers who do not have disabilities (Mesibov, Adams, & Klinger, 1997).

Pharmacological interventions (i.e., medications) are useful in reducing impulsivity, overactivity, short attention span, and obsessive preoccupations. However, medications are usually not effective in treating impairments in social interaction and communication (Tanguay, 2000).

The following intervention suggestions are useful for anyone working with children with autism spectrum disorder, which includes autistic disorder and Asperger's disorder (Mesibov, Shea, & Adams, 2001. The suggestions recognize that children with autism spectrum disorder have difficulties (a) understanding both verbal and nonverbal aspects of language and related concepts of communication, (b) understanding social conventions and feelings, (c) modulating behavior, (d) sizing up situations and understanding quickly what should be done, and (e) dealing with sensory needs (e.g., they may have extreme sensitivity to sound or crave sensory experiences).

1. Supplement information provided orally with visual information (e.g., written information, photographs, pictures, drawings, small objects, symbols) or use visual information in place of verbal information.
2. Give explicit explanations and instructions.
3. Modify the circumstances surrounding a behavior of concern rather than focusing on the consequences of that behavior—that is, analyze the situation that led to the behavior of concern and make changes in the situation rather than withdrawing privileges.
4. Give repeated and explicit information about appropriate social behavior and the meaning of emotions.
5. Respect any idiosyncratic sensory needs.
6. Know when *not* to intervene—some behaviors are probably based on neurological factors (e.g., body-rocking, hand-flapping, length of monologues, lack of eye contact).
7. View special interests as strengths.

Suggestions for Teachers

Following are suggestions for teachers (Mesibov et al., 2001; Myles, 2005; Saskatchewan Education, 1999).

PRESCHOOL CHILDREN

1. Speak slowly, use short sentences, and emphasize key words.
2. Limit the length of your conversations.
3. Give one direction at a time.
4. Use pictures and words to provide information, especially when you are preparing children for transitions to new activities or helping them perform tasks that may not be enjoyable.
5. Limit children's exposure to sensory stressors such as noisy places, disliked food, or disliked clothing.

6. Encourage them to play, under your supervision, with children who do not have disabilities.

7. Incorporate any special interests that they may have into a broader range of activities.

VISUAL SUPPORTS

1. Adopt strategies for organizing the environment, such as labeling objects and containers; posting signs, schedules, lists, charts, calendars, and outlines; and using choice boards.

2. Use visual aids (e.g., handouts or posters that are written or in pictographic form) to (a) convey information about classroom rules or directions for specific tasks and activities, (b) encourage social development (e.g., teach social skills through the use of stories), (c) manage challenging behaviors and help children develop self-control (e.g., provide cues for expected behavior), and (d) teach abstract ideas and conceptual thinking.

3. Teach an augmentative communication system (e.g., a sign language) to children who are nonverbal.

CLASSROOM ENVIRONMENT

1. Make sure that the environment is consistently and clearly structured; for example, let children know where things belong, what is expected of them in a specific situation, and what to anticipate.

2. Vary tasks to prevent boredom, and alternate familiar experiences in which children can be successful with less preferred activities to reduce anxiety and prevent inappropriate behaviors.

3. Use reinforcers that are meaningful to the child, such as being left alone for a time, getting time to talk to a favorite staff member, making a trip to the cafeteria, going for a walk, playing with a favorite object, playing in water, performing a favorite routine, spending time with objects that provide specific sensory stimulation, or sitting at a window.

4. Use modeling, physical prompts, visual cues, and reinforcement to encourage attention, imitation, communication, and interaction.

5. Eliminate visual distractions such as excessive light, movement, reflection, or background patterns.

6. Eliminate auditory distractions such as noisy fans and loudspeakers.

7. Eliminate textures that seem to be aversive.

8. Make sure that the temperature in the room is appropriate.

9. Provide a designated quiet area where the child can go to relax.

10. Introduce unfamiliar tasks in a familiar environment when possible.

11. Modify tests and assignments as needed. For example, allow additional time on tests, reduce written homework assignments, allow children to dictate their work to a parent, modify testing arrangements (e.g., test in a separate room, allow oral instead of written answers, and use multiple-choice questions instead of essay questions).

SOCIAL SKILLS

1. Provide opportunities for meaningful contact with peers who have appropriate social behavior. Do not permit bullying in the classroom or other school facilities, arrange team games so that the child with autistic disorder is not always chosen last, and form cooperative learning groups in which the special skills of the child with autism spectrum disorder are useful and appreciated by the other children.

2. Use classroom situations to teach all children in the class about feelings and interpersonal relations, including positive emotions associated with sharing, taking turns, and working together and negative emotions associated with being teased, being ignored, being interrupted, not being selected for a team, and being criticized.

3. Pair the child with a buddy for unstructured activities such as walking down the hall or playing on the playground.

4. Vary peer buddies from time to time and from one activity to another to prevent dependence on one peer.

5. Provide opportunities for the child to interact in a variety of natural environments where appropriate models, natural cues and stimuli, and functional reinforcers are available.

6. To increase independence, teach self-management skills, such as having the child define a target behavior, identify reinforcers, and choose or design and learn an appropriate self-monitoring method (e.g., use of a wrist counter or stickers). Also facilitate the child's independence by gradually reducing prompts and increasing the time the child spends managing his or her own behavior.

7. Help the child learn how to take turns in playing games and in talking with others.

8. Encourage the child to play games with other children, including board games and card games.

9. Help the child learn to work and play quietly.

10. Help the child learn to accept that it is okay not to win at a game.

11. Help those with anxiety reactions by encouraging them to go somewhere where they can be alone briefly, to listen to soothing music, to do a favorite activity, to exercise, or to take prescribed medicines.

Suggestions for Professionals Working with Parents

The following suggestions will help you in your work with parents of children with autism spectrum disorder (Bloch, Weinstein, & Seitz, 2005; Morgan, 1984):

1. Give parents a realistic and cautious interpretation of autism spectrum disorder, presenting the child as a unique individual with a special set of problems. Parents may have misconceptions about the disorder, perhaps stemming from stereotyped images of autistic disorder derived from television or magazine articles. Help them recognize that symptoms such as bizarre responses to the environment,

insistence on sameness, attachment to objects, and deficient and unusual language are part of the syndrome of autism spectrum disorder.

2. Help parents to understand their child's level of functioning in cognitive and adaptive areas and the possibilities for improvement. Often, parents want to believe that their child's cognitive impairment is only temporary and that the child will return to normal when her or his behavioral and emotional problems are resolved. Caution parents that they should not equate the child's isolated abilities—such as early motor development or good rote memory—with general intelligence. Convey to the parents their child's strengths and weaknesses. By interpreting the child's relative skills, you may help the parents feel less threatened; as a result, they may become more receptive to your suggestions.

3. Assure parents that they are not responsible for their child's refusal to interact with the world. Parents often blame themselves for their child's condition, because autism spectrum disorder has such serious social and emotional overtones. For example, the child's inability to form affectionate family bonds and social relationships is likely to be most disturbing to parents. You can best deal with feelings of guilt by presenting parents with information about the diagnosis and the hypothesized causes of autism spectrum disorder. Knowing that they did not cause their child's disorder will enable them to move past their guilt and participate in intervention programs.

4. Help parents deal with anger, denial, or other reactions that may occur when they learn that their child has autism spectrum disorder.

5. Help parents put in proper context what they know about autism spectrum disorder.

6. Phrase statements about prognosis cautiously. Most cases of autism spectrum disorder are severe and long term.

7. Encourage the parents to play an active role in an intervention program. They can do this by collecting data about their child's behavior, observing their child's behavior, understanding early childhood development, recognizing behaviors that interfere with learning, monitoring their child's progress and change, and participating in team decisions about goals and remediation.

6. Help the child's siblings understand their brother's or sister's disorder. Families that gain an understanding of autism spectrum disorder will be in a better position to accept and help the child who has the disorder.

Suggestions for Parents

Following are suggestions for parents of children with autism spectrum disorder (Grandin, 2002; Ives & Munro, 2001):

SPEECH AND LANGUAGE

1. Speak in a calm voice.
2. Use your child's name to gain his or her attention.

3. Let your child know when an activity will be over. For example, say, "You have 5 minutes left to watch television."

4. Use concrete language and be concise and specific. Say, for example, "Take off your shoes and put on your slippers" instead of "Change into your slippers," because the child may take the latter remark literally and not understand it. Choose colloquial expressions carefully, because your child might interpret them literally. To help your child understand colloquial sayings, collect the more common ones in a notebook and describe what each one means. For example, for the saying, "I am hungry as a horse," you can write, "I am very hungry."

5. Avoid giving the child lengthy oral instructions.

6. Limit use of vague words like "maybe" or "we'll see." Say, for example, "We will do that after dinner tonight" instead of "Maybe we will do that later."

7. Make your instructions positive—thus, say what to do rather than what not to do. Say, for example, "Put your toys in the toy box" instead of "Don't leave your toys on the floor."

8. Accompany your verbal communication with nonverbal behaviors. For example, if you say, "Please drink your milk," point to the cup and move your hand to your mouth as if you were holding a cup.

9. If your child speaks, ask him or her to repeat what you said when you want to check on the child's understanding of your communication.

10. Use simple commands rather than questions. Say, for example, "Tell me the name of the animal from which we get milk" rather than "Where do we get milk?"

11. Provide straightforward and complete instructions. Say, for example, "Ask your father whether he got the tickets to the baseball game on Friday night, and then come and tell me his answer" instead of "Ask your father about the tickets."

12. Use specific questions rather than open-ended questions. Say, for example, "What happened at the softball game today?" rather than "How was school?"

13. Tell your child about the behaviors that you want him or her to do in the order in which they should be done. Say, for example, "First get your toothbrush, then put the toothpaste on your toothbrush, and then brush your teeth."

14. Arrange to have your child learn alternative means of communication, such as sign language, if he or she does not speak, and consider learning sign language yourself. You can also use electronic communication devices, such as voice synthesizers and special computers that can be programmed with spoken language.

SOCIALIZATION

1. Keep your promises.
2. Help your child understand what is expected of him or her in social situations.
3. Be consistent in your rules of social behavior.

4. When you use a reinforcer, make sure that it is available and use it without delay after the child performs the desired behavior.

5. Do not expect your child to understand emotional pleas.

6. Before you move into a new house, visit it with your child.

7. Before the first day in a new school, visit it with your child.

8. Allow your child to bring a comfort toy to school if he or she wants to.

TEACHING

1. Use concrete objects along with words when you are teaching your child. For example, use plastic letters to teach reading, utensils to teach table manners, and toy cars, airplanes, trains, and trucks to teach about transportation. Allow your child to touch the objects, because touching them might make it easier for your child to learn.

2. Teach vocabulary words by showing your child a flashcard with a photo of the object (or show the actual object) and the name of the object on the same side of the card. This technique is especially helpful if your child does not speak.

3. If your child has visual processing problems, reduce contrast on reading materials by using black print on colored paper. Try colors such as tan, light blue-gray, or light green, but experiment with other colors as needed. Avoid bright yellow, because this color might hurt your child's eyes.

4. Teach your child generalization skills by using several examples to illustrate a point. For example, if you want to teach your child not to run across the street, use several locations to teach this principle.

5. Use physical objects, such as blocks, to teach number concepts.

6. Teach your child how to type if he or she has poor handwriting.

7. Use things that the child strongly prefers as motivational tools. For example, if the child likes trucks, use toy trucks as aids to teach him or her reading and mathematics.

8. Avoid fluorescent lights if your child dislikes them.

9. Use a weighted vest (20 minutes on, 5 minutes off) to help your child calm down if he or she fidgets constantly.

10. Allow your child to swing on a swing or roll up in a mat, because the sensory input from swinging or pressure from the mat may improve his or her speech.

11. Sing to your child to improve his or her attention.

12. Do not ask your child to look and listen at the same time if he or she is unable to process visual and auditory input simultaneously.

13. Place the computer keyboard close to the monitor so that your child can see the keyboard and monitor almost simultaneously.

14. Use closed captions on the television set to teach your child reading. Recording your child's favorite program with captions is helpful, because you can use the videotape or DVD over again and stop it as needed.

15. Use an LCD monitor if the flicker from a CRT monitor annoys your child.

RETURNING TO SCHOOL

1. Establish or re-establish "school-year" home routines a few weeks prior to the beginning of a school year. This might mean having your child go to bed earlier, wake up earlier, or follow morning routines for getting ready to go to school.

2. Establish homework routines by having your child do quiet activities at a specific time and place every day. Encourage your child to read, write a journal, solve crossword puzzles, or perform other similar activities at these times.

3. Use reinforcements—such as watching TV shows, playing a favorite game, visiting a store, or earning tokens or points exchangeable for something your child wants—to motivate your child to perform needed activities.

4. If your child will be attending a new school, orient the child to the school by visiting it with the child several times over the summer so that he or she becomes familiar with the layout. Even if your child is returning to the same school, consider visiting it a few times during the summer. When your child knows his or her class schedule, practice routines that he or she will be following when school begins—for example, going from one class to another and going to the bus stop, home room, locker room, cafeteria, auditorium, and bathrooms.

5. Help your child become accustomed to school clothes by giving him or her a chance to wear the school uniform, if one is required, or to wear other school clothes a few times before the school year begins.

6. Meet with your child's teacher, if possible, before school starts. If you cannot meet with the teacher, prepare a one-page description of your child's strengths and weaknesses and give it to the teacher before school starts. Include any helpful information, such as your child's stress signs and what triggers stress, how to reduce your child's anxiety, and challenges that the teacher might face.

7. Remain in close contact with school personnel throughout the school year to discuss how your child is adjusting to school and what steps are needed to improve his or her performance.

8. Establish a collaborative relationship with school personnel and look for opportunities to show them your appreciation and support.

9. Invite one or two other children to your home a week or two before school starts. Consider enlisting the help of a parent of a child without a disability to encourage his or her child to act as a peer buddy for your child.

10. Remember to take the time you need to relax, to ensure that you can maintain the energy needed to help your child.

COMMENT ON AUTISTIC DISORDER

Research on autistic disorder is still needed, in order to identify the genetics underlying the disorder, refine early screening instruments, develop cognitive tests appropriate for very young children, identify subgroups so as to develop more individualized treatment strategies, and "identify the links among underlying neurofunctional abnormalities, information-processing impairments, and behavioral symptoms of autism" (Klinger et al., 2003, p. 443).

THINKING THROUGH THE ISSUES

1. Do you know a child with autistic disorder? If so, what have you observed?
2. If you know of any families who have a child with autistic disorder, what has it been like for the family to raise the child?
3. What pressure might parents face from relatives, spouses, and members of the community in raising a child with autistic disorder?
4. In what way might raising a child with autistic disorder be different from raising one with attention-deficit/hyperactivity disorder?

SUMMARY

1. The five pervasive developmental disorders are autistic disorder, Rett's disorder, childhood disintegrative disorder, Asperger's disorder, and pervasive developmental disorder not otherwise specified.

Pervasive Developmental Disorders

2. Autistic disorder is a lifelong neurodevelopmental disorder that is evenly distributed across socioeconomic and educational levels.
3. Although there are no biological markers or laboratory tests that reliably diagnose the disorder, genetic factors play a dominant role in its etiology.
4. Similarly, there is no widely accepted theory that explains the characteristic symptoms of autistic disorder (such as difficulties in development and use of language, imitation, affective expression, sharing, attention, and social comprehension), which can vary from mild to severe.
5. A few children with autistic disorder have special skills, such as the ability to dismantle and reassemble a complicated mechanical apparatus or the ability to memorize mathematical tables, bus schedules, and calendars.
6. The incidence of autistic disorder has been rising precipitously and mysteriously; recent prevalence estimates have ranged from 1 in 160 to 1 in 200 children.
7. Rett's disorder involves the loss of several functions after the first 5 months of normal development.
8. Childhood disintegrative disorder involves the loss, after the age of 2 years (but before the age of 10 years), of previously acquired skills in expressive or receptive language, social or adaptive behavior, bowel or bladder control, play, and motor coordination.
9. Children with a diagnosis of Asperger's disorder (also referred to as Asperger's syndrome) function at the higher levels of the autistic continuum. The essential features of Asperger's disorder are severe and sustained impairment in social interactions and development of restricted, repetitive patterns of behavior and interests.
10. Pervasive developmental disorder not otherwise specified is the diagnostic classification used for children who have severe and pervasive impairment in social interaction, verbal communication, and nonverbal communication or who display stereotyped behaviors, interests, and activities, but not to the extent needed to fully meet the criteria for any of the other types of pervasive developmental disorders or any other *DSM-IV–TR* classification.

Symptoms of Autistic Disorder

11. Symptoms of autistic disorder vary as a function of level of cognitive development and age. As level of intelligence increases, symptoms tend to decrease; in addition, children with higher IQs usually are identified as having an autistic disorder at a later age than children with lower IQs.
12. About 31% to 55% of children with autistic disorder show symptoms of the disorder in the first year of life, and about 75% to 95% show symptoms by the end of the second year of life.
13. The most common early symptoms are language and speech problems, failure to respond to one's name, failure to engage in imitation play behavior, and failure to switch the gaze to follow pointing.
14. A diagnosis of autistic disorder is arrived at when a child has impairments in each of three areas: social interaction, communication, and behavior.
15. Impairments in social interaction include marked impairment in the use of nonverbal behaviors; failure to develop peer relationships; and lack of social and emotional reciprocity and of spontaneous efforts to share enjoyment or interests with others.
16. Impairments in communication include delay in or lack of development of spoken language, which is not compensated for by other modes of communication; marked impairment in the ability to initiate or sustain conversation with others; and stereotyped and repetitive language or idiosyncratic language.
17. Impairments in behavior include lack of varied, spontaneous make-believe play or social imitative play appropriate to developmental level; stereotyped and restricted patterns of interest; inflexible adherence to specific nonfunctional routines or rituals; stereotyped and repetitive motor movements; and persistent preoccupation with parts of objects or things that move.

Etiology of Autistic Disorder

18. Autistic disorder has a strong genetic component.
19. Other explanations for autistic disorder include "viral exposures, vaccination, immunologic factors, autoimmune disorders, gastrointestinal disorders, prenatal exposure to thalidomide, anticonvulsants, and food allergies. The interaction between a genetic predisposition and early environmental insults has also been suggested" (M.I.N.D. Institute, 2002, p. 11).

20. It also has been hypothesized that autistic disorder is due to early developmental failures of the mirror neuron system located in the frontal cortex.

Co-Occurring Disorders

21. The estimated prevalence rates of co-occurrence of autistic disorder with other disorders are 40% to 69% for autistic disorder and mental retardation, 4% to 58% for autistic disorder and depression, 7% to 84% for autistic disorder and anxiety disorders, 30% for autistic disorder and tic disorders, and 11% to 39% for autistic disorder and seizure disorders.

Prognosis

22. The prognosis for children with autistic disorder is poor; academic achievement is likely to lag, and children may have difficulty acquiring independent living skills.
23. The prognosis is more favorable for children who receive intensive early interventions.
24. The most favorable prognostic signs are an IQ above 70 and the presence of some communicative speech before the age of 5 years.

Assessment of Autistic Disorder

25. The evaluation of children for autistic disorder is similar to evaluations for other exceptionalities. The assessment should include interviewing the child, parents, and teachers; observing the child; administering a battery of psychological tests; having the parents complete the Background Questionnaire; and having teachers complete the Teacher Referral Form.
26. The inherent disabilities of children with autistic disorder—such as their difficulty establishing social relationships, their impaired communication skills, and their unusual responses to sensory stimuli—may tax your skills as an examiner. As many as 50% of individuals with autistic disorder remain mute or nonverbal.
27. In interviewing a child with autistic disorder, talk slowly and simply, use short sentences, be concrete, omit unnecessary words and complex grammatical forms, and repeat sentences or rephrase them to make them simpler, if necessary.
28. Under no condition should you use facilitated communication to interview a child with autistic disorder.
29. Facilitated communication appears to be a pseudoscientific procedure and a hoax.
30. If you are reviewing a report based on information obtained by means of facilitated communication, ignore the information.
31. It is a dangerous, ineffective procedure that is inadvertently being used to disrupt families, ruin reputations, and waste the time, energy, and money of all those involved in helping communicatively handicapped individuals.
32. When you observe children who may have autistic disorder, note how they make eye contact, interact with toys, interact with parents, and interact with you, and observe their speech patterns, affect, motor patterns, and activity level.
33. In each case, consider the type of behavior displayed, the situations in which the behavior is displayed, the quality of the behavior displayed, the antecedents and consequences of the behavior, and the appropriateness of the behavior.
34. Research on the intellectual functioning of children with autistic disorder indicates that their IQs have the same properties as the IQs obtained by other children.

35. Several checklists are useful for the assessment of autistic disorder.

Interventions for Autistic Disorder

36. There are no cures for autistic disorder; the focus of any intervention is on reducing symptoms and encouraging desirable behaviors.
37. Interventions should begin early in life, and parents should be actively involved in the treatment process.
38. Early and intense interventions in some cases can help children with autistic disorder to perform at normal levels and to appear normal to all but the most expert observers.
39. Behavioral techniques, cognitive approaches, social-learning approaches, and pharmacological interventions all have their place in the treatment of children with autistic spectrum disorders.

Comment on Autistic Disorder

40. Research on autistic disorder is still needed, in order to identify the genetics underlying the disorder, refine early screening instruments, develop cognitive tests appropriate for very young children, identify subgroups so as to develop more individualized treatment strategies, and "identify the links among underlying neurofunctional abnormalities, information-processing impairments, and behavioral symptoms of autism" (Klinger et al., 2003, p. 443).

KEY TERMS, CONCEPTS, AND NAMES

Pervasive developmental disorders (p. 494)
Autistic disorder (p. 494)
Rett's disorder (p. 494)
Childhood disintegrative disorder (p. 494)
Asperger's disorder (p. 494)
Pervasive developmental disorder not otherwise specified (p. 494)
Symptoms of autistic disorder (p. 495)
Impairments in social interaction (p. 495)
Impairments in communication (p. 496)
Pronominal reversal (p. 496)
Prosodic features (p. 496)
Metaphorical language (p. 496)
Immediate echolalia (p. 496)
Delayed echolalia (p. 496)
Impairments in behavior (p. 496)
Etiology of autistic disorder (p. 497)
Co-occurring disorders (p. 497)
Prognosis (p. 497)
Assessment of autistic disorder (p. 497)
Peabody Picture Vocabulary Test–Third Edition (PPVT–III) (p. 497)
Listening Comprehension Scale of the Oral and Written Language Scales (OWLS) (p. 497)
Comprehensive Assessment of Spoken Language (CASL) (p. 497)
Bracken Basic Concept Scale–Revised (BBCS–R) (p. 497)
Peabody Individual Achievement Test–Revised Normative Update (PIAT–R/NU) (p. 497)
Leiter International Performance Scale–Revised (LIPS–R) (p. 497)
Universal Nonverbal Intelligence Test (UNIT) (p. 497)
Interviewing (p. 498)

Facilitated communication (p. 498)
Observations (p. 498)
Cognitive functioning (p. 499)
Gilliam Autism Rating Scale (GARS) (p. 500)
Autism Diagnostic Observation Schedule–WPS (ADOS–WPS) (p. 500)
Childhood Autism Rating Scale (CARS) (p. 500)
Screening Tool for Autism in Two-Year-Olds (STAT) (p. 500)
Autism Screening Instrument for Educational Planning (ASIEP) (p. 500)
Autism Diagnostic Interview–Revised (ADI–R) (p. 500)
Social Communication Questionnaire (SCQ) (p. 500)
Modified Checklist of Autism in Toddlers (M-CHAT) (p. 500)
Autistic Disorder Questionnaire (p. 500)
Asperger's Disorder Questionnaire (p. 500)
Asperger's Syndrome Diagnostic Scale (p. 500)
Autism Spectrum Screening Questionnaire (p. 500)
Australian Scale for Asperger's Syndrome (p. 500)
Autism Screening Questionnaire (p. 500)

Gilliam Asperger's Disorder Scale (p. 500)
Childhood Asperger Syndrome Test (p. 500)
Autism-Spectrum Quotient (p. 500)
Interventions for autistic disorder (p. 502)
Intervention suggestions for teachers (p. 502)
Suggestions for professionals working with parents (p. 503)
Suggestions for parents (p. 504)

STUDY QUESTION

Discuss children with autistic disorder. Include in your discussion a description of the disorder and how it differs from other pervasive developmental disorders; symptoms; etiology; co-occurring disorders; prognosis; assessment considerations, including interviewing issues, observational guidelines, and special instruments; and interventions.

23

BRAIN INJURIES: THEORY AND REHABILITATION

Do not mistake a child for his symptom.
—Erik Hamburger Erikson, German-born American
psychoanalyst (1902–1994)

Goals and Objectives

This chapter is designed to enable you to do the following:

- Become familiar with how the brain works

- Describe common causes of brain injury in children

- Describe the cognitive, behavioral, and emotional effects of brain injury on children

- Identify rehabilitation strategies for children with brain injuries

- Work effectively with families of children with brain injuries

This chapter covers theoretical and rehabilitation issues for children with brain injuries; the next chapter covers assessment issues, formal batteries, and informal measures. The two chapters provide a general introduction to neuropsychological assessment and rehabilitation. You will need to review texts on biological psychology and neuropsychology to gain a full appreciation of neuropsychological assessment.

Traumatic brain injuries are not inevitable. As a society, we can do several things to prevent brain injuries from occurring (Centers for Disease Control and Prevention, 2003):

- Automobile manufacturers should construct vehicles that are as safe as possible, protecting drivers and passengers.
- City planners should consider pedestrian safety and bicycle rider safety when they design streets, sidewalks, and crosswalks.
- Playground equipment should be designed to prevent serious injuries to children (by, for example, incorporating shock-absorbing materials).
- Infants should never be left unattended on a table, bed, or other elevated surface.
- Safety straps should be used to secure children in strollers, shopping carts, and infant carriers.
- Children should always be secured with a safety seat, booster seat, or seat belt when they ride in a motor vehicle.
- No one should ride in a vehicle whose driver is under the influence of alcohol or drugs.
- Children should wear helmets when riding bicycles, motorcycles, snowmobiles, or all-terrain vehicles; using roller skates or skateboards; playing a contact sport (such as football, hockey, boxing); batting and running bases (such as in baseball or softball); riding a horse; or skiing or snowboarding.
- Window guards should be installed to keep young children from falling out of open windows.
- Safety gates at the top and bottom of stairs should be used in homes where there is a young child.
- Tripping hazards (such as small area rugs and loose electrical cords) should be removed from homes.
- Nonslip mats should be used and grab bars installed in bathtubs and on shower floors.
- Firearms should be stored unloaded, and with trigger guards installed, in a locked cabinet or safe, and bullets should be stored in a separate secured location.
- Swimming and wading pools should be protected with high, locked fences, and children should be closely supervised whenever they are near water.

Brain injury refers to any disruption in brain structure (anatomy) or brain function (physiology). *Brain dysfunction* refers to symptoms that are associated with processing difficulties of any brain structure, including the cerebrum, midbrain, and brain stem structures. Evaluating children with brain injuries requires knowledge of (a) the types and causes of brain injuries and their effects on children's cognitive, behavioral, social, and affective processes, (b) how to communicate with children with brain injuries, (c) how to recognize their acquired deficits as well as their intact abilities, (d) how to select, administer, score, and interpret neuropsychological tests and procedures, (e) the various ways families relate to their children with brain injuries, and (f) effective rehabilitation strategies and other interventions useful for children with brain injuries.

The assessment of brain injury is a complex and exacting process. It requires extensive specialized knowledge and interdisciplinary cooperation. A multidisciplinary team is usually involved in the assessment of children with brain injuries and in the formulation of rehabilitation programs. Multidisciplinary teams may include neurologists, neurosurgeons, orthopedists, neuropsychologists, speech/language pathologists, educators, physical therapists, occupational therapists, school psychologists, and social workers.

Psychologists can help children with brain injuries, as well as their parents, families, and teachers, in several ways. They can use the results arrived at by the multidisciplinary assessment team to explain to those involved with the child's care how brain injury may affect the child's cognitive functioning, affective reactions, personality, and temperament, as well as the rehabilitation efforts necessary to improve the child's functioning. They can assist families in understanding and dealing with the often difficult day-to-day struggles that children with brain injuries have. Although the behaviors of children with brain injuries vary greatly, there are similarities in the ways these children function, particularly in their patterns of neuropsychological deficits.

OVERVIEW OF BRAIN FUNCTIONS

The following are some basic facts about the human brain and its development (Begley, 2002; Elias, 2005; Haier, Jung, Yeo, Head, & Alkire, 2004; Hotz, 1996a, 1996b, 2005; Williams, Whiten, Suddendorf, & Perrett, 2001):

- There is no center of consciousness, no single clearinghouse for memory, no one place where information is processed, emotions generated, or language stored, although some of these functions are processed in fairly discrete locations. Instead, the human brain is a constantly changing constellation of connections among billions of cells. Complex networks of neurons are linked by pathways that are forged and then continually revised in response to interactions with the environment.
- In an adult in the prime of life, the cerebral cortex contains about 25 billion neurons linked through approximately 164 trillion synapses. Neurons communicate with each other by secreting messenger chemicals, or neurotransmitters, that cross the synaptic gulf between cells and bind to receptors on neighboring cell membranes. Thus, neurotransmitters serve as the vehicles of information processing within the cortex.
- Thoughts thread through about 7.4 million miles of dendrite fibers and about 62,000 miles of axons so miniatur-

ized and compacted that the entire neural network is no larger than a coconut.

- During growth and development, the feedback between the brain and its environment is so intimate that there is no way to separate the effects of development of a brain's neural structure from the influence of the environment that nurtures it. For example, at birth infants can detect differences between the speech sounds of any human language. However, by 12 months, they have lost sensitivity to the sound contrasts in languages to which they are not exposed. Thus, they become most efficient at differentiating the sounds in their environment.

- There is no single, predetermined blueprint for the brain. More than half of all human genes are involved in laying the brain's foundation. Collectively, they exert a powerful influence over temperament, learning ability, and personality.

- Multiple regions throughout the brain are related to intelligence. Patterns of intellectual strengths and weaknesses are related to the volume and pattern of gray matter and white matter in the brain. Both white and gray matter are implicated in intelligence, but they perform different functions. Gray matter is involved in information processing centers in the brain, whereas white matter is involved in the network of connections between those processing centers.

- No two brains are identical. The complex connections of each brain are so individual that it is unlikely that any two people perceive the world in quite the same way.

- Subtle differences in brain anatomy affect the ways men and women process information, even when thinking about the same things, hearing the same words, or solving similar problems. Men and women appear to use different parts of the brain to encode memories, sense emotions, recognize faces, solve certain problems, and make decisions. Still, for many problem-solving activities, men's and women's brains work in the same way.

- Men and women appear to achieve similar intelligence with different brain regions. Women have a higher percentage of gray matter but more white matter related to intelligence than men. In contrast, men have a higher percentage of white matter but more gray matter related to intelligence than women.

- The most efficient brains—that is, those that use the least energy—appear also to be the most intelligent. Formal education, mental and physical stimulation, aerobic exercise, and antioxidant-rich foods improve brain efficiency.

- The complex circuitry of the brain reorganizes itself in response to sensory stimulation. Regions of the brain receiving maximum stimulation are larger and more active than regions receiving minimal stimulation. For example, the area of the brain devoted to finger movements is much larger in musicians who play string instruments than in nonmusicians. Even mental rehearsal of finger movements triggers changes in the regions of the brain devoted to finger movements.

- Special cells called *mirror neurons,* located in the frontal lobe, process visual information about the actions and intentions of others. Some mirror neuron cells code the posture and movements of the face, limbs, or whole body, whereas other mirror neuron cells code goal-directed movements. Mirror neurons may play important roles in the development of imitation skills, understanding of the actions of others, and social interactions.

- Structural abnormalities can develop in the brain long before any noticeable behavioral symptoms can be diagnosed; however, structural abnormalities do not always result in cognitive or behavioral symptoms or deficits.

- Minor alterations in neural circuits for vision and hearing (and perhaps other areas) may be responsible for dyslexia.

- Abnormalities in regions of the brain involved in inhibiting mental and behavioral activity could be the cause of attention-deficit/hyperactivity disorder.

As the above list suggests, our senses depend on the brain. The brain is the most complex computational device known. Although even desktop computers are much faster than the brain, the brain is unequaled in the complexity of its operations. Perception, cognition, affect, and behavior all depend on the brain, and the brain, in turn, depends on genetic endowment and the effects of experience.

LATERALIZATION

Lateralization refers to the specialization of the two hemispheres of the cerebral cortex for cognitive, perceptual, motor, and sensory activities. In general, the side of the brain that controls a *sensorimotor activity* (an activity that combines the functions of the sensory and motor portions of the brain) is opposite to the side of the body that carries out the activity. Consequently, damage to the right side of the brain may result in deficits on the left side of the body, whereas damage to the left side of the brain may produce deficits on the right side of the body. Examples of sensorimotor deficits are limb weakness, poor coordination, and insensitivity to stimulation. Subcortical (below the cortex) damage, especially damage to the cerebellum, may produce deficits on the side of the body where the damage occurred.

Lateral specialization (also referred to as cerebral specialization or hemispheric specialization) for all cognitive, sensory, and motor functions cannot be clearly established, for several reasons. First, the role of lateralization in visuoconstructional skills (skills related to visual and motor integration) is less clear than it is in language skills. Second, some tasks whose components are encoded both verbally and nonverbally, such as tasks involving easily recognizable figures with familiar names, may be bilaterally represented. For such tasks, some individuals may use verbal mediational strategies while others may use nonverbal mediational strategies. Third, there are individual variations in lateral specialization, including those related to left- and right-hand dominance.

Finally, although language and speech may be lateralized at birth (in the sense that the left hemisphere more readily supports these functions), complex changes in the direction and strength of hemispheric specialization occur as development proceeds (Lewkowicz & Turkewitz, 1982).

Hemispheric Higher-Level Functions

The two cerebral hemispheres—the left hemisphere and the right hemisphere—are specialized to varying degrees for higher-level functions, such as language and memory. Because the two hemispheres of the brain differ somewhat in their normal functioning, injuries to the left hemisphere are likely to have different effects than injuries to the right hemisphere.

The *left cerebral hemisphere* in most people is specialized for language functions—including reading, writing, speaking, verbal ideation, verbal memory, and certain aspects of arithmetic ability (such as skilled math analysis and computation). Left hemisphere processing has been described as analytic, temporal, sequential, serial, logical, and differential.

The *right cerebral hemisphere* in most people is specialized for nonverbal, perceptual, and spatial functions—including spatial visualization, visual learning and memory, arithmetical calculations involving spatial organization of the problem elements, vocal inflection nuances, complex visual-motor organization, and nonverbal sequencing. Right hemisphere processing is considered holistic (i.e., emphasizing the importance of the whole and the interdependence of its parts), simultaneous, Gestalt-like, intuitive, parallel, and integrative.

For simple tasks, nonverbal stimuli can be processed holistically by either hemisphere. The right hemisphere is generally inferior to the left hemisphere in the expressive functions of speech and writing but is not as inferior in the comprehension of language.

Four Lobes of the Cerebral Hemispheres

Within each hemisphere are four lobes: frontal, parietal, temporal, and occipital (see Figure 23-1).

- The *frontal lobes* are associated with general intelligence and play an important role in personality and emotional control. Specific functions include planning, initiation, and modulation of behavior (including self-control), as well as expressive verbal fluency, control of motor functions, and motor planning.
- The *parietal lobes* are associated with somatosensory functions, visual-spatial ability, and the integration of visual, somatosensory, and auditory stimuli.
- The *temporal lobes* are associated with auditory perception, auditory comprehension, verbal memory, visual memory, and visual processing.
- The *occipital lobes* are associated with visual perception, elaboration and synthesis of visual information, and the

integration of visual information with information gathered by other sensory systems.

Injuries to the frontal, parietal, temporal, and occipital lobes and to the subcortical centers (such as the basal ganglia and hippocampal structures) may produce disorders in cognition, affect, memory, motor output, and motivation. Following are examples of symptoms associated with injury to the cerebral lobes (adapted from Hickey, 1992, p. 493).

FRONTAL LOBES

- Inappropriate social behavior
- Emotional lability
- Loss of self-restraint
- Indifference
- A quiet, flat affect
- Inattentiveness, difficulty concentrating, and distractibility
- Confusion when confronted with choices
- Difficulty correcting mistakes or optimizing performance
- Difficulties with abstraction, generalizing, and setting goals
- Inflexibility in thinking
- Limited foresight
- Impaired short-term memory
- Denial of deficits

PARIETAL LOBES

- Abnormal sensations involving the skin (*paresthesia*)
- Tactile insensitivity (*hypoesthesia*)
- Loss of ability to distinguish two points when they are touched on the skin (*2-point sensation*)
- Visual difficulties
- Difficulty using numbers (*acalculia*)
- Difficulties recognizing, localizing, or naming body parts (*autotopagnosia*)
- Difficulty writing (*agraphia*)

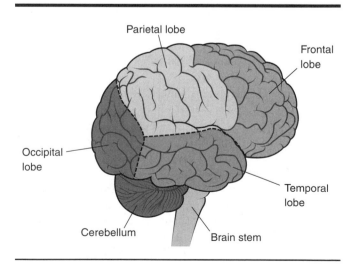

Figure 23-1. Drawing of brain and beginning of spinal cord.

- Difficulty with construction activities that require spatial abilities, such as drawing or assembling two- and three-dimensional objects (constructional apraxia)
- Disorientation and neglect of external environmental space

TEMPORAL LOBES

- Altered personality and affective behavior, including increased aggressive behavior
- Altered sexual behavior
- Disturbance of auditory sensation and perception
- Disturbance of language comprehension
- Disturbance of selective attention to auditory and visual input
- Disturbance of visual perception
- Impaired long-term memory
- Impaired organization and categorization of verbal material
- Loss of use of the upper quadrant of the body on the side opposite to the damage
- Psychomotor seizures (impaired consciousness with amnesia, emotional outbursts, and automatic behavior)

OCCIPITAL LOBES

- Defects in vision
- Difficulty reading and writing
- Difficulty recognizing objects, faces, and drawings
- Difficulty locating objects in space
- Difficulty identifying colors
- Difficulty recognizing movements of objects
- Visual hallucinations

Development of Lateralization

Lateralization begins in utero and continues through childhood into adulthood (Spreen, Risser, & Edgell, 1995). For most children of both sexes, linguistic functions are localized in the left hemisphere at birth (Hahn, 1987; Paquier & Van Dongen, 1993). Lateralization of functions in the right hemisphere is less straightforward—certain abilities are lateralized at birth (e.g., processing nonlinguistic stimuli), whereas others become lateralized during development (e.g., processing spatial information). Research on cerebral lateralization in childhood is continuing.

Comment on Lateralization

Once language develops, the left hemisphere is dominant for language in most individuals; the right hemisphere usually has limited potential for language functions. Thus, language disorders in children, like those in adults, are associated more frequently with left hemisphere damage than with right hemisphere damage. A child with left hemisphere damage may exhibit continuing deficits in grammatical, reading, and writing skills (Moscovitch, 1981; Whitten, D'Amato, & Chittooran, 1992).

Although the right hemisphere is less well understood than the left, its primary function may be to integrate information into meaningful wholes. The right hemisphere does not support the specific analytic skills required to process linguistic input phonetically or to decode complex syntax, but it does support communication (Moscovitch, 1981). Impairments of the right hemisphere may interfere with communication, conceptual skills, memory, and other cognitive functions, especially when a task requires the integration of multiple sources of information or the comprehension of nonliteral language, such as metaphor or sarcasm. Additionally, the right hemisphere appears to be important in prosody (rhythmic patterns of speech), allowing for the recognition of emotional expression in one's own speech and that of others.

Frank and Ernest

© 1994 Thaves / Reprinted with permission. Newspaper dist. by NEA, Inc.

ATTENTION AND MEMORY

Attention and memory are critical for processing information, and children with brain injuries may have difficulty with one or more types of attention and/or memory, as noted below. Attentional skills show gradual development during the period between about 5 and 13 years (Helland & Asbjørnsen, 2000). By about 5 years, children can effectively scan their environment. By about 7 years, children have the ability to focus attention. From about 7 years to early adolescence, children develop sustained attention.

Four types of attention can be delineated (Baron, 2004):

1. *Focused attention* (also referred to as *selective attention*) is useful for monitoring information and for maintaining a focus in the presence of distracting stimuli.
2. *Divided attention* is useful for attending to more than one task or event simultaneously.
3. *Sustained attention* is useful for responding consistently during a long or repetitive activity.
4. *Alternating attention* is useful for shifting from one task to another.

Children use mnemonic (memory) strategies infrequently before the age of 6 years. Between 7 and 10 years of age, mnemonic strategies, such as rehearsal and chunking, begin to emerge. After 10 years of age, mnemonic strategies mature and become increasingly refined, flexible, and effective. Thus, as children develop, they are increasingly able to use strategies to encode and retrieve information.

Three stages characterize the process of memory (Baron, 2004):

1. In the *stage of encoding,* a stimulus representation is built into memory. Encoding will not be successful if children have poor attention and cannot register the information.
2. In the *stage of consolidation and storage,* the new information is maintained, elaborated, and stored in long-term memory. Consolidation (retention) will not occur if children forget the information rapidly, have poor retrieval skills, and have poor delayed recognition memory (e.g., ability to identify a picture previously seen).
3. In the *stage of retrieval and recognition,* information may be freely recalled or be in the form of recognition memory.

The following types of memory can be delineated (note that both short-term working memory and long-term memory can be in the form of verbal memory, visual memory, or both verbal and visual memory; Baddeley, 1992; Baron, 2004; Gianutsos, 1987).

SENSORY MEMORY

- *Echoic memory* is useful for short-term auditory storage; it allows us to perceive speech sounds. Five or six bits of auditory stimuli (such as words) are stored in echoic memory for about 3 to 4 seconds.
- *Iconic memory* is useful for storage of visual images over a period of about half a second; it makes cinematography

possible. "A series of separate and discrete still pictures, each separated by a blank period, is perceived as a single moving figure since the information is stored during the blank interval and integrated into a single percept" (Baddeley, 1992, p. 6).

SHORT-TERM WORKING MEMORY

- *Primary memory* (also termed *intermediate memory* or *working memory*) is useful for temporary storage of information acquired while learning, reading, reasoning, or thinking. Although the working memory is limited in size, the information stored there can be used for the execution of complex cognitive tasks. The longer information is maintained in short-term memory and the more it is rehearsed, the more likely it is to be transferred to long-term memory.

LONG-TERM MEMORY

- *Declarative memory* (also termed *declarative knowledge*) is useful for storing memories of facts, concepts, and events. The two types of declarative memory are episodic memory and semantic memory. *Episodic memory* (also termed *biographical memory* or *autobiographical memory*) is useful for storing memories of personal events, including time, place, and associated emotions (e.g., what you ate for breakfast or the details of a birthday party you attended last year). *Semantic memory* is useful for storing information independent of content and not associated with particular events, times, or places (e.g., the name of the president of the country, a telephone number, the population of a city).
- *Procedural memory* (also termed *procedural knowledge, implicit memory,* or *nondeclarative memory*) typically involves motor tasks and is useful for recalling how to perform an action, such as going to the library, riding a bicycle, or playing a piano. In most cases, learning occurs without awareness.
- *Prospective memory* refers to memory for planned or anticipated future events or phenomena and may be defined as remembering to remember. It is useful for helping us remember to do something at a later time, such as remembering to go to the library after school or to call a friend about an assignment. There are three forms of prospective memory: *time-based prospective memory* (remembering to do something at a specified time), *event-based prospective memory* (remembering to interrupt a present activity in order to perform another activity), and *activity-based prospective memory* (remembering to take an action after finishing an activity). Both internally generated cues and external cues can trigger prospective memory.

As a result of brain injuries, children may develop amnesia (Baron, 2004). Those with *anterograde amnesia* will have difficulty forming new and lasting memories or lose the ability to recall events that occur after the onset of the amnesia. Those with *retrograde amnesia* will have difficulty recalling information that was encoded in memory prior to the injury.

CAUSES OF BRAIN INJURIES

Brain injuries can result from factors present in the period between conception and birth (*prenatal period*); from injuries sustained in the period around childbirth, especially the five months before and one month after birth (*perinatal period*); or from injuries sustained at any point after birth (*postnatal period*). (Note that the perinatal period overlaps with both the prenatal period and the postnatal period.)

Prenatal Period

Conditions that may contribute to brain injury during the prenatal period include the following:

- Congenital disorders (such as cerebral palsy or spina bifida)
- Maternal exposure to toxic substances (such as lead, asbestos, chlorines, fluorides, nickel, or mercury)
- Maternal infections caused by viruses or bacteria (such as rubella or syphilis or other sexually transmitted diseases)
- Maternal illnesses (such as hypertension or diabetes)
- Maternal use of alcohol or other drugs (whether prescribed or illegal) or tobacco
- Physical injury to the uterus
- Exposure to radiation
- Severe maternal malnutrition

Perinatal Period

Conditions that may lead to brain injury during the perinatal period include the following (see Chapter 21 for a description of asphyxia, kernicterus, meningitis, and Rh incompatibilities).

- Asphyxia
- Kernicterus
- Meningitis
- Rh incompatibilities
- Hypoglycemia
- Encephalitis

Hypoglycemia refers to an abnormally low concentration of glucose in the blood. The condition starves the brain of glucose energy, which is essential for proper brain function. Symptoms include anxiety, sweating, tremor, palpitations, nausea, pallor, headache, mild confusion, and abnormal behavior and can lead to loss of consciousness, seizures, coma, and even death. Hypoglycemia can be caused by various drugs, liver disease, tumors that release excess amounts of insulin, and prediabetes.

Encephalitis is an inflammation of the brain caused primarily by viral infection. Symptoms include fever, headache, vomiting, confusion, stiff neck and back, drowsiness, clumsiness, unsteady gait, and irritability and, when severe, loss of consciousness, seizures, muscle weakness, memory loss, and impaired judgment.

Postnatal Period

Conditions that may result in brain injury during the postnatal period include the following (see Chapter 18 for a description of congenital hypothyroidism, galactosemia, phenylketonuria, and Tay-Sachs disease).

- Congenital hypothyroidism
- Galactosemia
- Phenylketonuria (PKU)
- Tay-Sachs disease
- Hydrocephalus
- Niemann-Pick disease

Hydrocephalus is a condition marked by increased accumulation of fluid within the ventricles of the brain. Symptoms of hydrocephalus vary with age (National Institute of Neurological Disorders and Stroke, 2005). In infants, symptoms include rapid increase in head circumference or an unusually large head size, vomiting, sleepiness, irritability, downward deviation of the eyes, and seizures. In older children, symptoms include headache, nausea, papilledema (swelling of the optic disk, which is part of the optic nerve), blurred vision, diplopia (double vision), downward deviation of the eyes, problems with balance, poor coordination, gait disturbance, urinary incontinence, slowing or loss of development, lethargy, drowsiness, irritability, memory loss, and/or other changes in personality and cognition.

Niemann-Pick disease is a hereditary disorder involving lipid metabolism (the breakdown and use of fats and cholesterol in the body), in which harmful amounts of lipids accumulate in the spleen, liver, lungs, bone marrow, and brain. The disease may result in mental retardation, anemia, dark pigmentation of the skin, and enlarged liver, spleen, and lymph nodes.

Infancy, Early Childhood, and Adolescence

Conditions that may lead to brain injury during infancy, early childhood, and adolescence include the following (see Chapter 18 for a description of human immunodeficiency virus type I infection and neurofibromatosis 1).

- Trauma to the brain
- Brain tumors
- Deficiency of nutrients (such as iodine, protein, or vitamin A, B_1, B_2, or D)
- Diabetes
- Drug and alcohol abuse
- End-stage renal disease
- Epilepsy

- Exposure to *neurotoxins* (such as lead, arsenic, mercury, carbon disulfide, or manganese)
- Human immunodeficiency virus type I (HIV-I) infection
- Infections (such as scarlet fever, rabies, Rocky Mountain spotted fever, encephalitis, or meningitis)
- Neurofibromatosis 1
- Exposure to radiation

TRAUMATIC BRAIN INJURY

Each year, approximately 1 million children in the United States sustain head injuries from falls, physical abuse, recreational accidents, or motor vehicle accidents (Beers, 2003). Although trauma to the head does not always lead to brain injury, traumatic brain injury results in an estimated 2,685 deaths, 37,000 hospitalizations, and 435,000 emergency department visits among children ages 0 to 14 years (Centers for Disease Control and Prevention, 2003).

IDEA (Code of Federal Regulations 300.7(c)(12)) defines traumatic brain injury as follows:

> . . . an acquired injury to the brain caused by an external physical force, resulting in total or partial functional disability or psychosocial impairment, or both, that adversely affects a child's educational performance. The term applies to open or closed head injuries resulting in impairments in one or more areas, such as cognition; language; memory; attention; reasoning; abstract thinking; judgment; problem-solving; sensory, perceptual, and motor abilities; psychosocial behavior; physical functions; information processing; and speech. The term does not apply to brain injuries that are congenital or degenerative, or to brain injuries induced by birth trauma.

Although most children survive traumatic brain injuries because of advances in medical treatment and increased availability of trauma care, they often have residual cognitive, language, somatic, and behavioral difficulties. Traumatic brain injury is a threat to a child's quality of life—including life style, education, physical and recreational activities, interpersonal relationships, and self-control. Approximately 70% of children with severe traumatic brain injury continue to receive special education services 5 years after the injury (Massagli, Michaud, & Rivara, 1996).

Traumatic brain injury is associated primarily with physical abuse (shaken baby syndrome or thrown infant syndrome) in infants under the age of 1 year; with falls and physical abuse in toddlers and preschoolers; and with bicycle, motor vehicle, and sports-related accidents and injuries in children over the age of 5 years. Motor vehicle accidents, bicycle accidents, and falls account for between 75% and 80% of brain injuries in children (Yeates, 2000).

Incidence of Traumatic Brain Injuries

The incidence of traumatic brain injuries varies with sex and age (Yeates, 2000). Boys are more at risk for traumatic brain injuries than are girls, with the ratio of boys to girls rising from approximately 1.5:1 among preschool children to approximately 2:1 among school-age children and adolescents. The incidence is relatively stable from birth to 5 years of age, with injuries occurring in about 160 per 100,000 children in this age group. After 5 years of age, the overall incidence gradually increases until early adolescence and then shows rapid growth, reaching a peak of approximately 290 per 100,000 by 18 years of age.

Primary and Secondary Effects

Traumatic head injuries produce both primary effects (resulting directly from the trauma) and secondary effects (resulting indirectly from the trauma). *Primary effects* include skull fracture, penetration of brain tissue by skull fragments, lacerations of various layers of brain tissue, intracranial contusions and hemorrhage, focal compression of brain tissue, and microscopic damage resulting from twisting or shearing of the nerve fibers associated with violent movement of the brain within the skull. Disruption in brain function at a cellular level may cause excessive production of free radicals (byproducts of metabolism) or excitatory amino acids (a type of neurotransmitter) and disruption of the calcium balance inside cells (Yeates, 2000).

Secondary effects include cerebral edema (swelling in the cerebrum), diffuse brain swelling, elevated intracranial pressure, degeneration of nerve tissue, mass lesions (*hematoma*), *hypoxia* (deficiency of oxygen in the tissues of the body), and infection. Over time, severe traumatic brain injuries can result in a gradual and prolonged process of white matter degeneration, as well as cerebral atrophy and ventricular enlargement (Yeates, 2000).

Focal and Diffuse Head Injuries

Two major types of head injury are focal head injuries and diffuse head injuries. *Focal head injuries* (also referred to as open-head injuries or penetrating head injuries) usually involve a circumscribed area of the brain. In a focal head injury, the skull may be penetrated by a high-velocity projectile, such as a bullet, and brain tissue comes into contact with the outside environment. The damage is usually confined to the site of the injury.

Diffuse head injuries (also referred to as closed-head injuries, nonpenetrating head injuries, bilateral injuries, or multifocal injuries) usually involve multiple areas of the brain. In a diffuse brain injury, such as a brain injury caused by a motor vehicle accident, the force of the trauma affects the brain within the closed, bony space of the skull.

Brain tissue may be bruised at the point of impact (referred to as *coup*) and in an area opposite to the point of impact (referred to as coup-contrecoup). The *coup-contrecoup effect* occurs because the brain, which is enclosed in a fluid sac inside the skull, moves with the impact of the injury. The brain is bruised when it hits against the skull at the point of impact and then again when it hits the skull on the opposite side. If an *intracranial hematoma* (a collection of blood within the brain or between the brain and the skull) results, there may be damage to adjacent areas as well. Diffuse head injuries—particularly those caused by motor vehicle accidents—also may result in micro shearing of the nerve fibers, especially in vulnerable areas of the brain such as the inferior (underside) frontal lobes and the mesial (middle) temporal lobes.

Children with diffuse head injuries usually have more cognitive difficulties than children with focal head injuries (Aram & Eisele, 1992). The greater or the more widespread the damage, the more limited are the possibilities for neural reallocation of functions. Injury to the frontal lobes, for example, reduces the volume of its gray matter and increases the volume of cerebrospinal fluid (Levin, Hanten, Zhang, Swank, Ewing-Cobbs, Dennis, Barnes, Max, Schachar, Chapman, & Hunter, 2004). However, even focal head injuries may result in impairment not only of functions associated with the specific site of injury, but also of the acquisition of new cognitive skills.

SPECIFIC EFFECTS OF BRAIN INJURY IN CHILDREN

A physician should be contacted immediately if a child has any of the following symptoms after sustaining a head injury (adapted from Centers for Disease Control and Prevention, 2003):

- Changes in play
- Changes in school performance
- Changes in sleep patterns
- Tiredness or listlessness
- Irritability or crankiness
- Lack of interest in favorite toys or activities
- Loss of balance or unsteady walking
- Loss of newly acquired skills
- Refusal to eat or nurse
- Vomiting

The specific effects of brain injury in children depend on (a) the location, extent, and type of injury, (b) the child's age, (c) the child's preinjury temperament, personality, and cognitive and psychosocial functioning, (d) the child's familial and environmental supports, and (e) the promptness and quality of treatment. Symptoms of brain injury are usually directly related to the functions mediated by the damaged area. For example, damage to the occipital lobe may result in difficulties with visual perception, whereas damage to the frontal-temporal area may result in behavior problems and memory deficits. There may be a general deterioration in all or most aspects of functioning or highly specific symptoms when the injuries are in specialized locations. In some cases, there are no observable symptoms; in other cases, symptoms are quite obvious. Some symptoms may not be observed until several years after the injury. Overall, brain injuries may produce physical symptoms, cognitive disturbances, behavioral disturbances, and language and symbolic disorders.

Physical Symptoms

The physical symptoms associated with mild to severe brain injuries include the following (Mild Traumatic Brain Injury Committee, 1993).

MILD BRAIN INJURIES

- Nausea
- Vomiting
- Dizziness
- Headache
- Blurred vision
- Sleep disturbance
- Fatigue
- Lethargy
- Abnormalities of senses of smell and hearing
- Other sensory losses that cannot be accounted for by peripheral injury or other causes

SEVERE BRAIN INJURIES
(in addition to the above)

- Skull fracture
- Bruised brain tissue
- Cerebral laceration
- Intracranial hematoma
- Seizures
- Paralysis
- Balance and other coordination problems
- Drainage of cerebrospinal fluid from the nose to the mouth
- Collection of blood behind the eardrum or in the sinuses

Cognitive Disturbances

Cognitive disturbances after brain injury may be evident in the following areas:

- Attention and concentration
- Executive functions
- Judgment and perception
- Learning and memory
- Language and communication
- Speed of information processing

In school, cognitive disturbances may cause children with brain injuries to have difficulties with the following:

- Completing their work and understanding tasks
- Locating classrooms, getting to classes on time, and following schedules
- Remembering what they have learned in class or what they have studied at home
- Avoiding potentially dangerous situations
- Organizing thoughts, planning, and processing information

- Shifting from one activity to another
- Taking initiative or acting independently
- Connecting old with new information
- Generalizing

Cognitive disturbances may also cause children with brain injuries to have difficulties with the following communication tasks (Adamovich, 1991):

- Understanding the point of view of others
- Modifying an opinion
- Recognizing the main point of a conversation
- Sticking to the topic
- Joining an ongoing conversation appropriately
- Asking for clarification necessary to form an appropriate conclusion
- Taking turns
- Giving and receiving feedback
- Accepting group decisions
- Presenting an appropriate amount of information
- Switching from one topic to another

Children with brain injuries may have cognitive impairments that are not evident during an evaluation. For example, they may perform better when the conditions are structured than when they are unstructured. Similarly, although they may be able to converse adequately during an evaluation, they may become distracted easily when several people are talking.

Behavioral Disturbances

Following are behavioral symptoms associated with brain injury:

- Anxiety (e.g., restlessness, fatigue, concentration problems, irritability, sleep disturbances)
- Denial of illness (or *anosognosia*, which is an inability to recognize recent deficits in physical or psychological functioning)
- Depression and amotivational states (e.g., feelings of worthlessness, helplessness, or guilt; loss of interest in school, work, or family activities; decreased interest in social activities; decreased sexual drive in adolescents)
- Emotional lability (e.g., a lowered tolerance for frustration, rapid mood shifts, temper outbursts, demanding behavior, excessive dependence on others, talkativeness)
- Paranoid ideation (e.g., suspiciousness, hypervigilance, distrust of others)
- Psychomotor agitation (e.g., restlessness, excessive motor movements, fear, tension)
- Psychosocial disturbances (e.g., socially inappropriate behavior [such as saying embarrassing things and performing actions that embarrass others], reduced awareness of one's impact on others, insensitivity to others, difficulty making friends, social withdrawal, forgetting school responsibilities)

Behavioral symptoms may reflect impairments directly associated with the brain injury, emotional reactions to the acquired deficits, exaggeration of preexisting personality patterns, or a combination of these factors. Of particular importance are how the child perceives her or his limitations, the severity of these limitations, and what interventions are needed. These considerations, in turn, are related to the child's age, cognitive ability, social skills, family and environmental supports, schooling, ethnicity, and social status.

Some children with brain injuries show a pattern of behavior characterized by *overarousal* (such as inattentiveness, irritability, distractibility, hyperactivity, impulsivity, inappropriate behavior, aggressiveness, and, among adolescents, increased sexual drive), whereas other children with brain injuries show a pattern of behavior characterized by *underarousal* (such as apathy, poor motivation, social withdrawal; Filley, Cranberg, Alexander, & Hart, 1987). Overall, behavior problems are more likely to result from severe brain injury than from mild or moderate brain injury (Fennell & Mickle, 1992).

Some prescribed medications may cause psychological disturbances. For example, antiseizure medication can produce or exacerbate learning, attention, or memory disturbances; antipsychotic medication may produce blunted affect; and both types of medications may produce psychomotor retardation.

Brain injury may lead to losses in automatic processing—the ability to perform habitual and overlearned responses such as those involved in buttoning clothing, dialing a telephone, or brushing teeth. These overlearned and automatic sequential activities, which were carried out quickly and easily before the injury, may be performed slowly and require much effort and concentration after the injury. With the loss of automatic processing, children with brain injuries have less flexibility and less ability to adjust rapidly to environmental changes, which places them at a disadvantage in novel situations. In addition, deficits in one area of functioning may impair their performance in other areas. Changes in reasoning, judgment, cognitive efficiency, vigilance, reaction time, and temperament also may make children with brain injuries more vulnerable to sustaining subsequent head injuries.

Language and Symbolic Disorders

The major types of language and symbolic disorders associated with brain injuries are agnosia, apraxia, and aphasia.

Agnosia. Agnosia refers to a disturbance in the ability to recognize familiar stimuli despite intact sensory and perceptual functions. Following are several forms of agnosia:

- *Auditory agnosia* is impaired ability to identify sounds.
- *Autotopagnosia* is impaired ability to name body parts.
- *Finger agnosia* is impaired ability to identify or select specific fingers of the hands.
- *Prosopagnosia* is impaired ability to recognize familiar faces.

- *Tactile agnosia* is impaired ability to identify familiar objects by touch with the eyes closed.
- *Visual agnosia* is impaired ability to name or recognize objects by sight.
- *Visual-spatial agnosia* is impaired ability to follow directions, to find one's way in familiar surroundings, and to understand spatial details (such as left-right positions or the layout of a classroom).

Apraxia.   Apraxia refers to disturbance in the ability to execute learned movements or to carry out purposeful or skilled acts. Apraxia is not due to muscle weakness, sensory defects, comprehension deficits, or intellectual deterioration. Some forms of apraxia are as follows:

- *Bucco-facial apraxia* is impaired ability to perform facial movements (e.g., to whistle, pucker lips, protrude tongue, cough, sniff) in response to commands, although the movements can be executed spontaneously.
- *Constructional apraxia* is impaired ability to construct objects (e.g., to construct a pattern with blocks or to copy a drawing).
- *Dressing apraxia* is impaired ability to put on clothing correctly.
- *Ideomotor apraxia* is impaired ability to carry out an action (e.g., to brush teeth) on verbal command, although the action can be performed automatically.
- *Ideational apraxia* is impaired ability to execute a series of acts (e.g., to fold a letter, place it in an envelope, seal it, and stamp it), although each step can be performed separately.
- *Imitative apraxia* is impaired ability to repeat actions performed by others despite adequate motor control of the limbs.
- *Limb-kinetic apraxia* is impaired ability to use a single limb, resulting in clumsiness or in the inability to carry out fine-motor acts with the affected limb (e.g., to grasp an object).

Aphasia.   Aphasia refers to a disturbance in the ability to comprehend or produce symbolic language, caused by brain injury (and not caused by speech defects or motor difficulties). The following three types of childhood aphasia differ from one another mainly in the severity and age of onset of the language difficulty:

- *Congenital aphasia* is a language deficit present at birth, marked by an almost complete failure to acquire language.
- *Developmental language disorder,* a less pervasive cognitive and developmental impairment than congenital aphasia, is characterized by late onset of language and failure to develop language fully.
- *Acquired aphasia* is a language deficit resulting from brain injury following normal language development.

Aphasia may involve expressive components, receptive components, or both. *Expressive aphasia* (also called *nonfluent aphasia* or *Broca's aphasia*) is an impaired ability to use spoken and/or written language. The effects of the spoken language disability range from completely losing the ability to speak to simply having difficulty finding or retrieving the appropriate word. Writing is highly susceptible to disruption by brain injury because of the complex nature of the task; writing requires the coordinated activity of linguistic, motor, spatial, and perceptual systems. Children with expressive aphasia may have a restricted vocabulary; may use words repetitively; may have difficulty formulating grammatically correct, complete, or meaningful sentences; and may pause for long periods between words or phrases. Expressive aphasia primarily affects the symbolic use of language, with some aphasic disturbances involving word usage and order. Following are some forms of expressive aphasia:

- *Acalculia* refers to an inability to carry out simple mathematical calculations.
- *Agrammatism* refers to difficulty using grammatical constructions; a paucity of connecting and modifying words may give speech a telegraphic quality (e.g., "I work factory make steel").
- *Agraphia* refers to a loss or impairment of the ability to express language in written or printed form.
- *Anomia* refers to word-finding difficulty. In *verbal paraphasia* (also termed *semantic paraphasia*), an inappropriate word is unintentionally used in lieu of the target word (e.g., "I went to the store . . . no, the school"). In *phonemic paraphasia,* unintended sounds or syllables appear in the utterance of a recognizable word (e.g., "paker" for "paper" or "sisperos" for "rhinoceros"). In *phonosemantic blending,* the substitution of a phonemic sound in the target word creates another real word, related in sound but not in meaning (e.g., "cable" for "table" or "television" for "telephone"). In *neologistic paraphasia,* nonsense words are used but are not recognized as errors (e.g., "tilto" for "table").
- *Paragrammatism* refers to employing an incoherent and aimless syntactic structure in speech, with nouns appearing in verb slots and vice versa (e.g., "Runs he fast").

Receptive aphasia (also called *fluent aphasia* or *Wernicke's aphasia*) is impaired ability to understand spoken and/or written language. Speech may be relatively intact, although dysfluencies (use of incomplete sentences, sentences that do not hang together, irrelevant words, or phrase repetitions, especially in severe cases) may be present. Forms of receptive aphasia include the following:

- *Auditory aphasia* refers to an impaired ability to comprehend the meaning of spoken words, although the ability to hear remains intact.
- *Alexia* refers to an impaired ability to comprehend written or printed language, despite adequate vision and intelligence.

In children with brain injuries, auditory comprehension may be disturbed for several reasons. First, the brain injury may impair recognition of speech sounds and word meanings. Second, the child may suffer from attentional and short-term auditory memory problems. Third, situational variables—such as the personal relevance and emotional significance of the subject matter—may affect comprehension. Finally, all of these factors may interact to affect comprehension.

Disorders of auditory comprehension can involve problems with the comprehension of individual words, certain categories of words (such as names of body parts or letters of the alphabet), and sentences. A rare disorder of auditory comprehension, referred to as *pure word-deafness,* involves the inability to perceive speech sounds, while other language processes such as speaking, writing, and reading remain intact.

Global aphasia, or *mixed-type aphasia,* refers to impaired abilities in both expressive and receptive domains. It is the most severe form of aphasia because children produce few recognizable words and understand little or no spoken language. Table 24-2 in Chapter 24 illustrates procedures used to evaluate agnosia, apraxia, and aphasia.

Children older than 10 years of age have symptoms of aphasia similar to those of adults, whereas children younger than 10 years of age are more likely to have delays in the development of verbal and nonverbal communication (Aram & Eisele, 1992; Paquier & Van Dongen, 1993). Children and adults acquire aphasia in similar ways—as a result of trauma, vascular damage, tumors, infection, or seizure disorders. However, traumatic events are the main cause of brain injury in children, whereas strokes are the main cause of brain injury in adults. Because traumatic events are more likely than strokes to produce diffuse injuries, children have fewer clear-cut symptoms of aphasia than do adults.

Children under the age of 10 years with aphasia are usually alert, attentive, and eager to communicate their thoughts and reactions. The prognosis for recovery from aphasia is more favorable for young children than for adults. When recovery is not complete, children with aphasia may have long-term deficits, including naming and writing disorders and impaired use of syntax, all of which can disrupt academic performance. Improvement depends on the etiology of the brain injury, the age at which the injury occurred, and the size, location, and nature of the damage. Seizures, in particular, can impede recovery. Even when children recover from aphasia, they may still perform poorly in school or have verbal skill deficits (Martins & Ferro, 1992).

Exercise 23-1
Identifying Language and Symbolic Disorders in Children with Brain Injuries

Read each statement and indicate which one of the following types of language or symbolic disorders it exemplifies: acalculia, agraphia, agrammatism, auditory aphasia, alexia, visual agnosia, prosopagnosia, auditory agnosia, tactile agnosia, visual-spatial agnosia, constructional apraxia, bucco-facial apraxia, ideational apraxia, ideomotor apraxia, or dressing apraxia.

1. A 9-year-old child is shown a baseball bat, and she calls it "a piece of wood."

2. An 11-year-old adolescent is asked to touch a doll's right ear, and he says, "I don't know where to touch it."
3. An 8-year-old child is asked to put her hands in the air, and she stares out the window.
4. A 9-year-old child is asked to put on a sweater, and he fails in his attempt to do so. However, he can clap his hands when he is asked to do so.
5. An 8-year-old child is shown a picture of three blocks that are stacked in a tower from largest to smallest. She is asked to build the same tower. The child puts her three blocks in a row.
6. A 13-year-old adolescent is shown a picture of his brother, and he calls it "a picture of someone."
7. A 10-year-old child, when asked to write his name, makes random marks.
8. A 15-year-old adolescent is asked to identify, without looking at it, a coin placed in her hand, and she says, "It is something."
9. A 16-year-old adolescent with adequate vision, speech, and intelligence is asked to read aloud a paragraph from a third-grade reader but is unable to do so.
10. A 10-year-old child is asked to drink from a cup filled with water, and she complies with the request. She is then shown another cup that is empty. When she is asked to show how she would drink out of the cup, she looks puzzled and does not perform the action.
11. An 8-year-old child is asked to identify the sound of a drum, and he says, "I don't know what it is."
12. A 12-year-old adolescent says, "I go store buy candy."
13. A 9-year-old child is asked to add 4 + 3 + 2, and she says, "432."
14. A 13-year-old adolescent is asked to show his tongue, and he simply stares ahead.
15. A 10-year-old child is asked to do three things in order: open the door, pick up a pencil from the table, and then put it on the chair. The child says, "I don't know."

Answers

1. Visual agnosia or anomia 2. Visual-spatial agnosia 3. Auditory aphasia 4. Dressing apraxia 5. Constructional apraxia 6. Prosopagnosia 7. Agraphia 8. Tactile agnosia 9. Alexia 10. Ideomotor apraxia 11. Auditory agnosia 12. Agrammatism 13. Acalculia 14. Bucco-facial apraxia or auditory aphasia 15. Ideational apraxia (if a comprehension deficit has been ruled out as the cause)

To acquire aphasia is to suddenly lose both an important part of oneself and one's attachment to reality with no readily available means of compensation.
—Pierre Y. Létourneau, French-Canadian psychologist

Differential Effects of Traumatic Brain Injury in Young Children and in Adults

Traumatic brain injuries usually produce less specific effects in young children than in adults. In young children, brain injury may alter the basic pattern of cognitive development in many areas, rather than produce a striking loss of function in one area. Large unilateral injuries in infants usually result in a more widespread deficit in intellectual functions (e.g., mental retardation) than do similar injuries in adults. When adults sustain a brain injury, there may be a striking loss of previously acquired functions (in language, memory, perceptual-motor functions, social relations, or general intelligence).

The principles of behavior development, and the relationship between neural structures and behavior, are helpful in understanding traumatic brain injury in children. The first 5 years of life constitute the period of greatest cortical development. The process of myelination in various brain regions affects behavioral and cognitive development. In *myelination,* the axon of a neuron becomes insulated or coated, which increases the speed with which messages are transmitted among neurons. Myelination occurs in different areas at different times (Harris, 1995b):

1. At 40 weeks' gestation, in the spinal tract areas involved in postural control
2. At ages 2 to 3 months, in the midbrain areas involved in smiling
3. At the end of the first year of life, in the spinal tract areas involved in fine-motor control
4. During the second year of life, in the brain areas involved in motor control and coordination
5. During school years and later in life, in the brain areas involved in learning motor programs and higher mental processing

Conceivably, the behavioral difficulties that occur among children with brain injuries could be related to the neurostructural components undergoing the most rapid development at the time of the injury.

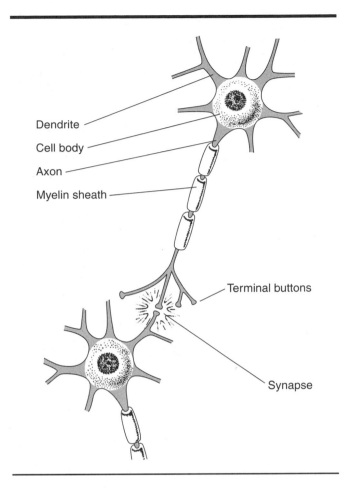

Figure 23-2. Typical structure of a neuron.

> *Dear, dear! How queer everything is today! And yesterday things went on just as usual. I wonder if I've been changed in the night? Let me think: Was I the same when I got up this morning? I almost think I can remember feeling a little different. But if I'm not the same, the next question is "Who am I?" Ah that's the great puzzle.*
> —Lewis Carroll, English writer (1832–1898)

Outcomes of Traumatic Brain Injuries

The ability of the brain to change in order to compensate for loss of function (referred to as *cerebral plasticity*) will, in part, determine the outcome of traumatic brain injury. The change may involve the taking over, by one part of the brain, of functions impaired by damage to another part of the brain or the functional reorganization of the brain to restore impaired functions. The brain is quite plastic and is capable of extensive reorganization and modification in response to injury. Children have more cerebral plasticity than do adults; however, there are limits to the degree of neuroanatomical plasticity attainable following brain injury. Recovery of function depends in part on the ability of the neurons in the damaged area to regenerate terminals and produce new terminals (see Figure 23-2). Reorganization is beneficial when the sprouting of intact axon collaterals (branches of an axon) facilitates the processing of information, but reorganization is harmful when anomalous neuronal connections are made that interfere with the processing of information (Taylor, 1991). Exhibit 23-1 describes some of the events associated with a traumatic brain injury and how the brain may repair itself.

About 75% to 95% of children with traumatic brain injuries either have a good recovery (resuming most activities and schooling with minimal neurobehavioral or functional impairments) or have mild disabilities (resuming most activities and schooling but still experiencing cognitive, behavioral, physical, and/or social problems; Barry, Taylor, Klein, & Yeates, 1996; Kinsella, Prior, Sawyer, Ong, Murtagh, Eisenmajer, Bryan, Anderson, & Klug, 1997; Yeates, 2000). If they need to be hospitalized, young children who sustain mild head injuries are more likely to show adverse psychosocial outcomes (e.g., hyperactivity, inattention, conduct disorder) at ages 10 to 13 years than those who did not need to be hospitalized (McKinlay, Dalrymple-Alford, Horwood, & Fergusson, 2002).

Exhibit 23-1
When the Brain Takes a Bump

To understand how the brain may repair itself, it's necessary to know how brain injury typically occurs. Usually, it's a consequence of several events. The first event is the actual trauma, such as a hard blow to the skull that ruptures the blood-brain barrier. The latter is the network of vessels carrying oxygen and fuel to the brain. These arteries and capillaries are tightly constructed of endothelial cells that permit only select substances such as glucose (sugar) to pass through their walls and into the brain itself. If the blood-brain barrier is breached by injury, whole blood, proteins, and other materials that normally circulate throughout the rest of the body can pour into the brain's cellular spaces, where neurons and supporting glial cells reside. These substances, which probably also include charged particles of oxygen and iron called free radicals, are poison to neurons. Direct contact with ordinary blood kills nerve cells. The blood flood causes swelling, or edema. Glial cells attempt to counteract the growing damage by absorbing unwanted chemicals, but if the blood flow is too great, the glial cells quickly become overloaded, rupture, and re-release their toxic contents into the brain, where the neuron-killing can begin anew.

At the same time that glial cells are struggling to clear away killer debris, injured, dying, or traumatized nerve cells are releasing their stores of neurotransmitters—the chemicals used to communicate with other nerve cells—and the calcium ions needed to activate them. This sudden, massive release of neurotransmitters can decimate nearby neurons, corroding their membranes or overstimulating them to the point of fatal burnout, a phenomenon called excitotoxicity. It can also activate enzymes within neurons, effectively signaling them to kill their makers.

The scene in a newly injured brain is, in some ways, like that of a major traffic accident. Some neurons die immediately; others suffer grave wounds that will kill them shortly. Yet other neurons seem to escape with only minor injuries or a simple case of shock. These latter neurons can appear normal, but many never fully regain their original functions. Some, for example, are permanently weakened, vulnerable to stress, or prone to failure at inappropriate times. On the whole, the brain adapts to trauma as best it can, re-establishing as quickly as possible its vital biochemical stability. The blood-brain barrier is repaired posthaste. All able neurons are called upon to resume ordinary duties without delay.

The architecture of a typical, living, healthy neuron resembles a bush. From the central cell body, an axon extends like a taproot. The axon's job is to carry messages away from the body of the cell toward neighboring cells. Branchy dendrites elsewhere on the cell stretch out to receive incoming communications. The axon is usually covered with smaller rootlets. If some, perhaps even most, of these rootlets are damaged or destroyed, the neuron will probably still be OK. Repairs can be made. But if too much of the axon is damaged by trauma, the remaining section retreats back into the body of the cell, a process called retrograde degeneration. The neuron, unable to draw sustenance, isolated from its neighbors, withers and dies, not unlike a tree chopped away from its root system.

Many variables, of course, affect whether a neuron successfully overcomes trauma or not, among them the age of the person injured (old cells don't fare as well as young ones), the type of cell damaged (neuron varieties with short axons tend to be more vulnerable), the distance between the brain lesion or injury and the cell body (the farther away the injury, the better), and the presence of healthy, neighboring cells capable of providing vital nutrients, called trophic factors.

Source: Adapted from LaFee (1999).

About 10% of children with traumatic brain injuries have moderate disabilities. They can function independently, but at a reduced level relative to their preinjury status, and they need special education or rehabilitation services. About 1% to 3% of children with traumatic brain injuries have severe disabilities even 2 years after returning to school. They are unable to function independently and require substantial assistance with self-care. Fewer than 1% of children with traumatic brain injuries remain in a persistent vegetative state (unable to function without a life-support system) or die.

The physical, intellectual, and emotional development of children who sustain severe brain injury is seriously compromised (Beers, 2003). For example, they may have sleep disturbances, memory loss, behavior problems, emotional instability, problems in adaptive functioning, and intellectual deficits. If they are unconscious for more than 24 hours, 50% are likely to have longer-term complications and 2% to 5% of these children may remain severely disabled.

Research findings about the relationship between recoverability and the child's age when he or she suffers a brain injury include the following (Middleton, 2004; Taylor & Alden, 1997):

1. Traumatic brain injuries in infancy or early childhood are likely to result in more impaired cognitive and academic functioning than traumatic brain injuries sustained during middle childhood or adolescence. However, if damage is discrete and occurs early, language functions may improve. Recovery is less possible when the damage is pervasive.

2. Cognitive impairments sustained as a result of early brain injuries become more prominent as children age. Complex, higher-level cognitive and behavioral skills that were relatively undeveloped at the time of injury may appear initially to have been spared; however, they may not develop fully later in life.

3. Skills undergoing active development at the time of the brain injury are more susceptible to disruption than previ-

ously established skills. For example, diffuse brain injuries may affect cognitive development in different ways at different times:

- Speech and language during the second year
- Spatial-symbolic processing during the third year
- Expressive and receptive language functions during the preschool years
- Written language during middle childhood (particularly between ages 6 and 8 years)
- Verbal processing, nonverbal processing, and visuospatial processing during adolescence

Overall, studies show that children do not necessarily completely recover all of their functions after traumatic brain injury (Johnson, 1992; St. James-Roberts, 1981; Taylor & Alden, 1997). Thus, there is little reason to believe that young children with traumatic brain injuries *always* or *usually* make a better recovery than older children with brain injuries. In fact, early brain injury may result in greater impairment than later brain injury. Generally, however, recovery is variable within each age group, depending on several factors, including the child's age at the time of the brain injury, preinjury status, experiential history, preexisting problems, education, type and severity of the brain injury (including the nature, locus, extent, and progression of the brain injury), stress level, promptness and quality of treatment, age at the time of treatment, time since treatment, and family and community supports. The correlation between severity of initial injury and neurodevelopmental outcome is far from perfect. Some functions may improve more than others, and some anatomical areas may be more susceptible to permanent deficits than others. Overall, changes in cognitive development after brain injury may best be viewed as involving cumulative interactions among etiological variables, recovery-period variables, and experiential variables.

No simple statement can capture the complex relationship between cerebral plasticity and recovery of function in children, although additional research should tell us more about the details of the relationship. Prognoses about a child's ability to recover from brain injury should be made carefully; evaluating language, speech, and other cognitive functions is more difficult in children than in adults. The available research does, however, indicate that there is little support for the concept of unlimited potential for neural reorganization in the immature brain (Aram & Eisele, 1992; Middleton, 2004).

REHABILITATION PROGRAMS

Rehabilitation programs should be based on the results of a comprehensive, multidisciplinary team assessment. In designing a rehabilitation program, consider when it would be best to begin the program and whether there is a critical period when rehabilitation efforts might be most effective. The following example shows why it may be necessary for a rehabilitation program to focus on each step of a retraining activity (Kay & Silver, 1989).

The child with a brain injury is likely to have the physical ability to perform activities of daily living. The child is able to pick up a toothbrush, squeeze the toothpaste tube, execute the requisite motor movements, rinse, and put things away; yet, the spontaneous integrated sequencing of these activities into a smooth continuity from beginning to end may not be possible. The toothbrush cannot be located. Enormous amounts of toothpaste are squeezed out; the behavior is not terminated at the appropriate point. Brushing is done in a cursory, repetitive, incomplete fashion. Rinsing is forgotten. The brush and toothpaste are left on the sink. And even if brushing one's teeth can be carried out in a reasonable fashion, it does not occur to the child to do so each morning unless prompted. When questioned, the child dutifully reports having brushed, with possibly no recollection of (or concern for) whether the activity was actually performed that day or not. (adapted from p. 146)

Among the most perplexing symptoms of some brain injuries is neglect of part of the visual field or part of the body. Even though both eyes are intact and the child is capable of moving his or her head to scan the entire visual field, the child may not notice things on one side and may fail to complete dressing that side of his or her body. A child may even be unaware of loss of motor control of one side of the body and may think a limb has been moved when it has not.

The following propositions provide a useful underpinning for rehabilitation efforts in cases of traumatic brain injury (Alfano & Finlayson, 1987; Cicerone & Tupper, 1986; Jacobs, 1993; Milton, 1988).

BACKGROUND PROPOSITIONS

1. Rehabilitation programs are designed to help children with brain injuries improve their cognitive and behavioral skills, learn new and compensatory skills, regulate their behavior, and understand and manage emotional reactions to changes in their functioning. Successful rehabilitation efforts will improve the functional and daily living skills of children with brain injuries.

2. Some rehabilitation goals may be difficult to achieve because children with brain injuries may have limited understanding of their condition. They may be poorly informed about basic brain functioning, how their injuries were sustained, how their problems developed, and how their injuries affect their cognitive processes and social interactions. They may show confusion about the passage of time, and they may believe that their difficulties are primarily physical. To make sense of their brain injury, they may hold contradictory ideas about their normality (e.g., recognizing that they lose their temper easily, but attributing the behavior to being tired or to the actions of others).

3. Neuropsychological deficits usually are most prominent during the first 6 months after a brain injury. Although most of the recovery occurs within the first 12 to 18 months after the brain injury, subtle changes may still occur several years after the injury, and changes in temperament and personality may persist even after neurological functions have recovered.

4. Cognitive functions are differentially affected by traumatic brain injury.
5. Each affected cognitive function may exhibit a different potential for recovery, rate of recovery, and remediation.
6. Rehabilitation efforts may be hampered by deficits in speed of processing, attention and concentration, memory and learning, and executive functions.
7. Rehabilitation goals should be appropriate to the child's physical and neuropsychological status and specific injury and should be geared to the child's readiness and motivation to reach the goals.

INTERVENTIONS

1. Alter the physical environment to help the child who has the additional burden of physical disabilities become more mobile and independent. Use adaptive equipment, such as voice-activated computers, page-turning machines, and voice synthesizers, whenever appropriate.
2. Create an environment that is highly organized, contains few distracting stimuli, and provides functional cues (such as timers and lists).
3. Help the child reduce symptoms of social withdrawal, interpersonal isolation, paranoid ideation, hyperactivity, and emotionality.
4. Try to increase the child's awareness of his or her current deficits and strengths, help the child accept his or her limitations, and teach the child to apply compensatory strategies to solve problems: using his or her remaining functions effectively, learning new skills to compensate for lost or impaired ones, and transferring and generalizing skills to new situations and contexts.
5. Try to reduce cognitive confusion by improving attention, concentration, learning, memory, and information-processing skills.
6. Focus on improving impaired areas of functioning by applying educational and other intervention procedures, including speech therapy, occupational therapy, and physical therapy.
7. Help the child being discharged from a hospital or rehabilitation center gradually make the transition back to his or her natural environment, where things are less structured and more demanding.
8. Modify goals based on the child's progress. For example, an early goal to improve oral-motor skills may be replaced by a later goal to improve functional language skills (e.g., using the telephone and the computer).
9. Evaluate the child's ability to use problem-solving strategies and to generalize newly learned skills to new situations.

EVALUATING THE INTERVENTIONS

1. How much did the child benefit from the rehabilitation program?
2. How long should the rehabilitation program continue?
3. How much additional training does the child need to improve and/or maintain his or her skills?
4. What additional techniques should be considered?

Effects of Alcohol on Rehabilitation Efforts

Consumption of alcohol can complicate both physical and cognitive recovery from a brain injury (Miller, 1989). Adolescents admitted to hospitals with a positive blood alcohol level have lower levels of consciousness, remain in a coma longer, and have longer hospital stays than those who have not consumed alcohol. In addition, excessive blood alcohol can lead to fluid and electrolyte abnormalities that exacerbate cerebral edema, alter blood-clotting mechanisms, and increase the risk of brain hypoxia, respiratory depression, and infection.

Chronic abuse of alcohol can produce cognitive deficits that interact with those produced by the traumatic brain injury and interfere with the recovery process. Adolescents who abuse alcohol may be less able to compensate for the effects of a head injury and may have fewer intact abilities to rely on in their rehabilitation than those who do not abuse alcohol. Perhaps even more important is their increased potential for resuming the abuse of alcohol and other drugs because of the stresses inherent in coping with a brain injury. Obviously, drug and alcohol abuse will interfere with the effectiveness of any rehabilitation and recovery program.

> " . . . because life after head injury may never be the same."
>
> —Logo of the New York State Head Injury Association

Rehabilitation Programs in Schools

Returning to school presents several difficulties for children with brain injuries (Roberts, 1999). They may have difficulty taking notes (because the teachers' lectures go too fast), catching on to new concepts and newly presented information, finishing assignments or tests on time, beginning and completing projects, coping with changes in the daily schedule, performing tasks that have multiple components, retrieving previously learned facts, giving detailed and meaningful responses to questions, taking part in conversations with peers, and maintaining friendships. These difficulties may lead to distress, brief staring spells, unexplained emotional outbursts, headaches, irritability, and confusion.

Teachers, other school personnel, and peers may not realize the magnitude of the child's struggles. They may need help in understanding that memory deficits, confusion, emotional outbursts, and other behavioral problems are not purposeful or due to poor attitude. Even the child may not understand the reason for his or her behavior. Consequently, the child needs counseling, not disciplinary action (Roberts, 1999). Be prepared to meet with teachers, specialists, and administrators to explain the situation and be the child's advocate.

Before the child returns to her or his classroom, visit the classroom and consult with the school staff about what modifications are needed to facilitate the child's learning and adjustment. (Chapter 8 presents useful guidelines for observing a classroom.) Finally, help the teacher carry out appropriate strategies for (a) reducing or eliminating barriers to learning, (b) reintegrating the child into the classroom, (c) establishing objectives, and (d) using effective instructional procedures. Review the child's educational placement periodically, especially during the early stages of recovery, because her or his needs are likely to change. If the child has more than one teacher, be sure to meet with all of them. Table 23-1 provides suggestions for teachers of children with brain injuries. The suggestions focus on emotional lability, motor restlessness, inattentiveness, language processing, memory and learning, executive functioning and problem-solving skills, using direct instruction, handling intervention difficulties, and working with the family and monitoring progress.

Table 23-1
Suggestions for Teachers of Children with Brain Injuries

Emotional Lability
- Provide a structured environment.
- Reduce the child's course load so the work does not become overwhelming.
- Reduce stressful experiences, such as being required to take pop quizzes and to perform in front of the class.
- Find ways to help the child calm down when frustrated, such as by giving the child extra time to respond or by having the child take a deep breath.
- Allow the child to rest as needed.
- Be alert to any signs that the child is reaching his or her frustration level.
- Understand that the child's outbursts are not deliberate and are not intended to embarrass anyone in class.
- Don't let the child perform any actions that might hurt another child; instead, redirect the child to an acceptable activity.
- Avoid overstimulating the child.
- Avoid overloading the child with information.

Motor Restlessness
- Plan extracurricular activities tailored to the child's physical and emotional capabilities and interests.
- Encourage the child to stand while reading or performing other activities.
- Assign the child active jobs in the classroom.

Inattentiveness
- Speak slowly and distinctly.
- Look at the child when you speak to him or her.
- Guide the child to listen for specific information.
- Gradually increase the amount of information you present to the child.
- Keep assignments to a reasonable level, fitted to the child's ability.
- Use frequent rest periods.
- Select simple tasks.
- Present one task at a time.
- Be prepared for delays in the child's responses.
- Provide the child with advance notice when schedule changes are to occur.
- Alert the child to the topic being taught ("I'm going to tell a story and then we'll discuss where it takes place").
- Keep classroom distractions to a minimum.
- Allow additional time to complete tests.

Language Processing
- Speak slowly and distinctly to the child.

- Use concrete language when you talk with the child; avoid figurative, idiomatic, ambiguous, ironic, or sarcastic language.
- Guide the child to listen for specific information.
- Gradually increase the amount of information you give the child.
- Learn to read the child's nonverbal cues.
- Encourage the child to communicate on his or her own.
- Establish (if needed) a system of verbal or nonverbal signals to cue the child to attend, respond, or alter her or his behavior.
- Provide clear, concrete instructions.
- Accompany verbal instructions with written instructions.
- Increase communication activities gradually and systematically.
- Make sure that you have the child's attention before you give him or her directions.
- Break complex instructions down into small, well-defined steps.
- Repeat instructions as needed.
- Limit the number of choices you give the child.
- Allow the child to use a calculator, tape recorder, computer, and other augmentative communication devices.

Memory and Learning
- Encourage the child to make a weekly calendar.
- Encourage the child to carry a written log of activities, a schedule of classes, a list of assignments and their due dates, and a list of classroom locations.
- Take baseline measures of the child's performance in each academic area.
- Slow the pace at which you present information.
- Give directions one step at a time.
- Pause frequently when you give classroom instructions.
- Present information in a controlled and manageable fashion.
- Determine the child's optimum rate of reception of information.
- Repeat instructions as needed.
- Use orientation and memory cues liberally.
- Break complex behaviors down into small, well-defined steps.
- Summarize frequently.
- Focus on activities that the child likes, that are neither too easy nor too boring, and that have a chance of being completed successfully.
- Use multimodal cuing (i.e., more than one sensory modality), as needed.
- Allow the child as much time as he or she needs to complete assignments and tests.
- Limit the amount of material you require the child to copy from the chalkboard.
- Use repetition and drilling.

(Continued)

Table 23-1 (*Continued*)

Memory and Learning (*cont.*)

- Present new information after the child has mastered previously learned information.
- Reintroduce facts in several different contexts.
- Record your lesson on tape for the child to replay later, thereby minimizing the need for extensive note taking.
- Provide written handouts whenever possible.
- Increase use of computer word processing when possible to avoid the need for extensive writing.
- Alert the child to what you expect him or her to do shortly before you talk to him or her.
- Gradually introduce tasks that require the child to remember longer pieces of information.

Executive Functioning and Problem-Solving Skills

- Help the child develop a system for maintaining organization.
- Plan small-group activities to facilitate learning.
- Select classroom buddies to keep the child aware of instructions, transitions, and assignments and to write for the child, if necessary.
- Keep choices to a minimum.
- Break down assignments into manageable parts.
- Encourage the child to monitor his or her behavior.
- Individualize the assignments and tests to accommodate the child's special needs.
- Establish specific goals for the child.
- Use positive reinforcement to increase desired behavior.
- Encourage the child to participate in programs that may help him or her overcome limitations.
- Use true/false or multiple-choice formats rather than lengthy essay questions.
- Explain the difference between the demands of new situations and old ones.

Using Direct Instruction

- Gain the child's attention before the lesson begins.
- Maintain a brisk instructional pace, require frequent responses from the child, provide adequate time for the child to process the information and to respond to questions, monitor the child's responses, and give the child feedback about any incorrect responses.
- Review prior lessons as appropriate.
- State the goals of the current lesson.
- Demonstrate the skill or strategy being taught.
- Provide sufficient practice and assistance at each stage of the lesson.
- Observe the child as she or he performs the new skill or strategy.
- Have the child apply the new skill or strategy to different problems and situations.
- Assign seatwork or independent practice.

- Review the lesson and what was learned.
- Provide a cumulative review of the material before introducing new material.
- Preview the next lesson for the child.
- Assign homework related to the current lesson.

Handling Intervention Difficulties

- If the child does not understand the task demands, provide clear, concrete instructions and, if needed, model the task yourself.
- If the child does not begin an assigned task, give the child prompts and reinforce each instance of initiative that the child shows, however minor.
- If the child is unable to do an assigned task, simplify the task, provide additional training to allow the child to perform the task successfully, teach each step of the task separately, and use "reverse chaining" to integrate the steps one at a time, beginning with the last step and working toward the first.
- If the child cannot find the right words to express herself or himself, use structured play and manipulative activities to help the child develop concrete verbal strategies to compensate for noticeable word retrieval difficulties.
- If the child is not motivated to perform the task, make the task more interesting and give the child rewards when she or he completes the task.
- If the child tries to avoid failure by not complying with the task, alternate difficult tasks with easy and enjoyable tasks.
- If the child avoids doing a task by complaining, inform the child that she or he must complete the assigned task, taking as much time as needed.
- If the child is noncompliant, use a time-out procedure or ignore the child's behavior.
- If the child is careless about safety, set firm limits on the child's behavior and establish specific rules of behavior.
- If the child argues and fights with peers on the playground, set firm limits on the child's behavior, select a buddy with whom the child gets along, encourage the buddy to be with the child during recess, and work with the child in small groups to encourage cooperative behavior.
- If the child forgets to do homework, develop with the child a daily written assignment sheet indicating dates and times when assignments are due.

Working with the Family and Monitoring Progress

- Involve the family in the educational program.
- Inform the family of the goals you have set and the methods you are using to meet the goals.
- Update the family about the child's progress.
- Make sure that knowledgeable staff members are available to answer the family's questions.
- Monitor the child's progress in order to make needed revisions in the educational program.

The Family's Role in a Rehabilitation Program

A child's recovery from a brain injury depends, in part, on family support and on the family's ability to manage the child's day-to-day problems. You will need to evaluate the family's ability to care for the child's physical, emotional, and behavioral needs. You will also need to evaluate the family's communication patterns, cohesion, adaptability, and level of adjustment (e.g., whether the family has a history of accidents, domestic violence, psychiatric disturbances, substance abuse, or child maltreatment). A family that was dysfunctional before the injury is likely to have a more difficult time coping with a child's injuries than a family that was not dysfunctional. (See Chapter 10 for ways to assess family functioning.)

When a child sustains a brain injury, family patterns may change. The family may suffer disruption of relationships, shifting of social roles and responsibilities, and adjustment problems. Sometimes, latent family strengths or weaknesses come to the surface. The behavioral, cognitive, and affective deficits that accompany the child's brain injury often are more distressing for the family than are the child's physical disabilities. Families may be concerned about children's irritability, inattentiveness, difficulties with social interaction, violence, aggression, immaturity, and dependency—characteristics that, in turn, are likely to diminish family harmony. Overall, families of children who sustain severe traumatic brain injury experience more stress than families of children who sustain moderate traumatic brain injury (Wade, Taylor, Drotar, Stancin, & Yeates, 1998).

Family stressors.   Families of children with traumatic brain injuries confront several types of stressors, including the following:

- Coping with the shock (in cases of sudden onset) of the traumatic brain injury
- Facing uncertainty about how well their child will recover
- Coping with dramatic changes in their child's cognitive abilities, personality, and temperament (such as diminished memory, problems with decision making, mood swings, limited motivation, decreased academic performance)
- Coping with their child's increased dependency and the constant struggle between the desire to foster their child's independence to speed recovery and the desire to provide control and structure to maintain their child's safety
- Coping with their child's symptoms associated with posttraumatic stress disorder (such as flashbacks, sleeping difficulties, anxiety reactions)
- Coping with siblings' jealousy, resentment about increased responsibilities, or anger at the changed family structure

- Working through possible feelings of blame or guilt and personal responsibility for their child's injury
- Working through grief reactions associated with loss of a normal life for their child
- Working out possible disagreements or misunderstandings with professionals about what actions to take to help their child
- Coping with the financial, time, and energy demands of a long-term rehabilitation program
- Facing the possibility that rehabilitation and educational resources in the community are inadequate
- Facing the possibility that their child may need to be placed in a long-term residential care facility

---

The uninjured sibling can become a potent source of help and support for the patient, or a target for clinical intervention [because of the stress of dealing with the patient]. It is the responsibility of the rehabilitation team to ensure that the former happens and not the latter.
—D. Neil Brooks, Scottish psychologist

Suggestions for working with families.   Helping families of children with brain injuries may take years, not just weeks or months (Brooks, 1991). Rehabilitation is best conceived of as a process involving three stages:

1. In the *stage of acute crisis,* families need help in learning to accept information about their child's brain injury. If they are in a state of shock, despair, or denial, they may not listen or understand what they hear. Gauge their ability to receive and understand the information, and, if necessary, delay the discussion until they appear able to listen.
2. In the *stage of prolonged rehabilitation,* families need information to help them make realistic plans. When possible, involve them in the treatment decisions.
3. In the *stage of disengagement,* families need to disengage from active professional intervention but maintain access to professional help for crises and guidance.

Following are suggestions for helping families of children with brain injuries (DePompei, Zarski, & Hall, 1988; Lezak, 1978; Miller, 1993; Rollin, 1987; Sachs, 1991).

EDUCATION

- Give the family accurate information about the nature of the trauma, their child's strengths and weaknesses, the types of problems their child may display, and the possible prognosis. Be sure that the information you give the family is consistent with that provided by other members of the health care team.
- Explain that there may be advances and setbacks during recovery.

Table 23-2
Suggestions for Parents of Children with Brain Injuries

Understanding Your Child

- Encourage your child to share her or his thoughts and feelings with you.
- Focus on your child's strengths.
- Recognize that your child may not be able to do things that he or she did before the injury and try to find alternative ways to accomplish the same goals.
- Allow your child to do things at her or his own pace.
- Set limits on your child's behavior as needed.
- Help your child understand her or his injury and what rehabilitation will be needed.

Handling Emotions and Avoiding Overstimulation

- Be alert to any signs that your child is reaching his or her frustration level.
- Understand that your child's outbursts are not deliberate and are not intended to embarrass you.
- Find ways to help your child calm down when frustrated, such as by giving the child extra time to respond or by having the child take a deep breath.
- Reduce stressful experiences that your child might face at home and with his or her friends.
- Don't let your child perform any actions that might hurt another person; instead, redirect your child to an acceptable activity.
- Avoid overstimulating your child.
- Avoid overloading your child with information.

Talking to Your Child

- Speak slowly and distinctly to your child.
- Look at your child when you speak to her or him.
- Use concrete language when you talk with your child and avoid idiomatic language.
- Guide your child to listen for specific information.
- Gradually increase the amount of information you give your child.
- Learn to read your child's nonverbal cues.
- Encourage your child to communicate on his or her own.
- Establish (if needed) a system of verbal or nonverbal signals to cue your child to attend, respond, or alter her or his behavior.
- Provide clear, concrete instructions.
- Accompany verbal instructions with written instructions.
- Increase communication activities gradually and systematically.
- Make sure that you have your child's attention before you give him or her directions.
- Break complex instructions down into small, well-defined steps.
- Repeat instructions as needed.
- Help your child remember longer pieces of information.
- Limit the number of choices you give your child.

Performing Activities

- Encourage your child to make a weekly calendar.
- Encourage your child to carry a written log of activities, a schedule of classes, a list of assignments and due dates, and a list of classroom locations.
- Permit your child to use a calculator, tape recorder, computer, and other devices to help him or her do school assignments.
- Encourage your child to develop computer word processing skills.
- Allow your child as much time as possible to complete homework assignments and chores.
- Encourage your child to write, such as by making a phone book of friends' phone numbers, addresses, and e-mail addresses; making a list of items to purchase from the store; or writing a letter to extended family members.
- Encourage your child to monitor his or her behavior.
- Encourage your child to participate in programs that may help him or her overcome limitations.
- Plan activities around the child's physical and emotional capabilities and interests.
- Assign your child jobs around the house, fitted to his or her ability.
- Encourage your child to lead a normal life style within the limits of his or her ability.
- Provide your child with advance notice when there will be changes in his or her schedule.
- Explain the difference between the demands of new situations and old ones.
- Alert your child to what you expect him or her to do shortly before you talk to him or her.
- Encourage your child to focus on one day at a time.
- Keep distractions to a minimum at home.

Increasing Social Skills

- Serve as a role model for your child for good social behavior.
- Give your child a choice about whether to participate in social activities, but encourage him or her to have friends.
- Supervise your child's social interactions with his or her friends.
- If your child is of preschool age, provide structured activities for her or him with one or two friends.
- Teach your child how to identify other people's facial expressions.
- Allow your child to become independent to the extent that this is possible.
- Provide praise and awards as appropriate.
- Instill confidence in your child.

- Explain why their child may have behavioral problems during the recovery period, and explain the relationship between behavioral problems and their child's brain injury.
- Explain the principles of behavioral interventions that they will need to use.

PROBLEM SOLVING

- Identify the child's problems and the possible effects of the problems on the family.
- Help the family become involved in the education and treatment of their child.
- Help the family establish goals consistent with their child's potential and with their own values and expectations.
- Elicit from the family their suggestions for positive reinforcers that can be used with their child.
- Help the family adjust to their child and to their changed roles.
- Encourage the family to approach seemingly insurmountable problems that they are having with their child by breaking the problems into manageable parts and by rehearsing and role-playing potentially stressful activities with their child.
- Help the family members to resolve their own differences over how to handle their child's problems.

SUPPORT

- Help the family work through their grief, anxiety, guilt, depression, and sense of hopelessness. They need to recognize that anger, frustration, and sorrow are natural emotions under the circumstances.
- Help the family become organized and focused on the actions needed to help their child.
- Enhance the parents' self-esteem and sense of well-being. Point out that they still have control over their lives. Encourage them to continue to pursue activities that they enjoy; they must take care of themselves if they are going to provide their child with good care. They will need to find respite care so that they can have some time alone and with other family members.
- Help the family develop realistic expectations about the length of time needed for their child to show improvements.
- Help the family accept their child at the level at which he or she is functioning.
- Recognize that some parents may resist your efforts to foster independence in their child. Caring for a child with a disability may give their lives added purpose. In such cases, you will need to work even harder to assist the parents in carrying out the rehabilitation program.
- Recommend that the parents seek drop-in counseling; brief, limited therapy to work through specific problems; support groups; parent training; or family therapy, as needed. Provide telephone numbers and addresses of local services, and help the family contact appropriate agencies that provide resources for persons with brain injuries, such as the Brain Injury Association of America.

Table 23-2 provides suggestions for parents of children with traumatic brain injuries. The suggestions are grouped into five categories: understanding your child, handling emotions and avoiding overstimulation, talking to your child, performing activities, and increasing social skills.

Comment on Rehabilitation Programs

Rehabilitation efforts should be monitored closely to determine children's progress and to ensure that programs are not placing undue stress on them or their families. If the rehabilitation goals are met, children will be better able to cope with the brain injury and improve the quality of their lives. Improved functioning would include having a more positive attitude toward school, achieving better grades in school, carrying out assignments with minimal help, participating in extracurricular activities, resuming and maintaining friendships, engaging in cooperative and dependable behavior, and assuming increased responsibility at home for personal and household chores. Many children with brain injuries make significant progress even though they may not become fully independent or regain their former level of skills. Rehabilitation efforts will improve as we learn more about how brain injury affects cognitive, linguistic, affective, and behavioral processes.

THINKING THROUGH THE ISSUES

1. Do you know someone who has had a brain injury? If so, what is the individual like? In what way has the brain injury affected him or her?
2. Why is it difficult to evaluate aphasic disturbances in young children?
3. What can you do to educate teachers and others who work with children with brain injuries about the relationship between brain injury and behavior?
4. Do you think that you have the patience to work with children with brain injuries? Why or why not?
5. Why do mental health professionals play an important role in the rehabilitation of children with brain injuries?
6. How likely is it that the incidence of brain injuries in children will be reduced in the future? What is the basis for your answer?

SUMMARY

1. Traumatic brain injuries are not inevitable. As a society, we can do several things to prevent brain injuries from occurring, including paying adequate attention to the construction of automobiles, to pedestrian safety, and to design of playground equipment.
2. Brain injury refers to any disruption in brain structure (anatomy) or brain function (physiology).
3. Brain dysfunction refers to symptoms that are associated with processing difficulties of any brain structure, including the cerebrum, midbrain, and brain stem structures.

4. The assessment of brain injury is a complex and exacting process. It requires extensive specialized knowledge and inter-disciplinary cooperation.

5. Psychologists can help children with brain injuries, as well as their parents, families, and teachers, by explaining to those in-volved with the child's care how brain injury may affect the child's cognitive functioning, affective reactions, personality, and temperament, as well as the rehabilitation efforts necessary to improve the child's functioning.

Overview of Brain Functions

6. There is no center of consciousness, no single clearinghouse for memory, no one place where information is processed, emo-tions generated, or language stored, although some of these functions are processed in fairly discrete locations.

7. In an adult in the prime of life, the cerebral cortex contains about 25 billion neurons linked through approximately 164 tril-lion synapses.

8. Thoughts thread through about 7.4 million miles of dendrite fibers and about 62,000 miles of axons so miniaturized and compacted that the entire neural network is no larger than a coconut.

9. During growth and development, the feedback between the brain and its environment is so intimate that there is no way to separate the effects of development of a brain's neural structure from the influence of the environment that nurtures it.

10. There is no single, predetermined blueprint for the brain.

11. Multiple regions throughout the brain are related to intelligence.

12. No two brains are identical.

13. Subtle differences in brain anatomy affect the ways men and women process information, even when thinking about the same things, hearing the same words, or solving similar problems.

14. Men and women appear to achieve similar intelligence with different brain regions.

15. The most efficient brains—that is, those that use the least energy—appear also to be the most intelligent.

16. The complex circuitry of the brain reorganizes itself in re-sponse to sensory stimulation.

17. Special cells called mirror neurons, located in the frontal lobe, process visual information about the actions and intentions of others.

18. Structural abnormalities can develop in the brain long before any noticeable behavioral symptoms can be diagnosed; how-ever, structural abnormalities do not always result in cognitive or behavioral symptoms or deficits.

19. Minor alterations in neural circuits for vision and hearing (and perhaps other areas) may be responsible for dyslexia.

20. Abnormalities in regions of the brain involved in inhibiting mental and behavioral activity could be the cause of attention-deficit/hyperactivity disorder.

Lateralization

21. Lateralization refers to the specialization of the two hemi-spheres of the cerebral cortex for cognitive, perceptual, motor, and sensory activities.

22. In general, the side of the brain that controls a sensorimotor ac-tivity (an activity that combines the functions of the sensory and motor portions of the brain) is opposite to the side of the body that carries out the activity.

23. Lateral specialization (also referred to as cerebral specialization or hemispheric specialization) for all cognitive, sensory, and motor functions cannot be clearly established.

24. The two cerebral hemispheres—the left hemisphere and the right hemisphere—are specialized to varying degrees for higher-level functions, such as language and memory.

25. The left cerebral hemisphere in most people is specialized for language functions—including reading, writing, speaking, verbal ideation, verbal memory, and certain aspects of arith-metic ability (such as skilled math analysis and computation).

26. The right cerebral hemisphere in most people is specialized for nonverbal, perceptual, and spatial functions—including spatial visualization, visual learning and memory, arithmetical calcu-lations involving spatial organization of the problem elements, vocal inflection nuances, complex visual-motor organization, and nonverbal sequencing.

27. The frontal lobes are associated with general intelligence; plan-ning, initiation, and modulation of behavior (including self-control); expressive verbal fluency; control of motor functions; and motor planning.

28. The parietal lobes are associated with somatosensory functions, visual-spatial ability, and the integration of visual, somatosen-sory, and auditory stimuli.

29. The temporal lobes are associated with auditory perception, au-ditory comprehension, verbal memory, visual memory, and visual processing.

30. The occipital lobes are associated with visual perception, elab-oration and synthesis of visual information, and the integration of visual information with information gathered by other sen-sory systems.

31. Injuries to the frontal, parietal, temporal, and occipital lobes and to the subcortical centers (such as the basal ganglia and hippocampal structures) may produce disorders in cognition, affect, memory, motor output, and motivation.

32. Lateralization begins in utero and continues through childhood into adulthood.

33. Once language develops, the left hemisphere is dominant for language in most individuals.

34. The primary function of the right hemisphere may be to inte-grate information into meaningful wholes.

Attention and Memory

35. Attention and memory are critical for processing information, and children with brain injuries may have difficulty with one or more types of attention and/or memory.

36. Types of attention include focused attention, divided attention, sustained attention, and alternating attention.

37. Children use mnemonic (memory) strategies infrequently before the age of 6 years.

38. Between 7 and 10 years of age, mnemonic strategies, such as rehearsal and chunking, begin to emerge.

39. After 10 years of age, mnemonic strategies mature and become increasingly refined, flexible, and effective.

40. Three stages characterize the process of memory: encoding, consolidation and storage, and retrieval and recognition.

41. Types of memory include echoic memory, iconic memory, pri-mary memory, declarative memory, procedural memory, and prospective memory.

42. Children with brain injuries may experience anterograde am-nesia or retrograde amnesia.

Causes of Brain Injuries

43. Brain injuries can result from factors present in the period between conception and birth (prenatal period), from injuries sustained in the period around childbirth, especially the five months before and one month after birth (perinatal period); or from injuries sustained at any point after birth (postnatal period).

44. Conditions that may contribute to brain injury during the prenatal period include congenital disorders, maternal exposure to toxic substances, maternal infections, maternal illnesses, maternal use of alcohol or other drugs or tobacco, physical injury to the uterus, exposure to radiation, and severe maternal malnutrition.

45. Conditions that may lead to brain injury during the perinatal period include asphyxia, kernicterus, meningitis, Rh incompatibilities, hypoglycemia, and encephalitis.

46. Conditions that may result in brain injury during the postnatal period include congenital hypothyroidism, galactosemia, phenylketonuria (PKU), Tay-Sachs disease, hydrocephalus, and Niemann-Pick disease.

47. Conditions that may lead to brain injury during infancy, early childhood, and adolescence include trauma to the brain, brain tumors, deficiency of nutrients, diabetes, drug and alcohol abuse, end-stage renal disease, epilepsy, exposure to neurotoxins, human immunodeficiency virus type I (HIV-I) infection, infections, neurofibromatosis 1, and exposure to radiation.

Traumatic Brain Injury

48. Each year, approximately 1 million children in the United States sustain head injuries from falls, physical abuse, recreational accidents, or motor vehicle accidents.

49. Although trauma to the head does not always lead to brain injury, traumatic brain injury results in an estimated 2,685 deaths, 37,000 hospitalizations, and 435,000 emergency department visits among children ages 0 to 14 years.

50. IDEA defines traumatic brain injury as " . . . an acquired injury to the brain caused by an external physical force, resulting in total or partial functional disability or psychosocial impairment, or both, that adversely affects a child's educational performance."

51. Although most children survive traumatic brain injuries because of advances in medical treatment and increased availability of trauma care, they often have residual cognitive, language, somatic, and behavioral difficulties.

52. Traumatic brain injury is a threat to a child's quality of life—including life style, education, physical and recreational activities, interpersonal relationships, and self-control.

53. Approximately 70% of children with severe traumatic brain injury continue to receive special education services 5 years after the injury.

54. Traumatic brain injury is associated primarily with physical abuse (shaken baby syndrome or thrown infant syndrome) in infants under the age of 1 year; with falls and physical abuse in toddlers and preschoolers; and with bicycle, motor vehicle, and sports-related accidents and injuries in children over the age of 5 years. Motor vehicle accidents, bicycle accidents, and falls account for between 75% and 80% of brain injuries in children.

55. Boys are more at risk for traumatic brain injuries than are girls.

56. Traumatic head injuries produce both primary effects (resulting directly from the trauma) and secondary effects (resulting indirectly from the trauma).

57. Focal head injuries (also referred to as open-head injuries or penetrating head injuries) usually involve a circumscribed area of the brain.

58. Diffuse head injuries (also referred to as closed-head injuries, nonpenetrating head injuries, bilateral injuries, or multifocal injuries) usually involve multiple areas of the brain.

59. Brain tissue may be bruised at the point of impact (referred to as coup) and in an area opposite to the point of impact (referred to as coup-contrecoup).

60. Children with diffuse head injuries usually have more cognitive difficulties than children with focal head injuries.

Specific Effects of Brain Injury in Children

61. A physician should be contacted immediately if a child has any of the following symptoms after sustaining a head injury: changes in play, changes in school performance, changes in sleep patterns, tiredness or listlessness, irritability or crankiness, lack of interest in favorite toys or activities, loss of balance or unsteady walking, loss of newly acquired skills, refusal to eat or nurse, or vomiting.

62. The specific effects of brain injury in children depend on (a) the location, extent, and type of injury, (b) the child's age, (c) the child's preinjury temperament, personality, and cognitive and psychosocial functioning, (d) the child's familial and environmental supports, and (e) the promptness and quality of treatment.

63. Symptoms of brain injury are usually directly related to the functions mediated by the damaged area.

64. There may be a general deterioration in all or most aspects of functioning or highly specific symptoms when the injuries are in specialized locations.

65. In some cases, there are no observable symptoms; in other cases, symptoms are quite obvious; in still other cases, symptoms may not be observed until several years after the injury.

66. Overall, brain injuries may produce physical symptoms, cognitive disturbances, behavioral disturbances, and language and symbolic disorders.

67. The physical symptoms associated with mild to severe brain injuries include nausea, vomiting, dizziness, headache, blurred vision, sleep disturbance, fatigue, lethargy, abnormalities in senses of smell and hearing, and other sensory losses that cannot be accounted for by peripheral injury or other causes.

68. The physical symptoms associated with severe brain injuries include those listed above as well as skull fracture, bruised brain tissue, cerebral laceration, intracranial hematoma, seizures, paralysis, balance and other coordination problems, drainage of cerebrospinal fluid from the nose to the mouth, and collection of blood behind the eardrum or in the sinuses.

69. Cognitive disturbances after brain injury may involve attention and concentration, executive functions, judgment and perception, learning and memory, language and communication, and speed of information processing.

70. In school, children with brain injuries may have difficulty completing their work and understanding tasks; locating classrooms, getting to classes on time, and following schedules; remembering what they have learned in class or what they have studied at home; staying out of potentially dangerous situations; organizing thoughts, planning, and processing information; shifting from one activity to another; taking initiative or acting independently; connecting old with new information; and generalizing.

71. Children with brain injuries may have difficulties with communication tasks such as understanding the point of view of others, modifying an opinion, recognizing the main point of a conversation, sticking to the topic, joining an ongoing conversation appropriately, asking for clarification necessary to form an appropriate conclusion, taking turns, giving and receiving feedback, accepting group decisions, presenting an appropriate amount of information, and switching from one topic to another.

72. Children with brain injuries may have cognitive impairments that are not evident during an evaluation.

73. Examples of behavioral symptoms associated with brain injury are anxiety, denial of illness, depression and amotivational states, emotional lability, paranoid ideation, psychomotor agitation, and psychosocial disturbances.

74. Behavioral symptoms may reflect impairments directly associated with the brain injury, emotional reactions to the acquired deficits, exaggeration of preexisting personality patterns, or a combination of these factors.

75. Some children with brain injuries show a pattern of behavior characterized by overarousal, whereas other children with brain injuries show a pattern of behavior characterized by underarousal.

76. Overall, behavior problems are more likely to result from severe brain injury than from mild or moderate brain injury.

77. Some prescribed medications may cause psychological disturbances.

78. Brain injury may lead to losses in automatic processing—the ability to perform habitual and overlearned responses.

79. The major types of language and symbolic disorders associated with brain injuries are agnosia, apraxia, and aphasia.

80. Agnosia refers to a disturbance in the ability to recognize familiar stimuli despite intact sensory and perceptual functions.

81. Apraxia refers to disturbance in the ability to execute learned movements or to carry out purposeful or skilled acts.

82. Aphasia refers to a disturbance in the ability to comprehend or produce symbolic language, caused by brain injury (and not caused by speech defects or motor difficulties).

83. Children older than 10 years of age have symptoms of aphasia similar to those of adults, whereas children younger than 10 years of age are more likely to have delays in the development of verbal and nonverbal communication.

84. Children under the age of 10 years with aphasia are usually alert, attentive, and eager to communicate their thoughts and reactions.

85. The prognosis for recovery from aphasia is more favorable for young children than for adults.

86. Traumatic brain injuries usually produce less specific effects in young children than in adults.

87. In young children, brain injury may alter the basic pattern of cognitive development in many areas, rather than produce a striking loss of function in one area.

88. The first 5 years of life constitute the period of greatest cortical development.

89. The process of myelination in various brain regions affects behavioral and cognitive development.

90. In myelination, the axon of a neuron becomes insulated or coated, which increases the speed with which impulses are transmitted among neurons.

91. The ability of the brain to change in order to compensate for loss of function (referred to as cerebral plasticity) will, in part, determine the outcome of traumatic brain injury.

92. Recovery of function depends in part on the ability of the neurons in the damaged area to regenerate terminals and produce new terminals.

93. About 75% to 95% of children with traumatic brain injuries either have a good recovery or have mild disabilities.

94. About 10% of children with traumatic brain injuries have moderate disabilities.

95. About 1% to 3% of children with traumatic brain injuries have severe disabilities.

96. Fewer than 1% of children with traumatic brain injuries remain in a persistent vegetative state.

97. The physical, intellectual, and emotional development of children who sustain severe brain injury is seriously compromised.

98. Traumatic brain injuries in infancy or early childhood are likely to result in more impaired cognitive and academic functioning than traumatic brain injuries sustained during middle childhood or adolescence.

99. Cognitive impairments sustained as a result of early brain injuries become more prominent as children age.

100. Skills undergoing active development at the time of the brain injury are more susceptible to disruption than previously established skills.

101. Children do not necessarily completely recover all of their functions after traumatic brain injury.

102. Recovery from brain injury depends on several factors, including the child's age at the time of the brain injury, preinjury status, experiential history, preexisting problems, education, type and severity of the brain injury, stress level, promptness and quality of treatment, age at the time of treatment, time since treatment, and family and community supports.

103. No simple statement can capture the complex relationship between cerebral plasticity and recovery of function in children, although additional research should tell us more about the details of the relationship.

104. Prognoses about a child's ability to recover from brain injury should be made carefully, as evaluating language, speech, and other cognitive functions is more difficult in children than in adults.

Rehabilitation Programs

105. Rehabilitation programs should be based on the results of a comprehensive, multidisciplinary team assessment.

106. In designing a rehabilitation program, consider when it would be best to begin the program and whether there is a critical period when rehabilitation efforts might be most effective.

107. Among the most perplexing symptoms of some brain injuries is neglect of part of the visual field or part of the body.

108. Rehabilitation programs are designed to help children with brain injuries improve their cognitive and behavioral skills, learn new and compensatory skills, regulate their behavior, and understand and manage emotional reactions to changes in their functioning.

109. Some rehabilitation goals may be difficult to achieve because children with brain injuries may have limited understanding of their condition.

110. Neuropsychological deficits usually are most prominent during the first 6 months after a brain injury.

111. Cognitive functions are differentially affected by traumatic brain injury.

112. Each affected cognitive function may exhibit a different potential for recovery.
113. Rehabilitation efforts may be hampered by deficits in speed of processing, attention and concentration, memory and learning, and executive functions.
114. Rehabilitation goals should be appropriate to the child's physical and neuropsychological status and specific injury and should be geared to the child's readiness and motivation to achieve the goals.
115. Alter the physical environment to help the child who has the additional burden of physical disabilities become more mobile and independent.
116. Create an environment that is highly organized, contains few distracting stimuli, and provides functional cues.
117. Help the child reduce symptoms of social withdrawal, interpersonal isolation, paranoid ideation, hyperactivity, and emotionality.
118. Try to increase the child's awareness of his or her current deficits and strengths, help the child accept his or her limitations, and teach the child to apply compensatory strategies to solve problems: using his or her remaining intact functions effectively, learning new skills to compensate for lost or impaired ones, and transferring and generalizing skills to new situations and contexts.
119. Try to reduce cognitive confusion by improving attention, concentration, learning, memory, and information-processing skills.
120. Focus on improving impaired areas of functioning by applying educational and other intervention procedures, including speech therapy, occupational therapy, and physical therapy.
121. Help the child being discharged from a hospital or rehabilitation center gradually make the transition back to his or her natural environment, where things are less structured and more demanding.
122. Modify goals based on the child's progress.
123. Evaluate the child's ability to use problem-solving strategies and to generalize newly learned skills to new situations.
124. Evaluate the interventions by considering how much the child benefited from the rehabilitation program, how long the rehabilitation program should continue, how much additional training the child needs to improve and/or maintain his or her skills, and what additional techniques should be considered.
125. Consumption of alcohol can complicate both physical and cognitive recovery from a brain injury.
126. Chronic abuse of alcohol can produce cognitive deficits that interact with those produced by the traumatic brain injury and interfere with the recovery process.
127. Returning to school presents several difficulties for children with brain injuries.
128. Teachers, other school personnel, and peers may not realize the magnitude of the child's struggles.
129. Before the child returns to her or his classroom, visit the classroom and consult with the school staff about what modifications are needed to facilitate the child's learning and adjustment.
130. A child's recovery from a brain injury depends, in part, on family support and on the family's ability to manage the child's day-to-day problems.
131. When a child sustains a brain injury, family patterns may change.
132. Families of children with traumatic brain injuries confront several types of stressors.
133. Helping families of children with brain injuries may take years, not just weeks or months.
134. Rehabilitation is best conceived of as a process involving a stage of acute crisis, a stage of prolonged rehabilitation, and a stage of disengagement.
135. Families of children with brain injuries need to be educated about brain injury, helped to solve problems associated with their child's brain injury, and provided with the support they need to help their child.
136. Rehabilitation efforts should be monitored closely to determine children's progress and to ensure that programs are not placing undue stress on them or their families.
137. Rehabilitation efforts will improve as we learn more about how brain injury affects cognitive, linguistic, affective, and behavioral processes.

KEY TERMS, CONCEPTS, AND NAMES

STUDY QUESTIONS

1. Discuss some pertinent facts about the brain and its development.
2. Discuss lateralization of the cerebral cortex.
3. Discuss attention and memory.
4. Discuss the causes of brain injury, using a developmental perspective. Include in your discussion factors that may cause brain injury during the prenatal period, the perinatal period, the postnatal period, infancy, early childhood, and adolescence.
5. Discuss traumatic brain injury. Include in your discussion the incidence of traumatic brain injury, types of traumatic brain injuries, and prognoses for recovery.
6. Brain injury produces specific as well as diverse effects. Describe some cognitive and behavioral symptoms of brain injury. Include in your discussion (a) symptoms associated with aphasia, agnosia, and apraxia and (b) possible interpretations of behavioral symptoms of brain injury.
7. Discuss how brain injury may affect children and adults in different ways.
8. Discuss why it is inappropriate to assume that children with brain injuries will enjoy complete recovery of brain functioning.
9. Explain several goals of a rehabilitation program for children with brain injuries. Include developmental issues in your discussion. Also discuss some important factors in designing a rehabilitation program.
10. If you were a consultant to a school, how would you advise school personnel about working with children with brain injuries?
11. Discuss the following proposition: "The recovery of a child with a brain injury will, in part, depend on the level of family support and on the family's ability to manage the child's day-to-day activities." Include in your discussion ways to help family members cope with both their child's brain injury and the changes within the family.

24

BRAIN INJURIES: ASSESSMENT

by Jerome M. Sattler and David Breiger

If the brain were so simple we could understand it, we would be so simple we couldn't.
—Lyall Watson, British naturalist (1939–   )

Goals and Objectives

This chapter is designed to enable you to do the following:

- Understand how to assess children with brain injuries
- Understand the basic concepts of neurological diagnostic techniques
- Understand the major neuropsychological test batteries
- Use informal techniques to assess children with brain injuries

The assessment of children with brain injuries focuses on their cognitive and behavioral skills, on their academic strengths and weaknesses, and on their interpersonal skills and social judgment. During the neuropsychological evaluation, be alert to the child's language, attention, memory, intellectual and cognitive functioning, emotions, executive functions, rate of information processing, and sensorimotor functioning. Because the effects of traumatic brain injury are multidetermined, the evaluation should be comprehensive. It should include an estimate of the child's preinjury functioning, as well as an evaluation of the child's postinjury functioning. Do not necessarily equate poor performance on a test with brain injury. You must also consider the possibility that the child's performance is related to situational factors, developmental immaturity, emotional impairments, or physical impairments.

Children who have sustained severe head injuries may be difficult to evaluate, especially if their speech is impaired, if they have aphasic disturbances, or if they have not fully regained consciousness. (In the latter case, the child is likely to be hospitalized.) A child who is confused and disoriented cannot participate fully in a formal assessment and therefore should be evaluated at a later date. Consequently, you will need to consider stage of recovery in your evaluation. The semicomatose child observed immediately after a blunt head injury, for example, usually bears little resemblance to the same child 2 months after injury.

SUGGESTIONS FOR CONDUCTING AN EVALUATION

You will need to consider several factors in conducting an assessment:

- The child's age
- The child's language ability
- Need for an interpreter
- Time available to conduct the assessment
- Which assessment procedures to use
- Need for adaptations in the selected assessment procedures
- Medicines the child is taking and how they might affect the child's performance
- Relevant compensation or legal factors that might affect how the child performs

Conduct the evaluation in a quiet room and minimize all potential sources of distraction. Some children with brain injuries respond to test questions without difficulty, whereas others are fearful, reticent, or emotionally labile, becoming easily aroused and shifting quickly from one emotion to another. Some children with brain injuries *perseverate* (persistently repeat the same thought or behavior), display inappropriate anger and hostility, withdraw from the situa-

tion, or give irrelevant responses, such as saying "I go to school" when asked to give their home address. Such behavior often is not under their willful control; rather, it reflects the effects of the brain injury. Still, these behaviors need to be reported, evaluated, and interpreted.

Seemingly irrelevant or disconnected responses may in fact be meaningful to the child and somewhat appropriate. For example, if a child says "George Washington" in response to a query about whether he or she likes school, when George Washington is the name of the child's school, consider the response as tangential rather than irrelevant. You may need to inquire further in order to understand the personal relevance of the child's response.

If the child is anxious about the evaluation, deal with her or his anxieties *before* you begin the formal evaluation. You can do this, for example, by working together on simple game-like materials; by increasing your use of praise, encouragement, and constructive comments; by keeping interview questions simple; and by beginning the assessment with relatively easy tasks to help the child experience initial successes.

Occasionally, a child may sit quietly for a long time before answering a question or make tentative, hesitant responses. In such cases, allow the child to proceed at his or her own pace. However, when the delay is excessive (say, over 30 seconds), repeat the question (except for memory items) or instructions, because the child may not remember what you said. If the child does not answer an important interview question, ask it again later in the examination, perhaps rephrasing it in a simpler form. Of course, you should not reword test items.

You need to be especially attentive to the reactions of children with brain injuries in order to minimize their frustration and fatigue. If a child shows signs of either, change the pace or content of the assessment, take a break, or make supportive comments, but do not pressure the child. If necessary, schedule another session.

Experiment with different communication methods, rates of communication, and types of content to find the most effective way to communicate with children with brain injuries. Following are some helpful guidelines (DePompei, Blosser, & Zarski, 1989; Lubinski, 1981):

1. Face the child when speaking with her or him. Eye contact promotes attention and helps the child take advantage of nonverbal cues.
2. Alert the child that communication is about to occur. For example, say the child's name and a few words of greeting before introducing a topic, question, or instruction.
3. Speak slowly and clearly.
4. Introduce questions slowly and casually.
5. Avoid sudden movements or noises.
6. Talk about concrete topics, such as objects and people in the immediate environment. Avoid figurative language.
7. Keep related topics together; do not jump from topic to topic.
8. Use short, grammatically correct, complete sentences.

9. Pause between comments to give the child time to comprehend and interpret the message.
10. Verify that the child understood your communication before proceeding. You can do this by asking the child to explain what you said.
11. Repeat important ideas several ways, if necessary; redundancy helps comprehension.
12. Use nonverbal cues to augment spoken communication.
13. Ask questions that require short responses or pointing responses.
14. Stop the evaluation if the child's emotional lability becomes too severe, and then sit quietly until the child seems ready to continue. Whatever happens, remain calm and take your time.
15. Understand that an in-depth assessment is a lengthy and sometimes tiring process. Therefore, consider conducting the assessment in several short sessions rather than one long session.
16. Allow the child to use any means to communicate, including speaking, writing, typing, using a computer or another augmentative communication device, pointing to letters, signing, or gesturing. Before the evaluation begins, determine the child's preferred communication method.
17. Use a multiple-choice procedure if needed. You can do this by employing a testing-of-limits procedure or by using a standardized test that has multiple-choice items, such as the WISC–IV Integrated or the Peabody Picture Vocabulary Test–III.
18. Tactfully ask the child to repeat unintelligible words or statements.
19. Encourage the child to express ideas in other ways when his or her communication is not clear. Say, for example, "Tell me about that in different words so that I can understand you better" or "Give me an example of. . . ." Occasionally, a child may be able to sing an answer when she or he cannot express it in any other way.
20. Be prepared to discuss communication difficulties openly. However, avoid pointing out any inadequacies in the child's responses. If necessary, switch to an easier topic or to a nonverbal activity.
21. Redirect the child to the topic at hand if perseveration occurs.
22. At various intervals, repeat what the child has said to help focus the conversation.
23. Recognize that the child may know what she or he wants to say but be unable to say it because of difficulty in recalling, in initiating a task, or in expressing himself or herself.
24. Recognize that the child may have difficulty in generalizing from one situation to another.
25. Recognize that inappropriate language, self-centeredness, and poor personal hygiene, for example, may be related to the brain injury and be difficult for the child to control.

BEHAVIORS ASSOCIATED WITH CHILDREN WITH BRAIN INJURIES

Parents of children with brain injuries may report concerns about some of the following behaviors in their children, or you may observe some of these behaviors during the assessment. Most parental concerns fall into one or more of the following categories: attention, memory and learning, language, visuoperception, and executive functioning. Although these problem behaviors can hinder the assessment process and be frustrating to you, they also constitute a valuable behavior sample that can help you understand and generate hypotheses about the child. The problem behaviors displayed during the assessment provide important information about how a child may function outside of the assessment. A child who has difficulty staying on task, who fatigues easily, and who becomes emotionally distraught when faced with difficult material will likely respond in a similar manner at school, at play, and at home.

ATTENTION

- Failing to stay on task, including being easily distracted and flitting from one activity to another
- Slowing down during timed tasks
- Completing visuospatial tasks more slowly than verbal tasks
- Frequently requesting that instructions be repeated
- Failing to understand questions
- Failing to attend to visual information
- Scanning pages poorly
- Looking at pages without taking in their content

MEMORY AND LEARNING

- Being absentminded or forgetful
- Failing to recall instructions
- Being unable to remember more than one thing at a time
- Forgetting homework or school assignments
- Forgetting where things are
- Forgetting what they need to bring to school
- Losing belongings
- Failing to remember what they have read; needing to reread material in order to remember it
- Being slow to learn new concepts, facts, and skills
- Failing to learn adequately
- Losing their place during tasks

LANGUAGE

- Having difficulty expressing themselves precisely
- Having difficulty understanding what people say to them
- Having difficulty understanding what they read
- Having difficulty speaking fluently
- Mispronouncing words frequently
- Having difficulty expressing themselves in writing
- Having difficulty understanding double meanings or verbal jokes
- Initiating conversation infrequently
- Displaying poor speech clarity and articulation

- Using inappropriate grammar
- Having difficulty recalling or choosing words
- Pointing to answers rather than giving answers orally
- Giving better single-word answers than answers requiring explanations
- Using circumlocutions or unnecessarily long explanations to convey ideas
- Failing to grasp communicative intent

VISUOPERCEPTION

- Writing too small, too large, or unevenly
- Drawing immaturely or poorly
- Doing puzzles poorly
- Playing sports poorly
- Bumping into things and tripping over things frequently
- Failing to respect other people's space
- Occluding one eye with hand or hair when drawing, writing, or reading
- Missing information on one side of the page or at the edge of the visual field
- Scanning information poorly
- Concentrating on the parts of a task rather than the whole

EXECUTIVE FUNCTIONING

- Having difficulty shifting from one task to another
- Being untidy
- Failing to plan homework or other activities
- Failing to initiate activities
- Failing to complete work once started
- Failing to complete work on time
- Going off on tangents on projects
- Making inferences or abstractions poorly
- Failing to organize work
- Failing to evaluate work
- Failing to control emotions
- Displaying disorganized behavior
- Perseverating

OBSERVING AND INTERVIEWING CHILDREN

Observe the child in several settings and at different times during the day, such as during the administration of tests, in an interview, and in natural settings. Chapters 8 and 9 provide detailed information about behavioral observations.

Chapters 5, 6, and 7 cover the principles of interviewing (see also Sattler, 1998). Appendix B contains three semistructured interviews useful for children with brain injuries. Table B-1 lists questions for school-age children. Table B-2 provides questions for a mental status interview. You can compare the responses given by a child 8 years old or older with those of a sample of 227 children without disabilities between the ages of 8 and 13 years (Iverson, Iverson, & Barton, 1994): (a) 100% knew their name, age, birthday, school, and grade, (b) 88% estimated the time of day within 1 hour of the correct time, (c) 98% knew the day of the week, (d) 97% knew the month, (e) 77% knew the day of the month, and (f) 99% knew the year.

Table B-8 is designed specifically for children with brain injuries. It has questions about the reasons for the brain injury, specific problem areas associated with brain injury, and changes, if any, in the child's behavior or relationships since the injury. Table B-8 contains both general questions and questions that focus on a traumatic event. Although children with brain injuries who are younger than 8 or 9 years of age may be difficult to interview, they should be able to respond to orientation questions and questions about how they are coping with their brain injury. Adolescents who know how to read can be encouraged to complete the Personal Data Form in Table A-2 in Appendix A.

INTERVIEWING PARENTS

Table B-10 in Appendix B contains a semistructured interview useful for obtaining an in-depth developmental history from a parent. Ask parents to complete the Background Questionnaire (see Table A-1 in Appendix A) and the Pediatric Inventory of Neurobehavioral Symptoms, which is discussed later in the chapter. If necessary, you also can use Table B-9 in Appendix B to obtain information about problem areas.

With minor modifications, most of the questions in Table B-8 in Appendix B can be used to interview parents about how their child is functioning. If you ask the child the questions in Table B-8 and then ask the parents the same questions about the child, you can compare their responses. In the interview, give parents an opportunity to express any concerns, including concerns about the child's attention, memory and learning, language, visuoperceptual skills, and executive functioning.

Parents may not always be objective in the information that they give you. They may describe the child's preinjury behavior and ability in an overly favorable light. And they may selectively disclose historical information or fail to disclose the child's preinjury problems because they have forgotten important details, they have vague recollections, they are experiencing emotional distress, or they are involved in litigation associated with the child's brain injury. If possible, interview persons outside the immediate family to document the information that you have obtained from the parents and the child. Again, recognize that extended family members and friends may not be objective for similar reasons.

NEUROLOGICAL EXAMINATION

A *neurological examination* includes a clinical history, a mental status examination, and a study of cranial nerves, motor functions (including muscle tone, dexterity, strength,

Frank and Ernest

and reflexes), coordination, sensory functions, and gait. A comprehensive neurological examination may include imaging and radiographic diagnostic procedures.

Imaging and Radiographic Methods

Various diagnostic methods provide information about the structure and function of the brain and its vasculature. Some methods yield a variety of information, whereas others focus on specific aspects of tissue anatomy, metabolism, or blood flow in the brain. Structural methods focus on identifying gross or subtle abnormalities in tissue, whereas functional methods record brain activity associated with cerebral metabolism, which in turn is related (directly or indirectly) to blood flow changes in parts of the brain that are engaged in a task (Mellers, 2004). Following are brief descriptions of eight imaging and radiographic methods:

- *Computed tomography (CT),* or *computerized axial tomography (CAT),* is an x-ray technique that uses a computer to scan objects in sequential slices. The high-resolution radiologic images produced by CT are useful in locating focal pathologies—such as tumors and hemorrhages—and in showing changes in brain structure. The disadvantages of CT scans are that they expose children to radiation and that the contrast material injected into the bloodstream may cause an allergic reaction; additionally, other structural imaging methods provide superior contrast between the gray and white matter of the brain.
- *Magnetic resonance imaging (MRI)* uses no radiation; instead, powerful electromagnetic gradients switch on and off at a resonant frequency, polarizing some of the body's water protons. As the protons spin with the magnetic field, they emit an electromagnetic signal that is detected by an antenna-like coil. The procedure is noninvasive and produces detailed anatomical images; however, the apparatus can be noisy and confining. As with CT, a contrast agent

may be injected to enhance the image. An advantage of MRI over CT is that it provides superior imaging of soft tissue, a feature that makes it particularly suitable for the investigation of tumors, edema, tissue pathology, and small lesions.

- *Functional magnetic resonance imaging (fMRI)* is an advanced imaging procedure that provides information about brain function rather than brain structure. It generates images much more quickly than conventional MRI; this feature allows clinicians to see metabolic changes that take place in an active part of the brain and locate regions associated with specific psychological functions. *Diffusion tensor imaging (DTI)* is a type of diffusion MRI that measures the direction as well as the magnitude of water diffusion in the brain. DTI can map subtle aspects of white matter and allows examination of functional connectivity of brain areas that work in concert during cognitive tasks.
- *Electroencephalography (EEG)* is a procedure in which electrodes are placed on the scalp to record the electrical activity of the brain. When a computer is used to collect and analyze data, the procedure is called *computerized electroencephalography (CEEG)* or *quantitative electroencephalography (QEEG).* EEG is relatively inexpensive, involves no radiation, and is noninvasive. An advantage of EEG is the ability to record subtle brain activity in real time. Disadvantages are that the recordings do not necessarily bear a specific relation to any brain structure, may pick up artificial signals of noncerebral activity, and may fail to identify abnormal signals that occur in lower brain structures (because the recordings are made at the surface of the brain). A related technique involving the analysis of EEG elicited in response to specific stimuli (e.g., a tone) is known as *event-related potential (ERP).* This technique provides information about how the brain responds to a specific event or stimulus.
- *Magnetoencephalography (MEG)* is a noninvasive scanning procedure that measures magnetic fields produced by

the electrical activity in the brain. Because the procedure is performed by a device that is located in a magnetically shielded room, there is less distortion of the electrical signal than with EEG, and thus MEG provides more accurate information. MEG can record from over 100 points across the entire skull. When MEG is combined with MRI, the process is referred to as *magnetic source imaging (MSI)*. A common clinical use of EEG and MEG is the diagnosis of seizures.

- *Positron emission tomography (PET)* produces a cross-sectional image of cellular activity or blood flow in the brain, following the intravenous injection of a radioactive substance. PET scans provide functional information about regional metabolic activity that occurs during the performance of behavioral and cognitive tasks. PET scans monitor a broad range of biochemical processes, including cerebral glucose utilization. Disadvantages of PET scans are that they are expensive and that they expose children to radioactive substances, either inhaled or injected. Also, the normative standards and clinical correlations are not as well established as they are for structural neuroimaging techniques such as CT and MRI.

- *Single photon emission computed tomography (SPECT)* provides a three-dimensional representation of regional cerebral blood flow. SPECT combines tomographic (structural) techniques with functional methods for measuring brain blood flow. Radioisotopes are inhaled or injected, and the radioactivity produced is monitored. Like PET, SPECT monitors a broad range of biochemical processes and indicates changes in brain activity during behavioral and cognitive tasks, including areas of hypometabolism and locations of seizure activity. SPECT is noninvasive, painless, and relatively safe. SPECT has some disadvantages: Its use per year must be restricted because of radiation exposure, spatial resolution is limited, the images may be contaminated by background radiation, and detecting lesions in white matter is difficult. Also, normative standards and clinical correlations for SPECT are not well established. However, progress is being made in addressing these limitations.

- *Cerebral angiography* is used to visualize the arterial and venous systems of the brain. A catheter is advanced through the carotid artery, and a series of radiographs is recorded while radiopaque dye (dye visible on x-rays) passes through the vasculature. Because the procedure is invasive, it presents a higher risk of complications such as stroke, as well as reaction to the contrast dye. An advantage of angiography is the possibility of performing interventions via the catheter to repair abnormalities such as malformations, aneurysms, and blockage.

Imaging techniques, in general, provide excellent detail about the gross anatomy of the brain and excel in depicting major structural and functional anomalies, including those associated with epilepsy, hydrocephalus, multiple sclerosis, and the degenerative effects of infectious disorders, tumors, congenital mishaps, and other childhood disorders. Although each method can be useful in the diagnostic process, imaging techniques do not provide reliable information about levels of cognitive functioning or about functional levels of performance—that is, how the child functions in everyday activities and situations.

Imaging and radiographic techniques, in general, vary along two distinct dimensions: temporal resolution and spatial resolution. Techniques with high temporal resolution provide information about the events within the brain on a millisecond to millisecond basis. Techniques with the best temporal resolution include MEG and EEG, followed by fMRI, DTI, PET, and SPECT. Techniques with high spatial resolution provide information about the location of events in the brain. Techniques with the best spatial resolution include MRI, fMRI, and DTI.

Neurological Signs

The neurological examination may reveal hard neurological signs and/or soft neurological signs. *Hard neurological signs* are those that are fairly definitive indicators of cerebral injury, such as abnormalities in reflexes, cranial nerves, and motor organization, as well as asymmetrical failures in sensory and motor responses. Hard neurological signs usually correlate with independent evidence of brain injury, such as the results of CT scans or EEGs.

Examples of hard neurological signs include the following:

- Seizures
- Cranial nerve abnormalities
- *Paresthesia* (tingling, crawling, or burning sensations on the skin)
- *Homonymous hemianopia* (blindness affecting the right halves or the left halves of the visual fields of the two eyes; it results from damage to the optic tract, thalamus, or visual cortex)
- *Hypoesthesia* (decreased tactile sensitivity)
- Loss of 2-point discrimination (inability to determine by feeling whether the skin is touched at one point or at two points simultaneously)

Soft neurological signs are mild and equivocal neurological irregularities, in primarily sensorimotor functions, that may not have any relationship to demonstrated neuropathology but may suggest neurological impairment, immaturity of development, or a mild injury. There is *no* direct relationship between soft neurological signs and specific neuropsychological impairments. Table 24-1 shows useful informal procedures for assessing soft neurological signs.

Examples of soft neurological signs include the following:

- *Astereognosis* (inability to identify three-dimensional objects when blindfolded, although sensory functions are intact)
- Atypical sleep patterns
- Awkwardness
- *Choreiform* (irregular, jerky) limb movements
- *Dysarthria* (disturbance in articulation)

Table 24-1
Informal Assessment of Soft Neurological Signs

Task	Description	Scoring	Ages 3 to 4 years	Ages 5 years and over
Walking on toes	Ask the child to walk across the room on his or her toes after you demonstrate the task.	The child must walk on the toes of both feet.	■	■
Walking on heels	Ask the child to walk across the room on his or her heels after you demonstrate the task.	The child must walk on the heels of both feet.	■	■
Tandem gait forward	Ask the child to walk forward, heel to toe, on a taped line after you demonstrate the task.	The child must walk forward with sufficient balance to avoid stepping off the line.	■	■
Tandem gait backward	Ask the child to walk backward, heel to toe, on a taped line after you demonstrate the task.	The child must walk backward with sufficient balance to avoid stepping off the line.		■
Touch localization	Ask the child to close his or her eyes and point to or report where he or she is touched. First touch the back of the child's right hand; second, the back of the child's left hand; third, the backs of both of the child's hands.	The child must report all localizations correctly, either verbally or nonverbally.	■	■
Restless movements	Ask the child to sit on a chair with feet off the floor and hands in lap for 1 minute (timed).	The child must remain seated for 1 minute and motionless for at least 30 seconds.	■	■
Downward drift	Ask the child to stand with outstretched hands for 20 seconds, with eyes closed.	The child must not allow either arm to drift downward.		■
Hand coordination	Ask the child to move his or her hand rapidly, alternating from palm up to palm down, one hand at a time.	The child must switch smoothly from palm up to palm down for at least three cycles with each hand.	■	■
Hopping	Ask the child to hop on one foot at a time; demonstrate if necessary.	The child must hop on each foot.		■
Alternate tapping	Ask the child to imitate three tapping tasks: (1) tap five times with right index finger (at a rate of about two taps per second); (2) tap five times with left index finger; (3) tap alternately with left and right index fingers for four cycles.	The child must perform all three tasks.		■
Complex tapping	Ask the child to imitate two tapping tasks: (1) tap twice with left index finger and then twice with right index finger, repeating the pattern five times (at a rate of about two taps per second); (2) tap once with left index finger and twice with right index finger, repeating the pattern five times.	The child must perform both tasks correctly.		■

Note. Score each item as pass or fail.
Source: Adapted from Huttenlocher, Levine, Huttenlocher, and Gates (1990).

- *Dysdiadochokinesia* (impairment in performing rapid, alternating movements in a smooth and rhythmic fashion)
- *Dysgraphesthesia* (impairment in identifying symbols traced on the palm surface when blindfolded)
- Impaired auditory integration
- Impaired fine-motor coordination; clumsiness
- Impaired memory
- Labile affect

- Mild word-finding difficulties
- Poor balance
- Slight reflex asymmetries
- Tremor
- Visual-motor difficulties (e.g., difficulty copying a circle or a square)

NEUROPSYCHOLOGICAL EXAMINATION

A neuropsychological examination complements a neurological examination. The information it provides about the child's adaptive strengths and weaknesses can be useful in assessing various neuropathological conditions, neurosurgical procedures, and trauma, as well as relatively isolated problems, such as learning disabilities. Neuropsychological evaluations generate baseline measures for evaluating the course of various neuropathological processes, aid in formulating appropriate treatment recommendations, and document the effects of therapeutic programs (e.g., behavioral or drug therapies) on cerebral functions.

A neuropsychological evaluation involves (a) reviewing the case history, including current medical records about the injury and prior medical history, (b) interviewing the child, (c) observing the child in one or more settings, (d) interviewing the parents to obtain detailed information about the child's development history and functioning, (e) interviewing teachers to obtain detailed information about the child's performance in school, and (f) administering a battery of neuropsychological tests.

Case History

The case history provides valuable information about the child's functioning both before and after the brain injury. As you review the case history, pay particular attention to such details as the following:

- Injuries to the head
- Use of anesthetics during surgery
- Blurred vision, loss of consciousness, or dilated pupils
- Changes in appearance, hygiene, social behavior, temperament, personality, energy level, work habits, or performance of daily routines, including sudden or progressive declines in cognitive, language, speech, memory, or motor functioning or in school performance
- Disruptive, aggressive, or confused behavior (including visual or olfactory hallucinations) that interferes with daily living activities, interpersonal relations, school performance, or work and/or unexplained instability, irritability, or lethargy
- Occasions of prolonged high fever, nausea, and vomiting that are not related to common illnesses
- Poisoning associated with foods, chemicals, or medications
- Significant delays in achieving developmental milestones

- Other medical conditions that might have associated cognitive impairments (e.g., epilepsy, toxic exposure, thyroid disorders, long-term substance abuse)
- Emotional or psychiatric disorders, especially those involving somatization, anxiety, or depression

Any sudden and inadequately explained changes in behavior are likely to be associated with acute, as opposed to chronic, brain disorders. Some of the above symptoms (e.g., prolonged nausea and vomiting and changes in behavior or school performance) can occur without the presence of brain injury and may be associated with drug use, depression, or other conditions. In addition, prior medical or behavioral disorders may interact with the current brain injury to compound assessment problems.

Areas Measured in a Neuropsychological Examination

The neuropsychological examination typically measures the following areas and functions (Mapou, 1995):

1. *General intellectual skills and academic achievement,* including evaluation of reasoning, problem solving, reading, writing, and mathematics abilities
2. *Arousal and attention,* including evaluation of level of alertness, focused attention, sustained attention, span of attention, and resistance to interference
3. *Sensory and motor functions,* including evaluation of visual functions, auditory functions, somatosensory functions (pertaining to bodily sensations, including those of touch, pain, pressure, and temperature), functional laterality (side of body preferred for sensory and motor tasks), motor strength, fine-motor skills (such as speed and dexterity), and sensorimotor integration
4. *Executive functions and problem-solving abilities,* including evaluation of planning, flexibility of thinking, sequencing and organizational skills, and verbal and nonverbal reasoning abilities
5. *Language functions,* including evaluation of both comprehension and production (see Table 24-2 for a list of informal procedures for testing agnosia, apraxia, and aphasia)
6. *Visuospatial functions,* including evaluation of perceptual skills, constructional skills, and spatial awareness
7. *Learning and memory,* including evaluation of the ability to learn new information, immediate and delayed recall, recognition, working memory, sequential memory, visual memory, and auditory memory
8. *Personality,* including evaluation of motivation, interests, impulsiveness, ability to tolerate changes in activities, temperament, mood, compulsions, and phobias
9. *Emotional functioning,* including evaluation of types of expressed affect, lability of affect, and modulation of emotional reactivity

Table 24-2
Informal Assessment of Agnosia, Apraxia, and Aphasia

Disorder	Ability	Procedure
Agnosia	Sound recognition	Ask the child, with eyes closed, to identify familiar sounds, such as a ringing bell or whistling.
	Auditory perception	Ask the child to repeat what you say.
	Auditory-verbal comprehension	Ask the child to answer questions and carry out instructions.
	Recognition of body parts and sidedness	Ask the child to point to her or his left and right sides and to name body parts.
	Visual object recognition	Ask the child to identify familiar objects, such as a pen or a wristwatch, placed in front of her or him.
	Color recognition	Ask the child to name colors.
	Facial recognition	Observe whether the child recognizes familiar faces.
	Tactile recognition	Ask the child, with eyes closed, to identify familiar objects placed in her or his hand, such as keys, a comb, and a pencil.
	Visual-spatial recognition	(For older child) Ask the child to walk to the left side of the room.
Apraxia	Bucco-facial movement	Ask the child to show you how to drink through a straw, blow out a match, cough, yawn, and stick out his or her tongue.
	Limb movement	Ask the child to wave good-bye, show you how to comb his or her hair, make a fist, throw a ball, and kick a ball.
	Bilateral limb movement	Ask the child to show you how to play a piano and file his or her fingernails.
	Whole-body movement	Ask the child to show you how to stand like a boxer, take a bow, and shovel dirt (or snow).
	Integrated skilled motor act (as well as memory)	Say to the child: "Here are three papers: a big one, a middle-sized one, and a little one. Take the biggest one, crumple it up, and throw it on the ground. Give me the middle-sized one. Put the smallest one in your pocket."
Aphasia	Verbal comprehension	Ask the child to name articles of clothing that she or he is wearing and to touch her or his nose, leg, mouth, eyes, and ears.
	Visual comprehension	Ask the child to tell you what you are doing. Pantomime such activities as writing, drinking, hammering a nail, combing hair, cutting with scissors, and waving.
	Visual-verbal comprehension	Ask the child to read a sentence from the newspaper and explain its meaning. If the child is unable to speak, print instructions on a sheet of paper and note whether the child can carry them out.
	Motor speech	Ask the child to imitate several sounds and phrases: "la-la," "me-me," "this is a good book," and others of increasing difficulty. Note abnormal word usage in conversation.
	Automatic speech	Ask the child to repeat one or two series of words that she or he has learned in the past, such as the days of the week or the months of the year.
	Volitional speech	Ask the child to answer questions. Note whether the answers are relevant.
	Writing	Ask the child to write (a) her or his name and address, (b) a simple sentence, and (c) the name of an object that you show her or him.

Note. All activities in the table should be used only with children who would be expected, based on their age, to have mastered the skill.

10. *Adaptive behavior skills* (e.g., self-help skills, communications skills)
11. *Environmental variables,* including evaluation of socioeconomic status and other family variables, quality of the neighborhood, and school environment

Uses of the Results of a Neuropsychological Examination

The results of a neuropsychological examination can be useful in the following ways:

- Identifying areas of brain injury that impair a child's ability to perform successfully
- Providing a cognitive profile of relative strengths and weaknesses
- Providing information about the functional consequences of impairments identified by neuroimaging techniques
- Documenting the deterioration (e.g., due to a progressive disease) or recovery of cognitive functions over time
- Providing information regarding changes in a child's capabilities and limitations in everyday functioning
- Differentiating behavioral disturbances that may stem from brain injury from those that may stem from other causes
- Planning for rehabilitation (e.g., estimating potential for recovery and improvement, describing management implications of the assessment findings, and designing interventions)
- Providing teachers with information on modifying the curriculum and on using teaching methods designed for children with brain injuries
- Helping courts determine levels of loss and compensation

Neuropsychological assessment of children differs from that of adults in several ways (Tramontana & Hooper, 1988). First, very young children have difficulty reporting their symptoms because their language ability has not yet fully developed. Therefore, parents (or other informants) must be relied on for information about their functioning. Second, environmental factors—particularly those related to the family—play a significant role in shaping outcomes. Third, in cases of early brain injury, it is difficult to evaluate children's preinjury levels of functioning. Fourth, deficits may be "silent" until later in life when cognitive demands increase (Anderson, Northam, Hendy, & Wrennall, 2001; Limond & Leeke, 2005). Finally, it is sometimes difficult to distinguish deficits associated with developmental delays and learning disabilities from those associated with brain injuries.

The aim of neuropsychological assessment has shifted from assisting in the diagnosis of cerebral damage to assisting in the assessment of the functional capacities of children with brain injuries and in rehabilitation efforts. This shift has taken place because brain-imaging techniques that provide accurate information about the location of brain injury have become more widely available.

Questions to explore during a neuropsychological assessment include the following:

- Which behavioral areas are intact, and which ones show a deficit?
- What changes in ability and personality can be expected of the child, and when might these changes occur?
- How can we determine whether the symptoms displayed by the child are associated with the recent brain injury or are related to past disorders?
- What can the teacher do to help the child learn better?
- What medical problems does the child have that will necessitate changes in the classroom?

- What type of rehabilitation program or special education services does the child need?
- How has the family been affected by the child's condition?
- Can the family support the child?
- What services does the family need?

The goal of both the neurological and the neuropsychological examination is to assess brain injury accurately. However, the neurological examination focuses on evaluating biological functions (e.g., motor system, perceptual system, and reflexes), whereas the neuropsychological examination focuses on cognitive processes (e.g., language and memory). A standard neurological examination—coupled with an EEG and other diagnostic studies—usually establishes the presence and locus of intracranial disease or damage. Because these procedures are not designed to evaluate functional impairment, they should be supplemented with a neuropsychological examination. A neuropsychological examination can help to confirm a diagnosis of brain injury and define the nature and the severity of defects in cognitive and motor and perceptual brain functions. Thus, a complete assessment of a child with brain injury includes a neurological examination, use of brain-imaging techniques when recommended by a neurologist, and a neuropsychological examination.

> *We are at the brink of enormous breakthroughs in this area—developmental neurobiology—and there is no longer a boundary between biology, psychology, culture and education.*
>
> —Bennett L. Leventhal, American pediatric and adolescent psychiatrist (1949–   )

HALSTEAD-REITAN NEUROPSYCHOLOGICAL TEST BATTERY FOR OLDER CHILDREN AND REITAN-INDIANA NEUROPSYCHOLOGICAL TEST BATTERY FOR CHILDREN

Two batteries useful for evaluating children suspected of having brain injury are the Halstead-Reitan Neuropsychological Test Battery for Older Children, designed for children ages 9 to 14 years, and the Reitan-Indiana Neuropsychological Test Battery for Children, designed for children ages 5 to 8 years (Reitan & Davison, 1974; Reitan & Wolfson, 1985, 1992; Selz, 1981). Both batteries contain cognitive and perceptual-motor tests, a few of which appear in the adult battery (Halstead-Reitan Neuropsychological Test Battery for Adults) and a few of which were especially designed for young children. (See Table 24-3 for a description of the batteries.) Table 24-4 gives the instructions for the Reitan-Indiana Aphasia Screening Test, and Figure 24-1 shows the stimulus figures for

Table 24-3
Description of the Halstead-Reitan Neuropsychological Test Battery for Older Children and the Reitan-Indiana Neuropsychological Test Battery for Children

Test	Description	H-R	R-I
Category Test	Measures concept formation; requires child to find a reason (or rule) for comparing or sorting objects	■	■
Tactual Performance Test	Measures somatosensory and sensorimotor ability; requires child, while blindfolded, to place blocks in appropriate hole using dominant hand alone, nondominant hand alone, and both hands	■	■
Finger Tapping Test	Measures fine-motor speed; requires child to press and release a lever, like a telegraph key, as fast as possible	■	■
Aphasia Screening Test	Measures expressive and receptive language functions and laterality; requires child to name common objects, spell, identify numbers and letters, read, write, calculate, understand spoken language, identify body parts, and differentiate between right and left	■	■
Matching Pictures Test	Measures perceptual recognition; requires child to match figures at the top of a page with figures at the bottom of the page	■	■
Individual Performance tests			
Matching Figures	Measures perception; requires child to match complex figures		■
Star	Measures visual-motor ability; requires child to copy a star		■
Matching Vs	Measures perception; requires child to match letter Vs		■
Concentric Squares	Measures visual-motor ability; requires child to copy a series of concentric squares		■
Marching Test	Measures gross-motor control; requires child to (a) use a crayon to connect a series of circles in a given order, first with right hand alone and then with left hand alone, and (b) reproduce examiner's finger and arm movements		■
Progressive Figures Test	Measures flexibility and abstraction; requires child to connect several figures, each consisting of a small shape contained within a large shape		■
Color Form Test	Measures flexibility and abstraction; requires child to connect colored shapes, first by color and then by shape		■
Target Test	Measures memory for figures; requires child to reproduce a visually presented pattern after a 3-second delay		■
Seashore Rhythm Test	Measures alertness, sustained attention, and auditory perception; requires child to indicate whether two rhythms are the same or different	■	
Speech Sounds Perception Test	Measures auditory perception and auditory-visual integration; requires child to indicate, after listening to a word on tape, which of four spellings represents the word	■	
Trail Making Test (Parts A and B)	Measures appreciation of symbolic significance of numbers and letters, scanning ability, flexibility, and speed; requires child to connect circles that are numbered or lettered	■	
Sensory-Perceptual Examination	Measures sensory-perceptual ability; requires child to perceive bilateral simultaneous sensory stimulation of tactile, auditory, and visual modalities in separate tests	■	■
Tactile Finger Recognition	Measures sensory-perceptual ability; requires child, while blindfolded, to recognize which finger is touched	■	■
Fingertip Number Writing	Measures sensory-perceptual ability; requires child, while blindfolded, to recognize numbers written on fingertips	■	■
Tactile Form Recognition	Measures sensory-perceptual ability; requires child to identify various coins through touch alone, with each hand separately	■	■
Strength of Grip	Measures motor strength of upper extremities; requires child to use Smedley Hand Dynamometer with preferred hand and nonpreferred hand	■	■

Note. H-R = Halstead-Reitan Neuropsychological Test Battery for Older Children, R-I = Reitan-Indiana Neuropsychological Test Battery for Children. The WISC–IV (or WAIS–III) is often administered as part of the complete battery.

Table 24-4
Instructions for the Reitan-Indiana Aphasia Screening Test

Task	Instructions
1. Copy square	"First, draw this [point to the square] on your paper. I want you to do it without lifting your pencil from the paper. Make it about the same size [pointing to the square]."
2. Name square	"What is that shape called?" or "What is the name for that figure?"
3. Spell *square*	"Would you spell that word for me?"
4. Copy cross	"Draw this [point to the cross] on your paper. Go around the outside like this [quickly draw a fingerline around the edge of the stimulus figure] until you get back to where you started. Make it about the same size [point to the cross].
5. Name cross	"What is that shape called?"
6. Spell *cross*	"Would you spell the name of it?"
7. Copy triangle	"Now I want you to draw this figure." Point to the triangle.
8. Name triangle	"What would you call that figure?"
9. Spell *triangle*	"Would you spell the name of it for me?"
10. Name baby	"What is this?" Show item 10.
11. Write *clock*	"Now I am going to show you another picture, but do NOT tell me the name of it. I don't want you to say anything out loud. Just WRITE the name of the picture on your paper." Show item 11.
12. Name fork	"What is this?" Show item 12.
13. Read *7 six 2*	"I want you to read this." Show item 13.
14. Read *M G W*	"Read this." Show item 14.
15. Reading I	"Now I want you to read this." Show item 15.
16. Reading II	"Can you read this?" Show item 16.
17. Repeat *triangle*	"Now I am going to say some words. I want you to listen carefully and say them after me as carefully as you can. Say this word: *triangle*."
18. Repeat *Massachusetts*	"The next one is a little harder, but do your best. Say this word: *Massachusetts*."
19. Repeat *Methodist Episcopal*	"Now repeat this one: *Methodist Episcopal*."
20. Write *square*	"Don't say this word out loud [point to the stimulus word *square*]. Just write it on your paper."
21. Read *seven*	"Would you read this word?" Show item 21.
21A. Repeat *seven*	Remove the stimulus card and say: "Now, I want you to say this after me: *seven*."
22. Repeat-explain *He shouted the warning*	"I am going to say something that I want you to say after me, so listen carefully: *He shouted the warning*. Now you say it. Tell me in your own words what that means."
23. Write *He shouted the warning*	"Now I want you to write that sentence on the paper."
24. Compute 85 – 27 =	"Here is an arithmetic problem. Copy it down on your paper any way you like and try to work it out." Show item 24.
25. Compute 17 X 3 =	"Now do this one in your head. Write down only the answer."
26. Name key	"What is this?" Show item 26.
27. Demonstrate use of key	Still presenting the picture of the key, say: "*If you had one of these in your hand, show me how you would use it.*"
28. Draw key	"Now I want you to draw a picture that looks just like this [pointing to the picture of the key]. Try to make your key look enough like this one [still pointing to the picture of the key] so that I would know it was the same key from your drawing. Make it about the same size."
29. Read	"Would you read this?" Show item 29.
30. Place left hand to right ear	"Now, would you do what it said?" Be sure to note any false starts or even mild expressions of confusion.
31. Place left hand to left elbow	"Now I want you to put your left hand to your left elbow."

Note. See Figure 24-1 for stimulus figures. The Reitan-Indiana Aphasia Screening Test is part of the Reitan-Indiana Neuropsychological Test Battery for Children. Considerable clinical experience is needed to administer and interpret the test or the battery. Two books that can assist you in interpreting the battery are *Aphasia and Sensory-Perceptual Deficits in Adults* by Reitan (1984) and *Aphasia and Sensory-Perceptual Deficits in Children* by Reitan (1985). Additionally, Reitan and Wolfson's (1985) *Halstead-Reitan Neuropsychological Test Battery: Theory and Clinical Interpretation* is an excellent source for information on how to integrate the findings of the Reitan-Indiana Aphasia Screening Test with the rest of the results of the Halstead-Reitan Neuropsychological Test Battery for a complete neuropsychological assessment. Separate kits for adults and children, which include the appropriate book, recording forms, and test booklet, are available from the Neuropsychology Press, 1338 E. Edison Street, Tucson, AZ 85719.
Source: Reprinted, with changes in notation and with permission of the publisher and authors, from R. M. Reitan and D. Wolfson, *The Halstead-Reitan Neuropsychological Test Battery* (Tucson, AZ: Neuropsychology Press, 1985), pp. 75–78. Copyright 1985 by Neuropsychology Press.

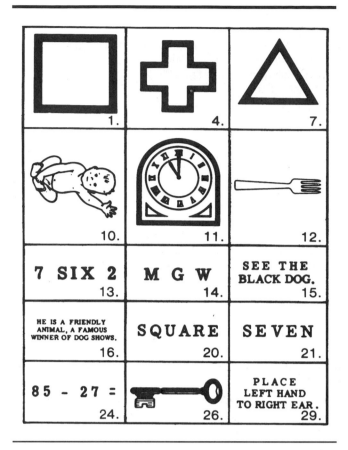

Figure 24-1. Stimulus figures for the Reitan-Indiana Aphasia Screening Test.

the test. The complete Halstead battery also includes an intelligence test and a measure of personality.

Although information about the reliability and validity of both batteries is limited, the available studies reveal several points. First, on the Halstead-Reitan Neuropsychological Test Battery for Older Children, there are clear developmental trends for all tests except for the Tactual Performance Test (Memory and Localization parts) and the Seashore Rhythm Test (Leckliter, Forster, Klonoff, & Knights, 1992). Second, research indicates that four tests may be unreliable: Tactual Performance Test (all timed measures and Memory and Localization tasks), Trail Making Test (Part B among younger children), Speech Sounds Perception Test, and Seashore Rhythm Test. Leckliter and colleagues suggest that clinicians may want to exclude the Speech Sounds Perception Test from the battery or at least interpret it with extreme caution. On the battery for older children, internal consistency reliabilities are relatively low for the Seashore Rhythm Test, moderate for the Aphasia Screening Test, and relatively good for the Speech Sounds Perception Test (Livingston, Gray, & Haak, 1999). The battery for older children appears to have seven factors: Spatial Processing, Motor Strength, Nonverbal Memory/Learning, Sensory-Perceptual, Auditory Processing, Motor

Speed, and Visual Attention (Livingston, Gray, Haak, & Jennings, 1997). Finally, the battery for younger children appears to have five factors: Tactile-Spatial, Concept Formation and Visual/Spatial, Motor Strength, Sensory Perception, and Motor Speed (Livingston, Gray, Haak, & Jennings, 2000).

Research indicates that the batteries are useful in distinguishing children with brain injuries from other children (Dalby & Obrzut, 1991) and that the Reitan-Indiana Aphasia Screening Test is useful as a screening procedure for identifying children with brain injuries (Dodrill, Farwell, & Batzel, 1987; Hynd, 1992; Reitan & Wolfson, 1992). Note, however, that the batteries cannot localize brain injury or predict recovery from brain injury (Hynd, 1992). A short form of the intermediate version of the Halstead Category Test, based on the first 15 items of every subtest, appears to be useful for screening purposes (Donders, 1996).

Normative data on several of the tests are available for children ages 5 to 14 years (unpublished norms provided by Findeis and Weight and reprinted in Nussbaum and Bigler, 1997) and for adolescents and adults (Yeudall, Reddon, Gill, & Stefanyk, 1987). In addition, norms are available for the Reitan-Indiana Neuropsychological Test Battery for Young Children based on a sample of 224 children ages 5 to 8 years who had academic or behavioral problems (Gray, Livingston, Marshal, & Haak, 2000). However, at age 5 years, the norms are based on small sample sizes (4 to 9 children), whereas at ages 6, 7, and 8 years, the norms are based on more adequate sample sizes (38 to 84 children). Overall, the batteries offer unique information not tapped by the Wechsler tests or by pediatric neurological examinations (Yi, Johnstone, Doan, & Townes, 1990) and can be useful for diagnosis and treatment planning (D'Amato, Gray, & Dean, 1988; Leckliter et al., 1992; Russell, 1998).

LURIA-NEBRASKA NEUROPSYCHOLOGICAL BATTERY–CHILDREN'S REVISION

The Luria-Nebraska Neuropsychological Battery–Children's Revision (LNNB–C) is designed to assess a broad range of neuropsychological functions in children ages 8 to 12 years (Golden, 1987). It can be considered a downward extension of the adult version, although items are not necessarily interpreted in the same manner on the two versions. The LNNB–C is designed to assess cognitive deficits and aid in planning rehabilitation programs.

The LNNB–C is individually administered. It contains 149 items, grouped into 11 clinical scales (see Table 24-5) and 2 optional scales. Additionally, the items are regrouped into 3 summary scales and 11 factor scales. The clinical scales are designed to assess sensorimotor, perceptual, and cognitive abilities. The summary scales provide information for discriminating between children with and without brain injuries. The factor scales are helpful in assessing specific neuropsy-

Table 24-5
Clinical Scales of the Luria-Nebraska Neuropsychological Battery–Children's Revision (LNNB–C)

Scale	Number of items	Description
C1: Motor Functions	34	Measures various motor functions, such as motor speed, kinesthetic movement, coordination, construction skills, motor imitation skills, and control of simple motor behaviors in response to verbal commands; requires child to perform various motor movements
C2: Rhythm	8	Measures auditory perception; requires child to hum, sing, report number of beeps heard, and reproduce a series by tapping
C3: Tactile Functions	16	Measures various aspects of tactile sensitivity; requires child to report skin sensation, discriminate being jabbed by a pin, discriminate pressure differentials, report direction of pressure, recognize various objects, identify a number written on wrist, and recognize objects placed in hand
C4: Visual Functions	7	Measures perceptual skills without involving motor movements; requires child to recognize objects visually and detect spatial positions of objects
C5: Receptive Speech	18	Measures ability to understand spoken speech; requires child to repeat spoken sounds and letters, discriminate phonemic sounds, comprehend words, understand simple sentences, and understand logical grammatical structures
C6: Expressive Speech	21	Measures fluency and articulatory speech skills; requires child to repeat spoken sounds and words, pronounce sounds and words that are read, repeat sentences from memory, count, and engage in spontaneous speech
C7: Writing	7	Measures ability to communicate in writing; requires child to spell, copy letters and syllables, and write from dictation
C8: Reading	7	Measures ability to read; requires child to read letters, syllables, words, phrases, and sentences
C9: Arithmetic	9	Measures arithmetic ability; requires child to write and read numbers; tell which number is larger; perform simple multiplication, addition, and subtraction; and count backwards
C10: Memory	8	Measures verbal and nonverbal memory; requires child to recall words presented orally, pictures, words presented visually, and a meaningful paragraph
C11: Intellectual Processes	14	Measures complex reasoning and problem-solving skills; requires child to describe pictures and put them in a meaningful order, indicate what is foolish about a picture, interpret a story, define words, identify the similarity and difference between two things, and answer arithmetic reasoning problems

Note. The optional scales are Spelling and Motor Writing; the summary scales group items into Pathognomonic, Left Sensorimotor, and Right Sensorimotor Scales; the factor scales group items into Academic Achievement, Integrative Functions, Spatial-Based Movement, Motor Speed and Accuracy, Drawing Quality, Drawing Speed, Rhythm Perception and Production, Tactile Sensations, Receptive Language, Expressive Language, and Word and Phrase Repetition Scales.
Source: Adapted from Golden (1987).

chological functions, although they must be interpreted cautiously. The LNNB–C takes approximately 2½ hours to administer.

Scoring

All items are scored 0, 1, or 2. A score of 0 indicates normal functioning, 1 indicates weak evidence of brain injury, and 2 indicates strong evidence of brain injury. Raw scores are transformed into T scores ($M = 50$, $SD = 10$), with higher T scores indicating poorer performance. You can classify errors by reference to 57 individual categories described in the manual—

such as attention difficulties, fatigue, jargon, perseveration, sequence errors, and tremors.

Standardization

The standardization sample consisted of 125 normal children (65 females, 60 males) between the ages of 8 and 12 years. An additional sample of 719 children, many of whom had disabilities, was used in the development and validation of the scales. Unfortunately, demographic information is scarce, and the manual gives no information about the representativeness of the normal group.

Reliability

Internal consistency reliability coefficients, based on 714 children (240 nonimpaired, 474 impaired), range from .67 to .90 (*Mdn* r_{xx} = .82) for the 11 clinical scales. Reliability coefficients are much higher for the group with brain injuries than for the group without brain injuries. Golden (1987) attributes this difference to the restriction in the range of scores in the group without brain injuries—children in this group made few errors. The manual provides standard errors of measurement for both the nonimpaired sample (SEM from 1.2 to 3.2) and the impaired sample (SEM from 1.4 to 3.6). Internal consistency reliability coefficients for the summary scales are similar to those for the clinical scales.

Validity

The manual, as well as a research review (Dalby & Obrzut, 1991), indicates that the LNNB–C is useful in distinguishing children with brain injuries from other children. However, the accuracy with which the LNNB–C classifies children as nonimpaired or brain injured depends on the number of scales used in the classification, the type of disorder the children have, and the critical level of the cutoff scores.

Comment on the LNNB–C

Overall, the LNNB–C may make a useful contribution to the field of neuropsychological assessment; however, more research is needed to evaluate its role. The LNNB–C should be used with caution, because the manual does not describe the standardization sample adequately and reliability is less than adequate. Each scale likely measures a heterogeneous group of skills, making interpretation difficult. Additionally, the test fails to consider maturational variables in assessing children and instead offers a shorter version of the adult battery with simplified items (Williams & Boll, 1997). Also, it is unclear whether the LNNB–C makes a distinct contribution to an assessment or whether a battery composed of the WISC–IV, WRAT–3, and other special ability tests would serve the same purpose. However, some LNNB–C scales, such as Motor Functions, Rhythm, and Tactile Functions, appear to make a unique contribution to an assessment battery (Hynd, 1992).

NEPSY—A DEVELOPMENTAL NEUROPSYCHOLOGICAL ASSESSMENT

NEPSY—A Developmental Neuropsychological Assessment is a neuropsychological test designed for children ages 3 to 12 years (Korkman, Kirk, & Kemp, 1998). It is an American adaptation of a Finnish test called the NEPSU (Korkman, 1990). There are a total of 27 subtests (see Table 24-6) di-

vided into a core battery and a full battery. The core battery contains 11 subtests for children ages 3 to 4 years and 14 subtests for children ages 5 to 12 years. The full battery contains 14 subtests for children ages 3 to 4 years and 26 subtests for children ages 5 to 12 years. The subtests comprise five domains: Attention/Executive Functions, Language, Sensorimotor Functions, Visuospatial Processing, and Memory and Learning. The NEPSY provides quantitative and qualitative information about neuropsychological processes.

Administration of the core battery takes approximately 45 minutes for preschoolers and about an hour for school-age children; administration of the full battery takes about 1 hour for preschoolers and about 2 hours for school-age children. The manual includes directions for administration, psychometric data, a sample clinical history form, a handedness inventory (with norms), an orientation questionnaire that focuses on the child's knowledge of self and place (with norms), and a table on suggested subtest usage with different disability populations.

Scoring

The NEPSY yields several types of scores. First, there are standard scores for the five domains (*M* = 100, *SD* = 15) and 27 subtests (*M* = 10, *SD* = 3). Second, there are supplementary standard scores for the Auditory Attention and Response Set, Memory for Faces, and Memory for Names subtests. The supplementary scores break down the child's performance into Attention versus Response Set components and Immediate versus Delayed Memory components. Third, information is provided about the behavior of the children in the standardization group during the administration of 19 of the 27 subtests, including the number of times they engaged in off-task behavior and made articulation errors, whether they exhibited hand tremors, and the type of pencil grip (mature, intermediate, immature) they demonstrated.

Standardization

The standardization sample consisted of 1,000 children ages 3 to 12 years, with 100 children in each of the 10 age groups, stratified according to 1995 U.S. Census data by age, gender, race/ethnicity, geographic region, and education of parents. Standardization data from an additional 500 children were collected for validation purposes.

Reliability

Average internal reliability coefficients in the five core domains for children ages 5 to 12 years range from a high of .87 on the Language and Memory and Learning Domains to a low of .79 on the Sensorimotor Domain. For children ages 3 to 4 years, average internal reliability coefficients range from

Table 24-6
Description of NEPSY Subtests by Domain

Subtest	Description
Attention/Executive Functions	
Tower	Measures the executive functions of planning, monitoring, self-regulation, and problem solving; requires child to move three colored rings to target positions on three pegs in a prescribed number of moves
Auditory Attention and Response Set	Measures vigilance, selective auditory attention, and ability to shift set, to maintain a complex mental set, and to regulate responses to contrasting and matching stimuli; requires child to shift set and respond to contrasting stimuli
Visual Attention	Measures the speed and accuracy with which child can scan an array and locate a target; requires child to scan an array of pictures and mark the targets as quickly and accurately as possible
Statue	Measures inhibition and motor persistence; requires child to stand still in a set position, with eyes closed, for 75 seconds and inhibit a response (opening eyes, moving body, vocalization) to distractors
Design Fluency	Measures ability to generate novel designs as quickly as possible on structured and unstructured arrays of dots; requires child to make as many different designs as possible by connecting two or more dots
Knock and Tap	Measures self-regulation and ability to inhibit immediate impulses evoked by visual stimuli that conflict with a verbal direction; requires child to learn a pattern of motor responses, maintain that cognitive set, and inhibit the impulse to imitate the examiner's action
Language	
Body Part Naming	Measures naming, a basic component of expressive language; requires child to name the parts of the body
Phonological Processing	(a) Measures phonological awareness (involves auditory discrimination); requires child to identify a picture from an orally presented word segment in one part and to analyze a phonemic pattern and produce a new word in the other part (b) Measures phonological segmentation at the level of letter sounds and word segments; requires child to create a new word by omitting a word segment (syllable) or letter sound (phoneme) or by substituting one phoneme for another
Speed Naming	Measures ability to access and produce familiar words rapidly; requires child to name items by size, color, and shape
Comprehension of Instructions	Measures ability to process and respond to verbal instructions of increasing syntactic complexity; requires child to point to objects and shapes of different sizes, colors, and positions
Repetition of Nonsense Words	Measures phonological encoding and decoding of a sound pattern, as well as articulation of complex nonwords; requires child to listen to nonsense words and repeat each word
Verbal Fluency	Measures ability to generate words according to semantic and phonemic categories; requires child to produce as many animal names as possible in 1 minute, name as many things to eat and drink as possible in 1 minute, and (older children only) produce words beginning with the letters *F* and *S* in 1-minute trials
Oromotor Sequence	Measures rhythmic oromotor coordination; requires child to repeat sound sequences and tongue twisters
Sensorimotor Functions	
Fingertip Tapping	Measures finger dexterity; requires child to tap index finger against thumb 32 times as quickly as possible and tap fingers sequentially against the thumb from index finger to little finger as quickly as possible
Imitating Hand Positions	Measures ability to imitate a hand position from a model; requires child to reproduce hand positions modeled by examiner
Visuomotor Precision	Measures fine-motor skills and hand-eye coordination; requires child to draw a line inside a track as quickly as possible

(*Continued*)

Table 24-6 (*Continued*)	
Subtest	*Description*
Sensorimotor Functions (*continued*)	
Manual Motor Sequences	Measures ability to imitate a series of rhythmic movements; requires child to produce hand movement sequences demonstrated by examiner
Finger Discrimination	Measures ability to perceive tactile input without the aid of vision; requires child to indicate which finger or fingers were touched by examiner (with the child's hand shielded from view)
Visuospatial Processing	
Design Copying	Measures visuomotor integration; requires child to copy two-dimensional geometric figures on paper
Arrows	Measures ability to judge line orientation; requires child to look at an array of arrows around a target and indicate the two arrows that point to the center of the target
Block Construction	Measures spatial-visual ability; requires child to reproduce, from models and from pictures, three-dimensional block constructions
Route Finding	Measures understanding of visuospatial relationships and directionality, as well as ability to transfer this knowledge from a simple schematic map to a more complex one; requires child to find a target in a schematic map
Memory and Learning	
Memory for Faces	Measures memory for faces; requires child to identify the gender of a series of faces, select the faces from three-face arrays, and, after a 30-minute delay, select the same faces from new three-face arrays
Memory for Names	Measures memory for names; requires child to learn, over three trials, the names of six or eight children depicted in line drawings and then, after a 30-minute delay, name the six or eight children
Narrative Memory	Measures narrative memory; requires child to listen to a story and recall it under free recall and cued conditions
Sentence Repetition	Measures memory of verbal material; requires child to recall sentences of increasing length and complexity
List Learning	Measures supraspan memory (i.e., the ability to learn and recall long lists) and ability to recall a list after interference; requires child to learn a list of 15 words, repeat the list after a new list is introduced, and repeat it again after 30 minutes

Source: Adapted from Korkman, Kirk, and Kemp (1998).

a high of .91 on the Memory and Learning Domain to a low of .70 on the Attention/Executive Domain. However, 13 of the 50 internal reliability coefficients in the five domains are below .80. Generally, the domain reliabilities are lowest at the upper age levels of the test, mainly at ages 10 to 12 years.

The subtest average internal consistency reliabilities for children ages 5 to 12 years range from a high of .91 on List Learning and Phonological Processing to a low of .59 on Design Fluency. For children ages 3 to 4 years, average internal consistency reliabilities range from a high of .91 on Sentence Repetition to a low of .50 on Statue.

Although there are 27 subtests, internal reliability coefficients are reported for only 22 of the subtests (the exceptions are Oromotor Sequence, Knock and Tap, Manual Motor Sequences, Finger Discrimination, and Route Finding). Of the

182 reliability coefficients reported for these 22 subtests, 105 are below .80. The subtests exhibiting the highest reliability coefficients are Phonological Processing, Memory for Names, and List Learning. Generally, the subtest internal reliabilities are lowest at the middle to upper age levels of the test, mainly ages 7 to 12 years.

Average standard errors of measurement (SEM) in the five domains for children ages 3 to 4 years range from a low of 4.43 on the Memory and Learning Domain to a high of 8.22 on the Attention/Executive Domain. For children ages 5 to 12 years, the average standard errors of measurement range from a low of 5.43 on the Language Domain to a high of 7.14 on the Sensorimotor Domain. The subtest average standard errors of measurement for children ages 3 to 4 years range from a low of .90 on Sentence Repetition to a high of 2.12 on

Statue. For children ages 5 to 12 years, the subtest average standard errors of measurement range from a low of .92 on List Learning to a high of 1.94 on Design Fluency.

Test-retest reliability coefficients were obtained from a sample of 168 children who were retested over a period of 2 to 10 weeks, with an average retest interval of 38 days. The 30 children ages 3 to 4 years had test-retest reliability coefficients that ranged from .63 on the Attention/Executive Domain to .90 on the Memory and Learning Domain. The median test-retest change was 3.76 points. The largest mean score change was 5.66 points on the Sensorimotor Domain ($M = 98.27$ on the first administration and $M = 103.93$ on the second administration), whereas the lowest mean score change was 3.13 points on the Memory and Learning Domain ($M = 103.70$ on the first administration and $M = 106.83$ on the second administration).

The 138 children ages 5 to 12 years had test-retest reliability coefficients that ranged from .47 on the Attention/Executive Domain to .84 on the Memory and Learning Domain. The median test-retest change was 6.81. The largest mean score change was 17.35 points on the Memory and Learning Domain ($M = 100.94$ on the first administration and $M = 118.29$ on the second administration, for children ages 7 to 8 years), whereas the lowest mean score change was $-.42$ point on the Visuospatial Domain ($M = 99.12$ on the first administration and $M = 98.70$ on the second administration, for children ages 11 to 12 years).

The largest test-retest changes were at ages 5 to 6 years (range of 6.36 to 15.98) and in the Memory and Learning Domain (11.78 to 17.35). The test-retest changes for the Attention/Executive Domain also were large (4.01 to 15.19).

Validity

The manual cites several studies that appear to support the content and construct validity of the NEPSY. However, fewer than 30 children were sampled in many of the studies. Therefore, more work is needed to evaluate the validity of the NEPSY. The validity studies indicate that three domains—Language, Memory and Learning, and Visuospatial—are moderately related to intelligence test scores and to school grades, whereas two domains—Sensorimotor and Attention/Executive—are not. A factor analysis did not support the construct validity of the NEPSY, as only a one-factor solution was found that best describes the test (Stinnett, Oehler-Stinnett, Fuqua, & Palmer, 2002).

Correlations between the NEPSY and various neuropsychological tests provide a mixed pattern of results. Generally, NEPSY subtests correlated moderately with other neuropsychological tests when the content was similar in the two tests. More research is needed to evaluate the relationship between the NEPSY and other neuropsychological instruments.

The clinical utility and sensitivity of the NEPSY were studied in several clinical groups—ADHD, ADHD and learning disability, reading disability, language disorder, autistic,

fetal alcohol syndrome, traumatic brain injury, and hearing impaired. Overall, the results indicate that NEPSY domain scores differentiate clinical groups from matched controls. However, some findings of interest were noted. First, children with a combined diagnosis of ADHD and learning disability were not significantly different from the control group on the Visuospatial Domain. Second, children with a reading disability were not significantly different from the control group on three domains: Attention/Executive, Sensorimotor, and Visuospatial. Third, children with autism were not significantly different from the control group on two domains: Sensorimotor and Visuospatial. Thus, the Visuospatial Domain least discriminates clinical groups from matched control groups. Other research suggests that selected components of the NEPSY—Phonological Processing, Speed Naming, and Sensorimotor subtests—are useful in differentiating children with neurological impairments from children with scholastic difficulties and from children without impairments (Schmitt & Wodrich, 2004).

Comment on the NEPSY

The NEPSY is a complex multidimensional instrument that provides useful information about neurodevelopmental functioning of children with brain injuries. However, it takes a significant amount of time to learn how to administer the test and interpret the results. Although the NEPSY is well standardized, its stability is questionable, particularly for the Memory and Learning and Attention/Executive Domains and for children ages 5 to 6 years. It may be, however, that these traits are unstable and that scores on the NEPSY just reflect the instability of the traits. Reliability is problematic because 13 out of 50 coefficients are below .80 and test-retest changes surpass 1 standard deviation in 4 of 25 instances. The NEPSY appears to have adequate content and construct validity, although a factor analysis is needed. In addition, research is needed to determine how well the NEPSY differentiates among clinical groups. The different levels of scoring and interpretation, particularly the supplemental scores and qualitative analyses, are useful. The test must be used with caution, and additional research is needed.

CONTRIBUTIONS TO NEUROPSYCHOLOGICAL ASSESSMENT BATTERY

The Contributions to Neuropsychological Assessment Battery (Benton, Hamsher, Varney, & Spreen, 1983) contains 12 individual tests designed to measure orientation, learning, perception, and motor ability. Five of the tests have norms for children (see Table 24-7). Although the manual does not give reliability data for any of the tests, the tests have a long history of use in neuropsychological assessment and have

Table 24-7
Tests with Children's Norms in the Contributions to Neuropsychological Assessment Battery

Test	Description
Facial Recognition	Measures sensory-perceptual ability; requires child to identify and discriminate photographs of unfamiliar human faces (norms for ages 6 to 14 years)
Judgment of Line Orientation	Measures spatial perception and orientation; requires child to select, from a stimulus array, a line that points in the same direction as the stimulus line (norms for ages 7 to 14 years)
Tactile Form Perception	Measures nonverbal tactile discrimination and recognition; requires child to touch concealed geometric figures made of fine-grade sandpaper and then visually identify the figures on a card containing ink-line drawings of the figures (norms for ages 8 to 14 years)
Finger Localization	Measures sensory-perceptual ability; requires child to identify fingers touched when hand is visible and then not visible (norms for ages 3 to 12 years)
Three-Dimensional Block Construction	Measures visuoconstructive ability; requires child to construct an exact replica of three block models—a pyramid; an 8-block, four-level construction; a 15-block, four-level construction (norms for ages 6 to 12 years)

Note. The total battery also includes seven other tests: Temporal Orientation, Right-Left Orientation, Serial Digit Learning, Visual Form Discrimination, Pantomime Recognition, Phoneme Discrimination, and Motor Impersistence.
Source: Benton, Hamsher, Varney, and Spreen (1983).

proven useful in the assessment process. Additional normative data for these measures can be found in Baron (2004). More research is needed, however, to examine the reliability and validity of the battery.

WECHSLER TESTS AS PART OF A NEUROPSYCHOLOGICAL TEST BATTERY

The Wechsler tests constitute a standardized series of tasks for evaluating the cognitive and visual-motor skills of children and adults with brain injuries. They are cornerstones of most neuropsychological test batteries. For individuals of any age, brain injury can impair the ability to learn, to solve unfamiliar problems, to remember, to perform subtle visual-motor activities, and to think abstractly. The Wechsler tests are sensitive to some of these abilities, but they do not provide a thorough measure of each. (The discussion below focuses on

the WISC–IV, but the general approach also applies to the WAIS–III and the WPPSI–III.)

The subtests that make up the Wechsler Verbal Comprehension Index rely heavily on retrieval of information acquired *before* the injury. However, these subtests do not sample important verbal abilities such as verbal learning, rapid and efficient processing and integration of large amounts of verbal information, verbal organization, and use and understanding of metaphors, verbal absurdities, synonyms, and antonyms. Also, the Wechsler tests do not probe adequately for subtle memory deficits and subtle visual-motor impairments that may occur as a result of brain injury. Overall, higher-level verbally mediated thinking—such as detecting and clearly stating main ideas in an essay, drawing appropriate inferences, and interpreting complex events correctly—is not measured by any current individually administered intelligence test. Thus, a comprehensive assessment of language ability must go beyond the administration of the Wechsler tests (or other individually administered intelligence tests) if language functioning and other functions are to be assessed fully.

An overall reduction in level of intelligence is a key finding in some cases of brain injury. However, there is no single pattern of subtest scores on Wechsler tests that reveals brain injury. In some cases, scores on the Verbal Comprehension Index and the Perceptual Reasoning Index differ greatly (e.g., by as much as 30 points); in other cases, they differ little, if at all.

Wechsler Index Score Discrepancies

Do discrepancies between scores on the WISC–IV Verbal Comprehension Index and the Perceptual Reasoning Index distinguish between right- and left-sided brain damage? The answer is likely no. Studies with prior versions of the Wechsler tests reported that the relationship between laterality of damage and Verbal Scale–Performance Scale IQs is tenuous (Aram & Ekelman, 1986; Aram, Ekelman, Rose, & Whitaker, 1985; Hynd, Obrzut, & Obrzut, 1981). Even among adults, discrepancies between Wechsler Verbal Scale and Performance Scale IQs do not occur regularly enough in patients with right- or left-hemisphere damage to be clinically reliable (Bornstein, 1983; Kljajic & Berry, 1984; Larrabee, 1986; Lezak, Howieson, & Loring, 2004). These findings do not mean that the relationship between verbal and nonverbal scores has no importance in assessing neurobehavioral deficits. The relationship can still provide important information about the behavioral consequences of brain injury for individual children, particularly when a Wechsler test is used along with tests of sensorimotor, language, and visual-spatial ability.

When brain injury has been documented (by history, CT, PET, MRI, or surgery), you can use the Wechsler tests to assess the cognitive sequelae of the neurological disorder and to identify adaptive deficits requiring more detailed analysis.

If the Verbal Comprehension Index score is 12 or more points lower than the Perceptual Reasoning Index score (or the Verbal Scale and Performance Scale scores), consider investigating linguistic abilities in more depth. (This discrepancy has less meaning for scores above 120.) Carefully analyze the child's verbal responses to questions on the Comprehension, Similarities, and Vocabulary subtests. You may need to administer specialized tests of naming, verbal fluency, and language comprehension if the child demonstrates word-finding difficulties, paraphasias, or inability to grasp the intent of the instructions or questions. The child's responses to the Arithmetic and Digit Span subtests will provide information about his or her ability to attend, concentrate, and deal effectively with numerical stimuli. Poor performance in these areas may suggest the need for additional tests and procedures to evaluate the extent of impairment.

If the Perceptual Reasoning Index score is 12 or more points below the Verbal Comprehension Index score, consider the possibility of impaired visual-spatial, constructional, or perceptual reasoning skills. An examination of the quantitative and qualitative features of performance on the Block Design, Picture Concepts, Matrix Reasoning, and Picture Completion subtests may reveal a need for further assessment focusing on graphomotor, spatial, and visual scanning abilities.

You should *not* consider a discrepancy of even 15 or more points between scores on the Verbal Comprehension Index and the Perceptual Reasoning Index as proof of brain injury, because about 13% of all children in the WISC–IV standardization group had differences of this magnitude or greater in either direction (see Table B.2 on pages 257 to 262 of the WISC–IV manual). A large Verbal Comprehension Index–Perceptual Reasoning Index discrepancy does not demonstrate brain injury; rather, it is an index of test performance that you should use to generate hypotheses for further investigation. In evaluating the child's cognitive abilities, consider, in addition to index or scale comparisons, subtest scores, qualitative features of the child's performance, observations of behavior, and the results of a neuropsychological and neurological assessment. (Note that similar considerations hold for all Verbal-Performance comparisons on Wechsler tests.)

Wechsler Subtest Interpretation

Detailed descriptions of the WISC–IV and the WPPSI–III can be found in Sattler and Dumont (2005); a detailed description of the WAIS–III can be found in Sattler (2001). The Wechsler subtests have neuropsychological implications. The following are interpretive suggestions for developing and testing clinical hypotheses; they are not meant to be diagnostic rules. Integrate the hypotheses you formulate about subtest scores (and all Wechsler scores) with the hypotheses you develop based on qualitative features of a child's performance, the results of specialized neuropsychological measures, the clinical history and background information, and the findings of the neurological evaluation.

1. *Information.* Performance on this subtest may be minimally affected by brain injury, except in cases of lesions involving the cortical or subcortical language areas. Scores on Information may provide an estimate of the examinee's preinjury level of functioning, particularly for older adolescents and adults. A pattern of failure on easy items and success on more difficult items suggests, for example, possible retrieval difficulties associated with long-term memory (Milberg, Hebben, & Kaplan, 1996), variable effort, or feigning. Retrieval difficulties may arise because the information was never learned, because the information is not accessible, or because there is a deficit in recalling specific types of information (e.g., history, geography, science).

2. *Comprehension.* Performance on this subtest may be minimally affected by brain injury, except in cases of lesions involving the cortical or subcortical language areas. However, in some cases, Comprehension may reveal difficulties with impulsivity, inattention, poor judgment, concrete thinking, perseveration, and disturbed associations. Examinees with brain injuries may fail the two proverb questions on the WAIS–III because they cannot understand the abstract nature of the proverbs; instead, they may offer a concrete explanation (e.g., "If the stone keeps rolling, moss will not stick to it").

3. *Similarities.* Performance on this subtest may reveal difficulties with verbal abstraction. In some cases, children with brain injuries show extremely concrete reasoning (e.g., "Orange and banana are not alike because one is long and one is round"). Children may be able to define each word but not integrate the pairs or may give differences between the words but not similarities. And some children may lose the set for responding. If this happens, you may need to repeat the instructions.

4. *Digit Span.* Performance on this subtest may reveal attention problems. Additionally, large differences between Digits Forward and Digits Backward (differences of three or more digits correctly recalled) may suggest a loss of flexibility or impaired attention (especially in more complex situations demanding the kind of attention associated with Digits Backward). Note whether the examinee begins the series before you are finished or repeats the digits at a rapid rate. Examine where the errors occurred: at the beginning, at the end, or in the middle. If there is a pattern of errors, it may suggest proactive interference (digits early in the series interfere with recall of later ones) or retroactive interference (digits later in the series interfere with recall of earlier ones).

5. *Arithmetic.* This subtest is good for evaluating attention, concentration, and cognitive reasoning. An examinee's anxiety about her or his arithmetical ability may result in low scores on this subtest. By using testing-of-limits procedures on this subtest, you may obtain valuable information about the examinee's writing skills, sequencing, and mastery of basic arithmetical processes. Note whether the examinee was impulsive in giving responses. Consider the possible reasons for any failures.

6. *Vocabulary.* Performance on this subtest may be minimally affected by brain injury, except in cases of lesions directly involving the cortical or subcortical language areas. Scores on Vocabulary (like those on Information and Comprehension) may provide an estimate of the examinee's preinjury level of functioning, particularly for older adolescents and adults. The subtest may reveal expressive difficulties, perseveration, distractibility, or association difficulties. If the examinee cannot define a word, you can ask him or her, after the test is completed, to use the word in a sentence.

7. *Word Reasoning.* Performance on this subtest may reveal difficulties with verbal comprehension, analogic and general reasoning abilities, ability to analyze and integrate different types of information, and short-term memory. Note the quality of the child's responses (concrete or abstract, precise or imprecise, normal or peculiar), when the child has problems (e.g., the number of clues needed for an item), and the child's overall performance on the subtest.

8. *Letter–Number Sequencing.* Performance on this subtest may reveal information about attention and memory, visuospatial functions, and processing speed. Note, for example, possible working memory deficits, anxiety, inattention, distractibility, impulsivity, or auditory sequencing problems.

9. *Picture Completion.* This subtest can be sensitive to visual difficulties and word-retrieval difficulties. For example, an examinee may give a response such as "nothing is missing" when his or her visual field is restricted or otherwise impaired. Children with visual agnosia may completely misidentify the stimulus picture, whereas those with expressive language difficulties may give an incorrect verbal response but correctly point to the missing part. Note whether the examinee has difficulty when a part is missing from the central portion of the figure but not when a part is missing from the edge or vice versa. Also note whether the difficulty is associated with "items requiring inferences about symmetry, inferences based on the knowledge of the object, or inferences based on knowledge of natural events" (Milberg et al., 1996, p. 66).

10. *Picture Arrangement.* Performance on this subtest can be sensitive to disturbances in serial ordering or sequencing. Children with brain injuries may leave the cards in the order in which they were placed or move the cards only minimally. This behavior may indicate deficits in attention to detail or impaired conceptual skills.

11. *Block Design.* Performance on this subtest may reveal visual-spatial and constructional difficulties. Note whether the examinee has difficulty in bringing the parts together to form a whole, fumbles, or has difficulties with angles. Are the reproductions grossly inaccurate? Breaks in a 2 × 2 or 3 × 3 block configuration may suggest visual-spatial difficulties. Children with brain injuries who have constructional apraxia may fail to produce the designs and yet be able to accurately describe the designs or the differences between the designs and their copies. This indicates intact perceptual ability but impaired ability to carry out purposeful movements.

12. *Object Assembly.* Performance on this subtest may reveal visual organization problems. Note which items the child passes and which ones he or she fails. Did the failed items require appreciation of contour and edge alignment or appreciation of internal details? What kind of test-taking strategies did the examinee use? Can the examinee say what the object is supposed to be, even though she or he cannot assemble the pieces accurately?

13. *Coding or Digit Symbol—Coding.* Performance on these subtests may reveal information about sequencing, speed, visual-motor functioning, new learning, scanning, and other related processes. Note, for example, the presence of perseveration, rotation of figures, transformation of figures (e.g., into perceptually similar letters), anxiety, extreme caution, slowness, or skipping of boxes.

14. *Matrix Reasoning.* Performance on this subtest may reveal information about perceptual reasoning ability, attention to detail, concentration, and spatial ability. Note, for example, possible reasoning difficulties, perseveration, anxiety, inattention, distractibility, impulsivity, or slow responding.

15. *Symbol Search.* Performance on this subtest may reveal information about perceptual discrimination, speed and accuracy, attention and concentration, short-term memory, and cognitive flexibility. Note, for example, the presence of perseveration, anxiety, confusion, visual-motor difficulties, extreme caution, slowness, or skipping of rows.

16. *Cancellation.* Performance on this subtest may reveal information about visual alertness and visual scanning ability, including information about perceptual discrimination, speed and accuracy, attention and concentration, and vigilance. Note any inattentiveness, distractibility, impulsivity, anxiety, extreme caution, slowness, or skipping of correct answers; also note whether the child makes more errors on the first half than on the second half of the tasks. Compare the child's performance on Cancellation Random and Cancellation Structured (Table A.8 in the WISC–IV manual provides separate scaled scores for each part).

Comment on the Wechsler Tests

Performance on intelligence tests (and other tests as well) is likely to be multidetermined. For example, the written responses to the WISC–IV Coding subtest are the end product of the integration of visual and fine-motor skills and several mental functions. Disturbances in any or all of these functions may result in poor performance. Consequently, to account for any observed deficits, you will need to identify the abilities related to performance on each subtest and consider which abilities may be intact and which abilities may be impaired. Hypotheses regarding the reason(s) for poor performance can be tested by using specialty tests (such as the WISC–IV Integrated) that isolate one or more of the abilities required. For example, poor performance on Block Design might be investigated further using tests that do not target motor or constructional skills or require speed.

Effects of brain injury on intelligence test performance may be general (i.e., a global reduction in intelligence) or specific (i.e., impairment of selective areas of cognitive functioning). Because of this variability, there are no patterns on the WISC–IV or the WAIS–III (such as process score discrepancies, subtest patterns, or specific subtest scores) that reliably distinguish children with brain injuries from children who are emotionally disturbed or normal. Perhaps the best single indicator of brain injury on the Wechsler tests (and on other measures of intelligence as well) is a lower-than-expected total score (such as the Full Scale IQ), given the child's age, education, socioeconomic status, and related factors.

The Wechsler Intelligence Scale for Children–IV Integrated (WISC–IV Integrated; Wechsler, Kaplan, Fein, Kramer, Morris, Delis, & Maerlender, 2004) is also useful in the assessment of children with brain injuries. The test contains 16 process subtests and is particularly useful in providing additional information about the cognitive processes that underlie performance on the WISC–IV subtests.

ADDITIONAL PROCEDURES FOR THE ASSESSMENT OF CHILDREN WITH BRAIN INJURIES

This section describes additional procedures useful for assessing children with brain injuries. Spreen and Strauss (1998) and Baron (2004) compiled normative data for several neuropsychological tests used with children and adults. Both books contain descriptions of the measures, the domains they are intended to measure, and validity information.

Testing-of-Limits

Testing-of-limits may include modifying instructions to involve more or fewer cues, adjusting the pace at which information is presented, modifying the modality of presentation, modifying the starting or discontinuance procedure by administering additional items, adjusting memory demands (e.g., using recognition instead of recall procedures), modifying the response format (e.g., allowing pointing instead of oral responses), adjusting task complexity (e.g., making tasks more concrete), and asking for explanations of responses. Testing-of-limits is used *after* a standardized test is administered. Here are some examples of testing-of-limits:

- On a memory test, you might compare the child's spoken responses with his or her written responses to determine which response modality may be more nearly intact.
- After asking the child to draw a circle, you might have the child copy a circle or imitate your drawing of a circle.
- When the child cannot recall a word, you might give him or her a choice of several words, using a multiple-choice procedure.

Scales for Assessing Levels of Consciousness and Amnesia

The Glasgow Coma Scale (GCS; Teasdale & Jennett, 1974) is widely used in hospitals for assessing levels of consciousness in children and adults with brain injuries. The scale is useful for monitoring changes during the first few days after injury, but it can also be used to describe posttraumatic states of altered consciousness. The GCS has three parts: Eye Opening, Best Motor Response, and Best Verbal Response or Best Behavior Response (see Table 24-8). When estimating level of consciousness, consider scores on each part of the GCS separately and supplement the scores with other clinical data. The Children's Orientation and Amnesia Test (COAT) is also used to evaluate cognition in children and adolescents during the early stages of recovery from traumatic brain injury (Ewing-Cobbs, Levin, Fletcher, Miner, & Eisenberg, 1991), as is the Westmead PTA Scale (Marosszeky, Batchelor, Shores, Marosszeky, Klein-Boonschate, & Fahey, 1993). Age norms have been published for the COAT (Iverson, Woodward, & Iverson, 2002).

Children who have sustained a brain injury may have *posttraumatic amnesia (PTA)*—that is, severe memory difficulties for a period of time after the injury. If so, they may not be able to recall many important details about their lives. Posttraumatic amnesia can be defined as incomplete registration of new events and information for a period of time following the injury (also known as time-limited anterograde amnesia). However, PTA may also involve a briefer period of retrograde amnesia—that is, difficulty in recalling the minutes to hours preceding the traumatic event. PTA can be affected by factors unrelated to the brain injury, such as concomitant drug or alcohol use.

Posttraumatic amnesia may be categorized on a time continuum that reflects the length of the amnesic episode (Jennett & Teasdale, 1981):

1. Very mild—less than 5 minutes
2. Mild—5 to 60 minutes
3. Moderate—1 to 24 hours
4. Severe—1 to 7 days
5. Very severe—1 to 4 weeks
6. Extremely severe—more than 4 weeks

Pediatric Inventory of Neurobehavioral Symptoms

The Pediatric Inventory of Neurobehavioral Symptoms (PINS; Roberts, 1992; Roberts & Furuseth, 1997) is a rating scale designed to be completed by parents or teachers of children who have sustained traumatic brain injuries (see Table 24-9). Items are scored on a scale that ranges from 0 to 3 points.

Self-Perceptions of Ability

The Pediatric Inventory of Neurobehavioral Symptoms–Self-Report (PINS–SR) is useful for obtaining information about

Table 24-8
Glasgow Coma Scale

Eye Opening

4 Spontaneously—opens eyes spontaneously when approached
3 To speech—opens eyes in response to speech (either normal volume or shout)
2 To pain—opens eyes only in response to painful stimuli
1 Not at all—does not open eyes, even in response to painful stimuli

Best Motor Response

6 Follows simple commands—obeys command to raise a hand or move lips or blink eyes
5 Localizes pain—pulls examiner's hand away in response to painful stimuli
4 Purposeful movement in response to pain—pulls part of his or her body away in response to painful stimuli
3 Flexion to pain—flexes body abnormally in response to pain
2 Extends upper and lower extremities in response to painful stimulation
1 None—no motor response to a painful stimulus

Best Verbal Response or Best Behavioral Response

5 Oriented—oriented to time, place, and person
4 Confused—converses, although seems confused or disoriented
3 Inappropriate—speaks only in words or phrases that make little or no sense
2 Incomprehensible—responds with incomprehensible sounds, such as moaning and groans
1 None—no verbal response

Note. The scale is appropriate for children 5 years of age and older and for adults. A score of 15 indicates a fully alert individual; a score of 3 indicates an individual in a deep coma. Scores between 13 and 15 indicate mild brain injury in individuals who are generally alert, who spontaneously open their eyes, and whose verbal responses vary from confused to oriented; scores between 9 and 12 suggest moderate brain injury; and scores 8 or lower suggest severe brain injury in individuals who cannot open their eyes, are unable to obey commands, and fail to utter recognizable words.
Source: Adapted from Reilly, Simpson, Sprod, and Thomas (1988) and Teasdale and Jennett (1974).

how adolescents perceive their abilities (see Table 24-10). If they have difficulty in reading the questionnaire, you can read the items to them. Compare their responses with results obtained from neuropsychological tests and with information provided by their parents and teachers on the Pediatric Inventory of Neurobehavioral Symptoms.

You can also ask adolescents with brain injuries to complete the Adolescent Brain Injury Symptom Checklist (see Table 24-11). The checklist has columns for rating the frequency, intensity, and duration of 18 physical, emotional, and cognitive complaints. If the adolescent has difficulty reading the items, you can read the items to him or her.

Questions for Determining Lateral Preference

With young children, use the following five instructions to determine lateral hand preference:

• Pick up this ball and throw it to me.
• Point to your nose.
• Pick up a crayon and draw a circle.
• Touch your nose with a finger.
• Pick up this tissue and wipe your face.

With children age 8 years and older, ask the following five questions to determine lateral hand preference:

• Which hand do you use to throw a ball?
• Which hand do you use to draw?
• Which hand do you use to write with?
• Which hand do you use to hold a toothbrush when you brush your teeth?
• Which hand do you use to hold an eraser when you erase a pencil mark?

To measure lateral foot, ear, and eye preferences, you can use the following items:

• Show me how you would kick a ball.
• Show me how you use a telephone.
• Show me how you would look through a telescope or microscope.

You can classify the child's responses using the following scale: 0 (never performed), 1 (always left), 2 (usually left), 3 (both equally), 4 (usually right), 5 (always right). Higher scores are associated with a right-hand preference (i.e., left hemisphere dominance). A standardized inventory with norms is also available for measuring lateral preference (Dean & Anderson, 1997).

Table 24-9
Pediatric Inventory of Neurobehavioral Symptoms

PEDIATRIC INVENTORY OF NEUROBEHAVIORAL SYMPTOMS

Child's name: _____   Date:_____

Sex: Male _____   Female _____   Birth date: _____   Age: _____

This form was completed by: Mother ☐   Father ☐   Teacher ☐   Other ☐ _____

Directions:
Please rate your child's (student's) behavior over the past two months using the following rating scale:

0	1	2	3
Almost never or not at all	Sometimes or just a little	Often or pretty much	Very often or very much

Items	Circle one
1. Has difficulty developing plans or setting a goal	0 1 2 3
2. Reacts to minor events as if they were catastrophes	0 1 2 3
3. Does not anticipate the consequences or outcomes of his or her actions	0 1 2 3
4. Swears or uses vulgar gestures	0 1 2 3
5. Complains of headaches or sharp head pains	0 1 2 3
6. Has difficulty accepting unexpected changes in schedule	0 1 2 3
7. Has difficulty with transitions from one activity to another	0 1 2 3
8. Does not perceive others' feelings accurately (for example, keeps talking when the other person is giving clear signals that it is time to be quiet)	0 1 2 3
9. Makes comments that are frequently irrelevant or off the topic being discussed	0 1 2 3
10. Blurts out tactless statements about others (for example, says aloud, "That person is fat")	0 1 2 3
11. Often moves too fast; seldom slows down	0 1 2 3
12. Has difficulty sustaining friendships; loses friendships after a short time	0 1 2 3
13. Has very little confidence in his or her own judgment	0 1 2 3
14. Lacks initiative (waits for directions before starting something)	0 1 2 3
15. Is unable to focus or stay on task without constant redirection	0 1 2 3
16. Smells or licks objects	0 1 2 3
17. Responds to changes in temperature differently from others (for example, is always cold when others are comfortable or warm)	0 1 2 3
18. Prefers spicier foods or asks for more seasoning on foods (compared to preferences in his or her younger years)	0 1 2 3
19. Complains of hearing ringing, buzzing, or tapping noises	0 1 2 3
20. Is impatient to have his or her needs met	0 1 2 3
21. Seldom changes his or her facial expression, even when he or she is mad, sad, or happy	0 1 2 3
22. Has difficulty memorizing even simple information	0 1 2 3
23. Is too easily led by other children or adolescents	0 1 2 3
24. Says or does things unexpectedly, or "out of the blue," that are unrelated to what is going on	0 1 2 3
25. Complains that food tastes or smells bad or rotten when the food is *not* bad or rotten	0 1 2 3
26. Has difficulty applying intelligence in practical ways	0 1 2 3
27. Misreads social situations	0 1 2 3
28. Puts nonfood items (for example, small toys) in mouth	0 1 2 3
29. Completes work appropriately only if the task is highly structured and predictable	0 1 2 3

(Continued)

Table 24-9 (*Continued*)				
Items	\multicolumn{4}{c}{**Circle one**}			
30. Sometimes stares off, unaware of what's going on around him or her	0	1	2	3
31. Has temper tantrums over things that are insignificant	0	1	2	3
32. Is restless or fidgety	0	1	2	3
33. Has decreased appreciation of dangerous situations	0	1	2	3
34. Tends to be withdrawn	0	1	2	3
35. Behaves like a child several years younger than he or she is	0	1	2	3
36. Complains of seeing things that other people cannot see	0	1	2	3
37. Checks the refrigerator or cupboards for snacks just a few minutes after eating a meal (never seems to be full)	0	1	2	3
38. Is puzzled when social situations do not go well	0	1	2	3
39. Is confused concerning time sequences	0	1	2	3
40. Has difficulty acting spontaneously; would prefer to just sit and do nothing	0	1	2	3
41. Sometimes seems confused, but confusion lasts only a short time	0	1	2	3
42. Seems unaware of others' feelings (for example, does not realize that someone is upset; does not understand why)	0	1	2	3
43. Completes school work too quickly	0	1	2	3
44. Overdoes or exaggerates expressions of emotion or expresses emotion inappropriate to the situation (for example, says "I love you" to a stranger)	0	1	2	3
45. Complains that food is tasteless	0	1	2	3
46. Feels sad or cries for no reason; has no explanation for the sad feelings	0	1	2	3
47. Is inflexible; insists on doing what he or she wants to do	0	1	2	3
48. Has difficulty modulating tone of voice appropriately (for example, shouts or uses harsh tone when only mildly irritated)	0	1	2	3
49. Has quick and dramatic mood changes (extremely happy one minute, extremely sad the next)	0	1	2	3
50. Fails to learn from positive or negative consequences	0	1	2	3
51. Seems to forget having had conversations with people	0	1	2	3
52. Repeats the same behavior over and over	0	1	2	3
53. Responds only to what is right here and now; does not think about what happened yesterday or what could happen tomorrow	0	1	2	3
54. Breaks into conversation abruptly or awkwardly	0	1	2	3

Note. Items are classified into the following five scales:

- Mental Inertia Scale: 1, 3, 13, 14, 22, 23, 26, 29, 34, 39, 40, 53
- Social Inappropriateness Scale: 4, 9, 10, 11, 12, 15, 20, 32, 33, 35, 43, 54
- Dissociation of Affect and Behavior Scale: 6, 7, 8, 21, 27, 38, 42, 44, 47, 48, 50, 52
- Episodic Scale: 2, 5, 19, 24, 25, 30, 31, 36, 41, 46, 49, 51
- Biologic Scale: 16, 17, 18, 28, 37, 45

The Mental Inertia Scale indicates reduced initiation of appropriate behavior. A student with problems on the Mental Inertia Scale would benefit from increased environmental structure and coaching or prompting. The Social Inappropriateness Scale indicates failure to inhibit inappropriate behavior. A student with problems on the Social Inappropriateness Scale would benefit from referral to a physician to assess the appropriateness of stimulant medication. Implementing positive daily routines also would be helpful. The Dissociation of Affect and Behavior Scale indicates inability to modulate emotional responses as well as reduced capacity to read other people's emotions or behavior. A student with problems on the Dissociation of Affect and Behavior Scale would benefit from structured social expe-

riences. The Episodic Scale indicates sensory, cognitive, and emotional symptoms that come and go for no apparent reason or with minimal provocation. A student with problems on the Episodic Scale would benefit from a neurobehavioral evaluation to assess the appropriateness of anticonvulsants or mood stabilizers. The Biologic Scale indicates alterations in basic biological functions. A student with problems on the Biologic Scale has a high probability of deficits in executive function and would benefit from of a more structured and safe environment. A functional academic program (e.g., practicing math skills in the real-world environment of the grocery store) is often beneficial, particularly as the student reaches junior high grades.

Source: Reprinted, with adaptations and with permission of the author, from M. A. Roberts, "Pediatric Inventory of Neurobehavioral Symptoms," unpublished manuscript, University Hospital School, University of Iowa, Iowa City, Iowa 52242. Copyright © 1992. From *Assessment of Children: Behavioral, Social, and Clinical Foundations (Fifth Edition)* by Jerome M. Sattler and Robert D. Hoge. Copyright 2006 by Jerome M. Sattler, Publisher, Inc. Permission to photocopy this table is granted to purchasers of this book for personal use only (see copyright page for details).

Table 24-10
Pediatric Inventory of Neurobehavioral Symptoms–Self-Report (PINS–SR)

PINS–SELF-REPORT

Name: _____   Date: _____

Sex: (Circle one) Male   Female   Birth date: _____   Age: _____

Directions: Please circle one—T (True), F (False), or DK (Don't Know)—for each item.

Circle One

T	F	DK	1. I get confused a lot.
T	F	DK	2. It is hard for me to keep friends.
T	F	DK	3. Other people get upset with the way I talk or with what I say.
T	F	DK	4. I get headaches that keep me from doing things I enjoy.
T	F	DK	5. Sometimes food just tastes blah to me.
T	F	DK	6. I have a tough time coming up with ideas for things to do.
T	F	DK	7. I get in trouble for not paying attention in school.
T	F	DK	8. I often do or say the wrong thing when I am with other kids.
T	F	DK	9. People tell me about having conversations with me that I don't remember at all.
T	F	DK	10. I am always hungry.
T	F	DK	11. I can do my best when other people show me exactly what to do.
T	F	DK	12. Sometimes I do things that other people think are dangerous.
T	F	DK	13. I don't get many phone calls from friends.
T	F	DK	14. I sometimes get really upset over little things.
T	F	DK	15. I just don't know why I get into trouble all the time.
T	F	DK	16. People tell me I rush through my school work.
T	F	DK	17. Other kids make fun of me.
T	F	DK	18. I sometimes hear ringing, buzzing, or tapping noises.

Note. The PINS–SR is based on the PINS (see Table 24-9). Items are classified into the following five scales:

- Mental Inertia Scale: 1, 6, 11, 15
- Social Inappropriateness Scale: 2, 7, 12, 16
- Dissociation of Affect and Behavior Scale: 3, 8, 13, 17
- Episodic Scale: 4, 9, 14, 18
- Biologic Scale: 5, 10

The note in Table 24-9 describes each scale and relevant intervention guidelines.
Source: The PINS–SR was developed by Mary Ann Roberts and Jerome M. Sattler.
From *Assessment of Children: Behavioral, Social, and Clinical Foundations (Fifth Edition)* by Jerome M. Sattler and Robert D. Hoge. Copyright 2006 by Jerome M. Sattler, Publisher, Inc. Permission to photocopy this table is granted to purchasers of this book for personal use only (see copyright page for details).

Bender Visual Motor Gestalt Test, Bender-Gestalt II, and Beery VMI–Fifth Edition

The Bender Visual Motor Gestalt Test, the Bender-Gestalt II, and the Beery VMI–Fifth Edition, covered in Chapter 12, are useful for assessing visual-motor skills, primarily for children between ages 5 and 12 years. All three tests provide norms. They can be administered twice—first as a memory test and then as a copying test—to screen different mental functions, including short-term visual memory and visual perception.

Rey-Osterrieth Complex Figure Test

The Rey-Osterrieth Complex Figure Test (ROCFT) is a measure of children's visual-motor ability (see Figure 24-2). Detailed scoring systems are available (Bernstein & Waber, 1996; Loring, Martin, Meador, & Lee, 1990; Spreen & Strauss, 1998; Stern, Singer, Duke, Singer, Morey, Daughtrey, & Kaplan, 1994; Taylor, 1959). Qualitative characteristics of the initial copy phase have been found to discriminate between a number of clinical groups (Baron, 2004). The

Table 24-11
Adolescent Brain Injury Symptom Checklist

ADOLESCENT BRAIN INJURY SYMPTOM CHECKLIST

Name: _____ Date: _____

Directions: Please read each item and circle one number in each column. Note that each column has a different scale. Use the description of each scale below to make your rating.

	Scale		
	Frequency	*Intensity*	*Duration*
	1 = Not at all	1 = Not at all	1 = Not at all
	2 = Seldom	2 = Vaguely present	2 = A few seconds
	3 = Often	3 = Clearly present	3 = A few minutes
	4 = Very often	4 = Interfering	4 = A few hours
	5 = All the time	5 = Crippling	5 = Constant

	Frequency	*Intensity*	*Duration*
Complaint	**Circle one**	**Circle one**	**Circle one**
1. Headache	1 2 3 4 5	1 2 3 4 5	1 2 3 4 5
2. Dizziness	1 2 3 4 5	1 2 3 4 5	1 2 3 4 5
3. Nausea and/or vomiting	1 2 3 4 5	1 2 3 4 5	1 2 3 4 5
4. Sleep disturbance	1 2 3 4 5	1 2 3 4 5	1 2 3 4 5
5. Easily fatigued	1 2 3 4 5	1 2 3 4 5	1 2 3 4 5
6. Blurred vision	1 2 3 4 5	1 2 3 4 5	1 2 3 4 5
7. Easily upset by bright light	1 2 3 4 5	1 2 3 4 5	1 2 3 4 5
8. Double vision	1 2 3 4 5	1 2 3 4 5	1 2 3 4 5
9. Memory problems	1 2 3 4 5	1 2 3 4 5	1 2 3 4 5
10. Difficulty concentrating	1 2 3 4 5	1 2 3 4 5	1 2 3 4 5
11. Judgment problems	1 2 3 4 5	1 2 3 4 5	1 2 3 4 5
12. Irritability	1 2 3 4 5	1 2 3 4 5	1 2 3 4 5
13. Aggravated by noise	1 2 3 4 5	1 2 3 4 5	1 2 3 4 5
14. Frustrated or impatient	1 2 3 4 5	1 2 3 4 5	1 2 3 4 5
15. Anxiety	1 2 3 4 5	1 2 3 4 5	1 2 3 4 5
16. Depressed or tearful	1 2 3 4 5	1 2 3 4 5	1 2 3 4 5
17. Temper outburst	1 2 3 4 5	1 2 3 4 5	1 2 3 4 5
18. Staring spells	1 2 3 4 5	1 2 3 4 5	1 2 3 4 5

Source: Adapted from Gouvier, Cubic, Jones, Brantley, and Cutlip (1992) and King (1996).
From *Assessment of Children: Behavioral, Social, and Clinical Foundations (Fifth Edition)* by Jerome M. Sattler and Robert D. Hoge. Copyright 2006 by Jerome M. Sattler, Publisher, Inc. Permission to photocopy this table is granted to purchasers of this book for personal use only (see copyright page for details).

ROCFT also can be used as a memory test, with the memory phase administered after the copying phase. A comparison of the initial drawing and the drawing recalled from memory may provide useful information. However, several well-standardized measures of learning and memory in children should be considered preferable for assessment of memory. The ROCFT memory trial should be considered supplemental to other formal assessments of memory and learning. Chil-

Courtesy of Herman Zielinski.

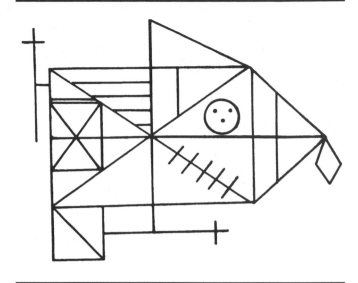

Figure 24-2. Rey-Osterrieth Complex Figure Test.

dren with brain injuries may do poorly on the test because of difficulties in organizing perceptual material or because of deficits in visual or spatial abilities, drawing, planning, or other factors. However, children with similar difficulties and no known brain injury may also do poorly on the ROCFT.

Benton Visual Retention Test–Revised–Fifth Edition

The Benton Visual Retention Test–Revised–Fifth Edition (BVRT; Sivan, 1992) assesses visual memory, visual perception, and visuoconstructive abilities in children 8 years old and older. It has three forms, with 10 designs in each form. The child copies the designs directly from the cards and also draws them from memory. You score the test by counting the number of correct responses or the number of errors. Norms are available in Baron (2004) for children ages 8 to 14 years. The Benton Visual Retention Test–Revised is similar to the Bender-Gestalt, but it contains more complex stimuli.

Bruininks-Oseretsky Test of Motor Proficiency

The Bruininks-Oseretsky Test of Motor Proficiency (see Chapter 12) contributes to the assessment of brain injury because it reliably measures fine- and gross-motor functions.

Purdue Pegboard

The Purdue Pegboard measures sensorimotor functions, particularly in the area of fine-motor coordination, that are essentially independent of educational achievement. In the first three 30-second parts of the test, the child places pegs in a pegboard, first with the preferred hand, then with the nonpreferred hand, and finally with both hands. In the fourth part of the test, which takes 60 seconds, the child forms "assemblies" out of a peg, a washer, a collar, and another washer. This test is a quick, simple instrument that has value for predicting the presence and laterality of cerebral injury. Norms are available for preschool children ages 2-6 to 5-11 years (Wilson, Iacoviello, Wilson, & Risucci, 1982), for school-age children ages 5-0 to 16-11 years (Gardner, 1979; Spreen & Strauss, 1998), and for adolescents ages 14-0 to 18-11 years (Mathiowetz, Rogers, Dowe-Keval, Donahoe, & Rennells, 1986). The Purdue Pegboard permits comparison of lower-level sensorimotor functions with higher-level cognitive functions, and it provides information about lateralized or bilateral deficits.

Grooved Pegboard Test

The Grooved Pegboard Test is a widely used test that assesses speed and eye-hand coordination (Baron, 2004). The grooved pegboard, containing five rows of keyhole shapes, is placed at the child's midline so that the peg tray is above the board. Children 9 years old and older place all 25 keyhole-shaped pegs into the holes on the board, beginning with their preferred hand. Following the trial with their preferred hand, the task is repeated with their nonpreferred hand. Children 5 to 8 years of age complete the first two rows. The child is instructed to place the pegs as quickly as possible without skipping any holes and using one hand at a time. Baron (2004) provides normative data for children.

Test of Right-Left Discrimination

Table 24-12 shows a set of instructions and questions that are useful for obtaining information about a child's understanding of right and left. You must consider the child's age when you interpret the results.

Finger Localization Test

Another procedure for evaluating soft neurological signs is the Finger Localization Test (see Table 24-13). Again, always keep the child's age in mind when considering the results.

Verbal Fluency Tests

Tests of verbal fluency are useful in assessing word-finding ability in children with brain injuries. Verbal fluency can be defined as the ability to retrieve words that belong to a specified category in a given time period. Note that the term *verbal fluency* also is used in speech and language pathology to reflect rate or rhythm of speech—relative to, for example, stuttering or aphasic disruption of phrasing. Factors associated with verbal fluency include the abilities to accumulate and store items and to access the stored information within a limited amount of time. The two different types of verbal fluency tests shown in Table 24-14 require different kinds of se-

---

Table 24-12
Right-Left Discrimination Test

1. "Raise your right hand."
2. "Touch your left ear."
3. "Point to your right eye."
4. "Raise your left hand."
5. "Show me your right leg."
6. "Show me your left leg."
7. "Point to your left ear with your right hand."
8. "Point to the wall on your right."
9. Examiner touches the child's left hand: "Which hand is this?"
10. Examiner touches his or her own right eye: "Which eye is this?"
11. Examiner touches his or her own right hand: "Which hand is this?
12. Examiner touches his or her own left ear: "Which ear is this?"
13. With the child's eyes closed, the examiner touches the child's left ear: "Which ear is this?"
14. Examiner touches his or her own left hand: "Which hand is this?"
15. Examiner touches his or her own left eye: "Which eye is this?"
16. Examiner touches child's right hand: "Which hand is this?"

Scoring: Give 1 point for each correct response.

Source: Adapted from Belmont and Birch (1965) and Croxen and Lytton (1971).

Table 24-13
Finger Localization Test

Directions: Show the child numbered diagrams of a right hand and a left hand. The child "localizes" by indicating the finger touched, either by pointing to it on the diagram, indicating its number, or naming it. You may touch the child's fingertips with a paper clip or pencil point.

Subtest	Instructions
I. Visual Subtest	Ask the child to extend her or his arm with the palm of the hand up. Allowing the child to see his or her hand, ask the child to localize single fingers that have been tactually stimulated. Give 10 stimulations to each hand. Touch each finger twice in a randomized order. Maximum score = 20.
II. Tactual Subtest	Ask the child to extend her or his arm with the palm of the hand up. Using a card as a shield to prevent the child from seeing her or his hand, ask the child to localize single fingers that have been tactually stimulated. Give 10 stimulations to each hand. Touch each finger twice in a randomized order. Maximum score = 20.
III. Tactual Pairs Subtest	This subtest is like the Tactual Subtest, but the child localizes two fingers that have been tactually stimulated simultaneously. Give 10 stimulations to each hand. Touch every possible combination on each hand. Maximum score = 20.

Scoring: Give 1 point for each correct response. For the Tactual Pairs Subtest, a misidentification of either one or both of the fingers is counted as a single error. Maximum score = 60.

Source: Adapted from Benton (1959) and Croxen and Lytton (1971).

---

mantic processing. The Animal-Naming Test requires retrieval from a narrowly defined category, with words accessed according to their meaning; this task involves a semantic factor. In contrast, the Controlled Word Association Test (naming as many words as possible that begin with a certain letter) requires retrieval from different logical categories, with word meanings becoming irrelevant or being suppressed; this task involves a symbolic factor. When you give both tests, you can make comparisons between the child's semantic and symbolic word-finding abilities. If a child cannot speak, the responses can be written. You must consider the child's age and intelligence when evaluating the results of verbal fluency tests.

The NEPSY Verbal Fluency subtest has normative data for children ages 3 to 6 years for responses to semantic cues and for children ages 7 to 12 years for responses to both semantic cues (animals, things to eat and drink) and phonemic cues (the letters S and F). The Delis-Kaplan Executive Function System (D-KEFS), discussed later in the chapter, con-

Table 24-14
Informal Measures of Verbal Fluency

Test	Directions
Animal-Naming Test	"Give the names of as many animals as you can think of. Begin." Allow 60 seconds.
Controlled Word Association Test	"Give as many words as you can think of that begin with the letter *F*. Do not give names of persons—like Frank or Florence—or names of states or cities—like Florida or Fresno—or other proper names. Begin." Allow 60 seconds. Then say, "Now give as many words as you can think of that begin with the letter *A*. Again do not give proper names. Begin." Allow 60 seconds. Then say, "Now give as many words as you can think of that begin with the letter *S*. Again do not give proper names. Begin." Allow 60 seconds.

Scoring: Give 1 point for each correct response. Do not count repetitions, proper nouns, or different forms of the same word.

Note. Verbal fluency tests can be administered either orally or in a written format. For children younger than 7 or 8 years of age, the written format generally is not appropriate. With older children, it may be valuable occasionally to compare oral and written performances on the same tests. The directions above are for the oral version. For the written version, substitute the word *write* for *give*. Tentative norms for the Animal-Naming Test, with a 1-minute time interval, are as follows (Levin, Culhane, Hartmann, Evankovich, Mattson, Harward, Ringholz, Ewing-Cobbs, & Fletcher, 1991): 7 to 8 years, $M = 14.4$ ($SD = 4.7$); 9 to 12 years, $M = 18.2$ ($SD = 4.5$); 13 to 15 years, $M = 21.1$ ($SD = 5.0$).

tains norms for fluency tests, as do the Kaufman Test of Educational Achievement II (KTEA II) and Barron (2004).

Picture Naming

You can measure *dysnomia* (difficulty in naming objects) with the WISC–IV Picture Completion subtest (or any other test that has pictures of objects). Use the following procedure to screen for dysnomia: Point to a part of a picture on each card and ask, "What is this called?" You can use a similar procedure with the WAIS–III and the WPPSI–R Picture Completion subtests. The Boston Naming Test is another procedure useful for evaluating naming ability (Kaplan, Goodglass, & Weintraub, 1983; Yeates, 1994).

Receptive vs. Expressive Vocabulary

The Peabody Picture Vocabulary Test–III and the Expressive Vocabulary Test allow comparison of performance on a receptive vocabulary test with that on an expressive vocabulary (picture naming) test normed on the same standardization group (see Sattler, 2001).

Informal Measures of Spatial Orientation

To evaluate a child's spatial orientation informally, you can ask the child to do the following (the age at which the ability emerges is shown in parentheses): (a) draw a person (about 5 years), (b) print numbers 3, 5, 6, 7, 9 (5 to 6 years), (c) print lowercase letters b, d, q, w, z, m, n (5½ to 6½ years), (d) draw a clock that shows 9 a.m. (7½ to 8½ years), and (e) print or write three sentences saying what he or she did last night (about 7½ years).

Informal Measures of Writing Ability

You can assess a child's writing ability in several ways (Rapcsak, 1997). You can ask her or him to (a) write individual letters, (b) write her or his name, (c) write a sentence, (d) write a paragraph that tells a story, (e) spell orally, type, and spell using blocks with letters, (f) write in a different case or style and transcribe from uppercase to lowercase and from print to script, and (g) copy letters, words, nonwords, and nonlinguistic visual patterns (e.g., Bender-Gestalt designs). These informal measures will help you clarify the relationships among the various output modalities and determine more precisely the nature of the child's functional impairment. For example, in certain cases a child with a brain injury cannot write letters from dictation but can copy letters. This, of course, also has implications for the child's educational program.

Informal Measures of Divergent Thinking

The assessment of divergent thinking provides information about the child's ability to formulate new ideas and produce a variety of responses. Supplementing standardized cognitive measures, which usually assess mainly convergent thinking, with informal measures of divergent thinking may yield additional information about a child's thinking style. These measures may be of special value in the assessment of children with brain injuries and culturally and linguistically diverse children, as well as in the general assessment of creativity. Table 24-15 illustrates a variety of informal divergent thinking tasks.

Raven's Progressive Matrices

The Raven's Progressive Matrices test provides an estimate of a child's nonverbal cognitive ability. A child suspected of having a brain injury who performs more poorly on Raven's Progressive Matrices (see Sattler, 2001) than on verbal intelligence tests may have nonverbal reasoning difficulties. The child may be able to concentrate on only one aspect of the stimulus array and thus may be unable to integrate the necessary spatial relationships to arrive at a correct response. In such cases, do not use the child's performance on Raven's

Table 24-15
Informal Measures of Divergent Thinking

Test	Description	Example
Unusual Uses	Child is asked to identify novel ways to use specific common objects.	Use the following instructions (Price-Williams & Ramirez, 1977, p. 7): "Let's see how clever you can be about using things. For instance, if I asked you how many ways an old tire could be used, you might say to fix up an old car, for a swing, to roll around and run with, to cut up for shoe soles, and so on. Now if I asked you 'How many ways can you use a pebble?' what would you say?" After you give these instructions, ask the child to give uses for a newspaper, a table knife, a coffee cup, a clock, and money. Two scores are obtained: an ideational fluency score (the sum of the uses mentioned for all five objects) and an ideational flexibility score (the sum of the different categories of usage for each object). The following examples illustrate the scoring. As a response to "newspaper," "to read, to make a mat, and to use as an umbrella" receives a fluency score of 3 and a flexibility score of 3. As a response to "table knife," "to cut your meat and cut other things" receives a fluency score of 2 and a flexibility score of 1. The two scores also form an efficiency index (ratio of flexibility score to fluency score).
Common Situations	Child is asked to list problems inherent in a common situation.	"Tell me some problems that someone might have while walking with a crutch."
Product Improvement	Child is asked to suggest ways to improve an object.	"Think of different ways to improve a toy car so that you would have more fun playing with it.'"
Consequences	Child is asked to list the effects of a new and unusual event.	"Just suppose that people no longer needed or wanted automobiles. What would happen? Tell me your ideas and guesses."
Object Naming	Child is asked to list objects that belong to a broad class of objects.	"Name as many objects as you can that cut."
Differences	Child is asked to suggest ways in which two objects are different.	"Tell me the ways in which a spoon and a ball are different."
Similarities	Child is asked to suggest ways in which two objects are alike.	"Tell me the ways in which cheese and vegetables are alike."
Word Arrangements	Child is asked to produce sentences containing specified words.	"Make up a sentence containing the words *dog* and *walked*."
Word Fluency	Child is asked to say words that contain a specified word or letter.	"What words have the /b/ sound in them?"
Possibilities	Child is asked to list objects that can be used to perform a certain task.	"Tell me as many different things as you can that can be used to write with."
Quick Response	Child is asked to say the first word that he or she can think of in response to words read aloud.	"What is the first word you think of when I say *run*?"
Associational Fluency	Child is asked to list synonyms for a given word.	"What words mean the same as *big*?"
Social Institutions	Child is asked to list two improvements for a social institution.	"Tell me two ways that you could improve or change marriage."

Table 24-15 (*Continued*)		
Test	*Description*	*Example*
Planning Elaboration	Child is asked to detail the steps needed to make a briefly outlined work plan.	"Your club is planning to have a party. You are in charge of the arrangements. What will you do?"
Ask and Guess	Child is encouraged to ask questions about a particular picture or to guess possible consequences of actions presented in the picture.	Show the child a picture of a boat. "Here is a picture of a boat. What are some questions that you can ask about the picture?"
What Would	Child is asked to think of items that could be improved if changed in a particular way.	"What would taste better if it were sweeter?"
Criteria	Child is asked to tell the criteria that might be used in judging an activity or object.	"Tell me some reasons why people might like to eat apple pie."
Questions	Child is asked to list questions related to specified words.	"What questions could you ask about the word *city*?"

Note. These measures are primarily useful for children ages 10 years and older.
Source: The tasks are from Guilford and Hoepfner (1971), Parnes (1966), and Torrance and Myers (1970).

Progressive Matrices to estimate his or her general intelligence. The strategies needed to solve Raven's Progressive Matrices are not unique to either hemisphere (Zaidel, Zaidel, & Sperry, 1981). For example, a child could solve the matrices either with an analytic strategy (i.e., sampling one element at a time) or with a synthetic strategy (i.e., grouping patterns into larger units or wholes). Consequently, do not assess lateralization of injury based on performance on Raven's Progressive Matrices. Note that the WISC–IV, SB:IV, DAS, WAIS–III, and K–BIT (see Chapter 16 in Sattler, 2001), for example, allow comparison of performance on a matrix subtest with that on verbal subtests normed on the same standardization group.

Token Test for Children

The Token Test for Children (DiSimoni, 1978) is useful as a screening test of receptive language (auditory comprehension) for children between 3-0 and 12-5 years of age. Other versions are available for older adolescents and adults (De Renzi, 1980; De Renzi & Faglioni, 1978). The test requires children to manipulate tokens in response to commands given by the examiner, such as "Touch the red circle." The commands vary in length and syntactic complexity. The 20 tokens vary in color, shape, and size. The Token Test is a sensitive indicator of mild receptive disturbances in aphasic children who have passed other auditory tests. The test is only a screening device, because its psychometric properties and norms are not well established; however, it is a useful instrument for the assessment of receptive aphasia. See Spreen and Strauss (1998) for normative data for children ages 6 to 13 years.

Reporter's Test

The Reporter's Test is a useful screening test for examining expressive language (De Renzi & Ferrari, 1978). You administer the test by performing various actions on an array of 20 tokens. The child is asked to report the performance verbally in a way that would enable a hypothetical third person to replicate your actions. For example, if you touch the large yellow square, the child must state the relevant information so that the imaginary third person can perform the action. A correct response would be "Touch the large yellow square." The child must produce an accurately connected sequence of words. Research suggests that the Reporter's Test provides useful information for assessing expressive language (Ballantyne & Sattler, 1991; Feldman, 1984; Hall & Jordan, 1985; Jordan & Hall, 1985). The Reporter's Test complements the Token Test and usually is administered after the Token Test.

Memory and Learning Tests

Impaired memory and learning ability are commonly observed in children who have experienced a traumatic brain injury (as well as in children with developmental disorders and, in some cases, with specific learning disabilities). Typically, the measures used to assess memory focus on explicit or episodic memory (see Chapter 23 for a discussion of several types of memory) or on the rate of learning and recall (retrieval) of material following a delay. For example, children are asked to remember a list of words read to them, remember the location of a series of dots, or learn and recall material (typically stories) following a single exposure.

The following tests are useful measures of memory and learning:

- California Verbal Learning Test–Children's Version (CVLT–C; Delis, Kramer, Kaplan, & Ober, 1994)
- Children's Auditory Verbal Learning Test–Second Edition (CAVLT–2; Talley, 1993)
- Children's Memory Scale (CMS; Cohen, 1997)
- Rey Auditory-Verbal Learning Test (RAVLT; Forrester & Geffen, 1991; Savage & Gouvier, 1992; Taylor, 1959)
- Tests of Memory and Learning (TOMAL; Reynolds & Bigler, 1994)
- Wide Range Assessment of Memory and Learning–Second Edition (WRAML–2; Adams & Sheslow, 2003)
- Rivermead Behavioural Memory Test for Children (RBMTC; Wilson, Ivani-Chalian, & Aldrich, 1991)

Attention Tests

Problems with attention and memory are common following traumatic brain injuries. Persistent difficulties with attention may continue long after an injury and may interfere with success in many settings, including school and leisure activities. Attention is a multidimensional construct and has such dimensions as the abilities to focus, execute, sustain, encode, and shift (Mirsky, Anthony, Duncan, Ahearn, & Kellam, 1991). The Test of Everyday Attention for Children (TEA-Ch; Manly, Robertson, Anderson, & Nimmo-Smith, 1999) is useful for measuring attention in children between the ages of 6 and 16 years. Continuous performance tests also provide information about attention, as do intelligence tests (see Chapter 15).

Tests of Executive Functions

As noted in Chapter 23, executive functions include a broad range of higher-order cognitive processes such as planning, set maintenance, impulse control, working memory, and attentional control. Baron (2004) has information and normative data on a large number of measures of executive functions.

The Delis-Kaplan Executive Function System (D-KEFS; Delis, Kaplan, & Kramer, 2001) contains nine individual tests designed to measure various aspects of executive functioning and covers ages 8 years to 89 years. The nine measures are as follows:

- Sorting Test (measures problem solving, verbal and spatial concept formation, and flexibility of thinking)
- Trail Making Test (measures flexibility of thinking on a visual-motor task)
- Verbal Fluency Test (measures fluent productivity in the verbal domain)
- Design Fluency Test (measures fluent productivity in the spatial domain)
- Color-Word Interference Test (measures verbal inhibition)
- Tower Test (measures planning and reasoning and impulsivity)

- 20 Question Test (measures hypothesis testing and verbal and spatial abstract thinking)
- Word Context Test (measures deductive reasoning)
- Proverb Test (measures metaphorical thinking and comprehending abstract thought)

The Behavior Rating Inventory of Executive Function (BRIEF; Gioia, Isquith, Guy, & Kenworthy, 2000) is a set of questionnaires designed to evaluate executive functions. They are completed by parents, teachers, and the child. The BRIEF includes normative data for children 5 to 18 years of age. It is based on a principal components analysis and has eight subdomains, two indices, and an overall composite. The BRIEF is useful in assessing and monitoring the progress of children who have experienced a traumatic brain injury, as well as children with a developmental disorder.

EVALUATING THE ASSESSMENT FINDINGS

A comprehensive neuropsychological evaluation may reveal disturbances in a child's motor, sensory, affective, cognitive, and social behavior and in the child's temperament and personality. For example, intellectual deficits may be revealed by a global reduction in IQ or by reduced efficiency in specific performance or verbal areas. During the early stages of brain injury, symptoms such as hallucinations may mimic the symptoms of psychiatric disorders. Brain injury itself may play a major role in predisposing children to severe forms of psychopathology, as well as to subtle changes in personality. Brain injury also may exacerbate a subclinical psychiatric condition that was present before the injury.

Inferential Methods of Test Analysis

You can use several inferential methods to analyze the data you obtain from a neuropsychological test battery.

1. *Level of performance.* This approach involves comparing the child's test scores with cutoff points based on a normative sample. The level-of-performance approach is based on quantification of behavioral data. However, establishing cutoff points is not easy, because the performances of normal children vary greatly. Additionally, poor scores might be caused by factors unrelated to the brain injury, such as behavioral problems, poor motivation, attention problems, sensory difficulties, other developmental disabilities, and testing conditions. The level-of-performance approach, if used exclusively, may generate high false positive rates—some children will be identified as brain injured when in fact they are not. However, the approach is useful for comparing a child's present performance with past performance in order to pinpoint changes.

When you do not have preinjury scores, estimates of a child's preinjury level can be made from scores on nationally standardized measures of intellectual ability, measures of achievement found on grade school and high school transcripts, Scholastic Aptitude Test scores, school grades, test scores, teachers' and parents' reports, special class placements, work products, and employment history (for adolescents). For example, a 10-year-old child in the fourth grade with an A average probably had at least average or high-average ability before the brain injury was sustained. If an intelligence test administered after the brain injury indicates an IQ in the 70 to 80 range (or below), there is a strong possibility that the child's ability has decreased considerably. You can also use test scores that are relatively resistant to the effects of brain injury, such as scores on tests of vocabulary ability and reading ability (assuming that the child does not have a history of dyslexia). Finally, you can consider the mean of the natural parents' educational or intelligence levels (assuming that the parents are not socioeconomically disadvantaged), although Redfield (2001) advises being cautious about drawing conclusions on the basis of discrepancies between familial IQ and the child's IQ.

2. *Pattern of performance.* The aim of this approach is to obtain information about functional deficits and strengths by considering the pattern of results among several tests and within each test.

3. *Pathognomonic signs of brain injury.* This approach focuses on signs of pathology in the test performance (such as aphasic or apractic disturbances, visual field defects, or severe memory disturbances) and on neurological tests (such as EEG abnormalities). The pathognomonic approach assumes that certain indices on neuropsychological tests and on the neurological examination reflect brain impairment. However, the pathognomonic approach, if used exclusively, may generate high false negative rates—some children will be identified as not brain injured when in fact they are. This is because the absence of signs is not necessarily an indication of health. The pathognomonic approach may also lead to false positives. For example, EEG abnormalities may not necessarily indicate the presence of brain injury, and a single anomalous score in the neuropsychological evaluation may be due to chance (error variance).

4. *Comparison of performance on the two sides of the body.* This approach relies on lateralization of deficits—the relative efficiency of the right versus the left side of the body. The focus, therefore, is primarily on tests of lower-level motor, sensory, and sensorimotor functioning. Although the child serves as his or her own control (one side of the body versus the other side), you will find that normative data are useful. The normative data, which should be age standardized, provide information about the absolute level of performance for each side of the body. Do not use this approach exclusively in the assessment, because unilateral injury may not always produce lateralized motor or sensory difficulties. Also, this approach tells only about lower-level brain functions, not about higher-level brain functions that are particularly important for learning and everyday functioning.

You should compare the findings resulting from each approach to arrive at a diagnostic impression; do not use one method exclusively.

Diagnostic Considerations

The diagnostic effort should be based on all of the information you have obtained from formal and informal assessment procedures, including information from the case history. You will want to consider the following questions:

1. What are the relevant background characteristics of the child?
   * Age at the time of the injury
   * Gender
   * Handedness
   * Cultural and linguistic background
   * Medical history
   * Educational history
   * Family history
   * Developmental history
   * Overall adjustment before the injury
   * Level of cognitive, perceptual-motor, and affective functioning before the injury
   * Behavior, temperament, personality, and interpersonal skills before the injury

2. What aspects of the developmental history are important (Middleton, 2004)?
   * Prenatal factors (mother's health and health-related behavior such as smoking, use of alcohol or other drugs, maternal trauma, or illnesses such as phenylketonuria or epilepsy)
   * Perinatal events (neurological damage associated with mechanical causes or hypoxia, difficult birth, very low birth weight, premature birth) and Apgar score (which indicates the physical status of the neonate)
   * Developmental milestones and increases or decreases in height and weight

3. What aspects of the medical history are important (Middleton, 2004)?
   * Sensory functioning (hearing, vision)
   * Systemic illness (illnesses that affect the entire body, such as high blood pressure or influenza)
   * Neurological illness
   * Previous head injuries
   * Epilepsy (seizures, febrile convulsion, infantile spasms)
   * Substance abuse
   * Toxic exposure
   * Allergies
   * Psychiatric disorders (such as depression, ADHD)
   * Interventions attempted and their outcomes

4. What aspects of the educational history are important (Middleton, 2004)?
   * School grades
   * Test scores
   * Teacher reports (such as reports about the child's attention, memory, planning, behavior, and social interactions)

5. What aspects of the family background are important (Middleton, 2004)?

- Education of the parents and siblings
- Any illnesses of a genetic origin in parents and siblings
- Any learning disabilities in parents and siblings
- Possible impact of cultural and linguistic factors on the child's neurological problems
- Behavior of siblings with child: Are siblings kind to the child (making sure that the child always has his or her books, repeating things often because the child tends to forget things, avoiding games that require kicking and throwing because the child has difficulty with them) or do siblings reject or tease the child?

6. What are the neurological/medical findings?
   - Type of brain injury
   - Lateralization of the brain injury
   - Location of the brain injury
   - Severity of the brain injury
   - Immediate effects of the brain injury (including loss of consciousness and duration of coma, if relevant)
   - Delayed effects of the brain injury (if relevant)
   - Diaschisis effects (effects of the brain injury on undamaged parts of the brain)
   - Treatment (including any hospitalization)
   - Prognosis

7. What are the results of the neuropsychological evaluation (Kay & Silver, 1989)? (See Table 24-16 for symptoms associated with brain injuries.)
   - *Affect, temperament, motivation, and behavior modulation* (ability to display the appropriate affect for the situation, display appropriate motivation, and behave in a planned, good-natured, and calm manner)
   - *Arousal level* (ability to initiate activities, including behaviors that are purposeful, thoughtful, consistent, and independent)
   - *Attention and speed of information processing* (ability to focus, sustain, shift, and divide attention)
   - *Compensatory functions* (awareness of and ability to compensate for deficits)
   - *Executive functioning* (ability to plan, organize, monitor, modulate, and adjust behavior; ability to perceive task elements accurately, select a strategy, integrate information, and reach a solution; awareness of behavior, including level of orientation and awareness of deficits)
   - *Higher complex cognitive functions* (ability to use words to convey desired meanings adequately; ability to think abstractly, integrate new information, and generalize and apply information flexibly across changing situations)
   - *Learning and memory* (ability to learn and retain new information and recall previously learned information)
   - *Interpersonal skills* (ability to interact with others in a meaningful way)
   - *Motor skills* (ability to perform fine- and gross-motor movements)
   - *Self-care skills* (ability to take care of personal needs, including dressing, feeding, bathing, and other aspects of personal hygiene)

The results of the neuropsychological evaluation should help you answer such questions as the following (Middleton, 2001):

- Has the child shown a loss of skills, failure to make progress since the brain injury, or a slow rate of learning?
- Is the child able to carry out everyday living tasks, grasp what is going on around him or her, process information in pressured as well as unpressured situations, gather and express thoughts, respond to questions or requests, and perform motor tasks such as catching a ball and walking across the street?
- Does the child forget simple instructions, have difficulty recalling instructions containing several items, lose belongings, forget homework, forget to bring home school announcements, forget what she or he has planned the next day, or forget where she or he has put things down?
- Does the child trip or bump into things, ignore things on one side of the field of vision, have difficulty writing (or drawing or copying), have problems doing puzzles or working with constructional toys, or have a poor aim while playing ball games?
- Is the child able to initiate conversations, speak clearly, express ideas clearly, follow conversations, understand jokes (and ambiguous and abstract concepts), express thoughts in writing, read with comprehension, and spell at a level commensurate with his or her age?
- Is the child able to organize his or her work (and room and clothes), plan homework and other activities, adhere to plans, initiate activities, and evaluate her or his work objectively?

8. How does the child's current level of functioning compare to her or his previous level of functioning? Information about the child's prior functioning is critical in evaluating the assessment results. For example, if a 6-year-old could not read *before* the accident, it's not surprising that the child cannot read *after* the accident. *You do not want to report a loss of functioning when the competency was never established in the first place.*

9. What resources do the family and community have to assist the child in his or her rehabilitation? Consider the family history, support systems available to the family, and the home, school, and community environment. Does the family have adequate transportation, insurance, and finances?

When you evaluate the information from the child's case history, use a normative-developmental framework (see inside front cover for developmental landmarks). For example, recognize that children usually crawl before they walk, babble before they say meaningful words, draw lines before they draw circles, and identify individual alphabet letters before they read whole words. A normative-developmental approach encourages you to consider, for example, that most children begin to use individual words by 18 months, draw circles by 3 years, and learn to read by 6 to 8 years. Answers to the questions in Table 25-1 will help you review the information obtained by the multidisciplinary health care team and

Table 24-16
Checklist of Symptoms Associated with Brain Injury

CHECKLIST OF SYMPTOMS ASSOCIATED WITH BRAIN INJURY

Name: _____   Date: _____

Physical	Y	N
1. Headaches	☐	☐
2. Vomiting	☐	☐
3. Seizures	☐	☐
4. Drowsiness	☐	☐
5. Psychomotor slowing	☐	☐
6. Slow reaction time	☐	☐
7. Hyperactivity	☐	☐
8. Muscle weakness	☐	☐
9. Stiffness	☐	☐
10. Paralysis	☐	☐
11. Dizziness	☐	☐
12. Head buzzing or tingling	☐	☐
13. Bowel problems	☐	☐
14. Bladder problems	☐	☐
15. Genital problems	☐	☐
16. Tics	☐	☐
17. Grimaces	☐	☐
18. Balance problems	☐	☐
19. Fatigue	☐	☐
20. Refusal to go to bed	☐	☐
21. Awakening frequently	☐	☐
22. Nightmares	☐	☐
23. Sleeping during the day	☐	☐
24. Loss of appetite	☐	☐
25. Overeating	☐	☐
26. Significant weight gain	☐	☐
27. Significant weight loss	☐	☐
28. Swallowing problems	☐	☐
29. Somatic concerns	☐	☐
30. Problems seeing	☐	☐
31. Problems hearing	☐	☐
32. Problems tasting	☐	☐
33. Problems speaking	☐	☐
34. Problems smelling	☐	☐
35. Abnormal sensations	☐	☐
36. Coordination problems	☐	☐

Affective

	Y	N
1. Difficulty modulating emotions	☐	☐
2. Marked shifts in mood	☐	☐
3. Depression	☐	☐
4. Anxiety	☐	☐
5. Irritability	☐	☐
6. Restlessness	☐	☐
7. Marked apathy	☐	☐

Affective (cont.)	Y	N
8. Inappropriate laughter	☐	☐
9. Talkativeness	☐	☐
10. Poor frustration tolerance	☐	☐
11. Guilt feelings	☐	☐
12. Moodiness	☐	☐
13. Anger	☐	☐
14. Aggression	☐	☐
15. Verbal outbursts	☐	☐
16. Indifference	☐	☐
17. Impulsiveness	☐	☐
18. Difficulty inhibiting actions	☐	☐
19. Quick temper	☐	☐
20. Agitation	☐	☐
21. Withdrawal	☐	☐
22. Boastfulness	☐	☐
23. Restricted emotions	☐	☐
24. Poor self-control	☐	☐

Cognitive

	Y	N
1. Alteration in consciousness	☐	☐
2. Confusion	☐	☐
3. Decreased intellectual efficiency	☐	☐
4. Difficulty generalizing	☐	☐
5. Problems following directions	☐	☐
6. Slow thought processes	☐	☐
7. Impaired orientation	☐	☐
8. Impaired judgment	☐	☐
9. Difficulties with spatial relationships	☐	☐
10. Inability to plan ahead	☐	☐
11. Concentration difficulties	☐	☐
12. Attention difficulties	☐	☐
13. Memory difficulties	☐	☐
14. Impaired organizational skills	☐	☐
15. Distractibility	☐	☐
16. Failure to learn from experience	☐	☐
17. Tangential communication	☐	☐
18. Irrelevant speech	☐	☐
19. Confabulation	☐	☐
20. Difficulties in understanding	☐	☐
21. Rigid and inflexible thinking	☐	☐

Cognitive (cont.)	Y	N
22. Deterioration of academic performance	☐	☐
23. Overly concrete thinking	☐	☐
24. Unusual thought content	☐	☐
25. Intrusive thoughts	☐	☐
26. Preoccupation with irrelevant details	☐	☐
27. Confusion when confronted with choices	☐	☐
28. Difficulty setting goals	☐	☐
29. Difficulty anticipating predictable outcomes	☐	☐

Social/Personality

	Y	N
1. Unkempt and careless appearance (when previously fastidious)	☐	☐
2. Performing crude bodily functions in public	☐	☐
3. Misperception of intentions of others	☐	☐
4. Making unusual remarks	☐	☐
5. Performing inappropriate actions	☐	☐
6. Difficulty in engaging in give-and-take conversations	☐	☐
7. Difficulty in respecting others' personal space	☐	☐
8. Loss of interest in friends	☐	☐
9. Regressive behavior	☐	☐
10. Bodily preoccupations	☐	☐
11. Lying	☐	☐
12. Stealing	☐	☐
13. Truancy	☐	☐
14. Sexual offenses	☐	☐
15. Uncooperativeness	☐	☐
16. Suspiciousness	☐	☐
17. Impolite speech	☐	☐
18. Coarse language	☐	☐
19. Poor table manners	☐	☐
20. Lack of concern for others	☐	☐
21. Limited initiative	☐	☐
22. Inaccurate insight and self-appraisal	☐	☐
23. Denial of deficits	☐	☐
24. Overdependence on parents	☐	☐
25. Difficulty accepting feedback	☐	☐

work with them to plan a rehabilitation program. Study each case thoroughly to identify the factors responsible for the behavioral effects shown by the child.

Qualitative analysis and testing-of-limits are primarily useful for generating, but not proving, hypotheses. These approaches are not standardized and do not have norms or validated guidelines for interpretation. Making interpretations from these approaches requires much experience. You must take care not to confuse an interesting hypothesis based on qualitative analysis with a finding that has received substantial empirical support. Nevertheless, qualitative analysis and testing-of-limits are important components of a neuropsychological assessment.

Brain injuries produce highly complex behavioral effects that lead to diagnostic difficulties. The reasons for the diagnostic difficulties are numerous.

1. Similar forms of brain injury do not always produce the same behavioral effects, nor do behavioral differences among children with brain injuries always relate directly to the severity of the injury or to their preinjury personality characteristics.
2. Some children with brain injuries are able to compensate for deficits and may not show markedly impaired performance on psychological or neuropsychological tests.
3. Conversely, because complex human behavior is multi-determined (e.g., by the integrity of the individual's brain, emotions, and motivational factors), impaired performance on psychological or neuropsychological tests does not necessarily mean that the individual has a brain injury.
4. Low test scores may be related to motivational difficulties, specific learning disabilities, anxiety, educational deficits, physical handicaps, cultural factors, developmental delays, or cerebral impairment. Thus, you cannot rely on level of performance as a key diagnostic sign in evaluating brain injury; you also must consider other factors.
5. Positive neurological findings may be present without observable behavioral correlates. For example, the brain injury may (a) affect specific deep reflexes or superficial reflexes only, (b) affect cranial nerves or other subcortical structures only, or (c) lead to transient epileptiform activity (brain waves that resemble those of an epileptic disorder but are not associated with any directly observable clinical indication of seizures). In addition, a child may develop successful compensatory strategies.
6. Neuropsychological tests may be insensitive to some subtle signs of behavioral disturbance.
7. Neuropsychological tests may reveal marked impairment in some areas of functioning, even though a neurological examination indicates intact functioning.
8. With evolving cerebral injury, there may be an interval when pathological brain processes develop without affecting the functions assessed by either the neurological or the neuropsychological examination.
9. Early in the development of pathology, the child's compensation for deficits may mask clinical manifestations of the injury.

10. It may be difficult to pinpoint the reasons for vague complaints, such as loss of memory, dizziness, or irritability.
11. Children with a hearing deficit, learning disability, mild mental retardation without brain injury, autistic disorder, emotional instability, or delayed speech may display symptoms similar to those of children with a brain injury, thus making a differential diagnosis difficult. For example, the emotionally disturbed behavior of a child with aphasia, which stems from the frustrating inability to communicate and understand language, may be difficult to distinguish from the behavior of a child with an emotional disturbance without brain injury. Children with aphasia and children with autism share abnormal responses to sounds, delay in language acquisition, and problems in articulation. Children with aphasia, however, usually do not manifest the perceptual or motor disturbances characteristic of children with autism. Furthermore, children with aphasia, in contrast to children with autism, relate to others through nonverbal gestures and expressions, are sensitive to gestures and expressions of others, learn to point toward desired objects, and show communicative intent and emotion when they acquire speech.
12. Deficits associated with a brain injury incurred at an early age may not become evident until several years later (as noted in Chapter 23).

Reliability of Information

Corroborate any information obtained from the child—such as the nature of the trauma, length of unconsciousness, perceived changes in functioning, and seizure history—with information obtained from the parents and from the child's medical records. Compare what the child tells you about himself or herself with what the parents tell you about the child. The extent of agreement between the child's and parents' reports is a useful measure of the validity of the child's (or the parents') report. Children with brain injuries sometimes underestimate the severity of their problems and may even deny having any. Because children with brain injuries may be unreliable reporters as a result of memory and attention problems, interviews with the parents and other informants take on added importance. Information from these sources may allow you to compare the child's preinjury level of functioning with his or her postinjury level of functioning.

Malingering

In addition to considering the information presented in Chapter 7 on malingering, watch for the following features in a child's performance, which may raise suspicions of malingering (Powell, 2004):

- Degree of deficit disproportionate to the severity of the injury
- Bizarre errors that are not seen when there are genuine deficits

- Patterns of test performance that do not make neuropsychological sense
- Failure to show expected patterns (failure to show any learning whatsoever on learning tasks; discrepancies in performance on similar tasks)
- Inconsistencies between information conveyed in the interview and information conveyed on tests (unable to repeat short sentences during the assessment but able to do so in a general conversation)
- Inexplicable claims of memory loss even for important life events by older children (e.g., an adolescent does not recall graduating from high school or getting married)

- Below-chance responding on forced-choice tests (suggesting that the child must know the right answer in order to choose the wrong one)
- Failure to report difficulties until long after the brain injury

Report Writing

Chapter 25 presents detailed guidelines for report writing. There may be occasions, however, when you will want to use a standardized format for reporting assessment results. Table 24-17 shows a general worksheet that you can modify to suit

Table 24-17
Neuropsychological Report Writing Worksheet for Children of School Age

WORKSHEET

Instructions: Insert applicable information in the spaces and cross out inapplicable phrases.

Reason for Referral

_____ is a _____ -year-old male/female who was born on _____. He/She was referred for a neuropsychological evaluation after a _____ on _____.

Tests Administered
The following records, tests, and assessment procedures were used [check appropriate ones]:

1. School records
2. Medical records
3. Interview with parents
4. Interview with child
5. Wechsler Intelligence Scale for Children–Fourth Edition (WISC–IV)
6. Wechsler Adult Intelligence Scale–Third Edition (WAIS–III)
7. Stanford-Binet: Fifth Edition
8. Bender Visual Motor Gestalt Test
9. Benton Visual Retention Test–Revised
10. Wide Range Achievement Test–Third Edition
11. Halstead-Reitan Neuropsychological Test Battery for Older Children
12. Reitan-Indiana Neuropsychological Test Battery for Children
13. Luria-Nebraska Neuropsychological Battery–Children's Revision
14. Contributions to Neuropsychological Assessment Battery
15. NEPSY—A Developmental Neuropsychological Assessment
16. Bruininks-Oseretsky Test of Motor Proficiency
17. Purdue Pegboard
18. Grooved Pegboard Test
19. Token Test for Children
20. Reporter's Test
21. Raven's Progressive Matrices
22. California Verbal Learning Test–Children's Version
23. Children's Auditory Verbal Learning Test–Second Edition
24. Children's Memory Scale
25. Rey Auditory-Verbal Learning Test
26. Test of Memory and Learning

27. Wide Range Assessment of Memory and Learning–Second Edition
28. Informal tests
29. Other tests: _____
_____

History
The child has noticed/parents have reported the following problems since the accident/onset of symptoms:

1. _____
2. _____
3. _____
4. _____
5. _____
6. _____
7. _____

These problems appear to be improving/getting worse/remaining the same.

The child is in the _____ grade and was performing at a satisfactory/an unsatisfactory level before the injury/onset of symptoms. Behavioral problems were/were not present before the brain injury. [If present, describe the behavioral problems: The child had difficulties in _____ _____.]

Birth was normal/abnormal. [If abnormal, describe what was abnormal: _____ _____.]

Achievement of developmental milestones was satisfactory/delayed. [It delayed, describe what milestones were delayed.
_____
_____
_____.]

Behavioral Observations
When seen for testing, _____ was/was not alert and well oriented. Difficulties were/were not observed during the evaluation. [If present, describe the difficulties: These difficulties included _____
_____.]

(Continued)

Table 24-17 (*Continued*)

Intellectual Functioning

The child achieved a Verbal Comprehension Index of_____ (_____ percentile), a Perceptual Organization Index of _____ (_____ percentile), a Working Memory Index of _____ (_____ percentile), a Processing Speed Index _____ (_____ percentile), and a Full Scale IQ of _____ ± _____ on the WISC–IV. His/Her overall score suggests that current intellectual functioning falls within the _____ range and at the _____ percentile. The chances that the range of scores from _____ to _____ includes his/her true IQ are about _____ out of 100. The results appear/do not appear to be reliable.

The Full Scale IQ appears/does not appear to reflect the child's level of functioning before injury/onset of symptoms. This estimate is based on parents' and teacher's reports/prior psychological tests. Thus, there is/is no evidence of a general loss of intellectual functioning. [If present, describe the estimated loss: The loss appears to be of approximately _____ IQ points.]

Marked intellectual impairments were/were not noted on the subtests of the WISC–IV. There was/was no evidence of clinically significant scaled score deviations. [If present, describe which subtest scores deviated significantly from the mean of each scale: Strengths were shown in_____

_____

Weaknesses were shown in_____

_____.]

Higher cognitive functions (comprehension, abstract thinking, and problem solving) appeared to be generally intact/impaired.

Educational Achievement

Reading skills are at the _____ grade level and the _____ percentile (standard score of _____); spelling skills are at the _____ grade level and the_____ percentile (standard score of_____); and arithmetic skills are at the _____ grade level and the_____ percentile (standard score of _____), as measured by the_____. These standard achievement scores are consistent/discrepant with _____'s level of scholastic attainment before injury/onset of symptoms. Writing ability was adequate/impaired and thus not indicative/indicative of dysgraphia. There is/is no evidence of a learning disability. [If present, describe the learning disability: The learning disability involves the child's reading/spelling/arithmetic, with difficulties in_____

_____

_____.]

Motor Functioning

_____ demonstrated consistent right/left/mixed hand dominance. Gross-motor coordination was intact/impaired. Fine-motor coordination was adequate/impaired. [Additional comments: _____

_____.]

Auditory Perceptual Functioning

Auditory perceptual functioning was intact/impaired. _____ had no/had difficulty in differentiating between pairs of words.

[Additional comments: _____

_____

_____.]

Tactile Perceptual Functioning

Tactile perceptual functioning was relatively intact/impaired. There were no/some errors indicating finger agnosia, no/some errors in graphesthesia, and no/some errors in stereognosis. [Additional comments: _____

_____

_____.]

Visuo-Spatial Functioning

Visuo-spatial functioning appeared to be adequate/impaired. Visuomotor speed was adequate/impaired. [Additional comments: _____

_____

_____.]

Oral Language Ability

Language ability was intact/impaired with respect to reading, writing, listening, and talking. There was no/was evidence of dysarthria. Motor aspects of speech were intact/impaired, as there was no/was evidence of disturbance in articulation and repetition. Comprehension of speech was adequate/ inadequate and thus not indicative/indicative of a receptive disorder. Word-finding fluency was intact/impaired and thus not indicative/indicative of an expressive disorder. [Additional comments:

_____

_____

_____.]

Memory Processes and Attentional Processes

_____'s immediate memory was intact/impaired. Recent memory, including the ability to learn both new verbal and new visual information, was adequate/impaired. Remote memory was satisfactory/impaired. Attentional processes were intact/impaired. There was no/was evidence of an impairment of concentration or attention. [Additional comments:

_____

_____

_____.]

Behavior

Parental reports indicate that _____ has satisfactory/unsatisfactory behavior patterns. [If unsatisfactory, include additional comments here: Parents report that _____

_____

School reports indicate that his/her behavior in school is satisfactory/unsatisfactory. [If unsatisfactory, include additional comments here: Teachers report that _____

_____.]

Comments

[Include additional comments and recommendations here:

_____

_____

_____.]

Source: Adapted from Gilandas, Touyz, Beumont, and Greenberg (1984).
From *Assessment of Children: Behavioral, Social, and Clinical Foundations (Fifth Edition)* by Jerome M. Sattler and Robert D. Hoge. Copyright 2006 by Jerome M. Sattler, Publisher, Inc. Permission to photocopy this table is granted to purchasers of this book for personal use only (see copyright page for details).

your needs. The worksheet outlines several standard procedures and provides appropriate spaces for recording the findings. Some items call for a checkmark (e.g., tests administered) or a number (IQ or percentile rank), whereas others require detailed comments (e.g., behavioral observations). You can compile a final report directly from the worksheet.

As in all clinical cases, you will want to base your interpretations, conclusions, and recommendations on a careful analysis of all available information. Focus on children's deficits and strengths; their awareness and acceptance of their deficits; their motivation; the environmental supports available to them; the degree of accommodation they (and their parents) have made to any changes in their personality, temperament, cognitive abilities, and social skills; and their goals and future plans. The behavior of children with brain injuries must be understood in relation to their organically based neuropsychological deficits. In addition, physical recovery does not guarantee cognitive recovery. Although a child's physical appearance may have returned to normal (e.g., scars may have healed, orthotic devices may no longer be needed), cognitive and neurobehavioral deficits may remain for a lifetime.

During the assessment, when distractions are minimized and the focus is on one task at a time, children with traumatic brain injuries sometimes perform at an average or above-average level. However, under real-world conditions, when distractions are present and multi-tasking skills are required, they may perform more poorly. Thus, it is sometimes difficult to generalize from the results obtained in a standard assessment situation to real-world situations. Observing the child in his or her natural environment (e.g., in school, at play with peers and siblings) may help you identify situational and environmental factors that are related to the child's behavior. Children sustaining brain injury early in life should be reassessed during early adolescence because, as noted previously, it is during these years that more complex and higher-level cognitive and behavioral processes emerge. Exhibit 24-1 provides an example of a psychological report in a form of a letter written to a physician

---

Exhibit 24-1
A Report to a Physician

BOSTONIA MEDICAL CENTER
Neuropsychology Center
1234 Main Street
Anywhere, WI 84632

Dr. Roberta Zelka
5678 Main Street
Anywhere, WI 85666
August 24, 2005

Dear Dr. Zelka,

I saw your patient Vincent Reese, who is 10 years, 9 months old, on August 23, 2005 for a neuropsychological evaluation. Vincent was struck by a car while riding his bicycle on July 9, 2005 and suffered a severe head injury. He was hospitalized for approximately 14 days. He suffered a midline skull fracture and a broken jaw, clavicle, and tibia. The CT/MRI scan showed pinpoint hemorrhaging throughout the brain, as well as trauma to the left frontal lobe.

For the initial six days of hospitalization, Vincent was unconscious, required life support, and often had seizures. Surgery has repaired Vincent's broken jaw, but he still has a cast on his left leg. He is currently seizure free and is not taking medications. Vincent's medical history indicates that he has a depressed immune system, which is a hereditary condition that has resulted in bronchitis and pneumonia. Prior to his head injury, Vincent was described as a mature, dependable preadolescent, with no history of behavioral problems. He was an excellent student, making straight As.

Since the accident, Mrs. Reese has noticed several changes in Vincent's behavior. He has difficulties in short-term memory, reading, and arithmetic and becomes mentally confused and disoriented at times. His moods fluctuate from fairly normal to a depressed, lifeless state, and he often bickers with his younger brother and friends and has outbursts of anger. He needs a great deal of time to complete daily activities such as eating and grooming.

In order to evaluate his general level of cognitive functioning, I administered the WISC–IV. On this test, Vincent obtained a Verbal Comprehension Index of 89 (23rd percentile), a Perceptual Reasoning Index of 79 (8th percentile), a Working Memory Index of 77 (6th percentile), a Processing Speed Index of 75 (5th percentile), and Full Scale IQ of 75 (5th percentile) ± 6 (95% confidence level). His Full Scale IQ is in the Borderline range.

To gain a more specific measure of Vincent's current level of achievement, I administered the Wide Range Achievement Test–Third Edition. It revealed below-average ability in arithmetic (standard score of 78, 7th percentile) but average ability in reading (standard score of 105, 57th percentile) and in spelling (standard score of 109, 63rd percentile). Given Vincent's prior history of excellent academic achievement, the discrepancy between his cognitive functioning and his achievement indicates that he likely has sustained substantial cognitive impairment.

Other tests of cognitive functioning reveal cognitive slowing and impaired short-term memory, mental manipulation, problem-solving skills, and learning efficiency. These deficits will probably interfere with Vincent's academic work. His mental confusion in part may be associated with his memory and organizational difficulties. The additional tests I administered were the Boston Naming Test, Verbal Fluency Test, Finger Localization Test, a lateral dominance test, Tactile Performance Test, Finger Oscillation Test, Grooved Pegboard Test, Category Test, Trails Test, Wide Range Assessment of Memory and Learning–Second Edition, Conners' Parent Rating Scale–Revised, and Missouri Behavior Checklist.

Vincent also has bilateral finger agnosia and dysgraphesthesia. His motor dexterity is relatively intact, although he shows some minor deficit in motor skills.

(Continued)

Exhibit 24-1 *(Continued)*

In summary, Vincent appears to have suffered substantial cognitive impairments as a result of his traumatic brain injury. He has deficits in memory, problem solving, and mental speed. His performance indicates some generalized cognitive slowing. It has been just over a month since Vincent's accident, and it is likely that he will continue to recover and progress.

When he returns to school next month, Vincent may have difficulty learning new material because of his short-term memory problems, organizational problems, and problem-solving difficulties. He will need special tutoring. The emotional distress that Vincent is experiencing may be caused by his recognition of and frustration at what has happened to him. It will be necessary to monitor his mood, especially after he re-enters school. Given his cognitive impairments, he will no doubt have some difficulty readjusting to the academic environment. Counseling and extensive support will be important parts of any rehabilitation, and his capabilities and limitations will need to be considered in his educational programming. Vincent should be re-evaluated in 6 to 12 months in order to monitor his progress and to make any needed adjustments in his academic program.

Specific recommendations follow:

1. The best strategy to help Vincent cope with his emotional lability or an outburst of anger is to reduce environmental inputs. This would include providing a quiet place where he can go where other people are not staring at him. His tutors will need to be patient with him and to reassure him. Punishment would only diminish his self-esteem further. Vincent's behavior is a manifestation of his brain injury and is not deliberate and intentional. Prior to his brain injury, he never displayed any emotional lability or outbursts of anger.
2. Because of his cognitive slowing, memory difficulties, and reduced capacity for attention, Vincent should be given one-on-one attention in a highly structured environment.
3. Individual instruction should be given in the morning or early in the day, when Vincent is less likely to be fatigued. Later in the day, he can join his regular class.
4. Every morning his tutor should cover the lessons that will be taught that day. This material will be reinforced when he attends his regular class later in the day.

Thank you for the opportunity to participate in this patient's care. Please don't hesitate to contact me if I can provide additional information or referral assistance.

William T. Bradford, Ph. D.
Clinical Psychologist

POSTSCRIPT

Vincent was reexamined 9 months after the accident. He showed substantial improvement in several areas. On the WISC–IV, Vincent obtained a Verbal Comprehension Index of 96 (39th percentile), a Perceptual Reasoning Index of 100 (50th percentile), a Working Memory Index of 95 (37th percentile), a Processing Speed Index of 94 (34th percentile), and a Full Scale IQ of 97 (42nd percentile) ± 6 (95% confidence level). His Full Scale IQ is in the Average range. On the Wide Range Achievement Test–Third Edition, he obtained an arithmetic standard score of 94 (34th percentile), a reading standard score of 112 (79th percentile), and a spelling standard score of 104 (61st percentile).

Vincent continues to show evidence of mild finger agnosia, dysgraphesthesia, and mildly impaired grip strength, but these difficulties are less pronounced than they were when he was examined previously. His manual speed and dexterity are bilaterally even and within the expected range.

Psychomotor and information processing speed are substantially improved relative to the previous examination and are within the average range. He still, however, has deficits in executive functioning requiring mental flexibility, as noted by his difficulties in shifting cognitive sets.

Vincent also shows substantial improvements in memory functions. Recall of visual and verbal material, both immediately and after a time delay, are within the average range, although recall of visual spatial memory is somewhat below average.

Mrs. Reese continues to report that Vincent displays emotional lability, has outbursts of anger, and is impulsive, although these behaviors have slightly improved over the past year. Despite his emotional outbursts (mostly tantrums), he is not violent toward others or destructive of property. Finally, Mrs. Reese reports that Vincent spends most of his time in the regular classroom, although he still receives some tutoring; in addition, he is allowed additional time to complete tests.

THINKING THROUGH THE ISSUES

1. Defend the proposition that intelligence tests are useful neuropsychological instruments.
2. Why is it difficult, if not impossible, to find uniform neuropsychological test profiles in children with brain injuries?
3. When would you use both formal and informal neuropsychological measures?

SUMMARY

1. The assessment of children with brain injuries focuses on their cognitive and behavioral skills, on their academic strengths and weaknesses, and on their interpersonal skills and social judgment.

2. Children who have sustained severe head injuries may be difficult to evaluate, especially if their speech is impaired, if they have aphasic disturbances, or if they have not fully regained consciousness.

Suggestions for Conducting an Evaluation

3. You will need to consider several factors in conducting an assessment, including the child's age, the child's language ability, the need for an interpreter, the time available to conduct the assessment, which assessment procedures to use, the need for adaptations in the selected assessment procedures, medicines the child is taking, and relevant compensation or legal factors that might affect how the child performs.
4. Conduct the evaluation in a quiet room and minimize all potential sources of distraction.

5. Seemingly irrelevant or disconnected responses may in fact be meaningful to the child and somewhat appropriate.

6. If the child is anxious about the evaluation, deal with his or her anxieties before you begin the formal evaluation.

7. You need to be especially attentive to the reactions of children with brain injuries in order to minimize their frustration and fatigue.

8. Experiment with different communication methods, rates of communication, and types of content to find the most effective way to communicate with children with brain injuries.

Behaviors Associated with Children with Brain Injuries

9. Parents of children with brain injuries may report various concerns about their children's behavior, and you may observe some of these behaviors during the assessment. Most parental concerns fall into one or more of the following categories: attention, memory and learning, language, visuoperception, and executive functioning.

10. Although these problem behaviors can hinder the assessment process and be frustrating to you, they also constitute a valuable behavior sample that can help you understand and generate hypotheses about the child.

Observing and Interviewing Children

11. Observe the child in several settings and at different times during the day, such as during the administration of tests, in an interview, and in natural settings.

12. Appendix B contains three semistructured interviews useful for children with brain injuries.

Interviewing Parents

13. Appendix B contains a semistructured interview useful for obtaining an in-depth developmental history from a parent.

14. The information that parents give you may not always be objective.

Neurological Examination

15. A neurological examination includes a clinical history, a mental status examination, and a study of cranial nerves, motor functions, coordination, sensory functions, and gait.

16. A comprehensive neurological examination may include imaging and radiographic diagnostic procedures.

17. Computed tomography (CT), or computerized axial tomography (CAT), is an x-ray technique that uses a computer to scan objects in sequential slices.

18. Magnetic resonance imaging (MRI) uses no radiation; instead, powerful electromagnetic gradients switch on and off at a resonant frequency, polarizing some of the body's water protons.

19. Functional magnetic resonance imaging (fMRI) is an advanced imaging procedure that provides information about brain function rather than brain structure.

20. Diffusion tensor imaging (DTI) is a type of diffusion MRI that measures the directionality as well as the magnitude of water diffusion in the brain.

21. Electroencephalography (EEG) is a procedure in which electrodes are placed on the scalp to record the electrical activity of the brain.

22. Magnetoencephalography (MEG) is a noninvasive scanning procedure that measures magnetic fields produced by the electrical activity in the brain.

23. Positron emission tomography (PET) produces a cross-sectional image of cellular activity or blood flow in the brain, following the intravenous injection of a radioactive substance.

24. Single photon emission computed tomography (SPECT) provides a three-dimensional representation of regional cerebral blood flow.

25. Cerebral angiography is used to visualize the arterial and venous systems of the brain.

26. Imaging techniques, in general, provide excellent detail about the gross anatomy of the brain and excel in depicting major structural and functional anomalies, including those associated with epilepsy, hydrocephalus, multiple sclerosis, and the degenerative effects of infectious disorders, tumors, congenital mishaps, and other childhood disorders.

27. Imaging and radiographic techniques, in general, vary along two distinct dimensions: temporal resolution and spatial resolution.

28. Techniques with the best temporal resolution include MEG and EEG, followed by fMRI, DTI, PET, and SPECT. Techniques with the best spatial resolution include MRI, fMRI, and DTI.

29. Hard neurological signs are fairly definitive indicators of cerebral injury.

30. Soft neurological signs are mild and equivocal neurological irregularities, in primarily sensorimotor functions.

Neuropsychological Examination

31. A neuropsychological examination complements a neurological examination. The information provided about the child's adaptive strengths and weaknesses can be useful in assessing various neuropathological conditions, neurosurgical procedures, and trauma, as well as relatively isolated problems, such as learning disabilities.

32. The case history provides valuable information about the child's functioning both before and after the brain injury.

33. Any sudden and inadequately explained changes in behavior are likely to be associated with acute, as opposed to chronic, brain disorders.

34. The neuropsychological examination typically measures the following areas and functions: general intellectual skills and academic achievement, arousal and attention, sensory and motor functions, executive functions and problem-solving abilities, language functions, visuospatial functions, learning and memory, personality, emotional functioning, adaptive behavior skills, and environmental variables.

35. The results of a neuropsychological examination can be useful in the following ways: identifying areas of brain injury that impair a child's ability to perform successfully, providing a cognitive profile of relative strengths and weaknesses, providing information about the functional consequences of impairments identified by neuroimaging techniques, documenting the deterioration or recovery of cognitive functions over time, providing information regarding changes in a child's capabilities and limitations in everyday functioning, differentiating behavioral disturbances that may stem from brain injury from those that may stem from other causes, planning for rehabilitation, providing teachers with information on modifying the curriculum and on using teaching methods designed for children with brain injuries, and helping courts determine levels of loss and compensation.

36. Neuropsychological assessment of children differs from that of adults.

37. The aim of neuropsychological assessment has shifted from assisting in the diagnosis of cerebral damage to assisting in the

assessment of the functional capacities of children with brain injuries and in rehabilitation efforts.

38. The goal of both the neurological and the neuropsychological examination is to assess brain injury accurately. However, the neurological examination focuses on evaluating biological functions, whereas the neuropsychological examination focuses on cognitive process.

Halstead-Reitan Neuropsychological Test Battery for Older Children and Reitan-Indiana Neuropsychological Test Battery for Children

39. The Halstead-Reitan Neuropsychological Test Battery for Older Children is designed for children ages 9 to 14 years.

40. The Reitan-Indiana Neuropsychological Test Battery for Children is designed for children ages 5 to 8 years.

41. Although information about the reliability and validity of both batteries is limited, research indicates that both batteries may include tests that are psychometrically sound. Overall, both batteries are useful in discriminating children with brain injuries from other groups.

Luria-Nebraska Neuropsychological Battery–Children's Revision

42. The Luria-Nebraska Neuropsychological Battery–Children's Revision (LNNB–C) is designed to assess a broad range of neuropsychological functions in children ages 8 to 12 years. The LNNB–C should be used with caution, because the manual does not describe the standardization sample adequately and reliability is less than adequate.

NEPSY—A Developmental Neuropsychological Assessment

43. NEPSY—A Developmental Neuropsychological Assessment is a neuropsychological test designed for children ages 3 to 12 years. The reliability of the NEPSY is problematic, but content and construct validity appear to be adequate. The test must be used with caution, and additional research is needed.

Contributions to Neuropsychological Assessment Battery

44. The Contributions to Neuropsychological Assessment Battery contains 12 individual tests designed to measure orientation, learning, perception, and motor ability in children. More research is needed to examine the reliability and validity of the battery.

Wechsler Tests as Part of a Neuropsychological Test Battery

45. The Wechsler tests constitute a standardized series of tasks for evaluating the cognitive and visual-motor skills of children and adults with brain injuries. They are cornerstones of most neuropsychological test batteries.

46. The subtests that make up the Wechsler Verbal Comprehension Index rely heavily on retrieval of information acquired *before* the injury. However, these subtests do not sample important verbal abilities.

47. A comprehensive assessment of language ability must go beyond the administration of the Wechsler tests (or other individually administered intelligence tests) if language functioning and other functions are to be fully assessed.

48. An overall reduction in level of intelligence is a key finding in some cases of brain injury.

49. However, there is no single pattern of subtest scores on Wechsler tests that reveals brain injury.

50. Discrepancies between scores on the WISC–IV Verbal Comprehension Index and the Perceptual Reasoning Index probably do not distinguish between right- and left-sided brain damage.

51. When brain injury has been documented, you can use the Wechsler tests to assess the cognitive sequelae of the neurological disorder and to identify adaptive deficits requiring more detailed analysis.

52. If the Verbal Comprehension Index score is 12 or more points lower than the Perceptual Reasoning Index score, consider investigating linguistic abilities in more depth.

53. If the Perceptual Reasoning Index score is 12 or more points below the Verbal Comprehension Index score, consider the possibility of impaired visual-spatial, constructional, or perceptual reasoning skills.

54. You should *not* consider a discrepancy of even 15 or more points between scores on the Verbal Comprehension Index and the Perceptual Reasoning Index as proof of brain injury, because about 13% of all children in the WISC–IV standardization group had differences of this magnitude or greater in either direction.

55. In evaluating the child's cognitive abilities, consider, in addition to index or scale comparisons, subtest scores, qualitative features of the child's performance, observations of behavior, and the results of a neuropsychological and neurological assessment.

56. Integrate the hypotheses you formulate about subtest scores (and all Wechsler scores) with the hypotheses you develop based on qualitative features of a child's performance, the results of specialized neuropsychological measures, the clinical history and background information, and the findings of the neurological evaluation.

57. Performance on intelligence tests (and other tests as well) is likely to be multidetermined.

58. Effects of brain injury on intelligence test performance may be general (i.e., a global reduction in intelligence) or specific (i.e., impairment of selective areas of cognitive functioning).

59. The Wechsler Intelligence Scale for Children–IV as a Process Instrument is also useful in the assessment of children with brain injuries.

Additional Procedures for the Assessment of Children with Brain Injuries

60. Testing-of-limits may include modifying instructions to involve more or fewer cues, adjusting the pace at which information is presented, modifying the modality of presentation, modifying the starting or discontinuance procedure by administering additional items, adjusting memory demands, modifying the response format, adjusting task complexity, and asking for explanations of responses.

61. The Glasgow Coma Scale (GCS) is widely used in hospitals for assessing levels of consciousness in children and adults with brain injuries.

62. Posttraumatic amnesia (PTA) can be defined as incomplete registration of new events and information for a period of time fol-

lowing the injury (also known as time-limited anterograde amnesia).

63. Posttraumatic amnesia may be categorized on a time continuum that reflects the length of the amnesic episode.

64. The Pediatric Inventory of Neurobehavioral Symptoms (PINS) is a rating scale completed by parents or teachers of children who have sustained traumatic brain injury.

65. The Pediatric Inventory of Neurobehavioral Symptoms–Self-Report (PINS–SR) is useful for obtaining information about how adolescents perceive their abilities.

66. The Adolescent Brain Injury Symptom Checklist is useful for having adolescents rate the frequency, intensity, and duration of 17 physical, emotional, and cognitive complaints.

67. Several questions are useful for determining lateral hand, foot, ear, and eye preferences.

68. The Bender Visual Motor Gestalt Test, the Bender-Gestalt II, and the Beery VMI–Fifth Edition are useful for assessing visual-motor skills.

69. The Rey-Osterrieth Complex Figure Test (ROCFT) is a measure of children's visual-motor ability.

70. The Benton Visual Retention Test–Revised–Fifth Edition (BVRT) assesses visual memory, visual perception, and visuo-constructive abilities in children 8 years old and older.

71. The Bruininks-Oseretsky Test of Motor Proficiency contributes to the assessment of brain injury because it reliably measures fine- and gross-motor functions.

72. The Purdue Pegboard measures sensorimotor functions, particularly in the area of fine-motor coordination, that are essentially independent of educational achievement.

73. The Grooved Pegboard Test is a widely used test that assesses speed and eye-hand coordination.

74. Several instructions and questions are useful for obtaining information about a child's understanding of right and left.

75. The Finger Localization Test is another procedure that is useful for evaluating soft neurological signs.

76. Tests of verbal fluency are useful in assessing word-finding ability in children with brain injuries.

77. You can measure dysnomia (difficulty in naming objects) with the WISC–IV Picture Completion subtest (or any other test that has pictures of objects).

78. The Peabody Picture Vocabulary Test–III and the Expressive Vocabulary Test allow comparison of performance on a receptive vocabulary test with that on an expressive vocabulary (picture naming) test normed on the same standardization group.

79. You can use several procedures to informally evaluate a child's spatial orientation.

80. You can assess a child's writing ability in several ways.

81. The assessment of divergent thinking provides information about the child's ability to formulate new ideas and produce a variety of responses.

82. The Raven's Progressive Matrices test provides an estimate of a child's nonverbal cognitive ability.

83. The Token Test for Children is useful as a screening test of receptive language (auditory comprehension) for children between 3-0 and 12-5 years of age.

84. The Reporter's Test is a useful screening test for examining expressive language.

85. Several tests are useful for the assessment of memory and learning.

86. The Test of Everyday Attention for Children (TEA-Ch) is useful for measuring attention in children between the ages of 6 and 16 years.

87. The Delis-Kaplan Executive Function System (D-KEFS) contains nine individual tests designed to measure various aspects of executive functioning and covers ages 8 years to 89 years.

88. The Behavior Rating Inventory of Executive Function (BRIEF) is a set of questionnaires designed to evaluate executive functions.

Evaluating the Assessment Findings

89. A comprehensive neuropsychological evaluation may reveal disturbances in a child's motor, sensory, affective, cognitive, and social behavior and in the child's temperament and personality.

90. Several inferential methods are used to interpret the results of a neuropsychological test battery, including (a) analysis of level of performance, (b) analysis of pattern of performance, (c) analysis of pathognomonic signs of brain injury, and (d) comparison of performance on the two sides of the body.

91. The diagnostic effort should be based on all of the information you have obtained from formal and informal assessment procedures, including information from the case history.

92. When you evaluate the information from the child's case history, use a normative-developmental framework.

93. Qualitative analysis and testing-of-limits are primarily useful for generating, but not proving, hypotheses.

94. Brain injuries produce highly complex behavioral effects that lead to diagnostic difficulties.

95. Corroborate any information obtained from the child—such as the nature of the trauma, length of unconsciousness, perceived changes in functioning, and seizure history—with information obtained from the parents and from the child's medical records.

96. Watch for particular features in a child's performance that may raise suspicions of malingering.

97. In writing your reports, focus on children's deficits and strengths; their awareness and acceptance of their deficits; their motivation; the environmental supports available to them; the degree of accommodation they (and their parents) have made to any changes in their personality, temperament, cognitive abilities, and social skills; and their goals and future plans.

98. During the assessment, when distractions are minimized and the focus is on one task at a time, children with traumatic brain injuries sometimes perform at an average or above-average level. However, under real-world conditions, when distractions are present and multi-tasking skills are required, they may perform more poorly.

99. Children sustaining brain injury early in life should be reassessed during early adolescence because it is during these years that more complex and higher-level cognitive and behavioral processes emerge.

KEY TERMS, CONCEPTS, AND NAMES

STUDY QUESTIONS

1. What should examiners consider in administering tests to children with brain injuries?

2. What are some behaviors exhibited by children with brain injuries?

3. What are some important factors in observing and interviewing children with brain injuries and interviewing their parents?

4. Describe a neurological examination. Include in your discussion (a) areas covered in the examination, (b) imaging and radiographic methods, and (c) examples of several hard and soft neurological signs of possible brain injury.

5. Describe a neuropsychological examination. Include in your discussion the ways in which a neuropsychological examination complements a neurological examination and how it contributes to the assessment process.

6. Discuss the place of neuropsychological test batteries in the assessment of children with brain injuries.

7. Discuss the role of the Wechsler tests in the assessment of children with brain injuries.

8. Describe additional assessment procedures—other than neuropsychological test batteries and the Wechsler tests—useful in the assessment of brain injury in children.

9. Discuss the inferential methods used to analyze the findings from a neuropsychological assessment.

10. What diagnostic considerations are important in the assessment of children with brain injuries? Include in your discussion (a) cases history and assessment results, (b) reliability of information, (c) malingering, and (d) report writing.

11. After you completed an evaluation of a child who was referred to you for psychological problems, under what circumstances would you refer the child to a neuropsychologist? to a neurologist?

12. Why is it preferable to have a child receive both a neuropsychological evaluation and a neurological evaluation in cases of suspected brain injury?

25

REPORT WRITING

A naturalist's life would be a happy one if he had only to observe and never to write.
—Charles Darwin, English naturalist (1809–1882)

Goals and Objectives

This chapter is designed to enable you to do the following:

- Understand the purposes of a psychological report

- Understand the sections of a psychological report

- Develop appropriate skills for communicating your findings and recommendations in a report

- Write a psychological report

This chapter presents an overview of report writing, then describes the nine sections of a report, and finally offers 13 principles of report writing. After reading this chapter, you should understand the fundamentals of psychological report writing. The final test of your skills, however, will be writing a good report yourself. Note that in this chapter we will use the term *report* or *psychological report* to refer to both psychological reports (the term used in mental health, medical, forensic, and similar settings) and psychoeducational reports (the term used in school settings).

Psychological reports may be based on information obtained from psychological tests; interviews with the child, his or her parents, teachers, and others; systematic behavioral observations; and school records, prior psychological reports, medical reports, psychiatric reports, and other relevant sources. If you are in training at a university or are a member of a multidisciplinary team, your report may be based on only one assessment tool (e.g., a test, an interview, or a systematic behavioral observation). However, when children are referred for a comprehensive evaluation, the report should be based on multiple assessment procedures. Ideally, the report should integrate all of the assessment information you obtain.

A comprehensive psychological report should discuss background information, presenting problems, health and developmental history, schools attended, attendance record, classroom behavior, academic performance, evaluation techniques and teaching methods in the classroom, homework and study habits, learning style, family factors, observations during the assessment, perceptual-motor ability, speech and language ability, attention, cognitive ability, memory ability, learning ability, affect, motivation, social interactions, and interventions. Table 25-1 lists topics to cover and questions to consider in developing a report. Additional questions that are relevant for children with specific types of disabilities are found in several chapters of this book.

Table 25-1
Questions and Topics to Consider in Preparing a Psychological or Psychoeducational Report

Note. Consider only those questions that pertain to the case.

Background Information
1. What is the reason for the referral?
2. What do the child and parents think about the referral?
3. What are the child's sex, age, ethnicity, and appearance?
4. What language does the child speak at home, in school, and in the neighborhood?
5. Has the child received a psychological or psychoeducational evaluation in the past? If so, when was the evaluation, and what were the results?
6. What assessment procedures will the report be based on?

Presenting Problems
1. What are the child's presenting problems?
2. What are the frequency, duration, and magnitude of the child's problems?
3. When did the problems begin?
4. Where do they occur?
5. Does the child have problems in a particular academic area such as reading, mathematics, or written expression? If so, what is the area, and what are the problems?
6. Does the child have behavior problems? If so, describe the problems.
7. Does the child abuse alcohol or drugs? If so, which substance is abused, how does the child obtain the substance, and how long has the child abused the substance?
8. Were there any significant events in the child's prenatal, perinatal, or postnatal development that may be related to the current problems? If so, describe the events.
9. How does the child describe his or her problems?
10. How does the child handle the problems?
11. How do the parents describe the child's problems?
12. How do the parents handle the child's problems?
13. How does the teacher describe the child's problems?
14. How does the teacher handle the child's problems?
15. What does the child believe might contribute to his or her problems?

16. What do the parents believe might contribute to the child's problems?
17. What does the teacher believe might contribute to the child's problems?
18. Can the child control his or her behavior? If so, in what situations and how does the child control the behavior?
19. Do the descriptions of the problems given by the child, parents, and teachers agree? If not, describe the disagreements.
20. What information have the parents received from teachers, psychologists, or physicians about the child's problems?

Health and Developmental History
1. What is the child's health history?
2. Is there a current medical evaluation? If so, what were the results?
3. If the child received any medical treatment, what was the child treated for, what was the treatment, and how effective was the treatment?
4. When did the child reach specific developmental milestones, such as smiling, sitting, crawling, walking, saying single words, making simple word combinations, reacting to strangers, becoming toilet trained, and acquiring dressing skills? Were there delays in the child's reaching developmental landmarks? If so, in what areas were the delays, and how long were they?
5. Did the parents suspect that something was wrong with the child's rate of development? If so, what did they suspect and when did they first suspect that something was wrong?
6. Does the child have visual or auditory difficulties? If so, describe the difficulties.
7. Does the child take medicine that might affect his or her school performance? If so, what is the medicine and what are its major side effects?
8. Was the mother exposed to alcohol or drugs during her pregnancy? If so, what was she exposed to and how did the exposure affect the infant?
9. Did the mother have amniocentesis or ultrasound during the pregnancy? If so, what did the tests indicate?

(Continued)

Table 25-1 (*Continued*)

10. What were the child's Apgar score and temperament as an infant?
11. Did the child have hypoxia, neonatal jaundice, brain injury, meningitis, epilepsy, or any other illnesses or conditions at birth or shortly thereafter? If so, what did the child have, what treatment did the child receive, and what was the outcome of treatment, including any residual symptoms?

Schools Attended
1. What school does the child attend, how long has the child been going to this school, and what grade is the child in?
2. What schools did the child previously attend and when, and what were the reasons for changing schools?

Attendance Record, Suspensions, and Promotions
1. What is the child's current school attendance record? If poor, what are the reasons for it?
2. Has the child had poor attendance in the past? If so, when and for what reason?
3. Has the child ever been suspended or expelled from school? If so, when and for what reason?
4. Has the child ever been retained in a grade? If so, when and for what reason?

Classroom Setting and Behavior
1. What classroom setting is the child in?
2. How many students, teachers, and teacher aides are in the classroom?
3. How many different classrooms does the child go to in a typical day?
4. Is the child grouped with students of similar abilities for particular academic subjects? If so, what is the basis for the grouping and at what level has the child been placed for each academic subject? If the child has been moved from one group to another, what was the reason for the move and in what academic subject(s) did the move occur?
5. How does the child perform in the classroom? For example, how does the teacher describe the child's ability to sit still, make friends, get along with other children, listen to stories, follow oral and written directions, skim reading selections, locate information in a textbook, take notes from a discussion, sustain attention over a protracted period, understand age-appropriate rule-governed behavior, take turns when playing with other children, understand and manipulate symbols, count, spell, read, carry through a series of goal-oriented moves, maintain appropriate spatial direction, understand the complexities of a short story, and understand the complexities of a long story?
6. Does the child's classroom behavior change? If so, how and under what circumstances does it change?
7. How well does the child follow the classroom rules?
8. In the past, what type of classroom setting was the child in?

Academic Performance
1. What is the child's current level of academic performance?
2. Has the child's academic performance changed during the academic year? If so, describe the changes.
3. How satisfied is the child with his or her grades?
4. Describe the assignments completed by the child in the classroom and at home.
5. Which subjects does the child like and dislike?

Evaluation Techniques and Teaching Methods in the Classroom
1. What basis does the teacher use for assigning classroom grades?
2. What evaluation techniques are used in the classroom?
3. Does the child have more difficulty with some evaluation techniques than with others? If so, describe the difficulties and the techniques that cause them.
4. Does the teacher make any special accommodations for the child when tests are administered? If so, describe the accommodations.
5. What teaching methods, materials, and strategies are used in the classroom?

Homework and Study Habits
1. How much time does the child spend on homework each night?
2. Is the time spent on homework sufficient to do the assignment?
3. What are the child's work habits, rate of learning, learning style, and ability to adapt to new situations?
4. Does the child have any work habits that interfere with his or her school work? If so, describe the habits.

Learning Style
1. Does the child seek information before undertaking an assignment? If so, how does the child do this?
2. Does the child keep notes of class lectures?
3. Does the child review his or her test results?
4. Does the child have a place to study at home that is free from distractions?
5. Does the child seek help with his or her school work from peers, teachers, siblings, parents, or other adults?
6. How does the child prepare for a test? For example, does the child read the assigned material, study it, reread notes, or review prior tests?
7. Does the child receive rewards from parents for good performance in school? If so, what are the rewards?

Familial Factors
1. What is the composition of the child's family?
2. Describe the relationship between the parents and the child and between the parents and the child's siblings.
3. Describe the relationship among the siblings in the family.
4. What is the socioeconomic status of the family?
5. Is there a history among the family members of child maltreatment, substance abuse, spousal abuse, medical disorders, psychiatric disorders, learning disorders, mental retardation, or other significant disorders? If so, which family members have which problems or disorders? If they received treatment, what treatments were given and how successful were the treatments? Which problems are still current and/or under treatment?
6. Are there any factors in the home that might affect the child's ability to study and learn? If so, describe the factors.
7. What is the parents' opinion about the child's school and teachers?
8. What have the parents been told about their child's school performance?
9. Do the parents desire any special program for their child? If so, describe the program and their reasons for wanting the program for their child.

Table 25-1 (*Continued*)

10. Does the teacher have an opinion of the family? If so, describe the opinion. (Consider carefully whether you want to include this information in the report.)

Observations During the Assessment

1. Describe the child's appearance, behavior, motor skills, attention level, activity level, and degree of cooperativeness during the evaluation.
2. What is the quality of the child's expressive and receptive language? For example, did the child understand the questions, make appropriate and coherent replies, seem to understand nonverbal messages, use correct grammar, listen appropriately, and understand idioms used in conversation?
3. What social skills did the child exhibit in interacting with the examiner?
4. Can the child sustain attention or concentration when mental processing is required, such as when reading or doing mental arithmetic?
5. Can the child shift back and forth between two or more tasks without becoming overwhelmed or confused?
6. Does the child return to the task at hand spontaneously after being distracted or interrupted?

Perceptual-Motor Ability

1. Describe the child's fine- and gross-motor coordination.
2. Describe the child's perceptual processes.

Language Ability

1. Describe the child's expressive language.
2. Describe the child's receptive language.

Attention and Concentration

1. Describe the child's attention span and concentration abilities.

Cognitive Ability

1. Describe the child's cognitive ability.

Memory Ability

1. Describe the child's short-term and long-term memory ability.

Learning Ability

1. Describe the child's learning ability.
2. Does the child benefit from both intrinsic and extrinsic rewards? If so, describe the rewards.
3. What are the optimal rates and duration for presenting material to the child?
4. Which of the child's sensory modalities best facilitates learning?
5. What methods used in the classroom best help the child learn?
6. What types of cues best help the child learn?
7. What schedule and type of reinforcement best help the child learn?
8. How do practice and rehearsal affect the child's learning?
9. Does the child use strategies to help him or her learn? If so, describe the strategies.
10. How well does the child learn new material, retain it, integrate the knowledge, and apply it to new situations?
11. What factors impede the child's learning?

Affect

1. Describe the child's affect.
2. Does the child become angry easily? If so, in what situations does this occur?

3. How often is the child angry?
4. What is the child's response to frustration?
5. Can the child bring his or her emotions under control if they get out of hand?
6. Can the child inhibit inappropriate behaviors or comments?
7. Does the child show rapid fluctuation in mood without environmental cause, frequent tearfulness, or situationally inappropriate affect (such as laughing at serious subjects or showing no emotional reaction to events to which others react)?
8. What factors precipitate, alleviate, or aggravate the child's affect or cause changes in the child's affect?

Motivation

1. Describe the child's motivation.

Social Interactions and Interests

1. Describe the child's social interactions.
2. How does the child perceive his or her relations with other family members?
3. How does the child get along with other children?
4. Have the child's interpersonal relations changed as he or she has developed? If so, in what way?
5. What responsibilities does the child have at home, and how does he or she fulfill these responsibilities?
6. Has the child shown any aggressive behavior during development? If so, what type of behavior and at what ages?
7. What are the child's general interests, academic interests, and hobbies?

Overall Assessment Results

1. If the child received a psychological evaluation in the past, how do the present results compare with previous results?
2. Do the assessment results suggest any diagnostic classification? If so, what is it?

Interventions

1. Has the child received special education services or psychological or psychiatric treatments in the past? If so, describe the services or treatments and their effectiveness.
2. Does the child have an IEP? If so, briefly describe the IEP.
3. Is the child currently receiving interventions for his or her problems? If so, describe their effectiveness. Also describe how the child, parents, and teachers view the interventions.
4. How willing are the child, parents, and teachers to cooperate with intervention efforts?
5. What interventions, including services, would the child, parents, and teachers like the child to receive?
6. Is the child eligible for special education services?
7. If the child has a disability, what supports will enable the child to attend general education classes with his or her nondisabled peers? Do you recommend these supports?
8. Can the child function in a regular education classroom, or is a self-contained classroom needed?
9. What other interventions do you recommend?
10. What family supports are available?
11. What transition services might the child need (if applicable)?
12. What supports will the child need to live and work independently (if applicable)?
13. What services are available in the community?

INTRODUCTION TO PSYCHOLOGICAL REPORT WRITING

A psychological evaluation is complete only after the obtained information has been organized, synthesized, and integrated. The traditional medium for presenting assessment information is a written report, although you may use other formal and informal means of presentation (e.g., recording forms or oral reports). The completion of a report is an integral part of the clinical or psychoeducational assessment process. The report should convey clearly and concisely the information obtained, the findings, clinical impressions (where applicable), and specific recommendations. A report may influence a child and family for years to come; its drafting deserves extreme care and consideration. Report writing is one of the defining activities of clinicians.

Qualities of a Good Report

Your report should be well organized and solidly grounded. A good report does not merely present facts. It integrates what you have learned about the examinee and presents the information in a way that shows respect for her or his individuality. This respect for individuality should permeate the entire assessment process; you should view the examinee as an individual in the context of her or his life and not simply as a stimulus for gathering data.

Purposes of the Report

A psychological report (a) provides accurate assessment-related information to the referral source and other concerned parties, (b) serves as a basis for clinical hypotheses, appropriate interventions, and information for program evaluation and research, (c) furnishes meaningful baseline information for evaluating the examinee's progress after the interventions have been implemented or changes that occur as a result of time alone, and (d) serves as a legal document.

Formulating the Report

In formulating and constructing your report, first consider who will be the primary audiences for the report. The target audience may be parents, a general education teacher, special education personnel, a health care provider, a probation officer, an attorney, a judge, or a colleague. In all cases, you want to ensure that nonprofessionals understand the report. Second, consider the circumstances under which the assessment took place, the number of opportunities for observation and interaction, and the behavioral basis for the judgments you made about the examinee. Third, include examples, as appropriate, to illustrate or document selected statements you make in the report. Fourth, make your recommendations with an appreciation of the needs and values of the examinee, the family, and the extended family; the family's resources; the examinee's

ethnic and cultural group; the school; and society. Throughout the process, consider how your values affected the way you conducted the assessment, arrived at conclusions and recommendations, and emphasized certain details in the report.

Subjective Elements in the Report

Although you should strive for objectivity and accuracy in writing the report, remember that no report can be completely objective. Every report has elements of subjectivity, because the information in it is open to different interpretations. Recognize that you introduce subjectivity with each word you use to describe the examinee, each behavior you highlight or ignore, each element of the history you cite, and the sequence you follow in presenting the information. The evaluation procedure also contains elements of subjectivity.

Promptness in Writing the Report

Write the report as soon as possible after you complete the assessment. You want to record all important details (and not forget any). The referral source needs a prompt reply. Unfortunately, in some settings, there is a delay between the time someone makes a referral and the initiation of the assessment. You, as the examiner, should not introduce further delay by putting off writing the report.

Contents of the Report

The psychological report should adequately describe the assessment findings, including information about the examinee's history, current problems, assets, and limitations; it should also include behavioral observations and test interpretations. The assessment instruments used should be noted. The value of the psychological report lies in the degree to which it addresses the referral question.

Each report should be an independent document—that is, its content should be comprehensive enough to stand alone. The reader should not need to refer to other materials for illustration or clarification. However, it is perfectly acceptable to refer the reader to past reports for purposes of comparison with the present findings. Test protocols, data sheets, and other assessment information should be filed in the child's private evaluation folder and not attached to the report or placed in the child's cumulative folder.

SECTIONS OF A PSYCHOLOGICAL REPORT

A typical psychological report has the following nine sections:

1. Identifying Information
2. Assessment Instruments

3. Reason for Referral
4. Background Information
5. Observations During the Assessment
6. Assessment Results and Clinical Impressions
7. Recommendations
8. Summary
9. Signature

Identifying Information

The first part of the report presents relevant identifying information. Include the examinee's name, date of birth, sex, age, and grade in school (if applicable); date(s) of the assessment; date of the report; and the examiner's name. You also may want to state the name of the child's teacher (if applicable) and the names of the child's parents. Provide information on the organization sponsoring the assessment (e.g., school, clinic, agency, private practice, or university), including the address, telephone number, and, if available, fax number, as well as the e-mail address, telephone extension, voice-mail-box, or other contact information for the examiner.

Determining the child's chronological age requires attention. Correctly subtracting the child's birthday from the date of testing is worthless if the child's date of birth is wrong. Young children make mistakes in giving their date of birth, and files may contain wrong information. It is a good practice to confirm the child's birthday with a parent.

Assessment Instruments

List both formal and informal assessment instruments and techniques that you used to conduct the evaluation. For example, include the names of standardized tests and informal tests and the names of any other techniques that you used, such as an interview and/or a systematic behavioral observation. Spell out all test names completely, followed by the acronym in parentheses.

Some examiners find it helpful to have on hand (either as hard copy or as computer files) brief descriptions of all the instruments they use. It is then easy to add an appendix to the report, either photocopying the hardcopy or cutting and pasting from the computer files to create a guide to the tests used in the evaluation. Such appendixes provide useful information to lay readers without cluttering the text of the report.

Reason for Referral

Citing the reason for referral helps document why the psychological evaluation was conducted. Consider including the following information: (a) name, position, and affiliation (if applicable) of the referral source, (b) why the referral source asked for the assessment, (c) specific questions the referral source has about the examinee, (d) a brief summary of the specific behaviors or symptoms displayed by the examinee that led to the referral, and (e) possible ways the assessment

may be used (e.g., to plan remedial measures, treatment, or educational programs).

Here are two examples of Reason for Referral sections.

The Planning and Placement Team of Central Elementary School referred Mikey for an assessment to gain a better understanding of his cognitive and behavioral strengths and weaknesses. This request was prompted by Mikey's distractible behavior, poor work completion, inadequate peer relations, and attention-seeking behaviors in his third-grade class.

Carl has recently completed a course of radiation therapy for a brain tumor. His physician requested that neuropsychological testing be conducted to assess cognitive and behavioral changes associated with his treatment and condition.

Background Information

In the Background Information section, you may include material obtained from interviews with the parents, teachers, and child; from the examinee's educational file; and from previous psychological, psychiatric, and medical accounts. Always acknowledge the sources of the information, and report the dates on which the accounts were written. You will probably need a signed release of information form (usually signed by a parent) to obtain previous psychological or medical reports or similar information from other agencies. You may want to include in this section demographic information, information about the current problems, historical information (including the child's developmental history), information about the family, and information about the parents.

As you review the material you obtained from the interviews with the child, parents, teachers, and other informants, estimate the accuracy of the information that they gave you. For example, were they cooperative, confused, or hostile? Was there anything in these interviews suggesting that an interviewee was slanting or distorting information, hiding information, or deliberately giving you misleading information? Were there any gaps in the information? These and similar questions should guide your evaluation of the material that you obtained.

You also will want to compare the information you obtained from different interviewees (see Chapter 6). What were the similarities and differences in the information obtained from the child, the parents, and the teacher about the child's problems and concerns? How did each interviewee describe the child's behavior? What trends were evident in the developmental history, observational findings, parental reports, teacher reports, medical reports, psychological and psychiatric reports, and police reports (if applicable), and how consistent were the trends?

Don't be surprised to find differences in the information given to you by children, parents, and teachers. For example, they may agree about external symptoms but not about internal ones. If there are differences between the accounts of the parents and child, teacher and child, parents and teacher, or two parents, what might account for the differences? Here are some questions for you to consider:

1. Do the parents and teacher differ in their ability to observe, evaluate, and judge the behavior of the child?

2. Could the variance be associated with different standards for judging deviant behavior or different tolerances for behavioral problems? For example, what the parents consider hyperactive, the teacher may consider normal, or vice versa.

3. Could differences in how the parents and teacher view the child's behavior be related to situational factors? For example, if parents report *fewer* problems than the teacher does, the child may be overindulged at home but treated normally at school. If parents report *more* problems than the teacher does, the child may be experiencing a stressful environment at home (e.g., unsympathetic parents, poor structure and discipline, conflicts with siblings) but a normal environment at school (e.g., even-handed discipline, consistency, clear and reasonable expectations).

Thus, discrepancies between interviewees may suggest that the behaviors of concern are not pervasive or generalizable—the child may actually behave differently at home than at school (Achenbach, McConaughy, & Howell, 1987). In addition, the demands on students of their home environments differ from those of school environments. Consider all of the information you have before arriving at an explanation for any discrepancies between informants.

When information is available from several sources, you will need to organize and interpret it to arrive at a systematic understanding of the child. You will need to consider the child as a whole, given his or her family, culture, and environment. Although the information may not always be clear, you still must sort out the findings and establish trends. Rather than ignoring discrepant information, try to account for it.

Following is a sample Background Information section. The examinee was admitted to a psychiatric hospital on an emergency basis because of bizarre, unpredictable, and out-of-control behavior. His mother reported that he had been talking to himself and may have been having delusions and hallucinations.

> Henry, a 12-year, 9-month-old adolescent, is the youngest of five children. He lives with his mother, who has been married three times. All of the background information was obtained from Henry's mother. Henry last saw his father when he was 5 months old and just beginning to crawl. He first walked alone at 15 months and achieved bowel control at 2 years of age. However, he never achieved full bladder control, and he remains enuretic at night.
>
> He attended a Head Start program at the age of 4 and was referred to a child guidance clinic by his Head Start teacher because of behavioral problems. He received a diagnosis of attention-deficit/hyperactivity disorder at that time from his health care provider. When Henry was 5 years old, his maternal grandmother died of a stroke, and Henry became extremely depressed. His mother noted that shortly afterward Henry told her that he knew in advance that his grandmother was going to die; he claimed that he knew what was going to happen in the future.
>
> At 6 years of age, Henry attempted suicide by throwing himself in front of a car after his mother was hospitalized for hypertension; however, he was not seriously injured. Henry told his mother that he believed that she was going to die and he wanted to die, too. This incident resulted in Henry's referral to Main County Mental Health Clinic, where he was treated for the suicide attempt and for hyperactivity and enuresis. At the clinic, he started taking medications for his depression and attention-deficit/hyperactivity disorder.
>
> When Henry was 9 years old, his 16-year-old sister attempted suicide by a drug overdose. Henry was depressed for several months. At the age of 10 years, he was expelled from school for alleged sexually inappropriate behavior, including touching other children's genitalia. He was subsequently transferred to another school, where he currently attends special education classes. He was classified by school personnel as having a behavior disorder. Academically, his grades were average in reading and spelling, but below average in mathematics and writing.
>
> The relationship between Henry and his mother has always been close, although recently he has become "difficult to get along with." His mother described Henry as a social isolate—having no friends and preferring to spend his time alone or only with her. No serious medical problems were reported.

Observations During the Assessment

One of the challenges in writing a report is to communicate what you have observed during the assessment. A good report carefully describes the examinee's behavior during the evaluation and any observations that you made in the examinee's classroom, home, or hospital setting. Your observations help the reader understand what you consider to be important features of the examinee's behavior. They also lend some objectivity to the report by providing information about what the examinee did that led you to form specific impressions. Finally, information obtained from behavioral observations may be used in the development of intervention plans.

In writing about your observations, recognize the differences between statements that *describe* behavior and those that *interpret* behavior (see Chapters 8 and 9). A statement that the child was tapping his or her feet during the evaluation describes the child's behavior. A statement that the child was anxious during the evaluation interprets the child's behavior. Both descriptive and interpretive statements are valuable to include in a report. Sometimes it is useful to include a descriptive statement followed by a statement interpreting the behavior or vice versa.

The child's behavior in the assessment setting may differ from behavior in other settings. Consequently, you must be careful in generalizing only from the child's behavior in the assessment setting. However, the behaviors that you observe during the evaluation are in the child's repertoire and should be reported.

In describing the child's behavior, focus on the *presence* of a behavior rather than on its *absence*. You can cite an almost infinite number of adjectives that did *not* characterize a child's behavior, but such descriptions are relatively useless. Instead, emphasize how the child actually performed. For example, instead of saying "The child was not hyperactive," say, "The child was quiet and calm" or "The child remained still." Similarly, focus on what the behavior suggests rather than on what it doesn't suggest. For example, instead of saying "Her agility while running suggests no obvious delays in gross-motor development," say, "Her agility while running suggests at least average gross-motor development." An exception is when the referral source asks you to comment on a specific problem or symptom. In such cases, include a statement about the specific problem or symptom, even if it did not occur. Another exception is if you fail to observe a behavior that normally would be expected to occur; you should note the absence of the behavior in that case.

In the Behavioral Observations section of the report, you can comment on the examinee's physical appearance, reactions to being evaluated, reactions to you, general behavior, activity level, language style, general response style, mood, response to inquiries, response to encouragement, attitude toward self, motor skills, and unusual habits, mannerisms, or verbalizations. You also can include your own reactions to the examinee. Four excerpts from Behavioral Observations sections follow.

William is a 5-year, 2-month-old child with blond hair and brown eyes. He was friendly and animated and appeared eager to talk. He was curious about the toys in the room, examining them in each cabinet. During the evaluation, he often squirmed in his seat, exhausting nearly every position possible while remaining on his chair. Despite his frequent squirming, William maintained a high degree of interest throughout the evaluation. He was attentive and followed the questions well, and he established excellent rapport with the examiner.

Regina is a 16½-year-old adolescent whose makeup and hairstyle make her look older than she is. She appeared anxious and somewhat sad throughout the evaluation. Her wide-eyed look and clenched hands underscored her anxiety and tension and suggested fearfulness. Although Regina seemed able to relax after talking with the examiner, she was extremely tense when some topics were discussed. In discussing her school performance, for example, she made many self-deprecating remarks, such as "I can't do well in most subjects" and "I'm terrible at that subject." She also responded repeatedly with "I don't know" rather than attempting to answer difficult or personal questions. Despite Regina's anxiety, she occasionally smiled and laughed appropriately.

Karl is a bright-eyed, amiable, 6-year, 3-month-old child of above-average height. He was eager to begin the evaluation and immediately took a seat when I asked him to do so. Initially, he chatted easily with me. However, when I gave him an opportunity to play with the toys in the room, he seemed unsure of himself. He wandered from activity to activity, never staying with any one toy or game. He seemed to be unable to focus his attention. His initial attitude of confidence and self-composure seemed to deteriorate, and he began to whisper his answers. It appeared that he was afraid to respond in the event that I might disapprove of his answers. He was concerned about and sensitive to my opinion of his responses and frequently asked, "Was that OK?" or "Is that right?" Karl appeared disappointed when he could not talk about some things that I asked him to discuss. Even when I gently encouraged him to tell exactly what he meant, he continued to use the same words or added, "I don't know." Karl appeared to relax somewhat as the evaluation progressed. When he realized that I was not critical of responses, he gave his answers in a normal voice and became more assertive. Karl was given a short break because of his restlessness, after which he seemed considerably more relaxed and comfortable.

Frank, a 17-year, 4-month-old adolescent, avoided eye contact with me and, at times, seemed to have difficulty finding the right words to express himself. He showed some signs of anxiety, such as heavy breathing, sniffling a great deal, mumbling, and making short, quick movements with his hands and head. He seemed to answer some questions impulsively, but he occasionally said quietly, "No, wait" and then gave another answer.

Assessment Results and Clinical Impressions

The Assessment Results and Clinical Impressions section consolidates the assessment information you have obtained and provides a comprehensive picture of the assessment findings. Topics covered include assessment findings, precision range of the major scores, reliability and validity of the test results, and clinical and diagnostic impressions.

Reliability and validity. Do not report assessment findings unless, in your opinion, they are a valid indication of the child's ability or behavior. If you have any concerns that a finding may not be reliable or valid, clearly state your concerns and the reasons for them at the beginning of the Assessment Results and Clinical Impressions portion of the report.

Of course, you also need to evaluate the reliability and validity of each assessment instrument before you use it by reading the relevant test manuals and other published literature. Do not use instruments with poor psychometric properties to make decisions about examinees. After you administer the instrument, evaluate the reliability and validity of the results, looking for any factors that might make the results questionable. As you may recall from Chapter 2, several factors affect reliability. Because reliability affects validity, an unreliable performance cannot be valid.

In reporting assessment results that you believe are valid (in which case they must be reliable), you might say, "The results of the present assessment appear to be valid, because Richard's motivation and attention were good throughout the assessment process." An appropriate way to report results that have questionable validity might be "The assessment results may not be valid, because Rebecca was ill on the day of the testing" or "Darleen often appeared confused and unwilling to discuss many facets of her life. Consequently, it is doubtful that the limited information she provided about herself was either reliable or valid."

Guidelines for reporting test results. Do not simply report test scores; you also need to integrate and interpret them. Important topics to cover in the Assessment Results and Clinical Impressions section are the following:

1. Factors that may have affected the assessment results
2. Names of the instruments you administered
3. Percentile ranks associated with the scores
4. Description of the child's strengths and weaknesses
5. Illustrative responses
6. Signs suggestive of psychopathology
7. Signs suggestive of exceptionality, such as creativity, giftedness, emotional maturity, or learning disability
8. Interrelationships among test findings
9. Interrelationships among all sources of assessment information
10. Implications of assessment findings
11. Diagnostic impressions

Whenever possible, provide several sources of information to substantiate your interpretations.

Consider what data you should include in or append to the report (Freides, 1993; Matarazzo, 1995). Some clinicians are reluctant to include technical assessment data in reports because readers may misunderstand or misinterpret the information. Other clinicians argue that such data should be included in or appended to the report so that qualified readers can evaluate the basis for the examiner's conclusions. You will need to be guided by your agency's policy on this matter. If technical assessment data are not included in the report, the data should remain readily available to future examiners.

Clinical and diagnostic impressions. When you develop hypotheses about an examinee's performance, consider the examinee's scores on the assessment instruments; patterns of scores; the relationships among the test scores; observations about the examinee's verbal and nonverbal behavior during the evaluation; information obtained from systematic behavioral observations; information obtained from interviews with the examinee, the examinee's parents, and the examinee's teachers; prior assessment findings; developmental history; family history; and other relevant case history information. You are on firmer ground for making interpretations when you have consistent findings from several sources. *Use extreme caution in making any interpretations or diagnostic formulations when you have inconsistent assessment information.* Inconsistent assessment information gives rise to questions that you might want to explore further. In any case, never make interpretative or diagnostic statements when there are major discrepancies in the findings or information that you have obtained.

Organizing the Assessment Results and Clinical Impressions section. You may choose to organize the assessment results on a *test-by-test basis* (e.g., WISC–IV, MMPI-A, CBCL), a *domain-by-domain basis* (e.g., intelligence, pathological states, behavioral adjustment), or a com-

bined test-by-test and domain-by-domain basis. In deciding how to organize a report, think about the nature of the referral question and about which approach is likely to provide the most clarity for the reader. A typical report based on the more common test-by-test organization includes a separate paragraph describing the results of each test or procedure—intelligence test results, visual-motor test results, achievement test results, personality test results, adaptive behavior inventory results, systematic behavioral observation results, and so on. A summary paragraph at the end of the section then integrates the main findings.

A typical report based on domain-by-domain organization includes a separate paragraph for each domain of interest—such as intelligence, pathology, and adaptive behavior. Each paragraph reports results from the different assessment procedures relevant to the child's functioning in that domain. For example, a paragraph on pathology and behavioral adjustment might include data from a personality test, a behavioral checklist completed by the teacher, and observations of the child in the classroom setting.

As a beginning examiner, you might find the test-by-test organization style easier to use than the domain-by-domain style. If you choose the test-by-test organization style, you should still comment on the relationships among related data—for example, you may have to explain why there are discrepancies in the reports of mother, father, and teacher. Whichever style you choose, organize and synthesize all of the assessment findings and present them clearly.

Recommendations

Recommendations are an important part of a psychological report. As with the Assessment Results and Clinical Impressions section, base your recommendations on all the information available to you, including the case history, the child's overall level of performance, and the child's strengths and weaknesses. Recommendations may focus on interventions, class placement, treatment, or rehabilitation. The intent is not to present a "cure" or a "label," but to offer a flexible approach for interventions and appropriate placements. Recommendations should take into consideration the resources of the family and school. If you believe that further assessment is needed before you can make a diagnosis or offer interventions, you may recommend, for example, a neuropsychological evaluation, a medical evaluation, a speech and language evaluation, or a psychiatric evaluation. With sufficient information, you will be in a better position to recommend appropriate interventions. When you make suggestions that involve others (e.g., teachers or parents), it is important that you collaborate with them, rather than telling them what to do.

Develop reasonable recommendations. Recommendations should describe realistic and practical intervention goals and treatment strategies. Questions to consider in developing the recommendations include the following:

1. How representative are the present assessment results?
2. Can the present assessment results be generalized?
3. Were *all* relevant factors considered in arriving at the recommendations, including test results, observations, parental reports, teacher reports, examinee's self-report, medical evaluations, school grades, prior history, previous psychological test results, and response to prior interventions (if applicable)?
4. What is the examinee's eligibility for special programs?
5. What type of intervention program does the examinee need (behavioral, academic, counseling, or a combination of these)?
6. What are the goals of the intervention program?
7. How can the examinee's strengths be used in an intervention program?
8. How might family members become involved in the treatment plan?
9. Can the recommendations be implemented, given the resources of the family, community, and school?
10. Who can carry out the recommendations?
11. Are the recommendations written clearly and understandably?
12. Are the recommendations sufficiently detailed that they can be easily followed but sufficiently broad to allow for flexibility in implementation?
13. Is there a need for further evaluation? If so, what is needed?
14. Are follow-up evaluations necessary? If so, when and by whom?

You should list the specific recommendations in order of priority. The highest priority recommendations usually address the referral question. However, if you find more pressing problems and have recommendations to alleviate these problems, emphasize them in this section of the report first, and address the referral concerns later. A useful strategy is to introduce each recommendation by stating the basis for your suggestion: "Because of Sarah's below-average reading comprehension skills, it is recommended that. . . ." "Because Arthur has difficulty memorizing new data, I suggest that. . . ." "Because of Amy's limited phonological awareness, she might. . . ."

Involve children, parents, and teachers in the recommendations. Two important aims in making recommendations (and carrying out the assessment as a whole) are to find ways to help the examinee help himself or herself and to involve parents and teachers directly in therapeutic and educational efforts. The emphasis, however, is on the examinee, on his or her situation, and on identifying avenues for growth and enrichment. Your suggestions for change should be practical, concrete, individualized, and based on sound psychological and educational practice. Because there are many demands on classroom teachers and on parents, your recommendations need to be realistic.

Use caution in making long-range predictions. Making predictions about future levels of functioning is difficult and risky. You don't want to lull the reader of the report into thinking that a course of development is fixed. Although you should always indicate the examinee's present level of functioning and make suggestions about what might be expected, any statements about the examinee's performance in the distant future should be made cautiously.

Write the recommendations so that the reader can clearly recognize your degree of confidence in any prediction. Cite test or behavioral data, when needed, to help the reader better understand the recommendations. Your recommendations should individualize the report, highlighting the major findings and their implications for intervention.

Summary

The Summary section reviews and integrates the information in the prior sections of the report. Ideally, the report itself should be a summary—that is, it should be precise and concise. When you write the Summary section, limit yourself to one or two short paragraphs. Consider including in the summary one key idea (or more as needed) from each part of the report. *Do not include new material in the summary.* The summary might reiterate the reason for referral and mention pertinent background information, behavioral observations, assessment results, reliability and validity of the assessment results, classification of scores, examinee's strengths and weaknesses, examinee's verbal and nonverbal abilities, interrelationship among assessment scores, special features of the examinee's performance, clinical impressions, and recommendations. You may want to include a single statement in the Summary section that reflects the major recommendation: "The reported findings indicate that Sarah may qualify for special education services under the learning disability [state code]."

Some people read only the Summary section or rely on it heavily. This is unfortunate, for the body of the report often contains critical information. Because a Summary section may give readers the idea that they can ignore the body of the report, some examiners choose not to include one. If you do include a Summary section, it may be prudent to refer explicitly to the body of the report at least once within it. We recommend that, while you are in training, you always include a Summary section.

Signature

Your name, professional title, and degree should appear at the end of the report, with your signature placed above your printed name. The professional title you use should be in compliance with your state laws. For example, in some states the title "psychologist" should be used only by those who are licensed psychologists. And the title "school psychologist" should be used by psychologists employed by schools. Get into the habit while you are in training of signing your reports, because an unsigned report may not be considered a legal document. If you are in training, your supervisor will also sign your reports. When a multidisciplinary team of examiners is involved in an assessment, the name and title of each member of the team, as well as the name and title of the person who synthesized or compiled the report, need to be included. The team report also may need to be signed by each examiner, although in some cases the signature of the compiler may suffice.

Comment on Sections of a Psychological Report

The preceding discussion on organizing a report is a good guide; however, there is no single, unalterable way to organize a report. The way you organize a report should be governed in part by who will make use of the report. The organization of the report should be logical and should convey the information as clearly as possible. Sometimes you may want to place the Recommendations section after the Summary section rather than before it. The summary would then focus on the assessment findings—not on the recommendations.

> *Sometimes one has to say difficult things, but one ought to say them as simply as one knows how.*
> —G. H. Hardy, English mathematician (1877–1947)

PRINCIPLES OF REPORT WRITING

We now consider 13 principles designed to help you write reports. The principles cover how to organize, interpret, and present the assessment findings. Exercises are included to help you evaluate your understanding of the principles.

Principle 1. Organize the assessment findings by looking for common themes that run through and across the assessment findings, integrating the main findings, and adopting a theoretical perspective.

Although there is no one best method for organizing the assessment findings, using a consistent three-step strategy and keeping goals clearly in mind will help. Ideally, the goal of the psychological assessment is to obtain a comprehensive view of the child and the child's life situation while at the same time responding to the referral question. Often, however, an assessment has the narrower focus of addressing a circumscribed referral question.

Before you write the report, look over all of the information you obtained. Consider the following questions:

1. What are the reasons for the referral?
2. What are the backgrounds of the persons for whom the report will be written?
3. What are the major findings you want to report?
4. How do the present results compare with previous ones?
5. What are the major themes you want to develop?
6. How have the findings answered the referral question?
7. What questions remain unanswered?
8. What are the major recommendations you want to present?

As a beginning student—or even as a practitioner—you may have difficulty making sense of the assessment results, especially when they are from several sources. Some findings may be clear, others murky. You may have obtained conflicting results from different tests purporting to measure the same ability or received conflicting information from the child, teachers, and parents. Discuss discrepant findings in the report and provide explanations, when possible. If you cannot explain the findings, report that there is no clear explanation for the discrepant findings. Caution the reader about the results where appropriate.

Calvin and Hobbes   by Bill Watterson

Once you have a general understanding of the assessment findings, you are ready to undertake the following three-step process for organizing and interpreting the findings.

Step 1. Look for common themes.   The first step is to detect any common themes and trends that appear in your results. The following questions may help you detect common themes.

1. Are there any consistent findings and/or patterns among the assessment data?
2. What are the divergent findings?
3. Which divergent findings are major and which are minor?
4. What do the themes suggest to you about the examinee's present problems, strengths, weaknesses, coping mechanisms, and possibilities for remediation or change?
5. How do family members, other children, and other adults contribute to the child's difficulties (e.g., anxiety attacks occur only when the examinee's father is present)?
6. What are some important environmental contingencies (e.g., the child has trouble eating in the cafeteria but not at home)?

Step 2. Integrate main findings.   The second step is to consider all the information you have—even information that seems contradictory—as you develop your clinical impressions and recommendations. Recognize that people rarely show the same behavior in every situation. Suppose, for example, that the examinee exhibits anxiety in some situations but not in others. Note this variability and take it into account in evaluating the extent of the child's anxiety disorder. Remember that variability in behavior may be associated with both individual and situational factors.

Earlier in this chapter we discussed several formats for organizing the Assessment Results and Clinical Impressions section of a report—a test-by-test format, a domain-by-domain format, and a combination of the two formats. Regardless of the format you choose, bring together findings that relate to common themes. For example, if a diagnosis of learning disability appears probable, discuss the findings that support this clinical impression. Or if the findings suggest the presence of neurological dysfunction, describe the pertinent facts that led you to this clinical impression. Show how the child's abilities are interrelated by using expressions signaling comparison and contrast, such as *however, but, on the one hand, on the other hand,* or *in comparison with.* When contrasting results, use comparative terms such as *higher, lower, stronger,* or *weaker.*

Be aware of two potential sources of error in integrating findings. One is forming hypotheses prematurely, which may lead you to ignore information that conflicts with your initial conceptualization and to seek data to confirm your premature hypothesis. The second is overgeneralizing based on limited findings. You should not draw conclusions about a child's everyday school behavior from a limited observation period or generalize from the child's behavior in the evaluation to how the child behaves in other settings.

Step 3. Adopt a theoretical perspective.   The third step is to interpret the material using a specific theoretical perspective or an eclectic theoretical perspective. The perspective you adopt may vary from case to case, depending on the context of the particular case, the referral question, and other relevant factors. The major theoretical perspectives related to the assessment focus of this text are developmental, normative-developmental, cognitive-behavioral, and eclectic perspectives (see Chapter 1). A cognitive-behavioral perspective, for example, may focus on the environmental contingencies related to the problem behavior; the child's and parents' views of themselves, others, and the environment; the child's and parents' attitudes and beliefs; and antecedent events that may be related to the problem behavior. If possible, use a theoretical perspective that not only sheds light on the examinee's behavior but also offers some strategies for remediation and treatment. Often it may be useful to use an eclectic perspective—that is, to interpret findings from more than one theoretical perspective.

Principle 2. Include only relevant material in the report; omit potentially damaging material not germane to the evaluation.

When you are deciding what material to include in the report, consider the accuracy, relevance, and fairness of the material and whether the material augments the reader's knowledge of the examinee. No matter how interesting the information is, if it does not contribute to an understanding of the examinee and the referral question, it is irrelevant and should be left out. Weigh the value of each statement. If you cite any highly sensitive information in the report, make its relevance clear and present supporting data. Consider the effect your report will have on various readers, including the child's parents.

Also discuss how much weight you gave to various factors in arriving at your clinical impressions, conclusions, and recommendations. This will help the reader understand your reasoning. In general, include in the report a mix of general implications, specific behavioral illustrations, and some testing details to help the reader understand how you arrived at your clinical impressions.

What information does the reader really need? The reader wants information about the referral question, the findings, your interpretation of the findings, and possible interventions. Do not include tangential information. For example, when is it worthwhile to note in a report whether the examinee is right handed or left handed or whether the examinee is well groomed? A discussion of the examinee's handedness is worthwhile if there is a question of mixed dominance, and a discussion of the examinee's grooming is useful if it helps the reader understand the examinee's self-concept, attitudes, or familial environment (e.g., parental care and guidance). In other cases, neither handedness nor grooming may be important. Similarly, in a report about a child referred for learning problems, information about the father's or mother's sex life usually would be tangential. In exceptional cases, when private information about family members has a direct bearing on a child's problem, think carefully about the most professional way to phrase the information so that it does not appear to be simply a bit of titillating gossip.

The following are examples of irrelevant or potentially damaging statements:

- "James told the examiner that his father frequently invited different women over to the house." This information is unlikely to add to an understanding of the child or the assessment results, and it is potentially damaging to the child and his father. *Suggestion:* Delete it, or, if you are convinced that this statement is relevant, replace it with a statement that may give some insight about the child's feelings—for example, "James expressed resentment about frequent female visitors to his house."

- "Tara is in excellent health but has food allergies. Some researchers have posited an association between learning disabilities and allergies." The last sentence is controversial. *Suggestion:* Delete the last sentence; however, you can recommend that Tara be referred to a health care provider if she is not already under treatment.

- "Joe appeared disheveled and dirty at times because his family is on welfare." Don't assume a strong relationship between grooming and limited income. This statement is prejudicial toward people who receive welfare aid. *Suggestion:* The problem here could be corrected by making the statements about Joe's appearance and his family's income separate sentences, to avoid implying a relationship between the two.

- "Jeffrey's mother has been seen leaving the house at odd hours." This statement may be irrelevant to the case. *Suggestion:* If this statement is relevant, say why it is relevant, explain the word *odd*, cite the source, use the qualifier *reportedly,* or convey the information orally to the referral source; otherwise, delete it.

Exercise 25-1
Evaluating the Relevance of Statements

Read the statements, evaluate them, and then compare your evaluations with those in the Comment section.

1. "Eileen did much better than expected in her communications with me, given the fact that she lives in an impoverished neighborhood."

2. "At one time, she wanted to use my pencil to write out a response, but I explained to her that she should try to talk about herself."

Comment

1. The assumption underlying this statement reveals the writer's prejudices. First, the writer labeled the neighborhood "impoverished." A more effective way of presenting information about the child's living conditions would be to describe what was observed in the neighborhood rather than simply labeling it. Second, the writer has made the assumption that poor living conditions lead to poor communications skills, which is a biased assumption. Thus, the writer made a value-laden judgment that the child did much better than expected without presenting a reasonable explanation for this interpretation.

2. Unless this statement illustrates a point, why include it? The statement may distract the reader. (In addition, the examiner's refusal to allow the examinee to write out a response may have been an unwise assessment decision, because the examinee may have wanted to divulge sensitive material that she was unwilling to say aloud. Examiners should be flexible in the ways they allow examinees to express themselves.)

Principle 3. Be extremely cautious in making interpretations based on a limited sample of behavior.

Be careful about any generalizations and inferences you make, especially about underlying traits or processes. For example, "Johnny refused to be interviewed and ran away from the office in tears" is better than "Johnny is a negative child who shows hostility toward those who wish to help him." If the latter statement was based only on the observation that the child ran away from the office in tears, it would be unacceptable, because it would be an unwarranted generalization. If, however, you can demonstrate that you have enough information to support an interpretation like this, then make it. Also avoid the temptation to assume that a behavior demonstrated in one setting will occur in another setting. For example, do not assume that an examinee who is impulsive in the classroom also is impulsive at home.

The following are examples of statements that may make incorrect inferences:

- "From the start, Derek tended either to repeat questions to himself or to ask the examiner to repeat the questions for him. This appeared to be Derek's attempt to structure or clarify the questions for himself." This behavior *could* reflect the child's attempt to structure the question, but it is not clear how repeating the question helped him to structure it. It also could be a means of controlling the situation, or it could suggest inattention. In addition, the behavior may reflect a delay tactic, a need for additional support, or a coping pattern associated with a hearing deficit. Consider everything you know about the child to arrive at the best interpretation (if you need to make one). *Suggestion:* Leave out the last sentence ("This appeared to be . . .") unless you have other supporting information.

- "As the assessment progressed, he tended to sit with his arms folded or to pick at and scratch his arm when responding to questions. Although at first these behaviors made John seem less interested, it appears that he was compensating for his low self-confidence." This interpretation seems to have little merit. How do folding arms and scratching arms reflect compensation for low self-confidence? Could these actions simply be a habit, a response to frustration, or a reaction to mosquito bites? *Suggestion:* Keep the first sentence and eliminate the second one. Then describe comments the child made about himself, if any, and note how cooperative he was.

- "Harry's statements about his inadequacies resulted in an increase in feelings of inferiority and self-deprecating behavior, as shown by an increase in nervous laughter and by impulsive answers." This inference is conjectural. It implies a cause-and-effect relationship between verbal expressions and behavior. There is no way of knowing how his own statements made the examinee feel, unless he told you explicitly about his feelings. *Suggestion:* Limit the statements to a description of the child's verbalizations and behavior: "When he was asked about his school work, Harry answered impulsively, laughed, and made self-deprecatory remarks." You also could include one of Harry's own comments: "He said, 'I'm a lousy student.' "

- "Perhaps she played independently because other children could not or did not want to keep up with her." This inference may or may not be correct. To make this statement, you must have supporting information about the other children's behavior and thoughts. *Suggestion:* Omit the sentence unless you have information about the behavior and thoughts of the other children.

- This statement was made about a young woman who was observed in a rehabilitation program for developmentally delayed individuals: "Her performance on the assembly line may be somewhat slower than what might be expected of a worker with average intellectual ability." This statement is fine if you know the performance rate of individuals with average intellectual ability. If you do not have this information, leave the statement out. Without the relevant information, it is prejudicial and based on stereotyped notions. You should make statements that compare the examinee with a relevant norm group only when you have information about that group.

Exercise 25-2
Evaluating Inferences

Read the statements, evaluate them, and then compare your evaluations with those in the Comment section.

1. "The child is small for his age and may feel a need to achieve."
2. "Her physical appearance suggested no behavioral problems."
3. "Since there is no evidence of Oedipal conflict in Gunnar's behavior, he must have completely repressed it."
4. "Bill is considered a troublemaker, and this may be due to good social judgment and grasp of social conventionality."
5. "It must be noted, however, that because Steve is a minority student, the low score of 68 on this intelligence test cannot be used as a valid input toward a nonbiased assessment of this youngster."

Comment

1. Without additional information, these two thoughts are unrelated. *Suggestion:* If the only information available to you about the child's achievement needs is that he is small, do not make this inference.
2. Rarely will a child's physical appearance suggest a behavioral problem. Additionally, this is an example of stating information in the negative. *Suggestion:* This sentence should be omitted.

3. The interpretation has little merit. *Suggestion:* Avoid making such speculative interpretations, especially when they are based on the absence of evidence.
4. "Troublemaker" implies a value judgment. *Suggestion:* Whenever you use such a label, cite the basis for using the label. Also, it is far from reasonable to assume that good social judgment and grasp of social conventionality might cause a child to become a "troublemaker."
5. This conclusion may be inaccurate. The minority status of the examinee is not a sufficient basis for concluding that the test results are biased. After all, you should not have administered a test that you know is biased. *Suggestion:* Consider all relevant information in arriving at a decision about the validity of the test results, such as whether the child could understand English (assuming the assessment was conducted in English) or comes from a background similar to that of the children in the standardization group. There are many reasons why an individual assessment might not be considered valid. Maybe the child was sick that day, or there was a tornado drill during the middle of the assessment, or something happened at home that disturbed the child. But minority status *alone* should not invalidate the test results if you have used an appropriately normed test (which you are ethically bound to do).

Principle 4. Use all relevant sources of information about the examinee in generating hypotheses, formulating interpretations, and arriving at recommendations.

Conclusions and generalizations should follow logically from the information in the report. Support your conclusions with reliable and sufficient data, and avoid unwarranted generalizations. You can base your inferences, diagnoses (or hypotheses about possible psychopathology or educational deficiencies), and conclusions on several factors, including the assessment results, quality of the interaction between you and the examinee, behavioral observations, case history, medical history, and previous assessment results. Always use test results in conjunction with other sources of information. Consider all relevant sources of information, and make generalizations only when you have a clear, consistent pattern of behavior. Describe cause-and-effect relationships only when the assessment information is substantial and clear.

Consider the following questions:

1. What are the similarities and differences in the information obtained from the child, parents, and teachers?
2. Are there consistent trends in the assessment data?
3. Does the child's behavior in the assessment correspond with her or his behavior in the classroom and at home?
4. Do the findings point to a clear diagnostic impression?
5. What interventions are likely to be both effective and feasible, given the assessment findings, available facilities and personnel, and family resources?

After you answer these questions, formulate hypotheses and organize the confirming evidence. Entertain alternative hypotheses and revise them as needed. Drop hypotheses supported by only one piece of minor evidence, or regard them as extremely tentative. Retain for further consideration hypotheses supported by more than one piece of evidence—especially if the supporting data come from several sources (e.g., from the child, parents, and teacher). Also, carefully review any evidence that may disconfirm hypotheses. Advance only those hypotheses that receive support. Although these hypotheses represent tentative explanations of a complex situation, they may help you in working with the referral source, the child, and the parents and in formulating treatment recommendations.

Statements in reports can reflect one of three levels of clinical inference:

First level. Take the assessment information at face value and keep interpretations to a minimum. *Example:* "Bill scored within the clinical range on the Externalizing Problems subscore of the Child Behavior Checklist–Teacher Report Form. His score was equal to or higher than the scores of 82% of children in his age range."

Second level. Present the assessment findings, draw generalizations, and present hypotheses about the causes of the behavior. *Example:* "Sylvia's parents and teacher report that she has mood changes and difficulty getting along with others. Several changes in her mood were observed during the evaluation. Her mood changes suggest that Sylvia may have difficulty controlling her emotions, which may, in part, contribute to her interpersonal difficulties."

Third level. Make the most inclusive interpretations, including explanatory speculations about the examinee's behavior; this level involves clinical hunches, insights, and intuitions. *Example:* "A pervasive pattern of neglect during his formative years, coupled with feelings of self-doubt, suggests a negative self-concept. A negative self-concept may, in part, contribute to his poor school performance."

You may use all three levels of clinical inference in the report. However, weigh the assessment information carefully before you decide to offer broad explanatory speculations. If you offer any speculations, label them as such in the report.

When you make a generalization, cite supporting data, particularly if the generalization has important consequences for the child. For example, you might support a statement that Johnny needs special education by stating "Johnny's academic achievement is significantly below that of his age peers, as demonstrated by his performance on the reading and mathematics sections of the Wide Range Achievement Test–3. His intellectual skills, as estimated by the WISC–IV, are in the Average range."

The following are examples of faulty diagnostic statements:

- "The score on the Child Behavior Checklist–Teacher Report Form indicates a diagnosis of attention-deficit/hyperactivity disorder." This statement is unwarranted, because you should never use a score from a single instrument to establish a diagnosis. To make a diagnosis of attention-deficit/hyperactivity disorder, you would need scores from a parent rating measure, observational data from several settings, and case history information.

- "The low Performance IQ and the high Verbal IQ indicate brain damage." This statement is inappropriate, because you must *never* consider a discrepancy between Verbal and Performance IQs by itself as an indication of brain damage. First, this discrepancy is only one of many possible indicators of brain dysfunction; some individuals with brain damage have a high Performance IQ and a low Verbal IQ. More important, discrepancies between Verbal and Performance IQs may have nothing to do with brain damage; normal children also have this pattern. The discrepancy may simply represent this individual's cognitive style.

Recommendations are a valuable part of the report. Develop one or more recommendations that you believe may be appropriate and feasible. You want to be on firm ground when you make recommendations. In other words, your recommendations should be based on assessment information, not on hunches or speculation. Be careful not to make any potentially misleading statements. You may find it appropriate to recommend one or more of the interventions listed in Table 25-2.

Principle 5. Be definitive in your writing when the findings are clear; be cautious in your writing when the findings are not clear.

Phrases and words such as *probably, it appears, perhaps,* and *it seems* are often used in reports when the writer is not completely sure about his or her conclusions, inferences, or predictions. When the assessment findings are definitive, however, present them confidently. For example, you might write: "The child's results on both the personality test and the behavioral checklists clearly reveal evidence of disturbance." Avoid using qualifiers redundantly, as in the following sentence: "It *appears* as though he *may* have a *possible tendency* toward *sometimes* saying the wrong thing."

The degree of certainty you convey in your statements should relate to the adequacy of your information. The more current, reliable, complete, and valid the information, the more definitive your statements should be. The degree of certainty also should relate to the type of assessment information you are considering. Assessment information gained through observation (what you saw an examinee doing) has a greater degree of certainty than prognostic statements (statements about what the examinee may do under other conditions or in the future).

Do not undermine your message by making excuses either for the measuring instrument or for the child's performance on the measure. Report, without apology, the results of the evaluation in as objective a manner as possible. The following are examples of apologetic statements:

- "Nora gave the impression of enjoying herself, and at the same time was willing to try to meet the challenge of the seemingly never-ending questions of the examiner." To whom did the questions seem never-ending? Do not apologize for the examination techniques; apologetic statements tend to belittle your professional status indirectly and may diminish the value of the report.

Table 25-2
Examples of Intervention Strategies Used in Schools

Environmental Strategies

1. Provide a structured learning environment.
2. Adjust class schedules.
3. Use classroom aides and note takers.
4. Modify non-academic times such as lunch break, recess, and physical education.
5. Change student seating.
6. Use a study carrel.
7. Alter location of personal or classroom supplies for easier access or to minimize distraction.
8. Reduce class size.

Organizational Strategies

1. Modify how tests are administered.
2. Provide a sample or practice test.
3. Use tape recorders, computer-aided instruction, and other audiovisual equipment.
4. Select special textbooks or workbooks.
5. Tailor homework assignments.
6. Use one-on-one tutorials.
7. Provide peer tutoring.
8. Set time expectations for assignments.
9. Highlight main ideas and supporting details in books.

Behavioral Strategies

1. Use behavioral management techniques.
2. Use behavioral contracts.
3. Use positive reinforcements (rewards).
4. Use negative consequences (punishments).
5. Confer with student.
6. Confer with student's parents.
7. Confer with student's teachers.
8. Establish a home/school communication system for behavior monitoring.
9. Post rules and consequences for classroom behavior.
10. Offer social reinforcers for appropriate behavior.
11. Put student on daily/weekly progress report.
12. Implement self-recording of behaviors.

Presentation Strategies

1. Tape record lessons.
2. Provide copies of material for extra practice (e.g., outlines, study guides).
3. Limit amount of material presented on a single sheet.
4. Use fewer drill and practice activities.
5. Give both oral and visual instructions for assignments.

6. Vary the method of lesson presentation (e.g., lecture, small groups, large groups, audiovisuals, peer tutors or cross-age tutors, demonstrations, experiments, simulations, games, and one-on-one instruction with adult).
7. Provide for oral testing.
8. Ask student to repeat directions/assignments to show understanding.
9. Arrange for a mentor to work with student in the student's interest area or area of greatest strength.

Methodology Strategies

1. Repeat and simplify instructions about in-class assignments and homework assignments.
2. Supplement verbal instructions with visual instructions.
3. Change instructional pace.
4. Change instructional methods.
5. Move about the room; sometimes stand directly behind inattentive students.
6. Vary speaking tone, volume, and tempo.
7. Make frequent use of maps, globes, charts, timelines, diagrams, illustrations, examples, and demonstrations.
8. Relate unfamiliar or abstract material to concepts familiar to the student.

Curriculum Strategies

1. Change instructional materials.
2. Use supplementary materials.
3. Assess whether the student has the prerequisite skills to complete a particular curriculum.
4. Determine whether materials are appropriate to the student's current interest and functioning levels.
5. Implement study skill strategies.
6. Provide appropriate instruction/materials based on the student's preferred learning style.

Study Skill Strategies

1. Teach the student how to read and survey the material first.
2. Teach the student how to develop questions about the material.
3. Teach the student how to learn the pertinent facts about the material.
4. Teach the student how to recite the pertinent facts learned about the material.
5. Teach the student how to review everything he or she has learned about the material.

Source: Adapted with permission of the Colorado Department of Education.

- "The examiner is sorry that Edward obtained scores reflecting a pathological condition." The word *sorry* reflects the examiner's personal feelings, and your personal feelings should not be imposed on the reader or projected onto the child.

Principle 6. Cite specific behaviors and sources and quote the examinee directly to enhance the report's readability.

When you describe the examinee's behavior, draw inferences, or make conclusions, add selected examples of the examinee's behavior to illustrate your points. For example, if you say that the examinee gave overly detailed replies, provide an illustration. Give sources for any information you did not obtain personally. Statements such as "his mother reported," "according to his classroom teacher," "according to the report prepared by the school psychologist," or "according to the police report" provide documentation for the source of your information.

Examples are a particularly valuable way to clarify technical terms. For instance, the statement that the child has poor sequential planning ability may not mean much to a reader. However, if you follow it with the comment that the child is "unable to recall more than two digits in the proper sequence or place four pictures in their proper sequence," the reader will have a better idea of what you mean.

The following are examples of undocumented statements:

- "Billy has uncontrolled temper tantrums." The source of the statement should be cited. *Suggestion:* "According to Billy's classroom teacher, he cries and stomps his feet when she denies him a privilege. All methods tried by the teacher to prevent these tantrums have proved unsuccessful."

- "The father has a drug-dependency problem." Either a source should be cited for this statement or the statement should be eliminated. Be careful about accepting such information from sources other than persons likely to have firsthand knowledge of the situation. *Suggestion:* "During an interview with the examiner, Arnold's father stated that he is dependent on heroin."

Principle 7. Interpret the meaning and implications of a child's scores, rather than simply citing test names and scores.

The preferred way to report assessment results is to use *child-oriented statements* (or child-focused statements); such statements focus on the child's performance based on her or his test scores. For example, "John displayed no evidence of pathology on the personality test" is a more child-oriented statement than "John obtained scores on all personality test subscales below the clinical cutoff range" which is a *test-oriented statement* (or score-focused statement). Test-oriented reports tend to lose sight of the child and the reason for referral and thus may mean less to parents, court personnel, and other readers. The data you report should clearly and accurately describe the child's performance.

> *Don't write merely to be understood. Write so that you cannot possibly be misunderstood.*
> —Robert Louis Stevenson, Scottish author (1850–1894)

Principle 8. Use scores obtained by extrapolation or interpolation with caution.

You diminish the validity of test scores when you obtain them by extrapolation or interpolation. *Extrapolation* refers to converting raw scores to standard scores not actually obtained in the standardization sample. Extrapolated standard scores, then, are an extension of the norms. However, there is no way to know the reliability and validity of the extrapolated standard scores. If you prefer not to use extrapolated standard scores and if a raw score is extremely high or extremely low, you can report the standard score as falling above or below the highest or lowest standard score given in the norms (e.g.,

"above an IQ of 154" or "below an IQ of 55"). Or, you can report the extrapolated standard score and follow it with the term *estimated. Interpolation* refers to estimating standard scores for raw scores that fall between scores listed in the conversion table in the test manual. If you report an interpolated score, follow it with the term *estimated.*

Principle 9. Communicate clearly, and do not include unnecessary technical material in the report.

Good writing is essential if you want your report to be useful. Present your ideas in a logical and orderly sequence, with smooth transitions between topics. You will impede communication if the report contains sentences with unfamiliar or highly technical words, excessive wording, test scores without interpretation, or irrelevant material. Use words that have a low probability of being misinterpreted, that are non-technical, and that convey your findings as clearly as possible. *Avoid psychological jargon.*

You want the reader to comprehend your report with a minimum of effort. Check carefully that you have written an understandable report, and revise any potentially confusing sentences. You will enhance communication if you write concisely, follow rules of grammar and punctuation, use a consistent style, make clear transitions between different ideas or topics, and give examples of the examinee's performance. Technical and professional writing should leave little room for misinterpretation. Because your report will likely be read by several people who have different levels of psychological knowledge, write it in a way that will be clear to all readers.

Use clear and accurate statements. Make your statements as direct and concrete as possible; avoid vague and abstract ideas and terms that may be difficult to follow. For example, the statement that an examinee's "enthusiasm was slightly off track" is vague, and the statement that an examinee "cultivated a recalcitrant pose" forces the reader to struggle to understand the meaning. If you use a word with multiple meanings, be sure that the meaning is clear from the context in which you use the word.

As noted in Principle 3, behavioral descriptions usually are preferable to interpretive statements. Describe the examinee's behavior accurately. Choose the term that best says what you want to say. For example, was the examinee *anxious, eager, uninterested,* or *depressed*? Did the examinee *walk, stomp, prance, saunter,* or *race* around the room? Do not say that an examinee *lacks* an ability when what you mean is that the examinee's ability is *weak*. Use *limited, restricted, weak,* or *less well developed* rather than *lack of,* unless *lack of* is literally correct. Also, avoid terms that have medical connotations (such as *diminished* or *depressed*) when you mean *low*.

The word *only*, as in "Sheila raised her hand only twice," may be misleading. If this behavior was the norm, the reader might be incorrectly led to believe that Sheila did not raise her hand as frequently as the other students. Use of the word *just* is similarly problematic. The words *very* and *quite* add little meaning to a sentence and are best left out.

Be careful with words that have special connotations, such as *intelligent, bright, average, psychopathic,* and *psychotic.* Use these words only when you have objective information to support their use. Use the word *thinks* or *believes* when you refer to a person's thoughts and the word *feels* when you refer to a person's feelings or emotions.

In professional writing, be precise when you discuss numbers. For example, in the statement "Most children were age three," *three* could refer to months, years, or even days. Although the context of the report will likely clear up the meaning, it is better add *years* if that is what you mean.

Be as specific as possible in your descriptions. For example, instead of saying "There was a small group of children," note the exact size of the group. More detail would enhance the following description: "Joseph is a somewhat apprehensive child, with brown eyes and brown hair." Although the term "apprehensive child" may be accurate, it would be helpful to cite the behaviors that led to this description. Don't use *tends to* or *has a tendency to* to describe a behavior when you have observed the specific behavior. For example, instead of saying "Tommy tends to hit other children," describe what you observed: "Tommy hit his younger brother three times during my visit to his home."

The following section from a hypothetical "politically correct" report is a humorous illustration of how jargon (or catch words) can reduce the clarity of a report and the reader's understanding. In your reports, you should use conventional terms that are accepted by your profession; avoid using a term simply because it is "PC."

A POLITICALLY CORRECT REPORT

John is a *cerebrally challenged child* (a slow learner) who is *uniquely coordinated* (clumsy) in his movements. In school, he *achieved deficiencies in* (failed) several subjects because of *differently logical* (wrong) answers. He *has an alternative body image* (is obese) and is *nasally gifted* (large nosed) and *vertically challenged* (short). When he sleeps, he *is nasally repetitive* (snores). Occasionally, he *engages in negative attention getting* (misbehaves) and is *temporally challenged* (late) in getting to his classes. His teacher says he is *motivationally deficient* (lazy) and *an expert at incorporating multiple viewpoints* (indecisive). He has been caught *committing an ethically different act* (stealing) and admits to *having an ethical disability* (lying) at times. In addition to his parents, John has a 6-month-old sister who *engages in precommunicative vocalizations* (babbles), is *orally challenged* (a messy eater), wears *temporary waste containment devices* (diapers), and is *periodontically oppressed* (teething). A grandfather who is *chronologically gifted* (old) also lives at home.

Use transition words. Transition words help achieve continuity in a report. Transition words may be time links (*then, next, after, while, since*), cause-effect links (*therefore, consequently, as a result*), addition links (*in addition, moreover, furthermore*), or contrast links (*however, but, conversely, nevertheless, although, whereas, similarly*).

Use standard terms. You weaken your presentation when you use informal meanings of terms, terms of approximation, empty phrases, and colloquial expressions to describe your observations and interpretations. These terms and expressions diminish the professionalism and readability of the report and should not be used unless, of course, you are quoting the examinee.

Avoid the following:

- Empty phrases (*in the event that* rather than *if*)
- Unnecessary jargon (*structural methodology*)
- Colloquial expressions (*right away* for *now, kids* for *children,* or *lots of* for *many*) and expressions that imply more than you mean (*gang* for *peer group*)
- Offensive terms (*drunk* for *has a drinking problem, retard* for *mentally retarded*)
- Disability-centered language (*learning-disabled child* for *child with a learning disability* or *brain-injured child* for *child with a brain injury*)

Avoid technical terms. To enhance the readability of your report, keep technical descriptions to a minimum. Whenever possible, use common expressions to present the information you have gathered. Technical jargon may confuse the lay reader. It also may communicate meanings different from those you intended to convey. Even professionals do not always agree on the interpretation of psychological terminology.

Be careful when you are using technical terms or concepts to describe the examinee's performance. For instance, do not say, "Mental ability was better than nonverbal ability," because *mental ability* includes both verbal and nonverbal cognitive ability. Likewise, do not say, "There was no significance to be found in the scores," because the term *significance* can be used either in a statistical sense (with respect to statistically significant differences between scores) or to mean importance. All scores are significant in the sense of being important, as they tell you something about the child's performance. If you are describing statistical significance, make sure that your description is clear.

The reader does not need to know about the procedures you used to interpret the child's performance or about the specific steps you used to arrive at your interpretations. Don't discuss the statistical methods you used to arrive at your conclusions, because you will confuse most readers. Leave references to standard deviations, raw scores, significance levels, scatter, and most other technical concepts out of the report. Focus instead on presenting the findings and their implications.

It is important to identify the scoring system and norms that you used for a particular test when there are several possible scoring systems or different sets of norms. For example, because there are several scoring systems used with the Bender-Gestalt, such as the Koppitz system and the Hutt system, note in the report which one you used to score the examinee's performance. This is essential for record keeping and will be invaluable in cases of litigation.

It is also important to tell whether test norms are based on the child's age or grade in school. For example, achievement tests usually offer both age and grade norms. You may want to report the results using both sets of norms.

The following are examples of unnecessary use of technical terms and information:

- "His attention to detail should be strengthened, as indicated by his performance on the Magic Window subtest." A subtest name is likely to have little, if any, meaning to the reader. If you refer to a specific subtest, describe what the subtest measures.
- "When she reached the ceiling level, she became more restless and serious." Some readers may not understand the term *ceiling level.* You could say instead, "When the more difficult levels of the test were reached, she. . . ." If you do use the term *ceiling level,* add "the level at which all or most tests were failed" in parentheses.

Exercise 25-3
Evaluating Statements Containing Technical
Terms and Information

Read the statements, evaluate them, and then compare your evaluations with those in the Comment section.

1. "The level of agreement for the two observers was >80%."
2. "His sometimes wandering attention may have contributed to the scatter of his subtest scores."

Comment

1. It is preferable to leave technical symbols such as > out of the report, because readers may not be familiar with them. You can, however, describe the symbol in words.
2. "Scatter" is a technical concept and may be misunderstood by lay readers. It is better to use the term *differences* (e.g., "contributed to the marked differences between his subtest scores"). Also, the phrase *sometimes wandering attention* could be replaced with the word *inattention.*

So far as most of us are concerned there are thousands upon thousands of words that are, with rare exceptions, better left in the dictionary where they won't be misused, waste time, and cause trouble.
    —Wendell Johnson, American speech pathologist
        and semanticist (1906–1965)

Avoid confusing and inappropriate writing techniques.   You may be tempted to inject excitement into your writing by using techniques appropriate to creative writing—shifts in topic, tense, or mood or surprising or ambiguous statements. These techniques may, however, confuse the reader and should be avoided (American Psychological Association, 2001). Also, do not use creative embellishments

or language that attracts undue attention to itself, such as heavy alliteration (repetition of initial consonant sounds in two or more neighboring words or syllables), rhymes, or clichés. If you do, you may distract readers and diminish the focus on your ideas. Use metaphors with care, and never use mixed metaphors, such as "She tends to go off the deep end and wind up clear out in left field." Simply say, "She is impetuous." Use figurative or colorful expressions (like "dog tired") sparingly; they can make your writing sound either labored and unnatural or too casual. When you use synonyms to avoid repetition of terms, choose your words carefully so that you do not unintentionally suggest a different meaning. Pronouns can sometimes be used to reduce repetition, but you must be certain that the pronoun's antecedent (the word it stands for) is perfectly clear.

Examples of unclear statements.   The following are examples of statements that can be misinterpreted or are not clear:

- "His performance is a submaximal representation of his intellectual ability." The word *submaximal* is a poor choice. *Suggestion:* "His ability may be greater than his scores indicate."
- "He had a tendency to elicit heavy sighs and become visibly frustrated when he had to discuss his home life." The word *elicit* is used incorrectly. *Suggestion:* Replace *elicit* with *emit* or say, "He sighed heavily and became frustrated when he discussed his home life."

"**It is recommended that hemispheric processing tasks be instituted that take into account the information processing components associated with Processing Speed and Perceptual Organization and disregarding the questionable scatter.**"

Gee, I'm sure glad that Dr. Wordiness didn't get too technical with that evaluation.

Courtesy of Joanne Davis and Jerome M. Sattler.

- "There was no evidence of abnormality in her conversation." The term *abnormality* is likely to be confusing to readers and is potentially misleading. *Suggestion:* "Her conversation was normal."
- "The seizure affected his behavior." The seizure is a behavior, so the statement is not clear. *Suggestion:* "He was unable to complete the examination because he had a seizure."
- "During the examination, Anna engaged in reactive behavior." The term *reactive behavior* is not clear. The sentence forces the reader to guess what the writer means. Instead, describe the child's behavior. *Suggestion:* "During the evaluation, Anna became upset when she discussed her parents' divorce."

Principle 10. Eliminate biased terms from the report.

Your report should avoid implications of bias. This may be difficult, as biased language is well established in U.S. culture. The use of *man* to denote *humanity* and the use of *he* as a generic pronoun are common examples of gender bias. These terms may convey to the reader an implicit message that women are not included in the reference or that females are less important. Where possible, eliminate gender-referenced nouns, pronouns, and adjectives, replacing them with terms that refer to people in general.

Refer to the examinee by the examinee's name or use the term *child* or *client* rather than the term *subject*. The terms *child* and *client* are more neutral and humanizing terms than the term *subject*. The term *subject* has more negative connotations, including the implication of a power difference between the client and the professional.

Implications of gender bias may also arise from the use of nonparallel terms. *Woman* and *husband* or *man* and *wife,* for example, are not parallel, and using them together may imply differences in the roles of women and men. The terms *husband* and *wife* are parallel, as are *man* and *woman* (American Psychological Association, 1994b). Guard against expressions and clichés that imply unequal roles for men and women.

Refer to members of ethnic groups with nouns and adjectives that are acceptable given current social trends, the preferences of members of the group being referred to, and the preferences of readers of the report. Consider carefully whether ethnic designations are needed in the report. For example, reporting that a child's teacher is Hispanic American may be important if you are discussing the child's response to the teacher, but not if you are merely citing the teacher as an informant about the child. Generally, the ethnicity of the examinee is useful information to include in the report. If you routinely mention the ethnicity of examinees from minority groups, be sure to note that an examinee is a member of the majority group when applicable.

Look for signs of stereotyping or prejudice in your writing. For example, avoid giving the impression that all welfare clients have limited education or intelligence or that all obese people are unhappy. Do not make inferences about an examinee's family or friends based on knowledge of the examinee's social class or ethnic group. Comparing two ethnic groups may result in irrelevant, negative evaluations of one of the ethnic groups. *Never make evaluative statements about social, ethnic, or gender groups or about members of these groups in a report.*

Principle 11. Write a report that is concise but adequate.

The following guidelines will help you write more concise reports.

1. *Avoid wordy sentences.* Say, "The patient is probably aphasic" rather than "Although it cannot be definitely established, it is quite probable that the patient is in all likelihood suffering some degree of aphasia." Say, "The patient's left leg was immobilized" rather than "The patient was positioned in bed in such a way that he could not move his left leg sideways or bend it at the knee." Say, "He is overweight" rather than "His weight is beyond the norms of a typical child." Say, "He wrote with his left hand" rather than "It was observed that he wrote with his left hand."

2. *Avoid trite phrases.* Say, "I learned" rather than "It has come to my attention" and "now" rather than "at to this point in time."

3. *Avoid useless repetitions.* Say, "The twins were identical" rather than "The twins were *exactly* identical," "He was small" rather than "He was small *in size,*" and "The family needs to make changes" rather than "The family needs to make *new* changes."

4. *Avoid abstract words or phrases.* Say, "She punched a younger child in the nose" rather than "She manifested overt aggressive hostility" and "Five of the 30 children were out of their seats and shouting to one another" rather than "A minority of the class was misbehaving."

5. *Avoid sentences that are either too long or too short.* The length of sentences is an important factor in readability. Numerous short, choppy sentences can make text sound disjointed and dull, but long, complicated sentences can render the text difficult to follow. Varying sentence length is a way of maintaining the reader's interest and aiding comprehension. When you need a long sentence to communicate a difficult concept, use simple words and sentence structure.

6. *Avoid long paragraphs.* Restricting the content and length of paragraphs in a report contributes to the report's readability. A paragraph should have a unifying theme and usually should run about four or five sentences. Ordinarily, a paragraph that runs longer than a quarter of a page strains the reader's attention span and impairs the reader's ability to recognize the unifying theme and ideas. If you have written a long paragraph, break it down and reorganize it.

If it is possible to cut a word out, always cut it out.
—George Orwell, British author (1903–1950)

Calvin and Hobbes

by Bill Watterson

Principle 12. Attend carefully to grammar and writing style.

Follow conventional grammatical rules in writing psychological reports. A good general reference for technical writing is the American Psychological Association's (2001) *Publication Manual.* For specific questions, consult a dictionary, style manual, or grammar text. Following are some important grammatical, stylistic, and structural aspects of report writing.

1. *Abbreviations.* In general, it is preferable not to use abbreviations in a report. Some abbreviations, such as *etc.,* can be misleading, and some readers may be confused by the use of *TA* for *target adolescent, CC* for *comparison child, E* for *examiner, EE* for *examinee,* or other similar types of abbreviations. If you do need to use abbreviations, anticipate problems the reader might have in understanding them. It is permissible to abbreviate the names of commonly used tests (e.g., *WISC–IV* for the Wechsler Intelligence Scale for Children–Fourth Edition). However, the first time you refer to a test, use its complete name, followed immediately by the accepted abbreviation in parentheses. Similarly, the first time you refer to a university, such as San Diego State University, add its abbreviation (*SDSU*) after its name if you plan to use the abbreviation later in the report. You can use an abbreviation such as *IQ,* however, because it is a familiar term. Always capitalize *IQ* and write it without periods. Avoid acronyms whenever possible.

2. *Capitalization.* Capitalize the first letter of each major word in a test or subtest name, such as Digit Span. Capitalization helps the reader distinguish a particular test or subtest, such as the WISC–IV Vocabulary subtest, from the skill that it measures, such as vocabulary. Capitalize the first letter of the child's IQ classification, as in Average classification or High Average classification. Do not capitalize terms that refer to abilities, such as language skills or visual-motor abilities,

unless they are part of the name of a test. Also, do not capitalize the terms *examiner* and *examinee.*

3. *Hyphens.* The rules for hyphenation are complex. It is helpful to consult a dictionary or other sources, such as *The Chicago Manual of Style,* 15th edition (2003). A term such as *7-year-old* is usually hyphenated, both as a noun (the 7-year-old) and as a compound adjective (a 7-year-old child). Whatever style you use, be consistent throughout the report.

4. *Punctuation.* Effective punctuation will help clarify your writing and enhance the report's readability. Punctuation cues the reader to the relationship between ideas, as well as to the normal pauses and inflections that help emphasize the main ideas and concepts in the report. The placement of quotation marks sometimes presents a problem. Always place a period or comma before the closing quotation mark. Place a colon, semicolon, or question mark after the closing quotation mark, unless it is part of the quoted material. Again, use a style manual or similar source to check your punctuation.

5. *Tense.* A problem you may encounter with tense is how to determine when to use the past tense and when to use the present tense. In general, refer to the examinee's enduring traits—such as physical characteristics, sex, ethnicity, and intelligence—in the present tense. For example, in the following sentence, the present tense is more appropriate than the past tense: "Leah is a dark-haired, 18-year-old female." However, describe behavior you observed during the evaluation in the past tense, because the child displayed the behavior on a specific past occasion: "John was cooperative during the evaluation" or "Martin held his pen in a firm grip."

In discussing a child's level of intelligence, usually use the present tense: "The child is currently functioning in the Average range of intelligence." If the past tense were used in this sentence, it would sound as if the child were deceased or no longer functioning in the Average range at the time the report was written.

When discussing the testing environment, use the past tense, as in "The classroom was brightly lit and had paintings by many children on the wall." The past tense is more appropriate because the room might not always be brightly lit or have children's paintings on the wall.

6. *Spacing.* When you are planning to send a report to an agency, use single spacing. During your training, however, double space your reports to allow for corrections and the instructor's comments.

The following are examples of statements with stylistic and grammatical difficulties:

- "His general performance would be described as being within the Average range." The phrase "would be described as" is unnecessary. *Suggestion:* "His general performance is within the Average range."

- "Phil constantly kept finding things in a drawer of the desk he was being evaluated at to play with throughout the interview, ie. Paper clips, rubber bands, pens, etc." This is an awkward sentence, and it contains punctuation mistakes. The abbreviation *i.e.* should have two periods and should be followed by a comma. However, *e.g.* (for example) would be a better choice than *i.e.* (that is). In clinical report writing, *etc.* should not be used—all relevant information should be presented and not left to the reader's imagination. *Suggestion:* "Throughout the evaluation, Phil played with paper clips, rubber bands, and pens that he found in the desk drawer."

- This statement appeared in a report about an 8-year-old with a WISC–IV Full Scale IQ of 101: "Within a single subtest, his behavior and even speech seemed to deteriorate as the problems got successively more difficult." There are several problems here. First, does the writer mean that the child's behavior and speech deteriorated during every subtest, during just one subtest, or during a few subtests? Second, how did the child's behavior deteriorate? The word *deteriorate* carries connotations of severe impairment and should be used with caution. Third, to obtain average IQs, the child must have been able to perform adequately on several of the subtests. Consequently, whatever deterioration occurred must have been short-lived. *Suggestion:* The writer should give examples of how the child's behavior and speech changed. Also, as discussed earlier, the writer should avoid using phrasing that attracts attention to itself or may cause confusion, such as "his behavior and even speech." Just saying "his behavior and speech" is sufficient.

- "She was observed in the outdoor, free play period." Be careful how you modify terms. *Suggestion:* "She was observed outdoors during a free play period."

- "When approached by a child whom he appeared to dislike, however, Albert threw a ball at the child with one fist." Grammatically, this sentence could mean either that the other child had only one fist or that Albert threw with one fist. *Suggestion:* "When approached by a child whom he appeared to dislike, Albert threw a ball at him."

Exercise 25-4
Evaluating Style and Grammar

Read the statements, evaluate them, and then compare your evaluations with those in the Comment section.

1. "John goes to HMMS."
2. "His mother said, that Fred is lazy".
3. "Ann has shown scores of average intelligence with a lack of intellectual maturity."
4. "He does not demonstrate good behavioral control at the automatic level yet."
5. "Although quite verbal, this 9-year-old girl did not exhibit the egocentric babbling of a less mature child."

Comment

1. This statement will not be clear to readers who are unfamiliar with the abbreviation. *Suggestion:* "John attends Horace Mann Middle School."
2. There is no need for a comma after the verb, and the placement of the period is incorrect. *Suggestion:* "His mother said that Fred is lazy" or "His mother said, 'Fred is lazy.' "
3. The two ideas in this sentence appear to be in conflict with each other. Although the term *intellectual maturity* is imprecise, average intelligence would seem to suggest intellectual maturity.
4. This statement is confusing because it is not clear to what "automatic level" refers. *A possible restatement:* "John's behavior in the classroom is sometimes a problem, as can be seen by his inability to follow the teacher's directions."
5. Observations of behavior should concentrate on what the child did, not on what the child did not do. Why does the writer include the phrase "egocentric babbling of a less mature child"? Why does the sentence begin with *Although*? *Suggestion:* "Jane used mature language in her conversation."

AAAAA—American Association Against Acronym Abuse

Principle 13. Develop strategies to improve your writing, such as using an outline, revising your first draft, and proofreading your final report.

You should develop writing strategies that suit your needs and style. Four effective methods for improving the quality of your writing are using an outline, rereading and editing your first draft, using a word processor to write your report, and proofreading your report.

Use an outline. Writing from an outline will help you maintain the logic of the report because you identify the main ideas and subordinate concepts at the outset (American Psychological Association, 1994b). An outline also will help you write more precisely and ensure that you include all pertinent assessment information. You can use the outline of the nine sections of a report shown earlier in the chapter as the basis for a more detailed report outline tailored to each case.

Reread and edit your first draft. Check your draft for errors and for vague, ambiguous, or potentially misleading material. A guiding theme underlying the 13 principles in this chapter is that someone who is not in the field of psychology should be able to understand any report you write.

The following questions may help you assess the quality of your report:

1. Are the identifying data correct (examinee's name, date of birth, chronological age, and sex; the date of the evaluation; your name; and the date of the report)?
2. Is the referral question stated succinctly?
3. Does the background material contain relevant historical information, such as developmental, educational, family, medical, and psychiatric history and prior test results and recommendations?
4. Do the statements containing behavioral observations enable the reader to form a clear impression of the examinee and his or her behavior?
5. Are the names of all the assessment procedures noted and spelled correctly in the report?
6. Are the reliability and validity of the assessment findings addressed?
7. Are the assessment scores, percentile ranks, and other assessment-related data correct?
8. Is the information obtained from various sources clearly organized, succinct, and integrated, and are the sources of the information noted?
9. Does the report answer the referral question?
10. Are the present results compared with past results (if available) and with the results of other current assessments, and are any discrepancies noted and discussed?
11. Are themes about the examinee's functioning clearly delineated?
12. Are illustrative examples and descriptions provided?
13. Are any doubts about the information, findings, or conclusions stated clearly?
14. Does the report identify questions that remain unanswered or that are answered incompletely?
15. Are the clinical impressions clearly stated?
16. Do the recommendations clearly follow from the findings?
17. Is a rationale provided for each recommendation?
18. Are the recommendations clear and practical?
19. Are speculations clearly labeled as such?
20. Is the summary accurate, succinct, self-contained, coherent, and readable?
21. Is the writing professional in style and grammatically correct?
22. Is the report free of jargon, biased wording, and ambiguities?
23. Is the report straightforward and objective?
24. Does the report focus on the strengths and weaknesses of the examinee, including adaptive capabilities as well as pathology?
25. Is the report of reasonable length? (The length will vary depending on the referral question, the number of tests administered, the number of people interviewed, the number of other procedures that were used, and so forth.)
26. Have you used a spelling and grammar checker to analyze the report?
27. Have you proofread the report carefully?

Table 25-3 will help you avoid some common pitfalls in report writing; study it carefully. Accompanying each guideline are examples of sentences that fail to meet acceptable standards of communication. Try to figure out the error in the sentence before you read the *Appropriate statement* column.

Use a word-processing program to write the report. Word-processing programs can help you in writing a report (Matthews, Bowen, & Matthews, 1996). If your computer's word-processing program has a thesaurus, use the thesaurus to make your writing more varied and interesting, but keep your language clear and understandable. The spell-check and grammar-check functions contained in many word-processing programs also are useful, but they can lull you into thinking that a report is in better shape than it really is. In the first-draft stage of development, grammar checkers are most helpful for picking up simple mechanical problems, such as a missing parenthesis or quotation mark, and for picking up writing quirks, such as too many short sentences or overuse of "to be" verbs. However, spell checkers and grammar checkers cannot evaluate the meaningfulness of your writing. You must make those judgments yourself.

When you use a word-processing program, save your work frequently and make a backup copy of the file on a disk (or other storage device) as a safeguard against inadvertently erasing the file. Remember to update the backup file each time you make revisions. When you are not working on the computer, store the backup disk (or other storage device) in a safe place (such as a locked file cabinet). *It is important to treat your computer files and disks (or other storage devices) as carefully as you would treat confidential paper files.*

Some writers prefer to make a printout of the draft and then make changes by hand, which they later enter into the computer. Use the spell-check function as one of the last steps after you have revised and edited the report and have made the necessary changes to the computer file.

Proofread your report.   As you proofread your report, look for spelling errors, grammatical errors, omitted phrases, and other typing errors. You will probably make fewer major revisions as you gain experience, but you will always need to proofread carefully. You may find it helpful to read your report aloud while proofreading.

Even if you use a spell checker, do not assume that your word usage is correct—you may have spelled words correctly but used them incorrectly. Also, you may have used a wrong word form (e.g., *difficulty* for *difficult*) that will elude a spell checker. If you have any questions about word usage, consult a dictionary or grammar text. If you have used a word-processing program to write the report, check the final copy to see that it is formatted properly.

Table 25-3
Some Guidelines for Good Report Writing

Guideline	Inappropriate statement	Appropriate statement
1. *Use language that is specific rather than general, definite rather than vague, concrete rather than abstract.*	"The child appeared to be mentally retarded."	"Tom obtained an IQ of 62 ± 5 on the Wechsler Intelligence Scale for Children–Fourth Edition. This level of intelligence falls within the Mentally Retarded range."
2. *Make the verb of a sentence agree with the subject.* Use singular verb forms with singular subjects and plural verb forms with plural subjects.	"All of the students in the class was able to answer the question but Joey." "Lisa's grades are below average but is an accurate reflection of her abilities."	"All of the students in the class except Joey were able to answer the question." "Lisa's grades are below average but appear to be an accurate reflection of her abilities."
3. *Avoid unnecessary shifts in number, tense, subject, voice, or point of view.*	"When he heard about his grade, he complains." "Tom was born in California, but New York was his home in later years."	"When he heard about his grade, he complained." "Tom was born in California but lived in New York in later years."
4. *Avoid sentence fragments.* Fragments often occur when syntax becomes overly complicated.	"Not being sure of himself, several items which should have been easy for him, though he said they were difficult."	"Not being sure of himself, James said that several items were difficult, even though they should have been easy for him."
5. *Avoid redundancies and superfluous material.*	"His confidence was congruent with his abilities, and although he realized he was intelligent, he did not appear to undervalue it or overvalue it but rather seemed to accept it without evaluating it." "He did not appear to be anxious or concerned but was willing to try to succeed within his normal pattern of motivation." "The client complained of numbness and loss of feeling." "The client was excited and agitated." "The client is doing well without problems."	"He displayed a great deal of confidence in his abilities." "His motivation was satisfactory." "The client complained of numbness." "The client was agitated." "The client is doing well."
6. *Make sure that any opening participial phrases refer to the grammatical subject.*	"Administering the Vineland Adaptive Behavior Scales, the mother admitted that enuresis was still a problem." "Analyzing the results of the two tests, the scores indicated below-average functioning." "After climbing the mountain, the view was nice."	"Replying to questions on the Vineland Adaptive Behavior Scales, the mother said that the child was enuretic." "The results of the two tests indicated below-average functioning." "After climbing the mountain, we enjoyed a nice view."
7. *Use verb forms of words rather than noun or adjective forms whenever possible.* Using verb forms puts life into reports and helps shorten sentences.	"The principal suggested the implementation of a point system for the improvement of Ricky's playground behavior." "The child is negligent in her work."	"The principal suggested implementing a point system to improve Ricky's playground behavior." "The child neglects her work."
8. *Do not overuse the passive voice.* Although use of the passive voice is acceptable, its overuse can make a report sound dull. To change a sentence from passive to active voice, make the actor the subject of the sentence.	"Authorization for the absence was given by the teacher."	"The teacher authorized the absence."

(Continued)

Table 25-3 (*Continued*)

Guideline	Inappropriate statement	Appropriate statement
9. *Provide adequate transitions.* Each sentence in a report should logically follow the previous one. The first sentence in a paragraph should prepare the reader for what follows.	"Richard is above average on memory items. He failed a memory item at an early level of the test."	"Richard's memory ability is above average relative to that of his age peers, even though he failed a memory item at an early level of the test."
10. *Express new thoughts in new sentences.*	"Mrs. James has not attended any teacher conferences this year, and she has been married four times."	"Mrs. James has not attended any teacher conferences this year. She has been married four times."
11. *Express similar ideas in parallel form.* The content, not the style, should protect the report from monotony.	"The patient sat alone at 6 months. At 8 months, crawling began. Walking was noted at 12 months." "The recommendations are to learn a phonics approach and attending an individualized reading class."	"The patient sat alone at 6 months, crawled at 8 months, and walked at 12 months." "The recommendations are to use a phonics approach within an individualized reading class."
12. *Combine or restructure sentences to avoid repeating the same word, phrase, or idea.* Consecutive sentences that have the same subject or describe the same process often require revision.	"Jim's mother said that he had been in an automobile accident last year. His mother also told me that Jim has had memory difficulties since the accident." "Hyperactivity characterized Jim's behavior. He was hyperactive in class and hyperactive on the playground, and he was also hyperactive in the interview."	"Jim's mother said that he has had memory difficulties since his automobile accident last year." "Jim was constantly in motion in the classroom, on the playground, and during the interview."
13. *Omit needless words and phrases.* Make every word count.	"the question as to whether" "due to the fact that" "pertains to the problem of" "at this point in time" "there were several members of the family who said" "four different teachers said"	"whether" "because" "concerns" "now" "several family members said" "four teachers said"
14. *Avoid misplaced modifiers.* Misplaced modifiers add to confusion and occasionally create unintended humor in a report. Be sure that modifiers qualify the appropriate elements in the sentence. Modifiers should be placed (a) close to the words they modify and (b) away from words that they might mistakenly be taken to modify.	"In response to my instructions, Aaron picked up the ball and walked around the room with his left hand." "Dr. Jones instructed the patient while in the hospital to watch his diet carefully."	"In response to my instructions, Aaron picked up the ball with his left hand and then walked around the room." "While visiting her patient in the hospital, Dr. Jones told him to watch his diet carefully."
15. *Avoid the use of qualifiers.* Words such as *rather, very, little,* and *pretty* are unneeded and are best left out of a report.	"The patient was very attentive." "She was a pretty good student." "a pretty important rule"	"The patient was attentive." "She was a good student" or "She was a mediocre student" or "She had a grade-point average of 3.4." "an important rule"
16. *Use words correctly.* Misused words reflect unfavorably on the writer and discredit the report. Two commonly misused words are *affect* and *effect.*	"The behavior modification approach used by the teacher seems to have had a favorable affect on Edward."	"The behavior modification approach used by the teacher seems to have had a favorable effect on Edward" or "The behavior modification approach used by the teacher seemed to affect Edward favorably."

Table 25-3 (*Continued*)

Guideline	Inappropriate statement	Appropriate statement
17. *Avoid fancy words.* The line between fancy words and plain words is sometimes alarmingly fine. The wise writer will avoid an elaborate word when a simple one will suffice. The report must not become an exhibition of the writer's professional vocabulary.	"The patient exhibited apparent partial paralysis of motor units of the superior sinistral fibers of the genioglossus, resulting in insufficient lingual approximation of the palatoalveolar regions. A condition of insufficient frenulum development was noted, which produced not only sigmatic distortion but also obvious ankyloglossia."	"The patient was tongue-tied."
18. *Do not take shortcuts at the expense of clarity.* Acronyms should be avoided unless they will be understood by all readers. (Even sophisticated readers appreciate having test names written out initially.)	"The PPVT–III, VABS, and WISC–IV were administered."	"The following tests were administered: Peabody Picture Vocabulary Test–Third Edition (PPVT–III), Vineland Adaptive Behavior Scales (VABS), and Wechsler Intelligence Scale for Children–Fourth Edition (WISC–IV)."
19. *Capitalize proper names of tests.*	"In a previous assessment, he was given the bender and the motor-free test."	"In a previous assessment, he was given the Bender Visual Motor Gestalt Test and the Motor-Free Visual Perception Test."
20. *Put statements in positive form, and make definite assertions.* Readers will be dissatisfied if they are told only what did not happen; they want to know what did happen.	"The child did not know his colors." "The child did not have good motor control."	"The child did not name the colors of the red and blue blocks. However, he did separate the blocks by color and matched them to other red and blue objects in the room." "The child stacked two blocks but was unable to stack three blocks."
21. *Do not affect a breezy manner.* Be professional, avoid pet ideas and phrases, and cultivate a natural rather than a flippant style of writing.	"Would you believe, Ma and Pa had a fuss right in the middle of the interview over when the child began to walk." "Mom said her child was sad."	"The child's parents disagreed as to when the child had first walked." "Mrs. Smith said her child was sad."
22. *Do not overstate.* If you overstate, the reader will be instantly on guard, and everything else you include in your report will be suspect in the reader's mind.	"There is no tension in the home." "The client is absolutely brilliant."	"Bill's father reported no tension in the home." "The student scored 141 on the Stanford-Binet Intelligence Scale: Fifth Edition, presented a report card with all As, and was voted 'most intelligent' by the high school faculty."

Source: Adapted from Bates (1985), Gearheart and Willenberg (1980), Kolin and Kolin (1980), and Moore (1969).

Spelling Chequer

Eye halve a spelling chequer
It came with my pea sea
It plainly marques four my revue
Miss steaks eye kin knot sea.
Eye strike a key and type a word
And weight four it two say
Weather eye am wrong oar write
It shows me strait a weigh.

As soon as a mist ache is maid
It nose bee fore two long
And eye can put the error rite
Its rare lea ever wrong.

Eye have run this poem threw it
I am shore your pleased two no
Its letter perfect awl the weigh
My chequer tolled me sew.

—Sauce Unknown

Here are some humorous examples of what can happen when writers fail to proofread and correct their work:

- It is important to proofread carfully!
- After a week of therapy, his back was better, and after two weeks it had completely disappeared.
- Why let worry kill you off—let our professional psychologists help!
- At the IEP meeting the student will need a disposition. We will get Ms. Blank to dispose of him.
- The preschooler has one teenage sibling, but no other abnormalities.
- The adolescent was alert and unresponsive.
- The medical history indicates that the X-rated picture of her brain is normal.
- The client has no past history of successful suicides.
- Mr. Jones has been depressed ever since he began seeing me in January 2005.
- The adolescent completed therapy feeling much better except for her original complaints.

Exercise 25-5
Evaluating and Rewriting Sentences

Evaluate the following statements and then rewrite them. Check your evaluations and revisions against those in the Comment section.

1. "This examination with Helen just flew by in terms of time, because the subject answered quickly and without any hitch."
2. "The mother currently shares an apartment with another woman which she doesn't get along with."
3. "He generally answered quickly while malingering over questions about his home."
4. This statement was made about a child with an IQ of 73: "Some consideration of not allowing Tom to do less than his potential should be kept in mind."
5. "Beth's overreaction to criticism very often leads to a type of perseveration that affects following behaviors until success is again achieved."
6. "Most of our LDs are resourced, but Mark is in a self-contained class because he's both LD and EMH."
7. "His score places him in the 92%ile."

Comment

1. The colloquial expressions "just flew by" and "without any hitch" are not appropriate; the phrase "in terms of time" is redundant. Also, as noted earlier, the term *the subject* is not recommended for use in a psychological report (or a research report). *Suggestion:* "Helen was cooperative and well motivated and answered questions quickly."
2. *Which* is not the correct pronoun for "another woman." The proper pronoun is *whom* (in the phrase "with whom"). Also, it is preferable to better identify "the mother" and to leave out the word *currently*. *Suggestion:* "Henry's mother and a woman with whom she doesn't get along share an apartment."

3. *Malingering,* which means pretending to be ill, is used incorrectly in this sentence. *Lingering* was probably intended.
4. This sentence is poorly written. *Suggestion:* "Every effort should be made to encourage Tom to work at a level commensurate with his abilities."
5. The phrase "type of perseveration" is vague. Because specific behaviors are not cited, the reader has little concrete information. The writer should describe the child's reaction to criticism and how the child's reaction affected her performance.
6. Some readers will not know what these abbreviations mean. The abbreviations are best left out; if they are needed, they should be described fully. In addition, it is inappropriate to describe children as "LDs" and "resourced." *Suggestion:* "Mark is in a classroom for children with learning problems."
7. The words *92nd percentile* should be written out.

CONCLUDING COMMENT ON REPORT WRITING

The overall goal of report writing is to use clear and precise language to write a well-integrated and logical report that will be meaningful to the reader and relevant to the child and his or her problems. In formulating the report, consider all

Courtesy of Herman Zielinski and Jerome M. Sattler.

sources of information, the possible implications of the information, and the possible interventions. As you work through this material carefully and logically, recognize which statements are based on observations and which are based on inferences. Clearly state any findings that are substantial and acknowledge those that are inconclusive, uncertain, or incongruous. Don't come to conclusions prematurely. Write a report that informs the reader of your findings and recommendations and responds to the referral question—not a report that becomes an assessment of the reader's ability to understand your language. If the grammar-check function in your word-processing program reports a readability level, try to keep this level at tenth grade or below.

Psychological and psychoeducational reports may have such problems as omission of supporting data or behavioral referents, poor expression (e.g., use of clichés and jargon, imprecise use of terms, vagueness), poor organization, inconsistencies, incorrect use of theory, poor differentiation between test data and other data, failure to answer the referral question, failure to explain the test data, recommendations that are too vague, unrealistic suggestions for the classroom teacher, and either excessive brevity or excessive length and irrelevance. In contrast, good reports are understandable and enjoyable to read, interpret test results well and explain them clearly, explain how the problem developed, answer specific referral questions, and provide recommendations that could be implemented in the classroom.

Many tests come with report-writing software. We believe that you should avoid relying on such software, as it is important for you to develop your own report-writing skills and learn to write a report independently. However, we suggest that you print out a computer-generated report as a working prototype. Then translate the information in the computer-generated report into your own words, as needed, and form your own hypotheses and interpretations. Every report must be individualized. Remember, *you* are responsible for the content of the report.

The following guidelines, in addition to other guidelines in the chapter, will help you write a clear, succinct, and engaging report:

1. Make your presentation straightforward and objective.
2. Base your interpretations on the assessment information that you obtained.
3. Include the rationale for each recommendation.
4. Do not allow personal biases to influence your interpretations or recommendations.
5. Do not overinterpret the assessment information.
6. Focus on both strengths and weaknesses and adaptive capabilities, as well as pathology.
7. Admit uncertainty if you are uncertain.
8. Be prepared to justify everything you say in the report, because readers may want clarification and because the report may be used in an administrative hearing or in court.

9. Avoid writing a report that is so bland it might represent anyone. Instead, try to describe a unique, specific child.
10. Make the report tight—strive for clarity and brevity.
11. Edit the report carefully to make certain that spelling, grammar, and punctuation are accurate.
12. Watch your semantics—avoid overused or nebulous words, colloquial expressions, and stereotyped phrases.
13. Avoid using the report as a place to display your learning or a large vocabulary.
14. Spell out abbreviated terms the first time you use them (with the abbreviation in parentheses).
15. Avoid jargon and arcane terms.
16. Refer to parents by name or as "Sam's mother," not "Mom," "Dad," "the mother," or "the father."

Report writing is a process of refining ideas, establishing clarity of expression, and applying expertise to make decisions. The ability to write a clear and meaningful report is an important skill. A good report will contribute to both the assessment and the treatment of the child and her or his family. Exhibit 25-1 provides an example of a psychological report.

Summer Vacation!
...but I have a few
more reports to do.

Courtesy of Daniel Miller.

Exhibit 25-1
Psychological Evaluation

PSYCHOLOGICAL EVALUATION

Name: Gregory
Date of birth: Oct. 10, 1995
Chronological age: 10-0

Date of examination: Oct. 10, 2005
Date of report: Oct. 15, 2005
Grade: Fourth

Tests Administered
Wechsler Intelligence Scale for Children–IV

VERBAL COMPREHENSION		PERCEPTUAL REASONING	
Similarities	7	Block Design	12
Vocabulary	7	Picture Concepts	10
Comprehension	7	Matrix Reasoning	10
Information	4	Picture Completion	14
Word Reasoning	6		

WORKING MEMORY		PROCESSING SPEED	
Digit Span	5	Coding	6
Letter-Number Sequencing	6	Symbol Search	7

Verbal Comprehension Index = 80
Perceptual Reasoning Index = 104
Working Memory Index = 71
Processing Speed Index = 80
Full Scale IQ = 83 ± 6 at the 95% confidence level

Wechsler Individual Achievement Test–II

	STANDARD SCORE	PERCENTILE
Basic Reading	67	1
Reading Comprehension	71	3
Listening Comprehension	83	13
Spelling	74	4
Written Expression	76	5
Numerical Operation	88	21
Mathematics Reasoning	94	34

Reading = 64 ± 6 at the 95% confidence level
Mathematics = 90 ± 7 at the 95% confidence level
Writing = 70 ± 8 at the 95% confidence level

Vineland Adaptive Behavior Scales (*Survey Form*)

Adaptive Behavior Composite = 76 ± 11 at the 95% confidence
level, 5th percentile

Bender-Gestalt

Standard score = 91
Percentile = 27th

Child Behavior Checklist

Teacher's Report Form

Reason for Referral
Gregory was referred by his teacher because of learning problems at school, particularly in reading, spelling, and language arts. His teacher noted that Gregory has specific problems such as substituting phonetically similar words when reading aloud (for example, *chair* for *cheer*, *then* for *when*), omitting inflectional endings (that is, *-s*, *-ed*, *-ing*) when reading, and misspelling words by attempting to spell them phonetically.

Background Information
Gregory, a 10-year, 0-month-old boy, is in the fourth grade. The recent divorce of his parents, the death of a grandfather, and the return home of Gregory's two older brothers have made for a tumultuous home setting. Gregory's mother seems to be trying to deal with numerous areas of frustration and tension.

Besides his two older brothers, Gregory has a 13-year-old sister with whom he is close. A physician's report indicated that Gregory is in good health. In addition, his mother stated that Gregory has had no serious childhood illnesses, although some motor and speech milestones were delayed. He has few friends but there are no reports of behavior problems.

Since kindergarten, Gregory's teachers have reported that he has difficulties with listening, oral language, reading, and writing. His overall grades have been in the C range. The school nurse screened Gregory's hearing and vision at the beginning of this school year and reported no difficulties.

Behavioral Observations
Gregory, who arrived with his mother, initially seemed shy with the examiner. Nevertheless, he willingly came with the examiner and, except for occasionally laughing anxiously, seemed relatively at ease. Gregory tended to be chatty, with a somewhat disconnected conversational style. Numerous sound substitutions and omissions (such as "vorsed" for *divorced* and "skies" for *disguised*) and syntax errors (often in tense as well as in subject-verb agreement) were noted in his spontaneous speech. He also displayed some word retrieval difficulties, such as labeling dresser knobs "holes"; auditory discrimination difficulties, such as mishearing *cow* as *car*; and difficulty repeating short sentences, such as rendering the question "How many things make a dozen?" as "How much make a bunch?"

Gregory's work style tended to be slow and cautious, and he seemed to want to avoid all errors. Although generally cooperative, he sometimes wanted to give up when tasks became difficult, but he persisted with mild verbal encouragement. Overall, his level of activity was age-appropriate, and he reacted appropriately to success and failure.

Assessment Results and Clinical Impressions
On the WISC–IV, Gregory, with a chronological age of 10-0, obtained a Verbal Comprehension Index score of 80 (9th percentile), a Perceptual Reasoning Index score of 104 (61st percentile), a Working Memory Index score of 71 (3rd percentile), a Processing Speed Index score of 80 (9th percentile), and a Full Scale IQ of 83 ± 6. The chances that his true IQ is be-

Exhibit 25-1 *(Continued)*

tween 77 and 89 are about 95 out of 100. His overall performance is classified in the Low Average range and is equal to or higher than that of 13% of children his age. These, as well as other test results, appear to be reliable and valid.

A significant difference of 24 points was noted between Gregory's Verbal Comprehension Index score and his Perceptual Reasoning Index score. A difference this large occurs in less than 4.0% of the population. Functioning was low average in verbal areas and in processing speed, average in nonverbal perceptual reasoning, and borderline in working memory. Gregory has a strength in spatial reasoning, average to above-average ability in visual-perceptual reasoning, and weaknesses in the areas of short-term auditory memory and processing speed. Thus, Gregory performs well on tasks requiring visual processing, while doing less well on tasks requiring verbal processing and perceptual speed.

Qualitatively, many of Gregory's answers on the WISC–IV tended to be concrete. For example, he said that shirt and shoe were alike because they are in his closet and that cat and mouse were alike because you see them in cartoons on television. He defined *hat* as something that tells you about different countries. Answers also tended to be poorly organized, with a loose, run-on sentence structure.

On the Wechsler Individual Achievement Test–II, Gregory's reading ability (that is, word recognition and passage comprehension) and writing ability (that is, spelling words and writing paragraphs) both rank at or below the 5th percentile. Although he knows numerous spelling rules, he has considerable difficulty in employing them appropriately. For example, he spelled the word *play* as *pla*. His reading does not reflect an effective use of phonic skills. For example, he read the word *now* for *know* and said *inside* for *instead*. He can identify letters reliably. In attempting to read words, he tends to separate out each phonetic unit and then is often unable to integrate the units effectively. The scores that Gregory obtained on his achievement testing, in both the Reading and Writing sections, were well below what would be expected based on his age, grade, and current cognitive ability.

Gregory's numerical operations skills and mathematics reading skills are at the 21st and 34th percentiles, respectively. Although he seems to have mastered simple addition and subtraction skills, including borrowing and carrying, he has difficulty with some age-appropriate arithmetic tasks.

It is not surprising that this student, who has difficulty in auditory discrimination (for example, saying "masic" for *magic* and "gammel" for *gamble*) and verbal and perceptual sequencing, also has difficulty spelling and reading phonetically. Gregory was unable to sequence all the sounds when asked the name of his school. Other common information that he seemed unable to give included his own address, his brother's age, and labels for familial relationships, such as *uncle*.

On the Vineland Adaptive Behavior Scales, with Gregory's mother as informant, Gregory was given an Adaptive Behavior Composite of 76 ± 11, which suggests adaptive functioning at the 5th percentile. This indicates that his adaptive level is moderately low. Gregory's freedom and responsibility are limited at home, as his mother does not allow him to leave the yard. His chores at home are few, and his mother still helps him with many self-care activities, including combing his hair.

His performance on the Bender-Gestalt suggested no perceptual-motor difficulties (errors = 3, standard score = 91, 27th percentile).

The results of the Child Behavior Checklist and Teacher's Report Form support the information provided by Gregory's mother and teacher. He is somewhat withdrawn, anxious, and depressed, but with no indications of aggressive behavior or other acting-out problems.

Gregory was also observed in his classroom for approximately 50 minutes from 9:30 to 10:20 a.m. on October 11, 2005. The class was engaged in a reading assignment for the first part of the period and in an arithmetic assignment for the second part of the period. During the entire time Gregory never raised his hand to answer a question; several other students did so. He often looked around the room, stared out the window, and played with his pencil. Only one other child was similarly distracted. When asked by his teacher to read, he was unable to sound out words correctly. However, he did answer a simple arithmetic problem correctly. His teacher was sensitive to his reading difficulty and complimented him on his correct arithmetic response.

Recommendations

Gregory may qualify for placement in a program for children with learning disabilities and for a speech/language therapy program. The scores that Gregory obtained on his achievement testing, in both the Reading and Spelling sections, were well below what would be expected based on his age, grade, and current cognitive ability. His school's special education multidisciplinary team should consider the current assessment results, along with other information available to them, when making an eligibility determination. Gregory is experiencing difficulty in school because of language processing difficulties.

The following recommendations are offered:

1. Because of Gregory's weakness in language skills, a program that places particular emphasis on language and language-related skills is recommended. The program should emphasize oral language, reading, and writing skills to improve Gregory's areas of academic weakness.
2. Speech and language therapy integrated into the education curriculum would be desirable. It appears that Gregory's weakness in auditory perception might be part of the basis for his difficulties with oral language, reading, and writing. If the speech-language pathologist's assessment supports this assumption, Gregory might profit from intensive work on phonemic awareness skills. The work on phonemic awareness skills would provide the underpinning to instruction in reading and writing skills.
3. It would be particularly beneficial for Gregory to work on learning to spell the same sounds, syllables, and words that he is learning to read. The spelling encoding and reading decoding would reinforce each other.
4. Gregory appears to have difficulty with memorization and retrieval of information. He may need particular help learning math facts and phonic rules. This is an area in which visual aids might be especially helpful.

Exhibit 25-1 *(Continued)*

5. Gregory's nonverbal spatial strengths should be used in the remediation program. Teachers can help by making special, additional efforts to use visual aids as much as possible. Charts, diagrams, models, timelines, maps, globes, illustrations, dioramas, and demonstrations might prove very helpful to Gregory.
6. Gregory's mother could use guidance in sorting out and resolving personal as well as family stress. Some areas on which she might focus are encouraging communication among family members, dealing with her hostility toward her ex-husband and older children, learning how to cope with being a single parent, and helping her children deal with the divorce.
7. Gregory's mother should be encouraged to help Gregory develop more independent daily living skills. A program emphasizing social skills should be considered.

Summary

Gregory, who is 10 years old, was referred because of educational difficulties. His medical history was normal, but there were some developmental delays. Gregory's cooperative behavior

and other factors suggest that the testing results are reliable and valid. Gregory showed some strengths as well as weaknesses across intellectual areas, with verbal ability, short-term memory ability, and processing speed ability at a below-average level and perceptual reasoning ability at an average level. Overall, Gregory obtained a WISC–IV Full Scale of IQ of 83 ± 6, which is at the 13th percentile and in the Low Average range. He has made little progress in developing skills in spelling and word recognition. These deficits are probably manifestations of his language processing difficulties. Socially, Gregory acts younger than his age. He appears to have a learning disability and language impairment. Recommendations are that he be provided with a program focusing on language and speech therapy. In addition, his family should be advised to seek counseling to help them resolve their problems in the home.

If there are any questions about this report or any of these findings, please feel free to contact me at (201) 123-4567.

(Signature of Examiner) _____

Examiner's name
Examiner's title

THINKING THROUGH THE ISSUES

1. What should be the function of a psychological report?
2. How might a teacher, a physician, and an attorney differ in the kinds of information they want in a psychological report?
3. Why do you think report writing is so difficult for many students?
4. How would you go about writing a report that was not likely to be misunderstood by the reader?
5. What other report formats, in addition to the one described in the chapter, might be useful for writing reports?
6. In addition to this book, what sources can you consult for help in writing better psychological reports?

SUMMARY

1. Psychological reports may be based on information obtained from psychological tests; interviews with the child, his or her parents, teachers, and others; systematic behavioral observations; and school records, prior psychological reports, medical reports, psychiatric reports, and other relevant sources.
2. A comprehensive psychological report should discuss background information, presenting problems, health and developmental history, schools attended, attendance record, classroom behavior, academic performance, evaluation techniques and teaching methods in the classroom, homework and study habits, learning style, family factors, observations during the assessment, perceptual-motor ability, speech and language ability, attention, cognitive ability, memory ability, learning ability, affect, motivation, social interactions, and interventions.

Introduction to Psychological Report Writing

3. A psychological evaluation is complete only after the obtained information has been organized, synthesized, and integrated.

4. The traditional medium for presenting assessment information is a written report, although you may use other formal and informal means of presentation.
5. A report may influence a child and family for years to come; its drafting deserves extreme care and consideration.
6. Your report should be well organized and solidly grounded.
7. A good report does not merely present facts. It integrates what you have learned about the examinee and presents the information in a way that shows respect for her or his individuality.
8. A psychological report (a) provides accurate assessment-related information, (b) serves as a basis for clinical hypotheses, appropriate interventions, and information for program evaluation and research, (c) furnishes meaningful baseline information for evaluating the examinee's progress after the interventions have been implemented or changes that occur as a result of time alone, and (d) serves as a legal document.
9. In formulating and constructing your report, first consider who will be the primary audiences for the report.
10. Every report has elements of subjectivity, because the information in it is open to different interpretations.
11. Write the report as soon as possible after you complete the assessment.
12. The psychological report should adequately describe the assessment findings, including information about the examinee's history, current problems, assets, and limitations; it should also include behavioral observations and test interpretations.
13. Each report should be an independent document—that is, its content should be comprehensive enough to stand alone.

Sections of a Psychological Report

14. A typical psychological report has nine sections: Identifying Information, Assessment Instruments, Reason for Referral, Background Information, Observations During the Assessment, Assessment Results and Clinical Impressions, Recommendations, Summary, and Signature.

15. The Identifying Information section presents relevant identifying information about the examinee and examiner.
16. The Assessment Instruments section lists the formal and informal instruments used to conduct the evaluation.
17. The Reason for Referral section helps document why the psychological evaluation was conducted.
18. The Background Information section includes material obtained from interviews with the parents, teacher(s), and child; from the examinee's educational file; and from previous psychological, psychiatric, and medical accounts.
19. The section on Observations During the Assessment provides a careful description of the child's behavior during the assessment.
20. The Assessment Results and Clinical Impressions section consolidates the assessment information you have obtained and provides a comprehensive picture of the assessment findings.
21. The Recommendations section should provide realistic and practical intervention goals and treatment strategies.
22. The Summary section reviews and integrates the information in the prior sections of the report.
23. The Signature section contains your name, professional title, and degree.

Principles of Report Writing

24. Thirteen principles of report writing cover how to organize, interpret, and present the assessment findings.
25. Principle 1: Organize the assessment findings by looking for common themes that run through and across the assessment findings, integrating the main findings, and adopting a theoretical perspective.
26. Principle 2: Include only relevant material in the report; omit potentially damaging material not germane to the evaluation.
27. Principle 3: Be extremely cautious in making interpretations based on a limited sample of behavior.
28. Principle 4: Use all relevant sources of information about the examinee in generating hypotheses, formulating interpretations, and arriving at recommendations.
29. Principle 5: Be definitive in your writing when the findings are clear; be cautious in your writing when the findings are not clear.
30. Principle 6: Cite specific behaviors and sources and directly quote the examinee to enhance the report's readability.
31. Principle 7: Interpret the meaning and implications of a child's scores, rather than simply citing test names and scores.
32. Principle 8: Use scores obtained by extrapolation or interpolation with caution.
33. Principle 9: Communicate clearly, and do not include unnecessary technical material in the report.
34. Principle 10: Eliminate biased terms from the report.
35. Principle 11: Write a report that is concise but adequate.
36. Principle 12: Attend carefully to grammar and writing style.
37. Principle 13: Develop strategies to improve your writing, such as using an outline, revising your first draft, using a word processor, and proofreading your final report.

Concluding Comment on Report Writing

38. The overall goal of report writing is to use clear and precise language to write a well-integrated and logical report that will be meaningful to the reader and relevant to the child and his or her problems.
39. Report writing is a process of refining ideas, establishing clarity of expression, and applying expertise to make decisions.

40. The ability to write a clear and meaningful report is an important skill.
41. A good report will contribute to both the assessment and the treatment of the child and her or his family.

KEY TERMS, CONCEPTS, AND NAMES

Psychological report writing (p. 586)
Qualities of a good report (p. 586)
Purposes of the report (p. 586)
Formulating the report (p. 586)
Subjective elements in the report (p. 586)
Promptness in writing the report (p. 586)
Contents of the report (p. 586)
Sections of a psychological report (p. 586)
Identifying information (p. 587)
Assessment instruments (p. 587)
Reason for referral (p. 587)
Background information (p. 587)
Observations during the assessment (p. 588)
Assessment results and clinical impressions (p. 589)
Test-by-test basis (p. 590)
Domain-by-domain basis (p. 590)
Recommendations (p. 590)
Summary (p. 591)
Signature (p. 591)
Principles of report writing (p. 592)
Three levels of clinical inference (p. 596)
Child-oriented statements (p. 598)
Test-oriented statement (p. 598)
Extrapolation (p. 598)
Interpolation (p. 598)
Bias (p. 601)
Writing strategies (p. 603)

STUDY QUESTIONS

1. What are the purposes of a psychological report?
2. What information is included in each of the following sections of a report: Identifying Information, Assessment Instruments, Reason for Referral, Background Information, Observations During the Assessment, Assessment Results and Clinical Impressions, Recommendations, Summary, and Signature?
3. What strategies can you use to organize assessment findings?
4. What guidelines should you use to decide which material to include in a report?
5. What are some guidelines for making generalizations, interpretations, and diagnoses?
6. What are some important factors to consider in communicating your findings?
7. How can you eliminate biased language from a report?
8. Describe some useful strategies for writing reports.
9. Develop a checklist for evaluating the quality of a psychological report.
10. What are some typical problems that readers of psychological reports encounter?

Appendix A

QUESTIONNAIRES

Table A-1
Background Questionnaire

BACKGROUND QUESTIONNAIRE

FAMILY DATA

Child's name _____ Today's date _____

Birth date _____ Age _____ Sex: ☐ Male ☐ Female

Home address _____

_____

School _____ Teacher _____

Person(s) filling out this form: ☐ Mother ☐ Father ☐ Stepmother ☐ Stepfather ☐ Caregiver

☐ Other (please explain) _____

Mother's name _____ Age _____ Education _____

Occupation _____ Phone: Home _____ Business _____

Father's name _____ Age _____ Education _____

Occupation _____ Phone: Home _____ Business _____

Stepmother's name _____ Age _____ Education _____

Occupation _____ Phone: Home _____ Business _____

Stepfather's name _____ Age _____ Education _____

Occupation _____ Phone: Home _____ Business _____

Marital status of parents _____ If separated or divorced, how old was the child when the separation occurred? _____

If remarried, how old was the child when the stepparent entered the family? _____

List all people living in the household (use an additional sheet if necessary):

Name	Sex	Relationship to Child	Age
_____	_____	_____	_____
_____	_____	_____	_____
_____	_____	_____	_____
_____	_____	_____	_____
_____	_____	_____	_____
_____	_____	_____	_____

List the name, sex, relationship to child, and age of any brothers, sisters, or other significant people living outside the home: _____

_____

_____

Dominant language spoken in the home_____ Other languages spoken in the home _____

What language does the child use to speak to you? _____

What language does the child use to speak with friends? _____

Was the child adopted? ☐ Yes ☐ No If yes, at what age? _____ Does the child know he or she is adopted? ☐ Yes ☐ No

Name of medical coverage group or insurance company (If none, write "none") _____

Name of medical provider_____

If insured, insured's name_____

If referred, who referred you here? _____

(*Continued*)

PRESENTING PROBLEM

Briefly describe the child's current difficulties: _____

_____

_____

_____

How long has this problem been of concern to you? _____

When was the problem first noticed? _____

What seems to help the problem? _____

What seems to make the problem worse? _____

Have you noticed changes in the child's abilities? ☐ Yes ☐ No

If yes, please describe: _____

Have you noticed changes in the child's behavior? ☐ Yes ☐ No

If yes, please describe: _____

Has the child received evaluation or treatment for the current problem or similar problems? ☐ Yes ☐ No

If yes, when and with whom? _____

Is the child being treated for a medical illness? ☐ Yes ☐ No

If yes, for what condition is the child being treated? _____

Is the child on any medication at this time? ☐ Yes ☐ No

If yes, please list names of medications: _____

SOCIAL AND BEHAVIORAL CHECKLIST

Place a check next to any behavior or problem that the child *currently* exhibits.

☐ Has difficulty with hearing

☐ Has difficulty with vision

☐ Has difficulty with coordination

☐ Has difficulty with balance

☐ Has difficulty making friends

☐ Has difficulty keeping friends

☐ Refuses to share

☐ Prefers to be alone

☐ Does not get along well with brothers/sisters

☐ Does not get along well with adults

☐ Fights verbally with adults

☐ Fights physically with adults

☐ Yells and calls children names

☐ Shows wide mood swings

☐ Is aggressive (describe)

_____

☐ Is withdrawn (describe)

_____

☐ Is shy or timid

☐ Clings to others

☐ Tires easily, has little energy

☐ Is more interested in things (objects) than in people

☐ Engages in behavior that could be dangerous to self or others (describe)

_____

_____

☐ Breaks objects deliberately

☐ Lies (describe)

_____

☐ Steals (describe)

_____

☐ Injures self often

☐ Runs away

☐ Has low self-esteem

☐ Blames others for his or her troubles

☐ Is argumentative

☐ Does not get along well with other children

☐ Fights verbally with other children

☐ Fights physically with other children

☐ Does not show feelings

☐ Has frequent crying spells

☐ Has unusual or special fears, habits, or mannerisms (describe)

_____

☐ Wets bed

☐ Bites nails

☐ Sucks thumb

☐ Has frequent temper tantrums

☐ Has trouble sleeping (describe)

_____

☐ Rocks back and forth

☐ Bangs head

☐ Holds breath

☐ Eats poorly

☐ Is stubborn

☐ Has poor bowel control (soils self)

☐ Is overactive

☐ Is fidgety

☐ Is easily distracted

☐ Is disorganized

☐ Is clumsy

☐ Is unusually talkative

☐ Is forgetful

☐ Has blank spells

☐ Daydreams frequently

☐ Worries a lot

☐ Is impulsive

☐ Takes unnecessary risks

☐ Gets hurt frequently

☐ Has many accidents

☐ Doesn't learn from experience

☐ Feels that he or she is bad

☐ Is slow to learn

☐ Moves slowly

☐ Stares into space for long periods

☐ Engages in stereotyped behavior (describe)_____

☐ Does not understand other people's feelings

☐ Has difficulty following directions

- ☐ Gives up easily
- ☐ Complains of aches or pains
- ☐ Is disobedient
- ☐ Gets into trouble with the law
- ☐ Constantly seeks attention
- ☐ Is restless
- ☐ Has periods of confusion or disorientation
- ☐ Is jealous (describe)

  _____

- ☐ Is extremely selfish
- ☐ Feels hopeless
- ☐ Is nervous or anxious

- ☐ Is immature
- ☐ Is easily frustrated
- ☐ Has difficulty learning when faced with distractors
- ☐ Is suspicious of other people
- ☐ Requires constant supervision
- ☐ Has difficulty resisting peer pressure
- ☐ Shows anger easily
- ☐ Has difficulty accepting criticism
- ☐ Feels sad or unhappy often
- ☐ Talks about wanting to die
- ☐ Has poor attention span
- ☐ Has poor memory

- ☐ Sets fires
- ☐ Is afraid of new situations
- ☐ Has trouble making plans
- ☐ Eats inedible objects
- ☐ Is not toilet trained
- ☐ Uses illegal drugs (describe)

  _____

- ☐ Drinks alcohol excessively
- ☐ Has difficulty recognizing that he or she has a drinking problem
- ☐ Other problems (describe)

  _____

  _____

Place a check next to any behavior or problem that the child has shown *within the last three months.*

- ☐ Shows sexually provocative behavior
- ☐ Has extreme fear of bathroom or bathing
- ☐ Has anxiety when separated from parents
- ☐ Has extreme anxiety about going to school
- ☐ Has fear at bedtime
- ☐ Is wary of any physical contact with adults in general

- ☐ Refuses to sleep alone
- ☐ Refuses to go to bed
- ☐ Has loss of bladder control
- ☐ Is fearful of strangers
- ☐ (In cases of divorce) Is fearful of visiting a parent or caregiver
- ☐ Overeats
- ☐ Is very eager to please others
- ☐ Refuses to undress for physical education classes at school

- ☐ Has compulsion about cleanliness— wanting to wash or feeling dirty all the time
- ☐ Appears dazed, drugged, or groggy upon return from visiting a divorced or separated parent
- ☐ Other recent behaviors or problems (describe) _____

  _____

  _____

LANGUAGE/SPEECH CHECKLIST

Place a check next to any language or speech problem that the child *currently* exhibits.

- ☐ Speaks in shorter sentences than expected for age
- ☐ Does not know names of common objects
- ☐ Has difficulty recalling familiar words
- ☐ Substitutes vague words (e.g., "thing") for specific words
- ☐ Responds better to gestures than to words

- ☐ Does not make appropriate gestures to communicate
- ☐ Uses gestures instead of words to express ideas
- ☐ Has difficulty making speech understood
- ☐ Speaks very slowly
- ☐ Speaks too fast
- ☐ Is often hoarse
- ☐ Has unusually loud speech

- ☐ Has unusually soft speech
- ☐ Makes sounds but no words
- ☐ Mixes up the order of events
- ☐ Seems uninterested in communicating
- ☐ Prefers to speak to adults only
- ☐ Prefers to speak to children only
- ☐ Prefers to speak to family members only
- ☐ Speaks in a monotone or exaggerated manner

EDUCATIONAL HISTORY

Place a check next to any educational problem that the child *currently* exhibits.

- ☐ Has difficulty reading
- ☐ Has difficulty with arithmetic
- ☐ Has difficulty with spelling
- ☐ Has difficulty with handwriting
- ☐ Has difficulty with other subjects (please list) _____

  _____

- ☐ Has difficulty paying attention in class
- ☐ Has difficulty sitting still in class
- ☐ Has difficulty waiting turn in school
- ☐ Has difficulty taking notes in class

- ☐ Has difficulty respecting others' rights
- ☐ Has difficulty remembering things
- ☐ Forgets homework
- ☐ Has difficulty understanding homework directions
- ☐ Has difficulty getting started on his or her homework
- ☐ Has difficulty asking for help when it is needed
- ☐ Has difficulty remembering to hand in homework

- ☐ Makes careless mistakes
- ☐ Has difficulty keeping notebooks organized
- ☐ Has difficulty finishing a project on time
- ☐ Has difficulty getting along with teacher
- ☐ Has difficulty getting along with other children
- ☐ Dislikes school
- ☐ Resists going to school
- ☐ Refuses to do homework

Did the child attend preschool? ☐ Yes ☐ No

If yes, at what ages? _____   How often? _____

Table A-1 (*Continued*)

At what age did the child begin kindergarten? _____   What is his or her current grade? _____

Is the child in a special education class? ☐ Yes ☐ No

If yes, what type of class?_____

Has the child been held back in a grade? ☐ Yes ☐ No

If yes, what grade and why? _____

Has the child ever received special tutoring or therapy in school? ☐ Yes ☐ No

If yes, please describe: _____

Has the child's school performance become poorer recently? ☐ Yes ☐ No

If yes, please describe: _____

Has the child missed a lot of school? ☐ Yes ☐ No

If yes, please indicate reasons: _____

DEVELOPMENTAL HISTORY

Pregnancy

Did the mother have any problems during pregnancy (for example, unusual bleeding, high blood pressure, an infection, or diabetes)?

☐ Yes ☐ No ☐ Don't know

If yes, what kind? _____

How old was the mother when she became pregnant? _____   Was this a first pregnancy? ☐ Yes ☐ No ☐ Don't know

If no, how many times was the mother previously pregnant? _____

During pregnancy, did the mother smoke? ☐ Yes ☐ No ☐ Don't know

If yes, how many cigarettes each day?_____

During pregnancy, did the mother drink alcoholic beverages? ☐ Yes ☐ No ☐ Don't know

If yes, what did she drink? _____   Approximately how much alcohol did the mother consume each day?_____

During which part of pregnancy—1st trimester, 2nd trimester, 3rd trimester—did the mother consume alcohol?_____

Were there times when the mother consumed five or more drinks in one session? ☐ Yes ☐ No ☐ Don't know

If yes, during which trimester—1st trimester, 2nd trimester, 3rd trimester? _____

During pregnancy, did the mother use drugs (including prescription, over-the-counter, and recreational)? ☐ Yes ☐ No ☐ Don't know

If yes, what kind? _____   How often? _____

During pregnancy, was the mother exposed to any x-rays or chemicals? ☐ Yes ☐ No ☐ Don't know

If yes, what kind? _____   How often? _____

During pregnancy, was the mother exposed to any infectious disease? ☐ Yes ☐ No ☐ Don't know

If yes, what disease or diseases?_____

During pregnancy, did the mother receive prenatal care? ☐ Yes ☐ No ☐ Don't know

Was delivery induced? ☐ Yes ☐ No ☐ Don't know

How long was labor? _____ Were forceps used during delivery? ☐ Yes ☐ No ☐ Don't know

Was a cesarean section performed? ☐ Yes ☐ No ☐ Don't know

If yes, for what reason? _____

Were there any complications associated with the delivery? ☐ Yes ☐ No ☐ Don't know

If yes, what kind? _____

Was the child premature? ☐ Yes ☐ No ☐ Don't know

If yes, by how many weeks? _____

Was neonatal care needed? ☐ Yes ☐ No ☐ Don't know

If yes, what kind of care and how long was it needed? _____

Table A-1 (*Continued*)

Infancy

What was the child's birth weight? _____ Were there any birth defects or complications? ☐ Yes ☐ No ☐ Don't know

If yes, please describe: _____

As an infant, did the child have any feeding problems? ☐ Yes ☐ No ☐ Don't know

If yes, please describe: _____

As an infant, did the child experience any sleeping problems? ☐ Yes ☐ No ☐ Don't know

If yes, please describe: _____

As an infant, did the child need oxygen? ☐ Yes ☐ No ☐ Don't know

If yes, please describe: _____

As an infant, did the child have jaundice? ☐ Yes ☐ No ☐ Don't know

If yes, please describe: _____

As an infant, did the child have infections? ☐ Yes ☐ No ☐ Don't know

If yes, please describe: _____

As an infant, did the child need blood transfusions? ☐ Yes ☐ No ☐ Don't know

If yes, please describe: _____

As an infant, did the child have seizures? ☐ Yes ☐ No ☐ Don't know

If yes, please describe: _____

As an infant, did the child need antibiotics? ☐ Yes ☐ No ☐ Don't know

If yes, please describe: _____

As an infant, did the child experience any other problems? ☐ Yes ☐ No ☐ Don't know

If yes, please describe: _____

As an infant, was the child quiet? ☐ Yes ☐ No ☐ Don't know

As an infant, did the child like to be held? ☐ Yes ☐ No ☐ Don't know

As an infant, was the child alert? ☐ Yes ☐ No ☐ Don't know

As an infant, did the child grow normally? ☐ Yes ☐ No ☐ Don't know

If no, please describe: _____

As an infant, was the child different in any way from siblings? ☐ Yes ☐ No ☐ Don't know ☐ Not applicable

If yes, please describe: _____

First Years

During the child's first years, did he or she show any of the following behaviors? Place a check next to each one that he or she showed.

☐ Did not enjoy cuddling
☐ Was not calmed by being held
☐ Was colicky
☐ Was excessively restless
☐ Had poor sleep patterns
☐ Banged head frequently
☐ Was constantly into everything
☐ Had an excessive number of accidents

☐ Was exposed to lead
☐ Had fine-motor problems
☐ Had gross-motor problems
☐ Did not babble
☐ Did not speak
☐ Had excessive fears
☐ Ignored toys
☐ Was attached to an unusual object (describe) _____

☐ Was unaware of painful bumps or falls
☐ Had peculiar patterns of speech
☐ Preferred to play alone
☐ Had poor eye contact
☐ Was not interested in other children
☐ Did not smile socially
☐ Was insensitive to cold or pain
☐ Did not wave bye-bye

Were there any other special problems in the growth and development of the child during the first few years?

☐ Yes ☐ No ☐ Don't know

If yes, please describe: _____

(*Continued*)

Table A-1 (*Continued*)

The following is a list of infant and preschool behaviors. Please indicate the age at which the child first demonstrated each behavior. If you are not certain of the age but have some idea, write the age followed by a question mark. If you don't remember or don't know the age at which the behavior occurred, please write a question mark. If the child has not yet demonstrated the behavior, write an X.

Behavior	Age	Behavior	Age	Behavior	Age
Showed response to mother	_____	Spoke first word	_____	Took off clothing alone	_____
Held head erect	_____	Showed fear of strangers	_____	Put on clothing alone	_____
Rolled over	_____	Used a two-word sentence	_____	Tied shoelaces	_____
Sat alone	_____	Put several words together	_____	Rode tricycle	_____
Crawled	_____	Became toilet trained during day	_____	Named colors	_____
Stood alone	_____	Stayed dry at night	_____	Said alphabet in order	_____
Walked alone	_____	Drank from cup	_____	Preferred one hand	_____
Ran with good control	_____	Fed self	_____	Buttoned clothes	_____
Babbled	_____	Played pat-a-cake or peek-a-boo	_____	Fastened zippers	_____

CHILD'S MEDICAL HISTORY

Place a check next to any illness or condition that the child has had. When you check an item, also note the approximate age of the child when he or she had the illness or condition.

Illness or condition	Age	Illness or condition	Age	Illness or condition	Age
☐ Measles	_____	☐ Hearing problems	_____	☐ Gonorrhea or syphilis	_____
☐ German measles	_____	☐ Ear infections	_____	☐ Anemia	_____
☐ Mumps	_____	☐ Seeing problems	_____	☐ Jaundice/hepatitis	_____
☐ Chicken pox	_____	☐ Fainting spells	_____	☐ Diabetes	_____
☐ Whooping cough	_____	☐ Loss of consciousness	_____	☐ Cancer	_____
☐ Diphtheria	_____	☐ Paralysis	_____	(list type) _____	
☐ Polio	_____	☐ Dizziness	_____	☐ High blood pressure	_____
☐ Scarlet fever	_____	☐ Frequent headaches	_____	☐ Heart disease	_____
☐ Meningitis	_____	☐ Difficulty concentrating	_____	☐ Asthma	_____
☐ Encephalitis	_____	☐ Memory problems	_____	☐ Bleeding problems	_____
☐ High fever	_____	☐ Extreme tiredness	_____	☐ Eczema or hives	_____
☐ Convulsions	_____	☐ Rheumatic fever	_____	☐ Suicide attempt	_____
☐ Hay fever	_____	☐ Epilepsy	_____	☐ Sleeping problems	_____
☐ Injuries to head	_____	☐ Tuberculosis	_____	☐ HIV	_____
☐ Seizures	_____	☐ Bone or joint disease	_____	☐ AIDS	_____
☐ Broken bones	_____				

Does the child have any allergies?   ☐ Yes ☐ No ☐ Don't know If yes, please describe:_____

Does the child have any disabilities?   ☐ Yes ☐ No ☐ Don't know If yes, please describe:_____

Has the child had any serious illnesses?   ☐ Yes ☐ No ☐ Don't know If yes, please list illnesses: _____

Has the child been hospitalized?   ☐ Yes ☐ No ☐ Don't know If yes, please list reasons: _____

Has the child had any operations?   ☐ Yes ☐ No ☐ Don't know If yes, please list reasons: _____

Has the child had any accidents?   ☐ Yes ☐ No ☐ Don't know If yes, please describe:_____

Are the child's immunizations up to date? ☐ Yes ☐ No ☐ Don't know   Child's height _____ Child's weight _____

Table A-1 (*Continued*)

FAMILY MEDICAL HISTORY

Place a check next to any illness or condition that any member of the immediate family has had. When you check an item, please note the family member's relationship to the child.

Relationship of family member to child

☐ Alcoholism _____
☐ Blindness _____
☐ Cancer _____
☐ Deafness _____
☐ Depression _____
☐ Developmental problem _____
☐ Diabetes _____
☐ Drug problem _____
☐ Emotional problem _____
☐ Epilepsy _____
☐ Genetic disorder _____

Relationship of family member to child

☐ Heart trouble _____
☐ Hyperactivity _____
☐ Learning disorder _____
☐ Mental illness _____
☐ Mental retardation _____
☐ Neurological disease _____
☐ Seizure _____
☐ Sleep problems _____
☐ Suicide attempt _____
☐ Other problems (please list) _____

OTHER INFORMATION

Child's Activities

What are the child's favorite activities?

1. _____ 2. _____ 3. _____
4. _____ 5. _____ 6. _____

What activities would the child like to engage in more often than he or she does at present?

1. _____ 2. _____ 3. _____

What activities does the child like least?

1. _____ 2. _____ 3. _____

What chores does the child do around the house?

Has there been any recent change in his or her ability to carry out these chores? ☐ Yes ☐ No ☐ Don't know

If yes, please describe the change: _____

What time does the child usually go to bed on weekdays? _____ On weekends? _____

Trouble with the Law

Has the child ever been in trouble with the law? ☐ Yes ☐ No ☐ Don't know

If yes, please describe briefly: _____

Referral to Child Protective Services or Similar Agency

Has the child ever been referred to Child Protective Services or another similar agency for having been maltreated?

☐ Yes ☐ No ☐ Don't know

If yes, please describe briefly: _____

(*Continued*)

Table A-1 (*Continued*)

Your Use of Disciplinary Techniques

Place a check next to each technique that you commonly use when the child behaves inappropriately. There also is space for writing in any other disciplinary techniques that you use.

☐ Ignore problem behavior   ☐ Reason with child   ☐ Take away some activity or food

☐ Scold child   ☐ Redirect child's interest   ☐ Other technique (describe)

☐ Spank child   ☐ Tell child to sit on chair   _____

☐ Threaten child   ☐ Send child to his or her room   ☐ Don't use any disciplinary technique

Which disciplinary techniques are usually effective? _____

_____

With what types of problems? _____

_____

Which disciplinary techniques are usually ineffective? _____

_____

With what types of problems? _____

_____

Which parent (caregiver) usually administers discipline? _____

Activities Checklist

Place a check next to each activity that the child can do by himself or herself (even if the child does not do the activity regularly).

☐ Sets table   ☐ Helps with grocery shopping   ☐ Puts clothes away

☐ Cooks meals   ☐ Unpacks groceries   ☐ Sews

☐ Cleans table   ☐ Does laundry   ☐ Empties garbage

☐ Washes dishes   ☐ Does ironing   ☐ Does homework alone

Child's Responsibilities

Can the child be trusted to care for a pet? ☐ Yes ☐ No ☐ Don't know

If no, why not? _____

Does the child handle his or her personal finances? ☐ Yes ☐ No ☐ Don't know

If no, why not? _____

Does the child take responsibility for his or her personal hygiene? ☐ Yes ☐ No

If no, why not? _____

Is the child's behavior generally age appropriate? ☐ Yes ☐ No

If no, please describe in what ways it is not age appropriate: _____

_____

Other Areas

What do you enjoy doing with the child? _____

_____

What have you found to be the most satisfactory ways of helping the child? _____

_____

What are the child's assets or strengths? _____

_____

Is there any other information that you think may help us in working with the child? _____

_____

What prompted you to seek help at this time? _____

_____

Table A-1 (*Continued*)

Family Stress Survey

Every family sometimes experiences some form of stress. Please put a check next to any event that you know the family has experienced *in the last 12 months.*

- ☐ Child's mother died.
- ☐ Child's father died.
- ☐ Child's brother died.
- ☐ Child's sister died.
- ☐ Parents divorced.
- ☐ Parents separated.
- ☐ Grandparent died.
- ☐ Someone in family was seriously injured or became ill (list person): _____

- ☐ Parent remarried.
- ☐ Father lost job.
- ☐ Mother lost job.

- ☐ Family moved to another city.
- ☐ Family moved to another part of town.
- ☐ Someone in family was in trouble with the law or police (describe person's relationship to child): _____

- ☐ Family's financial condition changed.
- ☐ Member of family was accused of child abuse or neglect (describe person's relationship to child): _____

- ☐ Neighborhood was changing for the worse.
- ☐ Child was a victim of violence.

- ☐ Family experienced a natural disaster (describe): _____
- ☐ Child started having trouble with parents (caregiver).
- ☐ Child started having trouble with sisters/brothers.
- ☐ Child started having trouble in school.
- ☐ Child changed schools.
- ☐ Child's close friend moved away.
- ☐ Child's pet died.
- ☐ Other forms of stress (list) _____

_____
_____

Parent Needs Survey[a]

Listed below are some needs commonly expressed by parents (caregivers). Please put a check next to each item that you feel you need help with.

- ☐ More information about the child's abilities
- ☐ Someone who can help me feel better about myself
- ☐ Help with child care
- ☐ More money/financial help
- ☐ Someone who can babysit for a day or evening so that I can get away
- ☐ Better medical care for the child
- ☐ Better dental care for the child
- ☐ More information about child development
- ☐ More information about behavior problems
- ☐ More information about programs that can help the child
- ☐ Help communicating with the child's school
- ☐ Someone to help with household chores
- ☐ Counseling to help me cope with my situation

- ☐ Better therapy services for the child
- ☐ Day care so that I can get a job
- ☐ A bigger or better house or apartment
- ☐ More information about how I can help the child
- ☐ More information about nutrition or feeding
- ☐ Assistance in handling other children's jealousy of their brother or sister
- ☐ Health insurance
- ☐ Vocational training for me
- ☐ Assistance in dealing with problems with in-laws or other relatives
- ☐ Assistance in dealing with problems with friends or neighbors
- ☐ Special equipment to meet the child's needs
- ☐ More friends who have a child like mine
- ☐ Someone to talk to about my problems

- ☐ Assistance in dealing with problems between me and my spouse/partner
- ☐ A car or other form of transportation
- ☐ Medical care for myself
- ☐ More time for myself
- ☐ More time to be with the child
- ☐ More time to be with my spouse
- ☐ More time to be with other adults
- ☐ A vacation
- ☐ Other needs (list)

_____
_____
_____
_____
_____
_____
_____
_____

Thank you.

[a]These items are modifications of items included in the Parent Needs Survey by M. Seligman and R. B. Darling in *Ordinary Families, Special Children: A Systems Approach to Childhood Disability* (New York: Guilford Press, 1989). The Parent Needs Survey is an instrument designed to identify the priorities and concerns of parents of young children with disabilities. Reprinted and adapted with permission of the publisher and author.

Table A-2
Personal Data Questionnaire

PERSONAL DATA QUESTIONNAIRE

Please complete this questionnaire as carefully as you can. Please print clearly. All information will be treated confidentially.

Name _____
            First   Middle   Last

Address_____
                                                        Street

_____
            City   State   Zip code

School _____ Grade _____ Age _____ Sex _____ Birth date _____

Phone number _____ Email address _____ Today's date _____

SCHOOL INFORMATION

	Name of school	Grades attended	Years attended	Course of study or special classes
Elementary school				
Middle school				
High school				
College				
Other				
Other				

Best-liked subjects _____

Least-liked subjects _____

Easiest subjects _____

Hardest subjects _____

Leisure-time (or free-time) activities _____

Hobbies_____

Favorite music group _____

Do you read newspapers or magazines? ☐ Yes ☐ No If yes, which ones? _____

Do you read books? ☐ Yes ☐ No If yes, what types? _____

(If you read books) Approximately how many books have you read in the last month?_____

Do you participate in sports or athletic activities? ☐ Yes ☐ No If yes, which ones?_____

SCHOOL ACTIVITIES

School activity	Number of years of participation	Positions held	Describe activity

Please note any awards received or class offices held: _____

Table A-2 (*Continued*)

WORK EXPERIENCE

Job held	When	What did you like best about your job?	What did you like least about your job?
_____	_____	_____	_____
_____	_____	_____	_____
_____	_____	_____	_____
_____	_____	_____	_____

FAMILY AND HOME

Name	Does this person live at your home? (yes or no)	Age	Occupation	Years of school
Father _____				
Mother _____				
Brother/Sister _____				
_____				
_____				
_____				

HEALTH

Current height _____ Current weight _____

Do you have normal eyesight? ☐ Yes ☐ No If no, do you wear glasses or contacts? ☐ Yes ☐ No

Do you have normal hearing? ☐ Yes ☐ No If no, do you wear a hearing aid? ☐ Yes ☐ No

Do you eat a healthy diet? ☐ Yes ☐ No If no, briefly indicate in what way your diet is not healthy: _____
_____

Briefly list important factors in your health history, including any serious illnesses or times in the hospital: _____
_____

List any health problems you have now: _____
_____

Are you taking any medications? ☐ Yes ☐ No If yes, list the medications and what you are taking them for: _____
_____

PERSONAL CHARACTERISTICS

Circle Y (yes) if the item describes you fairly well or N (no) if the item does not describe you very well.

Y N 1. Active	Y N 11. Imaginative	Y N 21. Submissive	Y N 31. Jittery
Y N 2. Ambitious	Y N 12. Original	Y N 22. Absentminded	Y N 32. Likeable
Y N 3. Self-confident	Y N 13. Witty	Y N 23. Orderly	Y N 33. Leader
Y N 4. Persistent	Y N 14. Calm	Y N 24. Timid	Y N 34. Sociable
Y N 5. Hard working	Y N 15. Easily discouraged	Y N 25. Lazy	Y N 35. Quiet
Y N 6. Nervous	Y N 16. Serious	Y N 26. Frequently gloomy	Y N 36. Self-conscious
Y N 7. Impatient	Y N 17. Easy-going	Y N 27. Tough	Y N 37. Lonely
Y N 8. Impulsive	Y N 18. Good-natured	Y N 28. Dependable	Y N 38. Fearful
Y N 9. Quick-tempered	Y N 19. Unemotional	Y N 29. Cheerful	Y N 39. Intelligent
Y N 10. Excitable	Y N 20. Shy	Y N 30. Sarcastic	

(*Continued*)

Table A-2 (*Continued*)

What do you like best about yourself? _____

What do you like least about yourself? _____

Do you use drugs? _____ If yes, what kinds? _____

How often? _____

Do you use alcohol? _____ If yes, what kinds? _____

How often? _____

Do you smoke? _____ If yes, how many cigarettes per day do you smoke? _____

List the stressful events that you have experienced in the past year: _____

HOW I DO THINGS

Circle Y (yes) if the item generally describes how you do things or N (no) if the item does not generally describe how you do things.

Y N 1. I usually can find my school supplies when I need them.
Y N 2. I usually remember to do my jobs at home.
Y N 3. I usually put my books in the same place every day when I come home from school.
Y N 4. I usually finish a project I start.
Y N 5. I usually think about something before I do it.
Y N 6. I usually use a planner or calendar.
Y N 7. I usually get to classes on time.
Y N 8. I keep a separate notebook for each class.
Y N 9. I usually remember to bring my homework back to school.
Y N 10. I usually remember to bring home things that I need for studying or for homework.
Y N 11. I usually complete tests on time.
Y N 12. I usually read directions and questions carefully.
Y N 13. I usually can stay focused when I study.
Y N 14. I usually have no difficulty taking notes.
Y N 15. I usually can write down the important things that the teacher says about a subject.
Y N 16. I usually have no difficulty writing assignments in class.
Y N 17. I usually have no difficulty organizing my ideas when I write.
Y N 18. I usually use a computer without having major problems.
Y N 19. I usually keep my clothes clean.
Y N 20. I usually keep my room neat.
Y N 21. I usually know what to study for tests.
Y N 22. I usually proofread my written assignment that I do at home.

STRESS

Circle Y (yes) if the item generally causes you stress now or N (no) if the item does not generally cause you stress now.

Y N 1. Examinations and tests
Y N 2. Parents who don't understand what it's like to be a student today
Y N 3. Having too much work to prepare for class
Y N 4. Poor relations with other students
Y N 5. Being picked out by the teacher for poor work
Y N 6. Being disciplined in school for doing things wrong
Y N 7. Being teased by other students
Y N 8. Being ignored by other students
Y N 9. Shortage of money
Y N 10. Having too many things to study
Y N 11. Cost of books and equipment
Y N 12. Cost of clothes I need
Y N 13. Wishing my parents were richer
Y N 14. Appearing foolish to others
Y N 15. Difficulty with a boy/girl relationship
Y N 16. No place to study at home
Y N 17. No time to relax between classes
Y N 18. Nobody to talk to about personal problems
Y N 19. Difficulties in travel to school
Y N 20. Being unable to really talk to my mother
Y N 21. Being unable to really talk to my father
Y N 22. Not knowing how to study properly
Y N 23. No time for leisure activities
Y N 24. Being asked to read aloud or talk in front of the class
Y N 25. Teachers who talk to other students rather than to me
Y N 26. Sexual problems
Y N 27. Watching so much TV that it affects my homework
Y N 28. Being neglected or abused emotionally at home
Y N 29. Being abused physically or subjected to excessive physical punishment at home

Table A-2 (*Continued*)

Y N 30. Being abused sexually by an older person	Y N 41. Father's drinking habit	Y N 56. Demands by parents on after-school time
Y N 31. Being unable to relate to people my own age	Y N 42. My own drinking habit	Y N 57. Shyness in social situations
Y N 32. Fear of asking teachers about school work	Y N 43. Worry that I may not get a good job when I leave school	Y N 58. Being abused sexually by someone close in age
Y N 33. Worry about part-time employment	Y N 44. Unemployment generally	Y N 59. Adults who don't listen when I talk about problems
Y N 34. Worry about entering senior high school	Y N 45. Pressure to smoke cigarettes	Y N 60. Uncertainty about what values are the correct ones
Y N 35. Worry about entering middle or junior high school	Y N 46. Pressure to have sex	Y N 61. Lack of self-confidence
Y N 36. Adults who treat me like a child	Y N 47. Pressure to drink alcohol	Y N 62. Rejection by a group I want to belong to
Y N 37. Pressure to behave in a way my parents won't approve of	Y N 48. Being unable to keep up with others in school work	Y N 63. Doubts about my religious beliefs
Y N 38. Feelings of loneliness	Y N 49. Pressure to use drugs	Y N 64. Lack of privacy at home
Y N 39. Worry about what others think of me	Y N 50. Parents being divorced or separated	Y N 65. Arguments between my parents
Y N 40. Mother's drinking habit	Y N 51. My smoking habit	Y N 66. Concern about my health
	Y N 52. Experience with drugs	Y N 67. Pressure from my parents to get on in life
	Y N 53. School classes that are too large	
	Y N 54. Classmates' jealousy of my success in school	
	Y N 55. Poor self-concept	

RELATIONSHIP WITH PARENTS

Circle Y (yes) if the item generally describes your parents or N (no) if the item does not generally describe your parents.

Y N 1. My parents are very affectionate with me.	Y N 9. My parents lose their temper with me when I don't help around the house.	Y N 15. My parents ask me to tell them everything that happens when I am away from home.
Y N 2. My parents enjoy talking things over with me.	Y N 10. When I am bad, my parents forbid me to do things I especially enjoy.	Y N 16. My parents let me off easy when I misbehave.
Y N 3. My parents comfort me and help me when I have troubles.	Y N 11. My parents won't let me roam around because something might happen to me.	Y N 17. My parents are consistent about punishing me when they feel I deserve it.
Y N 4. My parents are happy when they are with me.	Y N 12. My parents worry that I can't take care of myself.	Y N 18. My parents let me get away without doing work they tell me to do.
Y N 5. My parents smile at me very often.	Y N 13. My parents worry about me when I am away.	Y N 19. My parents find it difficult to punish me.
Y N 6. My parents punish me by making me do extra work.	Y N 14. My parents do not approve of my spending a lot of time away from home.	Y N 20. My parents excuse my bad conduct.
Y N 7. My parents scold and yell at me.		
Y N 8. My parents threaten to spank me.		

FAMILY

Circle Y (yes) if the item generally describes your family or N (no) if the item does not generally describe your family.

Y N 1. Family members pay attention to each other's feelings.	allowed to be special and different.	Y N 14. Our happiest times are at home.
Y N 2. Our family would rather do things together than with other people.	Y N 7. We accept each other's friends.	Y N 15. The grownups in my family are strong leaders.
Y N 3. We all have a say in family plans.	Y N 8. There is confusion in our family because there is no leader.	Y N 16. The future looks good to our family.
Y N 4. Grownups in the family understand and agree on family decisions.	Y N 9. Family members touch and hug each other.	Y N 17. We usually blame one person in our family when things aren't going right.
Y N 5. Grownups in the family compete and fight with each other.	Y N 10. Family members put each other down.	Y N 18. Family members go their own way most of the time.
Y N 6. There is closeness in my family, but each person is	Y N 11. We speak our minds, no matter what.	Y N 19. Our family is proud of being close.
	Y N 12. In our home, we feel loved.	Y N 20. Our family is good at solving problems together.
	Y N 13. Even when we feel close, our family is embarrassed to admit it.	

(*Continued*)

Table A-2 (Continued)

Y N 21. Family members easily express warmth and caring toward each other.

Y N 22. It's okay to fight and yell in our family.

Y N 23. One of the adults in my family has a favorite child.

Y N 24. When things go wrong, we blame each other.

Y N 25. We say what we think and feel.

Y N 26. Family members would rather do things with other people than together.

Y N 27. Family members pay attention to each other and listen to what is said.

Y N 28. We worry about hurting each other's feelings.

Y N 29. The mood in my family is usually sad and blue.

Y N 30. We argue a lot.

Y N 31. One person controls and leads our family.

Y N 32. My family is happy most of the time.

Y N 33. Each person takes responsibility for his/her behavior.

PLANS

What are your plans for the future? _____

_____

What occupation would you like to have?_____

_____

Are there issues bothering you that you would like to discuss with a professional? ☐ Yes ☐ No If yes, what are they?_____

_____

ANY OTHER COMMENTS?

_____

_____

_____

_____

Thank you.

Source: The section on stress adapted from "Life Stress: A Questionnaire" by C. Bagley (1992); the section on relationship with parents adapted from "A Brief Scale for Assessing Parental Child-Rearing Practice" by E. L. George and B. L. Bloom (1997); and the section on family adapted from *Successful Families: Assessment and Intervention* by W. Robert Beavers and Robert B. Hampson (1990).

Table A-3
School Referral Questionnaire

SCHOOL REFERRAL QUESTIONNAIRE

Student's name _____ Grade _____ Sex _____ Date _____

School _____ Teacher's name _____

PRESENTING PROBLEM

Briefly describe student's current problem: _____
_____
_____

How long has this problem been of concern to you? _____

When did you first notice the problem? _____

What seems to help the problem? _____

What seems to make the problem worse? _____

Have you noticed changes in the student's abilities?　☐ Yes ☐ No

If yes, please describe: _____

Have you noticed changes in the student's behavior?　☐ Yes ☐ No

If yes, please describe: _____

Has the student received evaluation or treatment for the current problem or similar problems?　☐ Yes ☐ No

If yes, when and with whom? _____

What are the student's current school grades? _____
_____

What do you want to learn from this evaluation? _____
_____

CHECKLIST

Directions: Place a check mark next to each item that accurately describes the student. If you can't evaluate an item, please write a question mark next to the box by the item number.

Cognitive

☐ 1. Has poor comprehension of material
☐ 2. Has poor short-term memory for verbal stimuli
☐ 3. Has poor short-term memory for nonverbal stimuli
☐ 4. Has limited attention span
☐ 5. Has difficulty understanding oral directions
☐ 6. Has difficulty understanding written directions
☐ 7. Has difficulty following a sequence of directions
☐ 8. Misunderstands material presented at a fast rate
☐ 9. Has difficulty recalling story sequences
☐ 10. Has difficulty understanding teacher when he or she moves
☐ 11. Has difficulty being adaptable
☐ 12. Has difficulty reasoning abstractly
☐ 13. Has difficulty conceptualizing material
☐ 14. Uses problem-solving strategies inefficiently
☐ 15. Learns very slowly
☐ 16. Has poor long-term memory
☐ 17. Forgets newly learned skills

Language/Academic

☐ 18. Has difficulty decoding words
☐ 19. Has poor reading comprehension
☐ 20. Has poor expressive language
☐ 21. Has poor listening comprehension
☐ 22. Uses gestures instead of words
☐ 23. Has difficulty rapidly naming objects
☐ 24. Has difficulty rapidly reading words
☐ 25. Has speech impairment
☐ 26. Has difficulty producing rhymes
☐ 27. Has difficulty recognizing similar phonemes
☐ 28. Has difficulty arranging phonemes into words
☐ 29. Has difficulty using verbal coding as an aid in memory
☐ 30. Has difficulty using verbal coding as an aid in rehearsal
☐ 31. Has poor grammar
☐ 32. Has poor math computation skills
☐ 33. Has limited math problem-solving skills
☐ 34. Does not retain math facts
☐ 35. Has poor spelling

(Continued)

Table A-3 (*Continued*)

☐ 36. Has fluctuating performance
☐ 37. Has difficulty writing compositions
☐ 38. Does not know names of common objects

Perceptual/Motor
☐ 39. Has poor auditory perception
☐ 40. Has poor visual perception
☐ 41. Has poor tactile discrimination
☐ 42. Has poor handwriting
☐ 43. Has clumsy and awkward movements
☐ 44. Has poor speech communication
☐ 45. Has difficulty putting objects in correct sequence
☐ 46. Has difficulty remembering sequence of objects
☐ 47. Has right-left confusion
☐ 48. Has poor gross-motor coordination
☐ 49. Has poor fine-motor coordination
☐ 50. Moves slowly

Behavioral
☐ 51. Avoids doing work in class
☐ 52. Gives up easily
☐ 53. Has difficulty beginning tasks on time
☐ 54. Has difficulty completing tasks on time
☐ 55. Asks questions constantly
☐ 56. Is impulsive
☐ 57. Has trouble starting and continuing tasks
☐ 58. Has difficulty changing from one assignment to another
☐ 59. Shifts often to other activities
☐ 60. Has difficulty working independently
☐ 61. Has difficulty playing quietly
☐ 62. Is easily distracted
☐ 63. Doesn't seem to listen
☐ 64. Shows aggressive behavior
☐ 65. Shows disruptive behavior
☐ 66. Talks excessively
☐ 67. Interrupts others often
☐ 68. Speaks out of turn (often blurts out answers)
☐ 69. Makes comments not related to topic being discussed
☐ 70. Has difficulty remaining seated
☐ 71. Fidgets often when seated
☐ 72. Does not arrive on time for class
☐ 73. Fails to return on time to class
☐ 74. Has limited persistence
☐ 75. Fails to do homework
☐ 76. Loses homework
☐ 77. Seeks attention constantly
☐ 78. Is unorganized
☐ 79. Uses immature vocabulary
☐ 80. Is slow to complete tasks
☐ 81. Behaves inappropriately

☐ 82. Uses drugs or alcohol
☐ 83. Hurts others
☐ 84. Is cruel to animals
☐ 85. Talks about suicide
☐ 86. Destroys others' property
☐ 87. Is out of chair when supposed to be doing work
☐ 88. Has constant and repetitive behavior
☐ 89. Speaks slowly
☐ 90. Shouts or yells for no apparent reason
☐ 91. Has hallucinations
☐ 92. Stutters
☐ 93. Injures self often
☐ 94. Bites nails
☐ 95. Bangs head
☐ 96. Holds breath
☐ 97. Does not tolerate changes in routine
☐ 98. Wanders aimlessly around room
☐ 99. Daydreams
☐ 100. Tires easily
☐ 101. Tells lies
☐ 102. Steals
☐ 103. Has numerous physical complaints
☐ 104. Is frequently absent
☐ 105. Has poor eye contact
☐ 106. Requires constant supervision
☐ 107. Engages in dangerous behaviors
☐ 108. Prefers not to try new activities

Social
☐ 109. Is immature
☐ 110. Is stubborn
☐ 111. Has low self-esteem
☐ 112. Is socially isolated
☐ 113. Has low popularity
☐ 114. Has difficulty communicating interests
☐ 115. Has difficulty accepting criticism
☐ 116. Has limited social perceptiveness
☐ 117. Gives in to peer pressure
☐ 118. Is uncooperative
☐ 119. Has poor skills on playground
☐ 120. Is overly compliant
☐ 121. Is selfish
☐ 122. Seems suspicious of other people
☐ 123. Refuses to share
☐ 124. Shows sexually provocative behavior
☐ 125. Blames others for problems
☐ 126. Has difficulty seeking help
☐ 127. Has difficulty accepting help from teacher
☐ 128. Has difficulty accepting help from peers

Table A-3 (*Continued*)

☐ 129. Does not get along with other children

☐ 130. Does not offer opinions and answers when asked

☐ 131. Does not enjoy group activities

☐ 132. Does not show concern for others' feelings and property

☐ 133. Solves conflicts by shouting, fighting, or intimidating others

☐ 134. Has difficulty making constructive contributions during group activities

☐ 135. Avoids others completely

☐ 136. Has anger management problems

☐ 137. Displays inappropriate humor

☐ 138. Seeks to manipulate others

☐ 139. Is rigid and opinionated

☐ 140. Has unusual interest in sensational violence

☐ 141. Is fascinated with violence-filled entertainment

Affect/Motivation

☐ 142. Is easily frustrated

☐ 143. Shows anger quickly

☐ 144. Has limited motivation

☐ 145. Is often anxious

☐ 146. Is depressed or unhappy

☐ 147. Has low interest in school work

☐ 148. Is self-critical

☐ 149. Is overexcitable

☐ 150. Is hyperactive

☐ 151. Has temper tantrums

☐ 152. Has unusual fears

☐ 153. Is easily annoyed

☐ 154. Frequently cries

☐ 155. Is tense and fearful

☐ 156. Seldom shows emotion

☐ 157. Is shy or timid

☐ 158. Is upset by changes in routine

☐ 159. Has wide mood changes

☐ 160. Appears to feel hopeless

☐ 161. Has difficulty recognizing that he or she has a problem

Self-Care Skills

☐ 162. Has poor personal hygiene

☐ 163. Has disheveled and unclean personal appearance

☐ 164. Fails to dress appropriately for weather

☐ 165. Has poor table manners in cafeteria

☐ 166. Fails to use free time appropriately

☐ 167. Engages in self-stimulating behaviors

☐ 168. Has slumped posture

☐ 169. Has rigid, tense posture

☐ 170. Has atypical, inappropriate posture

Other problems_____

_____

_____

Assets

Please list the child's assets or strengths in each of the following areas.

Cognitive_____

Language/academic_____

Perceptual/motor_____

Behavioral_____

Social_____

Affect/motivation_____

Self-care skills_____

Other Comments

Please list anything else about the child that you think may be helpful._____

_____

_____

Thank you.

Appendix B

SEMISTRUCTURED INTERVIEW QUESTIONS

Table B-1
Semistructured Interview Questions for a Child or Adolescent of School Age

Introduction
1. Hi! I'm Dr. [Ms., Mr.] _____. How are you today?
2. When you don't understand a question that I ask, please say "I don't understand." When you tell me that, I'll try to ask it better. OK?
3. Please tell me how old you are.
4. When is your birthday?
5. What is your address?
6. And what is your telephone number?

Information About Problem
7. Has anyone told you why you are here today?
   (If yes, go to question 8; if no, go to question 10.)
8. Who told you?
9. What did he [she] tell you?
10. Tell me why *you* think you are here.
    (If child mentions a problem or a concern, explore it in detail. Ask questions 11 to 40, as needed. If the child does not mention a problem or concern, go to question 41.)
11. Tell me about [cite problem child mentioned].
12. When did you first notice [cite problem]?
13. How long has it been going on?
14. (If relevant) Where does [cite problem] happen?
15. (If needed) Does it occur at home . . . at school . . . when you're traveling . . . at a friend's house?
16. (If relevant) When does the problem happen?
17. (If needed) Does it happen when you first get up in the morning . . . during the day . . . at night before bedtime . . . at mealtimes? . . . Does it happen when you are with your mother . . . your father . . . brothers and sisters . . . other children . . . other relatives . . . the whole family together . . . friends . . . at school?
18. (If relevant) How long does the problem last?
19. How often does [cite problem] occur?
20. (If relevant) Do your brothers and sisters also have [cite problem]?
21. (If yes) Is your [cite problem] worse than or not as bad as theirs?
22. In what way?
23. What happens just before [cite problem] begins?
24. What happens just after [cite problem] begins?
25. What makes [cite problem] worse?
26. What makes [cite problem] better?
27. What do you do when you have [cite problem]?
28. What seems to work best?
29. What do you think caused [cite problem]?
30. Was anything happening in your family when [cite problem] first started?
31. (If needed) Did your parents get separated or divorced . . . you move to another city or school . . . your dad or mom lose a job . . . someone in your family go into the hospital?
32. (If some event occurred) How did you feel when [cite event] happened?
33. How do your parents help you with [cite problem]?
34. (If relevant) How do your brothers and sisters help you with [cite problem]?
35. And your friends, do they help in any way?
36. Have you seen anybody for help with [cite problem]?
    (If yes, go to question 37; if no, go to question 41.)

37. Whom did you see?
38. What kind of help did you get?
39. Has it helped?
40. (If needed) In what way?

School
41. Let's talk about school. What grade are you in?
42. What is your teacher's name [are your teachers' names]?
43. How do you get along with your teacher[s]?
44. Who is your favorite teacher?
45. Tell me about him [her].
46. Who is the teacher you like the least?
47. Tell me about him [her].
48. What subjects do you like best?
49. What is it about these subjects that you like?
50. And what subjects do you like least?
51. What is it about these subjects that you don't like?
52. What grades are you getting?
53. Are you in any activities at school?
54. (If yes) What activities are you in at school?
55. How do you get along with your classmates?
56. Tell me how you spend a usual day at school.

Attention and Concentration at School
57. Do you have any trouble following what your teacher says [teachers say]?
58. (If yes) What kind of trouble do you have?
59. Do you daydream a lot when you are in class?
60. (If yes) Tell me about that.
61. Can you complete your assignments, or are you easily distracted?
62. (If distracted) What seems to distract you?
63. Do you have trouble sitting still or staying in your seat at school?
64. (If yes) Tell me about the trouble you're having.
65. Do you find it hard to sit still for a long time and do you need a lot of breaks while studying?
66. Do you like to leave your studies to go see what's going on, get a drink, or change rooms or positions?
67. (If yes) Tell me more about that.
68. Do you have any trouble copying what your teacher writes on the blackboard?
69. (If yes) What kind of trouble do you have?
70. Do you have any trouble remembering things?
71. (If yes) Tell me about the trouble you're having.
72. How is your concentration?
73. Do you like to keep at your work until it's done?
74. Tell me more about that.
75. Do you have trouble taking notes in class?
76. (If yes) Tell me about the trouble you're having.
77. Do you have trouble taking tests?
78. (If yes) Tell me about the trouble you're having.

Home
79. Now let's talk about your home. Who lives with you at home?
    (Many questions from 80 to 117 assume that the child lives in a family with two caregivers. Ask those questions that apply to the child or modify them as needed—for example, substituting "stepmother" for "mother" or "sister" for "brothers and sisters.")

80. Tell me a little about [cite persons child mentioned].
81. (If needed) What does your father do for work?
82. (If needed) What does your mother do for work?
83. Tell me what your home is like.
84. Do you have your own room at home?
    (If no, go to question 85; if yes, go to question 87.)
85. Whom do you share your room with?
86. How do you get along?
87. What chores do you do at home?
88. How do you get along with your father?
89. What does he do that you like?
90. What does he do that you don't like?
91. How do you get along with your mother?
92. What does she do that you like?
93. What does she do that you don't like?
    (If child has one or more siblings, go to question 94 and modify questions as appropriate; if child has no siblings, go to question 101.)
94. How do you get along with your brothers and sisters?
95. What do they do that you like?
96. What do they do that you don't like?
97. What do you argue or fight with your brothers and sisters about?
98. What does your mother or father do when you argue or fight with your brothers and sisters?
99. Do your parents treat you and your brothers and sisters the same?
100. (If no) Tell me about that.
101. Are there rules you must follow at home?
102. Tell me about those.
103. When you get in trouble at home, who disciplines you?
104. Tell me about how your father [mother] disciplines you.
105. How do your parents tell you or show you that they like what you have done?
106. When you have a problem, whom do you talk to about it?
107. How does he [she] help you?
108. Do you think your parents are worried about you?
109. (If yes) What are their worries about you?
110. Is there anyone else in your family whom you are close to, like a grandparent or other relative?
111. (If yes) Tell me about him [her, them].
112. Do you spend much time at home alone?
113. (If yes) Tell me about that.
114. Does your family eat meals together?
115. (If yes) Tell me about the meals you eat together.
116. (If needed) How often do you eat meals together?
117. In general, how would you describe your family?

Interests
118. Now let's talk about what you like to do. What hobbies and interests do you have?
119. What do you do in the afternoons after school?
120. What do you do in the evenings on school days?
121. Tell me what you usually do on Saturdays and Sundays.
122. Do you play any sports?
123. (If yes) Tell me what sports you play.
124. Of all the things you do, what do you like doing best?
125. And what do you like doing least?

126. Do you belong to any group like the Boy Scouts [Girl Scouts] or a church group?
127. (If yes) Tell me about the group you belong to.
128. How much TV do you watch in a day?
129. Would you like to watch more TV?
130. (If yes) About how much more would you like to watch?
131. What are your favorite programs?
132. What do you like about them?
133. Do you play games on a PlayStation or some similar system?
    (If yes, go to question 134; if no, go to question 137.)
134. Where do you play these games?
135. How many hours a day do you play them?
136. What are your favorite games?
137. Do you like music?
138. (If yes) What kind of music—what are your favorite groups?

Friends
139. Do you have friends?
    (If yes, go to question 140; if no, go to question 149.)
140. Tell me about your friends.
    (Ask questions 141 to 148, as needed.)
141. What do you like to do with your friends?
142. Are you spending as much time with your friends now as you used to?
143. When you are with your friends, how do you feel?
144. How are your friends treating you?
145. Who is your best friend?
146. Tell me about him [her].
147. What do you like to do together?
148. How many of your friends do your parents know?
    (Go to item 150.)
149. Tell me about not having friends.

Mood/Feelings
150. Tell me about how you've been feeling lately.
151. Do you have different feelings in the same day?
152. (If yes) Tell me about these different feelings.
153. Have you been feeling more nervous over the past couple of days, as though you can't relax?
154. (If yes) Tell me about that.
155. Nearly everybody feels happy at times. What kinds of things make you feel happiest?
156. And sometimes people feel sad. What makes you feel sad?
157. What do you do when you're sad?
158. Sometimes children [teenagers] begin to get less pleasure from things that they used to enjoy. Has this happened to you?
159. (If yes) Tell me about that.
160. Have there been times lasting more than a day when you felt very cheerful in a way that was different from your normal feelings?
161. (If yes) Tell me about these feelings.
162. Almost everybody gets angry at times. What kinds of things make you angriest?
163. What do you do when you are angry?
164. Do you ever get into fights?
165. (If yes) Tell me about the fights.

Table B-1 (*Continued*)

Fears/Worries

166. Most children [teenagers] get scared sometimes about some things. What do you do when you are scared?
167. Tell me what scares you.
168. Does anything else scare you?
169. Are you startled by noises?
170. (If yes) Tell me more about that.
171. Do you have any special worries?
172. (If yes) Tell me about what you are worried about.

Self-Concept

173. What do you like best about yourself?
174. Anything else?
175. Tell me about the best thing that ever happened to you.
176. What do you like least about yourself?
177. Anything else?
178. Tell me about the worst thing that ever happened to you.
179. If you had a child of the same sex as you, in what ways would you want the child to be like you?
180. How would you want the child to be different from you?

Somatic Concerns

181. Tell me how you feel about your body.
182. Have you been feeling that way lately?
183. Do you have any problems with not having enough energy to do the things you want to do?
184. (If yes) Tell me what problems you're having.
185. Tell me how you feel about eating.
186. Are you having problems sleeping enough?
187. (If yes) Tell me about your problems getting enough sleep. (Go to question 190.)
188. Are you sleeping too much?
189. (If yes) Tell me about your problems with sleeping too much.
190. Tell me about your health.
191. (If needed) Have you been sick a lot?
192. (If yes) Tell me about that. (Follow up as needed.)
193. Do you ever get headaches?
194. (If yes) Tell me about them.
195. (If needed) How often do you get them? . . . What do you usually do?
196. Do you get stomachaches?
197. (If yes) Tell me about them.
198. (If needed) How often do you get them? . . . What do you usually do?
199. Do you get any other kinds of body pains?
200. (If yes) Tell me about them.
201. Do you have any trouble seeing things?
202. (If yes) Tell me about the trouble you're having seeing.
203. Do you have any trouble hearing things?
204. (If yes) Tell me about the trouble you're having hearing.
205. Do you take medicine every day?
     (If yes, go to question 206; if no, go to question 210.)
206. What do you take the medicine for?
207. What medicine do you take?
208. How often do you take the medicine?
209. How does the medicine make you feel?

Obsessions and Compulsions

210. Some children [teenagers] have thoughts that they think are silly or unpleasant or do not make sense, but these thoughts keep repeating over and over in their minds. Have you had thoughts like this?
211. (If yes) Tell me about these thoughts.
212. Some children [teenagers] are bothered by a feeling that they have to do something over and over even when they don't want to do it. For example, they might keep washing their hands or checking over and over again whether the door is locked or the stove is turned off. Is this a problem for you?
213. (If yes) Tell me about it.

Thought Disorder

214. Do you ever hear things no one else hears that seem funny or unusual?
215. (If yes) Tell me about them.
216. (If a voice) What does it say? . . . How often do you hear it? . . . How do you feel about the voice? . . . What do you usually do when you hear it?
217. Do you ever see things no one else sees that seem funny or unreal?
218. (If yes) Tell me about them.
219. (If needed) How often do you see them? . . . How do you feel about them? . . . What do you usually do when you see them?
220. Do you ever feel as if someone's spying on you or plotting to hurt you?
221. (If yes) Tell me about these feelings.
222. Does your thinking seem to speed up or slow down at times?
223. (If yes) Tell me about that.
224. Is it hard for you to make decisions?
225. (If yes) Tell me about that.
226. Is it hard for you to concentrate on your reading?
227. (If yes) Tell me about that.
228. Is it hard for you to understand people when they talk?
229. (If yes) Tell me about that.
230. Does it seem as if your thoughts are getting more mixed up or jumbled lately?
231. (If yes) Tell me more about that.
232. Have you had experiences that seemed odd or frightening to you?
233. (If yes) Tell me about them.

Memories/Fantasy

234. What's the first thing you can remember from the time you were a little baby?
235. How old were you then?
236. Tell me about your dreams.
237. Do you ever have the same dream over and over again?
238. (If yes) Tell me about that.
239. Who are your favorite television characters?
240. Tell me about them.
241. What animals do you like best?
242. Tell me what you like about these animals.
243. What animals do you like least?
244. Tell me what you don't like about these animals.
245. What is your happiest memory?
246. What is your saddest memory?
247. If you could change places with anyone in the whole world, who would it be?

(*Continued*)

Table B-1 (*Continued*)

248. Tell me about that.
249. If you could go anywhere you wanted to right now, where would you go?
250. Tell me about that.
251. If you could have three wishes, what would they be?
252. What things do you think you might need to take with you if you were to go to the moon and stay there for six months?

Aspirations
253. What do you plan on doing when you're grown up?
254. Do you think you will have any problem doing that?
255. If you could do anything you wanted when you became an adult, what would it be?
     (If interviewee is an adolescent, go to questions following question 258.)

Concluding Questions
256. Do you have anything else that you would like to tell me about yourself?
257. Do you have any questions that you would like to ask me?
258. Thank you for talking with me. If you have any questions or if you want to talk to me, please call me or ask your teacher to let me know. Here is my card.

ADDITIONAL QUESTIONS FOR ADOLESCENTS
Jobs
1. Do you have an after-school job or a summer job?
2. (If yes) Tell me about your job.

Sexual Relations
3. Do you have a special girlfriend [boyfriend]?
4. (If yes) Tell me about her [him].
5. Have you had any sexual experiences?
6. (If yes) Tell me about them.
7. Do you have any sexual concerns?
8. (If yes) Tell me about them.
9. Are you concerned about getting a sexual disease?
10. Tell me about that.
11. Are you sexually active now?
    (If yes, go to question 12; if no, go to question 17 if adolescent is a female or question 51 if adolescent is a male.)
12. Tell me about your sexual activity.
13. Do you use birth control?
    (If yes, go to question 14; if no, go to question 16.)
14. What type?
15. (If needed) Do you [Does your partner] use a condom?
    (If adolescent is a female, go to question 17; if adolescent is a male, go to question 51.)
16. Tell me about not using birth control.
    (If adolescent is a female, go to question 17; if adolescent is a male, go to question 51.)

Questions for Adolescent Females Only
17. Have you ever been pregnant?
    (If yes, go to question 18; if no, go to question 86.)
18. Tell me about it.
    (Ask questions 19 to 50, as needed.)
19. How many times have you been pregnant?

(Ask questions 20 to 50 for each pregnancy, as needed.)
20. How old were you when you became pregnant [the first time, the second time, etc.]?
21. Did you have the baby?
    (If yes, go to question 22; if no, go to question 44.)
22. When was the baby born?
23. Did you have a boy or a girl?
24. How is the child?
25. Who helped you during the pregnancy?
26. Did you see a doctor for care during your pregnancy?
27. Were there any problems during your pregnancy?
28. And were there any complications while you were in labor?
29. And during delivery, were there any problems?
30. Did you have any problems soon after the baby was born?
31. How did you feel during the pregnancy?
32. How do you feel about your baby?
33. How did your family react to your being pregnant?
34. And how did the baby's father react to your being pregnant?
35. Are you raising the baby?
    (If yes, go to question 36; if no, go to question 40.)
36. What is it like being a mother?
37. What kind of help are you getting?
38. Does the baby's father contribute money?
39. Does the baby's father see the baby?
    (Go to question 86.)
40. Who is raising the baby?
41. How do you feel about that?
42. (If needed) Do you ever see the baby?
43. (If yes) Tell me about that.
    (Go to question 86.)
44. What happened during your pregnancy that you didn't have the baby?
    (If interviewee had an abortion, go to question 45; otherwise, go to question 86.)
45. Tell me about the abortion.
    (Ask questions 46 to 50, as needed.)
46. What were your feelings about the abortion before you had it?
47. And how did you feel afterwards?
48. What would having a baby have meant for your future?
49. Would your family have helped you if you had had the baby?
50. Tell me about that.
    (Go to question 86.)

Questions for Adolescent Males Only
51. Have you ever gotten anyone pregnant?
    (If yes, go to question 52; if no, go to question 86.)
52. Tell me about it.
    (Ask questions 53 to 55, as needed.)
53. How many times have you gotten someone pregnant?
    (Ask questions 54 to 85, as needed, for each time interviewee got someone pregnant.)
54. How old were you when you got someone pregnant [the first time, the second time, etc.]?
55. Did she have the baby?
    (If yes, go to question 56; if no, go to question 81.)

Table B-1 (*Continued*)

56. When was the baby born?
57. Was the baby a boy or a girl?
58. How is the child?
59. Who helped the mother during the pregnancy?
60. Did she see a doctor for care during her pregnancy?
61. Were there any problems during her pregnancy?
62. And were there any problems while she was in labor?
63. And during her delivery, were there any problems?
64. And were there any problems soon after the baby was born?
65. How did she feel during her pregnancy?
66. How did she feel about the baby?
67. And how did you react to her being pregnant?
68. Do your parents know that you got someone pregnant?
69. (If yes) How did your parents react to her being pregnant?
70. Who is raising the baby?
    (If the baby is being raised by the mother or by someone else the father knows, go to question 71; if the baby is being raised by the father, go to question 76; if the baby was given up for adoption, go to question 78.)
71. How is the baby doing?
72. Do you see the baby?
73. (If yes) Tell me about that.
74. Do you contribute financially to the baby's support?
75. Tell me about that.
    (Go to question 86.)
76. How is the baby doing?
77. What is it like being a father?
    (Go to question 86.)
78. How do you feel about the baby's being adopted?
79. Is there anything else you want to tell me about your feelings about the adoption?
80. (If yes) Go ahead.
    (Go to question 86.)
81. What happened during her pregnancy that she didn't have the baby?
    (If she had an abortion, go to question 82; otherwise, go to question 86.)
82. Tell me about the abortion.
    (Ask questions 83 to 85, as needed.)
83. What were your feelings about the abortion before it was performed?
84. And how did you feel afterwards?
85. What would having a baby have meant for your future?
    (Go to question 86.)

Eating Habits

86. Now I'm going to ask some questions about your eating habits. Tell me about what you eat.

87. Tell me where you usually eat your meals.
88. Tell me when you usually eat your meals.
89. Have you ever gone on eating binges—that is, eaten an abnormally large amount of food over a short period of time?
90. (If yes) Tell me about these eating binges.
91. Has there ever been a time when people gave you a hard time about being too thin or losing too much weight?
92. (If yes) Tell me about that.
93. Has there ever been a time when people gave you a hard time about being too fat or gaining too much weight?
94. (If yes) Tell me about that.

Drug/Alcohol Use

95. Do your parents drink alcohol?
96. (If yes) Tell me about their drinking.
97. (If needed) How much do they drink? . . . How frequently do they drink? . . . Where do they drink?
98. Do your friends drink alcohol?
99. (If yes) Tell me about their drinking.
100. Do you drink alcohol?
101. (If yes) Tell me about your drinking.
102. Was there ever a time when you drank too much?
103. (If yes) Tell me about the time[s] when you drank too much.
104. Has anyone in your family—a friend, a doctor, or anyone else—ever said that you drank too much?
105. (If yes) Tell me about that.
106. Has alcohol ever caused problems for you?
107. (If yes) Tell me about that.
108. Do your parents use drugs?
109. (If yes) Tell me about the drugs they use.
110. (If needed) How much of the drugs do they take? . . . How frequently do they take them?
111. Do your friends use drugs?
112. (If yes) Tell me about the drugs they use.
113. Do you use drugs?
114. (If yes) Tell me about the drugs you use.
115. Have you or has anyone else ever thought that you used drugs too much?
116. (If yes) Tell me about that.
117. Do your friends huff or use aerosols or inhalants?
118. (If yes) Tell me about that.
119. Have you ever huffed or used aerosols or inhalants?
120. (If yes) Tell me about that.
     (Go back to questions 256–258 in the main interview.)

Table B-2
Semistructured Interview Questions for an Older Child or Adolescent in a Mental Status Evaluation

1. Hi! I'm Dr. [Ms., Mr.] _____. I'd like to ask you some questions. OK?

General Orientation to Time, Place, and Person
2. What is your name?
3. How old are you?
4. What is today's date?
5. What day of the week is it?
6. What is the season?
7. What time of day is it?
8. Where are you?
9. What is the name of the state we are in?
10. What is the name of this city?
11. What is the name of this place?

Recent and Remote Memory
12. And your telephone number is . . . ?
13. What is your address?
14. What grade are you in?
15. What is my name?
16. What did you have for breakfast?
17. What did you do in school [at the hospital, at home] yesterday?
18. Who is the president of the United States?
19. Who was the president before him?
20. (If relevant) Where did you live before you moved to [cite city]?
21. Name three major cities in the United States.
22. What are two major news events that happened in the last month?
23. How did you get to this hospital [clinic, office]?
24. What is your father's name?
25. What is your mother's name?
26. When is your birthday?
27. Where were you born?

28. What school do you go to?
29. (If relevant) When did you finish elementary school?
30. (If relevant) When did you finish high school?

Immediate Memory
31. Say these numbers after me: 6-9-5 . . . 4-3-8-1 . . . 2-9-8-5-7.
32. Say these numbers backwards: 8-3-7 . . . 9-4-6-1 . . . 7-3-2-5-8.
33. Say these words after me: pencil, chair, stone, plate.

Insight and Judgment
34. What does this saying mean: "Too many cooks spoil the broth"?
35. What does this saying mean: "A stitch in time saves nine"?
36. How are a banana, a peach, and a pear alike?
37. How are a bicycle, a wagon, and a car alike?

Reading, Writing, and Spelling
38. Read these words. (Give interviewee a piece of paper with the following words on it: pat, father, setting, intervention.)
39. Now write these same words. (Give interviewee a blank piece of paper on which to write; show the same words as in question 38 for the interviewee to copy.)
40. Spell these words aloud: spoon . . . cover . . . attitude . . . procedure.

Arithmetical Concentration
41. (For children between 7 and 12 years) Subtract by 3s, starting with 30.
42. (For adolescents) Subtract by 7s, starting with 50.

Concluding Questions
43. Are there any questions that you would like to ask me?
44. (If yes) Go ahead.
45. Thank you for talking with me. If you have any questions or if you want to talk to me, please call me. Here is my card.

Table B-3
Semistructured Interview Questions for an Older Child or Adolescent with Depression

Introduction

1. Hi! I'm Dr. [Ms., Mr.] _____. I'd like to talk to you about how you're getting along. OK?
2. When you don't understand a question that I ask, please say "I don't understand." When you tell me that, I'll try to ask it better. OK?

Dysphoric Mood

3. Tell me how you're feeling.
   (If needed, ask questions 4 through 24; otherwise, go to directions preceding question 25.)
4. I'm going to name some feelings and reactions. Please tell me if you often feel this way. OK?
5. Sad. Do you feel sad?
6. (If yes) Tell me about feeling sad.
7. Lonely. Do you feel lonely?
8. (If yes) Tell me about feeling lonely.
9. Unhappy. Do you feel unhappy?
10. (If yes) Tell me about feeling unhappy.
11. Hopeless. Do you feel hopeless?
12. (If yes) Tell me about feeling hopeless.
13. Depressed. Do you feel depressed?
14. (If yes) Tell me about feeling depressed.
15. Pessimistic. Do you feel pessimistic?
16. (If yes) Tell me about feeling pessimistic.
17. Do you get moody?
18. (If yes) Tell me about the times you get moody.
19. Do you get easily annoyed?
20. (If yes) Give me some examples of what annoys you.
21. Do you cry easily?
22. (If yes) Tell me about the times you cry easily.
23. Are you hard to please?
24. (If yes) Give me some examples of how you are hard to please.
    (Ask questions 25 to 32 separately for each feeling or reaction mentioned by interviewee, as needed.)
25. In the last week, how often have you felt [cite feeling or reaction]?
26. When did you first notice being troubled by [cite feeling or reaction]?
27. Does this feeling ever go away for some time—say, for a few days or weeks?
28. (If yes) How do you feel when [cite feeling or reaction] goes away?
29. How does [cite feeling or reaction] start—does it start suddenly, or is there a slow build-up of feelings?
30. Is your [cite feeling or reaction] connected in some way with what you are doing at a particular time?
31. (If yes) Tell me about that.
32. Do you have any idea about why this [cite feeling or reaction] comes about?
33. Has anything happened to you lately that might be important to mention now?
34. When do you feel best during the day?
35. When do you feel worst during the day?
36. How much change do you notice in the way you feel from day to day?

37. (If relevant) When you are feeling really down, is there anything that can cheer you up?
38. (If yes) Tell me what can cheer you up.

Self-Deprecatory Ideation

39. How do you feel about yourself?
    (Ask questions 40 to 53, as needed.)
40. Do you feel that you are worthless?
41. (If yes) Tell me about your feelings of being worthless.
42. Do you feel that you are useless?
43. (If yes) Give me some examples of how you feel useless.
44. Do you feel that you are dumb or stupid?
45. (If yes) Give me some examples of when you feel dumb or stupid.
46. Do you feel that you are ugly?
47. (If yes) Tell me about your feelings of being ugly.
48. Do you feel guilty?
49. (If yes) Give me some examples of when you feel guilty.
50. Do you feel that you are to blame for something that happened?
51. (If yes) Tell me about your feelings.
52. Do you believe that you are being harassed or picked on?
53. (If yes) Tell me about these feelings of being harassed or picked on.
54. Do you feel that you want to die?
55. (If yes) Tell me about these feelings of wanting to die.
56. Have you thought about committing suicide?
57. (If yes) Tell me about these thoughts.
58. Have you attempted suicide?
59. (If yes) Tell me about your suicide attempt[s].
60. Have you thought about running away from home?
61. (If yes) Tell me about these thoughts of wanting to run away from home.

Aggressive Behavior (Agitation)

62. Do you think that you're difficult to get along with?
63. (If yes) Give me some examples of how you're difficult to get along with.
64. Do you argue a lot with anyone?
    (If yes, go to question 65; if no, go to question 67.)
65. Who do you argue with?
66. What do you argue about?
67. Do you have trouble getting along with people in authority, such as teachers, the school principal, or the police?
    (If yes, go to question 68; if no, go to question 70.)
68. Who do you have trouble getting along with?
69. Give me some examples of the trouble you have getting along with [cite person or persons named by interviewee].
70. Do you get into fights with people?
    (If yes, go to question 71; if no, go to question 73.)
71. Who do you fight with?
72. What do you fight about?
73. Do you feel angry sometimes?
    (If yes, go to question 74; if no, go to question 76.)
74. What do you feel angry about?
75. What do you do when you feel angry?

(Continued)

Table B-3 (*Continued*)

Sleep Disturbances

76. Do you need more sleep than usual lately?
77. (If yes) Tell me about that.
78. Do you have trouble sleeping?
79. (If yes) Tell me about your trouble sleeping.
80. (If needed) How many nights this week have you had trouble falling asleep?
81. Are you restless when you sleep?
82. (If yes) Tell me about your restlessness when you sleep.
83. Is it hard for you to wake up in the morning?
84. (If yes) Tell me about the difficulty you have waking up in the morning.

Change in School Performance and Attitude

85. How do you feel about school?
86. Has your attitude toward school changed recently?
87. (If yes) How has your attitude toward school changed?
88. Do you daydream in school?
89. (If yes) Give me some examples of when you daydream.
90. Do you have trouble concentrating in school?
91. (If yes) Tell me about your trouble concentrating in school.
92. How have your grades been?
93. Do you have a good memory or a poor memory for your schoolwork?
94. (If poor) Give me some examples of your poor memory for schoolwork.
95. Do you find that you usually get your homework done?
96. (If no) Tell me about that.
97. Have there been changes recently in your ability to do your schoolwork?
98. (If yes) Tell me about these changes.
99. Have you ever refused to go to school?
100. (If yes) Tell me about that.

Diminished Socialization

101. How are you getting along with your friends?
102. Do you have any close friends you can talk to?
103. Tell me about that.
104. Have there been any changes in your relationships with your friends?
105. (If yes) Tell me about these changes.
106. And how about school? How do you get along with other students at school?
107. (If needed) Have you lost interest in doing things with other people?
108. (If yes) Tell me about that.

109. How much time do you spend alone?
110. And how do you feel when you are alone?
111. Do you feel a need to be alone?
112. (If yes) Tell me about that.

Somatic Complaints

113. Tell me about your health.
     (Ask questions 114 to 121, as needed.)
114. Do you get headaches?
115. (If yes) Tell me about your headaches.
116. Do you get pains in your stomach?
117. (If yes) Tell me about the pains in your stomach.
118. Do you get muscle aches or pains?
119. (If yes) Tell me about your muscle aches or pains.
120. Do you have any other pains or physical problems?
121. (If yes) Tell me about these pains or physical problems.

Loss of Usual Energy

122. Have you lost interest in doing things, like your hobbies?
123. (If yes) Give me some examples of your loss of interest.
124. Do you feel as though you have less energy to do things?
125. (If yes) Give me some examples of your loss of energy.
126. Have you stopped doing anything you used to do?
127. (If yes) Tell me about that.
128. Do you often feel tired?
129. (If yes) Give me some examples of your feeling tired.
130. Is there anything you look forward to?
131. (If yes) Tell me what you look forward to.

Unusual Change in Appetite and/or Weight

132. Has there been a change in your appetite?
133. (If yes) Tell me about the change in your appetite. (If needed, ask questions 134 to 137.)
134. Have you had to force yourself to eat?
135. (If yes) Tell me about that.
136. Do you find yourself eating too much?
137. (If yes) Tell me about that.
138. Has there been a change in your weight?
139. (If yes) Tell me about the change in your weight.

Concluding Questions

140. Is there anything else you would like to talk about or tell me?
141. (If yes) Go ahead.
142. Is there anything you would like to ask me?
143. (If yes) Go ahead.
144. Thank you for talking to me. If you have any questions or if you want to talk to me, please call me. Here is my card.

Note. With modifications, these questions also could be used with a parent. You would need to substitute the child's name for "you" or "your" and make the appropriate grammatical changes. If interviewee expresses suicidal thoughts, consider asking the questions in Table B-4 in this Appendix.
Source: Adapted from Weinberg, Rutman, Sullivan, Penick, and Dietz (1973) and Wilson, Spence, and Kavanagh (1989).

Table B-4
Semistructured Interview Questions for an Older Child or Adolescent Who May Be Suicidal

Introduction

1. Hello. I'm Dr. [Ms., Mr.] _____. I'd like to talk with you about how you're getting along. OK?
2. When you don't understand a question that I ask, please say "I don't understand." When you tell me that I'll try to ask it better. OK?

Changes in Behavior and Feelings

3. Have you noticed any changes in the way you're feeling or acting recently?
   (If yes, go to question 4; if no, go to question 42 or ask questions 5 to 41, as needed.)
4. What changes have you noticed?
   (Ask questions 5 to 41, as needed.)
5. Do you feel that life is pretty hopeless?
   (If yes, go to question 6; if no, go to question 8.)
6. In what way?
7. What has happened to make you feel that life is hopeless?
8. Do you often feel so frustrated that you just want to lie down and quit trying altogether?
9. (If yes) Tell me more about that.
10. Do you ever feel that you are worthless?
11. (If yes) Tell me about these feelings.
12. Have you become quieter recently?
13. (If yes) Tell me about that.
14. Do you find yourself losing interest in things?
15. (If yes) What are you losing interest in?
16. And do you tend to stay by yourself?
17. (If yes) Tell me about that.
18. And how about crying—do you find yourself crying often?
19. (If yes) Tell me about that.
20. Do you find that you are blaming yourself for bad things that have happened?
21. (If yes) What do you blame yourself for?
22. Do you blame yourself for family problems?
23. (If yes) What family problems do you blame yourself for?
24. Have you become more irritable lately?
25. (If yes) Tell me about that.
26. Do you find that you get angry very easily?
27. (If yes) Tell me about that.
28. Have you been worried about losing your mother or father? [If applicable, add other close relatives, such as sister or brother.]
29. (If yes) Tell me about your worries.
30. Have you been worried about losing a close friend?
31. (If yes) Tell me about your worries about losing a close friend.
32. Have you recently changed the way you eat?
33. (If yes) In what way?
34. Have your sleep patterns recently changed?
35. (If yes) In what way?
36. Have your school grades recently changed?
37. (If yes) In what way?
38. Has your personality changed in any way recently?
39. (If yes) In what way?
40. Have you begun to use drugs or alcohol recently?
41. Tell me about that.

Actions Suggestive of Loss of Interest in Living

42. Have you recently given away possessions that are very special to you?
43. (If yes) What have you given away?
44. Have you done anything to hurt yourself?
45. (If yes) Tell me what you have done.
46. Do you tend to do dangerous things these days?
47. (If yes) What sorts of things are you doing?
48. Have you eaten or drunk anything that might harm you?
49. (If yes) What have you eaten or drunk?
50. Have you done anything that might cause you to die?
51. (If yes) What have you done?
52. Have you written anything that you think might be the last thing you will ever write?
53. (If yes) What have you written?

Traumatic Events

54. Have you been seriously sick recently?
55. (If yes) Tell me about your illness.
56. Has someone close to you been hospitalized?
57. (If yes) Tell me about his [her] hospitalization.
58. Have you lost a pet recently?
59. (If yes) Tell me about how you lost your pet.
60. Did you recently end a relationship with a good friend?
61. (If yes) Tell me about that.
62. Has someone close to you died recently?
63. (If yes) Tell me about who died.
64. Has anyone in your family attempted or committed suicide?
    (If yes, go to question 65; if no, go to question 67.)
65. Who was it?
66. Please tell me about it.
67. Have any of your friends attempted or committed suicide?
    (If yes, go to question 68; if no, go to question 70.)
68. Who was it?
69. Please tell me about it.
70. Is there anyone else you like or admire who has attempted or committed suicide?
    (If yes, go to question 71; if no, go to question 73.)
71. Who was it?
72. Please tell me about it.
73. Is there anything else that has happened to you or to someone close to you that you are concerned about?
74. (If yes) Tell me about what happened.

Preoccupation with Death

75. Do you think about dying?
76. (If yes) What do you think about?
77. Do you dream about dying?
78. (If yes) What do you dream about?
79. Have you ever seen a dead person?
80. (If yes) Tell me about that.
81. Do you dream about any of your relatives who are dead?
82. (If yes) What do you dream about?
83. What do you think happens to people when they die?
84. How would others feel if you were dead?
85. Does the idea of endless sleep appeal to you?
86. (If yes) Tell me more about that.

(*Continued*)

Table B-4 (*Continued*)

Family

87. How does your family feel about the way you have been feeling?
88. How are you getting along with your parents?
89. Do your parents fight a lot?
    (If yes, go to question 90; if no, go to question 92.)
90. What do they fight about?
91. How does their fighting make you feel?
92. Do your parents give you the help and encouragement you feel you need?
93. Do you feel pressured to do more or better than you are able to?
94. (If yes) Tell me about that.
95. (If appropriate) How have you been getting along with your sisters [brothers]?
96. Has anyone in your family been abused?
97. (If yes) Tell me about that.
98. Is there anyone in your family who is seriously ill?
    (If yes, go to question 99; if no, go to question 102.)
99. Who is ill?
100. What illness does she [he] have?
101. How do you feel about her [his] being ill?

Thoughts and Actions Related to Suicide

102. Have you recently thought about killing yourself?
    (If yes, ask questions 103 through 111, as needed; if no, go to question 112.)
103. How much do you want to die?
104. How serious are you about wanting to die?
105. Do you have a plan for how you will kill yourself?
    (If yes, go to question 106; if no, go to question 110.)
106. Tell me about your plan.
107. Do you have a way to carry out your plan?
108. (If needed) Do you think about using a gun, a knife, pills, or some other method?
109. (If yes) Tell me about that.
110. How do you think your family and friends would feel if you tried to take your life?
111. Tell me about that.
112. Have you wished that you were dead?
113. (If yes) Tell me about that.
114. Have you talked to anyone about killing yourself?
115. (If yes) Tell me about that.
116. Have you ever tried to commit suicide?
    (If yes, go to question 117; if no, go to question 123.)

117. Tell me about your suicide attempt.
    (Ask questions 118 to 122, as needed.)
118. What happened?
119. When did it happen?
120. Who found you?
121. What happened after he [she] found you?
122. How do you feel about what you did?
123. Do you want to live?
124. Tell me about how you feel about living.
125. Have you thought about hurting someone else in addition to hurting yourself?
    (If yes, go to question 126; if no, go to question 128.)
126. Who is this person?
127. What have you thought about doing to him [her]?

Concluding Questions

128. What are your future plans?
129. Is there anything else you would like to tell me?
130. (If yes) Go ahead.
131. How does talking about all this make you feel?
132. Can anyone do anything to make you feel better?
133. Tell me about that.
134. Do you have anyone you can talk to about your problems?
135. (If yes) Who is that?
136. Is there anything else you would like to talk about?
137. (If yes) Go ahead.
138. Is there anything you would like to ask me?
139. (If yes) Go ahead.
140. Can you promise me that you won't hurt yourself at least until you meet with me again?
    (If yes, go to question 144; if no, go to question 141.)
141. Because you can't promise me that you won't hurt yourself, I must call your parents [or appropriate authorities]. Please wait here until I call them. (Call parents or appropriate authorities.) Is there anything else you would like to discuss?
    (If yes, go to question 142; if no, go to question 143.)
142. Go ahead.
    (Go to question 144.)
143. Your parents [or cite representative of appropriate agency] will be here soon. Thank you for talking with me. If you have any questions or if you want to talk to me, please call me. Here is my card. (End interview.)
144. Thank you for talking with me. If you have any questions or if you want to talk to me, please call me. Here is my card.

Note. With modifications, these questions also could be used with a parent. You would need to substitute the child's name for "you" or "your" and make the appropriate grammatical changes.
Source: Adapted, in part, from Pfeffer (1986).

Table B-5
Semistructured Interview Questions for an Adolescent or Older Child Being Screened for Alcohol Abuse or Dependence

Introduction
1. Hi. I'm Dr. [Ms., Mr.] _____. I'd like to talk to you about how you're getting along. OK?
2. When you don't understand a question that I ask, please say "I don't understand." When you tell me that, I'll try to ask it better. OK?

Background Information
3. Tell me about your being here today.
   (If the adolescent does not mention problems with alcohol, go to question 4; if the adolescent does mention problems with alcohol, go to question 5.)
4. I understand that you are drinking alcohol. Is that right?
   (If the adolescent acknowledges alcohol use, go to question 5. If the adolescent refuses to acknowledge that he or she has a problem with alcohol, you may not be able to continue with this interview. Instead, consider asking the questions in Table B-1 in this Appendix that focus on general issues associated with adolescent adjustment. Begin with item 7.)
5. Tell me about your drinking.
   (Ask questions 6 to 28, as needed.)
6. What do you drink?
7. How much do you drink?
8. How often do you drink?
9. At what times during the day do you drink?
10. Do you ever drink just after you get up in the morning?
11. (If yes) Tell me about that.
12. Can you stop drinking after you've had one or two drinks if you want to?
13. (If needed) Where do you do your drinking?
14. Are you alone when you drink, or are you with other people?
15. (If with others) Tell me something about the people you drink with.
16. How do you get the alcohol?
    (If purchased, go to question 17; if not purchased, go to question 20.)
17. Who buys the alcohol for you?
18. Do you give this person money to buy the alcohol?
19. Where do you get the money to buy the alcohol?
20. How old were you when you first started drinking?
21. What did you drink when you first started?
22. How much did you drink at that time?
23. Have you ever been drunk?
    (If yes, to question 24; if no, go to question 26.)
24. Tell me about the times you have been drunk.
25. How old were you the first time you ever drank enough to get drunk?
26. How has your drinking changed since you first began to drink?
27. Do you think you are losing control over your drinking?
28. (If yes) Tell me about that.

Symptoms and Related Issues
29. Do you ever have hangovers?
30. (If yes) Tell me about the times you get hangovers.
31. Have you ever had blackouts while drinking—that is, have you ever drunk enough that you couldn't remember the next day what you said or did?

32. (If yes) Tell me about your blackouts.
33. Have you ever had the shakes after cutting down on your drinking or when you stopped drinking?
    (If yes, go to question 34; if no, go to question 37.)
34. Tell me about when you had the shakes.
35. How often have you had the shakes?
36. And what did you do about the shakes?
37. Have you ever had health problems because of your drinking, such as liver disease or stomach problems?
38. (If yes) Tell me about them.
39. Have you ever made any rules about drinking, like not drinking before 5 o'clock in the evening or never drinking alone?
40. (If yes) Tell me about them.
41. Have you ever continued to drink when you were in a situation that might be made worse by drinking, such as when you were taking medicine that was not supposed to be used with alcohol?
42. (If yes) Tell me about these times.
43. Have you ever gone on binges where you kept drinking for a couple days or more without sobering up?
44. (If yes) Tell me about these times.
45. Have your parents said anything to you about your drinking?
    (If yes, go to question 46; if no, go to question 49.)
46. What did they say?
47. When did they say this to you?
48. And what did you do about it?
49. Have other people said anything to you about your drinking?
    (If yes, go to question 50; if no, go to question 52.)
50. What did they say?
51. And what did you do about it?

Reasons for Drinking
52. People have different reasons for drinking. What reasons do you have for drinking?
53. (If needed) Is it because you like the taste . . . you are celebrating special occasions . . . your friends drink . . . you feel nervous and tense . . . you are upset . . . you feel lonely or sad . . . you want to get high? Are there other reasons?
54. Does alcohol ever allow you to do things that you wouldn't do if you weren't drinking?
55. (If yes) Tell me about these things.
56. Have you ever felt bad or guilty about your drinking?
57. (If yes) Tell me about your feelings.

Problems as a Result of Drinking
58. Have you ever gotten into fights while drinking?
59. (If yes) Tell me about these times.
60. Have you ever been arrested because of your drinking?
61. (If yes) Tell me about that.
62. (If adolescent has a driver's license) Have you ever been arrested for drunk driving?
63. (If yes) Tell me about that.
64. Have you ever had an accident because of drinking?
65. (If yes) Tell me about that.

(Continued)

Table B-5 (*Continued*)

66. Have you ever had school troubles because of drinking—like missing too much school, coming in late for classes, or not paying attention in class?
67. (If yes) Tell me about these times.
68. (If relevant) Have you ever had trouble on a job because of drinking—like missing work or coming in late for work?
69. (If yes) Tell me about these times.
70. Have you lost any friends because of your drinking?
71. (If yes) Tell me about what happened.
72. Has there ever been a period of your life when you could not go on with your daily activities unless you had something to drink?
73. (If yes) Tell me about that.

Family and Friends
74. Does your father drink alcohol?
75. (If yes) Tell me about that.
76. Does your mother drink alcohol?
77. (If yes) Tell me about that.
78. (If relevant) Do any of your sisters and brothers drink alcohol?
79. (If yes) Tell me about that.
80. Does anyone else in the family drink alcohol?
81. (If yes) Who?
82. Do your friends drink alcohol?
    (If yes, go to question 83; if no, go to question 85.)
83. Tell me about their drinking.
84. When you are drinking with your friends, do you ever try to drink a bit extra and hide it from them?
85. Does anyone in your family use drugs?
86. (If yes) Tell me about that.
87. Do your friends use drugs?
88. (If yes) Tell me about that.
89. Do you also use drugs?
90. (If yes) Tell me about the drugs you use.

Attempts to Seek Help
91. Have you ever felt the need to cut down on your drinking?
92. (If yes) Tell me about that.
93. Have you ever talked to your parents . . . your friends . . . your doctor . . . your clergyperson . . . your teachers . . . any other professional about drinking too much?
    (If yes, go to question 94; if no, go to question 97.)

94. Tell me about who you talked to.
95. What did you say?
96. And what did he [she, they] say?
97. Have you ever tried to stop drinking?
98. (If yes) Tell me about the times when you tried to stop drinking.
99. Do you think you have a drinking problem?
100. (If yes) Tell me about that.
101. Have you ever been in an alcohol treatment program? (If yes, go to question 102; if no, go to question 104.)
102. Tell me about when you were in the program.
103. Did it help?
104. What is your goal—what would you like to see happen with regard to your drinking right now?

Attitude Toward Treatment
(If the adolescent has said that he or she has a problem with alcohol, go to question 105; if not, go to question 109.)
105. Do you want help for your problem?
    (If yes, go to question 106; if no, go to question 109.)
106. What kind of help do you want?
107. How long do you think it will take to gain control over your drinking?
108. Are you prepared to work with people who are trained to help you?
109. If you did not drink alcohol, what would you miss most about it?
110. And what would be the best thing about not drinking alcohol?
111. How would your friends react if you did not drink alcohol?
112. And how would your family react if you did not drink alcohol?
113. How then do you see the role of alcohol in your life—that is, what part should alcohol play in your life?

Concluding Questions
114. Is there anything else you would like to tell me about your alcohol use?
115. (If yes) Go ahead.
116. Do you have any questions that you would like to ask me?
117. (If yes) Go ahead.
118. Thank you for talking with me. (Tell the interviewee what will happen next, as needed.) If you have any questions or if you want to talk to me, please call me. Here is my card.

Note. With modifications, these questions also could be used with a parent. You would need to substitute the child's name for "you" or "your" and make the appropriate grammatical changes. Table B-6 in this Appendix contains a semistructured interview useful for inquiring about drug use.
Source: Adapted, in part, from Robins and Marcus (1987).

Table B-6
Semistructured Interview Questions for an Adolescent or Older Child with a Drug Abuse Problem

Introduction

1. Hi! I'm Dr. [Ms., Mr.] _____. I'd like to talk to you about how you're getting along. OK?
2. When you don't understand a question that I ask, please say "I don't understand." When you tell me that, I'll try to ask it better. OK?

Background Information

3. Tell me about your being here today.
   (If the adolescent does not mention problems with drug use, go to question 4; if the adolescent does mention problems with drug use, go to question 5.)
4. I understand that you are using drugs. Is that right?
   (If the adolescent acknowledges drug use, go to question 5. If the adolescent refuses to acknowledge that he or she has a problem with drugs, you may not be able to continue with this interview. Instead, consider asking the questions in Table B-1 in this Appendix that focus on general issues associated with adolescent adjustment. Begin with item 7.)
5. Tell me about the drug[s] you use.
6. Where do you get it [them]?
7. How much does it cost?
8. About how much money do you spend each week on [cite drug]?
9. How do you pay for it?
10. Are you having financial problems because of your drug use?
11. (If yes) Tell me about that.
12. Have you ever done things you otherwise wouldn't do to get [cite drug]?
13. (If yes) Tell me about that.
14. (If needed) What do you do to get [cite drug]?
15. Do you have trouble turning down [cite drug] when it is offered to you?
16. Tell me about that.
17. Does the sight, thought, or mention of [cite drug] trigger urges and craving for it?
18. (If yes) Tell me about that.
19. Do you think about [cite drug] much of the time?
20. (If yes) Tell me about these thoughts.
21. Do you have any concerns about your drug use?
22. (If yes) Tell me about your concerns.
23. (If needed) Are you frightened by the strength of your drug habit?

Exposure to Drugs

24. Does anyone else in your family drink alcohol too much or use drugs?
25. (If yes) Tell me about that.
26. Do any of your friends regularly use alcohol or drugs?
27. (If yes) Tell me about that.
28. Do any of your friends sell or give drugs to other kids?
29. (If yes) Tell me about that.
30. When did you first learn about [cite drug]?
31. Who told you about [cite drug]?
32. What did he [she] tell you?
33. How old were you when you first tried [cite drug]?
34. Where were you when you first tried [cite drug]?

35. Was anyone else there?
36. (If yes) Tell me about who was there.
37. How much [cite drug] did you take?
38. How did you feel after you took [cite drug]?
39. As you look back on your first experience with [cite drug], do you have any thoughts about the experience now?

Drug Usage

40. How old were you when you first started using [cite drug] regularly?
41. How do you go about taking [cite drug]?
42. (If needed) Do you smoke it . . . eat or swallow it . . . inject it . . . snort it . . . inhale it?
43. How much [cite drug] do you take?
    (If drug is injected, go to question 44; if not, go to question 46.)
44. Do you use a sterile needle?
45. Do you share needles with other people?
46. Where are you when you take [cite drug]?
47. (If needed) Do you take it at home . . . at school . . . in the park . . . at friends' houses . . . in other places?
48. At what times during the day do you take [cite drug]?
49. Are you with anyone else when you take [cite drug]?
50. (If yes) Tell me about whom you're with.
51. About how many times have you used [cite drug]?
52. When was the last time you used [cite drug]?
53. How often do you use [cite drug]?
54. (If needed) On the average, how many days per week do you use [cite drug]?
55. How long have you been doing this?
56. Do you tend to use all the [cite drug] that you have on hand, even though you want to save some for another time?
57. Was there a particular time when you realized that you had begun to use [cite drug] more often?
    (If yes, go to question 58; if no, go to question 60.)
58. When was that?
59. Why do you think you started to use [cite drug] more often?
60. How do you feel when you don't have [cite drug]?
61. What do you do about it when you don't have [cite drug]?
62. Did you ever find you needed larger amounts of [cite drug] because you couldn't get high on the amount you were using?
63. (If yes) Tell me more about that.
64. (If needed) When did that begin to happen?
65. Would you use even more [cite drug] if you could get it?
66. Have you ever woken up the morning after taking [cite drug] and found you couldn't remember a part of what happened the night before, even though your friends tell you that you didn't pass out?
67. Do you often wish you could keep taking [cite drug] even after your friends have had enough?
68. (If yes) Tell me about that.

Drug Binges

69. Do you go on drug binges—that is, use a drug or drugs continually for a period of time?
    (If yes, go to question 70; if no, go to question 77.)
70. How many times have you gone on binges?

(Continued)

Table B-6 (Continued)

71. When was the last time you went on a binge?
72. What was happening in your life at that time?
73. How long does a binge last?
74. How much [cite drug] do you take during a binge?
75. How do you feel during the binge?
76. How do you feel after the binge?

Attempts to Stop Drug Usage

77. Has a friend or member of your family ever gone to anyone for help about your drug use?
78. (If yes) Tell me about that.
79. Have you ever attended Alcoholics Anonymous or Narcotics Anonymous meetings?
80. (If yes) Tell me about what happened.
81. Have you ever tried to stop taking [cite drug]? (If yes, go to question 82; if no, go to question 89.)
82. What did you do to try to stop taking [cite drug]?
83. How long did you go without taking [cite drug]?
84. What happened that you started taking [cite drug] again?
85. About how many times have you tried to stop taking [cite drug]?
86. What happened when you tried to stop?
87. (If needed) Did you have withdrawal symptoms—that is, did you feel sick because you stopped or cut down on [cite drug]?
88. (If yes) Tell me about your symptoms.
89. Do you have any idea why you haven't stopped using [cite drug]?
90. (If yes) Tell me about that.
91. Have you ever tried to limit your drug use to only certain times or certain situations?
92. (If yes) Tell me about that.

Symptoms Associated with Drug Usage

93. Do you have any health problems because of using [cite drug]? (If yes, go to question 94; if no, go to question 97.)
94. Tell me about your health problems.
95. Have you ever gone to a doctor about these problems?
96. (If yes) What did the doctor do?
97. How is your appetite?
98. Have you gained or lost weight recently?
99. (If yes) Tell me about that.
100. Tell me about what you ate yesterday and today.
101. Is that the usual amount you eat?
102. (If no) How did that differ from what you would eat other times?
103. When you are taking [cite drug] regularly, do you miss meals?
104. (If yes) Tell me more about that.
105. Have you ever been hospitalized for using [cite drug]?
106. (If yes) Tell me about that.
107. Have you ever overdosed on a drug?
108. (If yes) Tell me about that.
109. Has your use of [cite drug] caused you to miss school . . . do poorly in school . . . get into trouble with your teacher or principal . . . get into an accident . . . lose control . . . get the shakes or become depressed . . . get into trouble with your family . . . get into trouble with your

friends . . . get into trouble with the police . . . have sex with someone . . . be sexually abused by someone?
110. (If yes to any of the above) Tell me about how you happened to [name problem] and the role [cite drug] played. (Ask this question for each behavior mentioned by interviewee.)
111. Do people who don't know about the drug use tell you that your behavior or personality has changed?
112. Have your parents talked to you about your drug use?
113. Tell me about that.
114. (If adolescent has a driver's license) Do you ever drive a car when you're high on [cite drug]?
115. (If yes) Tell me about that.
116. (If needed) Have you neglected your schoolwork or any important responsibilities because of your drug habit?
117. (If yes) Tell me about that.
118. Have your values and priorities changed because of your drug use?
119. (If yes) Tell me about that.
120. Do you feel guilty or ashamed for using [cite drug]?
121. Do you like yourself less for using [cite drug]?
122. Do you tend to spend time with certain people or go to certain places because you know that [cite drug] will be available?
123. Do you have any strange or scary feelings or thoughts when you use [cite drug]?
124. (If yes) Tell me about them.
125. Do you find yourself lying and making excuses because of your drug use?
126. (If yes) Tell me about that.
127. Do you ever deny or downplay the severity of your drug problem?
128. Has taking [cite drug] interfered with your life or activities?
129. (If yes) Tell me about how taking [cite drug] has interfered.
130. Have you been spending less time with "straight" people since you've been using more [cite drug]?

Reasons for Taking Drugs

131. People have different reasons for taking drugs. What reasons do you have?
132. (If needed) Is it because you like the feeling it gives you . . . you need it to have a good time . . . you're afraid of being bored or unhappy without it . . . it makes you feel less nervous or tense . . . you feel lonely and sad . . . your friends take drugs . . . you feel you couldn't function well without it?
133. Have your reasons for taking [cite drug] changed since you began using it?
134. (If yes) Tell me about that.

Involvement with Other Drugs

135. Do you drink alcohol or use any other drugs in addition to [cite drug]? (If yes, go to question 136; if no, go to question 141.)
136. Tell me about what you take or drink.
137. How does it make you feel?
138. Do you do it at the same time you use [cite drug]?
139. (If yes) Are you concerned about how these drugs [the drugs and alcohol] interact with each other?
140. (If yes) Tell me about your concerns.

Table B-6 (*Continued*)

Attitude Toward Treatment

141. Do you think you have a problem with drugs?
(If yes, go to question 142; if no, go to question 146.)
142. Do you want help for your problem?
(If yes, go to question 143; if no, go to question 146.)
143. What kind of help do you want?
144. How long do you think it will take to gain some control over your drug use?
145. Are you prepared to work with people trained to help you?
146. If you became drug free, what would you miss most about [cite drug]?
147. And if you became drug free, what would be the best thing about being clean?

148. How would your friends react if you became clean?
149. And how would your family react if you became clean?

Concluding Questions

150. Is there anything else you'd like to tell me about your drug use?
151. (If yes) Go ahead.
152. Do you have any questions that you would like to ask me?
153. (If yes) Go ahead.
154. Thank you for talking with me. If you have any questions or if you want to talk to me, please call me. Here is my card.

Note. With modifications, these questions also could be used with a parent. You would need to substitute the child's name for "you" or "your" and make the appropriate grammatical changes. Table B-5 in this Appendix contains a semistructured interview useful for inquiring about alcohol abuse or dependence.

Source: Adapted, in part, from Roffman and George (1988) and Washton, Stone, and Hendrickson (1988).

Table B-7
Semistructured Interview Questions for a Child or Adolescent with a Learning Disability

Introduction

1. Hi! I'm Dr. [Ms., Mr.] _____. I'd like to talk to you about how you are getting along. OK?
2. When you don't understand a question that I ask, please say "I don't understand." When you tell me that, I'll try to ask it better. OK?

Attitude Toward School

3. How are you getting along in school?
4. What do you like about school?
5. What don't you like about school?
6. What are your favorite subjects?
7. What are your least favorite subjects?
8. Which subjects are easiest for you?
9. Which subjects are hardest for you?
10. Now I'd like to talk to you about some specific subjects. OK?

Reading

11. How well can you read?
12. Do you like to read?
13. Tell me about that.
14. When you read, do you make mistakes like skipping words or lines, reading the same lines twice, or reading letters backwards?
15. (If needed) Tell me about the mistakes you make when you read.
16. Do you find that you can read each line of every paragraph but, when you finish the page or chapter, you don't remember what you've just read?
17. Do you understand and remember better when you read aloud or when you read silently?

Writing

18. How good is your handwriting?
19. Do you find that you cannot write as fast as you think?
20. (If yes) Do you run one word into another when you're writing because you're thinking of the next word rather than the one you're writing?
21. How good is your spelling?
22. Tell me about that.
23. How good is your grammar?
24. Tell me about that.
25. How good is your punctuation?
26. Tell me about that.
27. Do you know how to type on a computer?
28. (If yes) Does using a computer make writing easier for you?
29. Tell me about that.
30. Do you have difficulty copying from the chalkboard?
31. Tell me about that.
32. Do you have difficulty taking notes when the teacher lectures?
33. Tell me about that.

Math

34. Do you know the multiplication tables?
35. (If no) Tell me about that.
36. When you do math, do you make mistakes like writing "21" when you mean to write "12," mixing up columns of numbers, or adding when you mean to subtract?

37. Tell me about the mistakes you make when you do math.
38. Do you sometimes start a math problem but halfway through forget what you were trying to do?

Sequencing

39. When you speak or write, do you sometimes find it hard to get everything in the right order—do you maybe start in the middle, go to the beginning, and then jump to the end?
40. Do you have trouble saying the alphabet in order?
41. (If yes) Tell me about that.
42. Do you have to start from the beginning each time you say the alphabet?
43. Do you have trouble saying the days of the week in order?
44. (If yes) Tell me about that.
45. Do you have trouble saying the months of the year in order?
46. (If yes) Tell me about that.

Abstraction

47. Do you understand jokes when your friends tell them?
48. (If no) Tell me about that.
49. Do you sometimes find that people seem to say one thing yet tell you that they meant something else?
50. (If yes) Tell me about that.

Organization

51. What does your notebook look like?
52. (If needed) Is it pretty neat and organized, or is it a mess, with papers in the wrong place or falling out?
53. Is it hard for you to organize your thoughts or to organize the facts you're learning into the bigger idea that the teacher is trying to teach you?
54. Can you read a chapter and answer the questions at the end of the chapter but still not be sure what the chapter is about?
55. (If yes) Tell me about that.
56. Do you have trouble planning your time so that things get done on time?
57. (If yes) Tell me about that.
58. What does your bedroom at home look like?

Memory

59. How is your memory?
60. Has it changed in any way?
(Ask questions 61 to 64, as needed.)
61. Do you find that you can learn something at night but, when you go to school the next day, you don't remember what you learned?
62. When talking, do you sometimes forget what you are saying halfway through?
63. (If yes) What do you do when this happens?
64. (If needed) Do you cover up by saying things like "Whatever," "Oh, forget it," or "It's not important"?

Language

65. When the teacher is speaking in class, do you have trouble understanding or keeping up?
66. (If yes) Tell me about that.
67. Do you sometimes misunderstand people and, therefore, give the wrong answer?

Table B-7 (*Continued*)

68. (If yes) When does this tend to happen?
69. Do you sometimes lose track of what people are saying?
70. (If yes) Does this sometimes cause you to lose your concentration in class?
71. Do you sometimes have trouble organizing your thoughts when you speak?
72. (If yes) Tell me about that.
73. Do you sometimes have a problem finding the word you want to use?
74. (If yes) When this happens, what do you do?

Study Habits

75. Now I'd like to ask you about your learning and study habits. Tell me about what happens when you study.
76. Do you learn better alone, with one friend, or in a group?
77. Tell me more about that.
78. When you study, do you like to have adults help you, only help you if you ask them to, or leave you alone?
79. Tell me about that.

Time Rhythm

80. At what time of day do you learn best?
81. (If needed) Do you learn best early in the morning, right before lunch, after lunch, after school, or right before bedtime?
82. After you wake up in the morning, how long does it take you to feel really awake?
83. Do you sometimes have trouble staying awake after lunch or dinner?
84. (If yes) Tell me more about that.
85. Do you like to get up early?
86. If you stay up late, do you feel "foggy" the next day—as if your head were in a cloud?
87. What time do you usually go to bed?
88. How long does it usually take you to fall asleep?

Environment

89. Where is the best place for you to study?
90. Tell me more about that.
91. Do you like to study in a room with bright lighting or low lighting?
92. Do you think you feel cold or hot more often than other people?
93. (If yes) Tell me about that.
94. Do you like the room you're in to be warm or cool?

Attention and Concentration

95. Do you prefer noise or silence when you are studying?
96. Can you study if you hear a radio or television in the background?
97. Are you distracted if you hear people talking or children playing?
98. Do you like to study with music playing?
99. (If yes) What kind of music?
100. Do you daydream a lot when you are in class?
101. (If yes) Tell me about that.
102. Do you have trouble sitting still or staying in your seat at school?
103. (If yes) Tell me about the trouble you're having.

104. And at home, do you have trouble sitting still or staying in your seat?
105. (If yes) Tell me about that.
106. How is your concentration?
107. Can you complete your assignments, or are you easily distracted?
108. (If distracted) What seems to distract you?
109. Do you like to leave your studies to go see what's going on, get a drink, or change rooms or positions?
110. (If yes) Tell me more about that.
111. Do you like to keep at your work until it's done?
112. Tell me more about that.

Study Habits

113. Do you like to eat, chew gum, or have a drink while you are studying?
114. (If yes) How does it help?
115. Do you overeat while you are studying?
116. (If yes) How does it help?
117. Do you have any nervous habits while you're studying, such as chewing your fingernails or a pencil?
118. (If yes) Tell me about your habits.

Motivation

119. How important is it for you to get good grades?
120. Tell me about that.
121. Do you think your grades are important to your parents?
122. Tell me about that.
123. Do you think your grades are important to your teachers?
124. Tell me about that.
125. When you try to get good grades, is it more to please adults or to please yourself?
126. Tell me about that.
127. Do you think that getting a good education is important?
128. Tell me about that.
129. Do you think reading is important for more things in life than just school?
130. Tell me about that.
131. Do you let things go until the last minute?
132. Tell me about that.
133. Do you feel responsible for your learning?
134. Tell me about that.
135. How do you feel when you don't do well in school?
136. How do you feel when you turn in an assignment late?
137. How do you feel when you don't finish an assignment?
138. Do you like solving problems on your own, or do you prefer being told exactly what is expected and how to do it?
139. Do you get upset easily when you are learning?
140. (If yes) Tell me about that.
141. Do you like to learn and find out things, even when you aren't in school and don't have to?
142. Tell me about that.
143. How do you feel when someone criticizes your schoolwork?
144. Tell me about that.
145. Do you usually try to do your very best in school?
146. Tell me about that.

(*Continued*)

Table B-7 (*Continued*)

Anxiety

147. Do you think that you worry more about school or tests than other kids do?
148. (If yes) Tell me about that.
149. Do you feel shaky when the teacher asks you to read aloud, get up in front of the class, or write on the board?
150. (If yes) Tell me about that.
151. How do you feel about surprise tests?

Concluding Questions

152. Is there anything else you would like to tell me or talk about?
153. Do you have any questions that you would like to ask me?
154. (If yes) Go ahead.
155. Thank you for talking with me. If you have any questions or if you want to talk to me, please call me. Here is my card.

Note. With modifications, these questions also could be used for a parent. You would need to substitute the child's name for "you" or "your" and make the appropriate grammatical changes.
Source: Adapted from Dunn and Dunn (1977) and Silver (1992).

Table B-8
Semistructured Interview Questions for an Older Child or Adolescent with Traumatic Brain Injury

These questions supplement those in Table B-1 in this Appendix.

Introduction

1. Hi, I'm Dr. [Ms., Mr.] _____. I'm going to be asking you some questions. When you don't understand a question that I ask, please say "I don't understand." When you tell me that, I'll try to ask it better. OK?
2. Has anyone told you why you are here today?
   (If yes, go to question 3; if no, go to question 5.)
3. Who told you?
4. What did he [she, they] tell you?
   (Go to question 6.)
5. Tell me why you think you are here. (If interviewee doesn't know, explain to her or him that you want to find out how she or he is getting along or something similar.)

General Problems

6. Please tell me anything you can about how you are getting along.
7. (If needed) Are you having any problems?
   (If child says that he or she is having problems, go to question 8; otherwise, go to question 19.)
8. Tell me about [cite problems mentioned by child].
9. How do you feel about [cite problems]?
10. What changes have you noticed since [cite problems] began?
11. In what situations do you have the most difficulty with [cite problems]?
12. What do you do in these situations?
13. Is there anything that helps?
14. (If yes) How does it help?
15. What kind of help would you like?
16. How do your parents feel about the problems you are having?
17. How do your friends feel about the problems you are having?
18. And how do your teachers feel about the problems you are having?

Specific Current Problems and Complaints

19. I'm going to name some areas in which you may have problems. If you have problems or complaints in any of these areas, please let me know by saying yes. After we finish the list, we'll go back to the beginning and I'll ask you more about these problems. OK?

   (*If the child previously told you about a problem, do not mention it again now.* Pause after you name each problem or complaint. From time to time, remind the child of the task by prefacing the name of the problem with "Are you having a problem with . . . ?" or "Do you have any complaints about . . . ?")

General Physical Problems
- bowel or bladder control
- seizures
- headaches
- dizziness
- pain
- sleeping
- numbness
- loss of feeling
- blackouts
- muscle strength
- endurance
- coordination

Sensory-Motor Problems
- seeing
- hearing
- smelling
- speaking
- balance
- movements you can't control or stop
- doing things too fast or too slowly
- standing
- walking
- running
- drawing
- handwriting
- eating
- dressing
- bathing
- recognizing objects
- building or constructing things
- hearing ringing sounds
- changes in taste
- tingling in your fingertips or toes

Cognitive Problems
- thinking
- planning
- concentrating
- remembering
- paying attention
- understanding directions
- giving directions
- learning
- judging
- reading
- writing stories, poems, and other things
- spelling
- doing simple arithmetic problems
- understanding what is read to you
- handling money
- finding your way around
- organizing things
- changing from one activity to another

Psychosocial-Affective Problems
- keeping up with your responsibilities at home
- staying interested in things
- getting along with other children
- getting along with friends and family members

(Continued)

Table B-8 (*Continued*)

- getting along with teachers
- controlling your temper
- feeling sad
- feeling anxious
- showing initiative
- realizing that another person is upset
- controlling your laughter
- being inconsiderate of others
- being impatient
- being inflexible
- becoming angry without cause
- changing moods easily
- being irritable
- being aggressive
- being uncooperative
- being negative
- lying
- stealing
- having to do things exactly the same way each time
- changes in your personality
- recognizing problems in yourself
- being insecure
- visiting friends
- keeping friends
- going shopping

Language and Communication Problems
- talking too much
- talking too little
- using the right word
- using peculiar words
- saying embarrassing things
- reversing what you hear
- defining words
- naming objects that are shown to you
- counting
- naming the days of the week
- repeating names
- carrying on a conversation
- recognizing mistakes that you make in speaking or writing or reading
- using the telephone
- looking up telephone numbers
- remembering telephone numbers
- watching television

Consciousness Problems
- feeling disoriented
- feeling that you are losing your body
- feeling that some unknown danger is lurking
- doing things that you are unaware of
- starting to do one thing and then finding yourself doing something else
- feeling that the size of your hands or feet or head is changing

(If the child responded "yes" to any of the above problems, go to question 20; otherwise, go to question 24.)

20. You told me that you have a problem with [cite area]. Tell me more about your difficulty with [cite area]. (Repeat for each problem.)
21. Which problems bother you most?
22. How do you deal with these problems?
23. How do your parents deal with these problems?

Accident or Injury

24. I'd like to learn about the accident [injury]. Please tell me about it.
    (Ask questions 25 to 36 as needed.)
25. What happened?
26. What were you doing at the time of the accident [injury]?
27. Who else was involved in the accident [injury]?
28. Were you unconscious?
    (If yes, go to question 29; if no, go to question 31.)
29. How long were you unconscious?
30. Where did you wake up?
31. What kind of treatment did you get?
32. How did the treatment help?
33. What kind of treatment are you receiving now?
34. What was your behavior like right after the accident [injury] happened?
35. What was your behavior like several days later?
36. And what is your behavior like now?

Adjustment to Brain Injury and Typical Activities

37. Have you noticed any changes since the accident [injury] in how you are getting along with your parents?
38. (If yes) Tell me what you have noticed.
39. (If relevant) Have you noticed any changes since the accident [injury] in how you are getting along with your brothers and sisters?
40. (If yes) Tell me what you have noticed.
41. Have you noticed any changes since the accident [injury] in how you are getting along with your friends?
42. (If yes) Tell me what you have noticed.
43. Have there been any changes in your schoolwork since the accident [injury]?
44. (If yes) Tell me about the changes in your schoolwork.
45. (If relevant) Have there been any changes in your work habits since the accident [injury]?
46. (If yes) Tell me about the changes in your work habits.

Concluding Questions

47. Is there anything else that you want to tell me or that you think I should know?
48. (If yes) Go ahead.
49. Do you have any questions that you would like to ask me?
50. (If yes) Go ahead.
51. Thank you for talking with me. If you have any questions, if you want to talk to me, or if you think of anything else you want to tell me, please call me. Here is my card.

Note. With modifications, these questions also could be used with a parent of a child with traumatic brain injury. You would need to substitute the child's name for "you" or "your" and make the appropriate grammatical changes.

Table B-9
Semistructured Interview Questions for a Parent of a Child Who May Have a Psychological or Educational Problem or Disorder

Some of the questions in this table (for example, those dealing with peer relationships, interests and hobbies, and academic functioning) are not applicable to infants, and other questions (for example, those dealing with academic functioning) are not applicable to toddlers. Therefore, use your judgment in selecting appropriate questions to use. This table can be used in conjunction with Table B-10 in this Appendix, which contains additional questions concerning specific areas of child development in infancy and the toddler/preschool years. At the end of this table are additional questions that you can use to inquire about adolescents.

Introduction

1. Hi! I'm Dr. [Ms., Mr.] _____. I'd like to talk to you about [cite child's name]'s adjustment and functioning. OK?

Parent's Perception of Problem Behavior

2. Please tell me your concerns about [cite child's name].
3. (If needed) Can you describe these concerns a little more?
4. Is there anything else that you are concerned about?
5. What concerns you most?
6. Let's discuss [cite problem] in more detail. How serious do you consider [cite problem] to be?
7. When did you first notice [cite problem]?
8. How long has [cite problem] been going on?
9. Where does [cite problem] occur?
10. (If needed) Tell me about how [cite child's name] behaves at school . . . in stores or other public places . . . in a car . . . at friends' houses . . . with visitors at home.
11. When does [cite problem] occur?
12. (If needed) Does it happen in the morning . . . in the afternoon . . . at bedtime? . . . Does it occur when [cite child's name] is with you . . . his [her] father [mother] . . . his [her] brothers and sisters . . . other children . . . other relatives?
13. How long does [cite problem] last?
14. How often does [cite problem] occur?
15. What happens just before [cite problem] begins?
16. What happens just after [cite problem] begins?
17. What makes [cite problem] worse?
18. What makes [cite problem] better?
19. What do you think is causing [cite problem]?
20. Was anything significant happening in your family when [cite problem] first started?
21. (If needed) For example, had you recently separated or divorced . . . moved to another city or school district . . . had financial problems . . . dealt with the serious illness of a family member?
22. (If some event occurred) What was [cite child's name]'s reaction to [cite event]?
23. How does [cite child's name] deal with [cite problem]?
24. Do any other children in your family also have [cite problem]?
25. (If yes) How does [cite child's name]'s [cite problem] compare with theirs?
26. Has [cite child's name] been evaluated or received any help for [cite problem]?
    (If yes, go to question 27; if no, go to question 29.)

27. What type of evaluation or help has he [she] received?
28. And what progress has been made?
29. Why do you think [cite child's name] has [cite problem]?
30. How do you deal with [cite problem]?
31. How successful has it been?
32. How do family members react to [cite child's name]'s [cite problem]?
33. Are any of the other problems you mentioned, such as [cite problem], of particular concern to you now?
    (If yes, repeat questions 6 to 32 as needed.)

Home Environment

34. Tell me what your home is like.
35. Where does [cite child's name] sleep?
36. Where does [cite child's name] play?
37. Who lives at your home?
38. (If needed) Do you have a husband [wife] or partner?
39. (If relevant) Tell me about your husband [wife, partner].

Neighborhood

40. Tell me about your neighborhood.
41. Do you know your neighbors?
42. (If yes) What do you think of your neighbors?
43. (If needed) How do you get along with them?

Sibling Relations (if relevant)

44. How does [cite child's name] get along with his [her] brothers and sisters?
45. What do they do that [cite child's name] likes?
46. What do they do that [cite child's name] dislikes?
47. How do they get along when you aren't around?
48. Do you think the children behave differently when you are there?

Peer Relations

49. Does [cite child's name] have friends?
    (If yes, go to question 50; if no, go to question 60.)
50. Tell me about [cite child's name]'s friends.
51. (If needed) About how many friends does he [she] have?
52. (If needed) What are their ages?
53. How does he [she] get along with his [her] friends?
54. What does [cite child's name] do with his [her] friends?
55. How does he [she] get along with friends of the opposite sex?
56. Do you approve of his [her] friends?
57. Does [cite child's name] usually go along with what his [her] friends want to do, or is [cite child's name] more likely to do what he [she] wants to do?
58. Does [cite child's name] have a problem keeping friends?
59. (If yes) Tell me about that.
    (Go to question 64.)
60. Tell me about [cite child's name]'s not having friends.
61. Does [cite child's name] have opportunities to meet other children?
62. (If needed) Tell me more about that.
63. Does [cite child's name] seem to want to have friends?
64. How do other children react to [cite child's name]?

(Continued)

Table B-9 (*Continued*)

Child's Relations with Parents and Other Adults

65. How does [cite child's name] get along with you?
66. What does [cite child's name] do with you on a regular basis?
67. How does [cite child's name] express his [her] affection for you?
68. What are the good times like for [cite child's name] and you?
69. What are the bad times like for [cite child's name] and you?
70. Are there times when both you and [cite child's name] end up feeling angry or frustrated with each other?
71. (If yes) Tell me more about that.
    (If there are other adults in the household, repeat questions 65 to 71 for each adult, substituting the adult's name, and then go to question 72; otherwise, go to question 78.)
72. When something is bothering [cite child's name], whom does he [she] confide in most often?
73. Who is responsible for discipline?
74. Who is most protective of [cite child's name]?
75. Do you have any concerns about how other adults interact with [cite child's name]?
76. (If yes) Tell me about your concerns.
77. (If needed) About whom do you have concerns?
78. Does [cite child's name] listen to what he [she] is told to do?
79. How is [cite child's name] disciplined?
80. Which techniques are effective?
81. Which are ineffective?
82. What have you found to be the most satisfactory ways of helping your child?
83. How do you express your affection for [cite child's name]?

Child's Interests and Hobbies

84. What does [cite child's name] like to do in his [her] spare time?
85. What types of games does [cite child's name] like to play?
86. How skilled is [cite child's name] at sports or other games?
87. Is [cite child's name] involved in any extracurricular activities?
88. (If yes) Tell me about that.
89. What does [cite child's name] like to do alone . . . with friends . . . with family members?
90. What activities does [cite child's name] like least?
91. How much television does [cite child's name] watch each day?
92. Do you think that is an acceptable amount of television?
93. (If no) Tell me about that.
94. What are his [her] favorite programs?
95. How do you feel about the programs he [she] watches?
96. Does [cite child's name] play video or computer games?
97. (If yes) How much time does [cite child's name] spend each day playing these games?
98. Do you think that is an acceptable amount of time?
99. (If no) Tell me about that.
100. (If needed) And how about listening to music? Does [cite child's name] listen to music?
    (If yes, go to question 101; if no, go to question 103.)
101. What kind of music does [cite child's name] listen to?
102. How do you feel about the music [cite child's name] listens to?

Child's Routine Daily Activities

103. How does [cite child's name] behave when he [she] wakes up?
104. What changes occur in [cite child's name]'s behavior during the course of a day?
105. (If needed) Does he [she] become more fidgety or restless as the day proceeds, or does he [she] become more calm and relaxed?
106. Does [cite child's name] do household chores?
107. (If yes) What chores does he [she] do?
108. What does [cite child's name] do before bedtime?
109. How does [cite child's name] behave when he [she] goes to bed?

Child's Cognitive Functioning

110. How well does [cite child's name] learn things?
111. Does [cite child's name] seem to understand things that are said to him [her]?
112. Does [cite child's name] seem to be quick or slow to catch on?
113. Does [cite child's name] stick with tasks that he [she] is trying to learn?

Child's Academic Functioning

114. How is [cite child's name] getting along in school?
115. What does he [she] like best about school?
116. What does he [she] like least about school?
117. What grades does [cite child's name] get?
118. What are [cite child's name]'s best subjects?
119. What are [cite child's name]'s worst subjects?
120. Are you generally satisfied with [cite child's name]'s achievement in school?
121. (If no) Tell me what you're not satisfied about.
122. How does [cite child's name] feel about his [her] schoolwork?
123. How does [cite child's name] get along with the other children at school?
124. How does [cite child's name] get along with his [her] teacher[s]?
125. What do you think of [cite child's name]'s school?
126. What do you think of [cite child's name]'s teacher[s]?
127. What do you think of the principal of the school?
128. Has [cite child's name] ever repeated a grade or attended a readiness or transition class?
129. (If yes) Tell me about that.
130. Has any teacher recommended special help or special education services for [cite child's name]?
    (If yes, go to question 131; if no, go to question 136.)
131. Tell me about the help that was recommended.
132. Please describe what help, if any, he [she] has received.
133. Does [cite child's name] attend a special class?
134. Have you needed to attend specially scheduled parent-teacher meetings because of [cite child's name]'s behavior?
135. (If yes) What did you learn at the meeting[s]?

Child's Behavior

136. Tell me about [cite child's name]'s attention span.
137. What kind of self-control does [cite child's name] have?
138. How well does [cite child's name] follow directions?
139. Tell me about [cite child's name]'s activity level.
140. Is [cite child's name] impulsive?
141. (If yes) Tell me about his [her] impulsiveness.

Table B-9 (*Continued*)

Child's Affective Life

142. What kinds of things make [cite child's name] happy?
143. What makes him [her] sad?
144. What does [cite child's name] do when he [she] is sad?
145. What kinds of things make [cite child's name] angry?
146. What does [cite child's name] do when he [she] is angry?
147. What kinds of things make [cite child's name] afraid?
148. What does [cite child's name] do when he [she] is afraid?
149. What kinds of things does [cite child's name] worry about?
150. What kinds of things does [cite child's name] think about a lot?
151. What sorts of things does [cite child's name] ask questions about?
152. How does [cite child's name] typically react to a painful or uncomfortable event, such as when he [she] gets an injection or has to take pills?
153. How does [cite child's name] feel about himself [herself]?
154. How does [cite child's name] behave when faced with a difficult problem?
155. What makes [cite child's name] frustrated?
156. What does [cite child's name] do when he [she] is frustrated?
157. Does [cite child's name] ever become annoyed when you try to help him [her] with something?
158. (If yes) Tell me about that.
159. What things does [cite child's name] do well?
160. What things does [cite child's name] really enjoy doing?
161. Tell me what [cite child's name] is really willing to work to obtain.
162. What do you do when [cite child's name] is sad . . . is angry . . . is afraid . . . worries a lot . . . is in pain?

Child's Motor Skills

163. Tell me about [cite child's name]'s ability to do things that require small motor movements, such as turning pages of a book, using scissors, and folding paper.
164. Tell me about [cite child's name]'s general coordination, such as his [her] ability to walk, jump, skip, and roll a ball.

Child's Health History

165. I'd like to ask you about [cite child's name]'s health history. What common childhood illnesses has [cite child's name] had?
166. And has [cite child's name] had any serious illnesses?
167. (If yes) Tell me about them.
168. (As needed) When did the illness start? . . . What was the treatment? . . . Was the treatment successful?
169. Has he [she] had any surgical procedures?
170. (If yes) Tell me about them.
171. How would you describe [cite child's name]'s usual state of health?
172. Do you believe that [cite child's name] has been growing adequately?
173. (If no) Tell me more about that.
174. How is [cite child's name]'s hearing?
175. How is [cite child's name]'s vision?
176. Did [cite child's name] ever have any serious accidents or injuries?
177. (If yes) Tell me about them.
178. Did [cite child's name] ever go to an emergency room for an accident or illness?
179. (If yes) Tell me about it.

180. Did [cite child's name] ever need any stitches?
181. (If yes) Tell me about it.
182. Has [cite child's name] ever had any broken bones?
183. (If yes) Tell me about it.
184. Did [cite child's name] ever swallow anything dangerous?
185. (If yes) Tell me about what happened.
186. Does [cite child's name] have any allergies?
187. (If yes) Tell me about them.
188. What immunizations has [cite child's name] had?
189. Does [cite child's name] eat well?
190. (If no) Tell me about that.
191. Does [cite child's name] sleep well?
192. (If no) Tell me about that.
193. Does [cite child's name] have nightmares or other sleep problems?
194. (If yes) Tell me about that.
195. Does [cite child's name] have problems with bowel or bladder control?
196. (If yes) Tell me about that.
197. Does [cite child's name] take any medicine regularly? (If yes, go to question 198; if no, go to question 204.)
198. What medicine does he [she] take regularly?
199. What does [cite child's name] take the medicine for?
200. Does [cite child's name] report any side effects from taking the medicine? (If yes, go to question 201; if no, go to question 204.)
201. What are the side effects?
202. Have you discussed them with your doctor?
203. (If yes) What did the doctor say?

Family

204. Tell me about your family. Does anyone in your immediate or extended family have any major problems?
205. (If yes) Tell me about them.
206. (If relevant) How are you getting along with your husband [wife, partner]?
207. (If relevant) In your opinion, how does your relationship with your husband [wife, partner] affect [cite child's name]'s problem?
208. Have you or members of your family had any serious medical or psychological difficulties?
209. Has anyone in the family whom [cite child's name] was close to died?
210. (If yes) Tell me about that.
211. How about a close friend? Have any of [cite child's name]'s friends died?
212. (If yes) Tell me about that.
213. Has the family lost a pet?
214. (If yes) Tell me about the loss.
215. Has anyone in your family been the victim of a crime?
216. (If yes) Please tell me about what happened.
217. Have you recently changed your place of residence?
218. (If yes) Tell me about your move.
219. (If relevant) Has [cite child's name]'s caregiver recently changed?
220. (If yes) Tell me about that.
221. Have any members of your family had a problem similar to [cite child's name]'s problem?
222. (If yes) Tell me about that.
223. Has anyone in the family shown a major change in behavior within the past year?

(*Continued*)

Table B-9 (*Continued*)

224. (If yes) Tell me about that.
225. (If needed) Do any members of your family have a problem with drugs or alcohol?
226. (If yes) Tell me about that.
227. Do you have any concern that [cite child's name] may have been physically abused or sexually abused?
228. (If yes) Tell me about your concern.

Parent's Expectations

229. Do you think that [cite child's name] needs treatment, special education, or special services?
230. (If yes) What do you expect such services to do for [cite child's name]?
231. What are your goals for [cite child's name]?
232. How would your life be different if [cite child's name]'s problems were resolved?
233. (If relevant) Do you desire treatment for your own difficulties? (If there are other adult members of the household, go to question 234; otherwise, go to instructions following question 239.)
234. Who in the family is most concerned about [cite child's name]'s problem?
235. Who is least concerned?
236. Who is most affected by the problem?
237. Who is least affected?
238. How does your view of [cite child's name]'s problem compare with that of [cite other adult members of household]?
239. How does your view about what should be done to help [cite child's name] compare with that of [cite other adult members of household]?
(Before concluding the interview with questions 240–244), ask the questions at the end of this table about the development of an adolescent or those in Table B-10 in this Appendix about the development of an infant or toddler/preschooler, as needed.)

Concluding Questions

240. Overall, what do you see as [cite child's name]'s strong points?
241. And overall, what do you see as [cite child's name]'s weak points?
242. Is there any other information about [cite child's name] that I should know?
243. Where do you see [cite child's name] five years from now?
244. Thank you for talking with me. If you have any questions or if you want to talk to me, please call me. Here is my card.

Additional Questions About Adolescent's Development

1. Is [cite child's name] involved in any dating activities?
2. (If yes) What kind of dating activities?
3. Are there any restrictions on his [her] dating activities?
4. (If yes) How does he [she] feel about them?
5. Have you talked with [cite child's name] about sexual behaviors?
(If yes, go to question 6; if no, go to question 10.)

6. Tell me what you've talked about.
7. What kinds of sexual concerns does [cite child's name] have?
8. Do you and [cite child's name] agree or disagree about appropriate sexual behavior?
9. Tell me about that.
10. So far as you know, does [cite child's name] use drugs? (If yes, go to question 11; if no, go to question 20.)
11. Tell me about his [her] drug use. (Ask questions 12 to 19, as needed.)
12. What kind of drugs does [cite child's name] use?
13. How does [cite child's name] get the drugs?
14. How does [cite child's name] pay for the drugs?
15. Has [cite child's name] ever gotten into trouble because of his [her] drug use?
16. (If yes) Tell me about that.
17. Has [cite child's name] received any treatment for his [her] drug use?
18. (If yes) Tell me about the treatment he [she] has received.
19. Is there anything else you want to tell me about [cite child's name]'s drug use?
20. So far as you know, does [cite child's name] drink alcohol? (If yes, go to question 21; if no, go to question 30.)
21. Tell me about his [her] drinking. (Ask questions 22 to 29, as needed.)
22. What kind of alcohol does [cite child's name] drink?
23. How does [cite child's name] get the alcohol?
24. (If relevant) How does [cite child's name] pay for the alcohol?
25. Has [cite child's name] ever gotten into trouble because of his [her] drinking?
26. (If yes) Tell me about that.
27. Has [cite child's name] received any treatment for his [her] use of alcohol?
28. (If yes) Tell me about the treatment he [she] has received.
29. Is there anything else you want to tell me about [cite child's name]'s drinking?
30. Does [cite child's name] get high by using other substances besides drugs or alcohol? (If yes, go to question 31; if no, go to question 240 in main interview.)
31. What does [cite child's name] use to get high?
32. Tell me about that. (Ask questions 33 to 39, as needed.)
33. How does [cite child's name] get [cite substance]?
34. (If relevant) How does [cite child's name] pay for [cite substance]?
35. Has [cite child's name] ever gotten into trouble because of his [her] use of [cite substance]?
36. (If yes) Tell me about that.
37. Has [cite child's name] received any treatment for his [her] use of [cite substance]?
38. (If yes) Tell me about the treatment he [she] has received.
39. Is there anything else you want to tell me about [cite child's name]'s use of [cite substance]? (Go to question 240 in main interview.)

Note. If you want to obtain information about other problems, repeat questions 7 through 33 in the main interview. Any responses given to questions in this interview can be probed further. If you want to ask additional questions about maternal obstetric history, pregnancy, or labor and delivery or if you suspect that the parent has minimal parenting skills, see Table B-10 in this Appendix.

Table B-10
Semistructured Interview Questions to Obtain a Detailed Developmental History from a Mother Covering Her Child's Early Years and to Evaluate Parenting Skills

The questions in this semistructured interview supplement those in Table B-9 in this Appendix, which should be used first. You then have the choice of following up in areas related to infancy and toddler/preschool years. The questions are designed not only to obtain information about the child but also to evaluate parenting skills. Select the questions that you believe are applicable to the specific case and that complement those in Table B-9. If you want information about the mother's obstetric history, you might say, for example, "I'd now like to get some more information about [cite child's name]'s development. I would first like to learn about the time before [cite child's name] was born." If you decide to begin the semistructured interview with another section, use an appropriate introduction. Sections that pertain specifically to infants or toddlers/preschoolers are so identified in the section headings.

Maternal Obstetric History
1. How old were you when [cite child's name] was born?
2. Have you had any other pregnancies?
   (If yes, go to question 3; if no, go to question 9.)
3. Tell me about them. (Pay particular attention to miscarriages, abortions, and premature births and their outcomes.)
4. How many living children do you have?
5. (If more than one child) How old are they now?
6. (If any child died) How did your child die?
7. (If needed) Tell me about what happened.
8. (If needed) How old was your child when he [she] died?
9. I'd like to talk to you about your pregnancy with [cite child's name]. What was your pregnancy like?
   (Ask questions 10 to 13, as needed.)
10. Was it planned?
11. (If yes) How long did it take you to become pregnant?
12. Did you have any illnesses or problems during pregnancy? (Pay particular attention to vaginal bleeding, fevers, rashes, hospitalizations, weight gain, weight loss, vomiting, hypertension, proteinuria [the presence of an excess of protein in the urine; also called albuminuria], preeclampsia [a toxemia of late pregnancy characterized by hypertension, albuminuria, and edema], general infections, and urinary tract infections.)
13. Were any sonograms performed?
    (If yes, go to question 14; if no, go to question 16.)
14. How many were performed?
15. What did it [they] show?
16. Was your blood type incompatible with that of [cite child's name]?
17. (If yes) Tell me about that.
18. Did you take any medications or street drugs during pregnancy?
19. (If yes) What did you take? (Any of the following may affect the development of the fetus: prescription drugs; over-the-counter pills; cocaine/crack; marijuana/pot; hallucinogens, such as LSD, PCP, DMT, mescaline, and mushrooms; stimulants, such as uppers, speed, amphetamines, crystal, crank, and Dexedrine; tranquilizers, such as downers, Valium, Elavil, Quaaludes, Stelazine, barbiturates, and

thorazine; and opiates, such as morphine, Demerol, Percodan, codeine, Darvon, Darvocet, heroin, and methadone. If the mother mentions one of these or any other drug that may affect the fetus, go to question 20; if not, go to question 25.)
20. How often did you take it?
21. When during your pregnancy did you take it?
22. How did it make you feel?
23. Did you tell your health care provider that you were taking [cite drug]?
24. (If yes) Tell me about that.
25. Did you drink alcohol during your pregnancy?
    (If yes, go to question 26; if no, go to question 32.)
26. What did you drink?
27. How often did you drink alcohol?
28. And how much did you drink each time?
29. When during your pregnancy did you start drinking?
30. Did you drink throughout your pregnancy?
31. Did you tell your health care provider that you were drinking alcohol during your pregnancy?
32. Did you smoke cigarettes during your pregnancy?
    (If yes, go to question 33; if no, go to question 39.)
33. Tell me about that.
34. How many cigarettes did you smoke each day?
35. When during your pregnancy did you start smoking?
36. Did you smoke throughout your pregnancy?
37. Did you tell your health care provider that you were smoking during your pregnancy?
38. (If yes) Tell me about that.
39. Did you have x-rays taken during your pregnancy?
40. (If yes) Tell me about them.
41. Were you exposed to chemicals or other potentially harmful substances during your pregnancy?
42. (If yes) Tell me about what you were exposed to.
43. Did you see a health care provider during your pregnancy?
    (If yes, go to question 44; if no, go to question 46.)
44. What kind of health care provider did you see during your pregnancy?
45. How many visits did you make?
    (Go to question 47.)
46. Why didn't you see a health care provider?
47. Did you see anyone else for care during your pregnancy?
48. (If yes) Tell me about whom you saw.
49. Overall, was your pregnancy with [cite child's name] a good experience or a bad experience?
50. Tell me about your answer.
51. In general, how would you rate your health during your pregnancy with [cite child's name]?
52. Tell me about your answer.

Labor, Delivery, Infant's Condition at Birth, and Immediate Postpartum Period for Mother
1. Now I'd like to talk to you about your labor and delivery. Tell me about your labor and delivery.
   (Ask questions 2 to 15, as needed.)
2. What were your thoughts and feelings during labor?
3. Was [cite child's name] born on time?

Table B-10 (*Continued*)

4. (If early) How early was [cite child's name] born?
5. (If late) How late was [cite child's name] born?
6. How long did the labor last?
7. What kind of delivery did you have?
8. (If needed) Was it normal . . . breech . . . cesarean . . . forceps . . . induced?
9. (If delivery was cesarean, forceps, or induced) Why was this type of delivery needed?
10. How did the delivery go?
11. (If needed) Were there any complications at delivery?
12. (If yes) Tell me about them.
13. Were you given anything for pain during labor?
14. (If yes) Tell me about it.
15. Were labor and delivery what you expected?
16. What were your first impressions of your new baby?
17. Was the baby's father present during delivery?
18. (If yes) What were his first impressions of the new baby?
19. How was [cite child's name] right after he [she] was born?
20. What was [cite child's name]'s weight at birth?
21. What was [cite child's name]'s length at birth?
22. What was [cite child's name]'s skin color?
23. Did [cite child's name] cry soon after birth?
24. Do you know [cite child's name]'s Apgar score?
25. (If yes) What was it?
26. Did you want to hold [cite child's name] right away?
27. Were you allowed to hold [cite child's name]?
28. (If father was present) Was the baby's father allowed to hold [cite child's name]?
29. Did you have any physical problems immediately after [cite child's name] was born?
30. (If yes) Tell me about them.
31. Did you have any psychological problems after [cite child's name] was born?
32. (If yes) Tell me about them.
33. Did you have a rooming-in arrangement with the baby?
    (If yes, go to question 34; if no, go to question 35.)
34. What was it like to have the baby in the room with you?
    (Go to question 36.)
35. Why didn't you have a rooming-in arrangement?
36. Did [cite child's name] have any health problems following birth?
37. (If yes) Tell me about them.
38. Was [cite child's name] in a special care nursery in the hospital for observation or treatment?
    (If yes, go to question 39; if no, go to question 47.)
39. Tell me about the reason [cite child's name] was in a special care nursery.
40. Did you visit [cite child's name] when he [she] was in the special care nursery?
41. Did you feed [cite child's name] when he [she] was in the special care nursery?
42. How did you feel about having [cite child's name] stay in the special care nursery?
43. And how many days old was [cite child's name] when he [she] went home from the special care nursery?
    (If the father is in the picture, go to question 44; if not, go to question 47.)
44. Did the baby's father visit [cite child's name] when he [she] was in the special care nursery?

45. Did the baby's father feed [cite child's name] when he [she] was in the special care nursery?
46. How did the baby's father feel about having [cite child's name] stay in the special care nursery?
47. How did you spend your time in the first few days at home with [cite child's name]?
48. After the first few days, how much time did you spend at home with [cite child's name]?
49. Was [cite child's name] breastfed or bottlefed?
50. How did that go?
    (If the father is in the picture, go to question 51; if not, end this section.)
51. Did [cite child's name]'s father also spend time with him [her]?
52. What was their relationship like at this time?
53. (If needed) How did he feel about the baby?
54. Did the baby's father help you during this time?
55. Tell me about that.

Infant's Attachment

1. When [cite child's name] came home from the hospital, what was it like to have him [her] home?
2. Did you feel you knew the baby?
3. Tell me about that.
4. Did you feel the baby knew you?
5. Tell me about that.
6. How were [cite child's name]'s first few weeks of life at home?
7. Did [cite child's name] have any problems?
8. (If needed) Did [cite child's name] have problems with eating . . . drinking . . . sleeping . . . alertness . . . irritability?
9. (If yes) Tell me about [cite child's name]'s problems.
    (Inquire about the types of problems, their severity, what the parent did, treatment, outcomes, and so forth.)
10. Was it easy or difficult to comfort [cite child's name]?
11. How did you go about comforting [cite child's name]?
12. Was [cite child's name] too good—that is, did he [she] demand little or no care?
13. (If yes) What did you think about this?
14. Was [cite child's name] alert as a baby?
15. (If no) Tell me about how [cite child's name] reacted.
16. What was [cite child's name]'s mood generally?
17. How well did he [she] adjust to new things or routines?
18. How did he [she] respond to new people?
19. Was he [she] cuddly or rigid?
20. Was he [she] overactive or underactive?
21. Did he [she] engage in any tantrums . . . rocking behavior . . . head banging?
22. Did [cite child's name] develop a regular pattern of eating and sleeping?
23. (If no) Tell me about that.
24. Were there any surprises during [cite child's name]'s first weeks of life at home?
25. What was most enjoyable about taking care of [cite child's name]?
26. And what was least enjoyable about taking care of [cite child's name]?
27. What was most difficult about taking care of [cite child's name]?

Table B-10 (*Continued*)

28. What was easiest about taking care of [cite child's name]?
29. How did you feel about [cite child's name] during his [her] first few weeks of life at home?
30. (If father is in the picture) How did his [her] father feel about [cite child's name] during his [her] first few weeks of life?
31. (If other children in family) How did the other children in the family react to [cite child's name]?
32. (If needed) Did the other children show any signs of jealousy?
33. (If yes) How did they demonstrate their jealousy, and how did you [you and your husband, you and the baby's father] handle the jealousy?
34. Did you have confidence in yourself as a parent during the first six months of [cite child's name]'s life?
35. Tell me about that.
36. What kind of adjustments did you [you and your family] have to make?
37. How did your extended family react to [cite child's name]?

Infant's Responsiveness (if infant is focus of interview)

1. Does [cite child's name] respond to your voice?
2. When you pick [cite child's name] up, does he [she] become quiet?
3. Does [cite child's name] smile?
4. Does [cite child's name] look at you when you try to talk to or play with him [her]?
5. (If no) What does [cite child's name] do instead?
6. What sounds does [cite child's name] make?
7. Does [cite child's name] reach out and grasp a person's face or finger?
8. Can [cite child's name] tell the difference between strangers and familiar people?
9. Does [cite child's name] play with other people?
10. How does [cite child's name] respond to new people?
11. How does [cite child's name] respond to being in a new place?
12. How often does [cite child's name] want to be held?
13. Does [cite child's name] like physical contact, such as when you gently touch his [her] face, hands, and arms?
14. Is there any physical activity that [cite child's name] seems to enjoy especially?

Infant's Crying, Adjustment to Caregiving Situation, Behavior in Public, and Unusual Behavior (if infant is focus of interview)

1. When does [cite child's name] cry?
2. What do you do when [cite child's name] cries?
3. Why do you think [cite child's name] cries?
4. (If needed) When [cite child's name] cries, does it usually mean that something is really wrong or is it that something is bothering him [her] only a little bit and he [she] wants attention?
5. Can you tell the difference between the types of crying [cite child's name] does?
6. (If yes) How?
7. (If no) What does he [she] do that makes it difficult to know what his [her] crying means?
8. With whom do you leave [cite child's name] when you go out?
9. How do you feel about leaving [cite child's name]?

10. Do you leave [cite child's name] at a day care center, at somebody's house, or at your house with a sitter during any part of the week?
    (If yes, go to question 11; if no, go to question 28.)
11. Where do you leave him [her]?
12. Tell me about the reason you leave [cite child's name] there.
13. (If day care center or someone's house) How did you find out about [cite place where child is cared for]?
14. Are you satisfied with the way [cite child's name] is cared for there?
15. How is [cite child's name] getting along at [cite place where child is cared for]?
16. (If needed) Is [cite child's name] having any problems there?
17. (If yes) Tell me about them.
18. (If needed) How does [cite child's name] get along with the child care provider[s]?
19. (If needed) How does [cite child's name] get along with the other children?
20. Do you have a chance to talk regularly about [cite child's name] with the person[s] taking care of him [her]?
21. How long does it take you to get to [cite place where child is cared for]?
22. How does [cite child's name] act when you leave him [her] at [cite place where child is cared for]?
    (If behavior is not satisfactory, go to question 23; if behavior is satisfactory, go to question 27.)
23. How do you feel when [cite child's name] acts this way?
24. Does [cite child's name] always show that he [she] is upset in the same way?
25. What do you do to quiet [cite child's name] when he [she] is upset?
26. Does it help?
27. How does [cite child's name] react when you pick him [her] up from [cite place where child is cared for]?
28. How do you feel about taking [cite child's name] out in public?
29. How does [cite child's name] behave when he [she] is outside the home?
30. How does [cite child's name] react when you take him [her] to a friend's home?
    (If there are problems or concerns, go to question 31; otherwise, go to question 33.)
31. How do you handle these problems?
32. What seems to work best?
33. Does [cite child's name] have any unusual behaviors?
    (If yes, go to question 34; if no, end this section.)
34. What unusual behaviors does [cite child's name] have?
35. How often does [cite child's name] exhibit [cite unusual behavior]?
36. What is most likely to bring on [cite unusual behavior]?
37. What situations seem to make [cite child's name]'s [cite unusual behavior] worse?
38. What do you do at these times?
39. What works best?
40. Is there any connection between what [cite child's name] eats and [cite unusual behavior]?
41. How do you feel about taking care of [cite child's name] when he [she] behaves in this way?

(*Continued*)

Infant's Play, Language, Communication, and Problem-Solving Skills (if infant is focus of interview)

1. What does [cite child's name] play?
2. What toys does [cite child's name] like to play with?
3. What is [cite child's name]'s favorite toy?
4. Does [cite child's name] like to do the same activity over and over again?
5. What sounds does [cite child's name] make?
6. How long has he [she] been making these sounds?
7. In which situations does [cite child's name] make sounds?
8. (If needed) Does he [she] makes sounds early in the morning in his [her] crib . . . while riding in the car . . . when other children are around . . . when playing by himself [herself] . . . when adults are talking . . . when someone is talking on the phone . . . when in a quiet room?
9. At what times during the day does [cite child's name] make the most sounds?
10. What is happening at these times?
11. Does [cite child's name] seem to be trying to tell you something as he [she] babbles or makes sounds?
12. (If yes) Do you have any idea what [cite child's name] is trying to say when he [she] makes sounds?
13. How does [cite child's name] let you know that he [she] wants something?
14. How does [cite child's name] let you know how he [she] feels?
15. (If relevant) About how many words does [cite child's name] understand?
16. (If relevant) Tell me about [cite child's name]'s ability to gesture or point.
17. Do you ever hear [cite child's name] making sounds a few minutes after an adult speaks to him [her]?
18. Was there a time when [cite child's name] made more sounds or babbled more?
(If yes, go to question 19; if no, go to question 21.)
19. When did he [she] babble more?
20. How long has it been since he [she] stopped babbling as much?
21. Has [cite child's name] had any recent illness with fever and earache?
22. Is [cite child's name] exhibiting any other behavior that concerns you?
23. (If yes) What is this behavior?
24. Have there been any changes or stressful events in your home recently?
25. (If yes) Tell me about them.
26. Does [cite child's name] say any words?
27. (If yes) How old was [cite child's name] when he [she] spoke his [her] first words?
28. How does [cite child's name] use his [her] hands, eyes, and body to solve problems?
29. Tell me about [cite child's name]'s attention span.

Infant's Motor Skills (if infant is focus of interview)
(Note that these questions are arranged in developmental sequence. If the child has not mastered a motor skill, it is unlikely that he or she will be able to perform the next motor skill. Therefore, you can stop your inquiry after you find that the child has not mastered a skill.)

1. Can [cite child's name] roll over?
(If yes, go to question 2; if no, go to question 3.)
2. How old was he [she] when he [she] first rolled over?
(Go to question 4.)
3. What progress is [cite child's name] making toward rolling over?
4. Can [cite child's name] crawl?
(If yes, go to question 5; if no, go to question 6.)
5. How old was he [she] when he [she] began to crawl?
(Go to question 7.)
6. What progress is [cite child's name] making toward crawling?
7. Can [cite child's name] sit up?
(If yes, go to question 8; if no, go to question 9.)
8. How old was he [she] when he [she] first sat up?
(Go to question 10.)
9. What progress is [cite child's name] making toward sitting up?
10. Can [cite child's name] pull himself [herself] up to a standing position?
(If yes, go to question 11; if no, go to question 13.)
11. How old was he [she] when he [she] first pulled himself [herself] up to a standing position?
12. Does [cite child's name] sometimes remain standing for a short time after he [she] has pulled himself [herself] up?
(Go to question 14.)
13. What progress is he [she] making toward pulling himself [herself] up to a standing position?
14. Can [cite child's name] walk?
(If yes, go to question 15; if no, go to question 16.)
15. How old was he [she] when he [she] first walked?
(Go to question 18.)
16. What progress is he [she] making toward walking?
17. (If needed) Does [cite child's name] seem to want to move and explore on his [her] own?
18. In what situations is [cite child's name] most active physically?
19. (If needed) Is he [she] most active when someone plays with him [her] . . . when other children are around . . . when he [she] is outdoors?
20. Tell me about [cite child's name]'s ability to do things that require small-motor movements, such as his [her] ability to grasp things, pick things up, hold onto things, and release things.
21. Is [cite child's name] able to transfer small objects from hand to hand?
22. Does [cite child's name] help you hold his [her] bottle?
23. Is [cite child's name] able to follow an object or face with his [her] eyes?
24. Does [cite child's name] use his [her] eyes to examine his [her] hands?
25. Does [cite child's name] reach for objects?

Infant's Temperament and Activity Level (if infant is focus of interview)

1. How would you describe [cite child's name] to someone who did not know him [her] well?
2. What moods does [cite child's name] have?
3. How would you describe [cite child's name]'s activity level?

Table B-10 (*Continued*)

4. Are there times when [cite child's name] engages in quiet activities?
5. (If yes) Tell me about these times.
6. When does [cite child's name] get overexcited?
7. When [cite child's name] gets overexcited, what do you do to calm him [her] down?
8. What kinds of comforting make [cite child's name] feel better?
9. How does [cite child's name] respond to new situations?
10. How does [cite child's name] respond to being separated from you?
11. (If relevant) And how does [cite child's name] respond to being separated from his [her] father?
12. (If child has trouble separating) How long does [cite response] last?
13. What do you do to help [cite child's name] with difficult changes?
14. (If responses to questions in this section do not give you the information you want about the child's temperament, ask more direct questions, such as the following.) Would any of the following terms be helpful in describing [cite child's name]—even-tempered . . . moody . . . independent . . . clinging . . . stubborn . . . flexible . . . active . . . calm . . . happy . . . sad . . . serious . . . carefree?
15. (If yes to any of the above) Please give me an example of why you would say [cite child's name] is [cite term].

Infant's Eating (if infant is focus of interview)
1. I'd like to learn about [cite child's name]'s eating. How is [cite child's name] eating?
2. What does [cite child's name] like to eat?
3. Is [cite child's name] a messy eater?
4. (If yes) Tell me about that.
5. How does [cite child's name] let you know that he [she] is hungry?
6. How does [cite child's name] show that he [she] likes certain foods?
7. How does [cite child's name] show his [her] dislike for certain foods?
8. Is [cite child's name] able to tolerate most foods?
9. Does [cite child's name] like warm foods or cold foods?
10. Does [cite child's name] like foods with any special flavors . . . special smells . . . special colors?
11. What does [cite child's name] seem to enjoy about being fed?
12. (If needed) Does [cite child's name] enjoy having you pay attention to him [her] . . . being at eye level with you while he [she] is in the high chair . . . having you talk to him [her] while he [she] eats . . . playing with the spoon?
13. What meals does [cite child's name] eat during the day?
14. What snacks does [cite child's name] eat during the day?
15. Are there certain times during the day when [cite child's name] makes excessive demands for food?
    (If yes, go to question 16; if no, go to question 18.)
16. At what times does this happen?
17. Do you think [cite child's name] is truly hungry, or is he [she] just asking for attention?
18. Does [cite child's name] skip meals and not ask to eat?
19. (If yes) Tell me about that.

20. Does [cite child's name] eat when you do or at different times?
21. (If at different times) Tell me about the reason [cite child's name] eats at different times.
22. How often does [cite child's name] see adults in the family eat?
23. Does [cite child's name] eat what he [she] is given at mealtimes?
24. Does [cite child's name] have any problems with eating?
25. (If yes) What are the problems?
26. Does [cite child's name] drink from a cup or bottle?
27. (If yes) Does [cite child's name] have any problems with drinking from a cup [bottle]?
28. (If yes) What are the problems?
    (If child has problems with eating, drinking, or both, go to question 29; otherwise, end this section.)
29. How do you handle the problems?
30. Do those methods work?
31. (If father is in the picture) What does [cite child's name]'s father think about how you handle the problems?

Infant's Sleeping (if infant is the focus of the interview)
1. How is [cite child's name] sleeping at night?
2. About how many hours of sleep does he [she] get at night?
3. Tell me what happens at night before bedtime.
4. (If needed) Does [cite child's name] go to sleep on his [her] own, or does he [she] need to be rocked, patted, or given some other kind of help from you?
5. Does [cite child's name] take a daytime nap or naps?
   (If yes, go to question 6; if no, go to question 9.)
6. Around what time[s] does he [she] nap?
7. And for how long?
8. Is there any connection between the amount of time he [she] sleeps during the day and his [her] sleeping at night?
9. Do you think that [cite child's name] is tired enough at bedtime to go to sleep easily?
10. What kind of routine do you have at night for putting [cite child's name] to bed?
11. What parts of the nighttime routine do you think [cite child's name] likes?
12. What parts of the nighttime routine do you think [cite child's name] dislikes?
13. What parts of the routine do you like?
14. And what parts of the routine do you dislike?
15. Does [cite child's name] wake up during the night?
    (If yes, go to question 16; if no, go to question 23.)
16. How often does [cite child's name] wake up during the night?
17. About what time does [cite child's name] wake up?
18. How does [cite child's name] act when he [she] wakes up?
19. (If needed) Does he [she] moan . . . scream . . . whimper occasionally . . . call you?
20. What do you do when [cite child's name] wakes up during the night?
21. What seems to work the best?
22. Have you noticed any changes in [cite child's name]'s behavior during the daytime since he [she] began to wake up at night?
23. Have you noticed any signs of physical discomfort, such as teething, earache, congestion from a cold, or general fussiness, during the day?

(Continued)

Table B-10 (*Continued*)

24. (If yes) What have you noticed?
25. Have there been any changes recently in your home or in the child's routine related to bedtime?
26. (If yes) Tell me about these changes.
27. Does anyone share [cite child's name]'s bedroom?
28. (If yes) Who shares his [her] bedroom?
29. Does [cite child's name] have any difficulties falling asleep?
30. (If yes) Tell me about them.
31. Does [cite child's name] have his [her] own bed?
32. (If no) With whom does [cite child's name] sleep?
33. When does [cite child's name] usually go to bed?
34. How do you know when [cite child's name] is tired?

Toddler's/Preschooler's Personal-Social-Affective Behavior
(if toddler/preschooler is focus of interview)
1. Does [cite child's name] take turns?
2. Can [cite child's name] point to body parts on a doll?
3. Can [cite child's name] name his [her] own body parts?
4. Can [cite child's name] identify himself [herself] in a mirror?
5. Does [cite child's name] use words like *I, me,* and *them* correctly?
6. Does [cite child's name] feed himself [herself]?
7. Does [cite child's name] use a spoon or a fork?
8. Does [cite child's name] imitate things you do, like sweeping the floor and making the bed?
9. Does [cite child's name] play with a doll and do such things as feed, hug, and scold the doll?
10. How does [cite child's name] handle common dangers, such as hot stoves, electrical outlets, sharp knives, crossing the street, and the like?
11. How does [cite child's name] behave when he [she] plays with another child?
12. Does [cite child's name] share his [her] toys?
    (If yes, go to question 13; if no, go to question 15.)
13. What toys does he [she] share?
14. And with whom does he [she] share them?
    (Go to question 16.)
15. What have you done to help him [her] learn how to share?
16. Does [cite child's name] have temper tantrums?
    (If yes, go to question 17; if no, go to question 26.)
17. Tell me about the temper tantrums.
18. What sets off the temper tantrums?
19. Are the temper tantrums more frequent at certain times of the day than at other times?
20. (If yes) Tell me about these times.
21. Where do the temper tantrums occur?
22. What happens when [cite child's name] has a temper tantrum?
23. How do you feel about the temper tantrums?
24. How do you deal with [cite child's name]'s temper tantrums?
25. Which methods seem to be most effective?
26. How does [cite child's name] get along with other children?
27. Is [cite child's name] stubborn at times?
    (If yes, go to question 28; if no, go to question 31.)
28. In what way is [cite child's name] stubborn?
29. How do you handle his [her] stubbornness?
30. Has it worked?
31. Does [cite child's name] hit, bite, or try to hurt other children?
    (If yes, go to question 32; if no, go to question 36.)

32. How does he [she] hurt other children?
33. Why do you think he [she] acts this way?
34. How do you handle these situations?
35. What seems to work best?
36. Does [cite child's name] have any fears?
    (If yes, go to question 37; if no, go to question 46.)
37. What fears does he [she] have?
38. What kinds of situations tend to make [cite child's name] fearful?
39. Are these unfamiliar situations or familiar ones?
40. What does [cite child's name] do when he [she] is fearful?
41. How long has [cite child's name] been fearful?
42. What do you do when [cite child's name] shows fear?
43. How does it work?
44. Have you found that some methods are more effective than others?
45. (If yes) Tell me about them.
46. How do you handle [cite child's name] demands for your attention?
47. What situations seem to cause [cite child's name] to demand your attention?
48. What kinds of things does [cite child's name] seem to want when he [she] asks for attention?
49. Does he [she] demand your attention for a long time, or will a short time do?
50. Have you noticed any changes during the past few months in how much attention [cite child's name] has demanded?
51. (If yes) Tell me about the changes you've noticed.
52. How does [cite child's name] react when he [she] meets new people?
53. How do you feel about [cite child's name]'s behavior when he [she] meets new people?
54. (If needed) Is there anything you can do to make [cite child's name] more comfortable when he [she] meets new people?
55. When does [cite child's name] cry?
56. What do you do when [cite child's name] cries?
57. Why do you think [cite child's name] cries?
58. (If needed) When [cite child's name] cries, does it usually mean that something is really wrong or is it that something is bothering him [her] only a little bit and he [she] wants attention?
59. How can you tell the difference between the types of crying [cite child's name] does?
60. Does [cite child's name] play with his [her] genitals?
    (If yes, go to question 61; if no, go to question 66.)
61. When does [cite child's name] play with his [her] genitals?
62. (If needed) Does this occur during any particular situations?
63. (If yes) In what situation[s] does he [she] play with his [her] genitals?
64. How do you feel about his [her] doing this?
65. And what do you do when you find [cite child's name] playing with his [her] genitals?
66. What kinds of activities does [cite child's name] seem to be interested in?
67. What does [cite child's name] like to do on his [her] own?
68. Are you having any difficulties getting [cite child's name] to perform daily routines, such as washing hands . . . dressing . . . picking up clothes . . . putting away toys?

Table B-10 (*Continued*)

69. Does [cite child's name] let you do things *with* him [her]?
70. Tell me about that.
71. Does [cite child's name] let you do things *for* him [her]?
72. Tell me about that.
73. How does [cite child's name] get along with adults?
74. Is [cite child's name] interested in people?
75. Tell me more about that.
76. How does [cite child's name] spend his [her] time during a typical weekday?
77. And on weekends, how does [cite child's name] spend his [her] time?
78. How does [cite child's name] feel about himself [herself]?
79. (If there are other siblings in family) How does [cite child's name] compare with his [her] sisters and brothers?
80. Is [cite child's name] interested in animals?
81. Tell me more about that.
82. Is [cite child's name] generally interested in things?
83. (If no) Tell me more about that.
84. At what time of the day is [cite child's name] most active?
85. When [cite child's name] needs to do things, like get dressed or put things away, does he [she] do them too fast, too slowly, or at just about the right pace?
    (If too fast, go to question 86; if too slowly, go to question 90; otherwise, go to question 94.)
86. What happens when you try to make [cite child's name] move more slowly?
87. What other things does [cite child's name] do too fast?
88. (If needed) Does [cite child's name] eat too fast . . . get ready for bed too fast?
89. Are you concerned that [cite child's name] may be hyperactive?
    (Go to question 94.)
90. What happens when you try to make [cite child's name] move faster?
91. What other things does [cite child's name] do slowly?
92. (If needed) Does he [she] eat slowly . . . get ready for bed slowly?
93. Are you concerned that [cite child's name] may be generally slow?
94. How does [cite child's name] react when his [her] play is interrupted?
95. How does [cite child's name] let you know when he [she] wants to keep doing an activity longer than you had planned?
96. Does [cite child's name] have any unusual behaviors?
    (If yes, go to question 97; if no, end this section.)
97. What unusual behaviors does [cite child's name] have?
98. How often does [cite child's name] exhibit [cite unusual behavior]?
99. What is most likely to bring on [cite unusual behavior]?
100. What situations seem to make [cite child's name]'s [cite unusual behavior] worse?
101. What do you do at these times?
102. What works best?
103. Is there any connection between what [cite child's name] eats and [cite unusual behavior]?
104. How do you feel about taking care of [cite child's name] when he [she] behaves in this way?

Toddler's/Preschooler's Play and Cognitive Ability (if toddler/preschooler is focus of interview)

1. How does [cite child's name] occupy himself [herself] during the day?
2. What does [cite child's name] like to play?
3. How would you describe [cite child's name]'s play?
4. (If needed) Is it quiet play . . . active play? . . . Does he [she] build things . . . color?
5. What toys or other objects does [cite child's name] play with?
6. What kinds of things does [cite child's name] do with the toys or other objects that he [she] plays with?
7. What toys seem to be particularly interesting to [cite child's name]?
8. And how does [cite child's name] play with the toys he [she] especially likes?
9. Is [cite child's name] interested in exploring objects?
10. (If yes) Tell me more about what [cite child's name] does.
11. What happens when [cite child's name] is left on his [her] own to play?
12. How long does [cite child's name] usually stay with an activity?
13. Does [cite child's name] seem to play better at certain times of the day than at others?
14. What is particularly distracting to [cite child's name]?
15. In what situations does [cite child's name] get the most out of his [her] play?
16. How does [cite child's name] let you know what he [she] is interested in?
17. Tell me more about that.
18. (If relevant) Can [cite child's name] find his [her] toys when they are mixed up with those of his [her] brothers and sisters?
19. Is [cite child's name] more interested in watching others play than in playing himself [herself]?
20. Do you think that [cite child's name]'s play is about the same as that of other children of his [her] age?
21. (If no) In what way is it different?
22. What changes have you noticed over the last few months in the way [cite child's name] plays?
23. Where does [cite child's name] play at home?
24. (If needed) Does he [she] play in different rooms?
25. Does he [she] have enough space to play?
26. (If no) What have you done to get more space for [cite child's name] to play in?
27. How long does [cite child's name] stay in his [her] own room to play?
28. Is this amount of time OK with you?
29. Does [cite child's name] prefer playing alone or with someone?
30. With whom does he [she] like to play?
31. Does [cite child's name] engage in any pretend play?
32. (If needed) Does he [she] play house . . . play school . . . play doctor?
33. Does [cite child's name] have any imaginary friends?
34. (If yes) Who are they?
35. How does [cite child's name]'s play change when an adult plays with him [her]?
36. What kinds of things does [cite child's name] like to do with you?

(*Continued*)

37. How does [cite child's name] react when you try to show him [her] how to use a toy?
38. How much fun is [cite child's name] to play with?
39. Have you ever wondered whether [cite child's name] enjoys playing with you?
40. Tell me about that.
41. How much time do you spend playing with [cite child's name]?
42. Does having [cite child's name]'s toys underfoot in the house bother you?
43. (If yes) Tell me about that.
44. Does [cite child's name] look at you when you try to talk to or play with him [her]?
45. (If no) What does he [she] do instead?
46. Is [cite child's name] responsive to you?
47. Is [cite child's name] responsive to other adults?
48. Does [cite child's name] like physical contact, such as when you gently touch his [her] face, hands, and arms?
49. (If no) Tell me about that.
50. Is there any physical activity that [cite child's name] seems to enjoy especially?
51. Does [cite child's name] like doing the same activity over and over again?
52. Does [cite child's name] like to spin objects?
53. (If yes) Tell me about that.
54. Does [cite child's name] play outdoors?
    (If yes, go to question 55; if no, go to question 60.)
55. Where does he [she] play outdoors?
56. (If needed) Do you take [cite child's name] to any parks or playgrounds?
57. How does [cite child's name] react when you take him [her] outdoors to play?
58. Does [cite child's name] behave differently outdoors than indoors?
59. (If yes) In what way?
60. Does [cite child's name] seem to be in constant motion?
61. (If yes) How do you handle that?
62. Tell me about [cite child's name]'s ability to pay attention.
63. Does [cite child's name] like to put puzzles together?
64. Tell me about that.
65. Can [cite child's name] construct things out of blocks?
66. Tell me about that.

Toddler's/Preschooler's Adjustment to Caregiving Situation
(if toddler/preschooler is focus of interview)

1. Do you leave [cite child's name] at a day care center, at preschool, at somebody's house, or at your house with a sitter during any part of the week?
   (If yes, go to question 2; if no, go to question 20.)
2. Where do you leave him [her]?
3. Tell me about the reason you leave [cite child's name] there.
4. How do you feel about leaving [cite child's name]?
5. (If day care center, preschool, or someone's house) How did you find out about [cite place where child is cared for]?
6. Are you satisfied with the way [cite child's name] is cared for there?
7. How is [cite child's name] getting along at [cite place where child is cared for]?

8. (If needed) Is [cite child's name] having any problems there?
9. (If yes) Tell me about them.
10. (If needed) How does [cite child's name] get along with the caregiver[s]?
11. (If needed) How does he [she] get along with the other children?
12. Do you have a chance to talk regularly about [cite child's name] with the person[s] taking care of him [her]?
13. How long does it take you to get to [cite place where child is cared for]?
14. How does [cite child's name] act when you leave him [her] at [cite place where child is cared for]?
    (If behavior is not satisfactory, go to question 15; if behavior is satisfactory, go to question 19.)
15. How do you feel when [cite child's name] acts this way?
16. Does [cite child's name] always show that he [she] is upset in the same way?
17. What have you done to try to help him [her]?
18. Does it help?
19. How does [cite child's name] react when you pick him [her] up from [cite place where child is cared for]?
20. How do you feel about taking [cite child's name] out in public?
21. How does [cite child's name] behave when he [she] is outside the home?
22. How does [cite child's name] react when you take him [her] to a friend's home?
    (If there are problems or concerns, go to question 23; otherwise, end section.)
23. How do you handle these problems?
24. What seems to work best?

Toddler's/Preschooler's Self-Help Skills
(if toddler/preschooler is focus of interview)

1. Is [cite child's name] toilet trained?
   (If yes, go to question 2; if no, go to question 5.)
2. How old was [cite child's name] when he [she] was toilet trained?
3. Does [cite child's name] have toilet accidents once in a while?
   (If yes, go to question 4; if no, go to question 13.)
4. Tell me about the toilet accidents [cite child's name] has.
   (Go to question 13.)
5. Have you begun to toilet train [cite child's name]?
   (If no, go to question 6; if yes, go to question 7.)
6. At what age do you think [cite child's name] should be toilet trained?
   (Go to question 13.)
7. Tell me how it's going.
   (Ask questions 8 to 12, as needed.)
8. Are you having any problems with the toilet training?
9. (If yes) Tell me about the problems you're having.
10. What training methods are you using?
11. What did [cite child's name] do to make you think that he [she] was ready to be toilet trained?
12. (If needed) Did he [she] come to you to be changed? . . . Was he [she] interested in watching others in the bathroom . . . imitating others . . . staying dry?

Table B-10 (*Continued*)

13. Tell me about how [cite child's name] dresses and undresses himself [herself].
    (Ask questions 14 to 17, as needed.)
14. What clothing can [cite child's name] put on?
15. What clothing can [cite child's name] take off?
16. (If child is older than 4 years) Can [cite child's name] tie his [her] shoes?
17. How much supervision does [cite child's name] need in dressing and undressing?
18. Tell me about [cite child's name] bath time.
19. (If needed) Does [cite child's name] wash himself [herself]?
20. Does [cite child's name] wash his [her] hands when necessary, such as when he [she] is dirty or after he [she] goes to the toilet?
21. (If no) Tell me about [cite child's name]'s not washing his [her] hands when necessary.
22. Does [cite child's name] brush his [her] teeth?
23. (If no) Tell me about [cite child's name]'s not brushing his [her] teeth.
24. Does [cite child's name] brush or comb his [her] hair?
25. (If no) Tell me about [cite child's name]'s not brushing or combing his [her] hair.

Toddler's/Preschooler's Language, Communication, Speech, Comprehension, and Problem-Solving Skills
(if toddler/preschooler is focus of interview)

1. Does [cite child's name] talk?
   (If yes, go to question 2; if no, go to question 20.)
2. When did [cite child's name] begin to talk?
3. Does [cite child's name] have any problems with his [her] speech?
4. (If yes) Tell me about [cite child's name]'s problems with speech.
5. (If needed) Is [cite child's name] having problems speaking clearly . . . forming grammatically correct sentences . . . saying the right words in order . . . stuttering?
6. About how many words can [cite child's name] say?
7. What kinds of words does [cite child's name] usually say?
8. Does [cite child's name] have any pet phrases?
9. (If yes) What are they?
10. Does [cite child's name] use action words?
11. Can [cite child's name] speak in sentences?
12. (If yes) How old was [cite child's name] when he [she] first combined words to make sentences?
13. Did [cite child's name] have any problems with speech in the past?
14. (If yes) Tell me about that.
15. Do you understand what [cite child's name] says?
16. (If no) Tell me more about that.
17. Do other people understand [cite child's name]'s speech?
18. (If no) Tell me more about that.
19. What kinds of things does [cite child's name] talk about?
    (Go to question 25.)
20. How is [cite child's name] able to tell you about what he [she] needs?
21. (If needed) Does [cite child's name] make any sounds?
22. (If yes) Tell me about the sounds that [cite child's name] makes.
23. Did [cite child's name] ever talk?

24. (If yes) Tell me about when he [she] talked.
25. Does [cite child's name] understand most things that are said to him [her]?
26. (If no) What problems does [cite child's name] have in understanding things that are said to him [her]?
27. Can [cite child's name] follow directions?
28. (If no) What problems does [cite child's name] have in following directions?

Toddler's/Preschooler's Motor Skills
(if toddler/preschooler is focus of interview)

1. Tell me about [cite child's name]'s ability to do things that require small motor movements, such as his [her] ability to grasp things, pick up things, hold onto things, and release things.
2. (If needed) Tell me about [cite child's name]'s ability to open doors . . . turn pages in a book . . . use scissors to cut paper . . . fold paper . . . build objects with blocks . . . use pencils . . . use crayons . . . draw . . . copy circles or squares . . . screw things . . . unscrew things . . . button . . . tie shoes . . . use a zipper . . . play with Lego-type toys . . . print letters.
3. What types of toys are most frustrating to [cite child's name]?
4. Tell me about [cite child's name]'s other motor skills, such as his [her] ability to walk, run, jump, skip, and play ball.
5. (If needed) Tell me about [cite child's name]'s ability to walk up steps . . . walk down steps . . . hop . . . roll a ball . . . throw a ball . . . climb . . . ride a tricycle . . . use a slide . . . use a jungle gym.

Questions for Pregnant Mother About Toddler's/Preschooler's Acceptance of the Arrival of a New Baby
(if toddler/preschooler is focus of interview)

1. How do you think [cite child's name] will handle the coming of the new baby?
2. What do you think will be most difficult for [cite child's name] to handle?
3. What might you do to help [cite child's name] adjust to the new baby?
4. Have you told [cite child's name] about the new baby?
   (If yes, ask questions 5 and 6; if no, end this section.)
5. What did you say to him [her]?
6. And how did he [she] react?

Questions About the Family Environment and Family Relationships

1. I'd now like to ask you about life at home. OK?
2. How does [cite child's name] get along with you?
3. (For older child) How did [cite child's name] get along with you when he [she] was younger?
4. Who else lives at home?
   (If father or other adult male is in the picture, go to question 5; otherwise, go to directions before question 7.)
5. How does [cite child's name] get along with [cite name of father or other adult male]?
6. With whom does [cite child's name] get along better, you or [cite name of father or other adult male]?
   (If child has siblings, go to question 7; otherwise, go to directions before question 12.)

Table B-10 (*Continued*)

7. How does [cite child's name] get along with his [her] sisters and brothers?
   (Ask questions 8 to 11, as needed.)
8. What situations tend to cause conflict between [cite child's name] and the other children?
9. What do you do when the children argue?
10. What have you found that works?
11. What do you think would happen if you let the children settle their arguments themselves—except when you thought that one child might hurt another?
    (If mother has a husband or partner, go to question 12; otherwise, go to question 14.)
12. How are you getting along with your husband [partner]?
13. (If needed) Is there anything bothering you about your relationship with your husband [partner]?
14. Do any relatives live in your home?
    (If yes, go to question 15; if no, go to question 18.)
15. How are things working out with your mother-in-law [father-in-law, mother, father, etc.] staying at your home?
16. Are there any problems with having her [him, them] there?
17. How does [cite child's name] get along with her [him, them]?
18. Do any relatives live nearby?
    (If yes, go to question 19; if no, end section.)
19. Where do they live?
20. How does [cite child's name] get along with them?

Questions to Evaluate Parent's Ability to Set Limits and Discipline Child

1. How do you make [cite child's name] mind you?
2. Do you feel that you are spoiling [cite child's name]?
3. Tell me about your answer.
4. Does anyone tell you that you are spoiling [cite child's name]?
5. (If yes) Tell me about that.
6. Do you believe that [cite child's name] acts spoiled?
7. (If yes) In what ways does he [she] act spoiled?
8. Do you ever give in to [cite child's name]?
   (If yes, go to question 9; if no, go to question 14.)
9. Give me some examples of how you give in to [cite child's name].
10. How often do you give in to [cite child's name]?
11. How do you feel about giving in?
12. Which things are you sorry you gave in to?
13. Which of the things you gave in to do you feel are disruptive to the family?
14. Do you believe that you are too easy with [cite child's name], too strict, or just about right?
15. Tell me about that.
16. Which of [cite child's name]'s behaviors are particularly irritating to you?
17. In which areas would you most like to set limits?
18. What things won't you let [cite child's name] do?
19. Overall, how satisfied are you with [cite child's name]'s behavior?
20. Are there times when [cite child's name] doesn't mind you or gets into trouble?
    (If yes, go to question 21; if no, go to question 32.)

21. Tell me about these times.
22. (If needed) What kind of trouble does [cite child's name] get into?
23. What do you do when [cite child's name] doesn't mind [gets into trouble]?
24. (If relevant) How does [cite child's name] react when he [she] is punished?
25. Which methods of discipline work best?
26. Which methods don't work?
27. How do you feel when you have to discipline [cite child's name]?
28. What problems are you most concerned about?
29. What does [cite child's name] do that makes you most angry?
30. Does [cite child's name] usually understand what is expected of him [her]?
31. How do you expect [cite child's name] to behave?
32. What does [cite child's name] do that leads you to think that he [she] can live up to your expectations?
    (If the child's father or stepfather or any other adult male lives at home or has visitation rights, go to question 33, substituting the appropriate name for "father" as necessary; otherwise, end this section.)
33. What about [cite child's name] makes his [her] father most angry?
34. What does his [her] father discipline him [her] for?
35. How does his [her] father discipline him [her]?
36. Does his method work?
37. How does [cite child's name]'s father feel when he has to discipline him [her]?
38. How does [cite child's name] respond to his [her] father's discipline?
39. Do you and [cite child's name]'s father agree about how to discipline him [her]?
40. (If no) How do you handle the disagreements?
41. How do you feel about what [cite child's name]'s father does when he is angry with him [her]?
42. Do you do anything about your feelings?

Environmental Safeguards and Neighborhood

1. What have you done to make the house safe for [cite child's name] and to keep him [her] from getting into things?
2. (If needed) Have you put covers on electric outlets? . . . Have you put safety latches on any drawers or cupboards that contain cleaning products or other poisons, knives, guns, or other dangerous things?
3. Does [cite child's name] get into things at home that he [she] is not supposed to?
   (If yes, go to question 4; if no, go to question 8.)
4. What does he [she] get into?
5. Have you been teaching [cite child's name] not to get into these things?
6. (If yes) How has it been going?
7. How do you feel when [cite child's name] wants to get into everything he [she] sees?
8. Does [cite child's name] ever break things?
   (If yes, go to question 9; if no, go to question 11)
9. How do you feel when this happens?

Table B-10 (*Continued*)

10. And what do you do when he [she] breaks things?
11. Does [cite child's name] seem to understand when you tell him [her] not to touch objects?
12. (If yes) Do you think that he [she] can remember not to get into things?
13. Which objects seem to be particularly attractive to [cite child's name]?
14. Why do you think [cite child's name] likes them so much?
15. How do you stop [cite child's name] when he [she] is about to do something dangerous?
16. How long have you lived in your present house [apartment]?
17. How do you like living there?
18. (If needed) Tell me about that.
19. How do you get along with your neighbors?
20. (If needed) Tell me about that.
21. Are there any problems in the neighborhood?
22. (If yes) Tell me about them.

Mother's Resources and Occupation
1. Do you have any living relatives?
   (If yes, go to question 2; if no, go to question 8.)
2. Tell me who your living relatives are.
3. How often do you see your relatives?
4. And how do you get along?
5. Do they give you help when you need it?
   (If yes, go to question 6; if no, go to question 8.)
6. Which relatives give you help when you need it?
7. How do they help you?
8. Do you have any close friends?
   (If yes, go to question 9; if no, go to question 12.)
9. Tell me about them.
10. Have you ever turned to them for help?
11. (If yes) And how did they respond?
12. To whom would you turn for help if your family needed it?
13. Do you have someone to talk to when you have a problem or are feeling frustrated and upset?
14. Tell me about it.
15. Do you have medical insurance?
16. (If no) How do you plan to take care of any hospitalizations?
17. Have you been in contact with any social agencies?
18. (If yes) Tell me about your contacts.
19. Are you a member of a religious group?
20. (If yes) Tell me about the group.
21. Do you have a job outside of the home?
   (If yes, go to question 22; if no, go to instructions following question 24.)
22. What is your occupation?
23. How do you like your job?
24. (If needed) Tell me more about that.
   (If father is in the picture, go to question 25; otherwise, end this section.)
25. What is [cite child's name]'s father's occupation?
26. And how does [cite child's name]'s father like his job?
27. (If needed) Tell me more about that.

Mother Who Stays at Home
1. What do you enjoy about being a full-time parent?
2. What do you find most difficult about being a full-time parent?

3. What made you decide to be a full-time parent?
4. (If needed) What were you doing before your child was [children were] born?
5. Are you occasionally able to get out of the house with [cite child's name]?
6. Are you able to get some time for yourself on a regular basis?
7. Tell me about your answer.
8. (If needed) Do you get a babysitter occasionally and go out by yourself or with a friend [with your husband]?
9. Do you know other parents with young children in the neighborhood?
10. (If yes) Have you worked out any cooperative babysitting arrangements with them?

Spending Time with Child (for mother who works)
1. How much time do you spend with [cite child's name]?
2. How do you feel about the amount of time you spend with [cite child's name]?
3. How do you spend time with [cite child's name] before you go to work?
4. And when you come home, how do you spend time together?
5. And on weekends, how do you spend time together?
6. Which times seem to be the most enjoyable for you and [cite child's name]?
7. Which times seem to be the most rushed and tense for you and [cite child's name]?
8. How do you feel about taking care of [cite child's name] when you return home from work?
9. What do you usually do when you pick [cite child's name] up after work?
10. Do you have any time alone when you come home after work?
11. How do you deal with [cite child's name] if he [she] cries and fusses in the evening?
12. How do you get [cite child's name] to relax when you get home after work?
13. How do you get to relax when you get home after work?

Family Medical History
1. I'd like to know about your health history. Have you had any serious illnesses, accidents, or diseases?
2. (If yes) Tell me about them.
3. (As needed) How was the diagnosis established? . . . Tell me about the course of your illness, its treatment, and the prognosis.
   (If father is in the picture, go to question 4; otherwise, go to question 7 if child has siblings or end section if child does not have siblings.)
4. And how about [cite child's name]'s father—has he had any serious illnesses, accidents, or diseases?
5. (If yes) Tell me about them.
6. (As needed) How was the diagnosis established? . . . Tell me about the course of his illness, its treatment, and the prognosis.
   (If child has siblings, go to question 7; otherwise, end section.)

Table B-10 (*Continued*)

7. And [cite child's name]'s sisters and brothers—have they had any serious illnesses, accidents, or diseases?
8. (If yes) Tell me about them.
9. (As needed) How was the diagnosis established? . . . Tell me about the course of the illness, its treatment, and the prognosis.

General Questions About Infant or Toddler/Preschooler and Mother

1. We've covered a lot of areas. Before we finish, I have just a few more questions I'd like to ask you. OK?
2. What experiences did you have with young children before you had a child?
3. What do you like about being a parent?
4. What do you dislike about being a parent?
5. Is being a parent what you expected?
6. Tell me about that.
7. (If needed) What about being a parent is as you expected? What is different from what you expected?
8. What would make it easier for you to be a parent?
9. What about [cite child's name] gives you the most pleasure?
10. What kinds of things do you do together that are fun?
11. Do you have quiet times when you relax together?
12. (If yes) Tell me about them.
    (If mother has other children, go to question 13; otherwise, go to the instructions before question 15.)
13. Do you spend about the same amount of time with [cite child's name] as you do with the other children?
14. (If no) Tell me about that.
    (If child's father or stepfather or any other adult male lives at home or has visitation rights, go to question 15, substituting the appropriate name for "father" as necessary; otherwise, go to question 19.)
15. What kinds of things does [cite child's name] do with his [her] father?

16. How much time do they spend together? (If father has other children, go to question 17; otherwise, go to question 19.)
17. Is this about the same amount of time as he spends with the other children in the family?
18. (If no) Tell me about that.
19. In general, does [cite child's name] act like other children of his [her] age?
20. (If no) In what way doesn't he [she] act like other children of his [her] age?
21. Is there anything else about [cite child's name] that you would like to tell me?
22. (If yes) Go ahead.
23. Is [cite child's name] having any problems that we didn't discuss?
24. (If yes) What are they?
25. (If not asked previously) Do you have any reason to think that [cite child's name] is under any particular stress at this time?
26. (If yes) Tell me about that.
27. (If not asked previously) Have there been any changes in the home or in the child's routine recently?
28. (If yes) Tell me about that.
29. Have you discussed your concerns about [cite child's name]'s problems with a health care provider?
30. (If yes) What did the health care provider say?
31. Is there anything else about your role as a parent that you would like to tell me?
32. (If yes) Go ahead.
33. Do you have any questions that you would like to ask me?
34. (If yes) Go ahead.
35. Thank you for talking with me. If you have any questions or if you want to talk to me, please call me. Here is my card.

Note. This table is designed for interviewing mothers about their young children. With some alterations, it also could be used to interview fathers or other caregivers. Use Table B-13 in this Appendix to interview a parent who has a child with a pervasive developmental disorder.
Source: Adapted from Bromwich (1981) and Ferholt (1980).

Table B-11
Semistructured Interview Questions for a Parent Regarding a Brief Screening of Her or His Preschool-Age Child

1. Hi! I'm Dr. [Ms., Mr.] _____. I'd like to talk to you about [cite child's name]. Tell me a little bit about him [her].
2. Please tell me what [cite child's name] has been doing and learning lately.
3. How well do you think [cite child's name] is doing now?
4. Do you have any concerns about [cite child's name]'s health?
5. (If yes) What are your concerns?
6. Are you concerned about [cite child's name]'s general physical coordination or his [her] ability to run, climb, or do other motor activities?
7. (If yes) What are your concerns?
8. How well does [cite child's name] seem to understand things that are said to him [her]?
9. How well does [cite child's name] let you know what he [she] needs?
10. How would you describe [cite child's name]'s speech?
11. Does [cite child's name] speak in sentences?
12. Does [cite child's name] have any unusual speech behaviors?
    (If yes, go to question 13; if no, go to question 15.)
13. Tell me what seems to be unusual about his [her] speech.
14. (If needed) Is [cite child's name]'s speech intelligible?
15. Do you have any concerns about [cite child's name]'s behavior?
16. (If yes) What are your concerns?
17. How well does [cite child's name] get along with other children . . . with adults . . . with his [her] brothers or sisters . . . with you [you and your spouse]?
18. How well does [cite child's name] feed himself [herself] . . . dress himself [herself] . . . go to the toilet by himself [herself]?
19. Is there anything else about [cite child's name] that you wonder or worry about?
20. Did [cite child's name] have any difficulties during his [her] first two years of life?
21. (If yes) Tell me about that.
22. Does [cite child's name] have any problems that we did not cover?
23. Do you have any questions that you would like to ask me?
24. (If yes) Go ahead.
25. Thank you for talking with me. If you have any questions or if you want to talk to me, please call me. Here is my card.

Note. You can use probing questions to follow up on any problem areas mentioned by the parent.
Source: Adapted from Lichtenstein and Ireton (1984).

Table B-12
Semistructured Interview Questions for a Parent Regarding How Her or His Preschool-Age or Elementary School–Age Child Spends a Typical Day

Introduction

1. Hi! I'm Dr. [Ms., Mr.] _____. I'd like to know how [cite child's name] spends a typical day. I'll be asking you about how [cite child's name] spends the morning, afternoon, and evening. OK? Let's begin.

Early Morning

2. What time does [cite child's name] usually wake up?
3. Does [cite child's name] wake up by himself [herself]?
4. How do you know [cite child's name] is awake?
5. What does [cite child's name] do after he [she] wakes up?
6. Where are the other members of the family at that time?
7. What is [cite child's name]'s mood when he [she] wakes up?
8. How does [cite child's name] get along with other members of the family right after he [she] wakes up?
9. When does [cite child's name] get dressed?
10. Does [cite child's name] dress himself [herself]?
11. (If no) What kind of help does [cite child's name] need? (Go to question 13.)
12. Can [cite child's name] manage buttons . . . manage zippers . . . tie his [her] shoes?
13. Does [cite child's name] choose his [her] own clothes?
14. Are there any conflicts over dressing?
15. (If yes) Tell me about that.

Breakfast

16. Does [cite child's name] usually eat breakfast? (If yes, go to question 17; if no, go to question 22.)
17. When does [cite child's name] usually eat breakfast?
18. What does [cite child's name] usually have for breakfast?
19. With whom does [cite child's name] eat breakfast?
20. Are there any problems at breakfast?
21. (If yes) Tell me about them. (Go to question 23.)
22. Tell me about [cite child's name]'s not eating breakfast.

Morning

23. What does [cite child's name] do after breakfast [in the morning]?
24. (If needed) Does [cite child's name] go to a day care center or preschool, a regular school, or a sitter's house, or does he [she] stay at home?
(For children who stay at home, go to question 25; for children who go to a sitter's house, go to question 30; for children who go to a day care center or preschool, go to question 43; for children who go to a regular school, go to question 78.)

Stays at Home

25. Who is at home with [cite child's name]?
26. (If parent stays at home with child) How do you feel about being at home with him [her] during the day?
27. How does [cite child's name] spend his [her] time at home?
28. Does [cite child's name] have any problems at home during the day?
29. (If yes) Tell me about them. (Go to question 107.)

Goes to Sitter's House

30. Tell me about the sitter who watches [cite child's name].

31. How long does it take you to get to the sitter's house?
32. What time does [cite child's name] go there?
33. What time does [cite child's name] leave the sitter's?
34. How many other children are at the sitter's house when [cite child's name] is there?
35. (If one or more children) Tell me about the other children.
36. (If needed) How old are the other children at the sitter's?
37. How does [cite child's name] like it at the sitter's?
38. What kinds of things does [cite child's name] do there?
39. How is [cite child's name] doing at the sitter's?
40. Are you satisfied with [cite child's name]'s care at the sitter's?
41. (If no) Tell me about why you're not satisfied.
42. What changes have you noticed in [cite child's name]'s behavior since he [she] has been at the sitter's? (Go to question 107.)

Goes to Day Care Center or Preschool

43. Tell me about the day care center [preschool] that [cite child's name] goes to.
44. How long does it take you to get there?
45. What time does [cite child's name] go there?
46. What time does [cite child's name] leave the center [preschool]?
47. How old are the other children at the center [preschool]?
48. How many children are in [cite child's name]'s group?
49. And how many caregivers are in [cite child's name]'s group?
50. How does [cite child's name] like it at the center [preschool]?
51. What kinds of things does [cite child's name] do there?
52. How is [cite child's name] doing at the center [preschool]?
53. Are you satisfied with the center [preschool]?
54. (If no) Tell me about why you're not satisfied.
55. What changes have you noticed in [cite child's name]'s behavior since he [she] has been at the center [preschool]?
56. How did you decide to send [cite child's name] to this center [preschool]?
57. Have you met with [cite child's name]'s teacher?
58. (If yes) Tell me what you learned in talking with the teacher. (Go to question 61.)
59. Do you believe that you need to meet with [cite child's name]'s teacher?
60. (If yes) Tell me about why you want to meet with [cite child's name]'s teacher.
61. Do you participate in any activities at the center [preschool]?
62. (If yes) Tell me about them.
63. Is [cite child's name] having any problems at the center [preschool]? (If yes, go to question 64; if no, go to question 107.)
64. Tell me about [cite child's name]'s problem[s].
65. What is being done about it [them]?
66. Is anything being accomplished?
67. (If needed) Have you discussed the problem[s] with the teacher?
68. (If answer to question 67 is yes) What did the teacher say?
69. How do you feel about how the center [preschool] is handling the problem[s]?

Table B-12 (*Continued*)

70. Has [cite child's name] had problems in a center [preschool] before?
    (If yes, go to question 71; if no, go to question 74.)
71. Tell me about them.
72. What did you do about the problems then?
73. How were the problems resolved?
74. (If relevant) Have any of your other children had problems in a center [preschool]?
75. (If answer to question 74 is yes) Tell me about that.
76. Is there anything you would like to ask me about [cite child's name]'s problem[s] at the center [preschool]?
77. Is there anything you think I might do to help you with [cite child's name]'s problem[s] at the center [preschool]?
    (Go to question 107.)

Goes to Regular School

78. Tell me about [cite child's name]'s school.
79. How is [cite child's name] doing at school?
80. What are [cite child's name]'s best subjects?
81. What are his [her] poorest subjects?
82. What activities does [cite child's name] like best at school?
83. How does [cite child's name] get along with the other children?
84. How does [cite child's name] get along with the teachers?
85. Are you satisfied with the school?
86. (If no) Tell me about that.
87. How did you decide to send [cite child's name] to this school?
88. Have you met with [cite child's name]'s teacher?
89. (If yes) Tell me what you learned in talking with the teacher. (Go to question 92.)
90. Do you believe that you need to meet with [cite child's name]'s teacher?
91. (If yes) Tell me about why you want to meet with [cite child's name]'s teacher.
92. Are you involved in any school activities?
93. Tell me about them.
94. Is [cite child's name] having any problems at school?
    (If yes, go to question 95; if no, go to question 101.)
95. Tell me about [cite child's name]'s problem[s].
96. What is being done about it [them]?
97. Is anything being accomplished?
98. (If needed) Have you discussed the problem[s] with the teacher?
99. (If answer to question 98 is yes) What did the teacher say?
100. How do you feel about how the school is handling the problem[s]?
101. Has [cite child's name] had problems in school before?
    (If yes, go to question 102; if no, go to question 107.)
102. Tell me about them.
103. What did you do about the problems then?
104. How were the problems resolved?
105. Is there anything you would like to ask me about [cite child's name]'s problem[s] at school?
106. Is there anything you think I might do to help you with [cite child's name]'s problem[s] at school?

Lunch

107. When does [cite child's name] usually eat lunch?

108. What does [cite child's name] usually have for lunch?
109. Does [cite child's name] usually eat his [her] lunch?
110. Who eats with [cite child's name] at lunchtime?
111. Are there any problems at lunchtime?
112. (If yes) Tell me about the problems.

Afternoon

113. How does [cite child's name] spend his [her] afternoons?
114. Are there any problems in the afternoon?
115. (If yes) Tell me about them.

Related Areas

(Ask about any of the following areas, as needed.)

116. Before we get to supper and the end of the day, I'd like to ask you about [cite child's name]'s eating, friends, play activities, TV watching, and behavior outside the home. Let's first turn to [cite child's name]'s eating. OK?

Eating

117. How is [cite child's name]'s diet in general?
118. What are [cite child's name]'s likes and dislikes in food?
119. What is [cite child's name]'s behavior like when he [she] refuses to eat something?
120. How do you handle that kind of situation?
121. What does [cite child's name] usually have for snacks?
122. Are there any problems about snacks?
123. (If yes) Tell me about them.

Friends

124. Tell me about [cite child's name]'s friends.
125. (If needed) How old are they?
126. Where do the children play?
127. What do they do together?
128. How do they get along?
129. Are they able to take turns and share toys?
130. (If no) Tell me about that.
131. Who supervises them?
132. What kind of supervision do they need?

Play Activities

133. Does [cite child's name] ride a tricycle or bicycle?
134. (If yes) How well does [cite child's name] ride the tricycle [bicycle]?
135. Is [cite child's name] reckless in his [her] play?
136. (If yes) Tell me about that.
137. Does [cite child's name] have any fears about climbing?
138. (If yes) Tell me about that.
139. What are some of [cite child's name]'s favorite toys?
140. What does [cite child's name] like to do with them?
141. Is [cite child's name] able to play alone?
142. Tell me about that.

TV Watching

143. Does [cite child's name] watch television?
    (If yes, go to question 144; if no, go to question 154.)
144. What TV programs does [cite child's name] watch?
145. How much time does [cite child's name] spend watching television in an average day?
146. Does anyone in the family watch television with him [her]?
147. Does [cite child's name] watch any adult shows?
148. (If yes) Which adult shows does he [she] watch?

(*Continued*)

Table B-12 (*Continued*)

149. Has [cite child's name] ever been frightened by any shows?
150. (If yes) Tell me about that.
151. How did you handle his [her] fear?
152. Do you supervise [cite child's name]'s TV viewing?
153. Tell me about that.

Behavior Outside the Home

154. I'd like to know how [cite child's name] gets along when you go out, such as to a store, friend's house, church or synagogue or mosque, or restaurant. First, does [cite child's name] go shopping with you?
     (If yes, go to question 155; if no, go to question 159.)
155. How does [cite child's name] behave in the stores?
156. Does [cite child's name] like to choose things to buy?
157. What happens if [cite child's name] wants things he [she] cannot have?
158. How do you handle it?
159. How does [cite child's name] behave at a friend's house?
160. And how does [cite child's name] behave at church or synagogue or mosque, if you attend?
161. And how does [cite child's name] behave if you go to a restaurant?

Supper

162. When does [cite child's name] usually eat supper?
163. What does [cite child's name] usually have for supper?
164. Does [cite child's name] usually eat all his [her] food?
165. Who eats with [cite child's name] at supper?
166. Are there any problems at suppertime?
167. (If yes) Tell me about them.

Evening

168. What does [cite child's name] usually do in the evening?
169. When does [cite child's name] usually go to bed?
170. Does [cite child's name] have any routines associated with going to bed?
171. (If yes) Tell me about them.
172. Does [cite child's name] have any problems around bedtime?
173. (If yes) Tell me about them.
174. How much sleep does [cite child's name] usually get?
175. Does [cite child's name] sleep through the night?
     (If no, go to question 176; if yes, go to question 179.)
176. How often does [cite child's name] wake up?
177. What does [cite child's name] do when he [she] wakes up?
178. How do you handle it?
179. Where does [cite child's name] sleep?
180. Does [cite child's name] share a room with anyone?
181. (If yes) With whom?
182. How does that arrangement work out?

Concluding Questions

183. Is there anything that we have left out about how [cite child's name] spends a typical day?
184. (If yes) Please tell me about that.
185. Is there anything that you would like to ask me?
186. (If yes) Go ahead.
187. Thank you for talking with me. If you have any questions or if you want to talk to me, please call me. Here is my card.

Source: Adapted from Ferholt (1980).

Table B-13
Semistructured Interview Questions for a Parent of a Child Who May Have a Pervasive Developmental Disorder

The questions in this table primarily apply to children who are at least toddlers (ages 1 to 3 years). If the child is an infant, use only those questions that are appropriate.

Introduction

1. Hi! I'm Dr. [Ms., Mr.] _____. I'd like to get from you as complete a picture of [cite child's name]'s development as possible. OK?

Developmental History

2. Did you [the mother] experience any problems during your [her] pregnancy?
3. (If yes) Tell me about the problems.
4. Did you [the mother] experience any difficulties during labor and delivery?
5. (If yes) Tell me about those difficulties.
6. After [cite child's name] was born, did you sometimes wonder whether he [she] might have problems?
7. (If needed) Did you sometimes wonder whether he [she] might be deaf or blind?
8. (If yes) Tell me what you were concerned about.
9. Do you recall when [cite child's name] sat unassisted for the first time?
10. (If yes) When was that?
11. Do you recall how old [cite child's name] was when he [she] took his [her] first steps?
12. (If yes) When was that?
13. How would you describe [cite child's name]'s emotional responses during infancy?

Social Behavior as Infant

14. Now please tell me how [cite child's name] responded to you when he [she] was an infant.
    (Ask questions 15 to 22, as needed.)
15. Was [cite child's name] overly rigid when you held him [her]?
16. Was [cite child's name] ever overly limp when you held him [her]?
17. Did [cite child's name] seem to resist being held closely?
18. Did [cite child's name] seem indifferent to being held?
19. Did [cite child's name] look at you when you spoke to him [her]?
20. Did [cite child's name] enjoy playing peek-a-boo?
21. Was [cite child's name] content to be alone?
22. (If no) Did [cite child's name] cry and demand attention if he [she] was left alone?
23. And now please tell me how [cite child's name] responded to other adults.
    (Ask questions 24 to 27, as needed.)
24. Was [cite child's name] frightened of other people?
25. (If yes) Tell me more about that.
26. Did [cite child's name] withdraw from people?
27. (If yes) Tell me more about that.

Social Behavior as Toddler, Preschooler, or School-Age Child

28. How does [cite child's name] interact with you now?
    (Ask questions 29 to 51, as needed.)

29. Does [cite child's name] look at you while you are playing with him [her]?
30. (If no) What does he [she] do?
31. Does [cite child's name] look at you when you are talking to him [her]?
32. (If no) What does he [she] do?
33. Does [cite child's name] make direct eye contact with you?
34. Does [cite child's name] point with his [her] finger to show you things or to ask for things?
35. What does [cite child's name] do when you smile at him [her]?
36. Does [cite child's name] look through you as if you weren't there?
37. Does [cite child's name] seem to be hard to reach or in his [her] own world?
38. (If yes) Give me some examples.
39. Does [cite child's name] bring you things to show you?
40. Does [cite child's name] want you for comfort when he [she] is sick or hurt?
41. (If no) Tell me more about that.
42. Does [cite child's name] enjoy being held or cuddled?
43. Does [cite child's name] enjoy being bounced on your knee or swung?
44. Does [cite child's name] hug or kiss you back when you hug or kiss him [her]?
45. Does [cite child's name] come to you for a kiss or hug on his [her] own, without your asking him [her] to?
46. Does [cite child's name] enjoy being kissed?
47. Is [cite child's name] particular about when or how he [she] likes affection?
48. (If yes) Give me some examples of this.
49. Does [cite child's name] go limp when you hold or hug him [her]?
50. Does [cite child's name] pull away from you when you are being affectionate with him [her]?
51. And how does [cite child's name] interact with other adults?
    (Ask questions 52 to 57, as needed.)
52. Does [cite child's name] ignore people who try to interact with him [her]?
53. (If yes) Tell me more about that.
54. Does [cite child's name] actively avoid looking at people during interactions with them?
55. (If yes) Tell me more about that.
56. Does [cite child's name] look at people more when they are far away than when they are interacting with him [her]?
57. Does [cite child's name] make direct eye contact with people other than you?

Peer Interactions

58. Now I'd like to talk to you about how [cite child's name] gets along with other children. Please tell me about that.
    (Ask questions 59 to 68, as needed.)
59. Does [cite child's name] prefer to play alone rather than with other children?
60. Does [cite child's name] like to watch other children while they are playing?
61. Will [cite child's name] ever join in play with other children?

(*Continued*)

Table B-13 (*Continued*)

62. Do other children invite [cite child's name] to play with them?
63. Does [cite child's name] play games with other children in which they each take turns?
64. (If yes) What games does he [she] play with other children?
65. Does [cite child's name] enjoy playing with other children?
66. How does [cite child's name] show his [her] feelings toward other children?
67. Does [cite child's name] seem to be interested in making friends with other children?
68. (If yes) How does [cite child's name] show this interest?

Affective Responses

69. Now I'd like to ask you about [cite child's name]'s feelings. Does [cite child's name] seem to understand how others are feeling?
70. Please give me some examples.
71. Does [cite child's name] seem to understand the expressions on people's faces?
72. Is it difficult to tell what [cite child's name] is feeling from his [her] facial expressions?
73. (If yes) What makes it hard to tell?
74. Does [cite child's name] smile during his [her] favorite activities?
75. Does [cite child's name] smile, laugh, and cry when you expect him [her] to?
76. Do [cite child's name]'s moods change quickly, without warning?
77. (If yes) Please give me some examples of these changes.
78. Does [cite child's name] become very frightened of harmless things?
79. (If yes) What does he [she] become frightened of?
80. Does [cite child's name] laugh for no obvious reason?
81. Does [cite child's name] cry for no obvious reason?
82. Does [cite child's name] shed tears when he [she] cries?
83. Does [cite child's name] make unusual facial expressions?
84. (If yes) Please describe them.

Communication Ability

85. Now I'd like to talk to you about [cite child's name]'s language. Does [cite child's name] currently speak or attempt to speak?
    (If yes, go to question 86; if no, go to question 92.)
86. Tell me about his [her] speech.
87. Does [cite child's name] repeat words or phrases spoken by others?
88. Does [cite child's name] refer to himself [herself] as "you" or by his [her] name?
89. Does [cite child's name] have any problems when he [she] speaks?
90. (If yes) Tell me about those.
91. Overall, how would you describe [cite child's name]'s language abilities?
    (Go to question 100.)
92. Has he [she] ever spoken in the past?
    (If yes, go to question 93; if no, go to question 100.)
93. When did [cite child's name] speak in the past?
94. What did he [she] say?
95. How old was [cite child's name] when he [she] stopped speaking?

96. Did anything happen at the time he [she] stopped speaking?
97. (If yes) Tell me about what happened.
98. What did you think when [cite child's name] stopped speaking?
99. Tell me about that.
100. In addition to talking, there are lots of other ways that children can communicate their needs and wants, such as making sounds, pointing, or gesturing. Does [cite child's name] communicate by any other method?
101. (If yes) Tell me about that.
102. Does [cite child's name] have a range of facial expressions?
103. (If yes) Tell me about them.
104. Does [cite child's name] nod or shake his [her] head, clearly meaning yes or no?
105. Does he [she] use other gestures such as "thumbs up" to indicate success or approval?
106. Can you understand what [cite child's name] is trying to communicate?
107. Can other people understand him [her]?
108. Does [cite child's name] become frustrated when he [she] tries to communicate?
109. (If yes) What does [cite child's name] do when he [she] is frustrated?
110. Does [cite child's name] respond when you say his [her] name?
111. Does [cite child's name] understand what you say to him [her]?
112. How can you tell?
113. Does [cite child's name] seem interested in the conversations other people are having?
114. (If yes) Tell me more about that.
115. Does [cite child's name] follow simple directions, such as "Get your coat"?
116. Does [cite child's name] respond to only one word in a sentence rather than to the whole meaning of the sentence?
117. (If yes) Please give me some examples of this.
118. Does [cite child's name] take some speech literally? For example, would [cite child's name] think that the saying "It's raining cats and dogs" literally meant that cats and dogs were falling from the sky?
119. Does [cite child's name] listen to you when you read him [her] short stories?
120. Do you ever send [cite child's name] out of the room to get one object?
121. Could [cite child's name] be sent to get two or three things?
122. Can [cite child's name] follow a sequence of commands, such as "First do this, then this, then this"?
123. Can [cite child's name] understand the past tense . . . the future tense . . . the present tense?
124. Does [cite child's name] have any problems with spatial words, such as *under, in,* or *above?*
125. Does [cite child's name] understand better if instructions are sung to a tune instead of spoken?
126. Do you have to point or use gestures to help [cite child's name] understand what you say?

Table B-13 (*Continued*)

127. (If yes) Please give me some examples of what you do.
128. Does [cite child's name] understand that a nod or a shake of the head means yes or no?
129. Does [cite child's name] understand your different tones of voice?
130. Please give me some examples.
131. Does [cite child's name] understand other gestures you use?
132. Please give me some examples.
133. When you point to something, does [cite child's name] look in the direction you point?

Using Senses and Responding to Environment

134. Now I'd like to ask you about the way [cite child's name] uses his [her] senses and how he [she] responds to the environment. First, how does he [she] react to painful events, such as falling down or bumping his [her] head?
135. Is [cite child's name] overly sensitive to being touched?
136. (If yes) How does he [she] show this?
137. Does [cite child's name] examine objects by sniffing or smelling them?
138. (If yes) Please give me some examples of this.
139. Does [cite child's name] put inedible objects in his [her] mouth?
140. (If yes) What are some of the inedible objects he [she] puts in his [her] mouth?
141. Does [cite child's name] examine objects by licking or tasting them?
142. (If yes) Please give me some examples of this.
143. Is [cite child's name] overly interested in the way things feel?
144. (If yes) Tell me about this.
145. Does [cite child's name] enjoy touching or rubbing certain surfaces?
146. (If yes) Give me some examples of this.
147. Is [cite child's name] oversensitive to sounds or noises?
148. (If yes) Give me some examples of his [her] oversensitivity.
149. Does [cite child's name] cover his [her] ears at certain sounds?
150. (If yes) Please give me some examples of when he [she] does this.
151. Does [cite child's name] become agitated or upset at sudden or loud noises?
152. (If yes) Give me some examples of when this happens.
153. Does it seem to you that [cite child's name] does not hear well?
154. (If yes) Tell me more about this.
155. Does [cite child's name] ever ignore loud noises?
156. (If yes) Give me some examples of when he [she] ignores loud noises.
157. Does [cite child's name] stare into space for long periods of time?
158. (If yes) When might he [she] do this?
159. Is [cite child's name] overly interested in looking at small details or parts of objects?
160. (If yes) Please give me some examples of this.
161. Does [cite child's name] hold objects close to his [her] eyes to look at them?

162. Is [cite child's name] overly interested in watching the movements of his [her] hands or fingers?
163. Is [cite child's name] overly interested in watching objects that spin?
164. (If yes) Give me some examples of what he [she] likes to watch spin.
165. Is [cite child's name] overly interested in looking at lights or shiny objects?
166. (If yes) Give me some examples of this.
167. Is [cite child's name] overly sensitive to bright lights?
168. (If yes) Tell me more about this.
169. Does [cite child's name] look at things out of the corners of his [her] eyes?
170. (If yes) Give me some examples of this.
171. Does [cite child's name] do things without looking at what he [she] is doing?
172. (If yes) Give me some examples of what he [she] does without looking.
173. Is [cite child's name] aware of dangers, such as from hot or sharp objects?
174. Tell me about that.

Movement, Gait, and Posture

175. The next topic I'd like to cover is the way [cite child's name] moves and uses his [her] body. First, does [cite child's name] walk?
(If yes, go to question 176; if no, go to question 183.)
176. How does [cite child's name] walk?
177. (If needed) Does he [she] walk with swinging arms . . . on tip toe . . . oddly and awkwardly . . . gracefully?
178. Can [cite child's name] walk upstairs without help?
179. Can [cite child's name] walk downstairs without help?
180. Is [cite child's name] able to climb well?
181. Can [cite child's name] pedal a tricycle or a bicycle?
182. Can [cite child's name] run as well as other children of his [her] age?
183. Is [cite child's name]'s posture odd or awkward in any way?
184. (If yes) In what way is his [her] posture odd or awkward?
185. Can [cite child's name] copy other people's movements?
186. Does [cite child's name] wave goodbye?
187. Does [cite child's name] clap his [her] hands?
188. Are [cite child's name]'s movements easy, or are they stiff and awkward?
189. How easily does he [she] learn gymnastic exercises, dances, or miming games?
190. Does he [she] confuse up/down, back/front, or right/left when trying to imitate others?
191. How does he [she] behave when excited?
192. Does excitement cause [cite child's name] to move his [her] whole body, including face, arms, and legs?
193. Does [cite child's name] spin or whirl himself [herself] around for long periods of time?
194. (If yes) Tell me more about that.
195. Does [cite child's name] rock back and forth for long periods of time?
196. (If yes) Tell me more about that.
197. Does [cite child's name] move his [her] hands or fingers in unusual or repetitive ways, such as flapping or twisting them?

(Continued)

Table B-13 (*Continued*)

198. (If yes) Please give me some examples.
199. How well does [cite child's name] use his [her] fingers?
200. Tell me about that.
201. Does [cite child's name] move his [her] body in unusual or repetitive ways?
202. (If yes) Please give me some examples.
203. Would you say that [cite child's name] is more active or less active than other children of his [her] age?
204. Tell me about that.

Need for Sameness

205. Now I'd like to talk to you about [cite child's name]'s flexibility in adapting to change. Tell me how [cite child's name] responds when something out of the ordinary happens and his [her] routines must be changed.
206. Does [cite child's name] insist on certain routines or rituals, such as wearing only certain clothes or types of clothing?
207. (If yes) Tell me more about that.
208. Does [cite child's name] become upset if changes are made in his [her] daily routines?
209. (If yes) Please give me some examples of how he [she] becomes upset.
210. Does [cite child's name] become upset if his [her] belongings are moved or disturbed?
211. (If yes) Please give me some examples of how he [she] becomes upset.
212. Does [cite child's name] become upset if changes are made in the household—for example, if furniture is moved?
213. (If yes) Please give me some examples of how he [she] becomes upset.
214. Does [cite child's name] have certain favorite objects or toys that he [she] insists on carrying around?
215. (If yes) Tell me more about that.
216. Does [cite child's name] become upset when things don't look right, such as when the rug has a spot on it or books on a shelf lean to the side?
217. (If yes) Please give me some examples of this.
218. Does [cite child's name] become upset when he [she] is interrupted before he [she] has finished doing something?
219. (If yes) Give me some examples of this.
220. Does [cite child's name] become agitated or upset by new people, places, or activities?
221. (If yes) Please give me some examples of this.
222. Does [cite child's name] insist on performing certain activities over and over again?
223. (If yes) Tell me more about these activities.
224. Does [cite child's name] become upset when he [she] puts on new clothes?
225. (If yes) Tell me more about that.
226. Does [cite child's name] have certain mealtime rituals, such as eating from only one specific plate?
227. (If yes) Tell me about [cite child's name]'s mealtime rituals.
228. Does [cite child's name] have unusual food preferences, such as foods of a certain color or texture?
229. (If yes) Please give me some examples of what foods he [she] prefers.

Play and Amusements

230. Now I'd like to talk to you about [cite child's name]'s play. What kinds of games does [cite child's name] play?
231. Does [cite child's name] ever pretend to do things, such as pretending to feed himself [herself] with pretend food?
232. Does [cite child's name] enjoy playing simple hide-and-seek games with you?
233. Does [cite child's name] like to play with toys?
234. Does [cite child's name] roll things along the floor?
235. How many blocks can [cite child's name] use to build a tower?
236. Can [cite child's name] put puzzles together?
237. (If yes) How large a puzzle—how many pieces—can he [she] put together?
238. Does [cite child's name] make things with Legos, Tinker Toys, or similar toys?
239. (If yes) Can [cite child's name] follow the printed diagrams that come with such toys?
240. Does [cite child's name] use toys in unusual ways, such as spinning them or lining them up over and over again?
241. (If yes) Tell me how he [she] uses toys in unusual ways.
242. Is [cite child's name] destructive with toys?
243. (If yes) Tell me about that.
244. Does [cite child's name] play with toys or other objects in exactly the same way each time?
245. Does [cite child's name] imitate what you do when you play with him [her]?
246. (If yes) Tell me about that.
247. Does [cite child's name] imitate what other children do in their play?
248. (If yes) Tell me about that.
249. Does [cite child's name] engage in make-believe play?
250. (If needed) Does he [she] pretend to be a cowboy [cowgirl], policeman [policewoman], or doctor while acting out an imaginary game?
251. (If yes) Tell me about that.
252. Does [cite child's name] play with cars or trains as if they were real, such as by putting cars into a garage or moving trains around on a track?
253. Does [cite child's name] play with toy animals, dolls, or tea sets as if they were real?
254. Does [cite child's name] kiss the toy animals and dolls, put them to bed, hold tea parties for them, or play school with them?
255. Does [cite child's name] engage in imaginative play with other children, such as pretending to be doctor and nurse, mother and father, or teacher and student?
256. Does [cite child's name] take an active part, contributing to the play fantasy, or is he [she] always passive?
257. Does [cite child's name] join in cooperative play that does not incorporate fantasy, such as tag, hide-and-seek, ball games, and table games?
258. What types of outings does [cite child's name] enjoy?
259. What does [cite child's name] watch on television?
260. How long does [cite child's name] watch at a time?
261. How much time does [cite child's name] spend watching television each day?
262. What are [cite child's name]'s favorite shows?

Table B-13 (Continued)

263. Does [cite child's name] enjoy listening to music?
264. (If yes) What kind of music does [cite child's name] like?
265. Can [cite child's name] sing in tune?
266. Can [cite child's name] play a musical instrument?
267. (If yes) What instrument?

Special Skills

268. I'd like to learn whether [cite child's name] is especially good at something. Does he [she] have any special skills?
269. (If yes) Tell me about his [her] skills.
270. (If needed) We talked earlier about working with puzzles. Now can you tell me whether [cite child's name] has an unusual talent for assembling puzzles?
271. (If answer to question 270 is yes) Tell me about that.
272. Does [cite child's name] show any unusual abilities in music?
273. (If yes) Tell me about his [her] unusual abilities in music.
274. Does [cite child's name] have a very good memory?
275. (If yes) Tell me about his [her] memory.

Self-Care

(Modify the following questions based on the child's age.)

276. Now I'd like to talk to you about how [cite child's name] can take care of himself [herself]. First, does [cite child's name] have to be fed, or can he [she] feed himself [herself] with his [her] fingers, a spoon, a spoon and a fork, or a knife and a fork?
277. Does [cite child's name] need a special diet?
278. (If yes) Tell me about his [her] special diet.
279. Can [cite child's name] help himself [herself] to food when at the table?
280. Can [cite child's name] cut a slice of bread from a loaf?
281. How good are [cite child's name]'s table manners?
282. Does [cite child's name] have any problems with chewing?
283. Does [cite child's name] drink from a cup?
284. Does [cite child's name] dribble?
285. Can [cite child's name] wash and dry his [her] hands?
286. Can [cite child's name] bathe himself [herself] without help?
287. Is [cite child's name] aware when his [her] hands or face is dirty?
288. Can [cite child's name] dress himself [herself]?
289. (If yes) Tell me what [cite child's name] can do.
290. Can [cite child's name] undress himself [herself]?
291. (If yes) Tell me what [cite child's name] can do.
292. Can [cite child's name] brush or comb his [her] own hair?
293. Can [cite child's name] brush his [her] own teeth?
294. Is [cite child's name] concerned if his [her] clothes are dirty or untidy?
295. What stage has [cite child's name] reached in his [her] toilet training in the daytime?
296. (If dry during the day) And at nighttime, does [cite child's name] stay dry?
297. (If answer to question 296 is no) Tell me more about this.
298. Can [cite child's name] get objects that he [she] wants for himself [herself]?
299. Does [cite child's name] look for things that are hidden?
300. Does [cite child's name] climb on a chair to reach things?
301. Can [cite child's name] open doors?

302. Can [cite child's name] open locks?
303. Is [cite child's name] aware of the danger of heights or of deep water?
304. Is [cite child's name] aware that traffic is dangerous?
305. Does [cite child's name] know how to cross a street safely?
306. How much does [cite child's name] have to be supervised?
307. Is [cite child's name] allowed to go alone into another room . . . outside . . . in the neighborhood . . . farther away?
308. (If child is older than 11 or 12 years) Can [cite child's name] travel on a bus or train alone?

Sleep

309. Let's talk now about [cite child's name]'s sleeping habits. What are [cite child's name]'s sleeping habits? (Ask questions 310 to 319, as needed.)
310. What time does [cite child's name] go to sleep?
311. Does [cite child's name] have any rituals before going to sleep?
312. (If yes) Tell me about them.
313. Does [cite child's name] have any problems going to sleep?
314. (If yes) Tell me about them.
315. About how many hours of sleep does [cite child's name] get at night?
316. Does [cite child's name] take a daytime nap or naps?
317. (If yes) Around what time[s] does he [she] nap?
318. For how long?
319. What time does [cite child's name] get up?

Behavior Problems

(Modify the following questions based on the child's age.)

320. Let's talk now about [cite child's name]'s behavior. Does [cite child's name] run away or wander?
321. (If yes) Tell me about that.
322. Is [cite child's name] destructive with toys or other things?
323. (If yes) Tell me about that.
324. Does [cite child's name] have severe temper tantrums?
325. (If yes) Tell me about them.
326. (If needed) When do they occur? . . . Where do they occur? . . . How long do they last?
327. Does [cite child's name] hurt other children by biting, hitting, or kicking them?
328. (If yes) Give me some examples of how [cite child's name] hurts other children.
329. Does [cite child's name] try to hurt adults by biting, hitting, or kicking them?
330. (If yes) Give me some examples of how [cite child's name] tries to hurt adults.
331. How does [cite child's name] behave in public?
332. (If needed) Does [cite child's name] grab things in shops . . . scream in the street . . . make nasty remarks . . . feel people's clothing, hair, or skin . . . do anything else that is annoying?
333. Does [cite child's name] resist whatever you try to do for him [her]?
334. Does [cite child's name] automatically say "no" to any suggestion?

(Continued)

335. Is [cite child's name] generally aggressive?
336. (If yes) Tell me about his [her] aggressiveness.
337. Is [cite child's name] generally manipulative?
338. (If yes) Tell me about that.
339. Does [cite child's name] comply with rules or requests?
340. (If no) Tell me about how he [she] responds to rules or requests.
341. Does [cite child's name] hurt himself [herself] on purpose, such as by banging his [her] head, biting his [her] hand, or hitting or deeply scratching any part of his [her] body?
342. (If yes) Please give me some examples.
343. How would you describe [cite child's name]'s overall behavior at home?

School and Learning Ability

344. (If relevant) Now I'd like to talk about school. Does [cite child's name] go to school?
    (If yes, go to question 345; if no, go to question 349. Modify questions 349 to 361 based on the child's age.)
345. Where does [cite child's name] go to school?
346. How is [cite child's name] doing in school?
347. What subjects does [cite child's name] study in school?
348. (If subjects named) Tell me about how [cite child's name] is doing in these subjects.
349. Tell me about [cite child's name]'s ability to recognize objects in pictures.
350. (If needed) What kinds of pictures does [cite child's name] recognize?
351. Tell me about [cite child's name]'s ability to read.
352. (If needed) What kinds of things does [cite child's name] read?
353. Tell me about [cite child's name]'s ability to write.
354. (If needed) What does [cite child's name] write?
355. Tell me about [cite child's name]'s ability to do arithmetic.

356. (If needed) What kind of arithmetic problems can [cite child's name] do?
357. Can [cite child's name] tell time?
358. Does [cite child's name] know the days of the week?
359. Does [cite child's name] know the months of the year?
360. Does [cite child's name] know dates?
361. Can [cite child's name] draw?

Domestic and Practical Skills

(Modify the following questions based on the child's age.)

362. Now let's talk about how [cite child's name] functions at home. Does [cite child's name] have any chores to do around the house?
363. (If yes) Tell me about what [cite child's name] does. (Ask question 364 as needed.)
364. Does [cite child's name] help set the table . . . clean the table . . . straighten up his [her] room . . . wash his [her] clothes . . . help with washing dishes . . . use a vacuum cleaner . . . help with shopping . . . help prepare food . . . cook . . . knit or sew . . . do woodwork . . . do any other kind of craft . . . help with gardening?

Concluding Questions

365. Is there anything else you would like to discuss?
366. (If yes) Go ahead.
367. Does [cite child's name] have any problems that we didn't discuss?
368. (If yes) Tell me about them.
369. Do you have any questions that you would like to ask me?
370. (If yes) Go ahead.
371. Thank you for talking with me. If you have any questions later or if you want to talk to me, please call me. Here is my card.

Source: Adapted from Schreibman (1988), Stone and Hogan (1993), and Wing (1976). Permission to use questions from the "Parent Interview for Autism" was obtained from W. L. Stone.

Table B-14
Semistructured Interview Questions for a Family

1. Hi! I'm Dr. [Ms., Mr.] _____. In order to try to work out the problems you're having as a family, I'd like to hear from everyone about what's going on. OK?
2. (Looking at each of the family members present) Would you like to tell me why you are here today?

Perception of Problem

3. What do you see as the problem? (Obtain each family member's view, if possible.)
4. When did the problem start?
5. How did the problem start?
6. What is the problem like now?
7. How has the problem affected all of you? (Obtain each member's view, if possible.)
8. How have you dealt with the problem? (Obtain each member's view, if possible.)
9. To what degree have your attempts been successful?
10. Have you had any previous professional help?
    (If yes, go to question 11; if no, go to question 15.)
11. What kind of help did you receive?
12. What do you think about the help you received?
13. Was it successful?
14. Tell me in what ways it was successful [unsuccessful].

Description of Family

15. What words would you use to describe your family?
16. How do you think other people would describe your family?
17. What's it like when you are all together?
18. (Looking at the other family members) What kind of a person is [cite father's name]?
19. (Looking at the other family members) What kind of a person is [cite mother's name]?
20. (Looking at the other family members) What kind of son is [cite each son's name in turn]?
21. (Looking at the other family members) What kind of daughter is [cite each daughter's name in turn]?
22. Do you agree with the description of yourself given by the other family members? (Obtain a response from each member.)
23. Which parent deals more with the children?
24. Do the children have any specific chores to do at home?
25. Are these arrangements satisfactory and fair?
26. (If no) How could they be better?
27. Do you find it easy to talk with others in your family? (Obtain a response from each member; explore any difficulties, including who is involved and what the problem is.)
28. What's it like when you discuss something together as a family?
29. Who talks the most?

30. Who talks the least?
31. Does everybody get a chance to have a say?
32. Do you find you have to be careful about what you say in your family? (Obtain a response from each member.)
33. Who are the good listeners in your family?
34. Is it helpful to talk things over with the family, or does it seem to be a waste of time?
35. Is it easy to express your feelings in your family?
36. Do you generally know how the others in your family are feeling?
37. How can you tell how they are feeling?
38. How much time do you spend together as a family?
39. What sorts of things do you do together?
40. Who does what with whom?
41. Is this okay with everybody?
42. Who is closest to whom in the family?
43. How are decisions made in your family?
44. Is this satisfactory?
45. (If no) What would be preferable?
46. Do you have disagreements in your family?
    (If yes, go to question 47; if no, go to question 52.)
47. Who has disagreements?
48. What are they about?
49. What are the disagreements like?
50. What happens?
51. Do they get worked out?
52. What kind of work do you do, Mr. [cite father's last name]?
53. What kind of work do you do, Mrs. [cite mother's last name]?
54. (Indicating the children) Do any of you have jobs?
55. (If yes) What kind of work do you do?

Extended Family

56. Are there any other relatives or close friends living at home or nearby?
    (If yes, go to question 57; if no, go to question 59.)
57. Who are they?
58. How do all of you get along with them [him, her]?

Concluding Questions

59. How might each of you change in order to improve the family situation?
60. Is there anything else that you would like to discuss?
61. (If yes) Go ahead.
62. Are there any questions that any of you would like to ask me?
63. (If yes) Go ahead.
64. Thank you for talking with me. If you have any questions or if you want to talk to me, please call me. Here is my card.

Source: This table is based on the Family Assessment Interview, which was prepared by Dr. Peter Loader for the Family Research Programme at Brunel–The University of West London. Work related to the interview schedule was published by Kinston and Loader (1984).

Table B-15
Semistructured Interview Questions for a Teacher of a Child Referred for School Difficulties

---

Introduction

1. Hi! I'm Dr. [Ms., Mr.] . Please tell me why you referred [cite child's name].
2. Before we talk about these problems, I'd like to ask you about how [cite child's name] functions in some general areas. Does [cite child's name] have any auditory problems that you have noticed?
3. Does he [she] have any problems in the visual area . . . in the motor area . . . with speech . . . with attention . . . with concentration . . . in getting along with other children . . . in getting along with you or other teachers?
4. How about [cite child's name]'s energy level? Does he [she] tire easily?
5. And how is [cite child's name]'s motivation?
6. How does [cite child's name] handle assignments that require organization . . . that require planning . . . that require independent effort?
7. Does [cite child's name] attend class regularly?
8. (If no) Tell me about that.
9. Does [cite child's name] arrive in class on time, or is he [she] frequently late?
10. (If late) Do you know why he [she] is late?
11. Tell me about how [cite child's name] does his [her] homework.
    (If academic problems are important, go to question 12 and then go to specific sections for problems in reading, mathematics, spelling, use of language, attention and memory, perception, and motor skills. If child has primarily behavioral problems, go to question 134. If needed, ask questions from both the academic and behavioral sections. To conclude the interview after you inquire about the child's academic and/or behavioral problems, go to question 183.)

Academic Problems

12. What types of academic problems is [cite child's name] having in the classroom?

Reading Difficulties

13. What types of reading difficulties does [cite child's name] have?
    (Ask questions 14 to 23, as needed.)
14. Does [cite child's name] have any problems with silent reading . . . oral reading . . . reading comprehension . . . reading speed . . . endurance . . . listening?
15. Does [cite child's name] have difficulty reading single letters . . . words . . . sentences . . . paragraphs . . . stories?
16. How accurately does [cite child's name] seem to hear sounds in words?
17. Does [cite child's name] have difficulty with specific parts of words, such as prefixes, suffixes, middle sound units, vowels, or consonants?
18. How does [cite child's name] go about attacking words?
19. Does [cite child's name] have receptive difficulties, such as difficulty in understanding what he [she] reads?
20. Does [cite child's name] have expressive difficulties, such as difficulty in telling you about what he [she] has read?

21. Is there a discrepancy between [cite child's name]'s silent and oral reading?
22. (If yes) Tell me about the discrepancy.
23. What do you think should be done to help [cite child's name] master reading skills?

Mathematics Difficulties

24. What types of mathematical difficulties does [cite child's name] have?
25. Tell me about [cite child's name]'s problem with [cite mathematical difficulty].
26. (Include only relevant items, based on the child's grade level and the information obtained in questions 24 and 25.) Does [cite child's name] have difficulty with addition . . . subtraction . . . multiplication . . . division . . . memorization or recall of number facts . . . word problems . . . oral problems . . . fractions . . . decimals . . . percents . . . measurement concepts such as length . . . area . . . liquid measures . . . dry measures . . . temperature . . . time . . . money . . . exponents . . . numerical reasoning . . . numerical application . . . story problems . . . algebra . . . geometry?
27. Is [cite child's name] careless when he [she] does mathematical problems?
28. Is [cite child's name] impulsive when he [she] does mathematical problems?
29. Is [cite child's name] unmotivated when he [she] does mathematical problems?
30. What do you think should be done to help [cite child's name] master mathematical skills?

Spelling Difficulties

31. What types of spelling difficulties does [cite child's name] have?
32. Tell me more about [cite child's name]'s problem with [cite spelling difficulty].
33. (If needed) Does [cite child's name] tend to insert extra letters . . . omit letters . . . substitute one letter for another one . . . spell phonetically . . . reverse sequences of letters . . . put letters in the wrong order?
34. What do you think should be done to help [cite child's name] master spelling skills?

Language Skill Difficulties

35. What types of language difficulties does [cite child's name] have?
36. Tell me more about [cite child's name]'s problem in [cite language skill difficulty].
    (Ask questions 37 to 49, as needed.)
37. Does [cite child's name] have oral expressive language difficulties?
38. (If yes) Tell me about them.
39. Does [cite child's name] have difficulty speaking in complete sentences . . . using correct words in speaking . . . writing expressive language?
40. (If yes) Tell me about his [her] difficulties.
41. Does [cite child's name] have difficulty with writing complete sentences . . . using correct words in writing . . . generating

Table B-15 (*Continued*)

ideas . . . grammar . . . punctuation . . . writing organized compositions?

42. How would you compare [cite child's name]'s oral and written language?
43. Does [cite child's name] have difficulty using nonverbal gestures or signs?
44. Does [cite child's name] have difficulty speaking?
45. (If yes) What kinds of difficulties does he [she] have speaking?
46. (If needed) Does [cite child's name] have problems with pronunciation . . . speed of talking . . . vocal tone . . . intonation?
47. Does [cite child's name] have receptive language difficulties, such as difficulty understanding what others say . . . what he [she] reads . . . gestures?
48. How well does [cite child's name] recognize pictures . . . environmental sounds . . . nonverbal signs?
49. What do you think should be done to help [cite child's name] master language skills?

Attention and Memory Difficulties
50. What types of attention and/or memory difficulties does [cite child's name] have?
51. Tell me more about [cite child's name]'s problem with [cite attention and/or memory difficulty].
(Ask questions 52 to 92, as needed.)

General Attention
52. Under what conditions does [cite child's name] have difficulty attending to things?
53. Is [cite child's name] able to concentrate for an amount of time that is appropriate for his [her] chronological age?
54. Can [cite child's name] focus on a specific task?
55. Is [cite child's name] able to sustain attention for the duration of a typical assignment?
56. Is [cite child's name] distractible?
57. (If yes) Tell me about that.
58. Does [cite child's name] talk excessively . . . have difficulty working or playing quietly . . . often fail to finish things or follow through . . . often seem not to listen . . . often act before thinking . . . excessively shift from one activity to another?
59. Does [cite child's name] have difficulty organizing work . . . often lose things necessary for activities at school or home, such as toys, pencils, books, or assignments?
60. Does [cite child's name] need a lot of supervision?
61. Does [cite child's name] call out in class or blurt out answers?
62. Is [cite child's name] able to filter out surrounding noises—such as pencil sharpening or noises in the hall—so that he [she] can concentrate on the assigned task?
63. Does [cite child's name] stare into space for relatively long periods of time . . . doodle frequently?
64. Can [cite child's name] sit still for a long period of time?
65. (If no) Tell me what he [she] does.
66. Can [cite child's name] sit still for a short period of time?
67. (If no) Tell me what he [she] does.
68. Does [cite child's name] repeatedly say "What" or "Huh"?
69. Does [cite child's name] seek quiet places to work . . . become very upset in noisy, crowded places?

70. Is [cite child's name] constantly in motion?
71. How tolerant of frustration is [cite child's name]?
72. Is [cite child's name] impulsive in his [her] behavior?

Auditory Attention
73. How does [cite child's name] attend to sounds . . . lectures . . . class discussions?
74. Can [cite child's name] shift his [her] attention from one sound to another?
75. Does [cite child's name] have difficulty maintaining his [her] focus on sounds?
76. (If yes) Are there any specific types of sounds that he [she] has difficulty focusing on?
77. Is it easier for [cite child's name] to attend to rhythmic sounds, like music, than to spoken language sounds?
78. Does [cite child's name] mistake words he [she] hears, like *rat* for *ran*?
79. Does [cite child's name] attend better when you speak slowly to him [her]?

Auditory Memory
80. Does [cite child's name] have a good memory for things that happened recently . . . for things that happened in the distant past . . . for present events?
81. Can [cite child's name] recall people's names easily?
82. Does [cite child's name] have difficulty learning telephone numbers . . . addresses . . . the alphabet?
83. Does [cite child's name] call common objects, such as buttons and zippers, by their correct names?
84. Does [cite child's name] hesitate to name objects when he [she] is asked to do so?
85. Does [cite child's name] often ask to have questions repeated?

Visual Attention
86. How does [cite child's name] attend to visual stimuli?
87. (If needed) How does he [she] attend to . . . pictures . . . words in print . . . TV presentations . . . movie presentations . . . information on a computer screen?

Visual Memory
88. Does [cite child's name] remember things that he [she] saw recently . . . things that he [she] saw in the distant past . . . present events?
89. Can [cite child's name] recall the names of people he [she] has seen?
90. Does [cite child's name] have difficulty associating names with pictures?
91. Does [cite child's name] have difficulty recognizing letters . . . numbers . . . shapes?
92. What do you think should be done to help [cite child's name] master attention and memory skills?

Perceptual Difficulties
93. What types of perceptual difficulties does [cite child's name] have?
94. Tell me more about [cite child's name]'s problem with [cite perceptual difficulties].
(Ask questions 95 to 111, as needed.)
95. Does [cite child's name] have difficulty with auditory perception?

(*Continued*)

Table B-15 (Continued)

96. Does he [she] have difficulty with localizing sounds . . . identifying sounds . . . distinguishing between sounds . . . auditory sequencing . . . sound blending . . . figure-ground identification of sounds—that is, identifying only the most important sounds and ignoring other potentially useful sounds?
97. Does [cite child's name] have difficulty with visual perception?
98. Does he [she] have difficulty with identifying visual stimuli . . . matching forms . . . discriminating figure from ground—that is, identifying only the key letter, shape, or form on a page . . . recognizing letters or words in different forms, such as lowercase versus uppercase or standard type versus italics?
99. Does [cite child's name] have difficulty with spatial perception?
100. Does he [she] have difficulty recognizing the position or location of an object on a page . . . in a room . . . in a building . . . on the playground?
101. Does [cite child's name] have difficulty with appreciating relative sizes . . . depth perception . . . perspective . . . recognizing whether objects differ in size?
102. Does [cite child's name] have difficulty distinguishing right from left?
103. Which modality—visual or auditory—does [cite child's name] prefer?
104. Does [cite child's name] prefer to look at pictures or at graphs?
105. Does [cite child's name] prefer making oral or written presentations?
106. Does [cite child's name] seem to have difficulty processing visual information . . . auditory information?
107. Can [cite child's name] copy material from a chalkboard . . . from an overhead . . . from dictation?
108. Can [cite child's name] keep his [her] place on a page while reading?
109. Can [cite child's name] find his [her] way around a school building?
110. Can [cite child's name] open his [her] locker?
111. What do you think should be done to help [cite child's name] master perceptual skills?

Motor Skill Difficulties
112. What types of motor difficulties does [cite child's name] have?
113. Tell me more about [cite child's name]'s problem with [cite motor difficulties].
(Ask questions 114 to 133, as needed.)
114. Does [cite child's name] have gross-motor problems?
115. (If yes) Please describe them.
116. Do they involve walking . . . running . . . sitting . . . throwing . . . balance?
117. Does [cite child's name] have fine-motor problems?
118. (If yes) Tell me about them.
119. Do they involve drawing . . . handwriting . . . coloring . . . tracing . . . cutting . . . pencil grip . . . hand dexterity?
120. Tell me more about these problems.
121. (If there are handwriting problems) Does [cite child's name] have problems in sequencing, such as transposing

letters . . . spatial orientation, such as placing a letter of one word at the end of the preceding word (for example, writing "goh ome" for "go home") . . . writing letters or words on the same line . . . writing letters of appropriate size?
122. Does [cite child's name] scrawl?
123. Does [cite child's name] make tiny compressed letters?
124. Are [cite child's name]'s papers messy or neat?
125. How would you compare how [cite child's name] writes on a spelling test with how he [she] writes spontaneously?
126. Is [cite child's name] able to clearly write single letters . . . uppercase letters . . . lowercase letters . . . words . . . sentences . . . paragraphs . . . short stories or themes?
127. Is [cite child's name]'s problem in remembering shapes or in reproducing letter shapes?
128. Does [cite child's name] have visual-motor integration difficulties?
129. (If yes) Tell me about them.
130. What do you think should be done to help [cite child's name] master motor skills?
131. Can [cite child's name] type?
132. (If yes) How well does [cite child's name] type?
133. Does [cite child's name] do better with a word processor than with handwriting?

Behavioral Difficulties
134. Now I'd like to talk with you about [cite child's name]'s behaviors that bother you most. I'd like to discuss these behaviors, when they occur, how often they occur, and what occurs in your classroom that might influence the behaviors. I also would like to discuss some other matters related to [cite child's name] that will help us develop useful interventions. Please describe exactly what [cite child's name] does that causes you concern.
135. Which behaviors bother you most?
136. Which behaviors, in order of most to least pressing, would you like to work on now?
137. Let's look into the first problem in more detail. How serious is the problem behavior?
138. How long has it been going on?
139. When does the problem behavior occur?
140. (If needed) Does it occur when the children are just arriving at school . . . at their desks in the classroom . . . in small groups . . . at recess . . . at lunch . . . on a field trip . . . at an assembly? . . . Does it occur on a particular day of the week?
141. What classroom activity is generally taking place at the time the problem behavior occurs?
142. (If needed) Does the problem occur when the child is . . . working on a reading assignment . . . working on a math assignment . . . working on a history assignment . . . working on a writing assignment . . . working on a spelling assignment . . . working on an art assignment . . . working on a music assignment . . . working on a social studies assignment . . . involved a lecture . . . in unstructured play . . . doing independent work . . . interacting with you . . . interacting with other children?
143. How does the problem behavior affect the other children in the class?

Table B-15 (*Continued*)

144. How long does the problem behavior last?
145. How often does the problem behavior occur?
146. How many other children in the class also have this problem?
147. How does the level of [cite child's name]'s problem behavior compare with that of other children in the class who show the same behavior?
148. What happens just before the problem behavior begins?
149. What happens just after the problem behavior begins?
150. What makes the problem behavior worse?
151. What makes the problem behavior better?

Teacher's Reactions to Problem Behavior and Child
152. What do you do when the problem behavior occurs?
153. What does [cite child's name] do then?
154. What have you done that has been even partially successful in dealing with the problem behavior?
155. What do you think is causing the problem behavior?
156. What is your reaction to [cite child's name] in general?

Child's Relationship with Peers
157. How does [cite child's name] get along with his [her] classmates?
158. Does [cite child's name] have many friends?
159. Do the children include [cite child's name] in their games and activities?
160. Is [cite child's name] disliked by other children?
161. (If yes) Tell me why other children dislike [cite child's name].
162. How do other children contribute to [cite child's name]'s problem?
163. What do they do when [cite child's name] engages in the problem behavior?
164. How do other children help reduce the problem behavior?
165. How do other children react to [cite child's name] in general?
166. (If relevant) How do other teachers perceive and react to [cite child's name]?

Child's Social-Interpersonal Difficulties
(If social-interpersonal difficulties were not discussed, use this section.)
167. Does [cite child's name] have social and interpersonal problems?
168. (If yes) Tell me more about [cite child's name]'s problem in [cite social-interpersonal difficulties].
(Ask questions 169 to 176, as needed. Whenever there is a yes response, you might say "Please tell me more about that.")
169. Does [cite child's name] cry easily . . . give up easily . . . fly into a rage with no obvious cause . . . fear trying new

games or activities . . . lie or cheat in games . . . have problems with losing . . . show overcontrolling tendencies . . . prefer the company of younger children . . . prefer to be alone?
170. Does [cite child's name] have difficulty waiting for his [her] turn in games or group situations?
171. Does [cite child's name] fight, hit, or punch other children?
172. Does [cite child's name] frequently interrupt other children's activities?
173. Is [cite child's name] bossy, always telling other children what to do?
174. Does [cite child's name] tease other children or call them names?
175. Does [cite child's name] refuse to participate in group activities?
176. Does [cite child's name] lose his [her] temper often and easily?

Teacher's Expectations and Suggestions
177. For what part of the day is [cite child's name]'s behavior acceptable?
178. What do you consider to be an acceptable level of frequency for the problem behavior?
179. What expectations do you have for [cite child's name]?
180. What suggestions do you have for remedying the problem behavior?
181. What would you like to see done?
182. How would your life be different if [cite child's name]'s problems were resolved?

Child's Strengths
183. What are [cite child's name]'s strengths?
184. In what situations does [cite child's name] display these strengths?
185. How can these strengths be used in helping [cite child's name]?

Teacher's View of Child's Family
186. How much contact have you had with [cite child's name]'s family?
187. What impressions do you have about [cite child's name]'s family?

Concluding Questions
188. Are there any questions that you would like to ask me?
189. (If yes) Go ahead.
190. Thank you for talking with me. If you have any questions or if you want to talk to me further, please call me. Here is my card.

Note. Questions 137 through 151 can be repeated for additional problem areas.
Source: Some questions in this table were adapted from McMahon and Forehand (1988) and Witt and Elliott (1983).

Appendix C

TABLES FOR ATTENTION-DEFICIT/HYPERACTIVITY DISORDER

Table C-1
Classroom Observation Code: A Modification of the Stony Brook Code

GENERAL INSTRUCTIONS FOR USING THE CLASSROOM OBSERVATION CODE

1. This observation coding system is used to record behaviors that occur during structured didactic teaching and/or during periods of independent work under teacher supervision. Behaviors that occur during free play periods, snack time, etc., are not recorded. In addition, observers should not code behaviors in the following situations: a) whenever the child is out of seat at the teacher's request to hand out or collect materials, read in front of the class, work at the blackboard, or wait in line to have work checked; b) whenever the child receives individualized instruction from the teacher; c) whenever there is no assigned task, including instances in which the child is not required to initiate a new task after completion of assigned work; and d) whenever the teacher leaves the room.

2. Observers must be aware of the specific task assigned to the child and must note the particular class activity on the observation sheet. In addition, observers must be familiar with the general rules in each classroom. These rules, obtained from the teacher, are used as guidelines for employing this coding system. For example, a child who leaves his or her seat to sharpen a pencil without asking the teacher will be scored as "Gross Motor–Standing" (*GMs*) only if this behavior requires teacher permission. (*See* the Classroom Observation Code Observer Data Sheet: Classroom Rules.)

3. When a behavior category is observed, *circle* the respective symbols on the coding sheet. If no behavior category is observed, then code "Absence of Behavior" (*AB*); draw a slash through this particular symbol.

4. In coding a particular category, it is essential that the observer be familiar with the timing requirements of each of the behavior categories. That is, non-timed categories are coded as soon as they occur within a 15-second interval, with only the first occurrence noted. Timed categories are coded only if the child engages in behavior for more than 15 consecutive seconds. For example, a child is scored as "Off-Task" in interval 2 if the behavior began in interval 1 and continued uninterrupted throughout interval 2. Continue coding the behavior in subsequent intervals as long as the behavior continues, uninterrupted, throughout these intervals. Each box on the observation coding sheet corresponds to a 15-second interval.

5. Any time the child leaves the room for more than one full interval without permission, those interval boxes on the coding sheet should be crossed out. (*See* "Non-Compliance" and "Off-Task" for further details.)

6. Each coding sheet is divided into two 4-minute blocks. Observe each child for a total of 16 minutes, alternating 4-minute observations on each child.

I. Interference—Symbol: *I*

Purpose: This category is intended to detect any verbal or physical behaviors or noises that are disturbing to others; the purpose here is to detect a discrete and distinct behavior that does not necessarily persist.

Timing: This category is coded as a Discrete, Non-Timed Behavior.

Description:
A. Interruption of the teacher or another student during a lesson or quiet work period.
Examples:
1. Calling out during a lesson when the teacher or another student has the floor (includes ooh's and ahh's when raising hand).
2. Initiating discussion with another child during a work period.

Note:
1. "Interference" is coded immediately within the interval in which it first occurs.
2. If the child initiates a conversation that overlaps two intervals, code *I* only in the first interval.
3. If conversation stops and then starts anew in the next interval, code that interval as *I* if conversation is initiated by the target child.
4. In most classrooms a child is scored as *I* if he or she calls out an answer to the teacher's question. However, *I* is *not* coded in classrooms where calling out answers is permitted.
5. If the child engages in a conversation overlapping two intervals that is initiated by another child, do *not* code *I* in either interval.
6. Do *not* score the child as *I* if there is uncertainty as to whether the child initiated conversation or is only responding to another child.
7. Do *not* score the child as *I* if there is uncertainty as to whether or not a sound (e.g., "ooh") was made by the child.

B. Production of Sounds
Examples:
1. Vocalizations: e.g., screams, whistles, calls across room. coughs, sneezes, or loud yawns.
2. Noises other than vocalization: slamming or banging objects, tapping ruler, foot tapping, hand clapping, etc.

Note: Do not code *I* if a sound is made accidentally (e.g., the child drops a book, knocks over a chair, etc.).

C. Annoying Behavior: This behavior refers to nonverbal interruption. The child interrupts another child during a teacher-directed or independent work lesson.
Examples:
1. Tapping lightly or making gentle physical movements or gestures toward another child.
2. Sitting on another's desk when that child is present at the desk.
3. Moving or lifting another's desk when the owner is present.

D. Clowning.
Examples:
1. Mimicking the teacher or another child.
2. Kicking an object across the floor.
3. Engaging in or organizing games and other inappropriate activities during a work period (e.g., playing kickball in the class, throwing and catching a ball).
4. Showing off his or her own work when not called on by the teacher.

(Continued)

Table C-1 (*Continued*)

5. Making animal imitations.

6. Calling out a wildly inappropriate answer or making an obviously inappropriate public statement.

7. Shooting paper clips, airplanes, spitballs, etc. (If aimed at someone, this behavior is coded as "Aggression," *A*.)

8. Standing on a desk, chair, or table when not requested to do so by the teacher, or in any other inappropriate situation.

9. Posturing (child acts to characterize an action, an object, or another person).

10. Dancing in the classroom.

11. Play-acting.

12. Making mock threats. (If this does not occur in a clowning situation, then it is coded instead as "Threat or Verbal Aggression," *AC*.)

Note: If clowning involving vigorous gross-motor movements (e.g., running, dancing) occurs while the child is out of chair, then code both *I* and "Gross Motor–Vigorous" (*GMv*).

II. Off-Task—Symbol: *X*

Purpose: This category is intended to monitor behaviors when the child, *after* initiating the appropriate task-relevant behavior, attends to stimuli other than the assigned work.

Timing: This category is coded as Timed Behavior.

Description:

A. Manipulation and/or attending to objects, people, or parts of the body to the total exclusion of the task for one full interval following the interval in which the behavior began.

Examples:

1. The child plays with a pencil for one full interval after the interval in which the behavior was initially seen, without visual orientation toward the assigned task.

2. The child engages in extended conversation when he or she is supposed to be working.

3. The child does a task other than the assigned one (e.g., reads a different book). It is therefore essential that the observer be aware of the classroom situation and the specific assigned task.

Note:

1. When the child is doing something under the desk or where the observer can't see and is not attending to the task, assume the behavior is inappropriate and code *X*.

2. If the teacher is conducting a lesson at the board such that the child is required to look at the teacher or the board, score the child as *X* if he or she does not look at the teacher and/or the board at any time during the interval after the interval in which he or she first looked away.

3. If the teacher or another student is lecturing, reading a story, issuing instructions, etc., such that the child's task is to listen to the speaker, then code *X* if the child, by his or her behavior, indicates that he or she is not listening (e.g., head down on the desk, doodling in book, looking in book, etc.). Do *not* code *X* if the child looks at the speaker at any time during the interval.

4. Do *not* code *X* if the child shows any visual orientation to the task. Do *not* code *X* if there is uncertainty as to his or her visual orientation.

5. Do *not* code *X* if the child, by his or her behavior, indicates that he or she is listening (e.g., the child looks at the speaker's subject matter).

6. Do *not* code *X* if the child plays with or manipulates an object while attending to the task.

B. Code as *X* those instances when the child is allowed to leave his or her seat (e.g., to throw something in the trash) but remains away from the seat for more than five consecutive intervals following the interval in which he or she first left the seat.

Example:

Leaves Seat	Out of Seat	Out of Seat	Out of Seat	Out of Seat	Out of Seat	Out of Seat
1	2	3	4	5	6	7

Interval 7 is coded as *X* and "Out-of-Chair" (*OC*). Continue coding *X* and *OC* as long as the child remains away from his or her desk. If the child engages in task-relevant behavior while out of seat (e.g., attends to a teacher lesson), then stop coding *X* but continue coding *OC*.

Note:

1. If after initiating the task the child leaves the classroom for more than one full interval without permission, code *X* and indicate that the child is out of the room by crossing out the interval box. Continue coding *X* as long as the child remains out of the room.

2. Do *not* code *X* if the child stops working and it is not clear whether he or she has completed the task. However, put a dot above the interval in which there is uncertainty. If the teacher then confirms that the child was off-task (e.g., she says: "Why aren't you working?"), then go back and code these "dotted" intervals as *X*. If the teacher gives no indication, do not code *X*.

3. Do *not* code *X* in any interval that has been coded as "Solicitation" (*S*).

III. Non-Compliance—Symbol: *NC*

Purpose: This category is intended to monitor behaviors that reflect a failure on the part of the child to follow teacher instructions.

Timing: This category is coded as a Timed Behavior.

Description: The child fails to initiate appropriate behavior in response to a command or request from the teacher. It is to be distinguished from "Off-Task" (*X*), which is coded when the child, *after initiating* task-relevant behavior, ceases this task-relevant behavior.

Example: After a command has been given by the teacher (e.g., "Copy the words on the board into your notebook"), the child has one full interval after the interval in which the command was given to initiate the behavior. If the child has not complied, begin coding *NC* and continue coding *NC* for each full interval in which the child fails to initiate the task.

Note:

1. When the teacher gives a specific command, write "T.C." above the interval box in which the teacher finished giving the command.

2. If the child indicates that he or she is carrying out the teacher's command (e.g., the child looks for his or her notebook), then allow the child *five* full intervals to comply. If after this time period he or she has not initiated task-relevant behavior (e.g., copying words), then begin coding *NC*.

Table C-1 (*Continued*)

3. If before initiating the task the child leaves the classroom for more than one full interval without permission, code *NC* and cross out the interval box. Continue coding *NC* as long as the child remains out of the room.

4. The teacher will often issue commands that are not task-related, but are instead related to the handling of materials (e.g., "Put down your pencils," "Put away your book"). If the child has not complied by the end of the first full interval following the interval in which the command was given, then code that interval as *NC*. Do *not* continue coding *NC*. If the teacher repeats the same commands, then note "T.C." and begin to time the child to see if he or she complies.

5. A teacher may issue more than one command (e.g., "Put down your pencils and look at the board"). The child should *not* be scored as *NC* if he or she looks at the board but does not put down his or her pencil. Therefore, do not code *NC* if the child follows the more salient, task-related aspect of the teacher's command. The child should be scored as *NC* if he or she does *not* follow the more salient command (i.e., "look at the board").

6. The teacher will often tell the class to take out a textbook and begin working independently on a particular page. Do *not* code *NC* if the child begins working in the book on the wrong page.

7. A child may not have a book in school or may be unable to find it. Give the child *five* full intervals to attempt to find the appropriate materials. If at the end of this time interval the child has not informed the teacher that he or she doesn't have the book (homework, crayons, etc.), then begin coding *NC* until he or she notifies the teacher.

Situations that arise in the classroom can make it difficult to decide whether a child is non-compliant or off-task. The following guidelines should be useful in clarifying some of these situations.

8. During a classroom lesson the teacher will often issue commands that are *specific to the ongoing lesson*. In these instances, a child who had been working on the lesson but who does not follow the new command should be scored as *X* rather than *NC*. For example, during a math lesson, the children have been working in their math workbooks. They have been following the teacher's directions and have worked on specific math examples. The teacher tells them to "Do example 10." The child has been working all along but does not do example 10. If the required time interval elapses and the child has not begun work on this example, he or she should be scored as *X*.

9. The following situation should be coded as *NC* and not "Off-Task" (*X*). During a classroom lesson, the teacher instructs the children to work on or direct their attention to a task different from the one on which they had been working. For example, during a math lesson, the children have been working in their math workbooks. The teacher now shifts the focus of the math lesson and instructs the children to work on set theory using colored blocks. If the child does not follow these instructions within the required time interval, he or she should be scored as *NC*.

IV. Minor Motor Movement—Symbol: *MM*

Purpose: There are two aspects to this category, both of which are intended to monitor behaviors of the child that are indicative of restlessness and fidgeting.

Timing: This category is coded as Discrete, Non-Timed Behavior.

Description: Minor motor movements refer to buttock movements and rocking movements of the child while he or she is in the seat and/or to buttock movements while he or she is in *non-erect* positions while out of seat.

A. The child engages in in-seat movements such that there is an *observable* movement of the lower buttock(s)—i.e., that part of the buttock(s) that is in contact with the seat of the chair.

Examples: The following pertain to movements of one or both buttocks.

1. Sliding in seat.
2. Twisting, turning, wiggling, etc.—coded only when accompanied by buttock movement.
3. Lifting one or both buttocks off the seat.
4. Buttock movements while kneeling or squatting in seat.

B. The child produces rocking movements of his or her body and/or chair. Body rocking movements are defined as *repetitive* movements (at least two complete back-and-forth movements) from the waist up in a back-and-forth manner. Movements of the chair are also coded as *MM* when the child lifts two chair legs off the floor.

Note:

1. Do *not* code *MM* if the child makes *just one* forward-leaning movement or *just one* backward-leaning movement. However, if this movement is accompanied by an observable buttock movement, then *MM* should be coded.

2. Code as *MM* any movement that takes the child from a seated position into a kneeling, squatting, or crouching position, either in or out of the seat.

3. If the child is kneeling in or out of his or her seat or *leaning* over a desk or table, then code as *MM* any observable movements of the lower and/or upper buttocks—i.e., that area from the upper thigh to the hip.

4. If the child goes from a standing to a kneeling or squatting position, code *MM*.

5. Do *not* code *MM* if the physical set-up is such that the child *must* move in order to work on a task. There are *two* specific situations where minor motor movements should not be coded.

(a) The position of the child's desk requires that he or she move in order to work on a task—for example, the child faces the side of the room and the blackboard is in front. In this situation, the child *must* move his or her buttocks in order to copy from the board.

(b) While the child is working on a task that requires his or her visual attention (e.g., copying from the board, watching the teacher), the child's view is obstructed, requiring him or her to move in order to maintain visual contact.

6. Do *not* code *MM* if the child moves from a standing or kneeling position to a sitting position in the chair.

V. Gross-Motor Behavior

Purpose: There are two aspects of this category which are intended to monitor motor activity that results in the child's leaving his or her seat and/or engaging in vigorous motor activity.

Timing: This category is coded as a Discrete, Non-Timed Behavior.

(*Continued*)

Table C-1 (*Continued*)

A. Gross Motor–Standing—Symbol: *GMs*

Description: GMs refers to motor activity that results in the child's leaving his or her seat and standing on one or both legs (on the floor, chair, or desk) in an erect or semi-erect position such that the child's body from the waist up is *at least* at a 135-degree angle with the floor.

Note:

1. Do *not* code GMs when the child has permission, specific or implied, to leave his or her seat (e.g., to sharpen a pencil, throw something away, get materials, go to the board, go to the teacher's desk, etc.). If the child leaves his or her seat without permission, then code *GMs*.

2. Do *not* code GMs if the physical set-up is such that the child *must* move in order to work on a task. For example, while the child is working on a task that requires his or her visual attention (e.g., copying from the board, watching a demonstration), the child's view is obstructed, requiring him or her to stand up in order to maintain visual contact.

3. If it is not clear whether the child had to stand up, then code *GMs*.

B. Gross Motor–Vigorous—Symbol: *GMv*

Description: This is coded when the child engages in vigorous motor activity *while not seated at his or her desk* or when the child *leaves* his or her seat in a sudden, abrupt, or impulsive manner.

Examples:

1. Jumping up out of seat.
2. Running away from seat.
3. Running in the classroom.
4. Crawling across the floor.
5. Twirling.
6. Acrobatics.
7. Swinging between two seats or desks.

VI. Out-of-Chair Behavior—Symbol: *OC*

Purpose: This category is intended to monitor extended out-of-seat behavior.

Timing: This category is coded as a Timed Behavior.

Description: The child remains out of chair for one full interval after the interval in which he or she first left the seat.

Note:

1. *OC* is coded for each complete interval that the child remains out of chair, irrespective of whether the child is standing, sitting, or kneeling on the floor or roaming around the classroom.

2. If while being coded as *OC* the child kneels or squats (out-of-chair) or sits on the floor, then code this movement as "Minor Motor Movement" (*MM*) and continue to code *OC*. Any buttock movements that occur while the child is seated on the floor are coded as *MM*. *OC* is discontinued only when the child sits or kneels in a chair—be it his or her own or someone else's.

3. If the child is out of a chair getting materials, sharpening a pencil, getting a drink of water, throwing something away, etc. (when these are permitted behaviors), then allow the child a maximum of five full intervals after the interval in which he or she first left the seat to complete this task. After these five intervals, if the child is still out of chair, then begin coding *OC*. If

the child is *not working* during this period, then also score him or her as "Off-Task" (*X*).

4. If fewer than five intervals have elapsed and the child has obtained his or her goal (e.g., gotten a book, thrown something away, etc.), then allow him or her one full interval to return to his or her seat. If at the end of that interval he or she has not returned to the seat, then code that interval as *OC*

5. It is essential to be familiar with classroom rules regarding leaving seat with and without permission.

VII. Physical Aggression—Symbol: *A*

Purpose: This category is intended to measure physical aggression directed at another person or destruction of other's property. This behavior is coded regardless of the accuracy of the intended assault.

Timing: This category is coded as a Discrete, Non-Timed Behavior.

Description:

A. The child makes a forceful movement directed at another person, either directly or by utilizing an object as an extension of the hand.

Examples:

1. Blocking someone with arms or body; tripping, kicking, or hitting another person.
2. Throwing objects at another person.
3. Pinching, biting.

Note:

1. In all of the above examples, even if the child misses his or her goal, the behavior should be coded as *A*.

2. Code *A* even when the physical aggression is initiated by another child and the target child defends himself or herself. However, this should be noted on the coding sheet.

B. Destruction of others' materials or possessions or school property.

Examples:

1. Tearing or crumpling others' work.
2. Breaking crayons, pencils, or pens of others.
3. Misusing others' books (ripping out pages, writing in them, etc.).
4. Writing on another child or on another child's work.
5. Writing on a school desk.
6. Writing in a school textbook.

Note:

1. Code *A* even if the owner of the material is not at his or her desk.

2. If the child engages in *continuous* destructive behavior (e.g., writes on a desk or in a school textbook for several consecutive intervals), then code *A* only in the first interval in which the behavior occurs. If the child *interrupts* this destructive behavior and then returns to it, then code *A* anew.

C. Grabbing material in a sudden manner.

Examples:

1. The child grabs a book out of the hands of another child.
2. The child grabs his or her own material from another child.

Note:

Exclude casually taking material out of another's hand.

Table C-1 (*Continued*)

VIII. Threat of Verbal Aggression—Symbol: to children = *AC*, to teacher = *AT*

Purpose: This category is intended to monitor verbalizations or physical gestures of children that are abusive or threatening.

Timing: This category is coded as a Discrete, Non-Timed Behavior.

Description:

A. The child uses abusive language and gestures to children

Examples:

1. The child curses at another, says "shut up" to another.

2. The child sticks out his or her tongue at another, makes a threatening gesture, etc.

3. The child threatens others.

4. The child teases others, criticizes others.

5. The child bullies others.

B. When asked to do something by the teacher, the child directly states, "No I won't; I'm not going to do that." This should be coded as "Interference" (*I*) and *AT*. Do *not* code "Solicitation" (*S*).

C. The child answers the teacher back when a reply is not acceptable.

Example:

The teacher states, "We are not going outside today." The child calls back in a defiant manner, "Why not? I want to."

IX. Solicitation of Teacher—Symbol: *S*

Purpose: This category monitors behaviors directed toward the teacher. It is important to note that this behavior is coded only when initiated by the target child.

Timing: This category is coded as a Discrete, Non-Timed Behavior.

Description: Behaviors directed at obtaining the teacher's attention.

Examples:

1. Leaving seat and going up to the teacher. (This would be coded as *S* and "Gross Motor–Standing" (*GMs*); if the child speaks to the teacher, "Interference" (*I*) is also coded.)

2. Raising hand.

3. Calling out to the teacher.

Note:

1. These behaviors are coded as *S* whether or not the teacher recognizes the child.

2. When a child calls out to the teacher by mentioning the teacher's name or directs a question or statement specifically to the teacher while the teacher is attending to another child or addressing the class, then the behavior is coded as both *S* and "Interference" (*I*).

3. If the child says "ooh," "ahh," etc., while raising his or her hand in response to the teacher's question, code this as "Interference" (*I*) but *not S*.

4. If the observation begins while a teacher-child interaction is taking place, assume that the teacher initiated the interaction and do *not* code *S*.

5. If the child raises his or her hand in order to solicit the teacher and keeps the hand raised for more than one interval, code *S only* in the first interval in which the behavior occurred.

6. "Solicitation" and "Interference"(*I*) are coded if the child calls out an answer to the teacher when another child has the floor.

7. "Solicitation" is *not* coded if the child raises his or her hand in response to a teacher's question.

8. "Solicitation" is *not* coded if the child calls out in response to a teacher's question. In most classrooms, "Interference" (*I*) is coded if the child calls out an answer to a teacher's question.

X. Absence of Behavior—Symbol: *AB*

If no inappropriate behaviors as defined by the above categories occur in an interval, then code *AB*.

(Continued)

Table C-1 (*Continued*)

CLASSROOM OBSERVATION CODE
OBSERVER DATA SHEET: CLASSROOM RULES

Child A: _____ Seat: _____

Child B: _____ Seat: _____

School: _____ Teacher: _____ Room #: _____ Date: _____

1. Must a child always raise his or her hand before asking or answering questions?

   a) During a teacher-conducted lesson _____

   b) During independent work _____

   c) Comments _____

2. May a child engage in conversation with other children?

   a) During a teacher-conducted lesson _____

   b) During independent work _____

   c) Comments _____

3. Must a child work after completion of assigned task? _____

   a) On what? _____

   b) Can this be done out of his or her assigned seat? _____

4. May a child leave the room without permission? _____

5. May a child leave his or her seat without permission to

   a) sharpen a pencil_____   e) get materials _____

   b) throw something away _____   f) stand while working_____

   c) get a drink _____   g) other _____

   d) speak to the teacher_____

6. Other classroom rules: _____

   _____

Table C-1 (Continued)

CLASSROOM OBSERVATION CODE
SCORING SHEET

	1		2		3		4		5		6		7		8	
A	X	I A	X	I A	X	I A	X	I A	X	I A	X	I A	X	I A	X	I A
	NC	AC	NC	AC	NC	AC	NC	AC	NC	AC	NC	AC	NC	AC	NC	AC
	MM	AT	MM	AT	MM	AT	MM	AT	MM	AT	MM	AT	MM	AT	MM	AT
	GMs	GMv	GMs	GMv	GMs	GMv	GMs	GMv	GMs	GMv	GMs	GMv	GMs	GMv	GMs	GMv
	OC	S	OC	S	OC	S	OC	S	OC	S	OC	S	OC	S	OC	S
		AB		AB		AB		AB		AB		AB		AB		AB

	1		2		3		4		5		6		7		8	
B	X	I A	X	I A	X	I A	X	I A	X	I A	X	I A	X	I A	X	I A
	NC	AC	NC	AC	NC	AC	NC	AC	NC	AC	NC	AC	NC	AC	NC	AC
	MM	AT	MM	AT	MM	AT	MM	AT	MM	AT	MM	AT	MM	AT	MM	AT
	GMs	GMv	GMs	GMv	GMs	GMv	GMs	GMv	GMs	GMv	GMs	GMv	GMs	GMv	GMs	GMv
	OC	S	OC	S	OC	S	OC	S	OC	S	OC	S	OC	S	OC	S
		AB		AB		AB		AB		AB		AB		AB		AB

	1		2		3		4		5		6		7		8	
C	X	I A	X	I A	X	I A	X	I A	X	I A	X	I A	X	I A	X	I A
	NC	AC	NC	AC	NC	AC	NC	AC	NC	AC	NC	AC	NC	AC	NC	AC
	MM	AT	MM	AT	MM	AT	MM	AT	MM	AT	MM	AT	MM	AT	MM	AT
	GMs	GMv	GMs	GMv	GMs	GMv	GMs	GMv	GMs	GMv	GMs	GMv	GMs	GMv	GMs	GMv
	OC	S	OC	S	OC	S	OC	S	OC	S	OC	S	OC	S	OC	S
		AB		AB		AB		AB		AB		AB		AB		AB

	1		2		3		4		5		6		7		8	
D	X	I A	X	I A	X	I A	X	I A	X	I A	X	I A	X	I A	X	I A
	NC	AC	NC	AC	NC	AC	NC	AC	NC	AC	NC	AC	NC	AC	NC	AC
	MM	AT	MM	AT	MM	AT	MM	AT	MM	AT	MM	AT	MM	AT	MM	AT
	GMs	GMv	GMs	GMv	GMs	GMv	GMs	GMv	GMs	GMv	GMs	GMv	GMs	GMv	GMs	GMv
	OC	S	OC	S	OC	S	OC	S	OC	S	OC	S	OC	S	OC	S
		AB		AB		AB		AB		AB		AB		AB		AB

Abbreviations: X = Off-Task; NC = Non-Compliance; MM = Minor Motor Movement; GMs = Gross Motor–Standing; OC = Out-of-Chair; I = Interference; A = Physical Aggression; AC = Threat of Verbal Aggression to Children; AT = Threat of Verbal Aggression to Teacher; GMv = Gross Motor–Vigorous; S = Solicitation of Teacher; AB = Absence of Behavior.

Observer_____   Date _____   Time _____

Source: Reprinted, with changes in notation, with permission of the authors from H. Abikoff and R. Gittelman, "Classroom Observation Code: A Modification of the Stony Brook Code," *Psychopharmacology Bulletin*, 1985, *21*, pp. 901–909.

Table C-2
Structured Observation of Academic and Play Settings (SOAPS)

INSTRUCTIONS FOR STRUCTURED OBSERVATION OF ACADEMIC AND PLAY SETTINGS

To conduct the observation, you will need two tables (or desks) and chairs, a popular toy (e.g., hand-held videogame), five double-sided worksheets, and three copies of the recording form. Before the child enters the room, place the five double-sided worksheets on one table (or desk) and the toy on a nearby table (or desk). The room should be equipped with a one-way mirror or with a mounted camera for observing the child from an adjacent room.

Bring the child into the room and say, "This is our classroom. Here is your table. Let me show you some worksheets and how to do them." Help the child do a sample item at the top of each worksheet. Then say, "There are too many problems here for you to complete them all. But while I am gone for 15 minutes, I want you to do as many of them as you can. Keep working, don't leave your chair, and don't play with the toy over there. I'll be next door to make sure you're okay. I'll let you know when the 15 minutes are over." Then leave the room.

Use a 5-second time interval to record five behaviors: attention, sitting, fidgeting, noisy, and toy play. Note that the first two behaviors are appropriate behaviors and the last three are inappropriate behaviors. Make an audiotape that gives you prompts indicating the beginning of each interval. Record the following: "Begin 1 [5 seconds], Begin 2 [5 seconds], Begin 3, . . . , Begin 60."

In each of the five behavior code columns on the recording form, circle the code that represents the behavior observed during each interval. Three recording forms are needed for each 15-minute session.

After the session, record the number of intervals in which the child was on-task. Convert the number of on-task intervals to a percentage (divide by 60). A general rule is that a minimum of 80% on-task behavior is expected for elementary-age children (Roberts, 1990). Also record the number of worksheet items correctly completed.

Definitions of Coded Behaviors

1. *Attention* (Attending = AT; Not Attending = /AT). Code Attention when the child's eyes are focused on one of the assigned worksheets. Momentary shifts in focus away from a worksheet as well as obvious scribbling and clear lack of engagement with the task are coded as Not Attending (off-task).

2. *Sitting* (Sitting = SI; Not Sitting = /SI). Code Sitting when the child is sitting in the chair or when the child's weight is supported by the chair (e.g., when the child is sitting on his or her legs on the chair or when the child stands on the chair).

3. *Fidgeting* (Fidgeting = FI; Not Fidgeting = /FI). Code Fidgeting when the child makes any repetitive movement that is not directed to the completion of worksheet items (e.g., tapping a pencil on the table).

4. *Noisy* (Noisy = NO; Not Noisy = /NO). Code Noisy when the child makes an audible vocalization, even if the vocalization is low in volume or is unintelligible (e.g., whispering, singing, yelling).

5. *Toy Play* (Toy Play = TO; Not Toy Play = /TO). Code Toy Play when the child plays with the toy or when the child is looking at the toy and is within arm's reach of it.

Table C-2 (*Continued*)

RECORDING FORM FOR STRUCTURED OBSERVATION OF ACADEMIC AND PLAY SETTINGS

Name: _____ Date: _____ School: _____

Sex: _____ Grade: _____ Birthdate: _____ Teacher: _____

Intervals on-task: AT_____/60 = _____%; SI_____/60 = _____%; /FI_____/60 = _____%; /NO_____/60 = _____%; /TO_____/60 = _____%

No. of items completed correctly: 1_____; 2_____; 3_____; 4_____; 5_____; 6_____; 7_____; 8_____; 9_____; 10_____

Interval	Attention		Sitting		Fidgeting		Noisy		Toy Play	
1	AT	/AT	SI	/SI	FI	/FI	NO	/NO	TO	/TO
2	AT	/AT	SI	/SI	FI	/FI	NO	/NO	TO	/TO
3	AT	/AT	SI	/SI	FI	/FI	NO	/NO	TO	/TO
4	AT	/AT	SI	/SI	FI	/FI	NO	/NO	TO	/TO
5	AT	/AT	SI	/SI	FI	/FI	NO	/NO	TO	/TO
6	AT	/AT	SI	/SI	FI	/FI	NO	/NO	TO	/TO
7	AT	/AT	SI	/SI	FI	/FI	NO	/NO	TO	/TO
8	AT	/AT	SI	/SI	FI	/FI	NO	/NO	TO	/TO
9	AT	/AT	SI	/SI	FI	/FI	NO	/NO	TO	/TO
10	AT	/AT	SI	/SI	FI	/FI	NO	/NO	TO	/TO
11	AT	/AT	SI	/SI	FI	/FI	NO	/NO	TO	/TO
12	AT	/AT	SI	/SI	FI	/FI	NO	/NO	TO	/TO
13	AT	/AT	SI	/SI	FI	/FI	NO	/NO	TO	/TO
14	AT	/AT	SI	/SI	FI	/FI	NO	/NO	TO	/TO
15	AT	/AT	SI	/SI	FI	/FI	NO	/NO	TO	/TO
16	AT	/AT	SI	/SI	FI	/FI	NO	/NO	TO	/TO
17	AT	/AT	SI	/SI	FI	/FI	NO	/NO	TO	/TO
18	AT	/AT	SI	/SI	FI	/FI	NO	/NO	TO	/TO
19	AT	/AT	SI	/SI	FI	/FI	NO	/NO	TO	/TO
20	AT	/AT	SI	/SI	FI	/FI	NO	/NO	TO	/TO
21	AT	/AT	SI	/SI	FI	/FI	NO	/NO	TO	/TO
22	AT	/AT	SI	/SI	FI	/FI	NO	/NO	TO	/TO
23	AT	/AT	SI	/SI	FI	/FI	NO	/NO	TO	/TO
24	AT	/AT	SI	/SI	FI	/FI	NO	/NO	TO	/TO
25	AT	/AT	SI	/SI	FI	/FI	NO	/NO	TO	/TO
26	AT	/AT	SI	/SI	FI	/FI	NO	/NO	TO	/TO
27	AT	/AT	SI	/SI	FI	/FI	NO	/NO	TO	/TO
28	AT	/AT	SI	/SI	FI	/FI	NO	/NO	TO	/TO
29	AT	/AT	SI	/SI	FI	/FI	NO	/NO	TO	/TO
30	AT	/AT	SI	/SI	FI	/FI	NO	/NO	TO	/TO
31	AT	/AT	SI	/SI	FI	/FI	NO	/NO	TO	/TO
32	AT	/AT	SI	/SI	FI	/FI	NO	/NO	TO	/TO
33	AT	/AT	SI	/SI	FI	/FI	NO	/NO	TO	/TO
34	AT	/AT	SI	/SI	FI	/FI	NO	/NO	TO	/TO
35	AT	/AT	SI	/SI	FI	/FI	NO	/NO	TO	/TO
36	AT	/AT	SI	/SI	FI	/FI	NO	/NO	TO	/TO
37	AT	/AT	SI	/SI	FI	/FI	NO	/NO	TO	/TO
38	AT	/AT	SI	/SI	FI	/FI	NO	/NO	TO	/TO
39	AT	/AT	SI	/SI	FI	/FI	NO	/NO	TO	/TO
40	AT	/AT	SI	/SI	FI	/FI	NO	/NO	TO	/TO
41	AT	/AT	SI	/SI	FI	/FI	NO	/NO	TO	/TO
42	AT	/AT	SI	/SI	FI	/FI	NO	/NO	TO	/TO
43	AT	/AT	SI	/SI	FI	/FI	NO	/NO	TO	/TO
44	AT	/AT	SI	/SI	FI	/FI	NO	/NO	TO	/TO
45	AT	/AT	SI	/SI	FI	/FI	NO	/NO	TO	/TO
46	AT	/AT	SI	/SI	FI	/FI	NO	/NO	TO	/TO
47	AT	/AT	SI	/SI	FI	/FI	NO	/NO	TO	/TO
48	AT	/AT	SI	/SI	FI	/FI	NO	/NO	TO	/TO
49	AT	/AT	SI	/SI	FI	/FI	NO	/NO	TO	/TO
50	AT	/AT	SI	/SI	FI	/FI	NO	/NO	TO	/TO
51	AT	/AT	SI	/SI	FI	/FI	NO	/NO	TO	/TO
52	AT	/AT	SI	/SI	FI	/FI	NO	/NO	TO	/TO
53	AT	/AT	SI	/SI	FI	/FI	NO	/NO	TO	/TO
54	AT	/AT	SI	/SI	FI	/FI	NO	/NO	TO	/TO
55	AT	/AT	SI	/SI	FI	/FI	NO	/NO	TO	/TO
56	AT	/AT	SI	/SI	FI	/FI	NO	/NO	TO	/TO
57	AT	/AT	SI	/SI	FI	/FI	NO	/NO	TO	/TO
58	AT	/AT	SI	/SI	FI	/FI	NO	/NO	TO	/TO
59	AT	/AT	SI	/SI	FI	/FI	NO	/NO	TO	/TO
60	AT	/AT	SI	/SI	FI	/FI	NO	/NO	TO	/TO

(*Continued*)

Table C-2 (*Continued*)

WORKSHEET FOR STRUCTURED OBSERVATION OF ACADEMIC AND PLAY SETTINGS

Note that each of the following worksheets is a condensed version and needs to be expanded to fill an 8½-by-11-inch page.

Name: _____ 1

Date: _____

FILL IN THE EMPTY BOXES

P	V	R	N	O	Z	B	U	H	X
1	2	3	4	5	6	7	8	9	10

V	P	Z	O	H	R	B	Z	N	X	U	R	Z	V

R	O	B	H	P	V	N	Z	U	X	R	U	Z	X

N	H	O	X	P	Z	R	B	H	P	V	R	U	B

O	X	Z	V	B	U	X	P	O	N	B	R	H	P

Z	P	B	R	U	V	N	Z	H	X	P	O	B	N

B	V	U	N	H	P	R	X	Z	H	U	V	N	X

U	R	H	O	X	P	Z	B	U	X	H	N	O	Z

FILL IN THE EMPTY BOXES 2

@	%	#	*	$	!	¢	=	?	+
1	2	3	4	5	6	7	8	9	10

$	¢	#	@	+	=	!	*	%	?	*	@	+	$

=	%	$	!	¢	#	?	!	@	+	*	?	%	#

$	%	+	¢	@	%	#	!	?	=	!	¢	@	*

=	$	#	*	¢	+	?	=	!	%	+	=	¢	#

@	+	$	*	=	$	#	%	+	?	!	¢	#	@

¢	+	=	%	@	?	!	$	*	#	?	%	@	=

+	¢	#	*	!	$	+	!	%	@	#	=	?	*

3

MARK OUT ALL OF THE A'S THAT YOU SEE

G K A B P L A

T R C A L J V A A L W Q P F

Q W R A N C K A F W T D V P

O E X S H A W Z N L P D A I

K A P T A D W Q L H N B F A

G F A B K Y U S A D A C D F

A J X W N D A N W A C Y S L

T H X A M V D E A H L I A N

F G A D R A U O P Q S A D R

P K T A Y D R A T A W N A A

J A G N U S R T A N C A R U

4

MARK OUT ALL OF THE H'S THAT YOU SEE

K J Y H U P N

U R E C N H T R S U N G A J

H H M W S T R H O Y T H K P

R D H S W P O U H R D G H F

N H I L S H B D V M H X A T

L S Y C H W M H D N S X J A

F D C A D G S Y T J B A F G

A F V N H L Q W D A T P A K

I A D P L N Z W A H S X B O

T Y J H L Y E S E L S N E O

Y U I R F G N M B C V D H H

Table C-2 (*Continued*)

5

FILL IN THE EMPTY BOXES

R	X	S	U	Z	Q	T	E	G	H
1	2	3	4	5	6	7	8	9	10

U	E	R	G	X	H	G	T	S	Q	E	Z	T	H

X	E	U	Z	R	T	S	X	Q	H	R	G	Z	Q

S	Z	R	H	Q	T	U	X	G	S	E	U	R	T

E	S	X	G	Q	U	H	Z	T	H	U	R	E	Z

S	X	E	Q	G	R	T	Z	U	H	G	X	Q	S

E	T	H	X	R	U	Q	G	S	Z	S	H	E	X

Q	U	R	T	G	Z	X	H	E	S	T	G	R	Z

6

FILL IN THE EMPTY BOXES

Q	W	R	T	Y	P	S	D	F	G
1	2	3	4	5	6	7	8	9	10

T	D	Q	F	W	G	F	S	R	P	D	Y	S	G

W	D	T	Y	Q	S	R	W	P	G	Q	F	Y	P

R	Y	Q	G	P	S	T	W	F	R	D	T	Q	S

D	R	W	F	P	T	G	Y	S	G	T	Q	D	Y

R	W	D	P	F	Q	S	Y	T	G	F	W	P	R

D	S	G	W	Q	T	P	F	R	Y	R	G	D	W

P	T	Q	S	F	Y	W	G	D	R	S	F	Q	Y

7

MARK OUT ALL OF THE 4'S THAT YOU SEE

2 5 6 8 4 3 0 4

4 5 6 8 4 4 9 0 3 1 5 4 6 7

6 7 3 2 4 8 1 4 0 9 8 5 4 4

7 5 4 6 8 4 9 0 7 4 5 7 3 2

4 4 9 8 0 6 4 5 7 3 7 3 7 4

3 7 5 4 8 0 1 2 4 4 4 7 5 4

2 3 7 5 6 8 9 0 7 5 6 8 9 0

5 8 9 4 6 5 2 1 0 3 0 9 8 4

5 7 6 8 9 0 1 2 3 7 5 8 9 0

4 6 5 7 4 8 9 0 3 2 7 1 6 9

0 9 2 3 6 4 7 8 1 4 5 6 2 9

8

MARK OUT ALL OF THE 3'S THAT YOU SEE

3 7 1 9 0 3 2 5

3 2 9 6 4 0 1 3 8 4 3 9 0 2

7 3 5 2 9 7 6 4 5 3 1 2 5 4

0 5 7 8 3 1 4 2 4 6 8 7 3 5

9 5 2 8 0 4 3 7 4 1 3 6 0 5

6 8 3 3 5 1 8 5 3 9 2 9 4 3

9 4 3 5 2 3 6 6 3 9 0 1 9 4

8 4 1 0 6 4 3 2 7 3 9 0 6 4

7 5 2 7 3 9 0 8 3 1 5 3 6 7

6 2 3 1 6 8 9 3 5 7 2 6 0 4

5 3 6 1 7 9 2 5 4 3 0 7 3 8

Table C-2 (*Continued*)

				9

FILL IN THE EMPTY BOXES

Y	O	I	C	D	J	T	B	L	S
1	2	3	4	5	6	7	8	9	10

I	D	T	B	L	O	Y	S	J	C	T	L	D	I

B	O	C	L	Y	S	O	J	C	B	J	Y	L	T

I	T	D	Y	L	S	O	J	C	B	J	Y	L	T

Y	D	O	J	I	S	C	T	L	B	I	Y	S	D

J	L	O	B	S	Y	I	L	T	D	C	B	J	O

D	T	S	L	Y	J	I	C	B	O	L	I	Y	S

L	C	Y	D	J	I	B	S	O	T	C	D	O	B

				10

FILL IN THE EMPTY BOXES

B	C	N	R	Z	J	P	K	A	G
1	2	3	4	5	6	7	8	9	10

P	J	N	R	C	G	A	B	Z	K	N	C	J	P

R	G	K	C	A	B	J	P	Z	N	G	R	K	B

P	N	J	A	C	B	G	Z	K	R	Z	A	C	N

A	J	B	Z	P	B	K	N	C	R	P	A	G	J

Z	K	G	B	R	P	A	C	N	J	K	R	Z	G

J	N	B	C	A	Z	P	K	R	G	C	P	A	B

C	K	A	J	Z	P	R	B	G	N	K	J	G	R

Source: Adapted from Roberts, Milich, and Loney (1984). Worksheets reproduced, with changes in notation, with permission from Mary Ann Roberts.

From *Assessment of Children: Behavioral, Social, and Clinical Foundations (Fifth Edition)* by Jerome M. Sattler and Robert D. Hoge. Copyright 2006 by Jerome M. Sattler, Publisher, Inc. Permission to photocopy this appendix table is granted to purchasers of this book for personal use only (see copyright page for details).

Table C-3
ADHD Questionnaire

ADHD QUESTIONNAIRE

Child's name: _____ Name of person filling out form: _____

Age: _____ Grade: _____ School: _____ Date: _____

Directions: Please read each item and check either Y ("Yes") or N ("No"). If you check "Yes," please answer the questions in the last three columns for that item. Be sure to indicate whether you are using years or months for your answers.

Behavior	*Check one*	*How old was the child when you first noticed the behavior?*	*How long has the behavior persisted?*	*In what settings does the child show this behavior (such as home, playground, school, or work)?*
1. Often fails to give close attention to details or makes careless mistakes in schoolwork, work, or other activities	☐ Y ☐ N			
2. Often has difficulty sustaining attention in tasks or play activities	☐ Y ☐ N			
3. Often does not seem to listen when spoken to directly	☐ Y ☐ N			
4. Often does not follow through on instructions and fails to finish schoolwork, chores, or duties in the workplace	☐ Y ☐ N			
5. Often has difficulty organizing tasks and activities	☐ Y ☐ N			
6. Often avoids, dislikes, or is reluctant to engage in tasks that require sustained mental effort (such as schoolwork or homework)	☐ Y ☐ N			
7. Often loses things necessary for tasks or activities, such as toys, school assignments, pencils, or books	☐ Y ☐ N			
8. Often is easily distracted by extraneous stimuli	☐ Y ☐ N			
9. Often is forgetful in daily activities	☐ Y ☐ N			
10. Often fidgets with hands or feet or squirms in seat	☐ Y ☐ N			
11. Often leaves seat in classroom or in other situations in which remaining seated is expected	☐ Y ☐ N			
12. Often runs about or climbs excessively in situations in which it is inappropriate	☐ Y ☐ N			
13. Often has difficulty playing or engaging in leisure activities quietly	☐ Y ☐ N			
14. Often is "on the go" or acts as if "driven by a motor"	☐ Y ☐ N			
15. Often talks excessively	☐ Y ☐ N			
16. Often blurts out answers before questions have been completed	☐ Y ☐ N			
17. Often has difficulty awaiting turn	☐ Y ☐ N			
18. Often interrupts or intrudes on others (e.g., butts into conversations or games)	☐ Y ☐ N			

Source: Adapted from American Psychiatric Association (2000).
From *Assessment of Children: Behavioral, Social, and Clinical Foundations (Fifth Edition)* by Jerome M. Sattler and Robert D. Hoge. Copyright 2006 by Jerome M. Sattler, Publisher, Inc. Permission to photocopy this appendix table is granted to purchasers of this book for personal use only (see copyright page for details).

Table C-4
DSM-IV–TR **Checklist for Attention-Deficit/Hyperactivity Disorder**

Child's name: _____ Parent's name: _____

Age: _____ Grade: _____ School: _____ Date: _____

Symptoms	Check one
A. Inattention and Hyperactivity-Impulsivity	
1. Inattention	
a. Often fails to give close attention to details or makes careless mistakes in schoolwork, work, or other activities	☐ Y ☐ N
b. Often has difficulty sustaining attention in tasks or play activities	☐ Y ☐ N
c. Often does not seem to listen when spoken to directly	☐ Y ☐ N
d. Often does not follow through on instructions and fails to finish schoolwork, chores, or duties in the workplace	☐ Y ☐ N
e. Often has difficulty organizing tasks and activities	☐ Y ☐ N
f. Often avoids, dislikes, or is reluctant to engage in tasks that require sustained mental effort (such as schoolwork or homework)	☐ Y ☐ N
g. Often loses things necessary for tasks or activities, such as toys, school assignments, pencils, or books	☐ Y ☐ N
h. Often is easily distracted by extraneous stimuli	☐ Y ☐ N
i. Often is forgetful in daily activities	☐ Y ☐ N
2. Hyperactivity-Impulsivity	
Hyperactivity	
a. Often fidgets with hands or feet or squirms in seat	☐ Y ☐ N
b. Often leaves seat in classroom or in other situations in which remaining seated is expected	☐ Y ☐ N
c. Often runs about or climbs excessively in situations in which it is inappropriate	☐ Y ☐ N
d. Often has difficulty playing or engaging in leisure activities quietly	☐ Y ☐ N
e. Often is "on the go" or acts as if "driven by a motor"	☐ Y ☐ N
f. Often talks excessively	☐ Y ☐ N
Impulsivity	
g. Often blurts out answers before questions have been completed	☐ Y ☐ N
h. Often has difficulty awaiting turn	☐ Y ☐ N
i. Often interrupts or intrudes on others (e.g., butts into conversations or games)	☐ Y ☐ N
B. Some hyperactive-impulsive or inattentive symptoms that caused impairment were present before age 7 years.	☐ Y ☐ N
C. Some impairment from the symptoms is present in two or more settings (e.g., at school [or work] and at home).	☐ Y ☐ N
D. There is clear evidence of clinically significant impairment in social, academic, or occupational functioning.	☐ Y ☐ N
E. The symptoms do not occur exclusively during the course of a pervasive developmental disorder, schizophrenia, or other psychotic disorder and are not better accounted for by another mental disorder (e.g., mood disorder, anxiety disorder, dissociative disorder, or personality disorder).	☐ Y ☐ N

Table C-4 (*Continued*)

Diagnostic Criteria	Check one

Attention-Deficit/Hyperactivity Disorder, Combined Type

a. Six or more items from numbers 1 and 2 present for at least 6 months to a degree that is maladaptive and inconsistent with developmental level ☐ Y ☐ N

b. Some items from numbers 1 or 2 present before age 7 years ☐ Y ☐ N

c. Some items from numbers 1 or 2 present in two or more settings ☐ Y ☐ N

d. Clear evidence of clinically significant impairment in social, academic, or occupational functioning ☐ Y ☐ N

e. Symptoms not occurring exclusively during the course of a pervasive developmental disorder, schizophrenia, or other psychotic disorder and not better accounted for by another mental disorder ☐ Y ☐ N

If above items a through e are checked *Yes*, criteria are fulfilled for a diagnosis of attention-deficit/hyperactivity disorder, combined type.

Attention-Deficit/Hyperactivity Disorder, Predominantly Inattentive Type

a. Six or more items from number 1 present for at least 6 months to a degree that is maladaptive and inconsistent with developmental level ☐ Y ☐ N

b. Six or more items from number 2 *not* present for at least 6 months ☐ Y ☐ N

c. Some items from number 1 present before age 7 years ☐ Y ☐ N

d. Some items from number 1 present in two or more settings ☐ Y ☐ N

e. Clear evidence of clinically significant impairment in social, academic, or occupational functioning ☐ Y ☐ N

f. Symptoms not occurring exclusively during the course of a pervasive developmental disorder, schizophrenia, or other psychotic disorder and not better accounted for by another mental disorder ☐ Y ☐ N

If above items a through f are checked *Yes*, criteria are fulfilled for a diagnosis of attention-deficit/hyperactivity disorder, predominantly inattentive type.

Attention-Deficit/Hyperactivity Disorder, Predominantly Hyperactive-Impulsive Type

a. Six or more items from number 2 present for at least 6 months to a degree that is maladaptive and inconsistent with developmental level ☐ Y ☐ N

b. Six or more items from number 1 *not* present for at least 6 months ☐ Y ☐ N

c. Some items from number 2 present before age 7 years ☐ Y ☐ N

d. Some items from number 2 present in two or more settings ☐ Y ☐ N

e. Clear evidence of clinically significant impairment in social, academic, or occupational functioning ☐ Y ☐ N

f. Symptoms not occurring exclusively during the course of a pervasive developmental disorder, schizophrenia, or other psychotic disorder and not better accounted for by another mental disorder ☐ Y ☐ N

If above items a through f are checked *Yes*, criteria are fulfilled for a diagnosis of attention-deficit/hyperactivity disorder, predominantly hyperactive-impulsive type.

Source: Based on *DSM-IV–TR* (American Psychiatric Association, 2000).
From *Assessment of Children: Behavioral, Social, and Clinical Foundations (Fifth Edition)* by Jerome M. Sattler and Robert D. Hoge. Copyright 2006 by Jerome M. Sattler, Publisher, Inc. Permission to photocopy this appendix table is granted to purchasers of this book for personal use only (see copyright page for details).

Appendix D

TABLES FOR LEARNING DISABILITY

Table D-1
Informal Tests of Word Prediction Abilities

CLOZE PROCEDURES

Name: _____ Date: _____

Sex: _____ Grade: _____ School: _____

Birthdate: _____ Teacher: _____

Score (number correct): Task 1 _____, Task 2 _____, Task 3 _____, Task 4 _____, Task 5 _____, Task 6 _____.

Task	*Procedure and examples*
1. Auditory Cloze with Oral Response Child is required to complete a spoken sentence or phrase orally with a word that is both semantically and syntactically correct. This is a good beginning task for children, regardless of age, because it defines the prediction abilities necessary for the subsequent tasks.	*Directions:* Say: "I am going to say a sentence that has a word missing. I want you to complete the sentence with a word that makes the most sense. For example, if I say *An airplane flies in the* _____ [pause], you could say *sky* or *air*. Do you have any questions? [Answer any questions.] Here is the first sentence." Administer all six items, but stop testing if the child becomes frustrated. Score the child's responses as 1 (correct) or 0 (incorrect). Give credit for any reasonable response. 1. Maria went to the lake to _____. (fish, swim, relax, etc.) 2. John used his money to buy some _____. (candy, clothes, food, etc.) 3. A horse can run very _____. (fast, quickly, slowly, etc.) 4. On a lonely farm in the country lived a man and his _____. (wife, child, donkey, etc.) 5. Mr. Cook was going to the _____ to get some eggs. (barn, store, market, shop, etc.) 6. Ray finished picking up the trash and walked back to the _____. (house, store, barn, etc.)
2. Auditory Cloze, Initial Grapheme, and Oral Response Child is presented with a spoken phrase or sentence with a single word omitted and is given the initial grapheme of the missing word. The prediction now involves an added constraint; not only must the response be semantically and syntactically acceptable, but it must also begin with the indicated grapheme. This task, unlike the auditory cloze, requires familiarity with letters and with oral response words.	*Directions:* Say: "I am going to say a sentence that has a word missing. The sentence will also have the first letter of the missing word. I want you to complete the sentence with a word that begins with that letter and makes the most sense. For example, if I say *In the morning I put on my shoes and s_____* [make the first *sound* of the missing word], you could say *socks* or *shirt*. Do you have any questions? [Answer any questions.] Here is the first sentence." Administer all six items, but stop testing if the child becomes frustrated. Score the child's responses as 1 (correct) or 0 (incorrect). Give credit for any reasonable response that begins with the appropriate letter. 1. My kitten drinks m_____. (milk) 2. Today, the mailman brought a l_____. (letter) 3. Sandy put the small rock in his p_____. (pocket, pack) 4. Last night for supper we had potatoes and b_____. (bread, beef, bacon, etc.) 5. The alligator was hiding in the w_____ of the swamp. (water, weeds) 6. When the car stopped, the old man got out and k_____ it. (kicked)

(Continued)

Table D-1 (*Continued*)	
Task	*Procedure and examples*
3. Visual Cloze with Alternatives and Oral Response Child selects, from two alternatives, the more appropriate word to complete the written sentence. This task, which assesses use of semantic and syntactic cues, relies heavily on a child's ability to read the target sentence and the alternatives. A child may err on this task even though he or she has adequate word prediction ability. The chance factor is much higher on this task than on the others.	*Directions:* Say: "I am going to show you a sentence and I want you to read it silently. When you come to the part that has two words in parentheses, tell me which word makes the most sense. For example, look at this sentence. [Show child this sentence: *The dog chased the (pat, cat).*] The word that makes the most sense is *cat*. Do you have any questions? [Answer any questions.] Here is the first sentence." Administer all six items, but stop testing if the child becomes frustrated. Score the child's responses as 1 (correct) or 0 (incorrect). Give credit only if the child chooses the correct word. 1. Mary can hit the (dill/ball). 2. Sam picked some (fingers/flowers) from his garden. 3. An old lady was in her (house/horse). 4. Kim will (come/came) home after the ballgame. 5. Because she was mad, Mom said, "Go to your room and don't come (out/our)." 6. On the way to school, Tim stopped to pick up a (life/leaf).
4. Visual Cloze with Oral Response Child is required to complete a written sentence orally with a word that is both semantically and syntactically correct. Odd responses may be based on a miscue of one of the words in the item, not on a misapplication of semantic and syntactic constraints. Scoring should be based on both semantic and syntactic acceptability.	*Directions:* Say: "I am going to show you a sentence that has a word missing. Read the sentence silently and then tell me what missing word makes the most sense. For example, look at this sentence. [Show child this sentence: *At night I go to _____ .*] You could say *sleep* or *bed*. Do you have any questions? [Answer any questions.] Here is the first sentence." Administer all six items, but stop testing if the child becomes frustrated. Score the child's responses as 1 (correct) or 0 (incorrect). Give credit for any reasonable response. 1. Run as fast as you _____. (can, want, etc.) 2. The baby was very _____. (happy, sad, etc.) 3. At breakfast Max spilled milk all over the _____. (table, floor, kitchen, etc.) 4. A red bird built a nest in the _____. (tree, chimney, etc.) 5. The dog is old, but he still _____. (runs, eats, etc.) 6. Every day I eat a big bowl of cereal _____ breakfast. (for, at)
5. Visual Cloze with Written Response Child is presented with a written phrase or sentence with a word omitted and is required to write an appropriate word in the space provided. Scoring should be based primarily on both semantic and syntactic acceptability.	*Directions:* Say: "I am going to show you a sentence that has a word missing. Read the sentence silently and then print on the blank line a word that makes the most sense. For example, look at this sentence. [Show child this sentence: *My mother likes to _____.*] You could print the word *cook* or *read* or *sew* here [point to the blank line]. Do you have any questions? [Answer any questions.] Here is the first sentence." Administer all six items, but stop testing if the child becomes frustrated. Score the child's responses as 1 (correct) or 0 (incorrect). Give credit for any reasonable response. 1. The boy kicked the _____. (ball, dog, car, etc.) 2. One day a _____ ran off the road. (car, bike, motorcycle, etc.) 3. I wanted to see if I could _____ fudge. (make, cook, etc.) 4. The duck flew over the water, and soon we could not _____ him. (see, find, etc.) 5. Once upon a time there was a king who was so _____ they called him King Fatso. (fat, big, heavy, etc.) 6. Texas Dan was the best cowboy around, and he could _____ a bucking bronco. (ride)

Table D-1 (*Continued*)

Task	Procedure and examples
6. Visual Cloze, Initial Grapheme, and Written Response Child is presented with a written sentence with a word omitted and is required to write an appropriate word using the grapheme shown. Providing the initial grapheme limits the range of acceptable responses. Some children give responses that meet the initial grapheme criterion but that do not follow the semantic and syntactic cues.	*Directions:* Say: "I am going to show you a sentence that has a word missing. The sentence will also have the first letter of the missing word. Read the sentence silently. I want you to complete the sentence by printing the rest of the missing word that makes the most sense. For example, look at this sentence. [Show child this sentence: *The lion was in a cage at the z_____ .*] You could print the rest of the word *zoo* here like this. [Print *oo* on the blank line.] Do you have any questions? [Answer any questions.] Here is the first sentence." Administer all six items, but stop testing if the child becomes frustrated. Score the child's responses as 1 (correct) or 0 (incorrect). Give credit for any reasonable response. 1. The girl eats the h_____. (hotdog, hamburger, etc.) 2. Peter named his dog B_____. (Bill, Boy, Ben, etc.) 3. My bike is r_____ and white. (red) 4. Mary didn't want her little brother playing w_____ her toys. (with) 5. Where could I go if I wanted t_____ hide? (to) 6. The artist could draw the most beautiful p_____ of flowers. (picture)

Note. Record the child's response. Also note if the child makes (a) no response, (b) an incorrect response that was related to the theme, or (c) an incorrect response that was not related to the theme. If the child gives more than one word, ask for a single word.

Source: Adapted from Allington (1979). The six items for each procedure were obtained from R. L. Allington, personal communication, April 1982.

Table D-2
Strip Initial Consonant Task

STRIP INITIAL CONSONANT TASK

Name: _____   Date: _____

Sex: _____   Grade: _____   School: _____

Birthdate: _____   Teacher: _____

Score (number correct): _____

As you present each sample and item, speak clearly and distinctly and emphasize the key word.

Say, "Listen carefully. I am going to say a word. If you take away the first sound of the word I say, you will find a new word. First, I'll show you how to do it. *Ball.* If you take away the first sound, the new word is *all.* Now let's try another." Give Sample Item 1.

Sample Item 1

Say, "Tell me what the new word is when you take away the first sound in *cat.* What is the new word when you take away the first sound?"

If the child succeeds, say, "That's right" and go to Sample Item 2.

If the child fails, say, "If you take away the first sound from the word *cat,* the new word is *at.*" Repeat Sample Item 1. Say, "*Cat.* What is the new word when you take away the first sound?"

If the child succeeds, say, "That's right" and go to Sample Item 2.

If the child fails, say, "If you take away the first sound from the word *cat,* the new word is *at.*" Proceed to Sample Item 2.

Sample Item 2

Say, "Let's try another one. What is the new word when you take away the first sound from the word *task*?"

If the child succeeds, say, "That's right" and go to Test Item 1.

If the child fails, say, "If you take away the first sound from the word *task,* the new word is *ask.*" Repeat Sample Item 2. Say, "What is the new word when you take away the first sound from the word *task*?"

If the child succeeds, say, "That's right" and go to Test Item 1.

If the child fails, say, "If you take away the first sound from the word *task,* the new word is *ask.*" Proceed to Test Item 1.

Test Items

Say, "If you take away the first sound in *pink,* what is the new word?" If necessary, repeat these instructions before you say each new word. Do not correct any answers or indicate whether they are correct. Give all nine items.

1. pink
2. man
3. nice
4. win
5. bus
6. pitch
7. call
8. hit
9. pout

Source: Adapted from Stanovich, Cunningham, and Cramer (1984).
From *Assessment of Children: Behavioral, Social, and Clinical Foundations (Fifth Edition)* by Jerome M. Sattler and Robert D. Hoge. Copyright 2006 by Jerome M. Sattler, Publisher, Inc. Permission to photocopy this appendix table is granted to purchasers of this book for personal use only (see copyright page for details).

Table D-3
Phonological Memory Test

PHONOLOGICAL MEMORY TEST

Name:_____   Date:_____

Sex:_____   Grade:_____   School:_____

Birthdate:_____   Teacher:_____

Score (number correct): Words_____   Nonwords_____

Directions

Word directions: "I am going to say some words. After I say
each word, you say it. Let's try one for practice: *big.* Now you
say it. . . . OK. Here is the first word. . . . Now you say it."
Introduce each item with "Here is the next word." If needed, also
say: "Now you say it."

Nonword directions: "I am going to say some made-up words.
After I say each made-up word, you say it. Let's try one for
practice: *kek.* Now you say it. . . . OK. Here is the first made-up
word. . . . Now you say it." Introduce each item with "Here is the
next word." If needed, also say: "Now you say it."

Words	Nonwords
1. Arm _____	16. Grall_____
2. Hate_____	17. Nate_____
3. Pot_____	18. Mot _____
4. Bird _____	19. Plurd _____
5. Pull _____	20. Tull _____
6. Rabbit _____	21. Rubid_____
7. Letter_____	22. Diller _____
8. Driver_____	23. Grindle_____
9. Picture_____	24. Fannock _____
10. Button _____	25. Yennet_____
11. Newspaper _____	26. Brastering _____
12. Alphabet _____	27. Dopelate _____
13. Holiday _____	28. Kannifer_____
14. Elephant _____	29. Tumperine_____
15. Potato _____	30. Parrazon _____

Source: Adapted from Gathercole and Adams (1993).
From *Assessment of Children: Behavioral, Social, and Clinical
Foundations (Fifth Edition)* by Jerome M. Sattler and Robert D. Hoge.

Table D-4
Phonological Oddity Task

PHONOLOGICAL ODDITY TASK

Name: _____   Date: _____

Sex: _____   Grade: _____   School: _____

Birthdate: _____   Teacher: _____

Score (number correct): Test 1 _____ Test 2 _____ Test 3 _____

Speak clearly and distinctly, at an even pace, and emphasize the four key words in each item or example.

TEST 1. FIRST SOUND DIFFERENT

Say, "Listen carefully. I am going to say four words. One of the words begins with a different sound from the other words. Here is an example. If I say *bag, nine, beach, bike,* the word that begins with a different sound is *nine.* Now you try one." Give Sample Item 1.

Sample Item 1
Say, "Which word begins with a different sound from the other words: *rat, roll, ring, pop*?"

If the child passes, say, "That's right" and go to Sample Item 2.

If the child fails, say, "*rat, roll, ring, pop.* The word that has a different beginning sound is *pop.*" Repeat Sample Item 1. Say, "Which word begins with a different sound from the other words: *rat, roll, ring, pop*?"

If the child passes, say, "That's right" and go to Sample Item 2.

If the child fails, say, "*rat, roll, ring, pop.* The word that has a different beginning sound is *pop.*" Go to Sample Item 2.

Sample Item 2
Say, "Let's try another one. Which word has a different beginning sound: *nut, sun, sing, sort*?"

If the child passes, say, "That's right" and go to Test Item 1.

If the child fails, say, "*nut, sun, sing, sort.* The word that has a different beginning sound is *nut.*" Repeat Sample Item 2. Say, "Which word has a different beginning sound: *nut, sun, sing, sort*?"

If the child passes, say, "That's right" and proceed to Test Item 1.

If the child fails, say, "*nut, sun, sing, sort.* The word that has a different beginning sound is *nut.*" Proceed to Test Item 1.

Test Items
Give Test Items 1 through 8. Say, "Which word has a different beginning sound?" Then say the four words. If necessary, repeat the instructions before each item. Do not correct any answers or indicate whether they are correct. Introduce each item with "Here are the next four words."

1. not no nice *son*
2. ball bite *dog* beet
3. girl *pat* give go
4. *yes* run rose round
5. cap *jar* coat come
6. hand hut *fun* here
7. *cat* tan time ton
8. luck like look *arm*

TEST 2. MIDDLE SOUND DIFFERENT

Say, "Listen carefully. I am going to say four words. One of the words has a different sound in the middle from the other words. Here is an example. If I say *tap, cap, tell, hat,* the word that has a different sound in the middle is *tell.* Now you try one." Give Sample Item 1.

Sample Item 1
Say, "Which word has a different sound in the middle from the other words: *mop, hop, tap, pop*?"

If the child passes, say, "That's right" and go to Sample Item 2.

If the child fails, say, "*mop, hop, tap, pop.* The word that has a different sound in the middle is *tap.*" Repeat Sample Item 1. Say, "Which word has a different sound in the middle from the other words: *mop, hop, tap, pop*?"

If the child passes, say, "That's right" and go to Sample Item 2.

If the child fails, say, "*mop, hop, tap, pop.* The word that has a different sound in the middle is *tap.*" Go to Sample Item 2.

Sample Item 2
Say, "Let's try another one. Which word has a different middle sound: *pat, fit, bat, cat*?"

If the child passes, say, "That's right" and go to Test Item 1. If the child fails, say, "*pat, fit, bat, cat.* The word that has a different middle sound is *fit.*" Repeat Sample Item 2. Say, "Which word has a different middle sound: *pat, fit, bat, cat*?"

If the child passes, say, "That's right" and proceed to Test Item 1.

If the child fails, say, "*pat, fit, bat, cat.* The word that has a different middle sound is *fit.*" Proceed to Test Item 1.

Test Items
Give Test Items 1 through 8. Say, "Which word has a different middle sound?" Then say the four words. If necessary, repeat the instructions before each item. Do not correct any answers or indicate whether they are correct. Introduce each item with "Here are the next four words."

1. lot cot pot *hat*
2. fun *pin* bun gun
3. *hug* dig pig wig
4. red fed *lid* bed
5. wag rag bag *leg*
6. fell *doll* well bell
7. dog fog *jug* log
8. fish dish wish *mash*

TEST 3. LAST SOUND DIFFERENT

Say, "Listen carefully. I am going to say four words. One of the words has a different sound at the end from the other words.

Table D-4 (*Continued*)

Here is an example. If I say *fog, tag, pig, let,* the word that ends with a different sound is *let.* Now you try one." Give Sample Item 1.

Sample Item 1
Say, "Which word has a different sound at the end from the other words: *hat, mat, fan, cat*?"

If the child passes, say, "That's right" and go to Sample Item 2.

If the child fails, say, "*hat, mat, fan, cat.* The word that has a different ending sound is *fan.*" Repeat Sample Item 1. Say, "Which word has a different sound at the end from the other words: *hat, mat, fan, cat*?"

If the child passes, say, "That's right" and go to Sample Item 2.

If the child fails, say, "*hat, mat, fan, cat.* The word that has a different ending sound is *fan.*" Go to Sample Item 2.

Sample Item 2
Say, "Let's try another one. Which word has a different ending sound: *doll, hop, pop, top*?"

If the child passes, say, "That's right" and go to Test Item 1.

If the child fails, say, "*doll, hop, pop, top.* The word that has a different ending sound is *doll.*" Repeat Sample Item 2. Say, "Which word has a different ending sound: *doll, hop, pop, top*?"

If the child passes, say, "That's right" and proceed to Test Item 1.

If the child fails, say, "*doll, hop, pop, top.* The word that has a different ending sound is *doll.*" Proceed to Test Item 1.

Test Items
Give Test Items 1 through 8. Say, "Which word has a different ending sound?" Then say the four words. If necessary, repeat the instructions before each item. Do not correct any answers or indicate whether they are correct. Introduce each item with "Here are the next four words."

1. sun run *tub* fun
2. *hen* peg leg beg
3. fin *sit* pin win
4. map cap gap *jam*
5. cot hot *fox* pot
6. fill *pig* hill mill
7. *peel* weed seed feed
8. pack lack *sad* back

Source: Adapted from Bradley (1980) and Stanovich, Cunningham, and Cramer (1984).
From *Assessment of Children: Behavioral, Social, and Clinical Foundations (Fifth Edition)* by Jerome M. Sattler and Robert D. Hoge. Copyright 2006 by Jerome M. Sattler, Publisher, Inc. Permission to photocopy this appendix table is granted to purchasers of this book for personal use only (see copyright page for details).

Table D-5
List of Regular Words, Irregular Words, and Nonsense Words

Regular words		Irregular words		Nonsense words	
Grade 2	Grade 3	Grade 2	Grade 3	Grade 2	Grade 3
up	best	was	glisten	lopeb	fidot
it	nostril	does	pleasure	pilk	peb
am	napkin	learn	prove	sut	ipcrot
crop	rid	one	doubtful	nintred	kaxin
went	scalpel	gone	honest	noxtof	stum
at	spun	lawn	lawn	skep	polt
ran	disc	work	shove	sopog	fisc
hand	drank	among	realm	lin	glin
silk	complex	early	gentle	sifton	cospim
tax	demanded	flood	cough	lemp	lemp
top	piano	there	pigeon	ig	hintred
dog	rustic	right	cupboard	tipik	gix
man	hundred	any	fought	flontel	yentop
pen	colt	sugar	rough	marpi	oxitac
get	custom	nothing	hour	lut	pontflact

Source: Adapted from Freebody and Byrne (1988).
From *Assessment of Children: Behavioral, Social, and Clinical Foundations (Fifth Edition)* by Jerome M. Sattler and Robert D. Hoge. Copyright 2006 by Jerome M. Sattler, Publisher, Inc. Permission to photocopy this appendix table is granted to purchasers of this book for personal use only (see copyright page for details).

**Table D-6
Auditory Analysis Test**

AUDITORY ANALYSIS TEST

Name: _____   Date: _____

Sex: _____   Grade: _____   School: _____

Birthdate: _____   Teacher: _____

Score (number correct): _____

Directions: Show the child the top half of a sheet of 8½ × 11-inch paper on which pictures of a cow and a boy's head are shown side by side. Say: "Say *cowboy*." After the child responds, cover the picture of the boy and say: "Now say it again, but without *boy*." If the response is correct (*cow*), expose the bottom half of the sheet on which drawings of a tooth and a brush are shown side by side. Say: "Say *toothbrush*." After the child responds, cover the picture of the tooth and say: "Say it again, but without *tooth*."

If the child fails either demonstration item, teach the task by repeating the demonstration procedures with the pictures. If the child again fails to make correct responses to both items, discontinue testing.

If both responses are correct, withdraw the picture sheet and proceed with the test. Say: "Say *birthday*." Wait for a response, and then say: "Now say it again, but without *day*." Continue with the test. Always pronounce the specific sound (*not the letter name*) of the item to be omitted. If the child has a speech articulation problem, take this into consideration when you score the response. If the child fails an item, repeat the item. If there is still no response, record a score of 0 and give the next item. *Discontinue after four consecutive scores of 0.*

Circle the items that the child correctly segments; record incorrect responses on the blank line following the item. Note that the correct responses for all items are real words, except for items 26, 30, and 33.

Items

A. cow(boy) _____
B. (tooth)brush _____
   1. birth(day) _____
   2. (car)pet _____
   3. bel(t) _____
   4. (m)an _____
   5. (b)lock _____
   6. to(ne) _____
   7. (s)our _____
   8. (p)ray _____
   9. stea(k) _____
  10. (l)end _____
  11. (s)mile _____
  12. plea(se) _____
  13. (g)ate _____
  14. (c)lip _____
  15. ti(me) _____
  16. (sc)old _____
  17. (b)reak _____
  18. ro(de) _____
  19. (w)ill _____

20. (t)rail _____
21. (sh)rug _____
22. g(l)ow _____
23. cr(e)ate _____
24. (st)rain _____
25. s(m)ell _____
26. Es(ki)mo _____
27. de(s)k _____
28. Ger(ma)ny _____
29. st(r)eam _____
30. auto(mo)bile _____
31. re(pro)duce _____
32. s(m)ack _____
33. phi(lo)sophy _____
34. s(k)in _____
35. lo(ca)tion _____
36. cont(in)ent _____
37. s(w)ing _____
38. car(pen)ter _____
39. c(l)utter _____
40. off(er)ing _____

Source: Adapted from Rosner and Simon (1971).

Table D-7
Yopp-Singer Test of Phoneme Segmentation

YOPP-SINGER TEST OF PHONEME SEGMENTATION

Name: _____   Date: _____

Sex: _____   Grade: _____   School: _____

Birthdate: _____   Teacher: _____

Score (number correct): _____

Directions: "We're going to play a word game. I'm going to say a word, and I want you to break the word apart. Do this by telling me each sound in the word in order. For example, if I say *old*, you should say /o/-/l/-/d/. [Be sure to say the sounds, not the letters, in the word.] Let's try a few together."

Practice items: *ride*, *go*, *man*. Assist the child in segmenting these items as necessary.

Circle the items that the child correctly segments. Record incorrect responses on the blank line following the item.

Items

1. dog _____	12. lay _____
2. keep _____	13. race _____
3. fine _____	14. zoo _____
4. no _____	15. three _____
5. she _____	16. job _____
6. wave _____	17. in _____
7. grew _____	18. ice _____
8. that _____	19. at _____
9. red _____	20. top _____
10. me _____	21. by _____
11. sat _____	22. do _____

Source: Adapted from Yopp (1995).
From *Assessment of Children: Behavioral, Social, and Clinical Foundations (Fifth Edition)* by Jerome M. Sattler and Robert D. Hoge. Copyright 2006 by Jerome M. Sattler, Publisher, Inc. Permission to photocopy this appendix table is granted to purchasers of this book for personal use only (see copyright page for details).

INFORMAL WRITING INVENTORY

Name: _____ School: _____

Sex: _____ Grade: _____ Teacher: _____

Birthdate: _____ Date: _____ Title of assignment: _____

Guidelines

A. Content

1. Development of Ideas—Does the writer have a theme or message to convey? Does the entire composition relate to these basic ideas? Are the ideas well developed?

2. Overall Organization—Are paragraphs and sentences logically ordered? Is there a thesis statement in the first paragraph? Do topic sentences follow thesis statement? Do supporting details follow topic sentences?

3. Comprehensibility—Is the message clear? Is the writing easy to understand? Will the reader have questions? Are gaps present?

4. Paragraph Development—Does each paragraph have a main idea? Do the sentences in the paragraphs relate to each other? Are sentences logically ordered?

5. Sentence Construction—Are all of the sentences complete (absence of fragments)? Does each sentence contain a single idea (absence of run-on sentences)?

6. Types of Sentences—What kinds of sentences are included (compound, complex, simple, declarative, interrogative)? Do sentences contain too few or too many words?

7. Use of Words—Are the words descriptive/vague, complex/simple, appropriate/inappropriate, formal/informal? Are words omitted or parts omitted from or added to words?

8. Length—Is the passage too long or too short? Does the length reflect a reasonable effort?

B. Grammar

9. Subject-Verb Agreement—Do subjects and verbs agree?

10. Verb Tense—Is the correct verb tense used?

11. Pronoun Antecedents—Do pronouns and antecedents agree?

12. Use of Adjectives/Adverbs—Are adjectives and adverbs used properly?

13. Syntax—Is the sentence structure correct (e.g., parallelism, use of modifiers)?

14. Consistency of Tense—Is the tense appropriate and consistent across sentences and paragraphs?

C. Mechanics

15. Capitalization—Are capital letters used appropriately? If not, what types of words need to be capitalized (e.g., proper nouns, first word in a sentence)?

16. Punctuation—Is correct punctuation used? If not, what types of punctuation are needed (e.g., periods, commas, apostrophes)?

17. Spelling—Is the spelling generally correct? What types of spelling problems occurred? Did the writer have problems with difficult or easy words?

18. Handwriting—Is the handwriting generally neat and readable, with adequate spacing and consistent letter size?

Area	Evaluation (check one)				Comments
	Excellent	Adequate	Fair	Poor	
A. Content					
1. Development of Ideas					
2. Overall Organization					
3. Comprehensibility					
4. Paragraph Development					
5. Sentence Construction					
6. Types of Sentences					
7. Use of Words					
8. Length					

(Continued)

Table D-8 (*Continued*)

Area	Excellent	Adequate	Fair	Poor	Comments
B. Grammar					
9. Subject-Verb Agreement					
10. Verb Tense					
11. Pronoun Antecedents					
12. Use of Adjectives/Adverbs					
13. Syntax					
14. Consistency of Tense					
C. Mechanics					
15. Capitalization					
16. Punctuation					
17. Spelling					
18. Handwriting					

Source: Adapted from Billingsley (1988).

DIAGNOSTIC SPELLING TEST

Directions: Give the child a sheet of paper and a pencil with an eraser. Say: "I am going to say some words, and then I want you to spell each one. I will say the word first and then use it in a sentence. Here is the first word." Say the first word in List 1 or List 2, as appropriate; then follow the word with its corresponding sentence. On the blank line following the sentence, record the child's response.

List 1 (grades 2 and 3)			List 2 (grade 4 and higher)		
Word	Illustrative sentence	Response	Word	Illustrative sentence	Response
1. not	He is *not* here.	_____	1. flower	A rose is a *flower*.	_____
2. but	Mary is here, *but* Joe is not.	_____	2. mouth	Open your *mouth*.	_____
3. get	*Get* the wagon, John.	_____	3. shoot	John wants to *shoot* his toy gun.	_____
4. sit	*Sit* down, please.	_____	4. stood	We *stood* under the roof.	_____
5. man	Father is a tall *man*.	_____	5. while	We sang *while* we marched.	_____
6. boat	We sailed our *boat* on the lake.	_____	6. third	We are in the *third* grade.	_____
7. train	Tom has a new toy *train*.	_____	7. each	*Each* child has a pencil.	_____
8. time	It is *time* to come home.	_____	8. class	Our *class* is reading.	_____
9. like	We *like* ice cream.	_____	9. jump	We like to *jump* rope.	_____
10. found	We *found* our lost ball.	_____	10. jumps	Mary *jumps* rope.	_____
11. down	Do not fall *down*.	_____	11. jumped	We *jumped* rope yesterday.	_____
12. soon	Our teacher will *soon* be here.	_____	12. jumping	The girls are *jumping* rope now.	_____
13. good	He is a *good* boy.	_____	13. hit	*Hit* the ball hard.	_____
14. very	We are *very* happy to be here.	_____	14. hitting	John is *hitting* the ball.	_____
15. happy	Jane is a *happy* girl.	_____	15. bite	Our dog does not *bite*.	_____
16. kept	We *kept* our shoes dry.	_____	16. biting	The dog is *biting* on the bone.	_____
17. come	*Come* to our party.	_____	17. study	*Study* your lesson.	_____
18. what	*What* is your name?	_____	18. studies	He *studies* each day.	_____
19. those	*Those* are our toys.	_____	19. dark	The sky is *dark* and cloudy.	_____
20. show	*Show* us the way.	_____	20. darker	This color is *darker* than that one.	_____
21. much	I feel *much* better.	_____	21. darkest	This color is the *darkest* of three.	_____
22. sing	We will *sing* a new song.	_____	22. afternoon	We may play this *afternoon*.	_____
23. will	Who *will* help us?	_____	23. grandmother	Our *grandmother* will visit us.	_____
24. doll	Make a dress for the *doll*.	_____	24. can't	We *can't* go with you.	_____
25. after	We play *after* school.	_____	25. doesn't	Mary *doesn't* like to play.	_____
26. sister	My *sister* is older than I.	_____	26. night	We read to Mother last *night*.	_____
27. toy	I have a new *toy* train.	_____	27. brought	Joe *brought* his lunch to school.	_____
28. say	*Say* your name clearly.	_____	28. apple	An *apple* fell from the tree.	_____
29. little	Tom is a *little* boy.	_____	29. again	We must come back *again*.	_____
30. one	I have only *one* book.	_____	30. laugh	Do not *laugh* at other children.	_____
31. would	*Would* you come with us?	_____	31. because	We cannot play *because* of the rain.	_____
32. pretty	She is a *pretty* girl.	_____	32. through	We ran *through* the yard.	_____

Note: See Table D-10 for the elements tested in the Diagnostic Spelling Test.

Source: Reprinted and adapted from *Teacher's Guide for Remedial Reading* by William Kottmeyer, © 1959, with permission of The McGraw-Hill Companies, pp. 88–89.

Table D-10
Elements Tested in the Diagnostic Spelling Test

List 1 (grades 2 and 3)		List 2 (grade 4 and higher)	
Word	Element tested	Word	Element tested
1. not 2. but 3. get 4. sit 5. man	Short vowels	1. flower 2. mouth	ow-ou spellings of ou sound, er ending, th spelling
6. boat 7. train	Two vowels together	3. shoot 4. stood	Long and short oo, sh spelling
8. time 9. like	Vowel-consonant-e	5. while	wh spelling, vowel-consonant
10. found 11. down	ow-ou spelling of ou sound	6. third	th spelling, vowel before r
12. soon 13. good	Long and short oo	7. each	ch spelling, two vowels together
14. very 15. happy	Final y as short i	8. class	Double final consonant, c spelling of k sound
16. kept 17. come	c and k spellings of the k sound	9. jump 10. jumps 11. jumped 12. jumping	Addition of s, ed, ing; j spelling of soft g sound
18. what 19. those 20. show 21. much 22. sing	wh, th, sh, ch, and ng spellings, ow spelling of long o	13. hit 14. hitting	Doubling final consonant before ing
23. will 24. doll	Doubled final consonant	15. bite 16. biting	Dropping final e before ing
25. after 26. sister	er spelling	17. study 18. studies	Changing final y to i before ending
27. toy	oy spelling of oi sound	19. dark 20. darker 21. darkest	er, est endings
28. say	ay spelling of long a sound	22. afternoon 23. grandmother	Compound words
29. little	le ending	24. can't 25. doesn't	Contractions
30. one 31. would 32. pretty	Nonphonetic spellings	26. night 27. brought	Silent gh
		28. apple	le ending
		29. again 30. laugh 31. because 32. through	Nonphonetic spellings

Note. See Table D-9 for the list of sentences.
Source: Reprinted and adapted from *Teacher's Guide for Remedial Reading* by William Kottmeyer, © 1959, with permission of The McGraw-Hill Companies, p. 90.
From *Assessment of Children: Behavioral, Social, and Clinical Foundations (Fifth Edition)* by Jerome M. Sattler and Robert D. Hoge. Copyright 2006 by Jerome M. Sattler, Publisher, Inc. Permission to photocopy this appendix table is granted to purchasers of this book for personal use only (see copyright page for details).

Table D-11
Informal Assessment of Arithmetic

Number System
Say: "I am going to say some numbers, and I want you to tell me what number comes next. Here is the first one." Introduce the next four items with "Here is the next one."

1. 1, 2, 3, 4, 5,
2. 2, 4, 6, 8,
3. 1, 5, 9, 13,
4. 63, 65, 67,
5. 100, 200, 300,

Counting
6. Say: "Count by tens starting with 10 and stop when I tell you. Go ahead; count by tens starting with 10." Stop the child after he or she says the fifth number.

7. Say: "Count by tens starting with 14 and stop when I tell you. Go ahead; count by tens starting with 14." Stop the child after he or she says the fifth number.

Writing Numbers from Oral Presentation
Say: "Write these numbers using this pencil. Here is the first number." Introduce the next four items with "Here is the next number." Give the child a blank sheet of paper on which to write the numbers.

8. 39
9. 400
10. 658
11. 303
12. 550

Reading Numbers
Say: "I am going to show you some numbers. I want you to tell me what the numbers are. Here is the first one." Make five 3 × 5 cards, one for each number. Show each card to the child.

13. 18
14. 40
15. 300
16. 509
17. 842

Addition
Say: "I would like you to do the following problems. Use this pencil to write your answers. Go ahead." Point to problems 18 to 25 or reproduce them on a separate piece of paper.

18. 4
    +45

19. 6
    +2

20. 8
    +9

21. 6
    +7

22. 17
    +22

23. 23
    + 3

24. 47
    +36

25. 439
    +596

Subtraction
Say: "Now, I would like you to do the following problems. Use this pencil to write your answers. Go ahead." Point to problems 26 to 35 or reproduce them on a separate piece of paper.

26. 6
    −5

27. 9
    −2

28. 16
    − 8

29. 14
    − 3

30. 34
    −13

31. 46
    −12

32. 87
    −49

33. 65
    −17

34. 504
    −383

35. 300
    −177

Multiplication
Say: "Now, I would like you to do the following problems. Use this pencil to write your answers. Go ahead." Point to problems 36 to 43 or reproduce them on a separate piece of paper.

36. 6
    ×4

37. 9
    ×0

38. 4
    ×1

39. 7
    ×6

40. 43
    × 2

41. 28
    × 5

42. 56
    ×22

43. 19
    ×10

Division
Say: "Now, I would like you to do the following problems. Use this pencil to write your answers. Go ahead." Point to problems 44 to 50 or reproduce them on a separate piece of paper.

44. 8 ÷ 4
45. 9 ÷ 3
46. 54 ÷ 6
47. 100 ÷ 2
48. 64 ÷ 7
49. 109 ÷ 5
50. 78 ÷ 46

Table D-12
Stories for Meaningful Memory Recall

Directions: Say: "I am going to read a story. Listen carefully. When I am through, tell me the story that I read to you." Give the child 1 point for each unit recalled correctly; exact wording or order is not important. Also consider how the child organizes various elements in the story, what particular features the child recalls in the story, and what features the child distorts in the story. Do not read the numbers. They represent each important element in the story.

STORIES

Bozo Story

1) Once there were three 2) thieves 3) named 4) Bozo, 5) Tommy, and 6) Frank. 7) Bozo 8) was their leader. 9) They were good 10) friends and 11) went everywhere 12) together. 13) One night the 14) three of them 15) sneaked 16) through 17) a window 18) into 19) a house 20) on a hill. 21) There were trees 22) around the house. 23) Suddenly a 24) light 25) came on 26) in another 27) room. 28) They quickly 29) climbed 30) out 31) of the window. 32) Bozo and 33) Tommy 34) ran 35) down 36) the hill. 37) The other thief 38) climbed 39) a tree. 40) When a man 41) came 42) to the door of the house, 43) he could see 44) no one.

Airplane Story

1) The airplane 2) was coming in 3) for a landing. 4) It was 5) full 6) of people. 7) Suddenly, 8) the airplane 9) leaned 10) far to 11) the left 12) side. 13) All of the passengers 14) were afraid. 15) The pilot 16) did not know 17) what was wrong 18) so he landed the plane 19) very carefully. 20) As he landed, 21) one wing of the plane 22) scraped 23) the ground. 24) The passengers 25) and the pilot 26) climbed out 27) and looked 28) at the plane. 29) To their surprise, 30) a large 31) group 32) of birds 33) was sitting 34) on the wing of the plane.

Linda Story

1) Linda 2) was playing 3) with her new 4) doll 5) in front 6) of her house. 7) Suddenly, 8) she heard 9) a strange 10) sound 11) coming from under 12) the porch. 13) It was the flapping 14) of wings. 15) Linda ran 16) inside 17) the house and 18) grabbed 19) a shoe 20) box 21) from the closet. 22) She found 23) some sheets 24) of paper 25) and cut 26) the paper 27) into pieces 28) and put them 29) in the box. Linda 30) gently 31) picked up 32) the helpless 33) animal 34) and took it 35) with her. 36) Her teacher 37) knew what to do.

Source: Reprinted with permission of E. H. Bacon and D. C. Rubin, unpublished material. These stories were used in research by Bacon and Rubin (1983).

Table D-13
Questions to Help You Learn About a Child's Attitude Toward Reading and Writing

ATTITUDE TOWARD READING AND WRITING

Name: _____   Date: _____

Sex: _____   Grade: _____   School: _____

Birthdate: _____   Teacher: _____

Reading

1. How did you learn to read? _____

2. Who helped you learn to read? _____

3. What did they do to help you? _____

4. Who is the best reader you know? _____

5. Why do you think he or she is the best? _____

6. Are you a good reader? _____

7. How do you know? _____

8. Do you like to read? _____

9. When do you read? _____

10. What is your favorite book? _____

11. What is the last book you read? _____

12. When did you read it? _____

13. When you are reading alone and you come to a word you don't know, what do you do? _____

14. Why do you read? _____

15. Tell me three words that describe how you feel about reading. _____

16. How do you decide what you will read? _____

17. Who is your favorite author? _____

18. Do you like to be read to? _____

19. How many books have you read over the past 6 months? _____

Writing

20. Tell me three words that describe how you feel about writing. _____

21. How did you learn to write? _____

22. Why do you write? _____

23. Are you a good writer? _____

24. What makes a good writer? _____

25. When do you write? _____

26. What do you like to write about? _____

27. How much have you written over the past 6 months? _____

28. (If appropriate) Tell me about what you have written. _____

29. When you have a writing assignment, how do you usually go about completing it? _____

(Continued)

Table D-13 (*Continued*)

30. Is there anything else that you do? _____

31. Do you like to write? _____

32. Tell me about that. _____

33. How good is your writing? _____

34. Tell me about that. _____

35. What are some things you think about before you write? _____

36. What are some things you do before you write? _____

37. Once you've written your assignment, what do you usually do? _____

38. Some writers make an outline before they begin writing. Do you do that? _____

39. What do you do after your first draft is completed? _____

40. (If needed) Do you edit the first draft? _____

41. (If yes) Tell me what you do when you edit it. _____

Source: Adapted from Deshler, Ellis, and Lenz (1996), Farnan and Kelly (1991), and Mather and Gregg (2003).

Table D-14
Sentence Completion Technique for Children Who May Have Learning Problems

SENTENCE COMPLETION TECHNIQUE FOR CHILDREN WHO MAY HAVE LEARNING PROBLEMS

Name: _____   Date: _____

Sex: _____   Grade: _____   School: _____

Birthdate: _____   Teacher: _____

Directions: Say: "I am going to start a sentence. Then I'd like you to finish it any way you want. Here is an example. If I say, 'When I am tired . . . ,' you can say, 'I go to bed,' 'I take a nap,' 'I sit down,' or anything else that you can think of. OK? Let's try the first one."

Reading

1. When reading in class, I become nervous if_____.

2. Reading is easiest when_____.

3. Jobs that require reading are _____.

4. My favorite reading activity is _____.

5. If I couldn't read,_____.

6. My favorite place to read is_____.

7. If I could do any type of reading, I would _____.

8. Reading reminds me of _____.

9. The worst place to read is _____.

10. Jobs that do not require reading are_____.

11. If you asked people what they thought of reading, most would say _____.

12. I would be less nervous about reading if _____.

13. The person with whom I would like to read is_____.

Mathematics

14. When doing mathematics in class, I become nervous if_____.

15. Mathematics is easiest when _____.

16. Jobs that require mathematics are _____.

17. My favorite mathematics activity is _____.

18. If I couldn't do mathematics,_____.

19. My favorite place to do mathematics is _____.

20. If I could do any type of mathematics, I would _____.

21. Mathematics reminds me of _____.

22. The worst place to do mathematics is _____.

23. Jobs that do not require mathematics are _____.

24. If you asked people what they thought of mathematics, most would say_____.

25. I would be less nervous about mathematics if _____.

26. The person with whom I would like to do mathematics is_____.

(Continued)

Table D-14 (*Continued*)

Spelling

27. When doing spelling in class, I become nervous if _____.

28. Spelling is easiest when _____.

29. Jobs that require spelling are _____.

30. My favorite spelling activity is _____.

31. If I couldn't spell, _____.

32. My favorite place to do spelling is _____.

33. If I could do any type of spelling, I would _____.

34. Spelling reminds me of _____.

35. The worst place to do spelling is _____.

36. Jobs that do not require spelling are _____.

37. If you asked people what they thought of spelling, most would say _____.

38. I would be less nervous about spelling if _____.

39. The person with whom I would like to do spelling is _____.

Writing

40. When doing writing in class, I become nervous if _____.

41. Writing is easiest when _____.

42. Jobs that require writing are _____.

43. My favorite writing activity is _____.

44. If I couldn't write, _____.

45. My favorite place to do writing is _____.

46. If I could do any type of writing, I would _____.

47. Writing reminds me of _____.

48. The worst place to do writing is _____.

49. Jobs that do not require writing are _____.

50. If you asked people what they thought of writing, most would say _____.

51. I would be less nervous about writing if _____.

52. The person with whom I would like to do writing is _____.

General

53. The best time for me to do homework is _____.

54. When I start my homework, I _____.

55. At home, I study _____.

56. When I finish my homework, I _____.

57. My favorite subject is _____.

58. My least favorite subject is _____.

59. I think school is _____.

Source: Adapted from Giordano (1987).

Table D-15
Reading Study Skills Questionnaire

READING STUDY SKILLS QUESTIONNAIRE

Name: _____   Class: _____

Date: _____   Teacher's name: _____

School: _____

Directions: Read each question and put a check mark in the box for Y (Yes), N (No), or DK (Don't Know).
Try to answer each question. Thank you.

	Check one		
	Yes	No	Don't Know
Part 1. *When I have a reading assignment, I usually . . .*			
1. preview the material by reading the heading and one or two sentences.	☐ Y	☐ N	☐ DK
2. think about what I already know about this topic.	☐ Y	☐ N	☐ DK
3. think about how much time it might take me to complete it.	☐ Y	☐ N	☐ DK
4. think about how much of the assignment I want to read on the first day.	☐ Y	☐ N	☐ DK
5. think about what the rest of the material might be about after I read the first few sentences.	☐ Y	☐ N	☐ DK
6. think about what might be easy to learn as I look it over.	☐ Y	☐ N	☐ DK
7. think about what might be difficult to learn as I look it over.	☐ Y	☐ N	☐ DK
8. ask myself who the main characters in the story are as I read it.	☐ Y	☐ N	☐ DK
9. ask myself what a paragraph is about after I have read the paragraph.	☐ Y	☐ N	☐ DK
10. think about how what I am reading relates to what I already know about the topic.	☐ Y	☐ N	☐ DK
Part 2. *When I am reading an assignment, I usually . . .*			
11. use a dictionary (either a book or a dictionary on a computer) to look up words that I don't know.	☐ Y	☐ N	☐ DK
12. know when I need to give more attention to some parts of the assignment than to other parts.	☐ Y	☐ N	☐ DK
13. get someone to help me with the assignment when I am having difficulty with it.	☐ Y	☐ N	☐ DK
14. wonder how each paragraph fits in with the paragraphs that came before and after it.	☐ Y	☐ N	☐ DK
Part 3. *After I finish a reading assignment, I usually . . .*			
15. think about whether it turned out the way I thought it would.	☐ Y	☐ N	☐ DK
16. ask myself whether the material made sense.	☐ Y	☐ N	☐ DK
17. think about whether I need to reread parts of it.	☐ Y	☐ N	☐ DK
18. think about how the people in the story would look if they were real.	☐ Y	☐ N	☐ DK
19. try to summarize what I read.	☐ Y	☐ N	☐ DK
20. think about what I have learned.	☐ Y	☐ N	☐ DK
21. think about how what I learned fits in with other information I know about the topic.	☐ Y	☐ N	☐ DK

Table D-16
Self-Evaluation of Note-Taking Ability

SELF-EVALUATION OF NOTE-TAKING ABILITY

Name: _____   Class: _____

Date: _____   Teacher's name: _____

School: _____

Directions: Use the following rating scale to evaluate your ability to take notes:

1 I don't do this very well.
2 I'm barely OK at this.
3 I'm OK at this.
4 I do this well.
5 I do this very well.

Circle one number for each item. Thank you.

When I take notes, I usually . . .	Circle one				
1. write fast enough.	1	2	3	4	5
2. pay attention.	1	2	3	4	5
3. am able to make sense of the notes after the lecture.	1	2	3	4	5
4. know what information is important to write down.	1	2	3	4	5
5. understand what the teacher is saying.	1	2	3	4	5
6. see the overheads clearly.	1	2	3	4	5
7. see the notes that the teacher writes on the board clearly.	1	2	3	4	5
8. hear the teacher clearly.	1	2	3	4	5
9. use my notes to study for tests.	1	2	3	4	5
10. find my notes helpful when I study.	1	2	3	4	5

Source: Adapted from Deshler, Ellis, and Lenz (1996).

Appendix E

TABLES FOR AUTISM SPECTRUM DISORDERS

Table E-1
Observation Form for Recording Symptoms That May Reflect Autistic Disorder and Positive Behaviors

OBSERVATION FORM FOR RECORDING SYMPTOMS THAT MAY REFLECT AUTISTIC DISORDER AND POSITIVE BEHAVIORS

Name: _____   Examiner's name: _____

Age: _____   Grade: _____   School: _____   Birthdate: _____

Direction: Place an X in a box to indicate that the behavior was observed during that period. For "Other," write in the name of the behavior.

	Period									Total
Sensory Modulation	1	2	3	4	5	6	7	8	9	
1. Bangs ear										
2. Grinds teeth										
3. Looks at hands										
4. Stares										
5. Rubs surfaces										
6. Sniffs objects										
7. Sniffs hands										
8. Switches light on and off										
9. Locks and unlocks door										
10. Spins objects for a long time										
11. Does not respond to name										
12. Other:										
13. Other:										
Motility										
1. Flaps hands										
2. Turns head often										
3. Flicks or wiggles finger										
4. Grimaces										
5. Whirls or spins										
6. Walks on toes										
7. Darts or lunges										
8. Engages in peculiar postures										
9. Rocks body										
10. Jumps repetitively										
11. Runs aimlessly										
12. Bangs head										
13. Taps back of hand often										
14. Other:										
15. Other:										
General Behavior										
1. Mouths objects										
2. Claps hands										
3. Mouths hands										
4. Lacks appropriate facial expressions										
5. Resists change										
6. Has tantrums										
7. Displays self-injurious behavior										
8. Displays rigidity										
9. Insists on sameness										
10. Over- or underreactive to sensory input										
11. Has difficulty processing sensory information										
12. Other:										
13. Other:										

Table E-1 (*Continued*)

Relation to Examiner	1	2	3	4	5	6	7	8	9	Total
						Period				
1. Makes no eye contact										
2. Does not smile										
3. Does not respond to his or her name when called										
4. Turns face away when called										
5. Clings in an infantile way										
6. Insists on being held										
7. Makes inappropriate attempts at contact										
8. Ignores examiner										
9. Asks the same questions repeatedly										
10. Does not share a toy or activity										
11. Other:										
12. Other:										
Relation to Toys										
1. Uses toys inappropriately										
2. Uses toys ritualistically										
3. Spins toys inappropriately										
4. Orders and reorders toys continuously										
5. Lets toys fall out of hand										
6. Throws toys inappropriately										
7. Ignores toys										
8. Uses toys in a restricted manner with few combinations and in few constructive ways										
9. Lines toys up obsessively										
10. Other:										
11. Other:										
Language										
1. Is mute										
2. Babbles										
3. Shouts										
4. Shows immediate echolalia										
5. Shows delayed echolalia										
6. Reverses pronouns										
7. Uses words in a peculiar fashion										
8. Has difficulty initiating or sustaining conversation										
9. Gives tangential details when answering questions										
10. Other:										
11. Other:										
Positive Behavior										
1. Shows examiner a toy										
2. Asks examiner to play with him or her										
3. Asks examiner questions										
4. Asks examiner for help										
5. Engages in pretend play[a]										
6. Takes turns rolling or throwing the ball										
7. Other:										
8. Other:										

[a]Examples are pretending to talk on the phone, fly the helicopter, cook, or feed the doll.
Source: Adapted from Adrien et al. (1987) and Filipek et al. (1999).

Table E-2
Childhood Autism Rating Scale (CARS)

Scale	Rating			
	1 *Age appropriate*	*2* *Mildly abnormal*	*3* *Moderately abnormal*	*4* *Severely abnormal*
I. Relationships with people	Age-appropriate degrees of shyness, guardedness, negativism	Some lack of eye contact; some negativism or avoidance; excessive shyness; some lack of responsiveness to the examiner	Considerable aloofness; intensive intrusion may be necessary to get a response; contact is not normally initiated by child	Intense aloofness, avoidance, obliviousness; child seldom responds to examiner; only the most intensive intervention produces a response
II. Imitation (verbal and physical)	Age-appropriate imitation (both verbal and physical)	Child imitates most of the time; occasionally prodding may be required or imitation may be delayed	Child imitates only part of the time; great persistence is required on the part of the examiner	Child seldom, if ever, imitates either verbally or physically
III. Affect	Age- and situation-appropriate affective responses—child shows pleasure, displeasure, and interest through changes in facial expression, posture, and manner	Some lack of appropriate responsiveness to changes in affective stimuli; affect may be somewhat inhibited or excessive	Definite signs of inappropriate affect; reactions are quite inhibited or excessive or are often unrelated to the stimulus	Extremely rigid perseveration of affect; responses are seldom appropriate to the situation and are extremely resistant to modification by the examiner
IV. Use of body	Age-appropriate use and awareness of body	Minimal peculiarities in body use and awareness—some stereotyped movements, clumsiness, and lack of coordination	Moderate signs of dysfunction—peculiar finger or body posturing, examination of body, self-directed aggression, rocking, spinning, finger-wiggling, toe-walking	Extreme or pervasive occurrence of those functions listed in previous column
V. Relation to objects	Age-appropriate interest in, use of, and exploration of objects	Mild lack of interest in materials or mildly age-inappropriate use of materials—infantile mouthing of objects, banging of materials, fascination with materials that squeak, turning lights on and off	Significant lack of interest in most objects or peculiar and obvious preoccupation with repetitive use of objects—e.g., picking at objects with fingernails, spinning wheels, becoming fascinated with one small part	Severely inappropriate interest in, use of, and exploration of objects—extreme or pervasive occurrence of those functions listed in previous column; child is very difficult to distract
VI. Adaptation to environmental change	Age-appropriate responses to change	Some evidence of resistance to environmental changes—staying with an object or activity or persisting in same response pattern; child can be distracted	Active resistance to change in activities, with signs of irritability and frustration; child is difficult to distract when intervention is attempted	Severe reactions to change that are extremely resistant to modification; child may engage in a tantrum if change is insisted upon
VII. Visual responsiveness	Age-appropriate visual responses used in an integrated way with other sensory systems	Child must be reminded occasionally to look at materials; some preoccupation with mirror image; some avoidance of eye contact; some staring into space; some fascination with lights	Child must be reminded frequently to look at what he or she is doing, likes to look at shiny objects, makes little eye contact even when forced, looks "through" people, frequently stares into space	Pervasive visual avoidance of objects and people; bizarre use of visual cues

	Rating			
Scale	1 Age appropriate	2 Mildly abnormal	3 Moderately abnormal	4 Severely abnormal
VIII. Auditory responsiveness	Age-appropriate auditory responses used in an integrated way with other sensory systems	Some lack of response to auditory stimuli or to particular sounds; responses may be delayed; stimuli may occasionally have to be repeated; child is hypersensitive to or distracted by extraneous noises	Inconsistent responses to auditory stimuli; stimuli may have to be repeated several times before child responds; child is hypersensitive to certain sounds (e.g., very easily startled, covers ears)	Pervasive auditory avoidance, regardless of type of stimulus, or extreme hypersensitivity
IX. Tactile and olfactory	Normal response to pain, appropriate to intensity; normal tactile and olfactory exploration, but not to the exclusion of other forms of exploration	Some lack of appropriate response to pain or evidence of mild preoccupation with tactile exploration, smelling, tasting, etc.; some infantile mouthing of objects	Moderate lack of appropriate response to pain or evidence of moderate preoccupation with tactile exploration, smelling, tasting, etc.	Excessive preoccupation with tactile exploration (mouthing, licking, feeling, or rubbing) for sensory rather than functional experience; child may either ignore pain or grossly overreact to it
X. Anxiety reaction	Age- and situation-appropriate reactions—reactions are not prolonged	Mild anxiety reactions	Moderate anxiety reactions	Severe anxiety reactions—child may not settle down during the entire session or may be obviously fearful, withdrawn, etc.
XI. Verbal communication	Age-appropriate speech	Overall retardation of speech; most speech is meaningful, but it may include remnants of echolalia	Absence of speech or a mixture of some meaningful speech with some inappropriate speech (e.g., echolalia, jargon)	Severely abnormal speech; virtual absence of intelligible words or peculiar and bizarre use of more recognizable language
XII. Nonverbal communication	Age-appropriate nonverbal communication	Overall retardation of nonverbal communication; communication may consist of simple or vague responses, such as pointing to or reaching for a desired item	Absence of nonverbal communication—child does not use or respond to nonverbal communication	Peculiar, bizarre, and generally incomprehensible nonverbal communication
XIII. Activity level (motility patterns)	Normal activity level—child is neither hyperactive nor hypoactive	Child is mildly restless or is somewhat slow to move about, but generally can be controlled; activity level interferes only slightly with performance	Child is quite active and hard to restrain, with a driven quality to activity, or quite inactive and slow-moving; examiner must either exert control frequently or exert a great effort to get a response	Extremely abnormal activity level—child is either driven or apathetic; child is very difficult to manage or to get to respond to anything; almost constant control by an adult is required
XIV. Intellectual functioning	Normal intellectual functioning—no evidence of retardation	Mildly abnormal intellectual functioning—skills appear fairly evenly retarded across all assessed areas	Moderately abnormal intellectual functioning—some skills appear retarded and others are at or very near age level (hints of potential)	Severely abnormal intellectual functioning—some skills appear retarded and others are above age level or are unusual
XV. General impression	No autism	Minimal or mild signs of autism	Moderate signs of autism	Maximum or extreme signs of autism

Source: This table is a condensed and modified tabular presentation of the Childhood Autism Rating Scale, which is described in the unpublished appendix that accompanies Schopler et al. (1980). See Schopler et al. (1993) for a more current version of the CARS. Permission to reprint this condensed version of the CARS was given by E. Schopler.

Table E-3
Modified Checklist for Autism in Toddlers (M-CHAT)

MODIFIED CHECKLIST FOR AUTISM IN TODDLERS

Child's name: _____   Parent's name: _____

Child's age: _____   Date: _____

Directions: Please fill out the following checklist about how your child **usually** is. Please try to answer every question. If the behavior is rare (for example, you've seen it once or twice), please answer as if the child did not do it by checking N ("No"). If the behavior is not rare, please check Y ("Yes").

Behavior	*Check one*
1. Does your child enjoy being swung or bounced on your knee?	☐ Y ☐ N
2. Does your child take an interest in other children?	☐ Y ☐ N
3. Does your child like climbing on things, such as stairs?	☐ Y ☐ N
4. Does your child enjoy playing peek-a-boo or hide-and-seek?	☐ Y ☐ N
5. Does your child sometimes pretend, for example, to talk on the phone or take care of dolls, or pretend other things?	☐ Y ☐ N
6. Does your child sometimes use his [her] index finger to point, to ask for something?	☐ Y ☐ N
7. Does your child sometimes use his [her] index finger to point, to indicate interest in something?	☐ Y ☐ N
8. Can your child play properly with small toys—such as cars or bricks—without just mouthing, fiddling, or dropping them?	☐ Y ☐ N
9. Does your child sometimes bring objects over to you to show you something?	☐ Y ☐ N
10. Does your child look you in the eye for more than a second or two?	☐ Y ☐ N
11. Does your child sometimes seem oversensitive to noise (for example, plugging ears)?	☐ Y ☐ N
12. Does your child smile in response to your face or your smile?	☐ Y ☐ N
13. Does your child imitate you (for example, if you make a face, will your child imitate it)?	☐ Y ☐ N
14. Does your child respond to his [her] name when you call?	☐ Y ☐ N
15. If you point to a toy across the room, does your child look at it?	☐ Y ☐ N
16. Does your child walk?	☐ Y ☐ N
17. Does your child look at things you are looking at?	☐ Y ☐ N
18. Does your child make unusual finger movements near his [her] face?	☐ Y ☐ N
19. Does your child try to attract your attention to his [her] own activity?	☐ Y ☐ N
20. Have you ever wondered if your child is deaf?	☐ Y ☐ N
21. Does your child understand what people say?	☐ Y ☐ N
22. Does your child sometimes stare at nothing or wander with no purpose?	☐ Y ☐ N
23. Does your child look at your face to check your reaction when faced with something unfamiliar?	☐ Y ☐ N

Source: Adapted from Robins et al. (2001).
From *Assessment of Children: Behavioral, Social, and Clinical Foundations (Fifth Edition)* by Jerome M. Sattler and Robert D. Hoge. Copyright 2006 by Jerome M. Sattler, Publisher, Inc. Permission to photocopy this appendix table is granted to purchasers of this book for personal use only (see copyright page for details).

AUTISTIC DISORDER QUESTIONNAIRE

Child's name: _____ Parent's name: _____

Age: _____ Grade: _____ School: _____ Date: _____

Directions: Please read each item and check either Y ("Yes") or N ("No"). If you check "Yes," please answer the questions in the last two columns for that item. Be sure to indicate whether you are using years or months for your answers.

Behavior	*Check one*	*How old was the child when you first noticed the behavior?*	*How long has the behavior persisted?*
1. Makes little eye contact when talking to others	☐ Y ☐ N		
2. Did not wave bye-bye as an infant	☐ Y ☐ N		
3. Has difficulty making friends	☐ Y ☐ N		
4. Is not interested in making friends	☐ Y ☐ N		
5. Does not spontaneously share experiences with other people	☐ Y ☐ N		
6. Prefers to play alone rather than with other children	☐ Y ☐ N		
7. Ignores people who are trying to interact with him or her or does not participate in cooperative play	☐ Y ☐ N		
8. Does not seem to understand how others are feeling or seems to live in a world of his or her own	☐ Y ☐ N		
9. Did not babble	☐ Y ☐ N		
10. Does not speak	☐ Y ☐ N		
11. Speaks, but has difficulty starting a conversation with people	☐ Y ☐ N		
12. Speaks, but has difficulty taking turns speaking	☐ Y ☐ N		
13. Has peculiar patterns of speech (such as odd tone or volume), repeats other people's phrases over and over again, or speaks in a repetitive and stereotyped way	☐ Y ☐ N		
14. Speaks, but confuses the word "I" with the word "he" or "she" or makes up new words that do not make sense	☐ Y ☐ N		
15. Does not engage in imaginative play or use toys in pretend play	☐ Y ☐ N		
16. Plays with toys in a rigid way	☐ Y ☐ N		
17. Has strong attachments to unusual objects (such as sticks or pieces of paper) rather than to teddy bears or dolls	☐ Y ☐ N		
18. Has a narrow and intense focus on a particular topic (for example, train schedules) or skill (for example, memorizing phone numbers)	☐ Y ☐ N		
19. Is preoccupied with things being done in a certain way (for example, insists on drinking from the same cup or plays with toys in the same way each time) and becomes upset if changes are made in his or her daily routines	☐ Y ☐ N		
20. Becomes upset if things don't look right (such as a stain on a table cloth), if something is out of place, or if there is a change in the way things are arranged or done	☐ Y ☐ N		
21. Does the same thing over and over again with his or her body (such as rocking, clapping hands, flapping arms, running aimlessly, walking on toes, or doing other odd movements)	☐ Y ☐ N		
22. Does the same thing over and over again with objects (such as opening and closing doors, flipping the tops of trash cans, turning a light switch on and off, flicking strings, transferring water from one container to another, or spinning objects)	☐ Y ☐ N		
23. Is overly interested in looking at small objects or parts of objects	☐ Y ☐ N		
24. Is preoccupied with parts of objects	☐ Y ☐ N		

Table E-5
Checklist of Possible Signs of an Autism Spectrum Disorder Obtained from the Case History

CHECKLIST OF POSSIBLE SIGNS OF AN AUTISM SPECTRUM DISORDER OBTAINED FROM THE CASE HISTORY

Child's name: _____   Parent's name: _____

Age: _____ Grade: _____ School: _____   Date: _____

Social Interaction	Check one
1. Child does not smile socially.	☐ Y ☐ N
2. Child is not interested in being held.	☐ Y ☐ N
3. Child is not interested in playing peek-a-boo games.	☐ Y ☐ N
4. Child prefers to play alone.	☐ Y ☐ N
5. Child fails to follow mother around.	☐ Y ☐ N
6. Child has an expressionless face.	☐ Y ☐ N
7. Child has poor eye contact.	☐ Y ☐ N
8. Child is in his or her own world.	☐ Y ☐ N
9. Child tunes parents out.	☐ Y ☐ N
10. Child is not interested in other children.	☐ Y ☐ N
11. Child has lost social skills.	☐ Y ☐ N

Communication	Check one
1. Child does not respond to his or her name.	☐ Y ☐ N
2. Child cannot tell parent what he or she wants.	☐ Y ☐ N
3. Child's language is delayed.	☐ Y ☐ N
4. Child does not follow directions.	☐ Y ☐ N
5. Child does not respond to sounds or names, and deafness is suspected.	☐ Y ☐ N
6. Child seems to hear sometimes but not at other times.	☐ Y ☐ N
7. Child does not point or wave bye-bye.	☐ Y ☐ N
8. Child used to say a few words but does not now.	☐ Y ☐ N
9. Child did not babble by 12 months.	☐ Y ☐ N
10. Child did not gesture (e.g., pointing, waving bye-bye) by 12 months.	☐ Y ☐ N
11. Child had no single words by 16 months.	☐ Y ☐ N
12. Child had no 2-word spontaneous phrases (in contrast to echolalic phrases) by 24 months.	☐ Y ☐ N
13. Child displays immediate echolalia.	☐ Y ☐ N
14. Child displays delayed echolalia.	☐ Y ☐ N
15. Child has stereotyped and repetitive use of language or idiosyncratic language.	☐ Y ☐ N
16. Child has odd or unusual voice.	☐ Y ☐ N
17. Child's language is too formal or "robotlike."	☐ Y ☐ N
18. Child makes naïve and embarrassing remarks.	☐ Y ☐ N

Communication (*Continued*)	Check one
19. Child fails to make language fit social contexts.	☐ Y ☐ N
20. Child has a literal understanding of ambiguous or metaphorical language.	☐ Y ☐ N

Restricted Repertoire	Check one
1. Child has tantrums.	☐ Y ☐ N
2. Child is hyperactive.	☐ Y ☐ N
3. Child is uncooperative.	☐ Y ☐ N
4. Child is oppositional.	☐ Y ☐ N
5. Child does not know how to play with toys.	☐ Y ☐ N
6. Child gets stuck on things over and over.	☐ Y ☐ N
7. Child toe-walks.	☐ Y ☐ N
8. Child has unusual attachments to objects.	☐ Y ☐ N
9. Child lines things up obsessively.	☐ Y ☐ N
10. Child has odd movement patterns.	☐ Y ☐ N
11. Child is hypersensitive to taste.	☐ Y ☐ N
12. Child is hyposenstive to cold or pain.	☐ Y ☐ N
13. Child is oversensitive to certain textures or sounds.	☐ Y ☐ N

Physiological Concerns	Check one
1. Child shows loss of skills.	☐ Y ☐ N
2. Child has poor muscle tone.	☐ Y ☐ N
3. Child has frequent ear infections.	☐ Y ☐ N
4. Child has difficulty sleeping or unusual sleep patterns.	☐ Y ☐ N
5. Child has frequent gastrointestinal problems (e.g., reflux, stomach pains, diarrhea, constipation).	☐ Y ☐ N
6. Child is a very picky eater or has unusual eating habits.	☐ Y ☐ N
7. Child has a rigid preference for certain foods.	☐ Y ☐ N
8. Child has seizures.	☐ Y ☐ N
9. Child has other disorders (e.g., tuberous sclerosis, fragile X, Landau Kleffner).	☐ Y ☐ N

Other Concerns	Check one
1. Child has a sibling with autism spectrum disorder.	☐ Y ☐ N
2. Child has family members with other significant disorders.	☐ Y ☐ N

Source: Adapted from Filipek et al. (1999), Gabovitch and Wiseman (2005), and Stone, MacLean, and Hogan (1995).
From *Assessment of Children: Behavioral, Social, and Clinical Foundations (Fifth Edition)* by Jerome M. Sattler and Robert D. Hoge. Copyright 2006 by Jerome M. Sattler, Publisher, Inc. Permission to photocopy this appendix table is granted to purchasers of this book for personal use only (see copyright page for details).

Table E-6
DSM-IV–TR Checklist for Autistic Disorder

***DSM-IV–TR* CHECKLIST FOR AUTISTIC DISORDER**

Child's name: _____   Parent's name: _____

Age: _____   Grade: _____   School: _____   Date: _____

Symptoms	Check one
A.	
1. Social Interaction	
a. Marked impairment in the use of multiple nonverbal behaviors	☐ Y ☐ N
b. Failure to develop peer relations	☐ Y ☐ N
c. Lack of spontaneous seeking to share enjoyment, interests, or achievements with other people	☐ Y ☐ N
d. Lack of social or emotional reciprocity	☐ Y ☐ N
2. Communication	
a. Delay in or total lack of spoken language	☐ Y ☐ N
b. Impairment in initiating or sustaining a conversation	☐ Y ☐ N
c. Stereotyped and repetitive use of language or idiosyncratic language	☐ Y ☐ N
d. Lack of varied, spontaneous make-believe play or social imitative play	☐ Y ☐ N
3. Restricted Repertoire	
a. Stereotyped and restricted pattern of interests	☐ Y ☐ N
b. Inflexible adherence to specific, nonfunctional routines or rituals	☐ Y ☐ N
c. Stereotyped and repetitive motor mannerisms	☐ Y ☐ N
d. Persistent preoccupation with parts of objects	☐ Y ☐ N
B. Delay or abnormal functioning must be present in at least one of the following three areas, with onset prior to age 3 years:	
a. Social interaction	☐ Y ☐ N
b. Language used in social communications	☐ Y ☐ N
c. Symbolic or imaginative play	☐ Y ☐ N

C. The disturbance is not better accounted for by Rett's disorder or childhood disintegrative disorder.

Diagnostic Criteria

a. Six or more items from numbers 1, 2, and 3	☐ Y ☐ N
b. At least two items from number 1	☐ Y ☐ N
c. At least one item from number 2	☐ Y ☐ N
d. At least one item from number 3	☐ Y ☐ N
e. Delay or abnormal functioning in at least one area covered in numbers 1, 2, and 3, with onset prior to age 3 years	☐ Y ☐ N
f. Not better accounted for by Rett's disorder or childhood disintegrative disorder	☐ Y ☐ N

If above diagnostic criteria a through f are checked *Yes*, criteria are fulfilled for a diagnosis of autistic disorder.

Source: Based on *DSM-IV–TR* (American Psychiatric Association, 2000).
From *Assessment of Children: Behavioral, Social, and Clinical Foundations (Fifth Edition)* by Jerome M. Sattler and Robert D. Hoge. Copyright 2006 by Jerome M. Sattler, Publisher, Inc. Permission to photocopy this appendix table is granted to purchasers of this book for personal use only (see copyright page for details).

Table E-7
Asperger's Disorder Questionnaire for Parents

ASPERGER'S DISORDER QUESTIONNAIRE

Child's name: _____ Parent's name: _____

Age: _____ Grade: _____ School: _____ Date: _____

Directions: Please read each item and check either Y ("Yes") or N ("No"). If you check "Yes," please answer the questions in the last two columns for that item. Be sure to indicate whether you are using years or months for your answers.

Behavior	Check one	How old was the child when you first noticed the behavior?	How long has the behavior persisted?
1. Makes little eye contact when talking to others	☐ Y ☐ N		
2. Did not wave bye-bye as an infant	☐ Y ☐ N		
3. Has difficulty making friends	☐ Y ☐ N		
4. Is not interested in making friends	☐ Y ☐ N		
5. Does not spontaneously share experiences with other people	☐ Y ☐ N		
6. Prefers to play alone rather than with other children	☐ Y ☐ N		
7. Ignores people who are trying to interact with him or her or does not participate in cooperative play	☐ Y ☐ N		
8. Does not seem to understand how others are feeling or seems to live in a world of his or her own	☐ Y ☐ N		
9. Has strong attachments to unusual objects (such as sticks or pieces of paper) rather than to teddy bears or dolls	☐ Y ☐ N		
10. Has a narrow and intense focus on a particular topic (for example, train schedules) or skill (for example, memorizing phone numbers)	☐ Y ☐ N		
11. Is preoccupied with things being done in a certain way (for example, insists on drinking from the same cup or plays with toys in the same way each time) and becomes upset if changes are made in his or her daily routines	☐ Y ☐ N		
12. Becomes upset if things don't look right (such as a stain on a table cloth), if something is out of place, or if there is a change in the way things are arranged or done	☐ Y ☐ N		
13. Does the same thing over and over again with his or her body (such as rocking, clapping hands, flapping arms, running aimlessly, walking on toes, or doing other odd movements)	☐ Y ☐ N		
14. Does the same thing over and over again with objects (such as opening and closing doors, flipping the tops of trash cans, turning a light switch on and off, flicking strings, transferring water from one container to another, or spinning objects)	☐ Y ☐ N		
15. Is overly interested in looking at small objects or parts of objects	☐ Y ☐ N		
16. Is preoccupied with parts of objects	☐ Y ☐ N		
17. Does not fit in social groups	☐ Y ☐ N		
18. Can't hold a job	☐ Y ☐ N		
19. Is very anxious or depressed	☐ Y ☐ N		
20. Language was not delayed during the first 3 years of development	☐ Y ☐ N		
21. Intellectual development was delayed during development	☐ Y ☐ N		
22. Self-help skills were delayed during development	☐ Y ☐ N		
23. Has not been curious about the environment	☐ Y ☐ N		

Table E-8
DSM-IV–TR **Checklist for Asperger's Disorder**

DSM-IV–TR CHECKLIST FOR ASPERGER'S DISORDER

Child's name: _____ Parent's name: _____

Age: _____ Grade: _____ School: _____ Date: _____

Symptoms	Check one
A. Social Interaction	
1. Marked impairment in the use of multiple nonverbal behaviors	☐ Y ☐ N
2. Failure to develop peer relations appropriate to developmental level	☐ Y ☐ N
3. Lack of spontaneous seeking to share enjoyment, interests, or achievements with other people	☐ Y ☐ N
4. Lack of social or emotional reciprocity	☐ Y ☐ N
B. Restricted Repertoire	
1. Preoccupation with one or more stereotyped and restricted patterns of interests that is abnormal either in intensity or in focus	☐ Y ☐ N
2. Inflexible adherence to specific, nonfunctional routines or rituals	☐ Y ☐ N
3. Stereotyped and repetitive motor mannerisms	☐ Y ☐ N
4. Persistent preoccupation with parts of objects	☐ Y ☐ N
Diagnostic Criteria	
a. At least two items from part A	☐ Y ☐ N
b. At least one item from part B	☐ Y ☐ N
c. Disturbance causes clinically significant impairment in social, occupational, or other important areas of functioning	☐ Y ☐ N
d. No clinically significant general delay in language	☐ Y ☐ N
e. No clinically significant delay in cognitive development or in development of age-appropriate self-help skills, adaptive behavior (other than in social interaction), and curiosity about the environment in childhood	☐ Y ☐ N
f. Criteria not met for another specific pervasive developmental disorder or schizophrenia	☐ Y ☐ N

If above diagnostic criteria a through f are checked *Yes*, criteria are fulfilled for a diagnosis of Asperger's disorder.

Source: Based on *DSM-IV–TR* (American Psychiatric Association, 2000).
From *Assessment of Children: Behavioral, Social, and Clinical Foundations (Fifth Edition)* by Jerome M. Sattler and Robert D. Hoge. Copyright 2006 by Jerome M. Sattler, Publisher, Inc. Permission to photocopy this appendix table is granted to purchasers of this book for personal use only (see copyright page for details).

Appendix F

MISCELLANEOUS TABLES

Table F-1
Abbreviated Coding System for Observing Children's Play

Definitions are as follows:

Functional Play: Child makes simple repetitive muscle movements with or without objects.

Constructive Play: Child manipulates objects to construct or create something.

Dramatic Play: Child uses imagery in play.

Games-with-Rules: Child accepts prearranged rules to follow in games.

I. **Solitary Play:** Target child plays alone, makes no attempt to communicate with other children, and is centered on his or her own activity.

a. *Functional Play.* Examples: Target child makes faces and dances while watching self in mirror, lies on back in the middle of the floor, spins truck wheels with fingers, runs around in a circle.

b. *Constructive Play.* Examples: Target child pushes car along a track, plays with puzzle pieces, places toy people in cars, plays with robot and punches button on robot, builds building using blocks, constructs an object with Legos.

c. *Dramatic Play.* Examples: (a) Target child plays alone with puppets, taking on the role of each puppet and making them talk to each other. (b) Target child plays in housekeeping area, talks to himself or herself, and takes on role of mother or father while feeding and dressing dolls.

d. *Games-with-Rules.* Example: Target child plays a board game, obviously adhering to the game rules.

II. **Parallel Play:** Target child plays in close proximity to another child, but each child works on his or her own task.

a. *Functional Play.* Examples: (a) Target child sits at a table with another child; both are drawing, but there is no interaction between the two children. (b) Target child and another child push button, open door, and ring bells on busy box, but they do not attend to each other's actions as they play.

b. *Constructive Play.* Examples: (a) Target child and another child paint together at a table, target child tells the other child that he or she is making a rainbow, and they trade paints. (b) Target child and another child sit at a table, and each makes his or her own construction out of Legos. (c) Target child and another child sit at a table working on a puzzle but do not interact.

c. *Dramatic Play.* Examples: Target child and another child are close to each other and play with puppets, but target child takes on the role of the puppet and the other child plays separately by just manipulating the puppet.

d. *Games-with-Rules.* Examples: Target child and another child play on the same game board, but they do not play together. The target child plays according to the game rules, but the other child moves the board pieces in no organized manner.

III. **Group Play:** Target child plays with another child or children. They borrow playthings from each other or follow each other's actions.

a. *Functional Play.* Example: Target child and another child are engaged in imitative behavior involving touching each other, smiling, and laughing.

b. *Constructive Play.* Examples: (a) Target child and another child exchange objects or offer objects to each other. (b) Target child throws a ball and waits for another child to retrieve it. (c) Target child and another child shovel sand into a toy truck and then dump the sand into a large pile.

c. *Dramatic Play.* Examples: (a) Target child and another child pretend to order pizza. Target child is the customer, and the other child has a puppet who manages the restaurant. Target child gives his or her order. (b) Target child and another child pretend to be dressed up. Target child begins to leave area, and the other child says, "Don't go without your hat."

d. *Games-with-Rules.* Example: Target child and another child play ball under a self-imposed, strict set of rules.

Source: Adapted from Guralnick and Groom (1988).

Table F-2
Social Competence Observation Schedule

Category	Description
Interacting with Peers	
1. Passively accepts aggression or domination from peer (Factor I)	Child allows another to boss, push, hit, or grab things from him or her without retaliation of any kind
2. Communicates in a positive way with peer (Factor I)	Child shows natural communication with peers; child appears at ease and comfortable in the situation
3. Is involved in cooperative activity with peer (Factor II)	Child voluntarily becomes involved with one or more children in an activity not required by the teacher
4. Shows successful leadership activity (Factor I)	Child initiates activity and makes suggestions that are followed by peers
5. Bosses or bullies peer—verbal (Factor II)	Child tells others what or what not to do, commands others
6. Exhibits physical aggression against peer (Factor II)	Child engages in aggression involving actual physical contact
Interacting with Teacher	
7. Clings to teacher (Factor I)	Child constantly stays by teacher's side or, for example, holds on to teacher's hand or clothes
8. Tenses or withdraws in response to teacher's approach (Factor I)	Child tenses body or moves farther away when approached by teacher
9. Communicates feelings to teacher in positive way (Factor I)	Child makes a positive statement to the teacher that is not related to classroom activities
10. Volunteers ideas or suggestions to teacher (Factor I)	Child makes suggestions or gives ideas during formal, teacher-directed classroom activities
11. Seeks attention of teacher while latter is interacting with another child (Factor II)	Child calls out to teacher, grabs teacher's arm, or performs similar actions when teacher is involved with another child
12. Exhibits physical aggression toward teacher (Factor II)	Child hits, kicks, or bites teacher
13. Seeks teacher attention—negative (Factor II)	Child uses inappropriate behavior to seek teacher's attention
14. Follows teacher request for help (Factor II)	Child follows teacher's directions willingly and immediately
15. Follows teacher suggestion regarding play activity (Factor II)	Child accepts and follows teacher's ideas or suggestions during informal, free activity
16. Exhibits other cooperative interactions with teacher (Factor II)	—
Child Is Alone	
17. Quietly listens to peer or teacher (Factor I)	Child is attentive to teacher while latter is giving instruction, reading a story, or performing a similar activity or when peer talks to him or her
18. Daydreams, stares into space, has blank look (Factor I)	Child has tuned out what is happening in the classroom, is unaware of what is going on, and looks sad
19. Puts things away carefully (Factor I)	—
20. Appears alone, confused, and bewildered (Factor I)	Child's face registers confusion; child appears not to understand or know how to organize or carry out an activity
21. Cries or screams—frightened (Factor I)	Child cries or screams to express some emotion other than, for example, anger or humiliation
22. Wanders aimlessly (Factor I)	—
23. Engages in task in positive manner (Factor II)	Child is actively involved in carrying out task sanctioned by teacher; he or she is concentrating, alert, and interested
24. Engages in task in negative manner (Factor II)	Child resists instructions, destroys an object, or engages in similar negative behaviors
25. Throws temper tantrum (Factor II)	Child screams or kicks

Table F-2 (*Continued*)

Category	Description

Child Is Alone (*Continued*)

Category	Description
26. Exhibits inappropriate verbal activity (Factor II)	Child expresses anger or frustration through words or gestures
27. Exhibits inappropriate gross-motor activity (Factor II)	Child runs around room, throws objects, jumps, or performs similar inappropriate gross-motor activity
28. Exhibits other isolated negative behavior (Factor I)	—

Note. Factor I refers to Interest-Participation vs. Apathy-Withdrawal and Factor II refers to Cooperation-Compliance vs. Anger-Defiance. Items 2, 3, 4, 9, 10, 14, 15, 16, 17, 19, and 23 are given 1 point, while items 1, 5, 6, 7, 8, 11, 12, 13, 18, 20, 21, 22, 24, 25, 26, 27, and 28 are given −1 point.

This schedule was designed to parallel the two teacher-judgment measures developed by Martin Kohn (the Social Competence Scales and the Problem Checklist). For additional information about the schedule, see Ali Khan and R. D. Hoge, "A Teacher-Judgment Measure of Social Competence: Validity Data," *Journal of Consulting and Clinical Psychology*, 1983, *51*, 809–814.

Source: Reprinted, with changes in notation, by permission of R. D. Hoge.

Table F-3
Standard Scores for the Koppitz Developmental Scoring System

	Chronological age												
Errors	5-0 to 5-5	5-6 to 5-11	6-0 to 6-5	6-6 to 6-11	7-0 to 7-5	7-6 to 7-11	8-0 to 8-5	8-6 to 8-11	9-0 to 9-5	9-6 to 9-11	10-0 to 10-5	10-6 to 10-11	11-0 to 11-11
0	160	143	139	131	126	125	125	118	119	116	115	115	115
1	155	138	135	127	122	119	119	112	112	109	107	107	104
2	150	134	130	122	117	114	113	106	105	102	99	98	94
3	146	130	125	118	113	109	107	100	99	95	91	90	83
4	141	125	121	114	108	103	101	94	92	88	83	82	72
5	137	121	116	109	104	98	95	88	85	81	76	73	61
6	132	116	112	105	99	92	89	82	78	74	68	65	51
7	128	112	107	101	95	87	83	76	71	66	60	57	
8	123	108	103	97	90	82	77	70	65	59	52		
9	119	103	98	92	85	76	71	64	58	52			
10	114	99	94	88	81	71	65	58	51	45			
11	110	94	89	84	76	66	59	52					
12	105	90	85	79	72	60	53	46					
13	100	85	80	75	67	55	47						
14	96	81	75	71	63	50							
15	91	77	71	67	58								
16	87	72	66	63	54								
17	82	68	62	58	49								
18	78	63	57	54	45								
19	73	59	53	49									
20	69	55	48	45									
21	64	50											
22	60	46											
23	55												

Note. These standard scores (*M* = 100, *SD* = 15) are based on a linear transformation of the data obtained from E. M. Koppitz's (1975) normative 1974 sample. Standard scores are useful primarily from 5 to 8 years of age. After the age of 8 years, the low ceiling and the skewed distribution of developmental scores make standard scores not very meaningful.

Table F-4
Achievement Scores Necessary to Establish a Significant ($p = .10$) IQ–Achievement Discrepancy Using Standard Scores with $M = 100$ and $SD = 15$

IQ	Correlation																
	.80	.79	.78	.77	.76	.75	.74	.73	.72	.71	.70	.69	.68	.67	.66	.65	.64
	Achievement test score necessary for discrepancy																
150	125	124	123	122	121	121	120	119	118	118	117	116	115	115	114	113	112
149	124	123	122	121	121	120	119	118	118	117	116	115	115	114	113	113	112
148	123	122	121	121	120	119	118	118	117	116	115	115	114	113	113	112	111
147	122	121	121	120	119	118	118	117	116	115	115	114	113	113	112	111	111
146	121	121	120	119	118	118	117	116	115	115	114	113	113	112	111	111	110
145	121	120	119	118	118	117	116	115	115	114	113	113	112	111	111	110	109
144	120	119	118	118	117	116	115	115	114	113	113	112	111	111	110	109	109
143	119	118	118	117	116	115	115	114	113	113	112	111	111	110	109	109	108
142	118	118	117	116	115	115	114	113	113	112	111	111	110	109	109	108	107
141	117	117	116	115	115	114	113	113	112	111	111	110	109	109	108	107	107
140	117	116	115	115	114	113	112	112	111	110	110	109	109	108	107	107	106
139	116	115	114	114	113	112	112	111	110	110	109	108	108	107	107	106	105
138	115	114	114	113	112	112	111	110	110	109	108	108	107	107	106	105	105
137	114	114	113	112	112	111	110	110	109	108	108	107	107	106	105	105	104
136	113	113	112	111	111	110	109	109	108	108	107	106	106	105	105	104	104
135	113	112	111	111	110	109	109	108	108	107	106	106	105	105	104	103	103
134	112	111	111	110	109	109	108	107	107	106	106	105	104	104	103	103	102
133	111	110	110	109	108	108	107	107	106	106	105	104	104	103	103	102	102
132	110	110	109	108	108	107	107	106	105	105	104	104	103	103	102	101	101
131	109	109	108	108	107	106	106	105	105	104	104	103	102	102	101	101	100
130	109	108	107	107	106	106	105	104	104	103	103	102	102	101	101	100	100
129	108	107	107	106	105	105	104	104	103	103	102	102	101	101	100	100	99
128	107	106	106	105	105	104	104	103	102	102	101	101	100	100	99	99	98
127	106	106	105	104	104	103	103	102	102	101	101	100	100	99	99	98	98
126	105	105	104	104	103	103	102	102	101	101	100	100	99	99	98	98	97
125	105	104	104	103	102	102	101	101	100	100	99	99	98	98	97	97	96
124	104	103	103	102	102	101	101	100	100	99	99	98	98	97	97	96	96
123	103	102	102	101	101	100	100	99	99	98	98	97	97	97	96	96	95
122	102	102	101	101	100	100	99	99	98	98	97	97	96	96	95	95	95
121	101	101	100	100	99	99	98	98	97	97	97	96	96	95	95	94	94
120	101	100	100	99	99	98	98	97	97	96	96	95	95	95	94	94	93
119	100	99	99	98	98	97	97	96	96	96	95	95	94	94	93	93	93
118	99	99	98	98	97	97	96	96	95	95	94	94	94	93	93	92	92
117	98	98	97	97	96	96	95	95	95	94	94	93	93	93	92	92	91
116	97	97	96	96	96	95	95	94	94	93	93	93	92	92	91	91	91
115	97	96	96	95	95	94	94	94	93	93	92	92	92	91	91	90	90
114	96	95	95	94	94	94	93	93	92	92	92	91	91	91	90	90	89
113	95	95	94	94	93	93	92	92	92	91	91	91	90	90	89	89	89
112	94	94	93	93	93	92	92	91	91	91	90	90	90	89	89	88	88
111	93	93	93	92	92	91	91	91	90	90	90	89	89	88	88	88	88

(Continued)

Table F-4 (Continued)

IQ	\.80	\.79	\.78	\.77	\.76	\.75	\.74	\.73	\.72	\.71	\.70	\.69	\.68	\.67	\.66	\.65	\.64
	Correlation																
	Achievement test score necessary for discrepancy																
110	93	92	92	91	91	91	90	90	90	89	89	88	88	88	88	87	87
109	92	91	91	91	90	90	90	89	89	88	88	88	87	87	87	87	86
108	91	91	90	90	89	89	89	88	88	88	87	87	87	86	86	86	86
107	90	90	89	89	89	88	88	88	87	87	87	86	86	86	86	85	85
106	89	89	89	88	88	88	87	87	87	86	86	86	85	85	85	85	84
105	89	88	88	88	87	87	87	86	86	86	85	85	85	84	84	84	84
104	88	87	87	87	86	86	86	86	85	85	85	84	84	84	84	83	83
103	87	87	86	86	86	85	85	85	84	84	84	84	83	83	83	83	82
102	86	86	86	85	85	85	84	84	84	83	83	83	83	82	82	82	82
101	85	85	85	84	84	84	84	83	83	83	83	82	82	82	82	81	81
100	85	84	84	84	83	83	83	83	82	82	82	82	81	81	81	81	80
99	84	84	83	83	83	82	82	82	82	81	81	81	81	80	80	80	80
98	83	83	82	82	82	82	81	81	81	81	80	80	80	80	80	79	79
97	82	82	82	81	81	81	81	80	80	80	80	80	79	79	79	79	79
96	81	81	81	81	80	80	80	80	79	79	79	79	79	78	78	78	78
95	81	80	80	80	80	79	79	79	79	79	78	78	78	78	78	77	77
94	80	80	79	79	79	79	78	78	78	78	78	77	77	77	77	77	77
93	79	79	79	78	78	78	78	77	77	77	77	77	77	76	76	76	76
92	78	78	78	78	77	77	77	77	77	76	76	76	76	76	76	75	75
91	77	77	77	77	77	76	76	76	76	76	76	75	75	75	75	75	75
90	77	76	76	76	76	76	75	75	75	75	75	75	75	74	74	74	74
89	76	76	75	75	75	75	75	75	74	74	74	74	74	74	74	74	73
88	75	75	75	74	74	74	74	74	74	74	73	73	73	73	73	73	73
87	74	74	74	74	74	73	73	73	73	73	73	73	73	72	72	72	72
86	73	73	73	73	73	73	72	72	72	72	72	72	72	72	72	72	72
85	73	72	72	72	72	72	72	72	72	71	71	71	71	71	71	71	71
84	72	72	72	71	71	71	71	71	71	71	71	71	70	70	70	70	70
83	71	71	71	71	70	70	70	70	70	70	70	70	70	70	70	70	70
82	70	70	70	70	70	70	70	69	69	69	69	69	69	69	69	69	69
81	69	69	69	69	69	69	69	69	69	69	69	68	68	68	68	68	68
80	69	69	68	68	68	68	68	68	68	68	68	68	68	68	68	68	68
79	68	68	68	68	67	67	67	67	67	67	67	67	67	67	67	67	67
78	67	67	67	67	67	67	67	67	66	66	66	66	66	66	66	66	66
77	66	66	66	66	66	66	66	66	66	66	66	66	66	66	66	66	66
76	65	65	65	65	65	65	65	65	65	65	65	65	65	65	65	65	65
75	65	65	65	64	64	64	64	64	64	64	64	64	64	64	64	64	64
74	64	64	64	64	64	64	64	64	64	64	64	64	64	64	64	64	64
73	63	63	63	63	63	63	63	63	63	63	63	63	63	63	63	63	63
72	62	62	62	62	62	62	62	62	62	62	62	62	62	62	62	62	63
71	61	61	61	61	61	61	61	61	61	61	62	62	62	62	62	62	62
70	61	61	61	61	61	61	61	61	61	61	61	61	61	61	61	61	61
69	60	60	60	60	60	60	60	60	60	60	60	60	60	60	60	61	61
68	59	59	59	59	59	59	59	59	59	59	59	60	60	60	60	60	60
67	58	58	58	58	58	58	58	58	59	59	59	59	59	59	59	59	59
66	57	57	57	58	58	58	58	58	58	58	58	58	58	58	58	59	59

(Continued)

Table F-4 (Continued)

							Correlation										
	.80	.79	.78	.77	.76	.75	.74	.73	.72	.71	.70	.69	.68	.67	.66	.65	.64
IQ						Achievement test score necessary for discrepancy											
65	57	57	57	57	57	57	57	57	57	57	57	57	58	58	58	58	58
64	56	56	56	56	56	56	56	56	56	57	57	57	57	57	57	57	57
63	55	55	55	55	55	55	55	56	56	56	56	56	56	56	56	57	57
62	54	54	54	54	55	55	55	55	55	55	55	55	56	56	56	56	56
61	53	54	54	54	54	54	54	54	54	54	55	55	55	55	55	55	56
60	53	53	53	53	53	53	53	53	54	54	54	54	54	54	55	55	55
59	52	52	52	52	52	52	53	53	53	53	53	53	53	54	54	54	54
58	51	51	51	51	51	52	52	52	52	52	52	53	53	53	53	53	54
57	50	50	50	51	51	51	51	51	51	52	52	52	52	52	53	53	53
56	49	50	50	50	50	50	50	50	51	51	51	51	51	52	52	52	52
55	49	49	49	49	49	49	50	50	50	50	50	51	51	51	51	51	52
54	48	48	48	48	48	49	49	49	49	49	50	50	50	50	51	51	51
53	47	47	47	48	48	48	48	48	48	49	49	49	49	50	50	50	50
52	46	46	47	47	47	47	47	48	48	48	48	48	49	49	49	49	50
51	45	46	46	46	46	46	47	47	47	47	48	48	48	48	49	49	49
50	45	45	45	45	45	46	46	46	46	47	47	47	47	48	48	48	48

							Correlation										
	.63	.62	.61	.60	.59	.58	.57	.56	.55	.54	.53	.52	.51	.50	.49	.48	.47
IQ						Achievement test score necessary for discrepancy											
150	112	111	110	110	109	108	108	107	106	106	105	104	104	103	102	102	101
149	111	110	110	109	108	108	107	106	106	105	104	104	103	103	102	101	101
148	111	110	109	109	108	107	107	106	105	105	104	103	103	102	101	101	100
147	110	109	109	108	107	107	106	105	105	104	103	103	102	102	101	100	100
146	109	109	108	107	107	106	105	105	104	104	103	102	102	101	100	100	99
145	109	108	107	107	106	105	105	104	104	103	102	102	101	101	100	99	99
144	108	107	107	106	105	105	104	104	103	102	102	101	101	100	99	99	98
143	107	107	106	106	105	104	104	103	102	102	101	101	100	100	99	98	98
142	107	106	106	105	104	104	103	103	102	101	101	100	100	99	99	98	97
141	106	106	105	104	104	103	103	102	101	101	100	100	99	99	98	97	97
140	105	105	104	104	103	103	102	101	101	100	100	99	99	98	98	97	96
139	105	104	104	103	103	102	101	101	100	100	99	99	98	98	97	97	96
138	104	104	103	103	102	101	101	100	100	99	99	98	98	97	97	96	96
137	104	103	102	102	101	101	100	100	99	99	98	98	97	97	96	96	95
136	103	102	102	101	101	100	100	99	99	98	98	97	97	96	96	95	95
135	102	102	101	101	100	100	99	99	98	98	97	97	96	96	95	95	94
134	102	101	101	100	100	99	99	98	98	97	97	96	96	95	95	94	94
133	101	101	100	100	99	98	98	97	97	96	96	96	95	95	94	94	93
132	100	100	99	99	98	98	97	97	96	96	95	95	95	94	94	93	93
131	100	99	99	98	98	97	97	96	96	95	95	94	94	94	93	93	92

(Continued)

Table F-4 *(Continued)*

	Correlation																
	.63	.62	.61	.60	.59	.58	.57	.56	.55	.54	.53	.52	.51	.50	.49	.48	.47
IQ	Achievement test score necessary for discrepancy																
130	99	99	98	98	97	97	96	96	95	95	94	94	94	93	93	92	92
129	99	98	98	97	97	96	96	95	95	94	94	93	93	93	92	92	91
128	98	97	97	97	96	96	95	95	94	94	93	93	92	92	92	91	91
127	97	97	96	96	95	95	95	94	94	93	93	92	92	92	91	91	90
126	97	96	96	95	95	94	94	94	93	93	92	92	91	91	91	90	90
125	96	96	95	95	94	94	93	93	93	92	92	91	91	91	90	90	89
124	95	95	95	94	94	93	93	92	92	92	91	91	90	90	90	89	89
123	95	94	94	94	93	93	92	92	91	91	91	90	90	90	89	89	88
122	94	94	93	93	92	92	92	91	91	91	90	90	89	89	89	88	88
121	94	93	93	92	92	92	91	91	90	90	90	89	89	89	88	88	88
120	93	92	92	92	91	91	91	90	90	89	89	89	88	88	88	87	87
119	92	92	91	91	91	90	90	90	89	89	89	88	88	88	87	87	87
118	92	91	91	91	90	90	89	89	89	88	88	88	87	87	87	86	86
117	91	91	90	90	90	89	89	89	88	88	88	87	87	87	86	86	86
116	90	90	90	89	89	89	88	88	88	87	87	87	86	86	86	85	85
115	90	89	89	89	88	88	88	87	87	87	86	86	86	86	85	85	85
114	89	89	88	88	88	87	87	87	87	86	86	86	85	85	85	85	84
113	88	88	88	88	87	87	87	86	86	86	85	85	85	85	84	84	84
112	88	88	87	87	87	86	86	86	85	85	85	85	84	84	84	84	83
111	87	87	87	86	86	86	85	85	85	85	84	84	84	84	83	83	83
110	87	86	86	86	85	85	85	85	84	84	84	84	83	83	83	83	82
109	86	86	85	85	85	85	84	84	84	84	83	83	83	83	82	82	82
108	85	85	85	85	84	84	84	83	83	83	83	83	82	82	82	82	81
107	85	84	84	84	84	83	83	83	83	82	82	82	82	82	81	81	81
106	84	84	84	83	83	83	83	82	82	82	82	81	81	81	81	81	80
105	83	83	83	83	82	82	82	82	82	81	81	81	81	81	80	80	80
104	83	83	82	82	82	82	81	81	81	81	81	80	80	80	80	80	80
103	82	82	82	82	81	81	81	81	80	80	80	80	80	80	79	79	79
102	82	81	81	81	81	80	80	80	80	80	80	79	79	79	79	79	79
101	81	81	80	80	80	80	80	80	79	79	79	79	79	79	78	78	78
100	80	80	80	80	80	79	79	79	79	79	79	78	78	78	78	78	78
99	80	79	79	79	79	79	79	78	78	78	78	78	78	78	77	77	77
98	79	79	79	79	78	78	78	78	78	78	77	77	77	77	77	77	77
97	78	78	78	78	78	78	77	77	77	77	77	77	77	77	76	76	76
96	78	78	77	77	77	77	77	77	77	77	76	76	76	76	76	76	76
95	77	77	77	77	77	76	76	76	76	76	76	76	76	76	75	75	75
94	76	76	76	76	76	76	76	76	76	75	75	75	75	75	75	75	75
93	76	76	76	76	75	75	75	75	75	75	75	75	75	75	74	74	74
92	75	75	75	75	75	75	75	75	74	74	74	74	74	74	74	74	74
91	75	75	74	74	74	74	74	74	74	74	74	74	74	74	74	73	73
90	74	74	74	74	74	74	73	73	73	73	73	73	73	73	73	73	73
89	73	73	73	73	73	73	73	73	73	73	73	73	73	73	73	73	72
88	73	73	73	73	72	72	72	72	72	72	72	72	72	72	72	72	72
87	72	72	72	72	72	72	72	72	72	72	72	72	72	72	72	72	72
86	71	71	71	71	71	71	71	71	71	71	71	71	71	71	71	71	71

(Continued)

Table F-4 *(Continued)*

IQ	Correlation																
	.63	.62	.61	.60	.59	.58	.57	.56	.55	.54	.53	.52	.51	.50	.49	.48	.47
	Achievement test score necessary for discrepancy																
85	71	71	71	71	71	71	71	71	71	71	71	71	71	71	71	71	71
84	70	70	70	70	70	70	70	70	70	70	70	70	70	70	70	70	70
83	70	70	70	70	69	69	69	69	69	69	70	70	70	70	70	70	70
82	69	69	69	69	69	69	69	69	69	69	69	69	69	69	69	69	69
81	68	68	68	68	68	68	68	68	68	68	68	68	69	69	69	69	69
80	68	68	68	68	68	68	68	68	68	68	68	68	68	68	68	68	68
79	67	67	67	67	67	67	67	67	67	67	67	67	68	68	68	68	68
78	66	66	66	67	67	67	67	67	67	67	67	67	67	67	67	67	67
77	66	66	66	66	66	66	66	66	66	66	66	66	66	67	67	67	67
76	65	65	65	65	65	65	65	66	66	66	66	66	66	66	66	66	66
75	65	65	65	65	65	65	65	65	65	65	65	65	65	66	66	66	66
74	64	64	64	64	64	64	64	64	65	65	65	65	65	65	65	65	65
73	63	63	63	64	64	64	64	64	64	64	64	64	64	65	65	65	65
72	63	63	63	63	63	63	63	63	63	64	64	64	64	64	64	64	64
71	62	62	62	62	62	63	63	63	63	63	63	63	63	64	64	64	64
70	61	61	62	62	62	62	62	62	62	62	63	63	63	63	63	63	64
69	61	61	61	61	61	61	61	62	62	62	62	62	62	63	63	63	63
68	60	60	60	61	61	61	61	61	61	61	62	62	62	62	62	62	63
67	59	60	60	60	60	60	60	61	61	61	61	61	61	62	62	62	62
66	59	59	59	59	59	60	60	60	60	60	60	61	61	61	61	61	62
65	58	58	59	59	59	59	59	59	60	60	60	60	60	61	61	61	61
64	58	58	58	58	58	58	59	59	59	59	59	60	60	60	60	61	61
63	57	57	57	58	58	58	58	58	58	59	59	59	59	60	60	60	60
62	56	57	57	57	57	57	58	58	58	58	58	59	59	59	59	60	60
61	56	56	56	56	57	57	57	57	57	58	58	58	58	59	59	59	59
60	55	55	55	56	56	56	56	57	57	57	57	58	58	58	58	59	59
59	54	55	55	55	55	56	56	56	56	57	57	57	57	58	58	58	58
58	54	54	54	55	55	55	55	55	56	56	56	57	57	57	57	58	58
57	53	53	54	54	54	54	55	55	55	55	56	56	56	57	57	57	57
56	53	53	53	53	54	54	54	54	55	55	55	55	56	56	56	57	57
55	52	52	52	53	53	53	54	54	54	54	55	55	55	56	56	56	57
54	51	52	52	52	52	53	53	53	54	54	54	54	55	55	55	56	56
53	51	51	51	52	52	52	52	53	53	53	54	54	54	55	55	55	56
52	50	50	51	51	51	51	52	52	52	53	53	53	54	54	54	55	55
51	49	50	50	50	51	51	51	52	52	52	53	53	53	54	54	54	55
50	49	49	49	50	50	50	51	51	51	52	52	52	53	53	53	54	54

(Continued)

Table F-4 (Continued)

									Correlation								
	.46	.45	.44	.43	.42	.41	.40	.39	.38	.37	.36	.35	.34	.33	.32	.31	.30
IQ							Achievement test score necessary for discrepancy										
150	101	100	99	99	98	97	97	96	96	95	94	94	93	93	92	91	91
149	100	99	99	98	98	97	96	96	95	95	94	93	93	92	92	91	91
148	100	99	98	98	97	97	96	95	95	94	94	93	93	92	91	91	90
147	99	99	98	97	97	96	96	95	94	94	93	93	92	92	91	91	90
146	99	98	98	97	96	96	95	95	94	94	93	92	92	91	91	90	90
145	98	98	97	97	96	95	95	94	94	93	93	92	92	91	90	90	89
144	98	97	97	96	96	95	94	94	93	93	92	92	91	91	90	90	89
143	97	97	96	96	95	95	94	93	93	92	92	91	91	90	90	89	89
142	97	96	96	95	95	94	94	93	93	92	92	91	91	90	89	89	88
141	96	96	95	95	94	94	93	93	92	92	91	91	90	90	89	89	88
140	96	95	95	94	94	93	93	92	92	91	91	90	90	89	89	88	88
139	95	95	94	94	93	93	92	92	91	91	90	90	89	89	89	88	88
138	95	94	94	93	93	93	92	92	91	91	90	90	89	89	88	88	87
137	95	94	94	93	93	92	92	91	91	90	90	89	89	88	88	87	87
136	94	94	93	93	92	92	91	91	90	90	89	89	88	88	88	87	87
135	94	93	93	92	92	91	91	90	90	89	89	89	88	88	87	87	86
134	93	93	92	92	91	91	90	90	90	89	89	88	88	87	87	87	86
133	93	92	92	91	91	90	90	90	89	89	88	88	87	87	87	86	86
132	92	92	91	91	90	90	90	89	89	88	88	88	87	87	86	86	85
131	92	91	91	90	90	90	89	89	88	88	88	87	87	86	86	86	85
130	91	91	90	90	90	89	89	88	88	88	87	87	86	86	86	85	85
129	91	90	90	90	89	89	88	88	88	87	87	86	86	86	85	85	85
128	90	90	90	89	89	88	88	88	87	87	86	86	86	85	85	85	84
127	90	90	89	89	88	88	88	87	87	86	86	86	85	85	85	84	84
126	89	89	89	88	88	88	87	87	86	86	86	85	85	85	84	84	84
125	89	89	88	88	88	87	87	86	86	86	85	85	85	84	84	84	83
124	89	88	88	87	87	87	86	86	86	85	85	85	84	84	84	83	83
123	88	88	87	87	87	86	86	86	85	85	85	84	84	84	83	83	83
122	88	87	87	87	86	86	86	85	85	85	84	84	84	83	83	83	82
121	87	87	87	86	86	86	85	85	85	84	84	84	83	83	83	82	82
120	87	86	86	86	85	85	85	85	84	84	84	83	83	83	82	82	82
119	86	86	86	85	85	85	84	84	84	84	83	83	83	82	82	82	82
118	86	85	85	85	85	84	84	84	83	83	83	83	82	82	82	82	81
117	85	85	85	84	84	84	84	83	83	83	83	82	82	82	81	81	81
116	85	85	84	84	84	83	83	83	83	82	82	82	82	81	81	81	81
115	84	84	84	84	83	83	83	83	82	82	82	82	81	81	81	81	80
114	84	84	83	83	83	83	82	82	82	82	81	81	81	81	81	80	80
113	84	83	83	83	82	82	82	82	82	81	81	81	81	80	80	80	80
112	83	83	83	82	82	82	82	81	81	81	81	81	80	80	80	80	79
111	83	82	82	82	82	81	81	81	81	81	80	80	80	80	80	79	79
110	82	82	82	81	81	81	81	81	80	80	80	80	80	79	79	79	79
109	82	81	81	81	81	81	80	80	80	80	80	79	79	79	79	79	79
108	81	81	81	81	80	80	80	80	80	79	79	79	79	79	79	78	78
107	81	81	80	80	80	80	80	79	79	79	79	79	79	78	78	78	78
106	80	80	80	80	80	79	79	79	79	79	79	78	78	78	78	78	78

(Continued)

Table F-4 *(Continued)*

IQ	.46	.45	.44	.43	.42	.41	.40	.39	.38	.37	.36	.35	.34	.33	.32	.31	.30
									Achievement test score necessary for discrepancy								
105	80	80	79	79	79	79	79	79	79	78	78	78	78	78	78	78	77
104	79	79	79	79	79	79	78	78	78	78	78	78	78	77	77	77	77
103	79	79	79	78	78	78	78	78	78	78	77	77	77	77	77	77	77
102	78	78	78	78	78	78	78	77	77	77	77	77	77	77	77	77	76
101	78	78	78	78	77	77	77	77	77	77	77	77	77	76	76	76	76
100	78	77	77	77	77	77	77	77	77	77	76	76	76	76	76	76	76
99	77	77	77	77	77	77	76	76	76	76	76	76	76	76	76	76	76
98	77	76	76	76	76	76	76	76	76	76	76	76	76	75	75	75	75
97	76	76	76	76	76	76	76	76	75	75	75	75	75	75	75	75	75
96	76	76	76	75	75	75	75	75	75	75	75	75	75	75	75	75	75
95	75	75	75	75	75	75	75	75	75	75	75	75	75	74	74	74	74
94	75	75	75	75	75	74	74	74	74	74	74	74	74	74	74	74	74
93	74	74	74	74	74	74	74	74	74	74	74	74	74	74	74	74	74
92	74	74	74	74	74	74	74	74	74	74	74	74	74	73	73	73	73
91	73	73	73	73	73	73	73	73	73	73	73	73	73	73	73	73	73
90	73	73	73	73	73	73	73	73	73	73	73	73	73	73	73	73	73
89	72	72	72	72	72	72	72	72	72	72	72	72	72	73	73	73	73
88	72	72	72	72	72	72	72	72	72	72	72	72	72	72	72	72	72
87	72	72	72	72	72	72	72	72	72	72	72	72	72	72	72	72	72
86	71	71	71	71	71	71	71	71	71	71	71	71	71	72	72	72	72
85	71	71	71	71	71	71	71	71	71	71	71	71	71	71	71	71	71
84	70	70	70	70	70	70	70	70	71	71	71	71	71	71	71	71	71
83	70	70	70	70	70	70	70	70	70	70	70	70	70	71	71	71	71
82	69	69	69	69	69	70	70	70	70	70	70	70	70	70	70	70	70
81	69	69	69	69	69	69	69	69	69	69	70	70	70	70	70	70	70
80	68	68	68	69	69	69	69	69	69	69	69	69	69	70	70	70	70
79	68	68	68	68	68	68	68	69	69	69	69	69	69	69	69	69	70
78	67	67	68	68	68	68	68	68	68	68	68	69	69	69	69	69	69
77	67	67	67	67	67	67	68	68	68	68	68	68	68	69	69	69	69
76	66	67	67	67	67	67	67	67	67	68	68	68	68	68	68	69	69
75	66	66	66	66	67	67	67	67	67	67	67	68	68	68	68	68	68
74	66	66	66	66	66	66	66	67	67	67	67	67	67	68	68	68	68
73	65	65	65	66	66	66	66	66	66	67	67	67	67	67	67	68	68
72	65	65	65	65	65	65	66	66	66	66	66	67	67	67	67	67	67
71	64	64	65	65	65	65	65	65	66	66	66	66	66	67	67	67	67
70	64	64	64	64	64	65	65	65	65	65	66	66	66	66	66	67	67
69	63	63	64	64	64	64	64	65	65	65	65	65	66	66	66	66	67
68	63	63	63	63	64	64	64	64	64	65	65	65	65	66	66	66	66
67	62	63	63	63	63	63	64	64	64	64	65	65	65	65	65	66	66
66	62	62	62	63	63	63	63	63	64	64	64	64	65	65	65	65	66

(Continued)

Table F-4 *(Continued)*

IQ	.46	.45	.44	.43	.42	.41	.40	.39	.38	.37	.36	.35	.34	.33	.32	.31	.30
	Achievement test score necessary for discrepancy																
65	61	62	62	62	62	63	63	63	63	64	64	64	64	65	65	65	65
64	61	61	61	62	62	62	62	63	63	63	63	64	64	64	65	65	65
63	61	61	61	61	61	62	62	62	63	63	63	63	64	64	64	64	65
62	60	60	61	61	61	61	62	62	62	62	63	63	63	64	64	64	64
61	60	60	60	60	61	61	61	61	62	62	62	63	63	63	64	64	64
60	59	59	60	60	60	61	61	61	61	62	62	62	63	63	63	64	64
59	59	59	59	60	60	60	60	61	61	61	62	62	62	63	63	63	64
58	58	58	59	59	59	60	60	60	61	61	61	62	62	62	63	63	63
57	58	58	58	59	59	59	60	60	60	61	61	61	62	62	62	63	63
56	57	58	58	58	59	59	59	60	60	60	61	61	61	62	62	62	63
55	57	57	57	58	58	58	59	59	60	60	60	61	61	61	62	62	62
54	56	57	57	57	58	58	58	59	59	59	60	60	61	61	61	62	62
53	56	56	57	57	57	58	58	58	59	59	59	60	60	61	61	61	62
52	55	56	56	57	57	57	58	58	58	59	59	60	60	60	61	61	61
51	55	55	56	56	56	57	57	58	58	58	59	59	60	60	60	61	61
50	55	55	55	56	56	56	57	57	58	58	58	59	59	60	60	60	61

Note. This table was constructed following Heath and Kush (1991). For this table to be used, the intelligence test and the achievement test must have $M = 100$ and $SD = 15$. The following procedure was used to obtain the observed achievement levels necessary for a significant IQ–achievement discrepancy.

1. All correlation values between .30 and .80 and all IQ values between 50 and 150 were selected.
2. The standard error of estimate for each correlation value was computed by using the following formula: $SEE = SD\sqrt{1 - r_{xy}^2}$.
3. The predicted achievement scores were then computed by using the following formula: $\hat{y} = r_{xy}(IQ - 100) + 100$.
4. A z value of 1.65 was used to establish confidence intervals about the predicted achievement scores. This z value at $p = .10$ is a reasonable compromise between too stringent and too lax a criterion. The formula used to establish the confidence interval was $15z\sqrt{1 - r_{xy}^2}$.
5. The lower limit of the confidence interval was then subtracted from the predicted achievement scores to obtain the minimal achievement level that represents a discrepancy at the $p = .10$ level.

An example of how the table is read follows: For a child with an IQ of 100 who is administered an achievement test that has a .65 correlation with the intelligence test (see 17th column on page 740), an achievement score of 81 or lower represents a significant discrepancy.

REFERENCES

Aaron, P. G. (1997). The impending demise of the discrepancy formula. *Review of Educational Research, 67,* 461–502.

Aaron, P. G., Joshi, R. M., Palmer, H., Smith, N., & Kirby, E. (2002). Separating genuine cases of reading disability from reading deficits caused by predominantly inattentive ADHD behavior. *Journal of Disabilities, 35,* 425–435.

Aaron, P. G., & Simurdak, J. (1991). Reading disorders: Their nature and diagnosis. In J. E. Obrzut & G. W. Hynd (Eds.), *Neuropsychological foundations of learning disabilities: A handbook of issues, methods, and practice* (pp. 519–548). San Diego: Academic Press.

Abidin, R. R. (1995). *Parenting Stress Index* (3rd ed.). Lutz, FL: Psychological Assessment Resources.

Abikoff, H., & Gittelman, R. (1985). Classroom observation code: A modification of the Stony Brook Code. *Psychopharmacology Bulletin, 21,* 901–909.

Abikoff, H., & Klein, R. G. (1992). Attention-deficit hyperactivity and conduct disorder: Comorbidity and implications for treatment. *Journal of Consulting and Clinical Psychology, 60,* 881–892.

Abramowitz, A. J., O'Leary, S. G., & Futtersak, M. W. (1988). The relative impact of long and short reprimands on children's off-task behavior in the classroom. *Behavior Therapy, 19,* 243–247.

Abramson, L. Y., Metalsky, G. I., & Alloy, L. B. (1989). Hopelessness depression: A theory-based subtype of depression. *Psychological Review, 96,* 358–372.

Achenbach, T. M. (1993). Implications of multiaxial empirically based assessment for behavior therapy with children. *Behavior Therapy, 24,* 91–116.

Achenbach, T. M., & Edelbrock, C. S. (1983). *Manual for the Child Behavior Checklist and the Revised Child Behavior Profile.* Burlington: University of Vermont, Department of Psychiatry.

Achenbach, T. M., & McConaughy, S. H. (1992). Taxonomy of internalizing disorders of childhood and adolescence. In W. M. Reynolds (Ed.), *Internalizing disorders in children and adolescents* (pp. 19–60). New York: Wiley.

Achenbach, T. M., McConaughy, S. M., & Howell, C. T. (1987). Child/adolescent behavioral and emotional problems: Implications of cross-informant correlations for situational specificity. *Psychological Bulletin, 101,* 213–232.

Achenbach, T. M., & Rescorla, L. A. (2000). *Manual for the ASEBA Preschool Forms & Profiles.* Burlington: University of Vermont, Research Center for Children, Youth, & Families.

Achenbach, T. M., & Rescorla, L. A. (2001). *Manual for the ASEBA School-Age Forms & Profiles.* Burlington: University of Vermont, Research Center for Children, Youth, & Families.

Ackerman, P. T., McPherson, B. D., Oglesby, D. M., & Dykman, R. A. (1998). EEG power spectra of adolescent poor readers. *Journal of Learning Disabilities, 31,* 83–90.

Adamovich, B. L. B. (1991). Cognition, language, attention, and information processing following closed head injury. In J. S. Kreutzer & P. H. Wehman (Eds.), *Cognitive rehabilitation for persons with traumatic brain injury: A functional approach* (pp. 75–86). Baltimore: Brookes.

Adams, W., & Sheslow, D. (2003). *Wide Range Assessment of Memory and Learning–Second Edition.* Wilmington, DE: Jastik Associates.

Adrien, J. L., Ornitz, E., Barthelemy, C., Sauvage, D., & LeLord, G. (1987). The presence or absence of certain behaviors associated with infantile autism in severely retarded autistic and nonautistic retarded children and very young normal children. *Journal of Autism and Developmental Disorders, 17,* 407–416.

Agency for Health Care Policy and Research. (1999). *Diagnosis of attention-deficit/hyperactivity disorder: Summary.* Retrieved June 20, 2005, from http://www.ahrq.gov/clinic/epcsums/adhdsutr.htm

Albano, A. M., Causey, D., & Carter, B. D. (2001). Fear and anxiety in children. In C. E. Walker & M. C. Roberts (Eds.), *Handbook of clinical child psychology* (3rd ed., pp. 291–316). New York: Wiley.

Albano, A. M., Chorpita, B. F., & Barlow, D. H. (1996). Childhood anxiety disorders. In E. J. Mash & R. A. Barkley (Eds.), *Child psychopathology* (pp. 196–241). New York: Guilford.

Alberto, P., & Troutman, A. (2003). *Applied behavior analysis for teachers* (6th ed.). Saddle River, NJ: Prentice Hall

Alessi, G. (1980). Behavioral observation for the school psychologist: Responsive-discrepancy model. *School Psychology Review, 9,* 31–45.

Alessi, G. (1988). Direct observation methods for emotional/behavior problems. In E. S. Shapiro & T. R. Kratochwill (Eds.), *Behavioral assessment in schools* (pp. 14–75). New York: Guilford.

Alfano, D. P., & Finlayson, M. A. J. (1987). Clinical neuropsychology in rehabilition. *Clinical Neuropsychologist, 1,* 105–123.

Allen, K. D., & Matthews, J. R. (1998). Behavior management of recurrent pain in children. In T. S. Watson & F. M. Gresham (Eds.), *Handbook of child behavior therapy* (pp. 263–285). New York: Plenum.

Allington, R. L. (1979). Diagnosis of reading disability: Word prediction ability tests. *Academic Therapy, 14,* 267–274.

Altmaier, E. M. (Ed.). (2003). *Setting standards in graduate education: Psychology.* Washington, DC: American Psychological Association.

Amabile, T. M. (1983). *The social psychology of creativity.* New York: Springer-Verlag.

Aman, M. G., Singh, N. N., Stewart, A. W., & Field, C. J. (1985). Psychometric characteristics of the Aberrant Behavior Checklist. *American Journal of Mental Deficiency, 89,* 492–501.

Ambrosini, P., & Dixon, J. F. (1996). *Schedule for Affective Disorders & Schizophrenia for School-Age Children (K-SADS–IVR).* Philadelphia: Allegheny University of the Health Sciences.

American Academy of Child and Adolescent Psychiatry. (1997). Practice parameters for the assessment and treatment of children and adolescents with anxiety disorders. *Journal of the American Academy of Child and Adolescent Psychiatry, 36,* 69–84.

American Academy of Pediatrics. (2001). *ADHD—treatment with medication.* Retrieved May 26, 2005, from http://www.aap.org/pubed/ZZZ98TFTXSC.htm?&sub_cat=18

American Academy of Pediatrics and National Initiative for Children's Healthcare Quality. (2002). *National initiative for children's healthcare quality (NICHQ) attention-deficit/hyperactivity disorder (ADHD) practitioners' toolkit: Diagnosis.* Retrieved May 26, 2005, from http://www.utmem.edu/pediatrics/general/clinical/behavior/index.php

American Association on Mental Retardation. (2002). *Mental retardation: Definition, classification, and systems of support* (10th ed.). Washington, DC: Author.

American Counseling Association. (2003). *Standards for qualifications of test users.* Alexandria, VA: Author.

American Educational Research Association, American Psychological Association, & National Council on Measurement in Education. (1999). *Standards for educational and psychological testing.* Washington, DC: American Educational Research Association.

American Prosecutors Research Institute. (1993). *Investigation and prosecution of child abuse* (2nd ed.). Alexandria, VA: Author.

American Psychiatric Association. (2000). *Diagnostic and statistical manual of mental disorders: Text revision (DSM-IV–TR)* (4th ed.). Washington, DC: Author.

American Psychological Association. (1986). *Guidelines for computer-based tests and interpretations.* Washington, DC: Author.

American Psychological Association. (1990). *Guidelines for providers of psychological services to ethnic, linguistic, and culturally diverse populations.* Washington, DC: Author.

American Psychological Association. (1993). Record keeping guidelines. *American Psychologist, 48,* 984–986.

American Psychological Association. (1994a). Guidelines for child custody evaluations in divorce proceedings. *American Psychologist, 49,* 677–680.

American Psychological Association. (1994b). *Publication manual of the American Psychological Association* (4th ed.). Washington, DC: Author.

American Psychological Association. (1996). *Book I: Guidelines and principles for accreditation of programs in professional psychology.* Washington, DC: Author.

American Psychological Association. (2001). *Publication manual of the American Psychological Association* (5th ed.). Washington, DC: Author.

American Psychological Association. (2002). Ethical principles of psychologists and code of conduct. *American Psychologist, 57,* 1060–1073.

American Psychological Association. (2004). *Code of fair testing practices in education.* Washington, DC: Author.

Anastasi, A., & Urbina, S. (1997). *Psychological testing* (7th ed.). Upper Saddle River, NJ: Prentice Hall.

Anastopolous, W. D., Spisto, M. A., & Maher, M. C. (1994). The WISC–III Freedom from Distractibility factor: Its utility in identifying children with attention deficit hyperactivity disorder. *Psychological Assessment, 6,* 368–371.

Anderson, C. M., & Stewart, S. (1983). *Mastering resistance: A practical guide to family therapy.* New York: Guilford.

Anderson, J. C. (1994). Epidemiological issues. In T. Ollendick, N. King, & W. Yule (Eds.), *International handbook of phobic and anxiety disorders in children and adolescents* (pp. 43–66). New York: Plenum.

Anderson, V., Northam, E., Hendy, J., & Wrennall, J. (2001). *Developmental neuropsychology: A clinical approach.* Hove, England: Psychology Press.

Andrews, D. A., & Bonta, J. (1998). *The psychology of criminal conduct* (2nd ed.). Cincinnati, OH: Anderson.

Angold, A., Cox, A., Rutter, M., & Simonoff, E. (1996). *Child and Adolescent Psychiatric Assessment (CAPA): Version 4.2—Child version.* Durham, NC: Duke Medical Center.

Annie E. Casey Foundation. (2001). *Kids count: Census data online.* Retrieved May 20, 2001, from http://www.aecf.org

Annie E. Casey Foundation. (2002). *Kids count: Census data online.* Retrieved February 1, 2002, from http://www.aecf.org

Annie E. Casey Foundation. (2003). *Kids count: Census data online.* Retrieved June 11, 2003, from http://www.aecf.org

Aram, D. M., & Eisele, J. A. (1992). Plasticity and recovery of higher cognitive functions following early brain injury. In I. Rapin & S. J. Segalowitz (Eds.), *Handbook of neuropsychology* (Vol. 6, pp. 73–92). Amsterdam, Netherlands: Elsevier Science.

Aram, D. M., & Ekelman, B. L. (1986). Cognitive profiles of children with early onset of unilateral lesions. *Developmental Neuropsychology, 2,* 155–172.

Aram, D. M., Ekelman, B. L., Rose, D. F. & Whitaker, H. A. (1985). Verbal and cognitive sequelae following unilateral lesions acquired in early childhood. *Journal of Clinical and Experimental Neuropsychology, 7,* 55–78.

Archer, R. P. (1992). *MMPI–A: Assessing adolescent psychopathology.* Mahwah, NJ: Erlbaum.

Archer, R. P. (1999). *MMPI–A interpretive system version 2.* Lutz, FL: Psychological Assessment Resources.

Ashton, C. (1996). In defence of discrepancy definitions of specific learning difficulties (A response to Frederickson and Reason). *Educational Psychology in Practice, 12,* 131–140.

Association for Assessment in Counseling. (2003). *Responsibilities of users of standardized tests.* Greensboro, NC: Author.

Athey, J. L., & Ahearn, F. L. (1991). The mental health of refugee children: An overview. In F. L. Ahearn & J. L. Athey (Eds.), *Refugee children: Theory, research, and services* (pp. 3–19). Baltimore: Johns Hopkins University Press.

Atkins v. Virginia, 536 U.S. 304 (2002).

Atkins, M. S., Pelham, W. E., & Licht, M. H. (1988). The development and validation of objective classroom measures for conduct and attention deficit disorders. *Advances in Behavioral Assessment of Children and Families, 4,* 3–31.

Attwood, T. (1998). *Asperger's syndrome: A guide for parents and professionals.* Philadelphia: Jessica Kingsley.

Atwater, J. B., Carta, J. J., & Schwartz, I. S. (1989). *Assessment Code/Checklist for the Evaluation of Survival Skills: ACCESS.* Kansas City: University of Kansas.

Aylward, E. H., & Schmidt, S. (1986). An examination of three tests of visual-motor integration. *Journal of Learning Disabilities, 19,* 328–330.

Bacon, E. H., & Rubin, D. C. (1983). Story recall by mentally retarded children. *Psychological Reports, 53,* 791–796.

Baddeley, A. D. (1992). Memory theory and memory therapy. In B. A. Wilson & N. Moffat (Eds.), *Clinical management of memory problems* (2nd ed., pp. 1–31). San Diego: Singular.

Badian, N. A. (1999). Reading disability defined as a discrepancy between listening and reading comprehension: A longitudinal study of stability, gender differences, and prevalence. *Journal of Learning Disabilities, 32,* 138–148.

Bagley, C. (1992). Development of an adolescent stress scale for use by school counsellors: Construct validity in terms of depression, self-esteem and suicidal ideation. *School Psychology International, 13,* 31–49.

Baird, S. M., Haas, L., McCormick, K., Carruth, C., & Turner, K. D. (1992). Approaching an objective system for observation and measurement: Infant-Parent Social Interaction Code. *Topics in Early Childhood Special Education, 12,* 544–571.

Bakeman, R., & Gottman, J. M. (1986). *Observing interaction: An introduction to sequential analysis.* New York: Cambridge University Press.

Baker, L., & Cantwell, D. P. (1989). Specific language and learning disorders. In T. H. Ollendick & M. Hersen (Eds.), *Handbook of clinical psychology* (pp. 93–104). New York: Plenum.

Ballantyne, A. O., & Sattler, J. M. (1991). Validity and reliability of the Reporter's Test with normally achieving and learning disabled children. *Psychological Assessment, 3,* 60–67.

Barker, P. (1990). *Clinical interviews with children and adolescents.* New York: Norton.

Barker, R. G., & Wright, H. F. (1954). *Midwest and its children: The psychological ecology of an American town.* Evanston, IL: Peterson.

Barker, R. G., & Wright, H. F. (1966). *One boy's day: A specimen record of behavior.* New York: Archon Books.

Barkley, R. A. (1981). *Hyperactive children: A handbook for diagnosis and treatment.* New York: Guilford.

Barkley, R. A. (1997). Behavioral inhibition, sustained attention, and executive functions: Constructing a unifying theory of ADHD. *Psychological Bulletin, 121,* 65–94.

Barkley, R. A. (1998). *Attention-deficit hyperactivity disorder: A handbook for diagnosis and treatment* (2nd ed.). New York: Guilford.

Barkley, R. A. (2000). *Taking charge of ADHD* (Rev. ed.). New York: Guilford.

Barkley, R. A. (2002). Psychosocial treatments for attention-deficit/hyperactivity disorder in children. *Journal of Clinical Psychiatry, 63,* 36–43.

Barkley, R. A. (2004). Attention-deficit/hyperactivity disorder and self-regulation: Taking an evolutionary perspective on executive functioning. In K. D. Vohs & R. F. Baumeister (Eds.), *Handbook of self-regulation: Research, theory, and applications* (pp. 301–323). New York: Guilford.

Barkley, R. A., Fischer, M., Smallish, L., & Fletcher, K. (2004). Young adult follow-up of hyperactive children: Antisocial activities and drug use. *Journal of Child Psychology and Psychiatry, and Allied Disciplines, 45,* 195–211.

Barkley, R. A., Grodzinsky, G., & DuPaul, G. J. (1992). Frontal lobe functions in attention deficit disorder with and without hyperactivity: A review and research report. *Journal of Abnormal Child Psychology, 20,* 163–188.

Barkley, R. A., & Murphy, K. R. (1998). *Attention-deficit hyperactivity disorder: A clinical work-book.* New York: Guilford.

Barnett, D. (1997). The effects of early intervention on maltreating parents and their children. In M. J. Guralnick (Ed.), *The effectiveness of early intervention* (pp. 147–170). Baltimore: Brookes.

Baron, I. S. (2000). Clinical implications and practical applications of child neuropsychological evaluations. In K. O. Yeates, M. D. Ris, & H. G. Taylor (Eds.), *Pediatric neuropsychology: Research, theory, and practice* (pp. 446–452). New York: Guilford.

Baron, I. S. (2004). *Neuropsychological evaluation of the child.* New York: Oxford University Press.

Baron-Cohen, S., Wheelright, S., Skinner, R., Martin, J., & Clubley, E. (2001). The autism-spectrum quotient (AQ): Evidence from Asperger syndrome/high-functioning autism, males and females, scientists and mathematicians. *Journal of Autism and Developmental Disorders, 31,* 5–17.

Barriga, A. Q., Gibbs, J. C., Potter, G. B., & Liau, A. K. (2001). *How I Think (HIT) Questionnaire manual.* Champaign, IL: Research Press.

Barry, C. T., Taylor, H. G., Klein, S., & Yeates, K. O. (1996). Validity of neurobehavioral symptoms reported in children with traumatic brain injury. *Child Neuropsychology, 2,* 213–226.

Barsky, A. E., & Gould, J. W. (2002). *Clinicians in court: A guide to subpoenas, depositions, testifying, and everything else you need to know.* New York: Guilford.

Baska, L. K. (1989). Characteristics and needs of the gifted. In J. F. Feldhusen, J. VanTassel-Baska, & K. Seeley (Eds.), *Excellence in educating the gifted* (pp. 15–28). Denver: Love.

Bates, J. D. (1985). *Writing with precision* (rev. ed.). Washington, DC: Acropolis Books.

Baumrind, D. (1967). Child care practices anteceding three patterns of preschool behavior. *Genetic Psychology Monographs, 75,* 43–88.

Baumrind, D. (1978). Parental disciplinary patterns and social competence in children. *Youth and Society, 9,* 239–276.

Bayley, N. (1993). *Bayley Scales of Infant Development* (2nd ed.). San Antonio, TX: The Psychological Corporation.

Beavers, W. R., & Hampson, R. B. (1990). *Successful families: Assessment and intervention.* New York: Norton.

Beck, A. T., Rush, A. J., Shaw, B. F., & Emery, G. (1979). *Cognitive theory of depression.* New York: Guilford.

Beck, J. S., Beck, A. T., & Jolly, J. B. (2001). *Beck Youth Inventories.* San Antonio, TX: The Psychological Corporation.

Beers, M. H. (2003). *The Merck manual of medical information* (2nd ed.). Whitehouse Station, NJ: Merck Research Laboratories.

Beery, K. E., & Beery, N. A. (2004). *Beery VMI* (5th ed.). Minneapolis: NCS Pearson.

Begley, S. (2002, October 11). Survival of the busiest. *The Wall Street Journal,* pp. B1, B4.

Begley, S. (2003, July 16). New insights into autism. *The Wall Street Journal,* pp. B1, B4.

Begley, S. (2005, April 22). Water-flea case shows that ability to adapt is what's really innate. *The Wall Street Journal,* p. B1.

Beiser, M., Dion, R., & Gotowiec, A. (2000). The structure of attention-deficit and hyperactivity symptoms among native and non-native elementary school children. *Journal of Abnormal Child Psychology, 28,* 425–437.

Bellack, A. S., & Hersen, M. (1980). *Introduction to clinical psychology.* New York: Oxford University Press.

Bellak, L., & Abrams, D. M. (1997). *The T.A.T., the C.A.T., and the S.A.T. in clinical use* (6th ed.). Boston: Allyn & Bacon.

Bellak, L., & Bellak, S. S. (1949). *The Children's Apperception Test.* New York: C.P.S.

Bellak, L., & Bellak, S. S. (1965). *The C.A.T.–H. —A human modification.* Larchmont, NY: C.P.S.

Belmont, L., & Birch, H. G. (1965). Lateral dominance, lateral awareness, and reading disability. *Child Development, 36,* 57–71.

Bender, L. (1938). A Visual Motor Gestalt Test and its clinical use. *American Orthopsychiatric Association Research Monograph, No. 3.*

Bender, W. N. (2001). *Learning disabilities: characteristics, identification, and teaching strategies.* Boston: Allyn & Bacon.

Bender, W. N., & Smith, J. K. (1990). Classroom behavior of children and adolescents with learning disabilites: A meta-analysis. *Journal of Learning Disabilites, 23,* 298–305.

Benjamin, A. (1981). *The helping interview* (3rd ed.). Boston: Houghton Mifflin.

Benson, P. L., Scales, P. C., & Mannes, M. (2003). Developmental strengths and their sources: Implications for the study and practice of community-building. In R. M. Lerner, F. Jacobs, & D. Wertlieb (Eds.), *Handbook of applied developmental science* (Vol. 1, pp. 369–406). Thousand Oaks, CA: Sage.

Benton, A. L. (1959). *Right-left discrimination and finger localization.* New York: Hoeber-Harper.

Benton, A. L., Hamsher, K. DeS., Varney, N. R., & Spreen, O. (1983). *Contributions to neuropsychological assessment: A clinical manual.* New York: Oxford University Press.

Bergan, J. R. (1977). *Behavioral consultation.* Columbus, OH: Merrill.

Berkow, R. (1997). *The Merck manual of medical information.* Whitehouse Station, NJ: Merck Research Laboratories.

Berninger, V. W., Mizokawa, D. T., & Bragg, R. (1991). Theory-based diagnosis and remediation of writing disabilities. *Journal of School Psychology, 29,* 57–59.

Bernstein, G. A., & Borchardt, C. M. (1991). Anxiety disorders of childhood and adolescence: A critical review. *Journal of the American Academy of Child and Adolescent Psychiatry, 30,* 519–532.

Bernstein, J. H., & Waber, D. (1996). *Developmental scoring system for the Rey-Osterrieth Complex Figure.* Lutz, FL: Psychological Assessment Resources.

Berument, S. K., Rutter, M., Lord, C., Pickles, A., & Bailey, A. B. (1999). Autism Screening Questionnaire: Diagnostic validity. *British Journal of Psychiatry, 175,* 444–451.

Besharov, D. J. (1990). *Recognizing child abuse: A guide for the concerned.* New York: Free Press.

Betancourt, H., & López, S. R. (1993). The study of culture, ethnicity, and race in American psychology. *American Psychologist, 48,* 629–637.

Bialystok, E. (1992). Selective attention in cognitive processing: The bilingual edge. In R. J. Harris (Ed.), *Cognitive processing in bilinguals* (pp. 501–513). Amsterdam: North-Holland.

Biederman, J., Spencer, T., & Wilens, T. (2004). Evidence-based pharmacotherapy for attention-deficit hyperactivity disorder. *International Journal of Neuropsychopharmacology, 7,* 77–97.

Bienenstock, M., & Vernon, M. (1994). Classification by the states of the deaf and hard of hearing students. *American Annals of the Deaf, 139,* 128–131.

Bierman, K. L. (1983). Cognitive development and clinical interviews with children. In B. B. Lahey & A. E. Kazdin (Eds.), *Advances in clinical child psychology* (Vol. 6, pp. 217–250). New York: Plenum.

Bierman, K. L. (1990). Using the clinical interview to assess children's interpersonal reasoning and emotional understanding. In C. R. Reynolds & R. W. Kamphaus (Eds.), *Handbook of psychological and educational assessment of children: Personality, behavior, and context* (pp. 204–219). New York: Guilford.

Bierman, K. L., & Schwartz, L. A. (1986). Clinical child interviews: Approaches and developmental considerations. *Journal of Child and Adolescent Psychotherapy, 3,* 267–278.

Bigler, E. D., Lajiness-O'Neill, R., & Howes, N. (1998). Technology in the assessment of learning disability. *Journal of Learning Disabilities, 31,* 67–82.

Biklen, D., Morton, M. W., Gold, D., Berrigan, C., & Swaminathan, S. (1992). Facilitated communication: Implications for individuals with autism. *Topics in Language Disorders, 12,* 1–28.

Billingsley, B. S. (1998). Writing: Teaching assessment skills. *Academic Therapy, 24,* 27–35.

Billingsley, B. S., & Wildman, T. M. (1990). Facilitating reading comprehension in learning disabled student: Metacognitive goals and instructional strategies. *RASE: Remedial & Special Education, 11,* 18–31.

Bird, H. R., Yager, T. J., Staghezza, B., Gould, M. S., Canino, G., & Rubio-Stipec, M. (1990). Impairment in the epidemiological measurement of childhood psychopathology in the community. *Journal of the American Academy of Child and Adolescent Psychiatry, 29,* 796–803.

Bishop, V. E. (1996). *Teaching visually impaired children* (2nd ed.). Springfield, IL: Charles C. Thomas.

Black, M. M., & Ponirakis, A. (2000). Computer-administered interviews with children about maltreatment: Methodological, developmental, and ethical issues. *Journal of Interpersonal Violence, 15,* 682–695.

Blackburn, A. C., & Erickson, D. B. (1986). Predictable crises of the gifted student. *Journal of Counseling & Development, 64,* 552–555.

Blaha, J., Fawaz, N., & Wallbrown, F. H. (1979). Information processing components of Koppitz errors on the Bender Visual-Motor Gestalt Test. *Journal of Clinical Psychology, 35,* 784–790.

Blakemore, B., Shindler, S., & Conte, R. (1993). A problem solving training program for parents of children with attention deficit hyperactivity disorder. *Canadian Journal of School Psychology, 9,* 66–85.

Bloch, J. S., Weinstein, J., & Seitz, M. (2005). School and parent partnerships in the preschool years. In D. Zager (Ed.), *Autism spectrum disorder: Identification, education, and treatment* (3rd ed., pp. 229–265). Mahwah, NJ: Erlbaum.

Boden, M. A. (1994). Dimensions of creativity. In M. A. Boden (Ed.), *The definition of creativity* (pp. 75–117). Cambridge, MA: MIT Press.

Bogdan, R. C., & Biklen, S. K. (1982). *Qualitative research for education: An introduction to theory and methods.* Boston: Allyn & Bacon.

Boggs, S. R., & Eyberg, S. M. (1990). Interview techniques and establishing rapport. In A. M. La Greca (Ed.), *Through the eyes of the child: Obtaining self-reports from children and adolescents* (pp. 85–108). Boston: Allyn & Bacon.

Bolen, L. M., Hewett, J. B., Hall, C. W., & Mitchell, C. C. (1992). Expanded Koppitz scoring system of the Bender Gestalt Visual-Motor Test for adolescents: A pilot study. *Psychology in the Schools, 29,* 113–115.

Boney-McCoy, S., & Finkelhor, D. (1995). Psychosocial sequelae of violent victimization in a national youth sample. *Journal of Consulting and Clinical Psychology, 63,* 726–736.

Borkowski, J. G., & Burke, J. E. (1996). Theories, models, and measurements of executive functioning: An information processing perspective. In G. L. Lyon & N. A. Krasnegor (Eds.), *Attention, memory and executive function* (pp. 235–261). Baltimore: Brookes.

Bornstein, M. H., Cote, L. R., Maital, S., Painter, K., Park, S., Pascual, L., Pêcheux, M., Ruel, J., Venuti, P., & Vyt, A. (2004). Cross-linguistic analysis of vocabulary in young children: Spanish, Dutch, French, Hebrew, Italian, Korean, and American English. *Child Development, 75,* 1115–1139.

Bornstein, M. H., & Lamb, M. (Eds.). (1999). *Developmental psychology: An advanced textbook* (4th ed.). Mahwaw, NJ: Erlbaum.

Bornstein, P. H., Hamilton, S. B., & Bornstein, M. T. (1986). Self-monitoring procedures. In A. R. Ciminero, K. S. Calhoun, & H. E. Adams (Eds.), *Handbook of behavioral assessment* (2nd ed., pp. 176–222). New York: Wiley.

Bornstein, R. A. (1983). Verbal IQ–Performance IQ discrepancies on the Wechsler Adult Intelligence Scale–Revised in patients with unilateral or bilateral cerebral dysfunction. *Journal of Consulting and Clinical Psychology, 51,* 779–780.

Borum, R. (2000). Assessing violence risk among youth. *Journal of Clinical Psychology, 56,* 1263–1288.

Boxer, R., Challen, M., & McCarthy, M. (1991). Developing an assessment framework: The distinctive contribution of the educational psychologist. *Education Psychology in Practice, 7,* 30–34.

Boyer, P., & Chesteen, H. (1992). Professional helpfulness? The experiences of parents of handicapped children with counsellors and social workers. *Journal of Child and Youth Care, 7,* 37–48.

Boyse, K. (2004). *Non-verbal learning disability (NLD or NVLD).* Retrieved June 28, 2005, from http://www.med.umich.edu/1libr/yourchild/nld.htm

Braden, J. P. (1994). *Deafness, deprivation, and IQ.* New York: Plenum.

Braden, J. P., & Hannah, J. M. (1998). Assessment of hearing-impaired and deaf children with the WISC–III. In A. Prifitera & D. H. Saklofske (Eds.), *WISC–III clinical use and interpretation* (pp. 177–202). San Diego: Academic Press.

Braden, J. P., Kostrubala, C. E., & Reed, J. (1994). Why do deaf children score differently on performance vs. motor-reduced nonverbal intelligence tests? *Journal of Psychoeducational Assessment, 12,* 357–363.

Bradley, L. (1980). *Assessing reading difficulties: A diagnostic and remedial approach.* London, England: MacMillan.

Bradley, R. H. (1994). The HOME inventory: Review and reflections. *Advances in Child Development and Behavior, 25,* 241–288.

Bradley-Johnson, S. (1994). *Psychoeducational assessment of students who are visually impaired or blind: Infancy through high school* (2nd ed.). Austin, TX: Pro-Ed.

Bramlett, R. K., & Barnett, D. W. (1993). The development of a direct observation code for use in preschool settings. *School Psychology Review, 22,* 49–62.

Brannigan, G. G., Aabye, S. M., Baker, L. A., & Ryan, G. T. (1995). Further validation of the qualitative scoring system for the Modified Bender-Gestalt Test. *Psychology in the Schools, 32,* 24–26.

Brannigan, G. G., & Brunner, N. A. (1989). *The Modified Version of the Bender-Gestalt Test for Preschool and Primary School Children.* Brandon, VT: Clinical Psychology Publishing Company.

Brannigan, G. G., & Brunner, N. A. (1996). *The Modified Version of the Bender-Gestalt Test for Preschool and Primary School Children–Revised.* Brandon, VT: Clinical Psychology Publishing Company.

Brannigan, G. G., & Brunner, N. A. (2002). *Guide to the qualitative scoring system for the Modified Version of the Bender-Gestalt Test.* Brandon, VT: Clinical Psychology Publishing Company.

Brannigan, G. G., & Decker, S. L. (2003). *Bender Visual-Motor Gestalt Test, Second Edition.* Itasca, IL: Riverside Publishing.

Breen, M. J. (1982). Comparison of educationally handicapped students' scores on the Revised Developmental Test of Visual-Motor Integration and Bender-Gestalt. *Perceptual and Motor Skills, 54,* 1227–1230.

Breen, M. J., Carlson, M., & Lehman, J. (1985). The Revised Developmental Test of Visual-Motor Integration: Its relation to the VMI, WISC–R, and Bender Gestalt for a group of elementary aged learning disabled students. *Journal of Learning Disabilities, 18,* 136–138.

Bregman, J. D. (1991). Current developments in the understanding of mental retardation: II. Psychopathology. *Journal of the American Academy of Child and Adolescent Psychiatry, 30,* 861–872.

Breslau, N. (1987). Inquiring about the bizarre: False positives in Diagnostic Interview Schedule for Children (DISC) ascertainment of obsessions, compulsions, and psychotic symptoms. *Journal of the American Academy of Child and Adolescent Psychiatry, 26,* 639–644.

Bretherton, I. (1993). Theoretical contributions from developmental psychology. In P. G. Boss, W. J. Doherty, R. LaRossa, W. R. Schumm, & S. K. Steinmetz (Eds.), *Sourcebook of family theories and methods: A contextual approach* (pp. 275–297). New York: Plenum.

Brewer, D. D., Hawkins, J. D., Catalano, R. F., & Neckerman, H. J. (1995). Preventing serious, violent, and chronic juvenile offending: A review of evaluations of selected strategies in childhood, adolescence, and the community. In J. C. Howell, B. Krisberg, J. D. Hawkins, & J. J. Wilson (Eds.), *Serious, violent and chronic juvenile offenders* (pp. 61–141). Thousand Oaks, CA: Sage.

Brockway, B. S. (1978). Evaluating physician competency: What difference does it make? *Evaluation and Program Planning, 1,* 211.

Brody, E. B., & Brody, N. (1976). *Intelligence: Nature, determinants, and consequences.* New York: Academic Press.

Brody, L. E., & Mills, C. J. (1997). Gifted children with learning disabilities: A review of the issues. *Journal of Learning Disabilities, 30,* 282–296.

Bromwich, R. M. (1981). *Working with parents and infants: An interactional approach.* Baltimore: University Park Press.

Brooks, D. N. (1991). The head-injured family. *Journal of Clinical and Experimental Neuropsychology, 13,* 155–188.

Brown, S. A., Aarons, G. A., & Abrantes, A. M. (2001). Adolescent alcohol and drug abuse. In C. E. Walker & M. C. Roberts (Eds.), *Handbook of clinical child psychology* (3rd ed., pp. 757–775). New York: Wiley.

Brown, T. E. (2001). *Brown Attention-Deficit Disorder Scales.* San Antonio, TX: Psychological Corporation.

Bruininks, R. H. (1978). *Bruininks-Oseretsky Test of Motor Proficiency.* Circle Pines, MN: American Guidance Service.

Bruininks, R. H., Woodcock, R. W., Weatherman, R., & Hill, B. (1996). *Scales of Independent Behavior–Revised.* Chicago, IL: Riverside Publishing.

Bruner, F. G., Barnes, E., & Dearborn, W. F. (1909). Report of committee on books and tests pertaining to the study of exceptional and mentally deficient children. *Proceedings of the National Education Association, 47,* 901–914.

Busch, B. (1993). Attention deficits: Current concepts, controversies, management, and approaches to classroom instruction. *Annals of Dyslexia, 43,* 5–25.

Buss, A. H., & Durkee, A. (1957). An inventory for assessing different kinds of hostility. *Journal of Consulting Psychology, 21,* 343–349.

Buss, A. H., & Warren, W. L. (2000). *Aggression Questionnaire manual.* Los Angeles: Western Psychological Services.

Butcher, J. N., & Williams, C. L. (1992). *Essentials of MMPI–2 and MMPI–A interpretation.* Minneapolis: University of Minnesota Press.

Butcher, J. N., Williams, C. L., Graham, J. R., Archer, R. P., Tellegen, A., Ben-Porath, Y. S., & Kaemmer, B. (1992). *Minnesota Multiphasic Personality Inventory–Adolescent.* Minneapolis: University of Minnesota Press.

Butler, S., Gross, J., & Hayne, H. (1995). The effect of drawing on memory performance in young children. *Developmental Psychology, 3,* 597–608.

Bütz, M. R., Bowling, J. B., & Bliss, C. A. (2000). Psychotherapy with the mentally retarded: A review of the literature and the implications. *Professional Psychology: Research and Practice, 31,* 42–47.

Campbell, S. B. (1989). Developmental perspectives. In T. H. Ollendick & M. Hersen (Eds.), *Handbook of child psychopathology* (pp. 5–28). New York: Plenum.

Canino, G., & Bravo, M. (1999). The translation and adaptation of diagnostic instruments for cross-cultural use. In D. Shaffer, C. P. Lucas, & J. E. Richtess (Eds.), *Diagnostic assessment in child and adolescent psychopathology* (pp. 285–298). New York: Guilford.

Canino, I. (1985). Taking a history. In D. Shaffer, A. A. Erhardt, & L. L. Greenhill (Eds.), *The clinical guide to child psychiatry* (pp. 393–407). New York: Free Press.

Canino, I., & Spurlock, J. (2000). *Culturally diverse children and adolescents: Assessment, diagnosis, and treatment* (2nd ed.). New York: Guilford.

Casey, R., Levy, S. E., Brown, K., & Brooks-Gunn, J. (1992). Impaired emotional health in children with mild reading disability. *Journal of Developmental and Behavioral Pediatrics, 13,* 256–260.

Caskey, W. E., Jr., & Larson, G. L. (1980). Scores on group and individually administered Bender-Gestalt Test and Otis-Lennon IQs of kindergarten children. *Perceptual and Motor Skills, 50,* 387–390.

Catalano, R. F., & Hawkins, J. D. (1996). The social development model: A theory of antisocial behavior. In J. D. Hawkins (Ed.), *Delinquency and crime: Current theories* (pp. 149–197). Cambridge, England: Cambridge University Press.

Ceci, S. J., Powell, M. B., & Crossman, A. M. (1999). Critical issues in children's memory and testimony. In D. L. Faigman, D. H. Kaye, M. J. Saks, & J. Sanders (Eds.), *Modern scientific evidence: The law and science of expert testimony* (pp. 40–69). St. Paul: Westgroup.

Center for Technology and Education. (1997). *Adapted pencils to computers: Strategies for improving writing.* Retrieved March 5, 2005, from http://cte.jhu.edu/adaptedpencils.pdf

Centers for Disease Control and Prevention. (2003). *Heads up: Preventing brain injuries.* Retrieved May 12, 2005, from http://www.cdc.gov/Migrated_Content/Brochures_and_Catalogs/tbi_preventing_brain_injuries.pdf

Centers for Disease Control and Prevention. (2004). *Mercury and vaccines (thimerosal).* Retrieved March 3, 2005, from http://www.cdc.gov/nip/vacsafe/concerns/thimerosal/thimerosal-vacs-facts.htm

Chandler, L. A., & Johnson, V. V. (1991). *Using projective techniques with children: A guide to clinical assessment.* Springfield, IL: Charles C. Thomas.

Chapman, R. S., Hesketh, L. J., & Kistler, D. J. (2002). Predicting longitudinal change in language production and comprehension in individuals with Down syndrome: Hierarchical linear modeling. *Journal of Speech, Language, & Hearing Research, 45,* 902–915.

Chess, S., & Thomas, A. (1986). *Temperament in clinical practice.* New York: Guilford.

Child Trends Data Bank. (2003a). *Suicidal teens.* Retrieved August 2, 2005, from http://www.childtrendsdatabank.org/pdf/34_PDF.pdf

Child Trends Data Bank. (2003b). *Teen homicide, suicide, and firearms death.* Retrieved August 2, 2005, from http://www.childtrendsdatabank.org/pdf/70_PDF.pdf

Christensen, C. A. (1992). Discrepancy definitions of reading disability: Has the quest led us astray? A response to Stanovich. *Reading Research Quarterly, 27,* 276–278.

Chung, R. C. Y., & Lin, K. M. (1994). Help-seeking behavior among Southeast Asian refugees. *Journal of Community Psychology, 22,* 109–120.

Cicchetti, D., & Toth, S. L. (1998). Perspectives on research and practice in developmental psychology. In I. E. Sigel & K. A. Renninger (Eds.), *Handbook of child psychology* (5th ed., pp. 479–582). New York: Wiley.

Cicerone, K. D., & Tupper, D. E. (1986). Cognitive assessment in the neuropsychological rehabilitation of head-injured adults. In B. P. Uzzell & Y. Gross (Eds.), *Clinical neuropsychology of intervention* (pp. 59–83). Boston: Martinus Nijhoff Publishing.

Clark, C. R. (1988). Sociopathy, malingering, and defensiveness. In R. Rogers (Ed.), *Clinical assessment of malingering and deception* (pp. 54–64). New York: Guilford.

Clark, H. H. (1985). Language use and language users. In G. Lindzey & E. Aronson (Eds.), *Handbook of social psychology* (3rd ed., Vol. 2). New York: Random House.

Clarke, A. M., & Clarke, A. D. B. (1994). Variations, deviations, risks, and uncertainties in human development. In W. B. Carey & S. C. McDevitt (Eds.), *Prevention and early intervention: Individual differences as risk factors for the mental health of children: A festschrift for Stella Chess and Alexander Thomas* (pp. 83–91). New York: Brunner/Mazel.

Cobb, H. C. (1989). Counseling and psychotherapy with handicapped children and adolescents. In D. T. Brown & H. T. Prout (Eds.), *Counseling and psychotherapy with children and adolescents: Theory and practice for school and clinic settings* (2nd ed., pp. 467–501). Brandon, VT: Clinical Psychology Publishing Company.

Cohen, D. H., & Stern, V. (1970). Observing and recording the behavior of young children. New York: Teachers College Press.

Cohen, D. H., Stern, V., & Balaban, N. (1997). *Observing and recording the behavior of young children* (4th ed.). New York: Teachers College Press.

Cohen, J. (1960). A coefficient of agreement for nominal scales. *Educational and Psychological Measurement, 20,* 37–46.

Cohen, J. (1968). Weighted kappa: Nominal scale agreement with provision for scaled disagreement or partial credit. *Psychological Bulletin, 70,* 213–220.

Cohen, J. (1988). *Statistical power analysis for the behavioral sciences.* Hillsdale, NJ: Erlbaum.

Cohen, L. M. (2003). A conceptual lens for looking at theories of creativity. In D. Ambrose, L. M. Cohen, & A. J. Tannenbaum (Eds.), *Creative intelligence: Toward theoretic integration: Perspective on creativity* (pp. 81–112). Cresskill, NJ: Hampton Press.

Cohen, M. J. (1997). *Children's Memory Scale.* San Antonio, TX: The Psychological Corporation.

Cohen, M. J., Becker, M. G., & Campbell, R. (1990). Relationships among four methods of assessment of children with attention deficit-hyperactivity disorder. *Journal of School Psychology, 28,* 189–202.

Cohen, P., & Kassen, S. (1999). The context of assessment: Culture, race, and socioeconomic status as influences on the assessment of children. In D. Shaffer, C. P. Lucas, & J. E. Richters (Eds.), *Di-*

agnostic assessment in child and adolescent psychopathology (pp. 299–318). New York: Guilford.

Cohen, S. B. (1991). Adapting educational programs for students with head injuries. *Journal of Head Trauma Rehabilitation, 6,* 56–63.

Colangelo, N., & Assouline, S. G. (2000). Counseling gifted students. In K. A. Heller, F. J. Mönks, R. J. Sternberg, & R. F. Subotnik (Eds.), *International handbook of giftedness and talent* (pp. 595–608). Oxford, England: Elsevier.

Coleman, L. J., & Cross, T. L. (2002). *Being gifted in school: An introduction to development, guidance, and teaching.* Waco, TX: Prufrock Press.

Collett, B. R., Ohan, J. L., & Myers, K. M. (2003). Ten-year review of rating scales. V: Scales assessing attention-deficit/hyperactivity disorder. *Journal of American Academy of Child & Adolescent Psychiatry, 42,* 1015–1037.

Compas, B. E., Hinden, B. R., & Gerhardt, C. A. (1995). Adolescent development: Pathways and processes of risk and resilience. *Annual Review of Psychology, 46,* 265–293.

Conduct Problems Prevention Research Group. (1992). A developmental and clinical model for the prevention of conduct disorder: The FAST track program. *Developmental and Psychopathology, 4,* 509–527.

Cone, J. D., & Foster, S. L. (1982). Direct observation in clinical psychology. In P. C. Kendall & J. N. Butcher (Eds.), *Handbook of research methods in clinical psychology* (pp. 311–354). New York: Wiley.

Conger, A. J. (1980). Integration and generalization of kappas for multiple raters. *Psychological Bulletin, 88,* 322–328.

Conger, R. D., Conger, K. J., Elder, G. H., Lorenz, F. O., Simons, R. L., & Whitbeck, L. B. (1993). Family economic stress and adjustment of early adolescent girls. *Child Development, 29,* 206–219.

Connecticut State Department of Education. (1999). *Guidelines for identifying children with learning disabilities* (2nd ed.). Hartford, CT: Author.

Conners, C. K. (1997). *Conners' Rating Scales–Revised: Technical manual.* North Tonawanda, NY: Multi-Health Systems.

Conners, C. K., March, J. S., Frances, A., Wells, K. C., & Ross, R. (2001). Treatment of attention-deficit/hyperactivity disorder: Expert consensus guidelines. *Journal of Attention Disorders, 4 (Suppl 1),* S-1–S-128.

Conners, C. K., & MHS Staff. (2000). *Conners' Continuous Performance Test II (CPT II).* North Tonawanda, NY: Multi-Health Systems.

Cook, R. E., Tessier, A., & Klein, M. D. (2004). *Adaptive early childhood curricula for children in inclusive settings* (6th ed.). Upper Saddle River, NJ: Prentice-Hall.

Cooper, H. M. (1989). *Integrating research: A guide for literature reviews.* Newbury Park, CA: Sage.

Corey, G., Corey, M. S., & Callanan, P. (1993). *Issues and ethics in the helping professions* (4th ed.). Pacific Grove, CA: Brooks/Cole.

Cormier, L. S., & Cormier, B. (1998). *Interviewing strategies for helpers: Fundamental skills and cognitive behavioral interventions* (4th ed.). Pacific Grove, CA: Brooks/Cole.

Cowen, E. L., Hightower, A. D., Pedro-Carroll, J. L., Work, W. C., Wyman, P. A., & Haffey, W. G. (1996). *School-based prevention for children at risk: The Primary Mental Health Project.* Washington, DC: American Psychological Association.

Crenshaw, T. M., Kavale, K. A., Forness, S. R., & Reeve, R. E. (1999). Attention deficit hyperactivity disorder and the efficacy of stimulant medication: A meta-analysis. *Advances in Learning and Behavioral Disabilities, 13,* 135–165.

Croxen, M. E., & Lytton, H. (1971). Reading disability and difficulties in finger localization and right-left discrimination. *Developmental Psychology, 5,* 256–262.

Csikszentmihalyi, M., & Wolfe, R. (2000). New conceptions and research approaches to creativity: Implications of a systems perspective for creativity in education. In K. A. Heller, F. J. Mönks, R. J. Sternberg, & R. F. Subotnik (Eds.), *International handbook of giftedness and talent* (pp. 81–94). Oxford, England: Elsevier.

Cuccaro, M. L., Wright, H. H., Rownd, C. V., Abramson, R. K., Waller, J., & Fender, D. (1996). Brief report: Professional perceptions of children with developmental difficulties: The influence of race and socioeconomic status. *Journal of Autism and Developmental Disorders, 26,* 461–469.

Cummings, E. M., Davies, P. T., & Campbell, S. B. (2000). *Developmental psychopathology and family process: Theory, research, and clinical implications.* New York: Guilford.

Cummings, J. A. (1986). Projective drawings. In H. M. Knoff (Ed.), *The assessment of child and adolescent personality* (pp. 199–244). New York: Guilford.

Cunnien, A. J. (1988). Psychiatric and medical syndromes associated with deception. In R. Rogers (Ed.), *Clinical assessment of malingering and deception* (pp. 13–33). New York: Guilford.

Cunningham, R. (1992). Developmentally appropriate psychosocial care for children affected by parental chemical dependence. *Journal of Health Care for the Poor & Underserved, 3,* 208–221.

Dadds, M. R., Schwartz, S., & Sanders, M. R. (1987). Marital discord and treatment outcome in the treatment of childhood conduct disorders. *Journal of Consulting and Clinical Psychology, 55,* 396–403.

Dalby, P. R., & Obrzut, J. E. (1991). Epidemiologic characteristics and sequelae of closed head-injured children and adolescents: A review. *Developmental Neuropsychology, 7,* 35–68.

Dalsgaard, S., Mortensen, P. B., Frydenberg, M., & Thomsen, P. H. (2002). Conduct problems, gender and adult psychiatric outcome of children with attention-deficit hyperactivity disorder. *British Journal of Psychiatry, 181,* 416–421.

D'Amato, R. C., Gray, J. W., & Dean, R. S. (1988). A comparison between intelligence and neuropsychological functioning. *Journal of School Psychology, 26,* 283–292.

Damico, J. S. (1991). Clinical discourse analysis: A functional language assessment technique. In C. S. Simon (Ed.), *Communication skills and classroom success: Assessment and therapy methodologies for language and learning disabled students* (pp. 125–150). Eau Claire, WI: Thinking Publications.

Dana, R. H. (1993). *Multicultural assessment perspectives for professional psychology.* Boston: Allyn & Bacon.

Danek, M. (1988). Deafness and family impact. In P. W. Power, A. E. Dell Orto, & M. B. Gibbons (Eds.), *Family interventions throughout chronic illness and disability* (pp. 120–135). New York: Springer.

Darley, F. L. (1978). A philosophy of appraisal and diagnosis. In F. L. Darley & D. C. Spriestersbach (Eds.), *Diagnostic methods in speech pathology* (pp. 1–60). New York: Harper & Row.

Davis, G. A. (1997). Identifying creativity students and measuring creativity. In N. Colangelo & G. A. Davis (Eds.), *Handbook of gifted education* (2nd ed., pp. 269–281). Boston: Allyn & Bacon.

Davis, J. L. (2005). *Choosing the right ADHD medication for your child.* Retrieved May 26, 2005, from http://my.webmd.com/content/article/106/108111.htm

Dawson, P., & Guare, R. (1998). *Coaching the ADHD student.* North Tonawanda, NY: Multi-Health Systems.

Dean, R. S., & Anderson, J. L. (1997). Lateralization of cerebral functions. In A. M. Horton, D. Wedding, & J. Webster (Eds.), *The neuropsychology handbook: Foundations and assessment.* (2nd ed., pp. 139–170). New York: Springer.

DeFries, J. C. (1989). Gender ratios in children with reading disability and their affected relatives: A commentary. *Journal of Learning Disabilites, 22,* 544–545.

DeFries, J. C., & Alarcon, M. (1996). Genetics of specific reading disability. *Mental Retardation & Developmental Disabilities Research Reviews, 2,* 39–47.

DeFries, J. C., Gillis, J. J., & Wadsworth, S. J. (1993). Genes and genders: A twin study of reading disability. In A. M. Galaburda (Ed.), *Dyslexia and development: Neurobiological aspects of extra-ordinary brains* (pp. 187–294). Cambridge, MA: Harvard University Press.

Delis, D. C., Kaplan, E. F., & Kramer, J. H. (2001). *The Delis-Kaplan Executive Function System.* San Antonio, TX: The Psychological Corporation.

Delis, D. C., Kramer, J. H., Kaplan, E. F., & Ober, B. A. (1994). *California Verbal Learning Test–Children's Version.* San Antonio, TX: The Psychological Corporation.

DeMers, S. T., Turner, S. M., Andberg, M., Foote, W., Hough, L., Ivnik, R., Meier, S., Moreland, K., & Rey-Casserly, C. M. (2000). *Report of the task force on test user qualifications.* Washington, DC: American Psychological Association.

DeMers, S. T., Wright, D., & Dappen, L. (1981). Comparison of scores on two visual-motor tests for children referred for learning or adjustment difficulties. *Perceptual and Motor Skills, 53,* 863–867.

DePompei, R., & Blosser, J. L. (1987). Strategies for helping head-injured children successfully return to school. *Language, Speech, and Hearing Services in Schools, 18,* 292–300.

DePompei, R., Blosser, J. L., & Zarski, J. F. (1989, November). *The path less traveled: Counseling family and friends of T.B.I. survivors.* Paper presented at the American Speech-Language-Hearing Association National Convention, St. Louis, MO.

DePompei, R., Zarski, J. J., & Hall, D. E. (1988). Cognitive communication impairments: A family-focused viewpoint. *Journal of Head Trauma Rehabilitation, 3,* 13–22.

De Renzi, E. (1980). The Token Test and the Reporter's Test: A measure of verbal input and a measure of verbal output. In M. T. Sarno & O. Hook (Eds.), *Aphasia: Assessment and treatment* (pp. 158–169). New York: Masson Publishing.

De Renzi, E., & Faglioni, P. (1978). Normative data and screening power of a shortened version of the Token Test. *Cortex, 14,* 41–49.

De Renzi, E., & Ferrari, C. (1978). The Reporter's Test: A sensitive test to detect expressive disturbances in aphasics. *Cortex, 14,* 279–293.

Deshler, D. D. (2002). Response to "Is learning disabilities just a fancy term for low achievement?" A meta-analysis of reading differences between low achievers with and without the label. In R. Bradley, L. Danielson, and D. Hallahan (Eds.), *Identification of learning disabilities: Research to practice* (pp. 763–772). Mahwah, NJ: Erlbaum.

Deshler, D. D., Ellis, E. S., & Lenz, B. K. (1996). *Teaching adolescents with learning disabilities: Strategies and methods.* Denver: Love.

DeSpelder, L. A., & Strickland, A. L. (1992). *The last dance: Encountering death and dying* (3rd ed.). Mountain View, CA: Mayfield.

Detterman, D. K., Gabriel, L. T., & Ruthsatz, J. M. (2000). Intelligence and mental retardation. In R. Sternberg (Ed.), *Handbook of intelligence* (pp. 141–158). New York: Cambridge University Press.

Diaz, R. M., & Klinger, C. (1991). Towards an explanatory model of the interaction between bilingualism and cognitive development. In E. Bialystok (Ed.), *Language processing in bilingual children* (pp. 167–192). Cambridge, England: Cambridge University Press.

DiMaio, S., Grizenko, N., & Joober, R. (2003). Dopamine genes and attention-deficit hyperactivity disorder: A review. *Journal of Psychiatry and Neuroscience, 28,* 27–38.

DiSimoni, F. G. (1978). *Token Test for Children.* Allen, TX: DLM Teaching Resources.

Dodrill, C. B., Farwell, J., & Batzel, L. W. (1987, September). *Validity of the Aphasia Screening Test for Young Children.* Poster session presented at the meeting of the American Psychological Association, New York.

Doll, E. A. (1946). *The Oseretsky Tests of Motor Proficiency: A translation from the Portuguese adaption.* Minneapolis: Educational Test Bureau.

Dolmage, W. R. (1996). One less brick in the wall: The myths of youth violence and unsafe schools. *Education and Law Journal, 7,* 46–54.

Donaghy, W. C. (1984). *The interview: Skills and applications.* Glenview, IL: Scott, Foresman.

Donders, J. (1996). Validity of short forms of the intermediate Halstead Category Test in children with traumatic brain injury. *Archives of Clinical Neuropsychology, 11,* 131–137.

Donovan, M. S., & Cross, C. T. (2002). *Minority students in special and gifted education.* Washington, DC: National Academy Press.

Downs, C. W., Smeyak, G. P., & Martin, E. (1980). *Professional interviewing.* New York: Harper & Row.

Drasgow, F. (1987). Study of the measurement bias of two standardized psychological tests. *Journal of Applied Psychology, 72,* 19–29.

Drell, M. J., Siegel, C. H., & Gaensbauer, T. J. (1993). Post-traumatic stress disorder. In C. H. Zeanah, Jr. (Ed.), *Handbook of infant mental health* (pp. 291–304). New York: Guilford.

Dresser, N. (1996). *Multicultural manners.* New York: Wiley.

Drotar, D., & Crawford, P. (1987). Using home observation in the clinical assessment of children. *Journal of Clinical Child Psychology, 16,* 342–349.

Dumas, J. E. (1987). Interact—A computer-based coding and data management system to assess family interactions. *Advances in Behavioral Assessment of Children and Families, 3,* 177–202.

Duncan, S. E., & DeAvila, E. A. (1990). *Language Assessment Scales–Oral.* Monterey, CA: CTB/McGraw-Hill.

Duncan, S. E., & DeAvila, E. A. (1994). *Language Assessment Scales–Reading and Writing.* Monterey, CA: CTB/McGraw-Hill.

Dunn, R., & Dunn, K. (1977). *How to raise independent and professionally successful daughters.* Englewood Cliffs, NJ: Prentice Hall.

Dunne-Maxim, K., Dunne, E. J., & Hauser, M. J. (1987). When children are suicide survivors. In E. J. Dunne, J. L. McIntosh, & K. D. Maxim (Eds.), *Suicide and its aftermath: Understanding and counselling the survivors* (pp. 234–244). New York: Norton.

DuPaul, G. J., & Eckert, T. L. (1997). The effects of school based interventions for ADHD: A meta-analysis. *School Psychology Review, 26,* 5–27.

DuPaul, G. J., Ervin, R. A., Hook, C. L., & McGoey, K. E. (1998). Peer tutoring for children with attention deficit hyperactivity disorder: Effects on classroom behavior and academic performance. *Journal of Applied Behavior Analysis, 31,* 579–592.

DuPaul, G. J., & Hennington, P. N. (1993). Peer tutoring effects on the classroom performance of children with ADHD. *School Psychology Review, 22,* 134–143.

DuPaul, G. J., Power, T. J., Anastopolous, A. D., & Reid, R. (1998). *ADHD Rating Scale–IV: Checklists, norms, and clinical interpretation.* New York: Guilford.

DuPaul, G. J., & Stoner, G. (2003). *ADHD in the schools* (2nd ed.). New York: Guilford.

Durston, S., Tottenham, N. T., Thomas, K. M., Davidson, M. C., Eigsti, I. M., Yang, Y., Ulug, A. M., & Casey, B. J. (2003). Differential patterns of striatal activation in young children with and without ADHD. *Biological Psychiatry, 53,* 871–878.

Edelbrock, C. S. (1984). Developmental considerations. In T. H. Ollendick & M. Hersen (Eds.), *Child behavioral assessment: Principles and procedures* (pp. 20–37). New York: Pergamon.

Edelbrock, C. S., & Costello, A. J. (1988). Structured psychiatric interviews for children. In M. Rutter, A. H. Tuma, & I. Lann (Eds.), *Assessment diagnosis in child psychopathology* (pp. 87–112). New York: Guilford.

Edelbrock, C. S., Costello, A. J., Dulcan, M. K., Conover, N. C., & Kalas, R. (1986). Parent-child agreement on child psychiatric symptoms assessed via structured interview. *Journal of Child Psychology and Psychiatry, 27,* 181–190.

Edelbrock, C. S., Costello, A. J., Dulcan, M. K., Kalas, R., & Conover, N. C. (1985). Age differences in the reliability of the psychiatric interview of the child. *Child Development, 56,* 265–275.

Editorial Board. (1996). Definition of mental retardation. In J. W. Jacobson & J. A. Mulick (Eds.), *Manual of diagnosis and professional practice in mental retardation* (pp. 13–53). Washington, DC: American Psychological Association.

Edwards, G., & Starr, M. (1996). Internalizing disorders: Mood and anxiety disorders. In M. J. Breen & C. R. Fiedler (Eds.), *Behavioral approach to assessment of youth with emotional/behavioral disorders: A handbook for school-based practitioners* (pp. 361–412). Austin, TX: Pro-Ed.

Edwards, H. P. (1994). Regulation and accreditation in professional psychology: Facilitators? Safeguards? Threats? *Canadian Psychology, 35,* 66–69.

Ehlers, S., Gillberg, C., & Wing, L. (1999). A screening questionnaire for Asperger syndrome and other high-functioning autism spectrum disorders in school age children. *Journal of Autism and Developmental Disabilities, 24,* 3–22.

Ehri, L. C. (1998). Grapheme–phoneme knowledge is essential for learning to read words in English. In J. L. Metsala & L. C. Ehri (Eds.), *Word recognition in beginning literacy* (pp. 3–40). Mahwah, NJ: Erlbaum.

Elbers, N. & Van Loon-Vervoorn, A. (1999). Lexical relationships in children who are blind. *Journal of Visual Impairment & Blindness, 93,* 419–421.

Elias, M. (2005). Want a sharp mind for your golden years? Start now. *USA Today.* Retrieved August 19, 2005, from http://news.yahoo.com/news?tmpl=story&u=/usatoday/20050818/ts_usatoday/wantasharpmindforyourgoldenyearsstartnow

Emmons, R. (1996, December 27). Black English has its place. *The Los Angeles Times,* p. B9.

Endres, J. (1997). The suggestibility of the child witness: The role of individual differences and their assessment. *Journal of Credibility Assessment and Witness Psychology, 1,* 44–67.

Engelberg, E., & Christianson, S. (2002). Stress, trauma, and memory. In M. Eisen, J. A. Quas, & G. S. Goodman (Eds.), *Memory and suggestibility in the forensic interview* (pp. 143–163). Mahwah, NJ: Erlbaum.

English, D. J., Widom, C. S., & Brandford, C. (2002). *Childhood victimization and delinquency, adult, criminality, and violent criminal behavior: A replication and extension.* Retrieved February 1, 2002, from http://www.ncjrs.org/pdffiles1/nij/grants/192291.pdf

Epstein, J. N., March, J. S., Conners, C. K., & Jackson, D. L. (1998). Racial differences on the Conners Teacher Rating Scale. *Journal of Abnormal Child Psychology, 26,* 109–118.

Epstein, N. B., & Bishop, D. S. (1981). Problem-centered systems therapy of the family. In A. Gurman & D. Kiniskern (Eds.), *Handbook of family therapy* (pp. 444–482). New York: Brunner/Mazel.

Erickson, L. G., Stahl, S. A., & Rinehart, S. D. (1985). Metacognitive abilities of above and below average readers: Effects of conceptual tempo, passage level, and error type on error detection. *Journal of Reading Behavior, 17,* 235–252.

Eth, S. (1990). Post-traumatic stress disorder in childhood. In M. Hersen & C. G. Last (Eds.), *Handbook of child and adolescent psychopathology* (pp. 263–274). New York: Pergamon.

Eth, S. (Ed.). (2001). *PTSD in children and adolescents: Vol 20. Review of the psychiatry series.* Washington, DC: American Psychiatric Association.

Evans, H. L., & Sullivan, M. A. (1993). Children and the use of self-monitoring, self-evaluation, and self-reinforcement. In A. J. Finch, Jr., W. M. Nelson, III, & E. S. Ott (Eds.), *Cognitive-behavioral procedures with children and adolescents: A practical guide* (pp. 67–89). Boston: Allyn & Bacon.

Everett, F., Proctor, N., & Cartmell, B. (1983). Providing psychological services to American Indian children and families. *Professional Psychology: Research and Practice, 14,* 588–603.

Ewing-Cobbs, L., Levin, H. S., Fletcher, J. M., Miner, M. E., & Eisenberg, H. M. (1991). The Children's Orientation and Amnesia Test: Relationship to severity of acute head injury and to recovery of memory. *Neurosurgery, 27,* 683–691.

Exner, J. E. (1993). *The Rorschach* (Vol. 1, 3rd ed.). New York: Wiley.

Exner, J. E. (1995). *Issues and methods in Rorschach research.* Mahwah, NJ: Erlbaum.

Exner, J. E., & Weiner, I. B. (1995). *The Rorschach: A comprehensive system: Vol. 3. Assessment of children and adolescents* (2nd ed.). New York: Wiley.

Eyberg, S., & Pincus, D. (1999). *Eyberg Child Behavior Inventory and Sutter-Eyberg Student Behavior Inventory–Revised professional manual.* Lutz, FL: Psychological Assessment Resources.

Eysenck, H. J. (1994). Dimensions of creativity. In M. A. Boden (Ed.), *The measurement of creativity* (pp. 199–242). Cambridge, MA: MIT Press.

Faraone, S. V., Biederman, J., Lehman, B. K., Spencer, T., Norman, D., Seidman, L. J., Kraus, I., Perrin, J., Chen, W. J., & Tsuang, M. T. (1993). Intellectual performance and school failure in children with attention deficit hyperactivity disorder and in their siblings. *Journal of Abnormal Psychology, 102,* 616–623.

Faraone, S. V., Doyle, A. E., Mick, E., & Biederman, J. (2001). Meta-analysis of the association between the 7–repeat allele of the dopamine D(4) receptor gene and attention deficit hyperactivity disorder. *American Journal of Psychiatry, 158,* 1052–1057.

Farmer, E. M. Z., Compton, S. N., Burns, B. S., & Robertson, E. (2002). Review of the evidence base for treatment of childhood psychopathology: Externalizing disorders. *Journal of Consulting and Clinical Psychology, 70,* 1267–1302.

Farnan, N., & Kelly, P. (1991). Keeping track: Creating assessment portfolios in reading and writing. *Journal of Reading, Writing, and Learning Disabilities International, 7,* 255–269.

Farrell, A. D. (1991). Computers and behavioral assessment: Current applications, future possibilities, and obstacles to routine use. *Behavioral Assessment, 13,* 159–179.

Fassnacht, G. (1982). *Theory and practice of observing behavior.* New York: Academic Press.

Favazza, P. C., & Odom, S. L. (1993). *CASPER: Code for Active Student Participation and Engagement Revised. Training manual for observers.* Nashville: Vanderbilt University, John F. Kennedy Center for Research on Human Development.

Fein, R. A., Vossekuil, B., Pollack, W. S., Borum, R., Modzelski, W., & Reddy, M. (2002). *Threat assessment in schools: A guide to managing threatening situations and to creating safe school climates.* Retrieved May 25, 2005, from http://www.secretservice.gov/ntac/ssi_guide.pdf

Feldhusen, J. F. (1998). A conception of talent and talent development. In R. C. Friedman & K. B. Rogers (Eds.), *Talent in context: Historical and social perspectives on giftedness* (pp. 193–209). Washington, DC: American Psychological Association.

Feldhusen, J. F., & Jarwan, F. A. (2000). Identification of gifted and talented youth for educational programs. In K. A. Heller, F. J. Mönks, R. J. Sternberg, & R. F. Subotnik (Eds.), *International handbook of giftedness and talent* (pp. 271–282). Oxford, England: Elsevier.

Feldhusen, J. F., Proctor, T. B., & Black, K. N. (2002). Guidelines for grade advancement of precocious children. *Roeper Review, 24,* 169–171.

Feldman, J. A. (1984). *Performance of learning disabled and normal children on three versions of the Token Test.* Unpublished master's thesis, San Diego State University, San Diego, CA.

Fennell, E. B., & Mickle, J. P. (1992). Behavioral effects of head trauma in children and adolescents. In M. G. Tramontana & S. R. Hooper (Eds.), *Advances in child neuropsychology* (pp. 24–49). New York: Springer-Verlag.

Ferholt, J. D. L. (1980). *Clinical assessment of children: A comprehensive approach to primary pediatric care.* Philadelphia: Lippincott.

Filipek, P. A. (1995). Neurobiologic correlates of developmental dyslexia: How do dyslexics' brains differ from those of normal readers? *Journal of Child Neurology, 10 (Supp.1),* 562–585.

Filipek, P. A., Accardo, P. J., Baranek, G. T., Cook, E. H., Jr., Dawson, G., Gordon, B., Gravel, J. S., Johnson, C. P., Kallen, R. J., Levy, S. R., Minshew, N. J., Prizant, B. M., Rapin, I., Rogers, S. J., Stone, W. L., Teplin, S., Tuchman, R. F., & Volkmar, F. R. (1999). The screening and diagnosis of autistic spectrum disorders. *Journal of Autism and Developmental Disorders, 29,* 439–484.

Filley, C. M., Cranberg, L. D., Alexander, M. P., & Hart, E. J. (1987). Neurobehavioral outcome after closed head injury in childhood and adolescence. *Archives of Neurology, 44,* 194–198.

Finger, P. T. (1998). *Retinoblastoma and secondary cancers.* Retrieved August 5, 2004, from http://www.eyecancer.com/Content.aspx?sSection=Patient&sSubSection=Conditions&sPage=ConditionList.ascx

Fischer, M., Barkley, R. A., Fletcher, K., & Smallish, L. (1990). The adolescent outcome of hyperactivity children diagnosed by research criteria, II: Academic, attentional, and neuropsychological status. *Journal of Consulting and Clinical Psychology, 58,* 580–588.

Fischer, M., Barkley, R. A., Smallish, L., & Fletcher, K. (2002). Young adult follow-up of hyperactive children: Self-reported psychiatric disorders, comorbidity, and the role of childhood conduct problems and teen CD. *Journal of Abnormal Child Psychology, 30,* 463–475.

Flanagan, N. M., Jackson, A. J., & Hill, A. E. (2003). Visual impairment in childhood: Insights from a community-based survey. *Child Care Health Development, 29,* 493–499.

Fletcher, J. M., Lyon, G. R., Barnes, M. A., Stuebing, K. K., Francis, D. J., Olson, R. K., Shaywitz, S. E., & Shaywitz, B. A. (2002). Classification of learning disabilities: An evidence-based evaluation. In R. Bradley, L. Danielson, & D. P. Hallahan (Eds.), *Identification of learning disabilities: Research to practice* (pp. 185–206). Mahwah, NJ: Erlbaum.

Foddy, W. H. (1993). *Constructing questions for interviews and questionnaires: Theory and practice in social research.* New York: Cambridge University Press.

Follete, W. C., & Houts, A. C. (1996). Models of scientific progress and the role of theory in taxonomy: A case study of the DSM. *Journal of Consulting and Clinical Psychology, 64,* 1120–1132.

Fombonne, E. (1998). Epidemiological surveys of autism. In F. R. Volkmar (Ed.), *Autism and pervasive developmental disorders* (pp. 32–63). New York: Cambridge University Press.

Forbes, C., Vuchinich, S., & Kneedler, B. (2001). Assessing families with the Family Problem Solving Code. In P. K. Kerig & K. M. Lindahl (Eds.), *Family observational coding systems: Resources for systemic research* (pp. 59–75). Mahwah, NJ: Erlbaum.

Ford, B. G., & Ford, R. D. (1981). Identifying creative potential in handicapped children. *Exceptional Children, 48,* 115–122.

Forrester, G., & Geffen, G. (1991). Performance measure of 7- to 15- year-old children on the Auditory Verbal Learning Test. *Clinical Neuropsychologist, 5,* 345–359.

Foster, S. L., & Cone, J. D. (1986). Design and use of direct observation systems. In A. Ciminero, K. Calhoun, & H. E. Adams (Eds.), *Handbook of behavioral assessment* (2nd ed., pp. 253–324). New York: Wiley.

Freebody, P., & Byrne, B. (1988). Word-reading strategies in elementary school children: Relations to comprehension, reading time, and phonemic awareness. *Reading Research Quarterly, 23,* 441–453.

Freedman, D. A., Feinstein, C., & Berger, K. (1988). The blind child and adolescent. In C. J. Kestenbaum & D. T. Williams (Eds.), *Handbook of clinical assessment of children and adolescents* (Vol. 2, pp. 864–878). New York: New York University Press.

Freeman, B. J., Rahbar, B., Ritvo, E. R., Bice, T. L., Yakota, A., & Ritvo, R. (1991). The stability of cognitive and behavioral parameters in autism: A twelve-year prospective study. *Journal of the American Academy of Child & Adolescent Psychiatry, 30,* 479–482.

Freides, D. (1993). Proposed standard of professional practice: Neuropsychological reports display all quantitative data. *Clinical Neuropsychologist, 7,* 234–235.

Fremouw, W. J., De Perczel, M., & Ellis, T. E. (1990). *Suicide risk: Assessment and response guidelines.* Elmsford, NY: Pergamon.

Frick, P. J. (1998). *Conduct disorders and severe antisocial behavior.* New York: Plenum.

Frick, P. J., & McCoy, M. G. (2001). Conduct disorder. In H. Orvaschel, M. Hersen, & J. Faust (Eds.), *Handbook of conceptualization and treatment of child psychopathology* (pp. 57–76). Amsterdam, Netherlands: Pergamon/Elsevier Science.

Frick, P. J., Silverthorn, P., & Evans, C. (1994). Assessment of childhood anxiety using structured interviews: Patterns of agreement among informants and association with maternal anxiety. *Psychological Assessment, 6,* 372–379.

Frick, P. J., Strauss, C. C., Lahey, B. B., & Christ, M. A. G. (1992). Behavior disorders of childhood. In P. B. Sutker (Ed.), *Comprehensive handbook of psychopathology* (pp. 765–789). New York: Plenum.

Friedman, M. C., Chhabildas, N., Budhiraja, N., Willcutt, E. G., & Pennington, B. F. (2003). Etiology of the comorbidity between RD and ADHD: Exploration of the non-random mating hypothesis. *American Journal of Medical Genetics, 120,* 109–115.

Frude, N. (1991). *Understanding family problems: A psychological approach.* New York: Wiley.

Fuchs, D., Mock, D., Morgan. P. L., & Young, C. L. (2003). Responsiveness to intervention: Definitions, evidence, and implications for the learning disability construct. *Learning Disabilities Research and Practice, 18,* 157–171.

Fuchs, L. S. (2003). Assessing intervention responsiveness: Conceptual and technical issues. *Learning Disabilities Research and Practice, 18,* 172–186.

Fuchs, L. S., & Fuchs, D. (1998). Treatment validity: A unifying concept for reconceptualizing the identification of learning disability. *Learning Disabilities Research and Practice, 13,* 204–219.

Fuligni, A. J. (1998). The adjustment of children from immigrant families. *Current Directions in Psychological Science, 7,* 99–103.

Fuller, G. B., & Vance, B. (1993). Comparison of the Minnesota Percepto-Diagnostic Test–Revised and Bender-Gestalt in predicting achievement. *Psychology in the Schools, 30,* 220–226.

Fuller, G. B., & Wallbrown, F. H. (1983). Comparison of the Minnesota Percepto-Diagnostic Test and Bender-Gestalt: Relationship with achievement criteria. *Journal of Clinical Psychology, 39,* 985–988.

Furlong, M., & Morrison, G. M. (2000). The school in school violence: Definitions and facts. *Journal of Emotional and Behavioral Disorders, 8,* 71–82.

Gable, R. A., Quinn, M. M., Rutherford, R. B., Jr., & Howell, K. (1998). *Addressing problem behaviors in schools: Use of functional assessments and behavior intervention plans.* Retrieved August 6, 2004, from http://www.ldonline.org/ld_indepth/special_education/quinn_behavior.html

Gabovitch, E. M., & Wiseman, N. D. (2005). Early identification of autism spectrum disorders. In D. Zager (Ed.), *Autism spectrum disorder: Identification, education, and treatment* (3rd ed., pp. 145–172). Mahwah, NJ: Erlbaum.

Gadow, K. D., & Sprafkin, J. (1997). *ADHD Symptom Checklist–4.* Stony Brook, NY: Checkmate Plus.

Gadow, K. D., Sprafkin, J., & Nolan, E. E. (1996). *ADHD School Observation Code.* Stony Brook, NY: Checkmate Plus.

Gallagher, J. J. (1991). Editorial: The gifted: A term with surplus meaning. *Journal for the Education of the Gifted, 14,* 353–365.

Gallagher, J. J. (1997). Issues in the education of gifted children. In N. Colangelo & G. A. Davis (Eds.), *Handbook of gifted education* (pp. 10–23). Boston: Allyn & Bacon.

Garb, H. N. (2000). Computers will become increasingly important for psychological assessment: Not that there's anything wrong with that! *Psychological Assessment, 12,* 31–39.

Garb, H. N., Wood, J. M., Lilienfeld, S. O., & Nezworski, M. T. (2002). Effective use of projective techniques in clinical practice: Let the data help with selection and interpretation. *Professional Psychology: Research and Practice, 33,* 454–463.

Garb, H. N., Wood, J. M., Nezworski, M. T., Grove, W. M., & Stejskal, W. J. (2001). Toward a resolution of the Rorschach controversy. *Psychological Assessment, 13,* 443–448.

Garbarino, J., Guttman, E., & Seeley, J. W. (1987). *The psychologically battered child: Strategies for identification, assessment and intervention.* San Francisco: Jossey-Bass.

Garbarino, J., & Stott, F. M. (1989). *What children can tell us: Eliciting, interpreting, and evaluating information from children.* San Francisco: Jossey-Bass.

Gardner, R. A. (1979). *The objective diagnosis of minimal brain dysfunction.* Cresskill, NJ: Creative Therapeutics.

Gathercole, S. E., & Adams, A. (1993). Phonological working memory in very young children. *Developmental Psychology, 29,* 770–778.

Gaub, M., & Carlson, C. L. (1997). Meta-analysis of gender differences in ADHD. *Attention, 2,* 25–30.

Gearheart, B. R., & Willenberg, E. P. (1980). *Application of pupil assessment information* (3rd ed.). Denver: Love.

Geary, D. C. (1994). *Children's mathematical development: Research and practical applications.* Washington, DC: American Psychological Association.

Geary, D. C., Hamson, C. O., & Hoard, M. K. (2000). Numerical and arithmetical cognition: A longitudinal study of process and concept deficits in children with learning disability. *Journal of Experimental Child Psychology, 77,* 236–263.

George, E. L., & Bloom, B. L. (1997). A brief scale for assessing parental child-rearing practice: Psychometric properties and psychosocial correlates. *Family Process, 36,* 63–80.

Gerard, A. B. (1994). *Parent-Child Relationship Inventory.* Los Angeles: Western Psychological Services.

Gershon, J. (2002). A meta-analytic review of gender differences in ADHD. *Journal of Attention Disorders, 5,* 143–154.

Geurts, H. M., Verte, S., Oosterlaan, J., Roeyers, H., & Sergeant, J. A. (2004). How specific are executive functioning deficits in attention deficit hyperactivity disorder and autism? *Journal of Child Psychology & Psychiatry and Allied Disciplines, 45,* 836–854.

Gianutsos, R. (1987). A neuropsychologist's primer on memory for educators. *Neuropsychology, 1,* 51–58.

Gibbs, J. T. (1988). Mental health issues of Black adolescents: Implications for policy and practice. In A. R. Stiffman & L. E. Davis (Eds.), *Ethnic issues in adolescent mental health* (pp. 21–52). Newbury Park, CA: Sage.

Giger, J. N., & Davidhizar, R. F. (Eds.). (1991). *Transcultural nursing: Assessment and intervention.* St. Louis: Mosby.

Gilandas, A., Touyz, S., Beumont, P. J. V., & Greenberg, H. P. (1984). *Handbook of neuropsychological assessment.* New York: Grune & Stratton.

Gilbert, R. K., & Christensen, A. (1988). The assessment of family alliances. *Advances in Behavioral Assessment of Children and Families, 4,* 219–252.

Gilhousen, M. R., Allen, L. F., Lasater, L. M., Farrell, D. M., & Reynolds, C. R. (1990). Veracity and vicissitude: A critical look at the Milwaukee Project. *Journal of School Psychology, 28,* 285–299.

Gillberg, C., & Billstedt, E. (2000). Autism and Asperger syndrome: Coexistence with other clinical disorders. *Acta Psychiatrica Scandinavica, 102,* 321–330.

Gillberg, C., Nordin, V., & Ehlers, S. (1996). Early detection of autism: Diagnostic instruments for clinicians. *European Child & Adolescent Psychiatry, 5,* 67–74.

Gilliam, J. E. (1995a). *Attention-Deficit/Hyperactivity Disorder Test.* Austin, TX: Pro-Ed.

Gilliam, J. E. (1995b). *Gilliam Autism Rating Scale.* Austin, TX: Pro-Ed.

Gilliam, J. E. (2001). *Gilliam Asperger's Disorder Scale.* Austin, TX: Pro-Ed.

Gilliam, J. E., Carpenter, B. O., & Christensen, J. R. (1996). *Gifted and Talented Evaluation Scales.* Austin, TX: Pro-Ed.

Gilmore, S. K. (1973). *The counselor-in-training.* New York: Appleton-Century-Crofts.

Gioia, G. A., Isquith, P. K., Guy, S. C., & Kenworthy, L. (2000). *Behavior Rating Inventory of Executive Function.* Lutz, FL: Psychological Assessment Resources.

Giordano, G. (1987). Diagnosing specific math disabilities. *Academic Therapy, 23,* 69–74.

Gittelman, R., & Abikoff, H. (1989). The role of psychostimulants and psychosocial treatments in hyperkinesis. In T. Sagvolden & T. Archer (Eds.), *Attention deficit disorder: Clinical and basic research* (pp. 167–180). Mahwah, NJ: Erlbaum.

Gittelman-Klein, R. (1988). Questioning the clinical usefulness of projective psychological tests for children. In S. Chess, A. Thomas, & M. Hertzig (Eds.), *Annual progress in child psychiatry and child development 1987* (pp. 451–461). New York: Brunner/Mazel.

Goldberg, R. J., Higgins, E. L., Raskind, M. H., & Herman, K. L. (2003). Predictors of success in individuals with learning disabilities: A qualitative analysis of a 20-year longitudinal study. *Learning Disabilities: Research & Practice, 18,* 222–236.

Golden, C. J. (1987). Screening batteries for the adult and children's versions of the Luria Nebraska Neuropsychological Batteries. *Neuropsychology, 1,* 63–66.

Goldenberg, H. (1983). *Contemporary clinical psychology* (2nd ed.). Monterey, CA: Brooks/Cole.

Goldman, S., & Beardslee, W. R. (1999). Suicide in children and adolescents. In D. G. Jacobs (Ed.), *The Harvard Medical School guide to suicide assessment and intervention* (pp. 417–442). San Francisco: Jossey–Bass.

Goldstein, D. E., Murray, C., & Edgar, E. (1998). Employment earning and hours of high school graduates with learning disabilities through the first decade after graduation. *Learning Disabilities Research and Practice, 13,* 53–64.

Gomez, R., Burns, G. L., Walsh, J. A., & De Moura, M. A. (2003). Multitrait-multisource confirmatory factor analytic approach to the construct validity of ADHD rating scales. *Psychological Assessment, 15,* 3–16.

Good, T. L., & Brophy, J. E. (1986). *Educational psychology: A realistic approach.* New York: Longman.

Goodman, J. D., & Sours, J. A. (1967). *The child mental status examination.* New York: Basic Books.

Goodman, S. A., & Wittenstein, S. H. (Eds.). (2003). *Collaborative assessment: Working with students who are blind or visually impaired, including those with additional disabilities.* New York: AFB Press.

Gorden, R. L. (1975). *Interviewing: Strategy, techniques and tactics* (Rev. ed.). Homewood, IL: Dorsey.

Gordon, M. (1988). *The Gordon Diagnostic System.* Dewitt, NY: Gordon Systems.

Goswami, U. (1992). Phonological factors in spelling development. *Journal of Child Psychology and Psychiatry, 33,* 967–975.

Gotlib, I. H., & Hammen, C. L. (1992). *Psychological aspects of depression: Toward a cognitive–interpersonal integration.* Chichester, England: Wiley.

Gouvier, W. D., Cubic, B., Jones, G., Brantley, P., & Cutlip, Q. (1992). Post-concussion symptoms and daily stress in normal and head-injured college populations. *Archives of Clinical Neuropsychology, 7,* 193–211.

Graham, S., Harris, K. R., & Larsen, L. (2001). Prevention and intervention of writing difficulties for students with learning disabilities. *Learning Disabilities Research & Practice, 6,* 74–84.

Graham, W. F., & Wexler, H. K. (1997). The Amity Therapeutic Community Program at Donovan prison: Program description and approach. In G. De Leon (Ed.), *Community as method: Therapeutic communities for special populations and special settings* (pp. 97–112). London, England: Praeger.

Graham-Bermann, S. (2001). Designing intervention evaluations for children exposed to domestic violence. In S. Graham-Bermann (Ed.), *Domestic violence in the lives of children: The future of research, intervention, and social policy* (pp. 237–267). Washington, DC: American Psychological Association.

Grandin, T. (2002). *Teaching tips for children and adults with autism.* Retrieved March 24, 2005, from http://www.autism.org/temple/tips.html

Gratus, J. (1988). *Successful interviewing.* Harmondsworth, England: Penguin Books.

Gray, R. M., Livingston, R. B., Marshal, R. M., & Haak, R. A. (2000). Reference group data for the Reitan-Indiana Neuropsychological Test Battery for Young Children. *Perceptual and Motor Skills, 91,* 675–682.

Green, M., Wong, M., Atkins, D., Taylor, J., & Feinlieb, M. (1999). *Diagnosis of attention deficit/hyperactivity disorder: Technical review 3.* Retrieved August 17, 2001, from http://www.ahrq.gov/clinic/epcsums/adhdsutr.htm

Greenbaum, A. (1982). Conducting effective parent conferences. *Communique, 10,* 4–5.

Greenberg, L. M. (1990). *Test of Variable of Attention (T.O.V.A).* Los Alamitos, CA: Universal Attention Disorders.

Greene, J. F. (1996). Psycholinguistic assessment: The clinical base for identification of dyslexia. *Topics in Language Disorders, 16,* 45–72.

Greenwood, C. R., Carta, J. J., & Dawson, H. (2000). Ecobehavioral Assessment System Software (EBASS). In T. Thompson, D. Felce, & F. J. Symons (Eds.), *Behavioral observation: Technology and applications in developmental disabilities* (pp. 229–251). Baltimore: Brookes.

Greenwood, C. R., Hops, H., Walker, H. M., Guild, J. J., Stokes, J., Young, K. R., Keleman, K. S., & Willardson, M. (1979). Standardized classroom management program: Social validation and replication studies in Utah and Oregon. *Journal of Applied Behavior Analysis, 12,* 235–253.

Gresham, F. M. (1983). Social skills assessment as a component of mainstreaming placement decisions. *Exceptional Children, 49,* 331–336.

Gresham, F. M. (1984). Behavioral interviews in school psychology: Issues in psychometric adequacy and research. *School Psychology Review, 13,* 17–25.

Gresham, F. M. (2002). Responsiveness to intervention: An alternative approach to the identification of learning disabilities. In R. Bradley, L. Danielson, & D. P. Hallahan (Eds.), *Identification of learning disabilities: Responses to treatment* (pp. 467–519). Mahwah, NJ: Erlbaum.

Groenveld, M., & Jan, J. E. (1992). Intelligence profiles of low vision and blind children. *Journal of Visual Impairment & Blindness, 86,* 68–71.

Gross, J., & Hayne, H. (1998). Drawing facilitates children's verbal reports after long delays. *Journal of Experimental Psychology: Applied, 5,* 265–283.

Grossberg, I. N., & Cornell, D. G. (1988). Relationship between personality adjustment and high intelligence: Terman versus Hollingworth. *Exceptional Children, 55,* 266–272.

Grossman, H. (Ed.). (1983). *Classification in mental retardation.* Washington, DC: American Association on Mental Deficiency.

Guida, F. V. (1987). Naturalistic Observation of Academic Anxiety Scale. *Journal of Classroom Interaction, 22,* 13–18.

Guidubaldi, J., & Cleminshaw, H. K. (1994). *Parenting Satisfaction Scale.* San Antonio, TX: The Psychological Corporation.

Guilford, J. P., & Hoepfner, R. (1971). *The analysis of intelligence.* New York: McGraw-Hill.

Guralnick, M. J., & Groom, J. M. (1988). Friendships of preschool children in mainstreamed playgroups. *Developmental Psychology, 24,* 595–604.

Hagopian, L. P., & Ollendick, T. H. (1993). Simple phobia in children. In R. T. Ammerman & M. Hersen (Eds.), *Handbook of behavior therapy with children and adults: A developmental and longitudinal perspective* (pp. 123–136). Boston: Allyn & Bacon.

Hahn, W. K. (1987). Cerebral lateralization of function: From infancy through childhood. *Psychological Bulletin, 101,* 376–392.

Haier, R. J., Jung, R. E., Yeo, R. A., Head, K., & Alkire, M. T. (2004). Structural brain variation and general intelligence. *NeuroImage, 23,* 425–433.

Hall, P. K., & Jordan, L. S. (1985). The Token and Reporter's Test: Use with 123 language-disordered students. *Language, Speech, and Hearing Services in Schools, 16,* 244–255.

Hallahan, D. P., & Kauffman, J. M. (2003). *Exceptional learners: Introduction to special education.* Boston: Allyn & Bacon.

Hallahan, D. P., Kauffman, J. M., & Lloyd, J. W. (1999). *Introduction to learning disabilities* (2nd ed.). Boston: Allyn & Bacon.

Hallahan, D. P., & Mercer, C. D. (2002). Learning disabilities: Historical perspective. In R. Bradley, L. Danielson, & D. P. Hallahan (Eds.), *Identification of learning disabilities: Research to practice* (pp. 1–67). Mahwah, NJ: Erlbaum.

Hammen, C. L., & Rudolph, K. D. (1996). Childhood depression. In E. J. Mash & R. A. Barkley (Eds.), *Child psychopathology* (pp. 153–195). New York: Guilford.

Hammer, R. (2002). *Stargardt's patients need special light protection.* Retrieved January 27, 2005, from http://www.mdsupport.org/library/stargardt.html

Happé, F. G. E. (1994). Wechsler IQ profile and theory of mind in autism: A research note. *Journal of Child Psychology and Psychiatry, 35,* 1461–1471.

Harms, T., & Clifford, R. (1998). *Early Childhood Environment Rating Scale* (revised edition). New York: Teachers College Press.

Harris, F. C., & Lahey, B. B. (1982). Subject reactivity in direct observational assessment: A review and critical analysis. *Clinical Psychology Review, 2,* 523–538.

Harris, J. C. (1995a). *Developmental neuropsychiatry, Volume 1: Fundamentals.* New York: Oxford University Press.

Harris, J. C. (1995b). *Developmental neuropsychiatry: Vol. 2. Assessment, diagnosis, and treatment of developmental disorders.* Cary, NC: Oxford University Press.

Harris, J. R. (2002). Beyond the nature assumption: Testing hypotheses about the child's environment. In J. G. Borowski, S. L. Ramey, & M. Bristol-Power (Eds.), *Parenting and the child's world: Influences on academic, intellectual, and social-emotional development* (pp. 3–20). Mahwah, NJ: Erlbaum.

Harris, M., & Coltheart, M. K. (1986). *Language processing in children and adults: An introduction.* London, England: Routledge & Kegan Paul.

Harris, S. L., Handleman, J. S., & Burton, J. B. (1990). The Stanford Binet profiles of young children with autism. *Special Services in the School, 6,* 135–143.

Harrison, P. L., & Oakland, T. (2000). *Adaptive Behavior Assessment System.* San Antonio, TX: The Psychological Corporation.

Harrison, P. L., & Oakland, T. (2003). *Adaptive Behavior Assessment System–II.* San Antonio, TX: The Psychological Corporation.

Hart, B., & Risley, T. R. (1995). *Meaningful differences in the everyday experience of young American children.* Baltimore: Brookes.

Hatlen, P. (1996). *The core curriculum for blind and visually impaired students, including those with additional disabilities.* Retrieved December 10, 2004, from http://www.afb.org/section.asp?Documentid=1349

Haynes, S. N. (1998). The changing nature of behavioral assessment. In A. S. Bellack & M. Hersen (Eds.), *Behavioral assessment: A practical handbook* (4th ed., pp. 1–21). Boston: Allyn & Bacon.

Haynes, S. N., & Horn, W. F. (1982). Reactivity in behavioral observation: A review. *Behavioral Assessment, 4,* 369–385.

Heath, C. P., & Kush, J. C. (1991). Use of discrepancy formulas in assessment of learning disabilities. In J. E. Obrzut & G. W. Hynd (Eds.), *Neuropsychological foundations of learning disabilities: A handbook of issues, methods, and practice* (pp. 287–307). San Diego: Academic Press.

Heath, S. B. (1989). Oral and literate traditions among Black Americans living in poverty. *American Psychologist, 44,* 367–373.

Hechtman, L. (1994). Genetic and neurobiological aspects of attention hyperactive disorder: A review. *Journal of Psychiatry & Neuroscience, 19,* 193–201.

Helland, T., & Asbjørnsen, A. (2000). Executive functions in dyslexia. *Child Neuropsychology, 5,* 37–48.

Henggeler, S., Schoenwald, S. K., Rowland, M. D., & Cunningham, P. B. (2002). *Serious emotional disturbance in children and adolescents: Multisystemic therapy.* New York: Guilford.

Hepworth, D. H., & Larsen, J. (1990). *Direct social work practice: Theory and skills* (3rd ed.). Belmont, CA: Wadsworth.

Herbert, M. (1994). Etiological considerations. In T. H. Ollendick, N. J. King, & W. Yule (Eds.), *International handbook of phobic and anxiety disorders in children and adolescents* (pp. 3–20). New York: Plenum.

Herring, R. D. (1992). Biracial children: An increasing concern for elementary and middle school counselors. *Elementary School Guidance and Counseling, 27,* 123–130.

Hickey, J. V. (1992). *The clinical practice of neurological and neurosurgical nursing* (3rd ed.). Philadelphia: Lippincott.

Hill, E. W., Guth, D. A., & Hill, M. M. (1985). Spatial concept instruction for children with low vision. *Education of the Visually Handicapped, 16,* 152–161.

Hiltonsmith, R. W., & Keller, H. R. (1983). What happened to the setting in person-setting assessment? *Professional Psychology: Research and Practice, 14,* 419–434.

Hirshberg, L. M. (1993). Clinical interviews with infants and their families. In C. H. Zeanah, Jr. (Ed.), *Handbook of infant mental health* (pp. 173–190). New York: Guilford.

Hocevar, D. (1981). Measurement of creativity: Review and critique. *Journal of Personality Assessment, 45,* 450–464.

Hodapp, R. M. (1998). *Development and disabilities: Intellectual, sensory, and motor impairments.* New York: Cambridge University Press.

Hodapp, R. M., & Dykens, E. M. (2003). Mental retardation (intellectual disabilities). In E. J. Mash & R. A. Barkley (Eds.), *Child psychopathology* (2nd ed., pp. 486–519). New York: Guilford.

Hodapp, R. M., & Zigler, E. (1999). Intellectual development and mental retardation—some continuing controversies. In M. Anderson (Ed.), *The development of intelligence* (pp. 295–308). Hove, England: Psychology Press.

Hodges, K. (1993). Structured interviews for assessing children. *Journal of Child Psychology & Psychiatry & Allied Disciplines, 34,* 49–68.

Hodges, K. (1997). *Child Adolescent Schedule (CAS).* Ypsilanti: Eastern Michigan University.

Hoge, R. D. (1988). Issues in the definition and measurement of the giftedness construct. *Educational Research, 14,* 12–17.

Hoge, R. D. (2001). *The juvenile offender: Theory, research, and applications.* Boston: Kluwer.

Hoge, R. D., & Andrews, D. A. (1992). Assessing conduct problems in the classroom. *Clinical Psychology Review, 12,* 1–20.

Hoge, R. D., & Andrews, D. A. (1996). *Assessing the youthful offender: Issues and techniques.* New York: Plenum.

Hoge, R. D., Andrews, D. A., & Leschied, A. W. (2002). *Youth Level of Service/Case Management Inventory (YLS/CMI).* North Tonawanda, NY: Multi-Health Systems.

Holland, J. C. (1989). Stresses on mental health professionals. In J. C. Holland & J. H. Rowland (Eds.), *Handbook of psychooncology: Psychological care of the patient with cancer* (pp. 678–682). New York: Oxford University Press.

Hops, H., Biglan, A., Sherman, I., Arthur, J., Friedman, I., & Osteen, V. (1987). Home observations of family interactions of depressed women. *Journal of Consulting and Clinical Psychology, 55,* 341–346.

Horowitz, F. D., & O'Brien, M. (1989). In the interest of the nation: A reflective essay on the state of our knowledge and the challenges before us. *American Psychologist, 44,* 441–445.

Horton, C. B., & Kochurka, K. A. (1995). The assessment of children with disabilities who report sexual abuse: A special look at those most vulnerable. In T. Ney (Ed.), *True and false allegations of child sexual abuse: Assessment and case management* (pp. 275–289). New York: Brunner/Mazel.

Hotz, R. L. (1996a, October 13). Deciphering the miracles of the mind. *The Los Angeles Times,* pp. A1, A20–A22.

Hotz, R. L. (1996b, October 16). Unraveling the riddle of identity. *The Los Angeles Times,* pp. A1, A10–A11.

Hotz, R. L. (1998, October 18). In art of language, the brain matters. *Los Angeles Times,* pp. A1, A38–A39.

Hotz, R. L. (2005, June 16). Deep, dark secrets of his and her brains. *The Los Angeles Times,* pp. A1, A20–A21.

Howard, M. E. (1988). Behavior management in the acute care rehabilitation setting. *Journal of Head Trauma Rehabilitation, 3,* 14–22.

Hunt, P. L. (1987). Black clients: Implications for supervision of trainees. *Psychotherapy, 24,* 114–119.

Hunter, J. E., & Schmidt, F. L. (1990). *Methods of meta-analysis: Correcting error and bias in research findings.* Newbury Park, CA: Sage.

Hutt, M. L. (1969). *The Hutt adaptation of the Bender-Gestalt Test* (2nd ed.). New York: Grune & Stratton.

Huttenlocher, P. R., Levine, S. C., Huttenlocher, J., & Gates, J. (1990). Discrimination of normal and at-risk preschool children on the basis of neurological tests. *Developmental Medicine & Child Neurology, 32,* 394–402.

Hynd, G. W. (1992). *Neuropsychological assessment in clinical child psychology.* Newbury Park, CA: Sage.

Hynd, G. W., Obrzut, J. E., & Obrzut, A. (1981). Are lateral and perceptual asymmetries related to WISC–R and achievement test performance in normal and learning-disabled children? *Journal of Consulting and Clinical Psychology, 49,* 977–979.

International Dyslexia Association. (2002). *What is dyslexia?* Retrieved June 6, 2004, from http://www.interdys.org/servlet/compose?section_id=5&page_id=95#What%20is%20dyslexia?

Iverson, G. L., Iverson, A. M., & Barton, E. A. (1994). The Children's Orientation and Amnesia Test: Educational status is a moderator variable in tracking recovery from TBI. *Brain Injury, 8,* 685–688.

Iverson, G. L., Woodward, T. S., & Iverson, A. M. (2002). Regression-predicted age norms for the Children's Orientation and Amnesia Test. *Archives of Clinical Neuropsychology, 17,* 131–142.

Iverson, T. J., & Segal, M. (1992). Social behavior of maltreated children: Exploring links to parent behavior and beliefs. In I. E. Sigel (Ed.), *Parental belief systems: The psychological consequences for children* (2nd ed., pp. 267–289). Hillsdale, NJ: Erlbaum.

Ives, M., & Munro, N. (2001). *Caring for a child with autism: A practical guide for parents.* London, England: Jessica Kingsley.

Jacobs, M. P. (1993). Limited understanding of deficit in children with brain dysfunction. *Neuropsychological Rehabilitation, 3,* 341–365.

Jacobson, J. W., Mulick, J. A., & Schwartz, A. A. (1995). A history of facilitated communication: Science, pseudoscience, and antiscience. *American Psychologist, 50,* 750–765.

Jamieson, S. (2004). Creating an educational program for young children who are blind and who have autism. *RE:view, 35,* 165–177.

Jansen, R. G., Wiertz, L. F., Meyer, E. S., & Noldus, L. P. J. J. (2003). Reliability analysis of observational data: Problems, solutions, and software implementation. *Behavior Research Methods, Instruments, & Computers, 35,* 391–399.

Jenkins, J. R., & O'Connor, R. E. (2002). Early identification and intervention for young children with reading/learning disabilities. In R. Bradley, L. Danielson, & D. P. Hallahan (Eds.), *Identification of learning disabilities: Research to practice* (pp. 99–149). Mahwah, NJ: Erlbaum.

Jenkinson, J. C. (1996). Identifying intellectual disability: Some problems in the measurement of intelligence and adaptive behavior. *Australian Psychologist, 31,* 97–102.

Jennett, B., & Teasdale, G. (1981). *Management of head injuries.* Philadelphia: Davis.

Jennings, R. L. (1982). *Handbook for basic considerations in interviewing children.* Unpublished manuscript, Counseling and Assessment Service, Independence, IA.

Jenson, J. M., Howard, M. O., & Yaffee, J. (1995). Treatment of adolescent substance abusers: Issues for practice and research. *Social Work in Health Care, 21,* 1–18.

Jesness, C. F. (2003). *Jesness Inventory–Revised.* North Tonawanda, NY: Multi-Health Systems.

Jitendra, A. K., Edwards, L. L., Starosta, K., Sacks, G., Jacobson, L. A., & Choutka, C. M. (2004). Early reading instruction for children with reading difficulties: Meeting the needs of diverse learners. *Journal of Learning Disabilities, 37,* 421–439.

Johnson, D. A. (1992). Head injured children and education: A need for greater delineation and understanding. *British Journal of Educational Psychology, 62,* 404–409.

Johnson, J. H., McCaskill, J. W., & Werba, B. E. (2001). Aggressive, antisocial, and delinquent behavior in childhood and adolescence. In C. E. Walker & M. C. Roberts (Eds.), *Handbook of clinical child psychology* (3rd ed., pp. 393–413). New York: Wiley.

Johnston, L. D., O'Malley, P. M., Bachman, J. G., & Schulenberg, J. E. (2005). *Monitoring the future national results on adolescent drug use: Overview of key findings, 2004.* Bethesda, MD: National Institute on Drug Abuse.

Jones, R. T., Kephart, C., Langley, A. K., Parker, M. N., Shenoy, U., & Weeks, C. (2001). Cultural and ethnic diversity issues in clinical child psychology. In C. E. Walker & M. C. Roberts (Eds.), *Handbook of clinical child psychology* (3rd ed.; pp. 955–973). New York: Wiley.

Jordan, L. S., & Hall, P. K. (1985). The Token and Reporter's Tests using two scoring conventions: A normative study with 286 grade and junior high students. *Language, Speech, and Hearing Services in Schools, 16,* 227–243.

Jordan, R. (1999). *Autistic spectrum disorders: An introductory handbook for practitioners.* London, England: David Fulton.

Kabot, S., Masi, W., & Segal, M. (2003). Advances in the diagnosis and treatment of autism spectrum disorders. *Professional Psychology: Research and Practice, 34,* 26–33.

Kadushin, A. (1983). *The social work interview* (2nd ed.). New York: Columbia University Press.

Kagan, A. (1991). Etiologies of adolescent risk. *Journal of Adolescent Health, 12,* 591–596.

Kahng, S., & Iwata, B. A. (2000). Computer systems for collecting real-time observational data. In T. Thompson, D. Felce, & F. J. Symons (Eds.), *Behavioral observation: Technology and applications in developmental disabilities* (pp. 35–45). Baltimore: Brookes.

Kaidar, I., Wiener, J., & Tannock, R. (2003). The attributions of children with attention-deficit/ hyperactivity disorder for their problem behaviors. *Journal of Attention Disorders, 6,* 99–109.

Kamphaus, R. W., & Pleiss, K. L. (1991). Draw-A-Person techniques: Tests in search of a construct. *Journal of School Psychology, 29,* 395–401.

Kamphaus, R. W., & Reynolds, C. R. (1998). *BASC Monitor for ADHD: Manual and software guide.* Circle Pines, MN: American Guidance Service.

Kanfer, R., Eyberg, S. M., & Krahn, G. L. (1983). Interviewing strategies in child assessment. In C. E. Walker & M. C. Roberts (Eds.), *Handbook of clinical child psychology* (pp. 95–108). New York: Wiley.

Kanfer, R., Eyberg, S. M., & Krahn, G. L. (1992). Interviewing strategies in child assessment. In C. E. Walker & M. C. Roberts (Eds.), *Handbook of clinical child psychology* (2nd ed., pp. 49–62). New York: Wiley.

Kansas State Department of Education. (n.d.). *Parent's companion to the effective practices for gifted.* Retrieved November 3, 2004, from http://www.kansped.org

Kaplan, E. F., Goodglass, H., & Weintraub, S. (1983). *The Boston Naming Test* (2nd ed.). Philadelphia: Lea & Febiger.

Karoly, P. (1981). Self-management problems in children. In E. J. Mash & L. G. Terdal (Eds.), *Behavioral assessment of childhood disorders.* (pp. 79–126). New York: Guilford.

Karpel, M. A., & Strauss, E. S. (1983). *Family evaluation.* New York: Gardner.

Kash, K. M., & Holland, J. C. (1989). Special problems of physicians and house staff in oncology. In J. C. Holland & J. H. Rowland (Eds.), *Handbook of psychooncology: Psychological care of the patient with cancer* (pp. 647–657). New York: Oxford University Press.

Katz, E. R., Kellerman, J., & Siegel, S. E. (1980). Behavioral distress in children with cancer undergoing medical procedures: Developmental considerations. *Journal of Consulting and Clinical Psychology, 48,* 356–365.

Kaufman, A. S., & Kaufman, N. L. (2001). Assessment of specific learning disabilities in the new millennium: Issues, conflicts, and controversies. In A. S. Kaufman & N. L. Kaufman (Eds.), *Specific learning disabilities and difficulties in children and adolescents: Psychological assessment and evaluation* (pp. 434–456). New York: Cambridge University Press.

Kaufman, J., Birmaher, B., Brent, D. A., Rao, U., & Ryan N. (1996). *Revised Schedule for Affective Disorders and Schizophrenia for School Age Children: Present and Lifetime Version (K-SADS–PL).* Pittsburgh: Western Psychiatric Institute and Clinic.

Kavale, K. A., & Forness, S. R. (1996). Social skill deficits and learning disabilities: A meta-analysis. *Journal of Learning Disabilities, 3,* 226–237.

Kavale, K. A., Kaufman, A. S., Naglieri, J. A., & Hale, J. B. (2005). Changing procedure for identifying learning disabilities: The danger of poorly supported ideas. *School Psychologist, 59,* 16–25.

Kay, T., & Silver, S. M. (1989). Closed head trauma: Assessment for rehabilitation. In M. D. Lezak (Ed.), *Assessment of the behavioral consequences of head trauma* (pp. 145–170). New York: Liss.

Kazdin, A. E. (1990). Childhood depression. *Journal of Child Psychology and Psychiatry, 31,* 121–160.

Kazdin, A. E. (1998). Conduct disorder. In R. J. Morris & T. R. Kratochwill (Eds.), *The practice of child therapy* (3rd ed., pp. 199–230). Boston: Allyn & Bacon.

Kazdin, A. E., & Marciano, P. (1998). Childhood and adolescent depression. In E. J. Mash & R. A. Barkley (Eds.), *Treatment of childhood psychopathology* (pp. 211–248). New York: Guilford.

Keane, K. J. (1987). Assessing deaf children. In C. S. Lidz (Ed.), *Dynamic assessment: An interactional approach to evaluating learning potential* (pp. 360–376). New York: Guilford.

Kearns, K., Edwards, R., & Tingstrom, D. H. (1990). Accuracy of long momentary time-sampling intervals: Implications for classroom data collection. *Journal of Psychoeducational Assessment, 8,* 74–85.

Kelley, P., Sanspree, M., & Davidson, R. (2000). Vision impairment in children and youth. In B. Silverstone, M. Lang, B. Rosenthal, & E. Faye (Eds.), *The Lighthouse handbook on vision impairment and vision rehabilitation* (Vol. 2, pp. 1137–1151). New York: Oxford University Press.

Kerig, P. K., & Lindahl, K. M. (Eds.). (2001). *Family observational coding systems: Resources for systemic research.* Mahwah, NJ: Erlbaum.

Keyser, D. J., & Sweetland, R. C. (1987). *Test critiques* (Vol. 6). Austin, TX: Pro-Ed.

Keyser, D. J., & Sweetland, R. C. (1994). *Test critiques* (Vol. 10). Austin, TX: Pro-Ed.

Khan, N. A., & Hoge, R. D. (1983). A teacher-judgment measure of social competence: Validity data. *Journal of Consulting and Clinical Psychology, 51,* 809–814.

Kim, S. H., & Arnold, M. B. (2002). Characteristics of persons with mental retardation. In M. Beirne-Smith, R. F. Ittenbach, & J. R. Patton (Eds.), *Mental retardation* (6th ed., pp. 276–309). Upper Saddle River, NJ: Merrill/Prentice Hall.

Kinard, E. M. (1999). Psychosocial resources and academic performance in abused children. *Children and Youth Services Review, 21,* 351–376.

King, N. S. (1996). Emotional, neuropsychological, and organic factors: Their use in the prediction of persisting postconcussion symptoms after mild head injuries. *Journal of Neurology, Neurosurgery, and Psychiatry, 61,* 75–81.

Kinsbourne, M., & Caplan, P. J. (1979). *Children's learning and attention problems.* Boston: Little, Brown.

Kinsella, G. J., Prior, M., Sawyer, M., Ong, B., Murtagh, D., Eisenmajer, R., Bryan, D., Anderson, V., & Klug, G. (1997). Predictors and indicators of academic outcome in children 2 years following traumatic brain injury. *Journal of the International Neuropsychology Society, 3,* 608–616.

Kinston, W., & Loader, P. (1984). Eliciting whole-family interaction with a standardized clinical interview. *Journal of Family Therapy, 6,* 347–363.

Kirsch, I. (Ed.). (1999). *How expectations shape experience.* Washington, DC: American Psychological Association.

Kleiger, J. H. (2001). Projective testing with children and adolescents. In C. E. Walker & M. C. Roberts (Eds.), *Handbook of clinical child psychology* (3rd ed., pp. 172–189). New York: Wiley.

Klein, R. G. (1991). Parent-child agreement in clinical assessment of anxiety and other psychopathology: A review. *Journal of Anxiety Disorders, 5,* 187–198.

Kleinmuntz, B. (1982). *Personality and psychological assessment.* New York: St. Martin's Press.

Klinger, L. G., Dawson, G., & Renner, P. (2003). Autistic disorder. In E. J. Mash & R. A. Barkley (Eds.), *Child psychopathology* (2nd ed., pp. 409–454). New York: Guilford.

Kljajic, I., & Berry, D. (1984). Brain syndrome and WAIS PIQ VIQ difference scores corrected for test artifact. *Journal of Clinical Psychology, 40,* 271–277.

Knauss, L. K. (2001). Ethical issues in psychological assessment in school settings. *Journal of Personality Assessment, 77,* 231–241.

Knight, G. P., & Hill, N. E. (1998). Measurement equivalence in research involving minority adolescents. In V. C. McLoyd & L. Steinberg (Eds.), *Studying minority adolescents: Conceptual, methodological, and theoretical issues* (pp. 183–210). Mahwah, NJ: Erlbaum.

Knoster, T. P., & Llewellyn, G. (1998a). *Functional behavioral assessment for students with individualized educational programs.* Harrisburg, PA: Instructional Support System of Pennsylvania, Pennsylvania Department of Education.

Knoster, T. P., & Llewellyn, G. (1998b). *Screening for an understanding of student problem behavior: An initial line of inquiry* (2nd ed.). Harrisburg, PA: Instructional Support System of Pennsylvania, Pennsylvania Department of Education.

Kolin, P. C., & Kolin, J. L. (1980). *Professional writing for nurses in education, practice, and research.* St. Louis: Mosby.

Koppitz, E. M. (1964). *The Bender Gestalt Test for young children.* New York: Grune & Stratton.

Koppitz, E. M. (1968). *Psychological evaluation of children's human figure drawings.* New York: Grune & Stratton.

Koppitz, E. M. (1975). *The Bender Gestalt Test for young children (Vol. 2): Research and application, 1963–1973.* New York: Grune & Stratton.

Koppitz, E. M. (1984). *Psychological evaluation of human figure drawings by middle school pupils.* Orlando, FL: Grune & Stratton.

Korkman, M. (1990). *NEPSY. Neuropsychologisk underskoning: 4–7 ar. Svensk version [NEPSY. Neuropsychological assessment: 4–7 years. Swedish version].* Stockholm: PsykologiForlaget AB.

Korkman, M., Kirk, U., & Kemp, S. (1998). *NEPSY: A developmental neuropsychological assessment.* San Antonio, TX: The Psychological Corporation.

Korotitsch, W. J., & Nelson-Gray, R. O. (1999). An overview of self-monitoring research in assessment and treatment. *Psychological Assessment, 11,* 415–425.

Kottmeyer, W. (1959). *Teacher's guide for remedial reading.* St. Louis: Webster.

Kovacs, M. (2001). *Children's Depression Inventory (CDI).* North Tonawanda, NY: Multi-Health Systems.

Krauft, V. R., & Krauft, C. C. (1972). Structured vs. unstructured visual-motor tests for educable retarded children. *Perceptual and Motor Skills, 34,* 691–694.

Krehbiel, R., & Kroth, R. L. (1991). Communicating with families of children with disabilities or chronic illness. In M. J. Fine (Ed.), *Collaboration with parents of exceptional chidlren* (pp. 103–127). Brandon, VT: Clinical Psychology Publishing Company.

Krisberg, B., & Howell, J. C. (1998). The impact of the juvenile justice system and prospects for graduated sanctions in a comprehensive strategy. In R. Loeber & D. P. Farrington (Eds.), *Serious and violent juvenile offenders: Risk factors and successful interventions* (pp. 346–366). Thousand Oaks, CA: Sage.

Krivitski, E. C., McIntosh, D. E., & Finch, H. (2004). Profile analysis of deaf children using the Universal Nonverbal Intelligence Test. *Journal of Psychoeducational Assessment, 22,* 338–350.

Kropenske, V., & Howard, J. (1994). *Protecting children in substance-abusing families.* Washington, DC: U.S. Department of Health and Human Services.

Krug, D. A., Arick, J. R., & Almond, P. J. (1980). *Autism Screening Instrument for Educational Planning.* Portland, OR: ASIEP Educational Company.

Kumabe, K. T., Nishida, C., & Hepworth, D. H. (1985). *Bridging ethnocultural diversities in social work and health.* Honolulu: University of Hawaii.

Lachar, D., & Gruber, C. P. (1995a). *Personality Inventory for Youth: Technical guide.* Los Angeles: Western Psychological Services.

Lachar, D., & Gruber, C. P. (1995b). *Personality Inventory for Youth: Administration and interpretation guide.* Los Angeles: Western Psychological Services.

Lachar, D., Wingenfeld, S. A., Kline, R. B., & Gruber, C. P. (2000). *Student Behavior Survey.* Los Angeles: Western Psychological Services.

LaFee, S. (1999, September 29). When the brain takes a bump. *The San Diego Union Tribune,* pp. E1, E5.

LaFromboise, T. D., Trimble, J. E., & Mohatt, G. V. (1990). Counseling intervetion and American Indian tradition: An integrative approach. *Counseling Psychologist, 18,* 628–654.

La Greca, A. M. (1983). Interviewing and behavioral observations. In C. E. Walker & M. C. Roberts (Eds.), *Handbook of clinical child psychology* (pp. 109–131). New York: Wiley.

Lahey, B. B., & Loeber, R. (1994). Framework for a developmental model of oppositional defiant disorder and conduct disorder. In D. K. Routh (Ed.), *Disruptive behavior disorders in childhood* (pp. 139–180). New York: Plenum.

Lambert, N., Nihira, K., & Leland, H. (1993). *AAMR Adaptive Behavior Scale–School* (2nd ed.). Austin, TX: Pro-Ed.

Landesman, S. (1987). The changing structure and function of institutions: A search for optimal group care environments. In S. Landesman, P. M. Vietze, & M. J. Begab (Eds.), *Living environments and mental retardation* (pp. 79–126). Washington, DC: American Association on Mental Retardation.

Langstrom, V. (2002). Child neuropsychiatric disorders: A review of associations with deliquency and substance use. In R. R. Corrado, R. Roesch, S. D. Hart, & J. K. Gierowski (Eds.), *Multi-problem violent youth: A foundation for comparative research on needs interventions and outcomes* (Vol. 324, pp. 91–115). Amsterdam, Netherlands: IOS Press.

LaRoche, C. (1986). Prevention in high risk children of depressed parents. *Canadian Journal of Psychiatry, 31,* 161–165.

Larrabee, G. J. (1986). Another look at VIQ-PIQ scores and unilateral brain damage. *International Journal of Neuroscience, 29,* 141–148.

Laucht, M., Esser, G., & Schmidt, M. H. (1993). Adverse temperamental characteristics and early behaviour problems in 3-month-old infants born with different psychosocial and biological risks. *Acta Paedopsychiatrica: International Journal of Child & Adolescent Psychiatry, 56,* 19–24.

Learning Disabilities Association of Canada. (2002). *Official definition of learning disabilities.* Retrieved July 28, 2005, from http://www.ldac-taac.ca/Defined/pdf/jan02eng.pdf

LeBaron, S., & Zeltzer, L. (1984). Assessment of acute pain and anxiety in children and adolescents by self-reports, observer reports, and a behavior checklist. *Journal of Consulting and Clinical Psychology, 52,* 729–738.

Leckliter, I. N., Forster, A. A., Klonoff, H., & Knights, R. M. (1992). A review of reference group data from normal children for the Halstead-Reitan Neuropsychological Test Battery for Older Children. *Clinical Neuropsychologist, 6,* 201–229.

Lederberg, M. (1989). Psychological problems of staff and their management. In J. C. Holland & J. H. Rowland (Eds.), *Handbook of psychooncology: Psychological care of the patient with cancer* (pp. 631–646). New York: Oxford University Press.

Ledingham, J. E. (1999). Children and adolescents with oppositional defiant disorder and conduct disorder in the community: Experiences at school and with peers. In H. C. Quay & A. E. Hogan (Eds.), *Handbook of disruptive behavior disorders* (pp. 353–370). New York: Kluwer Academic Press.

Lehman, J., & Breen, M. J. (1982). A comparative analysis of the Bender-Gestalt and Beery-Buktenica Tests of Visual-Motor Integration as a function of grade level for regular education students. *Psychology in the Schools, 19,* 52–54.

LePage, J. P., & Mogge, N. L. (2001). The Behavioral Observation System (BOS): A line staff assessment instrument of psychopathology. *Journal of Clinical Psychology, 57,* 1435–1444.

Lerner, J. W. (1997). Attention deficit disorder. In J. W. Lloyd, D. J. Kameenui, & D. Chard (Eds.), *Issues in educating students with disabilities* (pp. 27–44). Mahwah, NJ: Erlbaum.

Lerner, J. W. (2003). *Learning disabilities: Theories, diagnosis, and teaching strategies.* Boston: Houghton Mifflin.

Lesiak, J. (1984). The Bender Visual Motor Gestalt Test: Implications for the diagnosis and prediction of reading achievement. *Journal of School Psychology, 22,* 391–405.

Levin, H. S., Culhane, K. A., Hartmann, J., Evankovich, K., Mattson, A. J., Harward, H., Ringholz, G., Ewing-Cobbs, L., & Fletcher, J. M. (1991). Developmental changes in performance on tests of purported frontal lobe functioning. *Developmental Neuropsychology, 7,* 377–395.

Levin, H. S., Hanten, G., Zhang, L., Swank, P. R., Ewing-Cobbs, L., Dennis, M., Barnes, M. A., Max, J., Schachar, R., Chapman, S. B., & Hunter, J. V. (2004). Changes in working memory after traumatic brain injury in children. *Neuropsychology, 18,* 240–247.

Lewis, D. O. (1991). Conduct disorder. In M. Lewis (Ed.), *Child and adolescent psychiatry: A comprehensive textbook* (pp. 561–573). Baltimore: Williams & Wilkins.

Lewis, M. (1991). Psychiatric assessment of infants, children, and adolescents. In M. Lewis (Ed.), *Child and adolescent psychiatry: A comprehensive textbook* (pp. 447–463). Baltimore: Williams & Wilkins.

Lewkowicz, D. J., & Turkewitz, G. (1982). Influence of hemispheric specialization in sensory processing on reaching in infants: Age and gender related effects. *Developmental Psychology, 18,* 301–308.

Lezak, M. D. (1978). Living with the characterologically altered brain-injured patient. *Journal of Clinical Psychiatry, 39,* 592–598.

Lezak, M. D., Howieson, D. B., & Loring, D. W. (2004). *Neuropsychological assessment* (4th ed.). New York: Oxford University Press.

Lichtenstein, R., & Ireton, H. (1984). *Preschool screening: Identifying young children with developmental and educational problems.* Orlando, FL: Grune & Stratton.

Light, R. J., & Pillemer, D. B. (1984). *Summing up. The science of reviewing research.* Cambridge, MA: Harvard University Press.

Limbos, M. M., & Geva, E. (2001). Accuracy of teacher assessments of second-language students at risk for reading disability. *Journal of Learning Disabilities, 34,* 136–151.

Limond, J., & Leeke, R. (2005). Practitioner review: Cognitive rehabilitation for children with acquired brain injury. *Journal of Child Psychology and Psychiatry, 46,* 339–352.

Linnet, K. M., Dalsgaard, S., Obel, C., Wisborg, K., Henriksen, T. B., Rodriguez, A., Kotimaa, A., Moilanen, I., Thomsen, P. H., Olsen, J., & Jarvelin, M. R. (2003). Maternal lifestyle factors in pregnancy risk of attention deficit hyperactivity disorder and associated behaviors: Review of the current evidence. *American Journal of Psychiatry, 160,* 1028–1040.

Lipsey, M. W., & Wilson, D. B. (1998). Effective intervention for serious juvenile offenders: A synthesis of research. In R. Loeber & D. P. Farrington (Eds.), *Serious and violent juvenile offenders: Risk factors and successful interventions* (pp. 313–345). Thousand Oaks, CA: Sage.

Livingston, R. B., Gray, R. M., & Haak, R. A. (1999). Internal consistency of three tests from the Halstead-Reitan Neuropsychological Battery for Older Children. *Assessment, 6,* 93–99.

Livingston, R. B., Gray, R. M., Haak, R. A., & Jennings, E. (1997). Factor structure of the Halstead-Reitan Neuropsychological Test Battery for Older Children. *Child Neuropsychology, 3,* 176–191.

Livingston, R. B., Gray, R. M., Haak, R. A., & Jennings, E. (2000). Factor structure of the Reitan-Indiana Neuropsychological Battery for Children. *Assessment, 7,* 189–199.

Loeber, R., Farrington, D. P., & Waschbusch, D. A. (1998). Serious and violent juvenile offenders. In R. Loeber & D. P. Farrington (Eds.), *Serious and violent juvenile offenders: Risk factors and successful interventions* (pp. 13–29). Thousand Oaks, CA: Sage.

Lohrmann-O'Rourke, S., Knoster, T., Llewellyn, G. (1999). Screening for understanding: An initial line of inquiry for school-based settings. *Journal of Positive Behavior Interventions, 1,* 35–42.

Lonigan, C. J., Burgess, S. R., Anthony, J. L., & Barker, T. A. (1998). Development of phonological sensitivity in 2- to 5-year-old children. *Journal of Educational Psychology, 90,* 294–311.

Lord, C., Rutter, M., DiLavore, P. C., & Risi, S. (1999). *Autism Diagnostic Observation Schedule–WPS (ADOS–WPS)*. Los Angeles: Western Psychological Services.

Lord, C., & Schopler, E. (1989). Stability of assessment results of autistic and non-autistic language-impaired children from preschool years to early school age. *Journal of Child Psychology & Psychiatry & Allied Disciplines, 30,* 575–590.

Lord, R. G. (1985). Accuracy in behavioral measurement: An alternative definition based on raters' cognitive schema and signal detection theory. *Journal of Applied Psychology, 70,* 66–71.

Loring, D. W., Martin, R. C., Meador, K. J., & Lee, G. P. (1990). Psychometric construction of the Rey-Osterrieth Complex Figure: Methodological considerations and interrater reliability. *Archives of Clinical Neuropsychology, 5,* 1–14.

Lovell, K., & Shields, J. B. (1967). Some aspects of a study of the gifted child. *British Journal of Educational Psychology, 37,* 201–208.

Lubart, T. I. (2003). In search of creative intelligence. In R. J. Sternberg, J. Lautrey, & T. I. Lubart (Eds.), *Models of intelligence: International perspectives* (pp. 279–292). Washington, DC: American Psychological Association.

Lubinski, R. (1981). Environmental language intervention. In R. Chapey (Ed.), *Language intervention strategies in adult aphasia* (pp. 223–245). Baltimore: Williams & Wilkins.

Luiselli, J. K. (1989). Health threatening behaviors. In J. K. Luiselli (Ed.), *Behavioral medicine and developmental disabilities* (pp. 114–151). New York: Springer-Verlag.

Lynch, E. W., & Hanson, M. J. (Eds.). (1992). *Developing cross-cultural competence: A guide for working with young children and their families*. Baltimore: Brookes.

Lyon, G. R. (1995). Toward a definition of dyslexia. *Annals of Dyslexia, 45,* 3–27.

Lyon, G. R. (1996a). Learning disabilities. In E. J. Mash & R. A. Barkley (Eds.), *Child psychopathology* (pp. 390–435). New York: Guilford.

Lyon, G. R. (1996b). Learning disabilities. *Future of Children, 6,* 54–76.

Lyon, G. R., Fletcher, J. M., Shaywitz, S. E., Shaywitz, B. A., Torgesen, J. K., Wood, F. B., Schulte, A., & Olson, R. K. (2001). Rethinking learning disabilities. In C. E. Finn, Jr., A. J. Rotherham, & C. R. Hokanson, Jr. (Eds.), *Rethinking special education for a new century* (pp. 259–287). Washington, DC: Thomas B. Fordham Foundation and the Progressive Policy Institute.

Lyon, G. R., & Moats, L. C. (1988). Critical issues in the instruction of the learning disabled. *Journal of Consulting and Clinical Psychology, 56,* 830–835.

Maccoby, E. E. (1980). *Social development*. San Diego: Harcourt Brace Jovanovich.

Mace, F. C., & Kratochwill, T. R. (1988). Self-monitoring. In J. C. Witt, S. N. Elliott, & F. M. Gresham. (Eds.), *Handbook of behavior therapy in education* (pp. 489–522). New York: Plenum.

Macintosh, K. E., & Dissanayake, C. (2004). Annotation: The similarities and differences between autistic disorder and Asperger's disorder: A review of the empirical evidence. *Journal of Child Psychology and Psychiatry and Allied Disciplines, 45,* 421.

Maddox, T. (2003). *Tests: A comprehensive reference for assessments in psychology, education, and business* (5th ed.). Austin, TX: Pro-Ed.

Magnuson, K. A., & Duncan, G. J. (2002). Parents in poverty. In M. H. Bornstein (Ed.), *Handbook of parenting* (2nd ed., pp. 95–121). Mahwah, NJ: Erlbaum.

Mahoney, G., Powell, A., & Finger, I. (1986). The Maternal Behavior Rating Scale. *Topics in Early Childhood Special Education, 6,* 44–56.

Mainstream English Is the Key. (1996, December 22). *The Los Angeles Times,* p. M4.

Maller, S. J. (1996). WISC–III verbal item invariance across samples of deaf and hearing children of similar measured ability. *Journal of Psychoeducational Assessment, 14,* 152–165.

Maller, S. J., & Braden, J. P. (1993). The construct and criterion-related validity of the WISC–III with deaf adolescents. In B. A. Bracken & R. S. McCallum (Eds.), *Wechsler Intelligence Scale for Children: Third Edition. Journal of Psychoeducational Assessment Monograph Series—Advances in psychoeducational assessment* (pp. 105–113). Brandon, VT: Clinical Psychology Publishing Company.

Manly, T., Robertson, I. H., Anderson, V., & Nimmo-Smith, I. (1999). *The Test of Everyday Attention for Children*. Bury St. Edmunds, England: Thames Valley Test Company.

Mannuzza, S., Fyer, A. J., & Klein, D. F. (1993). Assessing psychopathology. *International Journal of Methods in Psychaitric Research, 3,* 157–165.

Mapou, R. L. (1995). A cognitive framework for neuropsychological assessment. In R. L. Mapou & J. Spector (Eds.), *Clinical neuropsychological assessment: A cognitive approach* (pp. 295–337). New York: Plenum.

March, J. S. (1997). *Multidimensional Anxiety Scale for Children*. North Tonawanda, NY: Multi-Health Systems.

Marin, G., & Marin, B. V. (1991). *Research with Hispanic populations*. Newbury Park, CA: Sage.

Marley, M. L. (1982). *Organic brain pathology and the Bender-Gestalt Test: A differential diagnostic scoring system*. New York: Grune & Stratton.

Marosszeky, N. E., Batchelor, J., Shores, E. A., Marosszeky, J. E., Klein-Boonschate, M., & Fahey, P. P. (1993). The performance of hospitalized, non head-injured children on the Westmead PTA Scale. *Clinical Neuropsychologist, 7,* 85–95.

Marschark, M. (1993). *Psychological development of deaf children*. New York: Oxford University Press.

Marston, D. (2002). A functional and intervention-based assessment approach to establishing discrepancy for students with learning disabilities. In R. Bradley, L. Danielson, & D. P. Hallahan (Eds.), *Identification of learning disabilities: Responses to treatment* (pp. 437–519). Mahwah, NJ: Erlbaum.

Martelle, S. (1999, July 28). Technology replacing braille. *The Los Angeles Times,* pp. A1, A15.

Martin, C. S., & Winters, K. C. (1998). Diagnosis and assessment of alcohol use disorders among adolescents. *Alcohol Health and Research World, 22,* 95–105.

Martin, D. A. (1988). Children and adolescents with traumatic brain injury: Impact on the family. *Journal of Learning Disabilities, 21,* 464–470.

Martins, I. P., & Ferro, J. M. (1992). Recovery of acquired aphasia in children. *Aphasiology, 6,* 431–438.

Mash, E. J., & Barkley, R. A. (1986). Assessment of family interaction with the Response-Class Matrix. *Advances in the Behavioral Assessment of Children and Families, 2,* 29–67.

Mash, E. J., & Dozois, D. J. A. (1996). Child psychopathology: A developmental-systems perspective. In E. J. Mash & R. A. Barkley (Eds.), *Child psychopathology* (pp. 3–60). New York: Guilford.

Mash, E. J., & Terdal, L. G. (1981). Behavioral assessment of childhood disturbance. In E. J. Mash and L. G. Terdal (Eds.), *Behav-*

ioral assessment of childhood disorders (pp. 3–76). New York: Guilford.

Mash, E. J., & Terdal, L. G. (1988). Behavioral assessment of child and family disturbance. In E. J. Mash & L. G. Terdal (Eds.), *Behavioral assessment of childhood disorders* (2nd ed., pp. 3–65). New York: Guilford.

Mash, E. J., & Wolfe, D. A. (2002). *Abnormal child psychology, Volume 2.* Belmont, CA: Wadsworth.

Massagli, T. L., Michaud, L. J., & Rivara, F. P. (1996). Association between injury indices and outcome after severe traumatic brain injury in children. *Archives of Physical Medicine and Rehabilitation, 3,* 13–25.

Masten, A. S. (1994). Resilience in individual development: Successful adaptation despite risk and adversity. In M. C. Wang & E. W. Gordon (Eds.), *Educational resilience in inner-city America* (pp. 3–25). Hillsdale, NJ: Erlbaum.

Masten, A. S. (2001). Ordinary magic: Resilience processes in development. *American Psychologist, 56,* 227–238.

Masten, A. S., & Braswell, L. (1991). Developmental psychopathology: An integrative framework. In P. R. Martin (Ed.), *Handbook of behavioral therapy and psychological science: An integrative approach* (pp. 35–56). New York: Pergamon.

Masten, A. S., & Curtis, W. J. (2000). Integrating competence and psychopathology: Pathways toward a comprehensive science of adaptation in development. *Development and Psychopathology, 12,* 529–550.

Mastropieri, M. A., & Scruggs, T. E. (1998). Constructing more meaningful relationships in the classroom: Mnemonic research into practice. *Learning Disabilities Research and Practice, 13,* 138–145.

Matarazzo, J. D. (1992). Psychological testing and assessment in the 21st century. *American Psychologist, 47,* 1007–1018.

Matarazzo, R. (1995). Psychological report standards in neuropsychology. *Clinical Neuropsychologist, 9,* 249–250.

Mather, N., & Goldstein, S. (2001). *Learning disabilities and challenging behaviors: A guide to intervention and classroom management.* Baltimore: Brookes.

Mather, N., & Gregg, N. (2003). "I can rite": Informal assessment of written language. In S. Vaughn & K. L. Briggs (Eds.), *Reading in the classroom: Systems for the observation of teaching and learning* (pp. 179–220). Baltimore: Brookes.

Mathiowetz, V., Rogers, S. L., Dowe-Keval, M., Donahoe, L., & Rennells, C. (1986). The Purdue Pegboard: Norms for 14- to 19-year-olds. *American Journal of Occupational Therapy, 40,* 174–179.

Matson, J. L. (1988). *The PIMRA.* Orland Park, IL: International Diagnostic System.

Matson, J. L. (1994). *The Diagnostic Assessment of the Severely Handicapped–II (DASH–II): User's guide.* Baton Rouge, LA: Scientific Publishers.

Matt, G. E., & Cook, T. D. (1994). Threats to the validity of research syntheses. In H. M. Cooper & L. V. Hedges (Eds.), *Handbook of research synthesis* (pp. 503–520). New York: Russell Sage.

Mattes, L. J., & Omark, D. R. (1984). *Speech and language assessment for the bilingual handicapped.* San Diego: College-Hill Press.

Matthews, J. R., Bowen, J. M., & Matthews, R. W. (1996). *Successful scientific writing: A step-by-step guide for the biological and medical sciences.* New York: Cambridge University Press.

Mattson, S. N., Riley, E. P., Gramling, L., Delis, D. C., & Jones, K. L. (1998). Neuropsychological comparison of alcohol-exposed children with or without physical features of fetal alcohol syndrome. *Neuropsychology, 12,* 146–153.

Maugh, T. H., II. (2005, May 6). Proteins may spot autism, researchers say. *The Los Angeles Times,* p. A20.

Mayberry, R. I. (1992). The cognitive development of deaf children: Recent insights. In S. J. Segalowitz & I. Rapin (Eds.), *Handbook of neuropsychology: Vol. 7. Child neuropsychology* (pp. 51–68). Amsterdam, Netherlands: Elsevier Science.

Mayes, S. D. (1991). Play assessment of preschool hyperactivity. In C. S. Schaefer, K. Gitlin, & A. Sandgrund (Eds.), *Play diagnosis and assessment* (pp. 249–272). New York: Wiley.

Mayes, S. D., & Calhoun, S. L. (2004). Influence of IQ and age in childhood autism: Lack of support for DSM-IV Asperger's disorder. *Journal of Developmental and Physical Disabilities, 16,* 257–272.

Mayes, S. D., Calhoun, S. L., & Crowell, E. W. (1998). WISC–III Freedom from Disctractibility as a measure of attention in children with and without attention deficit hyperactivity disorder. *Journal of Attention Disorders, 2,* 217–227.

Mazzeschi, C., & Lis, A. (1999). The Bender-Gestalt Test: Koppitz's Developmental Scoring System administered to two samples of Italian preschool and primary school children. *Perceptual and Motor Skills, 88,* 1235–1244.

McBride, G., Dumont, R., & Willis, J. O. (2004). Response to response to intervention legislation: The future for school psychologists. *School Psychologist, 58,* 86–91, 93.

McCarney, S. B. (1989). *Attention Deficit Disorder Evaluation Scale–Second Edition.* Columbia, MO: Hawthorne Educational Services.

McCarney, S. B. (1995a). *Behavior Dimensions Scale–Home Version.* Columbia, MO: Hawthorne Educational Services.

McCarney, S. B. (1995b). *Behavior Dimensions Scale–School Version.* Columbia, MO: Hawthorne Educational Services.

McCarney, S. B., & McCain, B. R. (1995). *The Behavior Dimensions Intervention manual.* Columbia, MO: Hawthorne Educational Services.

McCoach, D. B., Kehle, T. J., Bray, M., & Siegle, D. (2001). Best practices in the identification of gifted students with learning disabilities. *Psychology in the Schools, 38,* 403–411.

McComas, J. J., Hoch, H., & Mace, F. C. (2000). Functional analysis. In E. S. Shapiro & T. R. Kratochwill (Eds.), *Conducting school-based assessments of child and adolescent behavior* (pp. 78–120). New York: Guilford.

McConaughy, S. H. (1996). The interview process. In M. Breen & C. Fiedler (Eds.), *Behavioral approach to the assessment of emotionally/behaviorally disordered youth: A handbook for school-based practitioners* (pp. 181–223). Austin, TX: Pro-Ed.

McConaughy, S. H., & Achenbach, T. M. (2001). *Manual for the Semistructured Clinical Interview for Children and Adolescents* (2nd ed.). Burlington: University of Vermont, Research Center for Children, Youth, & Families.

McEachern, A. G., & Bornot, J. (2001). Gifted students with learning disabilities: Implications and strategies for school counselors. *Professional School Counseling, 5,* 34–41.

McGough, R. (2003, July 16). Is the autistic brain too masculine? *The Wall Street Journal,* pp. B1, B4.

McGraw, K. O., & Wong, S. P. (1996). Forming inferences about some intraclass correlation coefficients. *Psychological Methods, 4,* 390.

McIntosh, J. A., Belter, R. W., Saylor, C. F., & Finch, A. J. (1988). The Bender-Gestalt with adolescents: Comparison of two scoring systems. *Journal of Clinical Psychology, 44,* 226–230.

McKinlay, A., Dalrymple-Alford, J. C., Horwood, L. J., & Fergusson, D. M. (2002). Long term psychosocial outcomes after mild head injury in early childhood. *Journal of Neurology, Neurosurgery, and Psychiatry, 73,* 281–288.

McLean, M., Worley, M., & Bailey, D. B. (2004). *Assessing infants and preschoolers with special needs.* Upper Saddle River, NJ: Prentice-Hall.

McLoyd, V. C. (1998). Socioeconomic disadvantage and child development. *American Psychologist, 53,* 185–204.

McMahon, R. J., & Forehand, R. (1988). Conduct disorders. In E. J. Mash & L. G. Terdal (Eds.), *Behavioral assessment of childhood disorders* (2nd ed., pp. 105–153). New York: Guilford.

McWhirter, J. J., McWhirter, B., McWhirter, A. M., & McWhirter, E. H. (1993). *At-risk youth: A comprehensive response.* Pacific Grove, CA: Brooks/Cole.

Medoff-Cooper, B., Carey, W. B., & McDevitt, S. C. (1993). The Early Infancy Temperament Questionnaire. *Journal of Developmental and Behavioral Pediatrics, 14,* 230–235.

Mellers, J. D. C. (2004). Neurological investigations. In L. H. Goldstein & J. E. McNeil (Eds.), *Clinical neuropsychology: A practical guide to assessment and management for clinicians* (pp. 57–77). West Sussex, England: Wiley.

Melton, G. B. (1994). Doing justice and doing good: Conflicts for mental health professionals. *Future of Children: Sexual Abuse of Children, 4,* 102–118.

Mercer, C. D., & Mercer, A. R. (2005). *Teaching students with learning problems.* Upper Saddle River, NJ: Merrill/Prentice Hall.

Mercer, J. R., & Lewis, J. F. (1978). *System of Multi-Cultural, Pluralistic Assessment.* San Antonio, TX: The Psychological Corporation.

Merrell, K. W. (1993). Using behavior rating scales to assess social skills and antisocial behavior in school settings: Development of the School Social Behavior Scales. *School Psychology Review, 22,* 115–133.

Mesibov, G. B., Adams, L. W., & Klinger, L. G. (1997). *Autism: Understanding the disorder.* New York: Plenum.

Mesibov, G. B., Shea, V., & Adams, L. W. (2001). *Understanding Asperger syndrome and high functioning autism.* Norwell, MA: Kluwer Plenum.

Messick, S. (1989a). Meaning and values in test validation: The science and ethics of assessment. *Educational Researcher, 18,* 5–11.

Messick, S. (1989b). Validity. In R. L. Linn (Ed.), *Educational measurement* (3rd ed., pp. 13–103). Washington, DC: American Council on Education and National Council on Measurement in Education.

Messick, S. (1995). Validity of psychological assessment: Validation of inferences from persons' responses and performances as scientific inquiry into score meaning. *American Psychologist, 50,* 741–749.

Mick, E., Biederman, J., Faraone, S. V., Sayer, J., & Kleinman, S. (2002). Case-control study of attention-deficit hyperactivity disorder and maternal smoking, alcohol use, and drug use during pregnancy. *Journal of the American Academy of Child and Adolescent Psychiatry, 41,* 378–385.

Middleton, J. A. (2001). Practitioner review: Psychological sequelae of head injury in children and adolescents. *Journal of Child Psychology and Psychiatry, 42,* 165–180.

Middleton, J. A. (2004). Clinical neuropsychological assessment of children. In L. H. Goldstein & J. E. McNeil (Eds.), *Clinical neuropsychology: A practical guide to assessment and management for clinicians* (pp. 275–300). West Sussex, England: Wiley.

Milberg, W. P., Hebben, N., & Kaplan, E. F. (1996). The Boston process approach to neuropsychological assessment. In I. Grant & K. M. Adams, *Neuropsychological assessment of neuropsychiatric disorders* (2nd ed., pp. 58–80). New York: Oxford University Press.

Mild Traumatic Brain Injury Committee. (1993). Definition of mild traumatic brain injury. *Journal of Head Trauma Rehabilitation, 8,* 86–87.

Miller, J. A., Tansy, M., & Hughes, T. L. (1998). Functional behavioral assessment: The link between problem behavior and effective intervention in schools. *Current Issues in Education, 1(5).* Retrieved May 5, 2004, from http://cie.ed.asu/volume1/number5

Miller, J. H., & Milam, C. P. (1987). Multiplication and division errors committed by learning disabled students. *Learning Disabilities Research, 2,* 119–122.

Miller, L. (1989). Neuropsychology, personality and substance abuse: Implications for head injury rehabilitation. *Cognitive Rehabilitation, 7,* 26–31.

Miller, L. (1993). Family therapy of brain injury: Syndromes, strategies, and solutions. *American Journal of Family Therapy, 21,* 111–121.

Milling, L. S. (2001). Depression in preadolescents. In C. E. Walker & M. C. Roberts (Eds.), *Handbook of clinical child psychology* (3rd ed., pp. 373–392). New York: Wiley.

Millon, T. (1987). On the nature of taxonomy in psychopathology. In C. G. Last & M. Hersen (Eds.), *Issues in diagnostic research* (pp. 3–85). New York: Plenum.

Millon, T. (1993). *Millon Adolescent Clinical Inventory.* Minneapolis: National Computer Systems.

Millstein, S. G., & Irwin, C. E. (1983). Acceptability of computer acquired sexual histories in adolescent girls. *Journal of Pediatrics, 103,* 815–819.

Miltenberger, R. G. (1997). *Behavior modification: Principles and procedures.* Pacific Grove, CA: Brooks/Cole.

Milton, S. B. (1988). Management of subtle cognitive communication deficits. *Journal of Head Trauma Rehabilitation, 3,* 1–11.

M.I.N.D. Institute. (2002). *Report to the legislature on the principal findings from the epidemiology of autism in California: A comprehensive pilot study.* Davis, CA: University of California.

Mirsky, A. F., Anthony, B. J., Duncan, C. C., Ahearn, M. B., & Kellam, S. G. (1991). Analysis of the elements of attention: A neuropsychological approach. *Neuropsychology Review, 2,* 109–145.

Mitchell, R. E., & Karchmer, M. A. (2004). Chasing the mythical ten percent: Parental hearing status of deaf and hard of hearing students in the United States. *Sign Language Studies, 4,* 138–163.

Moats, L. C. (1998). Teaching decoding. *American Educator, 22,* 42–51.

Moats, L. C. (2001). Spelling disability in adolescents and adults. In A. M. Bain, L. L. Bailet, & L. C. Moats (Eds.), *Written language disorders: Theory into practice* (2nd ed., pp. 43–75). Austin, TX: Pro-Ed.

Moffitt, T. E. (1990). Juvenile delinquency and attention deficit disorder: Boys' developmental trajectories from age 3 to age 15. *Child Development, 61,* 893–910.

Mönks, F. J., & Mason, E. J. (2000). Developmental psychology and giftedness: Theories and research. In K. A. Heller, F. J. Mönks, R. J. Sternberg, & R. F. Subotnik (Eds.), *International handbook of giftedness and talent* (pp. 141–156). Oxford, England: Elsevier.

Moon, S. M., & Hall, A. S. (1998). Family therapy with intellectually and creatively gifted children. *Journal of Marital and Family Therapy, 24,* 59–80.

Moore, C. L., Feist-Price, S., & Alston, R. J. (2002). Competitive employment and mental retardation: Interplay among gender, secondary psychiatric disability, and rehabilitation services. *Journal of Rehabilitation, 68,* 14–20.

Moore, J. B., Reeve, T. G., & Boan, T. (1986). Reliability of the short form of the Bruininks-Oseretsky Test of Motor Proficiency with five-year-old children. *Perceptual & Motor Skills, 62,* 223–226.

Moore, M. (1987). Inter-judge reliability expressed as percent of agreement between observers. *Archivio di Psicologia, Neurologia e Psichiatria, 48,* 124–129.

Moore, M. V. (1969). Pathological writing. *ASHA, 11,* 535–538.

Morgan, A., & Vernon, M. (1994). A guide to diagnosis of learning disabilities in deaf and hard-of-hearing children and adults. *American Annals of the Deaf, 139,* 358–370.

Morgan, S. B. (1984). Helping parents understand the diagnosis of autism. *Developmental and Behavioral Pediatrics, 5,* 78–85.

Moritz, B., Van Nes, H., & Brouwer, W. (1989). The professional helper as a concerned party in suicide cases. In R. F. W. Diekstra, R. Maris, S. Platt, A. Schmidtke, & G. Sonneck (Eds.), *Suicide and its prevention* (pp. 199–210). New York: Brill.

Morris, E. F. (2000). An Africentric perspective for clinical research and practice. In R. H. Dana (Ed.), *Handbook of cross-cultural and multicultural personality assessment* (pp. 17–41). Mahwah, NJ: Erlbaum.

Morrison, G. M., & Cosden, M. A. (1997). Risk, resilience and adjustment of individuals with learning disabilities. *Learning Disability Quarterly, 20,* 43–60.

Morsbach, H. (1988). The importance of silence and stillness in Japanese nonverbal communication: A cross-cultural approach. In P. Fernando (Ed.), *Cross-cultural perspectives in nonverbal communication* (pp. 201–216). Gittingen, Germany: Hogrefe.

Moscovitch, M. (1981). Right-hemisphere language. *Topics in Language Disorders, 1,* 41–61.

Mostofsky, S. H., Cooper, K. L., Kates, W. R., Denckla, M. B., & Kaufmann, W. E. (2002). Smaller prefrontal and premotor volumes in boys with attention-deficit/hyperactivity disorder. *Biological Psychiatry, 52,* 785–794.

Mulick, J. A., Jacobson, J. W., & Kobe, F. H. (1993). Anguished silence and helping hands: Autism and facilitated communication. *Skeptical Inquirer, 17,* 270–280.

Muñoz-Sandoval, A. F., Cummings, J., Alvarado, C. G., & Ruef, M. L. (1998). *Bilingual Verbal Ability Tests.* Itasca, IL: Riverside.

Murphy, H. A., Hutchison, J. M., & Bailey, J. S. (1983). Behavioral school psychology goes outdoors: The effects of organized games on playground aggression. *Journal of Applied Behavior Analysis, 16,* 29–35.

Myles, B. S. (2005). *Children and youth with Asperger syndrome: Strategies for success in inclusive settings.* Thousand Oaks, CA: Corwin Press.

Myles, B. S., Bock, S. J., & Simpson, R. L. (2001). *Asperger Syndrome Diagnostic Scale.* Austin, TX: Pro-Ed.

Nader, K. O. (1997). Assessing traumatic experiences in children. In J. P. Wilson & T. M. Keane (Eds.), *Assessing psychological trauma and PTSD* (pp. 291–348). New York: Guilford.

Naglieri, J. A., LeBuffe, P. A., & Pfeiffer, S. I. (1994). *Devereux Scales of Mental Disorders.* San Antonio, TX: The Psychological Corporation.

Nass, C., Moon, Y., & Carney, P. (1999). Are people polite to computers? Responses to computer-based interviewing systems. *Journal of Applied Social Psychology, 29,* 1093–1110.

National Center for Educational Statistics. (2004). *Indicators of school crime and safety, 2003.* Retrieved March 25, 2004, from http://www.nces.ed.gov

National Center for Hearing Assessment and Management (NCHAM). (2005). *2004 State EHDI Survey.* Retrieved December 10, 2004, from http://www.infanthearing.org

National Center on Birth Defects and Development Disabilities (NCBDDD). (2005). *Mental retardation.* Retrieved January 27, 2005, from http://www.cdc.gov/ncbddd/dd/ddmr.htm

National Dissemination Center for Children with Disabilities. (2005). *Mental retardation.* Retrieved January 27, 2005, from http://www.nichy.org/pubs/factshe/fs8txt.htm

National Information Center for Children and Youth with Disabilities. (2004). *Learning disabilities.* Retrieved January 27, 2005, from http://www.nichcy.org/pubs/factshe/fs7txt.htm

National Institute of Mental Health. (1997). *What is autism?* Washington, DC: Author.

National Institute of Neurological Disorders and Stroke. (2005). *NINDS Septo-Optic Dysplasia information page.* Retrieved December 13, 2004, from http://www.ninds.nih.gov/disorders/septo_optic_dysplasia/septo_optic_ dysplasia.htm

National Institutes of Health. (2000). *Phenylketonuria: Screening and management.* Retrieved August 26, 2005, from http://consensus.nih.gov/2000/2000Phenylketonuria113html.htm

National Joint Committee on Learning Disabilities. (1991). Learning disabilities: Issues on definition. *ASHA, 33 (Suppl. 5),* 18–20.

National Reading Panel. (2000). *Teaching children to read: An evidence based assessment of the scientific research literature on reading and implications for reading instruction.* Washington, DC: National Institute of Child Health and Human Development.

Nay, W. R. (1979). *Multimethod clinical assessment.* New York: Gardner.

Neale, M. D., & McKay, M. F. (1985). Scoring the Bender-Gestalt Test using the Koppitz developmental system: Interrater reliability, item difficulty, and scoring implications. *Perceptual & Motor Skills, 60,* 627–636.

Newborg, J. (2005). *Battelle Developmental Inventory, 2nd Edition.* Itasca, IL: Riverside Publishing.

Nielsen, M. E. (2002). Gifted students with learning disabilities: Recommendations for identification and programming. *Exceptionality, 10,* 93–111.

Nielson, S., & Sapp, G. L. (1991). Bender-Gestalt developmental scores: Predicting reading and mathematics achievement. *Psychological Reports, 69,* 39–42.

Nihira, K., Leland, H., & Lambert, N. (1993). *AAMR Adaptive Behavior Scale–Residential and Community* (2nd ed.). Austin, TX: Pro-Ed.

Nishitani, N., Avikainen, S., & Hari, R. (2004). Abnormal imitation-related cortical activation sequences in Asperger's syndrome. *Annals of Neurology, 55,* 558–562.

Nonverbal Learning Disorders Association. (n.d.). *Diagnostic criteria.* Retrieved July 15, 2004, from http://www.nlda.org/content-page.asp?page=diagnostic

Northern, J. L., & Downs, M. P. (1991). *Hearing in children* (4th ed.). Baltimore: Williams & Wilkins.

Norvilitis, J. M., Scime, M., & Lee, J. S. (2002). Courtesy stigma in mothers of children with attention-deficit/hyperactivity disorder:

A preliminary investigation. *Journal of Attention Disorders, 6,* 61–68.

Nussbaum, N. L., & Bigler, E. D. (1997). Halstead-Reitan Neuropsychological Test Batteries for Children. In C. R. Reynolds & E. Fletcher-Janzen (Eds.), *Handbook of clinical child neuropsychology* (2nd. ed., pp. 219–236). New York: Plenum.

O'Brien, G. (2001). Adult outcome of childhood learning disability. *Developmental Medicine & Child Neurology, 43,* 634–638.

O'Connor, R. E. (2000). Increasing the intensity of intervention in kindergarten and first grade. *Learning Disabilities Research and Practice, 15,* 43–54.

O'Connor, R. E., Fulmer, D., Harty, K., & Bell, K. (2001, April). *Total awareness: Reducing the severity of reading disability.* Presented at the American Educational Research Conference, Seattle, WA.

O'Connor, R. E., & Jenkins, J. R. (1999). The prediction of reading disabilities in kindergarten and first grade. *Scientific Studies of Reading, 3,* 159–197.

O'Connor, R. E., Notari-Syverson, A., & Vadasy, P. F. (1996). Ladders to literacy: The effects of teacher-led phonological activities for kindergarten children with and without disabilities. *Exceptional Children, 63,* 117–131.

Odgers, C., Vincent, G. M., & Corrado, R. R. (2002). A preliminary conceptual framework for the prevention and management of multi-problem youth. In R. R. Corrado, R. Roesch, S. D. Hart, & J. K. Gierowski (Eds.), *Multi-problem violent youth: A foundation for comparative research on needs interventions and outcomes* (Vol. 324, pp. 302–329). Amsterdam: IOS Press.

Office of Juvenile Justice and Delinquency Prevention. (2004). *Juvenile offenders and victims: 2004 national report.* Retrieved January 11, 2005 from http://www.ojjdp.ncjrs.org

Okazaki, S., & Sue, S. (1995). Methodological issues in assessment research with ethnic minorities. *Psychological Assessment, 7,* 367–375.

Okun, B. (1982). *Effective helping: Interviewing and counseling techniques* (2nd ed.). Monterey, CA: Brooks/Cole.

Ollendick, T. H., & King, N. J. (1998). Empirically supported treatments for children with phobic and anxiety disorders. *Journal of Clinical Child Psychology, 27,* 156–167.

Ollendick, T. H., Oswald, D. P., & Ollendick, D. G. (1993). Anxiety disorders in mentally retarded persons. In J. L. Matson & R. P. Barrett (Eds.), *Psychopathology in the mentally retarded* (2nd ed., pp. 41–85). Boston: Allyn & Bacon.

Olson, D. H., & Portner, J. (1983). Family Adaptability and Cohesion Evaluation Scales. In E. E. Filsinger (Ed.), *Marriage and family assessment: A source book for family therapy* (pp. 299–315). Newbury Park, CA: Sage.

Olson, R. K. (1999). Genes, environment, and reading disabilities. In R. Sternberg & L. Spear-Swerling (Eds.), *Perspectives on learning disabilities* (pp. 3–22). New Haven: Westview Press.

Olweus, D. (1991). Bully/victim problems among school children: Basic facts and effects of a school based intervention program. In D. J. Pepler & K. H. Rubin (Eds.), *The development and treatment of childhood aggression* (pp. 411–448). Mahwah, NJ: Erlbaum.

Olweus, D. (1994). Bullying at school: Basic facts and effects of a school-based intervention program. *Journal of Child Psychology and Psychiatry, 35,* 1171–1190.

O'Neill, R. E., Horner, R. H., Albin, R. W., Sprague, J. R., Storey, K., & Newton, J. S. (1997). *Functional assessment and program development for problem behavior: A practical handbook* (2nd ed.). Pacific Grove, CA: Brooks/Cole.

Orel-Bixler, D. (2003). *Eye and vision function from birth to preschool.* Retrieved January 27, 2005, from http://spectacle.berkeley.edu/ class/opt10/lec_DOB.shtml

Ornstein, P. A., & Haden, C. A. (2002). The development of memory: Toward an understanding of children's testimony. In M. Eisen, J. A. Quas, & G. S. Goodman (Eds.), *Memory and suggestibility in the forensic interview* (pp. 29–61). Hillsdale, NJ: Erlbaum.

Orvaschel, H. (1995). *Schedule for Affective Disorders and Schizophrenia for School-Age Children–Epidemiological version 5 (K-SADS–E5).* Ft. Lauderdale, FL: NOVA Southeastern University.

OSEP Technical Assistance Center. (2001). *Functional assessment.* Retrieved September 26, 2004, from http://www.pbis.org

Oster, G. D., Caro, J. E., Eagen, D. R., & Lillo, M. A. (1988). *Assessing adolescents.* New York: Pergamon.

Oster, G. D., & Montgomery, S. S. (1995). *Helping your depressed teenager: A guide for parents and caregivers.* New York: Wiley.

O'Toole, M. E. (2000). *The school shooter: A threat assessment perspective.* Retrieved August 24, 2002, from http://www.fbi.gov/publications/school/school2.pdf

Oud, J. H., & Sattler, J. M. (1984). Generalized kappa coefficient: A microsoft BASIC program. *Behavior Research Methods, Instruments, & Computers, 16,* 481.

Paclawskyj, T. R., Matson, J. L., Rush, K. S., Smalls, Y., & Vollmer, T. R. (2000). Questions About Behavioral Function (QABF): A behavioral checklist for functional assessment of aberrant behavior. *Research in Developmental Disabilities, 21,* 223–229.

Paperny, D. M., Aono, J. Y., Lehman, R. M., Hammas, S. L., & Risser, J. (1990). Computer-assisted detection and intervention in adolescent high-risk health behaviors. *Journal of Pediatrics, 116,* 456–462.

Paquier, P., & Van Dongen, H. R. (1993). Current trends in acquired childhood aphasia: An introduction. *Aphasiology, 7,* 421–440.

Parnes, S. (1966). *Workshop for creative problem solving institutes and courses.* Buffalo, NY: Creative Educational Foundation.

Parsons, M. B., Reid, D. H., Green, C. W., Browning, L. B., & Hensley, M. B. (2003). Evaluation of a shared-work program for reducing assistance provided to supported workers with severe multiple disabilities. *Research in Developmental Disabilities, 23,* 1–16.

Pascal, G. R., & Suttell, B. J. (1951). *The Bender-Gestalt Test: Quantification and validity for adults.* New York: Grune & Stratton.

Paternite, C. E., Loney, J., Salisbury, H., & Whaley, M. A. (1999). Childhood inattention-overactivity, aggression, and stimulant medication history as predictors of young adult outcomes. *Journal of Child and Adolescent Psychopharmacology, 9,* 169–184.

Paulsen, J. S., & Altmaier, E. M. (1995). The effects of perceived versus enacted social support on the discriminative cue function of spouses for pain behaviors. *Pain, 60,* 103–110.

Pelham, W. E., Jr., Wheeler, T., & Chronis, A. (1998). Empirically supported psychosocial treatments for attention deficit hyperactivity disorder. *Journal of Clinical Child Psychology, 27,* 190–205.

Pendarvis, E. D., Howley, C. B., & Howley, A. A. (1990). *The abilities of gifted children.* Englewood Cliffs, NJ: Prentice Hall.

Pennington, B. F. (1999). Dyslexia as a neurodevelopmental disorder. In H. Tager-Flusberg (Ed.), *Neurodevelopmental disorders* (pp. 307–330). Cambridge, MA: MIT Press.

Pennington, B. F., & Welsh, M. (1995). Neuropsychology and developmental psychopathology. In D. Cicchetti & D. J. Cohen (Eds.), *Developmental psychopathology: Vol. 1. Theory and methods* (pp. 254–290). New York: Wiley.

Pericak-Vance, M. A. (2003). The genetics of autistic disorder. In R. Plomin, J. C. DeFries, & P. McGuffin (Eds.), *Behavioral genetics in the postgenomic era* (pp. 267–288). Washington, DC: American Psychological Association.

Perry, A., & Factor, D. C. (1989). Psychometric validity and clinical usefulness of the Vineland Adaptive Behavior Scales and the AAMD Adaptive Behavior Scale for an autistic sample. *Journal of Autism and Developmental Disorders, 19,* 41–55.

Peters, W. A. M., Grager-Loidl, H., & Supplee, P. (2000). Underachievement of gifted children and adolescents: Theory and practice. In K. A. Heller, F. J. Mönks, R. J. Sternberg, & R. F. Subotnik (Eds.), *International handbook of giftedness and talent* (pp. 609–620). Oxford, England: Elsevier.

Peterson, C., Dowden, C., & Tobin, J. (1999). Interviewing preschoolers: Comparisons of yes/no and wh-questions. *Law and Human Behavior, 23,* 539–555.

Peterson, J. S., & Colangelo, N. (1996). Gifted achievers and underachievers: A comparison of patterns found in school files. *Journal of Counselling and Development, 74,* 399–407.

Peterson, L., & Tremblay, G. (1999). Self-monitoring in behavioral medicine: Children. *Psychological Assessment, 11,* 458–465.

Petraitis, J., Flay, B. R., & Miller, T. Q. (1995). Reviewing theories of adolescent substance use: Organizing pieces of the puzzle. *Psychological Bulletin, 117,* 67–86.

Pezdek, K., & Taylor, J. (2002). Memory for traumatic events in children and adults. In M. Eisen, J. A. Quas, & G. S. Goodman (Eds.), *Memory and suggestibility in the forensic interview* (pp. 165–183). Hillsdale, NJ: Erlbaum.

Pfeffer, C. R. (1986). *The suicidal child.* New York: Guilford.

Phares, J. V. (2003). *Understanding abnormal child psychology.* New York: Wiley.

Phelps, J., Stempel, L., & Speck, G. (1985). The Children's Handwriting Scale: A new diagnostic tool. *Journal of Educational Research, 79,* 46–50.

Phelps, L., & Cox, D. (1993). Children with prenatal cocaine exposure: Resilient or handicapped? *School Psychology Review, 22,* 710–724.

Pianta, R. C., Smith, N., & Reeve, R. E. (1991). Observing mother and child behavior in a problem solving situation at school entry: Relations with classroom adjustment. *School Psychology Quarterly, 6,* 1–15.

Pisecco, S., Baker, D. B., Silva, P. A., & Brooke, M. (2001). Boys with reading disabilities and/or ADHD: Distinctions in early childhood. *Journal of Learning Disabilities, 34,* 98–106.

Plake, B. S., Impara, J. C., & Spies, R. A. (2003). *The fifteenth mental measurements yearbook.* Lincoln: University of Nebraska and Buros Institute of Mental Measurement.

Polansky, N. A., Borgman, R. D., & De Saix, C. (1972). *Roots of futility.* San Francisco: Jossey-Bass.

Politano, P. M., Nelson, W. M., Evans, H. E., Sorenson, S. B., & Zeman, D. J. (1986). Factor analytic evaluation of differences between Black and Caucasian emotionally disturbed children on the Children's Depression Inventory. *Journal of Psychopathology and Behavioral Assessment, 8,* 1–7.

Pope, K. S., Butcher, J. N., & Seelen, J. (1993). *The MMPI, MMPI–2, and MMPI–A in court: Assessment, testimony, and cross-examination for expert witnesses and attorneys.* Washington, DC: American Psychological Association.

Porter, G. L., & Binder, D. M. (1981). A pilot study of visual-motor development inter-test reliability: The Beery Developmental Test of Visual-Motor Integration and the Bender Visual Motor Gesalt Test. *Journal of Learning Disabilities, 14,* 124–127.

Powell, J. (2004). The effects of medication and other substances on cognitive functioning. In L. H. Goldstein & J. E. McNeil (Eds.), *Clinical neuropsychology: A practical guide to assessment and management for clinicians* (pp. 99–120). West Sussex, England: Wiley.

Poythress, N. G. (1992). Expert testimony on violence and dangerousness: Roles for mental health professionals. *Forensic Reports, 5,* 135–150.

Price-Williams, D. R., & Ramirez, M., III. (1977). Divergent thinking, cultural differences, and bilingualism. *Journal of Social Psychology, 103,* 3–11.

Prigatano, G. P., Fordyce, D. J., Zeiner, H. K., Roueche, J. R., Pepping, M., & Wood, B. C. (1986). *Neuropsychological rehabilitation after brain injury.* Baltimore: Johns Hopkins University Press.

Prior, M., & Ozonoff, S. (1998). Psychological factors in autism. In F. R. Volkmar (Ed.), *Autism and pervasive developmental disorders* (pp. 64–108). New York: Cambridge University Press.

Pryzwansky, W. B., & Wendt, R. N. (1999). *Professional and ethical issues in psychology: Foundations of practice.* New York: Norton.

Quay, H. C., & Hogan, A. E. (Eds.). (1999). *Handbook of disruptive behavior disorders.* New York: Kluwer Academic Press.

Quay, H. C., & Peterson, D. R. (1996). *Revised Behavior Problem Checklist–Par Edition: Professional manual.* Lutz, FL: Psychological Assessment Resources.

Quinn, K. M. (1988). Children and deception. In R. Rogers (Ed.), *Clinical assessment of malingering and deception* (pp. 104–119). New York: Guilford.

Rapcsak, S. Z. (1997). Disorder of writing. In L. J. G. Rothi & K. M. Heilman (Eds.), *Apraxia: The neuropsychology of action* (pp. 149–172). Hove, England: Psychology Press.

Rapoport, J. L., Swedo, S. E., & Leonard, H. L. (1992). Childhood obsessive compulsive disorder. *Journal of Clinical Psychiatry, 53,* 11–16.

Raskind, M. H., Goldberg, R. J., Higgins, E. L., & Herman, K. L. (1999). Patterns of change and prediction of success in individuals with learning disabilities: Results from a twenty-year longitudinal study. *Learning Disabilities Research and Practice, 14,* 35–49.

Raskind, W. H. (2001). Current understanding of the genetic basis of reading and spelling disability. *Learning Disability Quarterly, 24,* 141–157.

Redfield, J. (2001). Familial intelligence as an estimate of expected ability in children. *Clinical Neuropsychology, 15,* 446–460.

Reed, L. J., Carter, B. D., & Miller, L. C. (1992). Fear and anxiety in children. In C. E. Walker & R. C. Roberts (Eds.), *Handbook of clinical child psychology* (2nd ed., pp. 237–260). New York: Wiley.

Reich, W., Welner, Z., Herjanic, B., & MHS Staff. (1997). *Diagnostic Interview for Children and Adolescents–IV (DICA–IV).* North Tonawanda, NY: Multi-Health Systems.

Reiff, H. B., Gerber, P. J., & Ginsberg, R. (1997). *Exceeding expectations: Successful adults with learning disabilities.* Austin, TX: Pro-Ed.

Reilly, P. L., Simpson, D. A., Sprod, R., & Thomas, L. (1988). Assessing the conscious level in infants and young children: A paediatric version of the Glasgow Coma Scale. *Child's Nervous System, 4*, 30–33.

Reinecke, M. A., Beebe, D. W., & Stein, M. A. (1999). The third factor of the WISC–III: It's (probably) not freedom from distractibility. *Journal of the American Academy of Child & Adolescent Psychiatry, 38*, 322–328.

Reisman, J. M. (1973). *Principles of psychotherapy with children.* New York: Wiley.

Reiss, S. (1988). *Reiss Screen for Maladaptive Behavior.* Orland Park, IL: International Diagnostic Systems.

Reiss, S., & Valenti-Hein, D. (1994). Development of a psychopathology rating scale for children with mental retardation. *Journal of Consulting and Clinical Psychology, 62*, 28–33.

Reitan, R. M., (1984). *Aphasia and sensory-perceptual deficits in adults.* Tucson, AZ: Neuropsychology Press.

Reitan, R. M., (1985). *Aphasia and sensory-perceptual deficits in children.* Tucson, AZ: Neuropsychology Press.

Reitan, R. M., & Davison, L. A. (Eds.). (1974). *Clinical neuropsychology: Current status and applications.* Washington, DC: Winston.

Reitan, R. M., & Wolfson, D. (1985). *The Halstead-Reitan Neuropsychological Test Battery.* Tucson: Neuropsychology Press.

Reitan, R. M., & Wolfson, D. (1992). *Neuropsychological evaluation of young children.* Tucson, AS: Neuropsychology Press.

Repp, A. C. (1999). Naturalistic functional assessment of regular and special education students in classroom settings. In A. C. Repp & R. H. Horner (Eds.), *Functional analysis of problem behaviour: From effective assessment to effective support* (pp. 238–258). Belmont, CA: Wadsworth.

Repp, A. C., & Barton, L. E. (1980). Naturalistic observations of institutionalized retarded persons: A comparison of licensure decisions and behavioral observations. *Journal of Applied Behavior Analysis, 13*, 333–341.

Repp, A. C., & Horner, R. H. (Eds.). (1999). *Functional analysis of problem behavior: From effective assessment to effective support.* Belmont, CA: Wadsworth.

Reynolds, C. R., & Bigler, E. D. (1994). *Test of Memory and Learning.* Austin, TX: Pro-Ed.

Reynolds, C. R., & Kamphaus, R. W. (2004). *Behavior Assessment System for Children–Second Edition.* Circle Pines, MN: American Guidance Service.

Reynolds, C. R., Lowe, P. A., & Saenz, A. L. (1999). The problem of bias in psychological assessment. In C. R. Reynolds & T. B. Gutkin (Eds.), *The handbook of school psychology* (3rd ed., pp. 549–595). New York: Wiley.

Reynolds, C. R., & Paget, K. (1981). Factor analysis of the Revised Manifest Anxiety Scale for blacks, whites, males, and females with a national normative sample. *Journal of Consulting and Clinical Psychology, 49*, 349–352.

Reynolds, C. R., Plake, B. S., & Harding, R. E. (1983). Item bias in the assessment of children's anxiety: Race and sex interaction on items of the Revised Children's Manifest Anxity Scale. *Journal of Psychological Assessment, 1*, 17–24.

Reynolds, C. R., & Richmond, B. O. (1985). *Revised Children's Manifest Anxiety Scale.* Los Angeles: Western Psychological Service.

Reynolds, D., Creemers, B., Nesselrod, P., Schaffer, E., Stringfield, S., & Teddlie, C. (1994). *Advances and school effectiveness practice and research.* Oxford, England: Pergamon.

Reynolds, W. M. (1989). *Reynolds Child Depression Scale.* Lutz, FL: Psychological Assessment Resources.

Reynolds, W. M. (1992). Depressive disorders in children and adolescents. In W. M. Reynolds (Ed.), *Internalizing disorders in children and adolescents* (pp. 149–253). New York: Wiley.

Reynolds, W. M. (1998a). *Adolescent Psychopathology Scale: Administration and interpretive manual.* Lutz, FL: Psychological Assessment Resources.

Reynolds, W. M. (1998b). *Adolescent Psychopathology Scale: Psychometric and technical manual.* Odessa, FL: Psychological Assessment Resources.

Reynolds, W. M. (2000). *Adolescent Psychopathology Scale–Short Form.* Lutz, FL: Psychological Assessment Resources.

Reynolds, W. M. (2001). *Reynolds Adolescent Adjustment Screening Inventory: Professional manual.* Lutz, FL: Psychological Assessment Resources.

Reynolds, W. M. (2002). *Reynolds Adolescent Depression Scale–Second Edition.* Lutz, FL: Psychological Assessment Resources.

Reynolds, W. M., & Johnston, H. F. (1994). The nature and study of depression in children and adolescents. In W. M. Reynolds & H. F. Johnston (Eds.), *Handbook of depression in children and adolescents* (pp. 3–17). New York: Plenum.

Riccio, C. A., Cohen, M. J., Hall, J., & Ross, C. M. (1997). The third and fourth factors of the WISC–III: What they don't measure. *Journal of Psychoeducational Assessment, 15*, 27–39.

Rich, D., & Taylor, H. G. (1993). Attention deficit hyperactivity disorder. In M. Singer, L. Singer, & T. Anglin (Eds.), *Handbook for screening adolescents at psychosocial risk* (pp. 333–374). New York: Lexington Books.

Richard, D. C. S., & Bobicz, K. (2003). Computers and behavioral assessment: 6 years later. *Behavior Therapist, 26*, 219–223.

Richard, M. (1993, December). Ask CH.A.D.D. *CH.A.D.D.er*, p. 10.

Rief, S.F. (1993). *How to reach and teach ADD/ADHD children.* San Francisco: Jossey-Bass.

Rief, S.F. (2003). *The ADHD book of lists.* San Francisco: Jossey-Bass.

Rimm, S. B. (1997). Underachievement syndrome: A national epidemic. In N. Colangelo & G. A. Davis (Eds.), *Handbook of gifted education* (pp. 416–434). Boston: Allyn & Bacon.

Ritzler, B. A. (2001). Multicultural usage of the Rorschach. In L. A. Suzuki, J. G. Ponterotto, & P. J. Meller (Eds.), *Handbook of multicultural assessment: Clinical, psychological, and educational applications* (2nd ed.; pp. 237–252). San Francisco: Jossey-Bass.

Roberts, G. E., & Gruber, C. P. (2005). *Roberts–2 manual.* Los Angeles: Western Psychological Services.

Roberts, M. A. (1992). *Pediatric Inventory of Neurobehavioral Symptoms.* Unpublished manuscript, University of Iowa at Iowa City.

Roberts, M. A. (1999). Mild traumatic brain injury in children and adolescents. In W. R. Varney & R. J. Roberts (Eds.), *Mild head injury: Causes, evaluation, and treatment* (pp. 493–512). Hillsdale, NJ: Erlbaum.

Roberts, M. A. & Furuseth, A. (1997). Eliciting parental report following pediatric traumatic brain injury: Preliminary findings on the pediatric inventory of neurobehavioral symptoms. *Archives of Clinical Neuropsychology, 12*, 449–357.

Roberts, M. A., Milich, R., & Loney, J. (1984). *Structured Observation of Academic and Play Settings (SOAPS).* Unpublished manuscript, University of Iowa at Iowa City.

Robins, D., Fein, D., Barton, M., & Green, J. (2001). The Modified Checklist for Autism in Toddlers (M-CHAT): An initial study investigating the early detection of autism and pervasive developmental disorders. *Journal of Autism and Developmental Disorders, 31,* 131–144.

Robins, L. N., & Marcus, S. C. (1987). The Diagnostic Screening Procedure Writer: A tool to develop individualized screening procedures. *Medical Care, 25,* S106–S122.

Robins, P. M. (1992). A comparison of behavioral and attentional functioning in children diagnosed as hyperactive or learning-disabled. *Journal of Abnormal Child Psychology, 20,* 65–82.

Robinson, A., & Clinkenbeard, P. R. (1998). Giftedness: An exceptionality examined. *Annual Review of Psychology, 49,* 117–139.

Robinson, H. B. (1980, November). *A case for radical acceleration: Programs of the Johns Hopkins University and the University of Washington.* Paper presented at the meeting of the 1980 Symposium of the Study of Mathematically Precocious Youth, Baltimore.

Robinson, H. B. (1981). The uncommonly bright child. In M. Lewis & L. A. Rosenblum (Eds.), *The uncommon child: Genesis of behavior* (Vol. 3, pp. 57–81). New York: Plenum.

Robinson, N. M., & Noble, K. D. (1991). Social-emotional development and adjustment of gifted children. In M. C. Wang, M. C. Reynolds, & H. J. Walberg (Eds.), *Handbook of special education: Research and practice, Vol. 4: Emerging programs. Advances in education* (pp. 57–76). Oxford, England: Pergamon.

Robinson, N. M., Zigler, E., & Gallagher, J. J. (2000). Two tails of the normal curve: Similarities and differences in the study of mental retardation and giftedness. *American Psychologist, 55,* 1413–1424.

Roedell, W. C. (1980a). Characteristics of gifted young children. In W. C. Roedell, N. E. Jackson, & H. B. Robinson (Eds.), *Gifted young children* (pp. 7–26). New York: Teachers College Press.

Roedell, W. C. (1980b). Programs for gifted young children. In W. C. Roedell, N. E. Jackson, & H. B. Robinson (Eds.), *Gifted young children* (pp. 66–89). New York: Teachers College Press.

Roffman, R. A., & George, W. H. (1988). Cannabis abuse. In D. M. Donovan & G. A. Marlatt (Eds.), *Assessment of addictive behaviors* (pp. 325–363). New York: Guilford.

Rogers, R. (1988a). Current status of clinical methods. In R. Rogers (Ed.), *Clinical assessment of malingering and deception* (pp. 293–308). New York: Guilford.

Rogers, R. (1988b). Introduction. In R. Rogers (Ed.), *Clinical assessment of malingering and deception* (pp. 1–9). New York: Guilford.

Rollin, W. J. (1987). *The psychology of communication disorders in individuals and their families.* Englewood Cliffs, NJ: Prentice-Hall.

Romer, D., Hornik, R., Stanton, B., Black, M. M., Li, X., Ricardo, I., & Feigelman, S. (1997). "Talking" computers: An efficient and private method to conduct interviews on sensitive health topics. *Journal of Sexual Research, 34,* 3–9.

Rooney, K. J. (2002). Clinical judgement in the assessment of learning disabilities. In R. Brodley, L. Danielson, & D. P. Hallahan (Eds.), *Identification of learning disabilities: Research to practice* (pp. 713–722). Mahwah, NJ: Erlbaum.

Root, R. W., II, & Resnick, R. J. (2003). An update on the diagnosis and treatment of attention-deficit/hyperactivity disorder in children. *Professional Psychology: Research and Practice, 34,* 34–41.

Rorschach, H. (1942). *Psychodiagnostics* (5th ed.). Bern, Switzerland: Hans Huber.

Rosenthal, R. (1991). *Meta-analytic procedures for social research.* Applied Social Research Methods Series, Volume 6. Newbury Park, CA: Sage.

Rosner, J., & Simon, D. P. (1971). The Auditory Analysis Test: An initial report. *Journal of Learning Disabilities, 4,* 40–48.

Rotheram, M. J., & Phinney, J. S. (1986). Introduction: Definitions and perspectives in the study of children's ethnic socialization. In J. S. Phinney & M. J. Rotheram (Eds.), *Children's ethnic socialization: Pluralism and development* (pp. 10–28). Newbury Park, CA: Sage.

Rourke, B. P., & Conway, J. A. (1997). Disabilities of arithmetic and mathematical reasoning: Perspective from neurology and neuropsychology. *Journal of Learning Disabilities, 30,* 34–46.

Rourke, B. P., & Tsatsanis, K. D. (1996). Syndrome of nonverbal learning disabilities: Psycholinguistic assets and deficits. *Topics in Language Disorders, 16,* 30–44.

Rubba, J. (2003). *Phonological awareness skills and spelling skills.* Retrieved August 6, 2005, from http://www.cla.calpoly.edu/~jrubba/phon/phonaware.html

Rudel, R. G. (1988). *Assessment of developmental learning disorders: A neuropsychological approach.* New York: Basic Books.

Runco, M. A. (1992). Children's divergent thinking and creative ideation. *Developmental Review, 12,* 233–264.

Russell, E. W. (1998). In defense of the Halstead Reitan Batterey: A critique of Lezak's review. *Archives of Clinical Neuropsychology, 13,* 365–381.

Rutgers, A. H., Bakermans-Kranenburg, M. J., van IJzendoorn, M. H., & van Berckelaer-Onnes, I. A. (2004). Autism and attachment: A meta-analytic review. *Journal of Child Psychology and Psychiatry, 45,* 1123–1134.

Rutter, M. (1983). School effects on pupil progress: Research findings and policy implications. *Child Development, 54,* 1–29.

Rutter, M. (2000). Resilience reconsidered: Conceptual considerations, empirical findings, and policy implications. In J. P. Shonkoff & S. J. Samuel (Eds.), *Handbook of early childhood intervention* (2nd ed., pp. 651–682). New York: Cambridge University Press.

Rutter, M., Bailey, A. B., & Lord, C. (2004). *Social Communication Questionnaire (SCQ).* Los Angeles: Western Psychological Services.

Rutter, M., Giller, H., & Hagell, A. (1998). *Antisocial behavior by young people.* Cambridge, England: Cambridge University Press.

Rutter, M., LeCouteur, A., & Lord, C. (2004). *Autism Diagnostic Interview–Revised (ADI–R).* Los Angeles: Western Psychological Services.

Ryser, G., & McConnell, K. (2002). *Scales for Diagnosing Attention-Deficit/Hyperactivity Disorder.* Austin, TX: Pro-Ed.

Sachs, P. R. (1991). *Treating families of brain-injury survivors* (Vol. 9). New York: Springer.

Salend, S. J., & Salinas, A. (2003). Language difference or learning difficulties: The work of the multidisciplinary team. *Teaching Exceptional Children, 35,* 36–43.

Salvia, J., & Ysseldyke, J. E. (2001). *Assessment.* Boston: Houghton Mifflin.

Sanford, J. A., & Turner, A. (1995). *Intermediate Visual and Auditory Continuous Performance Test.* Richmond, VA: Brain Train.

Sanson, A., Smart, D., Prior, M., & Oberklaid, F. (1993). Precursors of hyperactivity and aggression. *Journal of the American Academy of Child and Adolescent Psychiatry, 32,* 1207–1216.

Saskatchewan Education. (1999). *Teaching students with autism: A guide for educators, 1999.* Retrieved November 15, 2002, from http://www.sasked.gov.sk.ca/branches/children_services/special_ed/docs/autism/Teaching%20Students%20with%20Autism%20Document.pdf

Sattler, J. M. (1992). *Assessment of children* (revised and updated 3rd ed.). San Diego: Sattler.

Sattler, J. M. (1998). *Clinical and forensic interviewing of children and families: Guidelines for the mental health, education, pediatric, and child maltreatment fields.* San Diego: Sattler.

Sattler, J. M. (2001). *Assessment of children: Cognitive applications* (4th ed.). San Diego: Sattler.

Sattler, J. M., & Dumont, R. (2004). *Assessment of children: WISC–IV and WPPSI–III supplement.* San Diego: Sattler.

Saudargas, R. A., & Lentz, F. E. (1986). Estimating percent of time and rate via direct observation: A suggested observational procedure and format. *School Psychology Review, 15,* 36–48.

Savage, R. M., & Gouvier, W. D. (1992). Rey Auditory-Verbal Learning Test: The effects of age and gender, and norms for delayed recall and story recognition trials. *Archives of Clinical Neuropsychology, 7,* 407–414.

Saywitz, K. J., & Lyon, T. D. (2002). Coming to grips with children's suggestibility. In M. Eisen, J. A. Quas, & G. S. Goodman (Eds.), *Memory and suggestibility in the forensic interview* (pp. 85–113). Hillsdale, NJ: Erlbaum.

Scarr, S. (1991). Theoretical issues in investigating intellectual plasticity. In S. E. Brauth, W. S. Hall, & R. J. Dooling (Eds.), *Plasticity of development* (pp. 57–71). Cambridge, MA: MIT Press.

Schachter, J. E., & Romano, B. A. (1993). Developmental issues in childhood and adolescent depression. In H. S. Koplewicz & E. Klass (Eds.), *Depression in children and adolescents: Monographs in clinical pediatrics* (Vol. 6., pp. 1–13). Philadelphia: Harwood.

Schmitt, A. J., & Wodrich, D. L. (2004). Validation of a developmental neurospsychological assessment (NEPSY) through comparison of neurological, scholastic concerns, and control groups. *Archives of Clinical Neuropsychology, 19,* 1077–1093.

Schneider, B. H., Clegg, M. R., Byrne, B. M., Ledingham, J. E., & Crombie, G. (1989). Social relations of gifted children as a function of age and school program. *Journal of Educational Psychology, 81,* 48–56.

Schopler, E. (1992). Facilitated communication—Hope or hype? *Autism Society of North Carolina, 8,* 6.

Schopler, E., Reichler, R. J., DeVellis, R. F., & Daly, K. (1980). Toward objective classification of childhood autism: Childhood Autism Rating Scale (CARS). *Journal of Autism and Developmental Disorders, 10,* 91–103.

Schopler, E., Reichler, R. J., & Renner, B. R. (1993). *The Childhood Autism Rating Scale (CARS).* New York: Irvington.

Schreibman, L. E. (1988). *Autism.* Newbury Park, CA: Sage.

Schultz, L. G. (1990). Social workers as expert witnesses in child abuse cases: A format. *Journal of Independent Social Work, 5,* 69–87.

Schwab-Stone, M., Fallon, T., Briggs, M., & Crowther, B. (1994). Reliability of diagnostic reporting for children aged 6–11 years: A test-retest study of the Diagnostic Interview Schedule for Children–Revised. *American Journal of Psychiatry, 151,* 1048–1054.

Schwab-Stone, M., Fisher, P., Piacentini, J., Shaffer, D., Davies, M., & Briggs, M. (1993). The Diagnostic Interview Schedule for Children–Revised version (DISC–R): II. Test-retest reliability. *Journal of the American Academy of Child & Adolescent Psychiatry, 32,* 651–657.

Schwartz, D., & Gorman, A. H. (2003). Community violence exposure and children's academic functioning. *Journal of Educational Psychology, 95,* 163–173.

Schwean, V. L., & Saklofske, D. H. (1998). WISC–III assessment of children with attention deficit/hyperactivity disorder. In A. Prifitera & D. H. Saklofske (Eds.), *WISC–III clinical use and interpretation* (pp. 91–118). San Diego: Academic Press.

Schworm, R. W., & Birnbaum, R. (1989). Symptom expression in hyperactive children: An analysis of observations. *Journal of Learning Disabilities, 22,* 35–40.

Scott, F. J., Baron-Cohen, S., Bolton, P., & Brayne, C. (2002). The CAST (Childhood Asperger Syndrome Test): Preliminary development of a UK Screen for mainstream primary-school-age children. *Autism, 6,* 9–13.

Scotti, J. R., Morris, T. L., McNeil, C. B., & Hawkins, R. P. (1996). DSM–IV disorders of childhood and adolescence: Can structural criteria be found? *Journal of Consulting and Clinical Psychology, 64,* 1177–1191.

Scruggs, T. E. (1987). Theoretical issues surrounding severe discrepancy: A discussion. *Learning Disabilities Research, 3,* 21–23.

Scruggs, T. E., & Mastropieri, M. A. (1992). Effective mainstreaming strategies for mildly handicapped students. *Elementary School Journal, 92,* 389–409.

Scruggs, T. E., & Mastropieri, M. A. (2002). On babies and bathwater: Addressing the problem of identification of learning disabilities. *Learning Disabilities Quarterly, 25,* 155–168.

Seligman, M., & Darling, R. B. (1989). *Ordinary families, special children: A systems approach to childhood disability.* New York: Guilford.

Selz, M. (1981). Halstead-Reitan Neuropsychological Test Battery for Children. In G. W. Hynd & J. E. Obrzut (Eds.), *Neuropsychological assessment and the school-age child: Issues and procedures* (pp. 195–235). New York: Grune & Stratton.

Semrud-Clikeman, M., Filipek, P. A., Biederman, J., Steingard, R., Kennedy, D., Renshaw, P., & Bekken, K. (1994). Attention deficit hyperactivity disorder: Magnetic resonance imaging morphometric analysis of the corpus callosum. *Journal of the American Academy of Child and Adolescent Psychiatry, 33,* 875–881.

Semrud-Clikeman, M., Hynd, G. W., Lorys, A. R., & Lahey, B. B. (1993). Differential diagnosis of children with ADHD and ADHD/with co-occurring conduct disorder. *School Psychology International, 14,* 361–370.

Shaffer, D. (1996). *Diagnostic Interview Schedule for Children (DISC–IV).* New York: New York State Psychiatric Institute.

Shane, H. C. (1993). The dark side of facilitated communication. *Topics in Language Disorders, 13,* ix–xv.

Shapiro, B. K. (1991). The pediatric neurodevelopmental assessment of infants and young children. In A. J., Capute & P. J. Accardo (Eds.), *Developmental disabilities in infancy and childhood* (pp. 139–164). Baltimore: Brookes.

Shapiro, E. S. (1984). Self-monitoring procedures. In T. H. Ollendick & M. Hersen (Eds.), *Child behavioral assessment: Principles and procedures* (pp. 148–165). New York: Pergamon.

Shapiro, E. S. (1996). *Academic skills problems workbook.* New York: Guilford.

Shapiro, E. S., & Cole, C. L. (1994). *Behavior change in the classroom: Self-management intervention.* New York: Guilford.

Shapiro, E. S., & Cole, C. L. (1999). Self-monitoring in assessing children's problems. *Psychological Assessment, 11,* 448–457.

Shapiro, E. S., DuPaul, G. J., & Bradley-Klug, K. L. (1998). Self-management as a strategy to improve the classroom behavior of adolescents with ADHD. *Journal of Learning Disabilities, 31,* 545–555.

Shapiro, S. K., & Simpson, R. G. (1994). Patterns and predictors of performance on the Bender-Gestalt and the Development Test of Visual Motor Integration in a sample of behaviorally and emotionally disturbed adolescents. *Journal of Psychoeducational Assessment, 12,* 254–263.

Share, D. L., Moffitt, R. E., & Silva, P. A. (1988). Factors associated with arithmetic-and-reading disability and specific arithmetic disability. *Journal of Learning Disability, 21,* 313–320.

Shaw, D. S., & Bell, R. Q. (1993). Developmental theories of parental contributors to antisocial behavior. *Journal of Abnormal Child Psychology, 21,* 493–518.

Shaywitz, B. A., Shaywitz, S. E., Blachman, B. A., Pugh, K. R., Fulbright, R. K., Skudlarski, P., Mench., W. E., Constable, T., Holahan, J. M., Marchione, K. E., Fletcher, J. M., Lyon, G. R., & Gore, J. C. (2004). Development of left occipitotemporal systems for skilled reading in children after a phonologically-based intervention. *Biological Psychiatry, 55,* 926–933.

Shaywitz, B. A., Shaywitz, S. E., Pugh, K. R., Mencl, W. E., Fulbright, R. K., Skudlarski, P., Constable, R. T., Marchione, K. E., Fletcher, J. M., Lyon, G. R., & Gore, J. C. (2002). Disruption of posterior brain systems for reading in children with developmental dyslexia. *Biological Psychiatry, 52,* 101–110.

Shaywitz, S. E., & Shaywitz, B. A. (2003). Neurobiological indices of dyslexia. In H. L. Swanson, K. R. Harris, & S. Graham (Eds.), *Handbook of learning disabilities* (pp.514–531). New York: Guilford.

Shea, S. C. (1988). *Psychiatric interviewing: The art of understanding.* Philadelphia: Saunders.

Shelton, T. L., & Barkley, R. A. (1994). Critical issues in the assessment of attention deficit disorders in children. *Topics in Language Disorders, 14,* 26–41.

Sheras, P. L. (2001). Depression and suicide in adolescence. In C. E. Walker & M. C. Roberts (Eds.), *Handbook of clinical child psychology* (3rd ed., pp. 657–673). New York: Wiley.

Sheras, P. L., Abidin, R. R., & Konold, T. R. (1998). *Stress Index for Parents of Adolescents.* Lutz, FL: Psychological Assessment Resources.

Shonk, S. M., & Cicchetti, D. (2000). Maltreatment, competency deficits, and risk for academic and behavioral maladjustments. *Developmental Psychology, 37,* 3–17.

Shoup, A. G., Owen, K. E., Jackson, G., & Laptook, A. (2005). The Parkland Memorial Hospital experience in ensuring compliance with universal newborn hearing screening follow-up. *Journal of Pediatrics, 146,* 66–72.

Shrout, P. E., & Fleiss, J. L. (1979). Intraclass correlations: Uses in assessing rater reliability. *Psychological Bulletin, 86,* 420–428.

Shrout, P. E., Spitzer, R. L., & Fleiss, J. L. (1987). Quantification in psychiatric diagnosis revisited. *Archives of General Psychiatry, 44,* 172–177.

Siegel, D. J., Minshew, N. J., & Goldstein, G. (1996). Wechsler IQ profiles in diagnosis of high-functioning autism. *Journal of Autism and Developmental Disorders, 26,* 389–406.

Siegel, L. S. (1999). Issues in the definition and diagnosis of learning disabilities: A perspective on Guckenberger v. Boston University. *Journal of Learning Disabilities, 32,* 304–319.

Siegler, R. S. (1998). *Children's thinking* (3rd ed.). Upper Saddle River, NJ: Prentice-Hall.

Silver, L. B. (1991). Developmental learning disorders. In M. Lewis (Ed.), *Child and adolescent psychiatry: A comprehensive textbook* (pp. 522–528). Baltimore: Williams & Wilkins.

Silver, L. B. (1992). *Attention-deficit hyperactivity disorder: A clinical guide to diagnosis and treatment.* Washington, DC: American Psychiatric Press.

Silverman, L. K. (1997). Family counseling with the gifted. In N. Colangelo & G. A. Davis (Eds.), *Handbook of gifted education* (pp. 382–397). Boston: Allyn & Bacon.

Silverstein, A. B. (1973). Note on prevalence. *American Journal of Mental Deficiency, 77,* 380–382.

Silverstein, A. B. (1982). Note on the constancy of the IQ. *American Journal of Mental Deficiency, 87,* 227–228.

Sincoff, M. Z., & Goyer, R. S. (1984). *Interviewing.* New York: Macmillan.

Singh, N. N., Oswald, D. P., & Ellis, C. R. (1998). Mental retardation. In T. H. Ollendick & M. Hersen (Eds.), *Handbook of child psychopathology,* (3rd ed., pp. 91–116). New York: Plenum.

Sink, C., & Tracy, L. (1988). Educating the head injured: A continuum of programs and services. *Cognitive Rehabilitation, 6,* 34-37.

Sisson, L. A., & Van Hasselt, V. B. (1987). Visual impairment. In V. B. Van Hasselt & M. Hersen (Eds.), *Psychological evaluation of the developmentally and physically disabled* (pp. 115–153). New York: Plenum.

Sivan, A. B. (1992). *Benton Visual Memory Test, Fifth Edition.* San Antonio, TX: The Psychological Corporation.

Skeen, J. A., Strong, V. N., & Book, R. M. (1982). Comparison of learning disabled children's performance on Bender Visual-Motor Gestalt Test and Beery's Developmental Test of Visual-Motor Integration. *Perceptual and Motor Skills, 55,* 1257–1258.

Slate, J. R., & Fawcett, J. (1995). Validity of the WISC–III for deaf and hard of hearing persons. *American Annals of the Deaf, 140,* 250–254.

Slate, J. R., & Saudargas, R. A. (1987). Classroom behaviors of LD, seriously emotionally disturbed and average children: A sequential analysis. *Learning Disability Quarterly, 10,* 125–134.

Smith, B. H., Pelham, W. E., Jr., Gnagy, E., Molina, B., & Evans, S. (2000). The reliability, validity, and unique contributions of self-report by adolescents receiving treatment for attention-deficit/hyperactivity disorder. *Journal of Consulting and Clinical Psychology, 68,* 489–499.

Smith, D., & Dumont, F. (1995). A cautionary study: Unwarranted interpretations of the Draw-A-Person Test. *Professional Psychology: Research and Practice, 26,* 298–303.

Smith, F., & Hardman, F. (2003). Using computerised observation as a tool for capturing classroom interaction. *Educational Studies, 29,* 39–47.

Smith, K. M., Daly, M., Fischer, M., Yiannoutsos, C. T., Bauer, L., Barkley, R. A., & Navia, B. A. (2003). Association of the dopamine beta hydroxylase gene with attention deficit hyperactivity disorder: Genetic analysis of the Milwaukee longitudinal study. *American Journal of Medical Genetics, 119,* 77–85.

Smith, T. C., & Smith, B. L. (1988). The Visual Aural Digit Span and Bender Gestalt Test as predictors of Wide Range Achievement Test–Revised scores. *Psychology in the Schools, 25,* 264–269.

Snell, M. E. (1988). Curriculum and methodology for individuals with severe disabilities. *Education & Training in Mental Retardation, 23,* 302–314.

Snyder, H. N., & Sickmund, M. (1999). *Juvenile offenders and victims: 1999 national report.* Washington, DC: Office of Juvenile Justice and Delinquency Prevention, U.S. Department of Justice.

Sohlberg, M. M., & Mateer, C. A. (2001). *Cognitive rehabilitation: An integrative neuropsychological approach.* New York: Guilford.

Spache, G. D. (1981). *Diagnosing and correcting reading disabilities* (2nd ed.). Boston: Allyn & Bacon.

Sparrow, S. S., Cicchetti, D. V., & Balla, D. A. (2005). *Vineland Adaptive Behavior Scales: Second Edition.* Circle Pines, MN: American Guidance Service.

Speece, D. L., Case, L. P., & Malloy, D. E. (2003). Responsiveness to general education instruction as the first gate to learning disabilities identification. *Learning Disabilities Research and Practice, 18,* 147–156.

Spencer, M. B., & Markstrom-Adams, C. (1990). Identity processes among racial and ethnic minority children in America. *Child Development, 61,* 290–310.

Spencer, T., Biederman, J., Wilens, T., Harding, M., O'Donnell, D., & Griffin, S. (1996). Pharmacotherapy of attention-deficit hyperactivity disorder across the life cycle. *Journal of the American Academy of Child & Adolescent Psychiatry, 35,* 409–432.

Spirito, A. (1980). Scores on Bender-Gestalt and Developmental Test of Visual-Motor Integration of learning-disabled children. *Perceptual and Motor Skills, 50,* 1214.

Spreen, O. (2001). Learning disabilities and their neurological foundations, theories, and subtypes. In A. S. Kaufman & N. L. Kaufman (Eds.), *Specific learning disabilities and difficulties in children and adolescents: Psychological assessment and evaluation* (pp. 283–308). New York: Cambridge.

Spreen, O., Risser, A. H., & Edgell, D. (1995). *Developmental neuropsychology.* New York: Oxford University Press.

Spreen, O., & Strauss, E. (1998). *A compendium of neuropsychological tests: Administration, norms, and commentary* (2nd ed.). New York: Oxford University Press.

St. James-Roberts, I. (1981). A reinterpretation of hemispherectomy data without functional plasticity of the brain. *Brain and Language, 13,* 31–53.

Stanovich, K. E. (1988). Explaining the differences between the dyslexic and the garden-variety poor reader: The phonological-core variable-difference model. *Journal of Learning Disabilities, 21,* 590–604, 612.

Stanovich, K. E. (1991). Discrepancy definitions of reading disability: Has intelligence led us astray? *Reading Research Quarterly, 26,* 7–29.

Stanovich, K. E., Cunningham, A. E., & Cramer, B. B. (1984). Assessing phonological awareness in kindergarten children: Issues of task comparability. *Journal of Experimental Child Psychology, 38,* 175–190.

Stanton-Chapman, T. L., Chapman, D. A., Bainbridge, N. L., & Scott, K. G. (2002). Identification of early risk factors for language impairment. *Research on Developmental Disabilities, 23,* 390–405.

State of Iowa, Department of Public Instruction. (1981). *The identification of pupils with learning disabilities.* Des Moines: Author.

Stein, J., Schettler, T., Wallinga, D., & Valenti, M. (2002). In harm's way: Toxic threats to child development. *Journal of Developmental and Behavioral Pediatrics, 23,* 13–22.

Stein, T. J., Gambrill, E. D., & Wiltse, K. T. (1978). *Children in foster homes: Achieving continuity of care.* New York: Praeger.

Steinberg, L. (1999). *Adolescence* (5th ed.). Boston: McGraw-Hill.

Steinberg, L., & Morris, A. S. (2001). Adolescent development. *Annual Review of Psychology, 52,* 83–110.

Stern, D. N., MacKain, K., Raduns, K., Hopper, P., Kaminsky, C., Evans, S., Shilling, N., Giraldo, L., Kaplan, M., Nachman, P., Trad, P., Polan, J., Barnard, K., & Spieker, S. (1992). The Kiddie-Infant Descriptive Instrument for Emotional States (KIDIES): An instrument for the measurement of affective state in infancy and early childhood. *Infant Mental Health Journal, 13,* 107–118.

Stern, R. A., Singer, E. A., Duke, L. M., Singer, N. G., Morey, C. E., Daughtrey. E. W., & Kaplan, E. F. (1994). The Boston Qualitative Scoring System for the Rey-Osterrieth Complex Figure: Description and interrater reliability. *Clinical Neuropsychologist, 8,* 309–322.

Stevenson, I. (1960). *Medical history-taking.* New York: Hoeber.

Stevenson, I. (1974). The psychiatric interview. In S. Arieti (Ed.), *American handbook of psychiatry* (2nd ed., Vol. 1, pp. 1138–1156). New York: Basic Books.

Stevenson, J., Pennington, B. F., Gilger, J. W., DeFries, J. C., & Gillis, J. J. (1993). Hyperactivity and spelling disability: Testing for shared genetic aetiology. *Journal of Child Psychology and Psychiatry, 34,* 1137–1152.

Stinnett, T. A., Fuqua, D. R., & Coombs, W. T. (1999). Construct validity of the AAMR Adaptive Behavior Scale–School: 2. *School Psychology Review, 28,* 31–43.

Stinnett, T. A., Oehler-Stinnett, J., Fuqua, D. R., & Palmer, L. S. (2002). Examinatiion of the underlying structure of the NEPSY: A developmental neuropsychological assessment. *Journal of Psychoeducational Assessment, 20,* 66–82.

Stoloff, M. L., & Couch, J. V. (Eds.). (1992). *Computer use in psychology: A directory of software* (Vol. 3). Washington, DC: American Psychological Association.

Stone, W. L. (1998). *Descriptive information about the Screening Tool for Autism in Two-Year-Olds (STAT).* Paper presented at the NIH State of the Science in Autism: Screening and Diagnosis Working Conference, Bethesda, MD, June 15–17.

Stone, W. L., & Hogan, K. L. (1993). A structured parent interview for identifying young children with autism. *Journal of Autism & Developmental Disorders, 23,* 639–652.

Stone, W. L., MacLean, W. E., Jr., & Hogan, K. L. (1995). Autism and mental retardation. In M. C. Roberts (Ed.), *Handbook of pediatric psychology* (2nd ed., pp. 655–675). New York: Guilford.

Strain, P. S., Sainto, D. M., & Maheady, L. (1984). Toward a functional assessment of severely handicapped learners. *Educational Psychologist, 19,* 180–187.

Strube, M. J. (1985). A BASIC program for the calculation of intraclass correlations based on fixed effects and random effects models. *Behavior Research Methods, Instruments, & Computers, 17,* 578.

Stuart, I. (1995). Spatial orientation and congenital blindness: A neuropsychological approach. *Journal of Visual Impairment & Blindness, 89,* 129–141.

Sturmey, P. (1996). *Functional analysis in clinical psychology.* New York: Wiley.

Subotnik, R. F., Karp, D. E., & Morgan, E. R. (1989). High IQ children at midlife: An investigation into the generalizability of Terman's genetic studies of genius. *Roeper Review, 11,* 139–144.

Substance Abuse and Mental Health Service Administration. (2004). *Overview of findings from the 2003 national survey on drug use and health* (Office of Applied Studies, NSDUH Series H–24, DHHS Publication No. SMA 04–3963). Rockville, MD.

Sue, D. W. (1990). Culture-specific strategies in counseling: A conceptual framework. *Professional Psychology: Research and Practice, 21,* 424–433.

Suicide Awareness Voices of Education. (2003). *Suicide: Identifying high risk children and adolescents.* Retrieved January 10, 2005, from http://www.save.org

Sullivan, P. M., & Montoya, L. A. (1997). Factor analysis of the WISC–III with deaf and hard-of-hearing children. *Psychological Assessment, 9,* 317–321.

Sulzer-Azaroff, B., & Reese, E. P. (1982). *Applying behavioral analysis: A program for developing professional competence.* New York: Holt, Rinehart and Winston.

Swanson, H. L., & Sáez, L. (2003). Memory difficulties in children and adults with learning disabilities. In H. L. Swanson, K. R. Harris, & S. Graham (Eds.), *Handbook of learning disabilities* (pp. 182–198). New York: Guilford.

Switzky, H. N., Haywood, H. C., & Rotatori, A. F. (1982). Who are the severely and profoundly mentally retarded? *Education and Training of the Mentally Retarded, 17,* 268–272.

Szapocznik, J., & Kurtines, W. M. (1989). *Breakthroughs in family therapy with drug abusing and problem youth.* New York: Springer.

Talley, J. L. (1993). *Children's Auditory Verbal Learning Test–Second Edition.* Lutz, FL: Psychological Assessment Resources.

Tanguay, P. E. (2000). Pervasive developmental disorders: A 10-year review. *Journal of the American Academy of Child and Adolescent Psychiatry, 39,* 1079–1095.

Tapp, J., & Walden, T. A. (2000). PROCORDER: A system for collection and analysis of observational data from videotape. In T. Thompson, D. Felce, & F. J. Symons (Eds.), *Behavioral observation: Technology and applications in developmental disabilities* (pp. 61–70). Baltimore: Brookes.

Tarbell, S. E., Cohen, I. T., & Marsh, J. L. (1992). The Toddler-Preschooler Postoperative Pain Scale: An observational scale for measuring postoperative pain in children aged 1–5: Preliminary report. *Pain, 50,* 273–280.

Tarnowski, K. J., & Rohrbeck, C. A. (1993). Disadvantaged children and families. *Advances in Clinical Child Psychology, 15,* 41–79.

Tasse, M. J., Aman, M. G., Hammer, D., & Rojahn, J. (1996). The Nisonger Child Behavior Rating Form: Age and gender effects and norms. *Research in Developmental Disabilities, 17,* 59–75.

Taylor, E. (1991). Developmental neuropsychiatry. *Journal of Child Psychology and Psychiatry and Allied Disciplines, 32,* 3–47.

Taylor, E. M. (1959). *Psychological appraisal of children with cerebral defects.* Cambridge, MA: Harvard University Press.

Taylor, H. G., & Alden, J. (1997). Age-related differences in outcomes following childhood brain insults: An introduction and overview. *Journal of the International Neuropsychological Society, 3,* 555–567.

Teasdale, G., & Jennett, B. (1974). Assessment of coma and impaired consciousness. *Lancet, 11,* 81–84.

Temple, E., Deutsch, G. K., Poldrack, R. A., Miller, S. L., Tallal, P., Merzenich, M. M., & Gabrieli, J. D. E. (2003). Neural deficits in children with dyslexia ameliorated by behavioral remediation: Evidence from functional MRI. *Proceedings of the National Academy of Sciences, 100,* 2860–2865.

Terman, L. M. (1925). *Genetic studies of genius* (Vol. 1). Stanford, CA: Stanford University Press.

Terman, L. M., & Oden, M. H. (1959). *The gifted group at midlife.* Stanford, CA: Stanford University Press.

Tharp, R. G. (1989). Psychocultural variables and constants: Effects on teaching and learning in schools. *American Psychologist, 44,* 349–359.

Tharp, R. G., & Wetzel, R. J. (1969). *Behavior modification in the natural environment.* New York: Academic Press.

Thompson, R. J., Merritt, K. A., Keith, B. R., Murphy, L. B., & Johndrow, D. A. (1993). Mother-child agreement on the Child Assessment Schedule with nonreferred children: A research note. *Journal of Child Psychology and Psychiatry, 34,* 813–820.

Thompson, T., Felce, D., & Symons, F. J. (Eds.). (2000). *Behavioral observation: Technology and applications in developmental disabilities.* Baltimore: Brookes.

Thompson, T., Symons, F. J., & Felce, D. (2001). Principles of behavioral observation: Assumptions and strategies. In T. Thompson, D. Felce, & F. J. Symons (Eds.), *Behavioral observation: Technology and applications in developmental disabilities* (pp. 3–16). Baltimore: Brookes.

Thomson, J. B., & Kerns, K. A. (2000). Mild traumatic brain injury in children. In S. A. Raskin & C. A. Mateer (Eds.), *Neuropsychological management of mild traumatic brain injury* (pp. 233–253). London, England: Oxford University Press.

Tidmarsh, L., & Volkmar, F. R. (2003). Diagnosis and epidemiology of autism spectrum disorders. *Canadian Journal of Psychiatry, 45,* 517–525.

Tilly, W. D., III, Knoster, T. P., Kovaleski, J., Bambara, L., Dunlap, G., & Kincaid, D. (1998). *Functional behavioral assessment: Policy development in light of emerging research and practice.* Alexandria, VA: National Association of State Directors of Special Education.

Torgesen, J. K. (1981). The relationship between memory and attention in learning disabilities. *Exceptional Education Quarterly, 2,* 51–59.

Torgesen, J. K. (2000). Individual differences in response to early interventions in reading: The lingering problems of treatment resisters. *Learning Disabilities Research and Practice, 15,* 55–64.

Torgesen, J. K. (2002). Empirical and theoretical support for direct diagnosis of learning disabilities by assessment of intrinsic processing weaknesses. In R. Bradley, L. Danielson, & D. P. Hallahan (Eds.), *Identification of learning disabilities: Research to practice* (pp. 565–613). Mahwah, NJ: Erlbaum.

Torgesen, J. K., Alexander, A., Wagner, R. K., Rashotte, C. K., Voellor, K., & Conway, T. (2001). Intensive remedial instruction for children with severe reading disabilities: Immediate and long-term outcomes from two instructional approaches. *Journal of Learning Disabilities, 34,* 33–58.

Torgesen, J. K., Wagner, R. K., Rashotte, C. K., Rose, E., Lindamood, P., Conway, T., & Garvan, C. (1999). Preventing reading failure in young children with phonological processing disabilities: Group and individual responses to instruction. *Journal of Educational psychology, 91,* 579–593.

Torrance, E. P. (1966). *Torrance Tests of Creative Thinking.* Princeton, NJ: Personnel.

Torrance, E. P., & Myers, R. E. (1970). *Creative learning and teaching.* New York: Dodd, Mead.

Tracy, E. M., Bean, N., Gwatkin, S., & Hill, B. (1992). Family preservation workers: Sources of job satisfaction and job stress. *Research on Social Work Practice, 2,* 465–478.

Tramontana, M. G., & Hooper, S. R. (1988). Child neuropsychological assessment: Overview of current status. In M. G. Tramontana & S. R. Hooper (Eds.), *Assessment issues in child neurospychology* (pp. 3–38). New York: Plenum.

Trapani, C., & Gettinger, M. (1996). Treatment of students with learning disabilities: Case conceptualization and program design. In M. A. Reinecke, F. M. Dattilio, & A. Freeman (Eds.), *Cognitive therapy with children and adolescents: A casebook for clinical practice* (pp. 251–277). New York: Guilford.

Treiman, R. (1998). Why spelling? The benefits of incorporating spelling into beginning reading instruction. In J. L. Metsala & L. C. Ehri (Eds.), *Word recognition in beginning literacy* (pp. 289–313). Mahwah, NJ: Erlbaum.

Treiman, R., & Bourassa, D. C. (2000). The development of spelling skill. *Topics in Language Disorders, 20,* 1–18.

Trevarthen, C., Aitken, K., Papoudi, D., & Robarts, J. (1998). *Children with autism: Diagnosis and interventions to meet their needs* (2nd ed.). Philadelphia: Jessica Kingsley.

Tripp, G., Ryan, J., & Peace, K. (2002). Neuropsychological functioning in children with DSM-IV combined type attention deficit hyperactivity disorder. *Australian and New Zealand Journal of Psychiatry, 36,* 771–779.

Tunks, E., & Billissimo, A. (1991). *Behavioral medicine: Concepts and procedures.* New York: Pergamon.

Turk, D. C., & Kerns, R. D. (1985). The family in health and illness. In D. C. Turk & R. D. Kerns (Eds.), *Health, illness and families: A life-span perspective* (pp. 1–22). New York: Wiley.

Turner, C. F., Ku, L., Rogers, S. M., Lindberg, L. D., Pleck, J. H., & Sonenstein, F. L. (1998). Adolescent sexual behavior, drug use, and violence: Increased reporting with computer survey technology. *Science, 280,* 867–873.

Turner, S. M., DeMers, S. T., Fox, H. R., & Reed, G. M. (2001). APA's guidelines for test user qualifications. *American Psychologist, 56,* 1099–1113.

Tuttle, D. W. (2004). *Self-esteem and adjusting with blindness: The process of responding to life's demands* (3rd ed.). Springfield, IL: Charles C. Thomas.

Uba, A. (1994). *Asian Americans: Personality patterns, identity, and mental health.* New York: Guilford.

Uebersax, J. S. (1982). A design-independent method for measuring the reliability of psychiatric diagnosis. *Journal of Psychiatric Research, 17,* 335–342.

Ullman, R. K., Sleator, E. K., & Sprague, R. L. (1991). *ACTeRS Teacher Form–Second Edition.* Champaign, IL: MetriTech.

Ullman, R. K., Sleator, E. K., Sprague, R. L., & MetriTech Staff. (1996). *ACTeRS Parent Form.* Champaign, IL: MetriTech.

U.S. Department of Education. (1999). *1999 annual report on school safety.* Washington, DC: Author.

U.S. Department of Education. (2001). *Twenty-third annual report to congress on the implementation of the Individuals with Disabilities Act.* Washington, DC: Author.

U.S. Department of Education. (2002). *To assure the free appropriate public education of all children with disabilities: Twenty-fourth annual report to Congress on the implementation of the Individuals with Disabilities Education Act.* Washington, DC: Author.

U.S. Department of Education. (2003). *Twenty-fourth annual report to Congress on the implementation of the Individuals with Disabilities Act.* Washington, DC: Author.

U.S. Department of Health and Human Services. (1999). *Mental health: A report of the Surgeon General–Executive summary.* Rockville, MD: U.S. Department of Health and Human Services, Substance Abuse and Mental Health Services Administration, Center for Mental Health Services, National Institutes of Health, National Institute of Mental Health.

U.S. Department of Health and Human Services. (2001). *Youth violence: A report to the Surgeon General.* Rockville, MD: Author.

U.S. Department of Justice. (2000). *Safe from the start: Taking action on children exposed to violence.* Washington, DC: Author.

U.S. Food and Drug Administration. (2004). *Class suicidality labelling language for antidepressants.* Retrieved April 5, 2005, from http://www.fda.gov/cder/drug/antidepressants/PI_template.pdf

Vance, B., Fuller, G. B., & Lester, M. L. (1986). A comparison of the Minnesota Perceptual Diagnostic Test Revised and the Bender Gestalt. *Journal of Learning Disabilities, 19,* 211–214.

Van Etten, G., Arkell, C., & Van Etten, C. (1980). *The severely and profoundly handicapped: Programs, methods, and materials.* St. Louis: Mosby.

VanTassel, J. (1979). A needs assessment for gifted education. *Journal of the Education of the Gifted, 2,* 141–148.

Vaughn, S., Bos, S. C., & Schumn, J. S. (2000). *Teaching exceptional, diverse, and at-risk students in the general education classroom.* Boston: Allyn & Bacon.

Vaughn, S., & Fuchs, L. S. (2003). Redefining learning disabilities as inadequate response to instruction: The promise and potential problems. *Journal of Learning Disabilities, 18,* 137–146.

Vellutino, F. R., Scanlon, D., & Lyon, G. R. (2000). Differentiating between difficult-to-remediate and readily remediated poor readers: More evidence against the IQ-achievement discrepancy definition of reading disability. *Journal of Learning Disabilities, 33,* 223–238.

Vellutino, F. R., Scanlon, D., Spay, E., Small, S., Pratt, A., Chen, R., & Denckla, M. B. (1996). Cognitive profiles of difficult-to-remediate and readily remediated poor readers: Early intervention as a vehicle for distinguishing between cognitive and experiential deficits as basic causes of specific reading disability. *Journal of Educational Psychology, 88,* 601–638.

Vellutino, F. R., & Shub, M. J. (1982). Assessment of disorders in formal school language: Disorders in reading. *Topics in Language Disorders, 2,* 20–33.

Venter, A., Lord, C., & Schopler, E. (1992). A follow-up study of high functioning autistic children. *Journal of Child Psychology and Psychiatry, 33,* 489–507.

Verderber, J. M., & Payne, V. G. (1987). A comparison of the long and short forms of the Bruininks-Oseretsky Test of Motor Proficiency. *Adapted Physical Activity Quarterly, 4,* 51–59.

Vignoe, D., & Achenbach, T. M. (1999). *Bibliography of published studies using the Child Behavior Checklist and related materials: 1999 edition.* Burlington: University of Vermont, Department of Psychiatry.

Wade, S. L., Taylor, H. G., Drotar, D., Stancin, T., & Yeates, K. O. (1998). Family burden and adaptation during the initial year after traumatic brain injury in children. *Pediatrics, 102,* 110–116.

Wadsworth, S. J., Olson, R. K., Pennington, B. F., & DeFries, J. C. (2000). Differential genetic etiology of reading disability as a function of IQ. *Journal of Learning Disabilities, 33,* 192–199.

Wagner, R. K., Torgesen, J. K., & Rashotte, C. K. (1999). *Comprehensive Test of Phonological Processing.* Austin, TX: Pro-Ed.

Wakefield, J. C. (1992). Disorder as harmful dysfunction: A conceptual critique of DSM-III–R's definition of mental disorder. *Psychological Review, 99,* 232–247.

Wallach, M., & Kogan, N. (1965). *Modes of thinking in young children.* New York: Holt, Rinehart, & Winston.

Wallbrown, F. H., & Fremont, T. S. (1980). The stability of Koppitz scores on the Bender-Gestalt for reading disabled children. *Psychology in the Schools, 17,* 181–184.

Washton, A. M., Stone, N. S., & Hendrickson, E. C. (1988). Cocaine abuse. In D. M. Donovan & G. A. Marlatt (Eds.), *Assessment of addictive behaviors* (pp. 364–389). New York: Guilford.

Waslick, B., Werry, J. S., & Greenhill, L. L. (1999). Pharmacotherapy and toxicology of oppositional defiant disorder and conduct disorder. In H. C. Quay & A. E. Hogan (Eds.), *Handbook of disruptive behavior disorders* (pp. 455–474). New York: Kluwer Academic Press.

Waterman, A. H., Blades, M., & Spencer, C. P. (2000). Do children try to answer nonsensical questions? *British Journal of Developmental Psychology, 18,* 211–226.

Watkins, E. O. (1976). *The Watkins Bender-Gestalt scoring system.* Novato, CA: Academic Therapy.

Webster, P. E., Plante, A. S., & Couvillion, M. L. (1997). Phonological impairment and prereading: Update on a longitudinal study. *Journal of Learning Disabilities, 4,* 365–375.

Wechsler, D. (1991). *Wechsler Intelligence Scale for Children–Third Edition.* San Antonio, TX: The Psychological Corporation.

Wechsler, D. (2004). *Wechsler Intelligence Scale for Children–Fourth Edition.* San Antonio, TX: The Psychological Corporation.

Wechsler, D., Kaplan, E. F., Fein, D., Kramer, J. H., Morris, R., Delis, D., & Maerlender, A. (2004). *Wechsler Intelligence Scale for Children Fourth Edition—Integrated.* San Antonio: Hartcourt Assessment.

Weinberg, W. A., Rutman, J., Sullivan, L., Penick, E. C., & Dietz, S. G. (1973). Depression in children referred to an educational diagnostic center: Diagnosis and treatment. *Journal of Pediatrics, 83,* 1066.

Weinfeld, R. (2003). *Programs for gifted students with learning disabilities.* Retrieved June 6, 2005, from http://www.mcps.k12.md.us/departments/eii/GTLD.html

Welsh, G. (1975). *Creativity of intelligence: A personality approach.* Chapel Hill: University of North Carolina Press.

Werner, E. E. (2000). Protective factors and individual resilience. In J. P. Shonkoff & S. J. Meisels (Eds.), *Handbook of early childhood intervention* (2nd ed., pp. 115–132). New York: Cambridge University Press.

Wesson, M. D., & Kispert, K. (1986). The relationship between the Test for Visual Analysis Skills (TVAS) and standardized visual-motor tests in children with visual perception difficulty. *Journal of the American Optometric Association, 57,* 844–849.

Westling, D. L. (1996). What do parents of children with moderate and severe mental disabilities want? *Education & Training in Mental Retardation, 31,* 86–114.

Wetherby, A. M., & Prizant, B. M. (1992). Facilitating language and communication development in autism: Assessment and intervention guidelines. In D. E. Berkell (Ed.), *Autism: Identification, education, and treatment* (pp. 107–134). Hillsdale, NJ: Erlbaum.

Weyandt, L. L. (2001). *An ADHD primer.* Boston: Allyn & Bacon.

Weyandt, L. L. (2004). The use of medication in the treatment of ADHD. *Communiqué, 33,* 35–38.

Weyandt, L. L., Iwaszuk, W., Fulton, K., Ollerton, M., Beatty, N., Fouts, H., Schepman, S., & Greenlaw, C. (2003). The Internal Restlessness Scale: Performance of college students with and without ADHD. *Journal of Learning Disabilities, 36,* 382–389.

Weyandt, L. L., Mitzlaff, L., & Thomas, L. (2002). The relationship between intelligence and performance on the Test of Variables of Attention (TOVA). *Journal of Learning Disabilities, 35,* 114–120.

Weyandt, L. L., Stein, S., Rice, J. A., & Wermus, C. (1994). Classroom interventions for children with attention-deficit hyperactivity disorder. *The Oregon Conference Monograph, 6,* 137–143.

Weyandt, L. L., & Willis, W. G. (1994). Executive functions in school-aged children: Potential efficacy of tasks in discriminating clinical groups. *Developmental Neuropsychology, 10,* 27–38.

Whalen, C. K. (1989). Attention deficit and hyperactivity disorders. In T. H. Ollendick & M. Hersen (Eds.), *Handbook of child psychopathology* (pp. 131–169). New York: Plenum.

Whalen, C. K., Henker, B., Swanson, J. M., Granger, D., Kliewer, W., & Spencer, J. (1987). Natural social behaviors in hyperactive children: Dose effects of methylphenidate. *Journal of Consulting and Clinical Psychology, 55,* 187–193.

Whitehurst, G. J., & Fischel, J. E. (1994). Early developmental language delay: What, if anything, should the clinician be doing about it? *Journal of Child Psychology and Psychiatry, 35,* 613–648.

Whitehurst, G. J., & Lonigan, C. J. (1998). Child development and emerging literacy. *Child Development, 69,* 235–357.

Whitman, T. L., Scibak, J. W., Butler, K. M., Richter, R., & Johnson, M. R. (1982). Improving classroom behavior in mentally retarded children through correspondence training. *Journal of Applied Behavior Analysis, 15,* 545–564.

Whitten, C. J., D'Amato, R. C., & Chittooran, M M. (1992). The neuropsychological approach to intervention. In R. C. D'Amato & B. A. Rothlisberg (Eds.), *Psychological perspectives on intervention: A case study approach to prescriptions for change* (pp. 112–136). Chicago: Waveland.

Widom, C. S., & Maxfield, M. G. (2001). An update on the "cycle of violence." *National Institute of Justice: Research in brief.* Retrieved February 28, 2001, from http://www.ojp.usdoj.gov/nij

Willcutt, E. G., Pennington, B. F., & DeFries, J. C. (2000). Etiology of inattention and hyperactivity/impulsivity in a community sample of twins with learning difficulties. *Journal of Abnormal Child Psychology, 28,* 149–159.

Willemsen-Swinkels, S. H. N., & Buitelaar, J. K. (2002). The autistic spectrum: Subgroups, boundaries, and treatment. *Psychiatric Clinics of North America, 25,* 811–836.

Williams, C. L., Butcher, J. N., Ben-Porath, Y. S., & Graham, J. R. (1992). *MMPI-A: Assessing psychopathology in adolescents.* Minneapolis: University of Minnesota Press.

Williams, J. H. G., Whiten, A., Suddendorf, T., & Perrett, D. I. (2001). Imitation, mirror neurons, and autism. *Neuroscience and Biobehavioral Reviews, 25,* 287–295.

Williams, M. A., & Boll, T. J. (1997). Recent advances in neuropsychological assessment of children. In G. Goldstein & T. M. Incagnoli (Eds.), *Contemporary approaches to neuropsychological assessment* (pp. 231–276). New York: Plenum.

Willis, D. J., & Walker, C. E. (1989). Etiology. In T. H. Ollendick & M. Hersen (Eds.), *Handbook of child psychopathology* (2nd ed., pp. 29–51). New York: Plenum.

Wilson, B. A., Ivani-Chalian, R., & Aldrich, F. (1991). *Rivermead Behavioral Memory Test for Children.* London, England: Harcourt Assessment.

Wilson, B. C., Iacoviello, J. M., Wilson, J. J., & Risucci, D. (1982). Purdue Pegboard performance of normal preschool children. *Journal of Clinical Neuropsychology, 4,* 19–26.

Wilson, J. J., & Howell, J. C. (1993). *A comprehensive strategy for serious, violent, and chronic juvenile offenders: Program summary.* Washington, DC: Department of Justice, Office of Juvenile Justice and Delinquency Prevention.

Wilson, P. H., Spence, S. H., & Kavanagh, D. J. (1989). *Cognitive-behavioral interviewing for adult disorders: A practical handbook.* London, England: Routledge.

Wing, L. (1976). Assessment: The role of the teacher. In M. P. Everard (Ed.), *An approach to teaching autistic children* (pp. 15–30). New York: Pergamon.

Winton, P. J. (1992). *Communicating with families in early intervention: A training module.* Chapel Hill, NC: Frank Porter Graham Child Development Center.

Wirt, R. D., Lachar, D., Seat, P. D., & Broen, W. E., Jr. (2001). *Personality Inventory for Children–Second Edition.* Los Angeles: Western Psychological Services.

Wistedt, B., Rasmussen, A., Pedersen, L., Malm, U., Traskman-Bendz, L., Wakelin, J., & Bech, P. (1990). The development of an observer-scale for measuring social dysfunction and aggression. *Pharmacopsychiatry, 23,* 249–252.

Witt, J. C., & Elliott, S. N. (1983). Assessment in behavioral consultation: The initial interview. *School Psychology Review, 12,* 42–49.

Witte, R. H., Philips, L., & Kakela, M. (1998). Job satisfaction of college graduates with learning disabilities. *Journal of Learning Disabilities, 31,* 259–265.

Wolf, F. M. (1986). *Meta-analysis: Quantitative methods for research synthesis.* Sage University Papers on Quantitative Applications in the Social Sciences, 07-001. Beverly Hills, CA: Sage.

Wolf, M. (2002). Response to "Clinical judgments in identifying and teaching children with language-based reading difficulties." In R. Brodley, L. Danielson, & D. P. Hallahan (Eds.), *Identification of learning disabilities: Research to practice* (pp. 725–735). Mahwah, NJ: Erlbaum.

Wolfe, D. A., & McGee, R. (1991). Assessment of emotional status among maltreated children. In R. H. Starr & D. A. Wolfe (Eds.), *The effects of child abuse and neglect: Issues and research* (pp. 257–277). New York: Guilford.

Wong, S. P., & McGraw, K. O. (1999). Confidence intervals and F tests for intraclass correlations based on three-way random effects models. *Educational & Psychological Measurement, 59,* 270–288.

Wood, J. M., Nezworski, M. T., Lilienfeld, S. O., & Garb, H. N. (2003). *What's wrong with the Rorschach? Science confronts the controversial inkblot test.* San Francisco: Jossey-Bass.

Wood, J. M., Nezworski, M. T., & Stejskal, W. J. (1996). The comprehensive system for the Rorschach: A critical examination. *Psychological Science, 7,* 3–10.

Woodcock, R. W., Muñoz-Sandoval, A. F., Ruef, M., & Alvarado, C. (2005). *Woodcock-Muñoz Language Survey–Revised.* Itasca, IL: Riverside.

Wright, D., & DeMers, S. T. (1982). Comparison of the relationship between two measures of visual-motor coordination and academic achievement. *Psychology in the Schools, 19,* 473–477.

Wright, D. L., Aquilino, W. S., & Supple, A. J. (1998). A comparison of computer-assisted and paper-and-pencil self-administered questionnaires in a survey on smoking, alcohol, and drug use. *Public Opinion Quarterly, 62,* 331–353.

Yarrow, L. J. (1960). Interviewing children. In P. H. Mussen (Ed.), *Handbook of research methods in child development* (pp. 561–602). New York: Wiley.

Yeates, K. O. (1994). Comparison of developmental norms for the Boston Naming Test. *Clinical Neuropsychologist, 8,* 91–98.

Yeates, K. O. (2000). Closed-head injury. In K. O. Yeates, M. D. Ris, & H. G. Taylor (Eds.), *Pediatric neuropsychology: Research, theory, and practice* (pp. 92–116). New York: Guilford.

Yeudall, L. T., Reddon, J. R., Gill, D. M., & Stefanyk, W. O. (1987). Normative data for the Halstead-Reitan Neuropsychological Tests stratified by age and sex. *Journal of Clinical Psychology, 43,* 346–367.

Yi, S., Johnstone, B., Doan, R., & Townes, B. D. (1990). The relationship between the pediatric neurological examination and neuropsychological assessment measures for young children. *International Journal of Neuroscience, 50,* 73–81.

Ylvisaker, M. (1986). Language and communication disorders following pediatric head injury. *Journal of Head Trauma Rehabilitation, 1,* 48–56.

Ylvisaker, M., Hartwick, P., & Stevens, M. (1991). School reentry following head injury: Managing the transition from hospital to school. *Journal of Head Trauma Rehabilitation, 6,* 10–22.

Yopp, H. K. (1995). A test for assessing phonemic awareness in young children. *Reading Teacher, 49,* 20–29.

Young, R. L., Brewer, N., & Pattison, C. (2003). Parental identification of early behavioural abnormalities in children with autistic disorder. *Autism, 7,* 125–143.

Yousefi, F., Shahim, S., Razavieh, A., Mehryar, A. H., Hosseini, A. A., & Alborzi, S. (1992). Some normative data on the Bender Gestalt Test performance of Iranian children. *British Journal of Educational Psychology, 62,* 410–416.

Zahn-Waxler, C., Cole, P. M., Welsh, J. D., & Fox, N. A. (1995). Psychophysiological correlates of empathy and prosocial behaviors in preschool children with behavior problems. *Development and Psychopathology, 7,* 27–48.

Zahn-Waxler, C., Iannotti, R. J., Cummings, E. M., & Denham, S. (1990). Antecedents of problem behaviors in children of depressed mothers. *Development and Psychopathology, 2,* 271–291.

Zahn-Waxler, C., McKnew, D. H., Cummings, E. M., Davenport, Y. B., & Radke-Yarrow, M. (1984). Problem behaviors and peer interactions of young children with a manic-depressive parent. *American Journal of Psychiatry, 141,* 236–240.

Zaidel, E., Zaidel, D. W., & Sperry, R. W. (1981). Left and right intelligence: Case studies of Raven's Progressive Matrices following brain bisection and hemidecortication. *Cortex, 17,* 167–186.

Zambrana, R. E., & Silva-Palacios, V. (1989). Gender differences in stress among Mexican immigrant adolescents in Los Angeles, California. *Journal of Adolescent Research, 4,* 426–442.

Zehnder, M. M. (1994). *Using expert witnesses in child abuse and neglect cases.* St. Paul: Minnesota County Attorneys Association.

Zigler, E. (1995). Can we "cure" mild mental retardation among individuals in the lower socioeconomic stratum? *American Journal of Public Health, 85,* 302–304.

Zigler, E., & Balla, D. (1981). Recent issues in developmental approach to mental retardation. In M. P. Friedman, J. P. Das, & N. O'Connor (Eds.), *Intelligence and learning* (pp. 25–38). New York: Plenum.

Zigler, E., & Hodapp, R. M. (1986). *Understanding mental retardation.* New York: Cambridge University Press.

Zima, J. P. (1983). *Interviewing: Key to effective management.* Chicago: Science Research Associates.

NAME INDEX

Harrison, P. L., 304, 315, 438
Hart, B., 394
Hart, E. J., 518
Hartmann, J., 565
Hartwick, P., 202
Harty, K., 412
Harward, H., 565
Hatlen, P., 473, 474
Hauser, M. J., 360
Hawkins, J. D., 355, 356
Hawkins, R. P., 14
Hayne, H., 149
Haynes, S. N., 247, 257
Haywood, H. C., 440
Head, K., 510
Heath, C. P., 746
Heath, S. B., 91
Hebben, N., 555
Hechtman, L., 377
Helland, T., 514
Hendrickson, E. C., 647
Hendy, J., 545
Henggeler, S., 355
Henker, B., 234
Hennington, P. N., 385
Henriksen, T. B., 377
Hensley, M. B., 441

SUBJECT INDEX

List of Tables in Appendixes A to F